Williams on Wills

Editors of previous editions

First edition	1952	W J Williams
Second edition	1961	W J Williams
Third edition	1967	W J Williams
Fourth edition	1974	C H Sherrin and R F D Barlow
Fifth edition	1980	C H Sherrin, R F D Barlow and R A Wallington
Sixth edition	1987	C H Sherrin, R F D Barlow and R A Wallington
Seventh edition	1995	C H Sherrin, R F D Barlow and R A Wallington

Williams on Wills

Eighth edition

C H SHERRIN
LLM Ph D
Professor of Law,
Department of Professional Legal Education,
University of Hong Kong

R F D BARLOW
MA (Oxon)
Barrister
A Bencher of Lincoln's Inn
10 Old Square, Lincoln's Inn, WC2A 3SU

R A WALLINGTON
MA (Cantab)
of the Middle Temple and Lincoln's Inn, Barrister
10 Old Square, Lincoln's Inn, WC2A 3SU

SUSANNAH L MEADWAY
MA (Oxon)
of the Middle Temple and Lincoln's Inn, Barrister
10 Old Square, Lincoln's Inn, WC2A 3SU

MICHAEL WATERWORTH
MA (Cantab)
of Lincoln's Inn, Barrister
10 Old Square, Lincoln's Inn, WC2A 3SU

Volume 2
Precedents and Statutes

Butterworths
London • Dublin • Edinburgh
2002

United Kingdom	Butterworths, a Division of Reed Elsevier (UK) Ltd, Halsbury House, 35 Chancery Lane, LONDON WC2A 1EL and 4 Hill Street, EDINBURGH EH2 3JZ
Australia	Butterworths, a Division of Reed International Books Australia Pty Ltd, CHATSWOOD, New South Wales
Canada	Butterworths Canada Ltd, MARKHAM, Ontario
Hong Kong	Butterworths Asia (Hong Kong), HONG KONG
India	Butterworths India, NEW DELHI
Ireland	Butterworth (Ireland) Ltd, DUBLIN
Malaysia	Malayan Law Journal Sdn Bhd, KUALA LUMPUR
New Zealand	Butterworths of New Zealand Ltd, WELLINGTON
Singapore	Butterworths Asia, SINGAPORE
South Africa	Butterworths Publishers (Pty) Ltd, DURBAN
USA	Lexis Law Publishing, CHARLOTTESVILLE, Virginia

A CIP Catalogue record for this book is available from the British Library

VOLUME 2 BARCODE/ISBN
ISBN 0-406-93393-6

9 780406 933935

COMPLETE SET BARCODE/ISBN
ISBN 0-406-93391-X

9 780406 933911

Typeset by Thomson Litho Ltd, East Kilbride, Scotland
Printed and bound in Great Britain by Clays Ltd, St Ives plc

Visit Butterworths LEXIS *direct* at: http://www.butterworths.com

Contents

Volume 2
PRECEDENTS AND STATUTES

Contents

Contents

B10 Pecuniary legacies

B12   Charitable gifts

Contents

Contents

Contents

B22 Testimonium and attestation clauses

Part C
COMPLETE WILLS

Contents

C11　Wills disposing of business property

C12　Wills disposing of farms and farming businesses

Contents

Part D
CODICILS

D   Codicils

Part E
STATUTORY WILL FORMS 1925

E Statutory Will Forms 1925

Part F
NON-TESTAMENTARY INSTRUMENTS

F1   Renunciation of probate and disclaimer of trusteeships

F2   Executors and trustees

F3   Disclaimers and variations of beneficial interests

Part G
STATUTES

Section 1
WILLS AND INTESTACY

Contents

MENTAL HEALTH ACT 1983

CHILDREN ACT 1989

LAW REFORM (SUCCESSION) ACT 1995

Contents

Section 3
MISCELLANEOUS PROVISIONS RELEVANT TO THE DRAFTING OF WILLS

Contents

Section 4
FAMILY PROVISION AND RELIEF FROM FORFEITURE

Contents

Form Finder

Form Finder

Form Finder

PECUNIARY LEGACIES—*contd*
Substitutional provisions with,
  Legacy to nieces, and the children of deceased nieces   B10.14   **[210.26]**
  Legacy with a clause of substitution in the case of an individual legatee   B10.13   **[210.25]**

PERSONL CHATTELS, GIFTS OF
  Articles of personal adornment to daughters as trustees shall determine   B4.8   **[204.22]**
  Articles with request to distribute them in accordance with testator's wishes   B4.9   **[204.23]**
  By reference to a document already in existence   B4.20   **[204.34]**
  Consumable stores   B4.21   **[204.36]**
  Furniture *see* FURNITURE
  Incorporation of definition in the Administration of Estates Act 1925   B4.2   **[204.16]**
  Incorporation of Statutory Will Forms 1925, Form 2   B4.1   **[204.15]**
  Item which might be conditionally exempt from inheritance tax   B4.14   **[204.28]**
  Letters and papers   B4.19   **[204.33]**
  Library   B4.16   **[204.30]**
  Located in specific dwellinghouse   B4.12   **[204.26]**
  Public collection or the nation of a work of art   B4.15   **[204.29]**
  Residuary estate paying costs of preservation, transport, packing and insurance   B4.13   **[204.27]**
  Selected by trustees on life interest trusts   B4.10   **[204.24]**
  Short form   B4.5   **[204.19]**
  Sporting implements   B4.17   **[204.31]**
  Statutory Will Forms 1925, Form 2: Meaning of 'personal chattels'   E3   **[238.8]**
  Stocks and Shares *see* STOCKS AND SHARES
  Trustees to, upon a short-term discretionary trust   B4.11   **[204.25]**
  Wearing apparel to servants   B4.18   **[204.32]**
  Wife, to   B4.3   **[204.17]**
  Wife to, —alternative form   B4.4   **[204.18]**
  Wife to, of such articles as she may select   B4.6   **[204.20]**
  Wife to, of such articles as she may select up to a stated amount and of the residue to daughters   B4.7   **[204.21]**

POWERS OF TRUSTEES
  Administrative powers, set for complete wills   C2.1(9)   **[224.30]**
  Appropriation *see* APPROPRIATION
  Borrowing
    Power to borrow   B20.20   **[220.69]**
  Business property, over
    No duty to intervene in the affairs of a private company   B21.17   **[221.21]**
    Power to carry on business   B5.13, B20.17   **[205.70]**, **[220.66]**
    Power to carry on farming business   B20.18   **[220.67]**
    Provision for exercise of powers though trustees interested in business   B5.18   **[205.75]**
    Power for some of the trustees only to carry on testator's business   B5.17   **[205.74]**
    Power to give guarantees for loans to companies wholly or substantially owned by trustees   B20.29   **[220.82]**
    Power to incorporate business   B20.19   **[220.68]**
    Power to trustees to carry on business where the will contains a general trust for conversion   B5.16   **[205.73]**
    Power to turn business into limited or unlimited company   B5.14   **[205.71]**
    Powers relating to sale of a business   B5.21   **[205.78]**
    Powers to give warranties etc on the sale of a business or private company shares   B5.22   **[205.79]**
    Retention of shares in family company   B20.5   **[220.44]**
    Set for complete wills   C11.1(6)   **[233.21]**
  Exercise and release of powers
    Powers and discretions exercisable in favour of a beneficiary trustee   B18.32   **[218.117]**
    Power to release powers   B18.33   **[218.118]**
    Testator's wishes as to the exercise of powers of maintenance and advancement [and power to make loans to guardians] during period of guardianship   B18.31   **[218.116]**

REVOCATION *see* COMMENCEMENT

RIGHTS OF RESIDENCE
Clause in will giving right to children to occupy residence   C7.5(5)   **[229.57]**
Clause in will giving right to sister to occupy home   C9.6(4)   **[231.67]**
Clause in will giving right to wife to occupy matrimonial home   C2.5(5)   **[224.85]**
Clause in will of widow or widower providing residence and furniture for children   B8.6   **[208.42]**
Clause where trustees are to have power to purchase property for use of beneficiary   B18.25   **[218.110]**
Gift of interest in dwellinghouse on trusts permitting wife to occupy dwellinghouse for life or during widowhood   C6.3(3)   **[228.37]**
Gift of residence for wife for life with the intention that she reside there—fuller form, providing for the possibility of a change of house by the testator before his death or by the trustees after his death   B8.5   **[208.41]**
Gift of the testator's interest as tenant in common in a house, the gift being postponed to allow the other tenants in common to continue to reside in the house   B8.10   **[208.46]**
Gift with the object of ensuring personal residence, giving the right to a series of short leases   B8.7   **[208.43]**
Gift with the object of ensuring personal residence by the devisee—alternative form using a periodic tenancy   B8.9   **[208.45]**
Gift with the object of ensuring personal residence in the form of a lease determinable on death with rentcharge to support residence   B8.8   **[208.44]**
Interest of beneficiary limited to right of residence, with the beneficiary's consent to a sale being required generally, with provision for changing residences   B8.2   **[208.38]**
Interest of beneficiary limited to a right of residence with provision for changing residences   B8.1   **[208.37]**
Powers to permit enjoyment in kind—restricted to prevent prejudice to inheritance tax status of beneficial trusts   B18.24   **[218.109]**
Power where wife is given residence for life or house is bought for beneficiary to invest trust money in purchase of furniture   B18.26   **[218.111]**
Trust for wife for life or until she remarries and then for son, with power to permit residence   B8.4   **[208.40]**
Trust to permit residence and use of furniture etc by the testator's wife   B8.3   **[208.39]**

SECRET TRUST
Declaration of trust of property devised or bequeathed by will on a secret trust   F2.5   **[240.5]**

SETTLED LAND
See also ENTAILS *and* LAND
Appointment of special executors of settled land   B3.25   **[203.42]**
Appointment of three persons, one of whom is abroad, to be executors and trustees, and also trustees for the purposes of the Settled Land Act 1925   B3.6   **[203.12]**
Gift of entailed property generally   B6.10   **[206.19]**
Gift of land of which the testator is tenant in tail   B6.9   **[206.18]**

SETTLED LEGACIES
Settled legacy—concise form   B16.25   **[216.30]**
Settled legacy—full form   B16.26   **[216.31]**

SOLICITORS
Executors and Trustees, appointment of *see* EXECUTORS, Appointment of

SPECIFIC GIFTS
See also BUSINESS PROPERTY, CONSUMABLES,DEBTS, FURNITURE, INTELLECTUAL PROPERTY, PERSONAL CHATTELS *and* STOCKS AND SHARES,
Clause exonerating specific gifts from charges   B4.54   **[204.76]**
Gift of a reversionary interest   B4.52   **[204.74]**

Form Finder

STATUTORY FORMS
  Clauses incorporating,
    Gift of furniture to wife for life and then to son, incorporating of Statutory Will Form as to inventory   B4.30   **[204.48]**
    Gift of personal chattels by incorporation of Statutory Will Forms 1925, Form 2   B4.1   **[204.15]**
    Gift of residue on trust for sale by incorporation of Statutory Will Forms 1925, Form 8   B14.11   **[214.20]**
    Gift of residue to children incorporating Statutory Will Forms 1925, Form 7, with modification   B16.21   **[216.26]**
    Trust for wife for life and then to children as she shall appoint incorporating Statutory Will Forms 1925, Form 9   B16.17   **[216.22]**
    Trust for wife for life and then to children in equal shares by incorporation of Statutory Will Forms 1925. Form 10   B16.11   **[216.16]**
  Forms,
    Statutory Will Forms 1925, Form 1: Confirmation of settlements   E1   **[238.7]**
    Statutory Will Forms 1925, Form 2: Meaning of 'personal chattels'   E2   **[238.8]**
    Statutory Will Forms 1925, Form 3: Inventories and provisions respecting chattels   E3   **[238.9]**
    Statutory Will Forms 1925, Form 4: Legacies to charities   E4   **[238.10]**
    Statutory Will Forms 1925, Form 5: Directions respecting annuities   E5   **[238.11]**
    Statutory Will Forms 1925, Form 6: Power of appropriation   E6   **[238.12]**
    Statutory Will Forms 1925, Form 7: Trusts of a settled legacy   E7   **[238.13]**
    Statutory Will Forms 1925, Form 8: Administration trusts   E8   **[238.14]**
    Statutory Will Forms 1925, Form 9: Trusts for spouse for life, with power to appoint to issue and gift over to them   E9   **[238.15]**
    Statutory Will Forms 1925, Form 10: Trusts for spouse and issue, without a power of appointment   E10   **[238.16]**

STOCKS AND SHARES
  Gift of shares held by testator at death and of shares to which he will be entitled at death   B4.33   **[204.55]**
  Gift of shares in public company   B4.34   **[204.56]**
  Gift of shares in public or private company—provision for only a lesser number of shares being available   B4.35   **[204.57]**
  Gift of shares with provision for amalgamation, reconstruction, reorganisation or demerger   B4.36   **[204.58]**
  Gift of stock as a general legacy   B4.31   **[204.53]**
  Specific gift of stock   B4.32   **[204.54]**
  Specific legacy of shares with added words negativing apportionment   B4.37   **[204.59]**

SUBSTANTIAL PROPERTY OWNERS, WILLS FOR
  Will of a bachelor landowner settling the principal family estate together with a share of residue on one nephew and his issue, creating a maintenance fund for the upkeep of the mansion house and settled chattels and settling substantial legacies on two nieces and their issue   C13.2   **[235.18]**
  Will of owner of substantial property with no immediate family containing specific gift of controlling shareholding in family company on trusts for the employees and leaving residue on charitable trusts   C13.1   **[235.2]**

SUBSTITUTION CLAUSES
  Substitution clause limited to children of deceased children   B19.5   **[219.18]**
  Trust for testator's children at twenty-five with substitution of issue of a child who predeceases the testator and further substitution of children on death after the testator's death without attaining a vested interest   B19.6   **[219.19]**

TESTIMONIUM AND ATTESTATION
  Alternative form of attestation clause   B22.3   **[222.5]**
  Attestation clause where the testator has an imperfect knowledge of English   B22.13   **[222.15]**
  Form of attestation where the testator acknowledges a signature which he has made previously—short form   B22.11   **[222.13]**

Table of Abbreviations

Abbreviation	Full Title
AA 1870	Apportionment Act 1870
AA 1976	Adoption Act 1976
AA 1984	Anatomy Act 1984
AEA 1925	Administration of Estates Act 1925
AHA 1986	Agricultural Holdings Act 1986
AJA 1969	Administration of Justice Act 1969
AJA 1970	Administration of Justice Act 1970
AJA 1982	Administration of Justice Act 1982
AJA 1985	Administration of Justice Act 1985
A(MP)A 1976	Agriculture (Miscellaneous Provisions) Act 1976
ATA 1995	Agricultural Tenancies Act 1995
AU 1662	Act of Uniformity 1662
BNA 1981	British Nationality Act 1981
BSA 1986	Building Societies Act 1986
CA 1881	Conveyancing Act 1881
CA 1960	Charities Act 1960
CA 1985	Companies Act 1985
CA 1992	Charities Act 1992
CA 1993	Charities Act 1993
CCA 1949	Consular Conventions Act 1949
CCA 1984	County Courts Act 1984
CDPA 1988	Copyright, Designs and Patents Act 1988
CEA 1968	Civil Evidence Act 1968
CEA 1995	Civil Evidence Act 1965
ChA 1989	Children Act 1989
CJA 1948	Criminal Justice Act 1948
CLA 1967	Criminal Law Act 1967
CLSA 1990	Courts and Legal Services Act 1990
CT(V)A 1954	Charitable Trusts (Validation) Act 1954
DMPA 1973	Domicile and Matrimonial Proceedings Act 1973
DVMPA 1976	Domestic Violence and Matrimonial Proceedings Act 1976
EA 1938	Evidence Act 1938
EPAA 1985	Enduring Powers of Attorney Act 1985
ERA 1996	Employment Rights Act 1996
FA 1870	Forfeiture Act 1870
FA 1965	Finance Act 1965
FA 1969	Finance Act 1969
FA 1975	Finance Act 1975
FA 1976	Finance Act 1976
FA 1980	Finance Act 1980
FA 1982	Finance Act 1982
FA 1985	Finance Act 1985
FA 1986	Finance Act 1986
FA 1988	Finance Act 1988
FA 1989	Finance Act 1989
FA 1994	Finance Act 1994
FA 1995	Finance Act 1995
FA 1996	Finance Act 1996
FA 1999	Finance Act 1999
FAA 1976	Fatal Accidents Act 1976
FoA 1982	Forfeiture Act 1982
FLA 1996	Family Law Act 1996

Table of Abbreviations

Volume 2 – Cumulative Table of Statutes

References in this Table to *Statutes* are to Halsbury's Statutes of England (Fourth Edition) showing the volume and page where the Act will be found.

[Entries up to and including (prefix) 105 are to volume 1. Entries from (prefix) 200 onward are to volume 2.]

References printed in **bold** type indicate where an Act is set out in part or in full.

Table of Statutes

Volume 2 – Cumulative Table of Cases

[Entries up to and including (prefix) 105 are to volume 1. Entries from (prefix) 200 onward are to volume 2.]

A

B

Table of Cases

Table of Cases

Table of Cases

PARA

PARA

PARA

Table of Cases

H

Table of Cases

PARA

M

Table of Cases

PARA

PARA

PARA

Table of Cases

Table of Cases

PARA

VOLUME 2

Precedents and statutes

Introductory note

Introductory note

I. GENERAL

[200.1]
The purpose of this note is to mention some of the practical matters that ought to be borne in mind when taking instructions for, preparing and executing wills and codicils. Most of these matters are fully considered in the text as well as in notes to the individual precedents and it is not proposed to touch on any of them more than briefly here. Nor is it claimed that the matters mentioned below constitute an exhaustive list but only that they are some of the matters more commonly encountered.

(a)   Capacity and freedom from influence

[200.2]
A person's capacity to dispose of his property by will is affected by a number of factors. Most obviously the would-be testator will need to be of full age (now 18 except in the case of privileged wills) and of a sound disposing mind. If instructions for a will are taken in circumstances where an attack on the testator's mental capacity is anticipated, it is a wise precaution for the will to be witnessed if at all possible by the testator's medical attendant and his solicitor and for these witnesses to make statements as to the testator's capacity: see Templeman J's remarks in *Kenward v Adams* [1975] CLY 3591; *Re Simpson* (1977) 121 Sol Jo 224; and see *Buckenham v Dickinson* [1997] CLY 4733. A solicitor may now witness a will appointing him an executor without forfeiting his right to the benefit of a charging clause: Trustee Act 2000 (TrA 2000), ss 28(4)(a) and 35(1) (Part G, paras **[246.143]** and **[246.150]**; see also the commentary at para **[221.42]** et seq).

[200.3]
Even if the testator's mental capacity is not in doubt, it is important to make sure that the testator fully and freely intends the dispositions proposed. The testator

should be seen on his or her own or, if that is not possible, in the absence of interested parties, and the instructions and attendance notes should be retained, especially where the testator is elderly or infirm, and even more so where the solicitor preparing the will has never acted for the testator before and has been instructed through someone who is a potential beneficiary under the will.

[200.4]
In any subsequent dispute the testator's solicitor may be called upon to give a statement to any interested party: see (1959) 56 Law Society's Gazette 619, and *Re Moss, Larke v Nugus* [2000] WTLR 1033 (also reported sub nom *Larke v Nugus* in (1979) 123 Sol Jo 337), CA. If a solicitor, or indeed any other person, preparing a will takes any substantial interest under it he must see that the testator obtains independent advice (see *Re a Solicitor* [1975] QB 475, [1974] 3 All ER 853; *Tristram and Coote's Probate Practice* (28th edn), para 33.50; and the Law Society's 'The Guide to the Professional Conduct of Solicitors' (8th edn, 1999), para 24.02, n 6).

[200.5]
The Law Society's 'The Guide to the Professional Conduct of Solicitors' (8th edn), para 24.02, has some further guidance in the commentary which should be noted. It states that if the client declines to take independent advice, the solicitor must refuse to act in drawing the will, that it is not sufficient just to have the will witnessed by an independent solicitor, and that the same rules apply to gifts to an employee of a solicitor. It also states that, where the client wishes to leave all or a substantial part of his or her estate to a solicitor to be dealt with in accordance with the testator's wishes as communicated to the solicitor either orally or in a document, or as a secret trust, independent advice is not needed if the solicitor will not benefit personally or financially, but that the solicitor should preserve the instructions (which is a sensible thing to do in relation to any will) and should make sure that the testator signs or initials a statement in writing of 'such secret trust'. It is not entirely clear from this statement whether independent advice is thought by the Law Society to be unnecessary where the solicitor will as a matter of strict law be entitled beneficially to property of the testator but intends in fact to distribute that property to others in accordance with a non-binding request of the testator, and we therefore recommend that independent advice is insisted on where it is proposed that this will be the case. An alternative, which would clearly not require independent advice, would be for the will to create a discretionary trust (under which the solicitor is not a beneficiary), combined with a non-binding memorandum of wishes. For secret trusts see Vol 1, paras **[36.1]–[36.13]** and for provision by will for discretionary distribution of chattels see the Preliminary Note on personal chattels in B4 at para **[204.7]**.

[200.6]
It often happens that a solicitor receives instructions to draft wills for husband and wife, which include an instruction that the wife's will is to contain a gift of all or nearly all her property to the husband if he survives her, but the instructions are communicated wholly by the husband. There is nothing especially suspect or unusual about this, but we do feel that a solicitor should in these circumstances make sure from direct contact with the wife that these really are her instructions.

[200.7]

A foreign domicile (or foreign matrimonial domicile) may affect a would-be testator's power to dispose by will of movables or even of English immovable property: *Re De Nicols, De Nicols v Curlier* [1900] 2 Ch 410. A wife's domicile will almost always be the same as her husband's, but as a result of the enactment of the Domicile and Matrimonial Proceedings Act 1973 this can no longer be taken for granted.

[200.8]

Other restrictions may be dictated by the nature of the testator's assets or of his interest in them (see generally Vol 1, paras **[7.1]–[7.32]**). The testator may own foreign property which is not freely alienable under the *lex situs*. He may be entitled to an interest in realty as a beneficial joint tenant in which case he will be unable to dispose of it by will unless he has first severed the joint tenancy (eg by notice) during his lifetime. He may be entitled to a capital sum under a pension scheme over which he has a power of nomination which must be exercised in accordance with the rules of the scheme or in respect of which his power of disposition may be restricted. He may have a limited interest in settled property or have a power of appointment limited to a particular class. In all cases the extent of the testator's property and his power of disposition over it must be carefully considered if possible by reference to the relevant documents.

(b)   Form of will

[200.9]

The will is a flexible instrument capable of accommodating the universal beneficiary at the one extreme and the large discretionary class at the other. Many considerations (some of which have been referred to above) will dictate the form of the will. The extent and nature of the testator's property (and liabilities) and the circumstances and needs of the members of his family or dependants will loom large. Unless a testator has a substantial estate he should be discouraged from making elaborate provision in his will which may make the administration of the estate difficult and expensive. A number of the more common forms of testamentary provision are briefly considered below together with some of the difficulties that may arise in connection with them.

[200.10]

Pecuniary legacies. These are frequently given as a token of friendship or for some charitable purpose which the testator has supported in his lifetime. There is a danger, however, that a testator's generosity in giving legacies may seriously prejudice the interests of the persons interested in residue who will ordinarily either be relatives or dependants. This danger may be aggravated by the fact that the testator's circumstances may deteriorate between the date of his will and the date of his death and by the fact that he may not fully appreciate either the extent of his existing liabilities or the effect or the incidence of inheritance tax. Where the estate is relatively small or the aggregate amount of the legacies relatively large, provision ought to be made for ensuring that residue does not fall below a certain value. See, eg Form B10.54 at para **[210.75]**.

[200.11]

Life interests. Life interests in residue or a settled fund are frequently employed as a means of giving income security to a surviving spouse or other relative. One of the difficulties that they pose is that it is not easy to predict what the amount of income is likely to be especially in the case of a life interest in residue. Further the amount of income may fluctuate with changing economic circumstances. One way of protecting the life tenant from a reduction in income is to empower the trustees to resort to capital for the benefit of the life tenant. It should be remembered, however, that such a power may be framed or exercised in such a way as to render capital paid over to the life tenant income in his or her hands and taxable accordingly. For suitable precedents see Forms B18.7 and B18.8 at paras **[218.37]** and **[218.38]** and the notes thereto, and Form C2.3 at paras **[224.51]–[224.65]** and for inheritance tax on settled property subject to a life interest see para **[200.85]** et seq.

[200.12]

Annuities. These have in the past been employed to make income provision for relatives or other dependants. In times of high inflation annuities will often fail to achieve their purpose, and the grant of an annuity to be charged on property may create inheritance tax problems which are avoidable if the annuity is provided for in some other way. Income tax considerations also arise. Is the annuity to be paid 'free of tax' and, if so, free of tax at the basic rate or at some higher rate? And what is to become of any tax repayments to which the annuitant may become entitled? These matters are best dealt with by express provision, as in the alternatives in Form B11.3 (at para **[211.10]**).

[200.13]

Specific gifts. Specific gifts of property, though frequently resorted to, are liable to ademption by a subsequent sale or other disposition during the testator's lifetime. This may not matter much where the gift is of some small personal item but where, for example, a specific gift of the testator's residence is adeemed, the testator's calculations (as well as the beneficiary's expectations) may be seriously upset. The testator may wish to include an express provision against such an event and Form B6.16 (at para **[206.25]**) may be used or adapted for this purpose. A testator should be informed that where property is specifically given the donee is liable to discharge any incumbrances, unless express provision is made to the contrary (AEA 1925, s 35: Part G, **[246.47]**). This is a particularly important point where a specific gift of a house which is subject to a mortgage is contemplated. The testator should also be informed that all foreign property prima facie bears its own inheritance tax, though this is now no longer true of UK real property, and has never been true of UK personalty (see the notes on incidence at paras **[214.55]–[214.71]**). He may wish to vary the incidence of inheritance tax on specific gifts: see eg Forms B6.30 and B6.31 (at paras **[206.39]** and **[206.40]**) and B14.31 and B.14.32 (at paras **[214.53]** and **[214.54]**).

[200.14]

Personal chattels. For obvious reasons these should not save in special cases be settled. A frequent device is to make an outright gift of such chattels coupled with a non-binding expression of desire as to their distribution. See the Note in B4 (at paras **[204.7]** and **[204.8]**) and Forms B4.6 to B4.11 (at paras **[204.20]**–**[204.25]**).

[200.15]
Business and partnership interests. These call for special care. If it is intended that the business should continue to be run by the beneficiary or the trustees suitable powers must be conferred and sufficient working capital made available. The incidence of inheritance tax and the interaction of business property relief and the spouse exemption, must also be considered. See the Preliminary Note to B5 at paras **[205.1]**–**[205.57]** and the Forms in B5 at paras **[205.58]**–**[205.79]**. See also C11 at para **[233.1]** et seq.

[200.16]
Rights of residence. Testators are often as much concerned to provide their dependants with a roof over their heads as to provide income. The use of a strict settlement coupled with a supporting rentcharge is no longer an option: see para **[200.52]**. But it can be effected in a number of other ways, and the Trusts of Land and Appointment of Trustees Act 1996 (TLATA 1996) has simplified the task. For alternative forms for the various options now available and a discussion of their respective merits, see the forms in B8 and the Preliminary Note to it at para **[208.1]** et seq. See also the notes on the TLATA 1996 at para **[200.48]** et seq.

[200.17]
'Commorientes' provisions. Particular care should be taken to ensure that spouses, or other couples making wills where each makes a will which leaves property to the other if the other survives, do not so dispose of their respective estates as to create additional and avoidable liabilities to inheritance tax t in the event of their dying simultaneously or within a short period of each other. Where the order of deaths is known, a survivorship condition (sometimes inaccurately called a 'commorientes clause'), ie a condition that the benefit given by will to the other is conditional on the other surviving the first to die by a specified period, will usually save inheritance tax. Where the order of deaths is not known, there is a greater inheritance tax advantage in there being no survivorship condition. See B19 at para **[219.1]** et seq and C2 at paras **[224.2]**–**[224.6]**. In cases where there are no issue or dependants, imposing a survivorship condition can also avoid the joint estate going entirely to the kin of the survivor, a consequence which neither testator may have envisaged. Even where there is a survivorship condition, this can happen if the second to die survives the relevant period, and it is much better for the dispositions in both wills to be so structured that this does not happen irrespective of the period by which one survives the other: see paras **[219.2]**, **[219.3]** and **[231.2]**.

[200.18]
Discretionary trusts. Once very popular on account of its inherent estate duty advantages, the discretionary trust lost most of its former appeal with the introduction of capital transfer tax (now inheritance tax) by the Finance Act 1975. This Act introduced a system of charging discretionary trusts to tax which was widely considered to be very unfavourable. But the law has since been

modified, and as now contained in the Inheritance Tax Act 1984 (ITA 1984), Part III, Ch III, has caused discretionary trusts to regain some of their popularity. See further the Note on discretionary trusts in B18 at para **[218.1]** et seq, where the circumstances in which a discretionary trust can be advantageous are considered. Some possible uses of discretionary trusts are also mentioned in B4 (at paras **[204.7]** and **[204.8]**) and in the note to Form C3.6 (at para **[225.83]** et seq).

[200.19]
Accumulation and maintenance trusts. These are trusts for persons under 25 which, if they fulfil certain conditions, attract the important inheritance tax advantages contained in the ITA 1984, s 71. Where any beneficiary under a will may still be a minor when the testator dies, consideration should be given as to whether the trusts for the beneficiary should be so structured as to satisfy s 71. See further, paras **[200.119]**–**[200.135]**. For examples of accumulation and maintenance trusts, see eg Forms C8.3 and C8.4 at paras **[230.30]** and **[230.45]**.

[200.20]
Protective trusts. If a testator is making a will for the benefit of anyone who might become insolvent, it will be a good idea to provide either a protective trust, where the beneficiary has a life interest until he goes bankrupt (or tries to dispose of the interest) to be followed after any such forfeiture by a discretionary trust for him and his family, or a fully discretionary trust from the outset. For appropriate clauses see Forms B16.1 and B16.2 at paras **[216.6]** and **[216.7]** (protective trusts), Form B18.1 at para **[218.31]** (discretionary trusts); and for relevant complete forms, see Forms C3.5 at para **[225.68]** et seq and C6.2 at para **[228.19]** et seq. For the statutory protective trusts, see the Trustee Act 1925 (TA 1925), s 33 (Part G, para **[246.28]**). For the inheritance tax treatment of protective trusts, see para **[200.116]**.

[200.21]
Additions to existing settlements and referential trusts. It is not uncommon for a testator to wish to transfer property by will to the trustees of an existing settlement rather than settle it on trusts declared by the will itself. It should be noted, however, that the addition of funds to a discretionary settlement made by the testator may be disadvantageous for inheritance tax purposes, particularly if the settlement was made before 27 March 1974; for the rather complex inheritance tax provisions relating to the addition of property to an existing discretionary settlement see *Foster's Inheritance Tax*, E4.15, E4.33. If the testator wishes to transfer property by his will to an existing settlement, the draftsman will need to take care to use appropriate language, eg 'I give my residuary estate to the trustees at my death of the settlement made by me on the — to hold on the trusts thereof and as an accretion to the trust fund therein defined for all purposes'. By contrast a gift of property 'on the like trusts as' or 'on similar trusts to' those contained in an existing settlement will not amount to a gift of property to the trustees of that settlement but a declaration of trusts of that property by reference to it, a rather inconvenient result as the trustees of the will will end up holding property on trusts contained not in the will but in another instrument. For examples of gifts of these kinds see Forms B6.22 (at para **[206.31]**), B6.23 (at para **[206.32]**) and B10.31 (at para **[210.45]**) respectively and the notes to those forms.

[200.22]
Precatory words. Testators often wish to make an absolute gift subject to a request, which is not intended to be legally binding, that the donee will use the gift to benefit others. It is important where this is being done to make the intention clear, because words of recommendation, confidence, request or desire have been construed as creating a legally-enforceable trust: see, eg *Comiskey v Bowring-Hanbury* [1905] AC 84, HL (and contrast *Re Williams, Williams v Williams* [1897] 2 Ch 12, CA). The only safe course is to negate any obligation by clear words such as 'I request, without imposing any trust or obligation'. The most common use of precatory words is in gifts of chattels: see, eg Form B4.9 at para **[204.23]**. For the law on whether words of request etc create a trust, see Vol 1, paras **[82.5]–[82.6]**, and Underhill & Hayton, *Law Relating to Trusts and Trustees* (15th edn), pp 111–116. Expressions of wishes may also influence how various provisions of the TLATA 1996 are to operate: see paras **[200.56]**, **[200.62]**, **[208.18]**, sub-para (6) and **[220.57]**.

[200.23]
Ademption, lapse and incidence of inheritance tax and other liabilities. Any one of these may defeat either wholly or partly a testator's intentions. Ademption, mentioned at para **[200.13]**, is fully considered in Vol 1 at para **[41.1]** et seq and for a precedent for its exclusion see Form B6.16 at para **[206.25]**. The effect of the incidence of inheritance tax and other liabilities has also been referred to at paras **[200.13]**, **[200.15]** and **[200.16]** and is further considered in the Preliminary Note to Form B14 at paras **[214.55]–[214.71]**. Lapse, which has not so far been mentioned, like ademption, often presents a trap for the unwary testator, for if the donee predeceases him then unless the donee is also a child or issue of the testator and leaves issue surviving the testator, the gift fails and there is no substitution of the donee's issue. If the donee is the testator's spouse the gift may fail as a result of a subsequent divorce (see para **[200.24]**; see also Vol 1, paras **[47.2]–[47.3]** and the Preliminary Note to Form C2 at para **[224.1]** et seq). If the testator's attention is drawn to these possibilities he may wish to make alternative or substitutional gifts so as to avoid them. These matters are more fully discussed in Vol 1 at para **[68.1]** et seq, and for relevant precedents see Forms B6.27 (at para **[206.36]**), B19.5 and B19.6 (at paras **[219.18]** and **[219.19]**) and B19.9 to B19.15 (at paras **[219.22]–[219.28]**).

[200.24]
Wills in favour of spouses. Where, as is commonly the case, a husband and wife have made at the same time wills in favour of each other and in the same terms mutatis mutandis, the question whether they intended the wills to be mutual wills (see Vol 1, paras **[2.1]–[2.10]**) sometimes arises, often years later after one of them has died. Where instructions are being taken for wills to be made at the same time by a husband and wife we recommend that they are asked whether they intend the wills to be mutual wills, and, whether they intend mutual wills or intend otherwise, that a declaration as to whichever is intended be included in both wills. It is particularly important to do this where there is any indication that there are circumstances of a sort which can give rise to succession disputes, eg the children being treated unequally, or the marriage being a second marriage for one or both parties and there being issue by a

previous marriage. For mutual wills see Form B1.6 at para **[201.10]** and for a declaration making it clear that wills are not mutual, see Form B1.7 at para **[201.11]**.

[200.25]
By virtue of the Wills Act 1837, s 18A, added by the Administration of Justice Act 1982, s 18(2) (see Part G, para **[244.18]** for the text of s 18A as currently in force; see also Vol 1, paras **[47.2]**–**[47.3]** and C2 at para **[224.1]** et seq for a commentary on it) a gift by will to the testator's spouse will lapse if the marriage has ended in divorce after the will was made (unless the will shows a contrary intention). For deaths on or after 1 January 1996, the amendments made to s 18A by the Law Reform (Succession) Act 1995, s 3 achieve this by deeming the spouse to have died on the date of the decree of divorce for the purposes of the devolution of property which the spouse was given (or was given an interest in). This means that an alternative gift to the spouse's gift which is expressed to take effect in the event of the spouse predeceasing the testator will take effect if there has been a divorce and the spouse survives the testator. In relation to deaths before 1 January 1996 such an alternative gift did not take effect in these circumstances (*Re Sinclair, Lloyds Bank plc v Imperial Cancer Research Fund* [1985] Ch 446, [1985] 1 All ER 1066, CA; see also Vol 1, para **[47.3]**)— although s 18A(3) made express provision for acceleration of remainders on a life interest given to the spouse (an effect now achieved by the deeming of the spouse to have died). Accordingly, it is no longer necessary to make express provision for the possibility of divorce in such gifts (or in an alternative appointment of an executor to one in favour of the testator's spouse): for a more detailed discussion see the Preliminary Note to C2 at para **[224.1]** et seq.

[200.26]
A special factor affecting the provision which a testator should make by will for his spouse is the exemption from inheritance tax for gifts to spouses, for which see further paras **[200.99]**–**[200.101]** and the problems which can arise for trying to make use of the inheritance tax nil rate band of the testator if he predeceases his spouse. For examples of the possible forms which the wills of married couples may take see C2 and C3 at paras **[224.1]** et seq and **[225.1]** et seq.

(c)   Other points

[200.27]
The age of majority. As from 1 January 1970, this was reduced from 21 to 18 by the Family Law Reform Act 1969 (FLRA 1969), s 1 (Part G, para **[246.74]**; see also Vol 1, para **[4.7]**). Testators had in the past very frequently adopted 21 as the age contingency which a beneficiary has to satisfy in order to attain a vested interest. No doubt some testators have begun to adopt 18 instead, but many will probably stick to 21. In most of the precedents which follow in which an age contingency is specified, 18 and 21 are inserted in the alternative. If a testator wishes to enable a minor to be able to give a good receipt then Form B10.19 (at para **[210.32]**), Form B21.18 (at para **[221.22]**) or Form C2.1, cl 8(3) (at para **[224.29]**) may be employed. It should be noted that the ChA 1989, s 3(3) (Part G, para **[244.119]**) provides that a parent or guardian of a minor with

'parental responsibility' for him or her (see Vol 1, para **[28.2]** for the meaning of this term) has the right to receive or recover for the benefit of the minor any property which the minor is entitled to receive or recover. This seems to mean that a trustee or personal representative can always accept a receipt from a parent or guardian with parental responsibility for a minor in respect of income or capital to which that minor is entitled. See also Vol 1, para **[9.42]**.

[200.28]
Children, issue and other words descriptive of relationship. The rules of construction relating to references in wills and other instruments to children and issue and to any other terms used to denote a blood relationship have undergone major reform in recent years. For the development of the new statutory rules and the application of the former rules to existing instruments, reference should be made to Vol 1 (at paras **[72.1]**, **[74.1]** and **[75.1]** et seq) and the statutes printed in Part G2 (at para **[245.1]** et seq) and the notes thereto. The current position as regards the devolution of property on death, under a will made now, may be summarised as follows:

(a) *Adoption.* The governing statute is the Adoption Act 1976 (the relevant provisions of which are printed at paras **[245.56]**–**[245.68]** and discussed in Vol 1 at paras **[75.1]**–**[75.7]** which provides that a child adopted under the Adoption Act 1976 or by any adoption recognised as valid by English law is to be treated for the purposes of the devolution of property, whether under a will or on an intestacy, as the legitimate child of his adoptive parent or parents. Effectively therefore any disability previously attaching to adopted status is removed. The one exception relates to property settled to devolve with a dignity or title of honour.

(b) *Legitimation.* The rights of persons who are legitimated by the subsequent marriage of their parents are governed by the Legitimacy Act 1976 (Part G, paras **[245.44]**–**[245.54]** and considered in Vol 1 at paras **[72.15]**–**[72.17]**) which provides that for succession purposes legitimated persons are to be treated as if born legitimate. There is a similar saving for property settled to devolve with a dignity or title of honour.

(c) *Illegitimacy.* The position is now governed by the Family Law Reform Act 1987 (FLRA 1987) (Part G, paras **[245.70]**–**[245.81]** and considered in Vol 1 at para **[72.14]**) which again effectively removes any disability to which persons who were either illegitimate or were claiming through illegitimate persons have in the past been subject, and in particular they are treated in the same way as legitimate children of the same parent when it comes to determining who is to benefit under a gift to, eg 'my children' or 'my nephews and nieces', unless a contrary intention is expressed. Again there is a saving for property settled to devolve with a dignity or title of honour. The FLRA 1987 replaces the FLRA 1969 and is wider in some respects than it (see para **[245.69]** for a summary of the main differences), although in the majority of cases where the meaning of a gift in a will is in issue the FLRA 1987 will have no different effect from that which the FLRA 1969 would have had.

(d) *Artificial insemination and in vitro fertilisation.* Recent medical developments have resulted in the enactment of special rules concerning the rights of succession of persons born in consequence of artificial insemination or other techniques designed to overcome infertility. These are now to be found in the Human Fertilisation and Embryology Act 1990 (Part G, paras **[245.83]–[245.91]** and considered in Vol 1 at paras **[74.5]–[74.7]**). Where a woman carries a child as a result of the use of any of these techniques, the child is treated as her child in law and no other woman's; her husband (or in certain cases her partner) will be treated as the father unless it is shown that he did not consent to the use of artificial insemination or other technique. If the man and woman are married, the child will seemingly be treated as their legitimate offspring. For the purposes of succession to property it is provided that any enactment, deed, instrument or other document (whenever made) is to be construed in accordance with the rules summarised above with the consequence that a child born as a result of one of the techniques in question will be eligible under a will or on an intestacy as if he were the legitimate or (as the case may be) the illegitimate child of his 'parent' or 'parents'. Again there is a saving for property settled to devolve with a dignity or title of honour.

[200.29]
The present position is thus that for all practical purposes children who are adopted, legitimated or illegitimate, and children who are born to 'parents' as a consequence of the medical techniques just mentioned, are treated for succession purposes on an equal footing with legitimate children. In the case of testamentary succession this is subject to any contrary intention being expressed in the particular will. The earlier law on the rights of adopted, legitimated or illegitimate children (Part G, para **[245.1]** et seq) remains relevant to the administration of estates or will trusts where the testator died or, in cases involving succession by illegitimate persons, made his will before the law on one or more of the above topics was changed, and to making an appointment under a special power of appointment where the power was created by a will or other instrument to which the earlier law applied (see B13 at para **[213.1]** et seq). Where illegitimate persons are involved, the earlier law remains relevant (irrespective of the date of death of the testator) to wills made before the FLRA 1987 came into force on 4 April 1988 (see FLRA 1987, s 19(7): Part G, para **[245.72]**), and, more importantly, to wills made before its predecessor the FLRA 1969 came into force on 1 January 1970 (see FLRA 1969, s 15(8): Part G, para **[245.39]**). It should be noted that a codicil which confirms a will made before one or both of these Family Law Reform Acts came into force does not by the fact of doing so cause the will to be treated as made after that or those Acts came into force (see the Preliminary Note to Part D at para **[237.6]**). By contrast, the rules in the Human Fertilisation and Embryology Act 1990 referred to at para **[200.28]**, sub-para (d) apply to any instrument, whenever made, and this includes all wills irrespective of their date or the date of death of the testator.

[200.30]
Drafting wills using words descriptive of relationship. The statutory rules just mentioned, so far as they relate to adopted or legitimated children, or ones born

as a result of the use of the medical techniques referred to above, will normally reflect what the testator would have wished anyway. This will not always be the case for the statutory rules relating to illegitimate children. The draftsman will need to bear in mind the new statutory rules, particularly those relating to the rights of illegitimate children, when taking instructions for a will. A married man with legitimate children may possibly have one or more illegitimate children as well, and not intend them to benefit to the same extent as his legitimate children, or at all. However, a gift to 'my children' without more will include the illegitimate children. Since it is now conclusively established that a solicitor taking instructions for a will owes a duty of care to take all usual steps to ensure that persons intended to benefit do in fact benefit and can be liable in damages to a disappointed beneficiary if he fails to discharge that duty (see *White v Jones* [1995] 2 AC 207, [1995] 1 All ER 691, HL; see also para **[200.46]**), the draftsman cannot leave the matter to chance. One way of dealing with the problem is to identify the children in the will by name, but this may not be convenient if the client is capable of having further children. Another possible course is to limit the gift to the children of the marriage. But the safest course (though not a very appealing one) is to enquire specifically of the client whether he has any illegitimate children and if he has (or may have) whether he wishes to exclude them, and, if he has and does, to exclude them expressly or exclude the Family Law Reform Acts from applying. For the latter purpose, we recommend the use of words such as 'Words descriptive of relationship shall be construed in all respects as if the Family Law Reform Act 1969, s 15 and the Family Law Reform Act 1987 had not been enacted'. A reference to the FLRA 1969 should be retained; since the FLRA 1987 repeals the FLRA 1969, s 15, such a provision which referred to the FLRA 1987 alone could be construed as a direction that the gift should be read as subject to the FLRA 1969.

[200.31]
Another point to remember is that where a testator leaves his estate to 'my children' without more, his executors will no longer be protected if they distribute to his legitimate children if unknown to them he happens to leave an illegitimate child: see the FLRA 1987, s 20 (Part G, para **[245.73]**) repealing the FLRA 1969, s 17 (Part G, para **[245.41]**). In such a case the executors are protected if they have advertised for claims pursuant to the TA 1925, s 27 (Part G, para **[246.23]**) and distributed the estate before becoming aware of the existence of the illegitimate child (*Re Aldhous* [1955] 2 All ER 80, [1955] 1 WLR 459).

[200.32]
Non-beneficial provisions and illegitimacy. As noted in Part G (at para **[245.69]**), there are few practical differences relevant to will drafting between the effect of the FLRA 1987, ss 1 and 19 (Part G, paras **[245.70]** and **[245.72]**) and the effect of its predecessor the FLRA 1969, s 15 (Part G, para **[245.39]**). However, one is that the FLRA 1969 only applied to provisions that were for the benefit of a person who was illegitimate or claimed through someone who was illegitimate (FLRA 1969, s 15(2)) while the FLRA 1987 is not so restricted. This means that the FLRA 1987 should be excluded in relation to a reference to the descendants of a named monarch when defining a royal lives perpetuity period, and that if there is a condition imposed on a gift such as 'if X shall predecease

me leaving issue' where no benefit is conferred on the issue of X, the reference to issue will now include illegitimate issue where it would not have done under the FLRA 1969.

[200.33]
Nephews, nieces and cousins. As mentioned at paras **[200.28]** and **[200.29]**, references to nephews, nieces and cousins and other classes of relative are now also construed in accordance with the statutory rules referred to above. References to relatives such as nephews, nieces or cousins may give rise to particular difficulty where relatives of the half-blood or spouses of relatives are or may be involved. (See generally Vol 1, para **[71.1]** et seq). It is advisable to take detailed instructions about such relatives, especially where a gift to a class rather than an individual is contemplated. Where possible, it is safer to refer to such relatives by name.

[200.34]
Family provision. Testators who anticipate that unwelcome claims may be made on their deaths under the Inheritance (Provision for Family and Dependants) Act 1975 (I(PFD)A 1975) (Part G, para **[247.2]** et seq; see also Vol 1, para **[105.1]** et seq) may seek to guard against the risk by inserting in their wills some form of declaration setting out the reasons for not making any or only limited provision for the potential claimant; for examples of such declarations see Form B2.15 at para **[202.40]**. The utility of such declarations is fairly limited, though they may be useful as a record of any special factors militating against the making of an award which might otherwise be overlooked. Perhaps a more effective way of deterring a possible claimant is for the testator to face up to the likelihood of a claim and make some provision for the potential claimant—potential claimants whom testators do not wish to provide for are usually former or separated wives, or in some cases children—but at the lower end of the scale in the hope that she will take what is offered rather than running the risk of making a claim and failing to establish that the will does not make reasonable provision for her. If the provision exceeds the capital limits for public funding for the claimant's claim that can also help to avert a claim. Special considerations apply in the case of a potential claimant under the I(PFD)A 1975, s 1(1)(e) (Part G, para **[247.2]**) as such claimant must show that he or she was being maintained by the deceased immediately before his death. If the testator wishes to ensure that such a person will be unable to claim he could do so, at least in theory, by ceasing to maintain such person.

[200.35]
Gifts to 'surviving' relatives. The words 'survive' and 'surviving' should be used with great care and deliberation as they, perhaps more than any other, frequently give rise to difficulty by limiting a gift in a way which is unexpected and which the testator would not have intended. The words 'survive' and 'surviving' in their natural meaning require that the person who is to survive must be living at the time of the event which he is to survive. Thus a gift to 'such of my grandchildren as survive me and attain 25' is prima facie confined to grandchildren living at the testator's death. There is a benevolent rule of construction which will let in a grandchild who is en ventre sa mère at the date of the testator's death (see *Villar v Gilbey* [1907] AC 139, HL, as explained in

Elliot v Joicey [1935] AC 209, HL), but otherwise after-born grandchildren will not be admitted to the class even though none of the grandchildren has attained 25 at the date of the testator's death. This may of course be what the testator intends, but frequently it is either contrary to his wishes or would be if his attention were drawn to the point. Again the word 'surviving' when used in a gift over in favour of a class may give rise to constructional problems if the time at which the surviving members of the class are to be ascertained is not clearly stated in the will. For a more detailed review of the relevant rules of construction see Vol 1, paras **[67.1]–[67.8]** and **[73.1]–[73.2]**.

[200.36]
Rules of apportionment. The rules of apportionment laid down by the Apportionment Act 1870, and the rules of apportionment between capital and income known as the rules in *Howe v Earl of Dartmouth* (1802) 7 Ves 137, *Re Earl of Chesterfield's Trust* (1883) 24 Ch D 643 and *Allhusen v Whittell* (1867) LR 4 Eq 295 are widely regarded as an administrative inconvenience, especially in the case of smaller estates, and are frequently excluded. For a more detailed discussion of these rules see B14 at paras **[214.35]–[214.38]**, **[214.43]** and **[214.44]** and for suitable precedents, see Forms B14.1 to B14.3 at paras **[214.10]–[214.12]**, B14.10 at para **[214.19]**, B14.24 to B14.27 at paras **[214.39]–[214.42]** and B14.28 to B14.30 at paras **[214.45]–[214.47]**.

[200.37]
'Free of tax'. 'Free of tax' in relation to annuities refers to income tax. It must not be confused with 'free of inheritance tax', which is a direction concerning the incidence of the inheritance tax on the testator's death (see further para **[214.55]** et seq). 'Free of duty' and 'free of capital transfer tax' are phrases that can still be used (ITA 1984, Sch 6, para 1 and Finance Act 1986 (FA 1986), s 100(1)(b)), but 'free of inheritance tax' is preferable.

[200.38]
Meanings given by statute. The Law of Property Act 1925 (LPA 1925), s 61 (Part G, para **[246.40]**) applies to wills, so that, in the absence of the context otherwise requiring, 'month' means calendar month, 'person' includes a corporation, the singular includes the plural and vice versa, and the masculine includes the feminine *and vice versa* (emphasis supplied). Thus a will need make no express provision for any of these matters. The statutory definitions in the Interpretation Act 1978 (IA 1978) do not apply to wills or other written instruments, but there is one provision of that Act which does apply to them, this is the IA 1978, s 23(3) (Part G, para **[246.81]**). The drafting of this provision by reference to the IA 1978, s 17(2)(a) (Part G, para **[246.80]**) is somewhat opaque, but the effect seems to be that if a will or other written instrument refers to a legislative provision, and that legislative provision is repealed and re-enacted (with or without modification), the reference in the will or other instrument to the original provision will operate as a reference to its re-enactment.

[200.39]
Capital gains tax. The death of a person does not constitute a chargeable disposal of all his assets for capital gains tax purposes, but it is an occasion on

which his assets are revalued without a tax charge: see the Taxation of Chargeable Gains Act 1992 (TCGA 1992), s 62(1). No special provision need therefore be made for the incidence of such tax. Where property is given to a minor contingently on attaining a specified age a charge will arise on the beneficiary's satisfying such contingency under the TCGA, 1992, s 71, on the ground that he then becomes absolutely entitled to the property as against the trustees: *Tomlinson (Inspector of Taxes) v Glyns Executor and Trustee Co* [1970] Ch 112, [1969] 1 All ER 700. Hold-over relief will be available only if business or agricultural assets are involved (TCGA 1992, s 165), or where it is an inheritance tax chargeable transfer which is not potentially exempt (TCGA 1992, s 260(1) and (2)(a)), or where it is the coming to an end of an accumulation and maintenance trust within the ITA 1984, s 71 (TCGA 1992, s 260(1) and (2)(d)). (For a fuller account of accumulation and maintenance trusts, see paras **[200.119]–[200.129]**.) It will be a chargeable transfer entitled to hold-over relief where it is an occasion of charge under the ITA 1984, s 65 on property leaving a discretionary trust (see the Preliminary Note to B18 at paras **[218.8]–[218.10]** and **[218.27]**), even where no inheritance tax is payable because the tax threshold is not exceeded. But hold-over relief will not be available on the coming to an end of an accumulation and maintenance trust where the beneficiary has already attained an interest in possession, ie a right to be paid the current income (see paras **[200.108]–[200.111]**), before becoming entitled absolutely to the capital. The limited availability of hold-over relief where a beneficiary becomes absolutely entitled to settled property means that it is good capital gains tax planning to settle property on children for life with flexible powers to pay them capital, rather than provide for absolute vesting at a specified age, so that there is maximum flexibility as to when, if at all, they become absolutely entitled and a capital gains tax charge arises. It should also be noted that the capital gains tax rate can be lower on settled property than it is on absolutely owned property (see para **[200.40]**). For examples of wills making this type of provision see Forms C2.2 (at para **[224.35]**) and C2.6 (at para **[224.95]**).

[200.40]
Capital gains tax rates. Capital gains realised by individuals are charged to capital gains tax as if they are income, and capital gains realised by settlements are charged to capital gains tax at a flat rate, currently (in 2001–02) 34 per cent: TCGA 1992, s 4. All these tax rates are applied to the gains after deduction of annual exemption, which is more generous for individuals than for settlements. The capital gains tax rates are thus neutral as between interest in possession and other kinds of settlement (whereas before 6 April 1998 interest in possession settlements were taxed at a lower rate). Whether it will be an advantage or disadvantage, with respect to the rate at which capital gains tax is charged, to settle property by will as compared with giving it absolutely, depends on what would be the personal rates of the tax of those to whom it would be given absolutely. One factor which can favour settling property as opposed to giving it absolutely is taper relief, under which a non-business asset held for more than three years, and a business asset held for more than one year, become subject to capital gains tax on any disposal on only a percentage of the gain realised, which percentage decreases year by year, down to a lowest percentage of 60 per cent after ten years (for a non-business asset) or 25 per cent after four years (for a

business asset). Trustees of a settlement are a single and continuing body of persons for capital gains tax purposes (TCGA 1992, s 69(1)), and it is possible for them to retain accrued entitlement to taper relief in respect of an asset through successive changes in beneficial interests, whereas successive individual owners of the asset would each have had to start again and build up his or her own entitlement.

[200.41]
Income tax. Different forms of disposition have different income tax consequences. Where a beneficiary is entitled to the income of an asset or a fund of assets, or to a fixed proportion or amount of such income (whether by virtue of an absolute or limited interest), that income will be taxed as his income (see *Simon's Direct Tax Service* C4.221), although income of a deceased person's residuary estate in the course of administration is only taxed as the beneficiary's when it is distributed to him, and what remains undistributed is taxed as his when the administration is completed (see *Simon's Direct Tax Service,* C4.107–111). Income which is accumulated or which is to be distributed under the exercise of a discretion is charged to income tax at the trust rate, currently (in 2001–02) 34 per cent, but can come to be treated for income tax purposes as the income of a beneficiary after it has been distributed to him: see B18 at paras **[218.28]** and **[218.29]** and *Simon's Direct Tax Service* C4.226. Discretionary trusts, and accumulation and maintenance trusts, now have the income tax disadvantage as compared with interest in possession trusts, that if there is dividend income which is then distributed to a beneficiary the tax credit on the dividend does not carry through to the beneficiary: see para **[218.30]**.

[200.42]
A reason in favour of 'generation skipping' dispositions in wills (see para **[200.91]**) is that they may avoid the income tax disadvantage of which the following is an illustration. If a testator, T, makes a gift by will of property to an adult, A, and after T's death A makes a lifetime gift or settlement of that property in favour of A's minor children, A will be the 'settlor' for income tax purposes of that gift or settlement and the income of the property will be treated as that of A so far as it is applied for the benefit of A's children (Income and Corporation Taxes Act 1988, s 660B: see *Simon's Direct Tax Service* at C4.315 et seq). This would be so even if A made the gift or settlement by deed of variation within two years of T's death; there is no relieving provision for income tax purposes corresponding with the ITA 1984, s 142 or the TCGA 1992, s 62(6) (see F3 at para **[241.19]**). The above income tax disadvantage would be avoided if T made a gift by will directly in favour of A's children.

[200.43]
Codicils. Codicils can be useful where a small variation of a testamentary provision is to be effected, eg the increase or reduction of a legacy. Where the changes are more substantial it is advisable where time permits for a fresh will to be prepared and executed, since the combined operation of will and codicil may produce unintended effects which a fresh will would have avoided. For the law relating to codicils, see Vol 1, paras **[20.1]**–**[20.9]** and for suitable precedents see the forms in Part D at para **[237.1]** et seq.

[200.44]

Execution. The formal requirements for the due execution of an English will are set out in Vol 1 at paras **[10.1]–[12.17]**. A testator who executes a will without a solicitor being present should be informed of these requirements in detail. He should also be warned that neither a witness to a will nor the spouse of such witness can in general take a benefit under the will. Such gifts will only be saved by the Wills Act 1968 (Part G, para **[244.82]** et seq) if such attestation is superfluous. To be valid, a will does not in general have to be dated (*Corbett v Newey* [1998] Ch 57, [1996] 2 All ER 914, CA), but it is preferable and usual for a will to be dated by the testator when it is executed, and if wills are undated it may be difficult to determine which is the last will and accordingly entitled to probate. However, there is a statutory exception for an appointment by will of a guardian, which to be valid must be dated: see Vol 1, para **[28.5]** and the ChA 1989, s 5(5), (Part G, para **[244.121]**).

[200.45]

Revocation. Testators should be discouraged from retaining custody of the executed will. If a testator insists on so doing he should be warned that if the will is not forthcoming on his death it will be presumed to have been revoked. Testators should also be advised that their subsequent marriage will automatically revoke their wills unless expressed to be made in expectation of the particular marriage. See generally as to revocation Vol 1, paras **[17.1]–[19.6]** and for wills made in expectation of marriage see Forms B1.2 and B1.3 at paras **[201.6]** and **[201.7]** and Form C6.1 at para **[228.5]**. It should also be noted that where a will contains an appointment of a guardian, that appointment can be revoked by a subsequent non-testamentary instrument: see Vol 1, para **[28.6]** and the ChA 1989, ss 5(3)–(5) and 6(1) and (2) (Part G, paras **[244.121]** and **[244.122]**).

[200.46]

Mistake. The court of probate has always possessed jurisdiction to rectify wills by omitting words if it can be shown that the testator either did not know or did not approve them: see, eg *Re Morris* [1971] P 62. But until the AJA 1982, s 20 (Part G, para **[244.96]**) came into force in relation to the wills of persons dying on or after 1 January 1983, there was no jurisdiction to add words. It should be noted, however, that the statutory jurisdiction is narrower than the equitable jurisdiction to rectify deeds and other instruments in that it is available only where the will fails to carry out the testator's intentions by reason of (a) a clerical error, or (b) a failure on the part of the draftsman to understand his instructions. There is no remedy where the draftsman understands his instructions but fails to employ language in the will which is appropriate to give effect to them, although there would be a remedy if the document was a deed: *Re Butlin's Settlement Trusts* [1976] Ch 251, [1976] 2 All ER 483. For a more detailed discussion of the jurisdiction to rectify wills see Vol 1, paras **[6.1]–[6.5]**. Mistakes can have other consequences. It is now conclusively established by the House of Lords that mistakes on the part of the draftsman can give rise to liability for damages in negligence at the suit of a disappointed beneficiary: *White v Jones* [1995] 2 AC 207, [1995] 1 All ER 691 (a case of delay on the part of the solicitor and the consequent failure of the client to execute the will for which he had given instructions thereby depriving the plaintiffs of their intended legacies) and see *Gartside v Sheffield Young and Ellis* [1983] NZLR 37, NZCA (referred to in *White v Jones*) and *Hooper v Fynmores (*2001) 145 Sol Jo LB 156 (also delay cases). For other instances of negligence see *Carr-Glynn v Frearsons (a firm)* [1999] Ch 326, [1999] 4 All ER 225, CA, and *Kecskemeti v Rubens Rabin & Co* (1992) Times, 31 December, (in both of which a solicitor instructed to draft a will who failed to advise the client to sever the beneficial joint tenancy of the matrimonial home was held liable in damages to the residuary beneficiary who was thereby deprived of an undivided half-share of the proceeds of sale). See also Vol 1, para **[1.5]**.

[200.47]
Custody of wills. In view of the presumption that a will which is traced to the custody of the testator but is not forthcoming on his death is revoked clients should be discouraged from retaining possession of their own wills. It is better to leave original wills where possible with the solicitors who drew them, though it is essential to ensure that the executors and other members of the family are fully informed of their whereabouts. Alternatively there is a system, not much used, for the deposit of wills at any probate registry and this facility will be extended under provisions contained in the Administration of Justice Act 1982 when (and if) these are brought into force. See generally Vol 1, para **[10.20]**.

(d) The Trusts of Land and Appointment of Trustees Act 1996 and the Trustee Act 2000

[200.48]
The Trusts of Land and Appointment of Trustees Act 1996. The TLATA 1996 (Part G, para **[246.86]** et seq) has made fundamental changes to the law relating to land held on trust, and has also effected limited, though significant, changes to the law relating to the appointment and retirement of trustees whether of realty or personalty. These changes have important consequences for dispositions of land by will, and for the drafting of wills. Attention is drawn to such changes, where appropriate, in the notes to the forms, but, to avoid excessive repetition of the same basic points, an outline is given below. With one minor exception (s 27(3)), the TLATA 1996 extends to England and Wales only. It came into force on 1 January 1997: The Trusts of Land and Appointment of Trustees Act 1996 (Commencement) Order 1996 (SI 1996/2974).

[200.49]
If a will draftsman goes on using pre-TLATA 1996 forms it is unlikely to have serious adverse consequences in most cases (except in the rare case of trying to create an entail—see para **[200.53]**). He will, however, be wasting the opportunities provided by the TLATA 1996 to make drafting simpler, more comprehensible, and more concise, by, eg not using trusts for sale, or omitting administrative powers or provisions as to occupation by beneficiaries, which are adequately covered by the statutory provisions.

[200.50]
One of the main ideas behind the TLATA 1996 is that a trust for sale is an inappropriate conveyancing fiction to use as a basis for co-ownership of houses

for the co-owners to live in. As a result, the trust of land has features, particularly the statutory right of occupation and the power to postpone sale implied in a trust for sale, which reflect a bias in favour of land which is being retained for occupation, but which create difficulties for trusts of land to be held as an investment, or for trusts for sale of land where the trust to sell is a reality rather than a fiction, such as a testamentary trust for several beneficiaries in undivided shares (where it is necessary to sell in order to be able to distribute to the beneficiaries).

[200.51]
Trusts of land. The major change made by the TLATA 1996 is a single system of trusts of land replacing the former trusts for sale and the Settled Land Act 1925 (SLA 1925) systems, with features of both but resembling the former trusts for sale system more than the settled land one. The SLA 1925 ceases to apply to new trusts, but continues to apply to ones to which it already applied (see para **[200.52]**), while all other trusts involving land fall within the TLATA 1996's provisions, whether or not there is a trust for sale. The TLATA 1996, s 1 defines 'trust of land' and 'trustees of land', and most of the operative parts of the Act legislate for trusts of land or trustees of land, and so the definitions in s 1 are what determine which trusts the Act applies to. 'Trust of land' is defined by TLATA 1996, s 1(1)(a) as 'any trust of property which consists of or includes land', and 'trustees of land' are defined as 'trustees of a trust of land': TLATA 1996, s 1(1)(b). For this purpose a 'trust' is defined as 'any description of trust (whether express, implied, resulting or constructive), including a trust for sale and a bare trust': TLATA 1996, s 1(2)(a). It includes a trust created before the commencement of the TLATA 1996 (s 1(2)(b)), but there is an exception for land which continues to be settled land under the SLA 1925 (TLATA 1996, s 1(3)) on or after that date. The TLATA 1996 thus applies to all trusts for sale of land created before 1 January 1997, and indeed to any other trust before that date apart from one which continues to be within the SLA 1925, and all trusts involving land of any kind created on or after that date. 'Land' here has the same meaning as in the LPA 1925: see TLATA 1996, s 23(2) (Part G, para **[246.109]**) and the LPA 1925, s 205(1)(ix) for the relevant definition. It apparently includes undivided shares of land.

[200.52]
Settled land. Strict settlements have not been abolished, but no new settlements can be created under the SLA 1925 on or after 1 January 1997, the commencement date of the TLATA 1996: TLATA 1996, s 2(1) (Part G, para **[246.87]**). There is a saving for SLA 1925 settlements in existence at the commencement of the TLATA 1996, and for any settlement which derives from such a settlement in existence at that date: TLATA 1996, s 2(2). (It is not clear when a settlement 'derives' from another as this term is not defined by the TLATA 1996, but it would seem to include settlements created in exercise of powers to resettle capital.) These settlements will continue to be governed by the SLA 1925 and to that extent the assimilation of SLA 1925 settlements and trusts for sale effected by the TLATA 1996 will not be completely achieved for many years to come. A settlement to which TLATA 1996, s 2(2) applies will cease to be a settlement governed by the SLA 1925 as soon as there is no 'relevant property' subject to the settlement after the commencement of the

TLATA 1996, 'relevant property' being land and heirlooms to which the SLA 1925, s 67(1) applies: TLATA 1996, s 2(4). The trustees of a such a settlement, after all 'relevant property' has been disposed of, will have a statutory power to buy more land by virtue of the Trustee Act 2000, s 8 if they do not have an express power to do so. Any land acquired by the trustees of such a settlement after the SLA 1925 has ceased to apply will be held on a trust of land within the TLATA 1996. Section 2(4) seems to have the following consequences—

(1) If trustees of a settlement subject to the SLA 1925 held no relevant property immediately after midnight of 31 December 1996, the SLA 1925 ceases to apply to it at that point and the TLATA 1996 applies to any land subsequently acquired.

(2) If trustees of a settlement subject to the SLA 1925 held relevant property immediately after midnight of 31 December 1996, but subsequently sell all relevant property either at once or in stages, the SLA 1925 ceases to apply when the last piece of relevant property is sold.

(3) If trustees of a settlement subject to the SLA 1925 held relevant property immediately after midnight of 31 December 1996, but subsequently sell the relevant property in stages, but as they sell some relevant property they buy other such property, in such a way that at all times they hold *some* relevant property, the SLA 1925 will continue to apply, and this seems to be so even if all the relevant property held when the TLATA 1996 came into force has been disposed of.

For a more detailed examination of the machinery of the strict settlement, reference should be made to *Cheshire & Burn's Modern Law of Real Property* (16th edn, 2000), pp 188–215.

[200.53]
Entailed interests. Entailed interests have suffered the same fate as strict settlements. Entails created prior to the commencement of the TLATA 1996 are not affected, but new entails cannot be created after the commencement of the Act and any entailed interest purportedly granted thereafter will take effect as an absolute interest: TLATA 1996, s 2(6) and Sch 1, para 5 (Part G, paras **[246.87]** and **[246.114]**).

[200.54]
Trusts for sale. Trusts for sale of land, whether created before or after the commencement of the TLATA 1996, have now become trusts of land. Statutory trusts for co-owners under the LPA 1925, ss 34 (tenants in common) and 36 (joint tenants), and of intestates' estates under the Administration of Estates Act 1925, s 33, have ceased to be trusts for sale and have become trusts of land without any duty to sell (but with a power of sale) by virtue of the amendments to those sections made by the TLATA 1996, Sch 2 (the sections are printed as amended in Part G at paras **[246.39I]**, **[246.39K]** and **[244.58]**). Trusts for sale are not abolished, but the TLATA 1996 tries to (and perhaps does) create a set of rules under which it makes no practical difference whether or not there is a trust for sale. The main way in which it does this is to provide a common set of powers and provisions which apply to all 'trusts of land' whether or not there is a trust for sale, but there are also two specific provisions which affect the operation and legal consequences of trusts for sale of land—

(1) In all trusts for sale of land created by a disposition a power to postpone sale is implied *despite any provision to the contrary made by the disposition* (emphasis supplied): TLATA 1996, s 4(1). This provision is worded in the same way as the LPA 1925, s 25(1) (which is repealed by the TLATA 1996 and replaced by the TLATA 1996, s 4(1)), but it differs from the SLA 1925, s 25(1) in that the latter only implied a power to postpone sale where no contrary intention appeared. The reasoning behind s 4(1) seems to be that a trust for sale of land should have the same consequences in practice as a trust of land with a power of sale, and that there should not be the presumption in favour of sale which there appeared to be under the pre-1 January 1997 law. The consequences of this power to postpone are discussed further at paras **[200.57]–[200.59]**.

(2) The other specific change made by the TLATA 1996 to trusts for sale is that the doctrine of conversion is abolished by TLATA 1996, s 3 in relation to express trusts for sale, whether made before or after the commencement of the Act, with the consequence that land held on trust for sale is no longer to be regarded as personalty. (There is an exception for trusts for sale created by the wills of testators dying before the commencement of the Act.) For consequences of this see Vol 1, para **[41.18]** and the notes to Forms B4.45 (at para **[204.67]**), B14.15 and B14.16 (at paras **[214.24]** and **[214.25]**).

[200.55]
Trusts for sale no longer necessary. In general, therefore, it is no longer necessary for gifts of land by will (or by inter vivos instrument) to be effected by way of disposition on trust for sale. Before 1 January 1997, if land was directed to be held on successive, contingent, discretionary or other trusts, but there was no direction to hold it on trust for sale, the SLA 1925 would apply. This reason for imposing a trust for sale has now been removed, and as explained above at para **[200.54]**, trusts for sale are made virtually if not totally indistinguishable in their practical consequences from trusts of land where there is no trust for sale. The objection to continuing to use the trust for sale is that it is an artificial and technical concept that is not readily comprehensible to the client, and is also counter-intuitive. Trustees do not in practice sit around considering whether to postpone sale all the time; they hold the property unsold without thinking about it at all until they have some reason for considering a sale. We therefore recommend that in general trusts for sale should not be included in trusts of land (and in particular not in administration trusts of residue). For administration trusts of residue after the TLATA 1996, see para **[214.1]** et seq.

[200.56]
A trust for sale might still be appropriate as follows—

(i) where the settlor or testator particularly wants there to be an early sale, an express trust for sale would emphasise his intention, but would not impose any greater legal obligation to sell (because the TLATA 1996, s 4 confers a non-excludable power to postpone sale);

(ii) where land is intended to be held as an investment, and not for the occupation of beneficiaries, again the traditional trust for sale wording might be a way of emphasising this (see the Preliminary Note to B8 at para **[208.1]** et seq concerning rights of occupation), although the strict legal position would probably be little or not at all different from one where there was no trust for sale; or

(iii)   where there is a gift of or including land, eg a gift of a residuary estate which includes land, to two or more persons as tenants in common (or joint tenants) absolutely and beneficially, the minority in terms of the aggregate value of their interests may have a stronger right to an immediate sale against the wishes of the majority if there is a trust for sale. If that is what is intended, the TLATA 1996, s 11 should be excluded (for which, see para **[220.58]**). See also paras **[200.58]** and **[200.59]** and Form B15.8 at para **[215.8]**.

In all the above cases an expression of intention should be included as well as a trust for sale (because a trust for sale may always have been included continuing to use old forms rather than because of a specific intent), and it may well be that the expressions of intention will be more decisive than the presence of a trust for sale. But the inclusion of a trust for sale can do no harm and may, at any rate in a case such as that described in sub-para (iii), turn out to make a real difference as to whether the court will order a sale on an application to it under the TLATA 1996, s 14: see paras **[200.59]** and **[200.62]**.

[200.57]
Distribution of land held in undivided shares—the need for a sale. Where property is held on trust for beneficiaries in absolute undivided shares and it is of a kind which is readily divisible, such as cash or stock exchange investments, and the trustees do not have a subsisting power to appropriate, each beneficiary is entitled to have transferred to him or her his or her proportionate share of each asset, but this is not so in the case of land, private company shares in special circumstances, and mortgage debts, where a sale or other conversion into cash is usually necessary before a beneficiary is entitled to a distribution (*Re Marshall* [1914] 1 Ch 192; *Re Weiner's Will Trusts* [1956] 2 All ER 482, [1956] 1 WLR 579; *Stephenson v Barclays Bank Trust Co Ltd* [1975] 1 All ER 625 at 637; *Lloyds Bank plc v Duker* [1987] 3 All ER 193, [1987] 1 WLR 1324). Thus where property given by will is or includes land, and it is given to a number of beneficiaries in equal or unequal undivided shares, a sale of that land is a necessary part of the working out of the trust, because usually the land cannot be finally distributed among the beneficiaries without a sale and distribution of the proceeds. There is also the possibility of partition (TLATA 1996, s 7: Part G, para **[246.92]**), or exercise of any available power of appropriation (see para **[220.70]** et seq), but this is often impracticable. If the trustees are different persons from the beneficiaries they can insist on conveying the land to the beneficiaries as co-owners under the power in the TLATA 1996, s 6(2), but this just transfers the problem of distribution to the beneficiaries to sort out among themselves.

[200.58]
Sale of land held in undivided shares. Before the TLATA 1996 came into force, the law in relation to a gift by will of land on trust to sell it and hold the proceeds of sale on trust for beneficiaries in undivided shares seems to have

been that the trustees' power to postpone sale came to an end when the beneficiaries' interests were absolutely vested and any prior life or other limited interest had come to an end (and the administration of the estate was complete): *Re Ball, Jones v Jones* [1930] WN 111. Although the LPA 1925, s 25 implied a power to postpone sale in any trust for sale of land, it yielded to a contrary intention, and it seems from *Re Ball, Jones v Jones* that a trust to sell with an express power to postpone sale excluded the statutorily implied power to postpone sale, at any rate once the moment for sale and division of the fund had arrived. Also, even where there was a continuing power to postpone sale, where the trustees were not unanimous in agreeing to do so, the trust to sell had to be executed, and the court would not interfere with that (*Re Mayo, Mayo v Mayo* [1943] Ch 302, [1943] 2 All ER 440), unless there was a continuing purpose of the trust, which is not usually the case with tenancies in common arising under a will. With effect from 1 January 1997 the position is altered significantly by the TLATA 1996 in a number of respects. The TLATA 1996, s 4 (Part G, para **[246.89]**; see also para **[200.54]**), by implying a power to postpone sale in any trust for sale of land *despite any provision to the contrary* made by the disposition creating the trust for sale, means that *Re Ball, Jones v Jones* [1930] WN 111 can no longer be good law according to its precise ratio decidendi. This is because whatever the express trusts under a trust for sale, and however imperative is the direction to sell, the trustees always have the statutorily implied power to postpone sale. Accordingly, when land becomes vested in beneficiaries absolutely in undivided shares under, eg a will trust, and there is no continuing trust purpose which justifies the continued retention of the land, the remedy of a beneficiary who wants a sale (if the trustees are refusing to sell) is to apply to the court for an order for sale under the TLATA 1996, s 14 (Part G, para **[246.100]**; see also para **[200.62]**). The power of the court to order a sale is discretionary and there is not the same certainty of outcome which an application for a sale based on *Re Ball, Jones v Jones* would have had before the Act came into force: see further paras **[200.59]** and **[200.62]**.

[200.59]
Whether someone with an undivided share can obtain an order for sale. It should be noted that the TLATA 1996, ss 14 and 15 (Part G, paras **[246.100]** and **[246.101]**; see also para **[200.62]**) give the court a wider discretion than the former LPA 1925, s 30, and would seem to override the former rule (see para **[200.58]**) that a sale must be ordered where the trustees cannot agree to postpone sale. It should also be noted that the TLATA 1996, s 15, which sets out the matters to which the court is to have regard on a s 14 application, also includes in sub-s (3) the wishes of any beneficiaries of full age and entitled to an interest in possession, or (in case of dispute) of the majority according to value. If the applicant for a sale under the TLATA 1996, s 14 is in a minority by value, the majority will argue that the TLATA 1996, s 15(3) means that the court should not order a sale. However, the court is only directed by s 15(3) to 'have regard' to the wishes of the majority, and that the weight to be given to those wishes will depend on the circumstances. It is tentatively suggested that if the time for distribution has arrived, and there is no continuing trust purpose which justifies further postponement of sale, and the TLATA 1996, s 11 (Part G, para **[246.97]**; see also para **[220.58]**) does not apply to the trust, then a sale should be ordered and the wishes of the majority should have little weight. If

this were not the case, the liberty given by TLATA 1996, s 11(2)(a) to exclude s 11 from applying would be of little consequence. On the other hand, if TLATA 1996, s 11 applies, it is arguable that the court should not order a sale if the majority of the beneficiaries by value do not want a sale. Section 11 can be excluded by the will or other disposition creating the trust (TLATA 1996, s 11(2)(a)), and this is something to consider doing in any will trust of land of this type where a sale and division of the proceeds is intended.

[200.60]
Repeal of trust for sale provisions of the Law of Property Act 1925. The TLATA 1996, Sch 4 repealed (without replacing) the following provisions of the LPA 1925 which were formerly relevant to will and other trust drafting—

(a) **Section 25(4)** – used to provide that a trust to retain or sell land took effect as a trust for sale with power to postpone sale. A trust to retain or sell land now has effect according to its terms.

(b) **Section 28(1)** – conferred various statutory powers set out in the SLA 1925 on trustees for sale, and is naturally repealed by the TLATA 1996 in view of the different and wider administrative powers conferred on trustees of land by the TLATA 1996, s 6. However, the SLA 1925, s 28(1) used also to provide that land acquired by trustees for sale should be conveyed to them on trust for sale, and that the statutory powers of leasing, improvement, etc of trustees for sale should be exercised with the consents (if any) required for a sale. The repeal of the SLA 1925, s 28(1) means that now trustees of land (including trustees for sale) whose power or trust to sell the land is subject to a requirement of obtaining the consent of someone do not need that person's consent to the exercise of their other powers over the land unless the will or settlement expressly says so.

(c) **Section 28(2)** – used to provide that subject to express provision to the contrary, the net rents and profits of land held on trust for sale, after payment for repairs insurance and other outgoings, should be paid or applied, except so far as liable to be set aside as capital money under the SLA 1925, in the like manner as the income of investments representing the purchase money would be payable or applicable if a sale had been made and the proceeds duly invested. This probably enacted what was broadly the position under the general law, but to be on the safe side any new will or settlement creating a trust for sale should now include an express trust of the net rents and profits of the land before sale. Further, the repeal of this provision for setting aside rents as capital money under the SLA 1925 means that there is now uncertainty as to whether any, and, if so, how much, of mining royalties and the proceeds of timber should be capitalised, and express provision should be made in this respect in any trust of land where there may be exploitation of minerals or sales of timber: see Form B20.12 at para **[220.61]** and the notes thereto.

(d) **Section 32** – used to provide that land acquired by a personalty settlement under an express power to do so was to be held on trust for sale (subject to an express contrary intention). This is repealed, although many personalty settlements contain express provision that any land acquired by the trustees shall be held on trust for sale.

[200.61]
Purchasers. The TLATA 1996, s 16 (Part G, para **[246.102]**) provides protection for purchasers dealing with trustees of unregistered land. A purchaser of land that is or has been subject to a trust of land need not be concerned to see that any requirement imposed on the trustees by the TLATA 1996, ss 6(5), 7(3) or 11(1) (all of which require the trustees to consult the beneficiaries or have regard to their rights) has been complied with: TLATA 1996, s 16(1). Further, a conveyance of land in contravention of any order, enactment or rule of law or equity to a purchaser who has no notice of the contravention is not invalidated by the contravention: TLATA 1996, s 16(2). In the case of registered land purchasers dealing with trustees need only have regard to restrictions registered on the title, there being a new restriction (Land Registry restriction no. 11A) to deal with cases where the statutory administrative powers are restricted by the will or settlement (the vendor trustees or their lawyers have to declare or certify that the restrictions have been complied with). The purchase money still has to be paid to or applied by the direction of two persons as trustees or a trust corporation (LPA 1925, s 27, as amended).

[200.62]
Powers of the court. The TLATA 1996, ss 14 and 15 (Part G, paras **[246.100]** and **[246.101]**) replace the LPA 1925, s 30, giving the court a wider jurisdiction than that under the LPA 1925, s 30 to make orders with respect to the exercise by trustees of land of any of their functions (whereas the LPA 1925, s 30 only applied where trustees were refusing to sell or exercise statutory powers over the land, or a beneficiary was refusing his consent to sale or such an exercise). The TLATA 1996, s 15 sets out the matters to which the court is to have regard, and they include the intentions of the testator (or settlor), and the purposes for which the land is held. The latter is an enactment of the case law principle under the LPA 1925, s 30 that sale would not be ordered where the land had been acquired for a purpose which had not come to an end, eg a house bought as a residence for a husband and wife (*Jones v Challenger* [1961] 1 QB 176, [1960] 1 All ER 785, CA), and will not usually be relevant in the case of property given in trust by will. The testator's expressions of intention, on the other hand, as to matters such as occupation by beneficiaries or sale, could be an important factor in such cases. The circumstances and wishes of beneficiaries will also be taken into account (see also para **[200.59]**).

[200.63]
Personal representatives. The provisions of the TLATA 1996 are declared to apply with exceptions and appropriate modifications to personal representatives: TLATA 1996, s 18(1), (2) (Part G, para **[246.104]**). The duty to consult beneficiaries under the TLATA 1996, s 11 and the right to apply to the court under s 14 are omitted from the list. The abolition of the doctrine of conversion does not apply to personal representatives if the death occurred before the commencement of the Act: TLATA 1996, s 18(3). The TLATA 1996 also amends the Administration of Estates Act 1925, s 39 (Part G, para **[246.48]**) so as to give personal representatives all the powers of trustees under the TLATA 1996 in relation to land.

[200.64]
Other provisions of the Trusts of Land and Appointment of Trustees Act 1996. Rights of occupation of trust land under the TLATA 1996 are discussed at para **[208.5]** et seq, powers of management of land under the Act at paras **[220.49]**–**[220.52]**, powers to delegate the powers of management of land to beneficiaries at paras **[220.54]**–**[220.56]**, consultation with beneficiaries at para **[220.58]** and the appointment of trustees under the Act in the notes at para **[221.39]**.

[200.65]
The Trustee Act 2000. The TrA 2000 is set out in Part G (at para **[246.115]** et seq). It confers on trustees and personal representatives newer and wider powers of investment, powers to delegate investment and investment-holding powers, and powers to charge, while imposing an excludable statutory duty of care. See paras **[220.12]**–**[220.18]** (powers of investment), **[220.36]**–**[220.38]** (delegation of investment powers), **[221.42]**–**[221.48]** (powers of charging) and **[221.15]** (statutory duty of care). One consequence of the Act is that it makes all kinds of investment (apart from equitable interests in land) authorised investments (see paras **[220.12]**–**[220.18]**). This may turn out to have consequences for other rules: for example, it may have the effect of abolishing or marginalising the rule in *Howe v Dartmouth* (1802) 7 Ves 137 (see para **[214.35]** et seq), or causing all trustees to have powers of appropriation (see para **[220.71]**).

[200.66]
Review of existing wills. In what circumstances (if any) should someone who made a will before the TLATA 1996 or the TrA 2000 came into force consider making a new will or a codicil by reason of the changes to the law made by these Acts? It seems that it is only in unusual circumstances that either or both of these Acts are likely to provide a compelling reason for reviewing an existing will. We suggest the following circumstances might justify revision in the light of the TLATA 1996 without other reasons for doing so—

(1)   Where SLA 1925 forms have been used, particularly if a will has used a form such as 'I give Blackacre to my wife for her life… I appoint X and Y to be the trustees for the purposes of the Settled Land Act 1925'. In such a case there could be doubt as to who are the trustees of the land in whom Blackacre should be vested by the executors. It would be a good idea to prepare a codicil substituting 'I give Blackacre to X and Y to hold it on trust for my wife for life' (or to my wife and X, or otherwise as appropriate – it may be that X and Y were willing to be SLA 1925 trustees but would not want the greater burden of being trustees of land under the TLATA 1996).

(2)   Where an entail is purportedly created. The prohibition of new entails, and conversion of purported entails into absolute interests (see para **[200.53]**) applies to trusts arising on a death on or after 1 January 1997 even though the will was made before that date. See Form C13.2 at para **[235.18]** et seq for a substitute for the traditional strict settlement.

(3)   It was intended that the trustees' powers over land should be more restricted than the powers of an absolute owner under the TLATA 1996, s 6(1) (Part G, para **[246.91]**; see also paras **[220.49]**–**[220.52]**). Express restriction of the TLATA 1996, s 6 should be made.

(4)   Where in a trust for sale a beneficiary's (or other person's) consent is required to a sale, and it was intended that other administrative powers of the trustees over the land should require the same consent by virtue of the LPA 1925, s 28(1) (now repealed). See Form B20.13 at para **[220.62]**. Revision of the will is probably not required simply to maintain as effective an express requirement of a beneficiary's consent to exercise of one of the trustees' administrative powers.

(5)   To exclude the TLATA 1996, ss 19 or 20 in a trust created to protect the beneficiaries from their own improvidence: see Form B21.34 at para **[221.39]**.

(6)   The rare case of a will which relies on the doctrine of conversion under a trust for sale for a particular disposition to be effective according to the testator's intention, eg which contains a gift of personalty which is intended to include an undivided share of land. See further, Vol 1, para **[41.18]**; and paras **[200.59]** and **[214.24]**.

(7)   There is a specific gift of an undivided share in land which might possibly be at risk of ademption by reverse application of *Re Newman* [1930] 2 Ch 409, ie because the gift is phrased as a bequest of personalty and the interest has been changed to an interest in realty by the TLATA 1996 (see Vol 1, para **[41.18]** and **[200.54]**). 'I give all my interest in Blackacre to X' should in our opinion remain effective; what is perhaps more at risk of ademption (but it is hard to believe that a court would now hold that there is ademption) is a gift of 'my interest in the proceeds of sale of Blackacre to X', and the undivided share of Blackacre is not under an express trust for sale but is governed by the LPA 1925, s 34 (which is now amended by the TLATA 1996 so as no longer to impose a trust for sale, even in relation to pre-1 January 1997 dispositions: see para **[200.54]**). A simple affirmatory codicil would deal with the point.

It is not necessary to make a new will or codicil simply in order to exclude the TLATA 1996, s 11 (consultation of beneficiaries) (see para **[220.58]**), as s 11 does not apply to wills made before 1 January 1997 even if the testator dies on or after that date (TLATA 1996, s 11(2)(b): Part G, para **[246.97]**). There does not seem to be anything in the TrA 2000 which might make a testator want to change his will, but a potential executor or trustee of a will of a testator who is still alive might want him to make a new will or codicil which excludes or restricts the statutory duty of care (see para **[221.15]**).

[200.67]
If a new will or a codicil is being made, consider eliminating trusts for sale and unnecessary duplication of the statutory powers over land, omitting powers of insurance (see para **[220.51]** for the statutory power of insurance introduced by the TrA 2000), remember that the TLATA 1996, s 11 (and ss 19 and 20) will apply unless excluded, make any restrictions on administrative powers relate expressly to the TLATA 1996, ss 6 and 7, and if you are creating a trust for sale, provide expressly that the net rents and profits pending sale are to be held on the same trusts as the income of the proceeds of sale (because of the repeal of the LPA 1925, s 28(2): see para **[200.60]**). If it is intended that the liability for negligence of all or any of the executors or trustees is to be limited or excluded, consider introducing wording to this effect which refers to the statutory duty of care under the TrA 2000.

II. INHERITANCE TAX

[200.68]
These introductory notes deal with more general topics; there are also notes to
particular groups of precedents or individual ones on inheritance tax points
which affect them.

(a) Main characteristics

[200.69]
Introductory. Inheritance tax is a tax which is imposed principally on the
property owned by a person at his death, or on gifts made by him within the
seven years preceding his death. It applies to deaths and lifetime gifts occurring
on or after 18 March 1986, and was introduced mostly by way of amendment of
the pre-existing capital transfer tax legislation, with the 1984 consolidation of
the capital transfer tax legislation being renamed the ITA 1984. There are
exemptions from the tax, principally for gifts to the spouse of the giver and to
charity (see para **[200.99]** et seq), and reliefs for agricultural and business
property (see paras **[205.1]**–**[205.57]**, **[233.1]** et seq and **[234.1]**–**[234.10]**).
Settled property where an individual is entitled to receive the income is
subjected to inheritance tax as if that individual owned it (see para **[200.114]**),
and other settled property is mostly either discretionary trust property subject to
a completely separate system of charging tax (see paras **[218.8]**–**[218.15]**) or
property held on accumulation and maintenance trusts with special privileges
(see paras **[200.119]**–**[200.136]**).

[200.70]
Lifetime gifts. These can be—

(i) wholly exempt transfers which are not charged to inheritance tax at all,
such as gifts to the donor's spouse or to charity (see para **[200.99]** et
seq) — there are certain categories of exemption specific to lifetime
transfers, such as annual exemption (see the ITA 1984, ss 19–22);

(ii) potentially exempt transfers which are only chargeable to tax if the
donor of the gift dies within seven years of it (ITA 1984, s 3A); or

(iii) immediately chargeable transfers, which are immediately chargeable to
inheritance tax at half the tax rate for transfers on death (but there may
be more tax to pay if the donor dies within seven years of the gift).

[200.71]
Potential exemption applies to gifts (other than wholly exempt ones) made by
one individual to another individual, or into an interest in possession trust (see
paras **[200.108]**–**[200.113]**), accumulation and maintenance trust (see paras
[200.119]–**[200.136]**), or a trust for a disabled person (see paras **[226.3]**–
[226.5]), and potential exemption also applies to the termination of an interest in
possession in settled property where it is succeeded by another interest in
possession, an absolute interest, accumulation and maintenance trusts, or a trust
for a disabled person.

The main category of immediately chargeable lifetime transfers is transfers of property onto discretionary trusts, or the termination of an interest in possession in settled property to be followed by discretionary trusts (for a full list of immediately chargeable transfers see *Foster's Inheritance Tax*, C3.19).

[200.72]
The inheritance tax charge on death. When someone dies, there is an inheritance tax charge imposed on the aggregate of the property to which he was beneficially entitled immediately before his death (ITA 1984, ss 4(1), 5(1)), including settled property in which he had an interest in possession (ITA 1984, s 49(1)) and certain property subject to a gift with reservation (see para **[200.58]**). The tax rate is calculated taking into account transfers made in the seven years preceding the death (see paras **[200.73]** and **[200.74]**), and where there is more than one fund, eg free estate and settled property subject to an interest in possession, the tax is apportioned rateably between them. The main exceptions or reliefs from this charge are as follows—

(i)   the deduction of debts and funeral expenses in determining the value of the estate (see para **[200.77]**);

(ii)   where the deceased was domiciled and resident outside the UK, property with a foreign situs, exempt UK government stock, and foreign currency bank accounts in the UK owned by him may be left out of account (ITA 1984, ss 6 and 157);

(iii)   exemptions for gifts to spouses, charities, political parties, housing associations, etc (see para **[200.99]** et seq);

(iv)   the exception from charge for the estate of someone who dies as a result of active service in the armed forces (ITA 1984, s 154);

(v)   certain exceptions relating to settled property: reversionary interests owned by the deceased (ITA 1984, s 48(1)), property in which the deceased had an interest in possession which on his death reverted to the settlor or the settlor's spouse (ITA 1984, s 54), and property in which the deceased had an interest in possession which was entitled to the estate duty surviving spouse exemption (ITA 1984, Sch 6, para 2);

(vi)   conditional exemption for works of art, land etc of historical artistic etc interest (ITA 1984, ss 30–34; see also the Note in B4 at para **[204.11]**);

(vii)   relief for business or agricultural property, which can be 100 per cent, ie amount to a complete exemption (see the Preliminary Notes to B5 at paras **[205.1]**–**[205.57]**; C11 at para **[233.1]** et seq and C12 at para **[234.1]** et seq);

(viii) relief for woodlands (ITA 1984, ss 125–130);

(ix)   relief in the form of a reduction of the taxable value where quoted shares which were owned by the deceased are sold within a year of death or land owned by him is sold within four years of death (ITA 1984, ss 178–198);

(x)   where the deceased died within five years of inheriting property on the death of someone else, there may be relief in respect of the inheritance tax paid on the earlier death (ITA 1984, s 141);

(xi)   where the deceased and another person died in circumstances that the order of deaths cannot be known they are treated as dying simultaneously, so that neither's taxable estate on death will be treated as including property inherited from the other (ITA 1984, s 4(2); see also B19 at para **[219.5]**);

(xii)   double tax relief where property in the estate is subject to foreign death duties (ITA 1984, s 158, 159).

There are complicated rules for establishing the taxable value of the estate where there is partial exemption: see para **[200.138]** et seq and the Preliminary Note to C11 at para **[233.1]** et seq.

[200.73]

Tax rates. There is a single tax-rate scale which applies in full to the estate on death and to lifetime transfers made within three years before death. It currently (in the tax year 2001–02) consists of a nil rate for the first £242,000 and a single rate of 40 per cent once the nil rate band is exceeded. The rate of inheritance tax on lifetime transfers is a percentage of a full charge where the period between the transfer and the transferor's death is more than three years but fewer than seven years, the percentage being reduced for every year beyond three years that the transferor has survived (ITA 1984, s 7). Transfers which are immediately chargeable (eg gifts into fully discretionary settlements) are charged to tax at half full rates initially, but if the transferor dies within seven years the tax charge is recalculated, taking into account among other things the date of the transferor's death, any loss of business or agricultural relief by virtue of the disposal of business or agricultural property before the transferor's death (see the ITA 1984, ss 113A, 113B, 124A, and 124B), and the tax rates prevailing at the transferor's death. If the tax so recalculated exceeds the tax already paid, the excess then becomes payable: ITA 1984, s 7(2), (4), and (5).

[200.74]

Aggregation. A potentially exempt transfer which becomes a chargeable transfer as a result of the transferor's death within seven years is not treated as forming part of the estate charged to inheritance tax on the transferor's death, although the tax on such a transfer becomes payable six months after the end of the month in which the death occurred (ITA 1984, s 226(3A)) and the rate-scale on which the tax is charged is that prevailing at the time of the death (ITA 1984, Sch 2, para 1A). A potentially exempt transfer which becomes chargeable is a lifetime chargeable transfer belonging, for the purposes of aggregation, to the time when it was made; it is one of the chargeable transfers which enters into the cumulative total of chargeable transfers of the previous seven years which is taken into account in calculating the inheritance tax charge on the transferor's estate on death (ITA 1984, s 7(1)). The tax charge on a potentially exempt transfer which has become chargeable is calculated taking into account the chargeable transfers made by the transferor in the seven years preceding it. These would include immediately chargeable transfers made in that period even though made more than seven years before the transferor's death and thus not taken into account when calculating the tax charge on the estate on death. It should be noted that the value transferred by a potentially exempt transfer is aggregated in full when calculating the inheritance tax charge on death unless the transferor survives a full seven years after the transfer. Therefore, where a lifetime transfer of value is made and the value transferred does not exceed the nil rate band (there being no previous transfers aggregable), there would be no advantage in that transfer being a potentially exempt transfer as opposed to an immediately chargeable transfer unless there were subsequent lifetime transfers of value.

[200.75]

The chargeable estate on death is aggregated with the lifetime chargeable transfers, if any, including any potentially exempt transfers, which were made by the deceased in the seven years preceding his death. Any of the nil rate band not used up by those lifetime transfers will be available in relation to the taxable estate on death, and the excess of the estate on death over the available nil rate band (if any) will be charged to inheritance tax at the 40 per cent rate (tax year 2001–02). Obviously if the nil rate band is entirely used up by lifetime chargeable transfers in the seven years preceding the death, the chargeable estate on death will all be taxed at 40 per cent.

[200.76]

Gifts with reservation. Property which has been the subject-matter of a gift, made on or after 18 March 1986, from the enjoyment of which or benefit from which the donor has not been entirely excluded after the gift was made ('property subject to a reservation') is taxed as if it had remained part of the donor's estate if the reserved enjoyment or benefit continues until his death, and if the reserved benefit or enjoyment ceased within seven years of his death the property is taxed as if he had made a potentially exempt transfer of it when the enjoyment or benefit ceased. The fact that the latter type of event is treated as a potentially exempt transfer means among other things that the inheritance tax on it becomes payable only after the donor's death and at the rates then prevailing, and the liability for the tax is the same as for potentially exempt transfers (see below). The essential legislative wording (FA 1986, s 102) and rules for tracing the property comprised in a gift (FA 1986, Sch 20) for the purposes of gifts with reservation are derived with very little modification, from the former estate duty rules on the subject. Most types of exempt gift, including ones within the spouse exemption, are excluded from being gifts with reservation (FA 1986, s 102(5)). There has been one major amendment to the legislation: the Finance Act 1999 inserted in the FA 1986 new ss 102A, 102B, and 102C, to counter the type of avoidance scheme where someone retains a lease of a house or other real property at a nominal rent but gives away the freehold, as was held to be effective to avoid the gift with reservation rules by the House of Lords in *Ingram v IRC* [2000] 1 AC 293, [1999] 1 All ER 297.

[200.77]

Deduction of liabilities on death. Liabilities of the deceased are deductible in determining his taxable estate on death for inheritance tax purposes, so far as they were incurred for consideration in money or money's worth or imposed by law (ITA 1984, s 5(5)), unless there is a right of reimbursement reasonably likely to be obtained (ITA 1984, s 162(1)) or the consideration was given by a person with property deriving from the deceased (see below). Liabilities which are incumbrances on property are deducted first from that property (ITA 1984, s 162(4)), and liabilities to persons outside the UK which do not fall to be discharged in the UK and are not charged on property in the UK are deducted so far as possible from property outside the UK: ITA 1984, s 162(5). Reasonable funeral expenses are deductible (ITA 1984, s 172) including a reasonable amount for mourning apparel (Inland Revenue Concession F1) and the cost of a tombstone or gravestone (Inland Revenue Statement of Practice

SP 7/87). The administration expenses are not deductible, save that the expenses of administering or realising foreign property may be deductible if attributable to the location of the property and subject to a limit of five per cent of the value of the property (ITA 1984, s 173), and the part of the estate spent on administration expenses apparently escapes being charged to inheritance tax so far as the expenses are paid out of exempt residue (see para **[200.143]**).

[200.78]
A liability incurred for no consideration, such as a deed of covenant, is not deductible for inheritance tax purposes. A liability incurred on or after 18 March 1986 for full consideration where the lender had previously been given property by the deceased is also not deductible, as a result of the reintroduction of some estate duty rules on this subject by the FA 1986: FA 1986, s 103(1)–(6). Also non-deductible is any liability connected with insurance made on or after 1 July 1986, unless the sums assured are part of the estate: FA 1986, s 103(7).

[200.79]
Liability for inheritance tax. Inheritance tax on potentially exempt transfers, and additional inheritance tax on chargeable transfers (never potentially exempt), made within seven years of the transferor's death, and inheritance tax on property subject to a reservation, is a liability of both the transferor's personal representatives (ITA 1984, ss 199(2) and 200(1)(a)), and of any person whose estate was increased by the transfer or in whom the property which was the subject-matter of the transfer or reservation is vested (ITA 1984, ss 199(1) and 200(1)). The liability of the transferor's personal representatives is, however, a secondary one, and which will in most cases only arise if such tax is unpaid twelve months after the end of the month in which the transferor or donor died (ITA 1984, s 204(8) and (9)).

[200.80]
Liability for the inheritance tax on a person's death is that of his personal representatives in relation to the deceased's free estate and any settled land in the UK which was comprised in a settlement before the death and which vests in them (ITA 1984, s 200(1)(a)), but not other settled property in which the deceased had an interest in possession. There is a concurrent liability of anyone who becomes interested in the property, and the trustees of a settlement in which the deceased had an interest in possession are primarily liable for the inheritance tax on the property in that settlement (ITA 1984, s 200(1)(b)–(d)). The personal representatives' liability is limited to the assets of the estate they have received or should have received (ITA 1984, s 204(1)), and where the primary liability for the inheritance tax on any property subject to the inheritance tax charge on death is not that of the residuary estate, the personal representatives may recover the tax from the person primarily liable (ITA 1984, s 211(3)). It should be noted that the personal representatives have no such right of recovery in relation to any inheritance tax paid by them on a lifetime potentially exempt or other transfer made by the deceased in the seven years before his death (see para **[200.79]**), in the absence of an express agreement having been made by the transferee with the deceased to pay it. For the incidence of inheritance tax on death see the Preliminary Note to B14 at para **[214.55]** et seq.

[200.81]
Valuation of the estate on death. The valuation is on the basis of a hypothetical sale on the open market immediately before the deceased's death (ITA 1984, ss 4(1) and 160), taking into account additions to the deceased's property and increases or decreases in the value of his property which have occurred by reason of his death, other than decreases arising from alterations in unquoted shares and any changes by way of accrual of property by survivorship or the termination of any interest:ITA 1984, s 171. Property subject to a restriction on alienation is valued on the assumption that it could be sold freely but that the purchaser will be subject to the same restriction when he has acquired it (*IRC v Crossman* [1937] AC 26, [1936] 1 All ER 762; *Alexander v IRC* [1991] STC 112), and it is assumed for the purposes of valuation that the hypothetical seller took the course of action which would get the largest price, such as, for example, dividing property up into lots, or selling separate items together, provided that this would not have entailed undue expenditure of time and effort (*Gray v IRC* [1994] STC 360).

[200.82]
The deceased's free estate and settled property in which he had an interest in possession (see para **[200.108]** et seq) will be valued together if that produces a higher value (ITA 1984, ss 4(1), 5(1) and 49(1)), and any property in the deceased's estate (including property in which he had an interest in possession) which has a higher value if it is valued as a proportionate part of the aggregate of it and related property will be so valued (ITA 1984, s 161(2)). Related property is property owned (absolutely or for an interest in possession) by the deceased's spouse, or which was owned at his death, or had during the preceding five years been owned, by a charity or similar body as a result of a post-15 April 1976 exempt transfer by the deceased or his spouse (ITA 1984, s 161(2)). Another category of property which may be valued in aggregation with the rest of the deceased's taxable estate is property subject to a reservation (see para **[200.76]**) at the deceased's death of which the deceased was the donor (FA 1986, s 102(3)). There is relief for falls in the value of property after death, in relation to quoted investments sold within one year of death (ITA 1984, ss 178–189) and land sold within four years of death: ITA 1984, ss 190–198.

[200.83]
Post-death rearrangement. It is often desired by the beneficiaries to alter the dispositions taking effect on the testator's death, sometimes to increase or alter the benefit taken by a particular beneficiary, sometimes to make better use of exemptions, reliefs or the nil rate band. It is often possible to rearrange the devolution of the estate within two years of the testator's death so that the rearrangement is treated for inheritance tax purposes as if done by the deceased, so that, for example, a rearrangement which gives more property to the deceased's surviving spouse obtains a corresponding increase in the amount of the estate which is exempt (see para **[200.99]** et seq for the spouse exemption). The main methods of making such rearrangements are disclaimers or instruments of variation under the ITA 1984, s 142 (see F3 at para **[241.1]** et seq) and distributions out of discretionary trusts created by will in accordance with the ITA 1984, s 144 (see C3 at para **[225.83]** et seq). There are also distribution in accordance with the deceased's wishes of personal property in

accordance with the ITA 1984, s 143 (see B4 at paras **[204.9]** and **[204.10]**) and court orders (including certain kinds of agreed order) under the I(PFD)A 1975 (see the I(PFD)A 1975, s 19: Part G, para **[247.21]**; and the ITA 1984, s 146; see also Vol 1, para **[105.49]**).

(b)   The consequences of inheritance tax for dispositions by will

[200.84]
Choice between lifetime and testamentary dispositions. Where the extent and nature of a person's assets enable him to make, and contemplate with equanimity making, potentially exempt transfers without any reservation of enjoyment or benefit, and that person has a reasonable chance of living for the next seven years, he has a strong incentive to make immediate lifetime gifts rather than retain property to devolve on his death. The provisions concerning gifts with reservation and non-deduction of debts, however, discourage lifetime gifts by persons with modest assets, who do not feel that they can afford to divest themselves completely of a significant part of what they have. Another problem for making lifetime dispositions can be capital gains tax, where the assets most suitable for giving away are ones which have gone up in value a lot since they were acquired. There will be a chargeable capital gains tax disposal on giving them away, unless they are put into a discretionary settlement with the result that the gift is an immediately chargeable transfer for inheritance tax purposes and hold-over relief can be claimed under the TCGA 1992, s 260; however, in such case there will be inheritance tax to pay if the value transferred (together with that of other immediately chargeable transfers made during the preceding seven years) exceeds the nil rate band. There are special considerations where a person has business or agricultural property: see the Preliminary Note to B5 at para **[205.1]** et seq.

[200.85]
Settlements by will. The inheritance tax rules are mostly neutral between making an absolute gift to a person and making a settlement under which that person has an interest in possession. The choice between these two will be largely determined by non-fiscal considerations, such as wishing to control the ultimate destination of the property on the death of the beneficiary, or wishing to protect the beneficiary from creditors. The capital gains tax rate on settled property is the trust rate, currently (2001–02) 34 per cent, which lies between the basic rate of 20 per cent and the higher rate of 40 per cent paid by individuals depending on their personal circumstances. A further point about capital gains tax which favours settling an asset (on any kind of trust), as compared with giving it absolutely, is that the trustees of a settlement will be treated as one continuing owner for the purposes of capital gains tax taper relief (under Taxation of Chargeable Gains Act 1992, s 2A and Sch A1, see *Simon's Direct Tax Service*, C2.14), irrespective of the beneficial interests from time to time. The relief increases in proportion to the period of a person's ownership of an asset, up to a maximum after 10 years in the case of non-business assets and after four years in the case of business assets. Trustees of a settlement can build up taper relief in relation to an asset, and retain the right to it once the maximum is reached, so long as the same settlement continues, while a series of successive

absolute owners will each have to start afresh building up his or her right to the relief.

[200.86]
Discretionary trusts have quite different fiscal implications, but can in some contexts offer advantages over interest in possession or absolute interests. Where one person intends to make a lifetime gift to or for the benefit of another, the inheritance tax rules discriminate between making a discretionary settlement on the one hand, where the gift will be an immediately chargeable transfer, and making an absolute gift or interest in possession settlement on the other hand, where the gift will be a potentially exempt transfer (see para **[200.70]** for these types of lifetime transfer). When it comes to making a testamentary disposition, however, there is not the same discrimination: broadly speaking the inheritance tax charge on death will be the same whatever the disposition in the will, save where the spouse exemption (see para **[200.99]**) is concerned – an interest in possession trust for the testator's spouse will qualify for the spouse exemption, but a discretionary trust under which the spouse is a discretionary beneficiary will not. A discretionary trust is a way of benefiting a beneficiary without the settled property becoming comprised in his estate for inheritance tax purposes and possibly being chargeable as such on his death; a particular application of this is the nil rate band discretionary trust under which the testator's spouse is a beneficiary (see the Note in B18 at para **[218.16]** et seq).

[200.87]
Although a beneficiary who is given an absolute interest or an interest in possession by will may be able to make potentially exempt transfers of the property he has inherited, it could still be an inheritance tax advantage for there to be a discretionary trust instead. Suppose a testator T wishes to provide a fund for B, but to enable the benefit of that fund to be passed on to B's child C. He can make an absolute gift of the fund to B, or give an interest in possession in it to B with remainder to C. In either case property can be passed on to C by means of a potentially exempt transfer during B's life, which will be free of inheritance tax if B survives it by seven years. On the other hand, the creation by T by his will of a discretionary trust under which both B and C were beneficiaries might be preferable. Where the tax rate on an exit charge would be low (see B18 at para **[218.11]** et seq), a distribution out of such a trust directly to C could have a number of advantages over a gift by will by T to B followed by a potentially exempt transfer by B to C. For example, there would be no further tax liability on B's death within seven years and no need to retain business or agricultural property for seven years to prevent loss of business or agricultural relief under the ITA 1984, ss 113A or 124A, as there would be in the case of a potentially exempt transfer, and B and C could share enjoyment of property so distributed without such property being at risk of being treated for inheritance tax purposes as being wholly part of B's estate (so long as B's enjoyment continued) under the gifts with reservation rules (for which see para **[200.76]**).

[200.88]
Continuing with the above example, another possible disposition T could make in his will would be a direct 'generation skipping' gift to C, which would normally be by means of accumulation and maintenance trusts where C is

under 25 – see para **[200.91]** and the notes on accumulation and maintenance trusts at para **[200.119]** et seq.

[200.89]
Other more specialised uses of discretionary trusts are in relation to the distribution of chattels (see B4 at para **[204.7]** et seq), trusts to enable rearrangement of the testator's dispositions within two years of his death (see C3 at para **[225.83]** et seq), and trusts for persons under a disability (see C4 at para **[226.1]** et seq).

It should be remembered that discretionary trusts have the disadvantage of loss of the benefit of dividend income tax credits when income is distributed to beneficiaries: see para **[218.30]**. The rate of capital gains tax on discretionary trusts, however, is now the same as it is for interest in possession trusts: see para **[200.40]**.

[200.90]
Gifts to spouses. The inheritance tax spouse exemption (see para **[200.99]** et seq) and the current inheritance tax rate structure of a wide nil rate band (£242,000 in the tax year 2001–02), with a flat 40 per cent rate once the nil rate band is exceeded, favours dispositions by will by married couples whereby the will of the first to die leaves a nil rate band's worth of property to the children or onto a discretionary trust, and leaves all his or her other property to the surviving spouse. In wills made by young or middle-aged couples to provide for an untimely death, an absolute gift of all the first to die's property to the other spouse will usually be preferred (see C2 at para **[224.1]** et seq), and the nil rate band using strategy is more for the older testator (see C3 at para **[225.1]** et seq). For nil rate band gifts see also B10 at para **[210.72]** and B18 at para **[218.16]** et seq.

[200.91]
Gifts to issue. Suppose a testator, T, is making his will. He has an adult child, B, who has two children, M and N. If he gives the property to B, B can make potentially exempt transfers in favour of M and N, but under inheritance tax there remain several good reasons why a 'generation skipping' disposition by T's will directly in favour of M and N could be an advantage. If M and N are minors, it will be an advantage if B is not the 'settlor' for income tax purposes of property given to M and N (see para **[200.42]**). A gift by T's will directly to M and N will ensure that some property reaches M and N instead of being squandered on riotous living by B. If T owns property which in aggregate has a value higher than the sum of the values of its parts, such as a majority holding of the ordinary shares of a property company, there may be advantages in the future if it has been split by T's will among separate gifts to B, M and N, each gift being of a minority holding. A direct gift by T's will to M and N will also avoid the disadvantage of potentially exempt transfers by B to M and N that perhaps substantial amounts of inheritance tax may be payable if B does not survive the transfer by seven years, and the disadvantage of lifetime transfers by B to M and N that the gifts with reservation rules could apply.

[200.92]
Where it is uncertain when T is making his will whether B will need the property which might be given directly to M and N, T's choice will lie between

making a gift to B, creating an interest in possession trust for B, and creating a discretionary trust under which B, M and N are beneficiaries. If T makes an absolute gift to B, or creates an interest in possession in his favour, B will still be able to make potentially exempt transfers in favour of M and N, and can make gifts to M and N by deed of variation within two years of T's death which will be treated for inheritance tax purposes as dispositions by T's will (see F3 at paras **[241.1]–[241.21]**). There will be the disadvantage, if M and N are minors, that B will be the 'settlor' for income tax purposes (see para **[200.42]** p 1018), and in the case of potentially exempt transfers the other disadvantages mentioned at para **[200.91]**. If T creates a discretionary trust by his will, distributions of capital in favour of B or M or N will give rise to an inheritance tax charge but this may be quite low or even nil, and in the case of distribution to M and N the inheritance tax position could in many circumstances be better than it would have been on a transfer by B from absolute property or settled property in which B had an interest in possession (see paras **[200.86]** and **[200.87]** and B18 at para **[218.6]** et seq).

[200.93]
For the form which gifts in favour of persons under the age of 25 may take, see the notes on accumulation and maintenance trusts at para **[200.119]** et seq.

[200.94]
Business and agricultural relief and partial exemption. See C11 at para **[233.1]** et seq.

[200.95]
Inheritance tax payable out of residue. The inheritance tax rules have the effect that the possible tax liabilities which may arise on death include the tax on potentially exempt transfers made within seven years of the transferor's death, additional tax on chargeable (not potentially exempt) transfers made within seven years before the transferor's death, and tax on property subject to a reservation within seven years of, or at, the donor's death. These tax liabilities are primarily payable by the transferees or donees or out of the property to which they relate (see paras **[200.79]** and **[200.80]**), and will not be borne by the transferor's or donor's residuary estate in the absence of express provision to that effect (see B14 at para **[214.60]**), except where the persons primarily liable fail to pay the tax and the personal representatives pay it and cannot recover it from them. However, any express direction in a will as to the incidence of inheritance tax needs to be considered carefully to see if it might unintentionally include within its scope any tax in these categories (see B14 at para **[214.70]**). The rules also include the special category of non-deductible debt where the creditor held property derived from the debtor (see para **[200.78]**), and the inheritance tax payable by reason of the debtor's death and attributable to such debts will be payable out of his residuary estate in the absence of provision to the contrary.

[200.96]
The inheritance tax rules may also make it more difficult to decide when making a will what inheritance tax on the estate should be borne by residue, in that the extent of the ultimate inheritance tax liability of a testator's estate, and therefore

the consequences of the various possible provisions he might make in his will for the incidence of inheritance tax, will be very uncertain at the time when his will is made if he has just made or is about to make substantial potentially exempt transfers. If he does not survive those transfers by seven years, not only will the rate of the inheritance tax charge on his death be much higher, but there will be the possibility that the estate may have to bear the tax on the lifetime transfers if the persons primarily liable do not or cannot pay (see paras **[200.79]** and **[200.80]**).

On these topics see, further, the Notes in B10 at paras **[210.64]–[210.67]** and B14 at para **[214.55]** et seq.

[200.97]

Administration of estates. Administration of estates may be seriously delayed by executors who are concerned about their liability for inheritance tax on lifetime gifts made by the deceased. Personal representatives can apply under the ITA 1984, s 239 for certificates of discharge in respect of such of these as they know about, and if the tax has been paid the Revenue has a duty to issue such a certificate if the transferor has died (ITA 1984, s 239(2)). Note that in the case of potentially exempt transfers which become chargeable an application for a certificate of discharge can only be made after two years have elapsed from the transferor's death, unless the Revenue think fit to entertain an earlier application made after the transferor's death (ITA 1984, s 239(2A)). However, neither s 239 nor any other provision of the ITA 1984 seems to make available any protection for personal representatives against inheritance tax liabilities in respect of lifetime transfers or property subject to a reservation of which they are wholly ignorant. Because a personal representative's liability for inheritance tax is an original liability and not a representative one (*IRC v Stannard* [1984] 2 All ER 105, [1984] 1 WLR 1039), it is submitted that personal representatives will not be protected against unforeseeable claims for inheritance tax by statutory advertisements under the TA 1925, s 27. However, the Inland Revenue have said that they will not usually pursue for further inheritance tax personal representatives who have done their best to discover lifetime transfers and disclose them to the Revenue, and have obtained a certificate of discharge and distributed the estate before a chargeable lifetime transfer comes to light (letter to the Law Society published in *Law Society's Gazette* 13 March 1991, reproduced in *Foster's Inheritance Tax*, X6.44).

[200.98]

Personal representatives who delay applying for a grant of representation for more than a year after the end of the month in which the deceased died may find that it is a condition of obtaining a grant of representation that they pay inheritance tax which is still unpaid in respect of lifetime gifts or property subject to a reservation of which the deceased was the donor. This is because it is a statutory precondition of obtaining a grant that they must pay all inheritance tax for which they are liable (Supreme Court Act 1981, s 109(1) and ITA 1984, s 226(2)), and they become liable for inheritance tax on lifetime gifts and property subject to a reservation if it remains unpaid after 12 months have elapsed from the end of the month in which the deceased died: ITA 1984, s 204(8) and (9).

(c)   Exemptions and reliefs relevant to testamentary dispositions

[200.99]
The exemption for gifts to spouses. A transfer of value between spouses is ordinarily exempt, to the extent of the value of property which thereby becomes comprised in the spouse's estate, or, where no property becomes so comprised, to the extent that the spouse's estate is thereby increased: ITA 1984, s 18(1). The exemption can thus apply to a transfer whereby the transferor's spouse acquires an interest in possession in settled property as well as to an outright gift to the transferor's spouse. However, there is no inheritance tax advantage in a testator giving his spouse a life interest as compared with giving an absolute interest (whereas there was such an advantage under estate duty), although the rate of capital gains tax on settled property can in some circumstances be a little lower (see para **[200.95]**).

[200.100]
The extent of the inheritance tax spouse exemption is restricted if the transferor but not the transferor's spouse is domiciled in the UK, for which see the ITA 1984, s 18(2). The overall limit for transfers in these circumstances is currently £55,000, although in some cases there is a greater amount of exemption under a relevant double tax treaty.

[200.101]
Making full use of the spouse exemption in testamentary dispositions will not always be the best course of action. For example, when a husband and wife have children to whom they intend their property ultimately to pass, if they make wills whereby the property of the first to die passes to the survivor the estates will be aggregated together on the second death for calculating the rate of inheritance tax. The optimum result in terms of tax rates will be achieved if both spouses have sufficient assets for whichever is the first to die to be able to give property of a taxable value equal to the inheritance tax nil rate band direct to the children, and if the first to die does give property of that value to the children by lifetime gift within seven years of his or her death or by will (or some combination of the two). Where it is desired for this purpose to transfer assets from the richer to the poorer spouse, it is best done by lifetime disposition because doing it by will is only effective if the wealthier spouse dies first. However, where the estates are unequal and the spouse with the smaller estate might outlive the spouse with the larger estate for a long time, the latter might well be advised to leave his or her spouse all of his or her estate in view of the likely long postponement of payment of inheritance tax and the possibilities of the surviving spouse making exempt lifetime dispositions in favour of the children, especially as any 'potentially exempt transfer' (see paras **[200.70]** and **[200.71]**) made by the surviving spouse will be free of tax if he or she survives it by seven years. See also para **[200.90]**.

[200.102]
Gifts to charities, political parties, housing associations, or for national purposes, and gifts to maintenance funds for historic buildings. There is exemption for all of these: ITA 1984, ss 23–25 and 27. A political party has to have attained a specified level of success in the most recent general election for

a gift to it to qualify for exemption: ITA 1984, s 24(2). 'Gifts for national purposes' for the purposes of the exemption means gifts to any of the institutions (such as national museums and galleries, universities, local authorities and government departments) specified in the ITA 1984, Sch 3: ITA 1984, s 25(1). For charitable gifts, see B10, and for a gift by will to provide a maintenance fund, see Form C13.2 at para **[235.18]**.

[200.103]
Sections 23(2) to (5), 24(3) and 25(2) of the ITA 1984 contain restrictions which ensure that these exemptions (subject to very limited exceptions) only apply to absolute gifts of the donor's entire interest in the property given.

For forms of charitable gifts and notes thereon, see B12 at para **[212.1]** et seq.

[200.104]
Gifts made by persons with a foreign domicile. Property situated outside the UK and beneficially owned absolutely by someone with a foreign domicile (the rules are quite different for settled property, for which see the ITA 1984, s 48(3)) is 'excluded property' (ITA 1984, s 6(1)), which does not form part of that person's estate for the purposes of the charge to inheritance tax on death: ITA 1984, s 5(1). It must always be remembered that under the ITA 1984, s 267 certain persons with a foreign domicile are treated as having a UK domicile for inheritance tax purposes; in particular, anyone now giving up his UK domicile has to have a foreign domicile and be a foreign resident for three years before he loses UK domicile for these purposes.

[200.105]
Persons with a foreign domicile but deemed to have a UK domicile under the ITA 1984, s 267 are, however, helped by the ITA 1984, ss 6(2) and 48(4)–(7). By virtue of those provisions, exempt government securities are 'excluded property' while beneficially owned by someone not domiciled or ordinarily resident in the UK and ITA 1984, s 267 does not apply for the purposes of that paragraph: ITA 1984, s 267(2). There is an additional exception for persons domiciled in the Channel Islands or the Isle of Man who are entitled to certain types of government bonds or rights under certificated contractual savings schemes: ITA 1984, s 6(3). The deemed domicile provisions are excluded in this case also: ITA 1984, s 267(2).

For the advantages of creating will trusts where the testator is domiciled outside the UK see C14 at para **[236.1]** et seq.

[200.106]
Exemptions and reliefs for particular kinds of asset. There are elaborate provisions for conditional exemption for works of art, historic buildings, etc (see the ITA 1984, s 30 et seq and B4 at para **[204.11]** et seq), and for relief for business property (ITA 1984, s 103), agricultural property (ITA 1984, s 115) and woodlands (ITA 1984, s 125) which are discussed in B5 at para **[205.1]** et seq, C11 at para **[233.1]** et seq and C12 at para **[234.1]** et seq.

(d) Will trusts (other than accumulation and maintenance trusts)

[200.107]

The rules for charging inheritance tax on settled property are set out in the ITA 1984, Part III. This Part provides two quite different methods of charging tax according to whether there is an interest in possession in the property or not. If there is an interest in possession (such as a life interest), the owner of that interest is treated for most inheritance tax purposes as if he were the owner of the settled property in which the interest subsists. Where there is no interest in possession in settled property (as is the case in the conventional form of discretionary settlement), inheritance tax is charged periodically during the subsistence of the discretionary trust; there is also an 'exit' charge whenever property ceases to be subject to the discretionary trust. The discretionary trust charging provisions, and the circumstances in which discretionary trusts may be advantageous, are considered at paras **[200.86]** and **[200.87]** and in B18 at para **[218.6]** et seq.

[200.108]

Interest in possession. This term is not defined in the legislation, but in their press notice dated 12 February 1976 the Inland Revenue expressed the view that:

'... an interest in possession in settled property exists where the person having the interest has the immediate entitlement (subject to any prior claim by the trustees for expenses or other outgoings properly payable out of income) to any income produced by that property as the income arises; but that a discretion or power, in whatever form, which can be exercised after income arises so as to withhold it from that person negatives the existence of an interest in possession. For this purpose a power to accumulate income is regarded as a power to withhold it, unless any accumulations must be held solely for the person having the interest or his personal representatives.

On the other hand the existence of a mere power of revocation or appointment, the exercise of which would determine the interest wholly or in part (but which, so long as it remains unexercised, does not affect the beneficiary's immediate entitlement to income) does not in the Board's view prevent the interest from being an interest in possession.'

[200.109]

After the notice quoted at para **[200.108]** was issued the meaning of 'interest in possession' for capital transfer tax (inheritance tax) purposes was authoritatively determined by a bare majority of the House of Lords (reversing the High Court and the Court of Appeal) in *Pearson v IRC* [1981] AC 753, [1980] 2 All ER 479. The House of Lords held that the Inland Revenue view is largely correct, and that where trustees have power, eg, to accumulate the income of any settled property, or to distribute such income among a class of beneficiaries, and subject to such power that income is held on trust for a specific person, the last-mentioned person does not have an interest in possession in the settled property for the purposes of the tax. The rationale of the decision is that a beneficiary has an interest in possession only if he is entitled to call for the income as it arises. Income which can be distributed to others or accumulated does not satisfy this test: see also *Re Trafford's Settlements, Moore v IRC* [1985] Ch 32, [1984] 1 All ER 1108. On the other hand an overriding power of appointment exercisable prospectively only is not inconsistent with the existence of an interest in possession. The House of Lords decision is also important in drawing a distinction between 'dispositive' powers, eg a power to distribute or accumulate income, and 'administrative' powers, eg a power to pay expenses, expressing the view that only powers of the former sort were capable of negativing interests in possession. For discussion of administrative powers and interests in possession, see B20 at para **[220.4]** et seq and for more detailed discussion of interests in possession generally, see *Foster's Inheritance Tax*, E1.41–E1.49.

[200.110]
A matter which formerly gave rise to some difficulty was whether an interest in possession is created if trustees allow a discretionary beneficiary to have the free use of a house or chattels or to borrow trust moneys interest free. The Inland Revenue originally indicated in 1975 that trustees allowing a beneficiary the free use of a house in normal circumstances would not be regarded as creating an interest in possession (see letter in the *Law Society's Gazette*, 6 August 1975). Subsequently the capital gains tax case of *Sansom v Peay* [1976] 3 All ER 375, [1976] 1 WLR 1073 was decided. In that case beneficiaries were permitted by the trustees of a discretionary settlement to occupy a house under a power contained in the settlement. It was held that such beneficiaries were 'entitled to occupy it under the terms of the settlement' within the Finance Act 1965, s 29(9) (now the TCGA 1992, s 225) with the consequence that the house was exempt from capital gains tax on its disposal by the trustees. The wording of that subsection is not identical with any provision in the capital transfer tax (inheritance tax) legislation but the similarities, especially with what is now the ITA 1984, s 50(5) are striking, and the Inland Revenue therefore announced that it would in future regard someone having the use of a house held on trust by permission of the trustee as having an interest in possession in many cases, particularly where the power is exercised to provide a permanent home for a beneficiary: see IR Statement of Practice SP10/79, 15 August 1979. Therefore, this type of power should only be exercised other than over assets in which a person already has an interest in possession and in favour of that person after careful thought for the inheritance tax consequences. See further B18 at para **[218.108]** and *Foster's Inheritance Tax* E1.47. For the difficulty caused for nil rate band discretionary trusts where the only significant asset is the matrimonial home, see para **[218.18]** et seq.

[200.111]
In spite of the rather narrower meaning put on the term 'interest in possession' by the House of Lords in *Pearson v IRC,* it is possible to retain some flexibility in a settlement by giving a life interest which constitutes an interest in possession but which is subject to overriding powers of appointment or application under which capital can be distributed to, or appointed on trust for, the life tenant or other specified persons. If such overriding powers are not capable of exercise in any manner which might affect the life tenant's right to income arising before such exercise, their existence will not prejudice the existence of an interest in possession (see the Inland Revenue statement quoted at para **[200.108]**). If such powers are exercised so that the life tenant becomes beneficially entitled to, or to another interest in possession in, property which was subject to his life interest, there is no inheritance tax charge: ITA 1984,

s 53(2). If such powers are exercised in favour of a person or persons other than the life tenant, the inheritance tax consequences are as if the life tenant had made a transfer of value of the capital over which the powers are exercised: ITA 1984, s 52(1). Such an event is capable of being a potentially exempt transfer (see para **[200.71]**). Examples of powers to pay capital to a life tenant will be found in B18 at paras **[218.37]**–**[218.39]** and Form C2.6 at para **[224.95]** is an example of interest in possession trusts combined with wide overriding powers.

[200.112]
Someone who has an annuity arising under a will and charged on the testator's estate, is treated as having an interest in possession in part of that estate for inheritance tax purposes. This may give rise to problems: see further B11 at para **[211.1]** et seq. If someone who is entitled to an interest in possession in some or all of a residuary estate dies, or assigns or surrenders the interest, before the administration of the estate has been completed, the same inheritance tax consequences follow as if the administration had been completed: ITA 1984, s 91. Thus if someone entitled under a will to a life interest in the testator's residuary estate dies while the estate is still being administered, the residuary estate will be taxed on his death as if he had had an interest in possession in it, even though the trust fund had not been constituted by the time of his death. However, someone entitled to an interest in possession in an estate may be able to assign or surrender the interest by instrument of variation or disclaimer under the ITA 1984, s 142 within two years of the testator's death without adverse inheritance tax consequences (see para **[241.1]** et seq).

[200.113]
Plainly one of the most important questions which now has to be answered in respect of any precedent for the creation of settled interests is whether it creates an interest in possession or not. A life or similar interest in income is on any view of the meaning of the term an interest in possession, and so is the interest of a person of full age with a presumptive interest in capital who is entitled to be paid the income of that capital until he attains an absolute interest or his interest fails. In the notes to the precedents in this work we only consider expressly the question whether any particular precedent creates an interest in possession where there is some doubt about it. For a discussion of the meaning of 'interest in possession' in the TLATA 1996, see para **[208.12]** et seq.

[200.114]
Inheritance tax on settled property subject to an interest in possession. If an individual is beneficially entitled to an interest in possession in settled property, he is treated for inheritance tax purposes as if he were beneficially entitled to the property: ITA 1984, s 49(1). If the interest comes to an end during his life without him becoming entitled to the property itself or another interest in possession in the property, eg as a result of a surrender of the interest or the exercise by the trustees of an overriding power, a set of inheritance tax charging provisions apply which parallel, but are not quite the same in some respects as, the provisions for charging inheritance tax on lifetime transfers of absolutely owned property (see the ITA 1984, ss 51–53 and *Foster's Inheritance Tax*, E2.21–30). The individual who was entitled to the interest is treated as having made a transfer of value of the settled property in which the interest in

possession subsisted (ITA 1984, s 52(1)), and this is capable of being a potentially exempt transfer: ITA 1984, ss 3(4), 3A(1) and (7) and see paras **[200.70]** and **[200.71]**. Where someone dies while beneficially entitled to an interest in possession in settled property, the settled property subject to the interest is charged to inheritance tax as part of his estate immediately before his death (ITA 1984, ss 4(1), 5(1) and 49(1)), and so on death settled property subject to an interest in possession is taxed under the rules for absolutely-owned property: see para **[200.72]**. However, the general personal representatives are not liable for the inheritance tax on such settled property unless it was settled land (see para **[200.80]**).

[200.115]
Will trusts of foreign domiciled testators. If a testator has a foreign domicile for inheritance tax purposes (see paras **[200.104]** and **[200.105]**), and some or all of the beneficiaries intended to benefit under his will are UK resident, he should consider making a will settling the property intended for UK beneficiaries so as to take advantage of the excluded property rules: see C14 at para **[236.3]**.

[200.116]
Protective trusts. These (see para **[200.20]**) receive special treatment under the ITA 1984, s 88, which eliminates the charge which would otherwise arise under the ITA 1984, s 52(1) on a forfeiture occurring by providing for the 'principal beneficiary' to be treated as continuing to have an interest in possession after forfeiture. A testator who feels that imposing protective trusts would be appropriate for a particular beneficiary need not be discouraged from doing so by the inheritance tax consequences. The Revenue have indicated that they do not accept as falling within ITA 1984, s 88 a protective trust which by comparison with the statutory form has a larger class of objects of the discretionary trust of income arising after a forfeiture, but do accept a power to pay capital to the principal beneficiary ([1976] BTR 421). We infer they would probably accept a trustee's power to lift the protection. The Revenue view cannot easily be reconciled with *Re Wallace's Settlements* [1968] 2 All ER 209, [1968] 1 WLR 711 (in which Megarry J said of the rather similar words of the Variation of Trusts Act 1958, s 1(2) that the word 'like' required not identity but similarity) or *Thomas v IRC* [1981] STC 382, but it is wiser not to depart from the TA 1925, s 33 (Part 6, para **[246.28]**) unless absolutely necessary. See B16 at paras **[216.6]** and **[216.7]** and Form C3.5 at para **[225.68]** for protective trust precedents.

[200.117]
Trusts for persons mentally disabled or in receipt of attendance allowance. If a testator wishes to make provision for someone in either of these categories a discretionary trust is the most appropriate method. Again there is special provision (see of the ITA 1984, s 89) so as to remove the inheritance tax disadvantages of discretionary trusts in the case of a trust primarily for the benefit of such a person. For a fuller discussion of this section, see C4 at para **[226.3]** et seq and for precedents see Forms B18.4 at para **[218.34]**, C4.1 and C4.2 at paras **[226.8]** and **[226.35]**.

[200.118]
Discretionary trusts. See paras **[200.86]–[200.89]** and B18 at paras **[218.6]–[218.15]** for discussion of these.

(e) Accumulation and maintenance trusts

[200.119]
For a more detailed account of accumulation and maintenance trusts in the contexts of inheritance tax see *Foster's Inheritance Tax*, E5. For precedents see, eg Forms C8.3 and C8.4 at paras **[230.30]** and **[230.45]**. Considerable inheritance tax advantages are conferred on settled property which satisfies all of the following three conditions now contained in the ITA 1984, s 71(1) and (2)—

   (a)   one or more persons (referred to as beneficiaries) will, on or before attaining a specified age not exceeding 25, become entitled to, or to an interest in, possession in the settled property or part of it;
   (b)   no interest in possession subsists in the settled property or part and the income from it is to be accumulated so far as not applied for the maintenance, education or benefit of a beneficiary; and
   (c)   either:
      (i)   not more than twenty-five years have elapsed since the day on which the settlement was made, or if it was later, since the time (or latest time) when the first two conditions above were satisfied with respect to the property or part, or
      (ii)   all the persons who are or have been beneficiaries are or were either grandchildren of a common grandparent or children, widows or widowers of such grandchildren who were themselves beneficiaries but died before the time when, had they survived, they would have become entitled as mentioned above.

[200.120]
The word 'will' in condition (a) above requires that the beneficiaries *are bound* under the trusts of the settlement to become entitled to or to an interest in possession in the settled property on attaining a specified age not exceeding 25 if they so long live. The existence of an overriding power of appointment exercisable in favour of persons who are not 'beneficiaries' is thus inconsistent with accumulation and maintenance trusts; see *Lord Inglewood v IRC* [1983] STC 133, CA.

[200.121]
The advantages noted at para **[200.132]** which are enjoyed by accumulation and maintenance trusts were intended to benefit relatively short term trusts in favour of children. However, as originally enacted the exemption was expressed too widely and relatively long term discretionary trusts fell within the qualifying definition. Accordingly, the third requirement noted at para **[200.119]** was added and it will be seen that the relief is limited to a 25-year period or to settlements in favour of one generation, in the latter case with the addition of certain substituted beneficiaries. Trying to frame trusts to fall within the ITA 1984, s 71(2)(b) (see para **[200.119]**, sub-para (c)(ii)) and so outside the 25-year

restriction is another task for the will draftsman. For example, if a testator wishes to benefit the children of two different families without the requisite common ancestry, there should be two different funds, one for each set of children, instead of a single one for all of them. For a point concerning substitution clauses and the ITA 1984, s 71(2)(b): see para **[200.131]**. It should be remembered that the 25-year restriction will not matter if the beneficiaries are a class of persons, such as the testator's own children, the membership of which will close on or shortly after the testator's death.

[200.122]

Three further points can be mentioned. First, there is nothing in ITA 1984, s 71 requiring the 'beneficiaries' to be identified otherwise than by description or their interest to be equal or quantified from the outset. Second, 'persons' include unborn persons, but the conditions noted at para **[200.119]** are not to be treated as satisfied unless there is or has been a living beneficiary: ITA 1984,s 71(7). If no children are born the conditions are not satisfied and a charge to tax may arise when the first child is born. Third, there is an important Inland Revenue concession that there need be no specified age if a beneficiary will become entitled on or before attaining 25, for which see B18 at para **[218.74]**.

[200.123]

The three requirements noted at para **[200.119]** are imperative and care is needed in drafting to ensure that they are satisfied. Powers of appointment, unless carefully restricted, may well jeopardise the trust's status as an accumulation and maintenance settlement and must be carefully considered.

[200.124]

Powers of appointment and revocation limited to the class of beneficiaries. It could be argued that even a power limited to members of the class is objectionable since the share of a particular beneficiary could be eliminated by its exercise and thus it cannot be said that he 'will' become entitled on or before attaining 25. However, the Revenue issued the following press release (19 January 1976):

'Where there is a trust for accumulation and maintenance of a class of persons who become entitled to the property (or to an interest in possession in it) at a specified age not exceeding 25 it would not be disqualified under para 15(1)(a) [now the ITA 1984, s 71(1)(a)] by the existence of power to vary or determine the respective shares of members of the class (even to the extent of excluding some members altogether) provided the power is exercisable only in favour of a person under 25 who is a member of the class.'

Thus, the imperative requirement that the class 'will' become entitled is viewed collectively not individually.

[200.125]

A power not limited to the class of beneficiaries will take the settlement outside the ITA 1984, s 71 because in such cases the vesting of capital, or of an interest in it, is capable of being defeated by an event other than death.

[200.126]

Although it is thus theoretically possible to have powers to vary the benefits taken by the beneficiaries while keeping within the scope of the ITA 1984, s 71, as a practical matter such powers are very difficult to draft, and the result is usually of some complexity, carrying with it the risk that there is some undetected flaw which takes the trust outside s 71. The main difficulty lies in ensuring that the power cannot be exercised or a revocation of an exercise cannot be made so as to benefit a beneficiary who has attained an interest in possession or absolute interest while there continue to be other beneficiaries whose shares are within the ITA 1984, s 71 and subject to the power. Such powers will be of limited utility if accumulation of the income of a beneficiary's share cannot continue beyond his attaining 18 (see B18 at paras **[218.72]**–**[218.74]**), because once a beneficiary has an interest in possession an exercise of a power so as wholly or partially to divest him of his interest can give rise to an inheritance tax charge on the termination of an interest in possession. For an example of a flexible accumulation and maintenance trust, see Form C8.4 at para **[230.45]**.

[200.127]

Statutory power of advancement. The view of the Inland Revenue is that the mere existence of a common form power of advancement (as in the TA 1925, s 32) does not prevent a settlement from satisfying the terms of the ITA 1984, s 71(1). This view has received the support of the Court of Appeal in *Lord Inglewood v IRC* [1983] STC 133. Nonetheless a cautious draftsman may wish to qualify the power of advancement by a proviso along the lines of that which appears in Form B18.20 at para **[218.104]**. For further notes on powers of advancement, see B18 at para **[218.85]** et seq.

[200.128]

Life interest. One point which the Revenue have clarified is that it is their view that the provisions of the ITA 1984, s 71 would be capable of operating after the death of a life tenant or any other event, provided that the conditions of the paragraph are then satisfied. If one had to look at the word 'will' by reference to the possibilities at the date of the settlement and there is a prior life interest under the terms of the settlement then clearly the life tenant might still be alive after the remaindermen had reached 25 so that (on that interpretation) the requirement of s 71(1)(a) would not be satisfied (see Law Society's Gazette, 7 May 1975, p 481.) This Inland Revenue view accords with the view that s 71 is to be applied from time to time rather than at a single point in time (see para **[200.132]**).

[200.129]

The treatment of income for Inheritance Tax Act 1984, s 71 purposes. In order to be sure of satisfying the ITA 1984, s 71(1)(b) as regards the trusts of income, the TA 1925, s 31 should always be permitted or (preferably) expressed to apply, or express accumulation and maintenance provisions should be drafted which follow the scheme of the TA 1925, s 31, that is to say, a *power* to pay or apply the income of each share of capital for the benefit of the person presumptively or certainly interested in that share, and a *trust* to accumulate the income not so paid or applied as an eventual accretion to the capital of that share (subject to certain qualifications). Full notes on the TA 1925, s 31 will be found in B18 at para **[218.41]** et seq.

[200.130]
Protective trusts. It is compatible with the ITA 1984, s 71 applying to provide trusts for the beneficiaries where what they will attain on or before attaining the age of 25 are protective life interests, even though a beneficiary might forfeit his life interest before becoming entitled to an interest in possession by virtue of it. This is because the ITA 1984, s 88 provides that the 'principal beneficiary' under a protective trust (see para **[200.116]** and the TA 1925, s 33: Part G, para **[246.28]**) is treated as having an interest in possession after a forfeiture.

[200.131]
Substitution clauses and the Inheritance Tax Act 1984, s 71. Because of the provision in the ITA 1984, s 71(7) that 'persons' in s 71(1) includes unborn persons, there is a possibility that a set of trusts for the grandchildren of a common grandparent will be outside the ITA 1984, s 71(2)(b) (and thus subject to the 25-year restriction) if there is a substitutional provision for children *and remoter issue*, even though remoter issue have not taken any interest and never had any real chance of doing so. We therefore recommend that in ITA 1984, s 71 trusts where the primary beneficiaries have a common grandparent, substitution clauses to take effect on the death of a beneficiary *after the death of the testator* should be limited to the substitution of children, widows and widowers of primary beneficiaries. Of course, there is not the same fiscal objection to the substitution of children and remoter issue in the event of a beneficiary predeceasing the testator, and provision for the substitution of remoter issue is much more important in such a case. An example of such double substitutional provision will be found in Form B19.6 at para **[219.19]**.

[200.132]
The advantages of settled property falling within the Inheritance Tax Act 1984, s 71. Where the requirements of the ITA 1984, s 71 are satisfied in respect of any settled property, there is no inheritance tax charge under the discretionary trust charging provision (ITA 1984, s 65) which would otherwise apply on a distribution of capital to a beneficiary or on a beneficiary becoming entitled to an absolute interest or an interest in possession, and no periodic charge under ITA 1984, s 64 is payable at a 'ten-year anniversary'; also, the death of a beneficiary does not give rise to an inheritance tax charge. Whether ITA 1984, s 71 applies has to be considered from time to time, and in particular at any time when an event happens on which there would be an inheritance tax charge if s 71 did not apply, such as a 'ten-year anniversary'. Once the ITA 1984, s 71 starts to apply to settled property it will usually only cease to do so through expiry of the 25-year period in ITA 1984, s 71(2)(a) where relevant before the beneficiaries have attained absolute interests or interests in possession (which would be an occasion of inheritance tax charge under the ITA 1984, s 71(3)), or through the class of beneficiaries dying out (which is not an occasion of tax charge: ITA 1984, s 71(4)(b)), or some one or more of its members attaining absolute interests or interests in possession, which as already mentioned is not an occasion of inheritance tax charge: ITA 1984, ss 58(1)(b) and 71(4)(a). The beneficiaries will usually attain absolute interests or interests in possession successively so that the settled property will cease to be within the ITA 1984, s 71 in stages, a share at a time, which is something to bear in mind when drafting powers to vary shares.

[200.133]

If there is no interest in possession in settled property and the ITA 1984, s 71 does not apply, and an event happens (such as the birth of the first beneficiary, or an exercise or release of a power of appointment) as a result of which s 71 commences to apply to that property, there will be a charge to inheritance tax under the ITA 1984, s 65(1)(a) on the property then ceasing to be 'relevant property'. It can therefore be important in drafting accumulation and maintenance trusts for a will to ensure that the ITA 1984, s 71 will apply from the beginning. If, for example, a testator wishes to benefit primarily the children of A, who has no children and might come to have some only after the testator's death, the class of beneficiaries should include some living young children (preferably with a grandparent in common with A's children if he has any: ITA 1984, s 71(2)(b) and paras **[200.119]** and **[200.121]**) who take only a nominal share of the fund if A has any children (see Form B17.21 at para **[217.26]** for a precedent).

[200.134]

It will be seen that the best results will often be obtained if accumulation and maintenance trusts are drafted when the circumstances at the death of the testator are known, and a will which takes advantage of the ITA 1984, s 144 (see C3 at para **[225.83]**) will make this possible. It is thought that the forms in this book for trusts for minor children satisfy the ITA 1984, s 71 except where a contrary view is stated.

[200.135]

Capital gains tax. Hold-over relief is available on a 'beneficiary' within the ITA 1984, s 71 becoming entitled to some or all of the settled property on or before attaining the specified age where he has not previously become entitled to an interest in possession in it (see the TCGA 1992, s 260(1) and (2)(d)), but is not otherwise generally available (see para **[200.39]**). It will thus be a good idea when putting accumulation and maintenance trusts in a will to include maximum flexibility, so that there can be an early distribution so as to obtain hold-over relief, or else the trusts can be left to continue for some time. See for examples Forms C2.6 at para **[224.95]** and C8.4 at para **[230.45]**.

[200.136]

Income tax. Accumulation and maintenance trusts share with discretionary trusts the disadvantageous income tax treatment of dividend income under the Income and Corporation Taxes Acts 1988, ss 686 and 687, outlined at para **[218.30]**. A way out of this is to provide that the beneficiaries are to have interests in possession so that they are entitled to the income as it arises. The trusts would then not be accumulation and maintenance trusts within the ITA 1984, s 71 but interest in possession trusts for inheritance tax purposes, with the consequence that if one of the minor beneficiaries dies it will be an occasion of inheritance tax charge on the share of the fund in which his interest in possession subsisted. Childhood deaths are now rare, and even if it happens there will not be any inheritance tax payable if the share is less than the amount of the nil rate band and he has no other taxable assets. For a method of achieving this, by way of amendment of the TA 1925, s 31 see Form B18.15 at para **[218.81]**.

(f)   Incidence of inheritance tax

[200.137]
The decision of the Court of Session in *Re Dougal* [1981] STC 514 to the effect
that capital transfer tax (now inheritance tax) on heritable property is prima facie
a testamentary expense payable out of residue gave rise to the enactment of what
is now the ITA 1984, s 211 (Part G, para **[246.83]**) giving legislative effect to
that decision throughout the UK in relation to deaths occurring on or after 26
July 1983. Incidence is more fully discussed in B14 at paras **[214.55]–[214.75]**
and there are also notes on provisions concerning incidence as follows: in
relation to specific bequests in B4 at para **[204.1]**; in relation to specific gifts of
land in B6 at para **[206.3]**; and in relation to pecuniary legacies in B10 at para
[210.3]. We would particularly draw attention to the absurd rule that in the
absence of contrary provision, pecuniary legacies charged on a mixed fund of
UK and foreign property bear their own tax to the extent that they are payable
out of the foreign property, and to possible methods of excluding the rule, for
which see B14 at paras **[214.64]** and **[214.71]**.

(g)   Partially exempt estates

[200.138]
The ITA 1984, Part II, Ch III contains rules to be applied when an estate is
partially exempt to determine the extent of the exempt part or parts and the
incidence of inheritance tax. As regards incidence, ITA 1984, s 41 has the effect,
overriding the terms of any will, that the recipients of the exempt parts of the
estate cannot be made to bear any of the inheritance tax on the non-exempt parts.
The only advantage gained by the beneficiaries interested in the non-exempt
parts is thus the reduction in the overall tax rate as a consequence of there being
parts of the estate which are exempt.

[200.139]
Another matter dealt with in the ITA 1984, Part II, Ch III is the allocation of
exemption where the total value of gifts of some exempt type exceeds the limit
for that exemption. The only types of testamentary gift to which this could now
be relevant (most of the former limits on exemptions having been removed) are
gifts by a person domiciled in the UK to a foreign domiciled spouse (limited to
an aggregate of £55,000: see the ITA 1984, s 18(2)). By the ITA 1984, s 38(2)
the excess over the exemption in these cases is attributed to gifts not bearing
their own tax before gifts bearing their own tax and otherwise attributed to the
relevant gifts in proportion to their values. This rule appears to be incapable of
variation by the terms of a will (though obviously it is the terms of the will
which determine which gifts bear their own tax and which do not).

[200.140]
The remainder of the ITA 1984, Part II, Ch III is mostly concerned with fixing
the extent of the exempt portion of any partially exempt estate. A full account of
these provisions is beyond the scope of this note, and we refer the reader to
Foster's Inheritance Tax, D2.31–43 for this. We can only mention a few
practical points for the draftsman.

[200.141]

Technical differences in drafting a will in ways relevant to the partial exemption rules can make only marginal differences to the amount of inheritance tax paid. The main point to bear in mind is that some fairly elaborate calculations are required if the will involves either of the following—

   (i) a wholly exempt residue combined with a mixture of specific gifts and/or legacies, some of which are free of and some subject to inheritance tax;

  (ii) a partially exempt residue combined with specific gifts and/or legacies of which some or all are free of inheritance tax.

[200.142]

The deterrent effect of the rules applicable here lies not in the advanced mathematics involved (the worst you have to do is gross up tax-free gifts) but the complexity of the rules which have to be mastered. In circumstances where these complex rules have to be mastered and applied there may be, it seems to us, a very small inheritance tax saving, which may pay for the extra administration costs involved.

[200.143]

Where residue is wholly or partially given to exempt beneficiaries, the partial exemption rules have some interesting consequences. One is that the amount of the estate which is chargeable to inheritance tax on the death can be affected, sometimes very much affected, where there are non-exempt specific gifts, by whether those specific gifts bear their own inheritance tax or not: see B14 at para **[214.74]**. Another is that where administration expenses such as legal fees are payable out of residue, it seems that the exempt residue used to pay them is still treated as exempt, so that in effect inheritance tax is not charged on the part of the estate used to pay such administration expenses so far as they are met out of exempt residue. This is because the partial exemption rules operate by determining the value for inheritance tax purposes of specific gifts (ITA 1984, s 38), and then providing that what is left of the value of the estate is attributed to residue (ITA 1984, s 39); the size of residue for the purposes of these rules is not affected by the payment of administration expenses out of it. By contrast, a liability of the estate which is not deductible (see para **[200.78]** for non-deductible debts) is treated as a specific gift under the partial exemption rules (ITA 1984, s 38(6)), so that the value of such a liability does not fall out of charge when it is paid out of exempt residue.

[200.144]

The ITA 1984, s 39A makes express provision for allocation of an estate between exempt and non-exempt gifts where there is business or agricultural relief. The relief is allocated rateably between the exempt and non-exempt parts of the estate, save that where there is a specific gift (whether or not to an exempt beneficiary) of business or agricultural property, the business or agricultural relief attributable to that property is allocated to that gift (see *Foster's Inheritance Tax* D2.40 and C11 at para **[233.1]** et seq). Thus, where a testator has any property which may qualify for business or agricultural relief on his death, and the estate will be partially exempt, it will save inheritance tax to make a specific gift of that property to a non-exempt beneficiary, or, if that is not practical, to avoid making a specific gift of that property to an exempt beneficiary. This is a topic with an even greater importance now that the higher rate of business and agricultural relief is 100 per cent (see B5 at para **[205.5]** and C12 at para **[234.7]**), and it is discussed at some length in the Preliminary Note to C11 at para **[233.1]** et seq.

[200.145]

Where a proportion of residue is exempt and the remainder of it is not exempt, it is a good practice to provide expressly how residue is to be divided between the different beneficiaries: see B14 at paras **[214.72]** and **[214.73]** and Forms B14.35 and B14.36 at paras **[214.78]** and **[214.79]** for examples of declarations to deal with this point.

Clauses in wills

B1 Commencement of will

PRELIMINARY NOTE

[201.1]
General words of commencement. A will should commence with the name of
the testator, a declaration that all former testamentary dispositions made by him
are revoked and a declaration that it is his last will. It is important that a will
should be dated, although it is not a legal requirement except where a guardian is
being appointed (see Vol 1, para **[28.5]**). Some practitioners place the date of the
will at the commencement, but the usual practice is to insert it in the
testimonium. In preparing the commencement of a will, care should be taken to
ascertain the correct full name of the testator as any inaccuracy will lead to the
probate having to be taken in both the correct full name of the testator and his
name as it appears in the will. If possible, it should be ascertained that the
testator's name and its spelling in the will agree with the name and spelling in
the testator's birth certificate. If the testator is commonly known by a name
which is not in his birth certificate, it is a good idea to put this in as well.

[201.2]
Revocation of previous wills. Every will should contain an express revocation
of all former testamentary dispositions. The declaration that a will is the
testator's 'last will' does not generally work a revocation and usually means no
more than that the document is intended to be the testator's will (see Vol 1,
paras **[1.6]**, n 7 and **[18.9]**). Although in a particular case it may be certain that
there are no former testamentary dispositions to revoke, it is usually safer to
include an express revocation. The term 'testamentary dispositions' is generally
used in this context in preference or in addition to the term 'wills', although the

only reason why it might be preferable or necessary is in the comparatively rare case these days where a testator has made an informal testamentary disposition while a serviceman on active service (see Vol 1, para **[16.1]** et seq).

[201.3]
Revocation of appointments of guardians. It is only necessary to include in a revocation clause an express revocation of a former appointment of a guardian of minor children (which appointment may have been included in a former will or in another written instrument which is not a will) where it is desired to revoke the appointment without making a new one. If a new appointment of a guardian is made in a will, a previous appointment contained in a former will or other instrument is thereby revoked without any express revocation: ChA 1989, s 6(1) (Part G, para **[244.122]**). For the revocation of appointments of guardians see Vol 1, para **[28.6]** and B3 at para **[203.43]** et seq. If an express revocation is required it could run as follows: 'I hereby revoke all former testamentary dispositions and appointments of guardians made by me.'

[201.4]
Wills made in expectation of marriage. As a general rule a will is revoked by the subsequent marriage of the testator. However, a will made on or after 1 January 1983 from which it appears that at the time it was made the testator was expecting to be married to a particular person and that he intended that the will should not be revoked by the marriage is not revoked by his marriage to that person: Wills Act 1837 (WA 1837), s 18 (as substituted by the Administration of Justice Act 1982 (AJA 1982), s 18), Part G, para **[244.16]**, replacing the Law of Property Act 1925 (LPA 1925), s 177 (Part G, para **[244.54]**) in respect of wills made on or after 1 January 1983. Therefore, if a will is not to be revoked by a subsequent marriage, it must appear from the will itself that the testator was expecting to marry a particular person and he intended that the will should not be revoked in that event. For wills made in expectation of marriage, see generally Vol 1 at para **[17.6]** et seq, and for the commencement of such a will see Forms B1.2 at para **[201.6]** and B1.3 at para **[201.7]**.

[201.5]

FORM B1.1:   Ordinary commencement[1]

I [*testator*] of [*address*] hereby revoke all former testamentary dispositions made by me and declare this to be my last will.

1   See the Preliminary Note at para **[201.1]**.

[201.6]

FORM B1.2:   Commencement of will made in expectation of marriage[1]

I [*testator*] of [*address*] hereby revoke all former testamentary dispositions made by me. I declare that I make this will in expectation of my intended marriage with [*name of intended wife or husband*] and that it shall not be revoked by reason of the said marriage. I further declare that it shall be effective even if the said marriage is not solemnised.

1   See the Preliminary Note at para **[201.1]** et seq. In this form the word 'expectation' is used in conformity with the WA 1837, s 18, as amended by the AJA 1982, s 18 (Part G, para **[244.16]**) but the word 'contemplation', as in the previous statutory provision (LPA 1925, s 177: Part G, para **[244.54]**) is probably still effective.

[201.7]

FORM B1.3:   Commencement of will made in expectation of marriage— conditional form[1]

I [*testator*] of [*address*] hereby make this will in expectation of my intended marriage with [*name of intended wife or husband*]. I declare that this will shall not be effective unless the said marriage is solemnised within —— months from the date hereof [or I die within —— months from the date hereof while still engaged to be married to [*name of intended wife or husband*]]. Upon this will so becoming effective, I declare that all former testamentary dispositions made by me shall be revoked and this will shall then be my last will.

1   See paras **[201.4]** and **[201.6]**, n 1. For conditional wills see Vol 1, para **[1.10]**.

[201.8]

FORM B1.4:   Commencement of will of testator with UK and foreign property confining the will to UK property[1]

I [*testator*] of [*address*] hereby make this my will which shall affect only my property of every kind in the United Kingdom of Great Britain and Northern Ireland and no other part of my property of any kind. I hereby revoke all former testamentary dispositions made by me to the extent that and so far only as they affect my property of every kind in the United Kingdom of Great Britain and Northern Ireland. I declare that I am domiciled in England[2] and that the proper law of this my will shall be the law of England and Wales.

1   Where a testator is possessed of property outside the United Kingdom and is able to dispose of such property and the greater part thereof to persons residing outside that area, there are obvious advantages in arranging for the distribution of such estate in the country outside the United Kingdom so far as possible in order to avoid the difficulties and expense of transferring such sums from one country to another. This is also true in the case of property situated in a dominion or colony, and it can often be appropriate to make separate and entirely independent wills with respect to the property in the United Kingdom and that situated outside the United Kingdom. Probate of a will granted in England does not extend to such property (*Re Murray's Goods* [1896] P 65), unless some of it is brought to England (*Stubbings v Clunies-Ross* (1911) 27 TLR 361). For the converse case of probate granted in a British possession, or by a British court in a foreign country, see the Colonial Probates Act 1892; and as to a limited colonial grant, see *Re Smith's Goods* [1904] P 114. (See generally as to probate *Tristram and Coote's Probate Practice* (29th edn).) See also C14 at para **[236.1]** et seq.
2   Such a declaration as to domicile will not be conclusive as to domicile at the date of death, nor indeed to domicile at the date of the declaration (see para **[236.10]**, n 1).

[201.9]

FORM B1.5:   Commencement of concurrent will of testator with UK and foreign property confining the will to UK property[1]

I [*testator*] of [*address*] hereby revoke all testamentary dispositions made by me prior to the date hereof and hereby declare that this will and another will of even

1103

date herewith together constitute my last will. This will shall affect only my property of every kind in the United Kingdom of Great Britain and Northern Ireland and no other part of my property of any kind. [*or* This will shall not affect my property of any kind in the United States of America [*or as the case may be*] which I have disposed of by the said will of even date herewith.]

1   Care must be taken that the will dealing with the foreign property should be properly executed to pass all kinds of property according to the law of the foreign country, and for this purpose a lawyer of the foreign country should be consulted. In some cases, eg the United States, it is necessary to consider the law of the particular State in which the property is situated. Though an English will may by its words imply that foreign property is excluded, yet those words may be inserted because the testator believes he has otherwise effectively disposed of such property. If that other disposition has failed, the foreign property will pass under the English will: *Re Duke of Wellington, Glentanar v Wellington* [1948] Ch 118, [1947] 2 All ER 854.

[201.10]

FORM B1.6:   Commencement of mutual will made in pursuance of an agreement that it shall not be revoked[1]

I [*testator*] of [*address*] hereby revoke all former testamentary dispositions made by me and declare this to be my last will. I declare that my wife [*name*] [*or as the case may be*] and I have agreed with one another to execute wills of even date and in similar terms and in consideration of such promise we have agreed that such respective wills shall not hereafter be revoked or altered either during our joint lives (so long as we shall remain married) or by the survivor of us (if surviving as the lawful spouse of the other).

1   As to mutual wills generally, see Vol 1, paras **[2.3]–[2.10]**. For the doctrine of mutual wills to apply it is not necessary for the second testator to die to have obtained a personal financial benefit under the will of the first testator to die: *Re Dale* [1994] Ch 31, [1993] 4 All ER 129. Careful thought should be given to the making of mutual wills because, for example, in the case of husband and wife, a remarriage by the survivor leads to obvious complications: see *Re Green, Lindner v Green* [1951] Ch 148, [1950] 2 All ER 913. If mutual wills are made by a husband and wife with their children as ultimate beneficiaries, the latter should be expressed to be the children of the marriage rather than eg 'my children'.

[201.11]

FORM B1.7:   Commencement of mirror but not mutual wills[1]

I [*testator*] of [*address*] hereby revoke all former testamentary dispositions made by me and declare this to be my last will. Notwithstanding that my wife [*name*] [*or as the case may be*] is making a will in similar terms to this will she and I have agreed that this my will and her said will are not mutual wills and accordingly that each of us shall be free to revoke his or her will at any time whether before or after the death of the other and shall not be under any obligation or trust to dispose of any of his or her property in accordance with the terms of the said wills.

1   The purpose of this form is to prevent argument or even litigation arising at a later date. Such an argument may not be limited to a claim that the wills were intended to be mutually binding but could extend to litigation under the Inheritance (Provision for Family and Dependants) Act 1975: see *Re Goodchild, Goodchild v Goodchild* [1996] 1 All ER 670; affd [1997] 3 All ER 63, CA. See also the Introductory Note on wills in favour of spouses in Part A at para **[200.24]** et seq. There should be a similar declaration in the other will.

[201.12]

FORM B1.8:   Commencement of will made on behalf of a mentally disordered person pursuant to an order of the Court of Protection[1]

This is the last will of me [*Name of Patient*] of [*address*] acting by [*name of authorised person*] of [*address of authorised person*] the person authorised in that behalf by an Order dated the [*date*] made by the Court of Protection pursuant to section 96(1)(e) of the Mental Health Act 1983. I hereby revoke all former Wills and Codicils made by me and declare this to be my last Will.

1   Part VII of the Mental Health Act 1983 (MeHA 1983) confers wide powers on the Court of Protection in relation to the property and affairs of any person who is found on medical evidence to be 'incapable, by reason of mental disorder, of managing his property and affairs', such person being defined as a 'patient': MeHA 1983, s 94(2). By the MeHA 1983, s 96(1)(e) (Part G, para **[244.112]**) the court may authorise the execution on behalf of a patient of a will (or codicil: see s 112) containing any provision (whether by way of disposing of property or exercising a power or otherwise) which could be made by a will executed by the patient if he were not mentally disordered. These powers are not to be exercised unless the patient is of full age (ie 18 or over) and the judge has reason to believe that he is incapable of making a valid will for himself: MeHA 1983, s 96(4). The mode in which a will made on behalf of a patient is to be executed is laid down in the MeHA 1983, s 97 (Part G, para **[244.113]**): see Form B22.14 at para **[222.16]** for a form of testimonium and attestation clause and see the note to that form for details of the requirements for due execution of a patient's will.

The wording set out in this form and in Form B22.14 at para **[222.16]** for the testimonium and attestation is based upon the statutory requirements and is intended to provide precedents for those parts of a will made under this jurisdiction which must necessarily differ from the corresponding parts of an ordinary will. Apart from them, it is thought, a will made under this jurisdiction need not differ in any way from a will made by a testator who is sui juris. These precedents are not in any sense official. In particular, it is a function of the Court of Protection to consider and criticise draft wills when they are submitted, and this function cannot be fettered in advance; but it is thought that objection would not normally be made to formal parts of a will couched in the terms set out in this form and Form B22.14.

The provisions relevant to the jurisdiction are to be found in the MeHA 1983, Pt VII (Part G, paras **[244.111]**–**[244.115]**), the Court of Protection Rules 2001 (SI 2001/824) and *Practice Direction* [1983] 3 All ER 255, sub nom *Practice Note* [1983] 1 WLR 1077.

B2 Miscellaneous declarations and desires sometimes included in wills

GENERAL NOTE

[202.1]
This Section brings together a number of provisions which have little in common with each other save that they are difficult to classify under any of the more conventional headings but are often found towards the beginning of a will.

Disposal of body

[202.2]
Note. The following declarations and expressions of desire should ideally be communicated to two or three near relatives or friends and confirmed by letter during the testator's lifetime. But it is not uncommon to confirm them also by will and to give the executors an express power to determine what is reasonable and proper and to incur any necessary expense in carrying out the testator's wishes. For the law relating to these matters see Vol 1, para **[7.33]**.

[202.3]
FORM B2.1:   Direction as to place of burial and tombstone

I desire that my body may be buried in my family grave in the —— Cemetery which is in the part of that cemetery for burials of deceased members of the [Church of England[1]] in Section —— Grave No ——[2] I further direct that my executors shall expend a sum of money [not exceeding £——] upon the erection of a suitable inscription upon a tombstone upon the said grave.[3]

1   Or such other part of the cemetery as may be desired.
2   A direction of this nature cannot be enforced: *Williams v Williams* (1882) 20 Ch D 659. The executors have a right to possession of the body and their duty is to bury it (*Williams v Williams*): see also Vol 1, para **[7.33]**. As to upkeep of graves, see paras **[202.18]** et seq.
3   For a direction that only necessary expense be incurred see Form B2.3 at para **[202.5]**; and for power to incur reasonable expense, see Form B2.5 at para **[202.7]**. Note that reasonable funeral expenses are allowed in valuing a deceased person's estate for inheritance tax purposes: ITA 1984, s 172. By Revenue concession such funeral expenses are taken to include the cost of a tombstone: SP7/87 (15 July 1987).

[202.4]

FORM B2.2:   **Expressions of desire as to cremation**

A.   I desire that my body may be cremated [in the crematorium at ——] and my ashes deposited at —— [or scattered on consecrated ground at ——][1] *or*

    B.   [*If the testator desires a more elaborate form of words, the following may be suggested:*] I desire that my trustees shall dispose of my remains by the cleansing fires of cremation and that my ashes shall be spread upon the garden of remembrance at ——[2] *or*

    C.   I direct that my body shall not be cremated.[3]

1   As to the law relating to cremation, see Vol 1, para **[7.33]**. Cremation must take place in a recognised crematorium. Written directions for cremation are not essential, see also n 3 infra. The Cremation Society of Great Britain, Second Floor Brecon House, 16-16A Albion Place, Maidstone, Kent, ME14 5DZ; tel: (01622) 688 292, issue a printed form of this direction, which, when completed, they undertake to register in their records; and they endeavour to give effect to the expressed desire. The printed form is in duplicate, one part for registration with the society and the other to be handed to the executor or selected relative.
2   This wording is based upon an actual will.
3   It is no longer unlawful to cremate a body where such a direction has been given, and whether cremation takes place is solely in the discretion of the deceased's executors or nearest relative, who are apparently free to disregard the deceased's wishes: see Vol 1, para **[7.33]**, n 4.

[202.5]

FORM B2.3:   **Direction that only necessary expense shall be incurred**[1]

I desire that at my death there shall be [no ostentation or show of any kind, that there shall be] no flowers and that mourning shall not be worn by my relatives and generally that no expense beyond what is necessary shall be incurred.

1   This direction is merely indicative of what some testators desire to be inserted and is, in fact based upon actual wills. Executors may incur all reasonable expenses in connection with the funeral and burial of the deceased without any direction or power in the will, though the amount they are allowed to spend is less where the estate is insolvent than where it is solvent: *Hancock v Podmore* (1830) 1 B & Ad 260; *Edwards v Edwards* (1834) 2 Cr & M 612 (where it is said that even in the case of an insolvent estate reasonable (as contrasted with necessary) expenses are allowed). Express directions, such as contained in this form, may limit the amount and, on the other hand, specific directions to spend large sums on tombs and monuments can be followed, certainly to any reasonable extent: *Paice v Archbishop of Canterbury* (1807) 14 Ves 364 at 372. At common law the husband was liable for the funeral expenses on the wife's death, but the Married Woman's Property legislation has removed the foundation of this rule and the wife's executors are now responsible for any expense so incurred: *Rees v Hughes* [1946] KB 517, [1946] 2 All ER 47.

[202.6]

FORM B2.4:   **Direction as to the ascertainment of the testator's death in order to prevent his being buried alive**[1]

I direct my executors to take all necessary steps and for this purpose to employ and pay such doctors or other skilled persons as they in their sole discretion may think proper for the purpose of ascertaining that I am in fact dead and not in any state having only the semblance of death in order so far as possible to avoid all risk of my being buried alive.

1   Although all necessary and proper expenses for this purpose are payable by the executor without express authority, it is wiser in this case to include in the will an express power as in Form B2.5 at para **[202.7]**.

[202.7]

FORM B2.5:   Power for executor to incur expense in respect of directions[1]

[Set out the directions in the will in addition to leaving such directions addressed to the executor and continue as follows] and I hereby authorise my executor to spend such sums in carrying out the above directions as may appear to him to be reasonable and his decision as to what is reasonable in the circumstances shall be final and binding upon all beneficiaries under this my will.

1   In order to avoid questions about incorporation of documents in the will and as to what documents should be admitted to probate, the directions should be set out in the will as well as in a letter to the executor or nearest relative. The executor under such a clause must act reasonably having regard to the directions given by the testator. The clause does not, of course, oust the jurisdiction of the court to determine what expenses it is proper to allow in all the circumstances, but it does show that the testator intended his bounty to the beneficiaries to be subject to these directions: see *Re Wynn's Will Trusts* [1952] Ch 271, [1952] 1 All ER 341; *Re Bromson* [1958] OR 367. Where it is alleged that there are customs relating to burial, such customs must be proved to be legal customs, and, if such is not shown, then only a reasonable sum can be claimed against the estate: *Tzedeck v Royal Trust Co* [1953] 1 SCR 31.

Anatomical research and organ transplantation

[202.8]
Donor cards. For obvious reasons it is essential that any directions concerning these matters should be given immediate effect. Such directions should therefore be communicated by the testator during his lifetime as well as incorporated in his will. Where appropriate, donor cards should be carried.

1.   Anatomical research

[202.9]
Arrangements for anatomical research. Anatomical research is quite distinct from organ transplantation in that it is limited in scope to the examination by dissection of a body for the purposes of teaching or studying or researching into morphology and does not involve the transfer or transplantation of tissue from one (deceased) body to a living person.[1] Before a body can be removed for anatomical examination various forms must be completed. These differ slightly depending on whether the deceased lived in the London area or in the provinces and practitioners asked to draw up a will with such a direction annexed to it would be well advised to obtain the necessary forms and notices from HM Inspector of Anatomy, Department of Health, Room 311, Wellington House, 135–155 Waterloo Road, London SE1 8UG (tel 0207 972 4551), and keep them with the will until required. The forms include a notice to be given to the Inspector 48 hours after death. A death certificate will also be required.

1   AA 1984, s 1(1).

[202.10]
As to procedure on death it is recommended that in London the executors should immediately telephone either HM Inspector of Anatomy at the above number or the London Anatomy Office and they will make the necessary arrangements to have the body removed.

[202.11]
Elsewhere in England and Wales the executors can either contact HM Inspector of Anatomy by telephone when he will at once assist them to make the necessary arrangements or they can get in touch with the Professor of Anatomy at the nearest Medical School who will supply the necessary forms to be filled in (if these have not already been obtained from HM Inspector of Anatomy as suggested above) and will arrange for the body to be collected. The following list of the principal University Medical Schools (with telephone numbers) may be of assistance in this connection:

[202.12]
Birmingham (0121 414 3858); Bristol (0117 928 9000); Cambridge (01223 336 700); Leeds (0113 243 2000 (switchboard); 0113 243 1751 (Dean)); Leicester (0116 252 2522); Liverpool (0151 794 2000); Manchester (0161 275 5027); Newcastle-upon-Tyne (0191 222 6000); Nottingham (0115 970 9381); Oxford (01865 221689); Sheffield (0114 271 3349); and Southampton (02380 595000); University of Wales College of Medicine (02920 747 747).

2.   Organ transplantation

[202.13]
Use of organs for therapeutic purposes. Section 1 of the Human Tissue Act 1961 authorises the use of the deceased's organs for therapeutic purposes subject to the following conditions. The deceased may authorise such use at any time in writing or orally in the presence of two witnesses during his last illness. The party lawfully in possession of the deceased's body may authorise such removal unless he has reason to believe that the deceased had expressed an objection and not withdrawn it or the surviving spouse or any surviving relative objects. The removal must be by a registered medical practitioner who has satisfied himself that life is extinct. No authority can be given where an inquest is likely to be held nor by a person entrusted by another with the burial or cremation of the body. Where the body is in hospital, the person having control and management of the hospital can authorise such removal or that person may delegate power to authorise such removal to any officer or persons designated by him. The use of organs for therapeutic purposes requires that the removal shall be effected on death or, in the case of eyes, within a few hours of death and therefore in most cases the deceased should give some oral indication of his wishes during his last illness in addition to this direction if it is to serve any practical purpose.

[202.14]
Eye hospitals. A list of Eye Hospitals which would probably be interested in receiving eyes for corneal grafting is set out below. It is not suggested that the list is complete but it is hoped that it may assist practitioners who may be asked to advise on this matter.

[202.15]

Birmingham and Midland Eye Hospital; Sussex Eye Hospital, Brighton; Bristol Eye Hospital; Royal Victoria Eye and Ear Hospital, Dublin; Glasgow Eye Infirmary; St Paul's Eye Hospital, Liverpool; Moorfields Eye Hospital, London EC1; Western Ophthalmic Hospital, London NW1; Kent County Ophthalmic and Aural Hospital, Maidstone, Kent; Manchester Royal Eye Hospital; North Riding Infirmary, Middlesbrough; Newcastle-upon-Tyne Ophthalmic Out-patients Department, Walkergate Hospital, Newcastle- upon-Tyne; Nottingham and Midland Eye Infirmary; Oxford Eye Hospital; Royal Eye Infirmary, Plymouth, Devon; Wolverhampton and Midland County Eye Infirmary, Wolverhampton; Eye, Ear and Throat Hospital, Shrewsbury.

[202.16]

FORM B2.6: Direction for anatomical examination and corneal grafting[1]

1. I desire that after my death my body may be made available [to ——] for such anatomical examinations as may be thought desirable but in accordance with the provisions of the Anatomy Act 1984 (AA 1984)[2] [and in due course the institution receiving it shall have it cremated[3]]. Such use may be made of all or any part thereof as may be lawful.

2. I hereby request that my body or any part thereof [*or if the testator so desires specify a particular part of the body*] may be used for therapeutic purposes or for the purposes of medical education or research.[4]

1 See Vol 1, para **[7.34]**. It must be remembered that the surviving spouse or nearest known relative can require interment without such examination. A direction of this nature need not be in writing but may be made orally provided it is made in the presence of two witnesses and during the illness from which the testator died. Here again it will be wiser to include an express power to pay expenses. See Form B2.5 at para **[202.7]**.

   As a deceased person has no power of disposition over his body it might perhaps be more suitable if this direction accompanied the will rather than being embodied in it although it is not suggested that it is of any great moment where the direction appears so long as it is kept in a place where it will be brought to the attention of the executors as soon as possible.

2 The AA 1984, which replaced the Anatomy Acts 1832 and 1871, came into force on 14 February 1988: SI 1988/81.

3 The institution receiving the body is responsible for seeing that it is decently interred in consecrated ground or in a public burial ground in use for persons of the religious persuasion to which the person whose body has been removed for examination belonged. Only a very simple funeral can be provided however and if any special arrangements (eg such as cremation) are required it is expected that the executors or next of kin will meet the additional cost so incurred.

4 For the law and other information concerning organ transplantation, see paras **[202.8]**–**[202.15]**.

[202.17]

FORM B2.7: Clause providing for the use of the testator's body for therapeutic purposes, but not for medical education or research[1]

(a) I desire that after my death any part or parts of my body which may be of use for therapeutic purposes (including corneal grafting in the case of my eyes and transplantation in the case of any other part of my body) shall be removed with a view to their use for those purposes.

(b) For the avoidance of doubt I declare that the foregoing provisions shall not authorise the use of my body or any part of it for medical education or research.

(c)   I desire that my body after the removal of such parts of it as may be removed with a view to their use for therapeutic purposes shall be cremated and I declare that arrangements for its cremation may be made either by my executors or (if my executors think fit) by any hospital or other institution which has custody of my body after such removal has been completed.

(d)   I authorise my executors to spend as much money from my estate as they may in their absolute discretion think fit in implementing the wishes which I have expressed in the foregoing provisions of this clause.

1   With the development of transplantation surgery, some testators wish to include in their wills a provision permitting their bodies to be used for the purposes of such surgery, but not for medical education or research. This clause is designed to fulfil these requirements. It is thus a variant of Form B2.6 at para **[202.16]**. It can of course be readily adapted to meet the needs of testators who wish to permit educational and research use as well as transplantation.

Maintenance of graves

[202.18]
Note. There are several methods of providing for the upkeep of a tomb or grave, none of them wholly satisfactory (See also Vol 1, para **[9.29]**).

[202.19]
Gifts for maintenance of graves are not charitable. A gift for the maintenance of a grave or family tomb (not being part of the fabric of a church) is not charitable, but such gift may be valid as a private trust if it does not infringe the rule against perpetuities: see *Pirbright v Salwey* [1896] WN 86, followed in *Re Hooper, Parker v Ward* [1932] 1 Ch 38. It is therefore possible to leave a legacy on trust to apply the income for the maintenance of a grave during a perpetuity period, as in Form B2.8 at para **[202.31]**. The disadvantage of a gift in this form is that it is of limited duration and that while it is lawful for the trustees to give effect to the trust, there is no beneficiary to enforce it and its efficacy therefore depends upon the goodwill and conscientiousness of the trustees. Doubts have been expressed as to whether it is possible to provide for such a gift to take effect for one of the perpetuity periods permitted by the Perpetuities and Accumulations Act 1964 (PAA 1964) because of the terms of s 15(4) of the PAA 1964. The authors take the view that s 15(4) does not prevent the 80-year perpetuity period from being employed in trusts such as these in Form B2.8 at para **[202.31]**.

[202.20]
Gifts for the upkeep of churchyards etc are charitable. Although a gift for the maintenance of a particular grave is not charitable, a gift for the upkeep of the churchyard of a parish church or church of any other religious denomination is a valid charitable gift: *Re Manser, A-G v Lucas*[1]. Further, such a gift will not be vitiated by the addition of words such as 'and in particular the grave of' a designated person[2] or some other merely precatory request for the maintenance of a particular tomb or grave. A gift in this form is contained in Form B2.9 at para **[202.32]**. It has the advantage over the gift in Form B2.8 at para **[202.31]** of not being of limited duration, but the extent to which effect is given to the wish

of the testator to have a particular grave maintained again depends entirely on the trustees.

1   [1905] 1 Ch 68.
2   [1905] 1 Ch 68, at 75.

[202.21]

Combined gifts are permitted. Where the grave is in a churchyard, a combination of the two forms of gift contained in Forms B2.8 and B2.9 at paras **[202.31]** and **[202.32]** can be employed: see Form B2.10 at para **[202.33]**.

[202.22]

Local Authority Cemeteries. Where the grave is in a cemetery maintained by a local authority, a charitable gift in the form sanctioned in *Re Manser*[1] is not available, but the local authority has power by statute to enter into arrangements for the maintenance of particular graves. The position is now governed by the Parish Councils and Burial Authorities (Miscellaneous Provisions) Act 1970 and the Local Authorities' Cemeteries Order 1977 (SI 1977 No 204), made under powers conferred by the Local Government Act 1972 and replacing earlier legislation. Article 10 of the 1977 Order provides that a burial authority may grant (inter alia) exclusive burial rights in any grave space or grave or the right to construct a walled grave or vault together with exclusive burial rights therein together with the right to place and maintain a tombstone or other memorial thereon. The authority may also enter into maintenance agreements for a period not exceeding 100 years, though there is power to extend this period.

1   [1905] 1 Ch 68.

[202.23]

The method of providing for the maintenance of a grave which the Order affords is clearly more simple, and probably more satisfactory, than the provisions to this end which have usually been employed in wills in the past. On the face of it, the testator need only direct his executors to enter into an agreement under the Order. But the following points should be noted.

[202.24]

(1) No agreement made under the Order may impose an obligation to maintain for longer than 100 years. It is conceivable that the authority might be prepared to indicate its willingness to continue maintenance beyond that period if circumstances permitted, particularly as there is now power to extend the period of maintenance, though it may not wish to impose upon itself a binding obligation. This would be a matter for discussion with the individual authority and might require the payment of an increased charge.

[202.25]

(2) The Order is permissive only and does not impose any obligation upon the authority to enter into such agreements. Even if the authority is willing to do so, it seems that it may limit its obligations to some period less than 100 years if it wishes to do this. Therefore a testator can do no more than direct that his executors shall enter into an agreement if the authority is willing, and that the agreement shall provide for maintenance for as long as the authority is prepared

to undertake it. With many Metropolitan authorities contemplating the future re-use of existing graves in order to alleviate overcrowding, lengthy maintenance agreements may become less common.

[202.26]
(3)   Although the Local Government Act 1972, s 214(3) confers a ministerial power to amend other Acts which are inconsistent with, or unnecessary in consequence of, the new provisions, it is possible that local Acts are still in operation in certain areas. It seems advisable, therefore, to permit the agreement also to be made under any local Act.

[202.27]
Form B2.11 at para **[202.34]** confers power on a deceased person's executors to enter into a maintenance agreement with a local authority under any statutory power.

[202.28]
Perpetual gifts from charity to charity are permissible. An alternative method of providing for the maintenance of a particular grave, which is embodied in Form B2.12 at para **[202.35]**, is also based on the law of charity but, unlike the provision contained in Form B2.9 at para **[202.32]**, is available wherever the grave is situated. The particular formula derives from the decision in *Re Tyler, Tyler v Tyler* [1891] 3 Ch 252, CA and involves: (i) an initial gift of property to a charity to be held on trust to apply the income in perpetuity either for its general purposes or for a particular charitable purpose administered by the selected charity; (ii) a condition requiring the charity to maintain the particular grave; and (iii) a gift over to a second charity on breach of that condition. The perpetuity rule does not apply to a gift from one charity to another, though it does apply where the gift over is from a charity to an individual (*Re Davies, Lloyd v Cardigan County Council* [1915] 1 Ch 543; *Re Talbot, Jubb v Sheard* [1933] Ch 895), or where the gift over is from an individual to a charity (*Worthing Corpn v Heather* [1906] 2 Ch 532). It must be noticed that the first gift must not be for the maintenance of the grave, as an indefinite gift for such a purpose will be invalid even though the first donee is a charity: see *Re Elliott, Lloyds Bank Ltd v Burton-on-Trent Hospital Management Committee* [1952] Ch 217, [1952] 1 All ER 145. Where the gift over is not to a charity it must be limited to take effect only within the perpetuity period, and, if the trust fails after the perpetuity period, the gift will automatically fall into residue. The efficacy of a gift in this form depends on the willingness of the second donee to enforce the condition. It is therefore advisable that the second donee should be a body having a permanent existence which is likely to be interested in ensuring that the grave is maintained. However, it should be noted that the decision of *Tyler v Tyler* was not followed by the High Court of Australia in *RSPCA of NSW v Benevolent Society of New South Wales* (1960) 102 CLR 629 where the non-charitable conditions imposed upon a charity to which property was left were considered to be part of the trust and the dominant purpose of the gift.

[202.29]
Reverter gifts no longer effective. A further device, based on the decision in *Re Chardon, Johnston v Davies* [1928] Ch 464, but now no longer available, was to

give a fund to trustees to pay the income thereof to a cemetery company or the persons responsible for the maintenance of the cemetery or burial ground so long as they should keep a particular grave or graves in repair. The efficacy of this method depended inter alia upon the rule that while a gift over on condition broken (other than a gift over as between charities) had to comply with the rule against perpetuities, a possibility of reverter did not. The PAA 1964, s 12(1) (Part G, para **[246.70]**) has now subjected possibilities of reverter to the perpetuity rule with the consequence that this method no longer works. The form based on *Re Chardon, Johnston v Davies* is accordingly omitted.

[202.30]
Value of gift for maintenance of grave. In the case of a gift from charity to charity the capital value of the gift to the charity should be substantially in excess of the cost of maintaining the grave so that the device works, because if the gift is small there is no incentive for the charity to enforce it and it may be invalid. However, in all cases where gifts are made for the maintenance of graves, care should be taken in calculating an appropriate capital value of the gift. There are two problems which may arise where the capital value of the gift is substantial. First, if excessive, it could be viewed as capricious thus rendering the whole of the gift void.[1] Secondly, if the capital value of the gift is such that it yields a greater income than that necessary for the maintenance of the grave the gift should specify what is to become of the excess income in the interim and, in particular, after the expiry of any accumulation period included in the terms of the gift.

1   There is no English authority on this point, but various US decisions have held gifts capricious. See, for example *Clark v Portland Burying Ground Association* 151 Conn 527 (1964); *In Filoon Estate* 71 D & C 506 (1950); and *In Shepp Estate* 29 D & C 2d 385 (1962).

[202.31]

FORM B2.8:   **Gift for the upkeep of a particular grave during a perpetuity period[1]**

I give to my trustees the sum of £—— upon trust to invest the same and during the period of eighty years[2] from my death (which period shall be the perpetuity period applicable to the disposition hereby effected)[3] to apply the income thereof in keeping the grave and gravestone of my late wife and of myself (if I shall be buried there) in good order and repair and in keeping the lettering thereon legible and causing the same to be re-cut from time to time when necessary for that purpose.

1   See para **[202.19]**.
2   For concerns about the permissible perpetuity period see para **[202.19]**.
3   See the PAA 1964, s 1(1): Part G, para **[246.59]**.

[202.32]

FORM B2.9:   **Perpetual gift for the upkeep of a churchyard with a request to maintain a particular grave[1]**

I give to the vicar and churchwarden of the parish church of —— and their successors the sum of £—— upon trust to invest the same and to apply the income thereof in keeping the graveyard of the said church in good order and repair and I request but without imposing any legal obligation on them that they will keep in good order and repair the grave and gravestones of my late wife and of myself (if I shall be buried there) and will keep the lettering thereon legible and will cause the same to be re-cut from time to time when necessary for that purpose.

1   For the general law relating to gifts in this form see para **[202.20]**.

[202.33]

FORM B2.10:   Gift for the upkeep of a particular grave in a churchyard during a perpetuity period followed by a perpetual gift for the upkeep of the churchyard with a request to maintain the particular grave[1]

(1)   I give to the vicar and churchwardens of the parish church of —— and their successors the sum of £—— upon trust to invest the same and during the period of eighty years[2] from my death (which period shall be the perpetuity period applicable to the disposition hereby effected[3] to apply the income thereof in keeping the grave and gravestone of my late wife —— and of myself (if I shall be buried there) in good order and repair and in keeping the lettering thereon legible and causing the same to be re-cut from time to time when necessary for that purpose and to apply any balance of the said income not required for such purpose in keeping the said graveyard in good order and repair.

(2)   After the expiration of the said period of eighty years the said vicar and churchwardens and their successors shall hold the said sum and the investments representing the same upon trust to apply the income thereof in keeping the said graveyard in good order and repair. And I request but without imposing any legal obligation on them that they will maintain the grave and gravestone of my said wife and of myself (if I shall be buried there) in the manner mentioned in subclause (1) hereof.

1   This form in effect combines the gifts contained in the two preceding forms: see paras **[202.19]–[202.21]**.
2   For concerns about the permissible perpetuity period, see **[202.19]**.
3   See para **[202.31]**, n 2.

[202.34]

FORM B2.11:   Direction to executors to enter into an agreement for the maintenance of a grave in a local authority cemetery[1]

If the burial authority or local authority which provides or maintains the burial ground where my body is buried [in accordance with the direction given in clause —— of this will] is willing to make an agreement (whether under the provisions of the Parish Councils and Burial Authorities (Miscellaneous Provisions) Act 1970 or any statutory modification or re-enactment thereof or under those of any local Act or other enabling power) with my executors [trustees] for the maintenance of my grave and of the tombstone or other memorial placed upon it then I direct my executors [trustees] to make an agreement with that authority providing for such maintenance to be carried out for the longest period for which the authority is prepared to undertake it and to pay from my estate the sum required by the authority as consideration therefor and any other costs which may reasonably be incurred in implementing the provisions of this clause.

1   For the general law on agreements for the maintenance of graves in local authority cemeteries, see para **[202.22]**. This Form provides for the care of a grave with a tombstone but can be readily adapted to meet the particular circumstances.

[202.35]

FORM B2.12:   Gift to a charity conditional upon the maintenance of a particular grave with a gift over on breach of the condition to another charity[1]

I give to [*charity*] the sum of £—— upon trust to apply the income thereof to its general purposes [*or name of particular purpose*] so long as the said [*charity*] shall maintain [*description of grave*] as the same has been maintained during my lifetime and upon the said [*charity*] failing so to maintain the said grave I give the said sum of £—— to [*second charity*] [*or* if before the expiration of twenty-one years from the death of the last survivor of all the descendants living and actually born at the date of my death of his late Majesty King George V the said [*charity*] shall fail so to maintain the said grave then I give the said sum of £—— to [*name of individual*] absolutely].

I declare that neglect to tend and replant the said grave for a period of [two] years shall constitute a failure to maintain the said grave and that allowing more than one third of the lettering of the tombstone on the said grave to be illegible for the same period shall also constitute such a failure.

The receipt of the proper officer of either the said [*charities*] or any person purporting to be such shall be a sufficient discharge to my trustees in respect of the said legacy.

1   For the law relating to gifts in this form see para **[202.28]**.

Maintenance of animals

[202.36]
Note. A gift, such as that contained in Form B2.13 at para **[202.37]**, for the upkeep of a particular animal is not charitable, but is valid if confined within perpetuity limits: see *Re Dean, Cooper-Dean v Stevens* (1889) 41 Ch D 552. In so far as this case decides that a dog's life is a life for the purposes of the perpetuity rule, it is generally considered to be wrong: see *Re Kelly, Cleary v James* [1932] IR 255 and Vol 1, para **[9.31]**. Since there is no beneficiary to enforce the trust, the efficacy of the gift depends entirely on the trustees' willingness to perform the trust. It may be preferable to give the pet animal together with a legacy to some person whom the testator can rely upon to look after it. It is possible to adapt Form B2.14 (at para **[202.38]**) for this purpose.

[202.37]

FORM B2.13:   Gift for the maintenance and upkeep of an animal

I give to my trustees the sum of £—— upon trust to invest the same and to apply the income therefrom for the upkeep and maintenance of my [dog *or other animal, describing it*] for the period of [twenty-one years[1]] from the date of my death if my said [dog] shall so long live and after the death of my said [dog] or after the expiration of the said period of twenty-one years whichever shall first happen the said sum shall fall into and form part of my residuary estate.

1   The period need not be confined to 21 years, provided that it does not exceed perpetuity limits.

[202.38]

FORM B2.14:   Combined gift of legacy and pet animal coupled with a non-binding expression of hope that the legatee will look after the animal[1]

I give to [*name*] a legacy of the sum of £—— together with my dog [or other animal, describing it] (if living at my death) and I express the hope (but without imposing any binding obligation on him) that the said [*name*] will look after the said dog [or other animal].

1   The legacy will take effect even if the dog or other animal is dead at the testator's death.

Declarations under the Inheritance (Provision for Family and Dependants) Act 1975

[202.39]
Note. The provisions of the Inheritance (Provision for Family and Dependants Act 1975 (I(PFD)A 1975)[1] are considered in more detail in Vol 1 at para **[105.1]** et seq. The court may receive in evidence oral and documentary statements by the deceased: Civil Evidence Act 1995, s 1. A testator may wish to take advantage of this provision by incorporating a statement in his will or by leaving a signed statement with his will. The court is not of course bound to accept the deceased's reasons as conclusive: see eg, *Re Preston, Preston v Hogarth* [1969] 2 All ER 961, [1969] 1 WLR 317. However, the court cannot entertain any application under the I(PFD)A 1975 made by the surviving party to a marriage or a former marriage, in contravention of an order made on the grant of a divorce, a decree of nullity of marriage or a decree of judicial separation that that party should not be entitled to apply for an order under the I(PFD)A 1975. Either party to a marriage may apply to the court for such an order excluding an application: I(PFD)A 1975, s 15[2].

1   See Part G, paras **[247.1]**–**[247.29]**.
2   See Part G, para **[247.16]**.

[202.40]

FORM B2.15:   Declarations under the Inheritance (Provision for Family and Dependants) Act 1975—Alternative forms

(1)   I hereby declare that no provision is hereby made for my wife [*name*] for the reason that by a deed of separation dated —— and made between [*parties*] I covenanted to pay her a clear annuity of £—— during her life and such annuity will after my death be a charge upon my estate.[1]

(2)   No provision is hereby made for my wife [*name*] for the reasons set out in a statement signed by me and deposited with ——.[2]

(3)   I hereby declare that my reason for making no provision for my present husband [*name*] or the infant children of my present marriage is that the whole of my real and personal estate was left to me by my first husband [*name*] and I consider that the whole of the beneficial interest therein should go to the children of my first marriage [more especially as my present husband is possessed of adequate means].

(4)   I hereby declare that the reason for making no provision in this my will for my unmarried daughter [*name*] is that she left home many years ago and I consider that my married daughter [*name*] with whom I have made my home for many years has a much greater claim on me.

(5)   I declare that my reason for making no provision in this my will for my infant son [*name*] is that he is already well provided for under the will of his godfather the late [*name*] while my other children have no means of their own.

(6)   I hereby declare that my reason for making no greater provision in this my will for [*name*] with whom I have lived for many years is that she has her own financial resources and has never been maintained by me during my lifetime.

---

1   Unless a contrary intention is expressed, an agreement for maintenance will bind the husband's estate: *Kirk v Eustace* [1937] AC 491, [1937] 2 All ER 715.

2   Where the testator's reasons for making no provision for any dependant are such that, if published, they would give rise to scandal, they should be stated in a separate document, for such matter is excluded from the probate: *Re Hall's Estate* [1943] 2 All ER 159.

Clause headings or marginal notes

[202.41]
Note. If clause headings or marginal notes are used in a will for more convenient reference it may be wise to include a declaration that they are not to be used in construing the will.

[202.42]

FORM B2.16:   Direction regarding clause headings or marginal notes

I declare that the [clause headings] *or* [marginal notes] added hereto are added for the sole purpose of more convenient reference and not for the purpose of the construction of the clauses herein.

B3 Appointment of executors, trustees and guardians

THE PUBLIC TRUSTEE

FORMS

SEPARATE EXECUTORS FOR PARTICULAR ASSETS

FORMS

GUARDIANS

FORMS

PRELIMINARY NOTE ON EXECUTORS AND TRUSTEES

[203.1]
Number of executors. In his will, a testator should appoint an executor or
executors to administer his property and carry into effect the provisions of the
will. The number of executors to be appointed needs to be considered. Probate
and letters of administration cannot be granted to more than four persons in
regard to the same part of a deceased's person's estate: Supreme Court Act 1981
(SCA 1981), s 114. A single executor can always take a grant of probate to a
will, although where a grant of administration has to be taken (for example,
where the executors named in the will have predeceased the testator) and a
minority or a life interest arises under a will, administration can only be granted
either to a trust corporation (with or without an individual) or to not fewer than
two individuals: SCA 1981, s 114(2). In many cases it may be wise to appoint at
least two executors. Two executors may exercise, by virtue of the Trustee Act
1925 (TA 1925), s 18(2), any trust or power which was vested in the testator as a
sole or last surviving trustee. If the will creates a trust for sale of land, although
one executor can sell as personal representative, there must be at least two
trustees if the sale is by trustees. In the case of settlements and dispositions on
trust for sale of land, the number of trustees is not to exceed four: TA 1925,
s 34(2) (Part G, para **[246.29]**).

[203.2]
Trust Corporations. A trust corporation may be an executor either alone or
jointly with another person: SCA 1981, s 115. For the meaning of 'trust
corporation' and other aspects of the appointment of corporations as executors
or trustees see para **[203.24]** et seq. See also Forms B3.11 to B3.13 at
paras **[203.28]–[203.30]** for examples of appointments of corporations.

[203.3]
Trustees. It is usually more convenient if the same persons are appointed both
executors and trustees. However, they need not necessarily be the same persons.
For a form appointing different persons as trustees see Form B3.4 at
para **[203.10]** and for an example of a complete will appointing trustees who are
not also the personal representatives see Form C5.4 at paras **[227.46]** et seq.

[203.4]
Executors and the Settled Land Act 1925. The Settled Land Act 1925 (SLA
1925) cannot apply to new settlements or trusts of land created on or after 1
January 1997, but existing Settled Land Act settlements continue to be subject to

the SLA 1925 unless and until sale of all the land (and heirlooms, if any). If a testator is the tenant for life of land under an existing strict settlement for the purposes of the SLA 1925, the settled land will normally be vested in him in fee simple. The Administration of Estates Act 1925 (AEA 1925), s 22 provides that a testator may appoint, and in default of appointment shall be deemed to have appointed, as his special executors in regard to settled land the persons who are trustees of the settlement at his death. These special executors will have the prior right to a grant of administration limited to the settled land: Non-Contentious Probate Rules 1987, r 29 (as amended with effect from 14 October 1991 by SI 1991/1876; before this amendment was made, *probate* limited to the settled land was granted to such special executors). For a form of appointment of special executors see Form B3.25 at para **[203.42]**. If there are no special executors, or there are but they do not take out a grant, the trustees of the settlement at the date of the grant are next in order of priority to take out a grant of administration, and failing them the testator's general personal representatives may take a grant: Non-Contentious Probate Rules 1987, r 29 (as amended by SI 1991/1876). In the case of the testator's personal representatives taking a grant, the Court has power to appoint a special or additional personal representative in respect of the settled land: AEA 1925, s 23. See further Vol 1, para **[26.1]** et seq.

[203.5]
Settled land to vest in tenant for life. The personal representatives in respect of the settled land (whoever they may happen to be) will hold the settled land on trust, if and when required to do so, to vest it in the person who under the trust instrument or by virtue of the SLA 1925, becomes the tenant for life or statutory owner. This right is subject to and without prejudice to the rights and powers of the personal representatives for the purposes of administration: SLA 1925, s 8(3). They may be liable for inheritance tax on the settled land (ITA 1984, s 200(1)(a), and may transfer or create legal estates pro tanto overriding the settlement for raising money or indemnifying themselves: SLA 1925, s 8(5) and (6).

[203.6]
Acceptance and renunciation. As to acceptance and renunciation or disclaimer of the office of executor or trustee, see Vol 1, paras **[25.12]**–**[25.13]**. For forms of renunciation of executorship and trusteeship see Forms F1.1 to F1.4 at paras **[239.2]**–**[239.5]**.

For executors generally, see Vol 1, para **[25.1]** et seq.

Individuals

[203.7]

FORM B3.1:   Appointment of wife as sole executrix and trustee with alternative appointment[1]

I appoint my wife [*name*] sole executrix and trustee of this my will but if my wife shall die in my lifetime or shall refuse or be unable to act as such executrix and trustee[2] then I appoint [*name*] of [*address*] and [*name*] of [*address*] to be the executors and trustees of this my will and I declare that in this will the expression 'my trustee' shall where the context so admits include my personal representatives or personal representative for the time being and the trustees or trustee for the time being of this will.

1   The appointment of a sole executor and trustee of a will is inadvisable except where there is a
     sole beneficiary of full age or the executor is a trust corporation. This Form assumes that the
     main gift in the will is to the testator's wife, with an alternative gift to take effect if the gift to
     her fails.
2   The appointment of a spouse as executor or as executor and trustee will fail, and the spouse will
     be deemed to predecease the testator for the purposes of the alternative appointment (testators
     dying on or after 1 January 1996), if the marriage is after the date of the will dissolved, annulled
     or declared void, unless a contrary intention appears by the will: WA 1837, s 18A (Part G,
     para [244.18]), see also Vol 1, para [47.2] and C2 at paras [224.12]–[224.19].

[203.8]

FORM B3.2:   Appointment of executors[1]

I appoint [*name*] of [*address*] and [*name*] of [*address*] to be the executors of this my will.

1   While a mere appointment of executors in this form may be sufficient where there is a universal
     beneficiary or all the gifts in the will are immediate and final distribution can be made as soon
     as the estate is cleared, it is always preferable that trustees of the will should be appointed as in
     the next following precedent. As to when executors, though not appointed trustees, become
     trustees, see *Re Ponder, Ponder v Ponder* [1921] 2 Ch 59 and Vol 1, para [27.1]. A grant will
     not be made to more than four persons in respect of the same part of a deceased person's estate
     but there is no longer any overall limit to the number of personal representations where separate
     grants are taken to different parts of the same estate: see s 114 (1) of the SCA 1981 reversing *Re
     Holland's Estate* [1936] 3 All ER 13.

[203.9]

FORM B3.3:   Appointment of same persons as executors and trustees[1]

I appoint [*name*] of [*address*] and [*name*] of [*address*] (hereinafter called 'my trustees' which expression shall include the trustees[2] for the time being hereof) to be the executors and trustees of this my will [and also to be the trustees hereof for the purposes of the Settled Land Act 1925][3] [If real or leasehold estate in Northern Ireland also is settled add: and of the Settled Land Acts 1882–1890, and section 42 of the Conveyancing Act 1881].[4]

1   It is usually convenient to appoint the same persons both executors and trustees though it is
     sometimes desired to appoint different persons, usually because the executors desire to be
     released from their duties as soon as possible. The following form is suitable where different
     persons are appointed, but such procedure will also entail some differences in the later part of
     the will, see paras [227.46]–[227.48]. As to the desirability of appointing at least two persons,
     see para [203.1].
2   Since the plural now includes the singular and vice versa (LPA 1925, s 61: Part G,
     para [246.40]) it is not strictly necessary to say 'the trustees or trustee' as in the common form
     before 1926, although it is still customary to do so. *Re Hayes' Will Trusts, Pattison v Hayes*
     [1971] 2 All ER 341, [1971] 1 WLR 758 establishes that where, as here, a will appoints the
     same persons as executors and trustees and defines them as 'my trustees', powers conferred on
     'my trustees' elsewhere in the will may be exercisable by those persons in either capacity. It is
     doubtful whether it is sufficient for the will to appoint the persons concerned as executors and
     trustees and then to contain a definition clause which merely makes it clear that 'my trustees'
     includes additional or substituted *trustees*. But each case must depend upon the intention of the
     testator to be deduced from the will as a whole.

3   These words will only be necessary where the provisions of the will are such that land becomes settled land within the SLA 1925. Their insertion is not essential as the SLA 1925, s 30(3), makes the personal representatives such trustees where none are appointed by the will and there are none by virtue of the provisions of the earlier part of that section. However, it is better practice to make an appointment in the will than to rely on the SLA 1925, s 30(3).

4   The changes made to the law of settled land by the English 1925 legislation have not been made to the law of settled land in any part of Ireland.

[203.10]

FORM B3.4:   Appointment of executors and of different persons as trustees[1]

I appoint [*name*] of [*address*] and [*name*] of [*address*] to be the executors of this my will and [*name*] of [*address*] and [*name*] of [*address*] (hereinafter called 'my trustees' which expression shall include the trustees for the time being hereof) to be the trustees of this my will [and I appoint my trustees to be the trustees hereof for the purposes of the Settled Land Act 1925].

1   See notes to last precedent. For a form of will where there are trustees who are different persons from the executors see Form C5.4 at para **[227.50]**.

[203.11]

FORM B3.5:   Appointment of wife during widowhood adult son and infant son when he attains majority to be executors and trustees

I appoint to be the executors and trustees of this my will my wife [*name*] [so long as she shall remain my widow][1] my son [*name*] and also my son [*name*] if and when such last-named son shall attain the age of eighteen years[2] who are hereinafter called 'my trustees' which expression where used throughout this my will shall (where the context permits) include the trustees for the time being of this my will whether original or substituted [and if there shall for the time being be no such trustees or trustee shall (where the context permits) include the persons or person empowered by statute to exercise or perform any power or trust hereby or by statute conferred upon my trustees willing or bound to exercise or perform the same][3] [and I appoint my trustees to be trustees hereof for the purposes of the Settled Land 1925].[4]

1   It is inadvisable to direct a person to cease to be an executor on the happening of a certain event or to become an executor on the happening of a certain event. If this clause is used at all, the wife and son should be trustees only, and even with this limitation, the clause is likely to cause difficulty and should be used only on the express instructions of the testator.

2   As to the effect of appointing an infant as a sole or joint executor, see s 118 of the SCA 1981.

3   See s 18(2) of the TA 1925 (Part G, para **[246.16]**) and s 30(3) of the SLA 1925. It is submitted that this addition is in law unnecessary because under these statutes the personal representative may either assume the position of trustee or appoint others to be trustees. If he assumes the position of trustee he becomes a trustee for the time being of the will. However, the words may be included if it is desired to make the position quite clear. As to executors generally, see Vol 1, para **[25.1]** et seq. As to the validity of appointment of a wife as executor during her widowhood see Wentworth, Off Ex 14th ed 29; Goldolphin, Part II, c 2, s 3. Probate or letters of administration will not be granted to more than four persons in respect of the same part of the estate of a deceased person, but there is no longer any limit to the total number of executors or administrators where separate grants are made to different parts of the estate: see para **[203.8]**, n 1. As to the position where an executor renounces, but is subsequently permitted to withdraw his renunciation and to prove, see s 6(1) of the AEA 1925.

4   See para **[203.9]**, n 4.

[203.12]

FORM B3.6:   Appointment of three persons, one of whom is abroad, to be executors and trustees, and also trustees for the purposes of the Settled Land Act 1925

I appoint [*name*] of [*address*] and [*name*] of [*address*] and also [*name*] of [*address*] [if and when such last-named person returns to England with the intention of permanently residing there][1] (hereinafter called 'my trustees'[2] which expression shall include the trustees or trustee for the time being hereof whether original or substituted) to be the executors and trustees of this my will and I appoint my trustees to be trustees hereof for all the purposes of the Settled Land 1925.[3] [If real or leasehold estate in Northern Ireland also is settled add: and of the Settled Land Acts 1882 to 1890 and section 42 of the Conveyancing Act 1881].[4]

1   An appointment of this kind is very inadvisable. For the difficulties that may arise under it, see *Re Arbib and Class's Contract* [1891] 1 Ch 601. If any named executor does not prove, those who do prove can validly execute a conveyance of real estate (AEA 1925, s 2(2), and note that 'real estate' in s 2(2) includes leaseholds: AEA 1925, s 3(1)).
2   See para **[203.9]**, n 3.
3   See para **[203.9]**, n 4. Settled Land Act trustees are also trustees for management of land during the minority of a person entitled in possession, unless their appointment provides to the contrary: SLA 1925, s 102.
4   The English 1925 legislation does not apply to any part of Ireland.

[203.13]

FORM B3.7:   Appointment of executors and trustees with provisions for substitution in case of vacancy[1]

I appoint [*name*] of [*address*] [*name*] of [*address*] and [*name*] of [*address*] to be executors and trustees of this my will and in case any one or more of them shall die in my lifetime or shall refuse or be unable to act in the office of executor and trustee then I appoint [*name*] of [*address*] [*name*] of [*address*] and [*name*] of [*address*] in the order named to fill any vacancy in the office of executor and trustee hereof that may occur by reason of such death refusal or inability as aforesaid. [And I declare that the expression 'my trustees' used throughout this my will shall include (where the context permits) my personal representatives for the time being and the trustees for the time being of this my will whether original or substituted. And if there shall for the time being be no such trustee the said expression shall (where the context permits) include the person empowered by statute to exercise or perform any power or trust hereby or by statute conferred upon my trustees and willing or bound to exercise or perform the same.] [I appoint my trustees to be the trustees hereof for the purposes of the Settled Land Act 1925.][2]

1   Where executors renounced, a grant was made to substituted executors: *Re Freeman's Estate* (1831) 146 LT 143. See also para **[203.9]**, n 3 as to the effect of the definition of 'my trustees'. For a form of appointment of a spouse as executor with an alternative appointment in case of a vacancy, see Form B3.1 at para **[203.7]**. The formula in this form can now be used where a spouse is initially appointed executor despite the possibility of the appointment failing by reason of the marriage ending in divorce, being annulled or being declared void: see para **[203.7]**, n 2.
2   See para **[203.9]**, n 4.

Solicitors

[203.14]
Partners in firms of solicitors. The two forms of B3.8 (at para **[203.21]**) are designed to cater for the wish of a client to appoint as executors and trustees of his will persons who will be partners in a firm of solicitors at the date of his death. Form A is based on a precedent which in the case of *Re Horgan* [1971] P 50, [1969] 3 All ER 1570 was considered by Latey J to be 'probably the best which could be devised'. It provides that all the partners at the date of death are appointed as both executors and trustees, but the intention is (if the precatory words in square brackets are included) that only two shall accept the appointment and that the remainder (if any) shall act neither as the executors nor as the initial trustees. It is important to phrase the appointment in this way to avoid uncertainty as to who has been appointed—a purported appointment of 'two of the partners in X firm' will be void: *Re Baylis' Goods* (1862) 2 Sw & Tr 613; *Re Blackwell's Goods* (1877) 2 PD 72.

[203.15]
Two partners as executors and trustees. Where Form A in B3.8 at para **[203.21]** is used, so far as the executorship is concerned, the two who decide to act can prove the will and the others can renounce probate or simply refrain from proving. But renunciation of probate or failure to prove the will does not necessarily amount to disclaimer of the trusteeship, so that when the administration is complete and the trusts begin to operate it is arguable that the trustees, prima facie, are all the partners and not merely the two who have proved the will. On the other hand, this difficulty may be more apparent than real. However, many people may be appointed trustees, the only people who actually become trustees are those who expressly or impliedly accept office, and if the other partners do not accept the trusteeship they will not become trustees. So far as conveyancing is concerned they will be hidden behind the curtain mechanism; the legal estate in the land will not leave the hands of the two proving executors unless and until they make an assent, and when they do make an assent the assent is, in favour of a purchaser, to be taken as sufficient evidence that the persons to whom it is made are those to whom it should have been made: AEA 1925, s 36(7). Nor is there any risk of the beneficiaries making the other partners liable as trustees unless they have actually intermeddled in the trusts (though having regard to the fact that they are partners in the same firm of solicitors as the 'real' trustees and might on occasion take on some of their work, there might be a slight risk that intermeddling could be inferred).

[203.16]
A drafting problem which can arise where Form A in B3.8 at para **[203.21]** is used in the more complicated type of will, where powers of appointment or application of capital are conferred on the executors and trustees, is avoiding the possibility that the powers can only be exercised by all the partners in the firm including those who do not take out a grant.

[203.17]
These difficulties with Form A appointment can be avoided by an appointment made along the lines of Form B of B3.8 at para **[203.21]**. This provides that the

only partners to be trustees are those who actually prove the will. It also provides a definition of 'my trustees', for use when conferring powers and creating trusts, which excludes from the definition persons appointed executors who do not take out a grant of probate.

[203.18]

Even where a definition of 'my trustees' is included on the lines of the one in Form B, this type of appointment is not a good one to choose if the will creates discretionary trusts with a view to taking advantage of the ITA 1984, s 144 (see C3 at paras **[225.83]–[225.91]**), at any rate where it may be desired to make an appointment under a power in the will before the grant of probate has been obtained, because the agreement to and execution of the appointment by all the partners in the firm at the testator's death will be needed for an appointment to be made before the grant of probate, even where Form B is used.

For forms of executors' oaths which may be applicable where partners of a firm of solicitors are appointed executors, see Form F2.3 at para **[240.3]**.

[203.19]

Solicitors' incorporated practices. By virtue of the Administration of Justice Act 1985, s 9 and the Solicitors' Incorporated Practice Rules 1988 solicitors may now act through bodies corporate rather than a partnership firms provided the body is recognised by the Law Society. The corporate body itself cannot take out a grant of probate or letters of administration to a person's estate because it is not a trust corporation, but its directors, members and the owners of its shares may. There are hardly any incorporated practices at present, but it is possible that the number will increase. Where Form B3.8 (at para **[203.21]**) has been used and the firm has become incorporated before the testator's death, there would be a question whether the appointment of executors was still effective.

[203.20]

Forms B3.9 and B3.10 (at paras **[203.22]** and **[203.23]**) are designed to cater respectively for a solicitors' practice which has already been incorporated, and for the possibility that what is at present a firm may become incorporated before the testator's death, where the testator wishes to appoint the members of the incorporated practice or firm as executors.

[203.21]

FORM B3.8:   Appointment of future partners in a solicitors' firm as executors and trustees

FORM A.   ORIGINAL FORM

I appoint the partners at the date of my death in the firm of [*name of firm*] of [*address*] or the firm which at that date has succeeded to and carries on its practice to be the executors and trustees of this my will [and I express the wish that no more than two of them shall prove my will and act initially in its trusts and that [*name*] if then a partner should be one of them].

FORM B.   ALTERNATIVE (PREFERRED) FORM

(a)   As executors of this will I appoint the partners at the date of my death in the firm of [*name of firm*] of [*address*] or the firm which at that date has succeeded to and carries on its practice [and I express the wish that no more than two of them shall prove the will and that [*name*] if then a partner should be one of them].

(b)   As trustees of this will I appoint the persons who take out a grant of probate [not being a grant limited to settled land][1] by virtue of the foregoing appointment of executors.[2]

(c)   The expression 'my trustees' in this my will means my personal representatives and the trustees of this will from time to time (whether original or substituted) but after there has been a grant of probate or letters of administration in respect of my estate [(other than a grant limited to settled land)][3] it shall not include, by virtue of the foregoing appointment of executors,[4] any person appointed an executor who for the time being has not proved this will.

1   These words could be included if the testator is a tenant for life under a SLA 1925 settlement which will continue after his death, because the first persons to take out a grant might be the trustees of the strict settlement. However, these words are now not strictly necessary in this context: as a result of the changes made to Non-Contentious Probate Rules 1987, r 29 by SI 1991/1876 (with effect from 14 October 1991) all grants in respect of settled land of which the deceased was the life tenant are now grants of *administration* not probate. See paras **[203.4]–[203.6]**.

2   This subclause is intended to include in the appointment of trustees anyone who takes out a grant including a grant subsequent to the first, eg where the partners in the firm who take out the initial grant and die while the estate is still in the course of administration, and another partner or partners take out a grant under the power reserved.

3   These words should be included if the testator is a tenant for life under a SLA 1925 settlement which will continue after his death, because the first persons to take out a grant of probate or letters of administration might be the trustees of the settled land. In contrast to these words in the preceding subclause these words are needed in this subclause despite the changes to Non-Contentious Probate Rules 1987, r 29 noted in n 1 supra because here there is a reference to grants of administration as well as probate.

4   The reason for including these words is to make it clear that someone who is initially appointed an executor, does not take a grant of probate, but is later appointed a trustee by, eg, an appointment under the TA 1925, s 36, is not excluded from the definition.

[203.22]

FORM B3.9:   **Appointment of members of solicitors' incorporated practice**

(a)   As executors of this will I appoint the persons who at the date of my death are the directors, members and beneficial owners of any share of the incorporated practice of [*name of incorporated practice*] of [*address of registered office*] and I express the wish that no more than two of them [including [*name*] if he/she should be a director, member or beneficial owner of any share at the time of my death] shall prove my will.

(b)   As trustees of this will I appoint the persons who take out a grant of probate [not being a grant limited to settled land][1] by virtue of the foregoing appointment of executors.

(c)   The expression 'my trustees' in this my will means my personal representatives and the trustees of this will from time to time (whether original or substituted) but after there has been a grant of probate or letters of administration in respect of my estate [(other than a grant limited to settled land)]^2 it shall not include, by virtue of the foregoing appointment of executors,^{3} any person appointed an executor who for the time being has not proved this will.

1   See para **[203.21]**, n 1.
2   See para **[203.21]**, n 3.
3   See para **[203.21]**, n 4.

[203.23]

FORM B3.10:   **Appointment of future partners in a solicitors' firm or future members of the body in the event of incorporation**

(a)   As executors of this will I appoint the partners at the date of my death in the firm of [*name of firm*] of [*address*] or the firm which has succeeded to and carries on its practice but in the event of such firm being incorporated at the date of my death I appoint the directors, members and beneficial owners of any share of the incorporated practice at the date of my death.

(b)   I express the wish that no more than two persons shall prove my will [including [*name*] if he/she should be partner, director, member or beneficial owner (as the case may be) at the time of my death].

(c)   As trustees of this will I appoint the persons who take out a grant of probate [not being a grant limited to settled land]^1 by virtue of the foregoing appointment of executors.

(d)   The expression 'my trustees' in this my will means my personal representatives and the trustees of this will from time to time (whether original or substituted) but after there has been a grant of probate or letters of administration in respect of my estate [(other than a grant limited to settled land)]^2 it shall not include, by virtue of the foregoing appointment of executors,^{3} any person appointed an executor who for the time being has not proved this will.

1   See para **[203.21]**, n 1.
2   See para **[203.21]**, n 3.
3   See para **[203.21]**, n 4.

Corporations

[203.24]
Trust corporations. A trust corporation may be an executor either alone or jointly with another person: SCA 1981, s 115. A trust corporation is the Public Trustee or a corporation appointed by the court as a trustee or entitled under the Public Trustee Rules to act as custodian trustee: TA 1925, s 68(18) (Part G, para **[246.36]**) and the LPA 1925, s 205(1)(xxviii) (Part G, para **[246.44A]**). For the last mentioned category, see r 30 of the Public Trustee Rules 1912 (SR & O 1912/348), as substituted by the Public Trustee (Custodian Trustee) Rules 1975 (SI 1975/1189) and subsequently amended (Part G, para **[246.58]**). Certain EC corporations can qualify as trust corporations. Any authorised officer of a trust corporation may on its behalf swear affidavits, give security, and do any other

act or thing which the court may require with a view to taking a grant, and the acts of such officer will be binding on the corporation.

[203.25]

Appointment of trust corporation. Most banks and insurance companies are trust corporations or have subsidiaries which are trust corporations. If it is proposed to appoint a bank or insurance company as executor or trustee, it must be ascertained whether the trustee department is a separate company, and if so, it must be referred to by its proper name. The institution's common form clauses should be obtained and agreed, with or without modification, together with the scale of fees. The will should be submitted to the institution in draft, so that it may inform the testator or those advising him whether it will accept office. Generally speaking all ordinary wills are accepted, but wills requiring the trustees to carry on a business are usually refused.

[203.26]

Charging clause. Where a will appoints a trust corporation as executor and/or trustee, a clause authorising it to charge for acting on its standard terms should be included. There is now a statutory power for a trust corporation to charge reasonable remuneration under the Trustee Act 2000, s 29 (Part G, para **[246.144]**), but it is not clear that it would include power to charge scale fees: see para **[221.48]**. Where a corporation is appointed administrator of an estate, the court can authorise remuneration both under the TA 1925, s 42 and its inherent jurisdiction: *Re Young's Estate* (1934) 103 LJP 75 and *Re Masters, Coutts & Co v Masters* [1953] 1 All ER 19.

[203.27]

Fees charged by banks. Where a bank was by codicil appointed executor and trustee of a will in place of a solicitor who was given the benefit of a charging clause, the bank was entitled to its ordinary scale of fees at the date of the codicil although nothing was said in the codicil as to charging: *Re Campbell's Estate* [1954] 1 All ER 448. Where a clause appointing a bank as executor and trustee included the following: 'and may without accounting for any resultant profit act as banker and perform any service on behalf of my estate on the same terms as would be made with a customer', it was held that where considerable funds of the estate remained uninvested for some four years while on deposit with the bank, the bank was under no duty to account for the profit gained by its employment of the money deposited with it, such procedure being justified by the charging clause: *Re Waterman's Will Trusts, Lloyds Bank Ltd v Sutton* [1952] 2 All ER 1054. The statutory power of a trust corporation to charge includes a power for one which is a bank to charge reasonable charges for its banking services: TrA 2000, s 29(3) (Part G, para **[246.144]**); see also para **[221.48]**.

[203.28]

FORM B3.11:   Appointment of a bank together with individuals as executors and trustees

I appoint [*names*] of [*address*] and the —— Bank plc to be executors and trustees of this my will.

[203.29]

FORM B3.12:   **Appointment of bank as sole executor and trustee**

I appoint —— Bank plc to be the executor and trustee [or the custodian trustee] of this my will. [*Add the clauses required by the bank.*] [I hereby also appoint the said bank to be the trustees hereof for the purposes of the Settled Land Act 1925.]¹

1   See para **[203.9]**, n 4.

[203.30]

FORM B3.13:   **Appointment of insurance company as executor and trustee**

I appoint —— Insurance Co plc to be the executor and trustee [*or* the custodian trustee] of this my will. If in relation to my will or the trusts thereof it shall become necessary to effect any policy of insurance such insurance may be effected with the said —— Insurance Co plc at their usual rates for such insurance and the said —— Insurance Co plc shall not be accountable to my estate in respect of any profit it may make in respect thereof. [*Add any special clauses required by the insurance company.*] [I hereby also appoint the said —— Insurance Co plc to be the trustee hereof for the purposes of the Settled Land Act 1925.]¹

1   See para **[203.9]**, n 4.

[203.31]

FORM B3.14:   **Remuneration clause for bank appointed as executor and trustee**

(a)   The bank shall have power to act by its proper officers and shall be entitled to remuneration for acting as executor and trustee [in accordance with the bank's published scale of fees contained in a letter dated —— written to me by the bank] *or* [in accordance with the bank's published scale of fees from time to time] *or* [in accordance with such scale of fees as may be agreed upon after my death between the bank and the other persons nominated herein as my executors and trustees or such of them as shall be living at my death].

 (b)   The bank may act as bankers to and make advances or loans to my trustees or my estate upon the usual terms as to interest and charges in the ordinary course of the bank's business and share stockbrokers' commissions and generally act as a banker may in relation to his customer and without accounting for any profit so made.

 [(c)   The bank shall hold all moneys deeds and documents relating to the trusts of this my will subject to proper facilities for my other trustees to inspect and verify the same and the name of the bank shall be placed first in the register of all registered securities or property.]¹

1   This subclause is not needed if the bank is sole executor.

The Public Trustee

[203.32]

FORM B3.15:   Application by an intending testator to the Public Trustee to act as executor and trustee under a will[1]

(*All information placed before the Public Trustee will be treated as confidential.*)

To the PUBLIC TRUSTEE,

81 Chancery Lane, London, WC2A 1DD.

DEAR SIR.

I shall be glad to learn if you will be prepared to act as

1. Executor [co-executor] *or*
2. Trustee [co-trustee] *or* } under my will.
3. Executor and trustee [co-executor and co-trustee]

I CONTEMPLATE disposing of my property in the following manner ——.

The original will (*with other testamentary documents, if any*) is [*will be*] deposited at ——.

My bankers are ——.

The stockbrokers I usually employ are Messrs —— of —— .

The solicitors whom I desire the Public Trustee to employ for any necessary professional work incidental to the administration of my estate are Messrs —— of ——.

Name of testator (in full) ——.

Signature ——.

Residence ——.

Occupation (if any) ——.

Date ——.

The property which will pass under the will will probably consist of the following:[2]

	Approximate value or amount.
Stocks and shares fully paid	£——
Stocks and shares partly paid	£——
Life insurances	£——
Real property in the United Kingdom	£——
Real property abroad	£——
Leasehold property in ——	£——
Mortgages on property in ——	£——
Other property ——	£——
Approximate total	£——

Part B   Clauses in wills

1   It is not essential to supply detailed information, but it is desirable that the form should be filled
    in and returned to the Public Trustee, who is then in the position to say, from the details
    submitted to him, whether he can act or not. On receipt of the form duly filled in, the Public
    Trustee's formal consent to act is forwarded to the applicant, and in this way a suitable record is
    established on either side. The submission of this form is in no way binding upon the applicant.
    The Public Trustee will not act where the carrying on of a business for an indefinite period is
    involved nor will he undertake a trust where the whole of the trust property is devoted to
    religious or charitable purposes, but this latter restriction does not apply to executorships. A
    testator may appoint the Public Trustee without first obtaining his consent, but the appointment
    does not have effect unless the Public Trustee consents to act: r 8 of the Public Trustee Rules
    1912 (SR & O 1912/348).
2   It is not essential to fill in this portion of the form, but it is convenient to the Public Trustee to
    see the general character of the estate with which it is proposed he shall deal.

[203.33]

FORM B3.16:   Clause in will appointing the Public Trustee as sole executor and trustee or jointly with others[1]

I appoint the Public Trustee [and [*first executor*] and [*second executor*] who and
the survivors and survivor of them are hereinafter referred to as 'my trustees'] to
be [sole] executor[s] and trustee[s] of this my will [and to be trustee[s] thereof
for the purposes of the Settled Land Act 1925].[2]

1   For power to appoint the Public Trustee either solely or jointly with others: Public Trustee Act
    1906 (PTA 1906), s 2(2).
2   It is desirable that the Public Trustee's name should appear first in order to secure that
    all communications, etc from companies should be addressed to him as the first-named
    holder.

[203.34]

FORM B3.17:   Clauses in will appointing executors and trustees, the Public Trustee being only a trustee or custodian trustee

I appoint [*first executor*] and [*second executor*] (hereinafter called 'my
executors') to be the executors of this my will and my executors and the Public
Trustee (who and the survivors and survivor of whom are hereinafter referred to
as 'my trustees') to be the trustees of this my will [and to be trustees thereof for
the purposes of the Settled Land Act 1925][1]

OR

I appoint [*first executor*] and [*second executor*] (who and the survivors and
survivor of whom and other the managing trustees for the time being hereof are
hereinafter referred to as 'my trustees') to be executors and the managing
trustees of this my will and the Public Trustee to be the custodian trustee thereof
[and I further appoint [*trustees, including Public Trustee if so desired*] to be the
trustees hereof for the purposes of the Settled Land Act 1925].[2]

On the death of the said [*first executor*] or [*second executor*] I appoint the
survivor and the Public Trustee to be the trustees of my will and the expression
'my trustees' shall thereafter mean and include such survivor and the Public
Trustee and other the trustees or trustee for the time being thereof provided
always that the trust funds and property from time to time subject to the trusts of
this my will shall be held in the sole name of the Public Trustee.[3]

1   See para **[203.9]**, n 4.
2   The Public Trustee may act as sole trustee including Settled Land Act trustee (PTA 1906, s 5(1); LPA 1925, s 27(2), as amended by the Law of Property (Amendment) Act 1926: Part G, para **[246.39D]**). See also para **[203.9]**, n 4.
3   The appointment of the Public Trustee as both managing trustee and custodian trustee might be ineffective: see *Forster v Williams Deacon's Bank Ltd* [1935] Ch 359, [1935] All ER Rep 374, and *Arning v James* [1936] Ch 158.

[203.35]

FORM B3.18:   **Clauses in will of a person domiciled elsewhere than in England and Wales appointing an individual executor and providing for transfer of the residuary estate or of a legacy to the Public Trustee to be held upon English trusts[1]**

I appoint [*executor*] to be executor of this my will and direct that my executor shall pay a legacy of £—— free from inheritance tax [*or* that after payment of my funeral and testamentary expenses and debts and the inheritance tax payable in respect of my death and all legacies given by this my will or any codicil thereto my executor shall pay or transfer the whole of my residuary estate] to the Public Trustee constituted by the Public Trustee Act 1906 to be held by him upon the trusts and with and subject to the powers and provisions hereinafter declared and contained concerning the same.

I declare that the trust to be created in respect of my residuary estate [or the said legacy of £——] shall be considered to be an English trust and that the Public Trustee in his character of trustee thereof shall be exempted from being subject to the process or decision of any tribunal other than the High Court of Justice in England.

[*Set out trusts upon which the legacy or share of residue is to be held.*]

1   The validity of the direction in favour of the Public Trustee may depend upon the law of the country of domicile of the testator.

[203.36]

FORM B3.19:   **Codicil revoking appointment of executors and trustees and appointing the Public Trustee sole executor and trustee in their place**

I [*Testator*] of [*address*] declare this to be a codicil (*or* the —— codicil) to my will dated ——.

I revoke the appointment contained in my said will [or in the —— codicil thereto] of [*names*] as executors and trustees [and also as trustees for the purposes of the Settled Land Act 1925] and in lieu thereof:

I appoint the Public Trustee to be sole executor and trustee of my said will [and the —— codicil[s] thereto] [and to be trustee thereof for the purposes of the Settled Land Act 1925].[1]

And in all other respects I confirm my said will [and —— codicils].

IN WITNESS ETC.[2]

1   See para **[203.34]**, n 2 and para **[203.9]**, n 4.
2   For a form of execution and attestation, see Form B22.9 at para **[222.11]**.

[203.37]

FORM B3.20:   Codicil appointing the Public Trustee as executor and trustee jointly with executors and trustees previously appointed or in place of one who has died

I [*Testator*] of [*address*] declare this to be a codicil [or the —— codicil] to my will dated ——.

[*Recite, if appropriate, the death of any executor and trustee previously appointed.*]

I appoint the Public Trustee to be an executor and trustee of my said will [and the —— codicil[s] thereto] [in place of [*name*] who has died and] jointly with [*names of surviving executors and trustees*] [and also as trustee of my said will jointly with [*names of surviving executors and trustees*] for the purposes of the Settled Land Act 1925].[1]

And I declare that my said will [and the —— codicil[s] thereto] shall be read and construed in all respects as if the official name of the Public Trustee had been inserted throughout as an executor and trustee [but so that the Public Trustee shall not be entitled to receive any legacy [*or* annuity] given to the said [*name of the deceased executor and trustee*] for acting as executor and trustee of my will].

And in all other respects I confirm my said will [and the —— codicil[s] thereto].

IN WITNESS ETC.[2]

1   See para **[203.9]**, n 4.
2   For form of execution and attestation, see Form B22.9 at para **[222.11]**.

[203.38]

FORM B3.21:   Clause in will prohibiting appointment of the Public Trustee as a trustee[1]

PROVIDED ALWAYS and I hereby direct and declare that the Public Trustee [or a trust corporation] shall in no event be appointed a new or additional trustee or custodian trustee of this my will or any codicil hereto or of any trust or duty by such will or codicil declared.

1   PTA 1906, s 5(3). A direction such as the above is not binding on the court (s 5(3)). Presumably the direction can be made in respect of trust corporations in general, though the subsection is confined to the Public Trustee.

Separate executors for particular assets

[203.39]

FORM B3.22:   Appointment of literary executors[1]

I hereby appoint [*name*] of [*address*] and [*name*] of [*address*] (hereinafter called 'my trustees') to be the executors and trustees of this my will except as to the part of my estate hereby given to my literary executors as hereinafter mentioned.

I appoint [*name*] of [*address*] and [*name*] of [*address*] (hereinafter called 'my literary executors') to be the executors of this my will to administer only the part of my estate hereinafter given to them [and I direct that the inheritance tax attributable to the said part of my estate and the expenses paid and incurred by them in taking out a limited grant of probate shall be borne by and payable out of the said part of my estate so given to them and as a first charge thereon].[2]

1   It is sometimes desired that special literary executors should be appointed. If so they should be persons having a special knowledge of the administration of literary assets or the interests in them under the will. The difficulties associated with a special grant make this a course which should not be adopted unless there are unpublished works likely from the reputation of the testator to be of considerable value and the publication of which require the supervision of a person experienced in such matters or where there are manuscripts of importance which are to be given to one person and it is desired to keep them separate from the general estate, see *Re Holland's Estate* [1936] 3 All ER 13. Where all the works have been published and it is merely a question of collecting royalties, the matter can in general be safely left to the general executors who can obtain such advice as they may require from qualified persons. A gift of an unpublished manuscript to literary executors carries with it the copyright unless a contrary intention is expressed; CDPA 1988, s 93. In the case where the literary assets are given to the executor for his absolute use and benefit, there is much more reason for adopting this course. As to the number of such executors to be appointed the following considerations may be relevant. If the literary assets are to be given to one person it seems best to appoint him the sole literary executor. If they are given upon special trusts or to be handed over to the general trustees to form part of the residue, then it seems better that there should be two such executors for the simple reason that one such may well predecease the testator and still more likely may die before the completion of his task and the whole object of the special appointment would be frustrated. There is no reason in law for the appointment of only one literary executor especially now that there is no limit to the overall total number of executors in cases where separate grants are made to different parts of the estate: see para **[203.8]**, n 1. See Forms B4.48 and B4.49 at paras **[204.70]** and **[204.71]**, for forms of gifts to and specific powers for literary executors.
2   In the absence of a direction such as this throwing the burden of inheritance tax attributable to the separate property upon the separate property, it would be borne by the testator's residuary estate, see the Preliminary Note to B14 at para **[214.55]** et seq.

[203.40]

FORM B3.23:   **Appointment of separate executors for testator's business[1]**

I hereby appoint [*name*] of [*address*] and [*name*] of [*address*] (hereinafter called my trustees) to be executors and trustees of this my will for all purposes other than the purpose of dealing with my business assets given by Clause [number] below and I appoint [*name*] of [*address*] and [*name*] of [*address*] (hereinafter called 'my business trustees') to be executors and trustees to administer and hold on trust my said business assets.

1   See Form B5.1 at para **[205.58]** for a gift of a business, and Form B5.6 at para **[205.63]** and Form C11.3 at paras **[233.36]**–**[233.51]** for other forms dealing with business property and appointing separate executors of it.

[203.41]

FORM B3.24:   **Appointment of separate executors for UK property and foreign property**

(a)   I hereby appoint [*name*] of [*address*] and [*name*] of [*address*] to be executors and trustees of this my will for the purpose of dealing with all real or personal property belonging to me and situate in the United Kingdom at my death [and for the purpose of receiving from my foreign trustees hereinafter appointed and dealing with the income and proceeds of sale and property vesting in my foreign trustees which my foreign trustees may hand over to them pursuant to the directions in that behalf hereinafter contained].

(b)   I hereby appoint [*names of individuals or of trust corporation*] [of] *or* [whose registered office is situate at] [*address*] to be executors and trustees of this my will in regard to and for the purpose of dealing with all property (movable or immovable) belonging to me and situate in [*name of country*] at my death.

[203.42]

FORM B3.25:   Appointment of special executors of settled land[1]

I appoint as my special executors in regard to settled land of which at my death I shall be the tenant for life or the person having the powers of a tenant for life the respective persons who shall be at the time of my death the trustees for the purposes of the Settled Land Act 1925 of such settlements provided the land settled thereby continues to be settled land after my death.

1   This form is included for completeness, but in the absence of an express appointment such an appointment is implied by statute: AEA 1925, s 22. See paras **[203.4]–[203.6]** generally on special executors.

Guardians

[203.43]
Note. The law of guardians has been much revised and completely restated by the Children Act 1989 (ChA 1989), and when it comes to drafting appointments of guardians the provisions of that Act are all that need to be considered. Its provisions are considered in detail in Vol 1, para **[28.1]** et seq and printed in Part G at para **[244.117]** et seq. For the power of a guardian to receive or recover the property of a minor see the ChA 1989, s 3(3) (Part G, para **[244.119]**) and Vol 1, paras **[9.38]–[9.42]**. Although the law has been made more complicated, its practical effect on the making of appointments of guardians is probably to simplify matters. Anyone making a will who has 'parental responsibility' (see Vol 1, para **[28.2]** for the meaning of this) for minor children should consider including in his will an appointment of a guardian to look after them in the event of his or her death. Anyone with parental responsibility for minor children who does not want to make a will should at least consider making an appointment of a guardian, which can be done by a signed and dated written instrument without observing the formal requirements for making a will, and which can like a will be revoked or changed subsequently (see Vol 1, para **[28.5]**). If a will is being made, we recommend putting any appointment of a guardian in it, since the appointment is more likely to be found and acted on after the appointor's death if it is in a will.

We have the following points and recommendations to make about the appointment of guardians.

[203.44]

(a)   Children with two parents with parental responsibility. This category comprises children of a marriage, children whom the law deems to be the children of both the parties to a marriage, and children whose parents are not and have not been married to each other but whose fathers have acquired parental responsibility (for which see Vol 1, para **[28.2]**). Children deemed to be children of both parties to a marriage include children legitimated by the subsequent marriage of their parents, adopted by a married couple, or conceived by artificial insemination or in vitro fertilisation in circumstances that they are treated as the child of both parties to a marriage (ChA 1989, s 2(1) and (3): Part G, para **[244.118]**; and HFEA 1990, ss 27 to 29: Part G, paras **[245.85]**–**[245.87]**).

[203.45]

An appointment of a guardian by the father of a child born out of wedlock will only be valid if it is made after he has acquired parental responsibility for the child, which he can do by agreement with the mother or a court order (see Vol 1, paras **[28.2]** and **[28.4]**), or by marrying the mother, which will have the effect that the child will be deemed to be the child of the marriage with both parents having parental responsibility (ChA 1989, s 2(1) and (3): Part G, para **[244.118]**; and FLRA 1987, s 1(2) and (3): Part G, para **[245.70]**). An appointment made by him before he has acquired parental responsibility will be of no effect even if he subsequently acquires it. It should be remembered that if he and the mother do decide to make a parental responsibility agreement the father will not acquire parental responsibility unless and until the agreement has been made in the prescribed form and has been registered with the Principal Registry of the Family Division of the High Court (see Vol 1, para **[28.2]**).

[203.46]

The main thing to bear in mind, and this is an innovation of the Children Act 1989, is that if one of two parents with parental responsibility for minor children dies leaving the other surviving, an appointment of a guardian made by the first to die will not take effect until the death of the other parent (unless the first to die had a residence order in his or her favour, to the exclusion of the other parent, at his or her death): see Vol 1, para **[28.4]** and ChA 1989, s 5(8) (Part G, para **[244.121]**). We recommend, at any rate where the parents' marriage or relationship is reasonably harmonious, for each parent's appointment of a guardian to be such that it will take effect only if the other has predeceased him or her, so that in the event of the death of both while any of the children are still under 18 it is only the appointment made by the second to die which will take effect. This will leave the survivor, after the death of the first to die, with a free hand as to the choice of a guardian to look after the children in the event of the survivor also dying while some of them are still minors, whereas if the first to die has left an effective appointment it will take effect on the death of the second to die and nothing (short of obtaining a court order) can be done to revoke or prevent it after the first to die's death. See Form B3.26 at para **[203.55]** for an example of an appointment which only takes effect if the other parent has predeceased the testator.

[203.47]

If an appointment of the kind just recommended has been made, it could have an effect which is not what the testator would have wanted if by the time of his or her death (predeceasing the other parent) there is a residence order made by the court in his or her favour (and which is not in favour of the other parent); an appointment of a guardian expressed to take effect only if the other parent predeceases the testator would not take effect in these circumstances, even though it could have taken effect immediately on the death of the first to die if it had been unconditional (see Vol 1, para **[28.4]** and ChA 1989, s 5(7) to (9): Part G, para **[244.121]**). See Form B3.27 at para **[203.56]** for an appointment which will take effect where there is a residence order at the testator's death, while still leaving the choice of guardian to the surviving parent if there is not a residence order.

[203.48]

A further point about leaving the surviving parent with a free hand as to the appointment of guardians is that he or she might not make any appointment, though appointing a guardian is perhaps unlikely to be neglected by someone who has had the experience of the death of the other parent. See Forms B3.26 and B3.27 at paras **[203.55]** and **[203.56]** for optional wording which will enable an appointment to take effect on the death of the survivor of the two parents if the survivor does not make an effective appointment. It seems unnecessary to include wording of this type where at the same time both parents are making wills containing appointments of guardians.

[203.49]

(b)   Children with only one parent with parental responsibility. This category includes children of a marriage where one parent has died, and children whose parents have never been married to each other and whose fathers have not acquired parental responsibility.

[203.50]

It is particularly important for a sole parent with parental responsibility of a child to make an appointment of a guardian. Where an unmarried couple are living together, and the father has not acquired parental responsibility, the mother should consider making an appointment of the father as guardian. She could also consider making a parental responsibility agreement giving the father parental responsibility; an important difference is that an appointment of a guardian is revocable by the appointor, while a parental responsibility agreement can only be terminated by a court order (see Vol 1, para **[28.2]**). On the other hand parental responsibility is a permanent acceptance of responsibility by the father, whereas he can always disclaim an appointment as guardian after the death of the mother (see Vol 1, paras **[28.6]** and **[28.7]**).

For forms for appointment of a guardian by a sole parent see Forms B3.29 and B3.30 at paras **[203.58]** and **[203.59]**.

Similarly, where a widow or widower has minor children by her or his first marriage, and marries again, she or he should consider making an appointment of her or his second spouse as guardian of the children: see Form B3.31 at para **[203.60]**.

[203.51]

(c)   Children in the care of guardians. A guardian of a minor child has power to appoint a successor to act as guardian in the event of his own death (see

Vol 1, para **[28.4]**). Such an appointment will take effect on his death even if the child has another guardian who is still living after the death, provided that there is no surviving parent with parental responsibility. For a form for an appointment by a guardian of a successor to himself see Form B3.32 at para **[203.61]**.

[203.52]
(d)   Number and identity of guardians. There is no limit to the number of guardians of the same child who may be appointed, and the ChA 1989 expressly contemplates that more than one may be appointed (ChA 1989, s 6(1): Part G, para **[244.122]**). As a practical matter the sensible course is to appoint one guardian, or at the most two who are eg a married couple. Only individuals may be appointed, and as the duties are looking after the child rather than looking after the child's property the chosen guardian will often be a different person from any of the executors, and it will normally be appropriate to appoint named persons, and not for instance 'my Executors' or 'my Trustees', especially when the latter are widely defined to include any personal representatives or trustees.

[203.53]
(e)   Alternative appointments; successive or delegated appointments. It will often be appropriate, eg when someone elderly is the first choice as the guardian of a child, to appoint a second guardian to act if the first one dies or disclaims before becoming a guardian. There is nothing in the ChA 1989 to prevent appointments of this kind being made. See Forms B3.29 and B3.30 at paras **[203.58]** and **[203.59]** for examples.

   The ChA 1989 does not enable a parent or guardian to appoint a guardian to act after the death of another guardian after the latter guardian has acted as guardian, nor does it enable a parent or guardian to authorise someone else to exercise his or her power of appointing a guardian. As mentioned above, a guardian has his own directly-conferred statutory power to appoint his own successor as guardian.

[203.54]
(f)   Revocation of previous appointments. The standard words of general revocation (see B1 at para **[201.2]** et seq) of previous wills or testamentary dispositions would probably not be effective by themselves to revoke any earlier appointments of guardians which were in a written instrument which was not a will. However, s 6(1) of the ChA 1989 provides that an appointment of a guardian under that Act revokes an earlier appointment by the same person in respect of the same child unless it is clear from the appointment that its purpose was to appoint an additional guardian. It should also be noted that if a previous will or codicil is revoked, as it will be by a general revocation clause revoking 'all former testamentary dispositions', any appointment of a guardian in that will or codicil is revoked (ChA 1989, s 6(4): Part G, para **[244.122]**). It is therefore not really necessary to provide expressly that earlier appointments of guardians are revoked when making an appointment of a guardian (unless there is something in the will which might suggest that the appointment was of an

additional guardian). Cautious draftsmen may wish to include such a provision, and an example is given in Form B3.31 at para **[203.60]**. Note also that an appointment of the spouse of the appointor as guardian is revoked by divorce or annulment of the marriage: see n 2 to Form B3.31 at para **[203.60]**.

For power to lend trust money to guardians, see Forms B18.30 and B18.31 at paras **[218.115]** and **[218.116]**. For examples of complete forms including the appointment of guardians see C2 at para **[224.20]** et seq, C6 at para **[228.5]** et seq and C7 at para **[229.2]** et seq.

[203.55]

FORM B3.26:   **Appointment of guardian to take effect only if the other parent predeceases the appointor, with optional wording making it also take effect if the other parent does not make an effective appointment**

If my [wife]/[husband] [*name*] dies before me [or survives me but does not make any effective appointment of a guardian of our minor children which is not disclaimed by the person appointed][1] then I appoint [*name*] of [*address*] to be the guardian of our minor children in the event of my death.[2]

1   The inclusion of these words in square brackets will allow the appointment to take effect if the other (surviving) parent fails to make an appointment.
2   For reasons given in the note at para **[203.46]** this is the recommended form for the appointment of a guardian where there are two parents with parental responsibility. The point is that after the death of one parent the survivor has a free hand as to the choice of guardian in the event of him or her also dying while the children are still minors.

[203.56]

FORM B3.27:   **Appointment of guardian which takes effect if the other parent predeceases the appointor or if there is a residence order in favour of the testator at his or her death, with optional wording making it also take effect if the other parent does not make an effective appointment**

I appoint [*name*] of [*address*] to be the guardian of the minor children of myself and [my husband [*name*]] in the event of my death Provided that if [my said husband] survives me and the foregoing appointment does not take effect on my death [and there is at least one effective appointment by [my said husband] of a guardian of our minor children which is not disclaimed by the person appointed][1] then the foregoing appointment of a guardian by me shall be void and of no effect.[2]

1   The inclusion of these words in square brackets will allow the appointment to take effect if the other (surviving) parent fails to make an appointment.
2   This is an alternative to the preceding form for cases where there is another parent with parental responsibility, and is appropriate where the testator is concerned about the possibility of the marriage or relationship breaking up. Again the other parent if surviving the testator has a free hand as to the choice of guardian in the event of he or she also dying while the children are still minors, but under this form this is subject to the testator's appointment taking effect if he or she is the first to die in circumstances that at his or her death there is a residence order relating to the children in his/her favour (which is not also in favour of the other parent). See the note to these forms at paras **[203.47]** and **[203.48]**.

[203.57]

FORM B3.28:   Appointment of two guardians with expression of wishes about religious education

I appoint [my sister [*name*] and her husband [*name*] both of [*address*]] to be the guardians of my minor children in the event of my death and it is my particular wish that my children shall be brought up [[in the Protestant religion] *or* [as members of the Church of England] *or* [as Roman Catholics] *or as may be*].[1]

> 1   The wishes of a parent as to the faith in which his or her child should be brought up after his or her death will be taken into account by the court if there are proceedings in which the court has to make a decision on the upbringing of the child, but such wishes will be considered along with the other relevant factors, including the child's own wishes, and it is the welfare of the child that is the paramount consideration: *Ward v Laverty* [1925] AC 101; *Re Collins* [1950] Ch 498, [1950] 1 All ER 1057. Given that this is the legal position, it will not make provisions of this kind any more effective to word them more strongly as, for example, directions as to the children's religious education, although this might give them a more persuasive effect.

[203.58]

FORM B3.29:   Appointment of a guardian with an alternative appointment if the first choice predeceases the testator or disclaims

I appoint [my mother [*name*] of [*address*]] to be the guardian of my minor children in the event of my death but if [she] shall die before me or disclaim the appointment then I appoint [*name*] of [*address*] to be such guardian.

[203.59]

FORM B3.30:   Appointment by the mother of illegitimate children, appointing the father as guardian with alternative appointment in the event of him predeceasing her

I appoint [*name*] of [*address*] to be the guardian of my minor children in the event of my death but if he shall die before me then I appoint [*name*] of [*address*] to be such guardian.[1]

> 1   This is for a case where the father has not acquired parental responsibility, which he can only do under a court order, or a parental responsibility agreement with the mother made in the prescribed form and registered with the Family Division of the High Court, or by marrying the mother: see Vol 1, para **[28.2]** and the notes at paras **[203.49]** and **[203.50]**. The conditions introducing the alternative appointment could also include the possibility of the father disclaiming (see the last preceding form), but the testator might not wish to contemplate, or wish to encourage the father to think, that he might disclaim. The alternative person chosen would very likely be appointed guardian by the court if the father did disclaim.

[203.60]

FORM B3.31:   Appointment of wife to be the guardian of children by a former marriage with general revocation of previous appointments

I appoint my wife [*name*] to be the guardian in the event of my death of such of my children [*names*] being children of my late wife [*name*] as may be minors at my death[1] and I revoke all previous appointments of guardians of my said children which I may have made.[2]

1   A step-parent would not become responsible for the children on the parent's death unless appointed a guardian, unless he or she had become a parent of them by legal adoption.
2   A general revocation clause is not really necessary: see the note at para **[203.54]**. Note that an appointment of this sort is revoked if the testator and his spouse are divorced (or the marriage is annulled), unless a contrary intention appears by the appointment: ChA 1989, s 6(3A) (Part G, para **[244.122]**) inserted by Law Reform (Succession) Act 1995, s 4 in relation to deaths on or after 1 January 1996 (see also Vol 1, para **[28.6]**).

[203.61]

FORM B3.32:   **Appointment of a guardian by a guardian**

I appoint [*name*] of [*address*] to take my place in the event of my death as the guardian of such of [*names*] as may be minors at my death, of whom I am the guardian appointed by the will of their [mother [*name*]] (who died on [*date*]).[1]

1   The details of the guardian's own appointment are not strictly necessary for the appointment to be valid. However, if any question arises after his death as to whether he had power to appoint a guardian, the provision of these details will make it easier for his own appointment to be checked. For the power conferred by the ChA 1989, s 5(4) (Part G, para **[244.121]**) for a guardian to appoint his own successor, see Vol 1, para **[28.2]** and the note at para **[203.53]**.

B4 Specific gifts

FURNITURE

STOCKS AND SHARES

DEBTS

UNDIVIDED SHARES AND CLAUSE DEALING WITH JOINT PROPERTY

FORMS

INTELLECTUAL PROPERTY

FORMS

MISCELLANEOUS GIFTS

FORMS

NOTE ON THE INCIDENCE OF INHERITANCE TAX

[204.1]
The incidence of inheritance tax payable on death on chattels and things in action is the same as in the case of estate duty: if they are situated in the United Kingdom the inheritance tax on them will be borne by residue as a testamentary expense, and if situated elsewhere they bear their own inheritance tax (see para **[214.55]** et seq), subject, of course, to any direction to the contrary.

However, a possible consequence of the Scottish case of *Re Dougal* [1981] STC 514 is that personal or movable property outside the United Kingdom does *not* bear its own tax (as to which see para **[214.58]**). It is also possible for a valuable chattel to be accidentally located outside the United Kingdom at the testator's death. It is therefore preferable to make express provision for the inheritance tax on property which will or might be outside the United Kingdom at the testator's death (see further paras **[214.63]** and **[214.71]**).

For circumstances in which it may be preferable to make chattels in the UK bear their own inheritance tax, see para **[204.28]**, n 1. Property located abroad will bear any foreign death duties payable in respect of it in the absence of a direction to the contrary: see Vol 1, para **[30.34]**.

Personal chattels

[204.2]
General considerations. Where a testator is giving all or nearly all his estate to his spouse or to his children absolutely, it will usually be unnecessary for his will to contain a separate disposition of his personal chattels, which will form part of his residuary estate. A separate gift is obviously needed where the testator wants to give his chattels to different persons from those who take residue, or to the same persons but for different interests from those they are given in residue. Where the testator's spouse, or any other person, is given a life or other limited interest in residue, it is better to make a separate absolute gift of the testator's personal chattels, because chattels, with the possible exception of things such as paintings and antique furniture, are most unsuitable for holding on trust. The expense, difficulty, and potential for dispute, when they are administered as part of a trust fund, is out of all proportion to their value. Trusts are sometimes created of, eg, furniture, or more valuable chattels: for examples see Form B4.10 at para **[204.24]** and Forms B4.26 to B4.30 at paras **[204.44]**–**[204.48]**. See also the Note on gifts of furniture at paras **[204.37]**–**[204.39]** concerning life interest trusts of chattels.

[204.3]
Choice of words. A mere gift of 'personal chattels' without more may involve a difficult question of what passes under those words, but the older practice of setting out a long list of such chattels can now be avoided either by incorporating the definition of such chattels in the Administration of Estates Act 1925 (AEA 1925), s 55(1)(x) (Part G, para **[246.52]**) or Form 2 of the Statutory Will Forms 1925 (reproduced at para **[238.8]**). The two forms are in practically the same terms save for the reference to 'wearing apparel' in the statutory will form. The will may, of course, come into the hands of persons who have no ready access to these definitions and it may be thought to be more convenient to set out one of the forms at length, though where wills have to be prepared hurriedly incorporation by reference may be unavoidable. There is some advantage in using forms rather than a specially prepared list of articles because they include many words which have already been judicially considered and which are likely from time to time to be construed by the court. Any such general gift must be made subject to specific dispositions of such or similar articles. These precedents may be adapted where the gift is to some person other

than the testator's spouse, but in that case more attention should be paid to the inheritance tax position (see para **[204.1]**). For gifts of individual chattels the draftsman must try to find a description which sufficiently identifies the item in question, making sure, where the testator has more than one item of the same kind, that there is no ambiguity as to which is meant. As to particular descriptions of property, see Vol 1, para **[64.1]** et seq.

[204.4]
Expenses of transport and preservation, and money charged on chattels specifically given. After the executor has assented to a specific gift of chattels, the cost of packing, transportation etc of them is normally borne by the legatee, including where they have to be transported from abroad: see Vol 1, para **[30.34]**. The cost of storing and preserving chattels specifically given is also probably something which should be borne by the legatee as from the testator's death (in the absence of contrary provision in the will), unless the legatee takes under a right of selection in which case such costs are borne by the estate until the selection takes place: see Vol 1, para **[30.34]**. For an example of a gift including the costs of transport see Form B4.13 at para **[204.27]**. A gift of a chattel, like a testamentary gift of any other property, is subject to any mortgage or charge on it which is outstanding at the testator's death, in the absence of an expression of a contrary intention: AEA 1925, s 35 (Part G, para **[246.47]**). However, a gift of a car (and this apparently applies to any other chattel) which has not been paid for or delivered is not a gift subject to a charge for the purchase price: *Re Coxen* [1948] Ch 747 [1948] 2 All ER 492.

[204.5]
Collections. Where a testator owns a valuable collection, for example, of stamps or coins, it is probably wise to make it the subject of a specific gift and not leave it to be decided following death whether it passes by a gift of personal chattels or not: see *Re Crispin's Will Trusts, Arkwright v Thurley* [1975] Ch 245, [1974] 3 All ER 772, CA and *Re Reynolds' Will Trusts, Dove v Reynolds* [1965] 3 All ER 686, [1966] 1 WLR 19, in which a valuable clock and watch collection and a valuable stamp collection respectively were held to pass under gifts of personal chattels.

[204.6]
Right of selection of chattels. A testator who is not living alone will normally want to leave all or most of his chattels to the person or persons he is living with. If he does not want to make a list of specific bequests of chattels, whether because he is uncertain as to who would like which of his chattels or for whatever reason, the testator can grant a right of selection. This can be in the form of a simple right of selection with a provision that those chattels not selected should fall into residue, as in Form B4.6 at para **[204.20]** or one with a gift over to other beneficiaries after selection is complete, as in Form B4.7 at para **[204.21]**. To avoid complications over rights of selection testators should provide, so far as they are able, that a selection exercised in a particular manner or before the expiration of a particular period is to be treated as irrevocable and executors should abide by such directions. For the sake of certainty testators and executors should make it quite clear that once a selection has been made and the executors notified that selection is irrevocable both as to the items selected and as to those over which no right has been exercised.

[204.7]
Discretionary distribution of chattels. The chattels of a testator who is living alone will be dispersed after his death. If he is concerned that these should be distributed among his friends or relations, and would prefer not just to leave his chattels to fall into residue to be sold, thrown away, or distributed among the residuary beneficiaries by the executors, then there are two main possibilities. One is to give the chattels to a particular legatee, with a precatory request that the legatee distribute the chattels in accordance with any written expression of wishes left by the testator, as in Form B4.9 at para **[204.23]**, the other is to give the chattels to the executors (or separate trustees) subject to a discretionary trust to distribute the chattels, with or without precatory expressions of wishes as to distribution (whether in the will or elsewhere), as in Form B4.11 at para **[204.25]** (for the inheritance tax implications see the notes on inheritance tax on discretionary distributions at paras **[204.9]** and **[204.10]**). A discretionary trust has the disadvantage that the discretion is limited to benefiting the beneficiaries specified in the will, but it is possible to define the objects widely, and to confer power to add to the class of objects (for an example of a very wide power see *Re Beatty's Will Trusts, Hinves v Brooke* [1990] 3 All ER 844, [1990] 1 WLR 1503).

[204.8]
In our opinion, where there is no relative or friend of the testator to whom it would be appropriate to bequeath the chattels beneficially in the hope that he or she will carry out a distribution in accordance with the testator's wishes, there should be a discretionary trust. It is not appropriate for professional executors who have no connection with the testator, except that of professional adviser, to take the chattels beneficially subject to precatory wishes as to distribution, at any rate where the chattels are of any significant value. There will be a serious question as to whether they, being persons appointed to act in a wholly fiduciary capacity, really are intended to take the chattels beneficially, and if in truth they are not intended to do so, then Inheritance Tax Act 1984 (ITA 1984), s 143 (see below) will not apply. If they really are intended to take the chattels beneficially, and they have also prepared the will, and the chattels are of significant value, they may be in breach of professional etiquette, or the gift may be overturned if the testator did not have independent advice on it (see Part A, para **[200.5]**).

[204.9]
Inheritance tax—discretionary distribution of chattels. Where a testator bequeaths property by his will, and leaves a memorandum or otherwise expresses a wish (not necessarily in writing) that any of the property should be transferred by the legatee to other persons, and the legatee transfers it in accordance with the testator's wishes within two years of the testator's death, there will be no inheritance tax charge on the transfers, and they are treated as having being made under the terms of the testator's will: see ITA 1984, s 143 (and s 17). The main purpose of s 143 is to provide for gifts of chattels, but it can apply to any gift by will of personal property; the use of the word 'bequeath' in s 143 implies that it would not apply to a gift of freehold land. It should be noted that a disadvantage of s 143 applying to any property given to the testator's spouse is that the spouse exemption from inheritance tax on the testator's death (see Part A, para **[200.99]** et seq) is lost in relation to that

property. Where the property is sufficiently valuable for there to be a significant amount of inheritance tax at stake, s 143 can be avoided by waiting for two years from the testator's death before making the transfer. It should, however, be borne in mind that this will mean that the distribution is a lifetime transfer by the spouse, chargeable to inheritance tax if the spouse dies within seven years of the distribution.

[204.10]
Section 143 of the ITA 1984 only applies where the legatee is given the property absolutely: *Harding (executors of Loveday) v IRC* [1997] STC (SCD) 321. Where property is given to trustees on trust to make a discretionary distribution, a similar result to the effect of s 143 can be achieved by ensuring that there is no interest in possession pending the distribution of the chattels, so that the ITA 1984, s 144 will apply so as to treat the distributions as if they were gifts in the testator's will: for s 144 see the Note in C3 at para **[225.83]** et seq and for a discretionary trust of chattels of this type see Form B4.11 at para **[204.25]**.

[204.11]
Inheritance tax—chattels of artistic or historic interest given to individuals.
Some personal chattels may qualify for conditional exemption from inheritance tax if they are works of art or otherwise of sufficient public interest to qualify to form part of the national heritage. In the case of chattels (unlike land) it is not possible to obtain from the Capital Taxes Office in advance an opinion as to whether any articles will qualify for conditional exemption. The relief is allowed on a conditional basis in return for undertakings from the legatee relating to the preservation of the property and for securing reasonable public access to it. Upon the sale of the property or upon any breach of an undertaking, the conditional exemption is withdrawn and a charge to tax arises. A claim for conditional exemption must be made to the Capital Taxes Office following the testator's death with full particulars being provided and, ideally, an opinion from an appropriate expert, together with the address at which the property can be inspected and details of any previous exemptions. The Capital Taxes Office refers the papers to an appropriate specialist, who inspects the items, gives his opinion, and the Capital Taxes Office informs the taxpayer if conditional exemption is to be granted and submits the appropriate undertakings for signature. The undertaking for reasonable public access may be that the object is lent to a public collection for display on a long-term basis, or perhaps, that details of the object and its location be listed on a register which is open for public inspection giving details of how the objects may be inspected. See cl 10 of Form C13.2 at para **[235.18]** for a gift of heirlooms, and *Foster's Inheritance Tax*, G5, for a more detailed treatment of the topic of conditional exemption for heritage property.

[204.12]
Where a will is being prepared containing a general direction to pay inheritance tax out of residue, and the testator has chattels which may qualify for conditional exemption, care should be taken to make sure that the tax payable in the event of a sale of the chattels after conditional exemption has been obtained is not within the scope of that general direction, since that could hold up the administration of the estate indefinitely and would anyway not be appropriate.

[204.13]

It is strongly recommended that any specific gift of a chattel (or any other property) which might qualify for conditional exemption should be made to bear its own inheritance tax: see para **[204.28]**, n 1 and para **[214.55]** et seq.

[204.14]

Inheritance tax—chattels of artistic or historic interest given to museums etc. If any property is given by will to a museum or other institution which is a charity or a public body listed in the ITA 1984, Sch 3 the gift is exempt from inheritance tax (see Part A, paras **[200.102]** and **[200.103]**), and so a gift of a chattel of historic or artistic interest to such an institution will be exempt. However, where the testator has chattels of historic or artistic etc interest which would be likely to qualify for conditional exemption, and they are of significant value, another option, which confers more benefit the non-exempt beneficiaries of the estate, is for such chattels to fall into residue with a view to their being accepted by the Revenue in satisfaction of inheritance tax on the other parts of the estate under the ITA 1984, s 230. The disadvantage of doing this is that the testator has no control over where the chattels will end up, and if the Revenue decide that they are not of sufficient interest for acceptance under s 230 they will probably not end up in a public collection at all. Where s 230 is to be relied on and residue will be settled on trusts, it is probably not necessary to provide express powers for the trustees to transfer assets in satisfaction of inheritance tax, as they are conferred by the ITA 1984, s 231.

[204.15]

FORM B4.1:   **Gift of personal chattels by incorporation of Statutory Will Forms 1925, Form 2**

I give to my wife [*name*] absolutely all my personal chattels and for the purposes of this gift Form 2 of the Statutory Will Forms 1925 is incorporated in this my will.[1]

1   The terms of this form are set out in Part E at para **[238.8]**.

[204.16]

FORM B4.2:   **Gift of personal chattels by incorporation of definition in the Administration of Estates Act 1925**

I give to my wife [*name*] absolutely all my personal chattels as defined in section 55(1)(x) of the Administration of Estates Act 1925,[1] but this gift shall take effect subject to any specific gift herein contained or made by any codicil hereto.

1   See Part G, para **[246.52]**. Where the will is being prepared in an emergency, the reference to the section can be omitted and a mere reference to the Act is sufficient. Included in this definition are a motor yacht used for pleasure purposes: *Re Chaplin* [1950] Ch 507, [1950] 2 All ER 155; racehorses: *Re Hutchinson Holt v Huchinson* [1955] Ch 255, [1955] 1 All ER 689; a stamp and coin collection and a motor car: *Re Collin's Settlement Trusts, Donne v Hewetson* [1971] 1 All ER 283, [1971] 1 WLR 37; and a collection of clocks: *Re Crispin's Will Trusts, Arkwright v Thurley* [1975] Ch 245, [1974] 3 All ER 772, CA.

[204.17]

FORM B4.3:   Gift of personal chattels to wife[1]

I give to my wife [*name*] absolutely all my horses, stable furniture and effects, motor cars and accessories, garden effects, domestic animals, plate,[2] plated articles, linen, china, glass, books,[3] pictures,[4] prints, furniture,[5] jewellery,[6] articles of household or personal use or ornament (including wearing apparel),[7] also musical and scientific instruments and apparatus, wines, liquors and consumable stores, but there is not included herein any chattels used at my death for business purposes, nor money[8] or securities for money,[9] and this gift shall take effect subject to any specific disposition.

1   This clause is in the terms of the Statutory Will Form, No 2, which follows the definition in the AEA 1925, s 55(l)(x) (Part G, para **[246.52]**), except for the addition of the words 'including wearing apparel.'
2   See Vol 1, para **[64.47]**.
3   See Vol 1, para **[64.6]**.
4   See Vol 1, para **[64.46]**.
5   See Vol 1, para **[64.27]**.
6   See Vol 1, para **[64.31]**.
7   See Vol 1, para **[64.45]**.
8   See Vol 1, paras **[64.35]–[64.40]**.
9   See Vol 1, para **[64.53]**.

[204.18]

FORM B4.4:   Gift of personal chattels to wife—alternative form[1]

I give all my household furniture plate plated articles linen wearing apparel china books stamp collections manuscripts pictures drawings prints photographs engravings etchings lithographs printed music musical instruments (including equipment for the reproduction of sound with all rolls tapes records or discs for the same) wireless and television sets works of art clocks watches jewellery articles of virtue clothing cycles motor cars motor cycles and garage furniture and other articles of household domestic garden or personal use or ornament to my wife [*name*] absolutely but this gift shall not include any article or thing used for business purposes or forming part of the stock in trade of any business in which I am interested nor shall it include any article fixed to the premises wherein it is situated even though the same would not be a fixture in law[2] and shall take effect subject to any specific disposition contained herein or in any codicil hereto.

1   For what has been held to fall within the various descriptions included in this gift, see Vol 1, para **[64.1]** et seq.
2   This seems a necessary addition in these days of built-in furniture and accessories: see *Gray v Fidler* [1943] KB 694, [1943] 2 All ER 289; *Property Holding Co Ltd v Mischeff* [1946] KB 645, [1946] 2 All ER 294.

[204.19]

FORM B4.5:   Gift of personal chattels—short form

I give to my wife [*name*] absolutely all articles of personal domestic household or garden use or ornament not hereby or by any codicil hereto specifically disposed of.

[204.20]

FORM B4.6:   Gift to wife of such articles as she may select[1]

I give to my wife [*name*] absolutely such of my furniture plate household linen and articles of personal domestic household or garden use[2] as she may select[3] within six months after my decease and any such articles not selected by her within the said time shall fall into and form part of my residuary estate provided always that this gift is subject to any specific disposition contained herein or in any codicil hereto

[Provided further that during the said period of six months from my decease my trustees shall pay or apply any income arising from the articles referred to above during such period to or for the benefit of all or any one or more of my wife and my issue as my trustees may in their absolute discretion think fit and no person shall be entitled to the enjoyment in specie of any such articles] *or*

[Provided further that during the said period of six months from my decease my wife shall be entitled to the enjoyment in specie of all articles to which this clause applies (whether or not for the time being selected by her) and she shall be entitled to be paid any income arising therefrom during such period].[4]

1   Since no limit except as to time is placed upon the right of selection, the wife is entitled to select the whole of such articles not specifically given: *Arthur v Mackinnon* (1879) 11 Ch D 385; *Re Sharland, Kemp v Rozey (No 2)* (1896) 74 LT 664; *Re Baron Wavertree of Delamere, Rutherford v Hall-Walker* [1933] Ch 837, [1933] All ER Rep 837. Should the wife die within the six months her right of selection ceases and cannot be exercised by her personal representatives: *Re Madge, Pridie v Bellamy* (1928) 44 TLR 372; *Skelton v Younghouse* [1942] AC 571, [1942] 1 All ER 650. See Vol 1, para **[8.7]**.
2   The list of articles may be expanded if desired as in Forms B4.1 to B4.4 at paras **[204.15]–[204.18]**.
3   For the need to ensure finality where rights of selection are exercised see para **[204.6]**. The executors should ensure that such a right is exercised with certainty by, for example, providing the widow with a comprehensive list of available items and requiring a written exercise of the right.
4   The two possible provisos have different inheritance tax consequences. The first proviso creates a discretionary trust of income during the selection period of six months so that the ITA 1984, s 144 should apply on the expiry of the period of six months, with the consequence that the resulting distribution will be treated as having taken effect on the testator's death, see paras **[204.10]** and **[225.83]** et seq. The second alternative proviso will give the surviving spouse an interest in possession for inheritance tax purposes from the testator's death until she makes a selection or the time runs out for doing so. This will mean that the spouse exemption will apply to all the chattels whether she selects them or not, but she will be deemed to make a transfer of value in respect of those which she does not select. This may not be too disadvantageous if the residue is given absolutely, or on interest in possession or accumulation and maintenance trusts, and the spouse survives the transfer by seven years, see Part A, paras **[200.70]** and **[200.71]**. Also the values involved may not be very great.

[204.21]

FORM B4.7:   Gift to wife of such articles as she may select up to a stated amount and of the residue to testator's daughters

I give to my wife [*name*] such of my furniture plate and household linen[1] as she may within six months after my decease select[2] to the value of £——[3] the value of the selected articles to be determined by my personal representatives and the whole of such property if my wife should not make any selection or the residue thereof not selected by her as the case may be[4] I give and bequeath to my daughters in equal shares [and in case any dispute shall arise with regard to the allotment of any of the above articles among my said daughters I direct that my personal representatives shall sell the same and divide the net proceeds after payment of the costs of such sale among my said daughters equally].[5]

1   See para **[204.20]**, n 2.
2   For the need to ensure finality where rights of selection are exercised see para **[204.6]**. The executors should ensure that such a right is exercised with certainty by, for example, providing the widow with a comprehensive list of available items and requiring a written exercise of the right.
3   See Vol 1, para **[8.7]**. In *Re Baron Wavertree of Delamere, Rutherford v Hall-Walker* supra, a right of selection 'of such effects as may be in either of my houses H or S' gave power to take all in both houses. If no provision had been made in case of disagreement, presumably the daughters would have had to draw lots as to who should have the first right of selection: see *Re Knapton, Knapton v Hindle* [1941] Ch 428, [1941] 2 All ER 573, though it may be that this being a gift to tenants in common, the division in default of agreement must be by sale and division of the net proceeds; see *Vanneck v Benham* [1917] 1 Ch 60. Daughters entitled to half or more of the furniture can apply to the court under the LPA 1925, s 188, for an order for division and the court can make such order and give such consequential directions as it thinks fit.
4   If the mother should predecease the testator so that she could not make a selection and only the residue after the mother's selection was given to the daughters, the gift to the daughters would fail: *Boyce v Boyce* (1849) 16 Sim 476.
5   See para **[204.20]**, n 2 and add one of the provisos at the end of Form B4.6 at para **[204.20]** if appropriate.

[204.22]

FORM B4.8: Gift of articles of personal adornment to daughters as trustees shall determine[1]

I give all my jewellery lace furs and all other articles of personal adornment to such of my daughters [*naming them*] as shall survive me to be divided among them as they shall agree and in default of agreement the same to be divided equally among my said daughters by my trustees as near as may be according to the value of the several articles the value thereof to be determined by my trustees and the division by my trustees shall be final and binding upon all my said daughters.

1   This form of gift is sometimes desired but it places an invidious duty upon trustees and the testatrix should if possible make specific gifts of the various articles, at least so far as they are of any substantial value.

[204.23]

FORM B4.9: Gift of articles with request to distribute them in accordance with testator's wishes[1]

I give to [*name*] absolutely my furniture plate and articles of household domestic or personal use or ornament and without imposing any trust or binding obligation upon [him]/[her] or conferring any interest upon any other person I request [him]/[her] to distribute the same in accordance with any existing or future memorandum of my wishes left by me and that in default of any such memorandum [he]/[she] will divide the said articles between [himself]/[herself] and [*names or descriptions*] as [he]/[she] thinks fit.

1   As any memorandum referred to may come into existence after the will is made it will not be incorporated in the will or included in probate (see Vol 1, para **[15.1]** et seq). This is in its legal effect an absolute gift and there is nothing to prevent the recipient from keeping the articles given, but if the recipient is someone the testator can trust to carry out his wishes this type of disposition enables him to retain a latitude as to the disposition of personal effects without the necessity for making a new will or codicil whenever he changes his mind. It should be emphasised to the testator that the persons whom he wishes to benefit are entirely at the mercy of the person to whom the assets are given. Since the transfer will be gratuitous, it may well constitute a disposal for capital gains tax purposes. But the articles will have been revalued on the death and if they are promptly distributed, no chargeable gain should in practice accrue on the disposal. In any event small gifts exemption under the Taxation of Chargeable Gains Act 1992 (TCGA 1992), s 262 may be available. A gain will not be chargeable if it arises from a disposal of any one chattel or set of chattels where the consideration or deemed consideration (ie. the market value where it is gratuitous) for the disposal is £6,000 or less. For inheritance tax purposes the distribution made by the legatee will be treated as made by the testator if the distribution is made within two years of the testator's death: see the ITA 1984, s 143. Section 143 apparently applies to any personal property given to a legatee where that legatee transfers it to another person or persons in accordance with wishes left by the testators. Other possibilities are a discretionary trust of chattels (see paras **[204.7]** and **[204.8]** and Form B4.11 at para **[204.25]**) and a disposition in accordance with a pre-existing memorandum (see Form B4.20 at para **[204.34]**).

[204.24]

FORM B4.10:   Gift of chattels selected by trustees on life interest trusts

I give to my trustees such of my jewels jewellery plate plated articles furniture pictures books prints china and glass as in the uncontrolled opinion of my trustees are suitable to be held upon the trusts set out below, and the following trusts powers and provisions shall apply:

(1)   My trustees shall hold the said articles and the assets from time to time representing the same on trust for the use and enjoyment of my daughter [*name*] during her lifetime or upon trust to pay the income thereof to my said daughter during her lifetime (according to the nature of the property) and subject thereto on trust for the children of my son [*name*] living at the death of my daughter in equal shares absolutely.

(2)   So soon as conveniently may be after my death my trustees shall cause an inventory to be made of the said articles and such inventory shall be retained by my trustees and a copy thereof signed by my trustees shall be delivered to my daughter who shall on the delivery to her of the said articles sign and deliver to my trustees a receipt therefor.

(3)   The said articles shall at all times during the lifetime of my daughter be kept insured to the full insurable value thereof against loss or damage by fire (so far as the same are capable of being insured) and properly preserved at the expense of my daughter.

(4)   After such receipt shall have been signed as aforesaid my trustees shall not be bound to see to the insurance or preservation of the said articles or any of them during the lifetime of my daughter and shall not be responsible for any omission or neglect on the part of my daughter with respect to the insurance or preservation thereof nor for any loss or damage occasioned by any other act or omission but nevertheless my trustees shall not be precluded from interfering for the protection of the said articles or any of them when and as they shall think fit.

(5)   The said articles or any of them may from time to time be exchanged for any other articles of a like nature or the form thereof altered at the expense of my daughter but so that the intrinsic value thereof shall not be diminished.

(6) My trustees may at their absolute discretion sell any of the articles held by them under this clause and shall in relation to the proceeds of sale have the same powers of investment and changing investments at their absolute discretion as a sole beneficial owner and shall also shall have power at their absolute discretion to apply the money arising from the sale of any articles held by my trustees under this clause or any investments made as aforesaid in the purchase of chattels to be held on the foregoing trusts.

(7) My trustees shall hold any investments made as aforesaid and the assets from time to time representing the same on trust to pay the income thereof to my daughter during her lifetime and subject thereto upon trust for the said children of my son [*name*] living at the death of my daughter in equal shares absolutely.

(8) My trustees may exercise the powers of appropriation conferred upon personal representatives by statute without the necessity of obtaining any consents.

[204.25]

FORM B4.11:   Gift to trustees of chattels upon a short-term discretionary trust[1]

(1) I give to my trustees my personal chattels as defined in section 55(1)(x) of the Administration of Estates Act 1925 to hold the same upon the following trusts and subject to the following powers.

(2) My trustees shall during the period of two years less one day from my death ('the relevant period') have power to distribute the said articles among the beneficiaries as hereinafter defined or any one or more of them in such manner as my trustees shall think fit.

(3) I request my trustees in exercising the said power to give effect to any memorandum of wishes left by me but no such memorandum shall have any testamentary character or create any trust right or obligation whatsoever.

(4) [Subject to subclause (5) below][2] the beneficiaries for the purposes of this clause are [my wife my children and remoter issue my parents my uncles and aunts my friends [*names*] and the children and remoter issue and spouses of all the foregoing] [and the public bodies specified in Schedule 3 to the Inheritance Tax Act 1984 as amended][3] and shall include all persons satisfying the foregoing descriptions at the date hereof or at any time hereafter not later than the date of my death.

[(5) My trustees shall have power [with the written consent of [*name*]] by written instrument to add any body of persons having wholly charitable purposes or any person other than one of my trustees to the beneficiaries for the purposes of this clause].[4]

(6) During the relevant period my trustees shall pay or apply any income arising from any of the said articles for the time being undistributed to or for the benefit of all or any one or more of the beneficiaries as my trustees may in their absolute discretion think fit and no person shall be entitled to enjoy in kind any of the said articles which are for the time being undistributed.

[(7) My trustees shall in relation to all or any of the said articles have power to delegate in writing their said power of distribution of the same to any one or more of the beneficiaries.][5]

(8)   My trustees shall during the relevant period have power at their absolute discretion to sell any of the said articles[6] and to dispose of any of the said articles which are of little value to whomsoever or in whatever manner (including for no consideration) as they think fit.[7]

[(9)   My trustees shall have power to insure the said articles against any risk and to any value and pay the premiums out of my residuary estate and to pay for the storage of the said articles out of my residuary estate.]

(10)   Subject as aforesaid the said articles or their proceeds of sale shall form part of my residuary estate.

1   This involves a discretionary distribution of chattels in relation to which there is or may be a memorandum of wishes of no legally binding effect. The persons who are to make the distribution are in a fiduciary position and will not benefit personally if the discretionary distribution does not occur. The ITA 1984, s 144 (see para [204.10]) will apply so that for inheritance tax the distribution (providing it is made more than three months after the testator's death) or the taking effect of the remainder trusts will be treated as occurring on the testator's death. Capital gains tax is unlikely to be a problem. The ultimate donees may be deemed to take as 'legatees' within the TCGA 1992, ss 62 and 64 if the distribution takes place during the course of administration, with the consequence that they will be deemed to acquire the chattels at the value at which the executors are treated as having acquired them, ie their market value at the date of the testator's death. If the administration is complete and the distribution constitutes a deemed disposal by the trustees under the TCGA 1992, s 71(1), the chattel exemption under s 262 of that Act (annually £6,000) will apply in most cases. The trustees would also be entitled to relief from tax on gains up to a fixed limit (£3,600 in 2001–02): TCGA 1992, s 3 and Sch 1, para 2.
2   To be omitted if sub-cl (5) is not included.
3   The ITA 1984, Sch 3 is a convenient list of public bodies, including museums, universities, conservation and heritage bodies, which might be appropriate to include where the testator has chattels of historic or artistic etc interest which he wishes to go to public collections. For the alternative possibility of taking advantage of the ITA 1984, s 230 (transfer of property of artistic etc interest in satisfaction of inheritance tax): see para [204.14].
4   This is thought to be valid despite the wide discretion involved: see para [225.92], n 2. Its purpose is to enable items to be distributed to persons who turn out to be deserving but not beneficiaries within the definition in the preceding subclause. However, for some testators it may be felt to give the trustees too wide a discretion.
5   This is a power which could be useful where there are professional executors and there may be a friend or relative of the testator who could, for example, distribute the testator's house contents, saving the considerable cost of the executors doing it and also having more idea of what would be an appropriate distribution.
6   There will often be items which for one reason or another should be sold immediately, eg because no beneficiary wants them and they are difficult to store or insure. This provision as it stands enables the trustees to sell everything without offering them to the beneficiaries first, but it is difficult to devise a restriction to make sure that the articles are first offered to the beneficiaries without imposing excessive restrictions on the trustees.
7   There will often be items which no beneficiary wants and which have no sale value. Further, since 1 March 1993, it has been illegal, other than for a private individual, to sell upholstered furniture which does not meet the Furniture and Furnishings (Fire) (Safety) Regulations 1988, SI 1988/1324. Therefore a professional trustee may be unable to sell such furniture.

[204.26]

FORM B4.12:   **Gift of chattels in specific dwellinghouse**

I give to [*name*] absolutely the whole of the chattels (including motor cars animals and consumable stores) in or about or used in connection with my dwellinghouse at —— or the garage outbuildings gardens or curtilage thereof with the exception of (a) money securities for money deeds contracts or other legal instruments[1] and (b) any chattels hereby or by any codicil hereto specifically given to any other person.

1   Such items would not normally pass under a gift of contents of a residence: see Vol 1, para [63.1].

[204.27]

FORM B4.13:   Gift of chattel with residuary estate paying costs of preservation, transport, packing and insurance

I give to my son [*name*] absolutely [my grand piano] and I direct that all costs of storage preservation and insurance of it while it remains in the control of my trustees and of transport packing and insurance in transit of it when it is transferred into the possession of my son shall be paid out of and borne by my residuary estate.[1]

1   Without these express provisions the legatee would bear the cost of transport etc: see Vol 1, para [30.34].

[204.28]

FORM B4.14:   Gift of item which might be conditionally exempt from inheritance tax

I give to my niece [*name*] [my picture by Rowlandson known as 'Landscape with Foxhounds Chasing an Attorney'] and I declare that the inheritance tax payable on my death which is attributable thereto (if any) shall be borne by my niece in exoneration of my residuary estate.[1]

1   See paras [204.11]–[204.13] generally for conditional exemption. A gift of property for which conditional exemption is claimed will, without express direction, be subject to any inheritance tax charge which arises from a subsequent sale or breach of undertaking. It would be better to make such a gift expressly subject to any inheritance tax which would arise on the testator's death if conditional exemption was not claimed, because otherwise the legatee might prefer that the exemption is not claimed (to which end he could refuse to give the appropriate undertakings) so that he takes the property free of a potential tax liability, at the expense of residue.

[204.29]

FORM B4.15:   Gift to a public collection or the nation of a work of art[1]

I give my [collection of antique snuff boxes] to the [British Museum].

1   A gift of an article pre-eminent for its national, scientific, historic or artistic interest to an institution named in or approved by the Treasury for the purposes of the ITA 1984, Sch 3 will be exempt from inheritance tax under s 25 of that Act. If a testator wishes such an article to pass into a public collection, but not any particular one, it will be advantageous if it passes into non-exempt residue and offered in satisfaction of tax under s 230 of the ITA 1984; if accepted it would find its way into an appropriate collection. See further para [204.14].

[204.30]

FORM B4.16:   Gift of a library

I give to [*name*] my bookcases and library books except such books as my wife may select for her own use within the period of six months from my decease [to a value not exceeding £———] which I give to her absolutely [and I direct that in case of disagreement such value shall be ascertained in such manner as my personal representatives shall determine] [and I direct that the value to be taken shall be the value agreed with the Capital Taxes Office for probate purposes].[1] [Provided that during the said period of six months from my decease no beneficiary under this will or any codicil hereto shall be entitled to the enjoyment in specie of any such articles and all income (if any) thereof shall be paid or applied at the absolute discretion of my trustees to or for the benefit of all or any one or more of [*names or descriptions of beneficiaries*]].[2]

1   The phrase 'taken at probate valuation' has been held to mean taken at the valuation put upon the gift in the Inland Revenue affidavit leading to probate: *Re Eumorfopoulos, Ralli v Eumorfopoulos* [1944] Ch 133, [1943] 2 All ER 719. But the phrase 'at the valuation agreed for probate' has been held to mean 'at the valuation ultimately agreed with the Estate Duty Office': *Re De Lisle's Will Trusts, White v De Lisle* [1968] 1 All ER 492, [1968] 1 WLR 322. It is better for the will to make the position absolutely clear as in this precedent. The first alternative appearing in this precedent is recommended on the grounds that a valuation inserted in an Inland Revenue account may be unrealistically low and may be rather arbitrary and the valuation ultimately agreed with the Capital Taxes Office may be on the low side.
2   See para [204.20], n 2.

[204.31]

FORM B4.17:   Gift of sporting implements

I give to [*name*] absolutely all my fishing tackle guns and sporting implements.

[204.32]

FORM B4.18:   Gift of wearing apparel to servants[1]

I give my wearing apparel to my indoor female servants in my service at my death to be distributed amongst them in such manner and in such shares as my trustees think fit.

1   As to gifts to servants see Vol 1, para [30.23] and see legacies to employees at paras [210.58]–[210.63].

[204.33]

FORM B4.19:   Gift of letters and papers[1]

I give to my wife [*name*] absolutely all my letters copies of letters papers personal manuscripts memoranda diaries and writings but not legal documents [paper money] securities for money or books of account.[2]

1   A gift of letters, papers and manuscripts does not include the copyright in any of them unless it is expressly given: *Re Dickens* [1935] Ch 267.
2   It is the duty of the executors to examine all letters and papers belonging to their testator. As to the meaning of 'books' see Vol 1, para [64.6]. If a testator possesses any documents which his executors are not to examine, he should bequeath them to the person whom he desires to have them, and appoint such a person a special executor as to them. This may sometimes be the case where the testator releases a debt, though he desires until his death to keep all the relevant documents. See para [203.11], n 3 as to the limitation of the number of executors who can prove. The appointment of a special executor should be avoided wherever possible. See also Form B3.22 at para [203.39].

[204.34]

FORM B4.20:   **Gift by reference to a document already in existence**

I give my watches jewellery trinkets and other articles of personal use and ornament unto [*name*] upon trust to distribute the same to the persons if living and in the manner set out in a list dated —— which I have already prepared and signed and which will be found with this my will at my death and in so far as the said articles are not subject to any directions contained in the said list I give the same to the said [*name*] absolutely.[1]

1   For the incorporation of documents see Vol 1, para **[15.1]** et seq. It is important to remember that future documents cannot be incorporated: *Re Jones, Jones v Jones* [1942] Ch 328, [1942] 1 All ER 642. The list will be admitted to probate as part of the will. This creates a binding obligation but the testator cannot change his mind without changing his will. Other forms offer greater flexibility but no binding obligation, as in Form B4.9 at para **[204.23]**, or create a discretionary trust as in Form B4.11 at para **[204.25]**.

Consumable stores

[204.35]
Note. In general a gift of successive interests in such things will fail and in a will where chattels, such as furniture or valuable ornamental articles, are given for successive interests, it may be advisable to make a separate absolute gift of consumable stores. The matter is dealt with in Vol 1 at para **[8.3]**.

[204.36]

FORM B4.21:   **Gift of consumable stores**

I bequeath to my wife [*name*] absolutely all my wines liquors and consumable stores [*add if such is the intention other articles such as a motor car, a particular picture or other article which it is desired that the wife should take absolutely*].

Furniture

[204.37]
Note. Where the gift of furniture is absolute there is not a great deal that requires consideration, and it is usual and preferable for gifts of furniture to be made absolutely. Under a gift of furniture generally only ordinary household and movable furniture will pass, and if there are books, fixtures, china, pictures or similar articles of any value, it will be of some importance to say whether these are included in or excluded from the gift (see Vol 1, para **[64.27]**). Where the donee or donees are to have a power of selection, the gifts will follow the forms already given for gifts of personal chattels (see paras **[204.20]** and **[204.21]**), care being taken to provide for any necessary valuation and for cases of disagreement. Where the gift is of furniture in a house regard must be had to the possibility of removal and to the fact that the furniture may at the time of death be in storage though, perhaps, the latter can be effectively dealt with only by a

codicil executed when the facts are known. Gifts of specific articles of furniture are necessarily liable to ademption by the testator parting with that article in his lifetime or the article ceasing to exist by wearing out or some form of destruction.

[204.38]

Furniture settled on trust. Where the gift is not absolute but gives successive interests in the furniture, there is the question whether there shall be an inventory of the furniture. Where the gift is to the wife for life or widowhood and the furniture on the cesser of that interest is to fall into residue, an inventory is often dispensed with and, in ordinary cases, this is the more reasonable course as the wife has treated the furniture as her own during the husband's life and it would be irksome to place restrictions upon her in the continued use of the furniture. In other cases it is probably desirable to provide for an inventory as in the following forms. In these cases of successive gifts, care should be taken not to include in the gift consumable goods, for these would vest in the first taker absolutely (see Vol 1, para **[8.4]**). It is also a good idea to provide an express power of sale and investment of the proceeds, in case some or all of the furniture becomes surplus to the life tenant's requirements. Prior to the commencement of the Trustee Act 2000 (TrA 2000) on 1 February 2001, where powers of sale and investment were not provided for expressly there was sometimes doubt as to whether any power of sale existed at all, and even if there was an implied or statutory power of sale the powers of investment were limited to those in Trustee Investments Act 1961. Trustees may now make any kind of investment that they could make if they were absolutely entitled to the assets of the trust ('the general power of investment'): TrA 2000, s 3 (see the Preliminary Note on Investment Powers in B20 at para **[220.11]** et seq). It is, however, sensible to provide an express power of sale. Insurance of the furniture should also normally be provided for and this is probably better left to the trustees until such time as the furniture vests absolutely in later donees. Apart from any direction by the testator, the trustees have a statutory power to insure: TA 1925, s 19 (as substituted by the TrA 2000, s 34(1): Part G, para **[246.149]**). However, it is advisable to provide for such insurance by a specific direction for there will be no income from the subject-matter of these gifts. A duty to repair is sometimes placed upon the limited owner, but with the greatly increased cost of such repairs this may now often become an impossible burden, having regard to the resources of the limited owner.

[204.39]

The subject-matter of the gift. In all cases it must be ascertained that the business of the testator in no way concerns the sale or use of furniture for where that is the case the furniture held or used for business purposes must usually be excepted from the gift though it may be assumed that a gift of 'household' furniture does not include furniture used for business purposes unless the latter is expressly mentioned: *Re Seton-Smith, Burnand v Waite* [1902] 1 Ch 717. There may thus be an automatic exception where the gift is of 'household furniture' or 'furniture for domestic use,' but even in the case of such gifts words of exception may be necessary and are certainly advisable where the testator is concerned with such occupations as boarding-house proprietor, private hotel proprietor or the letting of furnished accommodation. Again, it must be ascertained that the furniture is the testator's absolute property and not subject to a hire-purchase agreement. If a house and the furniture in it are given to different persons, it may well be the case that certain items now classed as furniture will be fixtures and pass with the house and not under a gift of furniture. Further it is possible that many such articles may be easily removable (eg by taking out a few screws), but such removal might reduce considerably the value of the house and it may be preferable for such articles of furniture to be excepted from the clause giving the furniture and made to pass with the house.

See the text on Personal Chattels at paras **[204.2]–[204.14]** for other aspects.

[204.40]

FORM B4.22: **Gift of furniture to wife**

I give to my wife [*name*] absolutely all my furniture except such as shall be used for business purposes and such as is fixed to the premises [whether or not the same is in law a fixture].[1]

1 See para **[204.18]**, n 2.

[204.41]

FORM B4.23: **Gift of furniture in a certain house**

I give to [*name*] absolutely all articles of household or domestic furniture which shall be in or about my house —— [or such other house as I may reside in] at my death.[1]

1 For a discussion as to what passes under such a gift, see *Re Baroness Zouche, Dugdale v Baroness Zouche* [1919] 2 Ch 178; see also Vol 1, para **[64.27]**. If instead of the words 'at my death,' the words 'now' or 'at present' are used, the will may still speak from death: *Re Ashburnham, Gaby v Ashburnham* (1912) 107 LT 601; see also Vol 1, paras **[59.1]–[59.3]**. Where the testator has two houses, furniture, etc, may be moved from one house to another. For a consideration of these circumstances, see *Re Earl of Stamford, Hall v Lambert* (1906) 22 TLR 632; see also Vol 1, para **[63.1]**.

[204.42]

FORM B4.24: **Gift of furniture to such of testator's children as survive him**

I give all my household furniture and effects to such of my children as shall survive me if more than one to be divided among them as nearly as may be in equal shares in such manner as my trustees in their absolute discretion think fit.[1]

1 It may be that the absolute discretion of the trustees would not in every case prevent children entitled to half or more of the furniture applying to the court under the LPA 1925, s 188, but they would have to make out a strong case against the trustees before any relief could be obtained.

[204.43]

FORM B4.25: **Gift to a daughter of furniture and effects in her bedroom**

I give to my daughter [*name*] all household furniture pictures and other effects whatsoever ordinarily used by her in her bedroom in my house known as —— [or such other house as I may reside in at my death].

Part B   Clauses in wills

[204.44]

FORM B4.26:   Gifts of furniture and effects to daughters contingently on their attaining eighteen or twenty-one or marrying[1]

I give all my household furniture [but excluding such furniture as is fixed to the premises whether or not the same is in law a fixture] to such one or more of my daughters as shall survive me and attain the age of [eighteen] [twenty-one] years or marry under that age if more than one to be divided between them in equal shares or as nearly thereto as my trustees in their absolute discretion think fit[2] and I declare that my trustees may at their sole discretion permit any of my daughters to have the use and enjoyment of any of such furniture to which she is for the time being presumptively entitled under the foregoing trust or may deposit the same for safe custody in such place or places as they think fit and also may make such provisions for the insurance repair and preservation thereof [out of the income or capital of my residuary estate] as they think fit but without being liable for any omission or neglect so to do or for any loss or damage that may happen to any of the said furniture in any manner whatsoever[3] and all insurance moneys received shall be held on the same trusts and subject to the same powers as proceeds of sale of the said furniture.

I declare that my trustees may with the consent of my daughters who have attained the age of [eighteen] [twenty-one] years or married under that age but otherwise at their discretion sell any part or parts of the said furniture and my trustees shall in relation to the proceeds of sale have all the powers of investment, changing investments, and purchase of further chattels of a sole beneficial owner and shall hold the net proceeds of sale and the assets from time to time representing the same upon the trusts applicable to the furniture given by this clause (which shall be deemed to carry the intermediate income).

[I direct that an inventory of the furniture subject to this gift shall be made by my trustees and copies thereof delivered to all my daughters benefiting thereby who are of full age or married under age. Where any daughter is permitted to have the use and enjoyment of any such furniture she shall sign a list of the articles she is permitted so to use and enjoy and deliver the same to my trustees and, if she so desires, she shall be entitled to a copy of such list signed by my trustees. On any change of the right to use and enjoy a new list or lists shall be signed and delivered as aforesaid. My trustees may exclude from any such list any articles of such trifling value or wearing out nature as they may consider should be so excluded. After delivery of such articles my trustees shall not be liable for any unauthorised dealing with such articles but shall keep up the policy of insurance (if any) which they have effected in respect of such articles.]

1   At the cost of reducing the trustee's discretion over the division of the furniture among the beneficiaries this form has been revised in an attempt to satisfy the requirements of the ITA 1984, s 71(1): see para **[200.119]** et seq.
2   See para **[204.42]**, n 1. It should be remembered, however, that actual use and enjoyment of any articles of furniture by a beneficiary presumptively entitled to it will probably give rise to an interest in possession. While the creation of an interest in possession will have no inheritance tax consequences in the present case, the termination of such interest before the beneficiary attains an absolute interest may have adverse consequences, at any rate in theory.
3   As to the application of the insurance money, see the TA 1925, s 20 (as amended by the TrA 2000, s 34(2): Part G, para **[246.18]**); as to the statutory power of insurance, see s 19 of the same Act (substituted by the TrA 2000, s 34(1): Part G, para **[246.17]**).

1164

[204.45]

FORM B4.27:   Gift of furniture and effects to wife for life or during widowhood; no inventory[1]

I give all my household furniture to my wife during her life [so long as she shall remain my widow] she keeping the same in good repair and insured so far as practicable against fire to the full value thereof at her own cost in the names of my trustees and after her decease [or remarriage whichever shall first happen] I direct that the same shall fall into and form part of my residuary estate and I declare that my wife shall not be bound to sign an inventory of such furniture and that it shall not be obligatory on my trustees to make an inventory[2] or to see to the repair or insurance of the said furniture and that they shall not be personally liable by reason of the neglect or omission of my wife to repair or insure such furniture or by reason of any loss resulting therefrom but that nevertheless my trustees may take such steps as they think fit for the protection and preservation of the said furniture[3] [but all moneys received in respect of any insurance of the said furniture shall be applied in the replacement and reinstatement thereof].

1   In this form it will be noticed that the furniture is not (as it is in the next form) given in the first place to the trustees. It is permissible to give chattels in this way to a tenant for life with a remainder to another person or as here to residue, though the first taker appears in strictness not to be a tenant for life but a trustee for himself and the remainderman. See *Re Swan, Withan v Swan* [1915] 1 Ch 829; see also Vol 1, para **[8.1]**. This form is generally only suitable for use in simple wills. Articles which are consumed in their use cannot be given in this way. It would be unwise to include a direction to keep up the value of the property given, for if the value increased during the lifetime of the widow, her estate would be entitled to the increase in value: *Re Powell, Dodd v Williams* [1921] 1 Ch 178. It should be noted that no power of sale is conferred, and it is not clear whether one is implied by statute or the general law. This clause confers an interest in possession on the widow for inheritance tax purposes. Note that if the interest is limited to widowhood there will be a lifetime termination of an interest in possession if there is a remarriage, although this will be a potentially exempt transfer if the gift of the testator's residuary estate is to a person or persons absolutely, or if it is held on interest in possession or accumulation and maintenance trusts, see Part A, para **[200.119]** et seq.
2   Apart from a special direction of this nature, a tenant for life is bound to sign an inventory: *Foley v Burnell* (1783) 1 Bro CC 274; *Conduitt v Soane* (1844) 1 Coll 285.
3   As to insurance moneys, see the TA 1925, s 20 (as amended by the TrA 2000, s 34(2): Part G, para **[246.18]**).

[204.46]

FORM B4.28:   Gift of furniture to wife during widowhood; repairs and insurance to be provided for by her, and an inventory made[1]

(1)   I give my furniture to my trustees upon trust to permit my wife to have the use and enjoyment thereof so long as she shall remain my widow she keeping the same in good repair and condition (reasonable wear and tear excepted)[2] and insured at her own cost but in the names of my trustees so far as is practicable against loss or damage by fire [and theft] in such an amount as my trustees may think proper and from and after the death or remarriage of my wife the said furniture shall fall into and form part of my residuary estate.

(2)   I direct that as soon as conveniently may be after my death my trustees shall cause an inventory to be made of the said furniture and that the same shall be signed by my wife and retained by my trustees and that a copy of such inventory signed by my trustees shall be delivered to my wife and that when an inventory has been duly signed and a copy thereof delivered as aforesaid my trustees shall not be bound to see to the repair or insurance of the said furniture and shall not be subject to any liability whatsoever by reason of the neglect of my wife to do such repairs or effect such insurance[3] and all insurance money received shall be held on the same trusts and subject to the same powers as proceeds of sale of the said furniture.

(3)   My trustees may with the consent of my wife during her life and thereafter at their absolute discretion sell any of the said furniture and my trustees shall in relation to the proceeds of sale have the same powers of investment and changing investments and purchase of further chattels as a sole beneficial owner and shall hold the net proceeds of sale and the assets from time to time representing the same upon the same trusts as the furniture given by this clause.

1   This clause is also thought to confer an interest in possession on the widow for inheritance tax purposes. See also the final sentence of para **[204.45]**, n 1.
2   As to the liability to repair under this exception, see *Brown v Davies* [1958] 1 QB 117, [1957] 3 All ER 401; *Regis Property Co Ltd v Dudley* [1959] AC 370, [1958] 3 All ER 491.
3   As to insurance moneys, see the TA 1925, s 20 (as amended by the TrA 2000, s 34(2): Part G, para **[246.18]**).

[204.47]

FORM B4.29:   Gift of furniture to wife during life and thereafter for children: directions for inventory, and for repairs and insurance out of wife's income during her life[1]

I bequeath all my household furniture to my trustees upon trust that they shall permit my wife to have the use and enjoyment thereof during her life and after her decease shall divide the same equally between such of my children[2] as survive her in such manner as my trustees in their uncontrolled discretion shall think proper. And I direct as follows:

(1)   So soon after my death as may be convenient my trustees shall cause an inventory to be made of the said furniture and the same shall be signed by my said wife and retained by my trustees and a copy thereof signed by my trustees shall be delivered to my wife [and to any child of mine surviving me who shall require a copy thereof such child paying the reasonable costs of making a copy].

(2)   My trustees shall during the life of my wife out of the income payable to her under the trusts hereinafter declared repair the said furniture so far as may in their opinion be necessary and insure the same against any risks they think fit in their names to the full value thereof such value to be determined by them in any manner they think proper. All moneys received in respect of any insurance of the said furniture shall be held on the same trusts and subject to the same powers as proceeds of sale of the said furniture.

(3)   [*Power of sale with consent of wife as in paragraph (3) of* Form B4.28 *at para* **[204.46]**.]

1   It is thought that this form will be the most satisfactory arrangement where the wife is given the
     income of the whole residuary estate during her life and such income is amply sufficient for her
     needs. However, it is really only if the residue is to be subject to different remainder interests
     from those intended for the furniture that this separate provision is necessary (instead of the
     furniture being included in residue). It is thought that this clause also confers an interest in
     possession on the widow.
2   For the construction of this word see Vol 1, paras **[72.1]–[72.18]** and **[74.1]–[75.9]**.

[204.48]

FORM B4.30:   **Gift of furniture to widow for life and then to son,
incorporation of Statutory Will Form as to inventory**[1]

I bequeath all my furniture to my trustees upon trust that they shall permit my
wife [*name*] to have the use and enjoyment thereof during her life and after her
decease to hold the same for my son [*name*] absolutely and Form No. 3 of the
Statutory Will Forms 1925 is hereby incorporated in this my will. My trustees
may [*continue as in third paragraph of* Form B4.28 *at para* **[204.46]**, *giving the
trustees a power of sale with the consent of the wife*].

1   For the terms of the statutory form, see Part E at para **[238.9]**.

Stocks and shares

[204.49]
Note. In the case of these gifts, the great difficulty is to decide whether they are
specific or general gifts. The matter is discussed with the authorities in Vol 1 at
para **[30.8]**. If it is desired that the gift shall be specific the following appear to
be the most suitable expressions to use: (a) 'all my stock' or 'shares' of a stated
description; (b) the use of 'my' or any possessive word; (c) the use of the words
'standing in my name.' If the gift is intended to be a general gift then apparently
it may be made so by adding the words 'as a general and not as a specific gift.'
But whether the gift is specific or general ultimately depends on the wording of
the particular will, for any rule there may be necessarily yields to any indications
in the will construed with reference to such surrounding circumstances as may
be legitimately taken into account: *Re Hawkins, Public Trustee v Shaw* [1922] 2
Ch 569. As to what passes under such words as 'investments,' 'securities,'
'shares,' stock,' etc, see Vol 1, paras **[64.30]**, **[64.53]** and **[64.54]**.

[204.50]
Inheritance tax relief. Shares in a company of which the business is something
other than dealing in or holding property or investments can be the subject of
business relief if owned for two years: relief is given by means of a reduction in
value of 100 per cent where the testator held securities forming part of a
controlling holding of unquoted shares and securities or held unquoted shares,
and 50 per cent for quoted controlling holdings of shares or securities. For fuller
details of this relief see *Foster's Inheritance Tax*, G1, and for more detailed
discussion of the drafting of wills when the testator has shares qualifying for
business relief see the Notes to B5 at paras **[205.5]–[205.16]** and **[205.29]–
[205.33]** and C11 at paras **[233.1]–[233.13]**. See Forms B5.9 and B5.10 at
paras **[205.66]** and **[205.67]**, for gifts of shares with a business relief element.

[204.51]

Shares in a farming company of which the testator had control and in which agricultural land is vested can qualify for agricultural relief to the extent that the value of the shares is attributable to the land: see *Foster's Inheritance Tax*, G3 for a full account of the relief and paras **[234.1]–[234.10]** for will drafting points in relation to assets qualifying for agricultural relief.

[204.52]

Situs of shares and inheritance tax. By virtue of the ITA 1984, s 211, personalty situated within the United Kingdom does not bear its own inheritance tax but personalty situated outside the United Kingdom does so (see B14 at paras **[214.55]–[214.72]**), though slight doubt remains as to the incidence of tax on foreign movable property in consequence of the decision in *Re Dougal* [1981] STC 514 (see B14 at para **[214.63]**). It should be noted that in general the situs of registered shares and securities is determined by the location of the register (see *Foster's Inheritance Tax*, J4.11), but that this rule is often displaced for the purposes of double taxation relief by Double Taxation Conventions so as to be determined by the place of incorporation (see *Foster's*, J5.32).

[204.53]

FORM B4.31:   **Gift of stock as a general legacy**

I give to [*name*] £—— 2½ per cent consolidated stock as a general and not as a specific legacy.[1]

1   As to the last words, see *Re Compton, Vaughan v Smith* [1914] 2 Ch 119, where such words converted an otherwise specific legacy into a general legacy. The legatee under such a gift in the case of abatement has to bring the legacy in at the value of the stock at one year after the testator's death and without any of the income from the stock in the interval (*Re Compton, Vaughan v Smith*). See generally Vol 1, paras **[30.1]–[30.9]**. See Forms B5.9 and B5.10 at paras **[205.66]** and **[205.67]**, for gifts of stocks and shares with business or agricultural property relief.

[204.54]

FORM B4.32:   **Specific gift of stock**

I bequeath to [*name*] all my £—— 4 per cent consolidated stock now standing in my name.[1]

1   Whether a legacy is specific or general is in every case a question of construction, but the above wording combined with the fact that it is all the stock of the designated kind the testator has will generally make the legacy specific: see generally Vol 1, paras **[30.1]–[30.9]**.

[204.55]

FORM B4.33:   **Gift of shares held by testator at death and of shares to which he will be entitled at death**

I give to [*name*] all of the shares in [*name of company*] which I shall hold at the date of my death and all of the shares in such company which I shall not hold but to which I shall be entitled at the date of my death.

[204.56]

FORM B4.34:   **Gift of shares in public company**[1]

I give to [*name*] absolutely [20] of my shares in —— plc [and if I do not at my death hold sufficient shares in the said company to satisfy this gift I give to the said [*name*] in lieu of said gift the sum of £——]. I declare that any charge on the said shares existing at my death shall be paid out of my residuary estate.[2]

1   This will normally be a general legacy of the shares (see Vol 1, paras **[30.8]** and **[30.9]**). Any difficulty arising from the fact that the testator does not hold such shares at his death is provided for by the substitutionary money gift which here replaces the whole gift of the shares. For a form replacing a partial failure, see the next following form.

2   Charges on personalty are on the same footing as those on realty and the gift is subject to them unless a contrary intention is shown: AEA 1925, s 35 (Part G, para **[246.47]**); the declaration here included is a clear expression of a contrary intention. See para **[204.75]**, n 1 and para **[206.22]**, n 1.

[204.57]

FORM B4.35:   **Gift of shares in public or private company—provision for only a lesser number of shares being available**[1]

I give to my son [*name*] absolutely [50] of my shares in —— [plc] [Limited] and if and in so far as I do not at my death hold sufficient shares to answer the above gift in lieu of each share by which my holding in the said company falls short of the said number of shares I give to my said son a sum equivalent to the mean market value of such share on the day of my death [*if the shares are not officially quoted* equivalent to the value of such share at my death such value to be certified by the secretary of the said company or if he refuses to certify to be fixed by my trustees]. I declare that any charge which at my death may be existing upon the shares hereby given shall to the extent to which it affects the said shares be paid out of my residuary estate.

1   See para **[204.56]**, nn 1 and 2.

[204.58]

FORM B4.36:   **Gift of shares with provision for amalgamation, reconstruction, reorganisation or demerger**

I bequeath all my [*number*] ordinary shares in —— [plc] [Limited] now standing in my name to [*name*] and declare that if at my death the said shares shall by virtue of any amalgamation reconstruction or reorganisation of the capital of the said company or sale of the said company's business or demerger of the said company (whether direct or indirect) be represented by a different capital holding or holdings whether in the said company or in any other company or in government local authority or other public stock to which I am entitled or which I possess at my death then the said gift shall take effect as if it had been a gift of the capital holding or capital holdings which as the result of such amalgamation reconstruction or rearrangement of capital or sale or demerger took the place of such shares.[1]

1   The purpose is to prevent ademption, but the gift will still be adeemed if the testator in his lifetime disposes of the substituted capital. As to ademption in such cases see Vol 1, para **[41.11]**.

[204.59]

FORM B4.37:   **Specific legacy of shares with added words negativing apportionment**

I give to [*name*] all my [ordinary shares] *or* [[——] 5 per cent preference shares] in —— [plc] [Limited] now standing in my name together with all dividends thereon received after my death (which shall not be apportioned to any period before my death).[1]

1   In the ordinary way accruing dividends must be apportioned upon the death of the testator, the specific legatee taking only such dividend as accrues subsequent to the death (Apportionment Act 1870: Part G, para **[246.2]** et seq; see also B14 at paras **[214.48]**–**[214.52]**). The above addition excludes such apportionment: *Re Lysaght, Lysaght v Lysaght* [1898] 1 Ch 115. The necessity for apportionment is not restricted to preference shares, but applies generally to securities of both public and private companies: *Re White, Theobald v White* [1913] 1 Ch 231. In the case of loan securities, such as debentures, it will be necessary to change the word 'dividends' to 'interest'. Arrears of dividends on cumulative preference shares are not apportioned, see *Re Wakley, Wakley v Vachell* [1920] 2 Ch 205; followed in *Re Buck* [1964] VR 284; *Re Marjoribanks, Marjoribanks v Dansey* [1923] 2 Ch 307. As to a gift of shares with 'current' dividends: see *Re Raven, Spencer v Raven* (1914) 111 LT 938, and compare *Re Joel, Johnson v Joel* [1936] 2 All ER 962, and *Re McCutcheon's Will* [1960] VLR 289. In the case of a general legacy of shares the legatee is not entitled to any dividends until the shares are transferred to him. If this is not done before the expiration of a year from the testator's death, the legatee gets neither dividends nor interest on the value of his legacy, but after the expiration of one year, he is entitled to interest on the value of the legacy until such time as the shares are transferred to him: *Re Hall* [1951] 1 All ER 1073. See Vol 1, para **[32.4]**, n 1 for the rate of interest.

Debts

[204.60]

FORM B4.38:   **Gift of a debt[1]**

I give to [*name*] all sums of money owing to me at the date of my death from [*name of debtor*] and all interest due and unpaid at the date of my death and to become due thereafter in respect thereof and all mortgages or other securities for the same [and I appoint him executor of this my will so far as regard the said sums of money interest mortgages and securities[2]].

1   For what passes under such a gift, see Vol 1, para **[7.28]** (choses in action). It is important to make clear whether arrears of interest are included or not in a gift of a debt, because the law on whether they are (in the absence of express provision) is most unclear: see Vol 1, para **[64.39]**.
2   The legatee, being appointed executor as regards the particular debt, can sue for it in his own name, if he proves the will; as to arrears of interest, see *Re Ford* [1911] 1 Ch 455.

[204.61]

FORM B4.39:   **Gift of principal of a debt but not of arrears of interest**

I give to [*name*] all principal sums of money owing to me at the date of my death from [*name of debtor*] but not any arrears of interest thereon which shall be outstanding at the date of my death.

[204.62]

FORM B4.40:   **Release to a debtor of debts present or future**

I forgive and release unto [*name*] [free of inheritance tax] all sums whether for principal or interest which at my death may be owing by him to me on the security of any mortgages bills bonds or other security or otherwise and I direct that all such mortgages bills bonds or other securities shall as soon as may be after my death be delivered by my executors to the said [*name*] or cancelled and that for the purposes aforesaid my personal representatives shall at the cost of my estate execute and deliver to the said [*name*] all necessary receipts reconveyances or reassignments and I declare that if the said same [*name*] shall predecease me his legal personal representatives shall be entitled to the benefit of this gift as if he had died immediately after my death.[1]

---

1   A general forgiveness of debts should never be inserted in a will. Such a clause raises questions of difficulty about debentures owned by a testator and his balances at a bank, etc (*Re Neville, Neville v First Garden City Ltd* [1925] Ch 44, [1924] All ER Rep 377; *Midland Bank Executor and Trustee Co Ltd v Yarners Coffee Ltd* [1937] 2 All ER 54). There may also be a doubt as to whether both secured and unsecured debts are included: *Re Coghill* [1948] 1 All ER 254; *Re Leach* [1948] Ch 232, [1948] 1 All ER 383 (direction to pay son's debts). As to business debts where there are running accounts, see *Crane v Maritime Trust Co* (1954) 33 UPR 15. Since the release of a debt is a specific gift, it abates as such (*Re Wedmore* [1907] 2 Ch 277 at 283) and lapses if the debtor predeceases the testator unless, as here, there is express provision against lapse.

[204.63]

FORM B4.41:   **Release of children's debts with optional provision for hotchpot**

I release each of my children [and their spouses] from any legal liability to pay any debt which may be due from him or her to me at the date of my death together with any arrears of interest thereon [but each of my children shall bring into hotchpot against the capital of his or her share of my residuary estate such total sum from which such child and/or such child's spouse shall have been released as aforesaid].

[204.64]

FORM B4.42:   **Gift of debt to a legatee of a share of residue with provision for hotchpot[1]**

I forgive and release unto [*name*] all sums whether for principal or interest which at my death may be owing by him to me whether secured by mortgage bills bonds covenants or otherwise or unsecured and I direct that all such securities shall as soon as may be after my death be cancelled and delivered up by my trustees to the said [*name*] and that at the cost of my estate my trustees shall execute and deliver to the said [*name*] all necessary receipts reconveyances or reassignments Provided always that all sums of money hereby released (whether or not the same constitute legal debts) with interest thereon at the rate of —— per cent per annum from the date of my death but not in any case for any period prior to my death shall be brought into hotchpot as against the said [*name*] in the share of my residuary estate hereby given to him [*or if the named person takes a life interest in a settled share of residue:* as against the share of my residuary estate in which the said [*name*] takes a life interest hereunder].

1   Release of debts of 'pecuniary beneficiaries' includes the release of debts of beneficiaries entitled to residue. Such forgiveness could not be defeated by distribution of the estate in specie: *Re Epstein* [1963] 2 OR 276.

[204.65]

FORM B4.43:   **Gift of mortgage debt to the mortgagor**

I bequeath to [*mortgagor*] absolutely all sums both for principal and interest which shall be due or accruing due at the date of my death and secured on property situate at —— by a mortgage dated —— and made between [*parties*] [and the further charges endorsed thereon dated —— and ——] [and I direct my trustees at the cost of my residuary estate to execute in favour of the said [*mortgagors*] a full discharge of the said mortgage and of all claims thereunder and to deliver up to him all title deeds and other documents held by me in respect thereof] *or* [and subject to the said [*mortgagor*] paying or providing for the costs thereof I direct my trustees to execute in his favour a full discharge of the said mortgage and of all claims thereunder and to deliver up to him all title deeds and other documents held by me in respect thereof].[1]

1   The usual form of indorsed receipt would, it is thought, be effective for the discharge of the mortgage, the trustees stating that they had received all moneys due under the mortgage, but it is obviously more proper to execute a surrender since there will in fact be no payment. There will be no stamp duty in either case.

[204.66]

FORM B4.44:   **Declaration that sums advanced were by way of gifts**

I declare that the various sums of money that have from time to time or at any time been given by me to or on account of [*name*] were gifts and nothing is now due to me in respect thereof and no claim can be made and no such claim shall be made against the said [*name*] or his personal representatives nor shall the said [*name*] be liable to bring into account any such sum or sums.

Undivided shares and clause dealing with joint property

[204.67]

FORM B4.45:   **Gift of undivided share in equity of real property[1]**

I hereby give unto [*name*] all that my share and interest in equity of and in [parcels] *or* [all that my one equal third share and interest of and in [*parcels*]] absolutely [subject to and charged with the recoupment to my residuary estate of the proper proportion of the inheritance tax leviable on my death attributable to such share and interest and with interest on such proportion].

1   A devise in a will executed before 1926 of 'all my freehold property' or of 'all my moiety or equal half part and all other my share in' freehold property was not effective to pass an

undivided share in the property owing to the conversion of the 1925 legislation of such interests into interests in the proceeds of sale: *Re Kempthorne, Charles v Kempthorne* [1930] 1 Ch 268, [1929] All ER Rep 495; and *Re Newman, Slater v Newman* [1930] 2 Ch 409, [1930] All ER Rep 617. Where, however, a codicil was executed after 1925, not dealing with the particular devise but confirming the will, it was held that the devise was not adeemed and the devise of the undivided share was effective to pass the corresponding interest in the proceeds of sale: *Re Warren, Warren v Warren* [1932] 1 Ch 42, [1931] All ER Rep 702. By virtue of the Trusts of Land and Appointment of Trustees Act 1996 (TLATA 1996) an undivided share is now an equitable interest in land whether under a trust for sale or not. It follows that: (a) a gift of an undivided share in land ought to be expressed as a gift and not a gift; and (b) following the abolition of the doctrine of conversion, no reference should be made to an interest in the 'proceeds of sale' of land. There has thus been a partial reversion to the position as it was before 1 January 1926.

Inheritance tax on undivided shares of the proceeds of sale of land in the UK held on trust for sale is borne by residue in the absence of a direction to the contrary: See B14 at para **[214.55]** et seq.

Note that this form and the next one will not operate as intended if the testator is in fact a joint tenant of the relevant property, and that making a will does not effect a severance. The testator's title should always be examined carefully when a will is being prepared containing a disposition of this kind, and a notice of severance served where appropriate. If it is not, and the beneficiary named in the will is disappointed at the expense of the surviving joint tenant, the legal adviser may be held liable in negligence to the disappointed beneficiary, see *Kecskemeti v Rubens Rabin & Co* (1992) Times, 31 December and *Carr-Glynn v Frearsons (a firm)* [1998] 4 All ER 225, [1999] Ch 326, CA.

For another form of gift of an undivided share in land see Form B8.10 at para **[208.46]**.

[204.68]

FORM B4.46: Gift of undivided share in personal property[1]

I hereby bequeath unto [*name*] all my share and interest in any [*description of personal property*] owned by me as tenant in common with [*co-owner*] or with any other person.

1 An undivided share in racehorses will not pass under a gift of horses (*Re Sykes, Skelton and Dyson v Sykes* [1940] 4 All ER 10). See *Re Lewis's Will Trusts, Lewis v Williams* [1984] 3 All ER 930, [1985] 1 WLR 102. Note that for the reasons given in the note to para **[204.67]** an undivided share in land is no longer personal property and this form should not be used to dispose of such an interest.

[204.69]

FORM B4.47: Clause dealing with property held in joint tenancy[1]

As to [*Whiteacre*] of which I and A are beneficial joint tenants in fee simple in possession I make the following provisions:

(a) If there is in my lifetime a severance of the said joint tenancy then I give all my interest in the said property to my nephew X.

(b) If there is no such severance and I survive the said A then I give the said property to my nephew X.

1 The provision here made is unusual, but it seems necessary as a precautionary measure in case on the severance it should be forgotten to make the necessary provision. A testator cannot sever an equitable joint tenancy by will and it would be left until the happening of one of the events mentioned in the clause before any such provision would be made. It has, however, been rightly pointed out that circumstances may arise in which there would be no opportunity of making these later provisions by codicil and it is as well to provide contingently for such events. In the ordinary case it would be simpler to sever by notice (as provided by the LPA 1925, s 36(2), proviso) and to dispose of the severed share by will.

Intellectual property

[204.70]

FORM B4.48:   Absolute gift of copyrights and unpublished works to literary executor[1]

I bequeath unto my literary executor absolutely all my published and unpublished works together with all manuscripts letters notes and other writings including those in electronic form [together also with including sound recordings films and other visual recordings howsoever recorded and stored][2] and the copyrights and all other rights and privileges therein for his own absolute use and benefit and declare that all administration expenses other than those arising out of the special grant of probate and the payment of inheritance tax necessary to secure such grant shall be borne by my general estate in exoneration of the gift hereby made and further that all debts and inheritance tax (except as already provided) shall also be borne by my general estate.

1   In this form the donee of the copyrights of unpublished works is the person appointed sole literary executor. For a form appointing the literary executor, see Form B3.22 at para **[203.39]**. It is not necessary to expressly provide that the copyright in unpublished works is to pass with the gift since a gift of an unpublished manuscript will carry with it the copyright unless a contrary intention is expressed: Copyright, Designs and Patents Act 1988, s 93. See also Vol 1, para **[61.2]**.
2   Similar provisions as to copyright apply to sound recordings and films: Copyright, Designs and Patents Act 1988, s 93. See also Vol 1, para **[61.2]**.

[204.71]

FORM B4.49:   Same—proceeds to be transferred to general executors[1]

(1)   I bequeath unto my literary executors all my published and unpublished works together with all manuscripts letters notes and other writings including those in electronic form[2] [together also with including sound recordings films and other visual recordings howsoever recorded and stored][3] (except those necessary to the administration of my general estate) and the copyright and all other rights and privileges therein with full right to publish any such unpublished works and to complete or have completed any unfinished work and to publish the same in such manner and subject to such terms and conditions as my literary executors may in their uncontrolled discretion determine.

(2)   Any loss sustained in the exercise of the foregoing discretion shall be borne by the literary assets hereby given to my literary executors or in case of deficiency of such assets by my general estate to the exoneration of my literary executors who shall not be accountable for any loss so incurred.

(3)   My literary executors shall be entitled to receive all payments of every kind made in respect of my published or unpublished works and after defraying thereout all expenses incurred in the carrying out of this gift shall transfer the net proceeds to my trustees to hold upon the same trusts as are herein declared in respect of the settled legacy hereinafter called the —— Fund *or* [upon the trusts herein declared in respect of my residuary estate].

[(4)   I declare that for the proper execution of any trust or duty hereby vested in my literary executors my trustees in their discretion may but shall not be bound to lend to my literary executors any sum or sums of money not exceeding in the whole the sum £—— (that being the total amount to be advanced irrespective of the fact that some sums may have already been repaid)].

1   In this case it may be advisable to appoint more than one literary executor but the total number of literary executors should not exceed four. The former restriction on the *total* number of executors to prove where separate grants are made to different parts of the same estate has now been abolished: see para **[203.8]**, n 1. See para **[203.39]**, n 1 for the appointment of literary executors. See also para **[204.70]**, n 1 and Vol 1, para **[61.2]**.
2   Letters pertaining to the general estate and necessary to its administration must be available to the general executors. The literary executors on the other hand may need private correspondence for the preparation of a biography.
3   See para **[204.70]**, n 2.

[204.72]

FORM B4.50:   Gift of patents

(1)   I bequeath all patents and interest in patents to which I am entitled to my trustees. I direct that my trustees shall have the fullest powers to sell and deal with the same including power to grant licences or rights (whether exclusive or not) of manufacturing selling using or working the subject-matter of any such patents and that any such sale or dealing may be made wholly or partly in consideration of royalties to be paid to my trustees: and I declare that my trustees may join with other persons interested in any such patent in any such sale or dealing as aforesaid.

(2)   My trustees shall hold the said patents upon the same trusts as are herein declared in respect of the settled legacy hereinafter called the —— Fund [*or* upon the trusts herein declared in respect of my residuary estate] *or* [upon the following trusts and subject to the following powers and provisions:][1]

1   For a wasting asset like a patent there could be an inheritance tax advantage in a discretionary trust of income, particularly where the patent would expire before the first ten-yearly periodic charge occurred. In the latter case the income can be distributed according to maximum income tax advantage, and there need be no inheritance tax charge unless income is accumulated. For further points on the advantages and disadvantages of discretionary trusts, see para **[218.6]** et seq.

Miscellaneous gifts

[204.73]

FORM B4.51:   Gift of entailed personalty[1]

I give all my personal property of which I am tenant in tail in possession under [*particulars of will or settlement*] to [*name*] absolutely.

1   The express reference to entails is not superseded by the TLATA 1996, although the creation of new entails on or after 1 January 1997 is prevented by the TLATA 1996, Sch 1, para 5 and any attempt to create one gives rise to an absolute interest. It is, however, still possible for a testator to be a tenant in tail under a pre-1997 disposition by which a tenant in tail in possession has power to dispose by will of entailed property referring specifically either to the property or the instrument under which it was acquired or to entailed property generally: LPA 1925, s 176 (Part G, para **[244.53]**). The gift takes effect as if the entail had been duly barred. There must be a reference either to the property or the document under which the interest arises. A reference to

the property sufficiently refers to an entailed interest in an undivided share: *Acheson v Russell* [1951] Ch 67, sub nom *Re Manor Farm, Kytes Hardwick, Acheson v Russell* [1950] 2 All ER 572. It should be remembered, however, that this power of disentailing is available only if the testator is tenant in tail in possession at the date of his death.

[204.74]

FORM B4.52:   Gift of a reversionary interest[1]

I give unto [*name*] of [*address*] all that the one equal [fifth] part or share and all other the share (if any) to which under the trusts of the will date —— of —— deceased I am at my death or thereafter entitled in reversion expectant on the death [or remarriage] of —— of and in the investments and property representing the residuary estate of the said —— deceased and all other the reversionary interest or interests under the said will to which whether at the time of my death or thereafter I may be or become entitled under the trusts of the said will.

1   Where the reversionary interest may be affected by advances or the operation of accruer clauses, it is necessary in order to avoid disputes to include words in this clause which will make it certain that the beneficiary is to take the whole benefit of the reversionary interest subject to advances received by the present testator in his lifetime. This gift is confined to reversionary interests and will not include eg interests vested in possession under the will which have not been distributed at the time of the present testator's death. A reversionary interest under a trust is 'excluded property' for inheritance tax purposes (unless purchased for a consideration at any time or vested at present or previously in the settlor or his wife) and is left out of account in charging inheritance tax on death: ITA 1984, ss 5(1) and 48(1).

[204.75]

FORM B4.53:   Gift of money secured by an insurance policy on testator's life

I give to [*name*] absolutely the policy of assurance on my life for the sum of £—— —— effected with the —— Life Assurance Society dated —— and numbered —— —— and the said sum of £—— and all bonuses and other sums payable in respect thereof. [Any charge upon the said policy including any charge made in connection with any charge upon any freehold or leasehold property shall be discharged out of my residuary estate[1]].

1   See the AEA 1925, s 35 (Part G, para **[246.47]**). In the absence of such a clause as above, any property or interest in property charged with the payment of money has to bear the charge. A letter saying how the charge is to be met will be insufficient to show a contrary intention unless it shows how that charge is to be met between the specific donee and the residuary estate: *Re Wakefield* [1943] 2 All ER 29; *Re Birmingham, Savage v Stannard* [1959] Ch 523, [1958] 2 All ER 397. Particular care should be exercised in the case of specific gifts of shares, etc, and policy moneys which are in practice frequently used to secure a temporary loan, see *Re Turner* [1938] Ch 593, [1938] 2 All ER 560. Where a testator has made a gift of land contracted to be purchased and dies before completion, the unpaid purchase money becomes a charge on the property: *Re Birmingham, Savage v Stannard*; see also n 1 to Form B6.13 at para **[206.22]**.

[204.76]

FORM B4.54:   Clause exonerating specific gifts from charges

I direct that if at the date of my death any property comprised in any specific gift made by this my will or any codicil thereto is charged with the payment of money such charge shall be discharged primarily out of my residuary estate in exoneration of the property so charged.[1]

1   See the AEA 1925, s 35 (Part G, para [246.47]). In the absence of such a clause as above, any property or interest in property charged with the payment of money has to bear the charge. A letter saying how the charge is to be met will be insufficient to show a contrary intention unless it shows how that charge is to be met between the specific donee and the residuary estate: *Re Wakefield* [1943] 2 All ER 29; *Re Birmingham, Savage v Stannard* [1959] Ch 523, [1958] 2 All ER 397. Particular care should be exercised in the case of specific gifts of shares, etc, and policy moneys which are in practice frequently used to secure a temporary loan, see *Re Turner* [1938] Ch 593, [1938] 2 All ER 560. Where a testator has made a gift of land contracted to be purchased and dies before completion, the unpaid purchase money becomes a charge on the property: *Re Birmingham, Savage v Stannard*; see also n 1 to Form B6.13 at para [206.22].

[204.77]

FORM B4.55:   **Gift of live and dead stock**

I give to my wife all my cows pigs and poultry and all my plants garden stock gardening implements and all other my live and dead stock [in or about my house —— or the grounds and other buildings occupied therewith].

[204.78]

FORM B4.56:   **Gift of farming stock**[1]

I give to my son [*name*] absolutely all my stock of cattle corn hay and grain horses cows calves sheep lambs swine live stock and animals of all kinds and also my farming utensils and implements of husbandry tools haymaking harvesting and other agricultural machines whether self propelled or not tractors lorries wagons carts trailers harness saddles and other accoutrements [and the motor car which I use in connection with my farming business] and all other my live and dead stock whatsoever which shall at my decease be used on my farm at —— [or any other farm belonging to me at the date of my death].

1   A gift of 'all my horses' will not pass an interest in horses owned as tenant in common. There is quite commonly a partnership in racehorses and sometimes in other pedigree stock. See *Re Sykes, Skelton and Dyson v Sykes* [1940] 4 All ER 10. See also *Cochrane v Moore* (1890) 25 QBD 57 at 73 and *Re Lewis's Will Trusts, Lewis v Williams* [1984] 3 All ER 930, [1985] 1 WLR 102.
     In *Re Sykes* it was held that extrinsic evidence that the testator owned no horses but owned half shares of three horses was not admissible in evidence to assist in the interpretation of 'all my horses,' in contrast to the position where the testator is referring to some specific item of property but what he owned did not exactly fit the description. It is thought that the new rules for the admission of extrinsic evidence contained in the AJA 1982, s 21 (see the commentary on it in Vol 1, paras [57.22]–[57.26], and the text of it in Part G at para [244.97]) do not alter this rule.

[204.79]

FORM B4.57:   **Gift of ready money**

I give to my wife absolutely all ready money[1] which at my death may be in or about my place of residence and also all money standing to my credit on current account at the —— Bank [or at my banker's *or* at any bank].

1   A gift of 'money' is a form of gift likely to cause difficulty owing to the numerous decisions construing such a gift. For a consideration of the cases, see Vol 1, paras [64.35]–[64.40]. As to gifts for immediate necessities, see the Note to B10 at paras [210.15]–[210.18].

[204.80]

FORM B4.58:   Gift of proceeds of premium savings bonds and prizes received or awarded since the testator's death[1]

I direct my trustees to encash all premium savings bonds which I may own at my death and to give the net proceeds thereof and any prize money in respect of them received after my death (whether awarded before or after my death) to [*name of beneficiary*].

1   Premium bonds are not transferable: see reg 3(4) of the Premium Savings Bonds Regulations 1972 (SI 1972/765). It is not therefore possible to give them away, but it is possible to direct that they be encashed and the proceeds given away.

B5 Gifts and other provisions relating to business property

Part B   Clauses in wills

TRUSTEES' POWERS

FORMS

PRELIMINARY NOTE

[205.1]
There is (for deaths, transfers and other events after 9 March 1992) 100 per cent business relief (in effect complete exemption) for many types of business asset: Inheritance Tax Act 1984 (ITA 1984), s 104(1). This means that the incentive to dispose of them by lifetime gift is less than it was previously (see para **[205.46]**) and that testamentary gifts of such property assume a greater importance.

[205.2]
B5 is concerned with testamentary dispositions of business assets, and powers and other ancillary provisions which may be relevant to such dispositions, and mentions some of the inheritance tax aspects which should be borne in mind. For testamentary options relating to business property see B9 at para **[209.1]** et seq and for a right of a beneficiary to have particular property appropriated to his share see Form B17.20 at para **[217.25]**. For further trustees' powers relevant to business property see Forms B20.17 to B20.19 (at paras **[220.66]**–**[220.68]**) and for complete wills involving business and agricultural assets, and the attendant problems of providing appropriately for the whole of the testator's family and avoiding waste of business and agricultural relief, see C11 (business) and C12 (agricultural) at paras **[233.1]** and **[234.1]** et seq and the Preliminary Notes thereto. For inheritance tax agricultural relief, see the Preliminary Note to C12 at para **[234.1]** et seq.

[205.3]
The main kinds of business asset which can qualify for business relief and which may be disposed of by will are sole traders' businesses, partnership shares,

company shares (typically shares in a private family company), and assets owned personally by the testator which are used in a business carried on by a partnership or company in which he is interested.

Business assets and inheritance tax—general points

[205.4]
For a complete account of inheritance tax on business assets we refer the reader to *Foster's Inheritance Tax*, in particular Divisions G1 (business relief), G3 (agricultural relief), H2 (principles of valuation), H3 (valuation of particular types of property) and L5 (payment by instalments). The notes in this work concentrate on inheritance tax aspects of business assets which are relevant to drafting wills and advising persons who are making wills.

[205.5]
Assets qualifying for relief and the rates of relief. There is at the moment (in relation to transfers after 5 April 1996) 100 per cent relief, subject to satisfying the preconditions mentioned further below, for the following types of business property:

(a)   businesses of sole traders;
(b)   partnership shares;
(c)   holdings of unquoted voting securities of a company controlled by the transferor;
(d)   holdings of unquoted shares.

[205.6]
There is at the moment (in relation to transfers after 9 March 1992) 50 per cent relief, subject to satisfying the preconditions mentioned further below, for the following types of business property:

(a)   holdings of quoted shares or securities giving control of the company;
(b)   land, buildings, machinery or plant owned personally and used in the business of a company which the owner of the asset controls or a partnership in which he is a partner, provided that the testator's interest or shares in the business in which it is used also qualify for business relief: ITA 1984, s 105(6);
(c)   land, buildings, machinery or plant comprised in a settlement and used in a business carried on by someone who has an interest in possession in such land, buildings, machinery or plant. On the death of someone with an interest in possession in settled property used in a business carried on by him there will normally be 100 per cent business relief on the business itself and the settled property used in it taken together as 'a business' (*Finch v IRC* [1985] Ch 1, sub nom *Fetherstonaugh v IRC* [1984] STC 261), and this separate 50 per cent relief category is only relevant where the settled property is comprised in a transfer of value which does not also include the business itself. Accordingly, this business relief category will not often be relevant to the inheritance tax charge on a person's death.

[205.7]
See the ITA 1984, ss 104(1) and 105(1). 100 per cent relief means that the value transferred is reduced by 100 per cent of the value of the asset qualifying for relief, and 50 per cent relief means that the value transferred is reduced by 50 per cent of that value: ITA 1984, s 104(1). For the allocation of the reduction where parts of an estate or transfer are exempt and parts not exempt, under the ITA 1984, s 39A see the Preliminary Note to C11 at para **[233.2]** et seq.

[205.8]
Types of business qualifying for business relief. Subject to the exceptions mentioned below, any trade or profession can qualify for inheritance tax business relief, either where it (or a partnership share of it) is directly owned by the testator, or where it is carried on by an unquoted company in which he has shares or a quoted company which he controls. The exceptions to this are for businesses of dealing in securities, stocks or shares, or land or buildings, or making or holding investments (ITA 1984, s 105(3)), but that itself is subject to exceptions for UK discount houses, and market makers on the stock exchange or the London International Financial Futures and Options Exchange: ITA 1984, s 105(4), (7) and SI 1992/3181. The Special Commissioners have held that ownership and management of land let to tenants is making or holding investments within the above exception and does not qualify for business relief, and this approach has been approved by the High Court in *Weston v IRC* [2000] STC 1064 (see for the now numerous cases in this area *Foster's Inheritance Tax*, G1.12). There is no territorial limit on the location of the business, and it can be anywhere in the world (whereas agricultural relief can apply only to land in the UK, Channel Islands, or Isle of Man). The assets of a farming business other than the agricultural land itself can only qualify for business relief not agricultural relief, as the latter relief is confined to land and buildings etc attached to land. See para **[205.15]** and C12 at para **[234.8]** for what happens when both reliefs might apply to agricultural land.

[205.9]
Excepted assets. The value of individual assets is excepted from the relief if they have not been used in the business for two years and are not required for use in it at the time of the transfer or death (ITA 1984, s 112), and land, buildings, plant or machinery personally owned and used in a business by a company which the testator controls or a partnership in which he is a partner is excepted unless it has been used in the business for two years or it and an asset it replaced have together been used in it for two out of the previous five years: ITA 1984, s 112(3).

[205.10]
Liabilities. Section 162(4) of the ITA 1984 provides that a liability which is an incumbrance on any property shall, so far as possible, be taken to reduce the value of that property. Liabilities incurred for the purposes of a business will be taken into account in valuing it (or the company or partnership shares which it underlies) whether or not charged on the business assets, but s 162(4) could reduce relief further where borrowing for some other purpose is charged on

business property. Where there is a choice between charging a liability on business or non-business property it may thus be better to choose the latter.

[205.11]
Required period of ownership, and succession. To qualify for business relief on a testator's death, business property must have been owned by the testator throughout the two years preceding his death: ITA 1984, s 106. If he inherited it he can count in the whole period from the death of the person from whom he inherited it, and if that person was his spouse he can count in the spouse's period of ownership as well as his own: ITA 1984, s 108. If he was given the business property by lifetime gift or inherited it, and business relief applied to the transfer by which he acquired it, the relief will also apply on his death if the only obstacle to it applying under the main rules is that he has not owned the property for two years by that time: ITA 1984, s 109.

[205.12]
The Inland Revenue regard these provisions as applying where the succession is by virtue of a gift by will of residue, notwithstanding that for a period after the death the business property will have been comprised in an estate in the course of administration and not strictly speaking held on trust for the person entitled to residue (*Stamp Duties Comr (Queensland) v Livingston* [1965] AC 694: see Vol 1, para **[1.12]**). This is because the ITA 1984, s 91 applies to treat the situation as the same as it would have been if the residue had been ascertained as from the relevant death.

[205.13]
For possible provision in a will where business property has not been owned for two years by the time of making a will, see paras **[205.31]** and **[205.50]**.

[205.14]
Contracts of sale and company liquidations. If business property is under contract of sale at the time of the death of its owner or any other occasion of inheritance tax charge, business relief does not apply to that property on that death or other occasion unless the contract provides for the transfer of the business to a company in return for shares in it, or for the reconstruction or amalgamation of a company: ITA 1984, s 113. This is a point of particular concern in relation to partnership shares which are subject to rights of acquisition vested in the other partners: see para **[205.28]**. Similarly, business relief does not apply to company shares on a death or other occasion of inheritance tax charge if at that time the company has gone into liquidation, unless it has done so as part of a reconstruction or amalgamation after which its business will continue: ITA 1984, s 105(5).

[205.15]
Relationship with agricultural relief. Where both reliefs are capable of applying, it is agricultural relief alone which applies: ITA 1984, s 114. There are notes on agricultural relief in the Preliminary Note to C12 at para **[234.1]** et seq.

[205.16]
Testamentary options. For the inheritance tax aspects of these, see the Preliminary Note to B9 at para **[209.1]** et seq.

Payment of inheritance tax by instalments

[205.17]
Under ss 227 and 228 of the ITA 1984 there is provision for payment by instalments over ten years, at the option of the person paying it, of the inheritance tax on death on the types of asset listed below. In addition, for certain categories, which almost but not quite coincide with the types of property which may qualify for business or agricultural relief, there is a right to pay by instalments which are *interest-free* under the ITA 1984, s 234, ie interest is only payable if an instalment is paid after it has become due (as opposed to interest being payable on an instalment from what would have been the due date for payment of the tax if there was no instalment option). Property with an interest-free instalment option for the payment of the inheritance tax on death is as follows:

    (a)   sole traders' businesses: ITA 1984, ss 227(2)(c) and 234(1)(a);
    (b)   partnership shares: ITA 1984, ss 227(2)(c) and 234(1)(a);
    (c)   land subject to agricultural relief: ITA 1984, ss 227(2)(a) and 234(1)(a);
    (d)   controlling shareholdings, quoted or unquoted (ITA 1984, ss 227(2)(b), 228(1)(a) and 234(1)(a)), provided that the company's business is not one of the kinds excluded from business relief by reason of being a land or investment dealing or holding company (ITA 1984, s 234(3); see also para **[205.8]**), and in judging whether the deceased had control, related property and settled property in which he had an interest in possession will be taken into account (ITA 1984, s 269(2), (3);
    (e)   unquoted shareholdings, which do not give control, again provided that the company's business is not one of the kinds excluded from business relief by reason of being a land or investment dealing or holding company (ITA 1984, s 234(3); see also para **[205.8]**) in any of the following three categories:
        (i)   if the tax on them, together with the tax on any other property to which the instalment payment option applies, represents at least 20 per cent of the tax on the deceased's death for which the person paying the tax on the shares is liable in the same capacity: ITA 1984, s 228(1)(b), (2);
        (ii) if they have a taxable value on the death of more than £20,000, *and* either were in their nominal value at least ten per cent of the nominal value of the capital of the company at the time of the deceased's death, *or* are ordinary shares which in their nominal value were at least ten per cent of the nominal value of the ordinary share capital of the company at that time: ITA 1984, s 228(1)(d), (3);
        (iii) if the Inland Revenue are satisfied that the tax on them cannot be paid in one sum without due hardship: ITA 1984, s 228(1)(c).

Shares which would fall within the above-listed categories qualifying for interest-free instalment payment if it were not for the fact that the company's business is land or investment dealing or holding, will qualify for *interest-bearing* instalment payment. Land or buildings not falling within categories (a), (b) or (c) above also qualify for *interest-bearing* instalment payment.

[205.18]
Payment by instalments and 100 per cent relief property. It will be apparent from the above that business or agricultural property of a kind which can qualify for 100 per cent relief will all qualify also for interest-free instalment payment, save for certain shareholdings (see further para **[205.34]** et seq). Property subject to 100 per cent business relief is of course property on which there should be no inheritance tax at all, but the right to pay inheritance tax by instalments can be relevant to it, for the reasons given at para **[205.51]**.

[205.19]
Payment by instalments and 50 per cent relief property. The only category of business property qualifying for 50 per cent relief which coincides more or less with a category of property qualifying for interest-free instalment payments is controlling shareholdings of *quoted* shares. The categories of unquoted shares which qualify for interest-free instalment payment are quite differently defined from those which qualify for 50 per cent business relief, and some 50 per cent relief unquoted holdings will qualify for interest-free instalment payment and some will not: see further para **[205.34]** et seq. Land, buildings, machinery or plant owned personally by the deceased or subject to an interest in possession of his, and qualifying for 50 per cent business relief (in the circumstances summarised at paras **[205.6]** and **[205.41]** et seq) does not qualify for interest-free instalment payment, but land and buildings can qualify for *interest-bearing* instalment payment: ITA 1984, s 227(2)(a) and IA 1978, Sch 1 (definition of 'land').

[205.20]
Subsequent sale. The unpaid instalments or an appropriate part of them become due immediately on a sale of all or a part of the property: ITA 1984, s 227(4) and (6). This can have implications for testamentary options: see the Preliminary Note to B9 at para **[209.1]** et seq.

Sole traders

[205.21]
In modern conditions limited companies tend to be preferred for any but the smallest businesses, and farms and shops are probably now the most common examples of businesses carried on by sole traders.

[205.22]
Business relief for a sole trader. A business of a sole trader qualifies for business relief at the 100 per cent rate, but it must be emphasised that to qualify for the relief the testator must at his death own a business which is *his*

business—this does not mean that he is necessarily working very hard in it (he could employ a manager), but the risk of loss and the hope of profit must be his, and a bundle of assets which adds up to being a business must be his property, although property he uses in the business and is deemed to own by virtue of it being settled property in which he has an interest in possession may be treated as part of the business assets for relief purposes (*Finch v IRC* [1985] Ch 1, sub nom *Fetherstonaugh v IRC* [1984] STC 261). An individual business asset which is not part of the assets of a business owned by the testator, eg because it is used by somebody else in that other person's business, will not qualify for the relief. Where someone wishes to hand over his business to someone else while retaining a stake in it which will qualify for business relief he should consider forming a partnership or a company.

[205.23]
As has been established in a number of cases on capital gains tax retirement relief, an asset used in a business is not 'a business': see, eg *McGregor v Adcock* [1977] STC 206, *Pepper v Daffurn* [1993] STC 466, and *Jarmin v Rawlings* [1994] STC 1005. Thus a lifetime gift by a sole trader of a single asset used in his business will not qualify for business relief. This is a less significant point in relation to inheritance tax on death, because if a person is in business as a sole trader at his death the entire business will be included in his deemed transfer of value on death. However, it is significant in relation to inheritance tax on death where the estate is partially exempt, because it affects the application of the ITA 1984, s 39A (business or agricultural relief and partial exemption), and specific gifts by will of individual assets of the business should be avoided where there are exempt gifts: see the Preliminary Note to C11 at para **[233.6]**.

[205.24]
The value for relief purposes. The business relief is on the net value of the business, ie the value of the assets owned by the testator and used in the business (including goodwill) less the liabilities incurred for the purposes of the business: ITA 1984, s 110. This deduction of liabilities occurs whether or not they are charged on the business assets; if there are any liabilities incurred other than for the purposes of the business which are charged on the business assets, then those liabilities will also go to reduce the amount of relief by virtue of the ITA 1984, s 162(4), which provides that an incumbrance on any property is (so far as possible) taken to reduce the value of that property.

[205.25]
Dispositions of businesses: executors' and trustees' powers. For specific dispositions of businesses see Forms B5.1 to B5.4 at paras **[205.58]–[205.61]**.

The addition of specific powers for running the testator's business should be considered where there is any possibility that it might be necessary or convenient for the executors or trustees to carry it on. Executors or trustees do not have power to carry on the testator's business in the absence of authority, express or implied, to do so (*Kirkman v Booth* (1848) 11 Beav 273), except that they may carry on a business for a reasonable time with a view to a beneficial sale (*Garrett v Noble* (1834) 6 Sim 504). A power to postpone sale and conversion of the testator's estate may authorise the carrying on of a business not only with a view to sale but so long as the power to postpone continues (*Re Crowther, Midgley v Crowther* [1895] 2 Ch 56), but not where there is a direction to sell the business as well as a power to postpone sale (*Re Smith, Arnold v Smith* [1896] 1 Ch 171). A direction in a will to carry on the testator's business does not of itself authorise the employment therein of more of the testator's assets than were employed in it at his death (*M'Neillie v Acton* (1853) 4 De GM & G 744). In the absence of express authority to write off losses against capital, a loss in one year must ordinarily be made good out of the profits of future years and not out of capital and a provision enabling the trustees to make reserves for depreciation reinforces this view: *Rutherford v IRC* [1965] NZLR 444. For power to carry on a business and employ capital of the estate in doing so see Form B5.13 at para **[205.70]**.

Partnership interests

[205.26]
Partnership, like sole trading, is not very often used for trading or manufacturing, the private company usually being preferred. Partnership has always been the rule for many professions which perform services rather than trade, for example, solicitors, doctors, accountants, architects, and surveyors, although incorporation is becoming an option for many professions, including solicitors. However, in many cases farming is still carried on in family or other partnerships. When preparing a will for someone who is a partner in a firm it is important to look at the terms of the partnership agreement and the partnership accounts to see whether the testator's partnership share is likely to have any significant value on his death, because if it will not there is no need to make any special provision. Further, partnership agreements usually contains terms as to what happens in the event of the death of a partner, and these need to be considered both for their inheritance tax implications (see para **[205.28]**), and for what (if anything) may be disposed of by the testator's will.

[205.27]
Business relief. Business relief, if it applies, is at the rate of 100 per cent on a partnership share. The value on which it is calculated will be based on the net value of the partnership share, ie the testator's appropriate part or portion of the net value of the partnership assets (after deduction of partnership liabilities). If the testator owns personally assets which are used in the partnership business, those assets and the partnership share may be valued as if sold together and the combined value apportioned between them: *IRC v Gray* [1994] STC 360.

[205.28]
Buy and sell agreements. Provision in a partnership agreement for the death of a partner often provides for the purchase by the surviving partner or partners of the testator's interest. This can take the form of automatic accruer of his share to the other partners with an obligation on them to make a payment to his personal representatives, an obligation by the surviving partners to buy and the testator's personal representatives to sell his share, or an option for the surviving partners to buy his share. Clearly the obligation to buy and sell will prevent business

relief from applying if it causes the share to be under contract of sale at death: ITA 1984, s 113. There has been some uncertainty as to whether the Revenue regarded in the same way automatic accruer provisions, but it now seems clear the Revenue's view is that s 113 does not apply to them. An option provided in the partnership agreement for the surviving partners to acquire the share will not affect the availability of business relief. The right to payment by instalments of the inheritance tax on the partnership share will be terminated by the exercise of an option, but of course this is inevitable in any arrangement whereby the surviving partners buy the testator's share.

Private company shares

[205.29]
Any unquoted shares, and this includes shares dealt in on the Alternative Investment Market (ITA 1984, s 105(1ZA)), can qualify for business relief, although the exclusions of land or investment dealing or holding businesses, value attributable to excepted assets, assets held for fewer than two years, etc should not be overlooked.

[205.30]
100 per cent relief shareholdings. There are two categories of holding which get 100 per cent relief, both unquoted: securities forming part of a controlling holdings of unquoted shares and securities (ITA 1984, s 104(1)(b)) and unquoted shares: ITA 1984, s 104(1)(bb). It is thought that 'securities' includes things like debenture stock, but it is not common for these to carry any votes.

[205.31]
Ownership requirement. Unquoted shares, in common with the other categories, have to have been owned for two years to qualify for the relief (see para **[205.11]**). Form B5.9 at para **[205.66]** is a gift of such of a particular class of share as the testator has owned for two years, which could be used in a case where he is continuing to buy more shares but wishes to make a non-exempt specific gift of only those which qualify for relief. There could, however, be difficulties of identification of the shares which have been held for two years if the testator has at his death shares of the same kind which have been owned for fewer than two years, and the shares of the class in question are not numbered by the company which issued them. It will anyway be important for him to keep careful records of his purchases if he is making a disposition of this type.

[205.32]
50 per cent relief shareholdings. The holdings of shares or securities which qualify for 50 per cent relief are quoted controlling holdings of shares or securities, subject to the qualifying conditions noted at para **[205.8]** et seq as to type of business, length of ownership, etc.

[205.33]
Quoted controlling holdings, as is the case with unquoted controlling holdings, can qualify for relief where they have been owned for two years and are part of a

controlling holding at the testator's death, even if he has not had control for as long as two years, and related property and settled property in which the testator has an interest in possession is taken into account.

[205.34]
Payment by instalments and shareholdings qualifying for business relief. The types of shareholdings in relation to which the option to pay the inheritance tax on death by interest-free instalments is available are listed at para **[205.17]**. Where shares qualify for business relief and instalment payment, the instalments are interest-free: ITA 1984, s 234. However, not all shareholdings which qualify for business relief do qualify for payment by instalments. Where the relief will be 100 per cent, there may not be any tax to pay and, if so, the availability of the instalment option will not matter, but this is not always the case: see para **[205.51]**.

[205.35]
A controlling quoted or unquoted holding of shares or securities qualifies for instalment payment: ITA 1984, s 228(1)(a).

[205.36]
As regards unquoted non-controlling holdings there are three possible ways of qualifying for payment by instalments, one of which, the discretion of the Revenue to allow it in a case of hardship (ITA 1984, s 228(1)(c)), cannot be relied on in advance as being something which will apply. When a will is being made, attention should be focused on whether the case will fall within one of the two categories where payment by instalments is available as of right.

[205.37]
The first question is whether the testator's shareholding is likely at the testator's death to be worth more than £20,000, and to represent in its nominal value either ten or more per cent of the nominal value of the company's share capital, or (being ordinary shares) ten or more per cent of the nominal value of the company's ordinary shares: ITA 1984, s 228(1)(d) and (3). Ordinary shares are defined here as ones which are entitled to dividends other than ones restricted to a fixed rate (ITA 1984, s 228(4)), and so voting powers are not relevant. It should also be noted that related property will not be taken into account in assessing the size of the testator's shareholding for this purpose, although it is possible that shares in which he has an interest in possession and ones in his free estate would be aggregated for this purpose when it comes to the inheritance tax charge on death under the general rule that the tax charge is on the value of the estate, which is defined as the aggregate of all property to which he is beneficially entitled (ITA 1984, ss 4(1) and 5(1)) and includes property in which he has an interest in possession to which he is beneficially entitled: ITA 1984, s 49(1).

[205.38]
However, it is also possible (from the wording of the ITA 1984, s 227(1)), and the Inland Revenue's attitude to this point is not known, that where different people are liable for the tax on different parts of a holding, the part of the

holding which each person is liable to pay the tax on has to be considered separately to see if it passes the ten per cent test, and, if that is so, interest in possession property would not be likely to be aggregated in this way (as the persons liable will not usually be the same). Thus making a number of different gifts of part of a holding, some or all of which bear their own inheritance tax, may reduce the chances of the shareholding or parts of it qualifying for instalment payment under this head (though it may increase the chances of it doing so under the other head discussed below). Even if a holding is prima facie likely to qualify for payment by instalments under the ten per cent of nominal capital rule, it is possible that it will cease to do so by the time of the testator's death, eg by the company increasing the amount of other classes of ordinary share capital, and where a will is made on the basis that shares will fall into this category the testator needs to be warned that he may need to review his will if there is alteration in the company's capital.

[205.39]
If there is or might be difficulty about an unquoted holding qualifying for instalment payment on the testator's death under the ten per cent of capital qualification described above, the other possibility is that it could qualify on the basis (which is only available in relation to the charge on death) that 20 per cent or more of the tax on the testator's death for which the person paying the tax is liable (in the same capacity) is the tax on the holding in question and on any other property on which payment by instalments is available: ITA 1984, s 228(1)(b) and (2). This appears to mean that if the holding is given free of tax (expressly or by reason of the ITA 1984, s 211 for which see para **[214.55]** et seq), whether the tax on it amounts to the necessary 20 per cent will be assessed with reference to the tax being paid by the personal representatives, but that if the holding or a part of the holding is given subject to tax this will be assessed with reference to the tax being paid by the person it is given to. If this is correct, a reason for making a subject to tax gift of unquoted shares (see para **[205.52]** et seq for other reasons) can be, in an appropriate case, to increase the chances of the right to pay by instalments being available. Note that the calculation is by reference to relative amounts of tax, not property values, so that the tax on shares on which there will be business relief will be a smaller proportion of the entire tax on the estate than the proportion which the actual value of the underlying property is of the entire value of the estate. If there are exempt gifts and the unquoted shares are the subject of a non-exempt gift, the greater the proportion of the estate which is exempt the greater will be the proportion of the tax payable on death which is represented by the shares.

[205.40]
What dispositions to make of shares qualifying for business relief. This topic is discussed at para **[205.46]** et seq.

Land, buildings, plant and machinery

[205.41]
Land, buildings, plant and machinery which is owned by the testator but used by a partnership in which he is a partner or a company which he controls can

qualify for business relief on his death, but, if it does, only 50 per cent relief will be available (unless it is farm land, in which case it might get 100 per cent agricultural relief—see the Preliminary Note to C12 at para **[234.1]** et seq). For such assets to qualify for the relief under this head the testator's relevant company shares or partnership interest must themselves be property which qualifies for business relief (ITA 1984, s 105(6)), and the land, buildings, machinery or plant must have been used in the business for the two years preceding the testator's death, or it and property it replaced must have been used in the business for two years or more in the five years preceding the testator's death: ITA 1984, s 112(3). In determining whether the testator has control of a company for this purpose, related property and interest in possession property are taken into account: ITA 1984, s 269. It should be noted that if land, buildings, machinery or plant are used by a company in which the testator has shares but not control, then the land, buildings, machinery or plant will get no business relief, even though the shares themselves may get business relief at the rate of 100 per cent.

[205.42]
One tax planning move to consider making with this type of asset is therefore a lifetime transfer of it to the partnership or company which uses it for business purposes, so as to get the higher rate of relief for it on the testator's death; as just mentioned, there are particularly strong reasons for doing so where it is used by a company in relation to which the testator does not have control. However, the capital gains tax consequences, and inheritance tax consequences (if it is to be done by gift), of doing so need to be analysed carefully, particularly where it is a transfer to a company which is contemplated.

[205.43]
Instalment payment of the inheritance tax on this type of asset is available for land and buildings, but not plant and machinery unless it counts as land. If the inheritance tax on land or buildings is paid in instalments, and the land or buildings do not qualify for agricultural relief (see para **[234.1]** et seq), the instalments are not interest-free, ie they all carry interest from what would be the due date for payment if there were no instalment option (see paras **[205.17]** and **[205.19]**).

[205.44]
Valuation and aggregation. It has now been held in *IRC v Gray* [1994] STC 360, by the Court of Appeal reversing the Lands Tribunal, that land owned by a deceased person and used by a partnership in which he was a partner can be valued as part of the aggregate of it and the partnership share, so that, for example, if the testator is in partnership with his spouse in a business which uses land owned by him alone there would be a vacant possession valuation of the land valued in aggregation with the partnership shares, and the total value apportioned between the testator's interest in the land, his partnership share, and his spouse's partnership share. This is another reason, in a case of this kind, to make the land a partnership asset so that it qualifies for 100 per cent relief, if it can be done without undue capital gains tax cost and the testator is prepared to allow his spouse or other partners to acquire an interest in it. It should be

remembered, however, that if the land owned by the testator and used by a partnership is agricultural land it can qualify for 100 per cent agricultural relief without being a partnership asset: see the Preliminary Note to C12 at para **[234.1]** et seq.

[205.45]
Options. Where the partnership or company has other partners or shareholders who are outside the testator's family, it may be desired to give the other partners or the company the option to purchase the land etc being used in the business. For options see B9 at para **[209.1]** et seq and note that the exercise of an option may terminate any right to pay the inheritance tax by instalments.

Implications of inheritance tax business relief and instalment payment for what dispositions to make

[205.46]
Whether to make lifetime gifts of business property. Where someone has property which qualifies for 100 per cent relief, ie in effect a complete exemption from inheritance tax, the obvious strategy, other things being equal, is for him to retain the property, in a state which continues to attract the relief at this rate, until his death, and, where there is a choice between exempt and non-exempt gifts, to make a specific gift of it by his will to a non-exempt beneficiary (ie his children or relatives, but not his spouse or charity). The main reasons are that although a lifetime gift of the property would also qualify for 100 per cent relief, the inheritance tax position is just as good on death, the capital gains tax position is often better if the property is retained until death (a complete rebasing instead of hold-over relief, unless there is retirement relief), and the testator may come to need the money before he dies. When it comes to making a will, business relief is wasted if it is made the subject of a gift which would be exempt anyway. For the rules governing the allocation of business relief between exempt and non-exempt parts of an estate see the Preliminary Note to C11 at para **[233.2]** et seq.

[205.47]
Considerations which weigh against retaining 100 per cent relief property until death are the possibility that the 100 per cent rate of relief might be replaced with a lesser relief (or none at all) before the testator's death (whereas a lifetime gift made by him now is more likely to retain the right to 100 per cent relief), and the possibility that the testator may want to retire and hand over ownership and running of the business to others.

[205.48]
Whether shareholdings of private company shares which attract 100 per cent relief should be kept together is considered at para **[205.56]**.

[205.49]
Where property qualifies for only 50 per cent relief there is more incentive to give it away by lifetime gift in the hope of surviving the gift by seven years so

that it becomes wholly free of inheritance tax. There are also special reasons for making a lifetime disposition of land, buildings, machinery or plant used by a company or partnership in which the testator has a stake: see paras **[205.41]** and **[205.42]**. If 50 per cent relief property is to be retained, and given by will, it is worth considering whether to make the gift bear its own inheritance tax, and, where there may be exempt gifts (to the testator's spouse or charity), whether to make it a non-exempt specific gift: see para **[205.52]** et seq and for business relief and exempt gifts see the Preliminary Note to C11 at para **[233.2]** et seq.

[205.50]
Property not owned for long enough. Where a testator acquires business property to which business relief will apply when it has been owned long enough, but makes a will before he has owned the business property for two years (and none of the succession provisions apply), he might be advised to do either or both of two things. One is to leave the business property to a non-exempt beneficiary contingently on the testator having survived the acquisition of the business property by two years (see Form B5.9 at para **[205.66]** for a disposition of this type, but note the possible problem of identification mentioned at para **[205.31]**), and the other is to leave the business property to his spouse, if he has one, in the event of his dying within two years of acquiring the property. The point of the latter is not only to make an exempt gift, but also to take advantage of the rule (see para **[205.11]**) that one spouse who inherits the other spouse's business property also inherits the other spouse's period of ownership for business relief purposes: ITA 1984, s 108.

[205.51]
When there may be inheritance tax on relieved property. When a will is being made by a party to a marriage who has substantial property prima facie attracting 100 per cent relief, and he or she is inclined to make a specific gift of that property to a non-exempt beneficiary, leaving most or all the remainder of the estate as an exempt gift to his or her spouse, some thought should be given to the possibility that there may in the event be inheritance tax on the non-exempt gift on his or her death. Possible circumstances in which this might occur are as follows:

(a) such property may not have been owned long enough for business or agricultural relief to apply (see para **[205.11]**), or may fail to qualify for relief by being under contract of sale or by the company being in liquidation: the property not having been owned for long enough will not exclude the right to pay by interest-free instalments except in the case of agricultural land, where it will mean that there will be an instalment option, but not interest-free;

(b) there may be 'excepted assets' (ITA 1984, s 112; see also para **[205.9]**) in relation to the value of which there is no relief;

(c) even if the asset in question wholly qualifies for 100 per cent relief at the time of making the will, the position could change before the testator's death, particularly in the case of private company shares: the company's business might be sold and the proceeds invested, substantial profits might come to be invested in 'excepted assets', or the company's share capital may be diluted or the rights attached to it altered;

(d) the 100 per cent rate of business relief might have been replaced by a lesser rate for the type of asset in question by the time of the testator's death;

(e) in the case of property to which 100 per cent agricultural relief applies, the relief only relates to the agricultural value of it, and if it has hope value arising from a possibility of planning permission for another use that will not qualify for agricultural relief. Other possibilities are that the farmhouse may have a value in excess of agricultural value or not be occupied for agricultural purposes for the relevant period (see para **[234.3]**), or that the land or some of it may be used for a non-agricultural purpose (see para **[234.4]**).

One possibility to consider is to make such a gift subject to tax, if any (see para **[205.52]** et seq), and another is to make the gift conditional on there being substantial or total relief from inheritance tax. See Forms B5.9 and B5.10 at paras **[205.66]** and **[205.67]**. See also the Preliminary Note to C11 at para **[233.10]**.

[205.52]
Subject to tax gifts. A specific gift by will of any property situated in the UK is prima facie free of tax, so that any inheritance tax on it is paid out of residue, unless the will directs to the contrary or the property was comprised in settled property immediately before the testator's death; property situated outside the UK bears its own inheritance tax unless the will directs to the contrary: ITA 1984, s 211 and see B14 at para **[214.55]**. Assets outside the UK can qualify for business relief, but cannot qualify for agricultural relief unless they are in the Isle of Man or Channel Islands.

[205.53]
There are often good reasons for a specific gift of business property to be made to bear its own inheritance tax. These include the following:

(1) Where substantial property prima facie entitled to 100 per cent business relief is being given by specific gift to a non-exempt beneficiary, or property prima facie entitled to 50 per cent relief is being given by such a gift having a prospective taxable value falling within the inheritance tax nil-rate band, with in either case most or all of the remainder of the estate being given to the testator's spouse, with the intention that the estate will not be charged to inheritance tax, it would be a sensible precaution to make the gift subject to tax, if any, in case there is tax on it. See para **[205.51]** for the circumstances in which there might be tax on apparently 100 per cent relief property, and in the case of 50 per cent relief property it could turn out to have a taxable value in excess of the nil-rate band or the nil-rate band might come to be wholly or partly used up in making lifetime gifts. Making such a gift subject to tax means that the taxable estate will be smaller than it would be if the specific gift were tax-free and grossed up (see B14 at para **[214.74]**). Further, if there does turn out to be substantial tax on the gift the beneficiary can disclaim or assign the property to the surviving spouse under a Deed of Variation (see F3 at para **[241.1]** et seq). If the gift to him is made tax-free (or the

property is in the UK and there is no direction as to incidence) the benefit and the burden will be separated and he can elect to take the gift and leave residue to pay the tax, even though the tax is more than the testator had contemplated.

(2)   Where the testator is contemplating a specific gift of business assets to a non-exempt beneficiary, and there is likely to be, or might be, inheritance tax on it, but which could be paid by instalments, one possible way in which the tax might be funded is for the donee to retain the property and pay the inheritance tax himself by instalments. This is of course most likely to be a viable option if the instalments will be interest-free instalments (see paras **[205.17]** et seq and **[205.34]** for what is meant by this and the types of property where it is available). If this is likely or appropriate, the gift should be made expressly subject to its own inheritance tax. Whether to do so depends on many factors, such as the value of the property, whether any of the estate will be exempt and the intended size of the non-exempt part, and what exactly the testator is trying to achieve. See further the Preliminary Note to C11 at paras **[233.7]–[233.11]** for relevant factors where the estate is partially exempt.

(3)   In the case of some unquoted shareholdings it seems that the chances of there being a right to pay the inheritance tax by instalments can be increased by making a gift of them subject to tax: see para **[205.39]**.

(4)   Where there is a right to pay inheritance tax on a specific gift by instalments, and the tax is to be paid out of residue, the final distribution of the residuary estate could be held up for years—the instalments are ten annual ones—while the executors retain enough from the residuary estate to pay the instalments and any interest on them.

For subject to tax gifts of business property, see Forms B5.1 (at para **[205.58]**), B5.4 (at para **[205.61]**), B5.9 (at para **[205.66]**) and B5.10 (at para **[205.67]**).

[205.54]
Where a specific gift of business property is directed to bear its own inheritance tax, the tax it bears ought on equitable principles to be the inheritance tax at the estate rate attributable to the taxable value of the business after the deduction of business relief, and in the event of a dispute we would expect a court so to hold, in the absence of clear contrary directions. However, it can save argument to deal with such a point expressly, and there are examples of clauses which do so in Forms B5.9 and B5.10 (at paras **[205.66]** and **[205.67]**) and Forms C11.1, cl 2(1)(a) (at para **[233.17]**) and C11.3, cl 2 (at para **[233.40]**).

[205.55]
Nil-rate band gifts and property qualifying for business relief. See the Preliminary Note to C11 at paras **[233.8]–[233.10]**.

[205.56]
Dividing up or keeping together shareholdings. On death a large shareholding can be divided among a number of different legatees or kept together and given to a single legatee, and whichever is done will usually make no difference to the

amount of the inheritance tax charge on the testator's death (except so far as an exempt legatee or exempt legatees are involved in either alternative). Where the testator owns a majority or large minority holding which does not qualify for business relief (eg a holding in a property company), dividing up ownership will have the advantage that each legatee will have a holding which will on a future occasion of inheritance tax charge be valued at a lower, sometimes a very much lower, amount per share than that of the single holding held by the testator. Now that 100 per cent business relief applies to unquoted holdings irrespective of the amount of votes (if any) controlled by the transferor, there is no longer any compelling inheritance tax reason for keeping a holding which qualifies for the relief together in order to maintain qualification for the relief. Capital gains tax business assets taper relief also no longer requires unquoted holdings to be of a minimum size to qualify for the relief.

[205.57]
Shareholdings where the relief depends on control. Agricultural relief for shares in a company owning agricultural property (see para **[234.6]**), business relief for land, building, plant or machinery owned by the testator and used but not owned by a company in which he is a shareholder (see para **[205.41]**), and the rare cases of business relief on securities forming part of an unquoted controlling holding or quoted shares forming part of a controlling holding (see paras **[205.5]** and **[205.6]**), depend on the testator having control of the company (taking into account related property and settled property in which he has an interest in possession). Where a testator has a controlling holding which qualifies for the relief of any of these kinds it will often be desirable to keep the holding together after his or her death so as to maintain the qualification for the relief on future occasions of inheritance tax charge. If it is desired to keep the holding together but enable many people to benefit, a possible solution is a discretionary trust as in Form C11.1 at para **[233.13]** et seq. Where spouses between them have control, a gift by the first to die to the survivor so as to enable the survivor to have control after the death of the first to die, with the balance going into a non-exempt gift, is a possible option, based on Form C11.2 at para **[233.26]** et seq.

[205.58]

FORM B5.1:   **Bequest of a sole trader's business**[1]

I give to [*name*] the goodwill of my business[2] of a *description of business*] carried on by me at *location*] and all the [equipment plant stock-in-trade][3] vehicles and all other assets of any kind employed or used in carrying on the same at my death and all book debts then owing to me in respect of such business together with the then balances (if any) to the credit of the current [and business reserve] accounts of the said business at the [*name*] Bank Plc[4] and the benefit of all contracts relating thereto but subject to taking over all my liabilities in connection with the said business existing at my death and indemnifying my estate against the same but subject as follows:

    (1)   [the foregoing gift shall include the freehold or such other estate or interest I may have at my death in the premises in which the said

business is carried on but subject to any mortgage charge or other liability on or of such premises subsisting at my death][5] *or where the premises are leasehold* [the foregoing gift shall include the lease or tenancy of the premises on which the said business is carried on but subject to accepting the covenants liabilities and obligations thereunder and keeping my estate indemnified against all liability under the said lease or tenancy whether or not such liability has arisen in my lifetime or arises from acts or omissions done or occurring during my lifetime] *or where the donee is not to be given the testator's interest in the premises* [the foregoing gift shall not include my interest in the premises in which the said business is carried on but the said [*name*] shall be entitled to a non-assignable [monthly] tenancy thereof [without any obligations in respect of external or structural repair] on such terms and at such market rent as shall be determined by my Trustees (and the said [*name*] may disclaim the foregoing gift at any time up to four weeks after being notified by the trustees of the rent and other terms which they have determined upon for such tenancy)];[6]

(2)   if there is any inheritance tax payable on my estate by reason of my death which is attributable to the foregoing gift (after allowing for any reduction in value for inheritance tax purposes which is attributed thereto) then the foregoing gift shall be subject to such inheritance tax and it shall be borne by the said [*name*] in exoneration of the rest of my estate.[7]

---

1   The rate of business relief should be 100 per cent if the business has been owned for two years: see the Note at para [205.22] et seq. For complete wills where there is business relief: see C11 at para [233.1] et seq. This Form is not intended for use as a gift of a farming business (for wills disposing of farms, see C12 at para [234.1] et seq) nor for a partnership share (for a gift of which see B5.6 at para [205.63]). In order to avoid disputes, it is better to give a business to one person who takes the benefit and assumes the liabilities. For an appointment of a separate executor of the testator's business, see Form B3.23 at para [203.40].

2   The word 'business' has no definite legal meaning. In its narrowest sense it may pass the mere right to carry on the business as the testator's successor and to use his trade name; in its widest sense it may include everything enumerated in this Form: see generally Vol 1, para [64.7]. The draftsman should consider in each case which of the things enumerated in this Form are intended to pass and specify them. It is important to state whether the gift of the business is subject to trade liabilities (see *Re Timberlake, Archer v Timberlake* (1919) 63 Sol Jo 286).

3   The list may need amendment depending on the kind of business.

4   Banking arrangements vary, and the conscientious will-draftsmen should enquire into those of his client's business and get instructions on what bank balances to include in the gift.

5   A bequest of a business prima facie passes all the testator's interest in all the assets of the business, including the business premises: *Re Rhagg, Easton v Boyd* [1938] Ch 828, [1938] 3 All ER 314, and under the AEA 1925, s 35 (Part G, para [246.47]) a gift is subject to any mortgages or charges on the property in the absence of the expression of a contrary intent. However, to avoid doubt and possible dispute, we recommend that express provision is made about the business premises, and charges on it where relevant. There may need to be amendment where the business is carried on on part only of premises owned or leased by the testator, and the donee of the business is not intended to receive the whole of the premises.

6   The third option given here is an example and many other possible arrangements can be made. Excluding the testator's interest in the business premises from the gift may mean that business relief is not fully utilised, particularly where the gift of the business is not exempt and the premises themselves fall into an exempt residue. It should be remembered that a tenancy will have security of tenure under the LTA 1954, Pt II and that the trustees may need special powers or directions as to, eg how often to seek a rent increase if the premises which they will hold subject to the tenancy are to be held on trust.

7   There should be no inheritance tax on the gift because of 100 per cent business relief (see the
     Note at para **[205.22]**), but for the circumstances in which tax may be paid on such property see
     para **[205.51]**. Adding this subclause is a precaution, for use particularly where much or all of
     the remainder of the estate may be exempt.

[205.59]

FORM B5.2:   Bequest to trustees of a business carried on on leasehold premises upon trust to carry on for a limited period

I bequeath my leasehold premises at *address of business premises*] for all my
estate term and interest therein and the goodwill of my business[1] of a —— now
carried on there by me and all the machinery plant stock-in-trade and effects
employed or used in carrying on the same and all book debts owing to me in
respect of my said business together with the balance (if any) to the credit of my
said business at the —— Bank [*or if the business account is not kept separately*
together with the sum of £—— for carrying on the business[2]] and the benefit of
all contracts relating thereto but subject to all my liabilities in connection with
the said business unto my trustees[3] upon the trusts hereinafter declared
concerning the same (that is to say):

(1)   upon trust that my trustees shall continue to carry on the said business on
       the said premises or any other suitable premises during such period as
       they in their sole discretion may think fit and subject thereto—

(2)   upon trust to sell the said premises on which the said business may be
       carried on and the said business as a going concern with the goodwill
       thereof and all the then existing assets thereof or such of them as my
       trustees think fit but subject to the liabilities thereof or such of them as
       my trustees think fit upon such terms as they may in their sole discretion
       think proper [*add such of* Forms B5.14 *at para* **[205.71]**, B5.15 *at
       para* **[205.72]**, B5.17 *at para* **[205.74]**, B5.18 *at para* **[205.75]**, B5.20 *at
       para* **[205.77]** *and* B5.21 *at para* **[205.78]** *as may be necessary*].

1   The bequest of a business prima facie passes all the testator's interest in all the assets of the
     business, including the business premises (*Re Rhagg, Easten v Boyd* [1938] Ch 828).
2   See para **[205.58]**, n 4.
3   Care should be taken to choose trustees who will be prepared to carry on the business even if
     only with a view to its sale. It may be appropriate for the gift to be subject to its own inheritance
     tax: see the Preliminary Note to B5 at paras **[205.52]**–**[205.54]** and the final subclause of Form
     B5.1 at para **[205.58]** for a form of words.

[205.60]

FORM B5.3:   Trusts of net profits and proceeds of sale of a business[1]

I declare that my trustees shall stand possessed of the said business and the
annual profits thereof after payment of all the expenses of carrying on the same
until the said business shall be sold and of the net proceeds of sale thereof after
the same shall be sold and of any other moneys arising therefrom or in
connection therewith and of the income of such proceeds of sale and other
moneys upon trust to pay such annual profits or income as the case may be to
my daughter [*name*] during her life and after her death as to the said business

and the said annual profits or (as the case may be) the said proceeds of sale and other moneys and the income thereof respectively upon trust etc.

1   This could be combined with Form B5.2 at para **[205.59]**.

[205.61]

FORM B5.4:   Gift of Lloyd's underwriting business[1]

I give to [*name*] of [*address*] the assets of my business as an underwriting member at Lloyd's subject to payment thereout of the liabilities of such business Provided that:

(1)   [subject as set out below][2] the assets given hereby shall include the following (as at or ascertained after my death):

    (a)   my syndicate capacity, all my investments and cash deposited at Lloyd's, all investments and cash comprised in my special reserve, personal reserve, and premiums trust funds, and any balances on my personal account with my underwriting agent;

    [(b)   any property charged as security for a guarantee or letter of credit provided by a bank or other financial institution to support my membership at Lloyd's in respect of my Lloyd's deposit or personal or other reserve;][3]

    (c)   all profits of the said business received after my death whatever the year to which they relate and any tax repayments received after my death attributable to my said business;[4] and

    (d)   the benefit of any stop loss insurance or estate protection plan.

(2)   [Subject as set out below][5] the liabilities to which the foregoing gift is subject shall include liabilities for income tax and capital gains tax on the foregoing assets and any losses paid after my death of the said business.

[(3)   The assets given hereby and liabilities to which they are subject shall exclude:

    [(a)   any property charged as security for a guarantee or letter of credit provided by a bank or other financial institution to support my membership at Lloyd's in respect of my Lloyd's deposit or personal or other reserve;][6]

    [(b)   any profits received on an underwriting year of account which shall have been closed before my death;]

    [(c)   any losses of the said business for any underwriting year of account which shall have been closed before my death].]

(4)   If the assets comprised in the foregoing gift are exceeded by the liabilities to which it is subject then this Clause shall be of no effect.

[(5)   If any of the assets comprised in the foregoing gift do not wholly qualify for business property relief under Chapter I of Part V of the Inheritance Tax Act 1984 or if any of the foregoing liabilities to which the foregoing gift is made subject are not wholly taken into account as a deduction from the assets qualifying for such relief in determining the amount of such relief then the foregoing gift shall comprise only such assets and/or parts of assets as qualify for such relief and shall be subject only to such liabilities and/or parts of liabilities as are a deduction in determining the amount of such relief.][7]

(6)   If there is any inheritance tax payable on my estate by reason of my death which is attributable to the foregoing gift (after allowing for any business property relief reducing its value for inheritance tax purposes which is attributed thereto) then the foregoing gift shall be subject to such inheritance tax and it shall be borne by the said [*name*] in exoneration of the rest of my estate.[8]

1   A Lloyd's underwriting interest will at least as to part enjoy 100 per cent relief as a 'business', and is thus something particularly worth making a specific gift of to a non-exempt beneficiary, especially because if it is given to the testator's spouse he or she may not become an underwriting member of Lloyd's (and so the business relief will not be carried forward to the spouse's death), and if he or she does become one he or she will have a new business and will not succeed to the testator's period of ownership for business relief purposes. However, not all the value of the Lloyd's deposit or the various reserves will necessarily be accepted by the Revenue as qualifying for the relief, on the grounds that they are in excess of what is really required for the business. It is important to investigate what the testator's underwriting assets consist of, and whether there is an estate protection plan, and consider to what extent these should be included in the gift. See further the footnotes on specific points below.
2   These words should be omitted if the exclusionary sub-cl (3) is omitted.
3   Before including this item consideration should be given to what it consists of and its value. The Revenue are unlikely to concede business property relief on it beyond the amount of the guarantee, and possibly not on any of it if it is in personal use, eg where it is the testator's residence, and this has now been confirmed by the decision in *IRC v Mallender* [2001] STC 514, High Court. This subclause should be omitted if sub-cl (3)(a) excluding such property is included.
4   There will be at least two, possibly more, underwriting years of account for which the profits will not have been received (or losses notified) by the time of the testator's death. It has been held by a Special Commissioner in *Hardcastle v IRC* [2000] STC (SCD) 532 that underwriting losses not notified at an underwriter's death were not liabilities deducted in valuing the business for relief purposes, but this may imply that profits not so notified would not qualify for the relief.
5   These words should be omitted if the exclusionary sub-cl (3) is omitted.
6   See n 3 supra. This subclause should be omitted if sub-cl (1)(b) including such property is included.
7   Such a provision may well be desirable for inheritance tax purposes, but there could be difficulty, where the Revenue only agree to relief on part of an asset or fund, as to whether it is possible to make a gift of only that part which gets the business relief: see the Preliminary Note to C11 at para **[233.10]**. Profits and losses of open years which have not been notified at the testator's death will apparently be excluded by this provision: see n 4 supra. There is thus a risk in this type of provision of throwing large liabilities on to the residuary estate, and, for example, reducing by too much the provision made for the testator's surviving spouse.
8   Where sub-cl (5) is not included it will often be appropriate to make the gift subject to inheritance tax, particularly where the residue is exempt and it is hoped to avoid inheritance tax on the estate (see the Note at paras **[205.52]–[205.54]**). Even where sub-cl (5) is included, it would be a sensible precaution to include this, in case the whole of the business relief on the underwriting assets cannot be marshalled against the gift.

[205.62]

FORM B5.5:   Clause providing that inheritance tax on business premises be paid by trustees and repaid to them by son[1]

I direct my trustees to pay out of my residuary estate all inheritance tax payable in respect of the said property in which the business of the said [*company*] is carried on and which is devised to my said son [*name*] as provided above.

Upon such payment in respect of inheritance tax being made by my trustees I direct that my son shall at the expiration of [six] months from the date of such payment repay the same to my trustees to be held by them as part of my residuary estate. PROVIDED always that such payment may at the election of my son be made by [ten] equal annual payments the first of such payments to be made at the expiration of the period of [six] months aforesaid. The said sum paid for inheritance tax by my trustees shall carry interest at the rate of [three] per cent until repayment and when paid by instalments such interest shall be charged only on the amount from time to time outstanding. If my trustees so require my son shall charge the said property with the repayment of the said sum or so much thereof as is for the time being outstanding and with the interest thereon. All instalments shall be held by my trustees as part of the capital of my residuary estate and the interest thereon shall be applicable as income of my residuary estate.

1   Where the inheritance tax will be payable by instalments (see paras **[205.17]–[205.20]**) the gift could simply be made subject to inheritance tax as in Form B5.1 at para **[205.58]**. The instalments would be interest-bearing ones (see para **[205.19]**), but would be ten annual instalments. This express provision could be used to give the son a lower rate of interest than that charged on inheritance tax, but the instalment number and period should be at least as generous as those under the ITA 1984, s 227 because the son will have a statutory right to repay in not less than the statutory instalments by virtue of the ITA 1984, s 213. If the testator controls the company which uses the property, the property could qualify for 50 per cent business relief: see para **[205.41]**.

[205.63]

FORM B5.6:   Nomination of a son to succeed testator in partnership and gift to him of partnership share if he becomes a partner

In exercise of the power contained in the Articles of Partnership[1] dated —— and executed by the partners in the firm of —— carrying on business as —— in which firm I am a partner and of every other power enabling me at my death in this behalf I hereby nominate my son [*name*][2] to succeed me as a partner in the said firm on the terms contained in the said articles of partnership or on the terms contained in any articles of partnership in force with regard to the said firm at the date of my death.

I bequeath unto my said son [*name*] in the event of his becoming a partner in the said firm under this clause all my share and interest of and in the capital goodwill stock-in-trade plant machinery and assets of the said firm but my said son [*name*] shall indemnify and keep indemnified my estate to the satisfaction of my trustees from all debts and liabilities of the said firm and shall account for any sum due or owing to me from the said firm by way of profit at my death.

[I appoint my said son [*name*] my special executor as to the said partnership share and the expenses of obtaining a grant limited to such property shall be paid by him][3].

[*Take in sub-cl (2) of* Form B5.1 *at para* **[205.58]**].

In the event of my said son [*name*] refusing or failing [within —— months from the date of my death] to become a partner in the said firm I direct that all my share and interest in the said business shall fall into my residuary estate and be held by my trustees upon the trusts and subject to the powers and provisions hereinafter declared concerning the same and in the like event I bequeath to my said son [*name*] a [further] legacy of £——.

1   This clause can be used only in the rare case where the partnership articles contain a special provision allowing such nomination and where the testator is at his death a partner in the firm.
2   The articles may allow the nomination of some relative other than a son. A nomination is not restricted to sons or even relatives but only persons who are mentioned in the articles can be nominated. The person to be nominated and his rights on nomination are fixed by the articles.
3   This is unnecessary if the partnership is a family one and the general executors are not likely to be adverse to the partnership. It is of importance only where the partners might object to the general executors seeing the private papers of the partnership.

[205.64]

FORM B5.7:   Clause giving effect to provision in partnership deed and granting widow a share of the profits during the joint lives of the widow and the surviving partner[1]

In exercise of the power in that behalf conferred on me by a partnership agreement dated —— and made between myself of the one part and AB of the other part I hereby direct that if I shall die during the continuance of the partnership thereby constituted and the said AB shall exercise the option given to him by the said agreement of purchasing my share in the capital and assets of the partnership business then there shall be paid to my wife [*name*] in accordance with the terms of the said agreement out of the net profits of the partnership business an annuity equal to —— parts of such net profits from time to time during the joint lives of my said wife and the said AB such annuity to commence from the date of my death and that my executors shall require the said AB to enter into a proper deed of covenant for payment of the said annuity to my said wife in a form to be approved by my executors.

1   This clause assumes that the partnership deed provides that, on the death of the partner, the other partner (usually the original owner of the partnership business) shall instead of paying a capital sum for the deceased's share in the partnership provide an annuity out of the partnership profits for the deceased's widow. Notice that the annuity is for the joint lives of the surviving partner and the widow and is, therefore, liable to cease during the widow's lifetime on the death of the surviving partner. Apparently the annuity is not part of the testator's estate and is free from the claims of his creditors: see *Re Flavell, Murray v Flavell* (1883) 25 Ch D 89, nor does the annuity render the widow liable as a partner: Partnership Act 1890, s 2(3)(c).

[205.65]

FORM B5.8:   Clauses giving assistance to son in acquiring partnership share, with alternative provision for realisation of the share[1]

POWER TO TRUSTEES TO LEAVE CAPITAL IN BUSINESS IF SON BECOMES A PARTNER

(1)   In the event of my dying while I am a member of the firm of [*firm name*] I direct my trustees to allow any capital of mine which at my death is invested in the business carried on by the said firm to remain in such business as a loan at [£5] per cent per annum until the expiration of three months from the date of my death or from the date of my son [*name*] attaining the age of [18]/[21] years whichever is later. If on or before the expiration of the period applicable in the event which happens the then members of the said firm enter into articles of

partnership with my said son upon the terms (inter alia) that my said son shall have not less than a [one-fourth] share of the profits of the said partnership then and in that event I direct my trustees to authorise the members of the said firm to retain a sum of £[10,000] out of my capital employed in the said business such sum of £[10,000] to belong to my said son as his share in the capital of the said business. And I further authorise and empower my trustees to allow the residue of my capital to remain in the said business upon the terms of the same being paid out to my trustees by the said firm by equal annual payments extending over a period of not more than [six] years from the admission of my said son into partnership with interest on the capital for the time being unpaid at [£5] per cent per annum.[2]

SON TO BRING AMOUNT OF CAPITAL INTO ACCOUNT IN DISTRIBUTION OF RESIDUE

(2)   In the event of my said son being admitted as a partner in the said firm as aforesaid and receiving the said sum of £[10,000] as his share in the capital of the said business I direct that neither he nor his children shall take anything under the residuary gift hereinbefore contained without bringing such sum of £[10,000] into hotchpot and accounting therefor and further that in the event of the said sum of £[10,000] exceeding the respective shares of my other children in my residuary estate my said son or his personal representatives shall repay to my trustees a capital sum equal to the difference between the said sum of £[10,000] and the sum which on an equal division of my residuary estate (including for the purpose of computation the said sum of £[10,000]) my said son would receive [or would (if he had survived me and my said wife) have received][3] as his share thereof such capital sum to be paid by equal yearly instalments extending over a period of not more than —— years with interest at the rate of [five] per cent per annum on such part of the said capital sum as for the time being remains unpaid and I direct that my son shall secure such payment as aforesaid by his personal covenant. And I direct that such capital sum when paid and the interest thereon or on such part thereof as for the time being remains unpaid shall be paid and divided by my trustees to and among the persons other than my said son who are entitled under the residuary gift hereinbefore contained in favour of my children and issue in the proportions in which they respectively benefit under such residuary gift.

POWERS TO TRUSTEES IF SON DOES NOT BECOME PARTNER

(3)   As and when it appears that such partnership as aforesaid has become impossible of effectuation (either through the refusal of the then partners or of my said son to entertain the proposition or by reason of the death of my said son or otherwise) I authorise my trustees:

(a)   To ascertain my share in the said business and either to procure immediate payment to them of the value of the same or in their discretion to allow the whole or any part of my share to remain in the said business as a loan bearing interest at [five] per cent per annum for any period not exceeding —— years from the date of my death and to arrange for the payment of my said share by instalments either with or without taking security for payment thereof and without being responsible for any loss occasioned thereby.

(b) To sell or concur with other partners or partner in selling the said business to any company or individual or in winding up the affairs thereof and on any sale to agree that the purchase money therefor shall remain on loan for any period not exceeding —— years from such sale or shall be payable by instalments and on every sale to a company to accept in payment [of an amount not exceeding one-half] of the purchase-money for my share in the said business fully paid preference or ordinary shares or debentures or debenture stock of such company and to retain the same as authorised investments under this my will.

(c) In winding up such business to pay compound or submit to arbitration all accounts debts or other sums due to or owing from such business upon such evidence whether strictly legal or not as to them may seem satisfactory and to sell upon such credit and give time for payment of any sums due to my estate from any person or persons upon such terms as my trustees may think fit and generally to enter into execute and do all such agreements releases and acts as may be necessary to wind up the same in the manner most beneficial to my estate.

DEFINITION OF FIRM, ETC

(4)   Any reference in this my will to the said firm of [*name*] or the business thereof or partnership therein shall be deemed to extend to and include the firm howsoever varied or constituted as to the members or member thereof for the time being and from time to time carrying on the business howsoever varied extended or limited now at the date of execution of this my will carried on by the said firm [*name*] and the business thereof and partnership therein.

1   This form assumes that residue has been given to the testator's children in equal shares, and that that gift might be subject to a life interest given to his widow.
2   The terms of the partnership articles, particularly in relation to repayment of capital and to interest on capital, should be ascertained, and considered. When this provision takes effect in favour of the son while the widow has a life interest it could cause a partial termination of the widow's interest in possession, which could be unsatisfactory in its inheritance tax consequences: see Part A, para [200.114].
3   These words should be included if the son's interest in the residuary estate is contingent on surviving the widow.

[205.66]

FORM B5.9:   Gift of such of unquoted shares as shall have been owned for two years by the time of testator's death, subject to inheritance tax

I give to [*name*] such [25p ordinary shares in ABC Ltd] as I shall have owned throughout the period of two years immediately preceding my death[1] (if any) subject to the said [*name*] paying any inheritance tax which is payable in respect of such shares by reason of my death (taking into account any business property relief reducing the value of such shares for inheritance tax purposes which is attributed thereto).[2]

1   The gift is thus contingent on the shares having been owned long enough to qualify for business relief: see the Preliminary Note at para [205.11]. There may be difficulties of identification of the shares in some circumstances: see the Note at para [205.31], in which case it may be better not to use this form. It is not necessary to provide an express alternative gift if falling into

residue is what is wanted in the event of this gift not taking effect, and the wording of the residuary gift is wide enough. The main point of a gift of this type is to make an inheritance tax-free gift to a non-exempt beneficiary, where the residue of the estate is given to the testator's spouse. This form does not allow for subsequent company or capital reconstruction: see Form B5.10 at para [205.67] for a form which does this.

2   There are various ways in which property apparently attracting 100 per cent business relief may give rise to an inheritance tax charge. For reasons for making the gift subject to inheritance tax, see the Note at paras [205.52]–[205.54]. Where this is the only (or only significant) non-exempt gift, the legatee can choose between taking a larger gift subject to paying some tax or assigning shares in excess of the nil-rate band to the widow by Deed of Variation within two years of the testator's death so as to eliminate the inheritance tax liability. To make this even easier, power to disclaim part of the gift could be included as in Form B5.10, sub-cl (3) at para [205.67].

[205.67]

FORM B5.10:   Gift of unquoted shares or any substitute shares on condition that they qualify for business relief, subject to inheritance tax, and with power to disclaim part of the gift[1]

(1)   If at my death I own any [ordinary shares in ABC Ltd] or any substitute shares (as defined below) which at my death qualify for any business property relief under Chapter I of Part V of the Inheritance Tax Act 1984 then I give such shares to [name] subject to [his] bearing any inheritance tax which is payable (after making allowance for such business property relief as is attributed thereto) in respect of such shares by reason of my death.[2]

(2)   For the foregoing purposes substitute shares are any ordinary shares which at my death would under any of the provisions of sections 126 to 136 of the Taxation of Chargeable Gains Act 1992 be identified with [ordinary shares in ABC Ltd] previously owned by me.[3]

(3)   The said [name] may by written instrument made within two years of my death disclaim irrevocably the foregoing gift of any one or more of the foregoing shares without disclaiming the entire gift, and any of the said shares which are so disclaimed shall devolve as if the said [name] had predeceased me.[4]

1   See Form B5.9, nn 1 and 2 at para [205.66] and the Preliminary Note at para [205.11]. This form is similar in its effect to B5.9, but it will fail if any factor, not just period of ownership, prevents any business relief from being available. It also makes provision for alterations in the company's capital, takeovers, etc and provides power to disclaim part of the gift.

2   For reasons for making the gift subject to inheritance tax, see the Note at paras [205.52]–[205.54].

3   These are the provisions which, for capital gains tax purposes, identify one shareholding with an earlier one where there has been a reorganisation of share capital, conversion of securities, or company reconstruction or amalgamation.

4   If the total of the value of this gift, and the value of any other parts of the estate which are chargeable to inheritance tax, exceeds the available nil-rate band, the legatee may wish to reduce this gift to a size which does not give rise to an inheritance tax charge, making use of the ITA 1984, s 142 (see F3 at paras [241.1]–[241.15]). This provision makes a tax-effective reduction in the size of the gift easier for the legatee to accomplish, assuming that residue is given to the testator's spouse. Even if this provision were not included in the testator's will the legatee could still effect such a reduction of the size of the gift by an instrument of variation, but a disclaimer is simpler and involves fewer parties than an instrument of variation, and no election is needed for the ITA 1984, s 142 to apply. However, a disclaimer of part of a gift is thought not to be possible, in the absence of a provision of this kind: see the Preliminary Note to F3 at para [241.16].

[205.68]

FORM B5.11:   Bequest of an annuity to widow of principal director from shares in a family company, the shares being given to sons on the widow's death[1]

I bequeath my —— shares in —— Company Limited to my trustees upon trust during the lifetime of my wife [*name*] to pay from the income accruing therefrom an annuity[3] to my said wife of £—— per annum [free of all deductions whatsoever and free of income tax at the basic rate] and subject thereto during the lifetime of my said wife to divide the said income equally between my sons —— and —— and after the death of my said wife the said shares shall be held in trust for my said two sons equally, provided always that in the event of the income therefrom in any year providing insufficient to satisfy the said annuity to my said wife the deficiency shall be raised by charges upon or sale of the said shares or some part thereof.

I direct that any rebate allowance or repayment of income tax which may be made or allowed to my said wife shall enure for her own benefit.

1   This clause is designed to provide for the widow of a principal director of a small company. Though not in strictness a bequest of the business, it will in many cases amount to much the same thing in practice. The wife's income may be raised from capital, but any capital so raised will be subject to income tax: *Cunard's Trustees v IRC* [1946] 1 All ER 159.
2   The gift of an annuity has certain fiscal disadvantages which are discussed in B11 at para **[211.1]** et seq. Also, changing an annuity in favour of the testator's widow on property entitled to business relief is wasteful of the relief and better avoided if possible: see C11 at para **[233.1]** et seq.

[205.69]

FORM B5.12:   Appointment by will of permanent director of private company[1]

In pursuance of article—of the articles of association of the —— Company Limited I hereby appoint [*widow or one of the trustees or as otherwise authorised by the article*] to be a permanent director of the said company subject always to the provisions of the said articles of association.[2]

1   For an article giving power to make such an appointment, see 9 Encyclopaedia of Forms and Precedents (5th edn, 2000 Reissue), Form 219 at para [1362].
2   Such an article may limit such an appointment to the duration of the life of the surviving original permanent director, and any director so appointed is liable to removal by simple resolution of the company in general meeting under the Companies Act 1985, s 303 though it is possible to provide by the articles for the weighting of votes on a resolution for the removal of a director so as in effect to entrench a director's position: *Bushell v Faith* [1970] AC 1099, [1970] 1 All ER 53.

Trustees' powers[1]

[205.70]

FORM B5.13:   Power to carry on business[2]

My trustees may carry on any business either alone or in partnership and may employ in it any capital of my residuary estate [*an indemnity as in* Form B5.15 *at para* **[205.72]** *could be added*].

1   See also Forms B20.17 to B20.19 at paras **[220.66]–[220.68]**, Forms B21.9 to B21.11 at paras **[221.10]–[221.12]**, B21.17 at para **[221.21]** and Form C11.1, cl 6(f)–(i) at para **[233.21]**.
2   See the Note at para **[205.25]** for trustees' powers to carry on a business.

[205.71]

FORM B5.14:   Power to turn business into limited or unlimited company

I declare that my trustees may form or join in forming a limited or unlimited company to take over or purchase such business or may sell the said business to a limited or unlimited company and I direct—

(a)   that all or any part of the expenses in connection with such formation and sale may be paid out of my residuary estate;

(b)   that my trustees or any of them may become directors or servants of the company and may receive the remuneration attaching to such office without being liable to account for the same and that any trustee may become qualified as a director (if the articles so allow) by the holding in his own name of shares belonging to my estate provided that he executes a declaration of trust thereof in favour of my trustees generally accompanied by the certificates of such shares and that he accounts to my estate for all dividends and bonuses payable in respect thereof;

(c)   that the consideration for any such sale may comprise either cash debentures or debenture stock, preference or ordinary or deferred shares [fully paid] [whether fully or partly paid] or may comprise all or any of the aforesaid in such proportions as my trustees may think fit;

(d)   that the sale may comprise the whole or some part only of the assets and liabilities of the said business;

(e)   that the price shall be fixed in such manner as my trustees may determine;

[(f)   that any debentures, debenture stock or shares of any kind in such company shall be an authorised investment under this my will][1].

1   This subclause will only be needed if there is a restricted power of investment which would not include such debentures, stock, or shares. For powers of investment see B20 at para **[220.1]** et seq.

[205.72]

FORM B5.15:   Indemnity to trustees carrying on business[1]

I declare that every trustee hereof shall be fully and effectually indemnified out of my estate and every part thereof in respect of any personal liability which he may incur in connection with the said business and I further declare that no trustee hereof shall be liable to my estate or to any person claiming any interest under this my will for any loss which may be incurred in carrying on the said business.

1   For a more general form of indemnity see Form B21.12 at para **[221.16]**.

[205.73]

FORM B5.16:   **Power to trustees to carry on business where the will contains a general trust for conversion**[1]

I declare that notwithstanding the trust for sale hereinbefore contained[2] it shall be lawful for my trustees to carry on [with a view to selling the same as a going concern] the business of a —— carried on by me at ——[3] and that in carrying on the said business they shall be free from the control or interference of any person or persons beneficially entitled under this my will and may employ in it any capital of my residuary estate.

1   See the Note at para **[205.25]**. Trustees carrying on a business under such a power are in a fiduciary relationship to the beneficiaries and cannot set up a competing business on their own account without severing all connection with the trust (*Re Thomson, Thomson v Allen* [1930] 1 Ch 203).

2   If a power to postpone sale is conferred the trustees would have an implied power to continue the business in the meantime: *Re Crowther, Midgley v Crowther* [1895] 2 Ch 56. But it is preferable to make express provision.

3   Under a direction to carry on the testator's business, the trustees or executors are entitled to the free use of the business premises and the fixed plant and machinery therein so long as they are entitled under the will to carry on the business (*Re Cameron, Nixon v Cameron* (1884) 26 Ch D 19). The trustees will be entitled to set aside sums for depreciation of assets and a reserve fund: *Re Crabtree, Thomas v Crabtree* (1911) 106 LT 49; *Re Robertson* [1953] 2 SCR 1. Such a setting aside is not an accumulation and is not subject to the LPA 1925, s 164 (Part G, para **[246.42]**).

[205.74]

FORM B5.17:   **Power for some of the trustees only to carry on testator's business**

I declare that in case any one or more of my trustees shall be unwilling to carry on such business then it shall be lawful for the others or other of such trustees to carry on such business and to exercise alone all powers authorities and discretions hereby conferred on my trustees in relation to carrying on the said business or winding up the affairs thereof or otherwise howsoever in respect thereof[1] and I declare that any one or more of my trustees may act as manager or managers of the said business at such salary[2] as may be agreed upon by the other or others of my trustees for the time being without being liable to account to my estate in respect thereof.

1   See *Re Mellor, ex p Butcher* (1880) 13 Ch D 465.

2   The salary would technically be legacy: *Re Salmen, Salmen v Bernstein* (1912) 107 LT 108.

[205.75]

FORM B5.18:   **Provision for exercise of powers though trustees interested in business**[1]

All or any of the above powers granted to my trustees in relation to the said business and premises may be exercised [by my executors and][2] by any of my trustees and may be exercised although he or she may be interested as a partner in the said business or as a beneficiary under this my will.

1   For a clause practically in these terms, see *Re Sykes, Sykes v Sykes* [1909] 2 Ch 241.
2   Where the will appoints the same persons both executors and trustees and defines them as 'my trustees,' these words are not necessary, but they might be of importance where different persons were so appointed in a case where the powers had to be exercised during the ordinary administration of the estate by executors as such.

[205.76]

FORM B5.19:   Power to lend money to legatee of business

My trustees may at any time lend trust moneys to my said son to whom my business is bequeathed to an amount not exceeding £—— at any one time and not exceeding £—— in all such loan or loans to be for such period or periods and at such commercial rate or rates of interest [not being less than—per cent per annum] and upon such other terms as my trustees may think fit and my trustees shall not in any event be under any liability in respect of money so advanced or the interest thereon.

[205.77]

FORM B5.20:   Power to employ a manager

My trustees may appoint any person (including any one or more of themselves) manager servant or agent to act in [the said business] at a salary or otherwise.

[205.78]

FORM B5.21:   Powers relating to sale of a business

My trustees shall have the following additional powers in any sale of [the said business]:

(1)   to allow the purchase money to remain on loan for any period not exceeding [five] years payable by instalments at such rate of interest as they may think proper and to pay compound or submit to arbitration all accounts debts or other sums due or owing from such business upon such evidence whether strictly admissible in a court of law or not as to them may seem proper and to sell upon credit and give time for payment of any sums due to [the said business] from any person or persons upon such terms as they may think fit;

(2)   in the event of [the said business] being sold to any company to accept, in satisfaction of the whole or any part of the purchase money payable in respect of such sale, shares in such company (whether wholly or partly paid up or preference or ordinary shares) or debentures or debenture stock in such company.

[205.79]

FORM B5.22:   Powers to give warranties etc on the sale of a business or private company shares

My trustees may in connexion with the sale of any assets of my estate (in particular the sale of any business or any private company shares) give any warranty indemnity or other agreement or covenant whatever and shall be fully indemnified out of [my residuary estate] against any liability they may incur thereunder.

B6   Gifts of freehold land

Part B   Clauses in wills

CROSS REFERENCES

For rights of residence see B8 at para **[208.1]** et seq. For testamentary options see
B9 at para **[209.1]** et seq. For gifts of land into trust see Forms B17.33 to B17.35
at paras **[217.38]–[217.40]**. For trustees' powers to permit enjoyment in kind see
Forms B18.24 to B18.26 at paras **[218.108]–[218.111]**. For trustees' powers in
the management of land see Forms B20.10 to B20.13 at paras **[220.49]–
[220.62]**. For discussion of trusts of land under the Trusts of Land and
Appointment of Trustees Act 1996 see Part A, para **[200.48]** et seq.

PRELIMINARY NOTE

[206.1]
Strictly, the correct term for a gift of real property as opposed to personal
property is a 'devise', and so apt to describe a gift of freehold land but not of
leasehold land (which is, properly speaking, 'a bequest'). However, in this
edition the words 'bequeath' and 'devise' have both been replaced with 'give'
which is now in common usage.

[206.2]
In the case of an absolute gift there is probably little that need be considered
save that testators are often misinformed as to the description of their interest in
property and are apt to describe properties in terms which are difficult to
reconcile with the title deeds. Where time permits, therefore, these matters
should be checked with the deeds in order to prevent later dispute.

[206.3]
Inheritance tax. Whether the gift is to be free of, or subject to, inheritance tax,
should also be given careful consideration. In the absence of contrary provision
inheritance tax on a specific gift of land in the United Kingdom is now a
testamentary expense payable out of residue: Inheritance Tax Act 1984 (ITA
1984), s 211 (Part G, para **[246.83]**). This is subject to the point that s 211 does
not treat as a testamentary expense the inheritance tax attributable to property
comprised in a settlement immediately before the testator's death. The relevant
definition of settlement (ITA 1984, s 43(2)) would include entailed property.
Therefore, property disposed of by will by virtue of a special or general power
of appointment of settled property, or by virtue of the power conferred by the
Law of Property Act 1925 (LPA 1925), s 176 (Part G, para **[244.53]**) to dispose
of entailed property by will, bears its own inheritance tax in the absence of an
expression of a contrary intention in the will. See C11 at para **[233.1]** et seq for

business relief and C12 at para **[234.1]** et seq for agricultural and woodlands relief.

[206.4]
Gifts to minors. A minor cannot have a legal estate vested in him. A gift of land to a minor under a will of a person dying on or after 1 January 1997 will have effect as a trust for the minor and the Settled Land Act 1925 (SLA 1925) will no longer apply: TLATA 1996, Sch 1, para 2 (Part G, para **[246.114]**). The personal representatives will hold the land on trust for the minor as a trust of land (TLATA 1996, s 2) and will transfer it to him when he attains 18 (the age of majority pursuant to Family Law Reform Act 1969 (FLRA 1969), s 1). The conveyancing is now much simplified and it makes no practical difference whether or not a trust for sale is included in the gift. While the donee is a minor the personal representatives no longer need to set up a settlement subject to the SLA 1925 by execution of a vesting assent, but will be able to assent to the vesting of the land in themselves as trustees and to appoint new trustees of land under the TA 1925, s 36 (Part G, para **[246.31]**).

[206.5]
If a minor dies on or after 1 January 1997 without having been married and without issue, any fee simple estate or absolute interest in freehold land to which he would otherwise have been entitled under a trust or settlement (including a will) he will be deemed to have had a life interest in and the trust or settlement is to be construed accordingly. Any freehold land so given to such a minor will accordingly revert to the testator's estate on the minor's death (see the AEA 1925, s 51(3), as amended by the TLATA 1996, s 25(1), Sch 3, paras 6(1), (4)(a): Part G, para **[244.66]**). In this respect an absolute gift of land to a minor without the interposition of a trust for sale is less 'absolute' than a gift of the proceeds of sale of land subject to a trust for sale.

[206.6]
Successive interests. Following the commencement of the TLATA 1996 on 1 January 1997, where a gift of freehold land is not absolute but creates successive interests it takes effect as a trust of land under that Act. It was at one time thought desirable that successive interests should be effected by creating a trust for sale in order to avoid the necessity for a special grant but because the SLA 1925 cannot apply it now makes little or no difference whether or not there is a trust for sale.

[206.7]
Administrative powers. Subject to the application of the duty of care under the Trustee Act 2000, s 1 (if not excluded by the will), for the purpose of exercising their functions as trustees, the trustees of land have in relation to the land subject to the trust all the powers of an absolute owner (TLATA 1996, s 6: Part G, para **[246.91]**) and if the land is sold the trustees have a general power of investment (TrA 2000, s 3: Part G, para **[246.118]**). Thus, the need to confer express administrative powers is much reduced and in many cases it will not be necessary to include any express powers at all. For examples of express powers

see paras **[220.49]–[220.58]** and Forms B20.10 to B20.13 at paras **[220.59]–[220.62]**.

[206.8]
Existing liability for repairs. When a testator is the owner in fee simple of property and gives it subject to a lease in which he has covenanted to keep the exterior in repair, the cost of such repairs necessary at the date of death, if executed after the death of the testator, must (in the absence of any direction to the contrary) be met out of the residue of the estate and not paid for by the donee. In one case the repairs had been discussed by the testator with builders but no definite order for their execution was given: *Re Day's Will Trusts, Lloyds Bank Ltd v Shafe* [1962] 3 All ER 699, [1962] 1 WLR 1419.

[206.9]
Ademption. It must be remembered that a sale of the property given after the execution of the will will result in ademption. For a codicil for use where there has been such a sale, see Form D7 at para **[237.14]**.

[206.10]

FORM B6.1:   **Absolute general gift of freeholds or lands generally**

I give all my freehold property[1] [including all my undivided shares therein][2] whatsoever and wheresoever whether in possession reversion remainder or expectancy or over which I may have any general power of disposition [including all freehold land of which I am tenant in tail in possession under [*describe the will or settlement*]] to [*name*] absolutely.[3]

1   Since the change in the law of intestacy and the abolition of descent to the heir, rendering the word 'heir' obsolete, the word 'hereditaments' has become rather meaningless. The word 'property' is here substituted but some may think that that word is insufficient in the case of incorporeal hereditaments and for the sake of completeness there may be added after the word property 'including incorporeal hereditaments'.
2   By virtue of the TLATA 1996 an undivided share is now an equitable interest in land. This does not mean that a phrase such as 'freehold property' will now include an undivided share of a freehold, because it is an interest in a freehold rather than being itself a freehold. However, it could save argument to make it clear whether or not undivided shares are included in the gift by including the words in parenthesis.
3   The express reference to entails is not superseded by the TLATA 1996, although the creation of new entails on or after 1 January 1997 is prevented by Sch 1, para 5 of that Act, and any attempt to create one gives rise to an absolute interest. It is, however, still possible for a testator to be a tenant in tail under a pre-1997 disposition. As to a gift of property of which the testator is tenant in tail in possession, see the LPA 1925, s 176 (Part G, para **[244.53]**). Such a gift operates as if the tenants in tail in possession had barred the entail and become owner of the fee simple. A reference to entailed property generally would be sufficient.
        A gift of the land of the testator or of the land of the testator described in a general manner is to be construed to include leasehold estates of the testator unless a contrary intention appears (WA 1837, s 26: Part G, para **[244.26]**), see Vol 1, paras **[64.32]–[64.34]**. If the words were 'all my lands', they would pass a testator's freeholds and leaseholds, and also, by virtue of the WA 1837, s 27 (Part G, para **[244.27]**), pass all similar property over which he has a general power of appointment, but this clause is restricted to freeholds.

[206.11]

FORM B6.2: **General gift of lands in a particular place**[1]

I give all my freehold property in the parish of —— *or* in the county of ——]
including all my undivided shares therein[2] to [*name*] absolutely [in fee simple
for his own absolute use and benefit].

1 The properties should be specified if possible but such general gifts may be used in cases where
   no better description is possible. They have in the past, however, often led to difficulty and
   contention: see Vol 1, para **[63.1]** et seq. See notes to the immediately preceding precedent.
2 See para **[206.10]**, n 2.

[206.12]

FORM B6.3: **Gift of freehold lands purchased in a certain year**[1]

I give my freehold lands[2] at —— which I purchased from —— in the year ——
to my daughter [*name*] absolutely.

1 See the notes to the immediately preceding precedents.
2 See para **[206.10]**, n 2.

[206.13]

FORM B6.4: **Specific gift of freeholds**[1]

I give to [*name*] in fee simple my freehold property[2] situate at —— in the
county of —— and known as —— [together with all easements appurtenances
and other rights thereto belonging or appertaining or reputed to appertain thereto
or to any part thereof or enjoyed or reputed or known as part or parcel thereof[3]].

1 While it will often not be possible to describe the property in the terms of the description in the
   title deeds, it is most desirable that whatever short description is adopted is part of the fuller
   description in those deeds so that the property is identified with the property there described.
2 See para **[206.10]**, n 2.
3 The words in brackets are required only where the testator owns adjoining property.

[206.14]

FORM B6.5: **Specific gift of property with provision against
apportionment**

I give to [*name*] in fee simple my freehold property[1] at —— in the county of —
— and known as —— together with the rents and profits due or accruing due[2] in
respect thereof at the date of my death but subject to the payment by him of all
outgoings and expenses usually chargeable against the income of such property.[3]

1 See para **[206.10]**, n 2.
2 Where rent is paid in arrear, these words will exclude the Apportionment Act 1870, s 2 (Part G,
   para **[246.3]**) which would otherwise require the rent to be considered as accruing from day to
   day and apportioned between the part of the rent period preceding the testator's death (that
   portion of rent passing with residue if not otherwise specifically given) and the part of the rent
   period following the testator's death (which portion of rent would pass with the specific gift).
   The Act does not apply where rent is paid in advance (*Ellis v Rowbotham* [1900] 1 QB 740) and

so the words 'or accruing due' should perhaps not be included where the gift is of land subject to a lease under which the rent is payable in advance because their inclusion might lead to a question over whether the gift is intended to carry rent for the part of the rent period following the testator's death.

3   As to outgoings usually chargeable against income, see *Eccles v Mills* [1898] AC 360; *Re Hughes, Ellis v Hughes* [1913] 2 Ch 491. In the case of land subject to leases, only expenses incident to the relationship of landlord and tenant are properly chargeable against income. This excludes expenses preparatory to the relationship of landlord and tenant such as expending money to put the property in a certain state of repair or condition required by the tenant as a condition of accepting a lease.

[206.15]

FORM B6.6:   Specific gift of registered land

I give to [*name*] [in fee simple] my freehold lands registered in HM Land Registry as County [*or* County Borough] —— Title No —— Property —— [and declare that all cost of the registration of the said [*donee*] with an absolute title thereto in the Land Register shall be payable out of my residuary estate].[1]

1   In the case of a specific gift the cost of vesting it in the beneficiary is to be borne by him in the absence of a direction to the contrary: *Re Grosvenor, Grosvenor v Grosvenor* [1916] 2 Ch 375.

[206.16]

FORM B6.7:   Gift to joint tenants or tenants in common

I give my freehold[1] house and premises known as —— and now in the occupation of [*tenant*] to my daughters [*name*] and [*name*] as joint tenants [*or* as tenants in common in equal shares[2]].

1   See para **[206.10]**, n 2.
2   See the LPA 1925, s 36, as to joint tenancy; and s 34, as to tenancy in common. A joint tenancy may be severed either expressly by service of a notice under LPA 1925, s 36, or by operation of law, eg by the beneficiary charging his interest in favour of a third party, and after severance the party severing will be a tenant in common with the other or others: that is, if there are two joint tenants, they become tenants in common; but if there are more than two, then the severer is a tenant in common with the others who remain joint tenants among themselves. The personal representatives will hold the land on trust for the beneficial tenants in common or joint tenants (LPA 1925, ss 34(2), (3) and 36(1)), but they can require the beneficiaries to accept a transfer of the land (TLATA 1996, s 6(2)). For a gift of the beneficial interest of a tenant in common, see Form B4.46 at para **[204.68]** and for a clause dealing with property held in joint tenancy, see Form B4.47 at para **[204.69]**.

[206.17]

FORM B6.8:   Gift to minor[1]

I give my freehold land[2] at —— in the county of —— known as —— to [*minor*] absolutely provided that if the said [*minor*] shall predecease me without leaving issue[2] living at my death or then en ventre but born thereafter or if he shall survive me and die under the age of [eighteen] [twenty-one] years without leaving children[2] living at his death then I give the said land unto —— and provided further that if the said [*minor*] shall predecease me leaving issue[3] living at my death or then en ventre but born thereafter then I give the said land to such issue and if more than one as tenants in common in equal shares per stirpes but so that no issue shall take whose parent is living at my death and so capable of taking.[4]

1   As to effect of such a gift, see the General Note to gifts at paras **[206.4]** and **[206.5]**. If the primary donee is under 18 at the testator's death the ITA 1984, s 71 (for which see Part A, paras **[200.119]–[200.136]**) will apply. Even if the gift over takes effect on the donee's death without issue at any age under 21, he will attain an interest in possession at 18. There will thus be no further inheritance tax charge on the primary donee becoming entitled to an interest in possession or absolute interest at a time subsequent to the testator's death as he has a vested interest (though subject to possible defeasance) and the accumulation and maintenance trusts of the TA 1925, s 31 (Part G, para **[246.26]**) will cease when he attains 18.

2   See para **[206.10]**, n 2.

3   Any reference to issue or children will, in the absence of a contrary intention, be construed as including illegitimate and adopted issue and children. For wills made after 3 April 1988 the inclusion of illegitimate issue and children will be by virtue of the FLRA 1987, ss 1 and 19 (Part G, paras **[245.70]** and **[245.72]**). (For wills made prior to that and after 1 January 1970, see FLRA 1969, s 15(1): Part G, para **[245.39]**). The inclusion of adopted children and issue is by virtue of Adoption Act 1976, ss 39 and 42, replacing (by way of consolidation) the Children Act 1975, Sch 1, paras 3 and 5 as from 1 January 1976, and brought into force on 1 January 1988. The Human Fertilisation and Embryology Act 1990, as from 1 August 1991, also affects the meaning of 'children' and 'issue' in some circumstances (see Part G, para **[245.83]** et seq). See generally Vol 1, paras **[71.1]–[76.6]**, for the meaning of the terms 'children' and 'issue'.

4   It seems that these words are necessary to avoid any question arising in the rare case where there is a child and grandchildren or other issue of differing generations.

[206.18]

FORM B6.9:   Gift of land of which the testator is tenant in tail[1]

I give all the land of which I am tenant in tail in possession under [*particulars of will or settlement*] to [*name*] in fee simple.

1   The express reference to entails is not superseded by the TLATA 1996, although the creation of new entails on or after 1 January 1997 is prevented by Sch 1, para 5 of that Act, and any attempt to create one gives rise to an absolute interest. It is, however, still possible for a testator to be a tenant in tail under a pre-1997 disposition by which a tenant in tail in possession has power to dispose by will of entailed property referring specifically either to the property or the instrument under which it was acquired or to entailed property generally: see the LPA 1925, s 176(1) (Part G, para **[244.53]**). A tenant in tail in this section includes the owner of a base fee in possession (sub-s (3)). This gift will bear its own inheritance tax unless there is some provision to the contrary in the will: see para **[206.3]** and paras **[214.4]–[214.7]**.

[206.19]

FORM B6.10:   Gift of entailed property generally[1]

I give all entailed property whatsoever and wheresoever of which, by virtue of section 176 of the Law of Property Act 1925, I have power to dispose by will to [*name*] absolutely [*or* in fee simple *or* for all the residue of the several terms of which the same are held *or* absolutely *according to the nature of the property*].

1   See para **[206.18]**, n 1. The LPA 1925, s 176 (Part G, para **[244.53]**), gives power not only to dispose by will of property of which the testator is tenant in tail in possession, but also of money (including the proceeds of property directed to be sold) subject to be invested in the purchase of property, of which, if it had been so invested, he would have been the tenant in tail in possession at his death. This gift will bear its own inheritance tax unless there is some provision to the contrary in the will: see paras **[206.3]** and **[214.4]–[214.7]**.

[206.20]

FORM B6.11:   **Gift of freeholds subject to the payment of a legacy[1]**

I give my lands situate at —— to [*donee*] subject to and charged with the payment of [the clear sum of] £—— to [*legatee*] and the [*donee*] accepting this gift shall [not] be personally liable for such payment.

[*OR*

I charge my lands situate at —— with payment of [the clear sum of] £—— to etc and subject to such charge give the same to etc.[2]]

1   A gift of land upon the condition that certain payments are made is usually construed as constituting those payments a charge upon the land. If, therefore, the words 'and charged with' were omitted from the above clause, the payment would probably still be a charge upon the land, but whether it was so or not would be a question of construction of the will taken as a whole. The inclusion of these words, therefore, will remove any difficulty of this nature which might arise. See *Re Lester, Lester v Lester* [1942] Ch 324, [1942] 1 All ER 646, and the cases there reviewed. As to such a gift creating a trust, see Vol 1, para **[91.2]**. A legacy charged on realty will not, as was formerly the case, bear a due proportion of the inheritance tax attributable to such realty, as tax on realty is now prima facie a testamentary expense: see the ITA 1984, s 211 (Part G, para **[246.83]**; see also paras **[214.4]**–**[214.7]** and **[214.55]**–**[214.74]**).
2   This form removes any doubt as to the land being charged with the legacy and is preferable to that first given.

[206.21]

FORM B6.12:   **Gift subject to the payment of debts, funeral, and testamentary expenses**

I give my freehold lands situate at —— but subject to and charged [in exoneration of my personal estate[1]] with the payment of my debts funeral and testamentary expenses and the legacies and annuities given by this my will or any codicil hereto and the inheritance tax on any legacy or annuity given free of inheritance tax to [*donee*] absolutely [and I declare that all inheritance tax payable in respect of any such legacy or annuity shall be born or paid by the said [*donee*] or the said lands in exoneration of the legatees or annuitants[2]].

1   These words must be inserted if such is the testator's intention (*Bootle v Blundell* (1815) 1 Mer 193 at 219), even if the land is outside the jurisdiction (*Re Smith, Smith v Smith* [1913] 2 Ch 216). The general practice now is to make the residuary realty and personalty subject to a trust for sale and to pay all these sums out of the proceeds in priority to all other sums.
2   A legatee whose legacy is charged on land is no longer liable to bear a proportion of the inheritance tax (see para **[206.20]**, n 1) and this express exoneration is therefore not strictly necessary.

[206.22]

FORM B6.13:   **Gift subject to a mortgage**

I give my freehold land situate at —— subject to and charged with the payment of all principal sums and interest secured thereon by way of mortgage or otherwise at my death to [*name*] absolutely.[1]

1   Every kind of property which a person dies possessed of or entitled to, or which he disposes of by his will under a general power of appointment (including entailed property under the statutory power) is now, in the absence of a contrary intention as between the different persons claiming through the deceased, primarily liable for the payment of any money charged on that property at the time of the deceased's death. See the AEA 1925, s 35 and the definition of 'property' in s 55(1)(xvii) (Part G, paras **[246.47]** and **[246.52]**). The results would, therefore, be the same if the land were given without reference to the mortgage, but it may be convenient to refer to it. The gift of an option to purchase at a price below the portion of a mortgage debt attributable to the specifically given property does not show a contrary intention within this section: *Re Biss, Heasman v Biss,* infra.

Where the property here specifically given has been mortgaged or charged with other property which is included in the residue, then the specifically given property must bear a proportionate part of the mortgage debt or charge: *Re Neeld, Carpenter v Inigo-Jones* [1962] Ch 643, [1962] 2 All ER 335, overruling *Re Biss, Heasman v Biss* [1956] Ch 243, [1956] 1 All ER 89, and *Re Cohen, National Provincial Bank Ltd v Katz* [1960] Ch 179, [1959] 3 All ER 740 on this point.

[206.23]

FORM B6.14:   Gift freed from a mortgage debt

I give my freehold lands situate at —— to [*name*] absolutely freed and discharged from all sums secured thereon by way of mortgage or otherwise at my death and I direct that such sums and all interest in respect thereof and costs and expenses relating to the discharge thereof shall be paid out of my residuary estate.[1]

1   See para **[206.22]**, n 1. There must be express words making this gift free of the mortgage or charge on the property.

[206.24]

FORM B6.15:   Gift of lands, and in the event of such lands being sold during testator's lifetime, bequest of the proceeds of sale of such lands

I give my freehold land at —— in the county of —— and known as —— to [*name*] absolutely and in case the said land [or any part thereof] shall be sold or contracted to be sold[1] by me in my lifetime then in lieu thereof [or of such part thereof] I give to the said [*name*] free of inheritance tax[2] the sum of £—— [*or* a sum equal in amount to the sum received as purchase-money in respect of such sale after the deduction of all expenses of such sale] [and I direct that in the event of there being an insufficiency of assets in my estate the legacy hereby given shall be treated as if it were property specifically given for the purposes of abatement[3]].

1   A binding contract for sale will effect an ademption: *Farrar v Lord Winterton* (1842) 5 Beav 1 and see Vol 1, paras **[41.1]–[41.8]**.
2   Inheritance tax on land is now prima facie payable out of residue, but a legacy may have to contribute to the payment of inheritance tax if residue includes foreign property: see para **[214.62]**.
3   But for these words the legacy would abate rateably other general legacies, whereas the specific gift of the property, had it not been adeemed, would have abated only with property specifically given.

[206.25]

FORM B6.16:   **Gift of lands which the testator has contracted to purchase**

I give the freehold lands at —— which I have lately agreed to purchase from [*vendor*] of etc to [*donee*] absolutely and I direct that the purchase-money payable in respect thereof and the costs of and incidental to such purchase or so much thereof respectively as shall remain unpaid at my death shall be paid out of my residuary personal estate.[1] [And in case the said contract shall be determined either in my lifetime or after my death I give to the said *donee*] in lieu of such lands a sum equal in amount to the agreed purchase money in respect of such purchase.]

1   The devisee takes subject to the vendor's lien for the purchase money: *Re Cockcroft, Broadbent v Groves* (1883) 24 Ch D 94, and *Re Birmingham, Savage v Standard* [1959] Ch 523, [1958] 2 All ER 397, unless there is an express direction for it to be paid out of the personal estate. See *Re Rix, Steward v Lonsdale* (1921) 90 LJ Ch 474, as to the position if the contract goes off before testator's death. See also *Re Riddell, Public Trustee v Riddell* [1936] Ch 747, [1936] 2 All ER 1600, where the balance of the purchase money on completion was paid by the testator's solicitors shortly before his death.

[206.26]

FORM B6.17:   **Gift of certain freehold lands to a charity**

I give my freehold lands at —— in the county of ——[1] and known as —— to the [*charity*] absolutely[2] [and I accordingly direct my personal representatives to vest the same in or cause the same to be vested in the trustees of the said [*charity*].[3]

1   If the gift is to be limited to such lands as the testator owns at the date of his will, the lands must be accurately described, as in a conveyance.
2   Such a gift was subject to the Mortmain and Charitable Uses Act 1891, s 5 but that provision has been repealed by the Charities Act 1960, s 38 and this gift now takes effect according to its terms. The gift will be free of inheritance tax under the ITA 1984, s 23(1): see further Part A, paras **[200.102]** and **[200.103]** and **[212.2]**.
3   Land held for charitable purposes is land subject to a trust of land within the meaning of the TLATA 1996, ss 1 and 2(5) (Part G, paras **[246.86]** and **[246.87]**). Accordingly the charity trustees will have all the powers of an absolute owner (s 6(1)) and these cannot be restricted or excluded by the instrument creating the trust (s 8(3)). The gift should not name the Official Custodian for Charities. If the charity so desires then it is for the charity to have the land vested in the Official Custodian for Charities as custodian trustee.

[206.27]

FORM B6.18:   **Gift subject to a condition as to taking a name**

I give my freehold lands at —— to [*donee*] in fee simple on condition that he shall within —— months after my death unless already using the surname of —— take and use upon all occasions the surname of —— in addition to [*or* in substitution for] his own surname but if the said [*donee*] shall neglect or refuse within such period as aforesaid to take and use the said surname or if the said [*donee*] using such surname shall discontinue such use then and in every such case immediately after the expiration of the said period of —— months or immediately after such discontinuance as aforesaid the estate of the said [*donee*] shall immediately cease and determine and I give the said lands unto my trustees in fee simple upon the trusts and with and subject to the powers and provisions hereinafter declared and contained of and concerning my residuary estate or such of the same as may for the time being be subsisting and capable of taking effect.[1]

1   See generally Vol 1, paras **[35.39]**–**[35.44]**. See also Form C13.2, cl 9 at para **[235.27]** and the notes thereto. Where this clause included the provision against discontinuance of the use of the name it had been held to be void for uncertainty: *Re Lewis' Will Trust, Whitelaw v Beaumont* [1951] WN 591; *Re Bouverie, Bouverie v Marshall* [1952] Ch 400, [1952] 1 All ER 408; *Re Wood's Will Trusts, Wood v Donnelly* [1952] Ch 406, [1952] 1 All ER 740, but these cases have been over-ruled by the decision in *Re Neeld, Carpenter v Inigo-Jones* [1962] Ch 643, [1962] 2 All ER 335.In the case of the will of a person dying on or after 1 January 1997 the land will be held on a trust of land within the meaning of the TLATA 1996. The land would otherwise have been settled land.

[206.28]

FORM B6.19:   Gift to a person with a gift over on death without issue

I give my freehold lands at —— to [*name*] absolutely but if he predeceases me without leaving [male] issue[1] living at my death or then en ventre but born thereafter or if he shall survive me and die under the age of [eighteen] [twenty-one] years without leaving [male] issue[1] living at his death then I give the said lands to [*name*] in fee simple[2] and if he predeceases me leaving [male] issue[1] living at my death or then en ventre but born thereafter then I give the said lands to such issue in equal shares per stirpes and that no such issue shall take whose parent is living at my death and so capable of taking.

1   For wills made after 3 April 1988 the inclusion of illegitimate issue and children will be by virtue of the FLRA 1987, ss 1 and 19 (Part G, paras **[245.70]** and **[245.72]**). (For wills made prior to that and after 1 January 1970, see the FLRA 1969, s 15(1): Part G, para **[245.39]**) The inclusion of adopted children and issue is by virtue of the AA 1976, ss 39 and 42, replacing (by way of consolidation) the Children Act 1975, Sch 1, paras 3 and 5 as from 1 January 1976, and brought into force on 1 January 1988. The HFEA 1990, as from 1 August 1991, also affects the meaning of 'children' and 'issue' in some circumstances (see Part G, paras **[245.83]** et seq). See generally Vol 1, paras **[72.1]**–**[76.6]**, for the meaning of the terms 'children' and 'issue'
2   Land given by a gift as in Form B6.19 is settled land in the case of a person dying before 1997 but in the case of a will of a person dying on or after 1 January 1997 the land will be subject to a trust of land within the meaning of the TLATA 1996.

[206.29]

FORM B6.20:   Gift in exercise of a special power of appointment[1]

In exercise of the power for this purpose given to me by the will dated —— of my deceased father [*name*] who died on —— and whose said will was proved in the [Principal] [—— District] [Registry of the Family Division] on —— [*or* by deed dated —— and made between [*parties*]] and of every or any other power enabling me in this behalf I give and appoint [all the freehold lands [capital moneys and investments][2] which may at my death be subject to such power of appointment to my sons [*name*] and [*name*] in equal shares as tenants in common absolutely[3]] [the freehold lands known as [*description*] to my son [*name*] and the freehold lands known as [*description*] to my son [*name*] and all

1221

the remainder of the freehold lands which may at my death be subject to such power of appointment to my said two sons in equal shares as tenants in common absolutely[4]].

1 If, as would normally be the case, the property subject to the power is settled property for inheritance tax purposes in which the testator has an interest in possession immediately before his death, it will bear its own inheritance tax unless there is express provision in the will to the contrary: see the Preliminary Note at para **[206.3]** and para **[208.41]**, n 1.

2 *Mills v Fox* (1887) 37 Ch D 153 at 162, shows the advantage of including these words for the property may be sold or compulsorily acquired before the death of the testator.

3 LPA 1925 undivided shares in land remain equitable interests but, as of 1 January 1997, if they do not arise under an express trust for sale they no longer take effect under a statutory trust for sale (LPA 1925, s 34, as amended by the TLATA 1996). The personal representatives will hold the land on trust for the beneficial tenants in common, but they can require the beneficiaries to accept a transfer of the land (TLATA 1996, s 6(2): Part G, para **[246.91]**).

4 A sale of any of the specific lands before the testator's death will vitiate the intention. If thought fit, express provision may be made for the death of one of the sons before the testator.

[206.30]

FORM B6.21:   Expression of testator's intention not to exercise a general power of appointment over land

Whereas under and by virtue of the will dated —— and duly proved in the [Principal] [—— District] [Registry of the Family Division] on —— of [*testator*] who died on ——I have a general power of appointment over certain freehold lands in the parish of —— in the county of —— now I hereby declare that it is not my intention to exercise the said power and that no clause of this my will shall operate as an exercise thereof.[1]

1 See the WA 1837, s 27 (Part G, para **[244.27]**) and Vol 1, paras **[39.8]**–**[39.15]**. This declaration is a clear expression of a contrary intention within the section so that the general power is not exercised by a general gift of real estate.

[206.31]

FORM B6.22:   Gift of lands upon the trusts of a settlement[1]

I give [*description of land*] to my trustees upon the same trusts and subject to the same powers and provisions [(including the trust for sale)][2] as are declared in the settlement [dated etc] of and concerning the property thereby settled so far as the same shall at my death be still subsisting and capable of taking effect.

1 This form should be used where the trustees of the settlement are the same as those of the will or where, for any reason, such as urgency, although there are different trustees it is desired to use this short form. It is, of course, highly inconvenient where trustees do not hold the document setting out the trusts which they are to administer. Adding property to existing settlements should be avoided if possible: see Part A, para **[200.21]** generally, and see paras **[218.11]**–**[218.14]** for the addition of property to settlements where the settled property is held on discretionary trusts.

2 The trust created by this clause will now (from 1 January 1997) be a trust of land within the TLATA 1996, whether or not it creates a trust for sale, and even if the settlement by reference to the trusts of which property is settled is a pre-1997 one to which the SLA 1925 applies.

[206.32]

FORM B6.23:   **Gift by reference to a settlement on trust for sale[1]**

I give all my real estate unto my trustees upon trust that they shall convey the same to or otherwise vest the same in the trustees for the time being of a conveyance dated —— and made between [*parties*] upon trust for sale and to hold the rents profits and other income thereof until sale and the net proceeds of sale and the income thereof upon the trusts declared by the trust instrument in the said conveyance referred to or such of the same as are for the time being subsisting and capable of taking effect in like manner in all respects as though the property hereby given had formed part of the property assured by the said conveyance.

1   See Part A, para **[200.21]** generally for the addition of property to existing settlements and paras **[218.11]**–**[218.14]** for the addition of property to settlements where the settled property is held on discretionary trusts.

[206.33]

FORM B6.24:   **Gift of lands to testator's sons, with successive gifts over if sons predecease testator without issue [male]**

I give my freehold lands at —— in the county of —— known as the —— Estate to my eldest son [*name*] in fee simple but if my said son dies in my lifetime leaving [male] issue living at my death or then en ventre but born thereafter[1] then to his personal representatives as part of his estate and in default of my said son or his personal representatives becoming entitled thereto hereunder I give the same to my second son [*name*] in fee simple but if my said son dies in my lifetime leaving [male] issue living at my death or then en ventre but born thereafter then to his personal representatives as part of his estate and in default of my said son or his personal representatives becoming entitled thereto hereunder [I give the same [*similarly for third son if required*]] and subject as aforesaid I declare that the said lands shall fall into and form part of my residuary estate.

1   As this is a gift to the testator's child, the WA 1837, s 33, as substituted by the AJA 1982, s 19 (see the commentary in Vol 1 at paras **[47.11]**–**[47.16]** and the text in Part G at para **[244.34]**) would apply so as to confer an interest on the issue by substitution in the event of the son predeceasing the testator, if it were not for the provisions of this clause vesting the gift in this event in the son's estate. This clause is similar in effect to the former s 33 of the WA 1837 (see Vol 1, paras **[47.11]**–**[47.16]** and Part G, para **[244.33]**) but with the difference that, unlike the former s 33, the gift to the testator's son's estate takes effect if the son predeceases the testator leaving only issue en ventre at the testator's death. It is thought that no inheritance tax will be payable on the estate of the son if predeceasing the testator: see para **[219.21]**, n 1. For substitution of children, see Form B17.1 at para **[217.6]** and the note thereto. For alternative forms of declaration against lapse, see Forms B19.10 to B19.16 at paras **[219.23]**–**[219.29]**.

[206.34]

FORM B6.25:   **Gift for the benefit of testator's children and the issue of deceased children at eighteen or marriage**

I give all my real estate whatsoever and wheresoever [*or* my freehold houses known as etc] unto my trustees upon the same trusts for my own issue as if I had died possessed thereof intestate leaving no wife surviving me.[1]

1   The above clause carries the sub-division of the property through all the generations living at the testator's death in the proper shares. The intestacy rules now in force give vested interests to all issue, whether male or female, legitimate or illegitimate, attaining eighteen or marrying under that age: AEA 1925, s 46(1)(i) and s 47(1)(i), as amended (Part G, paras **[244.60]** and **[244.61]**).

[206.35]

FORM B6.26:   Gift with provision against lapse

I give my freehold lands at —— and known as —— to my nephew [*name*] absolutely and if my said nephew shall die in my lifetime [leaving issue living at my death or then en ventre but born afterwards[1]] then to his personal representatives as part of his estate as if his death had happened immediately after mine.[2]

1   See para **[206.33]**, n 1.
2   For substitution of children, see Form B17.34 at para **[217.39]** and the note thereto. See also as to such provisions against lapse as this Vol 1, para **[47.23]** and the various alternative forms of declaration against lapse in Forms B19.7 to B19.16 at paras **[219.20]–[219.29]**.

[206.36]

FORM B6.27:   Clause creating an easement over land given to one person in favour of devisee of other land

I direct that the said [devisee of Blackacre] and his successors in title and all persons authorised by him or them shall have the right in fee simple in common with the said [devisee of Whiteacre] and his successors in title and all persons authorised by him or them at all times and either with or without animals or vehicles of any kind to pass and repass over and along the private road constructed by me and leading from —— to —— for the purpose of access thereby to [Blackacre] subject to the payment of a fair proportion of the expense of maintaining and keeping the said private road and the gates and fences thereof in repair and my personal representatives shall if so required by the said [devisee of Blackacre] give effect to this direction in their assents to the said gifts or otherwise as may be necessary subject to the payment of the costs incurred therein by the said [devisee of Blackacre].

[206.37]

FORM B6.28:   Gift of part of land to one person and the other part to another by reference to a plan, with cross easements

(1)   I give to my son [*name*] that part of my freehold land at —— and known as —— which part is more particularly described in the plan[1] entitled [Freehold land at —— and known as ——'] dated —— and signed by me and which part is delineated by being hatched black in such plan.
(2)   I give to my daughter [*name*] all the rest and residue of my said freehold land.
(3)   I direct that my son and his successors in title and all persons authorised by him or them shall have the right in fee simple in common with my daughter and her successors in title and all persons authorised by her or them at all times

to run electricity mains water soil and surface water and other services through any sewers drains water courses pipes cables wires or other channels or conductors which are now in under or over the land hereby given to my daughter for all purposes in connection with any user of the land hereby given to my son.

(4) I direct that my daughter and her successors in title and all persons authorised by her or them shall have the right in fee simple in common with my son and his successors in title and all persons authorised by him or them at all times to run electricity mains water soil and surface water and other services through any sewers drains water courses pipes cables wires or other channels or conductors which are now in under or over the land hereby given to my son for all purposes in connection with any user of the land hereby given to my daughter.

1   A plan may be admitted to probate with the testator's will if it is referred to in the will, the reference being sufficient to identify it, and if it is already in existence at the date of the will (for incorporation of documents generally, see Vol 1, para [15.1] et seq). It may save trouble in obtaining probate if colour is not used on the plan.

[206.38]

FORM B6.29:   **Declaration as to payment of inheritance tax on specific gifts**

I declare that the inheritance tax payable on my death in respect of the lands and hereditaments hereinbefore given to —— and —— respectively [and the inheritance tax payable on my death in respect of the lands and hereditaments hereinbefore given to my trustees in trust for my daughter and —— her issue] shall be a charge on such specifically given lands and hereditaments in exoneration of my residuary [personal] estate.[1]

1   For the incidence of inheritance tax see para [214.55] et seq. As mentioned there, inheritance tax on land in the UK is, in the absence of any expressed intention to the contrary, now prima facie payable out of residue, unless the land is comprised in a settlement immediately before the testator's death (see paras [206.3] and [214.58] and [214.59]). See also para [206.39], n 1.

[206.39]

FORM B6.30:   **Specific gift subject to inheritance tax**

I give to [*name*] in fee simple my freehold property at —— in the county of —— —— and known as —— subject to all inheritance tax (of any) attributable thereto and payable by reason of my death.[1]

Land which may be conditionally exempt under ITA 1984, s 30 (ie because of some scenic, artistic, historic, etc interest) should normally be given subject to payment of the inheritance tax attributable to it.

1   This form can be used to exclude the ITA 1984, s 211 (inheritance tax on UK free estate payable out of residue: see para [214.55] et seq and Part G, para [246.83]) in relation to a particular gift, and may also be used to qualify a general direction as to inheritance tax such as that in Form B14.33 at para [214.76].

[206.40]

FORM B6.31:   Specific gift of land which may qualify for agricultural property relief subject to inheritance tax[1]

I give to [*name*] my freehold farm land situate at —— and known as —— and I declare that the proportion of the inheritance tax payable on my estate by reason of my death which is attributable to the value of the said land (allowing for any reduction in value for inheritance tax purposes) shall be charged upon the said land and shall be borne by [*name of devisee*] in exoneration of my residuary estate.

1   The 'subject to tax' formula used in this form may also be used where business property relief may be grd. For agricultural and business property relief generally, see para **[233.1]** et seq. If the testator's estate may be partially exempt and include agricultural or business property other than the property specifically given, consider using the 'subject to tax' formula in Form B14.34 at para **[214.79]**; see also para **[214.73]**.

B7 Gifts of leasehold land

CROSS REFERENCES

For rights of residence see B8 at para **[208.1]** et seq, especially Forms B8.5 at
para **[208.41]**. For trustees' powers to permit enjoyment in kind see Note and
Forms B18.24 to B18.26 at paras **[218.108]–[218.111]**. For trustee's powers in
the management of land see Note and Forms B20.10 to B20.13 at
paras **[220.49]–[220.62]**.

PRELIMINARY NOTE

[207.1]
Leaseholds are personalty. Since leaseholds are personalty, it is common
practice to 'bequeath' leaseholds rather than 'devise' them, though it is generally
unimportant which term is used but see para **[207.3]**. However, in this edition
the words 'bequeath' and 'devise' have been replaced with 'give' which is now
in common usage. Care should of course be taken in distinguishing gifts of a
freehold and a leasehold interest in the same property. There is no harm in
continuing to use the term 'bequeath' in the context of leaseholds except where
there is a possibility that the freehold reversion will be acquired before death
under, for example, the Leasehold Reform Act 1967 (LRA 1967) (see

para **[207.9]** et seq). Leaseholds, though not real property, are commonly included in the term 'land' (see Vol 1, para **[64.33]**) and for that reason the word 'land' should not in general be used without some qualification restricting it to freehold land or to leasehold land depending on the testator's intention. The form of a gift of leaseholds has varied from time to time but at the present time such a gift seldom contains more than the following: 'I give to —— my leasehold premises at ——.' It necessarily follows that the donee takes them subject to the rent, the lessee's covenants and the conditions in the lease and these are now seldom referred to. There may be special cases where the lease requires to be specifically referred to, but having regard to the fact that every properly drawn assignment of leaseholds commences with a recital of the lease, this can seldom be of any practical value. A gift of leaseholds has since 1877 borne its own charges and there can be no question of a mortgage being paid off out of the personal estate unless the will contains a direction to that effect. Inheritance tax in respect of leaseholds in the UK is prima facie a testamentary expense (see para **[214.55]** et seq) and it will not normally be necessary to include a direction expressly freeing a gift of leasehold property from inheritance tax.

[207.2]
Liability for repair. In the case of an absolute donee of leaseholds, he will be bound to perform the tenant's continuing obligations under the lease, including repair, which arise after the testator's death: *Re Betty, Betty v A-G* [1899] 1 Ch 821. He usually takes the property as he finds it though it has been suggested that he has a remedy against the residuary estate of the testator in respect of dilapidations in the testator's lifetime: see *Harris v Poyner* (1852) 1 Drew 174 doubting *Hickling v Boyer* (1851) 3 Mac & G 635 on this point to the contrary. He can disclaim the gift and thus free himself from liability, but he may not be able to disclaim onerous leaseholds if the gift of them is only part of the bounty of the testator towards himself and it appears that other property has been given to him because the gift of the leaseholds carried heavy burdens without disclaiming all such other property also: see *Re Baron Kensington, Earl of Longford v Baron Kensington* [1902] 1 Ch 203, and see generally Vol 1 at para **[46.3]**, but see *Re Lysons, Beck v Lysons* (1912) 107 LT 146, where a donee was allowed to disclaim the leaseholds but to take the chattels given with it. Where, however, the gift is to a tenant for life and then to a remainderman the position is different. A trust for persons in succession of any leasehold property will (after 1 January 1997) be a trust of land under the TLATA 1996. Whereas the leasehold would formerly have vested in the tenant for life under a Settled Land Act settlement it now vests in the trustees who are thus liable to the landlord on the covenants for repair and the like. The trustees will have power to effect repairs, and a discretion as to how the repairs are paid for (under s 6(1) of the TLATA 1996: Part G, para **[246.91]**). If the life tenant has a right of occupation under s 12 of the 1996 Act, and exercises it, the trustees will be able to require him to accept the obligation to repair if it is reasonable to require this (s 13(3) and (5) of the TLATA 1996: Part G, para **[246.99]**). The extent to which the life tenant and/or the trustees under a trust of land will be liable to the remaindermen for non-repair depends on what exoneration from or imposition of liability (if any) there is in the will or settlement, and, subject to that, in the case

of trustees will depend on whether they have acted prudently and carefully and in the case of the life tenant it will depend on whether any obligation has been imposed as a condition of occupation. In general trustees cannot be expected to effect repairs at their own personal expense, and their liability to beneficiaries for non-repair will depend on (inter alia) the extent to which there is available income or capital of the trust fund to pay for the repairs. See further paras **[208.26]–[208.28]**.

[207.3]
Changes in the asset after the will is made. It is usually the sale during the testator's lifetime of property specifically given by his will which gives rise to questions of ademption. In the case of leaseholds additional problems may arise as a leasehold interest in property may cease to exist by merger on the purchase of the reversion expectant on the determination of the lease. However, merger has generally been construed as not amounting to an ademption. In some cases it has been considered as falling within the WA 1837, s 23 (Part G, para **[244.23]**), which provides that no alteration of the testator's interest shall operate to revoke a devise or bequest, be it greater or smaller at the time of his death than at the date of his will, and by the WA 1837, s 24 (Part G, para **[244.24]**) the will as to the property included within any devise or bequest speaks as from the testator's death. Again what passes under a gift is a question of construction of the words used by the testator and if he merely 'devises' his interest in certain lands, clearly this may pass the fee and this has been held to be so even where the testator has included the word 'term' in his description: see *Saxton v Saxton* (1879) 13 Ch D 359 ('all his term and interest') and an even stronger case: *Struthers v Struthers* (1857) 5 WR 809 (where the devise was for all the residue of the terms). Other cases in this line of cases are *Miles v Miles* (1866) LR 1 Eq 462; *Cox v Bennett* (1868) LR 6 Eq 422 and most recently of all *Re Fleming's Will Trusts, Ennion v Hampstead Old People's Housing Trust Ltd* [1974] 3 All ER 323, [1974] 1 WLR 1552 ('my leasehold house, 54 Narcissus Road'). A case contrary to the foregoing is *Emuss v Smith* (1848) 2 De G & Sm 722, which is generally explained as being a devise of specific property. In that case a testator by his will as varied by a codicil gave all his freehold property at B which he had purchased from C. A small part of the land purchased was leasehold of which he purchased the freehold after the date of the codicil, but this was held not to pass under the devise.

[207.4]
Renewed leases. In the case of a specific gift of 'my present lease' where the lease has expired but been renewed the donee may take the renewed lease: *Re Reeves, Reeves v Pawson* [1928] Ch 351, [1928] All ER Rep 342 (the will was confirmed by a codicil executed after the renewal); but where the old lease was surrendered, the donee took only so much of the new term as corresponded with the unexpired part of the old on surrender: *Wedgwood v Denton* (1871) LR 12 Eq 290.

[207.5]
For a form of declaration which makes it clear that the freehold or a successor lease is carried by the gift, see Form B7.6 at para **[207.20]**. For a form of a gift

of a leasehold flat which will carry with it any new lease with an extended term and any interest in the freehold obtained under the provisions of the LRA 1967 or the Leasehold Reform, Housing and Urban Development Act 1993 (LRHUDA 1993), see Form B7.2 at para **[207.16]**.

[207.6]
Settled leaseholds. The Settled Land Act 1925 (SLA 1925) can no longer apply to new trusts of land created on or after 1 January 1997 all of which are trusts of land within the meaning of the TLATA 1996 (see para **[207.2]**).

[207.7]
Old settled leaseholds. In relation to Settled Land Act settlements which existed and held land on 31 December 1996 and which have continued to do so the old learning still applies. In such cases under the SLA 1925, s 79, if the tenant for life of such leaseholds exercises his power of sale, the trustees may, notwithstanding anything in the SLA 1925, require the purchase money to be laid out, invested, accumulated or paid in such manner as in their judgment will give to the parties interested in that money the like benefit as they might lawfully have had from the lease. Parties interested may apply for an order of the court in these terms. In general the operation of the section is to give the tenant for life not only the income from the purchase money or the investments representing it but also in each year a part of the capital so that the fund will be exhausted at the time when the lease would have expired (see *Re Simpson, Clarke v Simpson* [1913] 1 Ch 277). This power is wholly discretionary in the trustees or in the court (*Re Duke of Westminster Settled Estates, Duke of Westminster v Earl of Shaftesbury* [1921] 1 Ch 585 at 599, [1921] All ER Rep 702 at 707), and a declaration to the contrary in the will would seem a sufficient safeguard against the exercise of such a power. Where the lease is short, the exclusion of the power may result in harsh treatment of the life tenant, for, having regard to allowance for dilapidations, the lease will not realise a great sum and the interest on the purchase money will be much less than the rent. A rather similar provision in principle provides for the capitalisation of the rent of a mining lease: SLA 1925, s 47. Under the new regime applicable to trusts of land there is no equivalent to the SLA 1925, s 79 which was a provision which went with the tenant for life having a power of sale.

[207.8]
A testator wishing to leave a leasehold upon trust for successive interests may wish to establish a sinking fund to secure the replacement of the wasting value of the leasehold. If the sinking fund is to be funded from the rents and profits of the leasehold before payment of the net rents and profits to the person entitled to the same for the time being, unless the direction for the establishment of the sinking fund is regarded as an administrative provision rather than a dispositive provision the settled leasehold will be treated for inheritance tax purposes as if there was no interest in possession in at least a part, and possibly the whole, of it. However, it seems that such a direction can be regarded as an administrative provision rather than a dispositive provision so that the person entitled to the net rents and profits should be regarded as having an interest in possession in the whole, see *Miller v IRC* [1987] STC 108. For a discussion of the difference

between dispositive provisions and administrative provisions, see *Foster's Inheritance Tax*, E1.42 and E1.43, and for the charge to inheritance tax where there is no interest in possession, see paras **[208.30]–[208.34]** and **[218.6]** et seq. For two forms establishing sinking funds, see Forms B7.11 and B7.12 at paras **[207.25]** and **[207.26]**.

[207.9]
The Leasehold Reform Act 1967. The LRA 1967 (whose scope has been extended by the LRHUDA 1993 and the Housing Act 1996 (HA 1996) to cover high value houses and those which fail the low rent test of the LRA 1967), the terms of which have been held by the European Court of Human Rights not to infringe the European Convention on Human Rights, allows certain tenants, occupying under long leases at low rents, either to purchase the freehold of their premises or to extend their leases for a further period of 50 years. One of the conditions to be fulfilled is that the tenant must, when he gives notice under the LRA 1967, have been occupying the premises as his only or main residence (s 1(2)) for the last three years or for periods amounting to three out of the last ten years (s 1(1)(b) as amended by the Housing Act 1980). Section 6 is relevant to cases involving the occupation of premises by beneficiaries under trusts, created by will or otherwise. The primary relevance of s 6 is to strict settlements under the SLA 1925 (which cannot be created after 1 January 1997). Briefly it provides:

(a) That a tenant who currently occupies premises as a direct tenant and who formerly occupied them either as a sole tenant for life under a strict settlement or as a beneficiary under a trust for sale, who was entitled or permitted to occupy the premises by reason of his beneficial interest, may treat periods of occupation in the earlier capacity as qualifying periods under the Act. It is not clear whether this includes an interest in an estate in the course of administration; where the person entitled under the will to a lease of a house is already in occupation, the executors should consider making an early assent in his favour.

(b) That an individual who is currently a sole tenant for life under a strict settlement shall have the same rights in respect of his occupation as if the tenancy belonged to him beneficially.

(c) That where premises are vested in trustees and a beneficiary under the trust is entitled or permitted to occupy them by reason of his beneficial interest, the *trustees* shall have the same rights as the occupant himself would have had if he were occupying in right of the tenancy.

(d) That without prejudice to any powers exercisable under the SLA 1925 by tenants for life or statutory owners, where the tenancy of premises is vested in trustees, then unless the instrument regulating the trusts (made after the passing of the Act) provides to the contrary the trustees shall have power to acquire and retain the freehold or an extended lease under the Act.

(e) That the purposes authorised for the application of capital money under a strict settlement or a trust for sale, and the purposes for which money may be raised by mortgage, shall include the payment of any expenses incurred in or in connection with proceedings taken in virtue of the provisions summarised in sub-paras (b) and (c) supra.

[207.10]
Testator's period of residence may count in favour of successor. If the
testator had a lease of a house such that enfranchisement under the LRA 1967
would have been possible if the residence condition had been fulfilled, anyone
who inherits the lease from the testator under his will or intestacy, and is a
member of the testator's family (within the definition in the LRA 1967, s 7(7))
who has been living with him in the property, may be able to count his or her
period of residence with the testator in the house as part of his or her three-year
period of residence as tenant, for the purposes of qualifying for enfranchisement:
see the LRA 1967, s 7, which applies even where the lease is inherited as a part
of a residuary gift (s 7(2)(b)). It is therefore advisable, where practical, for a
testator to leave a lease which could qualify for enfranchisement to a member of
the testator's family who has been living with him, especially if it is a lease with
only a few years to run which might run out before someone who inherited it
had himself lived there for three years.

[207.11]
The Leasehold Reform, Housing and Urban Development Act 1993.
Sections 1 to 38 give to long leaseholders of flats paying a low rent in a
predominantly residential building ('qualifying tenants') the right to purchase
collectively at market value the freehold of the building. The LRHUDA 1993
provides that at least one-half of qualifying tenants must satisfy the residence
condition of either having occupied their flats as their only or principal home for
the last 12 months or for periods amounting to three years in the last ten years.
Such occupation does not have to have been in right of the lease by virtue of
which the tenant is a qualifying tenant: LRHUDA 1993, s 6(3). Where the lease
is vested in trustees (other than a sole tenant for life within the meaning of the
SLA 1925), the right arises if an individual having an interest under the trust
(whether or not also a trustee) satisfies the occupation conditions: LRHUDA
1993, s 6(4)–(6), as inserted by the HA 1996. So if a testator bequeaths a lease to
someone who has lived with him in his flat as a licensee, that legatee's period as
licensee will count towards his residence, and so too, presumably, will his
occupation by permission of the personal representatives during the
administration of the estate prior to their assenting to the vesting of the lease in
him (assuming they have power under the will to give such permission). Where
trustees are a qualifying tenant of a flat their powers include the participation in
a claim to collective enfranchisement or to apply for a new lease unless the trust
instrument was made on or after 1 October 1996 and contains an explicit
direction to the contrary: LRHUDA 1993, s 93A, as inserted by the HA 1996.

[207.12]
Death of participating tenant. Where an initial notice has been given for
collective enfranchisement and one of the participating tenants dies his personal
representatives must within 56 days of his death notify the nominee purchaser
who is conducting the sale on behalf of the participating tenants of his death and
whether or not they are electing to withdraw from participation in the proposed
transaction, and unless they elect to withdraw they will be regarded as a
participating tenant as from the death of the tenant and so long as the lease is
vested in them: LRHUDA 1993, s 14(5) and (6). Where personal representatives

then assent to the vesting of the lease in any person, that person must within 14 days notify the nominee purchaser of the assignment and whether or not he is electing to participate in the proposed transaction: LRHUDA 1993, s 14(2).

[207.13]
Acquisition of new lease. Sections 39 to 62 of the LRHUDA 1993 give to a tenant who has occupied his flat as his only or principal home for the last three years or for a total of three years in the last ten the right to acquire a new lease of his flat: LRHUDA 1993, s 39(2) and (5). As in the case of the occupation conditions for collective enfranchisement mentioned above, a tenant's occupation for the requisite period or periods of time does not have to have been in right of his lease. Where the lease by virtue of which the qualifying tenant is a qualifying tenant is vested in trustees (other than a sole tenant for life within the meaning of the SLA 1925), the right arises if an individual having an interest under the trust satisfies the occupation conditions: LRHUDA 1993, s 39(2A), as inserted by the HA 1996. If a tenant who has given notice of his claim to acquire a new lease dies, his personal representatives and their assigns stand in his place: LRHUDA 1993, s 43.

[207.14]
Inheritance tax relief. As already mentioned, inheritance tax payable on a specific gift of a leasehold property is prima facie a testamentary expense payable out of residue. For notes on business relief see C11 at para **[233.1]** et seq and for notes on agricultural and woodlands relief see C12 at para **[234.1]** et seq.

[207.15]

FORM B7.1:   **Gift of leaseholds**

I give to [*name*] my leasehold property [together with the outbuildings and garage thereto] situate at —— in the county of —— and known as No —— Street[1] [for all the residue which shall at my death be unexpired of the term for which the same are held [*or* of the term created by the lease dated —— and made between *parties*] subject to the rent lessees' covenants and conditions therein reserved and contained]].

1   The bequest will normally end here for the donee could not take the benefit of the gift without assuming its burdens. The donee will be at liberty to disclaim the gift provided it is not associated with some other benefit given in consideration of his accepting the burden of this gift eg where the term is short and the liability for dilapidations may be heavy (see *Re Lysons, Beck v Lysons* (1912) 107 LT 146).

[207.16]

FORM B7.2:   **Gift of leasehold flat and devise of any interest in freehold of premises in which flat is contained[1]**

I give to [*name*] my leasehold flat known as —— and situate at —— for all the residue which shall at my death be unexpired of the term for which the same is held subject to the rent lessees' covenants and conditions therein reserved and contained and I also give all that my interest if any in the freehold of the premises in which the said flat is contained.

1   This gift would carry the residue of any lease which the testator has at his death in the named premises. So if, for example, he is granted before his death a new lease under the LRHUDA 1993, Pt I, Ch III extending his original term by 90 years this lease will pass under this gift. Also this gift will carry with it any interest in the freehold which the testator may have acquired by virtue of the exercise of the rights for collective enfranchisement under the LRHUDA 1993.

One of the conditions which must be met for a tenant to acquire a 90-year extension of the lease of his flat under the LRHUDA 1993 is that he must have occupied the flat as his only or principal home for three years or for periods amounting to three years in the last ten years. Such occupation does not have to have been in right of the lease, so if a testator bequeaths a lease to someone who has lived with him in his flat as a licensee, that legatee's period as licensee will count towards the residence condition if he wishes to apply for an extended lease. Similarly, the residence condition of 12 months or periods amounting to three years in the last ten years which must be met by at least half of the tenants applying for collective enfranchisement under the LRHUDA 1993, need not be residence by virtue of a lease.

[207.17]

FORM B7.3:   Gift of leasehold house free from mortgage

I give my leasehold residence and premises known as —— to my wife absolutely freed and discharged from any mortgage debt or other charge affecting the same which I direct shall be paid out of my residuary [personal] estate.[1]

1   See s 35 of the AEA 1925 (Part G, para **[246.47]**) under which section the property would bear its own charges if this contrary intention had not been shown. See also paras **[204.76]**, n 1 and **[206.23]**, n 1.

[207.18]

FORM B7.4:   Gift of leaseholds with a direction that the legatee is to pay all arrears of rent and cost of dilapidations

I give my leasehold residence and premises at —— to [name] absolutely he paying the rent payable in respect thereof and performing and observing the covenants in the lease thereof contained and on the lessee's part to be performed and observed and I declare that the rent in respect thereof owing or accruing at my death and the costs and expenses of putting the said premises into repair in compliance with the provisions of the said lease shall be borne and paid by the said [name] in exoneration of my residuary estate.[1]

1   As to disclaimer of onerous gifts, see *Guthrie v Walrond* (1883) 22 Ch D 573; *Re Loom, Fulford v Reversionary Interest Society Ltd* [1910] 2 Ch 230; *Re Lysons, Beck v Lysons* (1912) 107 LT 146 and Vol 1, para **[46.3]**. For forms of disclaimer see Forms F3.1 to F3.3 at paras **[241.22]–[241.24]**.

[207.19]

FORM B7.5:   Gift of leaseholds to trustees upon trust to pay rents and profits to a person for life, and after his death to assign to another

I give my leasehold property situate at —— in the county of —— known as —— and now in the occupation of —— [or all my leasehold property lands and hereditaments] to my trustees for all the residue unexpired of any term [or terms] for which I may hold the same [respectively] at my death. Upon trust that my trustees shall out of the rents and profits thereof pay the rent and all other expenses charges and outgoings payable from time to time in respect thereof and perform and observe the covenants on the part of the lessee to be performed or observed and shall pay the residue of such rents and profits to [*name*] during his life and after his death shall stand possessed of the said leasehold premises and the rents and profits thereof in trust for and shall assign the same to [*name*] absolutely.[1]

1   See para [207.6].

[207.20]

FORM B7.6:   Declaration that gift of lease includes the freehold reversion or any renewal if subsequently acquired

I declare that if in my lifetime I shall by purchase or otherwise become and be at my death the owner of the freehold reversion expectant on the determination of any leasehold term hereby given the same shall notwithstanding any gift in this my will or any codicil hereto contained enure for the benefit of the person or persons for the time being and from time to time beneficially entitled to such leasehold term and the property comprised therein and shall pass to or be held in trust for him or them as if included in the gift of such property hereinbefore contained and similarly if any such lease shall expire in my lifetime and shall be renewed by the lessor or if I shall surrender any such lease in consideration of the grant of a new lease, then such renewed or new lease shall pass to or be held in trust for him or them as if included in the gift of such property hereinbefore contained.[1]

1   See the Preliminary Note at paras [207.9]–[207.13]. The insertion of this clause prevents any question arising as to the testator's intention.

[207.21]

FORM B7.7:   Contingent gift of leaseholds

I give my leasehold house known as —— unto my trustees upon trust for my niece [A] if and when she attains the age of twenty-five years.[1]

1   A contingent or future specific devise or bequest carries the intermediate income (subject to the provisions as to accumulations contained in the Act) from the death of the testator, except so far as the income is otherwise *expressly* disposed of (LPA 1925, s 175: Part G, para [244.52]). During the minority of the beneficiary, the income will be available for maintenance; if the beneficiary on attaining eighteen has not yet obtained a vested interest, the whole income will be payable to the beneficiary until he attains a vested interest, or dies, or his interest is otherwise defeated (TA 1925, s 31, as amended by the FLRA 1969, s 1(3) and Sch 1, Pt 1: Part G, para [246.26]). By virtue of the LPA 1925, s 165 (Part G, para [246.43]) any period of minority during which accumulations are made under statutory power (eg the above section of the TA 1925) is not to be taken into account in determining whether a direction for accumulation goes beyond the period permitted by the LPA 1925, ss 164 or 166 (Part G, paras [246.42] and [246.44]) and the PAA 1964, s 13 (Part G, para [246.71]). See generally Vol 1, at para [95.1] et seq and the Note in B18 at para [218.41] et seq. There will thus be accumulation and maintenance trusts within the ITA 1984, s 71, for which see Part A, para [200.119] et seq.

[207.22]

FORM B7.8:   **Gift of undivided share in leaseholds**

I give all my undivided share[s] in the leasehold premises situate at —— in the county of —— known as ——to [*name*] absolutely [*or* to my trustees upon trust to etc].[1]

1   See para [204.67], n 1.

[207.23]

FORM B7.9:   **Gift of sinking fund policies in respect of leasehold properties**

I give to my trustees my sinking fund policies upon trust to hold the moneys received in respect of such policies and the proceeds of the sale or surrender of such policies under the power hereinafter contained on the trusts hereinafter declared concerning my residuary [personal] estate.

My trustees shall pay all premiums and other sums payable in respect of the said policies out of the income of my residuary [personal] estate.

If my trustees shall sell any leasehold property covered by any such policy they may at their absolute discretion sell or surrender any policy maintained in respect of the property so sold.

[207.24]

FORM B7.10:   **Declaration as to inheritance tax on settled leaseholds[1]**

I declare that the inheritance tax upon and by reason of my death attributable to the settled gift of leaseholds contained in clause —— hereof shall be borne by and paid out of the leasehold property thereby settled in exoneration of my personal estate and shall be raised by my trustees by mortgage or charge thereof or by a sale of a competent part thereof and be paid accordingly.

1   Inheritance tax on leaseholders will in the absence of a direction such as this be payable out of residue: see the Note to B14 at para [214.59] et seq.

[207.25]

FORM B7.11:   **Gift of leaseholds upon trust out of the rents and profits to form sinking fund[1]**

I give all my leasehold lands to my trustees upon the trusts and with the directions following:

(1)   In the first place to pay out of the rents and profits thereof the rents payable in respect of the leases under which the same are held and perform and observe the lessees' covenants therein contained.

(2)   In the next place to raise out of the said rents and profits any such annual sum (either for the premium or premiums in respect of a policy or policies of insurance to be effected by my trustees or by way of investment in their names and accumulation during any period allowed by law[2]) as shall be sufficient in

their opinion to provide at the expiration of the respective leases for which I hold the said leasehold lands a capital sum of £—— and to apply the annual sum so raised in paying the premiums for keeping on foot such policy or policies of insurance or by way of investment in the names of my trustees and accumulation accordingly.

(3)   Subject thereto to stand possessed of my said leasehold lands and the rents and profits thereof upon trust etc [*set out the trusts of the surplus rents and profits*]

(4)   My trustees shall invest the said sum of £—— as and when received or provided as aforesaid in manner herein mentioned and shall stand possessed thereof and of the investments for the time being representing the same and the income thereof upon the like trusts and subject to the like provisions in all respects as are hereinbefore declared and contained concerning my said leasehold lands and the rents and profits thereof so far as the same trusts and provisions may then be subsisting and capable of taking effect.

1   See para [207.6]. A clause of this kind could have adverse inheritance tax consequences in that it could be said that as part of the income of the trust property is to be accumulated there will be no interest in possession in at least a part of it, and possibly the whole, since the amount of income is decided by the trustees in their discretion. However, if the capital sum for which the trustees are to make provision at the expiry of the leases is no greater than the value of the leases as at the testator's death, so that the provision is merely one which directs the trustees to meet depreciation and not to increase the capital value of the trust assets, it may be that this can properly be regarded as an administrative provision rather than a dispositive provision, so that there will be an interest in possession in the whole: see *Miller v IRC* [1987] STC 108.

2   Accumulations are now governed by the LPA 1925, s 164 et seq (Part G, para [246.42] et seq) and the PAA 1964, s 13 (Part G, para [246.71]) but this clause seems to be valid for any accumulation and certainly in so far as it provides for keeping up a policy however long its provisions continue: *Re Gardiner, Gardiner v Smith* [1901] 1 Ch 697.

[207.26]

FORM B7.12:   **Alternative provision for sinking fund to replace leasehold value**[1]

I give all my leasehold lands unto my trustees upon the trusts and with the directions following:

(1)   Upon trust in the first place to pay out of the rents and profits thereof the rents payable in respect of the leases under which the same are held and to perform and observe the lessees' covenants therein contained and subject thereto to set aside out of the rents and profits of each such leasehold in each year such a sum and for such period as hereinafter directed.

(2)   Subject as aforesaid my trustees shall stand possessed of the said leasehold lands and the rents and profits thereof upon trust [*set out the trusts of the leaseholds and the rents and profits*].

(3)   The sum so to be set aside (as a sinking fund to secure the replacement of the wasting value of each leasehold) out of the net rents and profits of each leasehold in each year shall be calculated by dividing the net rents and profits of the year by one more than the number of complete years which at the date of my death the lease of that property has to run.

[(4)   But such setting aside shall not be made for a longer period than twenty-one years from my death.]

(5)   In respect of each such leasehold the said annual sums deducted or set aside as aforesaid shall be invested as one fund and shall be accumulated by investing the income thereof as an accretion to that fund.

(6)   Such accumulations shall cease [at the expiration of twenty-one years from my death *or*] upon the expiration of such lease while still held by my trustees or upon the sale of the leasehold in respect of which the said fund is being set aside and accumulated whichever period shall be the shortest.

(7)   Thereafter the fund so formed and the future income thereof shall be held by my trustees upon the same trusts (save for the setting aside of a sum out of income) as the leasehold itself is being held by my trustees or would be held if it had not expired or been sold, as the case may be, so far as the same trusts and provisions may then be subsisting and capable of taking effect.

(8)   And I specially declare that the fund so set aside and accumulated in respect of a leasehold shall be primarily liable for all claims for dilapidations and breaches of covenant if such leasehold shall be still held by my trustees at the date of expiration of the lease thereof.[2]

---

1   See para **[207.25]**, n 1. This form is preferable in that the sum to be set aside is expressly to form a sinking fund to meet depreciation, and so is arguably an administrative provision rather than a dispositive provision. But if it should be thought to be a dispositive provision rather than an administrative provision, since the amount to be accumulated is determined by a formula, there is less risk of the clause causing there to be no interest in possession in the entire property.

2   A direction to set aside annual sums out of rents to secure replacement is not within the Thellusson Act, whether the sums be expended in keeping up a policy or in actual investment; neither is the direction to accumulate the income of the sums invested, see *Re Gardiner, Gardiner v Smith* [1901] 1 Ch 697, and *Re Hurlbatt, Hurlbatt v Hurlbatt* [1910] 2 Ch 553, at any rate as long as it is made bona fide for replacement, and not for the purpose of evading the Act. The same principle applies to a reserve fund where the executors are empowered to carry on a business: *Re Crabtree* (1911) 106 LT 49; *Re Robertson* [1953] 2 SCR 1. Sections 164 et seq of the LPA 1925 (Part G, para **[246.42]** et seq) (which replace the Thellusson Act), do not appear to alter the position. For the taxation of accumulated income see the Note to B18 at para **[218.30]**.

B8 Rights of residence

PRELIMINARY NOTE

[208.1]
Cases often arise in which the testator wishes to provide a house for a beneficiary or beneficiaries to live in. Where the beneficiary or beneficiaries are also interested in residue a separate gift of a residence may be unnecessary; instead the trustees of residue can be given power to purchase, retain etc a residence for a beneficiary as in, eg Form C2.1, cl 9(3)(h) at para **[224.30]** or Forms B18.24 to B18.26 at paras **[218.109]–[218.111]**. However, a specific gift of the kind considered here can still be appropriate even if the beneficiary or beneficiaries are interested in residue, for example where it is desired to give provision of a residence priority over legacies and residuary gifts, or to make sure the property concerned is resorted to last to pay liabilities of the estate.

[208.2]
Two methods of providing a residence by specific gift are to be found in the forms in B8 as explained at paras **[208.3]** and **[208.4]**.

[208.3]
The first method—a trust of land under the Trusts of Land and Appointment of Trustees Act 1996. The Trusts of Land and Appointment of Trustees Act 1996 (TLATA 1996) (Part G, para **[246.86]** et seq) has, in relation to the creation of new trusts (whether by will or lifetime disposition), replaced the former alternative regimes of trusts for sale and settled land with a single trust of land, which can still be a trust for sale but it makes little or no difference whether there is a trust for sale or not. The basic scheme of the TLATA 1996 and its consequences are described in Part A at para **[200.48]** et seq. The notes below first discuss the rights of occupation given to beneficiaries by the TLATA 1996 (see paras **[208.5]–[208.18]**) and then more specific points to consider when getting instructions for and drafting trusts to provide a residence (see paras **[208.19]–[208.36]**). The TLATA 1996 is particularly orientated towards trusts of land for occupation by beneficiaries, and it does enable some simplification of the drafting of trusts of this type. For reasons given at paras **[200.55]** and **[200.56]** it is recommended that trusts for sale should not in general be used in trusts of land, and it is particularly inappropriate to provide a trust for sale where the purpose of the trust is or includes providing a property for residential or other occupation by a beneficiary.

[208.4]
The second method—grant of a lease by the trustees to the beneficiary. This may be a suitable method in some cases, but may in others be unsatisfactory. In particular, it should be noted that the gift of a lease terminable on or by reference to a death is now treated as the equivalent of a life interest in settled property for inheritance tax purposes (see the Inheritance Tax Act 1984 (ITA 1984), s 43(3)) and on disadvantageous terms compared with a true settlement since the reversion is not excluded property: ITA 1984, s 48(1)(c). It is thus better in general to create a life interest under a settlement, but we have retained the lease precedents for the sake of completeness and because some may fall outside the ambit of the ITA 1984, s 43(3). See Forms B8.7 to B8.9 at paras **[208.43]–[208.45]**.

The statutory right of occupation under a trust of land

[208.5]
The statutory right of occupation. The statutory rights of occupation described below are not confined in their application to residential property held on trust, but can be relevant to any kind of land in England and Wales held on trust which is capable of being occupied by a beneficiary, eg a farm or business premises. These rights are discussed in this part of this work because trusts to provide residences are probably the most common type of trust of land for occupation by a beneficiary created by will. Section 12(1) of the TLATA 1996 (Part G, para **[246.98]**) provides a right of occupation for a beneficiary 'who is beneficially entitled to an interest in possession' in land subject to a trust of land (see para **[200.51]** for the meaning of 'trust of land' and para **[208.12]** et seq for the meaning of 'interest in possession') at any time if at that time *either* (a) the purposes of the trust include making the land available for his occupation (or for the occupation of a class of which he is a member or of beneficiaries in general) *or* (b) the land is held by the trustees so as to be so available. This is subject to the right not being available if the land is either unavailable or unsuitable for occupation by him: TLATA 1996, s 12(2). The trustees may impose reasonable conditions on a beneficiary in relation to his occupation of land including payment of outgoings and assuming any other obligation in relation to the land or any activity conducted there (eg a farming business): TLATA 1996, s 13(3), (5) (Part G, para **[246.99]**). Where two or more beneficiaries are entitled to occupy land the trustees may exclude or restrict the entitlement to occupy of one or more but not all of them, but may not do so unreasonably (TLATA 1996, s 13(1), (2)), and the trustees can require compensatory provision to be made for anyone excluded: TLATA 1996, s 13(6). Section 13(6) contemplates two possibilities, that a beneficiary who occupies the land may be required to pay a 'rent' to an excluded beneficiary or beneficiaries, or that he forgoes benefit from another part of the trust fund so that a compensating additional benefit from that other part is received by the excluded beneficiary or beneficiaries.

[208.6]
Comparison with previous law. This right of occupation is completely new as compared with the previous statutory provisions concerning trusts for sale, under which there were no statutory rights of occupation for beneficiaries. The courts had held that beneficial joint tenants and tenants in common had rights of occupation (*Bull v Bull* [1955] 1 QB 234; *City of London Building Society v Flegg* [1988] AC 54), but it was not clear whether the same was true of someone with a life interest under a trust for sale of land, and it was common to provide expressly in trusts for sale for persons in succession that the trustees either should permit, or had a power to permit, occupation by a beneficiary or beneficiaries. The new statutory right of occupation puts someone with a life interest under a trust of land in a position similar (as regards the right to occupy trust property) to that of a tenant for life under a Settled Land Act 1925 settlement (because a tenant for life of settled land under that Act has a right of occupation of the land by virtue of having the legal estate vested in him).

[208.7]
Land available for occupation. There are two main requirements of the TLATA 1996, s 12 (Part G, para **[246.98]**) for a beneficiary to have the right to occupy trust land. First, he must be beneficially entitled to an interest in possession in it, a separate topic discussed at paras **[208.12]** and **[208.13]**. Second, either the purposes of the trust must include making the land available for occupation by the beneficiary (or beneficiaries of a class of which he is a member or of beneficiaries in general) (TLATA 1996, s 12(1)(a)), or the land must be held by the trustees so as to be so available: TLATA 1996, s 12(1)(b). Could s 12(1)(a) apply solely by virtue of the will or settlement conferring a standard-form administrative power to permit occupation by beneficiaries? The words in brackets in s 12(1)(a) suggest that this may be so, but it seems peculiar that the existence of express powers of this kind in the will or settlement could confer such a right when those powers duplicate powers which are conferred on all trustees of land by statute. Does s 12(1)(b) confer a right of occupation of any land held by the trustees which is for the time being vacant (subject to suitability, etc under the TLATA 1996, s 12(2)), or must the trustees make some decision or take some action to make it available first? We feel that the latter view would produce a more sensible result, but the position is unclear, and it is certainly possible that any beneficiary with an interest in possession can claim the right to occupy land which is for the time being vacant (again subject to suitability, etc within s 12(2)). This can be illustrated by the example of a residuary estate consisting of residential properties let to tenants, with the testator's widow having a life interest, and the purposes of the trust within s 12(1)(a) not including making land available for her occupation. A tenant of a residential property departs, leaving it vacant. Does the life tenant then have a right of occupation of that property, ie is it one which is held by the trustees so as to be available for occupation by her within s 12(1)(b), or does it only become so held if the trustees decide eg not to re-let and to repair it and offer it to the widow as a residence?

[208.8]
Suitability for occupation. Even where the requirements of the TLATA 1996, s 12(1) are met (see para **[208.7]**), s 12(2) qualifies the right by excluding it where the land is unavailable or unsuitable for occupation by him. The duplication of the availability test, ie that it appears in both s 12(1)(b) and in s 12(2), is slightly puzzling, but the explanation may be that 'unavailable' in terms of s 12(2) is intended for s 12(1)(a) cases, ie where the purposes of the trust are to make the land available. The exclusion by s 12(2) of a beneficiary's right of occupation where the land is unsuitable for that beneficiary's occupation is perhaps aimed at the kind of case where say the land is 6,000 acres of prime agricultural land and the beneficiary is bankrupt and has a drink problem. However, this would be better characterised as the beneficiary being unsuitable for occupation of the land rather than the land being unsuitable for the beneficiary's occupation. If the land is a light industrial unit and the beneficiary is looking for a residence, it seems clear that the right of occupation is excluded by s 12(2), although whether this is a case of unsuitability or unavailability it is probably not necessary to decide. A large country house would presumably be 'unsuitable' within s 12(2) for say an elderly widow who only needs a bed-sitting room. In general, s 12(2) is conceptually fuzzy and in many

circumstances will create uncertainty as to whether the right to occupy has arisen or not, and it has potential for dispute between trustee and beneficiary.

[208.9]
Two or more beneficiaries. A more complicated difficulty arises where there are beneficiaries with similar concurrent interests but only some of whom for the time being have interests in possession. This is best illustrated by an example. Suppose that there is an accumulation and maintenance trust of a farm for a class of four minor beneficiaries, who get vested interests in capital and income in equal shares at the age of 25 and attain interests in possession in their respective presumptive shares at the age of 18 under the Trustee Act 1925, s 31 by virtue of becoming entitled to be paid the current income of those shares (see para **[208.12]** as to whether this is an interest in possession in the land). The trustees farm the land themselves, employing a manager. The eldest of the beneficiaries then attains 18. Suppose that the TLATA 1996, s 12(1)(a) or (b) applies, either because a purpose of the trust is occupation by beneficiaries, or because (contrary to the tentative view expressed at para **[208.7]**) s 12(1)(b) is satisfied by the mere fact of there being vacant land in the trust. He then becomes a beneficiary entitled to occupy the land under the TLATA 1996, s 12 and cannot be prevented from doing so, subject only to the possible arguments that the land is not 'available' or not 'suitable' for occupation by him (TLATA 1996, s 12(2)) and to the right of the trustees to impose reasonable conditions on him in relation to his occupation: TLATA 1996, s 13(3) and (5). The trustees cannot exclude a beneficiary under the power in s 13(1) unless there are at least two beneficiaries with interests in possession, and then they cannot exclude all of them. It seems likely that 'reasonable conditions' would include requiring him to take over the farming business, including its liabilities, in particular the trustees' existing contractual liabilities to the farm manager: TLATA 1996, s 13(5)(b). The difficult question is whether he can be required to pay compensation for the benefit of the beneficiaries who are still under 18. Section 13(6) of the TLATA 1996 (under which the trustees can require a beneficiary who is in occupation to make compensation arrangements in favour of beneficiaries who are not) only applies where there are two or more beneficiaries with interests in possession, and it has no application to this example of one of a class of beneficiaries having an interest in possession while the others do not. There is thus a lack of specific express provision for such a case, but the question then arises of whether the trustees can impose compensatory provisions on the occupying beneficiary for the benefit of the other three beneficiaries under the general power to impose reasonable conditions in the TLATA 1996, s 13(3). The appropriate condition would be that an appropriate rent for three-quarters of the value of the land be paid to the trustees to be treated as income of the three-quarters of the fund still subject to accumulation and maintenance trusts. The occupying beneficiary could, however, put up a strong case for saying that a condition as to compensation of this kind can only be imposed to compensate other beneficiaries *who have a right of occupation under the Act which they are not able to exercise* (and this idea is supported by the TLATA 1996, s 15(2)). The trustees could reply that it is only fair to require compensation in circumstances where other beneficiaries have an interest in the property which would, in the absence of such compensation, bring them no

benefit, but which would bring them an income benefit if the property was yielding income.

[208.10]
Sub-trusts. Another somewhat unexpected result arises where there is a sub-trust of a beneficial interest, again best illustrated by an example. Suppose that a husband H and his wife W own a house as tenants in common. H dies, leaving his half share to his executors and trustees to hold it on trust for their daughter D for life. It seems from the TLATA 1996, ss 12(1) and 22(1), (2) (Part G, paras **[246.98]** and **[246.108]** respectively) that W has a right of occupation of the house under s 12 and D and H's will trustees do not have such a right. This is because s 22(1) provides that 'beneficiary' in relation to a trust means any person who *under the trust* (emphasis supplied) has an interest in property subject to the trust, which seems to exclude D from being a beneficiary under the trust of the house for the purposes of the TLATA 1996, s 12(1), and because, while s 22(1) provides that 'beneficiary' includes trustees of a sub-trust, s 22(2) provides that beneficiaries who are beneficially entitled do not include such trustees, with the consequence that the trustees of H's will do not have a right of occupation which they can allow D to use. As in the accumulation and maintenance trust example at para **[208.9]**, there is a question as to whether the trustees of the house could require W to pay compensation to the trustees of H's will for D's benefit, as a reasonable condition within the TLATA 1996, s 13(3) in relation to W's continued occupation of the house (subject to the possibility that s 13(7), discussed at para **[208.11]**, prevents its imposition). The arguments for and against are the same as in the accumulation and maintenance trust example given at para **[208.9]**.

[208.11]
Termination of occupation. A further point to note is that the termination of a beneficiary's occupation is made more difficult under the TLATA 1996 than it was under trusts for sale with a power to permit residence before 1 January 1997. Under the latter, the trustee could revoke the permission to reside and bring a possession action, whereas now the trustee will have to apply under the TLATA 1996, ss 13(7) or 14 (Part G, paras **[246.99]** and **[246.100]**) if there is some strong reason for the occupation to cease (eg the beneficiary is disabled or the house is falling into disrepair) and the beneficiary will not co-operate or is failing to fulfil obligations reasonably imposed by the trustee as a condition of occupation. Section 13(7) prohibits the powers of the trustees under s 13 being exercised so as to terminate the occupation of a beneficiary who is in occupation, or in a way likely to cause that beneficiary's occupation to cease, without that beneficiary's consent or the court's approval. Further, the right to occupy is not made conditional on observing the conditions reasonably imposed by the trustees under s 13(3), and the trustees cannot keep a beneficiary out of occupation while they decide on what conditions to impose. The trustees may well find that they have a more limited power to impose conditions if a beneficiary is in occupation than if he is not.

[208.12]
Meaning of 'interest in possession'. For a beneficiary to have a right to occupy trust land under the TLATA 1996, s 12(1) (Part G, para **[246.98]**) he must be

'beneficially entitled to an interest in possession' in it. This is perhaps the most important context in the TLATA 1996 where the expression 'interest in possession' appears, but it is also relevant to the power to delegate management of trust land in the TLATA 1996, s 9 (Part G, para **[246.94]**; see also para **[220.54]** et seq) and the duty to consult beneficiaries in the TLATA 1996, s 11 (Part G, para **[246.97]**; see also para **[220.58]**). As in the inheritance tax legislation, there is no definition of 'interest in possession'. The only express provision in the TLATA 1996 is the exclusion of annuitants from having interests in possession in land subject to a trust: see the TLATA 1996, s 22(3) (Part G, para **[246.108]**) for inheritance tax purposes an annuitant does have an interest in possession in a share of the trust property. The use of the term 'interest in possession' in the TLATA 1996 is probably influenced by the ITA 1984, but it does not follow that what is an interest in possession for the purposes of the ITA 1984 is also one within the TLATA 1996, as the statutory purposes of the use of the term are different. However, as a working hypothesis, anything which is an interest in possession in land for inheritance tax purposes is likely to be one for the purposes of the TLATA 1996, subject to the differences noted at para **[208.13]**. For the meaning of 'interest in possession' for inheritance tax purposes see paras **[200.108]**–**[200.113]** and *Foster's Inheritance Tax*, E1.41–E1.49.

[208.13]
The main differences between 'interest in possession' in the Trusts of Land and Appointment of Trustees Act 1996 and in the Inheritance Tax Act 1984—

(1)   A trust of a property for X and Y as beneficial joint tenants, or as beneficial tenants in common in equal (or unequal) shares, fairly clearly gives both X and Y interests in possession in that property for the purposes of the TLATA 1996. They may also have interests in possession within the meaning of the ITA 1984, but it is an academic question (except in relation to the ITA 1984, s 91) because they are not interests in possession *in settled property* for the purposes of the ITA 1984. Settled property in the ITA 1984 (see ITA 1984, s 43(2)) is trust property subject to interests other than absolute ones.

(2)   In *Pearson v IRC* [1981] AC 753 it was held that a right to the income of a fund, but subject to a trustees' power to accumulate that income, is not an interest in possession for inheritance tax purposes. It is, however, likely that this is an interest in possession for the purposes of the TLATA 1996, and in relation to the TLATA 1996, s 12 there is the further point that s 12 will only apply where the land is available for occupation and so unlet and not yielding income, so that for the time being there is no question of the trustees being able to exercise the power of accumulation (for possible inheritance tax consequences of this see para **[208.17]**).

(3)   Occupation of a trust property by a beneficiary under a discretionary trust as his permanent residence under an exercise of the trustees' powers to permit it is regarded by the Revenue as giving the beneficiary an interest in possession in that property for inheritance tax purposes (see Part A, para **[200.110]**). It may be that it is also an interest in possession for the purposes of the TLATA 1996, and in particular s 12, but this has

no practical consequences, since if there is an interest in possession within the meaning of s 12 it is co-terminous with the occupation, ie there is no interest in possession, distinct from the permission to occupy, which gives rise to a right of occupation independently of the permission given by the trustees.

(4) As already mentioned, an annuity is an interest in possession under inheritance tax, and is not for the purposes of the TLATA 1996: TLATA 1996, s 22(3).

(5) In the sub-trust example discussed at paras **[208.10]** and **[208.16]**, the daughter D who has a life interest under a sub-trust of a half undivided share of a property is not a beneficiary in relation to the underlying co-ownership trust of the property. The normal inheritance tax rule is that she is treated as entitled to half the property for inheritance tax purposes; she has an interest in possession in the sub-trust's share of the property, and so by the ITA 1984, s 49 she is treated as beneficially entitled to it. There is the possibility, discussed at paras **[208.10]** and [208.16], that the operation of the TLATA 1996, ss 12, 13 and 22 might deprive her of any benefit from the property while W is living in it, but it may well be that this would not prevent her from being entitled to an interest in possession in half the property for inheritance tax purposes: see *Foster's Inheritance Tax*, E1.46.

(6) The view has been expressed (see Kenny and Kenny, *The Trusts of Land and Appointment of Trustees Act 1996* (1997), pp 47–15 and 47–16) that where property is held on trust for sale to hold the proceeds of sale and the net rents and profits until sale on trust for X, X does not have an interest in possession in the land for the purposes of the TLATA 1996. If this were correct, this type of case would be one where there is an interest in possession for inheritance tax purposes but not under the TLATA 1996. However, it seems doubtful whether this is correct. It seems to us that to be entitled under a trust of land to be paid the current income of the land subject to the trust (other than by way of annuity) is to have an interest in possession in that land for the purposes of the TLATA 1996, irrespective of whether there is a trust for sale. If that were not the case, it would probably be unnecessary for the TLATA 1996, s 22(3) to exclude annuitants from the category of persons with interests in possession in land, and it would be the case that beneficial tenants in common or joint tenants under an express trust for sale would not have interests in possession in that land, and thus no right of occupation.

(7) Someone entitled to an interest in residue does not have a beneficial interest in the strict sense in the assets of the estate while it is in the course of administration: see Vol 1, para **[1.12]**. It therefore seems likely that a residuary beneficiary does not have an interest in possession giving him a right of occupation under the TLATA 1996, s 12 while the estate is in the course of administration, particularly as the TLATA 1996, s 18 provides that the TLATA 1996 applies to personal representatives without prejudice to their functions for the purposes of administration. On the other hand, the ITA 1984 has (in s 91) a provision that someone who would have an interest in possession in residue during the

administration of the estate is treated as having it for inheritance tax purposes. It is thought that someone with an interest in possession in a specific gift by will has it from the testator's death both under the TLATA 1996 and the ITA 1984.

[208.14]

Tax aspects of the right of occupation. If the trustees exercise their powers under the TLATA 1996, s 13 to exclude or restrict the rights of someone with an interest in possession, it might have the effect of terminating the excluded beneficiary's interest in possession. The Inland Revenue has expressed the tentative view that an administrative adjustment which does not affect the value of the respective interests (ie the excluded beneficiary receives full compensation from the occupying beneficiaries for his non-occupation) is not likely to be the termination of an interest in possession, and that the existence of the s 13 powers before they are exercised does not prejudice the existence of an interest in possession: see the Revenue's answers to questions put by Chris Jarman published in the *Tax Journal*, 30 January 1997, p 19 and 6 February 1997, p 19 (reprinted in *Foster's Inheritance Tax*, X6.69). If on the other hand a beneficiary with a right of occupation but out of occupation is not fully compensated, in their view he might have given up his interest in possession; but each case will depend on its own facts. These articles also discuss income tax aspects of beneficiary exclusion subject to compensatory rental payments under the TLATA 1996, s 13 and make the point that there would be no tax deduction for the compensation payments unless they were a business expense, and that they would be likely to be taxable income of the excluded beneficiary who received them. What is not discussed directly is the situation where a number of beneficiaries are entitled to occupy a property (typically this happens where a testator confers a right of residence on some or all of his children), and some live there and some do not, the ones out of occupation not being formally excluded and retaining the right of occupation. This situation was considered by a Special Commissioner in *Woodhall v IRC* [2000] STC (SCD) 558, in a case where under their father's will two brothers had rights of residence in a house (held on trust for sale), but only one had lived there. The one who lived there had died in April 1997. It was held that he had had an interest in possession in the house for inheritance tax purposes, but because his brother had an equal right (albeit unexercised) to occupy the house it was held (applying the ITA 1984, s 50(5)) that the deceased brother's interest in possession was in half the house, not the whole of it. This could offer a method of saving inheritance tax in some situations—see Form B8.3 at para **[208.39]**.

[208.15]

Tax aspects—accumulation and maintenance trusts and the right of occupation. The questions discussed in the *Tax Journal* articles mentioned at para **[208.14]** do not include whether the existence of the rights and powers under the TLATA 1996, ss 12 and 13 could prejudice the application of the ITA 1984, s 71 to accumulation and maintenance trusts. Reverting to the accumulation and maintenance trust example discussed at para **[208.9]**, the worst that could happen in that case is that the eldest attains an interest in possession for inheritance tax purposes in the entire property, by virtue of his rights under the TLATA 1996, s 12, when he attains 18. This possibility would not prevent the ITA 1984, s 71 from applying to the property before that happens. It could, however, be very unsatisfactory if he does acquire an interest in possession for inheritance tax purposes in the entire property in this way, because there will be a partial termination of this interest in possession when the next beneficiary attains 18 with possible adverse inheritance tax consequences, although we believe that he will not acquire an interest in possession in the entire property in this way if the trustees are able to require him to make compensatory payments as suggested at para **[208.9]**.

[208.16]
Tax aspects—sub-trusts. The sub-trust example discussed at para **[208.10]**, ie the house owned as to half by W and as to half by H's will trustees holding it on trust for D for life, is discussed in the *Tax Journal* articles mentioned at para **[208.14]**, on the assumption that W cannot be required to make compensation payments for the benefit of D. The Revenue accepts (see the *Tax Journal*, 30 January 1997, p 19 and 6 February 1997, p 19) that no taxable benefit flows from D to W in that example. There is a further question whether in these circumstances W has an interest in possession for inheritance tax purposes in H's former half of it with the result that it is subject to inheritance tax as part of W's estate on her death as well as her own absolute share. The Revenue's answer that W is entitled to occupy the property pursuant to her statutory right as tenant in common and beneficiary of the trust of land, and is not, therefore, in receipt of a benefit from either the trustees of H's will or D, would seem to imply that W's taxable interest continues to be limited to half the property only. If so, this arrangement is a way of using H's nil rate band up, while giving W security of exclusive possession of the house. If the trustees could require W to pay compensation for use of H's will trustees' half of the property but did not do so, the position might be different.

[208.17]
Interests in possession for inheritance tax purposes. As mentioned at paras **[208.12]** and **[208.13]**, the meaning of 'interest in possession' is not necessarily the same in the TLATA 1996 as it is in the ITA 1984. It is thus possible that a beneficiary might have a right of occupation under the TLATA 1996 by virtue of an interest which is an interest in possession for the purposes of the TLATA 1996, but which is not an interest in possession for inheritance tax purposes. For example, it is possible that an interest such as that which was the subject matter of *Pearson v IRC* [1981] AC 753, [1980] 2 All ER 479, [1980] STC 318, which was there held not to be an interest in possession for inheritance tax purposes (ie a right to the income of settled property subject to a trustees' power to accumulate the income), constitutes an interest in possession for the purposes of the TLATA 1996, s 12 where land is held on trusts of that kind. It is then possible that if a beneficiary takes up occupation by virtue of an interest of this type he becomes entitled to an interest in possession for inheritance tax purposes. Conversely, a beneficiary under a discretionary trust who is permitted to occupy the land in exercise of a trustees' power might then have an interest in possession for inheritance tax purposes (see para **[200.110]**), but would not have an interest in possession such as to give him a right of occupation under the TLATA 1996.

[208.18]
Drafting points concerning the right of occupation—

(1) The right of occupation cannot be excluded, and once it arises it will continue (while the conditions as to availability and suitability of land etc are fulfilled) so long as the beneficiary has an interest in possession. However, the TLATA 1996 places no constraints on when an interest in possession comes into existence or ceases, and, for example a trust will not give rise to rights of occupation under the Act if it is wholly discretionary and does not confer an interest in possession.

(2) In addition, the trustees' power to impose reasonable conditions on an occupying beneficiary under the TLATA 1996, s 13(3) is a discretionary power to be exercised from time to time taking into account the matters set out in s 13(4), which include the beneficiaries' circumstances and wishes as well as the intentions of the testator (or settlor) and the purposes for which the land is held, and which is subject to s 13(7) (protection of existing beneficiary occupation). It seems that the will (or settlement) cannot determine in advance what conditions it will be reasonable to impose. It is more realistic therefore to express an intention that occupation should be subject to repair, payment of outgoings, etc than to direct that it shall be. It would be possible to provide that the occupying beneficiary's interest in possession comes to an end in the event of, eg failure to repair or pay outgoings, but this could be excessively draconian in its practical operation, at any rate unless there was a relief from forfeiture provision, and if provision of the latter kind was included there could be inheritance tax problems, with an interest in possession terminating as a result of the failure and then starting again when the forfeiture was relieved.

(3) If problems under the TLATA 1996, ss 12 and 13 might arise, it will often not be an available option to provide eg a discretionary trust or some other non-interest in possession trust. Usually an interest in possession is wanted because of its tax consequences, and in particular the ITA 1984, s 71 (accumulation and maintenance trusts) requires an absolute interest or interest in possession to be obtained by the beneficiaries on or before attaining 25 for the provisions of that section to apply.

(4) Where an interest in possession is wanted, for tax or other reasons, it would still be possible to include an overriding power of appointment which enabled the interest in possession to be terminated if the exercise by a beneficiary of the right of occupation was causing problems for the administration of the trust. Such a power could, if so exercised, apparently be effective to give the trustee a right to possession, but of course there might be tax or other reasons for not wanting to exercise the power in this way, and if the trustee and beneficiary were already in dispute the trustee would be open to accusations of improper use of the power. However, the possible existence of rights under the TLATA 1996, ss 12 and 13 could be a reason for including a wide overriding power of appointment in an interest in possession trust of land.

(5) Whether the TLATA 1996, s 12(1)(a) applies to a will or settlement will be a matter of how it is worded, and this is a point where the drafting can

affect the operation of ss 12 and 13, but however strongly the wording prevents s 12(1)(a) from applying it cannot be sure of preventing s 12(1)(b) from ever doing so.

(6)　The TLATA 1996, s 13(4) declares that the matters to which trustees are to have regard when exercising their powers to impose conditions on occupying beneficiaries or to exclude beneficiaries from occupation include the intentions of the person creating the trust, the purposes for which the land is held, and the circumstances and wishes of each beneficiary entitled to occupy. These are also relevant under the TLATA 1996, s 15 to the court's decision in the event of a dispute. There is thus some scope for influencing the position in a will by including statements with regard to the testator's intention.

(7)　The problem discussed at para **[208.9]**, of some beneficiaries under an accumulation and maintenance trust having interests in possession and some not, is not solved by using a flexible accumulation and maintenance trust, ie with a power to vary shares, because the power to vary always has to run out at the point when the specified age (of 25 or less) is reached. The power could only be used to prevent the eldest claiming rights of occupation at a cost of depriving him of a share of the fund. What could be useful, where the beneficiaries might be less than seven years apart in age, are extended accumulation and maintenance trusts of income so that interests in possession arise after the age of 18. The trustees could be given a power to accelerate the attainment of interests in possession, and then could wait until the eldest was nearly 25 and the youngest over 18, and then exercise the power so that they all attained interests in possession simultaneously, or the trusts could be so constructed that they all (if they so long live) attain interests in possession on the same date. See Form B17.35, sub-cl (6) at para **[217.40]**.

(8)　On the positive side, the TLATA 1996, especially the trustees' powers in s 6 and the rights of occupation, makes it possible to have more concise forms of trust when the purpose of the trust is that a beneficiary or beneficiaries should occupy the trust property. See para **[208.19]** and Forms B8.1 and B8.5 at paras **[208.37]** and **[208.41]**.

Giving rights of residence by will

[208.19]
Main features of a trust to provide a residence. These should, we suggest, be the following—

(1)　An interest in possession in the property, either a life or similar interest or one ending when ceasing to reside in the property—see para **[208.21]**. Although the TLATA 1996 confers the right of residence on any beneficiary with an interest in possession, it does not impose any restrictions on the circumstances in which an interest in possession may come to an end.

(2)　No trust for sale (see Part A, paras **[200.55]** and **[200.56]**). Also unnecessary and probably redundant in an interest in possession trust are a power to permit occupation, because the beneficiary will have a statutory right of occupation (see para **[208.5]** et seq), or power to impose conditions as to repair, insurance, etc by the beneficiary (because that is provided for by the TLATA 1996, s 13(3), (5): Part G, para **[246.99]**). A power to permit occupation by a beneficiary and impose conditions on the beneficiary as to repair, insurance, etc should be included in a discretionary trust.

(3) An expression of intention that the trust is to provide a residence for the beneficiary, where the main trust does not make that clear, so as to make plain that the statutory right of occupation applies: TLATA 1996, s 12(1)(a) (Part G, para **[246.98]**; see also para **[208.7]**).

(4) No exclusion of the duty of trustees to consult beneficiaries who have an interest in possession in trust land about the exercise of powers or duties in relation to the land under the TLATA 1996, s 11 (Part G, para **[246.97]**; see also para **[220.58]**).

(5) The rights of the beneficiary can be further enhanced by providing that the trustees' powers of sale, and possibly other powers or discretions as well, may only be exercised with the consent of the beneficiary: the TLATA 1996, s 8(2) (Part G, para **[246.93]**) expressly contemplates that the statutory powers of management may be subject to consents. Where the interest in possession ceases on giving up residence in the property, consideration should be given to whether the requirement of consent should cease at the same time: see para **[208.21]**. If it becomes necessary for the trustees to sell the property against the wishes of the beneficiary, eg because of serious disrepair or, where the property is leasehold, failure to observe the lessee's covenants, then the trustees may apply to the court for an order under the TLATA 1996, s 14, in particular s 14(2)(a) (Part G, para **[246.100]**; see also Part A, para **[200.62]**). It is no longer the case that making sale of land subject to a beneficiary's consent causes the same consent to be required for the exercise of other powers over the land (see para **[220.62]**) and express provision must be made in relation to all powers or discretions which it is intended to make subject to a requirement of consent.

(6) The testator can also express a wish that the trustees should delegate all their powers of management of the land to the beneficiary under the TLATA 1996, s 9 (Part G, para **[246.94]**; see also para **[220.54]** et seq). An expression of wishes rather than a direction is appropriate because it appears that trustees cannot be obliged to exercise the power.

(7) Where the beneficiary's rights cease on giving up residence, it is preferable if the trusts provide for sale of one residence and purchase another with the proceeds.

[208.20]
Whether to provide a life interest or only a right to reside. When a testator wants to provide a right of residence, he usually intends that it should be no more than that, so that on the giving up of occupation by the beneficiary, or the sale of the property, the beneficiary's interest will terminate and the persons interested in remainder under the trusts of the property (often the persons interested in residue) will become entitled in possession to the property or its proceeds of sale. If such a testator could be persuaded to confer a full life

interest not dependent on continued residence it would be much kinder to the beneficiary, because it could be extremely hard on a beneficiary who wanted to live somewhere else but did not want to forfeit permanently a valuable right. The beneficiary's position is even worse where there is no provision for changing residences, so that the beneficiary might have to carry on living in a house which is in the wrong area or too large because leaving that particular house means forfeiture of all benefit. There could also be dilemmas for the trustees, who might for example find that there are grounds for thinking that the beneficiary has given up residence, but they are not sure, they are under pressure from the remaindermen to sell the property and hand the capital over to them, and do not have any funds (apart from the house) for legal proceedings (see further para **[208.21]**). Providing a full life interest, as in Form B8.4 at para **[208.40]** or B8.5 at para **[208.41]**, avoids these problems. It also means that the arrangements for residence do not need to be so tightly drafted, more can be left to the discretion of the trustees and to be taken care of by the TLATA 1996, and a much more concise clause is possible than in the case of trust to provide a right of residence only.

[208.21]
Interests ceasing on sale or on giving up residence. Where the testator particularly wants to create a trust for the beneficiary which terminates when the beneficiary gives up residence or the property is sold, the condition of obtaining the beneficiary's consent to a sale can either be general, ie a pre-requisite for a sale whether or not the beneficiary is living in the property, or only a pre-requisite for a sale so long as the beneficiary is in residence. If the beneficiary's consent is a general requirement, the beneficiary has more protection from precipitate action by the trustees, but there is more uncertainty about the position where the beneficiary leaves the property but will not consent to a sale. In these circumstances the trustees could have the dilemma that the property is a sterilised asset, perhaps a deteriorating one, particularly if the power to lease the property requires the beneficiary's consent and it is being withheld, and if they cannot be sure that they would be successful if they applied to the court under the TLATA 1996, s 14 to dispense with the beneficiary's consent to a sale. There might also be doubt as to whether the beneficiary's rights are really at an end or not.

[208.22]
Such possible difficulties could be reduced by not providing that *leasing* the property requires the beneficiary's consent after the beneficiary has given up residence (or at all), and/or by providing that any rents and profits of the property before it is sold should go to the beneficiary and not to the remainderman. Providing that the rents and profits before sale should go to the beneficiary rather than the remainderman in this situation would have a possible inheritance tax advantage (see paras **[208.31]** and **[208.32]**) and if the beneficiary's consent was needed for letting the property, it would of course encourage the beneficiary to consent to it. If the beneficiary's consent was not needed for letting the property when he or she was out of possession it would enable the trustees to obtain an income from which repairs, insurance, etc could be funded. These two provisions would also reduce ambiguity and make it fairly clear that the beneficiary, when out of residence, was entitled to block a sale

with a view to resuming occupation, but of course his or her rights would in effect be very similar to having a full life interest.

[208.23]
The potential difficulties just described are avoided if the requirement of the beneficiary's consent to a sale ceases on him or her ceasing to reside. The problem which could then arise for the trustees is whether the beneficiary has in fact ceased to reside, but if they can establish that he or she has ceased to do so they can at least be sure that the beneficiary's rights are at an end and the property should be sold. The authorities on construction of conditions as to residence, considered in Vol 1 at paras **[35.18]–[35.28]**, may provide some guidance as to when residence by the beneficiary should be regarded as having ceased. There is also the question whether involuntary cesser of residence should be declared not to amount to ceasing to reside. Without express provision involuntary cesser of residence would probably terminate the beneficiary's veto on sale. If words to this effect are included, it could be difficult for the trustees if the beneficiary is say taken to prison or hospital, or just disappears so that the trustees do not know what his or her circumstances are, and the house is in disrepair or perhaps at risk of vandalism or of being taken over by squatters and needs to be sold. In these circumstances the trustees would have to apply to the court for an order dispensing with the beneficiary's consent to a sale—either an application under the TLATA 1996, s 14 (Part G, para **[246.100]**) or if the beneficiary was mentally incapacitated, an application under the Mental Health Act 1983, s 96(1)(k) (Part G, para **[244.112]**). On the other hand, there could be unfairness in omitting this provision. The beneficiary might be taken to hospital and then recover, or be remanded in custody and then acquitted of the crime of which he or she was accused, and find that his or her residence had been sold. Deciding whether to include this provision is a matter of balancing the protection of the beneficiary's position against administrative convenience. A possible compromise is the provision in Form B8.1, sub-cl (8)(a) at para **[208.37]**, under which involuntary ceasing to reside does not terminate the beneficiary's interest, but does do so if he or she does not notify the trustees within a specified period that he or she intends to return.

[208.24]
Remainder trusts and avoiding gaps in the beneficial interests. Where the beneficiary has a life interest in the proceeds of sale the chances of failure to dispose fully of income or capital are small. Where the interest ceases on the remarriage of the beneficiary, however, the draftsman should make sure that the remainder trusts will take effect on his or her remarriage as well as his or her death. The chances of error are reduced by using remainder trusts of the kind which begin 'subject to the foregoing trusts', as opposed to those which begin 'on the death of the said ——'.

[208.25]
The chances of an accidental failure to dispose fully of the beneficial interest are increased where the beneficiary is only given a right of residence; it can sometimes happen that a will gives a beneficiary an interest in a house which ends when the beneficiary ceases to reside there, but then creates a remainder trust of the house which apparently only takes effect on the beneficiary's death.

Even where it is made clear that the remainderman becomes entitled when the property is sold, there can still be a question (which will not very often arise in practice, though it could) as to who is entitled to the rent if the property is let before it is sold. It is better to make express provision for this if there would otherwise be any ambiguity about it.

[208.26]
Repairs, payment of outgoings, etc. Where a residential property is held on trust for a beneficiary under a specific gift it is very often without any additional endowment of capital held on the same trusts which could be used to pay for repairs, insurance, etc. Where a beneficiary has an interest in possession in a residential property (or land of any other kind) which gives rise to a right of occupation of that land under the TLATA 1996, s 12 (Part G, para **[246.98]**) that right is subject to a power of the trustees to impose reasonable conditions on the beneficiary in relation to his occupation of that land under s 12: TLATA 1996, s 13(3) (Part G, para **[246.99]**; see also para **[208.5]**). It seems from the structure of the TLATA 1996, ss 12 and 13 and the lack of any provision permitting the exclusion of ss 12 and 13, that the right of occupation is subject only to the conditions which are reasonably imposed by the trustees under s 13(3) after taking into account not only the intentions of the testator and the purposes for which the land is held but also the circumstances and wishes of the beneficiaries: TLATA 1996, s 13(4). Accordingly, it seems that the will cannot predetermine what would be reasonable conditions for the trustees to impose, but that an expression of the testator's intentions as to the burdens to be assumed by an occupying beneficiary will carry weight under s 13(4) and, in the event of a dispute about the discharge of such burdens going to court, under the TLATA 1996, s 15(1) (Part G, para **[246.101]**).

[208.27]
Remedies for failure by a beneficiary to repair, pay outgoings, etc. It should be noted that the conditions imposed under the TLATA 1996, s 13(3) are not conditions for the right of occupation continuing to be exercisable; in other words the right of occupation does not come to an end if those conditions are broken. However, the practical position is likely to be that if an occupying beneficiary is in serious breach of reasonably imposed conditions relating to his or her occupation, one option will be for the trustees to apply to the court under the TLATA 1996, s 14 (Part G, para **[246.100]**) for an order for sale with vacant possession (and dispensing with the beneficiary's consent if the will makes that a requirement for a sale) on the grounds, for example, that the beneficiary cannot be relied on to observe the obligations which go with his or her occupation, the property is deteriorating, and the only hope of saving something for the remaindermen is a sale as soon as possible before the property deteriorates further. The trustees can also ask the court for directions as to what they should do if sale is not ordered. An alternative course of action would be proceedings against the beneficiary for compensation for failure to carry out the obligations imposed. It seems that by taking up occupation (or continuing in it after the testator's death) under a right given by the will (or an exercise of a power under the will) which is subject to repairing, insuring, etc the beneficiary cannot take the benefit without accepting the burden, so that for example, the trustees could sue the beneficiary for reimbursement of insurance premiums, or they (or

possibly the persons interested in remainder) could sue the beneficiary's estate for compensation after his or her death if he or she had failed to keep the property in repair. See *Re Williams* (1885) 54 LT 105; *Jay v Jay* [1924] 1 KB 826; *Re Field* [1925] Ch 636; and *Haskell v Marlow* [1928] 2 KB 45; these are all cases concerning obligations to repair of tenants for life of settled land (where the trusts expressly imposed a repairing obligation), but we can see no reason why the benefit and burden principle set out in those cases should not equally apply to someone with a life or lesser interest occupying property held on a trust of land subject to obligations to repair, etc reasonably imposed by the trustees under the TLATA 1996, s 13(3). The TLATA 1996 makes no express provision as to how conditions imposed on occupying beneficiaries are to be enforced, but the terms of the TLATA 1996, s 13(3) and (5) seem to imply that if a beneficiary breaks a condition reasonably imposed upon him he will be personally liable.

[208.28]
In practice, the lack of any additional endowment will make it extremely difficult for the trustees to take any steps to enforce the beneficiary's obligations, as there may be no funds even to pay for a simple application to the court for directions, without first selling the property. It is advisable to make it clear, where the trustees might be in this position, that they are not to be liable for any failure to enforce the beneficiary's obligations, although this would probably be implicit in trusts of this type. Other possibilities which could be considered are to restrict the liability to repair to keeping the property in the state it is in at the testator's death (where it is likely to be in a poor state of repair), and providing an endowment fund to pay for repairs, insurance, etc. Simply providing for expenses to be paid out of residue could hold up the distribution of residue for a long time. Where the beneficiary's own estate is likely to go on his or her death to the persons who are the remaindermen under the trusts of the residential property, precise definition of the beneficiary's obligations as to repair and outgoings is less important.

Other aspects

[208.29]
Freedom from liabilities. The intention of providing a residence could be frustrated if a gift for that purpose is burdened with a charge which is not directed to be paid out of residue (see the AEA 1925, s 35: Part G, para **[246.47]**). Inheritance tax in respect of land in the UK is now prima facie payable out of residue as a testamentary expense (ITA 1984, s 211: Part G, para **[246.83]**) and the incidence of inheritance tax no longer poses a problem in this respect. Where the beneficiary is the testator's widow or widower, and she or he becomes entitled to an interest in possession in the residence under the trusts of the will, the gift will normally be exempt from inheritance tax and the question of incidence will not arise: see Part A, para **[200.99]**.

[208.30]
Taxation. A beneficiary with a life interest in a property or its proceeds of sale will clearly have an interest in possession for inheritance tax purposes. The same

will almost certainly be true where the beneficiary is entitled to reside in the property but has no larger beneficial interest. Where the trusts are discretionary, or are fixed trusts in favour of persons other than the beneficiary, and the beneficiary occupies the property by virtue of the trustees' exercise of a power to permit him or her to reside there, it is likely that this will also give the beneficiary an interest in possession in the property for inheritance tax purposes, and the Inland Revenue are likely to so regard it: see *Foster's Inheritance Tax*, E1.47 and Part A, para **[200.110]**.

[208.31]
The beneficiary having an interest in possession in the property means that the death of the beneficiary while the interest in possession continues will give rise to an inheritance tax charge on the property (ITA 1984, ss 4(1), 5(1) and 49(1)), and that the termination of the interest in possession during his or her life will be an inheritance tax transfer of value, which may be a potentially exempt transfer if the termination of the interest is followed by an absolute interest or another interest in possession in it, or by an accumulation and maintenance trust: ITA 1984, s 3A. If it is a potentially exempt transfer, inheritance tax will only be payable in respect of the termination of the interest if the beneficiary dies within seven years of the termination.

[208.32]
It is therefore a bad idea for a will to create trusts of a residence which may give rise to a series of interests in possession for different people, with successive lifetime terminations of interests in possession, each with a potential for giving rise to an inheritance tax charge. This unsatisfactory result could arise if the beneficiary's interest in a property exclusively arises from a power to permit him or her to occupy, as the power will only come to be first exercised after some time has elapsed from the testator's death, and may not be exercised continuously thereafter, or from the beneficiary having a right of occupation which is interrupted by a period during which the property is let to a tenant and the rents are payable to the remainderman (who would thus have an interest in possession while entitled to the rents). On the other hand, giving concurrent rights of residence to a number of persons could effect an inheritance tax saving by dividing the value of the property among different estates (see para **[208.14]**), even though some of those persons will not exercise the right of residence. See Form B8.3 at para **[208.39]** and the notes thereto. Where the beneficiary is the testator's spouse, it is important that the beneficiary's interest in possession should commence from the testator's death, if it is desired that the spouse exemption (under the ITA 1984, s 18: see Part A, para **[200.99]**) should apply to the property on the testator's death; again this means that the will should provide a trust entitling him or her to occupation of the property, or a life (or until remarriage) interest.

[208.33]
Another inheritance tax problem for residences is the effectiveness of the nil rate band-using strategy of husband and wife owning the matrimonial home as tenants in common, and the first to die leaving his or her share of the home to a non-exempt beneficiary or beneficiaries such as their children, on the basis or with the intention that the surviving spouse will go on living there. An outright

gift to the children is probably effective to keep the first to die's share out of the taxable estate of the survivor, but at the cost of the survivor being at risk of the children seeking an order for sale. However, writing protection from this risk for the survivor into the trusts is likely to cause the survivor to have an interest in possession in the first to die's share. For example, the arrangement of this kind in Form B8.10 (at para **[208.46]**) was held to have this effect in *IRC v Lloyd's Private Banking* [1998] STC 559, High Court (see n 1 to para **[208.46]**). Another arrangement which might work is to give the child or children a life interest or interests in the share of the first to die, because the TLATA 1996, ss 12 and 13 seem to have the effect that the surviving spouse has security of exclusive possession of the property while having, it is hoped, a taxable interest in only half the property: see paras **[208.10]** and **[208.16]**. The latter scheme is untested and the Inland Revenue have not expressed views on it. The most popular method, and one which has the considerable advantage of having been accepted as effective, at least in some form, by the Inland Revenue, is a nil rate band discretionary trust fund under the first to die's will where the trust fund is constituted by a personal obligation of the surviving spouse or by a charge on the first to die's share of the matrimonial home: see para **[218.19]** et seq.

[208.34]
The capital gains tax private residence exemption should apply, as long as the property is the beneficiary's main residence: TCGA 1992, ss 222 and 225. This is likely to be so even where the beneficiary occupies by virtue of the exercise of a discretionary power: see *Sansom v Peay* [1976] 3 All ER 375, [1976] 1 WLR 1073, the decision on the basis of which the Inland Revenue regard occupation under the exercise of a power as giving rise to an interest in possession for inheritance tax purposes.

[208.35]
Administrative powers. Where a residence may be held on trust for some time there are various administrative powers and provisions which it might be appropriate to include in the will, such as: power to borrow (see Form B20.20 at para **[220.69]**), power to lend to the life tenant (see Form B18.27 at para **[218.112]**), power for a trustee to contract with the trust fund (see Form B21.7 at para **[221.8]**), power to appoint foreign trustees (see Form B21.36 at para **[221.41]**), and a professional trustee charging clause (see Forms B21.37 and B21.38 at paras **[221.49]** and **[221.50]**). An express power of investment is only needed if it is desired to confer on the trustees power to acquire land outside the UK or undivided shares of land (or other equitable interests in land), or unsecured loans—the statutory powers of investment enable purchase of most kinds of asset apart from these categories: see the Trustee Act 2000 (TrA 2000), ss 3 and 8 (Part G, paras **[246.118]** and **[246.123]**) and para **[220.12]** et seq. Express powers of management of land are needed if land outside England and Wales might be held, but for most purposes in relation to a trust to provide a residence the statutory powers over land in England and Wales are likely to be adequate: see the TLATA 1996, s 6(1) (Part G, para **[246.91]**) and para **[220.64]** et seq. Where any such provisions are being included in the will in relation to a residuary trust fund, it may be possible to make them applicable also to a specific gift of a residence, but care should be taken for inheritance tax reasons to make sure that powers over one fund or asset cannot be used to benefit

beneficiaries interested in another fund or asset (see the Note in B18 at para **[218.108]** and the General Preliminary Note to B20 at paras **[220.1]**–**[220.10]**).

[208.36]
Furniture. Sometimes it is desired to provide a life or other limited right to the use of some or all of the house contents along with the house. Except possibly in the case of really valuable furniture and fittings, it is better to make an absolute gift of chattels because the expense, difficulty, and potential for dispute of administering chattels as part of a trust fund is usually out of all proportion to their value. For forms for use in cases where the testator cannot be dissuaded from settling furniture and/or other chattels, see Forms B4.10 (at para **[204.24]**), B4.26 to B4.30 (at paras **[204.44]**–**[204.48]**), B8.3 (at para **[208.39]**) and B8.6 (at para **[208.42]**). For notes on settling chattels see the Note on furniture in B4 at para **[204.37]** et seq.

Trusts of land

[208.37]

FORM B8.1:   Interest of beneficiary limited to a right of residence with provision for changing residences[1]

(1)   I give my freehold dwellinghouse known as ————, or (if the same shall be sold or otherwise disposed of before my death) the dwellinghouse which I shall own at the date of my death, to my trustees free of all sums charged or otherwise secured thereon at my death (which sums shall be paid out of my residuary estate) to hold the same and any dwellinghouse acquired in substitution therefor (as provided below) upon trust to provide a residence for [my wife] so long as she wishes to reside there subject as provided below.
  (2)   If at my death I own more than one dwellinghouse the foregoing gift shall be of my principal place of residence at my death and if none of them is my principal place of residence then the foregoing gift shall be of the dwellinghouse which has the highest capital value (as determined by my trustees) at my death but [my wife] shall have the right to select by notice in writing to my trustees another dwellinghouse of mine to be the subject-matter of the foregoing gift in place that which would otherwise be the subject-matter of it provided that—

  (a)   the foregoing right of selection shall cease if such notice of selection has not been received by my trustees within one year of my death or within two months of the grant of probate or letters of administration to my estate if later;
  (b)   my trustees may extend the time for service of such notice of election for any period they think fit and if they do not inform [my wife] of her foregoing right of selection within six months of my death they shall extend the time for service thereof at least until the expiry of six months from her being so informed;
  (c)   if [my wife] is one of my trustees the references to my trustees in this subclause are to my trustees other than [my wife] and if [she] alone constitutes my trustees for the time being proviso (b) above to this

subclause shall not apply and [my wife] shall give notice of selection by endorsing notice of it on the probate or letters of administration;

(d) if more than one dwellinghouse of mine has the same capital value or if for any other reason there is a question as to which of my dwellinghouses is the subject-matter of the foregoing gift it shall be determined by notice of selection by my wife as set out above and if she shall not give valid notice of selection within the time for doing so it shall be determined by my trustees by notice in writing to [my wife].[2]

(3) My trustees shall not exercise their power to sell the said or any substitute dwellinghouse or their power to purchase any substitute dwellinghouse or exercise any of their other powers (conferred hereby or by law)[3] over any such dwellinghouse without the consent in writing of [my wife] so long as her interest continues and (if for the time being a dwellinghouse is held subject to the provisions of this clause) so long as she shall perform and observe any conditions reasonably imposed by my trustees in relation to her residence in any such dwellinghouse.[4]

(4) I wish my trustees to impose as a condition in relation to [my wife]'s residence in any such dwellinghouse that she should keep the same fully insured in the name of my trustees, keep the same in good repair, observe and perform the lessee's covenants (if the dwellinghouse is leasehold), and pay all taxes and other outgoings in respect thereof[5] and my trustees shall not be liable for lack of insurance repair or payment of outgoings or for not taking steps to enforce any reasonable conditions imposed in relation to [my wife]'s residence in any such dwellinghouse.[6]

(5) I also wish my trustees to delegate to [my wife] their powers of sale of any such dwellinghouse.[7]

(6) If [my wife] gives up residence in one dwellinghouse subject to this clause so as to enable it to be sold and some other dwellinghouse to be acquired for her to reside in then her interest shall not cease and she shall be entitled to be paid the income of the proceeds of sale of one dwellinghouse pending purchase of another,[8] and—

(a) my trustees may apply such proceeds of sale in the purchase of a dwellinghouse in any location they think fit (whether in England and Wales or elsewhere) to provide a residence for [my wife] and may apply some of the proceeds of sale of one dwellinghouse in the purchase of another dwellinghouse and some in the improvement and/or repair of that other dwellinghouse;[9]

(b) without prejudice to the generality of the foregoing, my trustees shall have power to purchase the substitute dwellinghouse together with [my wife] as tenants in common in such shares as my trustees may deem appropriate according to the respective contributions of my trustees and [my wife] and notwithstanding that [my wife] may be one of my trustees;[10]

(c) if my trustees decide to acquire an undivided share of a replacement dwellinghouse my trustees may join with [my wife] and/or the other co-owner or co-owners in charging the property to assist [my wife] or any other co-owner in borrowing money to finance the purchase of her or his share thereof on such times as my trustees think fit;

(d) my trustees shall have power to pay out of the proceeds of sale of the dwellinghouse sold any reasonable costs of temporary accommodation and/or storage of chattels for [my wife] between her moving out of the dwellinghouse sold and moving into the replacement dwellinghouse;

(e) any of the proceeds of sale of the dwellinghouse sold which are not applied in the purchase or purchase and improvement and/or repair of another dwellinghouse or in assisting [my wife] as aforesaid shall fall into my residuary estate;

(f) if the period of twelve months elapses after the sale of one dwelling-house without the acquisition of another dwellinghouse then [my wife]'s interest shall cease and all the proceeds of sale of the dwellinghouse sold shall fall into my residuary estate (but my trustees may by writing extend the period of continuance of [my wife]'s interest pending purchase of another dwellinghouse at any time or times when such period including any previous extension of it under this power has not expired).[11]

(7) On the death of [my wife] or (subject to subclause (6) above) in the event of her giving up residence, such dwellinghouse and any property representing it shall fall into my residuary estate.

(8) For the purposes of this clause—

(a) no involuntary ceasing by [my wife] to reside in a dwellinghouse subject to this clause shall be treated as ceasing to reside therein unless [my wife] shall have been out of residence continuously for six months and shall not have expressed in writing to my trustees her intention to take up residence again;[12]

(b) references to a dwellinghouse include a flat and an interest in, or undivided share of, a dwellinghouse.

(9) All the powers of my trustees may be exercised by them in favour of or for the benefit of [my wife] even though she may be one of my trustees but not if she is sole trustee.

[(10) My trustees shall have the same powers and [my wife] shall have the same rights in relation to any dwellinghouse subject to this clause which is situated outside England and Wales as they would have if it were situated in England and Wales.][13]

[Take in administrative powers and provisions as appropriate (see para **[208.35]***), such as Form B20.20 (borrowing) at para* **[220.69]***, Form B21.12 (trustee indemnity) at para* **[221.16]** *and Form B21.37 (trustee power to charge) at para* **[221.49]***.]*

1   This form is more complicated than the full life interest Form B8.5 (at para **[208.41]**), because it is essential in this type of trust to make provision for sale of one residence and purchase of another. If the client can be persuaded to give a full life interest, or at any rate an interest not ceasing on giving up residence, the drafting can be much simplified, and in some ways it is fairer on the beneficiary, since he or she will not be constrained to linger on in a property which he or she should move out of only because the benefit of it is lost if he or she does so. If the interest given is one which ceases on residence being given up by the beneficiary, where the beneficiary is someone with a claim on the testator, he or she may be able to apply under the I(PFD)A 1975 for the interest to be enlarged to a full life interest or even an absolute interest. Because the Form gives the widow a right of occupation over property comprised in a specific gift from the testator's death, an interest in possession in the property is almost certainly conferred on the beneficiary from the testator's death. Accordingly, where the beneficiary is the

testator's spouse the gift should be exempt from inheritance tax on the testator's death as a gift to a spouse, unless at the testator's death the testator is domiciled in the UK, his spouse is not, and the £55,000 limit for exempt gifts in such circumstances is exceeded (see Part A, para [200.100]). Where the property is or may be outside the UK, it may be appropriate to make the gift free of inheritance tax or foreign death duties: see Form B8.5, n 1 at para [208.41].

2   Subclause (2) can be omitted if it is likely that the testator will have only one dwellinghouse at his death. If it is omitted, the words 'or the principal dwellinghouse (if I have more than one)' could be inserted in sub-cl (1) between '... before my death) the dwellinghouse' and 'which I shall own at the date of my death ... '. It is not clear whether exercise of the right of selection will terminate the beneficiary's interest in possession in the whole of the property given under sub-cl (1), or whether the ITA 1984, s 52(3) will apply to relieve it from being an occasion of charge save in respect of the difference in value (if any) between the original property and the selected one. Any occasion of charge will be potentially exempt or immediately chargeable (see paras [200.71] and [200.114]) according to what the trusts of residue are.

3   This is no longer statutorily implied from the requirement of consent to a sale as a result of the repeal of the LPA 1925, s 28(1): see para [200.60]. The TLATA 1996, s 8(2) (Part G, para [246.93]) provides that exercise of the trustees' powers may be subject to consents (see para [200.66]).

4   Subclause (3) could be omitted, since so long as the beneficiary is in residence the trustees cannot sell the property without first applying to the court under the TLATA 1996, s 14 (Part G, para [246.100]) and making the requirement of her consent end if she does not fulfil the conditions of her occupation does not help the trustees much if she is still in occupation.

5   See para [208.18], sub-para (2) for the reasons for making this an expression of wishes rather than a direction that the beneficiary's occupation shall be subject to these burdens.

6   Although it is thought that the will cannot predetermine what obligations an occupying beneficiary will be subject to (see para [208.18], sub-para (2)) there is nothing to prevent the trustees being absolved from liability for want of repair, etc which it is contemplated will be the beneficiary's responsibility.

7   For the power of delegation, and the reasons for thinking that the most that can be provided in relation to it is an expression of wishes, see para [220.57] and the TLATA 1996, s 9 (Part G, para [246.94]).

8   The main reason for this provision is so that the beneficiary has an interest in possession in the proceeds of sale for inheritance tax purposes. It could have adverse inheritance tax consequences if the residuary beneficiaries had interests in possession in the proceeds of sale for a short period between the sale of one property and the purchase of another. See the note on taxation at para [208.30].

9   It is not clear that the proceeds of sale of one property could be spent on improving another property under the powers conferred by the TLATA 1996 or the TrA 2000 in the absence of express authorisation by the will. It is arguably not a power of an absolute owner in relation to the land within the TLATA 1996, s 6(1) since it is something done in relation to the cash received from a sale of the land, and it is not the purchase of a legal estate in land within the TrA 2000, s 8(1) (Part G, para [246.123]; see also para [220.52]).

10   The purchase of an undivided share in land is not authorised by the TrA 2000, s 8 (Part G, para [246.123]) and express power is needed to be able to do so. If an undivided share is subject to these trusts (either under the original gift or as a matter of subsequent acquisition) the beneficiary will apparently not have a right of occupation of the property under the TLATA 1996 in respect of that share: see para [208.10]. Usually the beneficiary will be the absolute owner of the other share, and have a right of occupation by virtue of owning it. If on a purchase of a substitute property the beneficiary is not one of the other co-owners the trustees should obtain the agreement of the other co-owners to the beneficiary's occupation before entering into the purchase.

11   Subclause (f) is a long stop provision to prevent the beneficiary refusing consent to purchase of a new property in order to go on enjoying the income. Some or all of sub-cls (a) to (d) of this proviso may in particular cases be unnecessary elaboration and if so can be omitted. If (a) and/or (d) are omitted there will be consequential amendment to make to (e).

12   The idea here is to protect the beneficiary against precipitate sale if she is hospitalised after an accident or illness, but if she is hospitalised and is mentally incapacitated she will not be able to express an intention to return and the trustees will be free to sell the property after six months. See also para [208.23]. This paragraph may be omitted if preferred.

13   The statutory rights and powers under the TLATA 1996, s 6(1) (Part G, para [246.91]; see also para [220.52]) only apply to land in England and Wales: TLATA 1996, s 27(3) (Part G,

para **[246.113]**). If land in Scotland or Northern Ireland is acquired under the statutory power to do so in the TrA 2000, s 8(1) (Part G, para **[246.123]**), they have the same statutory powers of management in relation to that land (TrA 2000, s 8(3)), but this will not apply to land in Scotland or Northern Ireland acquired under an express power or comprised in the testator's estate at his death. This subclause may be omitted if there is no likelihood of the beneficiary wanting to live outside England and Wales.

[208.38]

FORM B8.2:   **Interest of beneficiary limited to right of residence, with the beneficiary's consent to a sale being required generally, with provision for changing residences**

[(1)   *As sub-cl (1) of* Form B8.1 *at para* **[208.37]**.]
  [(2)   *As sub-cl (2) of* Form B8.1 *at para* **[208.37]**.]
  (3)   My trustees shall not during the lifetime of [my wife] sell the said or any substitute dwellinghouse or exercise their power to purchase any substitute dwellinghouse or exercise any of their other powers (conferred hereby or by law) over any such dwellinghouse without the consent in writing of [my wife] [Provided that while [my wife] is not in residence in any such dwellinghouse my trustees may grant leases or tenancies of it or of any part or parts of it without her consent].[1]
  [(4)   *As sub-cl (4) of* Form B8.1 *at para* **[208.37]**.]
  [(5)   *As sub-cl (5) of* Form B8.1 *at para* **[208.37]**.]
  [(6)   *As sub-cl (6) of* Form B8.1 *at para* **[208.37]**.]
  (7)   My trustees shall pay the net rents and profits of any such dwellinghouse arising before the sale thereof (if any) to [my wife].[2]
  [(8)   *As sub-cl (7) of* Form B8.1 *at para* **[208.37]**.]
  [(9)   *As sub-cl (8) of* Form B8.1 *at para* **[208.37]**.]
  [(10)   *As sub-cl (9) of* Form B8.1 *at para* **[208.37]**.]
  [(11)   *As sub-cl (10) of* Form B8.1 *at para* **[208.37]**.]

[*Take in administrative powers and provisions as appropriate (see para* **[208.35]***), such as* Form B20.20 *(borrowing) at para* **[220.69]**, Form B21.12 *(trustee indemnity) at para* **[221.16]** *and* Form B21.37 *(trustee power to charge) at para* **[221.49]**.]

1   On this subclause, see paras **[208.21]** and **[208.22]**.
2   See paras **[208.21]** and **[208.22]**. This subclause will prevent interests in possession stopping and starting where the beneficiary goes out of occupation, the property is let, and later the beneficiary returns to live there. It also will encourage the beneficiary to consent to a letting while she is out of residence, where her consent to such letting is not dispensed with.

[208.39]

FORM B8.3:   **Trust to permit residence and use of furniture etc by the testator's wife and children**[1]

(1)   I devise my freehold residence known as —— to my trustees upon trust for my wife and my children to reside therein so long as they so desire and so long as they or any of them shall so desire and so reside the said property shall not be sold without the consent of such one or more of them so desiring to reside.[2] I declare that no involuntary ceasing to reside in the said property shall be

construed as a ceasing to reside therein[3] and I wish my trustees to impose as a condition in relation to such residence that it shall be subject to the payment by those or the one so residing as the case may be of the council tax, cost of keeping the said property in reasonable repair and other outgoings. My trustees shall not be responsible for any neglect of the obligations of those or the one so residing. Subject as aforesaid my trustees shall hold the said property and any assets representing the same and the income thereof as part of my residuary estate as hereinafter defined.

(2)   If those so residing in —— aforesaid under the provisions of the last preceding subclause shall desire to reside in some other house then I hereby further authorise my trustees to sell the said house and out of the proceeds of sale thereof to purchase such other house as those so residing shall choose, provided always that no more than the proceeds of such sale shall be required to cover all the costs of sale and purchase and conveyance or transfer of the properties. In case immediate possession cannot be secured of such alternative residence I authorise my trustees at their absolute discretion to raise a sum not exceeding £—— out of my residuary estate and apply the same to the reasonable expenses incurred by those so residing in securing accommodation pending taking possession of the alternative residence. Such alternative residence [shall be situated in the United Kingdom and] may be freehold or leasehold the term of which has not fewer than 60 years unexpired and shall be vested in my trustees upon trust subject to the requirement of consent or consents to a sale as aforesaid such alternative residence to be held upon the trusts of this my will concerning —— aforesaid.

(3)   I bequeath to my trustees all my furniture and household and domestic effects upon trust with power to sell the same at their discretion and declare that no sale thereof shall be had without the consent of my wife and my children or such of them as shall for the time being be residing in —— aforesaid or the house substituted thereof under the provisions of the last preceding subclause. My trustees shall allow my wife and my children for the time being residing in the property specified in subclause (1) or subclause (2) of this clause the use of such furniture and they or such of them as shall for the time being be residing in the said property shall be responsible for the repair upkeep and insurance of such furniture. My trustees shall not be responsible for the neglect of the above obligations in respect of such furniture but nevertheless my trustees may take such steps as they think fit for the protection and preservation thereof. All moneys received in respect of any insurance of such furniture shall be applied in replacement or reinstatement thereof. Subject as aforesaid the said furniture or the proceeds of sale thereof shall fall into my residuary estate as hereinafter defined.[4]

---

1   The inheritance tax implications of this form need to be considered carefully if its use is contemplated—it could have advantages or disadvantages depending on the facts. The widow and children will have interests in possession in equal shares of the property: ITA 1984, s 50(5). It is not entirely clear whether one of them leaving to live elsewhere will cause a lifetime termination of his or her interest in possession. It seems from the Special Commissioner's decision in *Woodhall v IRC* [2000] STC (SCD) 558 that the interest in possession of one of them who is not living there may continue so long as at least one of them is still living in the house and the one not living there retains the right to return (see para **[208.14]**). This could have considerable advantages on the death of the widow as it would reduce the proportion of the house treated as part of her taxable estate on death if some or all of the children had interests in possession in the property even if not actually living there. There will clearly be lifetime

ceases and the house is sold, or where one of them irrevocably renounces the right. This will not matter if the termination is a potentially exempt transfer (see Part A, para **[200.70]**) and he or she survives the occasion by seven years or does not do so but does not turn out to have had taxable assets (including his or her estate on death and the capital value of his or her former deemed share of the property) in excess of the inheritance tax nil rate band. It should be remembered, however, that the spouse exemption (see Part A, paras **[200.90]** and **[200.99]**) will only apply on the testator's death as respects the part or share subject to the widow's interest in possession. This could give rise to unnecessary tax charges on the testator's death, but will not do so if the children's shares and any other non-exempt parts of the estate do not exceed the inheritance tax nil rate band. If the *Woodhall* decision stands this could be a tax efficient form of disposition to provide a residence for someone who is not the testator's spouse, eg by adding that person's children to the beneficiaries and so reducing the inheritance tax charge on that person's death.

For administrative powers which could suitably be added, see para **[208.35]**.

2   This sentence makes a distinction between the requirement as to when consent is needed, and the requirement as to whose consent is needed when it is needed. If at least one of the beneficiaries is residing in the property and the trustees wish to sell the house the trustees must get the consent of all those who wish to reside there, including those who wish to reside there but are not actually doing so. If none of the wife or the children is in residence the trustees are free to sell the property without the consent of any of them *whether or not any of them wants to reside there*. If the words 'and so reside' are omitted from this sentence the consent of all those who wish to reside is needed even when none of them is in residence, but the trustees' task is made more difficult in the event of them all ceasing to live in the property. If those words are omitted, the words in the next sentence from 'that no involuntary ceasing' to 'reside therein and' (inclusive) should also be omitted.

3   See para **[208.23]**.

4   For settlements of chattels, see also the Note on furniture in B4 at para **[204.37]** et seq and Forms B4.10 (at para **[204.24]**) and B4.26 to B4.30 (at paras **[204.44]**–**[204.48]**).

[208.40]

FORM B8.4:   Trust for wife for life or until she remarries and then for son, with power to permit residence[1]

I devise my freehold house and land known as No —— —— Street —— in the county of —— [free of all sums charged or otherwise secured thereon at my death (which sums shall be paid out of my residuary estate)] to my trustees to hold the same and the assets from time to time representing the same upon trust for my wife during her life [so long as she shall remain my widow] and after her death [or remarriage] my trustees shall hold the said property if unsold or the assets representing the same for my son CB absolutely. I intend the said property to be available for occupation by my wife and that my trustees should during the period of such occupation require her to pay all council tax and other outgoings payable in respect of the same and keep the said property in good repair and condition and refund to my trustees the cost of keeping the same insured. My trustees shall not be liable to see to such repair or the effecting or keeping up of such insurance or for any breach of the obligations hereby imposed on my wife.[2]

1   Unless the testator is domiciled in the UK and the wife has a foreign domicile, this gift will be exempt from inheritance tax on the testator's death (see Part A, paras **[200.99]** and **[200.100]**), but the property will be charged to inheritance tax on her death as part of her estate unless the interest ends on remarriage and she has remarried (see Part A, para **[200.101]**). If the interest is made to terminate on remarriage, and she remarries, the remarriage will cause a lifetime termination of an interest in possession, which will be treated as a lifetime transfer by her of the property, and which may be potentially exempt (see Part A, para **[200.70]**).

2   For administrative powers which could suitably be added, see para **[208.35]**.

[208.41]

FORM B8.5:   Gift of residence for wife for life with the intention that she reside there—fuller form, providing for the possibility of a change of house by the testator before his death or by the trustees after his death[1]

(1)   I give my [interest in the] freehold dwellinghouse known as ———, or (if the same shall be sold or otherwise disposed of before my death) the estate or interest owned by me at my death in my then dwellinghouse or my then principal dwellinghouse (if I have more than one),[2] to my trustees free of all sums charged or otherwise secured thereon at my death (which sums shall be paid out of my residuary estate) to hold the same and the assets from time to time representing the same on trust for [my wife] during her life and subject to [my wife's] said interest on trust as part of my residuary estate.

(2)   It is a purpose of the foregoing trust to provide a home for [my wife] so long as she so desires[3] and I declare that my trustees shall not be liable for lack of insurance repair or payment of outgoings of any home occupied by her under the foregoing trust or for not taking steps to enforce any reasonable conditions imposed by my trustees on [my wife] in relation to her occupation of any such home.[4]

(3)   In addition to their statutory powers of investment and acquisition of assets my trustees may acquire [land or buildings outside the United Kingdom or] any undivided share (whether in co-ownership with [my wife] or any other person) in land or buildings [in the United Kingdom or elsewhere] for any purpose including provision of a home for [my wife], and may apply capital in the improvement or repair of any land or buildings for the time being subject to the foregoing trust.[5]

[(4)   My trustees shall have the same powers and [my wife] shall have the same rights in relation to any property subject to this clause which is situated outside England and Wales as they would have if it were situated in England and Wales.][6]

(5)   All the powers of my trustees may be exercised by them in favour of or for the benefit of [my wife] even though she is one of my trustees, and at any time when she is not one of my trustees her consent shall still be required to any exercise of the trustees' powers of sale purchase or leasing in relation to any land or buildings or interest therein subject to this clause.[7]

[Other provisions of Form **B8.1** *at para* **[208.37]** *which could be added here are: sub-cl (4), (5)(c), (d), (7)(b) and (9). Take in administrative powers and provisions as appropriate (see para* **[208.35]***), such as* Form B20.20 *(borrowing) at para* **[220.69]***,* Form B21.12 *(trustee indemnity) at para* **[221.16]** *and* Form B21.37 *(trustee power to charge) at para* **[221.49]**.*]*

1   This Form shows the TLATA 1996 at its best. The removal of the need for a trust for sale (see para **[200.55]**), the statutory right of occupation (see para **[208.5]** et seq) and the wide administrative powers given to trustees of land (see para **[220.49]** et seq), reduce the amount of express provision needed and enable clauses of this kind to be more concise and comprehensible. The right of residence can also be made to terminate on, eg remarriage. Under this clause, if the house is sold and the beneficiary goes to live with a relative or in rented accommodation, she will be entitled to the income of the proceeds of sale as invested. Because this Form gives the widow an interest in possession in the property from the testator's death, the gift should be exempt from inheritance tax on the testator's death as a gift to a spouse, unless at the testator's death the testator is domiciled in the UK, his wife is not, and the £55,000 limit for

exempt gifts in such circumstances is exceeded: see Part A, para **[200.100]**. If the house is outside the UK (or might be replaced by a property outside the UK), the inclusion of a provision freeing the gift from foreign death duties should be considered. If the form is being adapted for use for someone other than the testator's spouse, or the testator is domiciled in the UK but his spouse is not (so that the gift will not necessarily be wholly exempt from inheritance tax—see Part A, para **[200.100]**), and the inheritance tax on the gift might not be borne by residue in the absence of express provision to that effect (eg the property is or might be outside the UK or the gift is an exercise of a general power of appointment over settled property: see the Preliminary Note to B14 at para **[214.60]**) a provision freeing the gift from inheritance tax should also be considered.

2   If the testator might have more than one property at his death, Form B8.1, sub-cl (2) (at para **[208.37]**) would provide more comprehensively for this eventuality. The words 'interest in the' in the first line, in square brackets, are to be left in or omitted depending on whether the testator owns an undivided share of the property or the whole of it at the time of making the will.

3   This should be sufficient to confer the statutory right of occupation on the beneficiary under the TLATA 1996, s 12(1)(a) (Part G, para **[246.127]**): see para **[208.7]**.

4   In the interests of economy there is no expression of wishes as to the conditions to be imposed on the beneficiary, but such could be included as in Form B8.1, sub-cl (4) at para **[208.37]**. See also nn 5 and 6 to that subclause.

5   These are all thought to be applications of capital money which are not authorised by the TLATA 1996 or the TrA 2000 (see para **[220.52]** et seq and Form B8.1, nn 9 and 10 at para **[208.37]**. This subclause can be omitted in whole or in part if there are provisions elsewhere in the will to the same effect which apply to this clause. See note 6 concerning the words in square brackets other than 'my wife'. The statutory powers of acquisition of assets are now in the TrA 2000, ss 3 and 8 (Part G, paras **[246.118]** and **[246.123]**; see also para **[220.11]** et seq).

6   The statutory rights and powers under the TLATA 1996, s 6(1) (Part G, para **[246.91]** and see para **[220.49]**) only apply to land in England and Wales: TLATA 1996, s 27(3) (Part G, para **[246.113]**). If land in Scotland or Northern Ireland is acquired under the statutory power to do so in the TrA 2000, s 8(1) (Part G, para **[246.123]**), they have the same statutory powers of management in relation to that land (TrA 2000, s 8(3)), but this will not apply to land in Scotland or Northern Ireland acquired under an express power or comprised in the testator's estate at his death. This subclause may be omitted if there is no likelihood of the beneficiary wanting to live outside England and Wales, and if it is omitted the words in square brackets other than 'my wife' in the preceding subclause should also be omitted.

7   The TLATA 1996, s 8(2) enables exercise of the trustees' powers over land to be made subject to consents. The repeal of the LPA 1925, s 28(1) (see para **[200.60]**) means that a requirement of consent to a sale is no longer applied by statute to other powers.

[208.42]

FORM B8.6:   Clause in will of widow or widower providing residence and furniture for children [1]

If any of my children are under [18]/[21] when I die then I give to my trustees free of [inheritance tax foreign death duties and][2] all sums of money charged or otherwise secured thereon at my death (which sums shall be paid out of my residuary estate) my freehold house known as [description] or other the house which I may own as my [principal] residence at the date of my death together with all my household furniture and household effects therein to hold such house furniture and effects and the assets from time to time representing the same ('the Fund') upon the following trusts and in accordance with the following provisions—

(a)   my trustees shall hold the Fund in trust for such of my children as [are under the age [18]/[21] at my death and][3] shall attain the age of 25 years if more than one in equal shares;

(b)   all of my children who have a vested or presumptive share under the foregoing trust shall be entitled to reside in the said house or any house representing the same free of charge and to use the said furniture and effects;[4]

(c)   my trustees may allow such other persons as they think fit to reside in the house free of charge with any of my children who are for the time being residing there;

(d)   my trustees shall keep the said house and the furniture and effects in good repair and insured comprehensively and to their full value and ensure that the rates and other outgoings are paid and the money required to discharge these obligations shall be found out of the income (or if that is insufficient then out of the capital) of the share or shares of my residuary estate in which the children who are residing in the house have for the time being a vested or contingent interest.

1   This clause contemplates a situation in which the testator's spouse is dead and in which he wishes to make express provision for his house to be used by his children while they are under 18 or 21. If the spouse is still alive the clause can be worded so as to take effect only if the spouse predeceases the testator, but it is not suitable for use in the event of the spouse surviving the testator.

The express right of occupation and the right of occupation under the TLATA 1996, s 12 (see para [208.5] et seq) mean that the beneficiaries will have interests in possession for inheritance tax purposes (see para [200.108] et seq). If the house is sold and the fund becomes one of investments, interests in possession in the more usual sense of being entitled to a share of the income (if any) will be attained at 18 (see the Note on maintenance in B18 at para [218.50]), this being a trust which carries the intermediate income: LPA 1925, s 175 (Part G, para [244.52]).

If full powers over residue are given to the trustees (eg as in Form C2.1 at para [224.20]), the trustees could allow the children to reside in the house. The main use of this clause will be where the trusts of residue are unsuitable for this purpose, the testator wishes to give priority to provision of a house, or there is a wide disparity in the ages of his children and it is desired to make this provision for younger children only (see n 3 infra).

The clause must, of course, be made consistent with the rest of the will. In particular, sub-cl (e) should be varied if necessary.

2   The words 'free of inheritance tax' will be unnecessary if the house is in the UK (see B14 at para [214.55] et seq).

3   Clearly if the ages of the testator's children are widely separated the eldest will attain an absolute interest well before the younger ones cease to need the house to live in. These parts in square brackets can be used to cut down the membership of the class of children interested under this clause, and so postpone absolute vesting, but of course they also have the effect of excluding the older children from participating in the capital.

4   The reason for this subclause is that without it interests in possession would probably only arise at 18 (see note 1), with the consequence that the children over 18 would apparently have a statutory right of occupation under the TLATA 1996, s 12 (see para [208.5] et seq) while those under 18 would not. This also means that those who are over 18 should not be able to argue that their statutory rights give them a right to occupy to the exclusion of those who are under 18 and do not have the statutory right to occupy. There might be difficulties about the interaction of the express and statutory rights of occupation, but it is submitted that this provision will give those under 18 interests in possession within the meaning of TLATA 1996, s 12.

Miscellaneous

[208.43]

FORM B8.7:   Gift with the object of ensuring personal residence, giving the right to a series of short leases[1]

I give my freehold residence situate at —— and known as —— to my trustees in fee simple upon trust that my trustees shall grant a lease thereof to my wife for a period not exceeding [three] years at a yearly rent of £[5] if she shall within one month from my death in writing request them so to do such lease to commence from my death and to contain an absolute covenant against assignment or underletting or parting with the possession thereof or any part thereof binding only on my said wife personally[2] and such other provisions as to my trustees shall seem reasonable including a proviso for re-entry on non-payment of rent or breach of any covenant or provision therein contained and to be renewable from time to time for like periods upon request in writing made by her to my trustees not less than one month before the expiration of each period unless any lease shall have been determined under such power of re-entry but without any fine being paid for such renewal and after the death of my wife or on her failing or becoming disentitled to request in manner aforesaid a grant or renewal of the said lease whichever shall first happen [and in the meantime subject to such lease and any renewal thereof under the aforesaid provisions] my trustees shall hold the said residence upon trust for [*name*] absolutely.

1   See the Preliminary Note at para **[208.4]**. This form makes the testator's wife a mere lessee for years at a rent. Now that new settled land See also Form B8.9 at para **[208.45]** and note thereto. The inheritance tax consequences of this form are obscure. The Inland Revenue would no doubt want to argue that the widow had an interest in possession in the property, but there are difficulties in such a view. The uncertainty makes this an inadvisable form to use in the present state of the law. It should be noted that if it does not create an interest in possession (so that there is no inheritance tax charge as a result of the death of the devisee) it will not be all fiscal gain, for the extent of the spouse's exemption on the testator's death will be much less. See also Part A, para **[200.99]**. It should also be noted that once the aggregate of the terms of the successive leases comes to exceed 21 years, the widow would be likely to become entitled to acquire the freehold under the LRA 1967 if the property is a house: see the LRA 1967, s 3(4). If the property is a flat she might similarly become entitled to a lease under the LRHUDA 1993, Pt I, Ch II: LRHUDA 1993, s 7(4).
2   *Seers v Hind* (1791) 1 Ves 294. Notwithstanding the covenant against assignment, the executors will be entitled to assign any part.

[208.44]

FORM B8.8:   The like—in the form of a lease determinable on death with rentcharge to support residence[1]

If within three months from my death my wife shall request my personal representatives so to do they shall grant to my wife a lease of my freehold residence [*description*] for the term of 90 years determinable after the death of my wife by one month's notice in writing at an annual rent of £1 [without impeachment of waste]. Such lease shall contain her absolute covenant against assignment underletting or parting with the possession of all or any part of the property so leased and such other covenants (if any) by her as lessee as my personal representatives shall in their uncontrolled discretion think fit and a proviso for re-entry on breach of any covenant and shall be made determinable at any time by my wife on three months' notice.

If my wife shall accept such lease she will be entitled to an annual rentcharge of £—— issuing out of and charged upon [*description of the property to be charged omitting therefrom the property comprised in the lease*] commencing as from the date of such lease and continuing so long only during her life as such lease shall remain subsisting and to be payable quarterly the first quarter's payment to be made at expiration of three months from the date of the commencement of said lease.[2]

[The said lease and rentcharge are given free of inheritance tax or contribution thereto [and as regards such rentcharge free of income tax at the basic rate but not at any higher rate] and the inheritance tax attributable to the said lease and rentcharge [and the said income tax] shall be exclusively charged on the property subject to such rentcharge [but as to income tax my wife shall account to my trustees for all tax repaid or otherwise allowed in account to her in respect of the tax on the said rentcharge]].[3]

1   This form undoubtedly creates a lease terminable on death within the ITA 1984, s 43(3) so that it is treated for inheritance tax purposes as a settlement. For the effect of this as compared with a true settlement see the Preliminary Note at para **[208.4]**.
2   See further the Preliminary Note to B11 at para **[211.1]** et seq and Form B11.6 at para **[211.13]**.
3   This paragraph shifts the inheritance tax liability from residue to the property subject to the rentcharge.

[208.45]

FORM B8.9:   Gift with the object of ensuring personal residence by the devisee—alternative form using a periodic tenancy

I give my freehold residence and land at —— and known as —— to my trustees in fee simple upon trust that my trustees shall if my wife so desire let the same to her on a yearly tenancy at a rent of £[1] per annum without power for her to assign sublet or part with the possession of the same premises or any part thereof except as a furnished house for a period or periods not exceeding —— months in any one year and upon the terms of my wife keeping the said premises in good and tenantable repair and insured against all damage by fire. Provided that so long as my wife [shall remain my widow and] shall duly observe and perform the conditions aforesaid a notice to determine such tenancy shall not be effectual unless signed by all my trustees for the time being but after the remarriage of my wife or any default on her part in observing and performing the conditions aforesaid such notice shall be effectual if signed by my trustees other than my wife.[1]

1   As with Form B8.7 (at para **[208.43]**) it is not clear whether this form creates a lease for a life for inheritance tax purposes; though we feel that the case for saying so is stronger here than in relation to Form B8.7. The remarks concerning inheritance tax in Form B8.7, n 1 at para **[208.43]** apply here also.
    In this case the wife could herself be made one of the trustees. By this means she cannot be given notice to quit against her will, whilst entitled to the tenancy.

[208.46]

FORM B8.10:   Gift of the testator's interest as tenant in common in a house, the gift being postponed to allow the other tenants in common to continue to reside in the house[1]

I give free of inheritance tax all my share as beneficial tenant in common in the freehold property known as [*description of property*] and all other (if any) my interest therein to my trustees to hold the same upon and subject to the following trusts and provisions—

    (a)   while any one or more of the following persons namely [*names of the other tenants in common*] remain alive and desire to reside in the property (and provided that the property is kept in good repair and insured comprehensively and to its full value with insurers approved by my trustees (their interest being noted on the policy) at no cost to my trustees and that my trustees are kept indemnified against all rates taxes and other outgoings in respect of the property) my trustees shall not make any objection to such residence and shall not disturb or restrict it in any way and shall not take any steps to enforce the trust for sale on which the property is held or to realise my share therein or to obtain any rents or profits from the property.

    (b)   subject as aforesaid my trustees shall hold the same as to both capital and income upon trust absolutely for [*name*].

---

1   Several people sometimes contribute to the purchase of a house as tenants in common, with the intention that all of them shall be allowed to live there for as long as they wish. Their rights in this respect may of course be defined in an agreement made between them at the time of purchase or at some later date. Failing this, however, it is necessary to include some suitable provision in their wills, and the clause which follows may be found appropriate for this purpose. From an inheritance tax point of view a provision of this kind is a 'settlement' (see the ITA 1984, s 43(2)(a)) under which the testator's co-tenants in common attain interests in possession: see *IRC v Lloyd's Private Banking Ltd* [1998] STC 559, High Court. This may not matter if their estates will be too small to attract inheritance tax charges on their deaths. Alternatively, if the co-owners are of commensurate age and hold in equal shares, an inter-vivos mutual agreement that there shall be no sale until they all die or cease to reside ought for each co-owner to be a restriction on dealing with his share incurred for full consideration, and which would minimise the incidence of inheritance tax. For trustees' powers in relation to undivided shares, see the TA 1925, s 24 (Part G, para **[246.20]**).

B9   Testamentary options

PRELIMINARY NOTE

[209.1]
Testamentary options generally. For an account of the general law relating to
testamentary options, see Vol 1, para **[92.1]** et seq. Testamentary options are a
peculiarity. The gift of an option to acquire property at its market value is not
really a gift at all and might be described as beneficial only in the sense that the
donee is given the opportunity of acquiring the property which he would not
otherwise have. An option might also be beneficial (and often is) in the sense
that it gives the donee the opportunity to acquire the property at an undervalue.
But the nature of a testamentary option itself is quite uncertain. The person
entitled to the option may not get the asset because the personal representatives
might have to sell it to pay debts or testamentary expenses (*Re Eve* [1956] Ch
479).

[209.2]
Validity of Testamentary options to purchase land. To be enforceable, an
option to purchase land must comply with the Law of Property (Miscellaneous
Provisions) Act 1989 (LP(MP)A 1989), s 2, which requires contracts for the sale
or other disposition of an interest in land to be made in writing signed by or on
behalf of each party to the contract. A Testamentary option to purchase land will
not, by its very nature, comply with that requirement. The donee could attest the
will but if he is a necessary witness the gift will be void: WA 1837, s 15 (Part G,
para **[244.12]**). However, a Testamentary option takes effect under the will and
not by way of contract, so the fact that it does not comply with the LP(MP)A
1989, s 2, would not seem to be fatal. Testamentary options are not really
options in the strict sense at all but fall somewhere between options and pre-

emption rights. It is advisable to ensure that a binding procedure for exercising the option is put in place by the will (see para **[209.5]**). Because of the decision in *Re Eve* [1956] Ch 479 it is also important to provide a relatively long period within which the personal representatives are required to set the option procedure in motion, so that they do not find that the will obliges them to sell property at a favourable price before ascertaining the debts and liabilities of the estate.

[209.3]
Inheritance tax and testamentary options. In estate duty days the grant of an option to purchase realty at an undervalue was treated as a gift of part of the interest in the property. Thus in the absence of a direction to the contrary in the will, the donee of the option was liable for the duty attributable to the excess value: *Re Lander, Lander v Lander* [1951] Ch 546. This was thought to have been the position for capital transfer tax until the Court of Session undermined that assumption with its decision in *Re Dougal* [1981] STC 514. The present position is that the inheritance tax attributable to *all* property in the UK (including realty) which on the death of a person vests in his personal representatives is prima facie a testamentary expense payable out of residue: see now the Inheritance Tax Act 1984 (ITA 1984), s 211 (Part G, para **[246.83]**); see also the Note at para **[214.55]** et seq for a general discussion of this topic. The tax attributable to any excess value conferred on the donee of the option is thus prima facie a testamentary expense whatever the nature of the property, provided that it is located in the UK. Foreign property, whether real or personal, prima facie bears its own tax (see para **[214.63]**) and where an option to buy foreign property at an undervalue is given but is not exonerated from inheritance tax the rule in *Re Lander* will apply.

[209.4]
Capital gains tax and testamentary options. On the transfer of an asset to a legatee, the personal representatives make neither gain nor loss for capital gains tax purposes and the legatee acquires the asset at the personal representatives' base value together with the expenses of effecting the transfer: TCGA 1992, ss 62(4) and 64(1). If the option permits the donee to acquire the asset at a favourable price he may well be regarded as a person taking under a testamentary disposition and would therefore be taken to have acquired the property at the value placed on it at the testator's death and the personal representatives will not make a gain. Some support for this view may be derived from *Re Lander, Lander v Lander* [1951] Ch 546 in which Roxburgh J held that the right to acquire property at a favourable value was a beneficial interest created by the will.

On the other hand, where the donee merely has the right to acquire the asset at market value the acquisition does not arise under the will but as a result of an independent transaction. The donee acquires the asset at its market value at the time the option is exercised, and the personal representatives dispose of it at that time and at that value. Any gain since the death it ought to be subject to capital gains tax: see Whiteman, *Capital Gains Tax* (4th edn), paras 28–45 and 28–46 and *Supplement*. This situation is not dissimilar to the case of a residuary beneficiary who makes a payment to the personal representatives in order to preserve a specific asset for his own use although he otherwise has no title to it: *Passant v Jackson* [1985] STC 133.

[209.5]
Drafting testamentary options. In drafting options the draftsman should bear the following points in mind:

(1) Although an option which does not specify a particular time for its exercise is valid, it is clearly desirable in the interests of a speedy and efficient administration for a time limit to be imposed. The Perpetuities and Accumulations Act 1964, s 9(2) (Part G, para **[246.67]**) imposes a maximum time limit of 21 years for options relating to land but a period of a month or so is all that will ordinarily be required. At the same time an option can be exercised only if the donee is aware of its existence. A time limit computed by reference to the death or the grant of probate may work unfairly if the donee is left in ignorance of his rights until too late. One method of reconciling the objectives of efficiency and fairness is to impose a primary duty on the trustees to give notice of the option to the donee and to compute the time for its exercise from the service of the notice. Forms B9.1 and B9.2 at paras **[209.6]** and **[209.7]** contain options in this form.

(2) Where options are granted to purchase property at a valuation rather than at a fixed price, it is essential to ensure that the gift contains adequate machinery for having the price determined. Thus, an option to purchase property at the value agreed with the district valuer for probate purposes will not be capable of operating in accordance with its terms if the district valuer declines to agree the value of the property, eg because the estate is exempt from inheritance tax: *Re Malpass, Lloyds Bank plc v Malpass* [1985] Ch 42 (where, however, Megarry V-C gave effect to the option by directing an inquiry as to the value of the property to which the district valuer could have been expected to agree for probate purposes). Care should also be taken to ensure that the testator owns the whole of the property concerned and, if not, that there is a proper mechanism for determining the value of his interest: *Dutton v Dutton* [2001] WTLR 553.

(3) Where an option is given to purchase property at a valuation, the testator may wish also to give the donee the right to resile from the option should the price be higher than expected by him. Subclause (e)(v) of Form B9.3 at para **[209.8]** can be used or adapted for this purpose.

(4) It is inadvisable to confer options to purchase foreign property, particularly immovable property and possibly also shares in a foreign company, without first taking the advice of a local lawyer. It may be preferable for the testator to execute a will in accordance with the local law disposing of such property: see generally the Preliminary Note to C14 at paras **[236.1]** et seq.

(5) Where an option is given to purchase business property and the property attracts an inheritance tax liability, eg because it qualifies only for 50 per cent relief or because there are 'excepted assets' which reduce the value to which the relief applies (as to which, see the Preliminary Note to B5 at para **[205.9]**) and the right to pay by instalments is available (see under

'Payment of inheritance tax by instalments' at paras **[205.17]–[205.20])** the right to pay by instalments will cease when a sale of the property pursuant to an exercise of the option takes place. This could cause particular difficulty where the option is to purchase at below market value as it is not clear that the option to pay by instalments will continue to be available in relation to that proportion of the market value which is effectively given to the option-holder.

(6)   Where an estate is partially exempt from inheritance tax, eg because part of it is given to the testator's spouse, it is not clear whether the gift by will of an option to purchase business or agricultural property qualifying for relief will constitute a specific gift of that property for the purposes of the ITA 1984, s 39A so as to attract all the relief attributable to the property. If it does not, the relief will be apportioned with a resultant reduction in the size of the exempt estate: see generally the Preliminary Note to C11 at para **[233.1]** et seq.

[209.6]

FORM B9.1:   Clause giving option to purchase land

I direct my trustees to offer my freehold property known as —— situate at —— in the county of —— to my son [*name*] for the purchase of the same by him at the price of £——[1] such offer to be made in writing within thirty-six[2] months of the date of my death or within twelve[2] months of the date of the grant of probate or administration to my estate (whichever shall be the longer period) and to be accepted in writing by my son within three months from the date on which such offer made by my trustees is received by my said son [but notwithstanding anything herein contained the option hereby conferred on my said son shall lapse and shall cease to be exercisable by him at the expiration of the period of thirty-nine months immediately following my death[3]].

And I declare that:

(i)   such option is personal to my son to be exercised by him during his lifetime and not by any person (not even his personal representative) after his death;

(ii)   the inheritance tax payable in respect of the said property on or by reason of my death or in the administration of my estate including any of the same payable by reason of the above price not being the full value of the said property shall be paid out of my residuary estate;[4]

(iii) if in their absolute and uncontrolled discretion they see fit to do so my trustees may accept from my said son a mortgage upon the said property for an amount not exceeding one-half of the above-stated option price upon such terms as to interest repayment and therein as my trustees think fit;

(iv)   upon my said son exercising the said option he shall be entitled to a conveyance of the fee simple of the said property free from incumbrances other than a mortgage to secure a part of the option price in accordance with the last foregoing provision my said son paying such costs as are paid by a purchaser for value. My said son shall not be entitled to any abstract of title but shall accept without investigation such title as my trustees have at the time of the exercise of the said option save that the property shall be vested in him free from incumbrances other than as aforesaid. The incumbrances other than as aforesaid (if any) upon the said property shall be discharged out of my residuary estate and all costs of such discharge shall also be borne by my residuary estate;[5]

(v)   upon any sale or other transaction by my trustees in respect of or relating to the said property any recital or statement in writing by my trustees that no offer as hereinbefore provided has been accepted by my said son shall in favour of a purchaser or other person dealing with my trustees for money or money's worth be conclusive evidence of the fact thus stated; and

(vi)   my trustees shall accumulate the income of the said property until the earlier to occur of the exercise of the said option or the expiry of the time for its exercise and hold such accumulations as part of my residuary estate.[6]

1   If the price is below the portion of a mortgage debt attributable to the property here in question, that fact does not show a contrary intention within the AEA 1925, s 35 (Part G, para **[246.47]**), ie an intention that the property shall be taken free from the charge: *Re Biss, Heasman v Biss* [1956] Ch 243, [1956] 1 All ER 89. The sale is expressly provided to be free from incumbrances in sub-cl (iv) of this form.

2   Long option periods are provided for because the personal representatives will not want to be compelled to sell before they know whether or not they need to sell the property on the open market in order to discharge liabilities so it is well to provide long periods within which the option should be exercised.

3   The words in square brackets if included, will enable the administration to be completed even though it proves impossible to trace the beneficiary.

4   If the stated price is not the full value of the property, there is a gift of the excess to the donee. Under estate duty law the donee would have been liable for the duty in respect of such excess: see *Re Lander, Lander v Lander* [1951] Ch 546. As mentioned in the Preliminary Note to this section (at para **[209.3]**) the inheritance tax position is now different as tax in respect of land in the UK is prima facie a testamentary expense payable out of residue: ITA 1984, s 211 (Part G, para **[246.83]**; see also para **[214.55]** et seq).

5   The donee would be entitled in any event to the property free from incumbrances created after the death of the testator: *Re Fison's Will Trusts, Fison v Fison* [1950] Ch 394. This clause entitles the donee to the property free from incumbrances created at any time other than a mortgage to secure part of the option price.

6   This provision is intended to prevent there being any interest in possession in the shares pending exercise of the option. It is thought that without such a provision it is possible to argue (though probably incorrectly) that before the option is exercised the shares are settled property and subject to an interest in possession if residue is subject to such an interest. If so, the interest in possession would terminate, with the usual inheritance tax consequences, when the option was exercised. The argument has more force where the option price is below the market value. If this subclause is included the ITA 1984, s 144 (see the Note in C3 at para **[225.83]** et seq) will apply when the option is exercised.

[209.7]

FORM B9.2:   Direction to trustees to offer farm and farming assets to the testator's sons successively at a valuation before selling under a trust[1]

I direct my trustees as soon as conveniently may be after my death to give in writing to my adult sons living at my death successively accordingly to seniority the option of purchasing my [freehold] farm and lands known as —— Farm and the live and dead stock farming machines implements and utensils therein or belonging thereto at a price to be determined by a valuer appointed by my trustees and I declare that each of my said adult sons shall have one month from the date of the giving of such respective options within which to give notice in writing to my trustees accepting the same and that my trustees shall not sell my said farm and effects unless and until all my said adult sons shall have neglected or refused to accept in writing such right of pre-emption within the time aforesaid but that no purchaser from my trustees shall be affected by the said right of pre-emption. [I declare that the right of pre-emption hereby granted is personal to my said sons and shall not be exercisable by their respective personal representatives.[2]]

1   For the inheritance tax implications of the grant of options over business or agricultural property see the Preliminary Note at para **[209.5]** and the Preliminary Note to C11 at para **[233.7]**.
2   The addition would avoid any suggestion that this option was exercisable after the decease of any such son, a contention which has often given rise to difficulty. See on this point *Skelton v Younghouse* [1942] AC 571, [1942] 1 All ER 650.

[209.8]

FORM B9.3:   **Devise of freehold property conditional upon the donee conferring a right of pre-emption on another person[1]**

(a)   Subject to the condition imposed by subclause (b) of this clause (if it arises under the provisions of that subclause) I give my freehold property known as, etc [and registered, etc] (in this clause called the property) absolutely to [*name*] of, etc [(hereinafter called the donee)] *or* if he predeceases me then to [*name*] of, etc (and such one of these two persons as becomes entitled (subject as aforesaid) to the property on my death is in this clause called the donee)].

(b)   If [*name*] of, etc (in this clause called the option holder) survives me then the gift made by subclause (a) of this clause shall be conditional upon the donee entering into an agreement with the option holder by deed signed by him or on behalf of each of them and embodying the terms set out in subclause (e) of this clause (the cost of its preparation and stamping to be paid out of my residuary estate) and if the donee refuses to accept this condition then the gift of the property to the donee shall not take effect and I give the same instead absolutely to the option holder [*or*, [*name*] of, etc] [*or*, it shall fall instead into my residuary estate].

(c)   My trustees shall within six months of my death give written notice to the donee of the contents of this clause and (unless in the meantime the donee has indicated his refusal to accept the condition imposed by subclause (b)) shall as soon as possible thereafter prepare an assent to vest the property in the donee and given written notice of its preparation to the donee informing him that they will deliver the assent or authorise its delivery duly executed to the donee or to the donee's agent if at the same time the donee will deliver to the option holder or to the option holder's agent the agreement referred to in subclause (b) of this clause duly executed by the donee and if the donee does not comply with the terms of such latter notice within two months of its receipt (he being given a reasonable opportunity to do so) then he shall be deemed to have refused to accept the condition imposed by subclause (b) of this clause.

(d)   My trustees shall accumulate the income of the said property until the earliest to occur of the donee's acceptance of the property on the foregoing terms the donee's rejection of the same (including any deemed refusal under the foregoing subclause) or the expiry of the period of two years less one day from my death and shall hold such accumulations on trust for the donee if he accepts the property as aforesaid and otherwise [upon trust for [the option holder] [*name of alternative donee*] [as an accretion to my residuary estate].[2]

(e)   The agreement referred to in subclause (b) of this clause shall embody the following terms:

(i)   That it shall remain binding and effective until the end of the period of 21 years from my death or until the death of the option holder (whichever shall happen first).

(ii)   That if the donee dies and the option holder within two months of the death gives written notice (in this clause called the option notice) to the donee's personal representatives of the option holder's desire to purchase the property then the terms set out in paragraphs (iv) and (v) of this subclause shall take effect.

(iii)   That if the donee desires to dispose (whether by sale letting gift or otherwise) in his lifetime of the property or any part of it he shall give written notice of such desire to the option holder and if the option holder within two months of the receipt of such notice gives written notice (in this clause called the option notice) to the donee of the option holder's desire to purchase the property then the terms set out in paragraphs (iv) and (v) of this subclause shall take effect.

(iv)   That if the option holder serves the option notice within the time prescribed by paragraphs (ii) or (iii) (as the case may be) of this clause then the option holder and the donee (or the donee's personal representatives) shall attempt to reach agreement on the value of the property in the open market and with vacant possession at the time of the service of the option notice and if such agreement has not been reached within one month from the service of the option notice then an independent surveyor shall be appointed to make a valuation binding on both parties and at their joint expense such appointment to be made by agreement between the parties or in default of agreement by the President for the time being of the Royal Institution of Chartered Surveyors to whom application may be made by either party.

(v)   That once such valuation has been agreed or made in the manner stated and communicated to both parties the option holder shall have one month in which to decide whether he wants to proceed with his intended purchase of the property at that valuation and if within that month he serves written notice on the donee (or his personal representatives) of his desire to proceed then he shall be entitled on paying the amount of the valuation to the donee (or his personal representatives) to a conveyance of the property free from all incumbrances (except for any exceptions reservations and restrictive or other covenants and conditions to which it is already subject at the date of my death) and the option holder shall not be entitled to any abstract of title but shall accept such title as the donee has (or his personal representatives have) to the property save that it shall be vested in him free from incumbrances (except as stated) that the title deeds shall be handed to him and that the donee (or his personal representatives) shall supply him with such other evidence required to perfect the title (if any) as he (or they) may be able to provide.

(vi) That if the option holder does not serve the option notice within the time prescribed by paragraphs (ii) or (iii) of this subclause or if having done so he does not serve written notice within the time prescribed by and under the provisions of paragraph (v) of his desire to proceed with the purchase then the donee (or his personal representatives) may deal with or dispose of the property free in all respects from the rights of the option holder and the option holder shall forthwith effect the cancellation of any entry which he may have made under the provisions of the Land Charges Act 1972 or the Land Registration Act 1925 (or any enactments amending or replacing them) in respect of his rights under the agreement.

(vii) That whilst the option holder has rights under the agreement the donee (or his personal representatives) shall keep the property in repair and insured comprehensively and to its full value (and with the option holder's interest noted on the policy) in some insurance office of repute and shall produce to the option holder on demand the insurance policy and the receipt for the last premium.

(viii) That the rights of the option holder under the agreement are personal to him and are not exercisable by his personal representatives.

(ix) That for the purposes of all the foregoing provisions time shall be of the essence of the contract.

1   Testators sometimes desire to make a gift of property to one donee but to ensure that if he wants to dispose of it he shall offer it first to some specified third party. The form which follows provides one method of carrying out such a desire. An advantage of requiring the donee to enter into an agreement with the third party lies in the fact that the third party can then register a class C (iv) land charge against the donee (or make an entry on the Register in the case of registered land) and thus safeguard his rights. The PAA 1964, s 9 (Part G, para [246.67]) provides that in the case of a disposition which consists in the conferring of an option to acquire for valuable consideration any interest in land, the perpetuity period shall be 21 years. It is assumed that the property will not be mortgaged on the testator's death: if it may be, special provision should be made (eg that any mortgage shall be discharged out of residue).

2   This is to prevent there being an interest in possession of the donee which terminates and gives rise to an inheritance tax charge if he refuses to accept the gift. If this subclause is included the ITA 1984, s 144 will apply: see further para [209.6], n 5 and the Note in C3 at para [225.83] et seq. As to length of option period, see para (1) of the Preliminary Note at para [209.5].

[209.9]

FORM B9.4:   Clause giving option to testator's wife to purchase retail business[1]

I grant to my wife the option of purchasing my retail business of —— carried on by me at [*address*] upon the following terms namely: my trustees shall either by themselves (and in such case in such manner as they shall in their absolute discretion think fit) or by an agent engaged by them for that purpose (and in such case at the cost of my residuary estate) fix the value of the said business as a going concern. If my wife shall desire to purchase the same she shall give to my trustees written notice of said intention within three months after they have been granted probate of this will and shall give such security for the payment of the sum so fixed as my trustees shall demand the sum so secured to be payable by weekly instalments of [£——] or such other instalments as my trustees may think fit without interest and either with or without a proviso that the unpaid amount for the time being shall become payable on default in the payment of any instalment or shall become payable if my wife shall sell the business or die before the price is fully paid provided that my trustees shall not be bound to enforce the payment of any instalment of purchase money if having regard to the circumstances my wife is in their opinion not in a position to pay the same. And I declare that for the purpose of this clause my business shall include all assets [including my interest in the premises on which the business is carried on] stock in trade book debts and goodwill [and moneys in the —— Bank standing to the credit of my [business] account] on the one hand and all liabilities in connection therewith on the other hand [but shall not include moneys at the bank] [nor shall it include the premises on which my said business is carried on].

1   The disposition of small businesses such as are carried on in retail shops requires very careful consideration in each individual case. The testator's wife may have taken a considerable part in the business and may frequently be capable of carrying it on. Indeed she may have become entitled to a beneficial interest in the business. In such circumstances the simplest course would be to give her the business outright. The testator may, however, wish to make provision for his children in which case a sale of the business to the wife provides a solution. Trustees cannot usually be advised to carry on the business themselves, even through the managership of the wife, as they may become personally liable for debts in the event of the failure of the business. The course suggested in this precedent is a sale to the wife on very easy terms, such as weekly payments made to a National Savings Bank account. If all goes well, the value of the business will gradually be restored for the benefit of the children, and there will be some salvage, even if the business ultimately comes to grief. Before the purchase price has been fully paid, the wife is entitled to the weekly profits which remain after the instalments have been paid to the trustees without any liability to account, and she therefore has every inducement to try and make a success of it. This clause is expressed in the simplest terms since it will obviously concern a small estate.

[209.10]

FORM B9.5:   Clause giving option to son to take lease or purchase freehold of business premises[1]

I direct my trustees if requested in writing so to do by my said son within six months after my death or within three months of the grant of probate or administration being taken to my estate (whichever shall be the longer period)[2] to grant to him a lease of the freehold premises on which my —— business is carried on at my death. And I further direct that such lease shall be for any term not exceeding [30] years from my death as my said son shall require and shall be at a yearly rent of £—— and shall contain all such covenants and conditions as my trustees shall think fit and such lease if and when granted shall be held by my said son as part of the assets of the said business. [And I authorise my said trustees if my said son shall be desirous of purchasing the said premises instead of taking a lease thereof and upon such a request in writing as aforesaid to sell the said freehold premises to my said son at the price of £—— or at such less price as some competent valuer to be nominated by my trustees other than my son shall determine to be the fair value thereof such determination to be conclusive and the basis or method of valuation not to be questioned and in the event of such sale being made I authorise my trustees to allow such part of the purchase money as my trustees other than my said son may think fit to remain on mortgage of the said freehold premises such mortgage to be upon such terms and to contain such provisions including a provision that the mortgage money shall not be called in for any fixed term as my trustees other than my said son may think fit.]

1279

1   This clause is intended for use in conjunction with a gift of the business itself. For a precedent for a gift of such a business see Form B5.1 at para **[205.58]**.
2   The grant of an option exercisable within a period measured by reference to the death only can cause difficulties if no grant is taken out within that time.

[209.11]

FORM B9.6:   Clause giving option to purchase shares in family company[1]

I direct my trustees as soon as conveniently may be after my death to give in writing to my son —— living at my death the option to purchase —— shares in the —— Company Limited at a price to be determined by an accountant to be agreed upon by my son and my trustees and in default of such agreement to be nominated by my trustees [*or other person*]. I declare that my son shall have one month from the date of the receipt of such notice[2] in which to exercise the same but no purchaser of the said shares shall be in any way affected by the terms of this clause.

1   For the inheritance implications of the grant of options to purchase business property, see the Preliminary Note to this section at para **[209.3]**. The company will be a private company and there will be some restriction on the transfer of shares which might interfere with the registration of transfers of shares to the sons. Restrictions which restrict the disposition by will are sometimes directed to the prevention of a substantial interest in the company becoming vested in a stranger.
2   It is assumed that the whereabouts of all the sons are known to the trustees. If not, the posting of such a notice addressed to his last known address should be made sufficient service of such a notice, and the period of one month should be made to run from the time of such posting. In such a case the period of one month may have to be lengthened if it is thought any son is in a part of the world difficult to reach by post. However, the only practical course in such a case is to make the period run from the date of posting.

[209.12]

FORM B9.7:   Clause giving option to purchase shares in private company (longer form)[1]

I direct my trustees to offer my shares in —— Limited (*if necessary limit the number and description of the shares*) to my son [*name*] for the purchase of the same by him at the price of £—— per share [*or at the current market value determined as provided below*] such offer to be made within twelve months of the date of my death or within six months of the grant of probate or administration to my estate (whichever shall be the longer period)[2] and to be accepted by my son within six months from the date on which such offer made by my trustees is received by my said son [but notwithstanding anything herein contained the option hereby conferred on my said son shall lapse and shall cease to be exercisable by him at the expiration of the period of two years immediately following my death[3]].
    And I declare that:

(i)   such option is personal to my son to be exercised by him during his lifetime and not by any person (not even his personal representatives) after his death;

[(ii) the inheritance tax payable in respect of the said shares on or by reason of my death including any payable by reason of the above price not being the full value of the said shares shall be paid out of my residuary estate;[4]]

(iii) if in their absolute and uncontrolled discretion they see fit to do so my trustees may accept from my said son a charge upon the said shares for an amount not exceeding one-half of the above-stated option price.

(iv) upon my said son exercising the said option he shall be entitled to a transfer of the said shares free from all liens and charges other than a charge to secure a part of the option price in accordance with the last foregoing provision my said son paying such costs and stamp duty as are paid by a purchaser for value. Any lien or charge other than as aforesaid (if any) upon the said shares shall be discharged out of my residuary estate and all costs of such discharge shall also be borne by my residuary estate;[5]

(v) upon any sale or other transaction by my trustees in respect of or relating to the said shares after the expiration of the above-mentioned period of two years a statement in writing by my trustees that no offer as hereinbefore provided has been accepted by my said son shall in favour of a purchaser or other person dealing with my trustees for money or money's worth be conclusive evidence of the fact thus stated;

[(vi) the current market value aforesaid shall be determined in accordance with subsection (3) of section 272 of the Taxation of Chargeable Gains Act 1992 (taking the day before the service of the notice exercising the said option as the 'relevant date' therein referred to) unless the said subsection does not apply in which case the said market value shall be determined as at the date of service of such notice by an accountant acting as expert and not as arbitrator to be agreed upon by my said son and my trustees or in default of agreement to be nominated upon the application of my said son or my trustees by the President of the Institute of Chartered Accountants in England and Wales the costs of such valuation to be borne equally by my said son and my estate;]

(vii) my trustees shall accumulate the income of the said shares until the earlier to occur of the exercise of the said option or the expiry of time for its exercise and hold such accumulations as part of my residuary estate.[6]

---

1 See para **[209.13]**, n 2.
2 See sub-para (1) of the Preliminary Note at para **[209.5]**.
3 See para **[209.6]**, n 2.
4 Where the option price is less than the full value of the shares there is a gift of the excess value to the donee, the inheritance tax in respect of which will prima facie come out of residue. In estate duty days where there was a beneficial option to purchase property which bore its own duty, the duty attributable to the excess value was payable by the donee: *Re Lander, Lander v Lander* [1951] Ch 546, [1951] 1 All ER 622.

Since real estate now bears its own tax, this principle will no longer apply save possibly in relation to foreign property: see Preliminary Note at para **[209.3]** and see generally the Note to B14 at para **[214.55]** et seq. The benefit of the option being exercisable at a price below the full value of the shares is not a specific gift. If the residue is insufficient to pay debts, etc, then the shares are the last property available for debts and as long as the other assets together with the purchase price of the shares are sufficient to meet the liabilities of the estate, then the purchase price and not the shares constitute part of the fund available for payment of debts, etc: *Re Eve, National Provincial Bank Ltd v Eve* [1956] Ch 479, [1956] 2 All ER 321.
5 The donee would be entitled in any event to the shares free from incumbrances created after the death of the testator: *Re Fison's Will Trusts, Fison v Fison* [1950] Ch 394, [1950] 1 All ER 501.

This clause entitles the donee to the property free from incumbrances created at any time other than a charge to secure part of the option price.

6   See para **[209.6]**, n 5.

B10 Pecuniary legacies

MINORS AND CHILDREN

FORMS

CONTINGENT AND CONDITIONAL LEGACIES

FORMS

LEGACIES TO EXECUTORS AND TRUSTEES

FORMS

LEGACIES FOR IMPROVIDENT PERSONS

FORMS

LEGACIES TO EMPLOYEES

FORMS

INHERITANCE TAX AND FOREIGN DEATH DUTIES

FORMS

NIL-RATE BAND LEGACIES

FORMS

MISCELLANEOUS

FORMS

PRELIMINARY NOTE

[210.1]
Legacies as gifts to relatives including minors. Legacies are generally a method of remembering the relatives and friends who are not included among the main beneficiaries of the estate, but they may in some cases be used for the purpose of increasing the benefit given to one of the principal beneficiaries. Particular types of legacy may require the insertion of special provisions. See, for example para **[210.33]**.

[210.2]
Legacies to debtors or creditors. A testator must be carefully questioned as to whether the intended beneficiaries either owe money to him, or, on the other hand, he owes money to them. The debts may have to be brought into account and the position in such cases should be made clear in the will.

[210.3]
Inheritance tax a testamentary expense payable out of residue. As stated in the note at para **[214.55]** et seq it is thought that the incidence of inheritance tax in respect of legacies is much the same as that of estate duty. But in one important aspect the law has changed. Under estate duty law it was settled that to the extent that a pecuniary legacy was payable out of realty (for which see below) it had to be considered as realty and bore the estate duty attributable to it: *Re Spencer Cooper, Poe v Spencer Cooper* [1908] 1 Ch 130; and *Re Owers* [1941] Ch 17. It was thought that inheritance tax payable in respect of real property was likewise prima facie payable out of the realty. But this assumption was not accepted in the context of Scottish Law by the Court of Session in *Re Dougal* [1981] STC 514. In the light of the uncertainties caused by that decision Parliament has intervened and the current position, now embodied in the Inheritance Tax Act 1984 (ITA 1984), s 211 (Part G, para **[246.83]**) is that tax on realty is prima facie a testamentary expense payable out of residue. The problems which used to arise in cases where legacies were changed on a mixed fund of realty and personalty are now largely a thing of the past. However, a rather similar problem remains where the fund includes foreign property. It is thought that in the absence of a direction to the contrary legacies charged on such a fund, unless they are given to charity, will be liable to contribute a rateable proportion of the tax attributable to the foreign property: see *Re Sebba, Lloyds Bank Ltd v Hutson* [1959] Ch 166 at 178 (declaration (3); not reported on this point in [1958] 3 All ER 393). A mixed fund of UK and foreign property is by no means an unlikely eventuality. It is therefore advisable to continue to include words expressly exonerating pecuniary legacies from inheritance tax, or to include a general declaration exonerating legacies from inheritance tax as in Forms B10.47 (at para **[210.68]**) and B14.33 (at para **[214.76]**).

[210.4]
Inheritance tax on legacies payable out of settled property. It is thought that legacies might also bear their own inheritance tax (in the absence of a direction to the contrary) to the extent that they are payable out of property which was settled property immediately before the testator's death, because the ITA 1984, s 211 does not treat the inheritance tax on such property as a testamentary expense (see s 211(1)(b): Part G, para **[246.83]**). This is a point which will not arise very often in modern conditions, but it could do so where legacies are payable out of residue, and residue includes formerly settled property over which the testator had a general power of appointment or the statutory power (under the Law of Property Act 1925 (LPA 1925), s 176: Part G, para **[244.53]**) to dispose of entailed property.

[210.5]
The funds from which legacies are payable. There is a considerable body of case law on this subject, much of which is superseded or has become of small practical importance, through changes in the customary patterns of disposition and changes in the law. The principal questions which have arisen are the following (references to realty and personalty below refer to realty and personalty which is not the subject of a specific gift):

(1) Whether the legacies are payable out of realty, or only out of personalty with the consequence that they abate if personalty is insufficient.
(2) Where the legacies are payable out of both realty and personalty, whether they are payable rateably out of both or only out of realty to the extent to which personalty is insufficient.
(3) Where there is an undisposed of share of residue, whether the legacies are payable out of it in priority over other shares of residue, or whether all shares of residue, disposed of or undisposed of, bear the legacies rateably.

Of these three questions, the third is the one which is most likely to arise in modern conditions, and the one which is affected by the 1925 property legislation, and it is discussed together with the similar problems which arise in relation to debts and administration expenses at para **[214.7]**. The law relevant to the first two questions was not altered by the 1925 property legislation (see *Re Thompson, Public Trustee v Husband* [1936] Ch 676, [1936] 2 All ER 141; *Re Rowe, Bennetts v Eddy* [1941] Ch 343; *Re Ridley, Nicholson v Nicholson* [1950] Ch 415, [1950] 2 All ER 1; and *Re Timson, Harper v Timson* [1953] 2 All ER 1252). The factors which have rendered the first two of the above questions less important than formerly are—

(a) it is now usual for a single combined residuary gift to be made of realty and personalty;
(b) it is very unusual to make separate gifts of residuary realty and residuary personalty; realty and personalty are, and have been since 1925, subject to a common set of intestacy rules; and
(c) the former rule that personalty was free of estate duty but realty bore its own duty (in the absence of express provision) has been altered in favour of both realty and personalty (situated in the UK) being free of inheritance tax in the absence of express provision (see para **[214.55]** et seq).

These are all factors which do not abolish the previous law on these topics, but which have the consequence either that the issues do not arise, or that where they could arise on the wording of the will, the determination of the issue does not matter because the outcome either way produces the same result for who gets what. On the other hand, in consequence of some of the changes to the law made by the TLATA 1996, it has become possible to abandon the former almost universal practice of imposing a trust for sale and conversion of the assets comprised in residue (see paras [214.5] and [214.6]). A check on the law concerning the burden of legacies is therefore called for, so as to make sure that this change in practice would not have unexpected consequences.

[210.6]
Liability of realty for legacies. Where the estate is wholly disposed of by will (for the effect of partial intestacy see paras [214.4] and [214.5]), in the absence of provision to the contrary, legacies are payable only out of personalty not specifically bequeathed: *Robertson v Broadbent* (1883) 8 App Cas 812; *Re Rowe, Bennetts v Eddy* [1941] Ch 343, [1941] 2 All ER 330; *Re Ridley, Nicholson v Nicholson* [1950] Ch 415. One very common form of contrary provision is where there is a gift of legacies followed by a residuary gift of real and personal estate, in which case either the real estate is liable for the payment of the legacies if personalty is insufficient (*Greville v Browne* (1859) 7 HL Cas 689; *Re Thompson, Public Trustee v Husband* [1936] Ch 676, [1936] 2 All ER 141), or, where the testator created by his will a mixed fund for such payment, realty and personalty are liable rateably to provide the legacies: *Roberts v Walker* (1830) 1 Russ & M 752; *Re Boards, Knight v Knight* [1895] 1 Ch 499. Where realty is liable for payment of legacies, and there is no difference in the destination of residuary realty and personalty, it will not usually matter whether realty is liable for them rateably with personalty or only after personalty is exhausted, but there could be exceptional circumstances where it would matter. One possible example is where there is a life interest in residue, the rule in *Howe v Earl of Dartmouth* (see para [214.35]) is not excluded, and there are wasting assets to which the rule applies which are comprised in the residuary personalty, with the consequence that the amount of income which is treated as capital is different according to whether the legacies are payable primarily out of personalty or rateably out of realty and personalty. Another possibility is where personalty includes assets situated outside the UK, the legacies are not expressed to be free of inheritance tax, and the circumstances are such that the legacies are liable to bear some inheritance tax so far as payable out of the foreign assets (see para [214.57]): in such a case the amount of inheritance tax borne by the legacies would be different according to whether the tax was borne rateably or by personalty before realty.

[210.7]
Liability of realty for legacies—what provision produces what result.

(1)   Gifts of legacies followed by a gift of all the testator's real estate and the residue of his personal estate (and without a trust for sale or any other relevant provisions) will usually mean that the legacies are payable only out of the personalty, and therefore abate if the personalty is insufficient to pay them all in full: *Re Rowe, Bennetts v Eddy* [1941] Ch 343, [1941]

2 All ER 330; *Re Wilson, Wilson v McKay* [1967] Ch 53; and *Re Ridley, Nicholson v Nicholson* [1950] Ch 415).

(2) Gifts of pecuniary legacies followed by a gift of the residue of both the testator's real and personal estate (and without a trust for sale or any other relevant provisions) will normally mean that the realty is available to pay legacies, but that the legacies will be payable primarily out of residuary personalty, and out of residuary realty only if the personalty is exhausted: *Re Thompson, Public Trustee v Husband* [1936] Ch 676, [1936] 2 All ER 141; *Re Anstead* [1943] Ch 161.

(3) However, a gift of residuary realty and personalty without a trust for sale can have the effect that legacies are payable rateably out of realty and personalty if an intention to create a mixed fund is shown: *Allan v Gott* (1872) 7 Ch App 439 (a number of factors showed this, including a power to sell realty and personalty as and when they thought fit), *Re Timson, Harper v Timson* [1953] 2 All ER 1252, [1953] 1 WLR 1361 (where the will gave the real estate and the residuary personal estate upon trust after payment thereout of debts, funeral and testamentary expenses, death and legacy duties to the daughter of the testatrix; by a codicil, the same property was given to trustees upon trust for sale; the codicil was in the events which happened ineffective, but it was held to show an intention to create a mixed fund and that the testatrix regarded her estate as a single indivisible entity and the pecuniary legacies were payable rateably out of the real and personal estate).

(4) A trust for sale and conversion of residuary realty and personalty together normally creates a mixed fund where the realty and personalty bear any legacies rateably: *Roberts v Walker* (1830) 1 Russ & M 752; *Tench v Cheese* (1855) 6 De GM & G 453; *Re Spencer Cooper, Poë v Spencer Cooper* [1908] 1 Ch 130.

(5) The above points are of course subject to any express direction as to how the legacies are to be paid. A direction to pay legacies out of particular property will often have the effect that they are not payable out of other assets of the estate if the particular property is insufficient: see *Halsbury's Laws of England*, vol 17(2) Reissue, paras 411 and 530. Where a testator gave three legacies and stated expressly that they were to be first second and third charges on his real estate, the legacies were payable in the first instance out of the proceeds of sale of his real estate and only so far as that proved insufficient out of personalty: *Re Pollock* [1964] VR 554.

(6) Where there is nothing in the will which varies the statutory rules in the AEA 1925 ss 33 and 34 and Sch 1, Pt II, and there is part of the estate which is not disposed by the will, the legacies are payable out of that part, including any realty comprised in it: see paras **[214.4]** and **[214.5]**.

[210.8]
Interest on legacies. The traditional fixed rates of interest on legacies (see Vol 1, para **[32.1]** et seq) may not be appropriate in times of very low or very high interest rates. Therefore, a testator may wish to direct that interest will be payable on legacies given by his will at a variable rate based on bank base rates (see Form B10.5 at para **[210.13]**). Where a legacy carries interest, that interest

is payable out of the income of the estate after payment of income tax. But the payment of interest to the legatee is gross, and the legatee will be liable to tax on that interest.

Absolute gifts

[210.9]

FORM B10.1:   Legacy to one individual

I.   GENERAL FORM

I give to [*name*] of etc the sum of £—— free of inheritance tax.[1]

II.   LEGACY PAYABLE AT FIXED TIME

I give to [*name*] of etc the sum of £—— free of inheritance tax[1] to be paid—— months[2] after my death.[3]

III.   LEGACY MAKING GIFTS TO CHARITY UP TO A NAMED AMOUNT

I give to the [*name of charity or similar body*] such a sum as will with the moneys I have already given to the said [*charity*] amount to £——.[4]

1   The inclusion of these words is still desirable; see the Preliminary Note at paras **[210.3]** and **[210.4]**.
     Where several legacies are given, all free of inheritance tax, it is a prudent course to give the legacies simply, and add immediately after the gift of them a direction that all the legacies are to be paid free of inheritance tax. This may save mistakes, as the words 'free of inheritance tax' might easily be omitted in reference to one among a number of legacies, and this might influence the construction of the will as to the incidence of inheritance tax: see *Re King, Barclays Bank v King* [1942] Ch 413, [1942] 2 All ER 182.
2   'Months' means 'calendar months' and it is unnecessary to insert the word 'calendar': LPA 1925, s 61 (Part G, **[246.40]**). See as to this section *Re Figgis, Roberts v Maclaren* [1969] 1 Ch 123, [1968] 1 All ER 999.
3   This will not make the legacy payable at the stated time if that time is within the executor's year: see Vol 1, para **[30.31]**, but interest on the legacy will run from the stated date. There is, however, nothing to prevent the executor paying the legacy at the stated time if he is satisfied that he has assets.
4   There is no cash limit on gifts for charitable purposes made on or within 12 months before death. A rule to this effect has been abolished and it is no longer important for inheritance tax purposes to impose a monetary limit or to provide that the legacy is to be free of inheritance tax. For the former law see *Re Dawson's Will Trusts, National Provincial Bank Ltd v National Council of the YMCA Inc* [1957] 1 All ER 177, [1957] 1 WLR 391, in which a clause in similar terms expressly free of tax was held to mean that the charity was to receive the clear sum without any deduction in respect of duty payable on the lifetime gift.

[210.10]

FORM B10.2:   Gift of a number of legacies[1]

I give to [*name*] the sum of £——.

I give to [*name*] the sum of £——.

I give to each of my trustees who shall prove my will and act in the trusts thereof the sum of £——.²
    All the above legacies are given free of inheritance tax.³

1   Where a number of legacies are given they are better set out in separate lines or paragraphs rather than in a schedule. For those who prefer a schedule, Form B10.3 (at para **[210.11]**) is included.
2   As to legacies to executors and trustees, see Form B10.35 at para **[210.49]**.
3   It is a wise precaution where all the legacies are to be free of inheritance tax to say so in an added sentence as here, for if the words are accidentally omitted in the case of one legacy then that legacy may not be free of tax; see *Re King, Barclays Bank Ltd v King* [1942] Ch 413, [1942] 2 All ER 182. See also paras **[210.3]** and **[210.9]**, n 1.

[210.11]

FORM B10.3:   **Legacies given by reference to a schedule¹**

I give to the several persons and institutions whose names are set forth in the first column of the schedule to this clause of my will the respective legacies set opposite to such names in the second column of the said schedule and I declare that all such legacies shall be paid free of inheritance tax and that the receipt of the treasurer or other proper officer for the time being of any institution named in the said schedule shall be a sufficient discharge for the legacy given to such institution.

THE SCHEDULE ABOVE REFERRED TO.

Name of Legatee.	Amount of Legacy.

1   See para **[210.9]**, nn 1 to 4. Notice that the schedule follows the clause giving the legacies and is not placed at the end of the will as is usual in the case of deeds. Care should be taken to see that the space in the schedule is either completely occupied by the names and amounts or else it is carefully ruled through so that there can be no question of further addition after the execution of the will.

[210.12]

FORM B10.4:   **Legacy to husband and wife or survivor**

I give to [*name*] and his wife [*name*] the sum of £—— in equal shares absolutely provided that if either of them shall predecease me I give to the survivor the whole of such legacy absolutely.

[210.13]

FORM B10.5:   **Direction as to payment of interest at a variable rate**

I hereby declare that interest shall be payable upon legacies given by this my will during the period between the first anniversary of the date of my death and the date of payment of such legacies and such interest shall be paid at the rate of —— per cent per annum above —— Bank's base rate from time to time during such period.

[210.14]

FORM B10.6:   Legacy uprated by reference to Index of Retail Prices[1]

I give to [*name*] free of inheritance tax a sum determined by dividing the sum of £—— by the index figure in the Index of Retail Prices for the month in which this my will is executed and (having made allowance for any re-basing of the Index which may have happened in the meantime) multiplying it by the index figure in that Index for the month in which my death occurs. For the purposes hereof the Index of Retail Prices shall mean the Index of Retail Prices published by HM Stationery Office or any official publication substituted therefor and in the event of any change after the date hereof in the reference base used to compile the said Index the figure taken to be that at which the said Index stands after such change shall be the figure at which the said Index would have stood if the reference base current at the date hereof had been retained.

1   The Index of Retail Prices is published monthly in the Department of Employment Gazette. The current index was introduced in 1956 and replaced earlier indexes to which it can be linked back (see Industrial Relations Handbook and a publication of the Stationery Office 'Method of Construction and Calculation of the Index of Retail Prices').

Provision for immediate needs

[210.15]
Date on which legacies payable. Where on the death of a spouse, more usually the husband, the income of the wife will practically cease for the reason that during marriage she was wholly dependent on him financially, it is advisable to provide for her immediate necessities until such time as the will can be proved and there are assets which can be made available to her, though now it must be remembered that a widow may be entitled to a pension or allowance under the Social Security Acts or under the pension scheme of the deceased husband's employers and most insurance companies have policies designed to meet this need. A pecuniary legacy given to her 'for her immediate necessities,' though a very usual provision, hardly fulfils this requirement, for such a legacy is not in strictness immediately payable. Payment could not even in the case of clearly solvent estates be required before the end of the executor's year and this is the case even where the will expressly provides for payment at some time within the year. Where, however, the legacy is to be paid immediately after the testator's death, it has been said that the legatee is entitled to immediate payment (see *Re Riddell, Public Trustee v Riddell* (1936), as reported in 155 LT 247; *Re Pollock, Pugsley v Pollock* [1943] Ch 338, [1943] 2 All ER 443), but the decision in these cases concerns the date from which interest is payable, so that it is clear that payment of the legacy was not in fact made until some time later. There appears to be a clear distinction between legacies 'immediately payable' and

those payable 'as soon as possible' after the testator's death. If it should happen that the assets are insufficient to pay all the legacies in full, such a legacy will (apart from some further provision) abate with other legacies (see Vol 1, paras **[31.1]–[31.5]**). This last difficulty may be overcome by giving the legacy express priority over all other legacies. The increase in the classes of possible claimants for family provision and the expansion of the court's jurisdiction made by the Inheritance (Provision for Family and Dependants) Act 1975 (Part G, paras **[247.2]** et seq), for which see Vol 1, para **[105.1]** et seq, make it more risky for personal representatives to make early distributions. They are only with certainty free from liability if they distribute at least six months after the date on which representation is first taken out, and without notice of any family provision claims (see s 20 of the I(PFD)A 1975). They would be wise to make a search for any proceedings which may have been issued within the time limit of six months after the date on which representation is first taken out, but which may not have been served (the period for service being four months after the date of issue).

[210.16]
Need for priority. These considerations make it essential that, if immediate necessities are to be met out of a legacy, the legacy must be made payable within a short time after the testator's death (this provision being inserted for what it is worth) but more particularly, it must be given priority over all other legacies, so that (in an ordinary case where no question of insolvency arises) it can be paid in full without any fear of questions of abatement arising. It is also important to make sure that the legacy does not bear any inheritance tax (see the note at para **[214.55]** et seq).

[210.17]
Alternative provision. The desire in general being to provide for the period immediately following the testator's death may be met in a much more practical way by the husband during his life opening a current account at a bank in the joint names of himself and his wife, and the mandate to the bank stating that cheques shall require the signature of only one of the persons in whose names the account stands. There will be no inheritance tax problem in view of the spouse exemption, and it will ensure that the wife will have funds available for her immediate day-to-day requirements which might not otherwise be available, for the property in such money passes to the wife by survivorship as a joint owner thereof and the will and the personal representative are not concerned in the matter at all: *Williams v Davies* (1864) 3 Sw & Tr 437; *Re Harrison, Day v Harrison* (1920) 90 LJ Ch 186; and see *Hirschhorn v Evans* [1938] 2 KB 801, [1938] 3 All ER 491.

[210.18]
Provision of funds for immediate payment of inheritance tax. Another immediate necessity is the obtaining of sufficient funds for the payment of the inheritance tax in order to obtain a grant of probate. Such funds are often supplied by a bank and the form of undertaking usually required is given below.

[210.19]

FORM B10.7:   Immediate legacy to wife or other person in charge of testator's household

I give to [my wife] *or* [my friend [*name*] *or as the case may be*] the sum of £—— [free of inheritance tax] to be paid to her immediately after my death in priority to all other bequests hereby or by any codicil hereto made such legacy to be a first charge upon my estate and to carry interest from the date of my death at the rate of [—— per cent per annum] *or* [—— per cent per annum above —— Bank's base rate from time to time between the date of my death and payment].[1]

1   The payment of interest from the testator's death is the law whenever the legacy is payable on death: *Re Pollock, Pugsley v Pollock* [1943] Ch 338, [1943] 2 All ER 443, but it is better stated in the will so that no question can arise, and the opportunity can be taken to fix a realistic rate of interest. A legacy for immediate needs has no priority over other legacies: *Re Schweder's Estate* [1891] 3 Ch 44, unless expressly provided, as here.

Deferred and prior legacies

[210.20]

FORM B10.8:   Legacy payable six months after the death of the survivor of testator and his wife

I give to each of my nephews and nieces [*names*] the sum of £—— free of all inheritance tax[1] to be paid within six months from the death of the survivor of myself and my said wife [and I direct that such legacies shall carry interest after but not before the expiration of the said period of six months].

1   It is a wise precaution where all the legacies are to be free of inheritance tax to say so in an added sentence as here, for if the words are accidentally omitted in the case of one legacy then that legacy may not be free of tax; see *Re King, Barclays Bank Ltd v King* [1942] Ch 413, [1942] 2 All ER 182. See also paras **[210.3]** and **[210.9]**, n 1.

[210.21]

FORM B10.9:   Legacy with priority

I give to [*name*] of etc the sum of £—— free of inheritance tax[1] to be paid in priority to all other legacies hereby or by any codicil hereto given.[2]

1   See paras **[210.3]** and **[210.9]**, n 1.
2   The effect of this provision is that the legacy will not abate with other legacies in the case of a deficiency of assets. Such a provision is not generally necessary except in the case of a legacy for immediate needs given to a wife: see paras **[210.16]** and **[210.17]**. A legacy does not take priority unless it is expressly given priority by the will: see *Re Schweder's Estate, Oppenheim v Schweder* [1891] 3 Ch 44, unless it was given in lieu of dower. A legacy to whomsoever given may be given such priority and the expression is not confined to gifts for immediate needs, though it would add to the difficulties of administration if such priority were given to a legacy payment of which was postponed for a long period.

[210.22]

FORM B10.10:   Declaration as to time of payment and priority of legacies

I give the following legacies which I declare shall be paid within [three] months of my death and in priority to all other legacies hereby or by any codicil hereto given [and shall be free of inheritance tax[1]] and shall carry interest from the day of my death at the rate of £—— per cent per annum that is to say [*specify the legacies intended to have priority*].

1   See paras **[210.3]** and **[210.9]**, n 1.

[210.23]

FORM B10.11:   Legacy payable on death of life tenant

I give to [*name*] of etc the sum of £—— and to [*name*] of etc the sum of £—— to be paid on the death of [*life tenant*] or if [*life tenant*] predeceases me to be paid on my death. And I direct that such legacies are to be paid free of all inheritance tax payable on my death or the death of the said [*life tenant*] and shall carry interest from the death of the said [*life tenant*] or if he predeceases me from the first anniversary of my death.[1]

1   Legacies of this nature are more commonly included at a later stage in the will. After a gift of immediate legacies and specific bequests, a trust for payment of debts immediate legacies and inheritance tax the income is given to the life tenant. Then follows a direction to hold the capital upon trust to pay these postponed legacies and further gifts of capital. There is, however, no objection to all the legacies being dealt with together. The postponed legacies will not be payable until the event happens upon which they are stated to be payable and they will carry interest only from the happening of that event. If the event happens in the lifetime of the testator, the legacies become immediate legacies and the better view seems to be that they then carry interest only from one year after the testator's death (as provided here): see *Re Palfreeman, Public Trustee v Palfreeman* [1914] 1 Ch 877, where certain earlier decisions were not followed. If the event happens after the death of the testator but within the executor's year, apparently interest runs from the happening of the event: *Re White, White v Shenton* (1909) 101 LT 780 (where the tenant for life died one month after the testator). It is desirable to exonerate the legacy expressly from inheritance tax on both deaths; see paras **[210.3]** and **[210.4]** and *Foster's Inheritance Tax*, K2.03.

[210.24]

FORM B10.12:   Power to trustees to postpone payment of legacies

I declare that the payment of the legacies hereinbefore given to [*names*] and to the trustees of the marriage settlement of my daughter [*name*] may if my trustees think fit be postponed for a period not exceeding [five] years from my death and shall until the same be paid carry interest at the rate of —— per cent per annum above —— Bank's base rate from time to time from the date of my death payable half-yearly [and in aid of my residuary personal estate I charge all my real estate with the payment of the said legacies and the interest thereon].[1]

1   Without such a power as this the trustees cannot ordinarily refuse to pay a legacy, if payment is demanded by a legatee of full age and there are assets available. See also paras **[210.34]**, n 1 and **[210.36]**, n 3. If any of the assets on which the legacies are charged or out of which they are payable are ones which ordinarily bear their own inheritance tax (see the Preliminary Note at

paras **[210.3]** and **[210.4]**), there should be included an express direction freeing the legacies from inheritance tax.

Legacies with substitutional provisions

[210.25]

FORM B10.13:   Legacy with a clause of substitution in the case of an individual legatee[1]

I give £—— free of inheritance tax[2] to AB but if the said AB be dead at the time of payment I give the said legacy to CD.

1   See Vol 1, paras **[30.30]** and **[30.31]** for the time of payment. A legacy of this nature does not lapse if AB, the original legatee dies in the lifetime of the testator but it is payable to CD in order to prevent a lapse; *Ive v King* (1852) 16 Beav 46, 54, and this is so whether AB the original legatee dies before the date of the will or after the date of the will and before the death of the testator or after the death of the testator and before the date of payment. In short it is immaterial when AB died so long as it is before the date of payment: *Ive v King* supra; *Ashling v Knowles* (1856) 3 Drew 593. See also Vol 1, para **[68.2]**.
2   See paras **[210.3]** and **[210.4]** and **[210.9]**, n 1.

[210.26]

FORM B10.14:   Legacy to nieces, and the children of deceased nieces

I give to each of the daughters living at my death [or born afterwards] of my brother [*name*] [except his daughter [*name*]] the sum of £—— free of inheritance tax[1] and if any daughter of my said brother [except the said [*name*]] shall have died in my lifetime leaving a child or children living at my death I give to such child or children the said sum of £—— free of inheritance tax[1] to be divided amongst them if more than one in equal shares.[2]

1   See paras **[210.3]**, **[210.4]** and **[210.9]**, n 1.
2   The benefit of the WA 1837, s 33, as substituted by the AJA 1982, s 19, is confined to children or issue of the testator: for the text of s 33, as substituted, see Part G, para **[244.34]**. For a discussion of the operation of the new s 33 see Vol 1, para **[47.14]**.

Legacies to debtors and creditors

[210.27]
Presumed satisfaction of debt. In the absence of a direction to pay debts, a legacy to a creditor of a sum equal to or greater than the debt is prima facie presumed to be in satisfaction of the debt: see *Re Rattenberr, Ray v Grant* [1906] 1 Ch 667. But the presumption may be rebutted on various grounds: see Vol 1, para **[44.14]**. The testator should, in order to avoid any question being raised, expressly direct whether the legacy is in satisfaction of the debt or not. A legacy to a creditor in satisfaction of his debt has no priority over other general legacies: see *Re Wedmore, Wedmore v Wedmore* [1907] 2 Ch 277, but it carries interest from the testator's death: see *Clark v Sewell* (1744) 3 Atk 96.

For forms relating to bequests and releases of debts, see Forms B4.38 to B4.44 at paras **[204.60]**–**[204.66]**.

[210.28]

FORM B10.15:   Legacy to a creditor[1]

I give to [*creditor*] free of inheritance tax[2] the sum of £—— and I declare that this legacy is not to be taken in satisfaction of the debt due by me to him but is additional thereto.

1   For the law relating to satisfaction of debts by legacies see Vol 1, para **[44.14]**.
2   The inclusion of these words is still desirable; see Preliminary Note at paras **[210.3]** and **[210.4]**. Where several legacies are given, all free of inheritance tax, it is a prudent course to give the legacies simply, and add immediately after the gift of them a direction that all the legacies are to be paid free of inheritance tax. This may save mistakes, as the words 'free of inheritance tax' might easily be omitted in reference to one among a number of legacies, and this might influence the construction of the will as to the incidence of inheritance tax: see *Re King, Barclays Bank v King* [1942] Ch 413, [1942] 2 All ER 182.

[210.29]

FORM B10.16:   Declaration as to legacies to creditors[1]

In so far as any of the legacies hereby given are given to persons to whom I am indebted, I declare that such legacies are given in addition to the payment of the debts owing to them and are not to be in satisfaction of such debts.

1   See para **[210.28]**, n 2.

[210.30]

FORM B10.17:   Legacy to debtor without forgiveness of debt[1]

I give to [*name*] free of inheritance tax[2] the sum of £—— and I declare (but without hereby releasing or forgoing the debt hereinafter mentioned) that this legacy shall be paid to him without requiring him to bring into account the debt of £—— now owing by him to me if the same shall remain undischarged at the time when this legacy is paid.

1   Where a legacy is given to a debtor of the testator, the personal representative has a right to set off the debt against the legacy and to pay to the legatee only such balance as may then remain (if any): see Vol 1, paras **[30.10]–[30.13]**. If this is not intended, the declaration above may be added. The result would be to leave the debt still recoverable provided it was not statute-barred. The above right of set-off extends to statue-barred debts. The alternative in brackets releases the debt and it will not then be recoverable at all. As to release of debts see Vol 1, para **[30.4]**.
2   See paras **[210.3]**, **[210.4]** and **[210.9]**, n 1.

[210.31]

FORM B10.18:   Legacy to debtor with forgiveness of debt

I give to [*name*] free of inheritance tax[1] the sum of £—— and I hereby forgive and release unto him free of inheritance tax[1] all principal sums owing by him to me at the date of my death on the security of any mortgages bills bonds or other securities or otherwise together with any arrears of interest thereon which shall be outstanding at the date of my death and I direct that all such mortgages bills bonds or other securities shall as soon as may be after my death be delivered by my trustees to the said [*name*] or cancelled and that for the purposes aforesaid my trustees shall at the cost of my estate execute and deliver to the said [*name*] all necessary receipts reconveyances or reassignments and if the said [*name*] shall predecease me his legal personal representatives shall be entitled to the benefit of this release and forgiveness as if the said [*name*] had died immediately after my death.

1   See paras **[210.3]**, **[210.4]** and **[210.9]**, n 1.

[210.32]

FORM B10.19:   Legacy to a son subject to deduction of sums owing[1]

I give to my son [*name*] the sum of £—— free of inheritance tax[2] subject to the deduction therefrom of any sums of principal and interest owing by him to me at my death [and in so far as the said sums may be secured but deducted as aforesaid I direct my personal representatives to hand over to my said son all documents and securities for the same and to execute [but only at the sole cost and expense of my said son] *or* [at the expense of my residuary estate] all proper releases surrenders or other necessary documents for the discharge of such security] and I declare that in the event of the sums owing exceeding the said sum of £—— that sum of £—— shall be deducted in full and the amount of the excess shall remain due and owing.

1   See para **[210.30]**, n 1. This form, though arranged for the case of a son which is the case most commonly occurring, may be used with proper adaptation in the case of any other person.
2   See paras **[210.3]**, **[210.4]** and **[210.9]**, n 1.

Minors and children

[210.33]

In the case of an absolute legacy to a minor, if the legacy is small and the minor nearing his or her majority, a testator may consider making provision in his will for the trustees to be fully discharged by a receipt given by the minor. However, it now seems that in contrast to the position in the past when trustees (in the absence of an express provision to the contrary) in order to get a sufficient discharge had to retain a minor's legacy until the minor was of full age (ie 18: FLRA 1969, s 1 (Part G, para **[246.74]**)) and able to give a good receipt, a person with parental responsibility for a minor can receive a legacy on the minor's behalf: see the ChA 1989, s 3(3) (Part G, para **[244.119]**), which came into force on 14 October 1991. A legacy which is contingent on the minor attaining full age must be retained until the attainment of that age or previous death. Where a legacy is contingent, express provision should be made as to intermediate income as a contingent legacy is not deemed to carry income under the LPA 1925, s 176 (Part G, para **[244.53]**).

[210.34]

FORM B10.20:   Legacy to minor[1]

I give to [*minor*] of etc the sum of £—— free of inheritance tax[2] and if at the time when such legacy would be paid the said [*minor*] shall not have attained the age of eighteen years then I declare as follows:

(i)   If the said [*minor*] shall at the time when the above legacy is paid have attained the age of sixteen years then the receipt of the said [*minor*] shall be a full and proper discharge to my trustees for the payment of the same.

(ii)   If the said [*minor*] shall at the time when the above legacy is paid not have attained the age of sixteen years then the receipt of his parent or guardian shall be a full and proper discharge to my trustees for the payment of the same.

1   This form enables the personal representatives to get a good receipt on payment to the minor after he or she has attained the age of sixteen. Otherwise it now seems that the person with parental responsibility for the minor can receive the legacy on the minor's behalf: See the ChA 1989, s 3(3) (Part G, para **[244.119]**) and para **[210.33]**. If, however, the person with parental responsibility will not accept the legacy (and the trustees do not pay it to the minor under an express power) then one of three courses is available to the trustees of the will: (i) they can retain the sum until the minor attains full age (now 18: FLRA 1969, s 1: Part G, para **[246.74]**); (ii) they can pay it into court under the TA 1925, s 63; (iii) the personal representatives can appoint trustees of the legacy under the AEA 1925, s 42 (Part G, para **[246.51]**). Trustees retaining such sums may invest them in some government stock redeemable at about the time the minor attains eighteen years. This would almost certainly ensure that the capital is intact.
2   See paras **[210.3]**, **[210.4]** and **[210.9]**, n 1.

[210.35]

FORM B10.21:   Small legacy to minor with provision for opening National Savings Bank account[1]

I give to [*minor*] of [*address*] the son of —— the sum of £—— free of inheritance tax[2] and I direct that my trustees may if in their absolute discretion they so decide open an account in the National Savings Bank in the name of the said [*minor*] and pay the said legacy and such interest (if any) as may be due thereon into such account. Thereupon my trustees may hand the National Savings Bank book relating to such account to the said [*minor*] and his acknowledgement of the receipt of the same shall be a full and proper discharge to my trustees in respect of the said legacy. If at the time when the said legacy falls to be paid there is an account in the said Bank in the name of the said [*minor*] it shall be sufficient if my trustees pay the legacy and interest into such account and such payment shall be a full discharge to my trustees in respect of the said legacy.

1   Where a minor is given a small legacy of the order of £50 or £100 it is a matter of inconvenience to the trustees to keep this sum until the minor attains eighteen years of age and the convenience of all parties is met by providing for the legacy to be paid into the National Savings Bank, see *Elliott v Elliott* (1885) 54 LJ Ch 1142. An alternative is by a similar clause to authorise the purchase of National Savings Certificates.
2   See paras **[210.3]**, **[210.4]** and **[210.9]**, n 1.

[210.36]

FORM B10.22:   Legacy to a minor who is married

I give to [*name*] the sum of £—— free of inheritance tax[1] and I declare that notwithstanding that the said [*name*] shall be under the age of eighteen years the same shall be paid to her or as she shall direct as soon as may be after my death and that her receipt shall be a sufficient discharge to my trustees for the same[2] [and this gift is additional to and not in [part] satisfaction of a sum I have covenanted to pay to the trustees of her marriage settlement dated ——].[3]

1   See paras **[210.3]**, **[210.4]** and **[210.9]**, n 1.
2   A minor who is married can give a receipt for income (LPA 1925, s 21: Part G, para **[246.39]**) but not for a capital sum. The form is drafted for a female minor but is equally applicable for a male minor. Payment may be made to the minor where the will so authorises: *Re Denekin, Peters v Tanchereau* (1895) 72 LT 220, but the trustee or personal representative has a discretion despite the direction to pay or to withhold payment until the infant attains the age of eighteen years. The same law applied to a legacy to a minor to be paid on marriage: *Re Somech, Westminster Bank Ltd v Phillips* [1957] Ch 165, [1956] 3 All ER 523. The will ought to add that the receipt of the minor shall be a sufficient discharge (*Re Somech*); and see *Re Robertson* (1908) 17 OLR 568.
     See also paras **[210.33]** and **[210.34]**, n 1. For a general receipt clause see Form B21.20 at para **[221.24]**.
3   It should be ascertained whether there is any sum of which the legacy could be in satisfaction (see Vol 1, para **[44.1]** et seq) and then if there is any such sum, it must be expressly stated whether the legacy is to be in satisfaction of that obligation or additional to it.

[210.37]

FORM B10.23:   Legacy to minor to be applied in maintenance[1]

I give to [*name*] the sum of £—— free of inheritance tax[2] and I declare that if the said [*name*] shall be under the age of eighteen years at my death my trustees may apply the same or any part thereof for the maintenance education advancement or benefit of the said [*name*] in such manner as they think proper or pay the same or any part thereof to the guardian for the time being of the said [*name*] without being responsible to see to the application thereof.

I direct that the said legacy shall carry interest at the rate of —— per cent per annum from the date of my death until the said sum shall be paid or invested and that section 31 of the Trustee Act 1925 shall apply to such interest and to the income of the said legacy when invested.

1   The statutory powers of maintenance and advancement (the TA 1925, s 31 being the statutory power of maintenance out of income, and trust to accumulate the surplus, relating to property held for a minor) are set out in Part G at para **[246.26]**. The power herein contained is wider than the statutory power of advancement. As to when a legacy to a minor carries interest from the death of the testator, see Vol 1, paras **[32.18]–[32.27]**, but, if it is intended that it should, it is better to avoid all question by saying so in express terms. A legacy to provide education carries interest from the testator's death: *Re Selby-Walker, Public Trustee v Selby-Walker* [1949] 2 All ER 178. We recommend, at any rate when such a legacy is of any size, that it carry income from the death of the testator, so that there is no argument that there is an occasion of inheritance tax charge at the point when the legacy begins to carry income with it. See also para **[210.46]**, n 1. It now means that a person with parental responsibility for the minor could call for the legacy on the minor's behalf, see para **[210.33]**. If a testator does not want this to

happen, the form below, which does not give the minor an absolute and indefeasible entitlement to the legacy prior to the age of eighteen, is to be preferred.

2 See paras **[210.3]**, **[210.4]** and **[210.9]**, n 1.

[210.38]

FORM B10.24: **Legacy to minor to provide an allowance for him**[1]

I give to my trustees the sum of £—— free of inheritance tax[2] to be invested in any manner they think fit with power to vary the investment of the same and to be held in trust for my son [*name*] and to be paid to him by way of allowance during his minority in such sums at such times or to be otherwise applied for his education or benefit in such manner as my trustees shall in the exercise of their absolute discretion determine and if all or any part of the said sum shall not be applied in the above manner during the minority of my said son [*name*] the said sum or so much thereof as shall not have been so applied shall be paid to my said son [*name*] on his attaining the age of eighteen years. If my said son [*name*] shall predecease me or having survived me die under the age of eighteen years the said sum or the unapplied part thereof shall fall into and form part of my residuary estate. I direct that the said legacy shall carry interest at the rate of —— per cent per annum from the date of my death until the said sum shall be paid or invested and that section 31 of the Trustee Act 1925 shall apply to such interest and the income of the said legacy when invested.

1 This form is in a sense alternative to the immediately preceding form but it is submitted that it meets the requirements of the testator more fully and is in a form more readily understood by him. The intended effect of this clause is that the son shall receive an annual allowance much in the same way as he would if the testator were alive. The son will not have any right to call for the capital until he is eighteen. If it is desired that he shall not receive the capital until he is of some greater age than eighteen, the gift over to residue must be adapted so that it operates on his death before attaining that later age, otherwise he would have a right to call for the capital at eighteen. The gift is not peculiar to the case of a son but is generally applicable to any minor either male or female.

   See para **[210.37]**, n 1 concerning inheritance tax, and the Note in B18 at paras **[218.41]**–**[218.76]** for the TA 1925, s 31 (set out in Part G at para **[246.26]**).

2 See paras **[210.3]**, **[210.4]** and **[210.9]**, n 1.

[210.39]

FORM B10.25: **Legacy of a capital sum for the education of children**[1]

I give to my trustees the sum of £—— free of inheritance tax[2] upon trust to invest the same on any investments hereby authorised with power to vary and transpose the same and to hold such investments and the income thereof upon the following trusts:

(a) Upon trust to apply the income thereof at the sole discretion of my trustees for the education of my children who shall be under the age of [thirty] years or any one or more of them to the exclusion of the other or others in such shares as my trustees shall in their absolute discretion deem proper.

(b) Upon trust in the event of the income of the said fund not proving sufficient for the purposes of the education of my said children to raise so much as in the absolute discretion of my trustees they shall deem necessary of the capital of the said fund and apply the same as aforesaid for the education of my said children.[3]

(c)   Until the expiration of twenty-one years from my death my trustees shall invest any surplus income from the fund in investments hereby authorised to be held as augmentations of the said fund and after the expiration of the said twenty-one years all surplus income shall be distributed as part of my residuary estate.

(d)   Without prejudice to their absolute discretion in the matter it is my desire that my trustees shall provide for the education of my said children at the following schools colleges or institutions ——.

(e)   In addition to providing for the education in schools colleges or institutions my trustees may provide out of the said fund for my said children such books of reference or of an educational nature and all such instruments and other things as may be reasonably required for purposes of such education and as my trustees in their absolute discretion think fit and in so far as my trustees in the exercise of such discretion think advisable and may apply the fund for securing any of the said children to become articled for the purpose of any profession or to be received as a pupil of any professional practitioner.

(f)   When all my children then surviving shall have attained the age of [thirty] years or all have died under that age the said fund or so much thereof as has not been expended in the execution of the foregoing trusts shall fall into and form part of my residuary estate.

1   This will be a trust without a 'qualifying interest in possession' for inheritance tax purposes (see the Note in B18 at paras **[218.8]–[218.18]**) without falling within the relieving provisions of the ITA 1984, s 71 (see Part A, para **[200.119]** et seq). It is also fairly restricted in the use to which it can be put.
2   See paras **[210.3]**, **[210.4]** and **[210.9]**, n 1.
3   Any capital so applied would be deemed to be income of the beneficiary concerned: see *Cunard's Trustees v IRC* [1946] 1 All ER 159.

[210.40]

FORM B10.26:   Legacy to grandchildren

I give the sum of £—— free of inheritance tax[1] to my trustees to invest the same in any manner they think fit with power to vary the investment of the same and to hold the same upon trust for such of my grandchildren as shall attain the age of [eighteen] [twenty-one] years or marry under that age if more than one in equal shares. For the avoidance of doubt I hereby declare that the class of my grandchildren shall not close on the attainment by any grandchild of the age of [eighteen] [twenty-one] years or marrying thereunder whether in my lifetime or after my death but shall include all my grandchildren whenever born.[2] The said sum shall carry interest at —— per cent per annum from the date of my death until the same shall be paid or invested and section 31 of the Trustee Act 1925 shall apply to such interest and the income of the said legacy when invested.

1   See paras **[210.3]**, **[210.4]** and **[210.9]**, n 1.
2   As to closing of classes under the rules of convenience, see Vol 1, paras **[65.1]–[66.23]**. Prima facie illegitimate grandchildren will be eligible: see generally Vol 1, para **[72.6]**. For the TA

1925, s 31 (Part G, para **[246.26]**) see B18 at paras **[218.41]**–**[218.76]** and Part A at para **[200.119]** et seq for inheritance tax and trusts of this type.

[210.41]

FORM B10.27:   Legacy to an adopted child[1]

I give to my adopted daughter [*or* son] [*name*] the sum of £—— free of inheritance tax[2] [*if the adopted child is still under age add provision for discharge of trustees as in* Form B10.20 *at para* **[210.34]**].

1   As to adopted children see Vol 1, para **[75.1]** et seq.
2   See paras **[210.3]**, **[210.4]** and **[210.9]**, n 1.

[210.42]

FORM B10.28:   Legacy to children and an illegitimate child[1]

I give to each of my children (including my child [*name*]) the sum of £—— free of inheritance tax.[2]

1   The expressions 'child', 'son', 'issue' and the like now prima facie include illegitimate children, sons or issue: FLRA 1987, ss 1 and 19(1) (Part G, paras **[245.70]** and **[245.72]**) and see generally Vol 1, para **[72.14]**. But it is wiser to be explicit, especially in the case of a father if there could be any doubt as to paternity.
2   See paras **[210.3]**, **[210.4]** and **[210.9]**, n 1.

[210.43]

FORM B10.29:   Legacy to illegitimate children of the testator, including one en ventre sa mère[1]

I give to each of the children whom I have or am reputed to have by [*name of mother*] (including the child of which she is now enceinte) the sum of £—— free of inheritance tax.[2]

1   See para **[210.42]**, n 1.
2   See paras **[210.3]**, **[210.4]** and **[210.9]**, n 1.

[210.44]

FORM B10.30:   Legacy to legitimate and illegitimate children of a brother of the testator

I give [to each of the children of my brother [*name*] and to each of his reputed children [*name*] and [*name*] now of the respective ages of —— and —— years] *or* [to each of the children of my brother [*name*] namely [*insert names*][1]] the sum of £—— free of inheritance tax.[2]

1   See para **[210.42]**, n 1.
2   See paras **[210.3]**, **[210.4]** and **[210.9]**, n 1.

[210.45]

FORM B10.31:   **Legacy to married daughters to become subject to the trusts of their respective marriage settlements, the amount of the legacies varying in order to equalise the provisions made by the testator for all his daughters**

I give to or for the benefit of each of my married daughters free of inheritance tax[1] [such a sum as with any sum paid by me to them or for their benefit in my lifetime or covenanted to be so paid on their respective marriages will make up] the clear sum of £—— and I declare that such respective legacies shall not be paid to my said respective daughters personally but shall (whether or not all or any of such daughters shall die in my lifetime) be paid clear of all deductions to the trustees or trustee for the time being of the respective marriage settlements of my said daughters and shall be held by them or him respectively upon the trusts and with and subject to the powers and provisions therein respectively declared and contained of and concerning the trust funds and property thereby settled by or for the benefit of my said daughters respectively and as an accretion to such respective trust funds.[2]

1   See paras **[210.3]**, **[210.4]** and **[210.9]**, n 1.
2   It should be ascertained whether the marriage settlements contain an ultimate trust for the testator or for the daughter, and generally what the provisions may be and what exercises of powers there have been. Questions may arise as to whether this bequest may not in the circumstances give the testator (ie his residuary estate) an interest on default of issue of the daughters (*Re Powell, Bodvel-Roberts v Poole* [1918] 1 Ch 407; or the principle of *Lassence v Tierney* (1849) 1 Mac & G 551, may apply; *Re Currie's Settlement, Re Rooper, Rooper v Williams* [1910] 1 Ch 329; *Re Burtons Settlement Trusts, Public Trustee v Montefiore* [1955] Ch 348, [1955] 1 All ER 433; compare also *Re Beaumont, Bradshaw v Parker* [1913] 1 Ch 325); see also Vol 1, para **[82.1]**; and the cases there cited. It is often better not to add property to existing settlements: see Part A, para **[200.21]** and the Preliminary Note at paras **[218.11]–[218.14]**.

Contingent and conditional legacies

[210.46]

FORM B10.32:   **Legacy contingent on attaining eighteen or twenty-one[1]**

I give the sum of £—— free of inheritance tax[1] to [*name*] if he shall attain the age of [eighteen] [twenty-one] years [or marry under that age and in the latter event his or her receipt shall be a sufficient discharge to my trustees[2]] [and I direct that such sum shall carry interest at the rate of —— per cent per annum from my death until the said [*name*] attains the said age of [eighteen] [twenty-one] years [or marries under that age]].

1   Normally a contingent pecuniary legacy does not carry interest and the LPA 1925, s 175 (Part G, para **[244.52]**) which enacts that certain contingent testamentary gifts shall carry the intermediate income, does not apply to pecuniary legacies (*Re Raine, Tyerman v Stansfield* [1929] 1 Ch 716). A contingent legacy given by the parent of, or a person *in loco parentis* to, the legatee carries interest for the purpose of maintenance (see the TA 1925, s 31(3): Part G, para **[246.26]**). The rate of interest is fixed in s 31(3) at five per cent per annum, but this is 'subject to any rules of court to the contrary'. CPR Sch 1 – RSC Ord 44, r 10 fixes the rate of

interest on legacies in accounts taken under judgment at six per cent. This provision is limited to accounts taken under judgment, and although it is widely thought that this is the rate governing interest on legacies generally (see Vol 1, para [**32.4**], n 1), it is submitted that this is not a rule of court to the contrary in the context of s 31(3), except where an account is directed by judgment, in which case the particular legacy will carry interest at the rate of six per cent rather than five per cent. A direction to set a legacy apart will usually cause it to carry interest or income (*Re Woodin, Woodin v Glass* [1895] 2 Ch 309); see also para [**218.57**]. This result can be effected by making the legacy a trust legacy as in the next precedent. See generally Vol 1, para [**32.1**] et seq. In the case of legacies of any size, we feel that there may be inheritance tax disadvantages if they do not convey the intermediate income from death. The fund out of which they are to be paid will be settled property for inheritance tax purposes (see the ITA 1984, s 43(2)), at any rate in the case of contingent legacies (the position as regards vested ones is less clear). If they do not carry the intermediate income there will apparently be no interest in possession in favour of the legatees, or a trust within the ITA 1984, s 71 under which there are 'beneficiaries', before they become entitled to be paid their legacies. There could thus possibly be a charge to inheritance tax on their becoming so entitled. This form accordingly provides for the legacy to bear interest until it vests.

2   The provision for vesting on marriage under the specified age contingency is often restricted to female legatees, but in this form male and female beneficiaries are treated on an equal basis in this respect as is done in the AEA 1925, s 47 (Part G, para [**244.61**]).

[210.47]

FORM B10.33:   Legacy contingent on attaining eighteen or twenty-one carrying interest[1]

I give to my trustees the sum of £—— free of inheritance tax[2] upon trust to invest the same in any investments authorised by law for the investment of trust moneys with power from time to time to vary such investments and to hold the said sum and the investments representing the same and the income therefrom in trust for [*minor*] if he shall attain the age of [eighteen] [twenty-one] years but if the said [minor] shall die under that age [*gift over or direction that the sum and the investments and any accumulations of income shall fall into residue*].

1   The direction to set apart the sum given will cause the legacy to carry interest and the provisions of the TA 1925, s 31 (Part G, para [**246.26**]), will apply to it: see *Re Raine, Tyerman v Stansfield* [1929] 1 Ch 716. When a legacy is payable at a certain age, but is, in terms, contingent, the legacy becomes vested when there is a direction to pay the interest in the meantime to the person to whom the legacy is given; and not less so when there is superadded a direction that the trustees shall pay the whole or such part of the interest as they shall think fit: *Re Parker, Barker v Barker* (1880) 16 Ch D 44, at 45, 46, approved in *Re Williams, Williams v Williams* [1907] 1 Ch 180 at 183. The effect, therefore, of an express gift of the income would be to make the legacy vest at the testator's death, with a result very different from that intended by the above clause.
     See generally Vol 1, para [**32.1**] et seq.
2   See paras [**210.3**], [**210.4**] and [**210.9**], n 1.

[210.48]

FORM B10.34:   Legacies to two persons contingently on their attaining eighteen or twenty-one years of age with survivorship

I give to each of [*name*] and [*name*] the sum of £—— free of inheritance tax[1] contingently on his attaining the age of [eighteen] [twenty-one] years and direct that interest thereon at the rate of —— per cent per annum shall be paid from my death until the said [*name*] and [*name*] respectively attain the said age and in the event of either of them dying under the said age the legacy hereby given to him with all interest thereon shall be paid to the survivor of them on his attaining the said age and in the event of both of them dying under the said age both the above legacies and all interest thereon shall fall into and form part of my residuary estate. Section 31 of the Trustee Act 1925 shall apply to the said interest.

1   See paras **[210.3]**, **[210.4]** and **[210.9]**, n 1.

[210.49]

FORM B10.35:   Legacy contingent on attaining twenty-five or marrying, relying on the statutory powers of maintenance

I give to [*name*] if he [she] shall attain the age of twenty-five years [or marry under that age] the sum of £—— free of inheritance tax[1] with interest thereon from my death at the rate of £—— per cent per annum until the same be set apart or invested. And I declare that if the said [*name*] shall die under the age of twenty-five years [and a spinster] the said legacy and all unapplied accumulations of the income thereof and the investments then representing the said legacy and the said accumulations shall fall into and form part of my residuary estate.[2]

1   See paras **[210.3]**, **[210.4]** and **[210.9]**, n 1.
2   The statutory power of maintenance will apply. After the age of eighteen the legatee will be entitled to payment of the full income both of the legacy and of the past accumulations of income (the TA 1925, s 31, as amended: Part G, para **[246.26]**; see also B18 at paras **[218.41]**–**[218.77]**).
      Where there is no gift over, a gift at twenty-five with a trust or direction to apply income for maintenance is a vested and not a contingent gift (*Re Gossling, Gossling v Elcock* [1903] 1 Ch 448), even if the direction is to apply such part only of the income as the trustees think fit (*Fox v Fox* (1875) LR 19 Eq 286; *Re Parker, Barker v Barker* (1880) 16 Ch D 44; *Re Ussher, Foster v Ussher* [1922] 2 Ch 321).
      In a gift to A when he shall attain the age (or at the age) of twenty-five, the attainment of that age may be a part of the description of the legatee, so that the gift is contingent on his attaining the age: *Re Francis, Francis v Francis* [1905] 2 Ch 295; *Re Astor, Astor v Astor* [1922] 1 Ch 364; see also Vol 1, para **[93.6]**. If the gift is a pecuniary legacy it only carries interest if directed to be set apart as in this precedent.

[210.50]

FORM B10.36:   Legacy subject to discharge of guarantee[1]

If the guarantee dated —— and entered into by me to secure the banking account of —— Co, Ltd at —— Bank (—— Branch) shall when the legacy hereby given becomes payable have been fully discharged otherwise than by payment by me in my lifetime or by my trustees [personal representatives] after my death then I give my husband a legacy of £—— free of inheritance tax. If the said guarantee shall not have been so fully discharged then I give my husband free of inheritance tax such sum (if any) as shall remain after deduction from the said sum of £—— of the amount or amounts paid by me or by my trustees [personal representatives] in discharge of the said guarantee.

1   The position here intended to be provided for is that the wife has guaranteed the banking account of a one-man company, of which the husband is the principal director. She wishes to give her husband a legacy provided she or her estate is not called upon to meet the liability under the guarantee. It is assumed that the guarantee is a limited one and that the legacy is of about the same amount as the total liability thereunder. Provision is made for a corresponding part of the legacy to be received if the wife or her estate have only to meet part of the total sum guaranteed.

Legacies to executors and trustees

[210.51]
Remuneration by way of lump sum and annuity. The duties of executors become more exacting with the increase of the number of statutory enactments affecting the proper administration of a testator's estate and in the case of a lay executor some recompense for the time and trouble spent in such matters should be given. At the same time it must be remembered that the duties of a trustee, though not inconsiderable, are much less arduous and generally capable of being spread over a much greater space of time and, therefore, not as likely to interfere with the personal affairs of the person appointed. It follows, therefore, that the executorship should attract higher remuneration than that of the trustee. The common practice is to grant a lump sum to a person who proves the will and accepts the trusts thereof. A more equitable practice is to give a lump sum to persons acting as executors and a small annuity to persons acting in the trusts thereof. It would not seem equitable to restrict such annuity to the first trustees, but, if later trustees are to receive payment, that should be expressly stated in the will, for a lay trustee can not receive any payment not provided for in the will; although a corporate trustee or a trustee acting in a professional capacity now can: TrA 2000, s 29 (Part G, para **[246.144]**). Note, however, that a trust corporation or a trustee who acts in a professional capacity will be entitled to receive 'reasonable remuneration' (TrA 2000, s 29(1) and (2)) but the provision of an annuity by the will denies that entitlement (TrA 2000, s 29(5)) and so may result in professional trustees refusing to take up the trusteeship. Remuneration to trustees in this way can only be given where the estate is a substantial one, and the annuity should bear a reasonable relation to the amount of the estate. A legacy given to an executor or trustee is presumed to be annexed to the office, and is forfeited if he does not prove or act in the trusts (*Re Appleton, Barber v Tebbit* (1885) 29 Ch D 893). The presumption may, however, be rebutted; the will should, therefore, contain an express statement whether the legacy is given conditionally on the legatee proving or acting in the execution of the trusts of the will, or otherwise. A legacy to an executor 'for his trouble' had, under the old law (prior to 1 February 2001 and the commencement of the TrA 2000), no priority over other legacies (*Duncan v Watt* (1852) 16 Beav 204) but the situation in respect of remuneration of professional and corporate trustees is now different: TrA 2000, s 28(4)(b) (Part G, para **[246.143]**).

[210.52]

FORM B10.37:   **Legacies to executors**

I give to each of my trustees[1] [*names*] free of inheritance tax[2] the sum of £——
if he shall prove my will and act in the administration thereof.[3]

1   It is assumed that the same persons are appointed executors and trustees and are stated to be
     referred to as 'my trustees'.
2   See paras **[210.3]**, **[210.4]** and **[210.9]**, n 1.
3   As to what amounts to acting in the administration of a will, see *Re Sharman's Will Trusts,
     Public Trustee v Sharman* [1942] Ch 311, [1942] 2 All ER 74 (where the legacy was £1,000
     and the trustee though he apparently continued to act for some years did little in the trusts) and
     see also *Re Parry, Dalton v Corke* [1969] 2 All ER 512, [1969] 1 WLR 614; see generally
     Vol 1, paras **[30.14]**–**[30.18]**.

[210.53]

FORM B10.38:   **Legacies to executors and annuities to trustees**

I give to each of my trustees[1] [*names*] free of inheritance tax[2] the sum of £——
if he shall prove my will and act as executor thereof.[3]

I give to each of the trustees for the time being of this my will[4] an annuity of
£—— per annum to be paid in equal quarterly payments and to be clear of all
deductions including income tax deductible at the source.

Such annuities shall in the case of the first trustees commence from the
expiration of one year from the date of my death and in other cases from the date
of the appointment of the trustee and continue as long as the trustee acts in the
trusts of my will.

The first payment to each trustee shall be made three months after the
commencement of the annuity and the payments shall accrue from day to day
and be apportionable in respect of any broken period.

Provided always that a trustee who acts in a professional capacity or is a trust
corporation shall be entitled to reasonable remuneration as defined by section
29(3) of the Trustee Act 2000 in place of the annuity hereinbefore provided for.[5]

1   See para **[210.52]**, n 1.
2   See paras **[210.3]**, **[210.4]** and **[210.9]**, n 1.
3   This sum is intended to be earned by merely proving the will, clearing the estate and executing
     any necessary assents.
4   Though this seems a very reasonable provision, a provision in these terms is seldom made. To
     the extent that the annuity represents reasonable remuneration its termination by the death of the
     trustee or otherwise is not an occasion of an inheritance tax charge: ITA 1984, s 90.
5   The purpose of this proviso is to ensure that corporate and professional trustees are entitled to
     their statutory reasonable remuneration without being limited to the annuity (which may be
     inadequate): TrA 2000, s 29 (Part G, para **[246.144]**).

Legacies for improvident persons

[210.54]
Settled legacies for children. The method of providing for children by means of
a settled legacy is not now as common as in the past but it is still an appropriate
course where the beneficiary is improvident or easily influenced, though, of

course, a share of residue can be settled in similar terms. Form 7 of the Statutory Will Forms 1925 (at para **[238.13]**) provides a means of greatly shortening the lengthy clause formerly necessary, but there is always the difficulty that trustees may not have a ready access to the form or know where to find it. For settled legacies see Forms B16.25 and B16.26 (at paras **[216.30]** and **[216.31]**) and C3.4 (at para **[225.57]** et seq).

[210.55]

FORM B10.39:   **Legacy with provision for forfeiture on alienation**[1]

I give to [*name*] a legacy of £—— free of inheritance tax[2] but if (whether before or after my death) any act or event shall have happened whereby the whole or any part of such legacy would but for this provision have before such legacy becomes payable at the expiration of one year from the date of my death become payable to or charged in favour of some person[3] other than the said [*name*] then the right of the said [*name*] to receive such legacy shall absolutely cease and determine and the same shall be held by my trustees as part of my residuary estate and subject to the trusts thereof.

1   The main object of this clause is to prevent a legacy becoming payable to the legatee's trustee in bankruptcy. It can be adapted to all legacies by commencing: 'Provided that in the case of every legacy hereby or by any codicil hereto given if whether before or after——.'
2   See paras **[210.3]**, **[210.4]** and **[210.9]**, n 1.
3   'Person' will include the plural 'persons' and also a corporation: LPA 1925, s 61 (Part G, para **[246.40]**).

[210.56]

FORM B10.40:   **Legacy to improvident person payable by instalments**[1]

I give to my trustees the sum of £—— free of inheritance tax payable on my death[2] as to the income thereof upon protective trusts for the benefit of [*A*] the wife of [*B*] during her life and my trustees shall until the failure or determination of the trust of income in favour of the said [*A*] have the further power at their absolute discretion and without being liable in any way for the exercise of such discretion to raise and pay to the said [*A*] for her absolute use and benefit at any time or times as my trustees shall determine any sum or sums not exceeding on any one occasion £—— clear of expenses out of the capital of the said sum of £—— and my trustees shall hold any part of the said sum of £—— not so transferred to the said [*A*] during her life as the said [*A*] shall by will or codicil appoint and in default of and subject to any such appointment [*gift over in default*] and I direct that my trustees shall on no account be liable or responsible for making any such payment whether of income or capital to the said [*A*] after the failure or determination of her said determinable life interest unless or until they shall have received express notice of the act or event causing such failure or determination.

1   The provisions of this clause make it possible for the capital of the legacy to be received by the legatee in instalments as required by her needs and are a safeguard against influence by her husband or others and generally against her own discretion. The clause can be used for any legatee who it is feared may squander the legacy. Obviously it will be required only where the income is insufficient for the support of the legatee. It must be remembered that the legatee can

combine with the person or persons entitled to the gift over and call upon the trustees to pay over the whole capital sum to them as the persons absolutely entitled, see *Re Smith, Public Trustee v Aspinall* [1928] Ch 915, [1928] All ER Rep 520. For the inheritance tax implications of protective trusts and in relation to powers to pay capital to a life tenant, see Part A, para **[200.116]**.
2   See paras **[210.3]**, **[210.4]** and **[210.9]**, n 1.

Legacies to employees

[210.57]
Legacies to employees. Many of the difficulties of legacies to servants or employees will now be non-existent because there are now few establishments with a large staff of indoor and outdoor servants; and as far as servants are concerned can now in practically every case be made as a legacy to a named person. They should be made additional to wages or other payment due to the servant or accruing due at the time of the testator's death but can be drafted so as to take into hotchpot any statutory redundancy payment.

[210.58]

FORM B10.41:   **Legacy to a servant, if not under notice to leave at testator's death**

I give to my butler [*name*] if he shall be in my service at my death and shall not then be under notice given by him or by me to quit my service the sum of £—— free of inheritance tax[1] in addition to any sums then owing to him for wages or otherwise.[2]

1   See paras **[210.3]**, **[210.4]** and **[210.9]**, n 1.
2   The bequest of a stated sum is preferable to 'a year's wages' since the latter has been held to restrict servants to those hired by the year: *Re Ravensworth, Ravensworth v Tindale* [1905] 2 Ch 1, but this rule does not apply to a gift of the amount of one year's wages: *Re Earl of Sheffield, Ryde v Bristow* [1911] 2 Ch 267. For a legacy intended to vary in accordance with size of redundancy payment, see Form B10.46 at para **[210.63]**.

[210.59]

FORM B10.42:   **Legacy to chauffeur with alternative gift if he shall have left the testator's service**

I give to my chauffeur [*name*] if in my service at the time of my death[1] the sum of £—— free of inheritance tax[2] in addition to any sums then owing to him for wages or otherwise and if he shall have left my service I give him the sum of £—— free of inheritance tax.[2,3]

1   Without the words 'at my death' a servant who has left the service can claim the legacy: *Re Sharland, Kempt v Rozey* [1896] 1 Ch 517. For provisions concerning redundancy payments see Form B10.46 at para **[210.63]** and as to redundancy payments generally, see **[210.63]**, n 1.
2   See paras **[210.3]**, **[210.4]** and **[210.9]**, n 1.
3   The bequest of a stated sum is preferable to 'a year's wages' since the latter has been held to restrict servants to those hired by the year: *Re Ravensworth, Ravensworth v Tindale* [1905] 2 Ch 1, but this rule does not apply to a gift of the amount of one year's wages: *Re Earl of Sheffield, Ryde v Bristow* [1911] 2 Ch 267. For a legacy intended to vary in accordance with size of redundancy payment, see Form B10.46 at para **[210.63]**.

[210.60]

FORM B10.43:   **Legacies to indoor servants**

I give to my maid [*name*] [in recognition of her long and faithful service] the sum of £—— free of inheritance tax[1] and if she shall still be in my service at my death the said legacy shall be in addition to any wages or other sums then owing to her.

I give to each of my indoor servants (other than my said maid) in my service at my death[2] the sum of £—— free of inheritance tax[1] such legacies to be in addition to any sums owing to them respectively for wages or otherwise.

1   See paras **[210.3]**, **[210.4]** and **[210.9]**, n 1.
2   Without the words 'at my death' a servant who has left the service can claim the legacy: *Re Sharland, Kempt v Rozey* [1896] 1 Ch 517. For provisions concerning redundancy payments see Form B10.46 at para **[210.63]** and as to redundancy payments generally, see para **[210.63]**, n 1.

[210.61]

FORM B10.44:   **Legacies to servants—longer form**

To each of my servants who shall be in my service at my death[1] and shall then have been in my service for one year or more continuously and shall not then be under notice to leave such service (whether given by him or her or me) and whether he or she be at yearly monthly weekly or other wages[2] a sum equal to the wages [net of income tax and national insurance contributions][3] earned by such servant for the last year preceding my death and to each of my servants who shall be in my service at my death and shall have been in my service for less than a year a sum equal to the wages [also net of income tax and national insurance contributions] earned by such servant up to the date of my death and I declare that such legacies shall be free of inheritance tax[4] and in addition to any sums then owing to them respectively for wages or otherwise.

1   See para **[210.60]**, n 2.
2   The form of this gift avoids the question whether only servants hired by the year can take: see *Re Ravensworth, Ravensworth v Tindale* [1905] 2 Ch 1; and *Re Earl of Sheffield, Ryde v Bristow* [1911] 2 Ch 267. This form is specially drawn to avoid the difficulties which have arisen in the construction of such gifts: see Vol 1, paras **[30.23]**–**[30.29]**.
3   'Wages' does not include extra allowances, perquisites and similar benefits: *Re Peacock* (1929) 45 TLR 301; *Re Smith, Phillips v Smith* [1915] WN 12 (commission). See Form B10.46 at para **[210.63]** as to redundancy payments.
4   See paras **[210.3]**, **[210.4]** and **[210.9]**, n 1.

[210.62]

FORM B10.45:   **Legacy to clerks**

To each of the clerks employed by me at my death in my business of —— if I shall then be carrying on such business who shall have been in my service for upwards of —— years the sum of £—— free of inheritance tax[1] and I declare that such legacies shall be in addition to any salaries or other sums owing to them at my death. [In computing such periods of service any temporary absence shall not be considered an interruption of service but the period of such absence shall be excluded when determining the length of such service.]²

1   See paras **[210.3]**, **[210.4]** and **[210.9]**, n 1.
2   Where the testator from a certain time carried on his business under a declaration of trust so that certain persons were entitled to certain shares in the profits but to all appearances and as far as his employees knew was carrying on the same for his own benefit it was held that the whole period could be included in such a computation: *Re Howell's Trusts, Barclays Bank Ltd v Simmons* [1937] 3 All ER 647. See Form B10.46 at para **[210.63]** as to redundancy payments.

[210.63]

FORM B10.46:   Adjustment of legacies to servants or employees occasioned by redundancy payments under the Employment Rights Act 1996¹

I
Such sum shall be in addition to any redundancy payment payable to the said [*employee or servant*] under the Employment Rights Act 1996 or any succeeding or supplementary Act.
II
Provided always as follows:

(i)   If the said *employee or servant*] shall be paid any redundancy payment under the Employment Rights Act 1996 or any succeeding or supplementary Act and such payment is equal to or more than the said sum of £—— then the above legacy shall not be payable.

(ii)   If the said payment under the said Act (which term includes any succeeding or supplementary Act) shall be less than the said legacy then I give the said [*employee or servant*] such sum free of inheritance tax as is equal to the difference between the said legacy and the redundancy payment and in addition to any sum then owing to him [her] for wages or otherwise.

[(iii)   If the said [*employee or servant*] shall within the terms of Chapter II of the said Act unreasonably refuse an offer to renew his employment or a re-engagement by my personal representatives then the above legacy and any addition thereto hereby authorised shall not be payable].

1   It has long been the custom to leave legacies to servants or employees of long standing but it may well be that with the enactment of the Redundancy Payments Act 1965, re-enacted in the Employment Rights Act 1996 that this custom may cease or testators may wish to leave only such sum as with the redundancy payment will amount to a stated sum. No payment is made where the contract of employment is renewed by the personal representative of the testator or the employee is re-engaged by the personal representative as long as such renewal or re-engagement takes effect within eight weeks of the death of the testator. Nor is any payment to be made where the personal representative has made the employee an offer in writing to renew the contract or to re-engage the employee where the renewal of re-engagement will take effect not less than eight weeks after the testator's death as long as the terms of the renewal or re-engagement are not different from those prevailing before the testator's death or the offer constitutes an offer of suitable employment of the employee and in either case the employee has unreasonably refused the offer. The substitution of the personal representatives for the deceased is not to be taken as making any material difference in the contract of employment nor whether the refusal was unreasonable. The proviso in respect of this renewal or re-engagement has been placed in brackets. It is a matter for the testator to decide whether he wishes payment to be withdrawn in these circumstances. It would seem that as the period of eight weeks is to be reckoned from the death of the testator, it is a very short period for any action to be taken as it may well be that eight weeks will have elapsed before a grant of probate can be obtained.

Inheritance tax and foreign death duties

[210.64]
Legacies free of or subject to inheritance tax. In the absence of express provision, pecuniary legacies bear inheritance tax or are free of it according to whether the assets out of which they are payable are of a kind which are tax-free or subject to tax. This means that pecuniary legacies will be free of inheritance tax to the extent that they are payable out of UK free estate (whether realty or personalty), and will be subject to tax to the extent that they are payable out of property which bears its own inheritance tax, such as foreign property or property which was comprised in a settlement immediately before the testator's death. See paras **[210.3]** and **[210.4]** and the note to B14 at para **[214.55]** et seq.

[210.65]
Freeing legacies from inheritance tax. Form B10.47 at para **[210.68]** (see also Form B14.33 at para **[214.76]**) is a direction freeing all legacies from inheritance tax and foreign death duties, for use in a case where the fund out of which legacies are payable (typically the testator's residuary estate) might be or include property which normally bears its own inheritance tax and Form B10.50 at para **[210.71]** is a form of direction that a legacy shall bear its own inheritance tax for use in the unusual case where that is desired. For incidence of inheritance tax and directions as to incidence see further the note at para **[214.55]** et seq and Forms B14.33 and B14.34 at paras **[214.76]** and **[214.77]**.

[210.66]
Gifts of the inheritance tax on lifetime transfers. As described in Part A at paras **[200.70]**–**[200.76]**, the Finance Act 1986 (FA 1986) has increased very significantly the potential for the death of a person to cause inheritance tax to become payable in respect of lifetime gifts which he has made. The possible categories of inheritance tax liability which may arise on a testator's death in respect of his lifetime gifts are as follows:

(i)   Until March 1989 there could arise additional inheritance tax on a lifetime transfer of value made before 18 March 1986 and three years or less before the testator's death. Where a testator died on or after 18 March 1986, the pre-18 March 1986 capital transfer tax rules were preserved in relation to any pre-18 March 1986 lifetime transfers he had made (FA 1986, Sch 19, para 40). Under these rules, if the testator died three years or less after a transfer, inheritance tax on the transfer was calculated on the rate scale applicable to the inheritance tax charge on death. The amount of tax then payable in respect of the transfer as a result of his death was the difference between that amount of tax and the tax already paid at the lifetime rates applicable to the transfer (ITA 1984, s 7(2) before it was amended by the FA 1986). There was no additional tax payable if he died more than three years after the transfer. This was subject to the tax rate table used for calculating the additional inheritance tax being that which was in force at the time of the testator's death, not that in force at the date of the transfer (ITA 1984, Sch 2, para 2 before it was amended by the FA 1986), and to the possibility of relief under the ITA 1984, Pt V, Ch IV where property subject to the transfer had gone down in value since the transfer was made. Since the death rates were reduced as from 18 March 1986, and the lifetime rates had been half the death rates, the amount of additional tax on a pre-18 March 1986 lifetime transfer where the transferor died within three years but after that date would thus be less, but not usually very much less, than the amount of tax already paid in respect of the transfer.

(ii) Inheritance tax on potentially exempt transfers (for which see Part A, para [**200.71**]) made by the testator on or after 18 March 1986 but which have become chargeable transfers as a result of the testator dying within seven years of the transfer (ITA 1984, s 3A(4)). Such transfers will include the making of an interest in possession settlement, the making of an accumulation and maintenance settlement, the termination of an interest in possession in favour of an absolute interest, or another or other interests in possession, or an accumulation and maintenance trust. Substantial liabilities could be involved here, since no tax will have been paid in respect of such a transfer. The tax rates are the full rates appropriate to the inheritance tax charge on death where the testator has survived the transfer by three years or less, but are a percentage of a full charge if the transferor has survived more than three years after the transfer, the percentage being reduced further for every year beyond three that he has survived the transfer (ITA 1984, s 7(1) and (4), as amended by the FA 1986, Sch 19, para 2). Again the rate table is that in force at the testator's death (ITA 1984, Sch 2, para 1A).

(iii) Additional inheritance tax payable in respect of chargeable (not potentially exempt) transfers made by the testator on or after 18 March 1986 and within seven years of his death. Such transfers will usually be the making of discretionary settlements, the termination of an interest in possession in favour of a discretionary trust or a transfer of value by a close company in which the testator was a participator, all of which are transfers or deemed transfers which are incapable of being potentially exempt transfers (ITA 1984, s 3A(1), (2), (3), and (6)). A chargeable (not potentially exempt) transfer is taxed at half rates initially (ITA 1984, s 7(2), as substituted by the FA 1986, Sch 19, para 2), but if the transferor dies within seven years of it, and the inheritance tax on it, recalculated on the same basis as the tax on a potentially exempt transfer (including the reducing percentages and the use of the rate table in force at the transferor's death) exceeds the inheritance tax already paid on it, the excess becomes payable (ITA 1984, s 7 and Sch 2, para 2, as amended by the FA 1986, Sch 19). It might be thought that, like the additional tax referred to under (i) above, this type of liability could never exceed the amount of tax already paid, but this is not so. First, the death of the transferor may cause potentially exempt transfers made before the chargeable transfer, but (as it turns out) within seven years before his death, to become aggregable with the chargeable transfer, and thus cause the chargeable transfer to be subject to a higher marginal rate when the amount of the inheritance tax charge on it comes to be recalculated as a result of the transferor's death. Such previous potentially exempt transfers would not have been aggregated with the chargeable transfer when the lifetime charge on it was calculated (see the ITA 1984, s 3A(5)). Secondly, there could have been business or agricultural relief on the chargeable transfer which is not available when the tax is recalculated on the transferor's death, because the transferee has disposed of the business or agricultural property in question before the transferor's death (see the ITA 1984, ss 113A and 124A).

(iv) Inheritance tax on property comprised in a gift with reservation made by the testator on or after 18 March 1986 (see the FA 1986, s 102), where the reservation continued until his death or ceased within seven years of it. If the reservation ceased during his life but within seven years of his death, he is treated as having made a potentially exempt transfer of the property at the time when the reservation ceased, and if the reservation continues until his death the property is taxed as if it was part of his estate on death (FA 1986, s 102(3) and (4)).

In all the above cases the inheritance tax or additional inheritance tax liability is prima facie borne by the donee (including within that expression the settlement trustees if the gift was by way of settlement), although the FA 1986 (in the amendments to the ITA 1984, ss 199 and 204) introduced a secondary liability on the part of the transferor's personal representatives. There is no reason why the donor should not direct that such liabilities should be paid out of his estate, such direction being in effect the gift of a pecuniary legacy of the amount of tax payable (see Form B10.48 at para **[210.69]**). Before directions are included in a will for the payment out of the testator's estate of any of these liabilities, careful consideration should be given to the sums possibly involved, which could be substantial, and the consequences of such a direction for the other dispositions intended to be made by the will, particularly in the case of transfers made on or after 18 March 1986 (see sub-paras (ii) to (iv)).

[210.67]

Gifts of the inheritance tax on property passing on death but not under the testator's will. There are various categories of property, notably settled property in which a testator had an interest in possession and a testator's severable share of property of which he was a joint tenant, which does not form part of his free estate disposed of by his will, but which devolves in some way on his death, and is charged to inheritance tax as if it was part of his estate on death. Property subject to a reservation of which the testator was the donor, and which remains subject to a reservation at his death, is also charged to inheritance tax as part of his estate on death (FA 1986, s 102). In the absence of express provision to the contrary, property in all these categories bears its own inheritance tax (see the Note at para **[214.70]** et seq.). Again, there is no reason why a testator should not make gifts of the inheritance tax arising on his death in respect of such property if he wants to, but again careful consideration should be given to the possibly substantial amounts involved. See Form B10.49 at para **[210.70]** which gives further examples of such property.

[210.68]

FORM B10.47:   **Legacies free of inheritance tax and duties payable outside Great Britain**[1]

All legacies and annuities hereby or by any codicil hereto given shall be paid free of inheritance tax and all duties or taxes upon or by reason of my death in whatsoever country or place the same may be payable.

1   'Death duties' will not prima facie include foreign duties (ie duties other than those leviable under UK legislation): *Re Goetze, National Provincial Bank Ltd v Mond* [1953] Ch 96, [1953] 1 All ER 76; see also *Re Cunliffe-Owen, Mountain v Comber* [1951] Ch 964, [1951] 2 All ER 220, and *Re Sebba, Lloyds Bank Ltd v Hutson* [1959] Ch 166, [1958] 3 All ER 393 (which latter decisions also considered the treatment of tax credits, whether concessionary or available under double taxation conventions). In Scotland the rule is different: *Maclean's Trustees v M'Nair* 1969 SC 65, expressly not following *Re Goetze*. A fortiori 'free of inheritance tax' will not include foreign death duties.

[210.69]

FORM B10.48:   Clause dealing with inheritance tax on lifetime gifts made by the testator[1]

(1)   I declare that if any additional taxes (as defined in subclause (2)) shall be payable by reason of my death then my trustees shall provide for the payment of such taxes (and any interest on them) [free of all taxes payable on my death][2] out of my residuary estate [except to the extent that the liability has been provided for by insurance effected for that purpose].[3]

(2)   'Additional taxes' shall mean the following liabilities to inheritance tax or additional inheritance tax payable by reason of my death:

- tax on any lifetime absolute gift made by me [except tax charged in respect of any settled property in which an interest in possession of mine shall have terminated during my lifetime][4];
- tax on any lifetime transfer by me of property into a settlement [except tax charged in respect of any settled property in which an interest in possession of mine shall have terminated during my lifetime][5];
- tax charged in respect of any settled property in which interest in possession of mine shall have terminated during my lifetime;
- tax charged under Part IV of the Inheritance Tax Act 1984 (close companies);
- in the case of property subject to a reservation in relation to me (within the meaning of sections 102 to 102C of the Finance Act 1986) at or within seven years of my death [any tax chargeable thereon by virtue of section 102(3) or (4) of the Finance Act 1986][6] *or* [an amount limited to the amount of inheritance tax (if any) which would have been chargeable if sections 102 to 102C of the Finance Act 1986 had not applied to such property].[7]

1   This clause can be modified to suit the testator's requirements, omitting those taxes which the testator does not wish to be paid from his residuary estate.
2   Since this is a pecuniary legacy, these words should be included where residue might include property which bears its own inheritance tax, eg foreign property, see the Preliminary Note at paras **[210.3]** and **[210.4]**.
3   A donee of a lifetime gift will often insure against the risk of inheritance tax or additional inheritance tax becoming payable by him on the donor's death. Therefore, the testator may wish to exclude from this provision for the payment of tax out of his residuary estate that tax which has been insured against.
4   If the testator does not wish tax charged in respect of the termination of an interest in possession to be paid from his estate, these words should be included to make this absolutely clear.
5   If the testator does not wish tax charged in respect of the termination of an interest in possession to be paid from his estate, these words should be included to make this absolutely clear.
6   Where a person has made a gift of property and reserved a benefit to himself, which benefit continues until his death, inheritance tax is charged as if he was beneficially entitled to the

property at his death (FA 1986, s 106(3)). If the benefit ceases within seven years of his death, he is treated as having made a potentially exempt transfer of the property at the time when the benefit ceases (FA 1986, s 106(4)). By virtue of the Inheritance Tax (Double Charges Relief) Regulations 1987, where there are two possible charges to inheritance tax in respect of property subject to a reservation of benefit, ie an inheritance tax charge as a result of the original lifetime gift (which may either have been a potentially exempt transfer or a chargeable transfer) and as a result of the FA 1986, s 106(3) or (4), only the higher amount of tax is charged. It is more likely that the tax charged as a result of the FA 1986, s 106(3) or (4) will be higher than that on the original gift, and so these words cover this tax.

7   See previous note. These words will only cover an amount up to the amount of tax which would be payable upon the original lifetime gift. So if under the Inheritance Tax (Double Charges Relief) Regulations 1987 such amount is the lesser amount of tax, the amount chargeable under the FA 1986, s 106(3) or (4) being higher and so the amount payable, the lesser amount will be payable out of the testator's residuary estate, and the balance due will be the primary liability of the donee of the gift.

[210.70]

FORM B10.49:   Clause providing for payment out of residue of inheritance tax on property not passing under the will[1]

Even though they do not pass under this will inheritance tax payable upon and by reason of my death on the following types of property shall be paid free of inheritance tax[2] out of my residuary estate:

(a)   Any interest which I may have at my death in any property of whatever kind [or, if the provision is to apply only to land, in the proceeds of sale of any freehold [or leasehold] property] as a beneficial joint tenant.

(b)   If and to the extent that it does not fall within the provisions of subclause (b) of this clause any money standing to the credit of any current [or deposit] bank account in the joint names of [name] and myself.

(c)   Any donationes mortis causa made by me or the property comprised in them.

(d)   Any lump sum payment annuity or other benefit arising under any life insurance or other policy effected by me to which any person becomes entitled on my death otherwise than by virtue of this will.

(e)   Any property of any of the following kinds to which a person becomes entitled on my death by virtue of a nomination made by me in my lifetime in favour of that person:

(i)   Money standing to the credit of any Trustee Savings Bank account of mine.

(ii)   Money standing to the credit of any National Savings Bank account of mine.

(iii)   Savings certificates of mine.

(iv)   Stock or securities of mine on the National Savings Stock Register.

(v)   Money payable on my death by any Friendly Society of which I am or may become a member.

(f)   Any property subject to an interest in possession (within the meaning of Part III of the Inheritance Tax Act 1984) to which I am beneficially entitled immediately before my death.[3]

(g)   Any property which immediately before my death is property subject to a reservation in relation to which I am the donor within the meaning of section 102 of and the Twentieth Schedule to the Finance Act 1986 where the inheritance tax is payable by virtue of section 102(3) or (4) of the Finance Act 1986.

1   This form is designed to cast onto residue the burden of certain inheritance tax which would not otherwise fall on it. It is assumed that the inheritance tax on any gifts actually made by the will has been dealt with elsewhere in the will. It is not suggested that the form should be adopted in its entirety: only those parts of it which are (or may be) relevant to the testator's circumstances should be used. For the incidence of inheritance tax see the Note at para **[214.55]** et seq.

Subclause (a) deals with the inheritance tax attributable to any interest of the testator in property as a joint tenant. Such an interest accrues automatically to the other joint tenant(s) who thus become(s) (unless provision is made to the contrary) liable for the tax.

Subclause (b) is designed to counter the result of *Re Figgis, Roberts v MacLaren* [1969] 1 Ch 123, [1968] 1 All ER 999, in which it was held that a gift of the duty on gifts inter vivos did not apply to money placed by the testator in a bank account in the joint names of himself and his wife. Such a provision is not always needed, of course: thus, if the other joint tenant receives the residuary estate in any case, there would be no point in including it. The spouse exemption will normally make it unnecessary in relation to the joint accounts of spouses.

Subclause (c) relates to donationes mortis causa for which see Vol 1, para **[1.14]**.

Subclause (d) relates to life insurance money, etc, which does not pass under the will: see further Vol 1, para **[7.11]**.

Subclause (e) deals with property which passes, by virtue of a nomination made by the testator in his lifetime, to the person nominated. A number of enactments permit or used to permit such nominations to be made in respect of certain types of property all of which, it is thought, are mentioned in this subclause; see further Vol 1, para **[7.9]**. Although it is no longer possible to make nominations in relation to any of the categories in sub-cl (e) apart from money in Friendly Societies (Vol 1, para **[7.10]**), nominations made before the right was withdrawn are still capable of taking effect. The fact that inheritance tax on nominated property should be expressly dealt with is demonstrated by *Re Walley, National Westminster Bank Ltd v Williams* [1972] 1 All ER 222, [1972] 1 WLR 257. Although on the particular facts of that case the estate duty on nominated property was held to be covered by the particular wording used, in relation to a general direction to pay estate duty or inheritance tax out of residue this would not normally be so.

Subclause (f) deals with settled property in which the testator had an interest in possession and sub-cl (g) deals with property subject to a reservation at the testator's death of which he was the donor. See the Note at para **[210.67]**.

2   See para **[210.69]**, n 2.

3   It is possible for settled property to be disposed of by will by virtue of a power of appointment or the statutory power to dispose of entailed property (LPA 1925, s 176: Part G, para **[244.53]**) and where this may happen care should be taken to see that a provision of this kind is consistent with the parts of the will which dispose of settled property.

[210.71]

FORM B10.50:   **Clause providing for payment by the donee of the inheritance tax on a testamentary gift which would otherwise be free of inheritance tax[1]**

I give [*subject matter of gift*] to [*donee*] absolutely but declare that the property [sum] comprised in this gift shall bear its own inheritance tax.

1   Most types of property now devolve free of inheritance tax unless a contrary intention is shown: see generally the Note at para **[214.55]** et seq. But testators may wish to direct that a particular gift should bear its rateable proportion of tax. This form is for use in such a case. If the estate will or may be partially exempt, and include business or agricultural property, consider the use of Form B14.36 at para **[214.79]** and see the Note at para **[214.73]**. See also Forms B5.1 at para **[205.58]** and B6.29 to B6.31 at paras **[206.38]**–**[206.40]**.

Nil-rate band legacies

[210.72]

FORM B10.51:   Nil-rate band legacy[1]

If the gift of my residuary estate to [my wife *or other exempt person, eg a charity*] shall take effect[2] I give to such of my children [*name*] [*name*] and [*name*] who shall survive me if more than one in equal shares absolutely a legacy of the maximum sum of money which can in the circumstances subsisting at my death be given by this clause without any liability being incurred for the payment of inheritance tax on or by reason of my death. And in particular but without prejudice to the generality of the foregoing the circumstances to be taken into account for the foregoing purpose shall include any chargeable transfers made by me during my lifetime (or events treated as such for inheritance tax purposes) the dispositions taking effect under this my will (apart from this present clause) or under any codicil hereto and any property treated as if it were part of my estate immediately before my death for inheritance tax purposes [provided that if such maximum sum exceeds [one-third] of the probate value of my estate (disregarding for this purpose any business [or agricultural] relief applicable thereto) then the amount of the foregoing legacy shall be equal to [one-third] of the said probate value] *or* [provided that if such maximum sum shall exceed [£242,000] I give instead of such maximum sum the said sum of [£242,000]].[3]

1   Where a testator's estate is likely to exceed the inheritance tax threshold, and his residuary estate will be exempt from inheritance tax because he is leaving it to an exempt person, for example, his spouse, he may wish to leave to non-exempt persons, such as his children, the maximum amount which he can leave without incurring any inheritance tax liability. This clause makes provision for this. See Part A, paras **[200.99]–[200.106]** on this topic generally, the Note to B18 at para **[218.16]** et seq and Form B18.2 at para **[218.32]** for nil-rate band discretionary trusts.
2   The gift should be made conditional upon the testator's residuary estate being exempt from inheritance tax because in the event of the testator's taxable estate exceeding the available nil-rate inheritance tax band, nothing will be payable according to the formula.
3   Where the testator's residuary estate may include property with the benefit of business or agricultural property relief, in particular property qualifying for such relief at the rate of 100 per cent, the maximum sum of money which could pass under this clause could exceed by a very considerable amount the sum which is the inheritance tax threshold, and leave the surviving spouse with less, perhaps much less, than the testator intends (see para **[233.9]**). The testator would be well advised to place a limit on the amount of the legacy in these circumstances, as provided here. For business relief see the Preliminary Notes to B5 at para **[205.1]** et seq, C11 at paras **[233.1]–[233.13]** and for agricultural relief, see the Preliminary Note to C12 at paras **[234.1]** et seq.

Miscellaneous

[210.73]

FORM B10.52:   Legacies with provision for some of the legatees not being able to be found

I give the sum of £—— free of inheritance tax to each of my nephews [*names*] provided that if the address of any such nephew is not known to my trustees and such nephew does not claim the said legacy within two years of my decease then the sum or sums given to that nephew or those nephews shall fall into or form part of my residuary estate.[1]

1   See *Hawkes v Baldwin* (1838) 9 Sim 355. The condition in this clause is binding on the legatee whether or not he is aware of it. He cannot claim the legacy after the expiration of the two years on the ground that he was ignorant of it nor is the executor bound to inform any such legatee of the terms of the legacy. See Vol 1, paras **[30.32]–[35.48]**.

[210.74]

FORM B10.53:   Demonstrative legacy[1]

I give to [*name*] the sum of £—— free of inheritance tax to be raised primarily out of my [4 *per cent Consolidated Stock*] but if I shall not have sufficient of such stock at my death then out of my residuary estate.

1   Such a legacy will not abate with the general legacies until after the particular fund out of which it is to be paid is exhausted: see Vol 1, para **[30.6]**.

[210.75]

FORM B10.54:   Bequest of legacies payable exclusively out of a particular property with provision for abatement and interest

I give to my trustees free of inheritance tax [my freehold property known as ——] upon trust to sell the same and from the net proceeds of sale (after payment of all of the costs of the sale including legal fees and estate agents' commission) I direct them to pay the following legacies to the following persons: [*set out the names of the legatees and the amounts of the legacies*] and I declare that if the net proceeds of sale of the property shall be less than the total of the said legacies (other than those that shall have failed or lapsed) such legacies shall abate between themselves rateably according to value and further I declare that such legacies shall carry interest from the first anniversary of my death until payment at the rate of —— per cent per annum such interest to be payable upon such payment and to be payable in the first place from the net rents and profits of the said property in the second place from the amount (if any) by which the net proceeds of sale exceed the total of such legacies and in the third place from my residuary estate.

[210.76]

FORM B10.55:   Clause providing for reduction of legacies where the testator's estate proves to have decreased in value[1]

In deciding on the amount of the above legacies I have estimated the net value of my estate after payment of my debts and the inheritance tax thereon on my death at about £100,000 at the time of making this my will and accordingly I declare that the said legacies to the said [*legatees*] given by me in this clause shall be subject to abatement and reduction as follows: if the value of my estate at the date of my death after payment of my funeral and testamentary expenses and debts and the inheritance tax in respect thereof shall amount to less than

£100,000 then the said pecuniary legacies given by this clause of this my will shall abate and be diminished so that the proportion of such legacies to be paid by my trustees to such legatees in satisfaction of their said legacies respectively shall be the same proportion as the net value of my estate (ascertained as aforesaid) shall bear to £100,000.

1   It is by no means impossible that the testator's estate will prove to be much less in value than could have been reasonably expected. The common practice is to give a number of legacies of stated amount and to divide the residue amongst the family. If the estate is greatly reduced, the legacies may exhaust the whole estate, and the family will in consequence be left unprovided for. This precedent provides for the reduction of the legacies, so that such a result may be avoided.

[210.77]

FORM B10.56:   Declaration as to currency in which legacies payable[1]

I declare that all legacies annuities and all other sums of money payable under this my will shall be paid in pounds sterling.

1   Prima facie the currency a legacy is to be paid in is that of the domicile of the testator, but where a different currency is expressly indicated in the will, the legacy is to be paid in that currency see Vol 1, para **[30.43]**. This clause will generally be required where there may be a doubt or there are legatees or annuitants resident in different countries or there are legacies charged on different properties in different countries.

[210.78]

FORM B10.57:   Direction as to rate of exchange for payment of legacies in a foreign currency[1]

I declare that all legacies payable under my will in a currency other than in pounds sterling although the same are expressed in pounds sterling shall be computed according to the applicable rate of exchange of the —— Bank prevailing [on such date prior to payment as my trustees shall in their absolute discretion (without being liable for loss) select] *or* [on the first anniversary of my death].

1   This direction should be used where a testator has expressly directed that certain legacies should be paid in a currency other than pounds sterling. In the absence of an express direction, the applicable rate of exchange is that prevailing on the first anniversary of the testator's death: see Vol 1, para **[30.43]**.

[210.79]

FORM B10.58:   Legacy for purchase of customary mourning

I give to my wife and to each of my sons such sums as shall in the absolute discretion of my trustees be sufficient to provide them with suitable mourning apparel.

B11   Annuities

PRELIMINARY NOTE

[211.1]
Annuities are unsatisfactory. Annuities used to be a convenient method of providing maintenance for persons to whom the testator felt an obligation but who were not primary objects of the testator's bounty. They are no longer very satisfactory, for two main reasons.

[211.2]
Inflationary devaluation of annuities. In a period of high inflation the real value of an annuity will decline rapidly, both between the making of the will and the testator's death, and during the period in which the annuity is payable. This can be compensated for by 'index-linking' the annuity (as in Form B11.4 at para **[211.17]**), but that could have the effect, if the value of the fund out of which the annuity is paid fails to keep pace with inflation, that the annuity grows to consume all the income, and possibly capital as well, of the fund.

[211.3]
Taxation problems of annuities. Inheritance tax on funds out of the income of which annuities are payable is charged in a manner which can operate unfairly, though it is also possible for it to be turned to advantage. An annuitant is treated as having an interest in possession in the same proportion of the capital fund as the proportion the annuity bears to the income of the fund (Inheritance Tax Act 1984 (ITA 1984), s 50(2)) but subject to prescribed maximum and minimum rates for the income of the fund (s 50(3)) which only apply when they favour the Inland Revenue. Thus, if the income of the fund is above the prescribed maximum or below the prescribed minimum there could be inheritance tax charges on more than the overall value of a fund if the annuitant and the person entitled to the rest of the income of the fund died within a short period of each other. Also the charge to inheritance tax on the death of the annuitant could be on a larger share of the settled property than was exempt on the testator's death, where the annuitant is his spouse. On the other hand, within the limits of these prescribed rates advantage can sometimes be obtained by deliberate re-investment to obtain a different income return for the fund or by appropriating an annuity to a small fund with a high income yield. The prescribed maximum and minimum rates for the purposes of s 50(3) after 15 August 1980 and before 18 February 2000 are contained in the Capital Transfer Tax (Settled Property Income Yield) Order 1980 (SI 1980/1000). The rates applicable after 17 February 2000 are contained in the Inheritance Tax (Settled Property Income Yield) Order (SI 2000/174). The latter Order designates the following rates of yield in the FT Actuaries Share Indices for the higher and lower rates: for the higher rate—the Irredeemables' yield shown in the indicies of FTSE Actuaries Government Securities UK Indices; for the lower rate—the rate of the All-Share actual dividend yield shown in the FTSE Actuaries Share Indices. In each case applicable rate is determined using the indices produced for the date on which the value in question is to be determined or, if those indices are not produced for that date, for the latest date preceding that date for which those indices are produced. There are also obscurities about these inheritance tax provisions: it is not clear what period is to be taken for the purposes of s 50(2), and although it

seems most unlikely that a change in the income rate of the fund or an appropriation of an annuity fund could be an occasion of an inheritance tax charge, the possibility cannot be finally ruled out. These inheritance tax problems of course relate only to annuities charged (wholly or partly) on the income of property, and do not apply to purchased life or covenanted annuities. See further *Foster's Inheritance Tax*, E 2.11–E2.14.

[211.4]
Alternatives. Other methods of providing maintenance are to give a life interest in a proportionate share of a fund (or a proportionate share of the income of a fund, ie so that there can be no appropriation of capital to the share of income— see *Re Freeston's Charity* [1979] 1 All ER 51, [1978] 1 WLR 741), or a life interest in a settled legacy, or a legacy of a capital sum with which the legatee may purchase an annuity: see further method (4) at para **[211.6]**.

[211.5]
General considerations. The various methods of providing annuities are discussed in detail at para **[211.6]**. The following general considerations should be mentioned:

(i)   An annuity is a form of pecuniary legacy, and it abates and bears inheritance tax in the same manner. It is important therefore to ensure that it is expressed to be free of inheritance tax, for, if it is not, administrative complications may ensue. This situation is less likely to arise now that tax on realty is prima facie treated as a testamentary expense. But although an annuity which is charged on a mixed fund of realty and personalty will no longer be required to contribute to the payment of inheritance tax, it will be otherwise if the fund includes foreign property: see the Preliminary Note to B10 at paras **[210.3]** and **[210.4]** and the Note to B14 at para **[214.63]**.

(ii) Where an annuity is charged on a fund, the extent to which the fund is liable to inheritance tax on the death of the annuitant can be a complex and difficult matter to determine: see *Foster's Inheritance Tax*, E2.12 and K2.03. From a fiscal and administrative point of view there is much to be said for giving annuities (if at all) only to individuals whose personal circumstances are such that no charge to inheritance tax on his death is likely to arise.

(iii) Annuities are payable subject to deduction of income tax at the basic rate. It is possible in wills, unlike other kinds of instrument, to provide income tax free annuities, and where the rule in *Re Pettit, Le Fevre v Pettit* [1922] 2 Ch 765 applies to such an annuity an annuitant whose personal circumstances entitle him to a refund of tax is required to account to the trustees for the proportionate part of such refund which is attributable to the annuity (see *Simon's Taxes*, E2.1119–E2.1128). While a testator who wants to ensure that the annuitant receives a net sum and no more may regard this as a fair arrangement, it will be an unwelcome administrative chore for all parties. Forms are given below which provide for the rule in *Re Pettit* to apply, but their use is not recommended.

(iv) Administrative difficulties may also arise if an annuity is given of a net amount computed by reference to tax rates which are higher than the basic rate. Effect can be given to such a direction only after the end of the relevant year of assessment when the annuitant's personal tax liability has been settled. Gifts of annuities on this basis are similarly not recommended.

[211.6]
Means of providing annuities. There are several methods of providing for the payment of an annuity given by will and these will be discussed in turn:

(1) The 'appropriated fund' method whereby the trustees have power to set aside part of the capital of the estate as an appropriated fund to answer the annuity by its income and, if necessary, by its capital. This has the disadvantages of inheritance tax on the annuitant's death and delay in the distribution of the estate. Furthermore, if the trustees are given power to resort to the capital of the appropriated fund in order to pay the annuity, and they exercise this power, the capital paid to the annuitant will be taxable in his hands as income.

(2) A *direction* to the trustees to purchase an annuity for the annuitant. This does avoid inheritance tax on the annuitant's death (since the annuity is not then supported by any slice of capital) – but see para (3) below – and it also avoids the delay in the distribution of the estate. But:

   (a) the annuitant can at once demand the capital which the trustees are directed to spend on the purchase of the annuity and can spend it as he likes, though this result can be avoided by a carefully-drafted provision in the will: see eg Form B11.12 at para **[211.25]**; and

   (b) the advantage of the normal rule applicable to a purchased annuity whereby the 'capital element' in the periodical annuity payments is exempt from income tax (Income and Corporation Taxes Act 1988 (ICTA 1988), ss 656 and 657) will be lost because this rule does not apply 'to any annuity purchased in pursuance of any direction in a will, or to provide for an annuity payable by virtue of a will or settlement out of income of property disposed of by the will or settlement (whether with or without resort to capital)' (ICTA 1984, s 657(2)(c)). It follows that the purchase of an annuity by the trustees is much less advantageous than the purchase of such an annuity by the annuitant himself.

(3) A gift of an annuity coupled with a *power* for the trustees to satisfy it by purchasing an annuity for the annuitant. The only difference here is that the right of the annuitant to demand the capital sum arises only when the trustees have decided to exercise their power to purchase the annuity. Otherwise, the position is the same as in (2) above. The purchased annuity to which the annuitant becomes entitled will normally be worth less than the share of capital in which the annuitant was treated as having an interest in possession for inheritance tax purposes (see above), so that arguably the purchase of the annuity could be an occasion of charge under the ITA 1984, s 52(4)(b). Although if there is an occasion of

charge under s 52, and the property released from the annuity vests absolutely in an individual, or becomes subject to an interest in possession to which an individual is beneficially entitled, or subject to accumulation and maintenance trusts, the deemed transfer of value may be potentially exempt and thus exempt if the annuitant survives it by seven years. As annuitants are usually elderly, this is perhaps of limited assistance. However, the Inland Revenue do not regard the substitution of a purchased annuity for an annuity paid out of the income of the testator's estate in exercise of a power given by the will, or in pursuance of a direction made by the will, as an occasion of charge under the ITA 1984, s 52 (see *Dymond's Capital Taxes*, para 16.509), although they do regard such a substitution as an occasion of tax charge where it is done by agreement with the annuitant (see *Dymond's Capital Taxes*, paras 16.510–16.512). A cautious draftsman could put the matter beyond doubt by creating an annuity fund in which there was no interest in possession until the trustees had decided how the annuities were to be met; if they did so within two years of the death their actions would be treated as those of the deceased for inheritance tax purposes under the ITA 1984, s 144 (see the Note in C3 at para **[225.83]** et seq).

(4) A simple gift to the annuitant of a lump sum, either without any further provision or with some purely precatory suggestion that he might use the money to buy an annuity; or else a gift to the annuitant of such a sum as in the opinion of the trustees, or of insurance brokers designated by trustees or in some other way, is sufficient to allow the annuitant to buy an annuity of specified amount. There is of course no way here of avoiding the risk that the annuitant may spend the money otherwise than in buying an annuity, but apart from that this method has the great advantage over methods (2) and (3) that the capital element of the annuity payments is not taxable in the hands of the annuitant, so that less capital needs to be spent to provide the annuitant with the same net income.

(5) A gift of an annuity coupled with a power for the trustees to *commute* the annuity by paying a lump sum to the annuitant. The idea behind this method is that the annuitant will, with the lump sum, purchase an annuity for himself and thus gain the income tax advantages which he would have lost if the trustees had purchased it for him. The results of this method, once the trustees exercise their power to commute, are the same as the results of method (4) but it may be preferred to method (4) because it gives the trustees a discretion as to whether, and if so when, to exercise the power, and they can make this decision in the light of all the circumstances which for the time being exist. This also has the tax disadvantage (although also the possibility of potential exemption) mentioned at (3) supra.

(6) A method whereby the annuity is neither purchased nor secured upon capital but payable by some third person as a personal obligation. This third person is usually a residuary beneficiary, because he is the person who stands to gain by accepting this obligation, and one difficulty in employing this method lies in the fact that there may be no residuary beneficiary who is adult, able and willing to undertake it. Assuming that there is, however, there are several ways in which the method may be

employed. The testator may, for instance, make the residuary gift conditional upon the residuary beneficiary (or beneficiaries) entering into a deed of covenant to pay the annuity. Alternatively, he may give the annuity and couple it with a power for the trustees to release the capital fund out of which it would otherwise be payable upon the residuary beneficiary (or beneficiaries) entering into such a deed of covenant or otherwise undertaking to pay it. This latter method is probably to be preferred because, again, it allows the trustees to make their decision in the light of current circumstances, but the inheritance tax disadvantage mentioned in (3) supra (although subject again to the availability of potential exemption) would be more serious in this case, as it could involve a charge on the whole of the share of the estate in which the annuity was treated as subsisting. For the purposes of this inheritance tax charge, the value of the covenant would apparently only be deductible from the value of the capital deemed to have been subject to the terminated annuity under the ITA 1984, s 52(2) if the *annuitant* agreed to the surrender of the annuity in return for the covenant. It should be emphasised that the use of this method provides less security for the annuitant than any of the others, because the continued payment of his annuity depends upon the residuary beneficiary's (and perhaps his personal representatives') continued goodwill and solvency. If these can be relied upon, however, it can be an advantageous method to adopt. It solves the two problems of inheritance tax on the annuitant's death and delay in distribution, but it enables the residuary beneficiary to obtain the whole of the residuary estate unencumbered and unreduced. The income tax rules for non-charitable covenants were altered by the Finance Act 1988 (adding new ss 347A and 347B to the ICTA 1984) so that they are not income tax deductible by the payer, but are not charged to income tax in the hands of the recipient. Since the covenantor would more likely be a higher rate taxpayer, and the convenantee not, this could be a disadvantage.

[211.7]

The draftsman will have to decide, in conjunction with the testator and in the light of the considerations outlined above, how best to provide for the annuity in question. Often it will be best to give the trustees several alternative powers, leaving them to decide between them when the time comes. They will then have an opportunity of assessing all the relevant points, including the age, health, wealth and character of the annuitant and of any person from whom a personal covenant may be taken, the size and nature of the estate as a whole, and any changes which may have been made in the law. Form B11.11 at para **[211.18]** is designed to give the trustees a fair range of alternative powers.

[211.8]

FORM B11.1:   Gift of simple annuity[1]

I give to [*name*] for [his]/[her] life[2] to be paid free of all deductions[3] by equal quarterly payments the first payment to be made at the end of three months after my death an annuity of £—— per annum.

1   See notes to Form B11.2 at para **[211.9]**. In this form the annuity is not tax-free and must be paid subject to deduction in respect of income tax. The word deduction does not include income tax, see note 3 below. For a tax-free annuity, see Form B11.2 at para **[211.9]**.

2   A gift of an annuity to a person without more is a gift of the annuity during the life of such person only (*Blight v Hartnoll* (1881) 19 Ch D 294), and see *Re Jackson, Day v Atkin* [1946] 1 All ER 327, where an annuity was coupled with a direction that it should be applied to the donee's maintenance and education until twenty-one, and it was held to be an annuity for life. But in order that no question may be raised, the duration of an annuity should always be expressed. As to duration of annuities, see Vol 1, paras **[33.11]**–**[33.22]** and as to annuities during widowhood or spinsterhood, see Vol 1, para **[33.20]**.

3   Words such as 'free of all deductions' or 'a clear annuity' were held in *Re Skinner, Milbourne v Skinner* [1942] Ch 82, [1942] 2 All ER 32 to exonerate an annuity from estate duty but not income tax. It is thought that such words will likewise exonerate annuities from inheritance tax. See also Vol 1, paras **[33.46]**–**[33.47]**. As to the importance of freeing annuities from inheritance tax, see the Preliminary Note to this section, sub-para (i) at para **[211.5]**.

[211.9]

FORM B11.2:   Gift of annuity tax-free[1]

I give to [*name*] for [his]/[her] life to be paid free of all deductions[2] whatsoever and free of income tax at the basic rate for the time being [*or if desired* free of income tax up to —— p in the £] by equal quarterly payments [the first payment to be made at the end of three months from my death an annuity of £—— per annum] *or* [the first payment to be made on the first usual quarter day occurring after the end of three months from my death such payment to include a proportionate payment in so far as the period for which it is paid exceeds the quarter ending on such day of payment].

[*Add one of the following as the intention may be*] I declare and direct that any rebate allowance or repayment of income tax which may be allowed or made to the said [*name*] shall enure for his [her] benefit [*or* shall be accounted for the said [*name*] to my trustees].[3]

1   A gift in this form provided the estate is sufficient will not allow the annuitant to claim the value of the annuity in a lump sum. Where, however, the estate is sufficient he can claim the lump sum, but the amount of it will, if necessary, have to abate in proportion to the abatement of other general legacies. See Vol 1, paras **[33.35]**–**[33.45]**.

2   See para **[211.8]**, n 3.

3   There are many decisions upon particular wording of the gifts as to whether there is liability to account for income tax repayments: see *Simon's Taxes*, E2.1122. The position can no doubt be made clear by adopting one of the special forms of words construed in the cases, but it seems preferable to put the question beyond doubt by expressly stating that the annuitant can retain the repayment or stating that it must be accounted for to the trustees. The annuitant must make the claim for the repayment where she is bound to hand it over to the trustees: *Re Kingcome, Hickley v Kingcome* [1936] Ch 566, [1936] 1 All ER 173.

[211.10]

FORM B11.3:   Gift of annuity with reference to liability of annuitant to account for reliefs and repayments—alternative forms[1]

I.   PROVISION FOR PAYMENT OF ANNUITY FREE OF INCOME TAX (THE RULE IN *RE PETTIT* BEING APPLICABLE) BUT NOT AT ANY RATE HIGHER THAN THE BASIC RATE

I give to A for [his]/[her] life an annuity of such sum as after deduction of income tax at the basic rate for the time being (but not at any higher rate)

amounts to clear^2 sum of £—— and I direct that any relief rebate allowance or repayment of income tax which may be allowed to A shall be accounted for by [him]/[her] to my trustees.

II.   PROVISION FOR PAYMENT OF ANNUITY FREE OF INCOME TAX AT THE BASIC RATE (THE RULE IN *RE PETTIT* NOT BEING APPLICABLE) BUT NOT AT ANY HIGHER RATE

I give to A for [his]/[her] life an annuity of such sum as after deduction of income tax at the basic rate for the time being amounts to the clear^2 sum of £—— and I direct that A shall be entitled to retain for [his]/[her] own benefit all reliefs rebates allowances and repayments of income tax made or allowed to [him]/[her].

III.   PROVISION FOR PAYMENT OF ANNUITY FREE OF INCOME TAX (THE RULE IN *RE PETTIT* BEING APPLICABLE) WHETHER AT THE BASIC OR AT ANY HIGHER RATE

My trustees shall pay to A for [his]/[her] life an annuity of such sum as after deduction of all income tax payable in respect thereof (whether at the basic or at any higher rate) amounts to the clear^2 sum of £—— and I direct that any relief rebate allowance or repayment of income tax which may be allowed to A shall be accounted for by [him]/[her] to my trustees.

IV.   PROVISION FOR PAYMENT OF ANNUITY FREE OF INCOME TAX AT THE BASIC RATE (THE RULE IN *RE PETTIT* NOT BEING APPLICABLE) AND OF INCOME TAX AT ANY HIGHER RATE

I give to A for [his]/[her] life an annuity of such sum as after deduction of income tax at the basic rate and of all income tax payable in respect thereof at any higher rate amounts to the clear^2 sum of £—— and I direct that A shall be entitled to retain for [his]/[her] own benefit all reliefs rebates allowances and repayments made or allowed to [him]/[her].

1   There are many decisions upon particular wording of the gifts as to whether there is liability to account for income tax repayments: see *Simon's Taxes*, E2.1122. The position can no doubt be made clear by adopting one of the special forms of words construed in the cases, but it seems preferable to put the question beyond doubt by expressly stating that the annuitant can retain the repayment or stating that it must be accounted for to the trustees. The annuitant must make the claim for the repayment where she is bound to hand it over to the trustees: *Re Kingcome, Hickley v Kingcome* [1936] Ch 566, [1936] 1 All ER 173.

2   For the effect of this word see para **[211.8]**, n 3.

[211.11]

FORM B11.4:   Gifts of annuity of such sum as after deduction of income tax at the basic rate for the time being will amount to a stated sum to be varied with reference to the Index of Retail Prices^1

I give to my wife [*name*] for her life an annuity of such sum as after deduction of income tax at the basic rate for the time being in force will amount to the clear^2 sum of £—— or such other clear^2 sum as may be substituted therefor as hereinafter provided such annuity to be paid in monthly instalments and the first payment to be made one month after my death.

As to such annuity I hereby declare and direct as follows:

(i)   The amount thereof shall be increased or decreased by dividing the sum of £—— by the index figure in the Index of Retail Prices for the month in which my will is executed and (having made allowance for any re-basing of the Index which may have happened in the meantime) multiplying it by the index figure in that Index for the month in which my death occurs.

(ii)   Any rebate allowance or repayment of income tax which may be allowed or made to my said wife [shall enure for her benefit] or [shall be accounted for by my said wife to my trustees].

(iii)   My trustees [shall]/[may] provide for the payment thereof by setting apart and appropriating in respect thereof such part of my residuary estate as shall in their opinion be sufficient by the income thereof to pay such annuity (hereinafter called the annuity fund). My trustees shall have absolute discretion in assessing the amount so to be set apart having regard to any possible increase in the said Index and shall not be liable for any loss incurred by the annuitant by reason of the annuity fund subsequently proving insufficient.[3]

(iv)   When such appropriation has been made the annuity shall be wholly charged on the annuity fund in exoneration of the rest of my estate but the capital of such fund may be resorted to in case at any time the income thereof is insufficient to pay the annuity.

(v)   In so far as the income from the annuity fund shall in any year exceed the sum required to pay the annuity my trustees shall accumulate the same during the lifetime of my said wife or for 21 years from the date of my death whichever period shall be the shorter by investing the same in any investments hereby authorised as my trustees shall think fit. Such accumulations and the interest or income thereof shall be held by my trustees to make up any deficiency of the annuity in any subsequent year and in so far as they are not so required they shall form an accretion to the annuity fund and on the determination of the said annuity shall with the annuity fund fall into and form part of my residuary estate.[4]

For the purposes hereof the Index of Retail Prices shall mean the Index of Retail Prices published by HM Stationery Office or any official publication substituted therefor and in the event of any change after the date hereof in the reference base used to compile the said Index the figure taken to be that at which the said Index stands after such change shall be the figure at which the said Index would have stood if the reference base current at the date hereof had been retained.

1   The Index of Retail Prices is published monthly in the Department of Employment Gazette. The current index was introduced in 1956 and replaced earlier indexes to which it can be linked back (see Industrial Relations Handbook and a publication of the Stationery Office 'Method of Construction and Calculation of the Index of Retail Prices').

2   See para **[211.8]**, n 3.

3   In economic conditions of high inflation and a tendency of most investments to fail to maintain their value in real terms, the use of this form is likely to present the trustees with considerable difficulty in deciding what size fund is appropriate, and a discretion not to do so may be preferred. In such economic conditions there is a serious risk of a large proportion of the estate being used up to meet an annuity in this form, with much capital being paid out, and charged to income tax, as income.

4   As to the right to 'hold up' income to meet future annuity instalments, see *Re Berkeley, Inglis v Countess Berkeley* [1968] Ch 744, [1968] 3 All ER 364, CA and see generally Vol 1, **[33.25]**. This subclause will mean that there is no interest in possession in the part of the annuity fund not treated as subject to the annuitant's interest in possession for inheritance tax purposes (see para **[211.3]**), and that that part will be subject to the 'discretionary trust' inheritance charging regime described in the Note to B18 at para **[218.1]** et seq.

[211.12]

FORM B11.5:   **Gift of several annuities**

I give free of all deductions[1] the following annuities to the following persons for their respective lives to be paid free of all deductions by equal half-yearly payments the first whereof respectively shall be made at the end of six months after my death. [*Add particulars of annuities and annuitants in separate paragraphs.*]

And I direct my trustees to appropriate in respect of each such annuity[2] [out of my personal estate] in their names investments of any nature hereinafter authorised of an amount sufficient at the date of such appropriation in the opinion of my trustees to answer out of the income thereof the annuity in respect of which such appropriation is made [and an increased margin of income not exceeding 10 per cent of that annuity] and I declare that such income shall be the primary fund for answering the said annuity and the capital of the said investments shall form the secondary fund for answering the same in the event of the income proving insufficient and further that after any such appropriation shall have been made my residuary estate or the income thereof shall no longer be liable to provide for the annuity in respect of which such appropriation shall have been made.

[*If annuities are to be charged on income only omit declaration as to primary and secondary fund and substitute*: And I declare that after such appropriation as aforesaid such income shall be the primary and only fund for answering the said annuity and that any deficiency of such income in any year shall be borne by the annuitant and shall not be made good to the annuitant.]

And I declare that the balance (if any) of the income of [the] [each] appropriated fund not required in any year for answering the annuity [in respect of which the fund was appropriated] shall form part of the income of my residuary estate and shall be distributed accordingly.

[*If an annuity is given free of income tax, add the following*: I direct that all rebates, allowances or repayments which may be made to or recovered by the said [*names*] in respect of income tax shall enure for the benefit of the said [*names*] [respectively] and that the said [*names*] shall not account to my trustees for the same or any part thereof *or* I direct that the said [*names*] shall respectively account to my trustees for all rebates allowances or repayments which may be made or allowed to them in respect of income tax.]

1   See para **[211.8]**, n 3.
2   It is probably convenient to have a separate fund for each annuity, so as to ensure that definite investments shall fall into residue automatically on the cesser of the annuity in question and be divisible as residue without question.

[211.13]

FORM B11.6:   Gift of annuities charged on land

I give the following annuities (that is to say) to [*names of annuitants and amounts and periods of duration of annuities*] and I hereby charge my lands and premises at —— in the county of —— with the payment of the said annuities [in exoneration of the rest of my estate[1]] and I direct that the said annuities shall be paid clear of all deductions[2] by equal quarterly payments the first whereof shall respectively be made three months after my death [and I further direct that no part of the inheritance tax payable by reason of my death in respect of such lands and premises shall be borne or paid by the said annuities or the said annuitants or any of them but all such tax shall be borne and paid by the person or persons entitled (subject to the said annuities) to the said lands and premises].

1   If the land is to be charged with the payment of the annuities in exoneration of the testator's personal estate, this must be expressly stated. Such a charge will result in the land being held on trust to give effect to the charge and there will be a trust of land within the TLATA 1996, s 2 and Sch 1, para 3 (Part G, paras **[246.87]** and **[246.114]**). Such an annuitant will not be regarded as having an interest in possession in the land within the meaning of the TLATA 1996 and so no question of a right to occupy the land or a right to be consulted or to have trustees' powers delegated to him can arise: TLATA 1996, ss 9, 11, 12 and 22 (Part G, paras **[246.94]**, **[246.97]**, **[246.98]** and **[246.108]**).
    An annuity charged only on land in the absence of any contrary intention was liable to bear a proportionate part of the interest on the sum required for estate duty upon the land (see Finance Act 1894, s 14; and *Re Parker-Jervis, Salt v Locker* [1898] 2 Ch 643), and the same used to be thought to be the case in relation to capital transfer (now inheritance) tax. However, as a result of legislative clarification following the Scottish decision in *Re Dougal* [1981] STC 514, it is now settled that tax on realty is prima facie a testamentary expense payable out of residue: see now the ITA 1984, s 211 (Part G, para **[246.83]**). Accordingly, an annuity charged on land will not now be burdened with payment of inheritance tax arising from the testator's death (unless there is some direction to that effect by the testator).
    The description of the land charged should be as specific as possible.
    If the land is eg agricultural land with a very low income yield there could be a serious inheritance tax disadvantage in the annuities being charged on it: see the Preliminary Note at para **[211.3]**
2   See para **[211.8]**, n 3.

[211.14]

FORM B11.7:   Power to purchase annuities, the capital cost being recouped out of income[1]

1.   I give free of all deductions[2] the following annuities [*particulars of names of annuitants and amounts and periods of duration of annuities*].

2.   I empower my trustees if in their discretion they think such a course in the best interests of my estate to purchase out of my residuary [personal] estate the above annuities from an insurance office of repute.

3.   In each of the twenty-one years from my death my trustees shall out of the income of my residuary estate add to the capital thereof a sum equal [either] to one twenty-first part of the sum required to purchase the annuities hereby bequeathed [or a sum equal to the balance of income remaining after paying to the person entitled from time to time to the income of my residuary estate the sum of £—— whichever shall be the less].[3]

1   For various reasons it is more convenient for purposes of administration to direct the purchase
     of an annuity than to charge it on the estate. In this form the trustees are given a discretionary
     power to purchase. For a direction to purchase, see Form B11.10 at para **[211.17]**. From the
     time when the trustees finally determine to exercise the power, the annuitant can claim to have
     the value of the annuity paid over to him. It may be desired to recoup the capital loss out of
     income. It is important to make sure that the income will be sufficient to stand this burden and
     provision is here made to ensure that the life tenant will receive a minimum sum. See however,
     sub-para (2)(b) of the Preliminary Note at para **[211.6]** and n 3 infra.

2   See para **[211.8]**, n 3.

3   Clause 3 apparently has the effect that a portion of the capital of the residuary estate will be
     treated as not being subject to an interest in possession for inheritance tax purposes, and thus
     subject to the 'discretionary trust' charging règime outlined in the Preliminary Note to B18 at
     para **[218.1]** et seq. For this reason it may in many cases be preferable to omit this clause when
     this form is used.

[211.15]

FORM B11.8:   Power to trustees to appropriate investments to answer annuities[1]—separate fund for each annuity

I authorise my trustees to provide for the payment of any annuity hereby or by
any codicil hereto bequeathed by setting apart and appropriating in respect of
each such annuity such part or parts of my residuary [personal] estate as shall in
their opinion be sufficient by the income thereof to pay such annuity.

I declare that when such appropriation shall have been made the annuity in
respect of which the appropriation shall be made shall be wholly charged on the
investments so appropriated (hereinafter referred to as 'the annuity fund') in
exoneration of the rest of my estate but that the capital of the annuity fund may
be resorted to in case at any time the income thereof is insufficient to pay such
annuity.

I further declare that on the cesser of any annuity the annuity fund
appropriated to such annuity shall revert to and form part of my residuary estate
and that any surplus income arising from any annuity fund shall be applied as
income of my residuary estate.

1   As stated in the Preliminary Note to these forms on annuities (see paras **[211.1]**–**[211.7]**), if this
     procedure is adopted the annuitant cannot claim to have the capital value of the annuity paid
     over to him unless the estate proves insufficient to set aside a sufficient sum to answer the
     annuities: see Vol 1, para **[33.3]**. In this form a separate fund is to be set aside to answer each
     separate annuity and then on the cesser of such annuity, that fund falls into residue. It is perhaps
     more economical to set aside an aggregate fund to answer all the annuities, but in that case,
     particularly where economy has been exercised, there may be a question as to how much of the
     aggregate fund can be released on the cesser of any particular annuity and this may lead to
     disputes between the trustees and those entitled to the residue in cases where the residuary
     legatees are entitled to immediate payment of the amount of the fund released.

[211.16]

FORM B11.9:   Power to trustees to appropriate investments to answer annuities—aggregate fund for all annuities[1]

[I authorise] *or* [I direct] my trustees to provide for the payment of the annuities
hereby or by any codicil hereto bequeathed by setting apart and appropriating in

respect of those annuities such part or parts of my residuary personal estate as shall in their opinion be sufficient by the income thereof to pay such annuities.

I declare that:

(i)   when such appropriation shall have been made the annuities shall be wholly charged on the investments so appropriated (hereinafter called 'the annuity fund') in exoneration of the rest of my estate but that the capital of the annuity fund may be resorted to if at any time the income thereof is insufficient to pay such annuities;

(ii) on the cesser of any annuity such part of the annuity fund as my trustees in their absolute and uncontrolled discretion shall determine shall be released to and thereafter be treated as part of my residuary estate my trustees retaining such part of the annuity fund as they may consider sufficient to produce by the income thereof an annual sum equal to the amount of any subsisting annuities;

(iii) any surplus income at any time arising from the annuity fund shall be applied as income of my residuary estate;

(iv) my trustees may from time to time vary any of the investments from time to time constituting the annuity fund in exercise of the general power of investment.[2]

OR

[Form 5 of the Statutory Will Forms 1925 is hereby incorporated in this my will.[3]]

1   See notes to Form B11.8 at para **[211.15]**. For the statutory will form, see Form E5 at para **[238.11]**. Since surplus income is applied as income of the residuary estate, this form is preferable to, eg Form B11.4 at para **[211.11]**, in its inheritance tax consequences: see para **[211.11]**, n 4.
2   For the general power of investment, see the TrA 2000, s 3 (Part G, para **[246.118]**).
3   For the text of this form, see Form E5 at para **[238.11]**. This form includes the usual provisions where one fund is made answerable for several annuities and by incorporating this Form it may well be that a number of annuities can be provided for more economically than by appropriating a separate fund to each annuity.

[211.17]

FORM B11.10:   Gift of annuity with direction to purchase[1]

I give free of all deductions[2] to A an annuity of £—— for the period of [his]/[her] life to commence from my decease and payable every three months the first payment to be made three months after my decease and I direct my executors to provide for the payment of the said annuity by purchasing the same from any public company.

1   Where there is a *direction* to purchase an annuity (as distinct from a *power* to purchase) the annuitant becomes immediately entitled if he or she so elects to be paid the sum necessary for such purchase and, even if he or she dies before any payment of the annuity becomes payable (but after the death of the testator), his or her personal representatives are entitled to the sum necessary for such purchase: *Re Robbins, Robbins v Legge* [1907] 2 Ch 8; *Re Brunning, Gammon v Dale* [1909] 1 Ch 276. In the case of a *power* to purchase the personal representatives of the annuitant have no such right.

This form may be both a grant of the annuity and a direction to purchase or merely a direction to purchase when the form will be: 'I direct my executors to purchase an annuity for A payable during her life of £—— per annum from any public company.'

If the will states that the purchase may be from any public company, the testator's executors have a discretion from whom they will purchase the annuity and, if a capital sum is claimed, it is only the sum required to purchase the annuity from the source chosen by the executors: *Re Smith, Royal Exchange Co v Lee* (1923) 130 LT 185. If for any reason the executors do not exercise that discretion or option, it is thought that the annuitant or his or her personal representatives could demand the cost of the annuity as determined in accordance with the Government annuity tables which remain in force despite the discontinuance of the sale of Government annuities in 1962. The tables now in force are those laid down by the following Government Annuity Table Orders: SI 1963/1178, SI 1968/1731, SI 1973/1407, SI 1974/1935, SI 1975/692, and SI 1977/1536.

The position where there is a power to purchase is rather different. It is not until the trustees have decided to exercise the power, that the annuitant can demand the sum required to purchase the annuity and in such a case the annuitant's personal representatives have no claim whatsoever in any event. See also Form B11.12 at para **[211.19]** and Vol 1, paras **[33.4]– [33.10]**.

2 See para **[211.8]**, n 3.

[211.18]

FORM B11.11: Annuity provisions designed to mitigate inheritance tax and income tax[1]

(a) I give free of inheritance tax[2] to [*name*] of [*address*] (in this clause called 'the annuitant') for his life and payable by equal quarterly instalments (the first payment to be made three months after my death) [an annuity of £——] *or* [an annuity of such sum as after deduction of income tax at the basic rate in force for the time being (the annuitant being entitled to retain any repayment of tax made to him) amounts to £——[3]].

(b) My trustees may provide for or in relation to the said annuity at their discretion at any time in any one or more of the following ways:

(i) By appropriating such part of my residuary estate as will in their opinion yield sufficient income to pay the annuity and the cost of paying it and if they exercise this power then the annuity shall be charged wholly on the appropriated fund (to which the powers of investment hereafter given shall apply) in exoneration of the rest of my estate but the capital of the appropriated fund may be resorted to if it is at any time insufficient to pay the annuity and when the annuity ceases the appropriated fund shall form part of my residuary estate and any surplus income which may arise from it in the mean time shall be applied as income of my residuary estate.[4]

(ii) By purchasing in their names an annuity from any public company and paying it to the annuitant but if my trustees exercise this power and the annuitant then does or permits any act or event or process by which the annuity thus provided would or might (but for this provision) become vested in or payable to any other person then his annuity shall immediately cease and the payments received during the remainder of his life under the purchased annuity shall be applied as income of my residuary estate and I declare that if my trustees decide to exercise this power the annuitant shall not be entitled to receive the capital value of the annuity given to him.[5]

(iii) By commuting the annuity with the annuitant's consent and paying to him such capital sum as they may in their discretion consider reasonable in all the circumstances (having regard in particular to the fact that any inheritance tax otherwise payable on the death of the annuitant may be avoided and that the administration of my estate may be simplified and to the position in relation to income tax) and if my trustees exercise this power the annuitant shall have no further claim against my estate in respect of this annuity.[6]

(iv) [By accepting from [name of residuary legatee]] or [By accepting from any one or more of the following persons namely [names of residuary legatees or others who might be willing to provide the annuity]] a Deed of Covenant in a form approved by my trustees and providing for the payment of the annuity by such person [or jointly and severally by such persons] and [his]/[her]/[their] personal representatives (and with any personal guarantees or sureties which my trustees may require) for the remainder of the annuitant's lifetime and if such a Deed is made and accepted by my trustees then the gift of the annuity made by subclause (a) of this clause shall not take effect or shall cease to have effect (as the case may be).[7]

1   See para **[211.6]** for a possible disadvantage of the powers to commute the annuity.
2   For the importance of this direction see para **[211.3]**.
3   For alternative forms of 'tax-free' annuity provisions see Form B11.3 at para **[211.10]**.
4   See para **[211.16]**, n 1.
5   This power is for the trustees to purchase an annuity and is worded in such a way that the annuitant cannot call for the capital even when they have decided to exercise it. Its use is virtually confined to circumstances in which the trustees feel that if the annuitant received a lump sum he might, to his own detriment, spend it otherwise than on an annuity. If they do not feel this, they would do better to act under the power to commute, which immediately follows. There would, it seems, be an inheritance tax charge on the forfeiture of a purchased annuity under this subclause under the ITA 1984, s 52(1). Potential exemption can now be available. For the circumstances in which it may be, see para **[211.6]**.
6   A power of this kind has been suggested by Messrs E F and J H George in *Brighouse's Short Forms of Wills*, where it is pointed out that since the use of the power will benefit the estate financially (by saving inheritance tax on the annuitant's death), and will benefit the annuitant as well (for the capital element in the annuity which he buys will be exempt from income tax), it may be possible for the trustees to grant a lump sum which will enable the annuitant to buy an annuity which gives him a higher net income than he would have had under the will and still leave the estate better off. For the inheritance implications of the exercise of such a power, see para **[211.6]**.
7   For an inheritance tax disadvantage of the exercise of such a power see para **[211.6]**.

[211.19]

FORM B11.12:   Gift of annuity and direction to trustees to purchase; the annuity to cease on alienation, and the annuitant not to be entitled to purchase-money in lieu of the annuity

I give to [*name of annuitant*] during [his]/[her] life an annuity of £—— [free of inheritance tax] to be paid by equal quarterly payments the first whereof shall be made three calendar months after my death and I direct my trustees [unless they see special reason to the contrary[1]] to purchase in their names and at the expense of my estate from some insurance office of repute an annuity for the life of the said [*annuitant*] of the above amount and I declare that my trustees shall stand possessed of such annuity when purchased upon trust to pay the same to the said [*annuitant*] in manner above directed and that until such purchase the said annuity shall be paid out of the income of my residuary estate. Provided always that if the said [*annuitant*] shall commit permit or suffer any act default or process whereby the said annuity or any part thereof would or might but for this present provision become vested in or payable to any other person or persons then such annuity shall immediately thereupon absolutely cease and determine as if the said [*annuitant*] were dead and any purchased annuity shall thenceforth during the life of the said [*annuitant*] be paid to [*name of person entitled on gift over*] and I declare that the said [*annuitant*] shall not be entitled to receive the capital value of the said annuity in lieu thereof.

1   If these words are omitted and the clause were ended at the words 'of the above amount' in the third line below these words, the annuitant would have the right to claim the cash value of the annuity. If the trustees had not, as here, been given the right to purchase from an insurance company, the cash value would have to be calculated by reference to the Government Tables: see para **[211.17]**, n 1 and Vol 1, paras **[33.4]**–**[33.10]**. The latter part of this clause makes the receipt of the capital sum altogether contrary to the intention of the testator and the right is in the last words of the clause expressly negatived; but these are insufficient to prevent the claim being sustained. The right to receive the capital sum can be prevented only by a gift over; see Vol 1, para **[33.7]**. As to valuation of annuities see Vol 1, paras **[33.35]**–**[33.43]**. For a possible inheritance tax disadvantage of this form see para **[211.6]**. Further, this would not seem to be a protective trust within the ITA 1984, s 88 (see Part A, para **[200.116]**) and there would be an inheritance tax charge under the ITA 1984, s 52(1) on a forfeiture occurring unless potential exemption was available.

[211.20]

FORM B11.13:   Proviso for cesser of annuities on alienation

Provided always that if any of the said annuitants [*or* any [*or* either] of them the said [*names of particular annuitants*]] shall commit permit or suffer any act default or process whereby but for this present provision the said annuity hereinbefore bequeathed to [him] *or* [her] or any part thereof would or might become vested in or payable to any other person or persons then such annuity shall immediately thereupon absolutely cease and determine as if such annuitant were dead.

[211.21]

FORM B11.14:   Declaration that annuities are to be paid clear of all deductions[1]

I declare that all the annuities bequeathed hereby or by any codicil hereto shall be paid clear of all deductions whatsoever [including income tax at the basic rate deductible at source] and that the expenses of and incidental to the purchase of any annuity under the provisions of this my will shall be borne by my residuary estate. I further declare that any rebate, allowance or repayment of income tax which may be allowed or made to any annuitant under this my will shall enure for the benefit of such annuitant[2].

1   See para **[211.5]**, sub-paras (iii) and (iv) and para **[211.8]**, n 2.
2   See para **[211.10]**, n 1.

[211.22]

FORM B11.15:   Gift of several annuities to same person, being annuities to widow with reduction on remarriage and provision for minor children residing with widow[1]

I give to my wife the following annuities [free of inheritance tax[2]] [and to have priority over all other pecuniary legacies and annuities hereby or by any codicil hereto bequeathed]:

(1)   as from my death so long as she remains my widow an annuity of £——[3]

(2)   as from her remarriage an annuity of £—— during the residue of her life and

(3)   as from my death so long as any child of mine[4] being a minor and unmarried resides with her[2] an annuity of £—— in respect of each such child. As to such annuities I declare as follows:

(a)   Such annuities if and when respectively payable shall be paid clear of all deductions[5] by equal quarterly payments on the usual quarter days with all necessary apportionments thereof respectively and my trustees shall not be bound to see to the application of any annuity payable under the trusts hereof to my said wife in respect of any child of mine.

(b)   My trustees shall as soon as conveniently may be provide for the payment of the said annuities by setting apart and appropriating a sufficient part of my residuary personal estate to produce by the income thereof such annuities and when that has been done such annuities shall be wholly charged on the investments so appropriated (hereinafter referred to as 'the annuity fund') in exoneration of the rest of my estate but the capital of the annuity fund may be resorted to if at any time the income thereof is insufficient to pay such annuities.

(c)   Till such appropriation the said annuities shall be paid out of [the income of] my residuary estate.

(d)   On the cesser of any of the said annuities the annuity fund or such part thereof as shall not in the opinion of my trustees be required for payment of the annuity or annuities for the time being remaining payable shall revert to and form part of my residuary estate and any surplus income arising from the annuity fund in each year shall be applied as income of my residuary estate.

---

1   These annuities are not given free of income tax. If the widow has little other income they will no doubt become virtually free of tax by reason that the widow's total income is not taxable. If the widow has an income of her own, a provision making them tax-free may lead to involved calculations if the widow is to account for reliefs, etc.

2   See para **[211.5]**, sub-para (i). These words should be omitted unless there are grounds for thinking that the gift might not be wholly exempt from inheritance tax, such as the testator being domiciled in the UK and his wife not.

3   The remarriage of the widow and the leaving home or coming of age of each child will be occasions of inheritance tax charge under the ITA 1984, s 52(1) unless potential exemption applies. See para **[211.6]** et seq.

4   Illegitimate and adopted children will be included: see Vol 1, paras **[72.1]** et seq and **[75.1]** et seq.

5   See para **[211.8]**, n 2.

[211.23]

FORM B11.16:   Gift of an annuity to a trustee in trust for a mentally disabled daughter[1]

I give to [*trustee*] during the life of my daughter [*name*] an annuity of £—— free of all inheritance tax[2] to be paid by equal quarterly payments the first whereof shall be made three months after my death and I authorise my trustees either to purchase from some insurance society of good repute an annuity of the above amount[3] or set apart and appropriate so much of my residuary estate (hereinafter called 'the annuity fund') as shall in their opinion be sufficient by means of the income thereof to pay such annuity and I direct as follows:

(1)   When the annuity shall have been provided for in either of the ways aforesaid the rest of my estate shall be exonerated from payment thereof and my trustees shall have recourse only to the annuity or the annuity fund to pay such annuity.

(2)   The capital of the annuity fund (if any) may be resorted to in case at any time the income thereof is insufficient to pay the said annuity.

(3)   On the cesser of the said annuity the annuity fund (if any) shall revert to my residuary estate and any surplus income arising in any year from the annuity fund shall be applied as income of my residuary estate.

(4)

(a)   The said [*trustee*] shall stand possessed of the said annuity of £—— upon trust to pay or apply the same for the maintenance or benefit of my said daughter [*name*] including the payment of all expenses of and incidental to the provision of a home for and the care and maintenance of my said daughter [*name*] and the said [*trustee*] shall have full and uncontrolled discretion with respect to the application of the said annuity and if and so long as my said daughter shall reside with the said [*trustee*] [he] *or* [she] shall be entitled to retain for [his] *or* [her] own benefit out of the said annuity the sum of £—— by way of rent in respect thereof.[4]

(b)   If at the date of the death of my said daughter there shall be any moneys resulting from any unapplied part of such annuity the same shall [fall as capital into my residuary estate]/[be paid by the said [*trustee*] to the treasurer for the time being of the —— Home for Incurables [*address*] whose receipt shall be a good discharge].

1   It is thought that this gives the annuitant an interest in possession for inheritance tax purposes. If it does not do so, the annuitant, if incapable of administering her property or managing her affairs within the meaning of the Mental Health Act 1983 at the date of the testator's death (or in receipt of an attendance allowance at that time), will be deemed to have an interest in possession under the ITA 1984, s 89. See also para **[226.3]** et seq.
2   See para **[211.5]**, sub-para (i).
3   For a possible inheritance tax disadvantage of the exercise of this power see para **[211.6]**.
4   Compare Form B18.4 at para **[218.34]**.

[211.24]

FORM B11.17:   Gift of an annuity upon trust for a spendthrift son and his wife and children

[*Gift of annuity, as in last form, down to the words* income of my residuary estate, *substituting* son *for* daughter *throughout.*]

(4)   [The said [*trustee*] shall stand possessed of the said annuity of £——
upon trust to pay or apply the same to or for the benefit of my said son during
his life or until he shall alienate or charge the same or become bankrupt or do or
suffer any act or thing whereby the same or any part thereof would or might but
for this present provision become vested in or payable to any other person or
persons.]

(5)   [*If the annuity is to cease on alienation*: After the happening of any of
the events hereinbefore mentioned the said annuity (if purchased) shall be
applied as income of my residuary estate].[1]

[*If the 'protected' interest is to continue during the life of the son substitute
the following for (4) and (5):* The said [*trustee*] shall hold the said annuity on
protective trusts for the benefit of my said son for the period of his life].[2]

1   Under this alternative there may be an occasion of inheritance tax charge when forfeiture occurs
    under the ITA 1984, s 52(1) (termination of an interest in possession) unless potential
    exemption is available. See para [211.6] et seq.
2   See the TA 1925, s 33 (Part G, para [246.28]), Part A, para [200.116] and Form B16.2 at
    para [216.7]. Where the annuitant was bankrupt at the death of the testator, but obtained his
    discharge before the first instalment of the annuity became payable, there was a forfeiture of the
    annuity (*Re Walker, Public Trustee v Walker* [1939] Ch 974, [1939] 3 All ER 902). A forfeiture
    of a protected life interest will not give rise to a charge to inheritance tax despite the termination
    of the life tenant's interest in possession: see the ITA 1984, s 88.

[211.25]

**FORM B11.18:   Direction as to payment of an annuity not created by the
will for insertion where the residue is settled**[1]

I direct that the payment of the annuity to [*name*] payable under a deed dated —
—— and made between —— shall be payable out of the capital of my residuary
estate.

1   Where an annuity not created by the will is payable out of settled residue the strict rule is to
    apply either of two complicated methods of calculation: see Vol 1, para [38.26]. This form will
    not make a great deal of difference unless the amount of the annuity is considerable but it is a
    far simpler method of dealing with the matter. The annuity could of course be made payable out
    of income only, but unless the annual income of the estate is considerable, this may place an
    unfair burden on the tenant for life.

B12 Charitable gifts

Part B   Clauses in wills

PRELIMINARY NOTE

[212.1]
For a statement of the general law relating to charities see Vol 1, paras **[102.1]**–**[103.21]**. And see the Note in B2 at para **[202.28]** et seq for charitable gifts for the maintenance of graves.

[212.2]
Charitable gifts are wholly exempt from inheritance tax: Inheritance Tax Act 1984 (ITA 1984), s 23. It is thought that, like the exemption for charities from income tax, the inheritance tax exemption is confined to charities established in the UK (see the income tax case of *Camille and Henry Dreyfus Foundation v IRC* [1956] AC 39, [1955] 3 All ER 97). Gifts to certain institutions, eg the British Museum, the National Gallery and the National Trust are wholly exempt: ITA 1984, s 25 and Sch 3. Gifts to political parties may in certain circumstances enjoy a similar exemption: ITA 1984, s 24. Gifts to housing associations may also be exempt: ITA 1984, s 24A. Many charitable gifts are concerned with quite small charities in which the testator has taken an active interest. It is with such charities that practical difficulties may occur: that is, that they have very little organisation and it may be difficult to find someone who can give a proper receipt for the legacy. It is wise in such cases to provide not only that the receipt of the treasurer or other proper officer shall be a full discharge, but to go further and say that the receipt of the person who professes to be the proper officer shall be such a discharge. In all cases it is important for those drawing the will to ascertain the precise name of the charity which the testator intends to benefit, for, on the one hand, there are many with very similar names and, on the other hand, testators commonly speak of a charity by a name which is quite different from its proper name. Failure to give the charity's correct name may result in the gift going to the wrong charity or even failing altogether. Now that most charities can be registered the name should be checked with the Charity Commission.

[212.3]

FORM B12.1:   Gifts to several charitable institutions[1]

I give[2] to the following institutions the sums set opposite their names and declare that the receipt of [the person who professes to be][3] the treasurer or other proper officer for the time being of the institution shall in each case be a sufficient discharge to my trustees
    To [*name of first institution*] the sums of £——
    To [*name of second institution*] the sum of £—— [*and similarly for all other institutions*].

1   The trustees should be discharged upon obtaining a receipt from an officer of the institution. Some small charities may not be constituted in any regular way and the trustees may have to accept the best receipt they can obtain for the legacy. The legacy, however, does not fail because there is no one who can give a receipt: *Re Meyers* [1951] Ch 534, [1951] 1 All ER 538; *Re Hutchinson's Will Trusts, Gibbons v Nottingham, Area No 1 Hospital Management Committee* [1953] Ch 387, [1953] 1 All ER 996. Another provision which can help in cases where there is a problem in identifying someone to whom a charitable gift can properly be paid is an anti-lapse clause as in Form B12.29 at para **[212.31]**.

2   The words 'free of inheritance tax' are not necessary now that the £100,000 limit on the exemption for gifts on or within one year of death has been removed: see para **[212.2]**. The words should be inserted at this point if the form is used for any gift to an institution which is not charitable, and the fund out of which the legacies will be paid includes assets which bear their own inheritance tax (see paras **[210.3]** and **[210.4]**).

3   To avoid practical difficulties in obtaining a receipt it is wise to include these words.

[212.4]

FORM B12.2:   Gifts of shares of residue to individual and charitable institutions

My trustees shall hold my residuary estate and the income thereof upon trust as to:

(a)   a one third share for my son for his own use and benefit absolutely;

(b)   a one third share for the charity known as [*name and address of charity*] for its general purposes (the receipt of the person who professes to be the treasurer or other proper officer for the time being of the charity to be sufficient discharge to my trustees); and

(c)   a one third share for such charitable institution or institutions in England [which have amongst their objects the relief of aged and infirm persons] as my trustees may in their absolute discretion within the period of one year from my death select and if more than one in such proportions as my trustees may think proper (the receipt of the person who professes to be the treasurer or other proper officer for the time being of any selected charitable institution to be sufficient discharge to my trustees) and in default of or subject to any such selection for the aforesaid charity [*name of charity*] for its general purposes.

And I hereby declare that in determining the said one third shares of my residuary estate my trustees shall divide my residuary estate into three shares without making any allowance for the inheritance tax payable by reason of my death and attributable to my residuary estate and then reducing such shares as are not exempt from inheritance tax by the inheritance tax attributable thereto.[1]

1   Where other shares of residue will not be exempt from inheritance tax, a declaration such as this should be included to avoid complicated calculations, see para **[214.72]**.

[212.5]

FORM B12.3:   Gift of a share of residue upon trust for charitable objects to be selected by trustees[1]

(1)   My trustees shall hold one equal [fourth] part of my residuary estate and the income thereof upon trust to apply the same for such charitable institutions or such other charitable objects in England as my trustees may in their absolute discretion select and to pay such share and income to or for such institutions or objects if more than one in such proportions as my trustees may think proper and I declare that the receipt of the [person who professes to be the][2] treasurer or other proper officer for the time being of any such charity shall be an effectual discharge to my trustees in respect of any sum (whether of capital or income) allocated under this gift.

(2)   I express the wish without imposing any binding trust or obligation that my trustees should distribute the whole of the said equal [fourth] part of my residuary estate and the income thereof within the period of two years from my death [and until such distribution is complete my trustees shall have power to invest all moneys liable to be invested in any property of whatever description or location as if they were a sole beneficial owner of such moneys][3].

(3)   The fractional shares of my residuary estate shall be determined by dividing my residuary estate into the fractional shares set out above without making any allowance for the inheritance tax payable by reason of my death and attributable to my residuary estate and then reducing such shares as are not exempt from inheritance tax by the inheritance tax attributable thereto.[4]

1   This form will be suitable where it is envisaged that the distribution will take place shortly after the testator's death. For a long-term discretionary trust, see Form C13.1 at para **[235.2]**. Care must be taken as to the description of the objects to be benefited in a gift such as this. It is clear that a gift for 'charitable objects' is good. A gift for 'charitable and benevolent objects' has also been held to be good (*Re Best, Jarvis v Birmingham Corpn* [1904] 2 Ch 354). On the other hand, a gift for 'charitable or benevolent objects' will be void for uncertainty (*Hunter v A-G* [1899] AC 309; *Re Horrocks, Taylor v Kershaw* [1939] P 198, [1939] 1 All ER 579; *Chichester Diocesan Fund and Board of Finance Inc v Simpson* [1944] AC 341, [1944] 2 All ER 60); but 'a gift for charitable or religious purposes' is good (*Re Ward, Public Trustee v Ward* [1941] Ch 308, [1941] 2 All ER 125, CA); the Charitable Trusts (Validation) Act 1954 validated certain existing charitable trusts that would otherwise have been void but did not have an effect on trusts created thereafter. See generally Vol 1, para **[102.23]**.
     There is a prima facie presumption that every power given to a trustee, even one involving the exercise of a very wide discretion such as the above is vested in them virtue officii and accordingly passes with the office to the holders for the time being thereof (*Re Smith, Eastick v Smith* [1904] 1 Ch 139). If, therefore, the testator desires that the power of selection is only to be exercised by the individuals named as trustees special provision must be made. A testator may leave the selection of charity beneficiaries to trustees see *A-G v National Provincial Bank* [1924] AC 262, [1923] All ER Rep 123 at 264 and 126 respectively.
2   To avoid practical difficulties in obtaining a receipt it is wise to include these words.
3   These words could be left out, because they are no broader than the general power of investment by which personal representatives can now make any kind of investment which they could make if they were absolutely entitled to the assets of the estate: TrA 2000, ss 3 and 35 (Part G, paras **[246.118]** and **[246.150]**)
4   If other shares of residue will not be exempt from inheritance tax, a declaration such as this should be included to avoid complicated calculations, see para **[214.72]**.

[212.6]

FORM B12.4:   Gift of residue upon a charitable trust[1]

I give my residuary estate (hereinafter called 'the trust fund') to my trustees to hold the same upon the following trusts with and subject to the following powers and provisions:

(1)   In this clause 'charity' means any purpose which is exclusively charitable according to the law of England and Wales and any institution whether corporate or not (including any trust or undertaking) which is established for purposes which are exclusively charitable according to the law of England and Wales and 'charities' has a corresponding meaning.[2]

(2)   My trustees shall pay the income of the trust fund to such charity or charities if more than one in such shares and in such manner generally as my trustees shall in their absolute discretion think fit provided that until the expiration of the period of 21 years from my death my trustees shall have power

to accumulate the whole or any part of such income by investing the same and the resulting income thereof in any manner hereby authorised so that any accumulations so made shall form an accretion to the capital from which such income arose for all purposes.

(3)   Notwithstanding the foregoing trust of income my trustees shall have power at any time or times to pay transfer or apply the whole or any part or parts of the capital of the trust fund to or for the benefit of such charity or charities in such shares if more than one and in such manner generally as my trustees shall in their absolute discretion think fit.

(4)   I express the wish without imposing any trust or legal obligation that my trustees should consider the purpose of the relief of poor persons resident in the county of —— and charities which have amongst their objects the relief of such persons as the principal beneficiaries of the trust fund and the income thereof.

(5)   The receipt of the person who professes to be the treasurer or other proper officer for the time being of any charity shall be sufficient discharge to my trustees.[3]

1   See also Form C13.1 at para **[235.2]**. The will should include suitable investment powers for the trustees as this trust may continue for some time.
2   This definition of charity is derived from the CA 1993, ss 96 and 97.
3   To avoid practical difficulties in obtaining a receipt it is wise to include these words.

[212.7]

FORM B12.5:   Gift to a Church of England Board of Finance[1]

I give the sum of £ —— to [the Central Board of Finance of the Church of England of Church House, Great Smith Street, London SW1[2]] [the Board of Finance of the Diocese of —— of [*address*][3]] for such ecclesiastical charitable purposes as the Board shall in its absolute discretion decide [*or* in aid of the fund for ——] [*or* for the following charitable purpose namely —— [*eg* the training of ordination candidates both male and female in the Church of England]] and I declare that the receipt of the secretary for the time being of the Board shall be a full and sufficient discharge to my trustees.

1   This form is based on forms recommended by the Central Board of Finance of the Church of England.
2   In *Re Barnes, Simpson v Barnes* [1930] 2 Ch 80n, it was held that a gift to 'the Church of England' was a good charitable gift, but the question whether the Central Board of Finance (a body incorporated in 1914 which administers the Central Church Fund which was established the year following) was entitled to call for the property given as of right was left undecided. If, therefore a gift for Church of England purposes is intended, it is advisable for the gift to be made in favour of the Central Board of Finance or one of the diocesan boards of finance (as to which see n 3 infra).
3   In every diocese there is a diocesan board of finance incorporated under the Companies Acts. A diocesan board of finance is empowered by its constitution to hold property for purposes connected with the Church of England.

[212.8]

FORM B12.6:   Gift to vicar for poor of a parish[1]

I give to the vicar [parish priest] for the time being of the parish of —— near —— — in the County of —— the sum of £—— to be used by him for the assistance in such manner in all respects as he shall determine of the poor of the said parish and the receipt of the said vicar [parish priest] shall be a full discharge to my trustees for the said sum and my trustees shall in no way be responsible for the application thereof.

1   It seems proper for such a gift to be made to the priest in charge, but it may, if the testator desires, be made to the parochial church council. As to gifts for parish purposes, see Form B12.8 at para [212.10] and Vol 1, para [102.16].

[212.9]

FORM B12.7:   Bequest coupled with a request to effectuate a purpose which the law will not enforce[1]

I give £—— [free of inheritance tax] to [*name of person or the holder of an office* at the date of my death or if the said office is then vacant to the first holder thereof within five years after the date of my death] absolutely. Without any intention of creating a trust or legal obligation I request the said —— to devote the said sum of £—— to [*the purpose desired*].

1   This is the form of bequest formerly in common use when it was desired to devote money to what were known as superstitious uses, such as the saying of masses for the dead. That purpose has now been held to be legal (see Form B12.11 at para [212.13]), but the form may still be wanted for some purposes. It can also be used for cases where the testator does not desire that the purpose shall be known except to some confidential agent who will apply the money according to his direction, though the purpose is one which the law allows. As this is not a charitable gift it will not be exempt from inheritance tax and the words 'free of inheritance tax' will be appropriate for inclusion where the legacy might be payable out of assets which bear their own inheritance tax. See paras [210.3], [214.59] and [214.60].

[212.10]

FORM B12.8:   Bequest for religious purposes in a particular parish[1]

I bequeath the sum of £—— to [the vicar and churchwardens for the time being] or [parochial church council] of the parish of —— on trust for such religious purposes in the said parish as [the said vicar and churchwardens] *or* [parochial church council] shall in their absolute discretion think fit and I declare that the receipt of [the said vicar and churchwardens] *or* [the treasurer of the said parochial church council] shall be a sufficient discharge to my trustees for the said sum and that my trustees shall not be bound to see to or inquire into the application thereof and I further declare that [the said vicar and churchwardens or their respective successors] *or* [the said parochial church council] shall be entitled at any time to expend the whole capital of the said sum in the manner aforesaid.

1   As to gifts for religious purposes, see Vol 1, paras [102.8] and [102.16].

[212.11]

FORM B12.9:   Bequest of legacy to provide Sunday school prizes[1]

1.   I give to my trustees the sum of £——.

2.   My trustees shall pay or transfer the said sum (which and the investments for the time being representing the same are hereinafter called the trust fund) to

or into the name of [the Parochial Church Council of ——] *or* [the vicar and churchwardens of the parish of ——²] *or* [the minister and deacons of the —— Congregational Church at ——] *or* [*as the case may be*] and [the Parochial Church Council] *or* [the vicar and churchwardens for the time being of the said parish] *or* [the minister and deacons for the time being of the said church] *or* [*as the case may be*] (hereinafter called the special trustees) shall hold the trust fund upon the trusts following:

(a)   Out of the yearly dividends of the trust fund the special trustees shall as they in their discretion think fit [grant prizes or awards] *or* [shall purchase prizes or awards of books] for deserving scholars attending a Sunday school in connection with [the church of St —— in the said parish] *or* [the said church] [for proficiency in religious knowledge] *or* [for good conduct regularity in attendance and progress in religious knowledge] provided that no one scholar shall receive any prizes or awards in respect of any one year exceeding in total [amount] *or* [value] the sum of ——.

(b)   If the whole of the dividends produced by the trust fund in any year shall not be applied in the [grant] *or* [purchase] of prizes or awards under the provision hereinbefore contained the special trustees shall at any time before the expiration of 21 years from my death invest and accumulate so much of the said dividends as is not so applied in their names [in any investments of whatever description or location as they may in their absolute discretion think fit]³ with power for the special trustees at their discretion to vary any investment for others of any nature hereby authorised and stand possessed of the said accumulations upon the same trusts as are hereby declared concerning the trust fund but so that the whole or any part of such accumulations may at any time be applied for the purposes aforesaid as if the same had been dividends arising in the year in which the same shall be so applied⁴ and after the expiration of 21 years from my death my special trustees shall pay or apply so much of the said dividends as is not applied as aforesaid for such religious purposes [in the said parish] *or* [of the said church] as they shall in their absolute discretion think fit.

1   The promotion of education in Christian knowledge is a charitable purpose: *A-G v Stepney* (1804) 10 Ves 22. See Vol 1, para [102.8].
2   It would seem the proper course to vest the legacy in the parochial church council, but, as the Parochial Church Councils (Powers) Measure 1956, s 5, is permissive in character, it may be that the legacy may still be vested in the vicar and churchwardens, as was the universal practice before 1921.
3   See para **[212.5]**, n 3.
3   As to this clause, see *Wharton v Masterman* [1895] AC 186 at 200.

[212.12]

FORM B12.10:   **Legacy to a religious community**¹

I give the sum of £—— to the person who at the time my trustees shall be ready to pay this legacy shall be or shall act as the [abbess] of the Convent of —— at —— in the county of —— [*or as the case may be*] upon trust to apply the income thereof for the general purposes of the said convent and the receipt of the said abbess or the person acting as such shall be a full discharge to my trustees for this gift.

1   The capital of the legacy is not disposed of, but a perpetual trust of income for charitable purposes is valid: *Re Levy, Barclays Bank Ltd v Board of Guardians and Trustees for the Relief of the Jewish Poor* [1960] Ch 346, [1960] 1 All ER 42. Those advising the testator must take particular care to obtain the correct name of the convent or community and the description of the person in charge. In many cases the person in charge will hold office for only a short period, a new head being elected or appointed from time to time. The descriptions of such persons vary considerably according to the religious order concerned. For a case where the will was witnessed by two nuns, one of whom had become abbess of the convent at the death of the testator, see *Re Ray's Will Trusts, Re Ray's Estate, Public Trustee v Barry* [1936] Ch 520, [1936] 2 All ER 93 (being a gift for the purposes of the convent and not a beneficial gift to either of the attesting witnesses, it was not rendered void by such attestation). If there is any doubt about the charitable status of the body in question, it would seem preferable to use a receipt clause in the terms of Form B12.1 at para **[212.3]** and to provide for the legacy to be free of inheritance tax where it may be payable wholly or partly out of assets which bear their own inheritance tax (see paras **[210.3]**, **[214.59]** and **[214.60]**).

[212.13]

FORM B12.11:   Bequests for masses[1]

I.   GIFT TO PARISH PRIEST

I give the sum of £—— to the priest in charge of the Roman Catholic Church at —— to be applied to the offering of masses in public for the repose of the soul[s] of —— and I declare that the receipt of the priest in charge of the said church at the time of the payment of the said sum of £—— shall be a full discharge to my executors in respect of the same.

II.   GIFT FOR A FOUNDATION MASS

[I give to the treasurer for the time being of the Roman Catholic diocese of the sum of £——] *or* [I direct my trustees to give to the treasurer for the time being of the Roman Catholic diocese of —— such sum as may be necessary] for the foundation of a [mass] *or* [masses] to be offered in public at the Roman Catholic church at —— for the repose of soul[s] of —— and I declare that the receipt of the treasurer for the time being of the said diocese shall be a full discharge to my executors in respect of the same.

III.   GIFT OF A SUM OF MONEY THE INCOME THEREOF TO BE APPLIED FOR THE OFFERING OF MASSES FOR THE DEAD

I give to the trustees of this my will the sum of £—— upon trust to apply the income thereof [for a period of —— years from the date of my death] in payment of the stipends [offerings][2] to the priest for the saying of masses in public for the repose of the soul[s] of —— such masses to be said as far as reasonably possible at the Roman Catholic church at —— the whole income in any one year being so expended as nearly as may be in the course of the year in which it is received and the receipt of the priest or priests saying such masses shall be a full discharge to my trustees in respect of the sums so paid [*add gift over if a limited period is provided for*].

1   At one time it was thought that a gift for masses was void as being for a superstitious use, but this view was held to be ill founded by the decision of the House of Lords in *Bourne v Keane* [1919] AC 815. It still remained to be decided whether such a gift was in law a charitable bequest, and it was decided to be so in *Re Caus, Lindeboom v Camille* [1934] Ch 162, [1933] All ER Rep 818. (This case was before the House of Lords in *Gilmour v Coats* [1949] AC 426, [1949] 1 All ER 848, and though it may be said that the House did not seem to regard the decision with any favour, their lordships refrained from expressing any definite view as to its correctness, and, indeed, the point of the decision did not arise in the case then decided.) The effect of the former decision was to confirm the validity of the bequest given in the first clause of this form. The latter decision made possible gifts, such as those in the remaining clauses, for the application of the income of an invested fund to defray the expenses of such masses. The more recent decision of *Re Hetherington* [1990] Ch 1, [1989] 2 All ER 129, has confirmed that a gift for the saying of masses in public, as opposed to in private, contains a sufficient element of public benefit to make the gift charitable. Where the gift is made by the payment of a lump sum to the parish priest, it will be presumably expended in defraying the mass stipends of the priest in saying masses within a short period of the date of the death of the person for whom they are to be said. A lump sum should be of a moderate amount. When a sum of £1,000 was given, it was decided by the diocesan authorities that such a gift was impossible of performance and the gift had to be refused. A foundation mass is a mass said once a year in perpetuity and is usually said upon the anniversary of the date of the death of the deceased, or possibly upon the Sunday nearest thereto. In such a case, a sum is paid to, and invested by, the diocesan treasurer, and out of the income thereof the treasurer for the time being pays the stipend of the priest saying the mass. The mass itself is usually said at the church which the deceased attended during his or her lifetime, which, of course, will be within the diocese. Where it is intended that the masses shall be paid for out of income, the arrangements for foundation masses will probably meet the desires of the testator and be the most convenient course to adopt. The third clause can be adopted where the arrangements for a foundation mass or foundation masses are thought to be insufficient, or where, for any other reason, they do not meet with the testator's approval. The third clause is also appropriate where the income is to be applied for the provision of masses for a limited time, after which the capital or the income of the fund is to be given over. Such a gift over must vest within the period limited by the rule against perpetuities, unless it is also in itself a charitable gift (*Re Tyler, Tyler v Tyler* [1891] 3 Ch 252).

2   Payment made to the priest for the saying of a mass is variously called a stipend or an offering. The amount of such stipend or offering is not invariable, and is often varied according to the means of the person desiring the mass to be said.

[212.14]

FORM B12.12:   Gift to the representative body of the Church in Wales[1]

I give [*description of property*] [the sum of £——] unto the representative body of the Church in Wales whose office is at 39 Cathedral Close, Cardiff, South Glamorgan CS1 9XF To be held and dealt with by them under and in accordance with the regulations and provisions contained in their charter of incorporation or otherwise for the time being in force respecting property held by them so far as the same are applicable Nevertheless upon trust that the said representative body shall from time to time apply at their discretion the income [and also if and when they see fit the capital] of the said [property] [sum] and of all or any property from time to time representing the same for the benefit of the bishop for the time being of [*or* for charitable Church purposes in] the diocese of —— [*or* the incumbent for the time being of [*or* for charitable Church purposes in] the parish of —— in the County of —— or any parish with or into which such parish may for the time being be united or merged] [*or* for charitable Church purposes in Wales] and the receipt of the treasurer or the other proper officer for the time being of the said representative body shall be an effectual discharge to my trustees in respect of this gift.

Part B   Clauses in wills

1   This form is based on precedents originally supplied by the Representative Body of the Church in Wales.

[212.15]

FORM B12.13:   Gift to the Salvation Army[1]

I give [the sum of £——] [*description of property*] to the Salvation Army for its general purposes[2] and direct that the receipt of the treasurer or finance secretary for the time being of the Salvation Army at its UK and International Headquarters, 101 Queen Victoria Street, London EC4P 4EP, shall be a good discharge to my trustees.

1   This form is based on a precedent supplied by the Salvation Army. Further information and advice regarding clauses making gifts for specific Salvation Army purposes is available from the Finance Secretary, The Salvation Army, 101 Queen Victoria Street, London EC4P 4EP.
2   Substitute here 'for its social work' if it is desired that the gift be used for Salvation Army social work.

[212.16]

FORM B12.14:   Bequest to the Trustees for Methodist Church Purposes on the model trusts of the Methodist Church Act 1976[1]

I give to the Trustees for Methodist Church Purposes of Central Buildings, Oldham Street, Manchester M1 1JQ (hereinafter called 'the Board') the sum of £—— to be held by the board as custodian trustees upon the model trusts for the time being contained in the Methodist Church Act 1976 and I desire the said sum to be applied for the ——[2] purposes (as defined in the said Act) of ——.[3]

1   This is based on a precedent provided by the Trustees for Methodist Church Purposes at the address given in the form (telephone no: 0161 236 5194). The model trusts referred to in this form are set out in Pt III of Sch 2 to the Methodist Church Act 1976, and are trusts generally for the purposes of the Methodist Church. However, declarations of preferences for particular churches or purposes may be included. Indeed where there is a gift of property in a will to any local Methodist church without any express declaration of trust effecting the property, then the Methodist Church Act 1976, s 15(2) provides that the gift will have effect as if the gift had been made to the Trustees for Methodist Church Purposes upon the model trusts containing a declaration of preference for the application of the property for the purposes of the local church referred to in the gift. Advice can be obtained on the wording of gifts for specific Methodist Church Purposes from the Trustees and from the Methodist Church Property Division (of the same address and telephone no). This form enables the testator to specify by precatory words some particular object which he or she wants the gift devoted to, but to avoid the danger of the gift failing by reason of the particular object ceasing before his or her death.
2   Insert 'local', 'circuit', 'district', 'connexional', or 'divisional' as required.
3   Insert name of church, circuit, district, division or fund.

[212.17]

FORM B12.15:   Bequest to the Baptist Union[1]

I give and bequeath to the Baptist Union of Great Britain and Ireland, the sum of £—— and I declare that the receipt of the treasurer for the time being of the said Baptist Union shall be sufficient discharge for the same. [I wish the said sum to be earmarked for the following purpose ——.[2]]

1   This form is based on a precedent supplied by the Bapist Union Corporation, Ltd. Any further information may be obtained from the Corporation at Baptist House, PO Box 44, 129 Broadway, Didcot, Oxon OX11 8RT.

2   A number of separate funds are mentioned as particular purposes and it may be important to make proper inquiries as to the proper name of the fund to which the legacy is to be applied. If no special fund is mentioned, the gift will be used for any of the purposes of the Union.

[212.18]

FORM B12.16:   Gift to the United Reformed Church[1]

I give to the United Reformed Church of 86 Tavistock Place, London WC1H 9RT for its general purposes (being charitable) [the sum of ——] [*description of property*] and I direct that the receipt of the treasurer for the time being of such church shall be a sufficient discharge for the same.

1   This form is based on a precedent supplied by the United Reformed Church of the address given in the form, from whom advice should be sought if it is desired to make a gift for some specific United Reformed Church purpose.

[212.19]

FORM B12.17:   Bequest to the Congregational Federation

I bequeath the sum of £—— to the Congregational Federation of 4 Castle Gate, Nottingham NG1 7AS and I declare that the receipt of the treasurer for the time being of the Federation shall be a sufficient discharge for the legacy.

[212.20]

FORM B12.18:   Bequest to the Presbyterian Church of Wales (Calvinistic Methodists)[1]

I give and bequeath to the treasurer for the time being of ——[2] in connection with the General Assembly of the Presbyterian Church of Wales (Calvinistic Methodists) the sum of £—— and the receipt of such treasurer to be sufficient discharge to my executors.

1   This form is based on a precedent supplied by the General Assembly of the Presbyterian Church of Wales, 53 Richmond Road, Cardiff CF2 3UP. The property of the Calvinistic Methodist or Presbyterian Church of Wales is by the Calvinistic Methodist or Presbyterian Church of Wales Act 1933 to be vested so far as it consists of land in the Properties Board of the Church but it is optional whether personal property is so vested unless the will expressly directs that the property be vested in the Properties Board. The above precedent is therefore applicable to personalty only.

2   Fill in here: 'for the general purposes of the connexion' or for a named church or for any of the particular funds administered by the connexion. In the last case it may be of importance to inquire as to the particular description of the fund.

[212.21]

FORM B12.19:   Devise for the Presbyterian Church of Wales (Calvinistic Methodists)[1]

I give to the Properties Board of the Calvinistic Methodist Church of Wales, or the Presbyterian Church of Wales as a custodian trustee [*describe property*] in trust for [*state specific connexional object or objects which it is desired to benefit*].

1   By the Calvinistic Methodist or Presbyterian Church of Wales Act 1933, s 7(2) (as to which see para [212.18], n 1), the transfer of property to the board by trustees or personal representatives is a good discharge to them for the property so transferred.

[212.22]

FORM B12.20:   Bequest to the Unitarian and Free Christian Churches[1]

I give to the society now known as the General Assembly of Unitarian and Free Christian Churches the sum of £—— and the receipt of the Treasurer or secretary of such society for the time being shall be a sufficient discharge to my executors.

1   This form and the following form are based on precedents supplied by the General Assembly of Unitarian and Free Christian Churches, Essex Hall, 1–6 Essex Street, London WC2R 3HY.

[212.23]

FORM B12.21:   Gift of land or houses to the Unitarian and Free Christian Churches

I devise to the society now known as the General Assembly of Unitarian and Free Christian Churches my house [*describe the premises*] upon trust for the general purposes of the said society.

[212.24]

FORM B12.22:   Gift to the United Synagogue[1]

I give to the United Synagogue [to be applied for the benefit of the synagogue at ——] the sum of £—— and I declare that the receipt of one of the treasurers for the time being of the United Synagogue shall be a sufficient discharge to my trustees.

1   This form is adapted from a form recommended by the United Synagogue, Woburn House, Upper Woburn Place, London, WC1H 0EZ. Many, though by no means all, Orthodox Jewish Synagogues in the United Kingdom are constituents of the United Synagogue, which is a corporate body. Gifts may be made to the United Synagogue either for its general purposes, or for the benefit of a constituent synagogue.

[212.25]

FORM B12.23:   Gift to a hospital supported by public funds[1]

I give the sum of £—— to the appropriate hospital authority (within the meaning of section 91(3) of the National Health Service Act 1977) for —— Hospital to be invested by the said authority in any investments [permitted by law for the investment of trust funds or by this my will] *or* [of whatever description or location as it may in its absolute discretion think fit] with power from time to time to transfer any such investments into others of a like nature upon trust to apply the income from such investments for any one or more of the following purposes [*insert such of the following purposes as may be desired*]:

  (i)   For the provision of prizes for student nurses undergoing training at the said —— Hospital.

(ii) For the provision of prizes or otherwise for the benefit of the —— Nurses' School attached to the said —— Hospital.

(iii) For the provision of extra comforts for the patients of the said —— Hospital including gifts of clothing or additional medical or surgical appliances on leaving the said —— Hospital.

(iv) For the provision of extra comforts for or the general welfare of the staff of the said —— Hospital.

(v) For the provision of accommodation for the use of the relatives who come from a distance of patients who are critically ill.[2]

(vi) For the purposes of any research [or name a particular branch of research] carried on at the said —— Hospital.

(vii) Generally for purposes relating to the said —— Hospital or any research carried out therein.

The above legacy is conditional upon the said authority undertaking [*or* It is my desire that in consideration of the said legacy the said authority shall undertake] to name and maintain in perpetuity a bed [cot] in the said hospital to be known as the —— Bed [Cot].[3]

I desire that the said gift shall always be known as the —— Fund [in memory of [my wife] who was for many years on the staff of the said hospital].

I declare that the receipt purporting to be signed by the treasurer or other proper officer of the said authority shall be sufficient discharge to my trustees in respect of the above legacy.

1   By the NHSA 1977, ss 90 and 91, a gift may be made to a health authority upon trust for purposes relating to the health service or to an NHS trust for purposes relating to the hospital aimed and managed by the NHS trust. This Form refers to 'the appropriate health authority' as defined by the NHSA 1977, s 91(3). This will be the appropriate NHS trust or area health authority save where there are special trustees for the hospital. This form is so worded that if the hospital to be benefited should become an NHS trust between the date of the will and the date of the death, the gift will be to the appropriate NHS trust.

2   See *Re Dean's Will Trusts* [1950] 1 All ER 882.

3   See *Re Ginger* [1951] Ch 458, [1951] 1 All ER 422; *Re Mills, Midland Bank Executor and Trustees Co Ltd v United Birmingham Hospitals Board of Governors* [1953] 1 All ER 835, [1953] 1 WLR 554. Where the gift was for providing beds for paying patients as to one-half at one hospital where there were none and as to the other half at another hospital where there were such beds it was held that both gifts were charitable: *Re Adams, Gee v Barnet Group Hospital Management Committee* [1968] Ch 80, [1967] 3 All ER 285.

[212.26]

FORM B12.24:   Bequest to school for provision of playing fields

I give the sum of £ —— free of inheritance tax to the governors of —— School to be applied by them in the purchase of a field or fields to be used for the school games and the school sports and similar purposes. [I also give to my trustees the sum of £—— free of inheritance tax [to invest in securities and investments of whatever description or location as my trustees shall in their absolute discretion think fit][1] and to pay the income therefrom to the said governors to be applied by them for the upkeep of the said playing fields and any buildings thereon. I empower my trustees as soon as the said playing fields have been purchased to transfer the said investments to trustees appointed by the said governors or to such persons as my trustees shall in their discretion think fit.][2]

1   See para **[212.5]**, n 3.
2   The first gift of a capital sum is good in any event, but the second gift is probably only
     charitable if the school is itself a charity, see *Re Mariette, Mariette v Aldenham School
     Governing Body* [1915] 2 Ch 284; *Re Gray, Todd v Taylor* [1925] Ch 362, [1925] All ER Rep
     250; for a case against such a gift being charitable where the school is not a charity, see *Re
     Nottage, Jones v Palmer* [1895] 2 Ch 649. See also *IRC v McMullen* [1981] AC 1, [1980] 1 All
     ER 884 (trust for the promotion of the physical education and development of pupils at schools
     and universities upheld as a valid charitable trust) and see generally Vol 1 at para **[102.7]**, and
     cases cited at para **[102.9]**, n 9.
        In case the gift is non-charitable (and thus not exempt from inheritance tax) and is payable
     wholly or partly out of assets which bear their own inheritance tax, a direction freeing the gift
     from inheritance tax may be appropriate (see paras **[210.3]** and **[210.4]** and **[214.59]** and
     [214.60]).

[212.27]

**FORM B12.25:   Bequest to school to be applied for the encouragement of
sport[1]**

I bequeath the sum of £—— free of inheritance tax to the governing body of —
— School at —— for the purpose of acquiring land and preparing and equipping
the same for the playing of [lawn tennis or *such other game for which amount of
the bequest may be sufficient*]. I also bequeath to the said governing body the
sum of £—— for providing by the income therefrom a prize or trophy for the
winner of [the 1,500 metres race] at the school's annual sports.

1   See para **[212.26]**, n 2.

[212.28]

FORM B12.26:   Gift of residue to found college fellowships

(1)   As to the net residue of the proceeds of my residuary real and personal
estate I give and bequeath the same unto my trustees upon trust subject to the
conditions hereinafter mentioned to pay the same to the treasurer or person or
persons for the time being authorised and acting as treasurer of —— College in
the University of —— for the purpose of founding fellowships in the said
college of not less than £—— per annum according to the following conditions
or provisions[1] namely:

   (a)   that the said fellowships shall [from time to time be given to such
          candidates as shall from time to time be adjudged to be the most fit and
          proper to receive the same upon the result of an examination in the
          higher branches of classics or of mathematics or of both combined all
          such candidates to] be confined to such persons as shall have been
          former students of the said college and shall have obtained certificates in
          the [tripos or final public] examination held in the said university for
          [classical or mathematical or medical or chemical or scientific or other
          honours] [provided also that the examiners for such fellowships shall be
          of opinion that such candidates possess sufficient merit and distinction].
   (b)   [That persons shall be selected for or elected to such fellowships from
          time to time in such manner as is usual in respect of other fellowships of
          the said college or in such special manner as the governing body of the
          college shall from time to time decide.]

(c) That such fellowships shall be tenable for [seven] years and not longer unless the governing body of the said college shall for special reasons consider that in any particular case the term [seven] years ought to be extended and in such case such term may be extended from time to time at the sole discretion of such governing body.

(d) [That such fellowships may be given to any such person as aforesaid who is undertaking or desires to undertake any branch of research or experimental work.]

(e) That the holders of such fellowships shall be styled Fellows of the said college and shall have a reasonable share in the government and management of the college pursuant to the constitution and regulations thereof as established [but need not be resident Fellows].

(f) [That the governing body of the college shall be at liberty to expend not only the income but also the capital of the said moneys in providing such fellowships as aforesaid since I consider it more beneficial to provide for the near than for the distant future, and I suggest to the said governing body that the whole of the said moneys both principal and interest might well be expended within the period of [twenty-one] years from the date of the receipt of the said moneys.]

(2) The offer and payment to the said treasurer or other persons acting as such shall be made subject to the acceptance by the said college and the governing body thereof of all and singular the above-mentioned conditions (with such modifications as may be approved by my trustees pursuant to clause (4) hereof) and in case of non-acceptance thereof within the period of three months from the date of such offer or within such extended period not exceeding twelve months as my trustees shall deem expedient my trustees shall make the same offer or payment to or in favour of [*name*] college upon the same conditions in all respects as if the name of the college lastly hereinbefore named were substituted for the college firstly hereinbefore named.

(3) In case neither of the said colleges shall accept the said conditions my trustees shall stand possessed of the said net residue of the proceeds of my real and personal estate upon trust for ——.

(4) I declare that my trustees shall have full power to vary or modify the said conditions of acceptance by [*name*] College and [*name*] College respectively provided that the paramount general intention of such conditions is effectuated.

1 Some of the following paragraphs are inserted as instances which have in fact proved useful, though in most cases the conditions will generally be left to the discretion of the governing body of the college. It may be mentioned that fellowships conferred after a qualifying examination are not usual at the universities.

[212.29]

FORM B12.27: Legacies in favour of the Scout Association[1]

I. LEGACY FOR THE GENERAL PURPOSES OF THE SCOUT ASSOCIATION

I hereby give to the Scout Association (incorporated by Royal Charter) the sum of £—— for the general purposes of such association and I declare that receipt of the treasurer for the time being of such association shall be a good discharge to my executors.

II.   LEGACY FOR THE BENEFIT OF A SCOUT GROUP OR DISTRICT OR COUNTY SCOUT COUNCIL[2]

I hereby give to the Scout Association (incorporated by Royal Charter) the sum of £—— for the general purposes of such association and I express the desire but without imposing any trust that the said sum shall be used for the —— [Group] [District/County Scout Council] of the Scout Association and I declare that the receipt of the treasurer for the time being of such association shall be a good discharge to my executors.

1   These forms are based on precedents supplied by the Scout Association.
2   In the event of the named group or district or council having ceased to exist at the date of the testator's death, it would be the normal practice of the association to apply the legacy for the benefit of scouting in the same locality.

[212.30]

FORM B12.28:   Legacies in favour of the Guide Association[1]

I.   LEGACY FOR THE GENERAL PURPOSES OF THE GUIDE ASSOCIATION

I hereby give to the Guide Association (incorporated by Royal Charter) the sum of £—— for the general purposes of such association and I declare that the receipt of the treasurer for the time being of such association shall be a good discharge to my executors.

II.   LEGACY FOR THE BENEFIT OF A UNIT OR AREA OF THE GUIDE ASSOCIATION[2]

I GIVE [the sum of £—— free of all tax] [a—— share of my Residuary Estate] to The Guide Association Trust Corporation of 17–19 Buckingham Palace Road London SW1W 0PT to hold the same upon the trusts of the Guide Association Trust Deed of 1938 as trustee for [—— County] of the Guide Association a registered charity number [——] or if the said Guide [County] has ceased to exist following amalgamation reorganisation disbandment or otherwise then for the Guide Association County [or Counties] which in the discretion of the Trust Corporation most nearly represents the present [—— County] as it exists at the date of this my will and I express the wish (but without imposing any binding trust or obligation) that the legacy shall be applied in or towards the [purchase and any subsequent improvement repairs and maintenance of a Pack Holiday House to belong to the Guide County but to be used particularly to enable inner city children to experience the fun of Pack Holidays].

1   These forms are based on precedents supplied by the Guide Association.
2   See para [212.29], n 2.

[212.31]

FORM B12.29:   General provision against lapse of charitable gifts

If any institution society or body of persons (incorporated or unincorporated) which is intended to be benefited by any gift made by me herein or in any codicil hereto [and which is referred to hereby or by such codicil as a charity or charitable[1]] shall be found never to have existed or to have ceased to exist or to have been amalgamated with another institution society or body of persons or changed its name or constitution before my death the benefit intended to be given under such gift shall be paid transferred or applied to such charitable institutions societies or bodies of persons established in the United Kingdom of Great Britain and Northern Ireland or for such charitable purposes in the said United Kingdom and if more than one in such shares as my trustees in their absolute discretion think fit and I express the wish without imposing any trust or obligation that in carrying out the foregoing trust my trustees should seek to benefit a charity or charities as close as possible in purpose to those of the institution society or body of persons intended to be benefited by my said original gift.

1   Some draftsmen may prefer to add these words, as otherwise a gift to any institution, even though not intended as a charitable gift, will be caught. But if such words are included, care must be taken to describe expressly all intended charitable objects as charities.

B13　Exercises of special powers of appointment

PRELIMINARY NOTE

[213.1]
Special powers of appointment may often be exercised by will. Where a
settlement, will or other instrument confers on any person a special power of
appointment, it is often the case that the donee is expressly authorised to execute
the power by will or codicil. In the absence of such express authorisation it is a
matter of construction of the instrument as a whole whether the donee may
exercise such a power validly by will or codicil. A power to be executed by 'an
instrument in writing' may be executed by will: *West v Ray* (1854) Kay 385.
When a testator desires to exercise a power of appointment, the terms of the
power must be carefully considered and followed.

[213.2]
For a full treatment of the exercise of special powers of appointment, see Vol 1,
[39.1] et seq. Some general observations on some points which often arise in
practice appear below.

[213.3]

OBJECTS OF POWER

Generally, a power may only be exercised for the benefit of the objects of the
power. A common special power of appointment is a power to appoint among a
person's 'children'. In this case, 'children' will have the same meaning as in the
instrument creating the power, so that even if before the date of exercise of the
power the law has changed the meaning of 'children' from the meaning it has in
the instrument creating the power, 'children' must still be identified according to
the meaning in the instrument creating the power. Where an appointment is
made to a person who is not a proper object according to the terms of the power,
it will be void, see *Re Hoff* [1942] Ch 298, [1942] 1 All ER 547 and *Re Brinkley*

[1968] Ch 407, [1967] 3 All ER 805. For the meanings of 'children' and 'issue' see Vol 1, paras **[74.1]–[74.9]** and **[76.1]–[76.6]**.

[213.4]
Death of appointee in testator's lifetime. Where a testator exercises a special power of appointment in his will and before his death the appointee dies, the appointment lapses, and the property which the appointee would have taken passes in default of appointment. Special powers are not within the WA 1837, s 33 (Part G, para **[244.34]**), so that appointments are not saved when made in favour of a child of the testator who predeceases him, *Holyland v Lewin* (1884) 26 Ch D 266. Neither is an appointment saved on the death of an appointee if the appointment is made to the appointee or his personal representatives, unless the personal representatives are objects of the power. To save against lapse, an appointment could contain a substitutional gift to other objects to take effect in the event of the death of a primary appointee during the testator's lifetime.

[213.5]
A special power of appointment often has as its objects the appointor's issue of all degrees, with a trust in default of appointment for the appointor's children. Such a special power can be usefully exercised to make an appointment in favour of the children of any child who has predeceased the appointor.

[213.6]

DELEGATION

A special power of appointment cannot be delegated and so on the exercise of such a power, trusts, powers and discretions should not be delegated to anyone unless the terms of the power authorise such a delegation. So, for example, an appointment should not (unless the power expressly or impliedly authorises it) appoint the settled funds upon discretionary trusts, or appoint the income upon protective trusts because of the discretionary trust arising on a forfeiture: *Re Boulton's Settlement Trust, Stewart v Boulton* [1928] Ch 703. However, some fairly standard special powers will authorise some delegation such as the inclusion of the statutory power of advancement (*Re Hunter's Will Trusts, Gilks v Harris* [1963] Ch 372, [1962] 3 All ER 1050) and new administrative provisions (*Re Rank's Settlement Trusts, Newton v Rollo* [1979] 1 WLR 1242). See also Vol 1, paras **[40.4]–[40.5]**.

[213.7]

PERPETUITIES

The perpetuity period applicable to the interests created under a special power of appointment is the perpetuity period applicable to the instrument creating the special power. So when exercising a special power of appointment, care must be taken to ensure that the interests which it creates vest in interest within the perpetuity period applicable to the instrument creating the power. This is particularly important where the instrument creating the special power of appointment took effect before 16 July 1964 because in this case there is no 'wait and see' rule which might save an otherwise perpetuitous appointment by enabling it to be treated as valid until it is apparent that the interests must vest, if at all, outside the perpetuity period. The 'wait and see' rule would only apply in relation to instruments creating a power which took effect on or after 16 July 1964, see the Perpetuities and Accumulations Act 1964 (PAA 1964), ss 3 and 15(5) (Part G, paras **[246.61]** and **[246.73]**). In some cases, instruments creating a special power of appointment will expressly define the applicable perpetuity period, for example, in the case of instruments taking effect on or after 16 July 1964 a period of 80 years or less may have been selected as provided by the PAA 1964, s 1(1), (Part G, para **[246.59]**). If there is no express perpetuity period in the instrument creating the power the period of a life or lives in being plus 21 years should be used. For perpetuities generally see Vol 1, para **[94.1]** et seq and for perpetuities in relation to powers of appointment see para **[94.41]** et seq.

[213.8]

ACCUMULATIONS

If a power expressly or impliedly authorises the appointment of a trust or power of accumulation, excessive accumulations should not be directed, ie accumulation for a longer period than that authorised by law and by the instrument creating the power. The periods of accumulation permitted by law are contained in the Law of Property Act 1925 (LPA 1925), s 164 (Part G, para **[246.42]**) and (for instruments taking effect on or after 16 July 1964) the PAA 1964, s 13 (Part G, para **[246.71]**). The instrument creating the power will sometimes expressly incorporate one of these periods of accumulation, otherwise it is a matter of construction of the instrument as a whole whether a period has been selected and which period it is. These periods, only one of which may apply in respect of any disposition, are in addition to any accumulations pursuant to the TA 1925, s 31 (Part G, para **[246.26]**), see the LPA 1925, s 165 (Part G, para **[246.43]**). For accumulations generally see Vol 1, para **[95.1]** et seq.

[213.9]

SOME TAX CONSIDERATIONS

Very often a person with a special power of appointment will have an interest in possession in the property over which the power is exercisable, and so on his death the value of the property will be treated as forming part of his estate for inheritance tax purposes. Therefore, if an appointor's spouse is an object of the power, it may be advantageous if an interest in possession (a life or lesser interest) is appointed to the spouse so that the spouse exemption will be available on the appointor's death. The partial exemption rules of the Inheritance Tax Act 1984 (ITA 1984), ss 36 to 42, for charging tax on death where the deemed transfer of value on death is partly exempt and partly chargeable will apply separately to such property from the appointor's free estate: ITA 1984, s 40.

[213.10]

Under the terms of a settlement, the settlor or the settlor's spouse may have an interest in possession in the settled property and a special power of appointment in respect of the settled property. If he exercises his special power to create discretionary trusts (assuming they are authorised by the power) to take effect immediately after his interest in possession, he will be regarded, for the purposes of the charging rules for relevant property (ie settled property in which there is no interest in possession), as the settlor of a new discretionary settlement at the time when his interest in possession ceases, see the ITA 1984, s 80 (but see also the ITA 1984, s 61(2)) which provides that for the purposes of calculating the ten year anniversary for the periodic charge to inheritance tax, the settlement should be regarded as having commenced when the property first became settled). In circumstances where s 80 applies, for the relevant property to qualify after the cessation of the interest in possession as excluded property under the ITA 1984, s 48(3)(a), or for the exemption in s 65(8) from an inheritance tax exit charge when relevant property becomes invested in exempt government securities, the condition as to the domicile of the settlor outside the UK at the time of his settlement must be satisfied both by the original settlor and his spouse at the times when their respective settlements were made or deemed to be made, see the ITA 1984, s 82. (See *Foster's Inheritance Tax*, E4.52, for a more detailed treatment of the ITA 1984, s 80, and its consequences.)

[213.11]

If an appointor has a life interest in the settled property over which he exercises, by will or codicil, his special power of appointment, his death will not usually be the occasion of a capital gains tax charge, whether he appoints the settled property on further trusts or absolutely, see the TCGA 1992, ss 72 and 73. There will usually be an uplift in the value of the assets on his death for capital gains tax purposes (the exception for reverter to the original settlor in the TCGA 1992, s 73(1)(b) not being relevant to a will trust where the settlor is ex hypothesi deceased).

[213.12]

FORM B13.1:   **Appointment by widow of her husband's residuary estate among children and issue**

In exercise of the power of appointment conferred on me by [the will of my late husband who died on —— which was proved *etc*] to appoint the capital and income of my late husband's residuary estate [to or for the benefit of our children and issue in such shares and with such trusts powers and provisions for their respective benefit exercisable at the discretion of any person or persons as I shall appoint[1]] I hereby direct that the trustees of the will of my said husband[2] shall after my death stand possessed of my late husband's residuary estate upon trust to divide the same into three equal parts and hold the same upon the trusts and with and subject to the powers and provisions following:

(1)   As to one equal third part and the income thereof upon trust for such of the children of my late son [*name*] as shall survive me and attain the age of twenty-one if more than one in equal shares absolutely provided that if

any of such children shall predecease me or survive me but die without having attained the age of twenty-one leaving a child or children living at my death or born thereafter such child or children shall take if more than one equally between them the share which his her or their parent would have taken if he or she had survived me and attained the age of twenty-one[3];

(2)   As to one equal third part and the income thereof upon trust for my daughter [*name*] absolutely;

(3)   As to the remaining one equal third part upon trust to pay the income thereof to my son [*name*] for his life[4] and subject thereto as to both capital and income for such of his children living at my death or born thereafter who shall attain the age of twenty-one if more than one in equal shares absolutely;

(4)   If the foregoing trusts herein declared of any equal third part of my late husband's residuary estate shall fail then each such part (together with any part or parts which may accrue thereto under this present provision) shall accrue to the other part or parts hereby appointed the trusts whereof shall not at the date of such accrual have failed;

(5)   The powers of section 32 of the Trustee Act 1925 shall apply to the foregoing trusts [as if the words 'one half of' were omitted from proviso (a) to subsection (1) thereof[5]].

---

1   The terms of this power are based on the power considered in *Re Hunter's Will Trusts, Gilk v Harris* [1963] Ch 372, [1962] 3 All ER 1050. They were held not to authorise the creation of an immediate discretionary trust for a class of appointees.

2   In exercising a special power of appointment the appointor should not (unless the power expressly or impliedly authorises it, see *Re Redgate, Marsh v Redgate* [1903] 1 Ch 356) appoint the settled funds to the trustees of the appointor's will. Under such an appointment the trustees of the settled property in respect of which the power is exercised are not bound to transfer the settled funds to the trustees of the will, but ought to carry out and execute the appointor's directions themselves (see *Busk v Aldam* (1874) LR 19 Eq 16; *Scotney v Lomer* (1886) 31 Ch D 380; *Re Tyssen, Knight-Bruce v Butterworth* [1894] 1 Ch 56; *Re Mackenzie, Bain v Mackenzie* [1916] 1 Ch 125).

3   Assuming that no perpetuity period has been defined in the husband's will, the common law perpetuity period will apply. Since the power is conferred by the husband's will which would only have come into force on his death his widow and the children of the marriage will be lives in being for the purposes of the common law rule against perpetuities. Therefore appointments to the children which vest in interest during their lifetimes will be valid, as will be appointments to their children which vest on the death of the widow or at or before they attain 21, and to the children of such a child who predeceases the widow or dies under 21 so long as there is no contingency such as the attainment of a specified age.

4   The terms of the power as recited would not permit an appointment of the income on protective trusts because the discretionary trust of income arising after any forfeiture would be an improper delegation of the power. It is not clear whether a power to pay or apply capital to a life tenant would be permitted.

5   The incorporation of the statutory power of advancement of the TA 1925, s 32 (Part G, para **[246.27]**) to pay one half of a beneficiary's presumptive share for his advancement or benefit, will not be an improper delegation, and it is thought that in the case of the terms of the recited power it will not be an improper delegation to extend the power to be exercisable in respect of the whole of a beneficiary's presumptive share.

[213.13]

FORM B13.2:   **Appointment by woman of fund in which she has a life interest in unequal shares, one child's share appointed direct to his own children, another's settled on him for life, the others appointed absolutely**[1]

In exercise of the power of appointment conferred on me by [the will of my late father who died on —— which was proved etc] to appoint the capital and income of his residuary estate in which I have a life interest [to all or any one or more exclusively of the others or other of my issue at such times and if more than one in such shares with such provisions for maintenance education and advancement and otherwise at the discretion of any person and with such gifts over and generally in such manner for the benefit of my issue or some or one of them as I shall appoint[2]] I hereby direct that the trustees of the will of my late father[3] shall after my death stand possessed of my late father's residuary estate upon trust to divide the same into five equal parts and hold the same upon the trusts and with and subject to the powers and provisions following:

(1)   As to two equal fifth parts upon trust to pay the income thereof to my daughter [*name*] for her life and subject thereto as to both capital and income for such of her children living at my death or born thereafter before the vesting day (as defined in my late father's will)[4] who shall attain the age of twenty-one or shall be living on the vesting day if earlier if more than one in equal shares absolutely.

(2)   As to one equal fifth part and the income thereof upon trust for such of the children of my daughter [*name*] living at my death or born thereafter before the vesting day who shall attain the age of twenty-one or shall be living on the vesting day (as defined in my late father's will)[5] if earlier if more than one in equal shares absolutely.

(3)   As to one equal fifth part and the income thereof upon trust for my son [*name*] absolutely.

(4)   As to the remaining one equal fifth part and the income thereof upon trust for my son [*name*] absolutely.

(5)   The powers and provisions of section 32 of the Trustee Act 1925 shall apply to the foregoing trusts as if the words 'one half of' were omitted from proviso (a) to subsection (1) thereof.

(6)   I declare that in the foregoing subclauses of this present clause the terms 'child' and 'children' shall have the same meanings as they have in my late father's will.[6]

(7)   The administrative powers and provisions of clauses —— of my late father's will shall continue to apply to my late father's residuary estate so far as consistent with the beneficial interests hereby appointed and the trustees of my late father's will shall have the following additional powers:[7]

(i)   power to invest trust moneys in any property of whatever description or location as if they were a sole beneficial owner of such moneys;

(ii)   power to borrow money with or without giving security and on such terms as to interest repayment and otherwise for any purpose connected with the trusts hereby appointed and no lender from whom the trustees borrow money in purported exercise of this power shall be concerned to enquire as to the propriety amount or purpose of any such borrowing.

1   For the purposes of this form it is assumed that the appointor's father died before 16 July 1964 and before the birth of any of the appointor's children. Therefore, the interests created must be certain to vest within the perpetuity period because there will be no 'wait and see' rule to save an otherwise perpetuitous appointment, see para **[213.7]**.

2   The terms of this power are based on the power considered in *Re Rank's Settlement Trusts, Newton v Rollo* [1979] 1 WLR 1242.

3   See para **[213.12]**, n 2.

4   It is assumed that the appointor's father's will contains an express perpetuity restriction, with a defined vesting day 21 years from the death of the last survivor of the appointor and Royal lives. If it is not defined the common law period of a life or lives in being plus 21 years will apply, so that if the appointor's grandchildren's interests were expressed to vest at the latest on the expiry of the period of 21 years from the death of the appointor there would be no perpetuity problem.

5   See n 4 supra.

6   See para **[213.7]**.

7   In *Re Rank's Settlement Trusts, Newton v Rollo*, supra, the terms of the power were held to authorise the creation of additional administrative powers.

[213.14]

FORM B13.3:   Exercise by married woman of powers of appointment contained in her marriage settlement in favour of her husband for life and if she has no children in favour of her husband absolutely

Whereas under a settlement dated —— and made between [*parties*] and executed in contemplation of my marriage with my husband [*name*] I have:

(a)   power to appoint to my said husband a life or less interest in the funds subject to the trusts thereof in the event of my husband surviving me; and

(b)   a general power of appointment by will in respect of the said funds in the event of no child of my said marriage attaining the age of twenty-one years or being female marrying subject to the interest so appointed to my said husband as aforesaid and also subject to any exercise of the special powers of appointment in favour of issue of our marriage conferred by such settlement on my husband and myself jointly and on the survivor of us.

Now in exercise of the said respective powers of appointment and of all other powers (if any) enabling me in this behalf I hereby direct and appoint that:

(1)   in the event of my said husband surviving me the trustees for the time being of the said settlement[1] shall from and after my death stand possessed of the said funds upon trust to pay the income thereof to my said husband during the residue of his life; and

(2)   in the event of my said husband surviving me and no child of our marriage attaining the age of twenty-one or being female marrying and subject to any exercise of such special powers conferred on my husband and myself jointly as aforesaid the trustees for the time being of the said settlement shall stand possessed of the capital and income of the said funds in trust for my said husband absolutely.

1   See para **[213.12]**, n 2.

B14 Residue

EXCLUSION OF APPORTIONMENT BETWEEN CAPITAL AND INCOME (RULES IN *HOWE V EARL OF DARTMOUTH* AND *RE CHESTERFIELD'S TRUSTS*)

FORMS

EXCLUSION OF RULE FOR APPORTIONMENT OF LIABILITIES BETWEEN CAPITAL AND INCOME (RULE IN *ALLHUSEN V WHITTELL*)

FORMS

EXCLUSION OF TIME APPORTIONMENT

FORMS

INCIDENCE OF INHERITANCE TAX

FORMS

Administration trusts

[214.1]

NOTE

Administration trusts and trusts of land. Residuary gifts are fully considered
in Vol 1, Ch 38. The coming into force of the Trusts of Land and Appointment
of Trustees Act 1996 (TLATA 1996) on 1 January 1997 has important
implications for the drafting of administration trusts. The Act prohibits the
creation of new settlements under the Settled Land Act 1925, although there is a
saving for existing strict settlements. The Act introduces the 'trust of land' as the
vehicle for all other settlements of land. The trust for sale of land is not
abolished but is largely assimilated. A particularly significant change in the
context of administration trusts is the abolition of the doctrine of conversion in
relation to trusts for sale of land. (For a fuller discussion of the changes effected
by the TLATA 1996, see Part A, para **[200.48]** et seq.) Under the former law it
was usual to include in an administration trust an express trust for sale and
conversion of all the property not otherwise disposed of, and to provide
expressly for the payment of debts, funeral and testamentary expenses,
inheritance tax and legacies out of it. This practice may well continue and in any
event, many pre-TLATA 1996 wills will remain unaltered. But a trust for sale is
no longer necessary and although forms of administration trust incorporating a
trust for sale are included in B14, we recommend administration trusts which
include a power of sale, rather than a trust for sale, unless there are special
reasons for including the latter: see paras **[200.55]**, **[200.56]** and **[214.2]**. This is
the formula which is adopted in the complete will forms in Part C.

[214.2]
Trust for sale and conversion or power of sale. It is now (ie from the
commencement of the TLATA 1996 on 1 January 1997) no longer necessary or
important to provide a trust for sale and conversion in administration trusts of
residue, because it is no longer the case that the Settled Land Act 1925 will
apply to land comprised in residue in the event of residue being subject to trusts
for persons in succession, subject to a contingency, etc: see paras **[200.51]** and
[200.52]). If there is land in residue is held on trust it will be a 'trust of land'
within the TLATA 1996, and it makes little or no difference whether or not there
is a trust for sale: see para **[200.54]**). We recommend that, in general, trusts for
sale are not provided (see paras **[200.55]** and **[200.56]**). We do, however,

recommend the express provision of a power of sale if there is no provision of a trust for sale, even though there are wide powers of sale conferred by the Administration of Estates Act 1925 (AEA 1925), ss 39 and 40 (Part G, paras **[246.48]** and **[246.49]**) and the TLATA 1996, s 6(1) (Part G, para **[246.91]**) for the purposes of the administration. This is because once the administration is over the trustees of the will are not given by the general law any general power of sale over residuary personalty (see para **[220.23]**), and it is an unusual residuary estate which does not contain some personalty, and because it is not clear to what extent s 39 of the AEA 1925 confers power to sell assets situated outside England and Wales, particularly land. For examples of administration trusts without a trust for sale, see Form B14.1 at para **[214.10]**, and the statutory administration trust for intestates' estates in the AEA 1925, s 33(1), as substituted by the TLATA 1996, Sch 2, para 5(2) which provides that the estate shall be held in trust by the personal representatives with the power to sell it (Part G, para **[244.58]**). For circumstances in which a trust for sale may still be appropriate see Part A, para **[200.56]** and Form B15.8 at para **[215.8]** for an example of use of a trust for sale to maximise the chances of an early sale. It seems that if all residuary realty and personalty are together disposed of, made subject to a power of sale and charged with payment of debts and testamentary expenses, this will still create a mixed fund from which the debts and testamentary expenses are payable generally rather than from an undisposed of share (ie the statutory order of application of assets under the AEA 1925, Sch I, Pt II is still varied to that extent): see *Allan v Gott* (1872) 7 Ch App 439 and para **[214.6]**. The provision of a power of sale rather than a trust for sale, together with an indication of intention that the time of sale should be within the trustees' discretion, may have the effect that the rule in *Howe v Dartmouth* does not apply: see para **[214.38]**. It is the provision of a power rather than a trust for sale which provides a concise method of excluding the rule in *Howe v Dartmouth*: see para **[214.38]**.

The Law of Property Act 1925 (LPA 1925), s 25(3) used to provide that a power to retain or sell land was to be treated as a trust for sale with power to postpone sale. This is now repealed with effect from 1 January 1997 by the TLATA 1996, Sch 4.

[214.3]
Power to sell or postpone sale. If the personal representatives and trustees are given a power of sale, as opposed to holding on trust for sale, they of course have a complete discretion as to whether and when to sell. Such a power is conferred on trustees in relation to land by the TLATA 1996, s 6(1) (Part G, para **[246.91]** and see generally para **[220.23]** et seq) unless excluded or restricted by the will, but because there is likely to be, or there could turn out to be, personalty in any residuary estate we recommend the provision of an express power of sale where no trust for sale is provided (see para **[214.2]**).

Where a trust for sale and conversion is provided in relation to land (in England and Wales) it is still the case, indeed it is even more the case, that statute implies a power to postpone the sale of that land, and provides that the trustees are not liable for postponing sale (in the exercise of their discretion) for an unlimited period. This is by virtue of the TLATA 1996, s 4(1) (Part G, para **[246.89]**; see also para **[200.54]**) which replaces the LPA 1925, s 25 in materially identical terms, with one crucial difference: the TLATA 1996, s 4(1) applies *despite any provision to the contrary made by the disposition*, while the LPA 1925, s 25(1) and (2) only applied so far as a contrary intention did not appear. The TLATA 1996, s 4(1) applies to personal representatives: TLATA 1996, s 18(1) (Part G, para **[246.104]**).

The TLATA 1996, s 4 means that a will cannot impose on the personal representatives a binding obligation to sell land at any particular point. Cases such as *Bate v Hooper* (1855) 5 De GM & G 338 (in which it was held that where a will contained a direction to sell and convert without conferring a power to postpone sale the conversion ought to take place within a year of the testator's death), *Re Rooke's Will Trust, Taylor v Rooke* [1953] Ch 716, [1953] 2 All ER 110 (in which a direction to sell land as soon as possible after the testator's death was held to to negative the implied power to postpone sale) and *Re Ball, Jones v Jones* [1930] WN 111 (in which it was held that the power to postpone sale ceased as soon all the beneficial interests vested absolutely) are superseded in relation to land. The *Bate v Hooper* point that there should be sale within a year of death if there is no power to postpone sale cannot arise in relation to land because there is now always power to postpone sale; and *Re Rooke* and *Re Ball* are decisions that the express provisions of the will in each case showed a contrary intention which excluded the LPA 1925, s 25(1). The grounds for those decisions are no longer available now that the power to postpone sale under the TLATA 1996, s 4(1) cannot be excluded or cut down. If a beneficiary is aggrieved that trustees are postponing sale of land for too long he should apply to the court for an order for sale under the TLATA 1996, s 14 (Part G, para **[246.100]**; see also paras **[200.57]** and **[200.59]**) if the administration is complete and the personal representatives have become trustees, or under the court's inherent jurisdiction over the administration of estates if the administration of the estate is still continuing (as s 14 of the TLATA 1996 does not apply to personal representatives: TLATA 1996, s 18(1) (Part G, para **[246.104]**)). For a form for a case where early sale is contemplated, see Form B15.8 at para **[215.8]** and the Note thereto.

It is still the case that no power to postpone sale is conferred on trustees holding personalty on trust to sell and convert, and so we still recommend the provision of an express power to postpone sale in relation to any mixed fund of realty and personalty held on trust for sale.

The TLATA 1996, s 4(1) provides (as had the LPA 1925) that where there is a power to postpone the sale of land, the trustees are not liable for postponing such sale for an indefinite period. The exercise of the power to postpone, as with the exercise of other fiduciary powers, requires the concurrence of all the trustees. Under the former law, in the absence of agreement to postpone a sale of property the sale generally had to take place: *Re Roth, Goldberger v Roth* (1896) 74 LT 50 and *Re Mayo, Mayo v Mayo* [1943] Ch 302 (decisions on the LPA 1925, s 25(2)). Neither of these decisions is a safe guide to the manner in which the court's jurisdiction will be exercised under the TLATA 1996, s 14: see Part A, paras **[200.59]** and **[200.62]**. Generally the power of postponement can be exercised only as a power of management for the general benefit of the estate and not so as to alter the rights of the parties: *Rowlls v Bebb* [1900] 2 Ch 107 at 116, but it seems it is no objection to the legitimate exercise of such discretion that it will benefit one beneficiary at the expense of another: *Re Sewell's Estate* (1870) LR 11 Eq 80; *Re Schneider, Kirby v Schneider* (1906) 22 TLR 223, and the court will not interfere with the bona fide exercise of the discretion: *Gisborne v Gisborne* (1877) 2 App Cas 300; *Re Burrage, Burningham v Burrage* (1890) 62 LT 752; *Re Charteris, Charteris v Kenyon* [1917] 2 Ch 257, and will presume that the discretion has been properly exercised: *Re Oddy, Connell v Oddy* (1911) 104 LT 128.

[214.4]
Order of application of assets to pay testamentary expenses, debts, etc.
Whether undisposed of residue is primarily liable for debts, administration expenses and legacies remains one question which sometimes still arises in modern conditions, where there is an undisposed of share of residue and the persons who take on intestacy are not the same as the persons who take the disposed of residuary estate, or if they are, do not take in the same proportions. The abolition of hotchpot in the partial intestacy rules (see Vol 1, paras **[104.13]** and **[104.14]**) means that where the testator leaves issue and an undisposed share of residue the chances of this question arising have slightly increased. The order of application of assets where the estate is solvent is laid down by the AEA 1925, Sch 1, Pt II (Part G, para **[246.54]**). By the AEA 1925, s 32 all liabilities of the testator have to be satisfied out of his estate, but by s 34(3) (Part G, para **[246.46]**) where the estate is solvent the real and personal property is subject to rules of court and the provisions as to charges on property in s 35 (Part G, para **[246.47]**) *and to the provisions, if any, contained in the will* applicable to the discharge of funeral testamentary and administration expenses debts and liabilities in the order mentioned in the AEA 1925, Sch 1, Pt II.

[214.5]
One of the main provisions of a will which may vary the statutory order of application is the creation of a mixed fund. Where a testator combines his real and personal estate into one general fund and states that the whole of that fund is to be applied for the payment of the liabilities of his estate including legacies the statutory order is excluded (*Re Petty, Holliday v Petty* [1929] 1 Ch 726, [1929] All ER Rep 493) so that debts, etc are not payable out of a lapsed share of residue (*Re Petty* supra, *Re Kempthorne, Charles v Kempthorne* [1930] 1 Ch 268, [1929] All ER Rep 495). The usual clause giving all property, subject to the exception of that specifically disposed of, to trustees upon trust for sale and conversion and for the payment of debts, etc, out of the proceeds, created a mixed fund for this purpose under the former law (*Bedford v Bedford* (1865) 35 Beav 584). It is not thought that the abolition of the doctrine of conversion in relation to trusts for sale of land will affect matters. A direction for real estate to be deemed to be personalty had a similar result (*Simmons v Rose* (1856) 6 De GM & G 411) The testator was also able to create a mixed fund by codicil (*Re Timson, Harper v Timson* [1953] 2 All ER 1252, [1953] 1 WLR 1361). But the mere gift of real and personal estate together coupled with a direction to pay debts, etc did not constitute a mixed fund (*Boughton v Boughton* (1848) 1 HL Cas 406); there had to be a direction to pay the debts, etc out of the mixed fund.

[214.6]
As mentioned in para **[214.2]** in relation to trusts for sale and conversion, it seems that if all residuary realty and personalty are together disposed of, made

subject to a power of sale, and charged with payment of debts and testamentary expenses, this still creates a mixed fund from which the debts and testamentary expenses are payable generally, rather than from an undisposed of share, the statutory order of application of assets under the AEA 1925, Sch I, Pt II being varied to that extent (*Allan v Gott* (1872) 7 Ch App 439). The question is whether the real and personal estate are intended to be combined into a general fund for the payment of liabilities: *Boughton v Boughton* (1848) 1 HL Cas 406 at 437; *Allan v Gott* (1872) 7 Ch App 439; *Re Timson, Harper v Timson* [1953] 2 All ER 1252, [1953] 1 WLR 1361.

[214.7]
Other matters by which the statutory order may be displaced are a direction for the payment of such expenses out of the proceeds of the conversion of the personal estate (*Re Atkinson, Webster v Walter* [1930] 1 Ch 47, [1929] All ER Rep 491; *Re Martin, Midland Bank Executor and Trustee Co Ltd v Marfleet* [1955] Ch 698, [1955] 1 All ER 865) or a gift of residue subject to such expenses (*Re Kempthorne, Charles v Kempthorne,* [1930] 1 Ch 268, [1929] All ER Rep 495; *Re Harland Peck, Hercy v Mayglothing* [1941] Ch 182, [1940] 4 All ER 347; *Re Berrey's Will Trusts, Greening v Warner* [1959] 1 All ER 15, [1959] 1 WLR 30). These provisions exclude the statutory order so far as it provides primarily for payment out of property undisposed of by the will. (In the case of a gift of residue subject to such expenses the presence or absence of a trust for sale is irrelevant.) On the other hand, a mere direction to pay such expenses followed by a residuary gift (*Re Lamb, Vipond v Lamb* [1929] 1 Ch 722, [1929] All ER Rep 82; *Re Kempthorne ; Re Tong, Hilton v Bradbury* [1931] 1 Ch 202, [1930] All ER Rep 262; *Re Worthington, Nichols v Harl* [1933] Ch 771, [1933] All ER Rep 189) or a gift of residue followed by a direction to pay duty (*Re Sanger, Taylor v North* [1939] Ch 238, [1938] 4 All ER 417) does not exclude the statutory order. An express charge of such expenses on specific gifts followed by a residuary gift to persons other than the specific legatees excludes the statutory order (*Re Littlewood, Clark v Littlewood* [1931] 1 Ch 443, [1930] All ER Rep 151; *Re James, Lloyds Bank Ltd v Atkins* [1947] Ch 256, [1947] 1 All ER 402; *Re Meldrum, Swinson v Meldrum* [1952] Ch 208, [1952] 1 All ER 274; *Re Ridley, Nicholson v Nicholson* [1950] Ch 415, [1950] 2 All ER 1) but a charge of such expenses on a legacy, the residue being undisposed of, does not exclude it (*Re Gordon, Watts v Rationalist Press Association Ltd* [1940] Ch 769, [1940] 3 All ER 205). (It is thought that these estate duty cases will apply equally under inheritance tax.)

[214.8]
It should be noted that where under the former law the residuary assets were directed by the will to be held on trust to sell or convert, and the debts, testamentary expenses, legacies, etc were directed to be paid out of the proceeds of such sale or conversion, the statutory order of application of assets to pay these would ordinarily be varied with the result that they would paid out of residue generally, rather than an undisposed of share of residue: see paras **[214.4]** and **[214.5]**. It is not thought that an administration trust which

confers a power of sale will have different consequences, provided that there is a clear intention to create a general fund out of which the liabilities are to be paid.

[214.9]
Order of application of the estate to pay legacies. There are two main issues which can arise: first, the extent to which real estate is available for payment of legacies, and, secondly, where there is a partial intestacy, whether legacies are payable out of the undisposed of residue or out of residue generally. The first of these is discussed in B10 at paras **[210.5]–[210.7]**. The second is a question of the extent to which the AEA 1925, ss 33(2), 34(3) and Sch 2, Pt II, para 1 (Part G, paras **[244.58]**, **[246.46]** and **[246.54]**) operate to direct payment of legacies primarily out of undisposed of estate, and what express provisions of a will are effective to displace those provisions. It should be noted that legacies for this purpose will include inheritance tax on specific gifts or general legacies which the will directs to be paid out of residue, and which would be borne by the gift itself in the absence of such direction, but not inheritance tax which is treated as a testamentary expense by the ITA 1984, s 211 (see para **[214.65]**). Subject to the provisions of the will, pecuniary legacies are first payable out of a lapsed share of residue or other property undisposed of by the will: *Re Worthington, Nichols v Hart,* [1933] Ch 771, [1933] All ER Rep 189; *Re Sanger, Taylor v North,* [1939] Ch 238, [1938] 4 All ER 417; *Re Gillett's Will Trusts, Barclays Bank Ltd v Gillett* [1950] Ch 102, [1949] 2 All ER 893; *Re Beaumont's Will Trusts, Walker v Lawson* [1950] Ch 462, [1950] 1 All ER 802; *Re Martin, Midland Bank Executor and Trustee Co Ltd v Marfleet,* [1955] Ch 698, [1955] 1 All ER 865; *Re Midgley, Barclays Bank Ltd v Midgley* [1955] Ch 576, [1955] 2 All ER 625; *Re Berrey's Will Trusts, Greening v Warner* [1959] 1 All ER 15, [1959] 1 WLR 30; and *Re Taylor's Estate and Will Trusts, Taylor v Taylor* [1969] 2 Ch 245, [1969] 1 All ER 113. The important question is what provisions of the will displace the statutory order. An express direction for payment of pecuniary legacies out of residue before it is divided into shares will naturally displace the statutory order, as in the case of liabilities (see para **[214.4]** et seq). The difficult point has been whether the presence of an express trust for sale in the will, without any express direction as to payment of legacies, excludes the statutory order so that the rule is that which prevailed before 1925, namely that the legacies are payable generally out of residue rather than out of the undisposed share. The most recent decision, *Re Taylor's Estate and Will Trusts* supra, following *Re Beaumont* supra, and not following *Re Midgley* supra, held that the presence of an express trust for sale was sufficient by itself to displace the statutory order. There are two main parts to the reasoning: first that the AEA 1925, s 33(2), which applied to undisposed of estate where s 33(1) imposing a statutory trust for sale applied, and which has the effect that the pecuniary legacies are primarily paid out of undisposed of property if it applies (see *Re Worthington* supra and *Re Berrey* supra), did not apply where there was an express trust for sale which displaced s 33(1), and secondly that AEA 1925, Sch 1, Pt II does not require the pecuniary legacies to be provided first out of undisposed of residue. This decision has been the subject of convincing criticism (see MJ Albery QC at (1969) 85 LQR 464), but even if it is not overruled the position may now be different after the coming into force of the TLATA 1996. This is because the AEA 1925, s 33 has been amended by the

TLATA 1996, s 5 and Sch 2, para 5 (see Part G, para **[244.58]**) so that the AEA 1925, s 33(1) does not contain a trust for sale and s 33(2) arguably is not dependent on s 33(1) applying, and because the former reason for providing an express trust for sale in administration trusts of residue no longer holds good as a result of the TLATA 1996 (see paras **[200.55]** and **[214.2]**). It is therefore possible that s 33(2) would now apply to an undisposed of share of residue even where there is a trust for sale of residue provided by the will, and even more likely that it would do so where, as in the form of administration trust recommended in para **[214.2]**, the will provides a power of sale not a trust for sale.

[214.10]

FORM B14.1:   Administration trust without a trust for sale

NOTE

For reasons mentioned at paras **[214.1]** and **[214.2]** it is no longer necessary for the administration trusts of residue to contain a trust for sale and conversion, and we recommend that they do not do so unless there is some specific reason for including a trust for sale. It is particularly appropriate not to provide one where there are life interest or other trusts which may continue for some time after the testator's death, and even more so where occupation of land by beneficiaries is contemplated. Where the gift of residue is into immediate and absolute fractional shares a trust for sale is arguably still appropriate: see Form B15.8 at para **[215.8]**.

If there is no trust for sale it is still appropriate to include an express power of sale, because the general law confers no general power to sell personalty (there is a power to sell it for purposes of administration under the AEA 1925, s 39 and a power to sell it in order to invest in investments authorised by the Trustee Act 2000 (TrA 2000)). The administration trust of an intestate's estate under the AEA 1925, s 33(1) has been amended by the TLATA 1996, Sch 2, para 5(2) so as to provide a power, not a trust, to sell: it is printed as so amended in Part G at para **[244.58]**.

The form below excludes the rules in *Howe v Dartmouth* and *Re Chesterfield's Trusts*, and statutory apportionment, but contains no directions as to the incidence of inheritance tax (except in so far as inheritance tax is a testamentary expense). It also provides a discretion as to the burden of liabilities as between capital and income instead of the total exclusion of the rule in *Allhusen v Whittell*. For a direction as to inheritance tax see eg Form C3.1, cl 5 at para **[225.15]**.

FORM

(1)   I give all my property not hereby or by any codicil hereto otherwise effectively disposed of [(including any entailed or other property over which I shall have at my death a general power of disposition by will)][1] to my trustees upon trust with power at their discretion to sell all or any of it when they think fit.[2]

(2)   My trustees shall pay my funeral and testamentary expenses my debts and any legacies given by this will or any codicil hereto out of such property or its proceeds of sale and shall have a discretion as to how such payments shall be borne as between capital and income.[3]

(3)   None of the equitable rules of apportionment between capital and income shall apply in any circumstances whatever.

(4)   Subject as aforesaid my trustees shall invest all money comprised in such property or arising from its sale in any of the investments hereby authorised with power to change such investments into any others hereby authorised and the said property and the assets from time to time representing the same (hereinafter called 'my residuary estate') shall be held on the trusts hereinafter declared.

(5)   All income of my residuary estate shall be treated as accruing on the date on which it becomes payable and there shall be no statutory apportionment of it to any other time or period.[4]

1   Subject to any express contrary intention property subject to a general power will be carried by a residuary gift under the WA 1837, s 27 (Part G, para [244.27]), but in the case of entailed property the will must refer to the property, or the instrument under which it was acquired, or entailed property generally for the statutory power of disposition to be exercised: LPA 1925, s 176(1) (Part G, para [244.53]). Although no new entails can be created on or after 1 January 1997 (see para [200.53]), entails created before that date can continue to exist and, if they do, the statutory power of disposition of them by will continues to be available.
2   This wording could be made even more concise, such as 'My trustees shall have power to sell all or any of such property'. One reason for using the slightly more elaborate wording in this Form is that it follows the wording which was held in *Re Pitcairn* [1896] 2 Ch 199 to prevent the rule in *Howe v Dartmouth* from applying, but out of caution sub-cl (3) is also included. See further, para [214.38].
3   The words from 'and shall have' are intended to exclude the rule in *Allhusen v Whittell* and give the trustees a complete discretion over the burden of debts and testamentary expenses as between capital and income. See paras [214.43] and [214.44] for exclusion of this rule.
4   For exclusion of statutory apportionment see paras [214.51] and [214.52].

[214.11]

Form B14.2:   Administration trust without A trust for sale, concise form[1]

(1)   My trustees shall hold all my property not hereby or by any codicil hereto otherwise effectively disposed of [(including any entailed or other property over which I shall have at my death a general power of disposition by will)][2] and the assets from time to time representing the same ('my residuary estate') with power to sell the same as and when they think fit upon the trusts set out below.

(2)   In the administration of my estate and the execution of the trusts hereof or of any codicil hereto:

(a)   none of the equitable rules of apportionment between capital and income shall apply in any circumstances whatever and my trustees shall have a discretion as to how expenses debts and legacies shall be borne as between capital and income;

(b)   my trustees shall treat all income as accruing on the date on which it becomes payable regardless of the period in respect of which it shall have accrued and shall not make any statutory apportionment of the same.[3]

1   This form omits any direction as to incidence of debts, administration expenses and legacies and leaves the incidence of them to statute. For the statutory order see paras **[214.4]–[214.9]**.
2   See para **[214.10]**, n 1.
3   See para **[214.10]**, nn 3 and 4.

[214.12]

FORM B14.3:   Residuary disposition to trustees on trust for sale, with administration trusts, directions as to inheritance tax, and exclusion of equitable and statutory apportionment

I give all my property not hereby or by any codicil hereto otherwise effectively disposed of (including any entailed or other property over which I shall have at my death a general power of disposition by will)[1] to my trustees to hold on trust as follows:

(1)   My trustees shall hold such property upon trust to sell the same[2] or such part thereof as shall not consist of money with full power to postpone the sale of all or any part thereof[3] without being responsible for loss;

(2)   Out of the net moneys to arise from such sale and any ready moneys comprised in my estate my trustees shall pay my funeral and testamentary expenses, my debts, any taxes or duties referred to in the next following subclause, and any legacies given by this will or any codicil hereto;

(3)   There shall be paid out of the said moneys (in addition to any inheritance tax on my death which is a testamentary expense) any inheritance tax or other tax or duty payable on or by reason of my death which is attributable to any gift in this will or any codicil hereto which is made free of such tax or duty;[4]

(4)   In the administration of my estate and the execution of the trusts hereof:

(a)   all income from my estate or any part thereof shall be treated as accruing on the date on which it becomes payable regardless of the period in respect of which it shall have accrued and it shall not be the subject of any statutory apportionment;[5]

(b)   the equitable rules of apportionment between capital and income shall not apply in any circumstances whatever and furthermore shall not apply to any assets in respect of which my trustees have not made any deliberate decision to postpone the sale thereof;[6] and

(c)   debts, testamentary expenses, inheritance tax or similar taxes, and legacies shall be paid out of capital but any interest on any such debts, expenses, taxes or legacies which may become payable in respect of any period falling after my death shall so far as possible be paid out of income;[7]

(5)   My trustees shall invest the residue of the said moneys in any of the investments hereby authorised with power to change the investment thereof into any other investment hereby authorised;

(6)   My trustees shall hold the residue of such moneys and the assets from time to time representing the same and all parts of my estate for the time being unsold (all of which property is hereinafter collectively referred to as 'my residuary estate') upon the trusts and with and subject to the powers and provisions hereinafter contained.

Part B   Clauses in wills

1   As to power to dispose by will of entailed property, see the LPA 1925, s 176 (Part G, para **[244.53]**) and Vol 1, para **[7.2]**; a general reference to entailed property is sufficient. Although entailed interests can no longer be created, existing interests can continue to exist, in which case this section will apply: see para **[200.53]**. For the exercise of general powers of appointment by will, see Vol 1, paras **[39.10]**–**[39.15]**.
2   Although we recommend the inclusion in administration trusts of a power of sale rather than a trust for sale (see para **[214.1]**), a trust for sale remains a perfectly acceptable alternative.
3   The power to postpone sale implied by the TLATA 1996, s 4(1) (Part G, para **[246.89]**) only applies in relation to *land* held on trust for sale.
4   See para **[214.71]**, sub-para (1).
    The inheritance tax on the testator's free estate in the UK will be paid out of residue as a testamentary expense, in the absence of the expression of a contrary intention: see para **[214.59]** et seq. Any inheritance tax which is not a testamentary expense (eg the tax on foreign property: see para **[214.63]**) and is attributable to a pecuniary legacy or specific gift which is made elsewhere in the will, or in a codicil to it, and which is expressed to be free of inheritance tax, will be payable out of residue by virtue of this subclause. The reason for the somewhat long-winded treatment of inheritance tax is so that what is a standard form is not construed so as to have an unintended effect where there are no gifts in the will to which it applies: see para **[214.70]**.
    It should therefore be noted that where this form is used, individual specific gifts or pecuniary legacies which prima facie bear some or all of their own inheritance tax (or foreign death duties) must be stated to be free of inheritance tax (and foreign death duties where appropriate) if the testator wants them to be free of such tax or duties. Pecuniary legacies should be expressed to be free of inheritance tax unless it is absolutely certain that there will be no property with a foreign location in the residuary estate: see para **[214.64]**.
5   For statutory apportionment, between different periods of time, see paras **[214.48]**–**[214.52]**.
6   For exclusion of the rules in *Howe v Dartmouth* and *Re Chesterfield's Trusts* see paras **[214.35]**–**[214.38]**. The words from 'and in particular' are intended to exclude what we refer to as the rule in *Re Rowlls* [1900] 2 Ch 107: see also para **[214.38]**.
7   For the reasoning behind this see para **[214.44]**.

[214.13]

FORM B14.4:   **Residuary disposition with power of sale with respect to personalty so as to prevent the rules in** *Howe v Dartmouth* **and** *Re Chesterfield's Trusts* **from applying, with administration trusts and exclusion of statutory apportionment and the rule in** *Allhusen v Whittell*

I give all my property not hereby or by any codicil hereto otherwise effectively disposed of (including any entailed or other property over which I shall have at my death a general power of disposition by will[1]) to my trustees upon trust as follows:

    (1)   My trustees shall have power to sell any of such property whenever they think fit but shall hold any freehold or leasehold land on trust for sale with full power to postpone the sale of all or any part thereof without being responsible for loss;[2]

    (2)   Out of the net moneys to arise from sale of such property and any ready moneys comprised in my estate my trustees shall pay my funeral and testamentary expenses, my debts, and any legacies given by this will or any codicil hereto;[3]

    (3)   In the administration of my estate and the execution of the trusts hereof:

    (a)   all income from my estate or any part thereof shall be treated as accruing on the date on which it becomes payable regardless of the period in respect of which it shall have accrued and it shall not be the subject of any statutory apportionment;[4] and

(b)   the rule of equity as to the apportionment between capital and income of payments made in the course of administration shall not apply to my estate, and debts, testamentary expenses, inheritance tax or similar taxes, and legacies shall be paid out of capital while any interest on any such debts, expenses, taxes or legacies which may become payable in respect of any period falling after my death shall as far as possible be paid out of income;[5]

(4)   [*As sub-clause (5) in* Form B14.3 *at para* **[214.12]**].

(5)   [*As sub-clause (6) in* Form B14.3 *at para* **[214.12]**].

1   See Form B14.1, n 1 at para **[214.10]**.
2   Where there is a power to sell personalty when the trustees think fit, it seems that the rules in *Howe v Dartmouth* and *Re Chesterfield's Trusts* cannot apply: see Vol 1, para **[38.23]**, n 11. For these rules and their exclusion see paras **[214.35]–[214.38]**. A disadvantage of using this method of excluding these rules is that it will not be as readily apparent that these apportionment rules do not apply as it would be if there were words of express exclusion of them. See further para **[214.38]**.
3   This form makes no provision for inheritance tax or foreign death duties from which specific gifts or pecuniary legacies are freed. See Form B14.3 at para **[214.12]** for an example of such provision.
4   For statutory apportionment, between different periods of time, see paras **[214.48]–[214.52]**.
5   For the reasoning behind this see para **[214.44]**.

[214.14]

FORM B14.5:   Residuary gift with no trust for sale and a power of sale which is to be used only if appropriation in specie not practicable[1]

(1)   I give all the rest of my property both real and personal whatsoever and wheresoever situate to [all my children] in equal shares if more than one.

(2)   My trustees may in extension of the power of appropriation conferred on personal representatives by section 41 of the Administration of Estates Act 1925 at any time or times without any of the consents required by that section appropriate any part of my residuary estate in its then actual condition or state of investment in or towards the satisfaction of the share of any infant beneficiary interested in my residuary estate.[2]

(3)   If at the expiration of three months after the submission of any proposal for appropriation by my trustees or such further period as my trustees in their absolute discretion shall allow the persons entitled thereto or whose consent is required as aforesaid have not consented in writing to such appropriation of any asset of my residuary estate under the preceding subclauses hereof such asset shall be sold by my trustees (with power at their absolute discretion to postpone such sale for so long as they shall think fit without being liable for loss) and the net proceeds of sale and the net income until sale shall be divided amongst [my said children].[3]

1   Although formerly less popular, the inclusion of a power of sale rather than a trust for sale in administration trusts is the authors' preferred option in the light of the changes in the law relating to settlements of land introduced by the TLATA 1996: see para **[214.2]**. This form leaves the incidence of debts, administration expenses etc to the general law, and if there is a

lapsed share of residue these will be primarily payable out of the lapsed share of residue rather than residue generally: see para **[214.5]**.

2   This provision only slightly extends the common law duty of executors. If an estate is given to a number of persons without any trust for sale, the duty of the executors is to appropriate the estate to the beneficiaries, and, if division of certain property is or becomes impossible, they must sell the property and divide the proceeds. See *Re Beverly* [1901] 1 Ch 681 at 685, and compare *Cooper v Cooper* (1874) LR 7 HL 53 at 65. If it was instead provided that exercise of the power of appropriation did not need any consents at all, not even those of the adult beneficiaries, it would make the administration of the estate easier, and might give a stamp duty advantage where there was land comprised in the residuary estate: see the Note and Forms concerning powers of appropriation in B20 at para **[220.70]** et seq.

3   See n 2 supra. This is a statement of what the executors would have to do anyway, in the absence of express provision, if they could not appropriate the entire estate, but its presence may reduce the scope for dispute.

[214.15]

FORM B14.6:   General residuary gift to trustees—direction to pay inheritance tax on specific gifts, pecuniary legacies, and lifetime gifts

I give my trustees all my real and personal estate whatsoever and wheresoever including both entailed[1] and all other property over which I have any power of disposition by will[2] excepting only the property hereby or by any codicil hereto specifically devised or bequeathed [*if the property is not to be made subject to a trust for sale, add* subject to the payment in due course of administration of my debts funeral and testamentary expenses inheritance tax and any death duties payable outside the United Kingdom in respect of any specific gift or pecuniary legacy hereby made[3] [and in respect of any gift or other transaction given or effected in my lifetime and giving rise to a claim for any inheritance tax or additional inheritance tax on my death[4]] and the legacies and annuities hereby or by any codicil hereto bequeathed].

1   As to power to dispose by will of entailed property, see the LPA 1925, s 176 (Part G, para **[244.53]**) and Vol 1, para **[7.2]**. A general reference to entailed property is sufficient. Although entailed interests can no longer be created, existing interests can continue to exist, in which case this section will apply: see para **[200.53]**.

2   This may include property subject to a general power of appointment: see Vol 1, paras **[39.10]**–**[39.15]**.

3   See the Note on the incidence of inheritance tax at paras **[214.55]** et seq and Forms B14.3 (at para **[214.12]**), B14.17 (at para **[214.26]**), B14.33 (at para **[214.76]**) and B14.34 (at para **[214.77]**) for alternative forms of direction concerning inheritance tax and foreign death duties.

4   The reference to inter vivos gifts should not be included without careful thought for the likely sums involved. It will refer to the inheritance tax or additional inheritance tax payable on any inter vivos chargeable or potentially exempt transfer made within seven years before the testator's death. See further the note in B10 at para **[210.66]**. A provision concerning the payment of inheritance tax on lifetime transfers such as this will in effect be one or more pecuniary legacies (eg for the purposes of abatement: see para **[214.65]**).

[214.16]

FORM B14.7:   Trust for conversion

I direct my trustees to sell call in and convert into money all such parts of my said real and personal estate as shall not consist of money or investments of the kinds hereinafter authorised[1] [*or* investments authorised by law for the investment of trust funds] with power to postpone such sale calling in and conversion for such time as my trustees in their absolute discretion and without being liable to account shall think fit.[2]

1   These words will be used where the will contains an express investment clause. Where there is no such clause, the words in brackets should be included.
2   See Note on power to postpone sale at para **[214.3]**. This form could be followed by Form B14.17 at para **[214.26]**.

[214.17]

FORM B14.8:   Trust to pay debts and invest residue—directions as to inheritance tax[1]

Out of my ready money and the clear moneys to arise from such sale calling and conversion as aforesaid my trustees shall pay or provide for my debts funeral and testamentary expenses (including inheritance tax treated as such by statute)[2] and the inheritance tax [and foreign death duties] payable on any gift caused to be free of inheritance tax [and foreign death duties] by any declaration in this will or any codicil hereto and the pecuniary legacies and annuities hereby or by any codicil hereto given (which shall not bear any inheritance tax [or foreign death duties] even if they are wholly or partly paid out of foreign assets and whether or not they are herein elsewhere expressed to be free of inheritance tax [or foreign death duties])[3] and subject thereto my trustees shall invest in manner hereinafter authorised with power to vary any such investments for others of a like nature the residue of the said moneys and stand possessed of such investments and of the residue of such investments as aforesaid which formed part of my estate at the time of my death and of all parts of my estate for the time being unsold and any ready money (hereinafter called 'my residuary estate') upon the trusts hereinafter declared concerning the same.

1   This form provides for all legacies and annuities to be free of inheritance tax, for specific gifts of property in the UK also to be free of it, but for specific gifts of foreign property to be free of inheritance tax only if specifically declared to be.
2   As to the meaning of 'testamentary expenses' see Vol 1, para **[55.7]**, and for the inheritance tax treated as such (ie that on UK property), see the ITA 1984, s 211 (Part G, para **[246.83]**) and paras **[214.55]** et seq.
3   The residue constitutes a mixed or blended fund and without these words, if the estate includes foreign assets, the legacies and annuities not expressed to be free of inheritance tax would be payable rateably out of UK and foreign assets and the part paid out of foreign assets would be liable to bear inheritance tax and foreign death duties paid in respect of it: *Re Spencer Cooper, Poë v Spencer Cooper* [1908] 1 Ch 130; *Re Owers* [1941] Ch 17, [1940] 4 All ER 225; *Re Sebba, Lloyds Bank Ltd v Hutson* [1959] Ch 166 at 178 (see the declaration on question (3)— the report at [1958] 3 All ER 393 does not report this point). See further para **[214.64]**. These words are not necessary if the legacies and annuities are all expressed to be free of inheritance tax, but the chances of error are less if a general provision of this type is used than if directions relating to individual gifts are used.

[214.18]

FORM B14.9:   Gift of residue to trustees who are different persons from the executors[1]

The executors after paying or satisfying my debts funeral and testamentary expenses inheritance tax and the aforesaid pecuniary and specific legacies shall transfer all the residue of my estate (including all property over which I have a power of appointment or disposition by will and all entailed property of which by virtue of section 176 of the Law of Property Act 1925 or any other statutory provision I can dispose by will[2]) to —— and —— (hereinafter called my trustees) to hold the same upon the following trusts: *[administration trusts]*.

1   Will forms generally assume that the same persons are appointed both executors and trustees of the will. Where different persons are appointed trustees, a variation of the residuary gift is necessary. If desired the following form may used: Subject to my debts funeral and testamentary expenses inheritance tax and the aforesaid pecuniary and specific legacies, I give all my real and personal property wheresoever situate and of whatsoever kind (including, etc) to —— and —— (hereinafter called my trustees) to hold, etc, as above.
2   See para [214.10], n 1.

[214.19]

FORM B14.10:   Gift of residue on trust for sale—exclusion of equitable apportionment rules[1]

I give all my real and personal movable and immovable property of whatever nature and wheresoever situate not hereby or by any codicil hereto otherwise disposed of unto my trustees upon trust to sell call in and convert the same into money with power to postpone such sale calling in and conversion as long as they shall in their absolute discretion think fit without being liable for loss and so that the income of all parts of my estate however constituted or invested (including the income of property required for the payments of debts and other payments made in due course of administration in payment whereof the proceeds of such sale calling in and conversion are hereinafter directed to be applied) shall as from my death be treated and applied as income and so that no reversionary or future interest shall be sold prior to the falling into possession thereof unless my trustees shall see special reason for an earlier sale and no such interest shall before falling into possession be treated as producing income and that the net rents and profits of my real and leasehold estate for the time being unsold after payment thereout of all outgoings which my trustees shall consider payable out of income shall go and be applied as if the same were income of authorised investments made of the proceeds of an actual sale thereof.

1   This form includes in a comprehensive paragraph several of the foregoing clauses, including a trust for sale (as to the implications of which see para [214.2]). It will then be followed by the trusts upon which the residue is to be held, for example, a trust to pay debts and expenses, a trust for investment where a short form of that trust is used, followed by the beneficial trusts of income and capital. Under this form the rule in *Howe v Earl of Dartmouth* (as to which, see paras [214.35]–[214.38]) is excluded in all its branches and the rule in *Allhusen v Whittell* (as to which, see paras [214.43] and [214.44]): see *Re Ullswater* [1952] Ch 105, [1951] 2 All ER 989 (the relevant words are the ones in brackets), but not apportionment under the Apportionment Act 1870 (Part G, para [246.2] et seq); see also paras [214.48]–[214.52].

[214.20]

FORM B14.11:   The same by incorporation of Statutory Will Forms 1925, Form 8

I devise and bequeath all my real and personal estate not hereby or by any codicil hereto specifically devised or bequeathed unto my trustees and the

Statutory Will Forms 1925, Form 8 (Administration Trusts) shall be incorporated herein and apply to this residuary gift.[1]

1   For Statutory Will Forms 1925, Form 8, see para **[238.14]**. If desired the Statutory Form can be incorporated with the exception or variation of certain parts. For example after the word 'incorporated' above may be inserted: 'with the exception of paragraph 7(b) of the said Form (Leasehold Sinking Fund).' For forms providing such a sinking fund, see Forms B7.11 and B7.12 at paras **[207.25]** and **[207.26]**.

[214.21]

FORM B14.12:   Definition of residuary estate

My trustees shall stand possessed of such investments and of the residue of such investments as aforesaid which form part of my estate at the time of my death and all parts of my estate for the time being unsold and any ready money and the assets from time to time representing the same all of which are together hereinafter referred to as 'my residuary estate' [and of the income thereof] upon the following trusts.[1]

1   Some of the more usual forms of these trusts are set out in B15 to B19 (at paras **[215.1]** et seq and **[219.1]** et seq) and see Statutory Wills Forms 1925, Forms 9 and 10 (Part E, paras **[238.15]** and **[238.16]**).

[214.22]

FORM B14.13:   Declaration negativing the exercise of the statutory power to dispose of entailed property or the exercise of a general power of appointment[1]

I hereby declare that nothing herein contained is intended to or shall operate as an exercise of any general power of appointment vested in me nor as the exercise of the statutory power to dispose of entailed property.

1   A general declaration in these terms is probably the most convenient way. For the power to dispose of entailed property by will see Vol 1, para **[7.2]** and for the exercise of general powers of appointment by will see Vol 1, paras **[39.10]**–**[39.15]**.

[214.23]

FORM B14.14:   Devise and bequest of residue charged with payment of debts

I devise and bequeath all my real and personal estate whatsoever and wheresoever not hereby or by any codicil hereto otherwise specifically disposed of (including any real or personal property over which I may have any general power of appointment [and including also any entailed property of which I have power to dispose by will]) unto [*donee*] absolutely but subject to and charged with the payment of my debts [including debts charged upon any property specifically devised or bequeathed] funeral and testamentary expenses and legacies and annuities bequeathed hereby or by any codicil hereto [and the inheritance tax on any such legacies or annuities].

[214.24]

FORM B14.15:   Bequest of residuary personal estate only

I bequeath all other personal estate (including [*or* except] leasehold property [and including also such part of any entailed property of which I have power to dispose by will as is in fact represented by personal estate]) not hereby or by any codicil hereto otherwise specifically disposed of to which I may be entitled at my death or over which I may have at my death any general power of appointment unto [*legatee*] absolutely.[1]

1   The effect of this Form and Form B14.16 at para **[214.25]** is probably altered by the TLATA 1996 in relation to undivided shares of land. Before the TLATA 1996 came into force an undivided share of land was an interest in the proceeds of sale of land held on trust for sale and was treated as an interest in personalty by virtue of the doctrine of conversion (*Re Kempthorne, Charles v Kempthorne* [1930] 1 Ch 268, CA). From the coming into force of the TLATA 1996 (1 January 1997) an undivided share of land is either an equitable interest in land directly (ie without the interposition of a trust for sale), or it is an interest under a trust for sale but with the doctrine of conversion abolished: see Vol 1, paras **[41.18]**, **[64.52]** and **[200.54]**. The only exception is an undivided share of land under an express trust for sale created by the will of a person who died before 1 January 1997 (in relation to which the doctrine of conversion still applies). Accordingly, it would seem that contrary to the position between 1 January 1926 and 31 December 1996 (inclusive), a gift as in Form B14.15 will not now include an undivided share of freehold land, and a gift as in Form B14.16 will do so. It is thought that an equitable interest in freehold land counts as real property, as such an interest devolved on the heir before 1926 (see, eg *Re Somerville and Turner's Contract* [1903] 2 Ch 583).

[214.25]

FORM B14.16:   Devise of residuary real estate only

I devise all the residue of the real estate other than [*or* including] leaseholds[1] not hereby or by any codicil hereto otherwise specifically disposed of to which I may be entitled at my death or over which I may have any general power of appointment [and all real estate other than [*or* including] leaseholds of which I am tenant in tail in possession under a settlement dated etc *or* under the will of etc] unto [*devisee*] absolutely.

1   See the WA 1837, s 26 (Part G, para **[244.26]**). Where there are freeholds, a devise of 'real estate,' without more, will not include leaseholds (*Butler v Butler* (1884) 28 Ch D 66), but if words of description are added to 'real estate', leaseholds may be included (*Moase v White* (1876) 3 Ch D 763).

      If there are no freeholds, a devise of 'real estate' will pass leaseholds (*Re Holt, Holt v Holt* [1921] 2 Ch 17). Undivided shares of real estate would probably now pass under this clause (see para **[214.24]**, n 1).

      As to whether this devise of residuary realty is a specific gift: see Vol 1, para **[30.3]**, nn 12 and 13.

[214.26]

FORM B14.17:   Trusts of proceeds of sale of residue with general direction to pay inheritance tax on free estate out of residue

I declare that my trustees shall stand possessed of the net moneys arising from the sale of my said residuary real and personal estate and of my ready money upon trust as follows:

(1)   To pay and discharge my funeral and testamentary expenses[1] and debts other than mortgage debts or charges on property specifically devised or bequeathed[2] which shall be paid out of the property charged therewith.

(2)   Except so far as is otherwise provided by this will or any codicil hereto to pay all inheritance tax [and foreign death duties (if any)] payable by reason of my death in respect of all property wherever situated disposed of by me by this will or any codicil hereto (other than property appointed under a special or general power of appointment or entailed property).[3]

(3)   To pay the legacies bequeathed hereby or by any codicil hereto and to provide for the annuities bequeathed hereby or by any codicil hereto

(4)   My trustees shall invest the residue of such moneys in their names in any of the modes of investment hereby authorised with power from time to time [with the consent of —— if living] to vary such investments for others of the nature aforesaid.[4]

1   As to the expression 'testamentary expenses.' See Vol 1, para **[55.7]**.
2   Specifically bequeathed personalty bears its own money charges: AEA 1925, s 35 (Part G, para **[246.47]**). If thought fit, property specifically given can be exonerated by a special direction. See Form B4.53, n 1 at para **[204.75]**.
3   See the Note on the incidence of inheritance tax at para **[214.55]** et seq and Forms B14.3 (at para **[214.12]**) and B14.33 and B14.34 (at paras **[214.76]** and **[214.77]**) for alternative forms.
4   These are the administration trusts. For beneficial trusts, see precedents in B15 to B19 (at paras **[215.1]**–**[219.1]** et seq). A devise of realty on trust to pay debts extended the period of limitation to twelve years as against the realty (*Re Balls, Trewby v Balls* [1909] 1 Ch 791).

Powers and directions for the administration of an estate

[214.27]

NOTE

Dispositions of residue. The beneficial interests commonly given in a residuary gift necessarily vary according to the circumstances of the testator. The common form in the case of a married person has changed as a result of the introduction of capital transfer tax (now inheritance tax). In the estate duty era the usual disposition was for the surviving spouse for life or until remarriage and then for the children of the marriage. Under inheritance tax there is no advantage in giving the testator's spouse a life interest (see para **[200.99]**), and it is now becoming more common to make an absolute gift to the surviving spouse with an alternative gift to the testator's children in case the spouse does not survive the testator. This is particularly the case with younger testators who are making wills principally to dispose of their property in the event of an unexpectedly early death. Older testators, in the interests of using up their inheritance tax nil-rate band (see para **[200.101]**), may wish to leave part of residue to their spouses and part to their children or on discretionary trusts under which the surviving spouse can benefit without the discretionary fund forming part of his or her taxable estate. They may also be more likely to want a traditional form of will which leaves only a life interest to their spouses, particularly if they have married a second time and wish to ensure that their property will go to their children by an earlier marriage after their spouses have died. Further, if they have grandchildren, there can be an inheritance tax advantage in leaving property on trust for their grandchildren so that it passes to them directly, missing out the intervening generation and an intermediate tax charge. For examples of such wills see C2 and C3 at paras **[224.1]** et seq and **[225.1]** et seq.

[214.28]
The types of trust most likely to be required are thus trusts for minors or young persons, which need to be drafted so as to satisfy the requirements of the ITA 1984, s 71 (see generally as to trusts of this description at para **[200.119]** et seq) and Forms B17.1 to B17.29 at paras **[217.6]**–**[217.34]**. There will be some demand for such things as life interests and protective trusts, for non-fiscal reasons. There has been a significant revival of interest in discretionary trusts as a result of the changes in the system of charging now inheritance tax on them introduced in 1982 and the subsequent reductions in inheritance tax rates: see the Note in B18 at para **[218.1]** et seq. In the case of unmarried persons, the residue, unless given to strangers must go to collaterals and then care should be taken to include or exclude, as the intention may be, those who are only collateral through marriage. For example, a nephew's wife may be commonly spoken of by a testator as his niece and, though she is not properly speaking his niece, it may be intended to include her. In such cases there may be much to be said for making the gifts to named persons rather than to classes, though this may involve more complication in making provision for those dying in the testator's lifetime or in infancy. For the simpler method of dealing with this difficulty, see Form B19.11 at para **[219.24]**. The statutory rules of construction including illegitimate children and issue, discussed in Vol 1 at para **[72.1]** et seq, should not be overlooked, nor should the rules including adopted children which are considered in Vol 1 at para **[75.1]** et seq.

Many examples of different dispositions of residue will be found in Part C, classified according to the family or other circumstances of the testator.

[214.29]

FORM B14.18:   Power to trustees to sell or mortgage for payment of incumbrances

I authorise my trustees at any time or times and from time to time in their discretion to sell or mortgage at such price and upon such terms and conditions as they may think fit all or any part of the real or leasehold property forming part of my residuary estate for the purpose of paying or of securing to the respective mortgagers or mortgagee for the time being any mortgage debt or debts owing by me at my death or to effect and keep on foot out of the income or if necessary out of the capital of my residuary estate any policy or policies of assurance for the purpose of discharging such mortgage debt or debts and I declare that no purchaser or mortgagee shall be concerned to inquire as to the propriety of any sale or mortgage under this power or as to the application of any money raised thereby.[1]

---

1   Under the TLATA 1996, s 6(1) (Part G, para **[246.91]**) trustees of land have all the powers of an absolute owner in relation to the land they hold.

[214.30]

FORM B14.19: Power to trustees to postpone conversion except as to certain property[1]

I declare that it shall be lawful for my trustees to postpone the sale calling in and conversion of my said residuary real and personal estate or any part thereof (except shares in companies with unlimited liability which I direct shall be sold as soon as conveniently may be after my death[2]) so long as my trustees shall in their uncontrolled discretion think proper.

1. A power to postpone sale is, in the case of every trust of land, implied despite any provision to the contrary made by the disposition: TLATA 1996, s 4(1) (Part G, para **[246.89]**). As to the effect of a power to postpone upon the application of the rule in *Howe v Earl of Dartmouth*: see *Re Berry, Lloyds Bank Ltd v Berry* [1962] Ch 97, [1961] 1 All ER 529 and Vol 1, para **[38.19]**. See also notes on the power to postpone sale at paras **[214.3]** and **[214.37]**.

2. As to the adequacy of these words, see *Re Rooke's Will Trusts, Taylor v Rooke* [1953] Ch 716, [1953] 2 All ER 110. (The decision in this case, which concerned land, has been superseded by the TLATA 1996, s 4(1) (Part G, para **[246.89]**), but remains good law as to other forms of property.)

[214.31]

FORM B14.20: Power to trustees to defer the calling in of certain debts

I authorise my trustees to defer the calling in of any debt or debts carrying interest which may be owing to me from [*name*] at my decease for any period not exceeding [five] years and I declare that my trustees shall not be bound to require any security or further security for such debt or debts provided such interest be regularly paid and that they shall not be responsible for any loss that may occur by reason of deferring such calling in or of any omission to require such security.

[214.32]

FORM B14.21: Direction to determine tenancy of a house

I direct that my trustees shall as soon as conveniently may be after my death use their best endeavours to sell or by surrender including a release from liability[1] thereunder determine the tenancy of my leasehold premises known as ——. They may for the purposes aforesaid pay out of the capital of my residuary estate to the purchaser or a reversioner as the case may be such sum as they in their uncontrolled opinion think reasonable not exceeding the clear sum of £——.

1. See *Richmond v Savill* [1926] 2 KB 530, [1926] All ER Rep 362.

[214.33]

FORM B14.22: Direction to trustees to convert foreign property, with powers of management[1]

With regard to property whether real or personal movable or immovable belonging to me or to which I may be entitled at the time of my decease in [Canada] I direct as follows:

(1)   My trustees shall sell convert into money and get in all such property at such time or times and in such manner and upon such terms and conditions as in their uncontrolled discretion they shall think fit with full power to buy in rescind or vary any contract of sale and to resell any property intended to be included in any such sale without being answerable for any loss and with power in the like discretion to postpone any such sale conversion or realisation for such periods as they may think fit.

(2)   Pending such sale conversion and realisation my trustees may let on lease for any term not exceeding [twenty-one] years manage and superintend the whole or any part of the said property and receive the rents and profits thereof and out of any moneys coming into their hands from my property in [Canada] execute and pay for all such cultivation improvements repairs insurances and other matters as my trustees may think expedient.

(3)   As regards any undivided share or interest to which I may be entitled at my decease in any property situate receivable or recoverable in [Canada] my trustees may concur with any person or persons entitled to or having power in that behalf over the other shares or interests in any such property in exercising any powers of sale leasing or managing hereinbefore conferred. And also if deemed expedient they may partition or concur in partitioning the same or any part thereof and for that purpose may agree to any apportionment of purchase-money rent expenses of sale or other matters and pay or receive money for equality of exchange or partition.[2]

1   See also Form C14.1 at para **[236.9]**.
2   The TrA 2000, Pt IV (Part G, paras **[246.126]**–**[246.142]**) gives to trustees and personal representatives very wide powers to delegate their functions which would include power to delegate their functions in relation to foreign property. Special power is therefore not required; it may, however, sometimes be advisable to insert full powers in order that persons in the foreign country may see upon the face of the will that the trustees have certain powers.

   If a will is being made in England of a person domiciled abroad, the section could easily be adapted so as to give the trustees of the will an express power of delegation in respect of land in England, if it were considered desirable for the powers to appear on the face of the will.

   A foreign country, as the words are used above, includes all countries except England and Wales, although they may be in the UK or the Commonwealth. The point is that such countries are not necessarily subject to precisely the same law, even though they may be common law jurisdictions. This form and adaptations of it may be useful where restrictions on foreign exchange make it difficult to send money from one jurisdiction to another. As far as possible all payments which can be made in the foreign jurisdiction should be made there and as little as possible remitted.

[214.34]

FORM B14.23:   Direction to foreign trustees to remit proceeds of sale to English trustees[1]

(1)   I declare that subject to the retention of such sums or sums as they may consider necessary for all or any of the purposes aforesaid in connection with any unrealised portion of my said real or personal estate in [*foreign country*] my foreign trustees shall from time to time hand over and remit to my English trustees through such bank as my English trustees may direct the net proceeds of all real and personal estate sold converted got in or realised by my foreign trustees in [*foreign country*] after paying all expenses of and incident to any such sale conversion and realisation and after deducting thereout the commission

payable to my foreign trustees for their services and all taxes and duties of whatsoever description which may be payable in [*foreign country*] in respect of my estate and also after paying thereout all pecuniary legacies bequeathed by this my will to any person or persons for the time being resident in [*foreign country*].

(2) I direct that as regards any income which may be received by my foreign trustees from any property of mine in [*foreign country*] pending the sale and conversion thereof and the handing of the proceeds of such sale and conversion over to my English trustees the same shall after payment thereout of all taxes and duties which may be payable in respect thereof in [*foreign country*] and subject to deduction therefrom of the commission payable in respect of such income to my foreign trustees be paid over to my English trustees and shall be applicable as income in their hands.

(3) The receipt of my English trustees [or other the trustees in England of this my will for the time being] shall be a good and complete discharge for all moneys paid over to them by my foreign trustees.

1   Compare Form C14.1, cl 5 at para **[236.15]**; see also Form B1.5, n 1 at para **[201.9]**.

Exclusion of apportionment between capital and income (rules in Howe v Earl of Dartmouth and Re Chesterfield's Trusts)

[214.35]

NOTE

The rules in *Howe v Earl of Dartmouth* and *Re Chesterfield's Trusts*. The rules in *Howe v Earl of Dartmouth* (income of assets of a wasting or hazardous nature or other unauthorised assets apportioned partly to capital) and the rule in *Re Chesterfield's Trusts* (reversions or other non-income yielding property apportioned retrospectively partly to income when they fall in or are sold) are commonly excluded. The rules, which are described in Vol 1 at paras **[38.17]**–**[38.27]**, only apply to personal property comprised in residue which is held on trust for persons in succession. There is copious case law on when the rules apply, and the rules concerning their exclusion are by now a nightmare of complexity and technicality. Indeed the precise basis of the rules is uncertain. The conventional view, adopted in the notes which follow, is that the rules apply in relation to investments which are unauthorised. On this view the introduction of a very wide statutory power of investment by the TrA 2000, s 3 (Part G, para **[246.118]**) will have excluded the rules in all but very exceptional cases. An alternative view is that the rules apply to assets which are of a wasting or hazardous nature, whether authorised or not: see Robert Mitchell 'Trusts for Sale in Wills – Excess Baggage' (1999) 63 Conv 84 at 98–103. This view, if correct, affords a further reason for excluding the rules. Note the following points:

(1) 'Personal property' here originally included leasehold land (but not of course freehold land), and a classic example of the type of wasting asset to which Howe v Earl of Dartmouth applied was a leasehold with only a few years to run. However, prior to 1 January 1997 the LPA 1925, s 28(2) effectively excluded the rule in relation to leaseholds held on

trust for sale, and it was arguable that because the Howe v Earl of Dartmouth rule applied to assets not expressly held on trust for sale by implying a trust for sale, s 28 (2) had the curious effect of also excluding the rule in relation to leaseholds not held on trust for sale (see Wolstenholme & Cherry's Conveyancing Statutes (13th edn), vol 1, pp 85–6), but the point was uncertain. The repeal of the LPA 1925, s 28(2) therefore may mean that leaseholds fall back into the rule in *Howe v Earl of Dartmouth*, unless it is the case that the rule does not apply to authorised investments (see supra), in which case the wide power to invest in leaseholds in TrA 2000, s 8(1) (Part G, para **[246.123]**; see also para **[220.17]**) has the effect (in relation to a will where this TrA 2000 power of investment is not excluded) that the rule in *Howe v Earl of Dartmouth* again does not apply to them.

(2)   If it is the case that the rule in *Howe v Earl of Dartmouth* does not apply to authorised investments (see supra), 'authorised investments' here includes investments authorised by the will (see *Brown v Gellatly* (1867) 2 Ch App 751 at 758–9) so that if the investment clause is wide enough to authorise investment in all the types of asset which are comprised in residue, as is now the case under the TrA 2000, ss 3 and 8 the rules will not apply. The main types of personalty which might be comprised in residue but still fall outside the new statutory power and some of the modern forms of wide investment powers are businesses (see eg *Re Berry, Lloyds Bank Ltd v Berry* [1962] Ch 97 at 111) and reversionary interests: see the Preliminary Note on Investment Powers in B20 at paras **[220.33]** and **[220.34]**.

(3)   'Trusts for persons in succession' here obviously includes a life interest with remainders and does not include an absolute interest. But what of eg a gift of capital contingent on obtaining the age of 30 and carrying the intermediate income? If the beneficiary dies at, say, 29 he will have been entitled to the current income since he attained 18 but the capital will go to somebody else. It may be that the equitable apportionment rules could apply to such a case; the only relevant authority seems to be *Re Bland, Miller v Bland* [1899] 2 Ch 336, where it was held that the rules did not apply on the particular facts of the case to a defeasible gift, but the judgment did not rule out the possibility that the rules could apply to such a gift. We recommend exclusion of the rules wherever the interests in residue are not immediate and absolute.

[214.36]
Why exclude the *Howe v Dartmouth* and *Re Chesterfield's Trusts* rules? The main reason for doing this is to avoid the administrative expense and difficulty in operating them. In addition they are out of date in various ways — the four per cent rate of assumed income yield is only occasionally in line with current interest rates, there is an assumption behind the rule in *Howe v Earl of Dartmouth* that rates of yield of unauthorised investments will be higher than those of authorised investments, and also an assumption that reversionary interests are readily saleable assets, which is no longer the case. It is also arguable in theory that the *Howe v Earl of Dartmouth* rule would prevent someone with a life interest from having an interest in possession for inheritance

tax purposes in the whole of the property to which the rule applied (since some of the income would be added to capital rather than paid to the life tenant) though we think it unlikely that such a point would be taken by the Inland Revenue in practice, and the Scottish decision of *Miller v IRC* [1987] STC 108, in which it was decided that a power to set aside income in a sinking fund to meet depreciation of capital value was compatible with there being an interest in possession for inheritance tax purposes, weighs heavily against this argument.

[214.37]
How to exclude the *Howe v Earl of Dartmouth* and *Re Chesterfield's Trusts* rules. The main traditional exclusionary formula is to direct that the actual income of the estate is from the testator's death to be treated as income: see Forms B14.10 (at para **[214.19]**) and B14.24 (at para **[214.39]**) and the AEA 1925, s 33(5) (Part G, para **[244.58]**) for the use of this formula for the estates of intestates. This formula excludes the rule in *Re Chesterfield's Trusts* as well as the rule in *Howe v Earl of Dartmouth* (see *Re Rowlls* [1900] 2 Ch 107), as does a declaration that the rule in *Howe v Earl of Dartmouth* in all its branches shall not apply (see *Re Hey's Settlement Trusts, Hey v Nickell-Lean* [1945] Ch 294). However, neither of these formulae excludes what might be called the rule in *Re Rowlls* [1900] 2 Ch 107, namely that where there is a trust for sale with power to postpone sale, and either of these exclusionary formulas is used, the rules in *Howe v Earl of Dartmouth* and *Re Chesterfield's Trusts* are only excluded in relation to any particular property which is an unauthorised investment, reversionary interest, etc if the trustees make a conscious discretionary decision to postpone its sale: see *Re Hey's Settlement Trusts, Hey v Nickell-Lean* [1945] Ch 294. If they did not know the property formed part of the estate (something which can easily happen in the case of a reversionary interest) or failed to address their minds to the point, equitable apportionment will still occur. We refer the reader whose reaction to this is disbelief to Vol 1, para **[38.23]**, n 15 for other decisions to the same effect.

[214.38]
It should be possible to exclude the rule in *Re Rowlls*, ie provide that even if the trustees fail to make an exercise of their discretion to postpone sale the equitable apportionment rules will still not apply. It would appear that the formula 'a reversionary interest shall not be sold unless the trustees see special reason for sale' which formerly appeared in the statutory trust for sale of the estates of intestates (AEA 1925, s 33(1) before its amendment by the TLATA 1996 and appears in Form B14.25 at para **[214.40]**) may well be effective to exclude the rule in *Re Rowlls* in relation to reversionary interests, but it should be remembered that 'reversionary interest' does not include every kind of interest to which the rule in *Re Chesterfield's Trusts* can apply (see eg *Re Fisher, Harris v Fisher* [1943] Ch 377—annuity paid under a life assurance policy). We put forward a suggestion for the exclusion of apportionment where residue is held on trust for sale, even if the trustees do not exercise their discretion to postpone sale, in Form B14.27 at para **[214.42]**. An alternative is to provide administration trusts of residue which do not include a trust to sell or convert, and which confer a power to sell the assets at the discretion of the trustees when they think fit (an administration trust which provides a power of sale rather than

a trust to sell is in general what we recommend on other grounds: see para **[214.2]**). The rule in *Howe v Dartmouth* apparently does not apply where there is a clear intention that the time of sale should be within the trustees' discretion: see Vol 1, para **[38.23]**, n 11 and the cases there cited, especially *Re Pitcairn, Brandreth v Colvin* [1896] 2 Ch 199. These decisions could still be overruled or held inapplicable, however, and it is not readily apparent to those who have not made a detailed study of this area of the law that the effect of such wording is to exclude the rule in *Howe v Dartmouth*. Accordingly, the cautious draftsman will prefer to use express exclusionary words (and see Robert Mitchell, 'Trusts for Sale in Wills – Excess Baggage' (1999) 63 Conv 84 at 99). See Forms B14.1 at para **[214.10]** and B14.4 at para **[214.13]** for examples of the *Re Pitcairn* formula.

[214.39]

FORM B14.24:   Exclusion of rule in *Howe v Earl of Dartmouth*[1]

The income of all parts of my estate for the time being unsold however constituted or invested shall as from my death be treated and applied as the income of investments authorised hereby or by the general law.

1   For a form incorporating much the same formula in a gift of residue on trust for sale see Form B14.10 at para **[214.19]**. Note also that this form is probably also effective to exclude the rule in *Re Chesterfield's Trusts*, but will exclude neither rule if there is a trust for sale with power to postpone sale and the trustees do not make a deliberate exercise of the latter power: see *Re Rowlls* [1900] 2 Ch 107; and para **[214.37]**. This form does not exclude the rule in *Allhusen v Whittell* (1867) LR 4 Eq 295 (*Re Ullswater, Barclays Bank Ltd v Lowther* [1952] Ch 105).

[214.40]

FORM B14.25:   Exclusion of rule in *Re Chesterfield's Trusts*[1]

No reversionary or future interest shall be sold prior to falling into possession unless my trustees see special reason for sale and no reversionary future or other property not producing income shall be treated as producing income.

1   For the rule itself see Vol 1, paras **[38.22]**–**[38.23]**: for notes on excluding it see para **[214.37]** and for much the same formula incorporated into a gift of residue on trust for sale, see Form B14.10 at para **[214.19]**. It may be that the direction not to sell in this form means that the rule in *Re Chesterfield* is excluded even if the trustees make no deliberate decision to postpone sale: see para **[214.37]**.

[214.41]

FORM B14.26:   Exclusion of rules in *Howe v Earl of Dartmouth* and *Re Chesterfield's Trusts*—short form naming case[1]

The rule in *Howe v Earl of Dartmouth* in all its branches shall not apply.

1   The authority that this excludes both rules is *Re Hey's Settlement Trusts, Hey v Nickell-Lean* [1945] Ch 294; it is also authority that if residue is held on trust for sale with power to postpone, the rules are only excluded by these words if the trustees make a deliberate decision to postpone sale: see para **[214.37]**.

[214.42]

FORM B14.27:   Exclusion of rules in *Howe v Earl of Dartmouth* **and** *Re Chesterfield's Trusts*—**alternative form**[1]

The rules of equity concerning the apportionment (between income and capital) of income from assets which are unauthorised investments or of capital arising from non-income yielding assets are hereby excluded from applying to any asset subject to the trusts of this will or of any codicil hereto in any circumstances whatever and notwithstanding that my trustees may not have made any deliberate decision to postpone the sale of such asset.[2]

1   This has the advantage over Form B14.24 (at para **[214.39]**) of being more direct and making its purpose clear, and has the advantage over Form B14.26 (at para **[214.40]**) of not using the case name and making some attempt to describe the rules it refers to. (Form B14.24 will convey nothing to non-lawyers, and little to many lawyers, and would be difficult to persuade some testators to accept.) This form also tries to exclude what we refer to as the rule in *Re Rowlls* (see para **[214.37]**). It has the disadvantage of not having been considered by the courts.
2   The words from 'notwithstanding' are our attempt to exclude what we refer to as the rule in *Re Rowlls* (see para **[214.37]**). A trust for sale with power to postpone sale affecting the whole of residue is assumed.

Exclusion of rule for apportionment of liabilities between capital and income (rule in Allhusen v Whittell)

[214.43]

NOTE

Exclusion of the rule in *Allhusen v Whittell.* This rule (apportionment of estate liabilities between income and capital) applies to the administration expenses, inheritance tax payable out of residue and legacies as well as debts and is described in Vol 1 at para **[38.25]**. It is again a rule which only has any relevance where residue is settled (so that income and capital will or may go to different beneficiaries), but it can apply to realty as well as personalty and is of course a rule which will apply to authorised and unauthorised investments alike. It is thus of potentially wider application than the rules in *Howe v Earl of Dartmouth* and *Re Chesterfield's Trusts*.

[214.44]
It is usual to exclude the rule to avoid intricate calculations, and it seems to us that in addition to just excluding it an express indication as to how liabilities etc are to be borne should be given. There are two main possibilities: the executors can be given a discretion as to the apportioning of liabilities etc between capital and income (see Form B14.28 at para **[214.45]**), or the liabilities can be directed to be paid out of capital (see Form B14.29 at para **[214.46]**). It should be noted that a likely consequence of a direction to pay debts and testamentary expenses out of capital is that interest on inheritance tax and on income tax arrears will be payable out of capital: *Re Hogg* (11 July 1983, unreported) Ch D (see McCutcheon 'Going the Whole Hogg?' [1986] *Capital Taxes* 27). This would seem to mean also that where a direction to pay liabilities etc out of capital

applies to legacies, the interest on the legacies should also be paid out of capital. It does seem inappropriate for interest on debts, administration expenses (in particular interest on overdue inheritance tax) and legacies, where the interest arises in respect of a period after the death of the testator, to be paid out of capital. A possible solution is to provide that the principal amounts are to be paid out of capital but that interest arising after the testator's death should as far as possible be paid out of income: see Forms B14.3 (at para **[214.12]**), B14.4 (at para **[214.13]**) and B14.30 (at para **[214.47]**).

[214.45]

FORM B14.28:   **Trustees given a discretion as to allocation**[1]

My trustees may at their absolute discretion allocate the burden of payments made in the due course of administration to or between income or capital of my estate and shall have no obligation to apply the rule [of equity as to such allocation[2]].

1   For the rule in *Allhusen v Whittell* see Vol 1, para **[38.25]** and the notes on excluding the rule at paras **[214.43]** and **[214.44]**. Form B14.10 at para **[214.19]** contains another formula for excluding the rule of a rather oblique kind – see n 1 thereto.
2   For the words in square brackets substitute 'in *Allhusen v Whittell*' if preferred.

[214.46]

FORM B14.29:   **Liabilities to be paid out of capital**[1]

My trustees shall pay all payments made in due course of administration of my estate out of capital and the rule [of equity as to the apportionment of the same between capital and income[2]] shall not apply.

1   For the rule in *Allhusen v Whittell* see Vol 1, para **[38.25]** and the notes on excluding the rule at paras **[214.43]** and **[214.44]**. Form 14.10 at para **[214.19]** contains another exclusionary formula – see n 1 thereto. Note that this form may cause interest on, eg inheritance tax, to be payable out of capital: see para **[214.44]**.
2   For the words in square brackets substitute 'in *Allhusen v Whittell*' if preferred.

[214.47]

FORM B14.30:   **Liabilities to be paid out of capital, but interest on them payable for periods after the testator's death to be paid out of income as far as possible**

The rule of equity as to the apportionment between capital and income of payments made in the course of administration shall not apply to my estate, and debts, testamentary expenses, inheritance tax or similar taxes, and legacies shall be paid out of capital while any interest on any such debts, expenses, taxes or legacies which may become payable in respect of any period falling after my death shall as far as possible be paid out of income.[1]

1   For the reasoning behind this see para **[214.44]**.

Exclusion of time apportionment

[214.48]

NOTE

The Apportionment Acts. The Apportionment Act 1870 (AA 1870) (Part G, para **[246.2]** et seq) provides that rents annuities dividends and other periodical payments in the nature of income are treated as accruing from day to day and apportionable in respect of time accordingly (AA 1870, s 1). This means that where an instalment of income is received after some change has occurred in the ownership of the right to receive the income, and the instalment is in respect of a period partly preceding the change, it is to be apportioned between the period before and the period after the change occurred.

[214.49]
The effect of the AA 1870 on dividends on ordinary shares is particularly notable, because the apportionment is to be to the period for which the dividend is declared (AA 1870, s 5 definition of 'dividends': Part G, para **[246.6]**), which is typically a period ending six months or so before the dividend becomes payable. The Act does not apply to the profits of a business, and does not apply to instalments of rent paid in advance (*Ellis v Rowbotham* [1900] 1 QB 740); since rent is almost invariably payable in advance under modern leases the Act has ceased to have much relevance to rent.

[214.50]
The AA 1870 is applicable on the death of the testator (see below), the death of a life tenant, and when there is a gift to a class of minor beneficiaries to which the Trustee Act 1925, s 31 (Part G, para **[246.26]**) applies and the class increases or decreases by birth or death (*Re Joel's Will Trusts, Rogerson v Brudenell-Bruce* [1967] Ch 14, [1966] 2 All ER 482). It does not apply in relation to the forfeiture of a protective life interest (*Re Jenkins, Williams v Jenkins* [1915] 1 Ch 46) or on the commencement or determination of any discretionary trust of income (*Weir's Settlement Trusts* [1971] Ch 145 at 167).
    The Apportionment Act 1834 (AA 1834) is superseded, but not repealed, by the AA 1870.

[214.51]
Exclusion of the Apportionment Acts. The Acts apply subject to a contrary stipulation: AA 1870, s 7 (Part G, para **[246.8]**) and AA 1834, s 3. The reason for excluding them is essentially the same as for excluding the other apportionment rules, namely to avoid troublesome calculations for no very advantageous result. In relation to the testator's own death the significance of the Acts applying to the income of residuary assets is that part of the income received shortly after death will be apportioned to capital, and the significance of it applying to assets comprised in a specific gift is that part of the income received shortly after death is likely to be apportioned to residue (as capital) instead of going to the person entitled to the specific gift. It is usual to exclude the Apportionment Acts in relation to the testator's death by a clause such as that in Form B14.31 at para **[214.53]**. For specific gifts including anti-

apportionment provision (so that the income payable after the testator's death goes to the specific legatee or devisee) see Forms B4.37 (at para **[204.59]**) and B6.5 (at para **[206.14]**). There could be some advantage in not excluding the Acts if the person who will be entitled to the income of residue will have a high personal income tax rate, since if some of the income is apportioned to capital it will not form part of that person's income for the purposes of higher rate income tax, although this may still be so where that person is entitled absolutely to the capital as well as the income.

[214.52]

If the will settles any property, Form B14.31 (at para **[214.53]**) will not exclude the Apportionment Acts in relation to any event subsequent to the testator's death, such as the death of a life tenant. We recommend excluding the Apportionment Acts in relation to such subsequent events, especially if there are accumulation and maintenance trusts (see *Re Joel's Will Trusts, Rogerson v Brudenell-Bruce* [1967] Ch 14, [1966] 2 All ER 482 mentioned at para **[214.50]**), by use of a general exclusion clause such as Form B14.32 at para **[214.54]**. If the AA 1870 is excluded by express reference to that Act, the AA 1834 might nevertheless still apply if not also expressly excluded. See also the exclusionary formula in Form B14.3 at para **[214.12]**.

[214.53]

FORM B14.31:   **Exclusion of Apportionment Acts as between before and after testator's death**[1]

All income of my estate (whether the same be received in respect of a period wholly or only partly prior to my death) which shall be actually received after my death shall be treated as accruing wholly after my death and shall not be apportioned to or treated as capital.

1   See para **[214.44]**. Exclusion of the Apportionment Acts will probably not prevent any of the income element of National Savings Certificates which has been capitalised before the testator's death from being treated as capital of his estate: *Re Holder, National Provincial Bank Ltd v Holder* [1953] Ch 468, [1953] 2 All ER 1.

[214.54]

FORM B14.32:   **Exclusion of Apportionment Acts generally**[1]

All income of my estate or of any property held from time to time on any of the trusts of this will or of any codicil hereto shall be treated as accruing at the time when it is payable and shall not be apportioned to any other time or period under the Apportionment Acts of 1834 or 1870.[2]

1   A general exclusion of this type is recommended where there is any interest in possession or accumulation and maintenance trusts: see para **[214.52]**. For an alternative form, see Form B14.3, sub-cl 4(a) at para **[214.12]**.
2   Specific reference to the Acts is preferable. The AA 1834 has never been repealed, although its provisions are duplicated by the more general provisions of the AA 1870. If the AA 1870 only is excluded there is a possibility that the AA 1834 might still apply. For the text of the AA 1870 see Part G, para **[246.2]** et seq.

Incidence of inheritance tax

[214.55]

NOTE

The Inheritance Tax Act 1984, s 211. The provisions now contained in the ITA 1984, s 211 (Part G, para **[246.83]**) apply in relation to deaths on or after 26 July 1983. They were previously contained in the Finance Act 1975, s 28, as amended by the Finance (No 2) Act 1983, s 13. We are here concerned with drafting wills for persons living after publication of this edition of this work, so we do not consider the previous law of incidence.

[214.56]
Section 211 of the ITA 1984 (Part G, para **[246.83]**) is a provision which was introduced to resolve the difficulties caused by the decision of the Court of Session in *Re Dougal* [1981] STC 514, a decision which contradicted the commonly held opinion that under Scottish law land comprised in a deceased person's free estate bore its own capital transfer tax (now inheritance tax) in the absence of express provision in the will, and instead held that the tax on it was to be paid out of residue. It had also been thought that land comprised in free estate bore its own capital transfer tax (now inheritance tax) in English law; it was possible that English law on the point might turn out to be different from the Scottish law, but there were sufficient resemblances between the two systems in material respects for there to be a real question as to whether *Re Dougal* might not be followed in England. The point has not been, and probably never will be, litigated, and the conclusion reached in *Re Dougal* has now been given statutory effect for the future by s 211 so that realty and personalty are now treated alike as regards incidence.

[214.57]
A slight doubt about s 211. The crucial part of the ITA 1984, s 211 is in sub-s (1); tax is treated as part of testamentary expenses *but only* so far as attributable to the UK free estate (real or personal). It thus expressly provides that the inheritance tax on assets other than UK free estate is not a testamentary expense. Subsection (3) provides for repayment of tax paid by personal representatives which is not a testamentary expense 'where occasion requires', but does not in any way determine what occasions do and do not so require, and it is really only sub-s (1) which has any effect on who should bear the inheritance tax on different parts of an estate.

[214.58]
However, the decision in *Re Dougal* [1981] STC 514 did not say anything about capital transfer tax (now inheritance tax) being a testamentary expense, but said that the tax is calculated by reference to the entire estate regardless of the nature of the chargeable property and that it is a debt for which the estate as a whole is liable and which the personal representatives are obliged to pay on all the estate, irrespective of the type of property; therefore there were no grounds for distinguishing land and other assets as regards incidence. There thus remains the possibility that it follows from *Re Dougal* that any inheritance tax for which the

personal representatives are liable is to be borne by residue, though not as an administration expense under the ITA 1984, s 211 and that this includes the inheritance tax on foreign property, or perhaps even the tax on property which does not vest in the personal representatives at all, such as the severable share of jointly tenanted property. The incidence of inheritance tax on any deceased person's estate could be put beyond all doubt by his will providing expressly for the incidence of all inheritance tax for which the personal representatives may be liable (see eg Form B14.33 at para [214.76]). However, in our view it is most unlikely that the courts of England and Wales would hold that the ITA 1984, s 211 does not exhaustively define the categories of property in respect of which the inheritance tax is borne by residue, as opposed to being borne by the property itself (in the absence of a contrary direction).

[214.59]
Inheritance tax which is a testamentary expense. Close examination shows that for inheritance tax to be a testamentary expense of a testator's estate by virtue of the ITA 1984, s 211(1) (Part G, para [246.83]):

(a) his personal representatives must be liable for the tax;
(b) the tax must relate to the inheritance tax charge on the testator's 'estate' immediately before his death for inheritance tax purposes (ie the charge under the ITA 1984, s 4);
(c) the property to which it relates must be in the UK (at the testator's death, it would seem);
(d) it must relate to property which vests in the testator's personal representatives; and
(e) it must relate to property which was not comprised in a settlement immediately before the testator's death.

[214.60]
Property which bears its own inheritance tax. The collection of often overlapping conditions (set out at para [214.59]) excludes from being a testamentary expense by virtue of the ITA 1984, s 211 any inheritance tax arising from a testator's death which falls into any of the following categories (with the result that such tax is borne by the property to which it relates in the absence of express provision):

(1) The inheritance tax on property of the testator situated outside the UK at his death.
(2) The inheritance tax on the testator's severable share of jointly tenanted property (see Vol 1, para [7.3]), property which devolves under a nomination (see Vol 1, paras [7.9]–[7.11]), or property comprised in a donatio mortis causa (see Vol 1, para [1.14]). Section 211(1) of the ITA 1984 does not apply to property devolving in any of these ways because such property does not vest in the testator's personal representatives, although such property is part of his estate on death for inheritance tax purposes and the personal representatives are liable for the inheritance tax on it.
(3) The inheritance tax on property which was comprised in a settlement immediately before the testator's death. The ITA 1984, s 211(1)

therefore does not apply to the inheritance tax which is charged by reason of the testator's death on settled property in which the testator had an interest in possession immediately before his death (ITA 1984, ss 4(1), 5(1) and 49(1)), and this is so even if such property vests in the testator's personal representatives or is disposed of by the testator's will. In particular, inheritance tax arising from the testator's death in respect of property which was settled immediately before the testator's death, but which is disposed of by his will in exercise of a general or special power of appointment, or in exercise of the statutory power to dispose of entailed property which is conferred by the LPA 1925, s 176 (Part G, para **[244.53]**; see also Vol 1, para **[7.2]**), will fall outside s 211(1). It will be recalled that property subject to a general power of appointment exercisable by a testator's will can very easily fall into his residuary estate by virtue of a general residuary gift which expresses no intention that the power should not be exercised: WA 1837, s 27 (Part G, para **[244.27]**; see also Vol 1, para **[39.2]** et seq).

(4) Inheritance tax or additional inheritance tax payable as a result of the testator's death in respect of potentially exempt transfers or chargeable transfers he has made during his life, but within seven years of his death (see paras **[200.70]** and **[200.71]** and B10 at para **[210.66]**). ITA 1984, s 211(1) will also not apply to the inheritance tax on events which are charged to inheritance tax as if they were lifetime potentially exempt transfers, such as property of which the testator was the donor ceasing to be subject to a reservation within seven years of his death (Finance Act 1986, s 102 (4): see para **[200.76]**), or the repayment by the testator within seven years of his death of a debt which would not have been a deductible liability on his death because the consideration for it derived from him (see the Finance Act 1986, s 103(1) to (6) and para **[200.77]**). This inheritance tax or additional inheritance tax arising on death in respect of lifetime transfers, or events treated as lifetime potentially exempt transfers, falls outside s 211(1) because it is not tax on the chargeable transfer on death, and the property concerned does not vest in the personal representatives.

(5) Inheritance tax on property comprised in a lifetime gift made by the testator which is property subject to a reservation (see para **[200.76]**) at the testator's death. Such property is comprised in the chargeable transfer made on death (see the Finance Act 1986, s 102(3)) and the personal representatives are liable for the tax on it, though as a secondary liability (see the ITA 1984, s 204(9) and para **[200.78]**). However, the property does not vest in the personal representatives and so ITA 1984, s 211(1) does not apply. The position is quite the opposite in relation to debts not deductible by virtue of the Finance Act 1986, s 103 (see para **[214.61]**).

(6) Inheritance tax on works of art, etc or woodlands where exemption or relief from the inheritance tax charge on death is obtained, but an inheritance tax charge arises from a subsequent sale or breach of undertakings. The ITA 1984, s 211(1) does not apply to the inheritance tax arising on such a subsequent event because it is not tax on the chargeable transfer on death and because the personal representatives are not liable for it: ITA 1984, ss 207 and 208.

[214.61]
Non-deductible liabilities. Debts or other liabilities of a testator's estate may not be deductible for inheritance tax purposes because they were not incurred or not wholly incurred for a consideration in money or money's worth (ITA 1984, s 5(5)), or because the consideration for the debt or other liability derived from the testator or came from a person who had property derived from the testator: Finance Act 1986, s 103(1)–(6). Whatever the inheritance tax treatment of such a liability, it remains a liability of the estate which is payable out of it in priority to all beneficial interests in the estate and it will not be subject to any deduction for the inheritance tax arising from the testator's death and attributable to such liability (*Re Gray* [1896] 1 Ch 620) unless the terms on which the liability was incurred provided for its payment or repayment to be subject to payment of such tax. If the liability was not incurred on such terms it is difficult to see how any provision of the testator's will could impose the burden of the inheritance tax attributable to such liability on the liability itself, although the burden could be thrown on to some other gift made by the will to the person to whom the liability is owed (unless that gift is exempt: see the ITA 1984, s 41).

[214.62]
What has just been said is subject to the possibility that where a non-deductible liability is payable out of property which bears its own inheritance tax, eg because the testator leaves no free estate in the UK or charges foreign property with the payment of his debts, the liability itself may bear its own inheritance tax, although the estate duty cases which suggest that this might be the case (*Re Hacket, Hacket v Gardiner* [1907] 1 Ch 385; *Re Hartland, Banks v Hartland* [1911] 1 Ch 459) depend on a provision of the estate duty legislation (Finance Act 1894, s 14(1)) which has no equivalent in the inheritance tax legislation and are concerned with non-deductible liabilities charged on real estate by a lifetime disposition. Where the total of non-deductible and other liabilities of an estate and the inheritance tax on the estate exceeds the value of the estate it seems that the estate is insolvent and that the inheritance tax which is a testamentary expense will have priority over the debts (under the Administration of Insolvent Estates of Deceased Persons Order 1986, SI 1986/1999, art 4 — in force from 29 December 1986). If in such a case there is inheritance tax which does not fall within the ITA 1984, s 211(1) and therefore is not a testamentary expense, such inheritance tax would presumably have priority over payment of non-deductible debts, perhaps by virtue of the Inland Revenue charge (under the ITA 1984, s 237) or on the basis that non-deductible liabilities bear their own inheritance tax where they are payable out of assets which bear their own inheritance tax.

[214.63]
Foreign property. At the time when the anomalous difference in the incidence of capital transfer tax (now inheritance tax) between realty and personalty was abolished by what is now the ITA 1984, s 211(1), an increase in ownership of foreign assets had been taking place as a result of the abolition of exchange control. Section 211(1) leaves foreign assets bearing their own tax, in the absence of an expressed contrary intention, just as under estate duty law, and it seems likely that many of the estate duty rules of incidence and cases on construction of free of duty provisions remain relevant. For many testators,

whether they want to make specific gifts free from or subject to inheritance tax will have little to do with the location of the assets. Further, it is most unusual for a testator to want pecuniary legacies to bear any inheritance tax or foreign death duties, which they might do in the absence of express provision to the contrary if they are payable wholly or partly out of foreign property (see para **[214.64]**). There is the further problem which could arise in relation to specific gifts of chattels that it is possible for chattels to be unexpectedly outside the UK at the testator's death, although it would be in an unusual case (yachts, aircraft, jewellery) that items of significant value would be involved. For possible methods of dealing with these problems see para **[214.71]**.

[214.64]
General and pecuniary legacies. Despite the ITA 1984, s 211 it remains probable that pecuniary or general legacies, in the absence of express provision to the contrary, are subject to inheritance tax as far as they are payable out of a fund which consists of or includes assets which bear their own inheritance tax, such as foreign property or property which was comprised in a settlement immediately before the testator's death. It was held in *Re Spencer Cooper, Poë v Spencer Cooper* [1908] 1 Ch 130 and *Re Owers, Public Trustee v Death* [1941] Ch 17, [1940] 4 All ER 225, CA that general or pecuniary legacies charged on a mixed fund of realty and personalty bore a proportion of the estate duty on the fund corresponding to the proportion of the fund that the realty represented, and in particular that this was so in the case of such legacies payable out of a mixed residuary fund directed to be held on trust for sale. The same principle applied to legacies charged on a mixed fund of British and foreign personalty: see *Re Sebba* [1959] Ch 166 at 178 (the declaration on question (3) — the reasoning is not reported, and the report at [1958] 3 All ER 393 does not report the decision on this point). Inheritance tax seems sufficiently similar to estate duty for it to be likely that this rule would apply to the incidence of inheritance tax on legacies paid out of a mixed fund of UK and foreign assets. It also seems likely that this rule would apply where residue (or some other fund out of which pecuniary or general legacies are to be paid) includes property which was comprised in a settlement immediately before the testator's death and was, eg subject to a general power of appointment which he exercised by his will (see para **[214.59]**, sub-para (c)).

[214.65]
Abatement. Inheritance tax on UK free estate will be a testamentary expense which will be satisfied out of the assets of the estate in the order prescribed by the AEA 1925, Sch 1, Pt II (Part G, para **[246.54]**) for debts and administration expenses. Inheritance tax on other assets, such as foreign assets, which the will directs to be paid out of residue, will constitute legacies (see the definition of 'pecuniary legacy' in the AEA 1925, s 55(1)(ix): Part G, para **[246.52]**) and will abate rateably with ordinary pecuniary legacies in the absence of a direction to the contrary. An example of a direction which would give priority over ordinary precuniary legacies to the inheritance tax on a specific gift of foreign property is contained in a proviso to Form B14.33 at para **[214.76]**.

[214.66]

Inheritance tax on events subsequent to the testator's death. There are some rather unreliable decisions from the 1914–18 War period (eg *Re Stoddart, Bird v Grainger* [1916] 2 Ch 444) which suggest that a general direction that duty be paid out of residue might easily include duty arising on the death of a tenant for life under the will trusts, but more recent cases (such as *Re Howell* [1952] Ch 264 and *Re Embleton's Will Trusts, Sodeau v Nelson* [1965] 1 All ER 771, [1965] 1 WLR 840) show the courts leaning heavily against such a conclusion. However, the possibility that a direction as to incidence might in some circumstances be interpreted as referring to tax on events subsequent to the testator's death should be borne in mind when drafting such directions.

[214.67]

Works of art, etc woodlands, and property on which the inheritance tax may be payable by instalments. Any testator who is thinking of making a specific gift of a work of art or other property which might qualify for conditional exemption under the ITA 1984, Pt II, Ch II ('heritage property'), or woodlands in the UK, could be well advised to make the gift bear its own inheritance tax. It will be apparent from what is said above that where there are no express directions about incidence, the effect of claiming exemption or relief from the inheritance tax charge on death in relation to either type of property is not only to defer the tax charge but to shift its incidence from residue to the property itself. If the specific legatee or devisee has not been given any share or interest in residue, he may prefer that the exemption or relief should not be claimed so that he takes the property free of the potential tax liability at the expense of residue. In the case of woodlands the decision whether to claim the relief would be the personal representatives' (ITA 1984, s 125(2)), and this could put them in an invidious position; in the case of heritage property the specific legatee could prevent conditional exemption being obtained by refusing to give the undertakings that he would almost certainly be asked to give as a condition of the exemption: ITA 1984, ss 30(1)(b) and 31(2)–(4). On the subject of heritage property, see also the Preliminary Note on chattels in B4 at para **[204.2]** et seq.

[214.68]

A testator might also consider whether it would be more appropriate to make subject to inheritance tax a specific gift of property in respect of which the inheritance tax might be paid by instalments, such as land, businesses, or majority shareholdings (see the ITA 1984, ss 227–229). This would enable the estate to be administered more rapidly, as the executors would be less likely to have to retain assets of the residuary estate with which to pay the instalments of tax for ten years after the testator's death. For further points favouring subject to tax gifts of business or agricultural property see the Note to B5 at paras **[205.52]**–**[205.54]** and the Preliminary Note to C11 at para **[233.10]**.

[214.69]

Partially exempt estates and incidence of inheritance tax. For points on incidence of inheritance tax specific to partially exempt estates, see paras **[214.72]**–**[214.75]**.

[214.70]

Drafting hazards. We suggest that the following are points to watch when formulating directions as to incidence of inheritance tax and foreign duties:

(1) There are many categories of property which are chargeable to inheritance tax or additional inheritance tax as a result of a testator's death which do not form part of his free estate disposed of by his will: see paras **[214.59]** and **[214.60]**. Formulae such as 'all the inheritance tax payable by reason of my death' without some words restricting the liability to the tax on the free estate, could be construed as including the inheritance tax on some or all of those categories of property, contrary to the likely intentions of the testator. References to 'my estate' could in some contexts be construed as having the extended meaning which the term 'estate' is given by the ITA 1984.

(2) A direction of the type often found in administration trusts to pay testamentary expenses and inheritance tax out of residue prima facie throws on to residue the burden of all the inheritance tax arising on the testator's death on his free estate, including the tax on property (such as foreign property) which normally bears its own inheritance tax (*Re Pimm, Sharpe v Hodgson* [1904] 2 Ch 345). However, such a direction may be construed as having a wider meaning and as including inheritance tax on death on property which is not part of the testator's free estate where all the inheritance tax on the free estate is a testamentary expense and the reference to inheritance tax would be redundant if not given the wider meaning: see *Re Walley, National Westminster Bank Ltd v Williams* [1972] 1 All ER 222, [1972] 1 WLR 257, where a direction to pay 'testamentary expenses ... and all death duties' out of residue was treated as including the estate duty on a Post Office Savings Bank account which devolved by nomination (see para **[214.60]**, sub-para (2)). The main ground for the decision was that the free estate consisted entirely of UK personalty, the duty on which was a testamentary expense anyway. Now that the ITA 1984, s 211(1) provides that inheritance tax on realty as well as personalty in the UK is a testamentary expense the possibility of a general reference of this kind to inheritance tax being redundant if not construed as referring to something other than the tax on free estate is much greater, and it is advisable to make clear what inheritance tax a general direction as to inheritance tax is intended to refer to.

(3) On the other hand, a general direction of the kind referred to under (2) above could be narrowed in its scope if the will also contains gifts of a kind which might otherwise be subject to tax which are specifically made free of tax and there are other gifts of the same kind which are not specifically made free of tax. In such cases the courts have tended to construe the general direction as referring only to the inheritance tax on those gifts which are specifically declared to be free of tax: see *Re Phuler's Will Trusts, Midland Bank Executor and Trustee Co Ltd v Logan* [1964] 2 All ER 948, [1965] 1 WLR 68 and *Re Neeld, Carpenter v Inigo-Jones* [1964] 2 All ER 952n, [1965] 1 WLR 73n. Therefore, any specific provisions as to inheritance tax made in relation to particular gifts need to be harmonised with any general directions as to incidence.

[214.71]
Recommendations for provisions as to incidence. Where there is no real possibility of the testator dying possessed of foreign property, or exercising by will any power of disposition over settled property, one course of action would be to rely entirely on the ITA 1984, s 211 refrain from including in the will any general direction as to the payment or incidence of inheritance tax, and include a specific direction only where a particular gift is to bear its own inheritance tax. If there is a possibility of there being any property comprised in the estate disposed of by will of a kind which bears its own inheritance tax (see para **[214.60]**, sub-paras (1) and (3)) the possibilities are to:

(1) Use 'free of inheritance tax and foreign death duties' or some such words in relation to individual gifts, such as pecuniary legacies and specific gifts of foreign property, which might otherwise bear inheritance tax, as far as it is desired that they should be free of tax and duties, and confine any general direction to referring to the tax on gifts made free of tax (see eg Forms B14.3 and B14.8 at paras **[214.12]** and **[214.17]**). This is the strategy adopted in the forms of complete wills in Part C.

(2) Include a general direction that all pecuniary and general legacies and gifts of personal chattels are free of inheritance tax and foreign death duties (see Form B14.34 at para **[214.77]**), with the result that specific gifts of foreign property (other than chattels) or settled property are subject to inheritance tax and foreign death duties unless specifically declared to be free of them.

(3) Include a general direction that the inheritance tax on the entire free estate is payable out of residue save in so far as it is declared to be subject to tax (see Forms B14.17 at para **[214.26]** and B14.33 at para **[214.76]**). If such a general direction is used, no individual gifts should be expressed to be free of inheritance tax. For specific gifts subject to inheritance tax, see Forms B5.1 (at para **[205.58]**), B5.4 (at para **[205.61]**), B6.31 (at para **[206.40]**), B10.50 (at para **[210.71]**) and B14.36 (at para **[214.79]**).

For directions for payment out of residue of inheritance tax on lifetime gifts and property not comprised in free estate, see Forms B10.48 and B10.49 at paras **[210.69]** and **[210.70]**. Most of the forms of complete will in Part C have directions as to incidence: see eg C3.1 at para **[225.9]** et seq and C11.1 at para **[233.13]** et seq.

[214.72]
Partially exempt residue. The special rules for partially exempt estates are described in outline in Part A at para **[200.138]** et seq. They give rise to a drafting problem where residue is given in fractional shares to different people, at least one of whom is an exempt beneficiary (most commonly the testator's spouse or a charity) and at least one of whom is not. Are the fractional shares to be calculated before deducting the tax attributable to the non-exempt shares so that the net benefit will not be in the proportions that the fractions prescribed in the will would suggest? Or are they fractional shares of the net benefit, and, if so, how is the inheritance tax charge to be calculated without throwing the burden of any of the tax on to exempt gifts (which is prohibited by the ITA

1984, s 41 notwithstanding the terms of any disposition)? In *Re Benham's Will Trusts* [1995] STC 210 the shares prescribed by the will were held to relate to the net benefit, with grossing up of the non-exempt shares to achieve this result. In *Re Ratcliffe* [1999] STC 262, however, it was held that the shares were to be ascertained first and tax imposed on the non-exempt shares so ascertained; *Re Benham* was regarded as a decision on its own special facts and can in practice now be disregarded. To eliminate any possible doubt on the point a declaration such as Form B14.35 at para **[214.78]** may be used. This makes it clear that the solution adopted in *Re Ratcliffe* is to prevail—it may not produce quite the result the testator wants, but it is probably the most practical and workable solution.

[214.73]
Gifts subject to inheritance tax where there is business or agricultural relief. The rules effective for occasions of tax charge on or after 18 March 1986 for partially exempt estates where there is business or agricultural relief (see the ITA 1984, s 39A, added by the Finance Act 1986, s 105; and the Preliminary Note to C11 at para **[233.1]** et seq) present a drafting problem for gifts subject to inheritance tax which is best explained by an example. Suppose a testator makes by his will a specific gift of his house to his son, and leaves residue to be divided equally between a charity and his daughter. Suppose also that the gift of the house is made subject to the inheritance tax attributable to it, and that the residuary estate turns out to include property on which there is business relief. Under the ITA 1984, s 39A the business relief will be apportioned rateably between the exempt and non-exempt parts of the estate in the process of determining the extent of the non-exempt part, and the house will be treated as having a value reduced by a rateable share of the business relief for this purpose. It seems to us that in these circumstances there could be doubt as to whether the tax attributable to the house which is to be borne by the son is the tax attributable to the value of the house as reduced by business relief under s 39A, or the tax attributable to its actual value. Form B14.36 (at para **[214.79]**) is an example of a declaration intended to deal with this point.

[214.74]
Subject to inheritance tax/free of inheritance tax specific gifts. Where some or all of residue is exempt, and there are any non-exempt specific gifts, the size of the non-exempt estate and thus the amount of tax payable on the testator's death will be much less if the non-exempt specific gifts bear their own inheritance tax. Inheritance tax free specific gifts are grossed up in the process of establishing the size of the chargeable estate: ITA 1984, s 38(3). There is nothing unfair about this, because the net amount after inheritance tax received by the persons entitled to the non-exempt specific gifts is correspondingly greater where the inheritance tax on those gifts is paid out of residue rather than out of their gifts, and the amount of net residue received by the exempt beneficiary or beneficiaries is correspondingly less. However, the fact that specific gifts of UK free estate are, in the absence of express provisions to the contrary, inheritance tax free and grossed up under the partial exemption rules can get overlooked when the inheritance tax consequences of proposals for a will which includes specific gifts to non-exempt beneficiaries and residuary gifts to exempt beneficiaries (ie the testator's spouse and/or charity) are being

considered, or when proposals for a deed of variation on these lines is being considered: see F3 at para **[241.12]**. For example, if the dispositions are calculated to use up the testator's nil rate band, and it is not intended that the non-exempt beneficiaries should receive more than they may receive without any inheritance tax being paid on the testator's death, the inheritance tax consequences of the gift to the non-exempt beneficiaries turning out to be over the inheritance tax threshold will be much less serious if the non-exempt gift is subject to inheritance tax.

[214.75]
Testamentary expenses. Where residue is wholly or partly exempt, and administration expenses such as legal fees are payable out of residue, it seems that the exempt residue used to pay them is still treated as exempt, so that in effect inheritance tax is not charged on the part of the estate used to pay such administration expenses as far as they are met out of exempt residue: see Part A, para **[200.143]**.

[214.76]

FORM B14.33:   **General declaration making all inheritance tax and foreign death duties on free estate payable out of residue**[1]

Except to the extent that provision to the contrary is made elsewhere in this will or any codicil hereto all inheritance tax [and foreign death duties] payable by reason of my death in respect of all property wherever situated which is disposed of by this will or any codicil hereto[2] (other than property which is disposed of in exercise of a special or general power of appointment or the statutory power to dispose of entailed property without becoming thereby comprised in my residuary estate[3]) shall be paid out of my residuary estate in exoneration of all specific gifts or general or pecuniary legacies (if any) and no inheritance tax on other property for which my personal representatives are liable shall be paid out of my residuary estate[4] [and the inheritance tax [and foreign death duties] payable out of my residuary estate shall be treated for all purposes (including abatement) as a testamentary expense[5]].

1   See paras **[214.55]**–**[214.71]**, in particular para **[214.71]**, sub-para (3). The main purpose of this form is to exonerate specific gifts of foreign property, and pecuniary legacies payable out of a residuary fund which contains foreign property or property which was comprised in a settlement immediately before the testator's death, from bearing any inheritance tax (or foreign death duties), except for specific gifts or pecuniary legacies expressly declared to be subject to tax or duties. See Forms B5.1 (at para **[205.58]**), B5.4 (at para **[205.61]**), B6.31 (at para **[206.40]**), B10.50 (at para **[210.71]**) and B14.36 (at para **[214.79]**) for specific gifts made subject to inheritance tax.
    If this form is used any woodlands, works of art etc which are specifically given by the will should be given subject to the tax attributable thereto and payable by reason of the testator's death. This is a sound idea anyway (see para **[214.67]**) and also there is a slight risk that unless such property bears its own inheritance tax it could be argued that under this form inheritance tax 'payable by reason of my death' includes the tax payable after the death of the testator on a sale of the property or (in the case of works of art etc) a breach of undertakings where exemption or relief from the charge on death has been obtained under the ITA 1984, s 30 (works of art etc) or s 125 (woodlands).
    See also Forms B14.6 (at para **[214.15]**), B14.8 (at para **[214.17]**) and B14.17 (at para **[214.26]**). For an alternative approach see Form B14.3 (at para **[214.12]**).

2   This slightly elaborate formula is used instead of 'comprised in my estate' because of the special meaning 'estate' has in the context of inheritance tax, including as it does settled property in which the testator had an interest in possession, any severable share of jointly tenanted property, and any property subject to a reservation at the testator's death of which he was the donor (see para **[214.60]**). This formula may make this clause unsuitable for a testator with a foreign domicile whose estate may be subject to compulsory portions.

3   These words are intended to exclude any property which was comprised in a settlement immediately before the testator's death which might be disposed of by the will, except for any such property which falls into residue. The latter exception is for the sake of drafting consistency with making pecuniary and general legacies free of inheritance tax. Property which was settled property immediately before the testator's death prima facie bears its own inheritance tax (see para **[214.60]**, sub-para (3)), and legacies prima facie bear their own tax to the extent that they are payable out of property which bears its own tax (see para **[214.64]**). Therefore, if tax-free legacies are payable out of a risduary estate which includes settled property it seems inconsistent for that property to be directed to bear its own inheritence tax.

For the statutory power to make a testamentary disposition of entailed property see the LPA 1925, s 176 (Part G, para **[244.53]**; see also Vol 1, para **[7.2]**).

4   The words 'And no inheritance tax ... residuary estate' are in our view unnecessary, but inclusion of them would eliminate the slight doubt about the effect of the ITA 1984, s 211(1) which arises from the decision in *Re Dougal* [1981] STC 514: see para **[214.58]**. It would not be appropriate to include these words if there were provision in the will for payment out of residue of the inheritance tax on lifetime gifts or on property charged to inheritance tax on death but not disposed of by the will, such as in Forms B10.48 at para **[210.69]** and B10.49 at para **[210.70]**.

5   Any inheritance tax on property which is freed from bearing it by express direction in a will is a pecuniary legacy for the purposes of abatement (see **[214.65]**), while inheritance tax which falls within the ITA 1984, s 211(1) (Part G, para **[246.83]**; see also paras **[214.55]**–**[214.65]**) is a testamentary expense which has priority over pecuniary legacies in the event of abatement. This proviso has the effect that the inheritance tax which is directed to be paid out of residue but which would otherwise not be so paid, and foreign death duties if that is desired, will have priority over ordinary pecuniary legacies if residue is insufficient to pay all debts administration expenses taxes and legacies, and the legacies have to abate. Whether to include this proviso is a matter for the testator's choice—whether he is more concerned about the donees of specific gifts of foreign or settled property receiving their gifts of tax or about the pecuniary legatees receiving maximum benefit.

[214.77]

FORM B14.34:   Declaration that inheritance tax and foreign death duties on pecuniary legacies and personal chattels shall be paid out of residue[1]

Any dispositions of any personal chattels (as defined in section 55(1)(x) of the Administration of Estates Act 1925[2]) or pecuniary or general legacies made or given by this will or any codicil hereto shall be free of any inheritance tax or foreign death duties payable by reason of my death and attributable thereto (which shall accordingly be payable out of my residuary estate) save in so far as any such dispositions or legacies are declared elsewhere in this will or any codicil hereto to be subject to inheritance tax or foreign death duties.

1   The purpose of this form is to prevent the pecuniary legacies being subject to any inheritance tax or foreign death duties in the event of their being paid out of a fund which includes property which bears its own inheritance tax and foreign death duties (see para **[214.60]**, sub-para (2), and to prevent specific gifts of personal chattels which are fortuitously outside the UK at the testator's death (see paras **[214.63]** and **[214.70]**, sub-para (2)) being subject to inheritance tax or foreign duties. If this form is used any specific gifts or dispositions made by the will of foreign property (other than chattels) or settled property will be subject to inheritance tax unless specifically directed to be free of it.

Any chattels which are works of art etc which are eligible for conditional exemption under the ITA 1984, s 30 and are specifically given (including ones comprised in a gift of 'my personal chattels') should be given subject to inheritance tax for the reasons given at para **[214.67]** and in Form B14.33, n 1 at para **[214.76]**.

2   See Vol 1, para **[64.44]** and Part G, para **[246.52]**.

[214.78]

FORM B14.35:   **Declaration concerning partially exempt residue**[1]

The entitlement of the [charities and][2] persons interested in [my residuary estate[3]] shall be determined by dividing [my residuary estate[3]] into the fractional shares set out above without making any deduction or allowance for the inheritance tax payable by reason of my death and attributable to [my residuary estate[4]] and then reducing such shares as are not exempt from inheritance tax by the inheritance tax attributable thereto.

1   See para **[214.69]** for the purpose of this form.
2   These words should be included if, as is likely in a case where this clause is relevant, charities are among the exempt beneficiaries interested in the residuary estate. If there is a residuary gift in favour of the testator's spouse it is usually a gift of the whole of residue, and cases where residuary estate is divided between exempt and non-exempt beneficiaries are usually ones where the exempt beneficiaries are charities.
        Further words may be needed if the residuary beneficiaries include a political party (a gift to which can also be exempt — see Part A, para **[200.102]**) or a non-charitable club or institution. In such circumstances a formula such as 'persons trusts and bodies of persons (corporate or unincorporated)' or 'societies trusts associations institutions and persons' could be used instead of 'charities and persons'.
3   It is assumed that the expression used here refers to the net residue after payment of debts, administration expenses, inheritance tax and legacies.
4   See the Preliminary Note to C11 at para **[233.1]** et seq for the ITA 1984, s 39A. See Form B5.1 at para **[205.58]** for a gift of business property bearing its own inheritance tax.

[214.79]

FORM B14.36:   **Specific gift subject to inheritance tax where the estate may turn out to be partially exempt and include business or agricultural property**[1]

I give to [*name*] my [house known as 'Laburnums', Acacia Avenue, Tuliptree Park, Sevenoaks, Kent] subject to payment of the inheritance tax attributable thereto and payable by reason of my death and I declare that if part of my estate is exempt from inheritance tax and the value of the foregoing gift is treated as reduced by virtue of section 39A of the Inheritance Tax Act 1984 the tax attributable to the foregoing gift for the foregoing purposes shall be the tax attributable to the value of the said gift as so reduced.[2]

1   See para **[214.73]** for the purpose of this form, and the Preliminary Note to C11 at para **[233.1]** et seq for the ITA 1984, s 39A. See Form B5.1 at para **[205.58]** for a gift of business property bearing its own inheritance tax.
2   It would be possible to provide that the donee pays the tax attributable to the full value of the gift, but it seems to us that this could cause uncertainty as to whether, when it comes to calculating the extent of the chargeable part of the estate under the ITA 1984, Pt II, Ch III (ss 36–42), the value of the gift should in some way be treated as reduced by the tax it bears in excess of the tax attributable to the value the property is treated as having by s 39A.

[214.80]

FORM B14.37:   Declaration that free of inheritance tax provisions relate only to tax on the testator's death

I declare that where any gift is hereby given free of inheritance tax, such gift shall be free only of inheritance tax payable on or by reason of my death.[1]

1   This expressly excludes any possibility that words freeing gifts of inheritance tax might be construed as including inheritance tax on events subsequent to the testator's death, although it is unlikely that words such as 'free of inheritance tax' would be so construed. See para **[214.66]**.

B15   Absolute and simple contingent gifts

CROSS REFERENCE

See also Form B19.16 at para [219.29]

[215.1]

FORM B15.1:   Residuary bequest to one person[1]

Subject to the payment of my debts funeral and testamentary expenses, inheritance tax legacies and annuities I devise and bequeath all my real and personal estate whatsoever and wheresoever of which I have any power of disposition by will whatsoever not hereby or by any codicil hereto specifically disposed of unto [*name*] absolutely.

1   Where there is an absolute gift to one person there is little point in interposing elaborate administration trusts. If the personal representatives need to realise assets for the payment of debt, they have power to do so under the AEA 1925, s 39 (Part G, para [246.48]) and the general law.

[215.2]

FORM B15.2:   Trusts of residue, as two persons jointly or the survivor of them shall appoint

I direct my trustees to stand possessed of the investments from time to time representing my residuary estate (hereinafter called the trust fund) and of the income thereof upon the following trusts. In trust for such persons and purposes and generally in such manner as —— and —— shall at any time or times by deed revocable or irrevocable jointly appoint and in default of and subject to any such appointment as the survivor of them shall [in manner aforesaid or] by will or codicil appoint.[1]

1   This form of disposition common in the case of a resettlement may be useful where the property is to go to an only son and his wife or only daughter and her husband who can then either take absolutely or settle it upon their children according to their own desires or the altered circumstances which may exist some years after the testator's death.

[215.3]

FORM B15.3:   Gift of residuary estate to three named persons[1]

My trustees shall hold my residuary estate in trust for A B and C as tenants in common in equal shares. In the event of the death of the said A B or C in my lifetime leaving issue[2] him or her surviving his or her share shall be held in trust for such issue living at my death and attaining the age of [eighteen] [twenty-one] years or marrying under that age in equal shares per stirpes but so that no issue shall take whose parent is alive at my death and so capable of taking.[3] In the event of any of the said A B or C dying in my lifetime leaving no issue living at my death [or then en ventre and born afterwards] or leaving such issue all of whom die under the age of [eighteen] [twenty-one] and unmarried the share of anyone so dying shall be held for the other persons entitled to my residuary estate as if the one or more so dying had been originally excluded from taking a share therein.

1   This form can be adapted for any number of named persons.
2   Illegitimate issue will prima facie be included. See Part A, para **[200.28]**.
3   For inheritance tax and substitution clauses see Part A, para **[200.131]**.

[215.4]

FORM B15.4:   Gift of residue to named children making provision for death in testator's lifetime or after his death in the latter case without leaving issue[1]

My trustees shall hold my residuary estate in trust for my three children [*names*] as tenants in common in equal shares. In the event of any of my said children dying in my lifetime leaving issue[2] him or her surviving his or her share shall be held in trust for such issue living or en ventre at my death and attaining the age of [eighteen] [twenty-one] years or marrying under that age as tenants in common in equal shares per stirpes. In the event of any of my said children dying in my lifetime without leaving any such issue as aforesaid the share of such child of mine so dying shall be held for the other persons entitled to my residuary estate as if the one or more so dying had for all the purposes of this clause been originally excluded from taking a share therein. In the event of [any of my said children dying after my death leaving no issue him or her surviving *or*[3]] none of the issue living or en ventre at my death of a child of mine who has predeceased me attaining a vested interest under the foregoing trust the share of such child of mine and any share which may accrue thereto by virtue of the provisions of this clause shall be held by my trustees as an accretion to the other shares (and equally if more than one) the trusts whereof shall not at the date of such accruer have failed or determined and upon the trusts powers and provisions applicable thereto herein contained or such of them as at the date of such accruer shall be capable of taking effect.

1   This clause makes a rather complicated provision and the complication can be avoided by the testator making a new will or codicil on the death of any child in his lifetime. Clauses of this nature are, however, often preferable because they are some protection against a testator neglecting to make new provisions on an alteration in the circumstances of his family.
2   Prima facie, illegitimate issue will be included: see Part A, para **[200.28]**.
3   If the part in square brackets is included, each child of the testator will have a vested interest subject to divestment on dying without issue, and distribution could be long postponed. We do not recommend its inclusion unless a power of advancement exerciseable over the whole of a presumptive share (see eg Form B18.20 at para **[218.104]**) is included as well.

[215.5]

FORM B15.5:   Clause disposing of residue in unequal shares, the interest of one of the beneficiaries being contingent, and with substitutional gifts to spouses and children and accruer provisions[1]

My trustees shall hold my residuary estate[2] upon trust to divide it or to treat it as being divided into fifteen shares of equal value and shall hold them upon the following trusts and subject to the following provisions:

(a)   My trustees shall hold such shares upon trust absolutely:
    (i)   As to three of them for [*donee*].
    (ii)   As to four of them for [*donee*].
    (iii)   As to one of them for such of my friends [*donees*] as survive me and if more than one in equal shares.
    (iv)   As to one of them for [*donee*] but if he predeceases me then for his wife [*donee*].
    (v)   As to two of them for [*donee*].
    (vI)   As to tour of them for [*donee*] contingently upon his reaching the age of [twenty-one] [eighteen] or marrying under that age.
(b)   Provided that if any of the persons named in paragraphs (i) (ii) and (v) or if both of those named in paragraph (iv) of subclause (a) of this clause predecease me leaving a child or children living at my death who reach the age of [eighteen] [twenty-one] or marry under that age then such child or children shall take absolutely and if more than one equally between them the share or shares of my residuary estate which his her or their parent would have taken if such parent had survived me.
(c)   Provided also that if at any time the trusts declared by subclause (a) read in conjunction with subclause (b) of this clause in respect of any share or shares of my residuary estate lapse or fail then from the date of such lapse or failure such share or shares (and any further share or shares or part thereof which may have accrued thereto by virtue of this provision) shall accrue to the other share or shares (and equally if more than one [or and if more than one in the proportions which they bear to each other][3]) the trusts of which have not at that date lapsed or failed and be held upon the trusts and with and subject to the powers and provisions from time to time affecting such other share or shares.

1   Testators often wish their estates to be divided into unequal shares, each affected by a different set of trusts. This form is designed to illustrate some of the many possible variations and the way in which they may be fitted together. To avoid disappointment or partial intestacy care should be taken to ensure that the sum of the fractional shares is singular. For problems, which can arise where residue is divided into fractional shares and some of the beneficiaries are exempt from inheritance tax see Part A, paras **[200.138]**–**[200.145]** and Form B14.35 at para **[214.78]**.
2   Or substitute 'the trust fund' or some similar expression if this has already been defined and use the same expression throughout the clause.
3   If the words 'and equally if more than one' are used then, although the property was originally divided into unequal shares, any share of which the trusts fail will be divided *equally* amongst the remaining shares. This is the simplest method to adopt. But if the testator wishes to perpetuate the original inequality, so that a share of which the trusts fail is divided amongst the remaining shares in the original *unequal* proportions, the words in square brackets should be substituted.

[215.6]

FORM B15.6:   Clause disposing of residue in percentage shares[1]

My trustees shall hold my residuary estate[2] upon trust to hold the same upon the following trusts and subject to the following provisions:

(a)
    (i)   As to forty per cent (40%) thereof for [*donee*].
    (ii)   As to fifteen per cent (15%) thereof for [*donee*].
    (iii) As to fifteen per cent (15%) thereof for [*donee*].
    (iv) As to ten per cent (10%) thereof for [*donee*].
    (v)   etc.

[(b)   Provided that if any of the persons named in paragraphs (i) (ii) and (iv) or if both of those named in paragraph (iii) of subclause (a) of this clause predecease me leaving a child or children living at my death who reach the age of [eighteen] [twenty-one] or marry under that age then such child or children shall take absolutely and if more than one equally between them the share or shares of my residuary estate which his her or their parent would have taken if such parent had survived me.][3]

(c)   Provided also that if at any time the trusts declared by subclause (a) read in conjunction with subclause (b) of this clause in respect of any share or shares of my residuary estate lapse or fail then from the date of such lapse or failure such share or shares (and any further share or shares or part thereof which may have accrued thereto by virtue of this provision) shall accrue to the other share or shares (and equally if more than one [*or and if more than one in the proportions which they bear to each other*][4]) the trusts of which have not at that date lapsed or failed and be held upon the trusts and with and subject to the powers and provisions from time to time affecting such other share or shares.][3]

1   To avoid disappointment or partial intestacy, care should be taken to ensure that the percentage shares add up to 100%. For problems which can arise where residue is divided into shares and some of the beneficiaries are exempt from inheritance tax see Part A, paras **[200.138]**–**[200.145]** and Form B14.35 at para **[214.78]**.
2   Or substitute 'the trust fund' or some similar expression if this has already been defined and use the same expression throughout the clause.

3   These provisions are similar to those included at para **[215.5]** but others could easily be devised in their place.

4   If the words 'and equally if more than one' are used, then although the property was originally divided into unequal shares, any share of which the trusts fail will be divided *equally* amongst the remaining shares. This is the simplest method to adopt. But if the testator wishes to perpetuate the original inequality, so that a share of which the trusts fail is divided amongst the remaining shares in the original *unequal* proportions, the words in square brackets should be substituted. See para **[215.5]**, n 3.

[215.7]

FORM B15.7:   Residuary gift without administration trusts[1]

(1)   I give all the rest of my property both real and personal whatsoever and wheresoever situate to all my children[2] in equal shares if more than one.

(2)   My executors may in extension of the power of appropriation conferred on personal representatives by section 41 of the Administration of Estates Act 1925, at any time or times with the consent in writing only of all other persons for the time being entitled to share in my estate who are of full age and capacity appropriate any part of my residuary estate in its then actual condition or state of investment in or towards satisfaction of the share of any infant beneficiary in my residuary estate.[3]

[(3)   If at the expiration of three months after the submission of any proposal for appropriation by my executor or such further period as my executor in his absolute discretion shall allow the persons entitled thereto or whose consent is required as aforesaid have not consented in writing to such appropriation of any article or other part of my estate under the preceding clauses hereof such article or part of my estate shall be sold by my executor (with power in his absolute discretion to postpone such sale for as long as he shall think fit) and the net proceeds of sale and the net income until sale shall be divided amongst my said children.][4]

[(4)   Provided that if any child of mine shall die in my lifetime leaving issue[2] living at my death such issue if and when they attain the age of [eighteen] [twenty-one] years or marry under that age shall take by substitution and if more than one in equal shares per stirpes the share of my estate which such deceased child of mine would have taken if he or she had survived me but so that no issue shall take whose parent is alive at my death and so capable of taking.][5]

1   This form of will avoids the conventional administration trusts, which are no longer as necessary as formerly because of the provisions of the TLATA 1996. See n 3 infra. This form is most suitable where all the gifts are immediate and of the simple nature here shown. See further para **[215.1]**, n 1.

2   References to children and issue in this clause will prima facie include illegitimate and legitimated children and issue: see Part A, para **[200.28]**.

3   This provision is designed for use where all the gifts under the will are immediate and the desire is to distribute the estate as far as possible at the earliest date. As soon as the estate is cleared the trustees (which by the usual express definition will include the executors, so that there is no question of the power of appropriation being given both to the executors and to the trustees and it is not necessary to show that the executors have become trustees before they are entitled to exercise this power) can proceed to distribution, except in the case of the shares of minors which must be held pending the attainment of full age. See Part G, para **[246.50]** for s 41 of the AEA 1925.

4   See n 3 supra. This in fact optional provision is only a statement of the duties of the executors but expressly stated in terms which may no doubt help to avoid disputes among the beneficiaries.

5   This provision is included for clarity and because of the option of providing that issue of
children who predecease the testator are to take other than at the age of 18 years, but the
statutory exception from lapse contained in s 33 of the WA 1837 renders the provision
otherwise unnecessary. See Part G, para **[244.34]** for s 33 of the WA 1837 (as substituted by the
AJA 1982, ss 19 and 73(6).

[215.8]

**FORM B15.8:   Absolute residuary gift to three children of the testator: land
to be sold**

NOTE

This form is an attempt to make as effective as possible within the constraints of
the Trusts of Land and Appointment of Trustees Act 1996 (TLATA 1996) a
residuary trust under which the trustees are to sell any land comprised in residue
and divide the proceeds: see Part A, paras **[200.57]**–**[200.59]** for the problems
which arise under the TLATA 1996 for making sure that a sale takes place. As
mentioned there, the key question is what happens should the majority by value
want to retain the property, but a minority want a sale so that they can have their
share in cash. The main matters in this form designed to maximise the chances
that there will be a sale are that there is a trust for sale; the provision for having
regard to majority wishes in the TLATA 1996, s 11 is excluded; and provisions
which might be thought to show that a long-term trust administration is
contemplated are tied specifically to the substitution clause. There is also an
express exclusion of occupation by beneficiaries as a purpose of the trust to
minimise the risk that a beneficiary who was in occupation of any property
comprised in residue could claim that he had a right of occupation (compare
Barclay v Barclay [1970] 2 QB 677 and see now the statutory right of
occupation discussed at para **[208.5]** et seq). It is not clear to what extent it
makes any difference to have a trust for sale in this context. It may well be that
the court, on an application for an order for sale under the TLATA 1996, s 14
would make the same decision on the basis of the same factors (such as the
beneficial trusts and the lack of a continuing trust purpose) whether there was a
trust for sale or a power of sale. However, the presence of a trust for sale may
make sale more imperative, and also may help to exclude any right of
occupation (see *Barclay v Barclay* [1970] 2 QB 677 at 684C–E).

FORM

I give all my property not hereby or by any codicil hereto otherwise effectively
disposed of [(including any entailed or other property over which I shall have at
my death a general power of disposition by will)][1] to my trustees upon trust as
follows—

(a)   my trustees shall hold the same upon trust to sell the same or such part
thereof as shall not consist of money with power to postpone such sale;

(b)   my trustees shall pay my funeral and testamentary expenses my debts
and any legacies given by this will or any codicil hereto out the proceeds
of any such sale and any ready money comprised in such property;

(c)   subject as aforesaid my trustees shall hold such moneys and any of my
said property for the time being unsold and any other assets for the time

being representing the foregoing (hereinafter called 'my residuary estate') upon trust for such of my three children AB CD and EF as shall survive me if more than one in equal shares absolutely;

(d)   all income of my residuary estate shall be treated as accruing on the date on which it becomes payable and there shall be no statutory apportionment of it to any other time or period;[2]

(e)   if any of my said children has already died or shall die before me leaving issue living at or after my death who shall satisfy the Vesting Condition (as hereinafter defined) then such issue shall take if more than one equally between them per stirpes the share of my residuary estate which such child of mine would have taken if he or she had survived me but so that no issue shall take whose parent is living at or after my death and satisfies the Vesting Condition;

(f)   for the purposes of the last foregoing subclause the Vesting Condition is attaining the age of [25] years before my death or before or at the expiry of the period of 80 years from the date of my death or being living but under the age of [25] years at the expiry of such period of 80 years from the date of my death which shall be the perpetuity period applicable to the foregoing disposition of my residuary estate;

(g)   if any substitutional trusts shall have effect under the foregoing subclauses in relation to any part or parts of my my residuary estate:

(i)   none of the equitable rules of apportionment between capital and income shall apply to such part or parts of residuary estate;

(ii)   section 31 of the Trustee Act 1925 (accumulation and maintenance trusts of income) shall apply to the income of such part or parts;

(iii) section 32 of the Trustee Act 1925 (payment or application of capital) shall apply to such part or parts as if the words 'one-half of' were omitted from proviso (a) to subsection (1) of the said s 32;

(iv)   my trustees shall have power to appropriate assets in their current state of investment to any share or shares of my residuary estate (whether the share or shares of any substituted beneficiaries or of any of my said children) without any consents being required to such appropriation;

(h)   section 11(1)(b) of the Trusts of Land and Appointment of Trustees Act 1996 (giving effect to beneficiaries' wishes) shall not apply to the exercise by my trustees of any of their functions relating to any land comprised in my residuary estate unless all my children or remoter issue who are for the time being interested under the foregoing trust and are of full age are unanimous as to their wishes and in particular I intend that after the expiry of one year from my death my trustees shall sell any land so comprised if requested to do so in writing by any one or more of my said children or remoter issue who are interested as aforesaid and of full age;[3]

(i)   it is not my intention that any land comprised in my estate at any time should be made available for the occupation of any beneficiaries under the foregoing trusts;[4]

(j)   my trustees shall have all the powers of a sole beneficial owner to invest trust moneys and change investments comprised in my residuary estate.

B15.8   Absolute residuary gift to three children of the testator

1   Subject to any express contrary intention, property subject to a general power will be carried by a residuary gift under the WA 1837, s 27 (Part G, para [244.27]), but in the case of entailed property the will must refer to the property, or the instrument under which it was acquired, or entailed property generally for the statutory power of disposition to be exercised: LPA 1925, s 176(1) (Part G, para [244.53]). Although no new entails can be created on or after 1 January 1997 (see Part A, para [200.53]), entails created before that date can continue to exist and, if they do, the statutory power of disposition of them by will continues to be available.

2   For exclusion of statutory apportionment of income over time see paras [214.48]–[214.52]. This clause has a function even if the substitution clause does not take effect in preventing apportionment as between before and after the testator's death.

3   For the TLATA 1996, s 11 see Part G, para [246.97] and B20 at para [220.58]. It does not apply insofar as provision that it does not apply is made by the disposition (s 11(2)(a)), and so it is thought that partial exclusion of it in this way is permitted.

4   For the statutory right of occupation see para [208.5] et seq and for drafting aspects see para [208.18].

B16 Life interests

PRELIMINARY NOTE

[216.1]
Using life interests. Although a testator's priority may be to ensure that following his death his spouse has adequate financial resources, he may also wish to ensure that so much of his property as is not needed by his spouse passes to his children and grandchildren, or perhaps other persons. This desire can often be best met by the conferral of a life interest in residue upon a spouse, with remainder trusts for children, more remote issue or other persons. The conferral of a life interest on a spouse may also have considerable inheritance tax advantages, particularly where the testator's estate exceeds the inheritance tax nil-rate threshold. The benefit of the spouse exemption can be claimed on the testator's death in respect of the property in which his spouse has a life interest, see Part A, paras **[200.99]–[200.101]**. On the death of the surviving spouse, if there is not much else which falls into the charge to inheritance tax other than the property in which her life interest subsists, the property may devolve with little or even no tax being payable (depending on its value). Alternatively, if the surviving spouse surrenders her life interest in part or parts of the property during her lifetime in favour of the remainder trusts she will be deemed to make transfers of value which may be potentially exempt from inheritance tax if the remainder gift is to persons absolutely or on interest in possession or accumulation and maintenance trusts, so that if she survives by seven years no tax is payable. Thus, it is possible that a testator's property may pass to his issue with no inheritance tax being payable.

[216.2]
Perpetuities. When drafting the trusts which are to take effect following a life interest, care must be taken that they do not infringe the rule against perpetuities. The rule, simply stated, is that every future interest in property must vest in interest (not necessarily in possession) within a perpetuity period allowed by law. The statutory perpetuity period is 80 years, and if this period (or a lesser period) is chosen by a will draftsman, it must be expressly stated to be the perpetuity period in the will: see the Perpetuities and Accumulations Act 1964 (PAA 1964), s 1 (Part G, para **[246.59]**). The common law perpetuity period is for a life or lives in being plus 21 years. The measuring life or lives may be, or may include, lives which have no connection with the trusts created, for example, those descendants of George V living at the testator's death, but then they must be expressly specified in the will as measuring lives. However, the more common and often more appropriate measuring lives are of those persons connected with the trusts. In this case it is not always necessary to specify expressly that those persons are the measuring lives. For example, a gift to such of the testator's grandchildren who attain the age of 21 and survive the testator's widow does not infringe the rule against perpetuities because the grandchildren's interests must necessarily vest within 21 years of the death of the last survivor of the testator's widow and children.

[216.3]
Wait and see rule. Although it is better if all interests created by will are certain to, or are expressly stated to, vest within the chosen perpetuity period (whether it be the statutory or common law period), since 1964 the 'wait and see' rule has meant that if it is not certain when a disposition takes effect that all of the interests will vest within a perpetuity period (before 1964 this lack of certainty was fatal to the interests which might not necessarily vest) then one can wait and see if the interest does in fact vest within an available perpetuity period (taking into account, if relevant, the lives specified in the PAA 1964, s 3(5) (Part G, para **[246.61]**). In none of the forms which follow has it been necessary to specify a perpetuity period because all of the interests must vest within the common law perpetuity period of a life or lives in being (of persons connected with the trusts), plus 21 years.

For a fuller account of perpetuities, see Vol 1, para **[94.1]** et seq.

[216.4]
Vesting. Where, as is commonly the case, a testator wishes to give a life interest to his spouse, with remainder to his children, the question arises as to whether the remainder gift should be contingent only on the children's surviving the testator so that the gift vests in interest absolutely on the testator's death and is not liable to divestment, or whether it should also be contingent on surviving the spouse (or liable to be divested on not surviving the spouse). In favour of the extra contingency (or the divestment) is the fact that by use of substitutional gifts or gifts over in the event of the contingency not being fulfilled (or the divestment), the destination of the testator's property can be determined by the testator's will instead of passing under the child's will or intestacy to persons whom the testator might not wish to benefit. The most common substitutional gift is for the children or issue of a child who does not satisfy all the conditions

of the gift. They usually take the share which that child would have taken if he had satisfied all of the conditions. This is often a preferable course to the trust property being divided between those children who do satisfy the conditions. If a substitution clause or gift over is incorporated in a will, care should be taken to ensure that it will take effect in whatever circumstances the primary gift fails.

[216.5]
However, the more contingencies or possibilities of divestment are introduced, the more difficult it is for the beneficiaries to terminate or rearrange the trusts by agreement, which may often be desirable in changing personal circumstances and a changing fiscal climate, and if children's interests remain contingent, it is more difficult for them to sell or raise a loan on their interests before they fall into possession. These disadvantages can to some extent be overcome if the trustees are given overriding powers to pay or advance capital or even alter the trusts.

[216.6]

FORM B16.1: Statutory protective trusts, varied by allowing accumulation for a period of years after a forfeiture has occurred[1]

I declare that the income hereinbefore directed to be held upon trust for or to be paid to the said [*name*] for life shall not vest absolutely in the said [*name*] but shall be held by my trustees [*or* I declare that the annuity hereinbefore bequeathed to the said [*name*] shall not vest in the said [*name*] absolutely but shall be received and held by my trustees] upon the statutory protective trusts (subject to the variations hereinafter mentioned) for the benefit of the said [*name*] for the period of his [*her*] life.

Provided however that in each year prior to the expiration of twenty-one years from my death during which my trustees under the said statutory trusts have a discretion as to the application of the said income [annuity] my trustees shall from time to time determine in their uncontrolled discretion how much (if any) part at all) of the income of the current year they will apply under the statutory trusts and the said trusts shall apply to the amount so determined and my trustees shall accumulate the balance of the said income [annuity] in the way of compound interest by investing the same and the resulting income thereof[2] but with power for my trustees in their uncontrolled discretion to determine from time to time during the said period of twenty-one years that any part of the past accumulations shall be income of the current year and be applicable accordingly at the discretion of my trustees, and I declare that after the death of the said [*name*] the said accumulations or the balance thereof shall be an accretion to the capital of the property from which such accumulations arose and be one fund with such capital for all purposes and shall be held by my trustees upon trust accordingly [*in the case of an annuity*, fall into the capital of my residuary estate and be distributed accordingly].[3]

---

1   See the TA 1925, s 33 (Part G, para **[246.28]**), which provides a statutory method of effecting a 'protected life interest'. The section contemplates that the whole of the yearly income (or annuity) must be applied every year, and does not provide for any accumulations (*Re Gourju's Will Trusts* [1943] Ch 24, [1942] 2 All ER 605; compare *Re Mellor, Alvarez v Dodgson* [1922] 1 Ch 312, [1922] All ER Rep 735; *Re Peel, Tattersall v Peel* [1936] Ch 161).

2   A period of 21 years from the testator's death is a permitted period of accumulation: see the LPA 1925, s 164(1)(b) (Part G, para **[246.42]**).

3   Although these variations of the trusts set out in the TA 1925, s 33 (Part G, para **[246.28]**) preserve its basic scheme, it seems that the Inland Revenue will not be prepared to accept these forms as 'to the like effect' for the purposes of inheritance tax relief under the ITA 1984, s 88 which disregards a forfeiture for inheritance tax purposes (for which see Part A, para **[200.116]**). Therefore, the occasion of the forfeiture of the life interest when such discretionary trusts take effect will be a chargeable transfer for inheritance tax purposes under the ITA 1984, ss 2(1) and 52(1). For some guidance on what trusts might be like to those of the TA 1925, s 33 (Part G, para **[246.28]**), see *Re Wallace's Settlements, Fane v Wallace* [1968] 2 All ER 209, [1968] 1 WLR 711. See also Form C3.2, cl 4(4) at para **[225.32]** and *Foster's Inheritance Tax*, E6.21.

[216.7]

FORM B16.2:   Protective income trusts for woman for life[1]

(A)   USING THE STATUTORY PROTECTIVE TRUSTS

My trustees shall hold the income of [my residuary estate] upon protective trusts for the benefit of [*name*] during her life provided that the discretionary trusts by statute implied to arise after the failure or determination during the life of the said [*name*] of the trust to pay such income to her shall be varied as follows:

  (i)   My trustees may in their discretion apply any income accrued but unapplied in any previous year for the purposes of such discretionary trusts in any subsequent year but at a time not exceeding twenty-one years after the date of my death.

 (ii)   After the death of any object of such discretionary trusts my trustees may in their discretion while [*name*] is still living within three years of the date of such death apply any income which accrued in his or her lifetime in or towards the discharge of any liability incurred by or on behalf of any such object which my trustees may think fit to satisfy.

(iii)   Notwithstanding the protective trusts hereinbefore declared and without determining her life interest thereunder the said [*name*] may by deed or deeds but with the consent of my trustees therein expressed (which consent my trustees shall have absolute power to give or withhold) assign any part or parts not exceeding in the whole one half of the income of [my residuary estate] to any her child children or issue[2] who shall at the date of such assignment have attained the age of [eighteen] [twenty-one] years or have married or shall marry within one month after such assignment.[3]

(iv)   Further and notwithstanding the protective trusts hereinbefore declared and without determining the life interest thereunder of the said [*name*] my trustees shall have power at any time or times during the lifetime of the said [*name*] either before or after her life interest shall have failed or determined to pay or apply the whole or any part or parts of the capital of [my residuary estate] to or for the benefit of the said [*name*].

 (v)   My trustees shall have power at any time or times before the life interest of the said [*name*] shall have failed or determined by deed or deeds to declare that they shall henceforth hold the income of [my residuary estate] or any part or share thereof upon trust to pay the same to the said [*name*] during her life and not upon protective trusts for her benefit.

(B)   ALTERNATIVE FORM—WITHOUT USING REFERENCE TO THE STATUTORY PROTECTIVE
TRUSTS[4]

My trustees shall pay the income of [my residuary estate] to the said [*name*]
during her life unless or until some act or event shall have happened or shall
happen whereby the said income or any part thereof if belonging absolutely to
her would become vested in or charged in favour of some other person.[5] And in
the event of the failure or determination during her life of the trust last above
declared in her favour my trustees shall during the remainder of her life pay or
apply such income unto or for or towards the personal support maintenance and
education of the said [*name*] [her husband] and her issue[6] for the time being and
the person who if she were dead would for the time being be interested in [my
residuary estate] or such one or more to the exclusion of the others or other of
such objects of this discretionary trust in such manner and if more than one in
such shares as my trustees shall think proper with power while [*name*] is still
living within three years after the death of any object of such discretionary trust
to apply any income which accrued in his or her lifetime in or towards the
discharge of any liability incurred by or on behalf of any such object which my
trustees shall think fit to satisfy.

[*Add sub-cls (iii), (iv) and (v) of alternative* Form (A) *supra.*]

1   Although these variations of the trusts set out in the TA 1925, s 33 (Part G, para **[246.28]**)
     preserve its basic scheme, it seems that the Inland Revenue will not be prepared to accept these
     forms as 'to the like effect' for the purposes of inheritance tax relief under ITA 1984, s 88
     which disregards a forfeiture for inheritance tax purposes (for which see Part A,
     para **[200.116]**). Therefore, the occasion of the forfeiture of the life interest when such
     discretionary trusts take effect will be a chargeable transfer for inheritance tax purposes under
     ITA 1984, ss 2(1) and 52(1). For some guidance on what trusts might be like to those of the TA
     1925, s 33 (Part G, para **[246.28]**); see *Re Wallace's Settlements, Fane v Wallace* [1968] 2 All
     ER 209, [1968] 1 WLR 711. See also Form C3.2, cl 4(4) at para **[225.32]** and *Foster's
     Inheritance Tax*, E6.21.
2   These words prima facie include illegitimate children or issue: see Part A, paras **[200.28]** and
     [200.29].
3   This provision will enable a settlement to be made on the marriage of a child of the protected
     life tenant .
4   See n 2 to Form B16.1 at para **[216.6]**. The differences between the trusts of this clause and
     those of the TA 1925, s 33 (Part G, para **[246.28]**) are the same as the differences between those
     of the preceding Form (A) and s 33 with the additional variation that the remainderman is an
     object of the discretionary trust of income even if the principal beneficiary has a spouse or issue
     living (compare s 33(1)(ii)(b)).
5   Singular includes plural and vice versa, and person a corporation (LPA 1925, s 61: Part G,
     para **[246.40]**). See on this clause, *Re Pilkington's Will Trusts, Pilkington v Harrison* [1937] Ch
     574, [1937] 3 All ER 213.
6   See n 2 supra.

[216.8]

FORM B16.3:   Determinable life interest

Until the death of my son [*name or as the case may be*] my trustees shall, if no
act or thing shall have been done permitted or suffered by my said son or shall
have been attempted to have been done and if no event shall have happened
(other than a consent to any advancement under any statutory or express power)
whereby the income of [my residuary estate *or as the case may be*] or some part

thereof would or might if belonging absolutely to my said son become vested in or charged in favour of some other persons or a corporation or my said son would or might be deprived of the right to receive the same or any part thereof, pay the said income to my said son during his life until some such act or thing as aforesaid shall be done permitted or suffered or be attempted to be done by my said son or some such event as aforesaid shall happen.

And after the death or earlier failure or determination in the lifetime of my said son of the trust in his favour hereinbefore contained my trustees shall stand possessed of [my residuary estate *or* his share of my residuary estate *or as the case may be*] and the income thereof in trust etc.[1]

1   TA 1925, s 33 (Part G, para [246.28]) cannot readily be adapted to the case considered in this form. This form may be adapted to a legacy (see Form B10.39 at para [210.55]) to prevent the legacy becoming payable, eg to a trustee on bankruptcy. This is not a protective trust for inheritance tax purposes.

[216.9]

FORM B16.4:   Life or widowhood interest to wife

My trustees shall pay the income of my residuary estate to my wife for her life [*or* as long as she shall remain my widow[1]].

1   As to the meaning of this term, see Vol 1, paras [80.1] and [80.2]. If the wife's interest is limited to her widowhood, her remarriage will determine her interest and may occasion an inheritance tax charge under ITA 1984, s 52(1) unless potential exemption is available, see Part A, para [200.114].

[216.10]

FORM B16.5:   Life interest to wife reducible on remarriage

My trustees shall pay the income of my residuary estate to my wife during her widowhood and after her remarriage they shall pay her the income from [one half of] my residuary estate during the remainder of her life.[1]

1   It is advisable following the widow's remarriage to give the widow the income of half the estate rather than half the income of the estate since this will allow one half of the estate to be distributed on remarriage. For this distinction see *Re Freeston's Charity, Sylvester v University College Oxford* [1979] 1 All ER 51, [1978] 1 WLR 741. There will of course be a partial termination of an interest in possession on remarriage which may attract a charge to inheritance tax under the ITA 1984, s 52(1) unless potential exemption is available, see Part A, para [200.114].

[216.11]

FORM B16.6:   Trust for wife during widowhood subject to an obligation to maintain children

In trust to pay the income thereof to my wife during her widowhood she thereout maintaining and educating my sons while under the age of twenty-five years and my unmarried daughters but my wife so long as she maintains and educates my children to the satisfaction of my trustees shall not be liable to account for the said income.[1]

1   *Re Booth, Booth v Booth* [1894] 2 Ch 282; *Re G (Infants)* [1899] 1 Ch 719; *Comiskey v Bowring-Hanbury* [1905] AC 84; *Re Ramsay, Thorpe v Ramsay* [1917] 2 Ch 64. This form imposes an obligation, and is not merely a precatory direction. If no obligation is to be imposed, this should be expressly stated as in the next following form. If the income in question is the income of a legacy, the legacy will carry interest from the testator's death where the primary object is maintenance (*Re Ramsay, Thorpe v Ramsay*), but not otherwise (*Re Crane, Adams v Crane* [1908] 1 Ch 379). For the purposes of inheritance tax this may create a discretionary trust (see para [218.8] et seq) and if this is not desired it will be safer to use the next following form instead.

[216.12]

FORM B16.7:   Same where no legal obligation imposed

In trust to pay the income thereof to my wife during her widowhood and I request her, but so as not to impose any legal obligation upon her, thereout to educate and maintain my sons while under the age of twenty-five years and my daughters while under that age and unmarried.

[216.13]

FORM B16.8:   Gift of income of residuary estate to a reputed wife as long as she is unmarried[1]

My trustees shall pay the income of my residuary estate[2] to my wife [*name of reputed wife*] during her life or until after my death she shall marry and from and after the death or such marriage of my said wife my trustees shall hold my residuary estate and the income thereof [*add gift over*].

1   This form will, it is thought, be found useful where the testator desires to conceal the true status of a reputed wife to whom he has never been legally married, but nevertheless wishes her interest to cease on her marriage after his death to any other person. See generally Vol 1, para [80.1] et seq. Her remarriage will determine her interest and may occasion an inheritance tax charge under the ITA 1984, s 52(1) unless potential exemption is available, see Part A, para [200.114].
2   It is assumed that the 'residuary estate' has been defined. In the event of the reputed wife marrying the testator, he will have to make a fresh will since marriage generally revokes a will, see Vol 1, para [17.1] et seq.

[216.14]

FORM B16.9:   Trust of income for several persons for life giving a general testamentary power of disposition to the survivor

In trust to pay the income thereof to my three daughters [*names*] and the survivors and survivor of them during their or her respective lives or life and after the death of such survivor in trust as to both the capital and income of the trust fund for such persons and in such manner as such survivor shall by will or codicil appoint [*add gift over in default of appointment as desired*].[1]

1   It is not unusual to make the ultimate gift to the last survivor absolutely but the result of giving him a general testamentary power of appointment is much the same as he can dispose of it as his property. If this form is used for the exercise of a special power of appointment care should be taken to keep within the common law perpetuity rule for the gift to the survivor is contingent: see *Re Legh's Settlement Trusts, Public Trustee v Legh* [1938] Ch 39, [1937] 3 All ER 823. An exercise of the power which is invalid at common law might nevertheless be saved under the 'wait and see' provision of the PAA 1964, s 3 (Part G, para [246.61]).

[216.15]

FORM B16.10: Trust for wife for life and then to children in equal shares[1]

(i) Upon trust to pay the income from my residuary estate to my wife for life [during her widowhood] [and I direct that if in any year the income of my residuary estate does not amount to £—— then my trustees shall resort to the capital of my residuary estate to make good the deficiency].

(ii) After the death [*or if wife's interest is restricted to widowhood,* After the death or remarriage] of my wife my trustees shall hold my residuary estate in trust in equal shares if more than one for all my children who attain the age of [eighteen] [twenty-one] years or marry under that age provided that if any child shall have died in my lifetime whether before or after the date hereof leaving issue living at my death such issue if and when they attain the age of [eighteen] [twenty-one] years or marry under that age shall take by substitution and if more than one in equal shares per stirpes the share of my residuary estate that such deceased child of mine would have taken had he or she survived me but so that no issue shall take whose parent is alive at my death and so capable of taking.

1 This is the common form of gift to wife for life and then for children in equal shares. Variations are shown for the case where the gift is for widowhood and where, as may be necessary in a small estate, there is a discretion to make the income up out of capital to a stated amount. Although these payments are made from capital, they attract income tax: *Cunard's Trustees v IRC* [1946] 1 All ER 159. There is no inheritance tax disadvantage in paying capital to someone who has an interest in possession in it: see Part A, para **[200.111]**. In this form male and female children are treated equally as to vesting on marriage. If such a clause as this is worded as a trust for the wife for life and then to children and the *issue* of any then dead, the issue must survive the wife: *Mousley v Rigby* [1955] Ch 139, [1954] 3 All ER 553, following *Re Embury* (1913) 109 LT 511; see also Vol 1, para **[68.11]**. Illegitimate children and issue will be eligible under this clause; see Part A, paras **[200.28]** and **[200.29]**.

[216.16]

FORM B16.11: Trust for wife for life and then to children in equal shares by incorporation of Statutory Will Forms 1925, Form 10

Statutory Will Forms 1925, Form 10, is hereby incorporated in this my will and shall apply to my residuary estate.[1]

1 This assumes that the term 'residuary estate' has already been defined. For Form 10 of the Statutory Will Forms 1925 see Part E, para **[238.16]**.

[216.17]

FORM B16.12: Trust for wife for life and then to unmarried daughters for life

My trustees shall hold my [residuary estate] upon the following trusts:

(i) Upon trust to pay the income thereof to my wife [*name*] during her life.
(ii) If both my daughters [*name*] and [*name*] shall be living and unmarried at the death of my said wife[1] to pay the income thereof to my said daughters in equal shares either for the period of their joint lives or until

the marriage of either of them whichever period shall be the shorter and on the death or marriage of one of my said daughters to pay the income of the appropriated fund hereinafter defined to my surviving or unmarried daughter (as the case may be) until her death or marriage.

(iii) If only one of my said daughters shall survive my said wife and shall at the death of my said wife be unmarried then to pay the income of the appropriated fund to such unmarried daughter until her death or marriage.

(iv) The appropriated fund hereinbefore mentioned shall be a fund set aside either at the death of my wife or at the death or on the marriage of the first of my said daughters to die or marry as the case may be and shall consist of investments sufficient at the time when such fund shall be set aside to produce the gross yearly sum before deduction of income tax of £——.[2]

(v) Subject to the above provisions and subject as hereinafter provided to hold [my residuary estate] in trust both as to capital and income in trust for all my children [who shall attain the age of [eighteen] [twenty-one] years or marry thereunder] in equal shares. Provided that if any child of mine has died or shall die in my lifetime leaving issue living at my death who attain the age of [eighteen] [twenty-one] years or marry thereunder such issue shall stand in the place of such deceased child and take per stirpes and equally between them if more than one the share of [my residuary estate] which such deceased child of mine would have taken if he or she had survived me [and had attained a vested interest] but so that no issue shall take whose parent is alive and capable of taking under this provision of my will.

(vi) So long as either of my said daughters remain unmarried such unmarried daughters shall not take any share or interest in the income of [my residuary estate] without bringing her share of the income of the appropriated fund into hotchpot and accounting for the same.

1   This clause assumes that the wife survives the husband, but if at this point and at corresponding points later in the clause, the words 'at the death of my said wife' are replaced by the words 'at the death of the survivor of myself and my said wife,' the clause will be applicable to the case where the wife predeceases the testator. There seems little reason to doubt that, as the clause stands, if the wife's interest fails, the later interests will be accelerated.

2   The unmarried daughter may not be entitled to much in the way of rebates or allowances, and it seems that a gross sum will be as convenient as any.

[216.18]

FORM B16.13:   Trust for wife for life and then to children as she shall appoint, with hotchpot provision[1]

(i)   Upon trust to pay the income thereof [of my residuary estate] to my wife for her life and subject thereto.

(ii)   Upon trust as to both capital and income for all or any one or more of my children and remoter issue in such shares and subject to such powers provisions and generally in such manner as my said wife shall by deed or will appoint and subject to any such appointment upon trust for all my children living at my death if more than one in equal shares as tenants in common.

(iii)   Any child who or whose issue takes any interest under the foregoing provision in default of appointment shall not take such interest in default of appointment without bringing into hotchpot any share or shares appointed to him or her or his or her issue and accounting for the same unless the appointment shall direct to the contrary.

1   This is a very short form and makes no provision under the trusts in default of appointment for children who die in the testator's lifetime leaving issue although the power of appointment can be exercised in favour of such issue. For a longer form, see Form B17.2 at para [217.7] and for a form with a wider power of appointment, see Form B16.14 at para [216.19] and Form C2.6 at para [224.95]. Illegitimate children will be eligible: see Part A, paras [200.28] and [200.29].

[216.19]

FORM B16.14:   Trust for wife for life and then to issue upon such trusts as she shall appoint[1]

(i)   Upon trust to pay the income thereof of [my residuary estate] to my wife for her life and subject thereto.

(ii)   Upon trust as to both capital and income for all or any one or more of my children and remoter issue for such interests at such ages or times in such shares and with and subject to such powers and discretions exercisable over capital or income by any person or persons as my wife shall by deed or will (without transgressing the rules against perpetuities) appoint.

(iii)   In default of and subject to any such appointment in trust for all my children living at my death if more than one in equal shares as tenants in common provided that if any child of mine shall have died in my lifetime whether before or after the date hereof leaving issue living at my death such issue shall take by substitution and if more than one in equal shares per stirpes the share of my residuary estate that such deceased child of mine would have taken in default or subject to any appointment as aforesaid had he or she survived me but so that no issue shall take whose parent is alive at my death and so capable of taking.

1   This form authorises the testator's widow to appoint new trusts, including discretionary trusts, for the benefit of the testator's issue. For another wide form of power of appointment, see Form C2.6 at para [224.95].

[216.20]

FORM B16.15:   Trust for wife during widowhood, then to son for life with remainder to his children

(i)   Upon trust to pay the income of [my residuary estate] to my wife during her widowhood.

(ii)   After the death or remarriage of my wife my trustees shall hold my residuary estate upon trust to pay the income thereof to my son [*name*] during his life and subject thereto upon trust in equal shares for all the children of my said son who shall attain the age of [eighteen] [twenty-one] years or marry thereunder.

[216.21]

FORM B16.16:   Trust for wife for life and then to children for life with substitution of their issue

My trustees shall hold my residuary estate and the income thereof upon the following trusts:

(a)   upon trust to pay the income thereof to my wife if she shall survive me during her life and subject thereto

(b)   upon trust to divide my residuary estate into equal shares the number of such shares being equal to the number of my children living at the death of the survivor of myself and my said wife together with the number of my children who have died (whether before or after the date hereof) prior to such date as aforesaid leaving issue living at such date. Such shares to be held upon the trusts and subject to the powers and provisions hereinafter contained.

(c)   in the case of each such living child of mine one share shall be held upon the following trusts:

   (i)   upon trust to pay the income thereof to such child during his or her life [*or* upon protective trusts for such child's benefit during his or her life] and after the death of such child

   (ii)   upon trust to pay the said income to any wife or husband of such child of mine who shall survive him or her during the residue of such wife's or husband's life.

   (iii)   upon trust as to both capital and income of such share for all or such one or more exclusively of the others or other of the children or remoter issue of such child of mine born within twenty-one years of the death of the survivor of myself and my said wife [and my children] at such times and if more than one in such shares and with such provisions for maintenance advancement and otherwise for the benefit of such children or remoter issue or some or one of them at the discretion of my trustees or any other persons and generally in such manner in all respects as such children of mine shall by deed revocable or irrevocable or by will or codicil appoint.[1] And subject to any such appointment

   (iv)   upon trust for the child or children of such child of mine who attain the age of [eighteen] [twenty-one] years or being female attain that age or marry under that age and if more than one in equal shares.

   (v)   provided always that no child of such child of mine who or whose issue shall take any part of such share by virtue of any appointment by such child of mine under the power aforesaid shall unless such child of mine so direct share in the unappointed part of such share without bringing the part so appointed into hotchpot and accounting therefor.

(d)   In the case of the issue of each such deceased child of mine one share shall be held upon the following trusts: upon trust in equal shares (if more than one) for all or any of the children or child of such deceased child of mine living at the date of the death of the survivor of myself and my said wife who attain the age of [eighteen] [twenty-one] years or marry under that age and for all or any of the issue living at the date aforesaid who attain the age of [eighteen] [twenty-one] years or marry under that age of any child (who dies before the aforesaid date leaving issue living at the aforesaid date) of such child of mine such issue to take through all degrees according to their stocks in equal shares (if more than one) the share which their parent would have taken if living at the aforesaid date and so that no issue shall take whose parent is living at the aforesaid date and so capable of taking.[2]

(e)   If the trusts of any such share as aforesaid shall fail by reason of no person attaining a vested interest therein then I direct that subject to the trusts powers and provisions herein contained or which may be applicable thereto by statute the said share and any share or shares which may accrue thereto by virtue of this present proviso shall be held by my trustees as an accretion to the other share or shares (and equally if more than one) the trusts whereof shall not at the date of such accruer have failed as aforesaid and upon the trusts powers and provisions applicable thereto herein contained or such of them as at the date of such accruer shall be capable of taking effect.

1   A joint power of appointment can be given to a daughter and her husband. At common law a power of appointment could not be given to the husband alone if he survived (*Re Abbott, Peacock v Frigout* [1893] 1 Ch 54), because such husband might be a person not born in the testator's lifetime, but would now be saved, at least partially, by the 'wait and see' provisions introduced by the PAA 1964, s 3 (Part G, para **[246.61]**).
2   Compare the AEA 1925, s 47(1) (Part G, para **[244.61]**).

[216.22]

FORM B16.17:   **Trust for wife for life and then to children as she shall appoint incorporating Statutory Will Forms 1925, Form 9**[1]

Statutory Will Forms 1925, Form 9, is hereby incorporated in this my will and shall apply to my residuary estate.

1   This statutory form makes provisions for children dying in the lifetime of the testator, for hotchpot and other matters. For the terms of this statutory will form, see Part E, para **[238.15]**.

[216.23]

FORM B16.18:   **Clause directing trustees to resort to the capital of residue in order to make up income to a minimum amount**[1]

I direct that if in any year the net income from [my residuary estate] in the hands of my widow she retaining all rebates allowances and repayments for her own benefit which shall be included in the computation of the said net income does not amount to £—— then my trustees shall [at the written request of my widow] resort to the capital of my residuary estate to make good the deficiency.

1   This clause directs trustees to make up income to a specified amount. It is thought that the total sum paid to the beneficiary is liable to income tax, see *Cunard's Trustees v IRC* [1946] 1 All ER 159, and see n 1 to Form B16.20 at para **[216.25]**.

[216.24]

FORM B16.19: Clause empowering trustees to resort to capital[1]

My trustees may at the written request of my widow at any time or times raise any sum or sums [(not exceeding £—— in any one year and not exceeding £—— in all)] out of the capital of my residuary estate and pay such sum or sums to or for the absolute benefit of my widow in addition to the income of my residuary estate hereinbefore given to her but in any such case my trustees shall have an absolute discretion whether or not they will raise such sums notwithstanding the written request of my said widow.

1 This form gives trustees power to resort to capital to make up income, rather than, as in the immediately preceding form, directing them to do so to make up income to a specified sum. The trustees must be satisfied that the raising of such sums is for the benefit of the wife or for that of the children whom the wife is supporting: *Re Powles, Little v Powles* [1954] 1 All ER 516, [1954] 1 WLR 336. It is not clear whether sums paid to the beneficiary will be liable to income tax, see n 1 to Form B16.20 at para **[216.25]**.

[216.25]

FORM B16.20: Clause empowering trustees to lend capital money to make up income of a share of residue to a stated amount[1]

I direct that if in any year during the lifetime of the said [*beneficiary*] the income of the share of residue hereinbefore bequeathed to the said [*beneficiary*] [*or for the benefit of the said [*beneficiary*] and [her]/[his] children [and issue]] shall after deduction therefrom of income tax at the basic rate for the time being in force but without taking into account rebates allowances or repayments of tax be less than £—— my trustees may in their absolute discretion out of the capital of the said residue lend to the said [*beneficiary*] upon her [his] written undertaking that such moneys shall be recoverable and that interest shall be paid thereon as hereinafter stated the difference between the net income of the said share of residue and the sum of £—— provided that the said [*beneficiary*] shall not be called upon by my trustees to repay any such moneys during [her]/[his] lifetime but that they shall be recoverable only after [her]/[his] death from [her]/[his] estate and provided that in arriving at the sum to be borrowed the interest on any previous loan shall not be taken into consideration.

[*Add rate and terms of payment of interest.*]

1 Form B16.18 at para **[216.23]** directs trustees to make up income to a stated amount by resorting to capital, and B16.19 at para **[216.24]** gives a power to trustees to make up income by resorting to capital. If an arrangement such as that of Form 16.18 is adopted (that is, directing a resort to the capital of the residuary estate) it is thought that the total sum paid to the beneficiary is liable to income tax, see *Cunard's Trustees v IRC* [1946] 1 All ER 159. It is less clear that this result follows if Form 16.19 is adopted, but it is possible that it does. It would seem that this result may be avoided by giving the trustees a right to recover the sums advanced from the beneficiary so advanced: see *Williamson v Ough* [1936] AC 384, HL.

[216.26]

FORM B16.21: Gift of residue to children incorporating Statutory Will Forms 1925, Form 7, with modification[1]

I give the residue of my real and personal estate to my trustees to hold the same upon trust for such of my children who shall be living at my death and if more than one in equal shares and I direct that Form 7 of the Statutory Will Forms 1925 (except clause (5) thereof) is hereby incorporated in my will and shall apply to the share in my residuary estate of each child of mine and to the investments representing the same as if such share were a legacy and instead of clause (5) of the said Form 7 I direct that if any such child of mine shall not have any child who under the incorporated trusts in default of appointment attains a vested interest in such child's share then subject to the incorporated trusts and powers in favour of such child and his or her issue the said share and the income thereof and all statutory accumulations (if any) of income and any share which shall accrue thereto under this present provision shall accrue to the other shares (and if more than one equally between them and whether such other shares are settled or not settled) in my residuary estate the trusts whereof shall not at the date of such accruer have failed or determined otherwise than by absolute vesting.

1   This statutory form makes provision for the payment of income to a life tenant, with remainder for the issue of the life tenant as he or she should appoint, with default provisions. For Form 7 see Part E, para **[238.13]**.

[216.27]

FORM B16.22:   Gift of residue incorporating intestacy provisions[1]

I devise and bequeath all the residue of my property to my trustees upon the same trusts and powers both as to the sale investment and administration thereof and as to the beneficial interests therein as if I had died intestate in respect thereof.

1   Subject to appointing executors and making some specific legacies, a person may wish his estate to pass as on an intestacy, or be prepared for this to happen if a will has to be made urgently. For the provisions which apply on an intestacy see the AEA 1925, ss 33 and 47 (Part G, paras **[244.58]** and **[244.61]**). If a testator leaves a spouse and issue, the spouse takes the personal chattels, a net sum currently of £125,000 with interest currently at 6% from the date of death, and a life interest in half the residue. Subject to the interest of the widow, the issue take the residue with stirpital substitution throughout.

[216.28]

FORM B16.23:   Settlement of child's share of residuary estate[1]

My trustees shall hold my residuary estate upon trust for such of my children who shall survive me if more than one in equal shares. Provided that the share of my residuary estate of all such children who shall survive me shall not vest absolutely in such child but shall be retained by my trustees and held upon the following trusts:

(1)   To pay the income from such share to such child for life and such child shall have power by will or codicil to appoint to any spouse who shall survive him or her a life or less interest in such income.[2]

(2)   From and after the death of such child [and subject to any such appointment as aforesaid to a surviving spouse] such share and the

income thereof shall be held upon such trusts for such one or more of his or her children and remoter issue as he or she may by deed with or without power of revocation and new appointment or by will or codicil appoint.

(3)   In default of any such appointment and so far as any such appointment shall not extend such share shall be held upon trust for all the children or any child of such child of mine who [being male] — shall attain the age of [eighteen] [twenty-one] years or [being female shall attain that age or] previously marry and if more than one equally as tenants in common. Provided that no child of any such child of mine shall take any part of my child's share in default of appointment under this present trust without bringing into hotchpot any part of the share of my child which he or she may have appointed in favour of such child or of any of such child's issue under the power in that behalf hereinbefore contained unless my child making the appointment shall direct to the contrary.

(4)   If the share of my child or any part thereof shall not vest absolutely in some person or persons under the foregoing trusts then after the death of my child his or her share or the part thereof which shall not so vest shall (subject to the trusts powers and provisions hereby or by statute vested in my trustees in respect of the income or the capital thereof and to every exercise of the same by my trustees) be held in trust for such persons or person as he or she shall by will or codicil appoint and in default of any such appointment in trust for the statutory beneficiaries entitled as if he or she had died intestate without ever having married and without leaving a parent and such share had formed part of his or her estate.

(5)   If at the date when such child of mine attains the age of [fifty] years he or she shall never have had a child or if at the said date all the children he or she shall then have had shall have died without attaining a vested interest in his or her share or if subsequently to the said date all the children he or she shall have had shall die without any of them attaining such a vested interest as aforesaid then my trustees may at any time or times after the date when such child of mine attains the age of fifty years or the subsequent date when his or her last surviving child shall die without attaining such a vested interest as aforesaid as the case may be and during the life of such child of mine transfer the whole or any part or parts of his or her share in its then actual state of investment to such child of mine absolutely freed and discharged from the trusts powers and provisions hereof.[3]

---

1   If this clause is used it will be advisable to add a clause expressly authorising the executors or trustees to appropriate; see Form B20.24 at para **[220.77]**. As to the construction of the words children and issue, see Part A, paras **[200.28]** and **[200.29]**.

2   Such an appointment would fail if a divorce takes place, since a divorced spouse cannot be a spouse who survives a named person: *Re Kettlewell, Jones v Kettlewell* (1907) 98 LT 23; *Re Williams' Settlement, Greenwell v Humphries* [1929] 2 Ch 361, [1929] All ER Rep 632; *Re Slaughter, Trustees Corpn Ltd v Slaughter* [1945] Ch 355, [1945] 2 All ER 214; *Re Allan, Allan v Midland Bank Executor and Trustee Co Ltd* [1954] Ch 295, [1954] 1 All ER 646. If a child does appoint an interest in possession to his or her spouse following his or her death, there will be no inheritance tax charge upon the child's share of residue on the child's death because the spouse exemption will apply.

3   See n 2 to Form B16.24 at para **[216.29]**.

[216.29]

FORM B16.24:   Provision directing payment of capital to a female life tenant having no likelihood of children, where she has herself a general power of appointment in default of children

If at the date when [*name*] [any daughter of mine] attains the age of [50] years she shall never have had a child[1] or if at the said date all the children[1] she shall then have had shall have died without attaining a vested interest in the [*property*] [*share of my residuary estate*] of which [she] [such daughter] is life tenant hereunder or if subsequently to the said date all the children [she] [such daughter] shall have had shall die without any of them attaining such a vested interest as aforesaid then my trustees shall at the date when the said [*name*] [such daughter] attains the age of [50] years or upon the subsequent date when the last surviving child of the said [*name*] [such daughter] shall die without attaining such a vested interest as aforesaid as the case may be transfer such [*property*] [*share*] as aforesaid in its then actual state of investment to the said [*name*] [such daughter] freed and discharged [from any life interest in the whole or a part thereof to which any husband of the said [*name*] [such daughter] who might survive her would or might have become entitled after her death whether under any appointment actually then made or otherwise and] from every [other] trust or power to take effect after her death under the trusts hereinbefore contained.[2]

1   Including an illegitimate child unless a contrary intention is shown: see Part A, paras **[200.28]** and **[200.29]**.
2   This precedent is for use when a female life tenant is entitled, in default of children attaining a vested interest, to a general power of appointment, or where in similar circumstances the property would otherwise go direct to her next of kin on her death. Any appointment to a surviving husband made under a power is overridden. It has been suggested that, where there is no longer any prospect of children, it is better that the life tenant should be able to break the trust even to the disadvantage of a husband who may survive her rather than that the money should go to (possibly) distant relatives. As to when the court used to presume a woman to be past child-bearing, see *Re Whichelow, Bradshaw v Orpen* [1953] 2 All ER 1558, [1954] 1 WLR 5; *Allen v Crane* [1953] ALR 959, St R Qd 95; *Re Pettifor's Will Trusts* [1966] Ch 257, [1966] 1 All ER 913; and *Re Westminster Bank Ltd's Declaration of Trust* [1963] 2 All ER 400n, [1963] 1 WLR 820; see also the PAA 1964, s 2(1)(a) (Part G, para **[246.60]**) for the presumption in the context of the rule against perpetuities. These authorities can no longer be relied on: see para **[221.34]**, n 1. For this form in the context of a set of beneficial trusts see Form B 16.23 at para **[216.28]**.

Settled legacies

[216.30]

FORM B16.25:   Settled legacy—concise form

(i)   I give to my trustees the sum of £—— [free of inheritance tax and foreign death duties[1]] upon trust to invest the same in any investments hereby authorised or authorised by law for the investment of trust funds with power to vary the same and to hold the same in trust to pay the income therefrom to A. during his life.

(ii)   Subject thereto as to both capital and income for all or any the children or child[2] of A. who attain the age of [eighteen] [twenty-one] years or marry under that age and if more than one in equal shares.[3]

[(iii)   I hereby declare that the administrative provisions of this my will relating to residue shall apply to this legacy].

[*If it is desired to impose protective trusts, substitute the following in clause (i) above*: and to hold the income of the same upon protective trusts for the benefit of A. during his life.[4]]

1   See paras **[210.3]**, **[210.4]** and **[214.64]** for inheritance tax and pecuniary legacies. These words are unnecessary if there is a general direction covering inheritance such as Forms B14.33 at para **[214.76]** or B14.34 at para **[214.77]** or the legacy will be payable wholly out of UK free estate.

2   Illegitimate and legitimated children will now be included; see Part A, paras **[200.28]** and **[200.29]**.

3   Where the income was given until marriage and upon marriage settled on the beneficiary and her children and in fact the beneficiary never married, the capital on the death of the beneficiary fell into residue: *Re Henry Will Trust, Mussett v Smith* [1953] 1 All ER 531, [1953] 1 WLR 376.

4   For the inheritance tax treatment of protective trusts, see Part A, para **[200.116]**. For TA 1925, s 33, which defines protective trusts, see Part G, para **[246.28]**.

[216.31]

FORM B16.26:   Settled legacy—full form

I.   FORM INCORPORATING STATUTORY WILL FORM

I give to [*legatee*] the sum of £—— [free of inheritance tax and foreign death duties[1]] and I declare that Form 7 of the Statutory Will Forms 1925 is incorporated in this my will and shall apply to this legacy [subject to the following modification, *add any necessary modification*].

II.   FORM SETTING OUT THE TRUSTS

I give to my trustees the sum of £—— [free of inheritance tax and foreign death duties] upon trust to invest the same in any investments hereby authorised [*or* authorised by law for the investment of trust funds] with power to vary and transpose the same and to hold such investments and the income thereof:

(a)   Upon trust to pay the income of the said investments to A. during his life and after his death;

[*or, if the life interest is to be protected*:

(a)   Upon trust to hold the income of the said investments on protective trusts for A. during his life[2]];

(b)   Upon trust if the said A. shall so direct by will to pay the income of the said investments or such part thereof as the said A. shall so direct to any wife of the said A. who shall survive him during the residue of her life or for such less period as the said A. shall so direct and subject thereto;

(c)   Upon trust as to both capital and income of the said investments for all or such one or more exclusively of the others or other of the children or remoter issue[3] of the said A. at such time and if more than one in such

1433

shares and with such provisions for maintenance advancement and otherwise for the benefit of such children or issues[3] or some or one of them at the discretion of my trustees or any other persons and generally in such manner in all respects as the said. A. shall by deed revocable or irrevocable or by will or codicil appoint And in default of and subject to any such appointment;

(d) Upon trust for all or any the children or child[3] of the said A. who shall attain the age of [eighteen] [twenty-one] years or marry under that age if more than one in equal shares as tenants in common;

(e) Provided always that no child of the said A. who or whose issue shall take by virtue of any appointment under the aforesaid power any share of the said investments shall unless the said A. so direct share in the unappointed part of the said investments without bringing the share so appointed into hotchpot and accounting therefor;

(f) If there shall be no child of the said A. who under the trust in default of appointment hereinbefore contained shall attain a vested interest in the said investments then the said investments and the income thereof and all accumulations of income shall be held upon trust for such persons and purposes and generally in such manner as the said A. shall by deed revocable or irrevocable by will or codicil appoint and subject to any such appointment;

(g) Upon trust for the next of kin of the said A. ascertained according to and in the shares provided by the law relating to intestacy as if the said A. had died intestate and a bachelor;

[(h) I hereby declare that the administrative provisions of this my will relating to residue shall apply to this legacy.]

1   See n 1 to Form B16.25 at para **[216.30]**.
2   See n 4 to Form B16.25 at para **[216.30]**.
3   Including an illegitimate child unless a contrary intention is shown: see Part A, paras **[200.28]** and **[200.29]**.

Ancillary provisions

[216.32]

FORM B16.27:   Trust for accumulation of income[1]

[Subject to the payment of the said annuity to my wife [*name*]] my trustees shall accumulate for the period of twenty-one years from the date of my death [if my wife shall so long live] the [surplus] income of my residuary estate by investing the same and the income therefrom in any investments hereby authorised with power to vary such investments as my trustees shall think fit until the termination of the said period of twenty-one years [or until the death of my wife whichever shall first happen] and shall then hold the accumulated fund as capital of my residuary estate but so that no part of such fund shall be invested in the purchase of land.

1   The periods allowed for accumulation are stated in the LPA 1925, s 164 (Part G, para **[246.42]**) and the PAA 1964, s 13 (Part G, para **[246.71]**). This clause assumes that the income of the

residuary estate is more than sufficient to maintain the widow and children and provides for the accumulation of the surplus income in order to provide more capital for the children.

For the taxation of accumulated income see paras **[218.28]–[218.30]**.

This clause could be unsatisfactory for inheritance tax reasons. Part of the residuary estate will be treated as subject to the annuitant's interest in possession (see the Preliminary Note to B11 at para **[211.1]** et seq) and the remainder will be taxed as a discretionary trust (see para **[218.8]** et seq).

[216.33]

FORM B16.28:   Payment of income to banker[1]

My trustees may and if any beneficiary entitled hereunder to receive any income so requests them in writing shall pay such income to any banker to be chosen from time to time by such beneficiary to be held by such banker for the account of such beneficiary and my trustees shall not be liable for any loss arising from payment so made but my trustees may from time to time if they think fit disregard in whole or in part any such request by such a beneficiary with respect to any income subject to a provision for forfeiture on alienation or to a discretionary trust or if at any time my trustees should not be satisfied as to the continued existence of such beneficiary.

1   This clause may be helpful on occasion, but in general this will be a matter for arrangement between the beneficiary and the trustees where the beneficiary is absolutely entitled to the income.

[216.34]

FORM B16.29:   Clause as to annual sums payable under an insurance policy[1]

I declare that the annual sums payable to my estate under a policy of insurance issued by —— and numbered —— shall [during the widowhood of my wife] be treated when received as income of my estate [and paid to my widow accordingly].

1   Insurance policies now often provide for the payment of a lump sum on death followed by an annual payment for a number of years and then, on the cesser of such payments, a final lump sum. These annual payments have been held to be capital of the testator's estate: *Re Fisher, Harris v Fisher* [1943] Ch 377, [1943] 2 All ER 615, and it therefore becomes necessary to include a clause such as this if such payments are to be treated as income. The same rule was applied where a testator was entitled to receive a percentage of the net profits of a business for some years after his death: see *Re Payne, Westminster Bank Ltd v Payne* [1943] 2 All ER 675. This clause is only necessary where the will gives a life interest. The wording here assumes that the will gives the income of the residuary estate to the widow during her widowhood. The wording must be adapted where the wife's interest is not restricted to widowhood and can be used where some person other than the wife takes a life interest in residue. It should be noted, however, that such sums may be taxable as income in the hands of the widow.

[216.35]

FORM B16.30:   No apportionment on death of life tenant[1]

I declare that the personal representatives of any person who under the trusts thereof is life tenant of any property shall not be entitled to receive any part of any dividends rents interest royalties or moneys of the nature of income which shall be actually received in respect of such property after the death of such life tenant, notwithstanding that the same be paid in respect of a period wholly or partly prior to the death of such life tenant; but the same when received shall belong to the person or persons who under the said trusts would have been entitled thereto if the same had been paid in respect of a period immediately subsequent to the death of such life tenant.

1   It seems that the general rule is that apart from express provision no apportionment is proper where shares are sold cum dividend on the death of the life tenant: see *Re Firth, Sykes v Ball* [1938] Ch 517, [1938] 2 All ER 217; distinguishing *Re Winterstoke's Will Trusts, Gunn v Richardson* [1938] Ch 158, [1937] 4 All ER 63. When, however, the shares are appropriated to beneficiaries in satisfaction of their interests on the death of the life tenant, an apportionment under the Apportionment Act 1870 is proper: *Re Henderson, Public Trustee v Reddie* [1940] Ch 368, [1940] 1 All ER 623, where the position is discussed and all the authorities considered. See Form B14.32 at para **[214.54]** for a shorter and more general form. See also the Note to B14 at paras **[214.48]–[214.52]** concerning the Apportionment Acts and their exclusion.

B17 Trusts for children

GIFTS OF LAND

FORMS

DECLARATIONS CONCERNING HOTCHPOT

FORMS

PRELIMINARY NOTE

[217.1]

Accumulation and maintenance trusts. The introduction of capital transfer tax, now inheritance tax, gave a new importance to trusts for children. If they satisfy the requirements the Inheritance Tax Act 1984 (ITA 1984), s 71 (for which see Part A, para **[200.119]** et seq) important advantages are conferred. Trusts which do satisfy these requirements are commonly known as accumulation and maintenance trusts. The requirements of s 71 relate both to the trusts of capital (sub-s (1)(a)) and the trusts of income (sub-s (1)(b)). This section of this book is principally concerned with the former, and the latter are considered at para **[200.129]** et seq and paras **[218.41]** et seq. The forms in this section are thought to satisfy s 71(1)(a) unless the contrary is stated, but it should be remembered that there must be at least one member of the class of beneficiaries already in existence at the testator's or life tenant's death (see para **[230.50]**). For complete forms of wills taking account of s 71 see eg Forms C2.2 at para **[224.35]** and C8.4 at para **[230.45]** et seq.

Where land which is available and suitable for occupation is held on accumulation and maintenance trusts, the statutory right of occupation of the Trusts of Land and Appointment of Trustees Act 1996 (TLATA 1996), s 12 can create a difficulty for trust administration and the tax effectiveness of the trust: see para **[208.15]** and Form B17.35 at para **[217.40]**.

[217.2]

Substitution. When trusts for the testator's children or remoter issue are being drafted it should be remembered that the new s 33 of the Wills Act 1837 (WA 1837) (substituted by the AJA 1982, s 19: Part G, para **[244.34]**) provides a statutory substitution clause in some circumstances, even in relation to class gifts: see Vol 1, para **[47.14]** et seq. The substitutional provisions for class gifts are of such uncertain application to the more common kinds of class gift that we recommend that express provision is made for substitution, or that s 33 is expressly excluded. Also, they can only apply where a child or remoter descendant of the testator predeceases him, and will not operate to substitute issue of someone who survives the testator but dies before attaining some age upon the attaining of which the gift is contingent. Express substitutional clauses can and should be made to apply in whatever circumstances a primary gift fails.

[217.3]

Perpetuities. When drafting trusts for children and issue care must be taken that they do not infringe the rule against perpetuities, see the Preliminary Note to B16 at paras **[216.2]** and **[216.3]** and for a fuller account of perpetuities, see Vol 1, para **[94.1]** et seq.

[217.4]

Vesting. If a gift to a minor is absolutely vested as from the testator's death, it now seems that in contrast to the position in the past when trustees (in the absence of an express provision to the contrary) in order to get a sufficient discharge had to retain the gift until the minor was of full age and able to give a good receipt, a person with parental responsibility for a minor can receive the gift on the minor's behalf: ChA 1989, s 3(3) (Part G, para **[244.119]**), which came into force on 14 October 1991 and Vol 1, para **[9.41]**.

For some considerations as to whether a gift to children should be made contingent upon their attaining a certain age or being living at a specified time, see the Preliminary Note to B16 at paras **[216.4]** and **[216.5]**.

[217.5]
Meaning of children and issue. When drafting a trust for a class of children, whether the testator's or someone else's, the testator should be asked to confirm that he wishes illegitimate, legitimated and adopted children and issue to be included because references to children and issue in wills will be construed as including such persons unless a contrary intention is expressed. For wills made after 3 April 1988 the inclusion of illegitimate issue and children will be by virtue of the Family Law Reform Act 1987 (FLRA 1987), ss 1 and 19 (Part G, paras **[245.70]** and **[245.72]**). (For wills made prior to that and after 1 January 1970, see the Family Law Reform Act 1969 (FLRA 1969), s 15(1): Part G, para **[245.39]**.) The inclusion of adopted children and issue is by virtue of the Adoption Act 1976 (AA 1976), ss 39 and 42, replacing (by way of consolidation) Children Act 1975, Sch 1, paras 3 and 5 as from 1 January 1976, and brought into force on 1 January 1988. The Human Fertilisation and Embryology Act 1990 (HFEA 1990), as from 1 August 1991, also affects the meaning of 'children' and 'issue' in some circumstances (see Part G, para **[245.82]** et seq). See generally Vol 1, Chs 71 to 76 for the meaning of the terms 'children' and 'issue'.

[217.6]

FORM B17.1:   Trust for children at twenty-five with substitutional trusts for those who die in testator's lifetime or after testator's death

In trust for such of my children as attain the age of twenty-five years and if more than one in equal shares absolutely provided always that if any child of mine shall die or has already died in my lifetime or shall die after my death under the age of twenty-five years leaving a child or children living at my death or born thereafter who attains or attain the age of twenty-one years then the share which such child of mine would have taken had such child survived me and obtained a vested interest in such share shall be held in trust for such child or children as aforesaid of such child of mine and if more than one in equal shares.

[217.7]

FORM B17.2:   Trust for children or issue as life tenant shall appoint: variation where there is a joint power of appointment[1]

In trust for all or such one or more exclusively of the others or other of the children or remoter issue[2] of the said —— [and ——] at such time and if more than one in such shares and with such provisions for maintenance advancement and otherwise for the benefit of such children or issue or some or one of them at the discretion of my trustees or any other persons and with such gifts over and generally in such manner as the said —— [and —— shall by deed revocable or irrevocable jointly appoint and in default of and subject to any such appointment as the survivor of them] shall by deed revocable or irrevocable or by will or codicil appoint and subject to any such appointment in trust for the child or children of the said —— [and ——] who shall attain the age of [eighteen] [twenty-one] years or [being female] previously marry and if more than one in equal shares as tenants in common provided that if any child of the said —— [and ——] dies in the lifetime of —— [*or* before the death of the survivor of —— and ——] leaving issue living at the death of [the survivor of —— and] —— then such issue if and when they attain the age of [eighteen] [twenty-one] years or marry thereunder shall take by substitution and if more than one in equal shares per stirpes the share of my residuary estate which such child would have taken had he or she survived [the survivor of —— and] —— but so that no issue shall take whose parent is alive and so capable of taking.

Any child who or whose issue take any interest under the foregoing provision in default of appointment shall not take such interest in default of appointment without bringing into hotchpot any share or shares appointed to him or her or his or her issue and accounting for the same unless the appointment shall direct to the contrary.

1   Though it may be more common to give the capital of the residue to children equally, it is certainly a wise precaution, where there is a life interest given to a wife, that she should be given a power of appointment, for this enables the division of the estate to be considered at the last possible moment. By this means those who have prospered or married well may be given less than those who have suffered misfortune and all inequalities of fortune may be compensated for to a great extent. *Class gifts* – The 'rules of convenience' are fully stated in Vol 1 at para **[66.1]** et seq.
2   Illegitimate children and issue will be objects of the power: see Vol 1, para **[72.14]**.

[217.8]

FORM B17.3:   **Trust for children at eighteen, with alternative contingency of previous marriage with consent of guardians**

In trust for my children[1] who [being male] attain the age of eighteen years or [being female either attain that age or[2]] marry under that age with the consent (if marrying after my death) of their [his] or her guardians or guardian[3] and if more than one in equal shares as tenants in common[4] provided always that if any child of mine shall die or has already died in my lifetime or shall die after my death without obtaining a vested interest leaving a child or children living at my death or born thereafter who attains or attain the age of eighteen years then the share which such child of mine would have taken had such child survived me and obtained a vested interest in such share shall be held in trust for such child or children as aforesaid of such child of mine and if more than one in equal shares.

1   Illegitimate children may share: see para **[217.7]**, n 2.
2   A child or daughter (as the case may be) who marries without the necessary consent will nevertheless attain a vested interest on attaining her majority. If the guardians die before the marriage, the law dispenses with their consent (*Dawson v Oliver-Massey* (1876) 2 Ch D 753).
3   A person under 18 who is not a widow or widower cannot marry without the consent of parents or guardians, though, if such consent is refused, it may be given by the court: see the Marriage Act 1949, ss 3 and 78(1) (27 *Halsbury's Statutes* (4th edn) (2000 Reissue) 622), as amended by the FLRA 1969, s 2(1). In the case of marriage after banns the marriage may be celebrated provided such persons do not dissent. To satisfy the clause consent is required though it may be presumed from conduct, see Vol 1, paras **[35.9]**–**[35.17]**.

4   If it is desired to substitute a higher age as the age contingency then the words 'under the age of
     eighteen years' should be added to the words in brackets 'if marrying after my death', since it is
     only in such a case that consent to a marriage will be required. If the sons and daughters are to
     be put on a level as regards marriage under eighteen, omit the first two parts in square brackets
     and include the third. This used not to be the usual practice, but was adopted in the statutory
     trusts for issue of an intestate (AEA 1925, s 47(1): Part G, para **[244.61]**) and now the desire to
     make no distinction between the sexes is almost invariable.

[217.9]

**FORM B17.4:   Trust for children; sons at twenty-five or on marriage after
twenty-one, and daughters at twenty-one or on previous marriage**

In trust for my children[1] living at my death who being male attain the age of
twenty-five years or marry under that age but over the age of twenty-one years
or being female attain the age of twenty-one years or marry under that age if
more than one in equal shares as tenants in common.[2]

1   Illegitimate and legitimated children will be eligible: see Part A, para **[200.28]** et seq.
2   It should be borne in mind that although the WA 1837, s 33 (as substituted by the AJA 1982,
     s 19: Part G, para **[24.34]**) can apply to a class gift, its application to contingent class gifts
     where a member of the class predeceases the testator is unclear, and it cannot apply where a
     member of the class survives the testator but dies without having attained a vested interest (see
     Vol 1, para **[47.14]** et seq). An express substitution clause should be included, such as in Forms
     B17.7 or B17.9 at paras **[217.12]**, **[217.14]**. Gifts to the testator's own children can of course be
     made to vest at any age, for the children are all 'lives in being.' For a clause where the children
     of a person other than the testator are to take, see Form B17.8 at para **[217.13]**. Testators should
     be warned that it is possible to defeat this clause so far as it postpones vesting until twenty-five,
     for a son could raise money on his interest by mortgaging it with the usual insurance policy. It
     may be preferable to settle the share and give trustees a power to determine the settlement on
     the son attaining twenty-five.

[217.10]

**FORM B17.5:   Trust for children at twenty-one by settling each child's
share and giving trustees power to pay or apply capital in favour of life
tenant[1]**

In trust for my children[2] living at my death who attain the age of twenty-one
years or marry thereunder if more than one in equal shares.
    Provided that the share of my residuary trust fund so given to every child of
mine who shall survive me and attain twenty-one years or marry shall not vest
absolutely in such child but shall be retained by my trustees upon the following
trusts:

  (i)   The income of such share shall be paid to such child during his or her
        life.
  (ii) Provided that my trustees shall have power in their absolute discretion
        from time to time during the life of such child after such child shall have
        attained the age of twenty-one years to pay transfer or apply to or for the
        benefit of such child the whole or any part or parts of the capital of such
        share freed and discharged from the trusts and powers hereof.
  (iii) Subject as aforesaid such share and the income thereof shall be held upon
        trust for such one or more of his or her issue[3] immediate or remote as he

1442

or she may by deed with or without power of revocation and new appointment or by will or codicil appoint.

(iv) In default of such appointment and in so far as any such appointment shall not extend and subject to the foregoing trusts and powers such share shall be held for all the children or the child of such child of mine who attain the age of twenty-one years or marry thereunder if more than one as tenants in common in equal shares provided that no such child shall take in default of appointment without bringing into hotchpot any part of such share my child may have appointed in his or her favour or in favour of his or her issue under the power in that behalf hereinbefore contained unless my child making such appointment shall direct to the contrary.

1   This may seem an involved provision but its purpose is to prevent a child raising money on the share contingent on attaining twenty-five years of age by mortgaging such share together with a policy of insurance against death before the share vests. It has the further advantage that, if on the child's attaining twenty years of age the trustees are convinced that the child is likely to waste the share coming to him, they can refuse to exercise their discretion and leave him with only the life interest. This may be of value where the child has married and has children.

2   Illegitimate and legitimated children will be eligible: see Part A, para **[200.28]**.

3   Illegitimate issue may take: see Part A, para **[200.28]**.

[217.11]

FORM B17.6:   Trust for children of a person who takes no life interest

In trust for all the children[1] of [*name*] [whenever born during the lifetime of [*name of parent*][2]] who attain the age of [eighteen] [twenty-one] years [or being female marry under that age] if more than one in equal shares as tenants in common.

1   See n 2 to Form B17.4 at para **[217.9]**. Illegitimate issue may take: see Part A, para **[200.29]**.

2   See Vol 1, para **[66.1]** et seq, on gifts to a class. If the gift is to children of a person who is not life tenant and the class is definitely extended to *all* his children, distribution will be delayed until his death, for until then the number cannot be ascertained. Where there is a life interest, words such as 'born or to be born' are referred to birth before the death of the life tenant and do not further extend the class (*Mogg v Mogg* (1815) 1 Mer 654), and so with 'all and every the children' (*Andrews v Partington* (1791) 3 Bro CC 401). If the class is to remain open indefinitely there should be a power of advancement exercisable over the whole of a presumptive share (see Form B18.20 at para **[218.104]**), so that the trusts can be terminated when it becomes reasonably certain that no more members of the class will be born.

[217.12]

FORM B17.7:   Trust for children of testator, including children dying in testator's lifetime leaving issue[1]

In trust for my children living at my death who attain the age of [eighteen] [twenty-one] years or die under that age leaving issue and for any children of mine who may have died in my lifetime whether before or after the date hereof leaving issue living at my death or then en ventre but born afterwards if more than one in equal shares as tenants in common but so that the share of any child of mine dying in my lifetime shall pass to his or her personal representatives as part of such child's estate as if such child had survived me.[2]

Part B   Clauses in wills

1   See n 2 to Form B17.4 at para **[217.9]**. Illegitimate issue may take: see Part A, para **[200.28]**.
2   It must be remembered that a share thus passing to the representatives of a deceased child
     becomes liable to the payment of the debts of that child. A direct gift to the child's issue may
     therefore in certain cases be more expedient. Forms B17.9 and B17.12 at paras **[217.14]** and
     [217.17] or Form B19.11 at para **[219.24]** may be used to prevent the share becoming available
     to satisfy the debts of a deceased child. Children of a deceased parent taking in substitution do
     not bring into account a debt owing by the deceased parent to the testator (*Re Binns, Public
     Trustee v Ingle* [1929] 1 Ch 677, [1929] All ER Rep 542). See also n 1 to Form B17.8 at
     para **[217.13]**.

[217.13]

FORM B17.8:   Trust for children of another, including children dying in testator's lifetime leaving issue[1]

In trust for the children of [*name*] living at my death or born afterwards who
attain the age of [eighteen] [twenty-one] years or die under that age leaving issue
and any children of the said [*name*] who may have died in my lifetime whether
before or after the date hereof leaving issue living at my death or then en ventre
but born afterwards if more than one in equal shares as tenants in common but
so that the share of any child of the said [*name*] dying in my lifetime shall pass
to his or her personal representatives as part of such child's estate and as if such
child had survived me.[2]

1   Illegitimate issue may take: see Part A, para **[200.28]**.
2   See n 2 to Form B17.7 at para **[217.12]**.

[217.14]

FORM B17.9:   Trust for children of testator living at his decease and issue of deceased children then living at eighteen or twenty-one or on previous marriage[1]

In trust in equal shares (if more than one) for all my children living at my and
for all or any of the issue living at my death who attain the age of [eighteen]
[twenty-one] years or marry under that age of any child of mine who
predeceases me or has already predeceased me leaving issue living at my death,
such issue to take through all degrees according to their stocks in equal shares (if
more than one) the share which their parent would have taken if living at my
death and so that no issue shall take whose parent is living at my death and so
capable of taking.

1   Illegitimate children and issue may take: see Part A, para **[200.28]**.

[217.15]

FORM B17.10:   The same by reference to the statutory trusts for issue[1]

Upon the same statutory trusts for my issue as if I had died possessed thereof
domiciled in England and intestate and without leaving a wife me surviving.[2]

1   Illegitimate children and issue may take: see Part A, para **[200.28]**.
2   See the statutory trusts of the AA 1976, s 47. The trusts give a vested interest not only to a
     female marrying under eighteen but also to a male marrying under that age. For deaths on or

after 1 January 1996 the trusts no longer provide for the bringing into hotchpot of money or property, etc, paid or settled or advanced or covenanted to be paid or settled to or on a child (see Vol 1, para **[104.7]**). If this is not desired, the following words excluding hotchpot should be added: 'Provided that the said statutory trusts shall apply as if the former s 47(1)(iii) of the AA 1976 (advances, gifts on marriage etc to be taken into hotchpot) had not been repealed'.

[217.16]

FORM B17.11: Trust for children at discretion of trustees until the youngest attains eighteen or twenty-one years of age[1]

Until my youngest surviving child shall attain the age of [eighteen] [twenty-one] years my trustees may at their absolute discretion apply the income of my residuary trust fund [*or as the case may be*] to or for the maintenance education and support or otherwise for the benefit of all or any to the exclusion of the others or other of my children for the time being living in such shares and manner as the trustee shall think fit with power to pay such income to and to accept the receipt of the guardian or guardians of my said children and shall accumulate as an accretion to the capital of the said fund for all purposes the balance of such income and upon the youngest surviving child[2] attaining the age of [eighteen] [twenty-one] years my trustees shall hold the said fund and the income thereof in trust for my said children in equal shares absolutely.

1 Illegitimate children and issue as well as children and issue adopted at any time will prima facie be eligible; see Part A, para **[200.28]**.
2 Where it is important that the trusts should satisfy the ITA 1984, s 71 (see Part A, para **[200.119]** et seq) this is not a very good form to use. If the eldest child will be over 25 when the youngest attains the age of vesting s 71 will clearly not be satisfied. But where the ages are sufficiently close together so that the oldest will not attain the age of 25 before the youngest attains the age of contingency, the Inland Revenue may accept that it satisfies s 71 (particularly in view of the liberal view now taken of 'specified age': see the Note in B18 at para **[200.122]**).

[217.17]

FORM B17.12: Remainder trust for children and issue of deceased children of life tenant at eighteen or twenty-one or on previous marriage[1]

In trust in equal shares (if more than one) for all or any the children or child of [*life tenant*] living at the date of the death of the survivor of myself and the said [*life tenant*] who attain the age of [eighteen] [twenty-one] years or marry under that age and for all or any of the issue living at the said date who attain the age of [eighteen] [twenty-one] years or marry under that age of any child of the said [*life tenant*] who dies before the said date or is already dead leaving issue living at the said date such issue to take through all degrees according to their stocks in equal shares (if more than one) the share which their parent would have taken if living at the said date and so that no issue shall take whose parent is living at the said date and so capable of taking.

1 Illegitimate children and issue as well as children and issue adopted at any time will prima facie be eligible; see Part A, para **[200.28]**. The possible inheritance tax disadvantages of a substitution clause for issue mentioned at para **[200.131]** is not relevant here because the substitution clause cannot have effect at any time after the death of the life tenant.

[217.18]

FORM B17.13:   The same by reference to the statutory trusts for issue

Upon the same statutory trusts for the issue of [*life tenant*] as if he had died at the date of the death of the survivor of himself and myself possessed thereof domiciled in England and intestate and without leaving a wife him surviving.[1]

1   Illegitimate children and issue may take: see Part A, para **[200.28]**. See n 2 to Form B17.10 at para **[217.15]** and n 1 to Form B17.12 at para **[217.17]**. As to the ascertainment of a class of next of kin at an artificial point in time, not being the date of the testator's death, see *Hutchinson v National Refugee for Homeless and Destitute Children* [1920] AC 795, [1920] All ER Rep 701 and Vol 1, paras **[77.2]** and **[77.3]**. In the absence of a contrary intention in a will the class will be ascertained at the testator's death, see *Gundry v Pinniger* (1852) 1 De GM & G 502.

[217.19]

FORM B17.14:   Trust for children of another person who attain twenty-five within the limits of the rule against perpetuities[1]

In trust for the children of [*name*] born in my lifetime or after my death[2] who before the expiration of the period of twenty-one years from the death of the survivor of myself and the said [*name*] attain the age of twenty-five years or marry under that age or are living but under the said age and unmarried at the expiration of such period if more than one in equal shares as tenants in common.

1   As to the construction of children and issue see Part A, para **[200.28]**.
2   The words 'after my death' extend the trust to children whenever born.

[217.20]

FORM B17.15:   Trust for children with entitlement to income during minority[1]

In trust for my children who attain the age of [eighteen] [twenty-one years] if more than one in equal shares absolutely and I declare that section 31 of the Trustee Act 1925 shall apply hereto as if in subsection (2) thereof the words 'as follows:– ' and paragraphs (i) and (ii) were replaced by the words 'upon trust for that person absolutely'.

1   If this form is used, the modification to the Trustee Act 1925 (TA 1925), s 31 (see paras **[218.51]**–**[218.54]** and Part G, para **[246.26]**) that any accumulations of income made by the trustees during a minority should belong to the minor absolutely, will mean that a child will be regarded by the Inland Revenue as having an interest in possession during his or her minority. Therefore, these trusts will not be accumulation and maintenance trusts within the ITA 1984, s 71 (considered in Part A, para **[200.119]** et seq). There is a possible advantage over accumulation and maintenance trusts in that income will not be taxed in accordance with the Income and Corporation Taxes Act 1988 (see paras **[218.28]**–**[218.30]**) but at the beneficiary's own rate of tax (which rate may well only be the lower or basic rate of tax depending upon the size of the fund) with his or her exemptions. However, there will be no hold-over relief in respect of any capital gains tax charge which arises when a beneficiary becomes absolutely entitled to his share of the settled property as would be available under the TCGA 1992, s 260(2)(d) (see para **[200.135]**) if the trusts were accumulation and maintenance trusts up to the time of the absolute entitlement. There may be an inheritance tax disadvantage in that there may be an inheritance tax charge if a beneficiary dies while entitled to an interest in possession,

although this will depend upon the size of the fund and whether or not it comes within the nil-rate inheritance tax threshold according to the beneficiary's circumstances.

[217.21]

FORM B17.16:   **Gift to children absolutely**[1]

In trust for my children living at my death if more than one in equal shares absolutely.

1   Like the previous form, this form will mean that a child will be regarded by the Inland Revenue as having an interest in possession during his or her minority. The same income tax and inheritance considerations will apply, but capital gains will be taxed at the beneficiary's own rate with his or her own personal exemption. A person with parental responsibility for a minor can now receive an absolute gift to a minor on the minor's behalf: ChA 1989, s 3(3) (Part G, para **[244.119]**), which came into force on 14 October 1991.

[217.22]

FORM B17.17:   **Trusts for children, sons taking double shares**[1]

In trust for my children who attain the age of [eighteen] [twenty-one] years or marry under that age if more than one as tenants in common in equal shares except that each son of mine entitled under this bequest shall take a share double the amount of the share of each daughter of mine [*or* except that my son [*name*] if he survives me and attains the age of [eighteen] [twenty-one] years shall take a share double the amount of the share of each of his brothers and sisters].

1   As to the construction of children and issue see Part A, para **[200.28]**.

[217.23]

FORM B17.18:   **Trusts for various persons unequally**[1]

In trust to divide the [trust] [said] fund into —— equal shares (and the words share or shares in this clause shall be always read as referring to such equal shares) and to hold —— shares in trust for [*name*] and if he shall die in my lifetime then in trust for such of his children who shall be living at my death who being male attain the age of [eighteen] [twenty-one] years or attain that age or marry and if there be more than one such child equally between them. And to hold —— shares in trust for [*name*] etc [*as above and continuing until all the shares are allotted*] Provided that if any of the trusts declared by this clause shall lapse or fail then the share or shares as to which the said trusts shall so lapse or fail (including any share or shares accruing by virtue of this provision) shall accrue to and be added equally to the other shares hereby given and be held in trust accordingly.

1   See also Form B15.5 at para **[215.5]**. As to the construction of children and issue see Part A, para **[200.28]**. The effect of this clause may be shown by a simple example. In the case of three nephews who are to take the fund thus: A taking 1/2, B1/3, and C1/6, it is clear that there must be 12 shares, of which A will take six, B will take four, and C will take two. As the word 'share' throughout refers to such equal twelfth part, if A's interest fails, then his six shares are added equally to the remaining six shares, so that B will still receive twice as much as C. For problems which can arise where residue is divided into fractional shares and some of the

beneficiaries are exempt from inheritance tax see the Note to B14 at para **[214.72]** and Form B14.35 at para **[214.78]**.

[217.24]

FORM B17.19:   **Trust for children in unequal shares**

In trust as to two equal sixth parts for my son [*name*] absolutely as to one other equal sixth part for my son [*name*] if and when he attains the age of [eighteen] [twenty-one] years and as to the remaining three equal sixth parts in trust in equal shares for my grandchildren —— and —— if and when they shall respectively attain the age of [eighteen] [twenty-one] years or marry under that age¹ [*add gift over of shares which fail to vest*].

1   A contingent gift of residuary personal estate has long since been held to carry the intermediate income. As to other gifts which now carry the intermediate income, see the LPA 1925, s 175 (Part G, para **[244.52]**). As to the statutory power of maintenance, see the TA 1925, s 31 (Part G, para **[246.26]**) and notes to B18 at para **[218.41]** et seq.

[217.25]

FORM B17.20:   **Gift to class of children with one child having the option to have assets appropriated in satisfaction of his share**

(i)   My trustees shall hold my residuary estate in trust for my children living at my death if more than one in equal shares absolutely.

(ii)   Provided that my trustees shall as soon as conveniently may be after my death give to my son [*name*] notice in writing of the option to have shares in the —— Company Limited which form part of my estate ('the Company Shares') to the value of his share of my residuary estate appropriated to him in satisfaction of his share of my residuary estate and [also the option to purchase such of the Company Shares not so appropriated at a price equivalent to their value] *or* [if the value of the Company Shares should exceed the value of my son's share of my residuary estate I give so many of the Company Shares as exceed that value to my son absolutely and the shares of my other children in my residuary estate shall abate equally amongst themselves by that excess value].

(iii)   The value of the Company Shares for the purposes of this clause shall be determined by an accountant nominated by my trustees as on the day of my death.

(iv)   I declare that my said son shall have one month from the date of receipt of such notice in which to exercise the option but no purchaser of the said shares shall be in any way affected by the terms of this clause.

[217.26]

FORM B17.21:   **'Peg life' trust¹**

In trust for such of [*name*] and the children of —— as attain the age of 25 years if more than one in equal shares provided that if the said [*name*] and any one or more of the children of —— shall attain the said age of 25 years such children or child of —— shall take (if more than one equally between them as tenants in common) a ninety-nine per cent share and the said [*name*] shall take a one per cent share.

1   The purpose of this type of trust is to create trusts which satisfy the ITA 1984, s 71 (see Part A, para **[200.119]** et seq) where none of the persons primarily intended to benefit has yet been born (see para **[200.122]**). If the 'peg life' does not have a grandparent in common with the primary beneficiaries the trust will only have the benefit of s 71 for 25 years from the testator's death, and it will be imperative for there to be a power of advancement exercisable over the whole of a presumptive share, so that absolute interests or interests in possession can be created if such interests have not been attained by the time the 25-year period is about to expire. Extended accumulation and maintenance provisions will also be an advantage (see the Note to B18 at paras **[218.72]**–**[218.76]**).

[217.27]

FORM B17.22:   Trust for children, in definite sums

In trust as to £[1000] or investments of that value for my daughter [*name*] if and when she attains the age of [eighteen] [twenty-one] years or marries under that age and as to £[1000] or investments of that value for my daughter [*name*] if and when she attains the age of [eighteen] [twenty-one] years or marries under that age and as to the residue (if any) for my son [*name*] absolutely.[1]

1   See n 1 to Form B17.19 at para **[217.24]**. The gift will carry the intermediate income, the beneficiaries being children of the testator. Such income will be available for maintenance purposes until the beneficiary attains majority. See the Note in B18 at paras **[218.55]**–**[218.59]** generally for what interests carry intermediate income.

[217.28]

FORM B17.23:   Trust for children other than a child who becomes entitled to settled estates[1]

In trust for the children of [*name*] who attain the age of [eighteen] [twenty-one] years or being female marry under that age if more than one in equal shares as tenants in common (other than and except any son or sons of the said [*name*] who on or before attaining the age of [eighteen] [twenty-one] years or any daughter or daughters of the said [*name*] who on or before attaining that age or marrying shall become entitled as tenant in tail [*or* in tail male] in possession or in remainder immediately expectant upon the determination of a life interest in possession to the —— Estates settled by etc *or* devised by etc) and if there shall be no child (other than and except as aforesaid) who shall attain the age of [eighteen] [twenty-one] years or being female shall marry under that age then in trust for such of the excepted children as attain the age of [eighteen] [twenty-one] years or being female marry under that age if more than one in equal shares.

1   If this form is used, and the age of vesting is greater than 18 years, accumulation and maintenance trusts of income should continue until the age of vesting (but not of course to an age greater than 25 or longer than a period of accumulation permitted by law), otherwise the termination of an interest in possession would be treated as a potentially exempt transfer for inheritance tax purposes (under the ITA 1984, ss 3A and 52(1)) where one of the beneficiaries comes to be within the exception after becoming entitled to be paid the income of his presumptive share. See Forms B18.11 to B18.13 at paras **[218.77]**–**[218.79]** for extended

accumulation and maintenance provisions. See also B18 at paras **[218.72]**–**[218.76]** on the advantages of extended accumulation and maintenance provisions.

[217.29]

FORM B17.24:   **Trust for two persons as tenants in common on attaining twenty-five, with a gift over on the death of either to the other of them**

In trust for [*name*] and [*name*] if and when they shall respectively attain the age of twenty-five years in equal shares as tenants in common and in case either of them is already dead or shall die in my lifetime or before attaining the age of twenty-five years I bequeath the share [of residue] hereinbefore bequeathed to the one so dying to the other of them if and when [he] shall attain the age of twenty-five years.

[217.30]

FORM B17.25:   **Trust for wife and children equally**[1]

In trust for such of my wife [*name*] and my children as survive me in equal shares as tenants in common.

1   All children alive at the testator's death will take. As to the construction of the word 'children', see Part A, para **[200.28]**. The gift to the wife is exempt from inheritance tax, the gifts to the children are not. For the problems this could cause see the Note to B14 at para **[214.72]** et seq and for a declaration to deal with the problem see Form B14.35 at para **[214.78]**.

[217.31]

FORM B17.26:   **Trust after life interest to a wife for nephews and nieces as wife shall appoint, and in default of appointment equally**[1]

In trust for all or any one or more exclusively of the others or other of my nephews and nieces children of my [deceased] brothers or sisters in such shares and generally in such manner as my wife shall by deed revocable or irrevocable or by will or codicil appoint and subject to any such appointment in trust for all my said nephews or nieces living at my death [*or* the death of my wife] if more than one in equal shares as tenants in common.

1   Nephews and nieces should always be carefully defined otherwise relations by marriage or even great-nephews and great-nieces may make a claim. As to the meaning of nephews and nieces, see Vol 1, para **[71.5]**.

[217.32]

FORM B17.27:   **Trust for brothers and sisters and children of deceased brothers and sisters**[1]

In trust for my brothers and sisters living at my death and the children then living of any then deceased brother or sister of mine who attain the age of [eighteen] [twenty-one] years or being female marry under that age if more than one in equal shares as tenants in common but so that the children of any such deceased brother or sister shall take equally between them as tenants in common only the share their parent would have taken had he or she survived me.

1   As to the construction of words describing a blood relationship, see Part A, para **[200.28]** et seq.

[217.33]

FORM B17.28:   **Trust of child's share by reference**

Upon the like trusts for the benefit of my daughter [*or* son] [*name*] and her [*or* his] children or issue and with the like gift over in favour of her [*or* his] [brothers and] sisters and their children and issue respectively as are herein-before expressed concerning the share of residue hereinbefore bequeathed for the benefit of my daughter [*or* son] [*name*] and her [*or* his] children or issue.[1]

1   This form is for use where children's shares are settled separately.

[217.34]

FORM B17.29:   **Trust of child's share by reference—another form**

Upon and subject to the same trusts powers and provisions as if clause —— of my will were herein repeated verbatim but with the substitution of the name of my daughter B. for that of my said son A. and of the word 'husband' for that of 'wife' and with the requisite change of genders.[1]

1   This form is for use where children's shares are settled separately.

[217.35]

FORM B17.30:   **Declaration excluding s 33 of the Wills Act 1837[1]**

Section 33 of the Wills Act 1837 (as substituted by section 19 of the Administration of Justice Act 1982) shall not apply to any of the foregoing trusts.

1   See the WA 1837, s 33, as substituted by the AJA 1982, s 19 (Part G, para **[244.34]**); see also Vol 1, para **[47.14]** et seq. The main use of this form would be where there is a gift to a class contingent on their attaining some specified age, and it is desired to eliminate the uncertainty as to whether and how s 33 would apply. (See Vol 1, para **[47.14]** et seq for the difficulties of applying s 33 to such a gift.)

[217.36]

FORM B17.31:   **Clause providing for forfeiture of gift on marriage to person not professing a certain religion[1]**

I hereby direct that if either[2] during my lifetime whether before or after the date of execution of this my will or after my decease any one or more of my children has or shall have married or shall marry a person who did not at the time of such marriage openly profess the —— religion then in every such case and in the case of marriage after my death as from the occurrence of such event such child or children shall absolutely forfeit and lose all interest in and right to the capital or income of any share in my residuary estate [gift hereby made] to such my child or children and the gift so forfeited shall [*add gift over*].

[But this clause shall have no operation in relation to any marriage that may have already occurred or shall hereafter in my lifetime occur and which in the uncontrolled opinion of my trustees I shall have approved at the time of marriage or shall have subsequently forgiven.]

For the purpose of deciding whether a person openly professes the —— religion my trustees shall accept a statement in writing by a priest or minister or any officer of a church of that religion and I declare that any such statement shall be final and binding upon all beneficiaries claiming under this my will.[3]

1   Such a forfeiture clause was held good in *Hodgson v Halford* (1879) 11 Ch D 959, and the decision of the House of Lords in *Clayton v Ramsden* [1943] AC 320, [1943] 1 All ER 16, which suggested that expressions referring to a particular religion are too uncertain, has been distinguished by the House of Lords in *Blathwayt v Baron Cawley* [1976] AC 397, [1975] 3 All ER 625, where a clause causing forfeiture on becoming a Roman Catholic was upheld as valid. A defining condition such as 'of the Jewish faith' without further definition of what is meant and without providing a procedure for determining whether it is broken, is at risk of being void, particularly if it is a condition subsequent, see *Re Tepper's Will Trusts* [1987] Ch 358, [1987], 1 All ER 970. If in themselves such conditions are too uncertain, it does not seem to be possible to make them certain by making the opinion of the trustees the criterion in such a case: see *Re Coxen, McCallum v Coxen* [1948] Ch 747 at 761, [1948] 2 All ER 492 at 502. The risk of the clause being void is best minimised by providing, as in the final paragraph of this form, for some kind of certification by an officer of the faith in question. Such a provision has recently been upheld as valid in *Re Tuck's Settlement Trusts, Public Trustees v Tuck* [1978] Ch 49, [1978] 1 All ER 1047, CA. The clause must be so drafted as not to interfere with the right of a parent or guardian in the exercise of his parental duty as regards the religious instruction of a child, see *Re Borwick, Borwick v Borwick* [1933] Ch 657, [1933] All ER Rep 737. See Vol 1, paras **[35.5]** and **[35.29]**.

2   There might have been a secret marriage before or after the date of the will, or the testator might have forgiven or approved a marriage. A clause of this nature may be so drawn that unintentionally the words apply only to marriage after the death of the testator, contrast *Re Evans, Hewitt v Edwards* [1940] Ch 629, with *Hodgson v Halford*.

3   It may be that in the case of some religions the proof can be much more precise, eg the person might shortly before marriage become a convert to the particular religion and have been baptised in that faith and these facts could be proved from the records of the church. See Vol 1, para **[35.29]** et seq.

[217.37]

FORM B17.32:   Child en ventre—general clause[1]

For the purposes of this my will any child en ventre at the date of my or any other death or other event referred to in my will but born alive[2] in due time[3] thereafter shall be deemed to be living at that date.

1   See generally Vol 1, paras **[73.1]** and **[73.2]** for the law relating to children en ventre.
2   A still-born child is not issue at all.
3   As to this expression, see *Re Watson, Culme-Seymour v Brand* [1930] 2 Ch 344. (It refers to the period of gestation and not to the period allowed by the perpetuity rule.)

Gifts of land

[217.38]

FORM B17.33:   Gift of land for the benefit of testator's children and issue of deceased children, sons taking at eighteen or twenty-one, daughters taking at eighteen or twenty-one or on marriage—variation for children of a person other than testator

I give my freehold lands and property at —— and known as —— to my trustees upon trust [to sell the same and to hold the net proceeds of sale both as to capital and income and the net rents and profits until sale on trust]¹ for all and every my children or child (if only one) [*or* the children or child (if only one) of —— deceased] who attain the age of [eighteen] [twenty-one] years or previously marry and if more than one in equal shares as tenants in common. Provided nevertheless that if any child of mine [*or* of the said ——] has died or shall die in my lifetime leaving issue living at my death who attain the age of [eighteen] [twenty-one] or previously marry such issue shall stand in the place of such deceased child and take per stirpes and equally between them if more than one the share of the proceeds of sale which such deceased child would have taken if he or she had survived me and attained a vested interest but so that no issue shall take whose parent is alive at my death and so capable of taking. [And provided further that the gift in this clause contained shall be construed as if section 15 (1) of the Family Law Reform Act 1969 and the Family Law Reform Act 1987 had not been enacted].²

1   A trust for sale is not strictly necessary in the light of the TLATA 1996, but may be desirable in any particular case where it is wished to emphasise that any beneficiary is entitled to a sale and the division of the proceeds of sale.
2   But for these words the references to children and issue would be deemed to include references to illegitimate children and issue: see generally Part A, para **[200.28]**. References to both statutes should be included because the FLRA 1987 repeals FLRA 1969, s 15 and so a provision which referred to the FLRA 1987 alone could be construed as a direction that the gift should be read as subject to the FLRA 1969, s 15 (Part G, para **[245.39]**). Adopted children and issue will be included by virtue of the AA 1976, ss 39 and 42. The HFEA 1990 also affects the meaning of issue in some circumstances: see Part G, para **[245.82]** et seq.

[217.39]

FORM B17.34:   Gift of land to minor with trust for sale and provision for his death under eighteen or twenty-one leaving issue¹

I give my lands at —— in the county of—— to my trustees in fee simple upon the following trusts.
    (i)   If [*minor*] shall predecease me without leaving issue living at my death [or then en ventre but born afterwards] upon trust for [*gift over*].
    (ii)   If the said [*minor*] shall predecease me leaving issue living at my death [or then en ventre but born afterwards] upon trust for such issue and if more than one in equal shares per stirpes as tenants in common but so that no issue shall take whose parent is living at my death and so capable of taking.
    (iii)   If the said [*minor*] shall be living at my death and have attained the age of [eighteen] [twenty-one] years upon trust for the said [*minor*] absolutely.

(iv)   If the said [*minor*] shall survive me but shall not at my death have attained the age of [eighteen] [twenty-one] years upon trust to apply such part or the whole of the income as my trustees shall in their uncontrolled discretion think proper for the maintenance education or benefit of the said [*minor*] and to accumulate any surplus income by way of compound interest by investing the same and the resulting income thereof from time to time in authorised investments but with power to apply any such surplus income or such accumulations or any part thereof as if they were income in the then current year until the happening of one of the following events.

(a)   If the said [*minor*] shall die under the age of [eighteen] [twenty-one] years leaving no children then surviving [or then en ventre but born afterwards] then all capital income and accumulations shall be held upon trust for *gift over*].

(b)   If the said [*minor*] shall die under the age of [eighteen] [twenty-one] years leaving children then surviving [*or* then en ventre but born afterwards] then all capital and accumulations and the income thereof (to which income section 31 of the Trustee Act 1925 as amended shall apply) shall be held upon trust for such children and if more than one in equal shares as tenants in common.

(c)   If the said [*minor*] being under [eighteen] [twenty-one] at the date of my death shall thereafter attain the age of [eighteen] [twenty-one] years then all capital income and accumulations shall be held upon trust for the said [*minor*] absolutely.

[The foregoing gift shall be construed in all respects as if section 15(1) of the Family Law Reform Act 1969 and the Family Law Reform Act 1987 had not been enacted.[2]]

1   The expressions 'issue' and 'children' in this form include illegitimate and adopted issue and children: FLRA 1987, ss 1 and 19 and AA 1976, ss 39 and 42. They will also be affected by the HFEA 1990 (Part G, para **[245.82]**). For inheritance tax purposes the ITA 1984, s 71 should apply to property held on these trusts if there is no absolute interest or interest in possession taking effect of the testator's death (for s 71 see Part A, para **[200.119]** et seq). See para **[206.4]** for gifts to minors of land.

2   The references to issue and children in this form will now be construed as including references to illegitimate issue and children unless the final words are added: see generally Part A, para **[200.28]**. References to both statutes should be included because the FLRA 1987 repeals the FLRA 1969, s 15 and so a provision which referred to the FLRA 1987 alone could be construed as a direction that the gift should be read as subject to the FLRA 1969, s 15. These references will also include children or issue by adoption, whenever the adoption occurs, see the AA 1976, ss 39 and 42. The HFEA 1990 also affects the meaning of issue in some circumstances (Part G, para **[245.82]**).

[217.40]

FORM B17.35:   Accumulation and maintenance trust of investment property

NOTE

This is a specific gift of a farm onto an accumulation and maintenance trust for the testator's grandchildren so as to fall within the ITA 1984, s 71 and where the farm is thought of as an investment property rather than one which the grandchildren or any of them might occupy (see para **[200.119]** et seq for accumulation and maintenance trusts within s 71). If the farm is not let but is farmed by a manager, there is a possibility of the grandchildren or some of them claiming a right of occupation under the TLATA 1996, s 12. Whether this really can be claimed depends on the facts and on the construction of s 12, which has its uncertainties (see para **[208.5]** et seq). There is no general power to exclude the rights of occupation under the Act, but this Form attempts to use what opportunities the Act presents to keep to a minimum the risk that rights of occupation can be claimed.

The scheme of the trusts is a primary trust for grandchildren vesting at 25 with substitution of children of any who die without attaining vested interests (sub-cl (3)), with the class of grandchildren who may take closing when the eldest attains 25. The accumulation and maintenance trusts of the income of each share extended beyond the age of 18 to the maximum age within the 21-year accumulation period from the testator's death (sub-cls (4)–(6)). The share of each grandchild is then settled on him for life with remainders to his own children, with a power to pay or apply capital of the share in his favour (sub-cl (7)), and there is an overriding power of appointment exercisable over any property in which for the time being there is an interest in possession (sub-cl (8)).

FORM

(1)   I give my freehold farm of approximately —— acres known as ——— unto my trustees [subject to any inheritance tax attributable thereto (after allowing for any reduction in value for inheritance tax purposes which is attributed thereto) payable by reason of my death][1] [and] [free of all sums charged or otherwise secured thereon at my death] upon trust to sell the same[2] and to invest the proceeds of sale in any investments hereby authorised with full power to change such investments into others hereby authorised, and to hold the proceeds of sale of the said farm and the assets from time to time representing the same (hereinafter called 'the Trust Fund') and the income thereof upon the following trusts.

(2)   For the purposes of this Clause the income of the Trust Fund includes the net rents and profits until sale of the said freehold farm, and 'the Closing Date' means the earlier to occur of the expiry of 55 years from the date of my death or the day on which the first grandchild of mine to attain the age of 25 years attains that age unless at the time of my death there is a living grandchild of mine who has already attained the age of 25 years in which case 'the Closing Date' means the date of my death.

(3)   My trustees shall hold the capital and income of the Trust Fund on trust for such of my grandchildren now living or born before the Closing Date and living at or after my death as have attained or shall attain the age of 25 years if more than one in equal shares Provided that if any grandchild of mine now living or born before the Closing Date shall predecease me or die after my death under the age of 25 years leaving a child or children living at or after my death who shall attain the age of 18 years before or on the Perpetuity Day (as hereinafter defined) or be living but under the age of 18 years on the Perpetuity Day such child or children shall take in equal shares the share of the Trust Fund

which such grandchild of mine would have taken if he or she had survived to attain a vested interest.

(4)   Section 31 of the Trustee Act 1925 (as amended by the Family Law Reform Act 1969) shall apply to the foregoing trust Provided that in relation to the presumptive share of any of my grandchildren in relation to whom the specified age (as hereinafter defined) exceeds 18 years the said section 31 (as amended as aforesaid) shall have effect as if the age of majority were the specified age (the expressions 'infant', 'infancy' and 'minority' therein being construed accordingly) and as if there were substituted the specified age for the words 'eighteen years' wherever the same occur in the said section 31 (as amended as aforesaid).

(5)   In the last preceding subclause 'the specified age' in relation to any of my said grandchildren means whichever is the lesser of:

(i)   the age which he or she will attain (if he or she so long lives) on his or her last birthday occurring not later than the expiration of 21 years from the date of my death, or

(ii)   the age of 25 years.[3]

(6)   Notwithstanding the foregoing my trustees shall have power to declare in relation to the presumptive share of any of my grandchildren in relation to whom the specified age is greater than 18 that subclause (4) above shall have effect in relation to that presumptive share as if the specified age were an age (not necessarily in whole years) stated in such deed being not less than 18 years and being less than the specified age as defined in subclause (5) above of that grandchild and also being an age which that grandchild has not attained at the time when such deed is made.[4]

(7)   The share of any of my grandchildren who attains a vested interest under the foregoing trust shall not vest in him or her but shall be retained by my trustees and held on trust to pay the income thereof to him or her during his or her life and subject thereto on trust for his or her children who attain the age of 18 years before or on the Perpetuity Day or are living but under the age of 18 years on the Perpetuity Day if more than one in equal shares absolutely, provided that:

(a)   until the Perpetuity Day my trustees shall have power at their discretion to pay or apply the whole or any part or parts of the vested or presumptive share of the Trust Fund of any grandchild of mine to him or her or for his or her benefit, but the foregoing power shall not be exercisable in favour of a grandchild of mine who is for the time being under the age of 25 years otherwise than so as to cause him or her to become immediately entitled to or to an interest in possession in the capital thereby paid or applied within the meaning of s 71(1)(a) of the Inheritance Tax Act 1984;

(b)   section 32 of the Trustee Act 1925 shall apply to any of the foregoing trusts for the children of any grandchild of mine as if the words 'one-half of' were omitted from proviso (a) to subsection (1) thereof; and

(c)   section 31 of the Trustee Act 1925 shall apply to the foregoing trusts for the children of any grandchild of mine.[5]

(8) Notwithstanding and in derogation of the foregoing trusts powers and provisions my trustees (being not fewer than two in number or a trust corporation) shall have power at any time or times and from time to time before the Perpetuity Day by deed or deeds revocable or irrevocable to appoint any part or share of the Trust Fund (up to the whole thereof) which is at the date of such exercise an appointable share (as defined below) upon trust for all or such one or more exclusive of the others or other of the discretionary beneficiaries (as defined below) if more than one in such shares and either absolutely or at such age or time or respective ages or times and with such trusts and powers for their respective benefit and such provisions as my trustees may think fit and my trustees may in exercise of the foregoing power delegate or create powers or discretions over capital or income including powers of further delegation or powers to create further powers or discretions over capital or income and create administrative powers or provisions of whatever nature provided that:

(a) no such appointment shall invalidate any payment transfer or application of capital or income previously made or any entitlement to income which has already accrued under any of the trusts or powers herein elsewhere contained;

(b) any such revocable appointment shall (so far as then unrevoked) cease to be revocable on the Perpetuity Day;

(c) 'the discretionary beneficiaries' means and includes my children and remoter issue and any spouse widow or widower of any of such children or remoter issue (and 'widow' and 'widower' shall include a widow or widower who has remarried);

(d) 'appointable share' means any part or share of the Trust Fund (up to the whole thereof) in which any beneficiary is for the time being beneficially entitled to an interest in possession within the meaning of Part III of the Inheritance Tax Act 1984 not being a part or share of the Trust Fund (up to the whole thereof) which has or would (but for this present subclause (8)) have vested indefeasibly in any person under the trusts hereinbefore declared;

(e) my trustees (being not fewer than two in number or a trust corporation) shall have power at any time or times and from time to time before the Perpetuity Day by deed or deeds to release or restrict the foregoing power either in whole or in part in any manner they think fit.[6]

(9) The perpetuity period applicable to the disposition made by this Clause shall be 80 years from the date of my death and 'the Perpetuity Day' referred to above means the day on which such period expires.

(10) Section 11(1) of the Trusts of Land and Appointment of Trustees Act 1996 (consultation with beneficiaries) shall not apply to the exercise by my trustees of any of their functions in relation to any land subject to the trusts of this Clause.[7]

(11) I declare (but not so as to impose any restriction on my trustees' powers) that all land comprised in the Trust Fund is intended to be held as investment property and is not intended for the occupation of any of the persons with a beneficial interest under the foregoing trusts and in particular I intend that any farmland in the Trust Fund which is not let to tenants should be managed by

a professional farm manager or by a company with an established farm management business.[8]

(12)   All income of the Trust Fund shall be treated as accruing on the date on which it becomes payable and there shall be no statutory apportionment of it to any other time or period.[9]

[Other powers or provisions which it may be useful to include are: administrative powers such as those in cl 9 of Form C3.1 at para **[225.19]**, *especially the power of investment in sub-cl (a), trustee indemnities and self-dealing provisions, provisions enabling powers to be exercised in favour of trustees who are beneficiaries, and a professional trustee charging clause (see eg Form C11.1, cls 7 to 9 at paras* **[233.22]–[233.24]***)].*

1   Making the gift subject to inheritance tax may be appropriate, particularly if the residuary gift is exempt and there will be inheritance tax agricultural relief on this property, and an option to pay any inheritance tax on it by interest-free instalments. For a discussion of making gifts of property which qualifies for business relief subject to inheritance tax, where the relevant factors are much the same as in relation to gifts of property qualifying for agricultural relief, see paras **[205.52]–[205.54]**.

2   A power to postpone sale is implied by the TLATA 1996, s 4. A trust for sale is provided here because it serves to emphasise that the property is held as an investment (see para **[200.56]**), and there is a possibility that an interest in possession in the proceeds of sale under a trust for sale is not an interest in possession in the land itself for the purposes of the TLATA 1996, s 12, with the consequence that it does not give rise to a right of residence, although on balance we do not share this view (see para **[200.13]**). It is quite possible that the legal consequences would be no different if there were no trust for sale, but this is not certain and its presence may make a difference.

3   Subclauses (4) and (5) extend accumulation and maintenance trusts of the income of each grandchild's share to the maximum available age in relation to that grandchild within the 21-year accumulation period from the death of the testator, while not doing so beyond the age of 25 because it is necessary for the beneficiaries to attain interests in possession no later than attaining the age of 25 for the ITA 1984, s 71 to apply. Subclauses (4) and (5) will have no effect in relation to the income of a share of a grandchild who is born three years or more after the death of the testator. See para **[218.72]** et seq for a discussion of extended accumulation and maintenance trusts of this type.

4   This is a power to vary the date on which beneficiaries attain interests in possession in their respective shares. The purpose of it is that if the ages of the eldest and youngest living members of the class are not more than seven years apart, and the eldest was aged seven or over at the testator's death, the trustees could use this power so as to cause all the living grandchildren to attain interests in possession at the same moment, and avoid the possible problems which might arise from the statutory right of occupation if there is a time when some but not all the beneficiaries have interests in possession: see paras **[208.9]** and **[208.15]**.

5   These engrafted trusts have the advantage of preventing the beneficiaries getting their hands on capital at too early an age, and have an advantage for capital gains tax purposes. If the property vested absolutely at a specified age, after a period of an interest in possession, there would be a capital gains tax charge under the TCGA 1992, s 71. Life interest trusts with a power to pay or apply capital enable the trustees to choose a good moment to distribute capital, eg when trust assets are sold and no additional capital gains tax charge will be incurred by making the beneficiary absolutely entitled to the proceeds of sale. The property in this case is agricultural land, so that there might be hold-over relief on the trust property vesting absolutely in the beneficiaries (TCGA 1992, s 165 and Sch 7), but it is possible that the original property will have been sold by the time that it does so.

6   The wide overriding power of appointment in sub-cl (8) increases flexibility, and might possibly be used to terminate a statutory right of occupation by terminating the relevant interest in possession (see para **[208.18]**). Note that proviso (d) confines it to being exercisable only over property in which there is for the time being an interest in possession. Subclause (8) can be omitted if that is preferred.

7   See Part G, para **[246.97]** for the TLATA 1996, s 11.

8   It is thought that an expression of intention of this sort is the most that can be done to exclude the statutory right of occupation, given that interests in possession of some sort are being created and that land will be comprised in the trust fund. See para **[208.18]**.

9   For exclusion of statutory apportionment see para **[214.48]** et seq.

Declarations concerning hotchpot

[217.41]

FORM B17.36:   Declaration that provisions made by will for testator's wife and children are in addition to and not in substitution for provisions made for them in his lifetime

I declare that the provisions hereby made for my wife and children [and their issue] are in addition to and not in substitution for the provisions in their favour respectively contained in my marriage settlement dated ―― [and in the settlement made by me upon the marriages of my daughters A and B] [*or as the case may be*].¹

1   In the absence of special provision a 'portion' given by will to a child will be presumed to be given in satisfaction or part satisfaction of the liability incurred by a testator in some former instrument to pay or provide a 'portion' for the same child.
      Having regard to the fact that the presumption against 'double portions' has the effect of depriving a child of one of the 'portions' without any word being said by the testator to that effect and to the fact that the presumption may be rebutted (in some cases by verbal evidence), it is advisable to inquire whether the testator has made any provision by covenant or gift for any of his children and to provide that the gift by will shall be in addition to the former provision or on the contrary shall be in substitution or part substitution therefor as the testator may desire.
      As to the presumption against 'double portions' see Vol 1, para **[44.1]** et seq. Form 1 of the Statutory Will Forms 1925, (Part E, para **[238.7]**), could be incorporated instead of this clause. The presumption only arises when the testator is the parent of or in loco parentis to the beneficiary.

[217.42]

FORM B17.37:   Declaration that provisions made by will for children are not to be in addition to provisions made for them by the testator's marriage settlement

(1)   Any child of mine [and any issue of a child of mine] who becomes entitled hereunder to a share in my residuary estate and who also becomes entitled under my marriage settlement dated . . . (either by appointment or in default of appointment) to a share in the property thereby settled shall upon the division of my residuary estate bring into hotchpot and account for the actual net value of such last-mentioned share such value to be ascertained as at the date when it becomes actually payable to him or her.

(2)   [If my residuary estate shall in the events which happen become divisible before the property settled by the said marriage settlement becomes divisible then the division of my said residuary estate shall not be deferred but any child [person] who under the aforesaid provisions is liable to bring into hotchpot a share in the property settled by the said settlement shall assign such last-mentioned share to my trustees and also if my trustees think fit execute to my trustees a bond in such form and for the payment of such sum as my trustees

may think fit before being entitled to receive his or her share in my residuary estate, and upon the said share in the property settled by the said settlement becoming payable my trustees shall receive and distribute the same among the persons entitled to my residuary estate under the provisions of this my will in such manner as to give effect as nearly as possible to the aforesaid provisions.[1]]

(3)   [Where any such child of mine is entitled hereunder to a life interest only in a share in my residuary estate and also where under the provisions hereof some other person or persons shall take by substitution the share in my residuary estate primarily given hereby to any such child the share in the property settled by the settlement directed to be brought into account by such child shall be brought into account as against such child and also as against all other persons interested in such share in my residuary estate.[2]]

1   If the division of the marriage settlement property may occur later than the division of the testator's residuary estate the administration of the latter will be rendered difficult. This clause may be adapted so as to enable the testator's estate to be distributed at once.
2   Where there are settled shares or a substitution in the case of the death before the testator of one of the primary residuary legatees provision should be made that the sums are still to be brought into account as against persons interested in the shares.

[217.43]

FORM B17.38:   **Declaration that certain children are to bring specified sums into hotchpot**

Having already transferred money or property to several of my children absolutely I direct that my children hereafter named shall bring into hotchpot upon the division of my residuary estate the respective sums following, namely, my son [A] the sum of £[X] my daughter [B] the sum of £[Y] etc. [And I direct that where any such child is entitled hereunder to a life interest only in a share of my residuary estate and where under the provisions hereof some other person or persons shall take by substitution the share in my residuary estate primarily given hereby to any such child the sum directed to be brought into account by such child shall be brought into account as against such child and also as against all persons interested in such share.[1]]

1   Gifts completely made over before the date of the will are not, in the absence of special directions, liable to be brought into account under the doctrine against double portions. As this clause is drafted the various persons will not be in a position to dispute the amount to be brought into account; see Vol 1, para **[44.2]**. If they are to have that privilege, as they might where the specified sums are stated to be loans and not gifts as in this case, add 'or so much of the said sums as remains unpaid'.

[217.44]

FORM B17.39:   **Declaration negativing ademption of a gift by will by subsequent gift**

I declare that no gift of money or property made by me after the date hereof to any child of mine and no covenant or obligation entered into by me after the date hereof for the benefit of any child of mine shall adeem in whole or in part any gift or provision made by this my will for such child or shall be brought into hotchpot by such child unless at the time of or within six months from the time of making such gift or entering into such covenant or obligation I shall in writing signed or initialled by me declare to the contrary.[1]

1 Under the doctrine of 'double portions' a cash payment of a 'portion' to, and an obligation entered into to provide a 'portion' for, a child of the testator is presumed to adeem, in whole or in part, a 'portion' provided for that child by a will already in existence.

[217.45]

FORM B17.40: Declaration that certain future gifts are to be brought into hotchpot

I declare that every gift at any one time of money or property of a greater amount or value at the time of such gift than £[—] made by me after the date of this my will to any child of mine and every sum of money or any property settled or agreed to be settled by me for the benefit of any child of mine after the date hereof shall be brought into hotchpot by such child upon the division of my residuary estate at the value thereof at the time of such gift or settlement and be accounted for accordingly, unless at the time of or within six months from the time of making such gift or settlement or agreement I shall in writing signed or initialled by me declare to the contrary[1] but save as aforesaid no future gift and no sum of money or property which I may hereafter give settle or agree to settle shall be brought into hotchpot by any such child.

1 See note to Form B17.39 at para **[217.44]**. The incorporation of a future declaration may be questioned: see *Re Deprez, Henriques v Deprez* [1917] 1 Ch 24, and *Re Jones' Will Trusts, Jones v Jones* [1942] Ch 328, [1942] 1 All ER 642. As to the calculation of shares on bringing money into hotchpot see Vol 1, paras **[100.1]–[100.7]**.

[217.46]

FORM B17.41: Express provision against satisfaction and ademption[1]

I expressly direct that no child or issue of mine taking any share or interest under the trusts aforesaid shall be liable to bring into account any sum of money or the value of any property or interest which I may have already paid or transferred to or settled upon such child or issue or for his her or their benefit or covenanted so to do or which I may hereafter pay or transfer to or settle upon such child or issue or for his, her or their benefit or covenant so to do [unless at the time of or within six months from the time of making such payment transfer settlement or covenant I shall in writing signed or initialled by me declare to the contrary].

1 As to bringing advances and settled shares into account see Vol 1, paras **[100.1]–[100.7]**.

B18   Discretionary trusts and powers

DISCRETIONARY TRUSTS

[218.1]
Note. Many kinds of trusts confer discretions on the trustees (and sometimes on beneficiaries) by means of which, to a greater or lesser extent, they may alter or determine what the beneficiaries will receive and when. What distinguishes a discretionary trust, as the term is commonly understood, is that the income is subject to the trustees' discretion to determine who receives it and in what shares, and none of the beneficiaries has an entitlement to any of the income as it arises (so that there is no interest in possession for inheritance tax purposes—see Part A, para **[200.108]**). Such a discretion as to income is of course usually combined with wide discretionary powers over capital and future income, so that the trustees can, in exercise of those powers, distribute capital to any of the beneficiaries, apply it for the benefit of any of them, or appoint other trusts.

[218.2]
There are both fiscal and non-fiscal reasons for providing discretionary trusts in wills. Some of their fiscal aspects are noted briefly below in this Note. The main non-fiscal reasons are to protect beneficiaries from their own improvidence, to prevent them (where they are children or young persons) from having too much money at too early an age, to prevent the creditors of a beneficiary who goes bankrupt from being able to get at the trust capital or income, and to maintain flexibility of responses to the different needs of the different beneficiaries from time to time. Another reason with the advent of the Trusts of Land and Appointment of Trustees Act 1996 (TLATA 1996) is to give trustees maximum discretion over the occupation and use of land comprised in the trust fund. If interests in possession are given, the beneficiaries could have statutory rights of occupation of the land under the TLATA 1996, s 12 (see para **[208.5]** et seq), but this may not be desirable where the property is essentially an investment property. A discretionary trust may be the solution since the beneficiaries will not automatically have rights of occupation. A discretionary trust may also be a good way of providing for someone who is disabled in some way and not able to manage his own property (see C4 at para **[226.1]** et seq). Form B18.1 at para **[218.31]** is an example of a straightforward discretionary trust of the usual type, and there are various examples of wills containing discretionary trusts in Part C, eg Forms C6.2 at para **[228.19]** and C10.2 at para **[232.15]**.

[218.3]
Discretionary trusts and the rule that a testator cannot delegate his power of testamentary disposition. In *Re Beatty's Will Trusts* [1990] 3 All ER 844, [1990] 1 WLR 1503 the creation by will of an extremely wide trustees' fiduciary power to distribute assets, which included power to distribute to themselves, was held to be valid and effective, and not an invalid attempt to delegate the testator's powers of testamentary disposition. It was held that a power which

would be valid if it was contained in a settlement is equally valid if it is contained in a will. The test as to whether the objects of a power are sufficiently certain for the power to be valid is a test which applies equally to powers created by will and those created by settlement. See further Vol 1, para **[9.45]**. At the end of his judgment in *Re Beatty's Will Trusts* Hoffmann J remarked that to hold otherwise would be an injustice to beneficiaries of testators who in reliance on earlier decisions to the same effect had conferred wide powers on their trustees. He gave as an example the wide power of appointment in the precedent in the sixth edition of this work ((6th edn), Vol 2, Form C10.2) which appears in this edition as Form C3.6 at para **[225.92]**, remarking that no warning was there given that such a power might be invalid, and that in his judgment there was no reason why there should have been.

[218.4]
Trustees as objects of powers. In framing discretionary trusts and powers the draftsman should bear in mind one particular application of the doctrine that a trustee may not profit from his trust, namely that the donee of a fiduciary power (ie a power given to trustees in their capacity as trustees, as opposed to one given to a beneficiary) may not exercise such a power for his own benefit unless authorised to do so by the settlement or will creating the power: see *Re Edward's Will Trusts, Dalgleish v Leighton* [1947] 2 All ER 521 at 524; and *Re Beatty's Will Trusts* [1990] 3 All ER 844, [1990] 1 WLR 1503 at 844–847 and 1506 respectively. It may be that when a power of appointment is conferred on trustees, a person who is named by the will or settlement as one of the original trustees and who is also a member of the class of objects of the power would be held to be impliedly authorised to join in an exercise of the power in his own favour, (see *Sargeant v National Westminster Bank plc* (1990) 61 P&CR 518 and *Edge v Pensions Ombudsman* [1998] Ch 512; [1998] 2 All ER 547), but a trustee who is not so named would not, it seems, be so authorised in the absence of an express provision to that effect. The same would probably apply to the exercise of a discretion over income under a discretionary trust of income, and to the exercise of the statutory power of advancement (ie the Trustee Act 1925 (TA 1925), s 32: considered at paras **[218.85]–[218.102]**).

[218.5]
This point, though frequently overlooked, is of particular relevance to discretionary trusts created by will, where it is often convenient and desirable that members of the testator's family should act as trustees. It is therefore advisable to remove any doubt by providing expressly that objects of a discretionary power or trust who agree to act as trustees are authorised to benefit under the exercise of any of the powers and discretions, subject to suitable safeguards, eg that the power can only be exercised if the trustees are not fewer than two in number or that the trustees exercising the power should include at least one person who is not interested in the exercise or not a beneficiary. See Form B18.32 at para **[218.117]** for a provision of this kind.

[218.6]
Inheritance tax advantages of discretionary trusts. Throughout most of the history of estate duty, discretionary trusts were an attractive option because they

were not subject to estate duty until the Finance Act 1969 introduced a not wholly successful attempt to subject them to it. Perhaps because of the difficulties which had been encountered in trying to subject discretionary trusts to estate duty, capital transfer tax (introduced by the Finance Act 1975) taxed them with particular severity, and their popularity was much reduced. A less severe set of rules for imposing capital transfer tax on discretionary trusts was introduced by the Finance Act 1982. The introduction of inheritance tax in 1986 made only minor differences to the position of discretionary trusts, but the subsequent reduction in inheritance tax rates and simplification of the rate bands to a single 40 per cent rate over and above a high tax threshold (from March 1988) on which the rates of tax on discretionary trusts are based (see paras **[218.11]–[218.14]**), have made discretionary trusts much more attractive.

[218.7]
The short point about a discretionary trust is that the property subject to it is not treated for inheritance tax purposes as if it were owned by one or more of the beneficiaries, whereas settled property subject to an interest in possession is so treated (see Part A, para **[200.107]** et seq). A discretionary trust forms an 'estate' by itself, though in some ways taxed as an emanation of the settlor or testator, and pays inheritance tax in fairly easy instalments which can be very small or nothing at all where the fund is of modest size. Particular uses of a discretionary trust are to provide a fund equal to the testator's nil-rate band from which the testator's spouse can benefit without it being treated as part of her estate (see paras **[218.16]–[218.18]** and Forms B18.2 at para **[218.32]** and C11.1 at para **[233.13]**) and to empower the executors to make the most tax-efficient distribution of the estate in reliance on Inheritance Tax Act 1984 (ITA 1984), s 144 (see Form C3.6 at para **[225.92]**).

[218.8]
Inheritance tax charges on discretionary trusts. The rules for charging inheritance tax on discretionary trusts apply to any settled property where there is no interest in possession, ie where no beneficiary is entitled to the income as it arises (see Part A, paras **[200.108]–[200.110]** for the meaning of interest in possession), subject to some exceptions. Some forms of trust where there is no interest in possession receive privileged treatment, such as accumulation and maintenance settlements for persons under 25 (see Part A, para **[200.119]** et seq), protective trusts (see Part A, para **[200.116]**), trusts for mentally disabled persons (see Part A, para **[200.117]** and C4 at para **[226.1]** et seq), discretionary will trusts lasting not more than two years (see C3 at para **[225.1]** et seq), charitable trusts, superannuation schemes, trusts for employees and trusts of shares in newspaper publishing companies: see *Foster's Inheritance Tax*, E5 and E6.

[218.9]
Where there is no interest in possession in settled property and the trusts do not fall into one of the privileged categories mentioned above, the rules now contained in ITA 1984, ss 58–69 apply. These rules are described in detail in

Foster's Inheritance Tax, E3 and E4. We can only give an outline of some of the main features of these rules here. There are two types of inheritance tax charge on settled property not subject to an interest in possession and not in one of the privileged categories mentioned above, which property is defined by s 58 as 'relevant property'. These are a periodic charge and an 'exit charge'. The periodic charge is imposed (s 64) at every tenth anniversary of the day on which property first became comprised in the settlement, on all property which immediately before the anniversary is comprised in the settlement and 'relevant property'. There is also an inheritance tax 'exit charge' on property ceasing to be 'relevant property' or dispositions which depreciate the value of relevant property (s 65), subject to certain exemptions, such as where relevant property goes to charity or a public body or authority specified in the ITA 1984, Sch 3 (s 76).

[218.10]
The rules for calculating the rate of periodic and exit charges are essentially similar. The periodic charge is the basic charge, and the exit charge can be looked upon as a means of collecting the periodic charge for which a potential liability has arisen since the last occasion of inheritance tax charge to affect the property, a potential liability which has arisen by virtue of the length of time for which that property has been relevant property.

[218.11]
Calculation of the rate of inheritance tax charge. There are two main stages to the calculation of the tax charge. First, the overall rate of inheritance tax on a hypothetical lifetime chargeable transfer is determined, the hypothetical value transferred and the hypothetical amount of previous chargeable transfers for this purpose being determined by reference to the history of the settlor and the settlement (see below). Secondly, the rate of tax so determined is reduced so that in the case of a periodic charge where the property has been relevant property comprised in the settlement for the previous ten years, the charge is 30 per cent of the overall rate at which inheritance tax would be charged on the hypothetical lifetime transfer (s 66(1)); in the case of a periodic charge where the property has not been relevant property comprised in the settlement for the previous ten years and in the case of any exit charge, the charge is that proportion of 30 per cent of the rate of inheritance tax on the hypothetical lifetime chargeable transfer which corresponds to the proportion of ten years represented by the period since the most recent occasion of periodic charge (if any) during which the property has been relevant property comprised in the settlement (ss 66(2), 68(1)–(3), 69(1) and (4)). The rate of inheritance tax on a lifetime chargeable transfer is half the death rates (ITA 1984, s 7(2)), and so relevant property bears tax at 15 per cent of a charge at death rates for every ten years that it is relevant property. This is 1.5 per cent of such a charge per year of property being relevant property, and would mean that a complete charge at death rates would be incurred in instalments if property remained relevant property for 67 years. As the highest marginal rate of inheritance tax at the rates charged on death is now 40 per cent, the highest marginal rate of a periodic charge on property which has been relevant property for a full ten years is now six per cent.

[218.12]

The hypothetical transfer used to calculate the tax rate in the case of a periodic charge at a ten-year anniversary is a transfer of the aggregate of the value of the relevant property on which tax is being charged, the value of any property comprised in the same settlement which has never been 'relevant property' comprised in the settlement (taken at its value when it first became comprised in the settlement), and any property comprised in a 'related settlement' (s 66(4)). The related settlement rules are of particular relevance to dispositions by will, and we mention them further below. The hypothetical previous transfers for calculating the rate of a periodic charge are the aggregate of the chargeable transfers made by the settlor in the seven years before he made the settlement, disregarding transfers made on the day he made the settlement (although a different period of aggregation of his transfers may be taken for this purpose where he has subsequently added property to the settlement—see s 67), and the values on which 'exit charges' have been charged on the settlement in the ten years preceding the anniversary (s 66(5) and (6)).

[218.13]

In the case of exit charges occurring after the first ten-year anniversary the calculations are based on the same hypothetical lifetime chargeable transfer as the most recent periodic charge was based, subject to adjustments for any property which may have been added to the settlement or become relevant property on or after the most recent occasion of periodic charge (s 69). In the case of an exit charge occurring before the first ten-year anniversary the tax rate is calculated on a hypothetical transfer of the value of the property comprised in the settlement immediately after it was made (whether relevant property or not), any property subsequently added to the settlement at its value when added, and the value of any related settlement (s 68(5)—see below for related settlements). The assumed previous chargeable transfers are those of the settlor in the seven years preceding the making of the settlement, not including the day on which the settlement was made (s 68(4)(b)).

[218.14]

Two settlements are 'related' to one another if neither is wholly and permanently charitable, they have the same settlor, and property first became comprised in both of them on the same day (ss 60 and 62). This is subject to the point that if the property first comprised in a settlement is subject to an interest in possession to which the settlor or his or her spouse (including his or her widow or widower) is beneficially entitled, that property will be treated for the purposes of the discretionary trust charging rules as not becoming comprised in that settlement at that time (s 80). Accordingly a settlement commencing with an interest in possession in favour of the settlor or his or her spouse will not be 'related' to a settlement in which property becomes first comprised at the same time. Where property comprised in a related settlement is taken into account for inheritance tax rate calculation purposes under the above rules it is taken at its value immediately after it first became comprised in the related settlement.

[218.15]
Inheritance tax on discretionary trusts created by will. Where property is settled by will it is treated as becoming comprised in the settlement when the testator dies (ITA 1984, s 83) and of course references to the settlor for the above purposes are to the testator (s 44). Some points to note about including discretionary trusts in wills are as follows:

(i)   As mentioned above, the rate of tax charged on an occasion of exit charge during the first ten years of a settlement is calculated by reference to a hypothetical chargeable transfer equal to the value of the settled property at the time when it first became comprised in the settlement (assuming that there is no related settlement and no subsequently added property). The relevant tax rate table is that which is in force at the time when the occasion of exit charge occurs (ss 66(3)(b), 68(4)(b) and Sch 2, para 3). Thus if the nil-rate band in the rate table in force at the time of an occasion of exit charge exceeds the value of the settled property when it first became comprised in the settlement, and there are no aggregable lifetime transfers made by the testator (see sub-para (iii) below) and no related settlement, no tax will be payable on such occasion of exit charge.

(ii) The tax rate calculations for any exit or periodic charge will not take into account any of the property passing under the testator's will except for property which goes into a related settlement. Thus where the testator by his will makes absolute gifts or settles property on trust for his or her widow or widower for life so that s 80 applies (see para **[218.14]**), the property so given or settled will not come into the calculations of periodic charges or exit charges on property settled on discretionary trusts by the same will.

(iii) Lifetime chargeable transfers (including of course potentially exempt transfers) made or treated as made by the testator during the seven years preceding his death will always be taken into account in calculating exit or periodic charges, but ones made seven years or more before his death will not be taken into account (unless property is added by the will to an existing discretionary settlement—s 66(5)).

[218.16]
Nil-rate band discretionary trusts. The inheritance tax nil-rate band is now (in tax year 2001–02) £242,000. If a testator leaves his entire estate to his spouse in the event of the spouse surviving him, and at the time of his death has not made any lifetime gifts in the previous seven years, his nil-rate band will be wasted in the event of his spouse surviving him. He could have left up to £242,000 to non-exempt recipients, eg his children, without any inheritance tax being payable. However, he will not want to leave £242,000 direct to the children in the event of his dying survived by his spouse if the spouse will or might need access to the income or even the capital of the whole of the testator's estate after his death. So, a testator who wishes to enable his spouse to be able to benefit from his entire estate and its income if need be, but who nevertheless wishes to provide for a nil-rate band's worth of his estate to devolve on eg his children, without it being charged to inheritance tax as part of the spouse's estate, can do so by means of a discretionary trust.

[218.17]
The usual method is for a legacy equal to the amount of the nil-rate band to be given by the will to trustees to hold it on discretionary trusts for his spouse and children. If the testator has by the time of his death made no lifetime transfers within the seven years before his death (apart from permanently exempt ones such as to his spouse or charity), and leaves no other non-exempt gifts by his will, his estate will not incur a liability for inheritance tax on his death. The income of the legacy can be paid to the spouse and, should the need arise, the capital also. But unless the capital of it is paid to the spouse, the legacy will not form part of the spouse's taxable estate and will escape being charged to inheritance tax in aggregation with the rest of the spouse's estate on death. The legacy will of course be liable to periodic charges to inheritance tax and to a charge when distributed. Such charges should amount to nothing or very little during the first ten years after the testator's death, and are unlikely to be very much even after that. See paras **[218.11]–[218.14]**.

[218.18]
The following further points should be noted:

- The tax effectiveness of a testamentary discretionary trust is normally increased if the testator does not by his will create any trusts of the balance of his estate, the reason being that the value of any such 'related settlement' will be taken into account in computing the rate of tax on the discretionary legacy: ITA 1984, s 68(5)(b); see also para **[218.15]**. However, trusts under which the surviving spouse takes an immediate interest in possession do not have this consequence, because of the provisions of the ITA 1984, s 80 (see para **[218.16]**). The testator's will could therefore give the spouse a life interest in residue instead of an absolute interest, when by the same will creating a nil-rate band discretionary trust with the objectives outlined above.
- The nil-rate band discretionary trust can only be relied on to work where the fund consists of income-yielding assets. If it were to consist of eg the matrimonial home, and the surviving spouse was permitted to occupy it as a residence under the terms of the trust, the surviving spouse would almost certainly be regarded by the Inland Revenue as having an interest in possession for inheritance tax purposes, so that the house would become part of the surviving spouse's 'estate' for inheritance tax purposes and chargeable to inheritance tax as such on the surviving spouse's death, and the objective of the discretionary trust would be frustrated: see Part A, para **[200.107]** et seq and *Sansom v Peay* [1976] 3 All ER 375, [1976] 1 WLR 1073. The strategy which has become popular for cases where there are insufficient assets apart from the matrimonial home to provide a nil-rate band trust fund is a debt or charge scheme, where the fund is constituted wholly or partly by a personal debt of the surviving spouse or a charge on the house or the first spouse to die's interest in the house (see para **[218.19]**).
- The device of the discretionary legacy, while advantageous for inheritance tax purposes, may be inconvenient and disproportionately expensive to administer. Testators may prefer the greater flexibility of the fully discretionary will or the will creating a two-year discretionary

trust of residue: see Forms B18.1 (at para **[218.31]**) and C3.6 (at para **[225.92]**) and for the rules for charging inheritance tax on discretionary trusts see paras **[218.11]**–**[218.14]**.

Form B18.2 at para **[218.32]** is an example of a nil-rate band legacy subject to discretionary trusts. Forms C3.4 at para **[225.57]** and C3.5 at para **[225.68]** are examples of complete wills incorporating such a legacy.

[218.19]
Nil-rate band discretionary trust funds constituted by a debt or charge.
Where it may not be possible to constitute the nil-rate band trust out of assets of the estate without using some or all of the matrimonial home, there is the problem that if the matrimonial home (or a share of it) is in the discretionary trust fund, and the surviving spouse is permitted to occupy the home, the latter may have an interest in possession in the discretionary trust fund, with the consequence that the inheritance tax-saving purpose of the arrangement is lost (see para **[218.18]**). A possible solution to this problem, which has become popular in recent years, is a debt or charge scheme, whereby the discretionary trust fund is constituted either by a personal obligation on the part of the surviving spouse to pay a sum of money to the trustees of the discretionary trust fund, or by a sum of money charged on the matrimonial home or a share of it. If the discretionary trust fund is a personal debt it is repayable on demand but interest free, and if it is a charge it is enforceable on demand or notice and interest free. The debt scheme is simpler and to be preferred, and the charge scheme is really something to fall back on if there appears to be a problem under the Finance Act 1986, s 103 for the debt scheme (see para **[218.21]**). Both schemes have the advantage that the house is owned by or held beneficially for the surviving spouse, so that the capital gains tax private residence exemption can (if the appropriate conditions are fulfilled) apply to the whole of it in the event of a decision to sell the existing one and buy another. For a will clause enabling such an arrangement to be entered into, see Form B18.2 at para **[218.32]** and for documentation putting such schemes into effect, see Forms F5.3 and F5.4 at paras **[243.4]** and **[243.5]**.

[218.20]
Debt or charge schemes have not so far been the subject of litigation, but they appear, at least in some forms, to be accepted as effective for inheritance tax purposes by the Capital Taxes Office. The theory behind them is that the debt or charge which constitutes the discretionary fund is a deduction from the surviving spouse's estate on the latter's death, but the surviving spouse does not have an interest in possession in the discretionary trust fund. In the case of a debt scheme, the surviving spouse has entered into the obligation in return for being distributed the residuary estate, and it is it is therefore incurred for full consideration, and deductible, if the estate distributed to him exceeds the amount of the debt. In the case of a charge scheme, the property in the residuary estate on which the charge is imposed is distributed to or held on trust for the surviving spouse subject to the charge (without the surviving spouse having a personal obligation), and should therefore be a deduction from the value of the property, but of course only to the extent that the amount of the charge does not exceed the unencumbered value of the property. Although allowing a beneficiary to

occupy trust property may create an interest in possession, the better view is probably that lending to a beneficiary all or part of a trust fund interest-free and repayable on demand does not give that beneficiary an interest in possession in the whole or part of the trust fund which is lent. Where a nil-rate band trust fund is constituted by a debt or charge of this type, it is thought that the inheritance tax status of the fund (as between being or not being subject to an interest in possession) is determined by reference to the trusts which would apply to the income which would be yielded by the debt or charge if interest were payable (see also *Foster's Inheritance Tax*, E1.45 and E1.46).

[218.21]
The reason for using the charge scheme—Finance Act 1986, s 103. If a simple personal obligation is entered into by the surviving spouse to pay the amount of the trust legacy to the trustees of it, there could be a question whether the debt is deductible on the death of the surviving spouse if the other spouse (ie the first to die) had during his life been given property by the surviving spouse. This is because the Finance Act 1986, s 103 may apply in these circumstance so as to abate the liability of the surviving spouse to the discretionary trust fund when it comes to determining the amount of the surviving spouse's taxable estate on the latter's death. The charge schemes are an attempt to get round this problem by creating a charge on one or more assets in the residuary estate, typically the first to die's share of the matrimonial home, which is not 'an incumbrance created by a disposition made by' the surviving spouse (see FA 1986, s 103(1) for the significance of this wording). It would be a charge on the property, but without the surviving spouse being personally liable. Where it is possible that the surviving spouse might want to change homes, it is advisable for the first to die's will to give the surviving spouse a life interest in residue rather than an absolute interest. This is because if the surviving spouse owns absolutely the house which is subject to the charge, a replacement charge on a new house (replacing that which passed on the death) will have to be imposed by the surviving spouse, and so the arrangement may then become caught by s 103 even though it was not so caught in relation to the original house (because the original charge was made by the executors of the first to die before distributing the original house to the surviving spouse). Where there is a life interest trust of residue for the surviving spouse, the trustees of the residuary estate are the appropriate persons to create the charge and they could also enter into a liability to pay the amount (and if they do, it should be limited to the amount of the available trust assets in their hands); alternatively they could enter into a personal liability (limited as just described) without charging the assets.

[218.22]
Debt and charge schemes—practical points.

(1) Specific powers to constitute the discretionary trust fund as a debt or charge are needed, since it is a form of investment of the discretionary trust fund which is disadvantageous to the beneficiaries of it compared with more conventional kinds of investment (see Form B18.2 at para **[218.32]** for an example).

(2) Similarly, it is important that all relevant trustees should be exonerated from liability for the fund being worth less than it would have been if conventionally invested, and from liability for a failure of the surviving spouse's resources (in the case of a debt) or the value of the property (in the case of a charge) to be sufficient to meet the amount of the debt or charge in full.

(3) For a debt scheme where the surviving spouse is to be the debtor, the legacy trustees should include at least one person who is not the surviving spouse, because a person cannot make a contract with himself. However, the legacy trustees and the general trustees could be the same persons. The surviving spouse can enter into a contract with himself and others: Law of Property Act 1925 (LPA 1925), s 82.

(4) Where the charge scheme might be used, the surviving spouse should not be one of the personal representatives or trustees who create the charge (but he could be a legacy trustee). This is so as to avoid any argument that the Finance Act 1986, s 103 applies to a charge created by trustees who include the surviving spouse among their number (see para [218.21]). As the charge would be created in exercise of a fiduciary power by trustees or personal representatives acting in that capacity, this seems unlikely to be correct, but the non-participation of the surviving spouse will reduce the number of contentious points to argue about.

(5) Where the charge scheme might be used, or there is a life interest trust of residue for the surviving spouse (so that the legacy fund will be a debt or charge, or both, incurred or made by the trustees of the residuary estate), the legacy trustees and the general trustees should not be exactly the same persons, again because of the problem of someone creating an interest in favour of himself. The LPA 1925, s 72(3) authorises a conveyance of land by a person to himself, but it is doubtful whether 'land' as defined for this purpose in the LPA 1925, s 205(1)(ix) (Part G, para [246.44A]), includes mortgages and charges (because they did not devolve on the heir before 1926 and are thus probably not 'hereditaments' within the definition). The LPA 1925, s 72(1), (2), and (4) makes it clear that if the two sets of trustees are not exactly the same persons, a charge will be valid even though one or more persons are members of both sets of trustees.

(6) Where the testator and spouse own the matrimonial home together, if they are joint tenants they need to sever the joint tenancy by agreement or notice before either has died (although it may be possible to remedy failure to do this by a deed of variation). The share of the first to die will form part of his residuary estate in which the surviving spouse will have an absolute or life interest. If a charge rather than debt scheme is used, the charge will be an equitable charge on the first to die's undivided share, not a charge on the house itself. This will mean that there will be a continuing trusteeship of the house itself, since one undivided share is subject to a charge and the other not.

(7) A personal debt will only be deductible to the extent that the surviving spouse has received property from the first to die's estate equal to the amount of the debt. A charge (without any personal liability) will only be deductible so far as it does not exceed the value of the property it is charged upon.

[218.23]
Discretionary trusts where there is no spouse exemption. There can be similar advantages to those of the nil-rate band discretionary trust as discussed above in having a discretionary trust in a will to which the spouse exemption is not relevant, particularly where the testator is elderly and making a will leaving all or most of his property in favour of a friend or relative who is also elderly. With a discretionary trust the income of the property of the testator can be enjoyed by the beneficiary without being charged to inheritance tax as part of the beneficiary's estate on his or her death, and is likely to be taxed much more lightly, if at all, when the discretionary trust terminates. This is particularly beneficial where the testator leaves an estate which is wholly or mostly free of inheritance tax, being within or mostly within the nil-rate band, and where the beneficiary already has property which will mostly or wholly use up the nil-rate band on his death, so that the testator's property, if it were added to the beneficiary's property and taxed as the latter's property on his death, would on the beneficiary's death give rise to an inheritance tax charge equivalent to 40 per cent of the testator's property . In this situation there would be no or hardly any successive charges relief under the ITA 1984, s 141 where the beneficiary died within five years, because little or no tax would have been paid on the testator's death. Even where there will be inheritance tax payable on the testator's death, creating a discretionary trust will often be likely to have an inheritance tax advantage over giving an absolute interest or interest in possession where the beneficiary is elderly and has property of his own exceeding or not much less than the nil-rate band.

[218.24]
Further, where a gift of an absolute interest or interest in possession to a beneficiary would not be exempt from inheritance tax, so that the inheritance tax charge on the testator's death is the same irrespective of the type of trust created for the benefit of the beneficiary, it is much less important to confine any discretionary trust to assets of the testator's estate equal to the nil-rate band. Doing so should ensure (where there are no aggregable lifetime chargeable transfers and no other property is settled by the will—see para **[218.15]**) that there is no inheritance tax charge on the termination of the discretionary trusts in the first ten years after the testator's death. However, avoiding an inheritance charge on the discretionary fund might be achieved at the cost of a much higher charge on absolute or interest in possession property on the death of the beneficiary. Where the fund intended to benefit the beneficiary will or may exceed the nil-rate band, it will often be the case that putting the whole of that fund into a discretionary trust will be likely to save inheritance tax on the beneficiary's death, as compared with a discretionary trust of part of the fund equal to the nil-rate band and the beneficiary being given an absolute interest or interest in possession in the remainder of the fund. See paras **[218.11]–[218.15]** and **[218.32]**, n 4. For a deed of variation which converts a life interest under a will to a discretionary trust see Form F3.9 at para **[241.30]**.

[218.25]
Two-year discretionary trusts to take advantage of ITA 1984, s 144. A distribution within two years after a testator's death out of a discretionary trust created by his will may be treated as a disposition by the will for inheritance tax

purposes, and a will can thus be made which subjects all or most of the testator's estate to a discretionary trust, with a view to the executors making the most tax-efficient disposition in the light of the circumstances at or shortly after the testator's death. This topic is discussed in more detail in the text in C3 at paras **[225.83]** et seq, an example of such a will is Form C3.6 at para **[225.92]**.

[218.26]
Capital gains tax and discretionary trusts. The rates of capital gains tax for an individual are arrived at by adding the capital gains made in a tax year to his or her income and charging them in effect to income tax. Capital gains tax on the gains of a settlement is charged at the income tax rate applicable to trusts under the Income and Corporation Taxes Act 1988 (ICTA 1988), s 686, currently 34 per cent in the tax year 2001–02 (see the Taxation of Chargeable Gains Act 1992 (TCGA 1992), s 4(1AA)(a)). The realisation of a chargeable gain on the sale of assets held in a discretionary trust will thus involve paying more capital gains tax than would be paid if the assets were owned absolutely by an individual who, after taking into the account the chargeable gain, was not a higher rate tax payer, but less capital gains tax than would be paid if they were owned absolutely by an individual whose highest marginal rate of capital gains tax was the higher rate of income tax, currently 40 per cent.

[218.27]
General capital gains tax hold-over relief for gifts and transfers in and out of settlements was abolished by the Finance Act 1989, leaving more limited hold-over reliefs for gifts of business and agricultural property (TCGA 1992, s 165 and Sch 7) and gifts on which inheritance tax is chargeable (TCGA 1992, s 260). The latter type of hold-over relief is available when property is distributed out of a discretionary trust and it is an occasion of inheritance tax 'exit charge' under ITA 1984, s 65, even if the hypothetical transfer on the basis of which the tax rate is calculated (see paras **[218.12]** and **[218.13]**) is such that no tax is in fact payable on the distribution. This is an advantage of a discretionary trust over an interest in possession one.

[218.28]
Income tax and discretionary trusts. Discretionary trusts still have some income tax advantages where the income received is not UK company dividends, in that the trustees are enabled to distribute income to those beneficiaries who pay least tax. However, the provisions for the taxation of the income of certain discretionary trusts contained in the ICTA 1988, ss 686 and 687, should be borne in mind, and there are now distinct disadvantages where the trust receives UK company dividends subject to the Schedule F trust rate of tax.

[218.29]
The ICTA 1988, s 686 provides that non-UK company dividend income is to be taxed on the trustees at 'the rate applicable to trusts' (currently 34 per cent) The income caught by the section includes inter alia income which falls to be accumulated and income which is payable to a beneficiary under a discretion (whether or not there is power to accumulate). Income applicable under the TA 1925, s 31 (Part G, para **[246.26]**) during the minority of a beneficiary would fall

within this definition. Various categories of income are excluded from the operation of s 686, of which it is sufficient to mention income applied in defraying trust expenses which are properly chargeable to income (or would be so chargeable but for some express provision of the trust): a restrictive interpretation of these words was adopted by the House of Lords in *Carver v Duncan* [1985] 2 All ER 645. The ICTA 1988, s 687 provides that income paid to a beneficiary as income is to be treated as income net of the rate applicable to trusts. The trustees are responsible for the payment of the amount of such tax subject to set off of the 'tax pool' which will include the income tax already paid to the Revenue. A beneficiary who receives income under a discretion and who pays tax at a rate below 34 per cent or who has unused personal reliefs available to him may be able to recover some part of the tax paid by the trustees in respect of such income. The ultimate burden of tax on income to which these sections apply is thus unaffected as long as such income is distributed as income, but if, for example, income is accumulated and subsequently distributed in the form of capital there can be no recovery of any part of the tax paid in respect of such accumulations. Now that investment income surcharge is abolished for individuals and the higher income tax rates for individuals are comparatively low accumulation of trust income (excluding UK company dividends) is fiscally unattractive in most cases.

[218.30]
If the trust includes UK company dividend income, however, new rules which came into force in 1999–2000 means that accumulation of such income will generally be preferable to distribution. A dividend from a UK company comes with a tax credit (currently 1/9 of the amount distributed), and under ICTA 1988, s 686, tax on such income is charged on the trustees at the Schedule F trust rate (currently 25 per cent). If the trustees distribute the dividend income, they are deemed to make a payment grossed up at the normal rate applicable to trusts (currently 34 per cent), and are liable under s 687 to tax on this grossed up amount. The tax credit on the dividends does not, however, go into the 'tax pool' to reduce this s 687 liability, so the trustees are only able to set-off the tax actually paid by them under s 686. The beneficiary who receives the dividend income is liable for tax on that payment at his own income tax rate, but with the benefit of a credit for the amount paid by the trustees, so he is entitled to a tax repayment or liable for further tax, as appropriate. The overall effect of the rules is that if a discretionary trust is to invest in UK company shares it will probably be better for the income produced thereby to be accumulated, rather than distributed, and for capital payments or loans to be made to the beneficiaries rather than income distributions.

[218.31]

FORM B18.1:   Discretionary trust for the testator's family

(1)   In this clause:
    (i)   'the trust period' means the period starting with the date of my death and ending 80 years afterwards (and that period shall be the perpetuity period applicable hereto);[1]

(ii)   'the beneficiaries' means [*here set out the persons comprising the class of beneficiaries. An example would be*: my wife my sister [*name*] and all the children and remoter issue of myself or of my said sister who may be born before the end of the trust period together with any spouse widow or widower of any such children or remoter issue (and so that the expressions 'widow' and 'widower' shall include a widow or widower who has remarried)].

(2)   My trustees shall hold the capital and income of the trust fund upon trust for all or such one or more of the beneficiaries at such ages or times in such shares and upon such trusts for the benefit of all or any one or more of the beneficiaries as my trustees (being at least two in number or a [trust] corporation)^2 may by deed or deeds^3 revocable or irrevocable at any time or times during the trust period appoint and in making any such appointment my trustees shall have powers as full as those which they could possess if they were the absolute beneficial owner of the trust fund and in particular (but without prejudice to the generality of the foregoing words) may:

(i)   appoint new trustees of the whole or any part or parts of the trust fund and provide for the remuneration of any who may be professional or corporate trustees;

(ii)   create or delegate powers and discretions over capital or income (including powers of further delegation) whether of a dispositive or administrative nature;

Provided that:

(a)   no appointment shall be capable of being made and no revocable appointment shall be capable of being revoked after the expiration of the trust period;

(b)   no appointment shall prejudice or affect any prior payment transfer or application of income or capital hereunder;

(c)   any appointment under the foregoing power may be made subject and without prejudice to any existing interests trusts or powers;

(d)   any such appointment may be made of income without any appointment of capital; and

(e)   my trustees (being at least two in number or a [trust]^4 corporation) may at any time or times by deed or deeds extinguish, or release or restrict the foregoing power in any manner and to any extent.^{5}

(3)   In default of and subject to and until any appointment made under the provisions of the preceding subclause:

(i)   during the trust period my trustees shall pay or apply the income of the trust fund to or for the maintenance or support or otherwise for the benefit of all or any one or more of the beneficiaries as my trustees may in their absolute discretion think fit; provided that during the 21 years immediately following my death^6 my trustees may if they in their absolute discretion think fit accumulate such income or any part of it by way of compound interest by investing the same and its resulting income in any way authorised by this will and if they do so they shall hold such accumulations as part of the capital of the trust fund but may nonetheless in any future year

1477

during the trust period apply them or any part of them as if they were arising in that year;

(ii)   upon the expiry of the trust period my trustees shall hold the trust fund as to both capital and income absolutely for [*here insert the dispositions to take effect at the end of the trust period in default of previous appointment. For example*: such of the beneficiaries as are then living and if more than one in equal shares.

or

such of my children and remoter issue as are then living and if more than one in equal shares according to their stocks and so that no issue shall take whose parent is still alive and so capable of taking].

(4)   [*As* Form B18.32 *at para* **[218.117]**.][7]

1   The disadvantage of adopting the 80-year (or lesser fixed term) perpetuity period for a discretionary trust is that it then becomes the *only* available perpetuity period when drafting an appointment in exercise of the power: see the PAA 1964, s 1 (Part G, para **[246.59]**). Accordingly, an appointment under the power of, say, a life interest to someone living at the testator's death, with remainder to someone born before the life tenant's death vesting at or before the age of 21, needs to be expressly limited so that all interests vest (in interest if not in possession) and all powers are exercised within the 80-year period, whereas no express perpetuity restrictions would be needed in such an appointment if the 80-year period (or a lesser fixed term) had not been adopted by the testator's will as the perpetuity period. We should add that if this is not done in an appointment where there is a relevant fixed-term perpetuity period, there will still be 'wait and see' under the PAA 1964, s 3 (Part G, para **[246.61]**), but it is better practice to draft trusts of which it is clear from the outset that they will vest within the relevant perpetuity period.

2   For the meaning of trust corporation see the Preliminary Note to B3 at para **[203.24]**. If a foreign corporate trustee might be appointed, the word 'trust' should be omitted.

3   For precedents, see Forms F4.1 to F4.4 at paras **[242.7]**–**[242.11]**.

4   See n 2 supra.

5   A power conferred on trustees in that capacity cannot be released by them unless they have express power to do so: see Vol 1, para **[40.10]**.

6   A period of 21 years from the testator's death is a permitted period of accumulation: see the LPA 1925, s 164(1)(h) (Part G, para **[246.12]**).

7   This will enable the trustees to exercise their powers and discretions in favour of one of their number.

[218.32]

FORM B18.2:   Legacy equal to inheritance tax threshold to be held on discretionary trusts[1]

(1)   In this clause the following expressions have the following meanings—

(a)   'the trust legacy' means the legacy by this clause bequeathed to my legacy trustees and the assets for the time being representing the same;

(b)   'the beneficiaries' means and includes [my wife [*name*]] and my children and remoter issue;[2]

(c)   'the trust period' means the period commencing on my death and expiring on the twenty-first anniversary of the death of [my wife];[3]

(d)   'the accumulation period' means the period commencing with my death and expiring on the twenty-first anniversary thereof;[4] and

(e)   'my legacy trustees' means [*name*] of [*address*] and [*name*] of [*address*] or other the trustee or trustees for the time being of the trust legacy].[5]

(2)   If [my wife] shall survive me[6] then I bequeath to my legacy trustees free of inheritance tax and foreign death duties[7] a legacy of [£242,000][8] *or* [the maximum sum of money (if any) which can in the circumstances subsisting at my death be given by this clause without any liability being incurred for the payment of inheritance tax on or by reason of my death. And in particular but without prejudice to the generality of the foregoing the circumstances to be taken into account for the foregoing purpose shall include any chargeable transfers made by me during my lifetime (or events treated as such for inheritance tax purposes) the dispositions taking effect under this Will (apart from this present clause) or under any codicil hereto and any property treated as if it were part of my estate immediately before my death for inheritance tax purposes].[9]

(3)   My legacy trustees shall hold the trust legacy and the income thereof upon such trusts for the benefit of all or any one or more exclusively of the others or other of the beneficiaries and if more than one in such shares and with such trusts and powers [(including trusts and powers conferring a discretion as to the distribution of capital or income exercisable by my legacy trustees or by any other person or persons)][10] and with such provisions generally as my legacy trustees (not being fewer than two in number or being a corporation) shall by any deed or deeds revocable or irrevocable appoint provided that no appointment shall be made and no revocable appointment shall be revoked after the expiration of the trust period.

[(4)   At any time or times during the trust period my legacy trustees (not being fewer than two in number or being a corporation) may raise the whole or any part or parts of the trust legacy and pay or apply the same to or for the advancement or benefit of any of the beneficiaries for the time being living in such manner as they think fit.][11]

(5)   Subject to any exercise of the foregoing power[s] my legacy trustees shall during the trust period hold the trust legacy upon trust to pay or apply the income thereof to or for the maintenance education or benefit of all or any one or more of the beneficiaries for the time being living in such shares if more than one and generally in such manner as they think fit provided that my legacy trustees may during the accumulation period accumulate the whole or any part of the income of the trust legacy by investing the same and the resulting income thereof in any of the investments hereby authorised and any accumulations of income so made shall form part of the capital of the trust legacy for all purposes.

(6)   Subject to any exercise of the foregoing powers the trust legacy and the income thereof shall be held at the expiration of the trust period in trust absolutely for such of my children and remoter issue as shall then be living in equal shares per stirpes.

(7)   Any capital or income of the trust legacy not otherwise disposed of by this clause shall be held in trust for such of my children as survive me if more than one in equal shares absolutely.

(8)   Any of my trustees or my legacy trustees may exercise any power or discretion hereby or by law conferred notwithstanding that he or she has a direct or indirect personal interest in the mode or result of such exercise.[12]

(9)   Instead of the trust legacy being satisfied by the payment of cash or by the appropriation of property—[13]

(a) my trustees may charge (with or without there being any personal liability of any person or persons) any property which is (or but for this clause would be) comprised in [my residuary estate] with payment of a sum of money equal to or less than the amount of the trust legacy to my legacy trustees and my legacy trustees shall accept such charge for such sum as the whole or a part (as the case may be) of the trust legacy; and

(b) my trustees may require my legacy trustees to accept in satisfaction of all or part of the trust legacy a binding promise of payment (secured or unsecured) made personally by [my wife] or by my trustees as trustees of [my residuary estate] which debt shall be payable on demand and my legacy trustees shall accept such debt as the whole or a part (as the case may be) of the trust legacy.

(10)   The following shall apply in relation to the powers in the last preceding subclause—

(a) my trustees may require to be included such terms if any as they think fit in relation to a charge under subclause (9)(a) above or a debt under subclause (9)(b) above including terms as to interest (if any) and terms linking the debt or sum charged to the index of retail prices or otherwise providing for its amount to vary with the passage of time according to a formula provided that the charge shall be enforceable by or the debt shall be payable to my legacy trustees on demand;

(b) my legacy trustees may leave the charge or debt outstanding for as long as they think fit and refrain from exercising their rights in relation to it and waive the payment of all or any part of any interest due in respect of it and may accept any substitute debt or charge undertaken or created by any person;

(c) my trustees may assent to the vesting of [my residuary estate] subject to an outstanding obligation to pay or satisfy the trust legacy and my legacy trustees may appoint new trustees in exercise of the statutory power to do so before the trust legacy has been paid or satisfied;[14]

(d) my legacy trustees and my trustees shall not be liable if [my wife] is or becomes unable to pay the debt or any security is or becomes inadequate or for any other loss or disadvantage which may occur as a result of their exercising or choosing not to exercise any of the foregoing powers; and

(e) the foregoing powers are in addition to any other powers given by this will or any codicil or by the general law and the foregoing powers may be exercised even though my trustees and my legacy trustees are the same persons or [my wife] is among either or both sets of trustees provided that such powers shall not be exercisable by a sole trustee who is [my wife].

1   See paras [218.16]–[218.19] for the purpose of this form. It is to go with a gift of the rest of the testator's estate to his spouse, either absolutely or for life (or other interest in possession). See Forms C3.4 at para [225.57] and C3.5 at para [225.68] for forms of complete wills incorporating a disposition of this type.

2   The definition of the discretionary class may need to be enlarged or adapted in individual cases. See also n 2 to Form C3.6 at para [225.100].

3   The trust period is longer than may be desired in most cases, but gives considerable flexibility.

4   A period of 21 years from the testator's death is a permitted period of accumulation: see the LPA 1925, s 164(1)(b) (Part G, para [246.42]).

5   The main circumstances in which there should be separate trustees of the legacy are where a charge scheme might be entered into, in which case the testator's spouse should not be one of the executors and trustees but could be a trustee of the legacy, or where the testator's spouse is or might be sole executor and a debt scheme might be entered into, or where there is a life interest trust of residue for the surviving spouse. See para **[218.22]**.

6   This form assumes an exempt gift of residue to the testator's spouse, or a gift of it on an interest in possession trust for the spouse (eg a life interest), so that the estate is wholly or mostly exempt apart from this gift. This gift of a nil-rate band fund on discretionary trusts should not be subject to a condition that the spouse survives the testator by a certain period (and note that an omnibus commorientes clause such as Form B19.2 at para **[219.15]** could have this effect). This is because the ITA 1984, s 92 would not apply to such a survivorship condition, since the condition would not be as to the survival of the beneficiary under the nil-rate fund, as the section appears to require; see para **[219.8]**.

7   See the Preliminary Note to B14 at para **[214.35]** et seq for the reasons for having these words if the testator has any foreign assets. It can be better to make this gift *subject* to tax. Making the gift subject to inheritance tax will, in the event of this gift taking the non-exempt estate over the inheritance tax threshold (eg because of changes in the law or the testator having made lifetime gifts during the seven years preceding his death), cause the size of the chargeable estate to be less than it would be if the gift was free of inheritance tax: see B14 at para **[214.74]**.

8   The current threshold is £242,000 (tax year 2000–01). If a legacy of £242,000 is settled on discretionary trusts and if, as in this form, all other benefits devolve on the spouse, no inheritance tax will be payable on the testator's death unless lifetime transfers fall to be taken into account or there is property treated as part of the testator's estate for inheritance tax purposes such as property subject to a reservation (see Part A, para **[200.76]**), or settled property in which he had an interest in possession.

9   The formula in square brackets is designed to ensure that the amount of the discretionary legacy does not exceed the inheritance tax threshold where other non-exempt gifts are made or where lifetime chargeable transfers fall to be taken into account on the death. Where a legacy subject to a discretionary trust is included in a will where the residuary gift will not be exempt from inheritance tax (see paras **[218.23]** and **[218.24]**), the second alternative formula for defining the amount of the settled legacy should not be used. This is because the amount of inheritance tax payable on the estate will be the same whatever the size of the legacy. The probable result of using the second alternative formula where none of the residue was exempt would be that if the taxable estate were within the nil-rate band and no inheritance tax was payable, the legacy would use up the entire residue, and that if any inheritance tax were payable on the estate the legacy would be nil. We suggest that where there is no exempt residue either a specified cash sum should be settled on discretionary trusts, or residue should be left on discretionary trusts with the idea that an appointment falling within the ITA 1984, s 144 (for which see the Note in C3 at para **[225.83]** et seq) can be made if the discretionary trust fund turns out after the testator's death to be larger than is appropriate.

10   The words in square brackets authorise the creation of discretionary powers, eg powers to advance capital to a life tenant, which may not otherwise be valid: see Vol 1, para **[40.5]**.

11   A power to pay or apply capital, being exercisable in a less formal manner than a power of appointment, may be a useful power to confer. It is essential that its exercise is adequately evidenced.

12   This will enable the trustees to exercise their powers and discretions in favour of one of their number.

13   These powers and the provisions of the next subclause are included so as to enable a debt or charge scheme to be used as a means of avoiding the surviving spouse having an interest in possession in the trust fund subject to the trusts of this clause, where there are insufficient assets other than the matrimonial home with which to constitute that trust fund. See paras **[218.19]**– **[218.22]**.

14   The purpose of this is so that new trustees of the residuary estate can be appointed before a charge is entered into, in a case where the surviving spouse is one of the personal representatives or the personal representatives and the trustees of the discretionary legacy are the same persons, and to make clear that new or additional trustees of the discretionary trust legacy can be appointed before the legacy is constituted as a debt from the surviving spouse where the surviving spouse is the sole trustee of it: see para **[218.22]** for the reasons for avoiding these states of affairs.

1481

[218.33]

FORM B18.3:   Devise to beneficiary on discretionary trusts[1]

I devise my freehold land at —— in the county of —— known as —— to my trustees upon trust to sell the same and to hold the rents and profits until sale after payment thereout of all outgoings usually chargeable against income and the net income from the proceeds of sale in trust for [*name*] during [his]/[her] life provided always that at any time or times instead of paying any such rents and profits or income accruing during the life of the said [*name*] to [him]/[her] my trustees may apply any such rents and profits or income for or towards the personal support maintenance and education of the said [*name*] or [his]/[her] issue for the time being or such one or more to the exclusion of the others or other of such objects of this discretionary power in such manner and if more than one in such shares as my trustees shall think proper with power within three years after the death of any object of such discretionary power to apply any income which accrued in his or her lifetime in or towards the discharge of any liability incurred by or on behalf of any such object which my trustees shall think fit to satisfy, and after the death of the said [*name*] [*gift over to remainderman or as the beneficiary shall appoint*].

---

1   This form may be appropriate as an alternative to a protected life interest, (see eg Forms B16.1 to B16.3 at paras **[216.6]–[216.8]** and Form B18.7 at para **[218.37]**) where a testator feels that the object of his bounty may be at risk of bankruptcy, divorce or some other calamity when it would be advantageous for the trustees to be able to divert income from the beneficiary to, eg persons dependent upon him. The trust for sale is not strictly necessary in the light of the TLATA 1996 (see para **[200.54]**), but since the purpose of the form is to provide the beneficiary with an income rather than a place to live, it may be appropriate The trusts of this clause, which give the beneficiary a life interest subject to power for the trustees to divert the income elsewhere, are of a type which does not confer an interest in possession on the married woman for inheritance tax purposes; see *Pearson v IRC* [1981] AC 753; see generally Part A, paras **[200.108]–[200.114]**. However, it is possible that she would have an interest in possession for the purposes of the TLATA 1996, so that unless the land devised was unavailable (eg let) or unsuitable (eg business premises) for her occupation, she might have a right to occupy the land under the TLATA 1996, s 12 (Part G, para **[246.98]**; see also para **[208.5]** et seq). Therefore, if the testator wishes to avoid this, a full discretionary trust form should be used, eg Form B18.1 at para **[218.31]**.
    For the taxation of the income and capital gains of discretionary trusts, see paras **[218.27]** and **[218.28]**.

[218.34]

FORM B18.4:   Trusts for a disabled person[1]

If my said son A (hereinafter called 'A') shall be living and [incapable by reason of mental disorder within the meaning of the Mental Health Act 1983 of administering his property or managing his affairs[2]]/[a disabled person within the meaning of the Inheritance Tax Act 1984, s 89][3] at the time of my death the said [share of my residuary estate] directed to be held upon trust for him as aforesaid (hereinafter called 'the share') shall not vest absolutely in A but shall be retained by my trustees and held upon the following trusts and with and subject to the following powers:

(1)   My trustees shall have power at their absolute discretion to pay or apply the whole or any part or proportion of the income of the share to or for the benefit of A during his life.

(2)   My trustees shall during the period of 21 years commencing with my death while A is living accumulate the income of the share which shall not be paid or applied for the benefit of A as aforesaid as an accretion to the capital of the share but shall have power to pay or apply such accumulations during the life of A as if the same were income of the then current year.

(3)   If A is still living at the expiration of the said period of 21 years my trustees shall from the expiration of such period during the remainder of the life of A pay or apply all income of the share arising after the expiration of the said period of 21 years which shall not be paid or applied to or for the benefit of A under the foregoing power to or for the benefit of all or any one or more of [my children and remoter issue for the time being living other than A] in such shares and proportions as my trustees think fit.

(4)   Notwithstanding the foregoing trusts and power my trustees shall have power during the life of A to pay or apply the whole or any part or parts of the capital of the share to or for the benefit of all or such one or more of [my children and remoter issue] and in such proportions as my trustees think fit provided that the foregoing power shall not be exercisable so as to cause the aggregate amount or value of the capital of the share which shall for the time being have been paid or applied to or for the benefit of persons other than A at any time to exceed the aggregate amount or value of such capital which shall for the time being have been paid or applied to or for the benefit of A.

(5)   Subject to the foregoing trusts and to any or every exercise of the foregoing powers my trustees shall hold the share or such part thereof as shall not have been paid or applied as aforesaid and the income thereof [upon trust for all or any my grandchildren or grandchild whenever born during the lifetime of the last of my children to die who shall attain the age of 18 years if more than one in equal shares].

(6)   Section 32 of the Trustee Act 1925 (relating to the payment or application of capital) shall apply to the last foregoing trust without modification during the life of A but after the death of A the said section 32 shall apply to the said trust in all respects as if the words 'one-half of' had been omitted from proviso (a) of subsection (1) thereof.

1   This form is intended to satisfy the conditions laid down in the ITA 1984, s 89 (see the Preliminary Note to C4 at paras [226.1] et seq). It assumes that the testator has made a gift in an earlier clause of the will to his disabled son, and that it is an absolute gift conditional only on surviving the testator. The trusts of the clause only come into operation if the disabled son 'A' is still disabled within the meaning of s 84(4) at the testator's death because it seems that the section will only apply if he is disabled at the time of the testator's death. During A's life current income is only paid for his benefit at the discretion of the trustees and is otherwise accumulated or distributed to other beneficiaries, but he will be deemed for inheritance tax purposes to have an interest in possession. Subclause (4) confers a wide power to apply capital with a proviso that is intended to 'secure that not less than half of the settled property which is applied during [A's] life is applied for his benefit' within the meaning of s 89(1)(b).
      Subclause (6) provides for the statutory power of advancement to apply without modification during A's life, so that the existence of the power does not prejudice the application of s 89: see sub-s (3). After A's death the power is made applicable to the whole of a presumptive share.
2   Such a person is one of the categories of disabled person within the ITA 1984, s 89. For the other categories, see n 3 infra.

3   A disabled person may be someone: (i) incapable by reason of mental disorder within the meaning of the Mental Health Act 1983 of administering his property or managing his affairs; (ii) in receipt of an attendance allowance under the Social Security Contributions and Benefits Act 1992, s 64 or the Social Security Contributions and Benefits (Northern Ireland) Act 1992, s 64; or (iii) in receipt of a disability living allowance under the Social Security Contributions and Benefits Act 1992, s 71 or the Social Security Contributions and Benefits (Northern Ireland) Act 1992, s 71, by virtue of entitlement to the care component at the highest or middle rate (ITA 1984, s 89(4)).

Powers

[218.35]

FORM B18.5:   Power to daughter to appoint life interest in a settled share to her husband[1]

Provided always and I hereby declare that notwithstanding the trusts hereinbefore contained my said daughter [*name*] shall have power[2] by deed revocable or irrevocable or by will or codicil to appoint to any husband who may survive her for the residue of his life or for any less period [the whole or] any part [not exceeding one-half] of the income of my said daughter's share[3] or the income of any asset or assets comprised in such share or of any part or share of such share [not exceeding one-half of the value at the date of such deed will or codicil of such share (all values for this purpose to be determined conclusively by my trustees)] and she may if she thinks fit appoint protective trusts of such income for his benefit during his life or any less period.

1   This could be a useful power for inheritance tax purposes in some circumstances since on the daughter's death there would (if she had had an interest in possession in all the settled property) be spouse exemption on property subject to a life interest appointed under this power and the charge on the husband's death would be as if the property subject to his life interest formed part of his estate. For the spouse exemption see Part A, paras **[200.99]–[200.101]** and for inheritance tax and protective trusts see Part A, para **[200.116]**. For an alternative form see Form 18.8 at para **[218.38]**.
2   If this power is only to be effectually exercised in default of children or issue attaining a vested interest, insert here: 'in case no child or other issue of such daughter shall attain a vested interest in such daughter's share.'
3   It is assumed that the fund is divided into shares, each of which is settled on a child of the testator with remainder to his or her own children. For examples see Forms C2.6 at para **[224.95]** and C7.4 at para **[229.37]**.

[218.36]

FORM B18.6:   Power to trustees to settle child's share[1]

Provided always and I hereby declare that in case any child of mine shall marry before attaining the age of [eighteen] [twenty-one] [*the age mentioned in the primary gift*] years my trustees shall have power in their absolute discretion until such child shall attain the said age to appoint by deed or deeds executed either before and contingent upon any such marriage or after such marriage to settle the whole or any part of the share of residue hereinbefore bequeathed to such child or the whole or any part of any specific property appropriated to the said share upon such trusts for the benefit of such child and his or her spouse or intended spouse and their children or issue or any of them in such manner and form and with such provisions stipulations and agreements as my trustees may think proper including discretionary trusts and powers and administrative powers and provisions as my trustees think fit provided that the foregoing power shall not be exercisable otherwise than so as to cause such child to become entitled to or to an interest in possession in the said share on or before attaining the age of 25 years within the meaning of section 71(1)(a) of the Inheritance Tax Act 1984[2] or otherwise than so as to cause the income of the said share to be accumulated so far as not applied for such child's maintenance education or benefit during such time as he or she shall not have become entitled as aforesaid.

1   This clause contemplates a compulsory settlement by the trustees before the child attains a vested interest, here supposed to be at eighteen or twenty-one years or on marriage. It is very inadvisable to attempt to give trustees power to make a settlement after the date of vesting; if the testator wishes the child to be protected, he should either settle the share himself, or make the age of vesting rather high and independent of marriage, and give his trustees power to settle the child's share before attaining the named age. A fiscal advantage of this form may be that it will enable the trustees to postpone the absolute vesting of the trust fund and so defer the capital gains tax charge under the TCGA, s 71 if hold-over relief would not be available on absolute vesting under the TCGA, s 260(2)(d) (see Part A, para **[200.135]**).

2   For s 71 see Part A, para **[200.119]** et seq. It is thought that this proviso will keep the trusts of the share within s 71.

[218.37]

FORM **B18.7:**   **Protective life interest with a power to raise and pay capital**[1]

I give to my trustees the sum of £—— free of inheritance tax payable on my death [*or* the residue of my property both real and personal wherever situate being or arising] as to the income thereof upon protective trusts for the benefit of A during his life and my trustees shall until the failure or determination of the trust of income in favour of the said A have the further power at their absolute discretion and without being liable in any way to account for the exercise of such discretion to raise and pay to the said A for his own absolute use and benefit at any time or times as my trustees shall determine [the whole or any part or parts of] [any sum or sums not exceeding on any one occasion £—— clear of expenses out of] the capital of the said fund [*or* residue] and my trustees shall hold any part of the said fund [residue] not so transferred to the said A during his lifetime as the said A shall by will or codicil appoint and in default of and subject to any such appointment [*set out trusts in remainder*] and I direct that my trustees shall on no account be liable or responsible for making any such payment whether of income or capital to the said A after the failure or determination of his said determinable life interest unless or until they shall have received express notice of the act or event causing such failure or determination.

1   The effect of this clause is that trustees can pay sums out of capital to the beneficiary and this may prove a very useful provision where the beneficiary has only a life interest whether protected or not. Care should be taken not to exercise the power in such manner as to encourage the Inland Revenue to claim that the capital advanced is liable to tax as income in the beneficiary's hands, eg by making advances of regular amounts at regular intervals to pay everyday living expenses. In *Stevenson v Wishart* [1987] STC 266 recurring payments of large sums out of trust capital for a discretionary beneficiary's nursing-home expenses were held not to be income, but the decision leaves open the question whether it is possible that recurring payments of capital made by trustees under a power of the kind in this Form could be taxed as income if they were intended to defray ordinary living expenses. The exercise of a power to pay

capital to a life tenant does not involve a charge to inheritance tax: see Part A, para **[200.114]** and the ITA 1984, s 53(2). For a shorter form of power to pay or apply capital for the benefit of a life tenant see Form B18.8 at para **[218.38]** and for a form by reference to the statutory power of advancement see Form B18.22 at para **[218.106]**.

[218.38]

FORM B18.8:   Life interest subject to trustees' power to pay or apply capital to or for the benefit of the life tenant, with remainders to the life tenant's children subject to powers of the life tenant to appoint a life interest to his spouse and to appoint capital among his issue

(1)   My trustees shall hold [the trust fund] on trust to pay the income thereof to [my son] during his life;

(2)   provided that my trustees shall have power in their absolute discretion from time to time during the life of [my son] to pay transfer or apply the whole or any part or parts of the capital of [the trust fund] in which [my son] has for the time being an interest in possession (within the meaning of Part III of the Inheritance Tax Act 1984)[1] to or for the benefit of [my son] in such manner as they shall in their absolute discretion think fit;[2]

(3)   subject to the foregoing trust and any or every exercise of the foregoing power my trustees shall hold [the trust fund] and the income thereof upon such trusts in such shares or proportions and with and subject to such powers and provisions (which may include discretionary trusts or powers or administrative powers or provisions) for the benefit of all or such one or more of [my son's] children and remoter issue as [he] may by deed (revocable or irrevocable) or by will or codicil appoint;

(4)   in default of and subject to any such appointment and subject to the foregoing trusts and any or every exercise of the foregoing powers my trustees shall hold [the trust fund] and the income thereof upon trust for the child or children of [my son] who shall attain the age of 21 years if more than one in equal shares;

(5)   notwithstanding the foregoing trusts and powers for the benefit of the issue of [my son] he shall have power by deed (revocable or irrevocable) or by will or codicil to appoint to any wife of his who may survive him as his widow a life or lesser interest (or a life or lesser interest on protective trusts) in the whole or any part or parts of [the trust fund] and the foregoing trusts for [my son's] children and any or every exercise of the foregoing power for the benefit of his issue shall take effect subject to such life or lesser interest;[3]

(6)   [*As* Form B18.32 *at para* **[218.117]**][4].

1   The point of restricting the power to property in which the life tenant has an interest in possession is that if his life interest is terminated by him, eg surrendering or assigning it in favour of the remaindermen, the power will automatically cease to be exercisable.

2   See n 1 to Form B18.7 at para **[218.37]**. This power would authorise lending capital to or for the benefit of the life tenant in an appropriate case (*Re Kershaw's Trusts* (1868) LR 6 Eq 322), although an express power to lend such as Form B18.27 at para **[218.112]** could usefully be incorporated. The case law on the scope of the statutory power of advancement, discussed at paras **[218.85]–[218.102]** is also relevant to an express power of this kind.

3   See n 1 to Form B18.5 at para **[218.35]**.

4   This will enable the trustees to exercise their power to pay or apply capital to the life tenant and the statutory power of advancement (for which see paras **[218.85]–[218.102]**) in favour of one of their number.

[218.39]

FORM B18.9:   Power to pay, to children who have life interests, increasing proportions of capital as they grow older[1]

Notwithstanding the trust hereinbefore declared my trustees may in the exercise of their absolute discretion as they think fit on or after the attainment of the age of [25] years by any child of mine pay transfer or apply to or for the benefit of such child one third or any less part of the share of such child and on or after the attainment of the age of [30] years by any child of mine pay transfer or apply to or for the benefit of such child a further third or any less part of the share of such child and on or after the attainment of the age of [35] years by any child of mine pay transfer or apply to or for the benefit of such child the whole or any part or parts of the share (or such of the same as has not previously been so paid transferred or applied) of such child [and I express the wish but without restricting my trustees' discretion in any way that each of my children shall receive all the capital of his share by the time he attains the age of 35 years].

> 1   This form presupposes a trust for the testator's children in shares which are settled on them for life with remainders to their own children. For a form of complete will containing a clause of this kind see Form C8.6 at para **[230.81]**.

[218.40]

FORM B18.10:   Power to trustees to vary trusts of child's settled share

Provided always and I hereby declare that my trustees shall have power during the lifetime of any child of mine by any deed or deeds to vary all or any of the trusts in this my will contained concerning the share of residue whether original or accruing hereby bequeathed to such child and to settle the whole or any part of such share upon such trusts for the benefit of such child etc [*Continue as in* Form B18.6 *at para* **[218.36]**].[1]

> 1   Care needs to be taken to make sure that the presence of this power will not prevent the ITA 1984, s 71 from applying (for which see Part A, paras **[200.119]** et seq. The proviso from Form B18.6 at para **[218.36]** should be sufficient for this purpose.

Maintenance

[218.41]
Note. The TA 1925, s 31 (Part G, para **[246.26]**) which contains the statutory power of maintenance was amended by the Family Law Reform Act 1969, s 1(3) and Sch 1, Part 1 which substituted for references therein to twenty-one years references to eighteen years. This amendment did not affect interests arising under instruments made *before* the commencement of the 1969 Act (ie before 1 January 1970), s 1(4) and Sch 3, para 5(1)(a) in which case the relevant age remained twenty-one years. For this purpose an interest created by an appointment made after 31 December 1969, under a special power is *not* an interest under an instrument made before the commencement of the Act, even if the power was created by an instrument made before then: see *Re Dickinson's Settlements, Bickersteth v Dickinson* [1939] Ch 27 (this is a decision on the TA

1925, s 31(5), but the relevant wording of the Family Law Reform Act 1969, Sch 3, para 5(1)(a) is virtually the same).

[218.42]
The TA 1925, s 31 applies where a trust carries the intermediate income and so should be read in conjunction with the LPA 1925, s 175 (Part G, para **[244.52]**), which extends the categories of interest which will now carry the intermediate income, unless that income is otherwise *expressly* disposed of. Our comments on the TA 1925, s 31 (the full text of which is set out in Part G at para **[246.26]**) are as follows:

[218.43]
(a)   Type of beneficiary. The section does not authorise maintenance when apart from the section the beneficiary on attaining a vested interest in capital would not be entitled to the income (*Re Raine, Tyerman v Stansfield* [1929] 1 Ch 716).

[218.44]
(b)   Commencement. The powers of maintenance contained in the TA 1925, s 31 do not apply where the will or instrument under which the interest arises came into operation before 1 January 1926. For this purpose a document exercising a special power of appointment is the instrument (*Re Dickinson's Settlements, Bickersteth v Dickinson* [1939] Ch 27). It is conceived that despite the repeal of the LPA 1925, Sch 7 (20 *Halsbury's Statutes* (2nd edn) 895) by the Statute Law Revision Act 1950 (41 *Halsbury's Statutes* (4th edn) 743), the Conveyancing Act 1881, s 43 (37 *Halsbury's Statutes* (4th edn) 59) still applies to instruments which came into operation before 1925.

[218.45]
(c)   Relationship to the terms of the will. The powers of maintenance are in addition to any powers conferred by the will. They apply without any incorporation in the will, but so far only as a contrary intention is not expressed in the will, and have effect subject to the terms of the will (TA 1925, s 69(2): Part G, para **[246.37]**). Where there is a specific direction to accumulate the whole income there is no power to apply it in maintenance: *Re Reade-Revell, Crellin v Melling* [1930] 1 Ch 52, [1929] All ER Rep 506; even where the direction to accumulate is void: *Re Erskine's Settlement Trusts, Hollis v Pigott* [1971] 1 All ER 572, [1971] 1 WLR 162. Where there is no direction to accumulate during a minority, the section allows maintenance even though there is a direction to accumulate after the attainment of the age of eighteen (or twenty-one): *Re Leng, Dodsworth v Leng* [1938] Ch 821, [1938] 3 All ER 181. The decision in *Re Reade-Revell, Crellin v Melling* was followed in *Re Stapleton, Stapleton v Stapleton* [1946] 1 All ER 323, where it was explained that in *Re Reade-Revell, Crellin v Melling* there was a specific direction to accumulate, but in *Re Leng, Dodsworth v Leng* there was only an implied direction. A positive direction to apply the entire income in maintenance precludes accumulation of surplus (*Re Peel, Tattersall v Peel* [1936] Ch 161).

[218.46]
(d) Prior interests. The provisions of the TA 1925, s 31 are subject to any prior interests or charges which affect the property: *Re Turner's Will Trusts, District Bank Ltd v Turner* [1937] Ch 15 at 28, [1936] 2 All ER 1435 at 1448.

[218.47]
(e) Interests to which s 31 of the TA 1925 applies. The provisions apply to any property held by trustees for any person for any interest, whether vested or contingent, but, in the case of contingent interests, only if the limitation or trust carries the intermediate income. As to what interests carry the intermediate income, see Vol I, paras **[32.3]**, **[32.15]**–**[32.17]** and **[218.51]**. As to the effect of s 31 on vested interests, see para **[218.50]**.

[218.48]
(f) Where income of another fund is also available. The statutory scheme is, in some respects, rather elaborate. Under its provisions, trustees, who have notice of any other income available for the maintenance of a minor, should attempt to agree with the trustees of the fund producing such other income upon a proper figure for the maintenance of the minor (a matter upon which there may be a divergence of opinion); the figure having been agreed each set of trustees is to apply, out of the income in their hands, a proportionate part only of the amount so agreed, the proportion being based on the incomes of the two funds. Where the two funds will, upon the failure of the minor's contingent interest, pass to different persons, the provision is eminently fair; but it may lead to difficulty and delay (eg where one set of trustees is in another country) in cases where it is essential that maintenance should be given promptly; however it only applies 'so far as practicable', and if difficulties arise it can be disregarded. The proviso to s 31(1) which provides for this is commonly excluded: see eg, Form B18.11 at para **[218.77]**.

[218.49]
(g) The trustees' discretion. Trustees must exercise a conscious discretion. They *are* to have regard to the age of the minor and his requirements and generally to the circumstances of the case. The trustees should take the income of a parent into account, for though they *may* apply income whether or not there is any person bound by law to provide, etc, yet it is only such part as may, in all the circumstances, be reasonable which may be applied. Where there is a discretionary trust to pay or apply income to or for the benefit of minors, who have only a contingent reversionary interest in the corpus which does not carry the intermediate income, any payment or application of income in pursuance of such discretionary trust is not made in pursuance of this section, for sub-s (3) excludes the case where there is no right to the intermediate income: *Re Vestey's Settlement, Lloyds Bank Ltd v O'Meara* [1951] Ch 209, [1950] 2 All ER 891.

[218.50]
(h) Income interests of contingent beneficiaries of full age. If a person on attaining eighteen has not a vested interest in the income (eg is still only entitled contingently as tenant for life or as owner of the corpus), he will be entitled personally to receive the income both of the property and of past accumulations

until he attains a vested interest (eg until he becomes a tenant for life or owner of the corpus), or until he dies, or until failure of his interest. This will be an interest in possession for inheritance tax purposes (see Part A, para **[200.108]** et seq). But an express direction for maintenance etc to continue to a later age will usually amount to a contrary intention within the TA 1925, s 69(2) (Part G, para **[246.37]**) so as to exclude the statutory entitlement to income: *Re Turner's Will Trusts, District Bank Ltd v Turner,* [1937] Ch 15 at 28, [1936] 2 All ER 1435 at 1448. The court has power, where the testator was a parent or in loco parentis, to allow maintenance in the case of a legacy contingent on the minor attaining an age other than full age (*Re Jones, Meacock v Jones* [1932] 1 Ch 642, [1932] All ER Rep 804).

[218.51]
(i)   Destination of accumulation of surplus income. Under the TA 1925, s 31(2) (Part G, para **[246.26]**) accumulations will cease in any event on the attainment of eighteen, unless there be an overriding direction in the will to the contrary (*Re Turner's Will Trusts, District Bank Ltd v Turner,* [1937] Ch 15 at 28, [1936] 2 All ER 1435 at 1448).

In three cases the accumulations will belong to the person who has been the object of the maintenance:

(i)   If the income during the minority or until marriage has been nominally vested in the minor (eg if he were—although still a minor—tenant for life or tenant in tail), and he attains eighteen or marries under that age.

(ii)   If the minor on attaining eighteen or on marriage under that age becomes entitled to the property itself either in fee simple, absolute or determinable, or absolutely, or for an entailed interest.

(iii)   He or his estate will be entitled to the accumulations even if he dies under eighteen if he had a vested annuity (TA 1925, s 31(4)), or an absolutely vested interest in capital (because the accumulations are added to capital but he is entitled to the capital), or there is some express provision of the trust instrument which has this effect (as in *Re Delamere's Settlement Trust, Kenny v Cunningham-Reid* [1984] 1 All ER 584, [1984] 1 WLR 813). It is thought that in any of these circumstances he will have an interest in possession for inheritance tax purposes during his minority. See Form B18.15 at para **[218.81]** for a variation of TA 1925, s 31 which provides for the accumulations to vest absolutely.

[218.52]
Where a minor child is absolutely and indefeasibly entitled to any of the income of a fund during his minority, he cannot insist on it being handed over to him while he is a minor, although the trustees will have power to pay it to him and accept his receipt if he marries while still a minor (LPA 1925, s 21) or there is specific power to accept his receipt in the will (such as Form B21.20 at para **[221.24]**). However, a parent or guardian with 'parental responsibility' (see Vol 1, para **[28.2]** for this term) for such a child could require such income to be handed over to the parent or guardian, and could give a good receipt where the trustees wish to hand it over, in reliance on the ChA 1989, s 3(3) (Part G, para **[244.119]**; see also Vol 1, para **[9.42]**).

[218.53]
If the person who has had income applied for his maintenance is not, and does not become, entitled to the accumulations in any of the ways described above, the accumulations are held as an accretion to 'the capital of the property from which such accumulations arose' and as one fund with it for all purposes, although the trustees have power to apply them as income of the current year while the beneficiary remains a minor and his interest continues (TA 1925, s 31(2)(ii): Part G, para **[246.26]**). What is 'the property from which such accumulations arose' presents difficulty in some circumstances. If there is eg a testamentary gift of a fund on trust for the children of A who attain the age of twenty-five in equal shares, with the TA 1925, s 31 applying, and A has two children X and Y of whom X is alive at the testator's death and Y is born five years after the testator's death, both of whom then attain the age of twenty-five, are the accumulations of the income of the fund which arose after the testator's death and before the birth of Y an accretion to the entire fund to which X and Y are both entitled, or are they an accretion to X's half share of the fund only? According to *Re Joel's Will Trusts* [1967] Ch 14 at 36–37, following *Re King* [1928] Ch 330 at 337–338, such accumulations would in this example be an accretion to X's half share of the fund only. See Form B18.14 at para **[218.80]** for a form which varies s 31 so that the accumulations go with the capital, with the result in this example that Y would get a half share of them.

[218.54]
It should be noted that a minor who is entitled to a defeasible interest in personalty does not have an 'absolute' interest so as to be entitled to the accumulation of income thereon on attaining full age or marriage, even though an equivalent interest in realty would so entitle him: *Re Sharp's Settlement Trusts, Ibbotson v Bliss* [1973] Ch 331, [1972] 3 All ER 151. The effect of s 31(2) is, however, to give a minor who would otherwise be entitled to a vested interest in income but not in capital only a contingent interest in the surplus income during his minority and he is not assessable to higher rate income tax in respect thereof: *Stanley v IRC* [1944] KB 255, [1944] 1 All ER 230. For the taxation of income in such a case see para **[218.65]**.

[218.55]
(j)   What interests carry intermediate income. The section must be read in conjunction with the LPA 1925, s 175 (Part G, para **[244.52]**). That section enacts that, except so far as the income or any part of it is otherwise *expressly* disposed of, the following interests *shall* (subject to statutory provisions as to accumulations: LPA 1925, ss 164–166: Part G, paras **[246.42]**–**[246.44]**; and the PAA 1964, s 13: Part G, para **[246.71]**) carry the intermediate income:

(a)   A contingent or future specific devise or bequest of any property: 'specific' applies to 'bequest' as well as to 'devise' (*Re Raine, Tyerman v Stansfield* [1929] 1 Ch 716), and consequently a contingent pecuniary legacy is not within these words.

(b)   A contingent residuary devise of freehold land.

(c)   A specific or residuary devise of freehold land to trustees upon trust for persons whose interests are contingent or executory.

[218.56]

Having regard to the rules under the general law (eg that a contingent residuary bequest and also a contingent residuary devise and bequest of mixed realty and personalty carry the intermediate income), it would appear that all contingent specific and residuary devises and bequests will now carry the intermediate income, unless that income is otherwise expressly disposed of.

[218.57]

The question of contingent or future pecuniary legacies to minors still remains to be considered under the general law. The testator may, or may not, be the parent of or in loco parentis to the legatee:

(a)   If he is a parent or in loco parentis (a grandfather is not usually in loco parentis as regards grandchildren; *Re Dawson, Swainson v Dawson* [1919] 1 Ch 102, and see generally, as to who is in loco parentis, Vol 1, para **[44.7]**), the general rule is that a contingent legacy to a minor carries interest:

   (i)   if the contingency is the attaining of full age or marriage. It appears that such a contingent legacy carries interest for the benefit of the legatee, even if there is another fund the income of which is available for his maintenance (*Re Moody, Woodroffe v Moody* [1895] 1 Ch 101; *Re Raine, Tyerman v Stansfield* [1929] 1 Ch 716 at 721). But if the contingency is the attaining of a greater age than full age, the legacy does not carry interest (*Re Abrahams, Abrahams v Bendon* [1911] 1 Ch 108).

   (ii)   in any case in which a contingent legacy to a minor, where the testator is not the parent of or in loco parentis to the legatee, would carry interest (see below).

   In all cases where the testator is the parent or in loco parentis to the minor legatee, and where the legacy carries interest under the general law, the rate of interest is 5 per cent per annum if the income is sufficient and subject to any rules of court to the contrary (TA 1925, s 31(3): Part G, para **[246.26]**), and the statutory rules of maintenance apply. It may be that the rate of interest on legacies provided by CPR 1998, Sch 1 – RSC Ord 44, r 10 (currently 6 per cent—see Vol 1, para **[32.4]**) for cases where the court orders an account of legacies, is a rate contained in a rule of court to the contrary for this purpose.

(b)   If the testator is not the parent or in loco parentis, still, under the general law, a contingent legacy to an infant carries interest if—

   (i)   the legacy is directed to be set apart; but in this case the court would not as a rule order maintenance if the father is living: *Re Boulter, Capital and Counties Bank v Boulter* [1918] 2 Ch 40 at 45; in cases of setting apart the general rule is that the income is added to and awaits the vesting of the capital; or

   (ii)   an intention is manifested in the will that the minor should be maintained; but if the income of any other fund under the will (residue for instance) is available for maintenance, the contingent legacy will not carry interest (*Re West, Westhead v Aspland* [1913] 2 Ch 345; *Re Raine, Tyerman v Stansfield* [1929] 1 Ch 716 at 720).

[218.58]
A future defeasible gift does not carry the intermediate income: *Re Gillett's Will Trusts, Barclays Bank Ltd v Gillett* [1950] Ch 102, [1949] 2 All ER 893 (gift of capital in default of appointment); *Re Geering, Gulliver v Geering* [1964] Ch 136, [1962] 3 All ER 1043 (where there was an express provision which carried the intermediate income), see also Vol 1, paras **[32.15]–[32.17]**.

[218.59]
Where income is available in such cases as these, the statutory rules as to maintenance will no doubt apply and carry interest. It should be noted that the general law does not give interest on a contingent legacy to a minor when there is a trust for accumulating the income which precedes the contingent gift (*Re George* (1877) 5 Ch D 837). On these subjects, see Vol 1, para **[32.1]** et seq.

[218.60]
(k)   Annuities. By s 31(4) of the TA 1925 (Part G, para **[246.26]**) a *vested* annuity is to be treated for the purpose of maintenance as if it were income of property, save that any accumulations during infancy belong in any case to the infant or his personal representatives.

[218.61]
(l)   Adaptations of the TA 1925, s 31. A number of testators will no doubt be content to rely on the statutory powers. Others may prefer to give their own trustees what may be a wider discretion by omitting the reference to other available income. Section 31(1)(i) (standing alone at any rate) gives the impression that the amount of income to be applied depends upon a standard of reasonableness, and that it cramps the discretion of the trustees (but see para **[218.49]**). Form B18.11 at para **[218.77]** meets this point by expressly giving an absolute discretion.

[218.62]
It will be appreciated that where the TA 1925, s 31 applies to property held on trust for a class of minors, several of whom are in existence, it applies severally to each presumptive share; that is, in each year all the income has to be divided up among the beneficiaries in accordance with their interests in capital, and then the share of income allocated to each beneficiary has to be applied for his benefit or accumulated for him in accordance with s 31.

[218.63]
Special provision will still have to be made if it is desired to use the income for the common maintenance of a class of individuals, and such provision may have inheritance tax disadvantages. See para **[218.67]** and Forms B18.16 at para **[218.82]** and B18.17 at para **[218.83]**. For extended accumulation and maintenance provisions continuing after the age of eighteen see para **[218.72]**. For provision in relation to an open class of beneficiaries of which new members are born after the trust for that class commenced, so that such new members participate in accumulations of income made before they are born, see para **[218.53]** and Form B18.14 at para **[218.80]**. For provision entitling a beneficiary absolutely to the accumulations of income of his share, and therefore

it seems conferring an interest in possession on him for tax purposes, see para **[218.51]** and Form B18.15 at para **[218.81]**.

[218.64]
(m)   The powers of the court. The court can order maintenance and, where there is already a provision for maintenance, increased maintenance. The court has jurisdiction with respect to the income of property belonging to or held in trust for a minor, to take care of it and apply it for his maintenance or otherwise for his benefit and accumulate any surplus not required to be so applied (*Havelock v Havelock, Re Allan* (1881) 17 Ch D 807; *Re Smeed, Archer v Prall* (1886) 2 TLR 535). Where, however, property is vested in trustees upon whom a power has been expressly conferred (which includes the statutory power) of applying at their discretion all or any part of the income for maintenance, education or benefit, the court will not override or interfere with that discretion, if the trustees actually exercise it (*Re Wells, Wells v Wells* (1889) 43 Ch D 281 at 286, 287) and are not doing so in a manner prejudicial to the infant's interests (*Re Lofthouse* (1885) 29 Ch D 921; *Re Bryant, Bryant v Hickley* [1894] 1 Ch 324). If there are two funds available for maintenance, the court orders maintenance from the fund from which it is most beneficial to the minor that it should be taken (*Re Wells*). Maintenance will be ordered out of income directed to be accumulated where there is a paramount intention that the beneficiary should be maintained (*Havelock v Havelock, Re Allan*; *Re Collins, Collins v Collins* (1886) 32 Ch D 229; *Walker v Duncombe* [1901] 1 Ch 879; *Re Wright* [1954] OR 755). Where necessary, maintenance will be ordered out of capital or income in which the minor has only a reversionary or contingent interest subject to the rights of creditors (*Revel v Watkinson* (1748) 1 Ves Sen 93 at 95) and recoupment of such expenditure may be secured by a policy of assurance (*Re Bruce* (1882) 30 WR 992; *Re Tanner* (1884) 53 LJ Ch 1108 at 1110) or by a charge on the property (*Re Colgan* (1881) 19 Ch D 305; *Re Tanner*; but see *Re Hambrough's Estate, Hambrough v Hambrough* [1909] 2 Ch 620, as explained in *Re Gower's Settlement* [1934] Ch 365 at 371, [1934] All ER Rep 796 at 798, but this difficulty has been removed by the enactment of the TA 1925, s 53). The jurisdiction under the TA 1925, s 53 is only applicable where money is required for the maintenance, education or benefit of a minor and cannot be used merely to put an end to a settlement (*Re Heyworth's Settlements* [1956] Ch 364, [1956] 2 All ER 21), but where the proceeds of a sale under that section are to be settled, it seems they are to be 'applied' for maintenance, education or benefit of a minor (*Re Meux, Gilmour v Gilmour* [1958] Ch 154, [1957] 2 All ER 630).

[218.65]
(n)   Income tax. It should be remembered that income which is to be accumulated or which is payable at the discretion of the trustees or any other person in so far as it is not used to defray trust expenses is taxable in the hands of the trustees at the rate applicable to trusts (currently 34 per cent), (unless it is UK company dividend income when it is taxable at the Schedule F trust rate, currently 25 per cent): ICTA 1988, s 686. This provision will apply to express discretionary and accumulation trusts, but it will also apply in cases where the maintenance and accumulation provisions of the TA 1925, s 31 apply, ie until the beneficiary has attained full age. Income applied for the benefit of a beneficiary under a power will be treated as such beneficiary's income for tax

purposes and he or she may be able to recover some part of the tax already paid by the trustees: ICTA 1988, s 687. See also paras **[218.28]** and **[218.29]**.

[218.66]
(o)   Time apportionment of income. Where the TA 1925, s 31 applies to property held on trust for an open class of minors contingently upon their attaining a particular age, the birth of an additional member of the class or the death of an existing one could cause elaborate apportionment calculations under the Apportionment Act 1870 if it is not excluded: see *Re Joel's Will Trusts; Rogerson v Brudenell-Bruce* [1967] Ch 14, [1966] 2 All ER 482. It is better to exclude the Act using eg Form B14.32 at para **[214.54]**.

[218.67]
(p)   Inheritance tax. One of the conditions which has to be satisfied if the ITA 1984, s 71 (for which see Part A, para **[200.119]** et seq) is to apply to any settled property, is that the income of that property is to be accumulated so far as not applied for the maintenance, education or benefit of a 'beneficiary' (s 71(1)(b): for this subsection and the meaning of 'beneficiary' see Part A, paras **[200.119]** et seq. This will clearly be satisfied where TA 1925, s 31 applies to the income. If express trusts of income during a minority are drafted we suggest they should follow the scheme of s 31, of a *power* to apply income for maintenance, education or benefit and a *trust* to accumulate the remainder. However, it is thought that the Inland Revenue take the view that a trust to accumulate without any power of maintenance would satisfy the ITA 1984, s 71(1)(b), and that a trust for maintenance with or without a power of accumulation would also do so.

[218.68]
Given that the application of the ITA 1984, s 71 is viewed collectively in relation to a class of 'beneficiaries' interested in settled property, a provision for maintenance and accumulation for a class of 'beneficiaries' out of a common fund of income is probably within s 71(1)(b), but care has to be taken to see that such a provision does not prejudice the application of s 71(1)(a) by postponing the time when some of the 'beneficiaries' attain absolute interests or interests in possession until after they attain the age of 25 or by allowing those who have attained 25 to benefit from income held for those who are under that age. We do not recommend the use of such provisions, even though they may be slightly more convenient administratively, because they increase the chances of something going wrong. See further, *Foster's Inheritance Tax*, E5.

[218.69]
(q)   Section 31 and the permitted periods of accumulation. It seems that accumulation under the TA 1925, s 31 during a minority is always valid, irrespective of whether a permitted accumulation period is available under the LPA 1925, s 164 (Part G, para **[246.42]**) or the PAA 1964, s 13 (Part G, para **[246.71]**) because it is directed by statute. Section 165 of the LPA 1925 (Part G, para **[246.43]**) provides that where accumulations of surplus income are made during a minority under any statutory power (or under the general law), the period for which such accumulations are permitted to be made is not to be taken into account in determining the periods for which accumulations are permitted to be made by the LPA 1925, s 164 (which is treated by the PAA

1964, s 13 as including those added by that section), and accordingly an express trust for accumulation for any other permitted period will not be invalidated by reason of accumulations also having been made during a minority under a statutory power (or the general law). It is not easy to work out exactly what the LPA 1925, s 165 is providing, and there is very little authority on it. The reference to a statutory power is a reference to the provisions for accumulation under the TA 1925, s 31; although the latter are strictly speaking a *trust* to accumulate, they are ancillary to the statutory power of maintenance (see *Re Turner's Will Trusts, District Bank Ltd v Turner* [1937] Ch 15).

[218.70]
Only one of the permitted periods of accumulation under the LPA 1925, s 164 is available in relation to any particular disposition, and it is a matter of construction of the instrument making the disposition to determine which period has seemingly been chosen: see eg *Jagger v Jagger* (1883) 25 Ch D 729; *Re Watt's Will Trusts, Watt v Watt* [1936] 2 All ER 1555, 1562, and *Re Ransome* [1957] Ch 348, 361. A possible interpretation is therefore that the LPA 1925, s 165 means no more than that a will or other disposition is not deprived of choice of accumulation period by providing trusts to which accumulation under the TA 1925, s 31 applies; for example, providing trusts to which s 31 applies does not amount to a selection of the duration of minorities of persons who would be entitled to the income if of full age (the period permitted by the LPA 1925, s 164(1)(d): Part G, para **[246.42]**), and the 21-year accumulation period can still be used.

[218.71]
There is a more radical interpretation of the LPA 1925, s 165, which is that it permits accumulation under the TA 1925, s 31 cumulatively with accumulation under the relevant period under s 164. This argument is really only of interest in relation to the 21-year period under s 165(1)(b) (or the PAA 1964, s 13(1)(a)); it would mean that the accumulation period was suspended during a period of accumulation under the TA 1925, s 31, but started again where it left off once the accumulation under s 31 had finished. If this was correct it would be possible for accumulation and maintenance trusts for a beneficiary to continue until he reached the age of 25 outside the period of 21 years from the testator's death, unless and until there had been accumulation other than under the TA 1925, s 31 for a total of 21 years, and this was the interpretation apparently accepted by Astbury J in *Re Maber* [1928] Ch 88 at 93, although it was not necessary for his decision in that case. This seems too good to be true, and it would have the inconvenient consequence that the 21-year period would apply differently to different parts of the same trust fund where there was a trust for eg the children of a named person. It is, however, an interpretation which cannot be completely ruled out on the wording of the LPA 1925, ss 164 and 165. From the point of view of drafting will (or any other) trusts it is not an argument which can safely be relied on unless and until there is a decision of the court more directly in point, particularly bearing in mind the often adverse consequences of provisions which go beyond the permitted accumulation periods (see Vol 1, paras **[95.8]** and **[95.13]**). For the practical purposes of will drafting, unless and until there is clear authority to the contrary, it should be assumed that the 21-year accumulation period under the LPA 1925, s 164(1)(b) (Part G, para **[246.42]**)

runs out 21 years from the testator's death, irrespective of whether there has been accumulation under TA 1925, s 31 during that period.

[218.72]
(r)   Extended accumulation and maintenance provisions. The accumulation and maintenance provisions of the TA 1925, s 31, as amended by the FLRA 1969 (Part G, para **[246.26]**), only apply during the minority of a beneficiary, that is, until the age of 18. Thus if there is a gift of capital to members of a class contingently on attaining 25, and s 31 as amended applies, each member of the class will be entitled to be paid the income of his presumptive share on attaining the age of 18, and will have an interest in possession in his presumptive share from that time. It is often desired to extend accumulation and maintenance provisions so as to continue to a greater age than 18. Apart from personal considerations (it is often felt that 18 is too early an age to start receiving a sometimes substantial income), and income tax advantages (the rate of income tax on accumulations may turn out to be lower than a beneficiary's personal tax rates), there is the inheritance tax advantage that an increase or decrease in the members of the class of beneficiaries, or the exercise of a power to vary the benefit taken, will not give rise to an inheritance tax charge on a part of the settled property which continues to be subject to accumulation and maintenance trusts (whereas such an event will give rise to a charge where an interest in possession is wholly or partially terminated).

[218.73]
If extended accumulation and maintenance provisions are to be included in a will, one of the accumulation periods permitted by the LPA 1925, s 164 will have to be used. The period of 21 years from the death of the testator will normally be the most appropriate: see paras **[218.69]–[218.71]** for its relationship with accumulation under TA 1925, s 31. If it is certain that all the beneficiaries will be over the age of 4 at the testator's death, the 21-year accumulation period will continue until all have attained 25 and accumulation and maintenance provisions can continue to that age. If the class is to consist only of persons living at the testator's death, accumulation and maintenance provisions can be made to continue until the age of 21. See Form B18.12 at para **[218.78]**.

[218.74]
Where the class of beneficiaries is to remain open after the testator's death, none of the above methods can be used for the presumptive shares of beneficiaries born after his death. Express accumulation and maintenance provisions could be drafted in respect of the income of the shares of such afterborn beneficiaries which continue to the end of the 21-year accumulation period. Strictly it has been argued that this would take the trusts outside the ITA 1984, s 71 because the attainment of an interest in possession does not occur at a specified age, and arguments of this kind have been advanced by the Inland Revenue. However, the Board of Inland Revenue have announced that they will regard the requirement of what is now the ITA 1984, s 71(1)(a) as being satisfied even if no age is specified in the trust instrument, provided that it is clear that a beneficiary will in fact become entitled to the settled property (or to an interest in possession in it) by the age of 25 (Press Release, 2 September 1977). Income trusts under which

an interest in possession arises at the end of an accumulation period and before the beneficiary attains 25 will thus be acceptable to the Inland Revenue as satisfying this requirement of s 71 but it will always be preferable (from abundance of caution) for absolute interest or interests in possession to be attained at a definite age where possible. Form B18.13 at para **[218.79]** varies the application of s 31 so that accumulation and maintenance trusts continue for each beneficiary until his last birthday before the expiration of the 21-year accumulation period, if he will be over 18 on that birthday.

[218.75]
It should be emphasised that extended accumulation and maintenance trusts will be of no effect if the capital vests indefeasibly in the beneficiary on or before he attains the age of eighteen. In these circumstances he will be able to call for the capital at that age, and since any accumulations would be added to that capital (see para **[218.51]**) he can call for the capital and the future income of it despite the fact that the future income has been directed to be accumulated. This is the rule in *Saunders v Vautier* (1841) Cr & Ph 240; affg 4 Beav 115.

[218.76]
The directory provisions of the TA 1925, s 31 (Part G, para **[246.26]**), eg the trust to accumulate, are capable of being varied by the provisions of a will or settlement creating the trusts to which s 31 applies, even though the TA 1925, s 69(2) only states that the *powers* conferred by the Act are subject to the terms of the trust instrument: see *Re Turner's Will Trusts, District Bank Ltd v Turner* [1937] Ch 15.

[218.77]

FORM B18.11:   Variation of the statutory provision for maintenance and accumulation to maximise the trustees' discretion

I declare that in the application to the trusts hereof of the statutory power of maintenance given to trustees by section 31 of the Trustee Act 1925 as amended[1] the proviso to subsection (1) of that section shall not apply and shall be deemed to be omitted[2] and that paragraph (i) of subsection (1) of the said section shall be read as if the words 'as the trustees think fit' were substituted for the words 'as may, in all the circumstances, be reasonable'.[3]

1   The section is set out as amended in Part G at para **[246.26]**. It should be remembered that the statutory power of maintenance will cease when the child attains 18, after which he or she will be entitled to the income: see para **[218.41]**.
2   This part of the clause excludes the reference in the section to the available income from another fund and the special statutory scheme where other available income exists; but it does not, of course, mean that the trustees are not to consider other available income as part of the 'circumstances'. See sub-para (f) of para **[218.48]**.
3   This part of the clause enlarges the discretion of the trustees. See para **[218.49]**.

[218.78]

FORM B18.12:   Statutory maintenance and accumulation to continue to the age of twenty-one[1]

Section 31 of the Trustee Act 1925 [as amended by the Family Law Reform Act 1969[2]] shall apply to the foregoing trust [provided that in relation to the presumptive share of any of [*beneficiaries*] who is actually in existence at the time of my death the said section 31 shall have effect[2]] as if section 1 of the Family Law Reform Act 1969 had not been enacted.

1   See paras [218.72]–[218.76]. The idea behind this clause is to allow maintenance and accumulation to continue for a period of 21 years from the testator's death, 21 years being a permitted period of accumulation: see LPA 1925, s 164(1)(b) (Part G, para [246.42]). The FLRA 1969, s 1 substituted in the TA 1925, s 31 references to 18 years for references to 21 years, so that if it is deemed not to have been enacted, the TA 1925, s 31 will apply as if the age up to which maintenance and accumulation is possible is 21. Any beneficiary actually in existence (and not merely en ventre sa mere) at the testator's death will necessarily attain 21 within the permitted accumulation period of 21 years from the testator's death, so that accumulation will be permissible until he attains the age of 21.

2   If it is certain that all the beneficiaries will be in existence at the testator's death, the parts in square brackets may be omitted.

[218.79]

FORM B18.13:   Statutory maintenance and accumulation to continue to maximum possible age[1]

(1)   Section 31 of the Trustee Act 1925 (as amended by the Family Law Reform Act 1969) shall apply to the foregoing trusts Provided that in relation to the presumptive share of any of the [*beneficiaries*] in relation to whom the specified age (as hereinafter defined) exceeds 18 years the said section 31 (as amended as aforesaid) shall have effect as if the age of majority were the specified age (the expressions 'infant' 'infancy' and 'minority' therein being construed accordingly) and as if there were substituted the specified age for the words 'eighteen years' wherever the same occur in the said section 31 (as amended as aforesaid).

(2)   In the last preceding subclause 'the specified age' in relation to any of the [*beneficiaries*] means whichever is the less of (i) the age which he or she will attain (if he or she so long lives) on his or her last birthday occurring not later than the expiration of 21 years from my death or (ii) the age of [25] years.[2]

1   See paras [218.72]–[218.76].

2   This definition has the function of preventing accumulation continuing beyond the permitted maximum of 21 years from the testator's death (see s 164(1)(b) of the LPA 1925: Part G, paras [246.42] and [218.69]–[218.71]), and also that of preventing accumulation and maintenance trusts continuing beyond the specified age. The latter should not exceed 25 years if the trusts are to satisfy the ITA 1984, s 71 (see Part A, para [200.119] et seq) and should not exceed the age of absolute vesting of capital if that is earlier than 25.

[218.80]

FORM B18.14:   Variation of the statutory provision for maintenance and accumulation—on the birth of a new member of the class existing accumulations are shared with the new member[1]

Section 31 of the Trustee Act 1925 shall apply to the foregoing trust[2] Provided that if after my death the class of [beneficiaries][3] interested or presumptively interested under the foregoing trust is increased by the birth of a further member of that class any accumulations of income which are held immediately before such birth on the trusts set out in subsection (2) of the said section 31 for any existing member of the class shall from such birth be held on those trusts for the respective benefit of such existing member and such new-born member in the same respective proportions as the proportions in which the share of capital in which such existing member is interested immediately before such birth comes to be held for such existing and new-born members respectively immediately after such birth.

1 Where there is an open class of beneficiaries, if there is no provision of this kind any accumulations of income held in relation to a beneficiary will continue to be held for him contingently on attaining 18 (or marrying) or as an accretion to his share after the birth of a further member of the class. The purpose of this provision is that accumulations made before the birth of a new member of the class are shared with that member in the same way as the underlying capital. See para **[218.53]** for further explanation of the effect of the TA 1925, s 31 (Part G, para **[246.26]**) which this form is intended to counteract. See n 2 infra for the type of trust to which this form is relevant.

2 This form assumes that the trust to which it applies is one for an open class of beneficiaries, eg a trust for the testator's grandchildren who attain the age of 25, so that it is possible for there to be members of it who are born after the testator's death. It also assumes that the trusts upon which any accumulations of income are to be held are those in the TA 1925, s 31(2) without any other variation. A provision of this kind is not relevant to a closed class, such as the testator's children, and it would be completely inconsistent with, and must not be combined with, a provision such as Form B18.15 at para **[218.81]** under which accumulations of income are vested absolutely in the beneficiaries from the outset. This provision could be combined with one that continued the accumulation and maintenance trusts of s 31 to an age greater than 18, such as B18.12 at para **[218.78]** and B18.13 at para **[218.79]**.

3 It will usually be appropriate to substitute a description of the class in question for 'beneficiaries', eg where the trust is for the testator's grandchildren who attain the age of 25 substitute 'my grandchildren' at this point.

[218.81]

FORM B18.15:   **Variation of the statutory provision for maintenance and accumulation—accumulations vesting absolutely**[1]

Section 31 of the Trustee Act 1925 shall apply to the foregoing trusts[2] as if in subsection (2) therereof there were substituted for the words from 'as follows' to the end of the subsection the words 'upon trust for such infant or his personal representatives absolutely'.

1 See para **[218.51]** for the trusts of accumulations of income under the TA 1925, s 31 (Part G, para **[246.26]**), which unless varied are such as usually to give minor beneficiaries a contingent interest in such accumulations, even if they have a vested interest in the income (unless they have an annuity). The purpose of this variation of s 31 is to cause the accumulations to be held on trust absolutely for the beneficiary in relation to whose interest the income arose, so as to confer an interest in possession for inheritance tax purposes. A minor cannot be paid income to which he is entitled (see Vol 1, para **[9.39]**) but it is thought that he has an interest in possession in income if it would form part of his estate if he died under the age of 18 (and unmarried).

2 This provision can be combined with any trust of capital but is not appropriate where the accumulations will vest absolutely without such a provision (see para **[218.51]**). It is inconsistent with, and should not be combined with, any provision extending the accumulation and maintenance trusts of TA 1925, s 31 to an age greater than 18, such as Forms B18.12 at para **[218.78]** and B18.13 at para **[218.79]**, nor with any provision altering the trusts of the accumulations such as Form B18.14 at para **[218.80]**.

[218.82]

FORM B18.16:   Maintenance of a class; applicable to shares in income as well as in capital[1]

With regard to maintenance I direct as follows:

(1)   Subject to any prior interests in the income hereinafter mentioned my trustees shall receive such part of the income arising from [my residuary estate] as is for the time being attributable to the shares or presumptive or prospective shares in my residuary estate or in the income thereof of such of [my children] [the children of the said [*name*]] as for the time being are under the age of [eighteen] [twenty-one] years and they may pay or apply the whole or so much thereof as they in their discretion think fit for or towards the maintenance education or benefit of such children for the time being under the said age of [eighteen] [twenty-one] years as a class and if my trustees think fit unequally as between such children and shall not be bound to consider whether or not there is any other income applicable for the same purposes or whether or not there is any person bound by law to provide for the maintenance or education of such children or any of them.

(2)   My trustees may pay the whole or any part of the said income to the parent or guardian or guardians of any of such children or to any such children if of the age of sixteen years or more without seeing to the application thereof and shall accumulate the surplus (if any) of the said income in each year by investing the same and the resulting income thereof in manner hereby authorised and subject to subclause (3) below my trustees may at any time apply such accumulations as if the same were income of the current year.

(3)   When and so often as any child of [mine] [the said [*name*]] attains the age of [eighteen] [twenty-one] years a share in the then existing accumulations corresponding to the share of my residuary estate to which or to the income of which such child shall then be entitled shall be transferred to the capital of such last-mentioned share and be dealt with accordingly and so that if any share in which or in the income of which any of the said children shall for the time being have a vested interest shall be increased by any event which may happen a share in the accumulations which exist at the date of such event proportionate to the increase in such share shall be transferred to the capital of such share and be dealt with accordingly.[2]

1   For consideration of this type of provision which can be used where a testator has left property to a class of beneficiaries in specified shares and the ITA 1984, s 71 see paras **[218.67]** and **[218.68]**. Twenty-one should only be chosen as the relevant age if all the children in question will be in existence by the time of the testator's death: see further n 2 to Form B18.17 at para **[218.83]**.
2   Paragraph (3) contemplates a division and transfer of the accumulations from time to time as and when any child becomes absolutely entitled.
    Under the usual form of maintenance clause (including the statutory clause: TA 1925, s 31 (Part G, para **[246.26]**)) trustees ought to keep the accumulated income of each child's share distinct, though they frequently do not do so.

[218.83]

FORM B18.17:   Another clause providing for maintenance out of a common fund[1]

With regard to maintenance I direct as follows:

(1)   Subject to any prior interests in the income hereinafter mentioned my trustees shall receive the income arising from my residuary estate or from so much thereof as shall not for the time being have become subject to an absolute interest or an interest in possession of any child[2] [of mine] [of the said [*name*]] under the trusts hereinbefore contained and may pay or apply such income or so much thereof as my trustees shall think fit for the maintenance education or benefit of such [of my children] [children of the said [*name*]] as shall for the time being be under the age of [eighteen] [twenty-one] years or any one or more exclusively of the others or other of such children in such proportions at such time and in such manner in all respects as my trustees shall in their sole discretion think proper with liberty to my trustees to pay the whole or any part of the said income to the guardian or guardians of any of the said children for the purposes aforesaid without seeing to the application thereof; and

(2)   My trustees shall invest the surplus (if any) of the said income in investments of the nature hereby authorised and shall accumulate the same at compound interest by investing the resulting income thereof as an accretion thereto and shall hold such accumulations as accretions to the capital of the whole part or parts of my residuary estate from which they arose and as one fund therewith for all purposes.[3]

1   For consideration of this type of clause in relation to the ITA 1984, s 71 see paras [218.67] and [218.68].
2   If the class has not closed at the death, eg because the gift is to the children of a person who may still be living at the testator's death, the age contingency specified throughout the clause should be 18 not 21. Otherwise the accumulation provision in sub-cl (2) may be invalid: see the LPA 1925, s 164(1)(d) (Part G, para [246.42]) restricting the power to accumulate to the minority (which now ends at 18) of any beneficiary otherwise entitled to income.
3   For fear of possible inheritance tax difficulties as regards the application the ITA 1984, s 71 (see Part A, para [200.119] et seq), there is no power to apply accumulations as income of the current year. We recommend that a power of advancement over the whole of a presumptive share is added to make up for this.

[218.84]

FORM B18.18:   Maintenance clause; simple express trusts[1]

(1)   Subject and without prejudice to any prior interest or charge affecting the income hereinafter mentioned, I empower my trustees during the minority [or minority and spinsterhood as the case may be] of any child [of mine] [*or* grandchild of mine] [*or* of the said [*name*]] to apply the whole or such part as my trustees shall think fit of the income of the expectant or presumptive share[2] of such child [*or* grandchild] for or towards his or her maintenance education or benefit with power to pay the same to the parent or to the guardian or guardians of such child [*or* grandchild] for the purposes aforesaid without seeing to the application thereof.[3]

(2)   My trustees may exercise the power aforesaid whether or not there is any other fund or income available for any of the aforesaid purposes and whether or not there is any person bound by law to provide for such maintenance or education.

(3)   The surplus income shall be accumulated by investing the same and the resulting income thereof in any investments of the kind hereby authorised and such accumulations shall be added to the property or to the share therein from which the same was derived and shall devolve therewith so as to follow the

destination of such property or share but my trustees shall be entitled at any time to apply any part of such accumulations for any of the purposes aforesaid as if the same were income arising in the then current year.

1   This form may be useful where the will may have to be acted on abroad, or where it is desired to express an ordinary maintenance clause in a will rather than to let the statutory clause apply. Further, it is a form which can be readily adapted to provide express accumulation and maintenance trusts to a higher age than 18. If, for example, it is desired to have these to the age of 21 for the testator's children, substitute for the words 'during the minority . . . of any child of mine' the words 'while any child of mine has not attained the age of 21 years'. There must of course be an available accumulation period for this to be valid: see paras **[218.72]–[218.76]**.
       It excludes the necessity of applying only a portion of the income where the trustees have notice of other available income (TA 1925, s 31: Part G, para **[246.26]**). In the Canadian case of *Re Larsen's Will* (1968) 66 WWR 358 a clause in similar terms was held wide enough to authorise the purchase by the trustees of an annuity for a beneficiary in need.
2   Where a woman was entitled to a share on birth of issue and, being over fifty years of age, had no children, the court refused to hold that she was past child-bearing, and she was, therefore, entitled to an expectant or presumptive share and to maintenance under an express maintenance clause: *Re Allen* [1953] ALR 959, St R Qd 95.
3   Giving a person power to maintain the minor out of income will not make the gift to the minor vested, if it is otherwise contingent: *Re Rogers, Lloyds Bank Ltd v Lory* [1944] Ch 297, [1944] 2 All ER 1.

Advancement

[218.85]
Note. TA 1925, s 32 (statutory power of advancement), as amended by the TLATA 1996, s 25(1), Sch 3, para 3(1), (8) subject to savings contained in s 25(4) thereof, is set out in Part G at para **[246.27]**. We have the following points concerning it:

[218.86]
(a)   Age. A 'specified age' in TA 1925, s 32(1) includes a double event, eg surviving another and attaining eighteen (or twenty-one): *Re Garrett, Croft v Ruck* [1934] Ch 477.

[218.87]
(b)   Extent of power. The amount which may be raised and applied is not to exceed one-half of the presumptive or vested share or interest of the person to be advanced; the amount advanced is to be brought into account if the person is or becomes absolutely entitled to a share in the property; but the advancement may be made notwithstanding that his interest is liable to be defeated by the exercise of a power of appointment, or to be diminished by an increase of the class to which he belongs. It will not therefore be necessary to make an absolute appointment to a person in order that he may be advanced; and again, if the class be merely the children of A, and A's wife dies, the whole class can be advanced up to the limit, notwithstanding that A might marry again and have a second family. We recommend that the power is always made exercisable over the whole of a presumptive share (see eg Form B18.20 at para **[218.104]**).

[218.88]
(c)   Effect of advancements on prior interests, including interests under protective trusts. The advancement cannot be made so as to prejudice any

person entitled to a prior life or other interest, vested or contingent: *Re Bainbridge* [1948] Ch 717, [1948] 2 All ER 657 (and see *IRC v Bernstein* [1960] Ch 444, [1960] 1 All ER 697, as to what is a prior interest), but any such person who is of full age may consent in writing. Objects of a discretionary trust do not have a vested or contingent interest within TA 1925, s 32(1)(c), though all together if of age they can put an end to the trust (*Re Beckett's Settlement, Re Beckett, Eden v Von Stutterheim* [1940] Ch 279). A married woman validly restrained from anticipation could give such consent (*Re Garrett, Croft v Ruck* [1934] Ch 477). It is clear that the consent of a life tenant whose interest is determinable on alienation, etc under protective trusts will not occasion a forfeiture in the following cases:

(i)   Where the provision for forfeiture in the protective trusts is expressly stated not to affect any steps taken by the life tenant to enable advances to be made by the trustees in accordance with the advancement clause contained in the settlement. This goes without saying, but the point is discussed in *Re Shaw's Settlement Trusts, Shaw v Shaw* [1951] 1 All ER 656 at 658.

(ii) Where the statutory protective trusts (TA 1925, s 33: Part G, para **[246.28]**) are incorporated because these trusts include a provision to that effect.

(iii) Where though the protective trusts do not include such a provision, there is an express protective trust and an express advancement clause in the settlement, because the whole document must be construed together and it is not to be supposed that it was intended that, if the advancement was to be made, the life tenant would forfeit his interest: *Re Hodgson, Weston v Hodgson* [1913] 1 Ch 34; *Re Shaw's Settlement Trusts, Shaw v Shaw* [1951] 1 All ER 656 at 659.

(iv) Where the settlement is made after 1925, and there is no express advancement clause and the provisions of the TA 1925, s 32 are implied, a consent to an advancement does not cause a forfeiture of the life interest because the draftsman must be deemed to have had in mind the statutory power and could not have intended that consent to its exercise should work a forfeiture: *Re Rees' Will Trusts, Lloyds Bank Ltd v Rees* [1954] Ch 202, [1954] 1 All ER 7. There remains the reported decision in *Re Stimpson's Trusts, Stimpson v Stimpson* [1931] 2 Ch 77, [1931] All ER Rep 809. This would not seem to be good law though it has not been expressly overruled. In this case the will was made in 1906 and the testatrix died in 1929. There was no express advancement clause, but, in the circumstances, the implied advancement clause under the TA 1925, s 32 applied, and it was held that a consent to an advancement would forfeit the life interest. No reasons for this are given and, it seems, that the only distinction which can be made is that the draftsman of the will in 1906 could not have had in mind and relied upon a clause in the 1925 Act.

[218.89]
(d)   The circumstances in which s 32 of the TA 1925 applies. Where the protective trusts were set out in the will and the trust after the cesser of the life interest was 'to apply any sums not exceeding in any one year the amount of the

annuity or life interest' for certain beneficiaries, this reference to 'the amount' is not an expression of a contrary intention within the TA 1925, s 69(2) (Part G, para **[246.37]**), which would exclude the application of s 32: *Re Rees' Will Trusts* [1954] Ch 202, [1954] 1 All ER 7.

[218.90]
The power given by s 32 of the TA 1925 is not applicable as long as a trust for accumulation is effective, since such a trust is inconsistent with an advance being made and a contrary intention within the TA 1925, s 69(2) is shown: *IRC v Bernstein* [1961] Ch 399, [1961] 1 All ER 320. The inclusion of an express power of advancement may also be evidence of a contrary intention within the meaning of the subsection: *Re Evans' Settlement, Watkins v Whitworth Jones* [1967] 3 All ER 343, [1967] 1 WLR 1294.

[218.91]
TA 1925, s 32 applies to all kinds of trust property other than capital money arising under the Settled Land Act 1925 (unless expressly declared to apply) (TA 1925, 32(2), as substituted by the TLATA 1996, s 25(1), Sch 3, para 3(1), (8) subject to savings contained in s 25(4) thereof). Since no new settlements can be created under the Settled Land Act 1925 on or after 1 January 1997, this exclusion will be of diminishing importance. Prior to 1 January 1997, when land was either held on trust for sale or was settled land, the section only applied where the trust consisted of money or securities, or property held upon trust for sale, calling in, and conversion where the money or securities, or proceeds of sale, were not by statute or in equity considered as land, or applicable as capital money under the Settled Land Act 1925, eg where there was no direction to reconvert into land (*Re Stimpson's Trusts, Stimpson v Stimpson* [1931] 2 Ch 77, [1931] All ER Rep 809, and Vol 1, para **[37.1]**).

The section does not apply to trusts constituted or created before 1 January 1926, and, contrary to the position under s 31, where the will comes into operation before 1926 does not apply where a special power of appointment arising under such a will is exercised after 1925 (*Re Batty* [1952] 1 All ER 425; see also *Re Leigh's Marriage Settlement* [1952] 2 All ER 57). The case is otherwise in the case of a general power of appointment: *Re Bransbury's Will Trusts, Grece v Bransbury* [1954] 1 All ER 605.

Under the TA 1925, s 69(2) (Part G, para **[246.37]**), the testator can negative or vary the statutory power; if he does not wish *any* power of advancement to apply, he should expressly negative the statutory power.

Section 32 is, speaking generally, a statutory enactment of the power of advancement which was usually inserted in settlements of personalty.

[218.92]
(e)   Meaning of 'benefit' in s 32. The power of advancement under the Act is a power the exercise of which must have some reference to the actual circumstances of the object of the power requiring to be benefited at the time of the exercise of the power. An advancement in its strict sense is something given by the parent to establish the child in life or to make what is called a provision for him; but where, as in the TA 1925, s 32 the power of application of capital may be exercised for advancement or benefit in such manner as the trustees may in their absolute discretion think fit, the power is not confined to the making of

advancements in the strict sense and is a very wide power indeed. The cited cases usually start with *Roper-Curzon v Roper-Curzon* (1871) LR 11 Eq 452, but that case merely decided that, while the advancement would not be authorised if the money were handed over to the son, it would be authorised if the money were settled upon himself, his wife and children upon the ordinary trusts of such a settlement. *Re Halsted's Will Trusts, Halsted v Halsted* [1937] 2 All ER 570, was a somewhat similar case on its facts but it was clearly held that, where the son had no other resources, such a settlement was for the 'benefit' of the son. In the first case the advancement was required for the pursuit by the son of the legal profession, but in the second there was no such requirement, the money being advanced merely for the purpose of the son making provision for his family. In *Re Ropner's Settlement Trusts, Ropner v Ropner* [1956] 3 All ER 332, the benefit was the possible avoidance of death duties in an otherwise similar case. The avoidance of death duties was the benefit in *Re Meux, Gilmour v Gilmour* [1958] Ch 154, [1957] 2 All ER 630 (a decision under the TA 1925, s 53 which does not deal with advancement) and in *Re Wills' Will Trusts, Wills v Wills* [1959] Ch 1, [1958] 2 All ER 472. Thus we have two points decided:

(i)   the avoidance of taxation may be a benefit within the meaning of that word in a power of advancement; and

(ii)   a settlement of the sum advanced is permissible under the power.

[218.93]
There has since been further authority on the scope of the power to settle capital in exercise of the power under the TA 1925, s 32. In *Re Wills' Will Trusts, Wills v Wills* [1959] Ch 1, [1958] 2 All ER 472, there was an express power of advancement which allowed application for the benefit of any child, children or wife of the person advanced and it was held that a provision for recently born twins of a beneficiary, whose interest might be defeated by his death under twenty-five, such beneficiary being engaged in war service, was a good exercise of the power. It was stated that such advancement though on contingent trusts was *in the circumstances* for the benefit of the twins. In *Pilkington v IRC* [1964] AC 612, [1962] 3 All ER 622, the statutory power was applicable. The beneficiary proposed to be advanced was a child of two years, the daughter of a wealthy parent well able to provide for her maintenance and education. The proposed trusts of the sum advanced were for the infant absolutely if she attained the age of thirty years and in the event of her death under that age leaving children then for such children on attaining twenty-one years of age and subject thereto for all the other children of the infant's father on attaining full age or marrying. It was held by the House of Lords that it was not possible to introduce into the statutory power a qualification which would exclude its exercise in such circumstances since the propriety of requiring a settlement of the money advanced had been recognised as lawful ever since *Roper-Curzon v Roper-Curzon* (1871) LR 11 Eq 452 was decided in 1871. It was also held that the statutory power of advancement must be treated as a provision written into the will and, therefore, so far as the rule of perpetuities is concerned, the trusts of the new settlement had to be read back into the will and their validity under the perpetuity rule decided as if they were contained in the will just as is done in the case of special powers. This is a matter of considerable importance, as the whole advance may fail if the trusts of the new settlement are substantially invalid: see

Re Hastings-Bass, Hastings-Bass v IRC [1975] Ch 25, [1974] 2 All ER 193, and
Re Abrahams' Will Trusts, Caplan v Abrahams [1969] 1 Ch 463, [1967] 2 All
ER 1175. Such invalidity may have serious fiscal consequences: *Spens v IRC*
[1970] 3 All ER 295, [1970] 1 WLR 1170.

[218.94]
Another point that has been discussed is whether the trustees of the settled
advanced sum can be given a discretion and more particularly whether that sub-
settlement can include discretionary trusts. In view of the extremely wide scope
of the powers under the TA 1925, s 32, as shown by *Pilkington v IRC* [1964] AC
612, [1962] 3 All ER 622 *Re Clore's Settlement Trusts, Sainer v Clore* [1966] 2
All ER 272, [1966] 1 WLR 955, and most recently by *Re Hampden Settlement
Trusts*, [1977] TR 177, we take the view that discretionary trusts could be
created in a proper case in exercise of the powers conferred by s 32. This has
certain inheritance tax consequences, for which see para **[218.99]**.

[218.95]
Other illustrations of applications of capital under a power to apply it for
someone's benefit are as follows. In *Re Kershaw's Trusts* (1868) LR 6 Eq 322
the court authorised trustees with such a power to make a loan of trust money to
the beneficiary's husband to provide him with capital to continue in business,
and in *Lowther v Bentinck* (1874) LR 19 Eq 166 payment of the beneficiary's
debts was held to be within such a power.

[218.96]
There are two important modern decisions on applications for a beneficiary's
benefit which take the form of the satisfaction of a moral or legal obligation of
his to others. In *Re Clore's Settlement Trusts, Sainer v Clore* [1966] 2 All ER
272, [1966] 1 WLR 955 the trustees were authorised to apply a proportion of a
beneficiary's presumptive share in donations to charity, the beneficiary being a
wealthy man who regarded himself as under a moral obligation to make
substantial charitable donations. In *Re Hampden Settlement Trusts* [1977] TR
177 the court held that the trustees had validly exercised an express power to
apply capital (in similar terms to the power under the TA 1925, s 32: Part G,
para **[246.27]**) for the benefit of an object of the power by settling the trust
property on immediate trusts for the benefit of his minor child and any future
children of his, again satisfying a moral (and legal) obligation of the beneficiary,
in this case to maintain and educate his own minor children. It should be noted
that in the *Clore* and *Hampden* cases the beneficiary was comfortably off
independently of the funds which were being applied to or on trust for others in
satisfaction of his obligations; the court would be unlikely to approve or uphold
an application of this type which stripped a beneficiary of all means of support.
    For the capital gains tax significance of the possibility of creating new trusts
in exercise of the power conferred by TA 1925, s 32, see paras **[218.100]**–
[218.102].

[218.97]
(f)   Transfers of property in specie under s 32. The trustees are empowered
by the section to pay or apply any capital money subject to the trust. The point
has arisen whether this provision allows the conveyance of land so subject. The

trustees could, of course, pay the purchase price to the beneficiary and with that money he could purchase the property. The court, however, has decided that such circuity of action would not be insisted on and the trustees might execute the conveyance forthwith under the terms of the power: see *Re Collard's Will Trusts, Lloyds Bank Ltd v Rees* [1961] Ch 293, [1961] 1 All ER 821 and *Pilkington v IRC* [1964] AC 612, [1962] 3 All ER 622, HL. In *Re Wills' Will Trusts, Wills v Wills* [1959] Ch 1, [1958] 2 All ER 472, the trustees were empowered to raise any part of his or her presumptive share and to pay or apply the same for the benefit of the beneficiary. Certain investments which had been appropriated to the beneficiary's share were directed to be held on certain new trusts and this was held to be a 'raising' within this special power of advancement.

[218.98]
(g)   Exercise of s 32 powers in breach of trust. Where trustees have a power of advancement with the consent of the tenant for life or other beneficiary, such exercise may be a breach of trust on the part of the trustees despite the consent of the tenant for life. The court has to consider all the circumstances in order to see whether it is fair and equitable that the person injured by such exercise should sue the trustees. It is not necessary that he should know that he is concurring in a breach of trust provided he fully understands in what he is concurring, nor is it necessary that he himself should have benefited by the breach of trust: *Re Pauling's Settlement Trusts, Younghusband v Coutts & Co* [1964] Ch 303, [1963] 3 All ER 1. In this case advances were made in respect of a child's share and applied for the benefit of the parents.

[218.99]
(h)   Inheritance tax. Where settled property is held on trusts of a type falling within the ITA 1984, s 71 (see Part A, para **[200.119]** et seq) s 32 or a similar express provision will commonly apply. As mentioned at para **[218.94]**, it is arguable that such powers could be exercised to create discretionary trusts, thus preventing the 'beneficiaries' from becoming entitled to, or to interests in possession in the settled property on or before attaining the age of 25, and prejudicing the application of s 71. However as mentioned in Part A (at para **[200.127]**), the Inland Revenue have never regarded the existence of a common form power of advancement (and we understand this includes one exercisable over the whole of a presumptive share) as preventing s 71 from applying. A restrictive proviso for use by the cautious draftsman appears in Form B18.20 at para **[218.104]**. The Revenue view has been upheld in *Lord Inglewood v IRC* [1983] STC 133, CA, but various problems remain. See *Foster's Inheritance Tax*, E5.15.

[218.100]
(i)   Capital gains tax. Where a power of application of capital, such as that conferred under the TA 1925, s 32, is exercised so as to create new trusts, this can be, for capital gains tax purposes, the creation of a new settlement (as opposed to being a continuation of the one under which the power arose). In such a case there is a deemed disposal for capital gains tax purposes of all the assets put into the new settlement under the TCGA 1992, s 71: see *Hoare Trustees v Gardner* [1979] Ch 10, [1978] 1 All ER 791. (New trusts created in

exercise of a special power of appointment, on the other hand, are in a normal case regarded as a continuation of the existing settlement, and no such deemed disposal arises on their creation—see *Bond (Inspector of Taxes) v Pickford* [1983] STC 517.) It has sometimes been thought that new trusts created under an exercise of the power of payment or application of capital conferred by the TA 1925, s 32 must always give rise to a new settlement, and thus to a deemed disposal, for capital gains tax purposes. However, it was held in *Swires v Renton* [1991] STC 490 that the question whether or not a new settlement was created, where new trusts were created in exercise of express power which in material respects resembled the wording of s 32, was a question of intention to be gathered from the language of the instrument exercising the power. Accordingly, with careful drafting it is possible to create new trusts in exercise of a power to pay or apply, such as s 32, without giving rise to a deemed disposal for capital gains tax purposes.

[218.101]
This possibility of creating new trusts under the TA 1925, s 32 without creating a new settlement is important now that general hold-over relief from capital gains tax has been abolished (see Part A, para **[200.135]**), because it means that, where a beneficiary with an interest in possession is about to reach an age of absolute vesting of capital which will be a capital gains tax deemed disposal under the TCGA 1992, s 71 it may be possible to defer the impending capital gains tax charge by a timely imposition of further trusts on the capital in exercise of the s 32 power (particularly where the power applies to the whole of a presumptive share), without this exercise of the power itself being a deemed disposal for capital gains tax.

[218.102]
By contrast, the deferment of capital gains tax may also be achieved by accelerating absolute vesting by a timely exercise of the s 32 power, where the trusts are accumulation and maintenance trusts falling within the ITA 1984, s 71 (for which see Part A, para **[200.119]** et seq). Where this is the case hold-over relief is available on the occasion of a 'beneficiary' under the accumulation and maintenance trust becoming absolutely entitled to capital (TCGA 1992, s 260(2)(d)). Where, as is often the case, the beneficiary becomes entitled to an interest in possession in the fund or his share of it before becoming entitled to receive the capital, this hold-over relief will not apply because the occasion of capital gains tax deemed disposal—him becoming absolutely entitled to the capital—occurs after the accumulation and maintenance trusts under the ITA 1984, s 71 have ceased. However, if the trustees had previously used the s 32 power to transfer the capital to him absolutely at a time when the accumulation and maintenance trusts of the income of that capital were still in operation, hold-over relief under this provision would be available.

[218.103]

FORM B18.19:   Statutory advancement clause restricted

I declare that the statutory power of advancement given to trustees by section 32 of the Trustee Act 1925,[1] shall apply to the trusts hereof as if incorporated herein save that the limit of advancement shall instead of being one-half of the value of the property or share be [one-third thereof] [the sum of £—— to be raised out of the property or share]

1   See Part G, para **[246.27]**.

[218.104]

FORM B18.20:   Statutory advancement clause varied to apply to the whole of a presumptive share, with restrictive proviso for inheritance tax purposes

Section 32 of the Trustee Act 1925 shall apply to the trusts hereof as if the words 'one-half of' were omitted from proviso (a) to subsection (1) thereof.[1] [Provided that the powers conferred by the said section 32 shall not be exercisable otherwise than so as to cause the person for whose benefit the same shall be exercised to become immediately entitled to or to an interest in possession in the capital thereby paid or applied within the meaning of section 71(1)(a) of the ITA 1984].[2]

1   In our view this is a better formula than declaring that proviso (a) to s 32(1) is to be treated as omitted, because a provision of the latter kind might permit the payment or application of *more than* a beneficiary's presumptive share for his advancement or benefit.
2   For the reasons for including such a proviso see para **[218.99]**. It will be noted that this proviso apparently does not permit the creation of further accumulation and maintenance trusts. For a form of proviso which does permit this see Form B18.6 at para **[218.36]**.

[218.105]

FORM B18.21:   Express Advancement clause; ordinary form

I declare that my trustees may raise any part or parts not exceeding altogether [one-half] [*or* any sum or sums not exceeding £—— in the whole] out of the then presumptive contingent expectant or vested [legacy or] share of any child [*or* grandchild] of mine [of the said [*name*]] under the trusts hereinbefore declared and may pay or apply the same as my trustees shall think fit for the advancement or benefit[1] of such child [*or* grandchild]. Provided that no such payment or application shall be made so as to prejudice any person entitled to any prior life or other interest whether vested or contingent in the money so to be paid or applied without the consent of such person.[2]

1   The essential wording of this power is the same as that of the statutory power under the TA 1925, s 32 (Part G, para **[246.27]**). For the scope of the power see paras **[218.92]**–**[218.96]** and for the capital gains tax aspects see paras **[218.100]**–**[218.102]**.
2   This may be usefully inserted in a will which may have to be acted upon abroad. The statutory power may be relied on in a simple case.

[218.106]

FORM B18.22:   Variation for advancement to life tenant

I declare that the statutory power of advancement given to trustees by section 32 of the Trustee Act 1925 shall apply to the trusts hereof and I declare that my trustees shall have a similar power of advancement out of the trust property or a share thereof in favour of a person who is entitled to a life interest only in the property or share or is contingently entitled to a life interest therein. Such power shall extend to [one-half of] the capital value of such property or share.[1]

1   See *Lowther v Bentinck* (1874) LR 19 Eq 166; *Re Brittlebank, Coates v Brittlebank* (1881) 30 WR 99 and paras **[218.92]**–**[218.95]**.

[218.107]

FORM B18.23:   **Expressions of desire for the guidance of trustees in exercising powers of advancement and of lending capital to the testator's spouse[1]**

In the hope that an indication of my own feelings in regard to the power conferred on my trustees by clause . . . of this will to raise capital for my wife [husband] may be of some help to them in exercising that power but without imposing any trust or obligation binding upon them at law or in equity or seeking to fetter their absolute discretion to exercise the power in such a way as may seem to them right in the light of current circumstances I would state that in conferring the power I contemplate that:

(a)   my trustees will be less ready to pay capital to my wife [husband] outright than to lend it to her [him]; and

(b)   subject to that they will not hesitate to exercise the power liberally for my wife's [husband's] benefit;

[OR

(b)   they will in any case regard the power as one to be exercised only in emergency].

1   Although it is not customary to include in a will provisions which are of no legal effect, there may sometimes be a case for doing so. One example arises in connection with the exercise of powers of maintenance and advancement during a period of guardianship: as to this, see Form B18.31 at para **[218.116]**. The point may also be illustrated in connection with the power commonly conferred on trustees to raise capital for a surviving spouse to whom a life interest is given. This power (partly for income tax reasons) normally contains no binding stipulation as to the exact extent to which it is to be exercised, and it is thought that trustees might welcome some indication of what the testator had in mind in this regard when he conferred it. The provision set out above may prove helpful in this connection. There is of course no need to include it in the will itself: it could (with any necessary variations) be the subject of a separate note addressed to the trustees. This form assumes that the will gives the trustees power either to give capital to the spouse outright or to lend it and will need amendment to fit it for other circumstances.

Enjoyment in kind

[218.108]

Note. Trustees' powers of investment are generally not sufficient to enable to acquire property for enjoyment in kind by a beneficiary (see the Preliminary Note to B20 at para **[220.30]**). However, trustees do now have statutory powers to acquire UK land for occupation by a beneficiary—under the Trustee Act 2000

(TrA 2000), any trustees (whether of land or not) may acquire freehold or leasehold land in the UK for occupation by a beneficiary: see TrA 2000, s 8(1)(b) (Part G, para **[246.123]**). Freehold or leasehold land in this context is defined to mean a legal estate in land or the equivalent in Scotland: TrA 2000, s 8(2) (Part G, para **[246.123]**). A beneficiary with an interest in possession in the land will be entitled to a right of occupation if the purposes of the trust include making the land available for his occupation, or it is held by the trustees so as to be so available (TLATA 1996, s 12: Part G, para **[246.98]**; see also the Preliminary Note to B8 at paras **[208.5]–[208.8]**). However, the trustees will require a specific power to enable a beneficiary of a discretionary trust, without an interest in possession, to occupy a property, and the statutory powers do not enable trustees to acquire an undivided share in a property to be occupied by a beneficiary (eg to purchase a property jointly with a beneficiary) or to purchase land outside the UK for such occupation, nor are there statutory powers to enable trustees to acquire chattels for use by a beneficiary. Therefore, express provision should still be made for these circumstances. When drafting powers to permit enjoyment in kind it is important to keep in mind the beneficial interests and their intended inheritance tax status, especially if there are accumulation and maintenance trusts intended to fall within the ITA 1984, s 71. The exercise of a power to provide a beneficiary with a residence or other assets to enjoy in kind is likely to be regarded by the Inland Revenue as creating an interest in possession for inheritance tax purposes in favour of that beneficiary if he does not already have one (Inland Revenue Statement of Practice SP 10/79 dated 15 August 1979). See further Part A, paras **[200.108]** et seq. Accordingly:

(1)   Where settled property is subject to an interest in possession, a power to permit the beneficiary entitled to that interest in possession to enjoy in kind assets comprised in that settled property (or the statutory right of occupation if it is land) should not cause any prejudice to the existence or continuance of that beneficiary's interest in possession. If the express power extended to permitting enjoyment in kind of assets comprised in the settled property by a person who did not already have the interest in possession in the settled property, the existence of the power would probably not prejudice the existence of that interest in possession, but its exercise would. If it is desired to provide power to benefit persons other than the life tenant in this way it would be better practice to provide an overriding power of appointment.

(2)   The existence of an express power to enjoy assets in kind should not prejudice a s 71 trust (see Part A, para **[200.119]** et seq) provided that the power cannot be exercised in favour of anyone who is not for the time being one of 'the beneficiaries' as defined in s 71.

(3)   The exercise of such a power in favour of a 'beneficiary' under a s 71 trust may create an interest in possession in his favour; that will not matter unless eg the 'beneficiary' then dies under the 'specified age' or it is subsequently decided, in exercise of some appropriate express power, to re-allocate the funds among the 'beneficiaries' (with the result that there is an inheritance tax charge which would not have occurred if such interest in possession had not been created).

(4)   Although it could be argued that the same considerations apply to trustees making a loan on beneficial terms to a beneficiary, the better

view is probably that doing this does not confer an interest in possession on the beneficiary, at any rate where the loan is repayable on demand (see para **[218.20]**). However, it may in many cases be preferable, in the interests of caution on this point, or in order to make sure that only a particular beneficiary or beneficiaries can benefit from a particular fund, to restrict the exercise of a power to make beneficial loans so that it can only be done in favour of persons with beneficial interests in the fund from which money is lent. There may be a stronger case for saying that an interest in possession is conferred where the right to repayment of the loan is restricted or deferred, but it seems more likely that in such a case no interest in possession is conferred, but that it is a transaction which diminishes the value of the settled property and gives rise to an inheritance tax charge under s 52(3) of the ITA 1984 (interest in possession property), s 65(1)(b) (non-interest in possession property) or s 71(3)(b) (accumulation and maintenance trust property).

See Form B18.24 at para **[218.109]** for restrictions which it is thought would prevent a power to permit enjoyment in kind from prejudicing the existence of an interest in possession or accumulation and maintenance trusts. See the Preliminary Note to B8 at para **[208.1]** et seq for specific gifts to provide a residence.

[218.109]

FORM B18.24:   Powers to permit enjoyment in kind—restricted to prevent prejudice to inheritance tax status of beneficial trusts[1]

My trustees may permit any beneficiary hereunder who for the time being is entitled to be paid the income of the whole or some part of [my residuary estate] (or would be so entitled if it yielded income) or to whom or for whose benefit for the time being the income of the whole or some part of [my residuary estate] may be paid or applied in exercise of a discretion (or might be so paid or applied if it yielded income) to have the use or enjoyment in kind of any land building chattel or other property which or the proceeds of sale of which or a share of which is comprised in such whole or part of [my residuary estate] upon such conditions as to payment by such beneficiary for outgoings insurance and repair as my trustees think fit (and my trustees shall not be liable for any failure to pay out-goings or insure or repair such property if a beneficiary is responsible for the same under the terms of such use or enjoyment).[2]

---

1   This express power is not necessary to enable a beneficiary with an interest in possession in land suitable and available for his occupation to occupy that land, since he has a right of occupation under the TLATA 1996, s 12 (Part G, para **[246.98]**; see also para **[208.5]** et seq). However, it will be necessary to enable a beneficiary without an interest in possession to occupy or enjoy land, and to enable any beneficiary (ie with or without an interest in possession) to use any chattel. For a corresponding power to purchase property for enjoyment in kind see Form B20.5 at para **[220.44]**. For the reasons behind the restrictions in this form, see para **[218.108]**.
2   See the Preliminary Note to B8 at para **[208.1]** et seq for a discussion of the effect of imposing these obligations on beneficiaries occupying trust property.

[218.110]

FORM B18.25:   Clause where trustees are to have power to purchase property for use of beneficiary[1]

The trustees shall have power to purchase land (or a share in land) situate in any part of the world for the purpose of providing a place of residence for one or more of the beneficiaries and to purchase chattels for the use and enjoyment of one or more of the beneficiaries with power from time to time to sell any property so purchased and to invest the proceeds of sale in the purchase of further property for the same purpose.

1   This clause is goes beyond the statutory powers to acquire land in that it permits the purchase of an undivided share in land, and also land in any part of the world.

[218.111]

FORM B18.26:   Power where wife is given residence for life or house is bought for beneficiary to invest trust money in purchase of furniture[1]

If my wife shall elect to reside in the said property [*or* If my trustees shall purchase property for providing a residence for the said [*beneficiary*]] my trustees may in their uncontrolled discretion purchase with any trust money in their hands for the time being such furniture as they think fit but not exceeding in value the sum of £ —— to be used and enjoyed by my wife [*or* the said [*beneficiary*]] during her life she keeping the same fully insured against fire and such other risks as my trustees may require and also keeping the same in good repair. Such furniture shall on the death of my wife [*or* the said [*beneficiary*]] fall into and form part of my residuary estate.

I direct that upon any such purchase my trustees shall cause an inventory to be made of the furniture so purchased and that the same shall be signed by my wife [*or* the said [*beneficiary*]] and retained by my trustees and that a copy of such inventory signed by my trustees shall be delivered to my wife [*or* the said [*beneficiary*]] and when such inventory and a copy thereof shall be signed and delivered as aforesaid my trustees shall not be bound to see to the repair and insurance of the said furniture and shall not be liable in any respect if my wife [*or* the said [*beneficiary*]] shall neglect to do such repairs or effect to keep up such insurance.

1   There is no statutory power for trustees to purchase chattels for a beneficiary's use, so an express power such as this should be conferred on trustees if they are to be able to make such purchases.

Loans to beneficiaries

[218.112]

FORM B18.27:   Loans to a life tenant

I declare that my trustees may lend money comprised in the whole or any part of my residuary estate to any person entitled for the time being to be paid the income of such whole or part of my residuary estate upon such terms as to the payment or non-payment of interest and otherwise as my trustees think fit.[1]

1   For the reasons for restricting the power to being exercisable in favour of someone who is already entitled to the income, see the Note on Enjoyment in Kind at para **[218.108]**. For a wider power, which also permits loans to discretionary beneficiaries, see Form C2.1, cl 9(3)(e) at para **[224.30]**, but note that such a power should be made subject to the inheritance tax restriction in cl 9(2) of Form C2.1.

[218.113]

FORM B18.28:   Loans to individuals without security

I declare that my trustees may make loans out of any moneys subject to the trusts hereof to [each of my sons A and B] to an amount not exceeding [£——] in respect of [each such son] upon [their] personal security only.

[218.114]

FORM B18.29:   Loans to beneficiary to whom a business is bequeathed

I declare that my trustees may lend out of any moneys subject to the trusts of this my will to the said *donee of business*] any sum or sums not exceeding in the whole the sum of £—— my trustees being satisfied that such sum or sums is or are required for and intended to be for the purposes of the said business. The rate of interest upon such sums shall not be less than the current base rate of the —— Bank subject however to a minimum rate of [10] per cent per annum and such sums shall be subject to such terms as to repayment and otherwise as my trustees shall think fit without being liable for loss *where the beneficiary is also a trustee add*: provided that my trustees other than the said *donee of business*] may call in and compel payment of such loan or loans as and when payment shall become due [but shall not be liable for loss for neglecting so to do]].

[218.115]

FORM B18.30:   Power for trustees to make loans to guardians[1]

My trustees shall have power at any time and from time to time if they consider it to be for the benefit of any minor child of mine to raise capital of the presumptive share of the trust fund[2] of such child and lend it to any person who is a guardian of such child of mine [(even though that person may also be a trustee)] with or without charging interest or taking security and on such terms as to repayment and otherwise as my trustees may in their discretion (without being liable for loss) think fit.

1   If an appointment of guardians is made, the testator should consider the practical problems with which the guardians may be presented in looking after the children and ensure that the other provisions of the will are calculated to minimise rather than to exacerbate these problems. The direct financial needs of the children themselves should be covered by the normal powers of maintenance and advancement, which apply automatically. But other problems may arise. To take one example, the guardians may find themselves compelled to have a larger house than they would otherwise need in order to provide adequate accommodation for the children, and they may have difficulty in finding the money to purchase and maintain it. Various detailed provisions could be designed to guard against possibilities such as this, but it is suggested that a

simple but wide power for the trustees to lend capital money to the guardians is not only desirable but also, in most cases, adequate. It is not thought that a power in this form would be inconsistent with the conditions specified in the ITA 1984, s 71(1), see Part A, para **[200.119]** et seq for accumulation and maintenance trusts. Attention is drawn also to Form B18.31 at para **[218.116]**. For the appointment of guardians see B3 at para **[203.43]** et seq.

2   It is assumed that 'the trust fund' has already been defined, (but if this is not so a suitable alternative, eg, 'my residuary estate', should be used), and that the fund is given to the children in specific shares contingently upon attaining 18 or some greater age.

Exercise and release of powers

[218.116]

FORM B18.31:   **Testator's wishes as to the exercise of powers of maintenance and advancement [and power to make loans to guardians] during period of guardianship**[1]

I should like my trustees to ensure (so far as seems to them reasonable having regard to the funds at their disposal and other relevant matters) that no guardian of any minor child of mine suffers any financial burden or loss by reason of anything he may do in the course of his guardianship (whether or not the act in question falls strictly within the ambit of his duties as guardian) and I therefore express the hope (but without imposing any trust or obligation binding at law or in equity) that my trustees will exercise any powers of maintenance and advancement or any similar powers which they may have in regard to that child by statute or under this will [and the power to lend money to the guardian which is given them by clause [*insert clause number*] of this will] in such a way as to ensure (so far as mentioned above) that no such burden or loss is suffered and I trust that the guardian himself will accept it as my wish that these powers should be exercised in that way.

1   If an appointment of guardians is made, doubt may arise during the period of guardianship as to how far the guardians should shoulder the financial burdens of caring for the children. They themselves may sometimes feel reluctant to accept money for this purpose from the trust set up by the will for the children's benefit. If the testator does not want the guardians to incur financial burdens in the performance of their functions (as normally, it is thought, he would not) it may therefore be useful to make this clear by including in the will some such provision as the following. The provision contains a variation designed to fit it for use in cases where the will gives the trustees power to make loans to guardians (see the preceding form). Of course the provision has no legal effect and so it could (with any necessary variations) be the subject of a separate note addressed to the trustees. It is not thought that a provision in this form, being merely precatory, would affect the status of accumulation and maintenance trusts: see also n 1 to Form B 18.30 at para **[218.115]**.

[218.117]

FORM B18.32:   **Powers and discretions exercisable in favour of a beneficiary trustee**

Any power or discretion hereby or by law vested in my trustees may be exercised in favour of a person who is an object of such power or discretion notwithstanding that he or she is one of my trustees provided that any such exercise of such a power or discretion is made by at least one of my trustees who does not have a personal interest in the mode or result of exercising the same.[1]

1   It is important to include a provision of this kind in wills under which significant discretions are conferred: see paras **[218.4]** and **[218.5]**.

[218.118]

FORM B18.33:   Power to release powers[1]

My trustees (being at least two in number or a [trust] corporation[2]) may at any time or times by deed release or restrict in any manner whatever and in whole or in part the future exercise of any powers or discretions hereby or by law conferred on them in such manner as to bind their successors as trustees hereof notwithstanding that the same shall be vested in them in a fiduciary capacity but no such release or restriction shall prejudice or affect any exercise of any of such powers made before any such release or restriction is made.

1   Trustees who have a power conferred on them virtute officii cannot release it unless they have express power to do so: see Vol 1, para **[40.10]**.
2   For the meaning of trust corporation see the Preliminary Note to B3 at para **[203.24]**. If there is a possibility of a foreign corporate trustee being appointed, the word 'trust' should be omitted.

B19   Provisions for failure of primary trusts

PROVISION CONCERNING DISCLAIMER

FORM

B19.17   Clause allowing for a partial disclaimer, the property disclaimed
devolving as if the person disclaiming had predeceased the testator ...... **[219.30]**

PROVISION CONCERNING FORFEITURE

FORM

B19.18   Forfeiture on contesting the will or attempting to intermeddle .... **[219.31]**

CROSS REFERENCES

For other survivorship or commorientes clauses see C2 at para **[224.1]**. For other
substitution clauses see Forms B6.19 at para **[206.28]**, B6.24 at para **[206.33]**,
B6.25 at para **[206.34]**, B10.13 at para **[210.25]**, B10.14 at para **[210.26]**, B17.7
to B17.13 at paras **[217.12]**–**[217.18]**, B17.33 at para **[217.38]** and B17.34 at
para **[217.39]**. For other declarations against lapse see Forms B6.27 at
para **[206.36]** and (for charitable gifts) B12.29 at para **[212.31]**. For declarations
against ademption see Forms B4.36 at para **[204.58]**, B6.15 at para **[206.24]** and
B7.6 at para **[207.20]**. For provision for forfeiture see Form B17.31 at
para **[217.36]**.

COMMORIENTES PROVISIONS

[219.1]
Note. Survivorship clauses—or commorientes clauses as they are commonly, if
less accurately known—ie provisions whereby a gift by will is made to take
effect only if the donee survives the testator by a given period, usually a
month—have become more popular in recent years. This is doubtless because
increased road and air travel has resulted in a greater risk of members of the
same family dying in a common accident. The principal purpose of
commorientes provisions is the practical one of enabling the testator to control
the devolution of his estate in circumstances in which the beneficiary dies either
at the same time as him or shortly thereafter. The justification on practical
grounds for such clauses is considered more fully below. Such clauses also have
fiscal implications and these are also considered.

[219.2]
(a)   Practical considerations. The LPA 1925, s 184 (Part G, para **[244.56]**)
provides that if two or more persons die in circumstances rendering it uncertain
which of them survived the other or others, their deaths are, for all purposes
affecting their title to property, presumed to have occurred in order of seniority.
Thus, if the donee is younger than the testator and the order of their deaths is
uncertain, the testator will be deemed to have died first. The statutory
presumption may have anomalous consequences as is demonstrated by the
classic case of *Re Rowland, Smith v Russell* [1963] Ch 1, [1962] 2 All ER 837.
In that case a husband and wife made wills leaving their estates to one another.
The husband's will went on to provide that 'in the event of the decease

of [his wife] preceding or coinciding with [his] own decease' his estate was to go to his brother and his wife's nephew. The wife's will correspondingly went on to provide that in a similar event her estate was to go to her niece. The parties died in circumstances rendering the order of their deaths uncertain but since there was no evidence that the deaths 'coincided', the wife, being the younger, was deemed to have survived the husband under s 184. Their combined estates accordingly passed to the wife's niece and the husband's beneficiaries took nothing. If the husband had died *intestate*, this unfortunate result would not have occurred as the statutory presumption as between the parties to a marriage where one of them dies intestate in circumstances rendering it uncertain which of them survived is that the other is *not* deemed to survive the intestate: AEA 1925, s 46(3): Part G, para **[244.60]**. The result would also have been avoided by a commorientes clause making the gift to the wife dependent upon her survival for a month (or some such period) because then she would never have become entitled under the husband's will: the husband's estate would have passed to his beneficiaries and hers to hers. Hence, the argument runs, commorientes clauses are desirable.

[219.3]
Useful though commorientes clauses may often be, it must be observed that they will not necessarily provide a complete answer. The fault in *Re Rowland* lay as much in the substantive provisions of the two wills as in the absence of commorientes provisions. It is never wise for a husband to leave his estate to his wife or, if she predeceases him, to the persons *he* wants to benefit and for the wife to leave her estate to him or, failing him, to the different persons *she* wants to benefit. In the nature of things one of them is bound to die first and the combined estates are (unless the surviving spouse has the opportunity to change his or her will in the meantime and does so) bound to devolve—later if not sooner—on the beneficiaries of the surviving spouse alone. This problem is further discussed, and forms providing solutions are printed in C9 at para **[231.1]** et seq. It follows that the unhappy results in *Re Rowland* could have been avoided by the draftsman without recourse to a commorientes clause—and they would have been better avoided without such recourse because even if a commorientes clause had been used it would not have helped if the wife had happened to die just outside the commorientes period.

[219.4]
Furthermore, although the trouble inherent in the ill-advised provisions of the two wills in *Re Rowland* would *in the circumstances which happened* have been avoided by a commorientes clause, cases can be imagined in which the trouble inherent in other ill-advised provisions would in certain circumstances be precipitated rather than avoided by such a clause. Suppose a widower left his estate equally between such of his children as survived him by one month, that one of his children survived him (or was presumed under s 184 to have survived him) but died within the month and that this child left a wife and young children of his own. The testator would (let us suppose) have wanted the bereaved family to take the share which his son would have had, but because he used a commorientes clause they cannot do so. If the testator had omitted the

commorientes clause the bereaved family would (assuming they were beneficiaries of the son's estate) have benefited as the testator would have wished. Here again, however, the trouble arises basically, not from the presence or absence of a commorientes clause, but from the substantive provisions of the will: a substitutional gift should have been included for the benefit of the family of any child who failed to take under the will; for a child might equally well have died just before the testator as just after him, and the former possibility needs to be guarded against just as much as the latter. But while commorientes provisions may not provide a complete answer, they can serve a useful function. A testator will usually want the beneficiaries named in his will themselves to enjoy the gifts thereby made and not the persons who may be entitled under their wills or intestacies. If the original donees cannot enjoy the gifts in this way, the testator would probably like them to pass instead to whoever would have had them if the donees had predeceased him. The inclusion of a commorientes clause may therefore be desirable because it goes some way towards ensuring that the only people who take the estate are those who are alive when it is actually distributed.

See also the Preliminary Note to C2 at para **[224.1]** et seq.

[219.5]

(b) Fiscal implications. The Inheritance Tax Act 1984 (ITA 1984), s 4(2) (42 *Halsbury's Statutes* (4th edn) (1996 Reissue) 603) provides that where it cannot be known which of two or more persons who have died survived the other or others they shall be assumed for the purposes of the charge to inheritance tax on death to have died at the same instant (ITA 1984, s 54(4)). Multiple charges to tax on simultaneous deaths are thus excluded. But this relieving provision does not extend to cases where the order of deaths is known however close in point of time they may be. In such cases relief may be available under the quick succession relief provisions contained in the ITA 1984, s 141, but such relief is at best only partial and in any event does not apply where the testator and beneficiary are married as the given property is ordinarily exempt from tax on the first death. In such cases the property will prima facie fall to be aggregated with the estate of the surviving spouse for tax purposes.

[219.6]

The effect of commorientes provisions in cases where deaths are close but not simultaneous is governed by the ITA 1984, s 92. Provided that the period for survival does not exceed six months from the testator's death, the dispositions taking effect at the end of that period or on the death of the beneficiary if earlier are to be treated as having had effect from the date of the death. It is not entirely clear from the wording of s 92 whether the provision extends to limited as well as absolute interests. The first reference to the word 'property' in the section might be taken to suggest that contingent income interests cannot fall within its terms. In view of the Inland Revenue's Statement in their Press Notice of 20 November 1975, in relation to the pre-existing law, it seems very unlikely that the section would be so narrowly construed. It is also to be noted that it appears not to matter whether or not the contingent gift carries the intermediate income. This again would be consistent with the terms of the Revenue Notice. However, where an immediate income interest eg, a life interest in residue, is given subject to a survival contingency, it would be wise to ensure that such contingent life interest did not itself carry the intermediate income of residue pending satisfaction of the contingency because an interest in these terms would have a decidedly artificial appearance being no different in effect from an immediately vested life interest.

[219.7]
Where the contingent beneficiary is the testator's spouse, special considerations apply. It should be noted that in these circumstances the spouse exemption under the ITA 1984, s 18 will be available if but only if the survival contingency is satisfied. This may be desirable if the aggregation of the property given to the spouse would have the effect of increasing the overall tax burden on the joint property eg, where the estates of the testator and the spouse are roughly equal in value. But where the testator's estate is more valuable it may be more advantageous for the testator to leave part of his property to his spouse unconditionally so that such property becomes taxable at a lower rate on the spouse's subsequent death whenever that may occur.

[219.8]
A circumstance where a survivorship condition should perhaps not be included is where the testator has left his estate to his spouse, subject to a legacy to non-exempt persons of the maximum sum he can leave without incurring inheritance tax (a "nil-rate legacy'). The nil-rate legacy will be subject to the condition that the gift to the spouse takes effect, so if the gift to the spouse is subject to a survivorship condition, then the gift of the nil-rate legacy is impliedly subject to the same condition. However, the ITA 1984, s 92 will not apply to this implied survivorship condition since the condition is not as to the survival of the beneficiary of the nil-rate gift, as the section appears to require. Nevertheless, where the spouse dies within a short period of the testator, there would appear to be no inheritance tax disadvantage in not having included a survivorship condition, since the testator will have fully utilised his nil-rate band by the nil-rate legacy. Furthermore there may be an inheritance tax advantage where the spouse's own estate does not exceed the nil-rate band.

[219.9]
A further point should be noted about inheritance tax where spouses die in circumstances where it cannot be known which of them survived the other. Where this happens, s 4(2) of the ITA 1984 applies, but it only applies for the purposes of s 4(1). It does not apply for the purposes of s 18 (the spouse exemption). Accordingly, if a husband and wife die in these circumstances, and they have each made a will leaving the other his or her entire estate (with no *commorientes* or survivorship provision) with, say, an alternative gift to their children, the estate of the older spouse will devolve on the younger spouse by virtue of Law of Property Act 1925, s 184; it will not be charged to inheritance tax on the death of the younger spouse because of the ITA 1984, s 4(2); and it will not be charged to inheritance tax as part of the estate on death of the older spouse because of the spouse exemption. If there had been a survivorship

condition in the older spouse's will this advantage would be lost because the older spouse's estate would not devolve on the younger.

[219.10]
Therefore if a survivorship clause, general or specific, is being included in a will so as to apply to gifts by the testator to his spouse, and the testator is older than the spouse, there could be an advantage in excluding the survivorship condition in the event of their dying in circumstances where it is uncertain which has survived the other. There has been no official pronouncement from the Inland Revenue on this point, although it is believed that it has been accepted in at least one case. Nevertheless, in case they do not accept the point in any particular case, it would be advisable to ensure that the will still contains gifts to non-exempt beneficiaries up to the inheritance tax threshold when the order of deaths is uncertain. We suggest as suitable wording (to go in the will of the older spouse only), where the gift incorporates a survivorship condition, Form B19.3 at para **[219.15]**.

A proviso to be added at the end of a general survivorship clause can be found in Form B19.4 at para **[219.16]**.

[219.11]
There is no capital gains tax provision corresponding with the ITA 1984, s 92. However, capital gains tax is unlikely to be a significant factor. If the property given subject to a survival contingency is a pecuniary legacy a charge to capital gains tax cannot in any event arise. Even if the gift is of a specific asset a charge to tax is unlikely to accrue during the contingency period which cannot exceed six months and is frequently no more than a month. The satisfaction of the contingency or the prior death of the beneficiary could be a deemed disposal under the settled property provisions. Since, however, the administration would very probably continue until after that time the settled property provisions would, it is thought, be excluded. Thus a beneficiary who became absolutely entitled to property one month after the death of the testator would ultimately take as 'legatee' under the Taxation of Chargeable Gains Act 1992, ss 62(4) and 64, ie he would be treated as having acquired it at its value at the testator's death, and there would be no deemed disposal under the TCGA 1992, s 71.

[219.12]
(c)   Conclusions. Commorientes provisions have a useful role to play but the substantive dispositions affected by the will should not be overlooked. Although deeds of variation and disclaimers (as to which see F3 at para **[241.1]** et seq) may be capable of rearranging beneficial dispositions in a more convenient or economic manner, this is not always the case. For an alternative approach to the problems which commorientes provisions are intended to solve the two-year discretionary trust might be considered: see C3 at para **[225.1]** et seq. Another alternative is the nil-rate band legacy, as in Form C3.4 at para **[225.57]**.

[219.13]
Of the first two forms which follow, Form B19.1 is specific, and Form B19.2 is general. In both cases it is provided that intermediate income should not be

carried. In view of the short period involved this seems the more convenient course administratively. For wills incorporating a survival contingency see C2 at para **[224.1]** et seq.

[219.14]

FORM B19.1:   Contingent gift of property which does carry intermediate income during the commorientes period

I give [*property*] to [*donee*] absolutely but contingently upon his surviving me for [one] calendar month and if he dies within the calendar month [*or as the case may be*] following my death he shall be treated as having predeceased me and the intermediate income from the said [*property*] shall not belong to him [*add alternative disposition, which should mention the intermediate income, thus*: and in that event I give the said [*property*] including the intermediate income thereof to [*alternative donee*] [*or* the said [*property*] including the intermediate income thereof shall form part of my residuary estate]].

[219.15]

FORM B19.2:   'Omnibus' commorientes provision extending to all gifts in the will

Every person who would otherwise benefit under this will but who fails to survive me for [three calendar months[1]] shall be treated for all purposes connected with the devolution of my estate[2] [[including] [but not including] section 33 of the Wills Act 1837[3]] as having predeceased me and my estate and the intermediate income thereof shall devolve accordingly to the intent that no such person shall be entitled to any intermediate income from my estate or any part of it if he dies within that period or acquire therein or in any part thereof a vested interest (or a vested interest subject to defeasance) before the end of it.

1   This period must not exceed six months.
2   These words cover the possibility of a partial intestacy.
3   For the operation of the new s 33 of the WA 1837 (as substituted by the AJA 1982, s 19 (Part G, para **[244.34]**)) see Vol 1, paras **[47.14]–[47.19]**. Since the new section creates what is in effect a substitutional gift in favour of the issue of a predeceasing child or remoter descendant of the testator, there may be advantages in preserving its effect. It is advisable to make the position absolutely clear by expressly including or excluding the section.

[219.16]

FORM B19.3:   Spouse survivorship clause for will of older spouse only[1]

I give [*property*] to my wife [*name*] if she shall survive me by the period of six months provided that if she and I shall die in circumstances where it cannot be known which of us survived the other then the foregoing survival condition shall not apply and the foregoing gift shall take effect.

1   For the possible inheritance tax advantage of including such a clause as this in the will of the older of two spouses, and what other gifts should be included in the will if this clause is used, see paras **[219.7]–[219.10]**.

[219.17]

FORM B19.4:   **Proviso for will of older spouse only to be added at the end of a general survivorship clause**[1]

Provided that if my wife [*name*] and I shall die in circumstances where it cannot be known which of us survived the other then the foregoing survival condition shall not apply and all gifts in her favour herein [other than ——] shall take effect.

1   For the possible inheritance tax advantage of including such a clause as this in the will of the older of two spouses, and what other gifts should be included in the will if this clause is used, see paras **[219.7]–[219.10]**.

Substitution clauses

[219.18]

FORM B19.5:   **Substitution clause limited to children of deceased children**[1]

Provided that if any of my said children is already dead or shall predecease me or shall die after my death without attaining the age of [eighteen] [twenty-one] [thirty] years leaving a child or children who shall attain the age of [eighteen] [twenty-one] years or marry thereunder such child or children shall take by substitution and if more than one in equal shares the share of my residuary estate [the trust fund] which his her or their parent would have taken if he or she had survived me and attained a vested interest.

1   As to the construction of children and issue see Vol 1, Chs 71 to 76.

[219.19]

FORM B19.6:   **Trust for testator's children at twenty-five with substitution of issue of a child who predeceases the testator and further substitution of children on death after the testator's death without attaining a vested interest**[1, 2]

(1)   My trustees shall hold [my residuary estate] in trust for such of my children as shall be living at or after my death and attain the age of [25] years if more than one in equal shares.

(2)   Provided that if any of my children is already dead or predeceases me the share of [my residuary estate] to which such child would be entitled if he or she survived me and attained a vested interest shall be held in trust for such of his or her children and remoter issue (if any) as shall be living at my death and attain the age of [25] years in equal shares per stirpes and so that no issue shall take whose parent is living at my death and capable of taking.

(3)   Provided further that if any child of mine or any remoter issue of mine presumptively entitled under the foregoing proviso is living at or after my death but dies without attaining a vested interest under the foregoing trusts the share of [my residuary estate] to which such child or issue of mine would be entitled if he or she lived to attain such a vested interest shall be held in trust for such of his

children (if any) as attain the age of 21 years or marry under that age if more than one in equal shares.

1   As to the construction of children and issue see Vol 1, Chs 71 to 76.
2   For the inheritance tax implications of this form see Part A, paras **[200.132]** and **[200.133]**.

Accruer clauses[1]

[219.20]

FORM B19.7:   Accruer of share[2]

If the gift of any such share as aforesaid shall fail by reason of no person attaining a vested interest therein then I direct that the said share and any share or shares which may accrue thereto by virtue of this present provision shall be held by my trustees as an accretion to the other share or shares [(and equally if more than one)] / [(if more than one in the proportion which such other shares bear to one another)][3] the gift or gifts whereof shall not at the date of such accruer have failed as aforesaid.

1   As to these clauses, see Vol 1, paras **[90.1]**–**[90.6]**.
2   This simple form is for use where the testator has left shares of residue or of a legacy to beneficiaries without any contingencies which might not be satisfied until after the testator's death (other than a survivorship condition). For a form for use where there are contingencies or the shares are settled, see Form B19.8 at para **[219.21]**.
3   Where shares are equal, the testator may wish any shares, the gifts of which have failed, to accrue equally to the others; but where the shares are initially unequal, he may wish the accrual to be in proportionate to the relative sizes of the remaining shares.

[219.21]

FORM B19.8:   Accruer of settled share[1]

If the trusts of any such share as aforesaid shall fail or determine (other than by absolute vesting) [before the vesting day][2] then I direct that subject to the trusts powers and provisions herein contained or which may be applicable thereto by statute the said share and any share or shares which may previously have accrued thereto by virtue of this present provision shall be held by my trustees as an accretion to the other share or shares [(and equally if more than one)] / [(if more than one in the proportion which such other shares bear to one another)][3] the trusts whereof shall not at the date of such accruer have failed or determined (other than by absolute vesting) as aforesaid and as one fund therewith for all purposes.

1   This form is for use where the testator has left a share or shares of residue or of a legacy subject to contingencies which might not be satisfied until after the testator's death, or has otherwise settled some or all of the shares. (For a simple form for use where there are no contingencies or settlements, see Form B19.7 at para **[219.20]**). Where beneficiaries are given an absolute interest and trusts are engrafted thereon and all die without issue, the absolute interests remain and, although the shares may have accrued as to income, the capital passes under the absolute interest of each beneficiary: *Re Atkinson's Will Trusts, Prescott v Child* [1957] Ch 117, [1956] 3 All ER 738.
2   This clause is contingent, and so should be confined to operating during a perpetuity period. These words would be appropriate where there are interests, such as life interests, which could

continue beyond the end of any available perpetuity period for the trusts. There is assumed to be a definition of the vesting day elsewhere in the will which is such that it falls within an appropriate perpetuity period.

3 Where shares are equal, the testator may wish any shares, whose trusts have failed, to accrue equally to the others; but where the shares are initially unequal, he may wish the accrual to be in proportionate to the relative sizes of the shares.

[219.22]

FORM B19.9: Accruer where shares given to named children

[Where residue divided into four shares, two for a named son and one each for each of two daughters.]

If my son [*name*] shall predecease me or shall survive me and fail to attain a vested interest in such two shares then I direct that my trustees shall stand possessed of one half of my said son's shares as an accretion to the share hereby given to and hereinafter settled on my said daughter [*name*] and her issue and of the other half of my said son's shares as an accretion to the share hereby given to and hereinafter settled on my said daughter [*name*] and her issue.

Provisions concerning lapse

[219.23]

FORM B19.10: Declaration against lapse in the case of a gift to a named person[1]

I declare that the [legacy of £——] [share of residue] hereinbefore bequeathed to [*name*] shall not lapse by reason of the death in my lifetime of the said [*name*] but shall in that event pass to his [*or* her] personal representatives as part of his estate.[2]

1 The words 'to the effect that my will shall take effect whether I survive or predecease my husband' are not sufficient to prevent lapse in the case of the husband predeceasing the testatrix (*Re Ladd, Henderson v Porter* [1932] 2 Ch 219). Where a person to whom a lapsed gift would pass also predeceased the testator, the the gift lapses in the testator's estate (*Re Cousen's Will Trusts, Wright v Killick* [1937] Ch 381, [1937] 2 All ER 276). It is thought that if the primary beneficiary dies before the testator there will not be a charge to inheritance tax on the gift as part of the primary beneficiary's estate as well as the charge as part of the testator's estate because the primary beneficiary will not at his death be beneficially entitled to anything under the testator's will.

2 This provision will not of course be inserted if issue are substituted, or if the WA 1837, s 33 (substituted by the AJA 1982, s 19: Part G, para [**244.34**]) can be relied on to effect the substitution which is desired: for the scope and effect of this provision see Vol 1, para [**47.14**].

[219.24]

FORM B19.11: Clause providing against lapse in the case of a gift to a named person and that the clause shall operate as a direct gift to the substituted persons[1]

I declare that if my said nephew or my said niece shall die in my lifetime [leaving issue[2] living at my death or then en ventre but born afterwards] the [devises and] bequests herein contained to him or her so dying shall not lapse but shall go and devolve in the same manner as if he or she had survived me and died immediately after my death provided that this direction shall take effect by way of direct gift to the persons (if any) beneficially interested under the will or on the intestacy (as the case may be) of my said nephew or niece and shall not make the said [devises or] bequests part of his or her estate so as to be liable for his or her debts or inheritance tax on his or her estate.

1   See para **[219.23]**, n 1.
2   Illegitimate issue are prima facie included: FLRA 1987; ss 1 and 19 (Part G, paras **[245.70]** and **[245.72]**). The HFEA 1990, as from 1 August 1991, also affects the meaning of issue in some circumstances: Part G, para **[245.82]** et seq.

[219.25]

FORM B19.12:   Declaration against lapse in the case of a class gift of residue

I declare that if any person who at or before the date of his or her death would have taken a vested interest in my residuary estate if the provisions of my will had at that date been operative shall die before me then the share which such person would have taken in my residuary estate if such person had survived me shall at my death pass to the personal representatives of such person as part of his or her estate as if such person had died immediately after me.[1]

1   See para **[219.23]**, n 1.

[219.26]

FORM B19.13:   Declaration against lapse of settled share

I declare that in case any daughter [*or* child] of mine shall die or has already died in my lifetime leaving issue living at my death or then en ventre but born afterwards [the legacy of £—— and] the share of residue hereinbefore bequeathed to her [*or* such child] whether original or accruing shall be retained by my trustees upon the like trusts in all respects as if such daughter [*or* child] had died immediately after me.[1]

1   For a case of lapse, see *Re Roberts, Tarleton v Bruton* (1885) 30 Ch D 234; for the more ordinary cases where there was held not to be a lapse, see *Re Pinhorne, Moreton v Hughes* [1894] 2 Ch 276; *Re Powell, Campbell v Campbell* [1900] 2 Ch 525; *Re Whitmore, Walters v Harrison* [1902] 2 Ch 66; *Re Harward, Newton v Bankes* [1938] Ch 632, [1938] 2 All ER 804.

[219.27]

FORM B19.14:   Clause as to application of lapsed share of residue[1]

I direct that any lapsed share of residue causing an intestacy as to that share shall be primarily applied in or towards the payment of debts funeral and testamentary expenses and pecuniary legacies hereby or by any codicil hereto bequeathed before recourse is had to any other property hereby or by any codicil hereto devised or bequeathed.

1   The order of application of assets where the estate is solvent is stated in the AEA 1925, Sch 1,
     Pt II (Part G, para **[246.54]**). Although the AEA 1925 provides for testamentary expenses, debts
     etc to be paid primarily out of a lapsed share, this can easily be displaced by the creation of a
     mixed residuary fund. Accordingly, this form could be used to prevent the creation of such a
     fund from having such an effect. See further the Preliminary Note to B14 at para **[214.4]** et seq.

[219.28]

FORM B19.15:   **General form of gift over on failure of the trusts of residue**[1]

If [any share or shares of] my residuary estate shall not vest absolutely in some
person or persons under the preceding trusts, then [such undisposed of share or
shares of] my residuary estate shall (subject to the trusts powers and provisions
hereby or by statute vested in my trustees in respect of the income or capital
thereof and to every exercise of the same by my trustees) be held by my trustees
[for such person or persons as *some previous beneficiary*] shall by will or codicil
appoint and in default of such appointment] in trust for my brothers and sisters
living at my death and the children of any then deceased brother or sister of
mine who attain the age of [eighteen] [twenty-one] years or marry thereunder if
more than one in equal shares as tenants in common but so that the children of
any such deceased brother or sister shall take between them as tenants in
common only the share their parent would have taken had he or she survived
me.

1   This form assumes that the residue is given to the testator's immediate family. It may readily be
     adapted to cases where the testator has no brothers or sisters and wishes to benefit more remote
     relatives or strangers.
         As to the construction of words denoting a blood relationship see Vol 1, paras **[71.1]–[71.5]**.

[219.29]

FORM B19.16:   **Gift to testator's wife with alternative gift to take on the
failure for any reason of the primary gift**[1]

I give [my residuary estate] to my wife [*name*] absolutely [if she shall survive
me by the period of [one month][2]] and if she shall predecease me [or fail to
survive me by the said period of [one month]s] or if the foregoing gift in her
favour shall lapse or fail for any other reason then [I give [my residuary estate]
to [*name*] absolutely] [my trustees shall hold [my residuary estate] upon the
following trusts namely [*specify desired trusts*]].

1   This form incorporates a primary absolute gift in favour of the testator's wife with a gift over on
     the failure for any reason of the primary gift. The wording of this form was designed to
     overcome the difficulties which could be encountered in relation to deaths before 1 January
     1996 if the parties were divorced after the date of the will. The primary gift lapsed under the
     WA 1837, s 18A (as introduced by the AJA 1982, s 18(2): Part G, para **[244.17]**), but if the ex-
     wife survived the testator and satisfied any survival contingency which might attach to the
     primary gift, the gift over would not take effect even though the primary gift had failed: see *Re
     Sinclair, Lloyds Bank plc v Imperial Cancer Research Fund* [1985] Ch 446, [1985] 1 All ER
     1066 and Vol 1, paras **[47.2]** and **[47.3]**. In relation to deaths on or after 1 January 1996 a
     divorced spouse is treated as having predeceased the testator for the purposes of a gift of this
     kind, and reference to failure of the gift to the spouse 'for any other reason', as here, is not
     necessary: see Preliminary Note to C2 at paras **[224.12]–[224.19]**.
2   A survival contingency may also be incorporated, if desired. The survival period should on no
     account exceed six months. There may be an inheritance advantage in excluding a survivorship

provision in the will of the older of two spouses in the event that the spouses die in circumstances where it cannot be known who died first. For clauses providing for this exclusion, see Forms B19.3 and B19.4. See generally the notes on commorientes provisions at paras **[219.7]–[219.10]**.

Provision concerning disclaimer

[219.30]

FORM B19.17:   Clause allowing for a partial disclaimer, the property disclaimed devolving as if the person disclaiming had predeceased the testator[1]

I declare that any person may disclaim in whole or in part any gift in his or her favour contained in this my will or any codicil hereto and in the event of such disclaimer either in whole or part the gift or part thereof disclaimed shall devolve as if the person disclaiming had predeceased me.

1   A disclaimer of a whole gift is possible in law and its effect is usually to accelerate gifts taking effect in remainder. So, for example, a disclaimed legacy falls into residue, and a disclaimed residuary gift passes as on an intestacy. This clause may vary the destination of a disclaimed gift. It is not possible as a matter of general law to disclaim a part of a gift (the position is otherwise in Scotland), so this clause expressly provides for it to be possible. For disclaimer generally, see Vol 1, paras **[46.1]–[46.6]**.

Provision concerning forfeiture

[219.31]

FORM B19.18:   Forfeiture on contesting the will or attempting to intermeddle

Provided that if any of *[names or description of beneficiaries]* shall either (i) dispute the validity of this will or any of the dispositions of my estate effected by it or (ii) at any time without reasonable cause interfere in or intermeddle with or attempt to interfere in or intermeddle with the administration or management of my estate then notwithstanding anything herein elsewhere provided that person shall forfeit his interest in [my residuary estate] and be deemed to have predeceased me for the purposes of the devolution of my estate.

B20   Administrative powers and provisions

Part B   Clauses in wills

CROSS REFERENCES

For powers relating to business property see B5 at para **[205.1]** et seq. For
administration trusts, declarations concerning apportionment and incidence of
inheritance tax see B14 at para **[214.1]** et seq. For maintenance and
advancement powers, powers to permit enjoyment in kind and general
declarations concerning the exercise of powers see B18 at para **[218.41]** et seq.
For trustees and executors—self-dealing, retention of benefits, indemnities,
appointment of new trustees and charging see B21 at para **[221.4]**. For complete
sets of administrative provisions see Form C2.1, cl 9 at para **[224.30]** and C11.1,
cl 6 at para **[233.21]**. For disclaimer and renunciation of probate or trusteeship
see F1 at para **[239.1]** et seq.

GENERAL PRELIMINARY NOTE

[220.1]
The extent of the administrative powers and provisions which need to be included in a will depends on the nature of the beneficial interests given; none (or none except perhaps a professional trustee charging clause) may be needed if the only gifts are absolute gifts to adults or to charity, while a variety of administrative provisions might be included where all or part of the estate is settled on trust. However, with the enactment of the Trusts of Land and Appointment of Trustees Act 1996 (TLATA 1996) and the Trustee Act 2000 (TrA 2000), the need to include express powers in the general run of cases is less pressing than was formerly the case. By virtue of the TLATA 1996, wide powers in relation to land are conferred on trustees of land, ie trustees of any trust of property which consists of or includes land (or the proceeds of sale of land): TLATA 1996, ss 1 and 3 (Part G, paras **[246.86]** and **[246.88]**). Subject to certain exceptions, these powers will also apply to personal representatives where the estate they administer includes land: TLATA 1996, s 18 (Part G, para **[246.104]**). The TrA 2000 is of wider application, and, with certain exceptions, applies to trustees (including personal representatives: TrA 2000, s 35, Part G, para **[246.150]**) whether they hold land or not. It provides a new wider statutory power of investment to replace the limited powers under the Trustee Investments Act 1961 (TIA 1961), and new powers to appoint agents (including investment managers), nominees and custodians, to insure trust property, and to pay professional trustees. These new powers generally apply to trusts whenever created. However, as under the present law, they will generally be in addition to any express powers and only apply to the extent that the will permits. Even after these two major enactments, however, there are still administrative powers and provisions which it might be considered advisable to include in any particular will. The preliminary notes to the sub-divisions of B20 indicate what may be lacking under the general law, even after the TLATA 1996 and the TrA 2000, in response to which the various categories of express provision might be considered useful.

[220.2]
B20 is concerned with powers and provisions relating to the administration of trust assets; powers and provisions concerning executors and trustees are in B21, and administration trusts of residue and directions concerning apportionment are in B14. The complete forms of will in Part C give examples of appropriate administrative provisions to combine with particular beneficial interests.

[220.3]
Where there are settled specific gifts or general legacies it is important to check that the administrative powers contained in the will apply to them and not just to the residuary trust fund. It is also important where there are any settled funds to make sure that provisions such as powers of appropriation, directions concerning the Apportionment Acts, and professional charging clauses will continue to apply after the administration of the estate is complete and the personal representatives give way to trustees.

[220.4]
Inheritance tax. A headache of which will draftsmen will be aware, is the danger that wide administrative provisions may prejudice the intended status of interest in possession trusts or of trusts intended to fall within the Inheritance Tax Act 1984, s 71 (accumulation and maintenance trusts).

[220.5]
In the case of interest in possession trusts (see Part A, para **[200.108]** et seq) the main concern is to avoid powers which, by their very existence, prevent the person prima facie entitled to the interest in possession from being entitled to the income of the relevant settled property as it arises. It is a natural incident of an interest in possession that it is subject to certain expenses being payable out of income: for example, rates, repairs and fire insurance premiums relating to land held on trust for sale, and income tax and interest on charges and incumbrances (see *Carver v Duncan (Inspector of Taxes)* [1985] AC 1082 at 1120, [1985] 2 All ER 645 at 652). It seems clear from *Pearson v IRC* [1981] AC 753, [1980] 2 All ER 479, HL, at 774–5 and 784–5 and 486 and 494 respectively that administrative powers to pay such expenses out of income do not prevent anyone from having an interest in possession for inheritance tax purposes. The passages in *Pearson v IRC* just cited, particularly the remarks of Lord Dilhorne, seem to be saying that a power to pay capital taxes out of income would not prejudice the existence of an interest in possession, but it is the authors' opinion that so liberal a view should not in the present state of authority (and bearing in mind *Carver v Duncan (Inspector of Taxes)*) be relied on.

[220.6]
What should be avoided is conferring express powers to pay capital expenses, such as life assurance premiums, capital taxes, or permanent improvements to land, or expenses attributable to some other share or fund, out of income. We should add that powers of this kind will not always prejudice the existence of an interest in possession, first, because a general discretion as to the burden of particular types of expense will not necessarily displace the trustees' normal duty to allocate the burden of expenditure equitably according to the various beneficial interests in the trust fund and its income; and second, because many such powers may not be exercisable until some other event happens, for example, life assurance premiums cannot be paid out of income until the trustees acquire or effect a life assurance policy.

[220.7]
There is a subsidiary category of administrative powers whose existence (unexercised) does not prevent some intended interest in possession from subsisting, but whose exercise might cause an interest in possession to terminate. The exercise of some powers to effect life policies might have this consequence, as might exercise of a power to allow a beneficiary other than the person entitled to an interest in possession to occupy a house comprised in the trust fund or have other enjoyment in kind of trust assets. (The Inland Revenue take the view that enjoyment in kind of trust assets by virtue of an exercise of a power of the trustees to permit it can give rise to an interest in possession, and there are

convincing reasons for their view—see Part A, para **[200.110]** and *Foster's Inheritance Tax*, E1.47.)

[220.8]
In the case of trusts intended to fall within the Inheritance Tax Act 1984 (ITA 1984), s 71 (see Part A, para **[200.119]** et seq) the requirements are more stringent and even more care must be taken to see that there are no administrative powers which prevent the conditions in paras (a) and (b) of s 71(1) from applying. It will be appreciated that a power to pay expenses not properly attributable to capital (or not properly attributable to the settled property in question), whether or not it is actually exercised, could prevent the 'beneficiaries' becoming entitled to, or to an interest in possession in, that capital on or before attaining the 'specified age'—ie it could prevent the trusts from satisfying s 71(1)(a). Further, the same would be the consequence of the existence of a power to permit enjoyment in kind of trust assets which was capable of being exercised in favour of persons other than the 'beneficiaries' as defined in s 71(1)(a). Similarly, a power that permitted the income to be applied in some way other than payment or application for the benefit of the 'beneficiaries' or accumulation would prejudice the application of s 71(1)(b).

[220.9]
On the other hand, the references to settled property and to the income from it in s 71(1) must be references respectively to the property net of the expenses properly attributable to it and to the income net of the expenses properly attributable to it.

[220.10]
We have tried in the forms in B20 to indicate what restrictions (if any) we regard as appropriate where there are interest in possession or accumulation and maintenance trusts. We have also included a form of general restriction intended to prevent any administrative powers from prejudicing the intended inheritance tax status of the beneficial trusts (see Form B20.28 at para **[220.81]** and Form C2.1, cl 9 at para **[224.30]**). For further discussion of these points, see *Foster's Inheritance Tax*, E1.43 and E5.14.

PRELIMINARY NOTE ON INVESTMENT POWERS

[220.11]
The main points to consider when drafting investment clauses seem to us to be as follows:

[220.12]
Statutory investment power. The TrA 2000 came into force on 1 February 2001 (Trustee Act 2000 (Commencement) Order 2001, SI 2001/49), and has replaced the provisions of the TIA 1961 as to trustees' powers of investment. The provisions of the TIA 1961 were widely considered to be too elaborate and troublesome to follow correctly, unduly restrictive, and particularly in relation to their policy of only permitting up to a specific proportion of a fund to be invested in ordinary shares, out-of-date. The power conferred on trustees (and

personal representatives) by the TrA 2000 is referred to as 'the general power of investment'. It is a power to make (subject to the further provisions of the TrA 2000, described below) any kind of investment, including loans secured on land but otherwise excluding land (power to invest in which is dealt with separately—see para **[220.17]**), that they could make if they were absolutely entitled to the assets of the trust: TrA 2000, s 3(1)–(3) (Part G, para **[246.118]**). By an irony of fate, the TrA 2000 conferred a full power to invest an entire fund in ordinary shares just in time to catch the substantial falls in the value of quoted shares in the summer and autumn of 2001. The new statutory power of investment is in addition to any other powers conferred on the trustees (eg by the will), but subject to any restriction or exclusion imposed by, eg the will: TrA 2000, s 6(1) (Part G, para **[246.121]**). It applies in relation to trusts whether created before or after the commencement of the Act on 1 February 2001, and in the case of a trust created by will, whenever the will was made or the testator died: TrA 2000, s 7(1) (Part G, para **[246.122]**). It applies to personal representatives as well as trustees: TrA 2000, s 35 (Part G, para **[246.150]**).

[220.13]
Duty to have regard to standard investment criteria. In exercising the general power of investment (or indeed any investment power, whether conferred expressly by the will or by some other statutory provision such as the TrA 2000, s 8(1)(a); for which see para **[220.17]**), trustees (or personal representatives) must have regard to 'the standard investment criteria'. These criteria are first, the suitability to the trust of investments of the same kind as any particular investment proposed to be made or retained and of that particular investment as an investment of that kind; and second, the need for diversification of investments of the trust, insofar as is appropriate to the circumstances of the trust. The trustees must also, from time to time, review the investments of the trust and consider whether, having regard to the standard investment criteria, they should be varied: TrA 2000, s 4 (Part G, para **[246.119]**). No indication is given as to how often trustees must review the investment, but once a year must surely be the minimum, and in the case of a large trust fund or one invested on the stock market at times of particular volatility, more reviews might be required. This in substance re-enacts the provisions of the TIA 1961, s 6(1), which also applied to express as well as statutory powers of investment. The only difference is that the wording of the TrA 2000, s 4 makes it even plainer than the TIA 1961, s 6(1) did that the requirement of having regard to the standard investment criteria applies to all powers of investment, and that it is not capable of being excluded. Although it cannot be excluded, trustees' liability for negligence, and therefore for negligent failure to have regard to the standard investment criteria, can be excluded or limited (see para **[221.15]**). Where it is intended that trustees should retain a particular asset, eg land or private company shares, thought should be given to adding an expression of wishes to that effect, by way of guidance on the question of whether diversification is 'appropriate to the circumstances of the trust'. More important than expressions of wishes, however, is the purpose of the trust. For example, if the purpose of a trust of family company shares is to retain it in the family while various members of the family work in it, or if the purpose of a trust of land is to provide a residence for a beneficiary or preserve a farm or landed estate for family business use or pleasure, those will be strong reasons

why diversification is not appropriate. For private company shares, see Form B20.5 at para **[220.44]**. For land, see Forms B8.1 to B8.6 at paras **[208.37]** to **[208.42]** and Form C13.2 at para **[235.18]** et seq.

[220.14]
Duty to take advice. Before exercising their statutory investment power (or indeed any investment power, whether conferred expressly by the will or by some other statutory provision such as the TrA 2000, s 8(1)(a); for which see para **[220.17]**) and when reviewing their investments, trustees must obtain and consider proper advice about the way in which, having regard to the standard investment criteria, their powers to invest or vary investments should be exercised. However, they do not need to obtain such advice if they reasonably conclude that in all the circumstances it is unnecessary or inappropriate to do so. Proper advice is the advice of a person who is reasonably believed by the trustees to be qualified to give it by his ability in and practical experience of financial and other matters relating to the proposed investment. (TrA 2000, s 5: Part G, para **[246.120]**). Circumstances where trustees might reasonably conclude that they do not need to obtain advice might be where one of their number is an investment specialist, or where the proposed investment is small in comparison to the size of the trust fund. This provision derives from the TIA 1961, s 6(2)–(4), but under that Act the duty to take advice applied only to making certain categories of investment, and when exercising the statutory powers of investment only. The change made by the TrA 2000, s 5 is that the duty applies to all types of investment and to the exercise of all powers of investment, not just the statutory one. As with the duty to have regard to the standard investment criteria (see para **[220.13]**), the duty to take advice cannot be excluded, but again the exclusion or limitation of liability for negligence (see para **[221.13]** et seq) will limit the practical effect of this duty.

[220.15]
Statutory duty of care. A concern that trustees might abuse the greater ambit of discretion given to them by 'the general power of investment', even with the requirement to take proper advice, has been met by the imposition on them when exercising those statutory powers, of a statutory duty of care. It is very important to note, however, that this statutory duty applies not only to trustees exercising the new powers conferred by the TrA 2000, but also to trustees exercising similar powers conferred on them expressly (eg by will) or by other Acts, whether before or after the passing of the TrA 2000. On the other hand, the TrA 2000 expressly permits the exclusion or limitation of the duty by express provision in the will. See para **[221.15]** et seq.

[220.16]
Mortgages. It is clear from the TrA 2000, s 3(3) that as part of their general power of investment, trustees may invest in loans secured on land, such loans being defined in the TrA 2000, s 3(4) and (5), as where one person provides another with credit, be it a cash or other money loan, or other financial accommodation, and the obligation of the borrower to repay is secured on land. 'Land' here includes buildings and other structures, land covered with water, and any estate, interest, easement, servitude or right in or over land:

Interpretation Act 1978 (IA 1978), Sch 1 (Part G, para **[246.81A]**). This power is subject to the trustees having regard to the standard investment criteria, the requirement to obtain proper advice and the statutory duty of care: see paras **[220.12]** and **[221.15]**. The former detailed rules relating to investment in mortgages in the Trustee Act 1925 (TA 1925), ss 8 and 10 are, along with the rest of Part I of that Act, repealed by the TrA 2000, Sch 2, para 18. Additionally, trustees of land have power to purchase a legal estate in any land in England and Wales (see para **[220.17]**) and the corresponding interests in land in Scotland or Northern Ireland: TrA 2000, s 8(1) (Part G, para **[246.123]**), which would include acquiring a legal mortgage or a charge by way of legal mortgage (taking into account the relevant definition of 'land' referred to above). This power is more limited than the power in the TrA 2000, s 3 in that it only permits trustees to lend on the security of land situated in the UK, but wider in that it permits trustees to lend on the security of land for purposes other than investment: eg trustees could make an interest-free loan to a beneficiary to enable him to purchase a property for his occupation, taking the property as security for the loan. In exercising the power for non-investment purposes, the trustees will not be under duties to have regard to the standard investment criteria or to obtain proper advice (but will be under such duties when doing so for investment): see paras **[220.13]** and **[220.14]**. They will be subject to the statutory duty of care (see the TrA 2000, Sch 1, para 2: Part G, para **[246.156]** and B21 at para **[221.15]**) unless it is expressly excluded.

[220.17]
Power to acquire land. Trustees may acquire freehold or leasehold land in the UK as an investment, for occupation by a beneficiary, or for any other reason: TrA 2000, s 8(1) and (2) (Part G, para **[246.123]**). 'Land' here includes buildings and other structures, land covered with water, and any estate, interest, easement, servitude or right in or over land (IA 1978, Sch 1: Part G, para **[246.81A]**), but 'freehold or leasehold land' for this purpose is specifically defined to mean, in relation to England, Wales and Northern Ireland, a legal estate (including in relation to Northern Ireland land held under a fee farm grant), and in relation to Scotland, the estate or interest of the proprietor if the dominium utile, or in the case of land not held on feudal tenure, the estate or interest of the owner, or a tenancy: TrA 2000, s 8(2). Therefore, it is clear that trustees are not permitted to acquire any undivided share in land in England and Wales under this power, since an undivided share exists only in equity and cannot subsist as a legal estate. If trustees are acquiring the land as an investment, they will be under duties to have regard to the standard investment criteria and to obtain and consider proper advice (see paras **[220.13]** and **[220.14]**), and also the statutory duty of care, if it has not been limited or excluded by the will or trust instrument. However, if they are acquiring it for a non-investment purpose, eg for occupation by a beneficiary, it seems that they will only be subject to the statutory duty of care (again, if it has not been limited or excluded by the will or other trust instrument): TrA 2000, Sch 1, para 2 (Part G, para **[246.156]**; see also para **[221.15]**). Prior to the enactment of the TrA 2000, there was no power to invest trust moneys in land (apart from mortgages) unless such power was expressly conferred, or the assets originally settled were land.

[220.18]
Express provision and the statutory powers. The general power of investment and the power to acquire land in the TrA 2000, ss 3 and 8 respectively (see paras **[220.12]** and **[220.17]**) are in addition to powers conferred on the trustees by the will or other trust instrument, and are subject to any restriction or exclusion imposed by the will or other trust instrument: TrA 2000, ss 6(1) and 9 (Part G, paras **[246.121]** and **[246.124]**). It is therefore possible to provide wider powers than the statutory powers, and to restrict the statutory powers. The main reasons for providing a wider express power are to enable the trustees to acquire land outside the UK, to acquire equitable interests in land such as undivided shares of land, and to acquire any other interests in or rights over land which are not legal estates (see para **[220.17]** for the limits of the statutory power to acquire land). There is also the possibility that the general power of investment does not include power to make unsecured personal loans or invest in non-income producing assets: see paras **[220.31]–[220.33]**. The TrA 2000, ss 6(1) and 9 also make it possible to impose a narrower choice of investments than that permitted by the statutory powers, eg to ensure a cautious, low-risk, investment policy, or to ensure an ethical investment policy. It is probably better to express wishes about investment policy than to deprive trustees completely of power to purchase particular types of investment, since doing the latter could put the trustees in a difficult position where, for example, a company whose shares were an authorised investment was taken over by one which was not. Where express powers are provided it is recommended that they are expressed to be in addition to those conferred by the general law, so as to avoid the possibility that a power which overlaps with the statutory power is intended to exclude it, just in case a situation arises where the statutory power enables something to be done which the express power does not.

[220.19]
It is no longer the case that land purchased in exercise of a power conferred by a settlement of personal property is, by the Law of Property Act 1925 (LPA 1925), s 32(1), directed to be held on trust for sale in the absence of contrary provision in the settlement. Nor is it any longer the case that land purchased by trustees for sale in exercise of their statutory powers is directed to be held on trust for sale by the LPA 1925, s 28(1) (both were repealed as from 1 January 1997 by the TLATA 1996). It is no longer necessary or desirable in clauses which confer power to invest in land to provide that any land in England and Wales acquired under the power shall be held on trust for sale. All land held on trust under a trust created on or after 1 January 1997 is subject to the trust of land provisions of the TLATA 1996, irrespective of whether there is a trust for sale: see Part A, para **[200.51]**.

[220.20]
Company shareholdings. The former provisions of the TA 1925, s 10(3) and (4) which gave extensive powers to trustees holding shares or other securities in a company to concur in schemes or arrangements for company reconstruction, etc have been repealed, along with the remainder of the TA 1925, Part I by the TrA 2000, Sch 2, para 18. This is because the point of the powers conferred by the TA 1925, s 10(3) and (4) was to permit acceptance and retention of new holdings which were not authorised investments but which replaced or arose

from old holdings which were authorised investments, and the powers are not needed now that the general power of investment conferred by the TrA 2000, s 3 (see para **[220.12]**) permits a complete discretion as to type of investment at any rate in relation to company shareholdings.

[220.21]
Bearer securities. The general power of investment in the TrA 2000, s 3 (Part G, para **[246.118]**; see also **[220.12]**) is clearly in wide enough terms to authorise investment in bearer securities. Where trustees hold bearer securities they are (unless express provision is made to the contrary in the will or other trust instrument) required to deposit them with a custodian: TrA 2000, s 18 (Part G, para **[246.133]**). Where this statutory requirement applies, the custodian must be someone who carries on business acting as a custodian, a body corporate controlled by the trustees, or an incorporated solicitors practice: TrA 2000, s 19(2) (Part G, para **[246.134]**), and there are statutory restrictions on the terms on which the custodian is appointed and requirements as to review of the appointment: TrA 2000, ss 20 and 22 (Part G, paras **[246.135]** and **[246.137]**).

[220.22]
Foreign investment. The investments authorised by the TrA 2000, s 3(1) (the general power of investment: see para **[220.12]** and Part G, para **[246.118]**) are not subject to any territorial limit. The power to acquire land conferred by the TrA 2000, s 8(1) (see para **[220.17]** and Part G, para **[246.123]**) is confined to the acquisition of land in the UK. Trustees can therefore under the statutory powers of investment acquire investments anywhere in the world, except for land and interests in land outside the UK, but with the latter exception being subject to an exception for loans secured on land (ie with the consequence that such loans outside the UK can be invested in), and with the power to acquire land in the UK being confined to the acquisition of legal estates.

[220.23]
Powers of sale. The TrA 2000, s 3(1) (the general power of investment—see para **[220.12]** and Part G, para **[246.118]**) by implication authorises the sale of the assets currently held so as to invest in other investments authorised under that power: compare *Re Pratt's Will Trusts, Barrow v McCarthy* [1943] Ch 326, [1943] 2 All ER 375 where the power of investment in the TA 1925, s 1 was held to authorise sale of assets in order to exercise that power of investment. The Administration of Estates Act 1925, s 39 (Part G, para **[246.48]**) confers power to sell personal estate for the purposes of the administration, but these powers cease when the administration is complete (see *Re Trollope's Will Trusts* [1927] 1 Ch 596). The TA 1925, s 16 (Part G, para **[246.14]**) authorises the sale of trust assets to raise money to pay or apply for any purpose or in any manner which the payment or application of capital money is authorised by the trust instrument or by law. Apart from these powers, there is no general power of trustees to sell property other than land.

[220.24]
Trustees of land which is located in England and Wales have in relation to the land all the powers of an absolute owner (TLATA 1996, s 6(1): Part G,

para **[246.91]**), and trustees who have acquired land in the UK under the power in the TrA 2000, s 8(1) (see para **[220.17]**) have in relation to it all the powers of an absolute owner: TrA 2000, s 8(3) (Part G, para **[246.123]**). Both powers clearly include a power of sale. The relevant definition of 'land' for the TLATA 1996 is that in the LPA 1925, s 205(1)(ix) (Part G, para **[246.44A]**) (incorporated by reference by the TLATA 1996, s 23(2): Part G, para **[246.109]**) and includes rights privileges or benefits in over or derived from land. The relevant definition of 'land' for the TrA 2000 is that in the IA 1978, Sch 1 and includes buildings and other structures, land covered with water, and any estate, interest, easement, servitude or right in or over land: IA 1978, Sch 1 (but it should be remembered that the power in the TrA 2000, s 8(3) is confined to being exercisable over land acquired under s 8(1) and the latter only confers power to purchase legal estates in land). These powers apply also to personal representatives: TLATA 1996, s 18 (Part G, para **[246.104]**, TrA 2000, s 35 (Part G, para **[246.150]**); and the AEA 1925, s 39 (Part G, para **[246.48]**) has been amended by the TLATA 1996, Sch 3, para 6 so that a personal representative's powers of sale, etc in relation to real estate for the purposes of administration are those of the TLATA 1996, s 6(1). The ancillary powers and provisions in relation to sale of property in the TA 1925, ss 12 and 13 (Part G, paras **[246.10]** and **[246.11]**) continue to apply.

[220.25]
The powers conferred by the TLATA 1996, s 6(1) can be restricted or excluded by the will or other trust instrument, and can be made subject to a requirement of consent to their exercise by some specified person (usually a beneficiary): TLATA 1996, s 8(1), (2), and the powers conferred by the TrA 2000, s 8(3) can be restricted or excluded: TrA 2000, s 9. It is therefore possible, though not advisable, to exclude the power to sell land, and render the land inalienable for a full perpetuity period. This would be subject to the possibility that the trustees could apply to the court to be given power to do so under the TA 1925, s 57 and also it is unlikely that an exclusion of power to sell land would be effective to prevent personal representatives from selling it to pay debts or administration expenses. As regards alienability of land, the previous law is therefore reversed. Before the TLATA 1996 came into force it was not possible to tie up land in trust and exclude the power to sell it, but it was possible to impose a binding obligation to sell. Now exclusion of all powers to sell land is permitted, but (because of the non-excludable power to postpone sale under the TLATA 1996, s 4, for which see paras **[220.28]** and **[200.54]**) it is no longer possible to impose an obligation to sell land without a power to retain it. For a discussion of ways of causing an early sale to take place, see paras **[200.56]–[200.59]**. The above described statutory powers in relation to land do not apply to land situated outside the UK, and only apply to land outside England and Wales where it has been acquired in exercise of the power in the TrA 2000, s 8(1).

[220.26]
Accordingly, where there are will trusts which include powers of investment that are wider than those conferred by statute, it is important to provide an express power or trust to sell the assets. For the usual trust for sale or powers of sale with respect to residue, see B14 at paras **[214.1]** et seq and **[214.10]** et seq and for powers of sale and changing investments, see Form B20.6 at para **[220.45]**.

[220.27]

There is normally implied in a power to invest trust moneys in investments of a particular kind a power to vary those investments (*Re Pope's Contract* [1911] 2 Ch 442), and so it is not so important to provide express power to vary investments, but it is better practice to do so.

[220.28]

Power to postpone sale. A trust to sell land is subject to a non-excludable power to postpone sale: TLATA 1996, s 4(1) (Part G, para **[246.89]**; see further Part A, para **[200.54]**).This is implied in a trust for sale of land in England and Wales, but not in a trust for sale of personalty. Express power to postpone sale is thus needed in relation to a trust for sale of personalty or a mixed fund of realty and personalty (see further B14 at para **[214.1]** et seq).

[220.29]

Construction of express powers. Despite the standard textbook proposition that powers of investment going beyond those conferred on trustees by the general law will be construed restrictively, in practice wide words will be given a wide meaning: see eg *Re Wragg, Wragg v Palmer* [1919] 2 Ch 58 ('. . . stocks funds shares securities or other investments of whatsoever nature and wheresoever . . . to the intent that the trustees should have the same full and unrestricted powers . . . as if . . . absolutely entitled . . .'—held to authorise purchase of land as an investment); *Re Harari's Settlement Trust, Wordsworth v Fanshawe* [1949] 1 All ER 430 ('shall invest . . . the moneys in or upon such investments as to them [the trustees] may seem fit'—not restricted to trust investments under the ordinary law); *Re Peczenik's Settlement Trusts, Cole v Ingram* [1964] 2 All ER 339, [1964] 1 WLR 720 ('in any stocks shares property' and an express declaration that trustees not restricted to 'trustee stocks'—held they could invest in any type of property which can properly be regarded as an investment). However wide and general the wording, specific provision may be needed as regards the matters mentioned in the succeeding paragraphs of this Note (see Form B20.2 at para **[220.41]** for an investment clause which makes provision for all these except for businesses).

[220.30]

Enjoyment in kind by beneficiaries. When exercising an *investment* power, however widely worded, the trustees must choose assets capable of being treated as investments ('not property which is acquired merely for use and enjoyment'—*Re Peczenik's Settlement Trusts, Cole v Ingram* [1964] 1 WLR 720 at 723), and choose and retain assets according to proper investment criteria, and may not, eg use investment powers to benefit particular beneficiaries, or, a fortiori, themselves. Hence, eg there must be express power for trustees to be able to purchase a residence for a beneficiary to live in (*Re Power, Public Trustee v Hastings* [1947] Ch 572), and the same must be so of the purchase of other types of asset for enjoyment in kind by a beneficiary; however, there is now an express statutory power to purchase a legal estate in land in the UK for occupation by a beneficiary: TrA 2000, s 8(1)(b) (Part G, para **[246.123]**). Express power is still needed for the purchase of land outside the UK for occupation by a beneficiary, purchase of an undivided share of land in the UK for this purpose, and for purchase of chattels for enjoyment in kind by a beneficiary. See further the Note and Forms concerning enjoyment of assets in kind in B18 at para **[218.108]** et seq and Form B20.2 at para **[220.41]**.

[220.31]
Loans. For the same sort of reason as that given above in relation to purchase of assets for enjoyment in kind, express power is needed to leave a loan outstanding to accommodate the borrower (Underhill and Hayton, *Law of Trusts and Trustees* (15th edn), p 595) and, it is submitted, to make loans to beneficiaries on other than commercial terms. See, further, the Note and Forms concerning enjoyment of assets in kind and loans to beneficiaries in B18 at para **[218.108]** et seq and Form B20.2 at para **[220.41]**.

[220.32]
Unsecured personal loans. Powers to invest are normally regarded as limited to the acquisition of some sort of property. Accordingly, unsecured personal loans are normally only permitted if the investment clause expressly says so (Underhill and Hayton, *Law of Trusts and Trustees* (15th edn), pp 594–595, and see *Re Peczenik's Settlement Trusts, Cole v Ingram* [1964] 1 WLR 720 at 723). It is possible, though not certain, that making unsecured personal loans is outside the statutory general power of investment in the TrA 2000, s 3(1) (Part G, para **[246.118]**; see also para **[220.12]**).

[220.33]
Non-income-yielding assets. The trustees must consider the interests of the beneficiaries as a whole, and in particular must hold the balance between the income and capital beneficiaries (Underhill and Hayton, *Law of Trusts and Trustees* (15th edn), pp 500–501). Prima facie they should be investing in income producing assets, and if it is intended that they should be able to acquire and retain non-income producing assets, or eg retain shares in a private company and permit the company to continue not to pay dividends, the will or settlement should say so. In practice the acquiescence of the life tenant may often be sufficient in the absence of such powers. If there is a good investment reason for acquiring a non-income-yielding asset, and it is not unfair on any category of beneficiary to do so, it seems likely that doing so would be within the general power of investment, but it is better to confer express authority to acquire non-income-yielding assets.

[220.34]
Businesses. Express power is always needed for trustees to be able to trade with trust assets: see eg *Re Berry* [1962] Ch 97 at 111, B5 at para **[205.25]**, Forms B5.13 to B5.22 at paras **[205.70]**–**[205.79]** and Forms B20.17 and B20.18 at paras **[220.82]** and **[220.83]**.

[220.35]
Delegation. It is becoming increasingly common for stock exchange investments comprised in trust funds to be managed by a professional fund manager, with the investments vested in nominees who are or are controlled by the fund manager. The fund manager makes the decisions as to purchase or sale without reference to the trustees, but in accordance with an investment policy

chosen by the trustees and periodically reconsidered by them. The conventional power of investment, however wide it may be as to the type of investment, confers the power to select investments and decide when to sell them on the trustees only, and it is not a power which the trustees can delegate in the absence of express authority to do so. However, the TrA 2000, Pt IV, ss 11–27, (Part G, paras **[246.126]–[246.142]**) now confers power on trustees and personal representatives to delegate investment functions to investment managers and to vest trust assets in nominees. The question from a draftsman's point of view is now whether to rely on the statutory powers or whether express provision should still be made.

[220.36]
The statutory power to delegate. The statutory power to delegate is contained in the TrA 2000, s 11(1) (Part G, para **[246.126]**), and in the case of non charitable trusts it enables trustees to authorise an agent to exercise any of their delegable functions—those are all functions other than those specified in s 11(2). The most important non-delegable functions specified in s 11(2) are those relating to asset distribution (eg powers of appointment), and the appointment of new trustees. The power to appoint nominees and vest assets in them is in TrA 2000, s 16 (Part G, para **[246.131]**). The power to remunerate agents and nominees, provided the terms of engagement include agreement to remunerate them, and the amount of the remuneration does not exceed what is reasonable in the circumstances, is in TrA 2000, s 32 (Part G, para **[246.147]**). The aspects of the statutory powers which might make express provision seem appropriate are—

(a)   Although trustees may delegate to an agent who is one or more of themselves, and to a person who is also acting as a nominee, they may not do so in favour of a beneficiary: TrA 2000, s 12 (Part G, para **[246.127]**).

(b)   The terms on which a delegation of powers to an agent is carried out may not include, *unless it is reasonably necessary for the trustees to agree to such terms* (emphasis supplied), a term permitting the agent to appoint a substitute, a term restricting the liability of the agent, or a term permitting the agent to act in circumstances capable of giving rise to a conflict of interest. See the TrA 2000, s 14 (Part G, para **[246.129]**). These last two are terms commonly sought to be imposed by professional investment managers. If all known fund managers seek to impose such terms, there will not be much difficulty in deciding that it is reasonably necessary to accept them. However, what is the position if trustees have a choice between investment manager A and investment manager B, where A insists on limitation of liability and self-dealing being permitted, and B does not, but A is thought to be a better investment manager who will achieve more capital growth? It might be thought desirable to give trustees an untrammelled discretion as to whether to accept terms such as these, but it is not at all clear that the requirements of s 14 can be excluded or by-passed by express provision in the will or other trust instrument: see para **[220.37]**.

(c)   Section 15 of the TrA 2000 (Part G, para **[246.130]**) imposes detailed requirements on agreements to delegate asset management functions to an agent, ie functions of acquiring and disposing of assets, and managing assets while they are held. The agreement must be or be evidenced in writing, the trustees must prepare a prior written policy statement, formulated with a view to ensuring that the asset management functions will be exercised by the agent in the best interest of the trust, and the agreement delegating these functions must include terms which secure compliance by the agent with the policy statement. It should be noted that these requirements can apply to, eg an estate agent to whom functions of management of commercially let land or buildings are delegated, as well as someone to whom investment of a stock exchange portfolio of shares is delegated. These are of course all things which it would be sensible for trustees to do in many or most cases, but it might be unduly constricting and expensive for the trust funds if the trustees are required to produce a policy statement whenever they delegate any of these matters. However, as with s 14, it is not at all clear that these requirements can be excluded or by-passed by express provision in the will or other trust instrument: see para **[220.37]**.

(d)   The persons who may be appointed nominees under the statutory power are confined to persons carrying on a business which consists of or includes acting as a nominee, a body corporate controlled by the trustees, or a body corporate which is an incorporated solicitors' practice: see TrA 2000, s 19(1), (2) (Part G, para **[246.134]**).

(e)   The terms on which a person may be appointed to act as nominee may not include, *unless it is reasonably necessary for the trustees to agree to such terms* (emphasis supplied), a term permitting the nominee to appoint a substitute, a term restricting the liability of the nominee, or a term permitting the nominee to act in circumstances capable of giving rise to a conflict of interest. See TrA 2000, s 20 (Part G, para **[246.135]**).

(f)   While an agent or nominee continues to act, the trustees must keep the arrangements under review, and must consider whether there is a need to intervene if circumstances make it appropriate to do so. If they do consider that there is a need to intervene, they must do so. Where the agent is managing trust assets, this duty includes considering whether to revise or replace the policy statement and doing so where this is considered by them to be needed, and assessing whether the policy statement is being complied with. See TrA 2000, s 22 (Part G, para **[246.137]**). These again are things which it will often be sensible for trustees to do, but which it may be unduly constricting and expensive for the trust funds if they are required to do these things in all cases all the time.

[220.37]
How far the statutory requirements can be excluded or restricted. It is clear that the provisions relating to the statutory powers of delegation and appointment of nominees listed at para **[220.36]** can all be excluded or restricted, or by-passed by an express power not subject to the same restrictions, apart from the TrA 2000, ss 14 and 15, referred to at para **[220.36]**, sub-paras (b) and (c). The excludability of the provisions other than ss 14 and 15 is clear either from the relevant provisions stating that they only apply to the statutory powers (see

TrA 2000, ss 12(1), 19(1) and 20(1)), or from express provision that may be excluded (see TrA 2000, s 21(3), which makes such provision in relation to s 22). Sections 14 and 15 are not expressly confined to imposing restrictions on the exercise of the statutory powers of delegation, but their context and wording suggest that they may have been intended to apply only to the statutory powers in s 11, and that any more general application may be an accident arising from the use of an economical drafting style. It is worth noting that in ss 4 and 5 (standard investment criteria and advice on investment: see paras **[220.13]** and **[220.14]**) the intention that those sections should apply to express powers of investment is made much more explicit by the wording of TrA 2000, ss 4(1) and 5(1) respectively (Part G, paras **[246.119]** and **[246.120]**). The TrA 2000, s 26 (Part G, para **[246.141]**) states that the statutory powers of delegation and appointing nominees are in addition to any express powers, and that they are subject to any restriction or exclusion by the trust instrument. This enables greater restrictions than the statutory restrictions to be imposed on the statutory powers, but does not permit exclusion of statutory restrictions imposed on express powers. Our conclusion is therefore that it is not clear whether ss 14 and 15 are excludable. If a will or other trust instrument purports to exclude them, or an express power is conferred which is so worded as to purport not to be subject to them, we recommend that the trustees act as if ss 14 and 15 apply unless and until it becomes clear from a court decision (or legislation) that they are not subject to them. See Form B20.8 at para **[220.47]** for a clause purporting to exclude the statutory restrictions on delegation and nomineeship.

[220.38]
Delegation, nomineeship, and liability. The statutory duty of care (see para **[220.15]**) applies to trustees when exercising powers of delegation or of appointing nominees, whether the powers exercised are those under the TrA 2000, ss 11 or 16, or are conferred by the will or other trust instrument, or otherwise: TrA 2000, Sch 1, para 3(1)(a), (b), (d), and para 3(2) (Part G, para **[246.156]**). It also applies when exercising the powers of review of delegation or nomineeship under the TrA 2000, s 22: Sch 1, para 3(1)(e). The duty of care can be excluded by the will or other trust instrument: TrA 2000, Sch 1, para 7 (Part G, para **[246.156]**). Trustees are not liable for any act or default of a person to whom powers have been delegated, or of a nominee appointed, under the powers in the TrA 2000 unless they have failed to comply with the duty of care when entering into the arrangements for the delegation or nomineeship, or when carrying out their duties of review etc under s 22: TrA 2000, s 23(1) (Part G, para **[246.138]**) and see s 21(1) for the confinement of s 23 to applying to the statutory powers (Part G, para **[246.136]**). This might appear to mean that trustees are not liable for the acts or defaults of a delegate or nominee where the trustees fail completely to carry out their duties of reviewing the delegation or nomineeship under s 22, as opposed to carrying out those duties without sufficient care, but this is probably illusory. Section 22 imposes a duty to review, and if trustees fail to do it, and the consequence is that, eg inadequately supervised investment managers cause a loss to the trust fund, the trustees will have an original (as opposed to vicarious) liability for a loss consequent on their own failure. What s 23(1) does is to make clear that there is no vicarious liability where trustees are not themselves at fault.

[220.39]

Other powers of delegation. The general power of delegation by trustees acting together as a body under the TrA 2000, s 11 should be distinguished from the power under the TA 1925, s 25 (as substituted by the Trustee Delegation Act 1999), which is a power of an individual trustee to delegate all his trusts powers and discretions by power of attorney for up to a year at a time, and is outside the scope of this work. There is also a power under the TLATA 1996, s 9 to delegate functions as trustees of land to a beneficiary entitled to an interest in possession in the land: see para **[220.54]** et seq.

Investment powers

[220.40]

FORM B20.1: Power of investment confined to fixed interest investments quoted shares and legal estates in land[1]

Trust moneys may be invested in any of the following (and the statutory general power of investment and power to acquire land shall not apply)—

(a) the public stocks funds or government securities of the United Kingdom of Great Britain and Northern Ireland or any member state of the British Commonwealth or any member state of the European Union or any province or state having a separate local legislature and forming part of any of the foregoing;

(b) bonds stocks debentures or other securities of any municipal or local body or authority in the British Commonwealth or the European Union;

(c) the units of any authorised unit trust scheme for the time being authorised under the Financial Services Act 1986 or the Financial Services and Markets Act 2000;

(d) the shares or deposits of any building society within the meaning of the Building Societies Act 1986 registered in the United Kingdom;

(e) in any investments of whatsoever nature which at the date of purchase are or on allotment will be listed on the Stock Exchange or on any of the stock exchanges of New York, Montreal, Paris, Frankfurt, Amsterdam, Milan, Madrid, Zurich, Tokyo, Hong Kong or Johannesburg;

(f) in the acquisition of freehold and leasehold legal estates (including legal mortgages or charges) in land situate in the United Kingdom including land for occupation by a beneficiary [pursuant to the power hereinafter contained][2] provided that—

    (i) leasehold estates in land shall be purchased only if at the date of the purchase the unexpired term exceeds fifty years,

    (ii) in relation to land in Scotland what may be acquired under the foregoing power is the estate or interest of the proprietor of the dominum utile or, in the case of land not held on feudal tenure, the estate or interest of the owner, or (subject to proviso (a) above) a tenancy, and

    (iii) 'land' includes buildings and rights over land.[3]

---

1   This is narrower than the statutory powers of investment (for which see paras **[220.12]** and **[220.17]**), for the cautious testator. It is intended to cover the main types of fixed interest

investment, quoted shares, and legal estates in land other than leases of 50 years or less unexpired. In practice these are probably all that prudent trustees with a fund of cash to invest, maintaining a balance of income and capital growth, would want to invest in, but it could turn out to be unduly restrictive. Where a testator is inclined towards something of this sort, it might be better to put it as an expression of wishes rather than a restriction on the trustees' powers. For the power to restrict or exclude the statutory powers of investment see the TrA 2000, ss 6(1) and 9 (Part G, paras **[246.121]** and **[246.124]**). For the non-excludable requirements of the TrA 2000, ss 4 and 5 as to having regard to the standard investment criteria and obtaining advice see paras **[220.13]** and **[220.14]**. The power permits investment in mortgages secured on UK land, whereas the statutory powers under the TrA 2000, s 3 (see para **[220.16]**) permit investment in mortgages secured on land anywhere.

2   The cautious draftsman will include this restriction for inheritance tax reasons: see para **[220.4]** et seq and the Note in B18 at paras **[218.67]** and **[218.68]**. For a power to permit beneficiaries to occupy or enjoy in kind trust assets, see Form B18.17 at para **[218.83]**.

3   This is based on the TrA 2000, s 8 (see para **[220.17]** and Part G, para **[246.123]**), but subject to the restriction (deriving from the more traditional investment clauses) that leasehold land with 50 or less years to run should not be acquired.

[220.41]

FORM B20.2:   Full discretion—long form[1]

Trust moneys may be invested in such stocks funds shares securities assurance policies land interests in land or other assets of any nature and wheresoever situate whether involving liability or not and whether yielding income or not including secured or unsecured loans [the purchase or improvement of dwellinghouses or other assets for occupation or enjoyment in kind by beneficiaries hereunder and secured or unsecured loans to beneficiaries hereunder[2]] as my trustees in their absolute discretion shall think fit and my trustees may grant indulgence to or release any debtor give and take guarantees enter into profit-sharing agreements or give and take options and accept substitution of any security for other security or of one debtor for another debtor to the intent that my trustees shall have the same unrestricted powers of investing and using trust moneys and managing investments as if they were absolutely entitled provided that:

(i)   no loan shall be made to a beneficiary hereunder unless it is either made for full consideration in money or money's worth or made in exercise of the power to make free or advantageous loans to beneficiaries hereinafter contained;[3]

(ii)   no beneficiary hereunder shall be permitted to have the occupation or enjoyment in kind of any asset except in exercise of the powers to permit such occupation or enjoyment hereinafter contained;[4] and

(iii)   in the professed exercise of the foregoing powers my trustees [and any person to whom such powers are delegated in pursuance of the power of delegation hereinafter contained[5]] shall not be liable for any loss arising from any purchase investment or other dealing made in good faith.[6]

1   This form is wider than the statutory powers in that it permits the acquisition of land outside the UK and equitable interests in land, and makes it clear that non income-yielding assets and unsecured loans may be acquired or made. See para **[220.18]**. For the non excludable requirements of the TrA 2000, ss 4 and 5 as to having regard to the standard investment criteria and obtaining advice, see paras **[220.13]** and **[220.14]**.

2   These words in square brackets are restricted by provisos (i) and (ii) and no amendment of these words should be considered without also considering those provisos and vice versa. See also the notes to the provisos.

3   This proviso is probably not needed for inheritance tax reasons, but together with an appropriately restricted power will ensure that the power is only exercised in accordance with the beneficial interests. See the Notes at para **[220.4]** et seq and the Note in B18 at paras **[218.67]** and **[218.68]**. For a power to make beneficial loans to a beneficiary entitled to an interest in possession see Form B18.26 at para **[218.107]**, and for a power to do so where a beneficiary has an interest in possession or has an interest in income as the object of a discretion see Form C2.1, cl 9 at para **[224.30]**.

4   This proviso is included for inheritance tax reasons. See the Notes at para **[220.4]** et seq and the Note in B18 at paras **[218.67]** and **[218.68]**. For a power to permit beneficiaries to occupy or enjoy in kind trust assets see Form B18.24 at para **[218.109]**.

5   Omit the words in square brackets if there is no power to delegate investment powers; see Form B20.8 at para **[220.47]** for such a power.

6   For a more general clause exonerating trustees from liability, see Form B21.12 at para **[221.16]**.

[220.42]

FORM B20.3:   **Full discretion—short form**[1]

My trustees may invest trust moneys in any property of whatever description or location including land buildings and interests in land or buildings, unsecured personal loans, non-income yielding property, and land or buildings or interests in land or buildings for occupation or use by beneficiaries pursuant to the power for that purpose set out below[2] as if they were a sole beneficial owner of such moneys.

1   This form is wider than the statutory powers in that it permits the acquisition of land outside the UK and equitable interests in land, and makes it clear that non-income-yielding assets and unsecured loans may be acquired or made. See para **[220.18]**. See also Form C2.1, cl 9 at para **[224.30]**. For the non excludable requirements of the TrA 2000, ss 4 and 5 as to having regard to the standard investment criteria and obtaining advice, see para **[220.13]** and **[220.14]**.

2   This assumes a separate power to permit the use of land and chattels by beneficiaries: see Form B18.24 at para **[218.109]**.

[220.43]

FORM B20.4:   **Statutory power subject to an ethical investment policy**[1]

(1)   Subject as set out below, my trustees shall have the general power of investment and the power to acquire land respectively conferred by sections 3 and 8 of the Trustee Act 2000.

(2)   [I request that my trustees do not] *or* [My trustees shall not][2] acquire or retain any shares securities bonds debentures land or other assets which are or include, or underlying which directly or indirectly are assets which include, any business which to a significant extent deals in, makes, promotes, provides services in respect of, or is otherwise commercially involved with, any of the following products—

(a)   cigarettes cigars pipe tobacco snuff or other tobacco products;

(b)   arms explosives mines bombs missiles or other weapons, or military or naval vehicles ships aircraft or other equipment, for use in or ancillary to the conduct of warfare, rebellion, suppression of rebellion or dissent, or other violent action against persons or property;

(c)   timber or timber products from non-renewable sources;

(d)   products which have been tested on live animals;

   (e)   products produced by the labour of children under the age of [15] years;
   (f)   alcoholic liquor of any kind;
   (g)   oil and petroleum products;
   (h)   chemical fertilisers or chemical pesticides or herbicides;
   (i)   plants or animals genetically modified by the manipulation of DNA.

   (3)   [I request that my trustees do not] *or* [My trustees shall not][3] acquire or retain any shares securities bonds debentures land or other assets which are or include, or underlying which directly or indirectly are assets which include, assets which are located in [*name(s) of country(ies)*] *or, eg* [any country state or territory where there is for the time being believed by my trustees to be abuse of human rights (as defined in the European Convention for the Protection of Human Rights and Fundamental Freedoms agreed by the Council of Europe in 1950 and the protocols thereto) or where there is capital punishment].

   (4)   I declare that my trustees shall not be liable for any loss which may arise from compliance or purported compliance with the foregoing, or from taking steps or refraining from taking steps in the belief that they are acting or refraining from acting in accordance with the foregoing, and that they shall be fully indemnified out of [my residuary estate] against the cost of obtaining information relevant to compliance with the foregoing.

1   This form in sub-cl (2) sets out a number of types of business which a testator might desire to exclude, either as the subject of precatory words of exclusion, or by express exclusion from the scope of the statutory powers of investment (on the relative merits of these alternatives see n 2 infra). From these, the provisions desired in any particular case can be selected, or others added or substituted. Subclause (3) excluding investments connected with particular countries or countries of a particular description, can be used either together with or separately from sub-cl (2). For the statutory powers of investment and purchase of land, and power to restrict them, see paras **[220.12]**, **[220.17]** and **[220.18]**.

2   One of these alternatives should be deleted. The use of precatory words is preferable because it is difficult to draft the descriptions of the excluded categories in a sufficiently definite and comprehensive manner to be workable as a matter of legal obligation, and because putting trustees under an obligation to avoid the specified types of investment puts a heavy burden on them, not only of interpreting the wording of the exclusion, but of obtaining sufficient information to establish whether particular investments fall within a prohibited category. The practical difference between imposing an obligation and using precatory words is not great, because if an obligation is imposed, the prohibited investments are not in a prohibited category because they carry a high risk of loss or poor prospects of income or capital profits, but because of moral disapproval. If trustees breach the obligation by investing in a company whose business is on the prohibited list, but the investment performs well as an investment, it is difficult to see how the trustees could be liable to the beneficiaries for the breach. The main things a testator should concentrate on if he wants an ethical investment policy is to absolve the trustees from liability for following it, and to choose trustees who share his outlook.

3   One of these alternatives should be deleted, and where sub-cl (2) is also included, it should be the same alternative. See n 2 supra for discussion of the relative merits of these alternatives.

[220.44]

FORM B20.5:   Retention of shares in family company

If I hold at my death any shares or securities in the [*name*] Company Limited (whether or not it has undergone any change of name) or in any company which as a result of any reconstruction amalgamation demerger or sale shall be a successor to any business of the said company or of any subsidiary of it, it is my wish that my trustees shall retain such shares or securities or any shares or securities they may come to hold in any successor company as aforesaid [if and so long as any of my children or remoter issue are employed in any of such businesses, and if and when none of them are so employed] unless and until it is in their opinion necessary in the interests of the beneficiaries to sell or otherwise dispose of such shares or securities or any of them and I declare that my trustees shall not be liable for any loss arising from investment in or retention of any shares or securities of the foregoing kinds.[1]

1   This form is for a testator who wants the trustees to continue to hold private company shares which he owns. The expression of a wish as to retention of the shares is intended as a counterweight to the duty to consider the need for diversification imposed by the TrA 2000, s 4 (see para **[220.13]**). This duty cannot be excluded, but diversification out of a holding of this kind may not be 'appropriate to the circumstances of the trust' (see the TrA 2000, s 4(3)(b): Part G, para **[246.119]**) where there is some special reason for retention, such as one or more beneficiaries working in the business. Although s 4 cannot be excluded, exclusion of liability for failure to diversify is possible, and the exclusion of liability for retaining the shares is perhaps the most effective step which can be taken towards bringing about retention of them. The specific exclusion of liability is not needed if there is a general exclusion of such liability elsewhere in the will.

[220.45]

FORM B20.6:   Powers of sale and transposing assets[1]

My trustees may at their discretion retain as invested or sell or otherwise convert into money [the property [other than money[2]] settled under clause —— of this will] and invest the moneys arising thereby [and such of the said property as may be money[2]] in any investments hereby or by law authorised with power from time to time to change such investments for others hereby authorised and in exercising the foregoing powers shall have all the powers of disposition and acquisition of an absolute owner.

1   A provision such as this is not necessary where the trust fund is net residue subject to administration trusts for conversion into money with power to postpone conversion, or subject to a power of sale, but such a provision is needed where specific property is settled on trust. Accordingly, this Form is assumed to refer to a clause of the will containing a specific gift. Powers of sale and changing investments are often integrated into the main trusts; see eg Form B16.26 at para **[216.31]**.
2   Omit 'other than money' and 'and such of the said assets as may be money' if the property settled does not include money.

[220.46]

FORM B20.7:   Power to give warranties on the sale of private company shares

My trustees shall have power on the sale or transfer of any private company shares to give any warranty indemnity guarantee or undertaking in relation to the shares and the company and any other matter in connection with such sale or transfer as they shall in their absolute discretion think fit and they shall be fully indemnified out of [my residuary estate] against any liability they may incur thereunder.

[220.47]

FORM B20.8: Power to delegate investment powers and vest assets in nominees[1]

(1) My trustees may delegate with respect to the whole or any part of [my residuary estate] their powers hereunder of investing trust moneys and changing trust investments and any other of my trustees' powers hereby or by law conferred relating to the management or administration of trust moneys or other trust assets to any person carrying on the business of management of investments to any extent for any period on any terms (which may include authorising self-dealing or limiting the liability of the person to whom such powers are delegated) and in any manner and may remunerate such person and section 22 of the Trustee Act 2000 shall not apply.

(2) My trustees shall have power to vest or register any property in any person or persons whether individual or corporate and whether or not an investment manager to whom powers have been delegated under the foregoing power (and who may be or include one or more of my trustees or the beneficiaries hereunder) as nominee or nominees for my trustees upon such terms as to remuneration or otherwise (including terms authorising self-dealing or providing for the limitation of the liability of the nominee) as my trustees think fit and section 22 of the Trustee Act 2000 shall not apply.[2]

1 Express provision for delegation of investment management powers is not as important as it formerly was because there is now the statutory power to appoint investment managers in the TrA 2000, Pt IV, ss 11–15 (Part G, paras **[246.126]–[246.130]**; see also para **[220.36]**). This clause differs from the statutory power in that the detailed procedural requirements of the TrA 2000, s 15 do not apply; the trustees have a wider discretion as to restricting an investment manager's liability or permitting self-dealing by him (compare the TrA 2000, s 14(2): Part G, para **[246.129]**, under which these can only be done if it is reasonably necessary); beneficiaries can be appointed (this is forbidden in exercise of the statutory power by the TrA 2000, s 12(3)); and the duty to review the arrangement from time to time under the TrA 2000, s 22 (Part G, para **[246.137]**) does not apply. The by-passing of the TrA 2000, ss 14 and 15 is only effective if those statutory provisions apply solely to the statutory powers of delegation, and do not apply to express powers to delegate investment management functions, something which is not at all clear (see para **[220.37]**). Even though trustees have an express power of this kind, unless and until there is either a definitive decision of the courts or amending legislation which makes it certain that ss 14 and 15 are excluded by such a power, trustees should regard themselves as bound by ss 14 and 15.

2 This is wider than the statutory power to appoint nominees in the TrA 2000, Pt IV, ss 16–20 (Part G, paras **[246.131]–[246.135]**; see also para **[220.35]** et seq), in that the trustees have a wider discretion as to restricting a nominee's liability or permitting self-dealing by him (compare the TrA 2000, s 20(2): Part G, para **[246.135]** under which these can only be done if it is reasonably necessary); the persons who may be appointed nominees are not confined to persons carrying on a business as nominees, a company controlled by the trustees, or a solicitors' incorporated practice (compare TA 2000, s 19(2): Part G, para **[246.134]**); and the duty to review the arrangement from time under the TrA 2000, s 22 (Part G, para **[246.137]**) does not apply.

[220.48]

FORM B20.9: Clause as to bonus shares[1]

If my trustees shall by virtue of any shareholding in any company for the time being held by my trustees upon the trusts hereof and listed on a stock exchange become entitled to any shares or stocks or securities distributed as dividend such that in the opinion of my trustees the capital value of the shares in respect of which the dividend is distributed is diminished by more than 10 per cent (comparing with their listed value immediately before and immediately after they became listed ex dividend but leaving out of account so far as possible any other factors influencing value other than the holdings becoming ex dividend) my trustees may apportion such whole or part of the said bonus shares stocks or securities to capital as in their opinion shall be just and reasonable.

1   For clauses negativing rules of apportionment generally, see Forms B14.24 to B14.29 at paras **[214.39]–[214.46]**. This clause is intended to deal with a case where a substantial dividend based on accumulated profits or capital profits of the company over a long period is declared in the form of distribution of a shares in a subsidiary in order to achieve a demerger or a reduction in capital. The law seems to be that if it is a direct demerger the shares distributed will be income, but if it is an indirect one they are capital: see *Sinclair v Lee* [1993] Ch 497, sub nom *Re Lee, Sinclair v Lee* [1993] 3 All ER 926. Thus what is in substance a capital split or repayment is treated under the general law in some situations as a distribution which constitutes income, and where this involves a substantial diminution of the capital value of the original holding this is unfair on the capital beneficiaries and a windfall to the income beneficiaries. There are objections to using this clause, however. First, its effects for inheritance tax purposes in relation to fixed interest trusts or accumulation and maintenance trusts are unclear and such effects may be adverse—treating what would otherwise be income as capital might affect the intended inheritance tax status of the trusts (but *Miller v IRC* [1987] STC 108, for which see n 1 to para **[220.61]** gives some support to the view that the intended inheritance tax status would not be prejudiced). Secondly, a clause in this form may involve an unlawful direction to accumulate after the expiration of the relevant accumulation period.

Management of land

[220.49]
The statutory powers. Trustees holding on trust land situated in England and Wales are given a wide power to manage that land by the TLATA 1996, s 6(1) (Part G, para **[246.91]**), and trustees holding on trust land in the UK which they have acquired in exercise of their powers to acquire land under the TrA 2000, s 8(1) are given the same power of management of such land by the TrA 2000, s 8(3) (Part G, para **[246.123]**). In both cases, they have in relation to the land all the powers of an absolute owner, for the purposes of exercising their functions as trustees. These powers apply also to personal representatives: TLATA 1996, s 18 (Part G, para **[246.104]**) and TrA 2000, s 35 (Part G, para **[246.150]**). For newly created trusts of land (see Part A, para **[200.51]** for this term) these powers replace the extensive and detailed powers of management of land which are conferred on tenants for life of settled land by the Settled Land Act 1925 (SLA 1925), and which also, before 1 January 1997 (the commencement of the TLATA 1996), applied to trustees for sale of land by virtue of the LPA 1925, s 28(1) (repealed by the TLATA 1996). The new statutory powers give the widest discretion in respect of such matters as sale, insurance, repair, improvement, mortgaging and leasing, and apply to all trusts of any kind involving land created on or after 1 January 1997, and all created before that date apart from ones to which the SLA 1925 continues to apply (see Part A, para **[200.48]** et seq).

[220.50]
Restrictions on the statutory powers. The powers may be restricted or excluded (TLATA 1996, s 8(1) and TrA 2000, s 9) or made subject to consents: TLATA 1996, s 8(2) (Part G, para **[246.93]**). It is thought that in relation to trusts created before the Act came into force the trustees will have the full s 6 powers, notwithstanding any express restriction on the trustees' powers in the disposition creating the trust, but that any requirement of consent will continue to be binding, because s 8(1) seems only to relate to specific exclusion of the powers conferred by the Act, whereas s 8(2) seems to refer to requirements of consent in relation to powers of a kind conferred by the Act. However, the LPA 1925, s 28(1) used to provide that land acquired by trustees for sale should be conveyed to them on trust for sale, and that the statutory powers of leasing, improvement, etc of trustees for sale should be exercised with the consents (if any) required for a sale. The repeal of the LPA 1925, s 28 from 1January 1997 by the TLATA 1996 means that now trustees of land (including trustees for sale) whose power or trust to sell the land is subject to a requirement of obtaining the consent of someone do not need that person's consent to the exercise of others of their powers over the land unless the will or settlement expressly says so.

[220.51]
Insurance. A new TA 1925, s 19 (power of insurance: see Part G, para **[246.17]**) is substituted by the TrA 2000, s 34 with effect from 1 February 2001, but in relation to trusts created before, on, or after that date. It provides that a trustee may insure any property subject to the trust against risks of loss or damage due to any event, and pay the premium out of any income or capital funds of the trust. This remedies the deficiencies of the previous statutory trustees' powers of insurance, and it is no longer necessary to make express provision. The power is also exercisable by personal representatives: TA 1925, s 69(1) and TrA 2000, s 35 (Part G, paras **[246.37]** and **[246.150]**). The TA 1925, s 20 makes full provision for the application of moneys received under a policy of insurance against loss, whatever the risk and whether the insurance was under an express or a statutory power.

[220.52]
The limitations of the statutory administrative powers. The limitations of the powers conferred by the TLATA 1996, s 6(1) and the TrA 2000, s 8(3) in relation to land which should in our opinion be borne in mind and which should be compensated for by express provision, either generally or in particular cases, are as follows—

(1) They only apply to land in England and Wales, and to land in Scotland and Northern Ireland acquired under the power in the TrA 2000, s 8(1) (see para **[220.17]** for this). Express powers are needed for management of any other land. Further, the meaning of 'land' in England and Wales for the purposes of the TLATA 1996, s 6(1) is that given by the LPA 1925, s 205(1)(ix) (see TLATA 1996, s 23(2)) and this is a definition which is difficult to construe and which possibly does not include mortgages or charges or all kinds of equitable interest in land (although it may include undivided shares of land). For an extended power of management see Form B20.10 at para **[220.59]**.

(2)   The TLATA 1996, s 6(1) and the TrA 2000, s 8(3) only apply 'in relation to the land'. It is not clear whether this would include power to use the capital or income of other trust assets, eg stock exchange investments, to pay for, eg repairs or improvements of the land. In the case of the construction of new buildings, it seems likely that the power of acquisition of land in the TrA 2000, s 8(1), which is of course a power to use any trust money to acquire land, would include power to pay for a new building on land already owned (provided the trustees own a legal estate in the land). This is because the verb is 'acquire' rather than 'purchase', and because the relevant definition of 'land' (IA 1978, Sch 1) includes buildings. The SLA 1925, s 73(1)(iii) did authorise capital money to be spent on improvements to land, and like other powers under that Act also applied to trusts for sale, and it is unlikely that the new powers are narrower than those which they replace. We recommend an express power in order to avoid uncertainty: see Form B20.11 at para **[220.60]**.

(3)   Similarly, it is not absolutely clear that the statutory powers in TrA 2000, s 6(1) would authorise borrowing on the security of the land held in trust to purchase, eg company shares as an investment, although again we think it likely that this is authorised. See Form B20.20 at para **[220.69]** for a power to borrow and note 1 thereto for the statutory powers to borrow.

(4)   It seems to us that the TLATA 1996, s 6(1) and TrA 2000, s 8(3) do not confer on the trustees of land sufficient powers to carry on a business such as farming on the land. They clearly authorise the use of the land in the business, but do not authorise the use of trust assets other than the land as capital for the business, or the incurring of business liabilities to be met out of the trust fund. A life tenant in occupation of land held on trust can of course carry on his own business there without special powers.

(5)   For the limitations of the statutory powers to purchase land see paras **[220.17]** and **[220.18]**.

[220.53]

Express provision. For the reasons given at para **[220.52]**, express powers of management should be conferred in relation to land outside England and Wales to which the statutory powers would not extend, and the recommended method is to follow the wording of the statutory powers: see Form B20.10 at para **[220.59]**. An express power to apply capital held on the same trusts as trust land in making improvements to the land is also recommended. Such a power is unlikely to cause inheritance tax difficulties of the kind considered at paras **[220.4]**–**[220.10]** since expenditure which increases the capital value of the trust fund is prima facie properly payable out of capital. On the other hand, it would be better not to confer express powers to pay for improvements out of income where there are intended to be interest in possession or accumulation and maintenance trusts for inheritance tax purposes. See Form B20.11 at para **[220.60]**. It would give greater flexibility for the trustees to be given a power to pay for repairs out of capital, but this is something better avoided in the case of accumulation and maintenance trusts; repair is something which is prima facie something to be paid for out of income and power to pay for it out of capital might prejudice the application of the ITA 1984, s 71 (see para **[220.4]** et seq).

[220.54]
Power to delegate powers of sale and management of land to a beneficiary.
By the TLATA 1996, s 9 (Part G, para **[246.94]**), trustees of land acting together jointly as trustees are given power to delegate by power of attorney to any beneficiary or beneficiaries of full age and beneficially entitled to an interest in possession in land any of their functions which relate to the land, for any period or indefinitely (but apparently not irrevocably—see para **[220.55]**). The corresponding power formerly vested in trustees for sale by the LPA 1925, s 29 was narrower in that it was only exercisable in respect of the trustees' powers of leasing and management, while the powers now delegable to a beneficiary include sale. The reason for this wider power of delegation is to make up for the non-availability of the SLA 1925 for trusts of land created after 1996 (for which see Part A, para **[200.52]**). After a full delegation of powers under the TLATA 1996, s 9 the beneficiary will be in a similar position to that of a tenant for life under the SLA 1925, but with the difference that he only gets in that position if the trustees make a discretionary decision to put him there, while a tenant for life under the SLA 1925 had the land vested in him and the powers of sale, leasing, etc as of right. Where the power of sale is delegated, the power to receive the purchase money cannot be delegated and remains in the hands of the trustees: TLATA 1996, s 9(7).

[220.55]
Delegation to beneficiaries—revocability. It seems from the TLATA 1996, s 9(3) and (4) (Part G, para **[246.94]**) that where the trustees decide to delegate to a beneficiary or beneficiaries, even if they express the delegation to be irrevocable, unless the power of attorney is given by way of security and is expressed to be irrevocable it can be revoked at any time by any one of the trustees, and is automatically revoked on appointment of a new trustee, or by the beneficiary's interest in possession coming to an end, or the beneficiary ceasing to be beneficially entitled to it. This underlines another essential difference between being a beneficiary with delegated powers under the TLATA 1996, s 9 and a tenant for life under the SLA 1925, because in the latter case the trustees have no power to terminate the tenant for life's powers. The TLATA 1996, s 9A(3) (inserted by the TrA 2000, s 40, Sch 2, para 47: Part G, para **[246.95]**) imposes duties on trustees to keep any delegation under review and intervene where it is needed, if the delegation is not irrevocable: TLATA 1996, s 9A(2)(b). Since no delegation under s 9 seems to be irrevocable unless done by way of security (which, it is suggested, would be a very unusual use of this power), these duties are more general than the wording of s 9A might suggest.

[220.56]
Delegation to beneficiaries—liability. A beneficiary in whose favour there is delegation under the TLATA 1996, s 9 (see para **[220.54]**) is liable as a trustee for his conduct in carrying out the delegated functions: TLATA 1996, s 9(7). The trustees are by the TLATA 1996, s 9A (inserted by the TrA 2000, s 40, Sch 2, para 47: Part G, para **[246.95]**) subject to the TrA 2000, s 1 duty of care (for which see para **[220.15]**) when deciding whether to exercise the power of

delegation: TLATA 1996, s 9A(1). Where the delegation is not irrevocable (see para **[220.55]** for what this seems to mean), trustees are under a continuing duty to review the delegation and intervene where needed, with the duty of care applying to carrying out the latter duties: TLATA 1996, s 9A(2)–(5). The trustees are not liable for the conduct of a beneficiary to whom they have delegated unless they have failed to comply with the duty of care in deciding to delegate or reviewing the delegation: TLATA 1996, s 9A(6). There is a question as to how far the statutory duty of care can be excluded or cut down by express provision in relation to the substituted TLATA 1996, s 9A. The duty of care is defined in the TrA 2000, s 1, and s 2 states that Sch 1 makes provision about when the duty applies to a trustee. Schedule 1 lists a number of situations where the duty of care applies, which do not in terms include the TLATA 1996, s 9A (but arguably it is one of the powers in relation to land referred to by Sch 1, para 2(c)), and Sch 1, para 7 (Part G, para **[246.114]**) states that the duty of care does not apply if or insofar as it appears from the trust instrument that the duty is not meant to apply. The application of the duty of care to the power of delegation in the TLATA 1996, s 9 is by virtue of the TLATA 1996, s 9A, not by virtue of the TrA 2000, Sch 1. The difficulty is whether TrA 2000, Sch 1, para 7 applies generally, or only in relation to the matters listed in Sch 1, and if the latter, whether the TLATA 1996, s 9A is among the powers referred to by Sch 1, para 2(c). It would be anomalous if the duty of care could not be excluded in relation to the power of delegation to a beneficiary, but could be excluded in relation to many equally important manners (and it would almost certainly arise from an accident of drafting), but it is possible.

[220.57]
Delegation to beneficiaries—express provision. It would seem that the power under the TLATA 1996, s 9 cannot be excluded or varied or its exercise made mandatory by express provisions of the will or other disposition, and there is the difficulty of construction as to whether the TrA 2000, s 1 duty of care can be excluded in relation to it (see para **[220.56]**). The most that can be done is to request the trustees to exercise the power (or not exercise it) in particular ways or in general, and if it is desired to encourage them to exercise it, to make the exercise of any of their powers over the land subject to obtaining the consent of the life tenant(s) in possession for the time being, and not to exclude the TLATA 1996, s 11 (see para **[220.58]**). Non-binding requests will not be legally binding on the trustees, but will be a factor to which the court is to have regard under ss 14 and 15 of the TLATA 1996 in the event of a dispute about the exercise or non-exercise of the power of delegation getting to court. For an example, see Form C13.2 at para **[235.18]** et seq, in particular cl 8 at para **[235.26]**.

[220.58]
Duty to consult beneficiaries. The TLATA 1996, s 11 (Part G, para **[246.97]**) imposes a duty on trustees of land in the exercise of any function relating to the land subject to the trust 'so far as practicable' to consult the beneficiaries of full age and beneficially entitled to an interest in possession, and so far as consistent with the general interest of the trust to give effect to the wishes of those beneficiaries, or (in the event of a dispute) the majority by value. This is in the same terms as the former LPA 1925, s 26(3) (which was repealed by the TLATA 1996). The difference between the TLATA 1996, s 11 and the former

LPA 1925, s 26(3) is that the latter only applied to an express trust for sale created by deed or will if it was expressly declared to apply, whereas the former will apply to any trust created on or after 1 January 1997, unless expressly excluded: TLATA 1996, s 11(2)(a). As it could add appreciably to the burdens and difficulties of the trustees, in general we recommend its routine exclusion unless there are special reasons for not doing so. Circumstances where it might be appropriate not to exclude it are a co-ownership trust of a house in which the co-owners are going to live, in a trust to provide a residence for, eg the testator's widow, or any other land where it is intended that a beneficiary will occupy it. It is particularly something to exclude in relation to a gift by will where it is intended that any land shall be sold and the proceeds divided (see further Part A, paras **[200.56]–[200.59]**). For a clause excluding s 11, see Form B21.23 at para **[221.27]**. It should be noted that s 11 does not apply to a will made before 1 January 1997 of a person who dies on or after that date: TLATA 1996, s 11(2)(b).

[220.59]

FORM B20.10:   **Power of management in relation to land in any location**[1]

My trustees shall have all the powers of an absolute owner in relation to any land held by them (wherever situated) and for this purpose 'land' includes buildings and estates interests or rights of any kind in or over land.

1   See para **[220.52]**, sub-para (1) for the reasons for this type of provision.

[220.60]

FORM B20.11:   **Power to apply other capital in improving land**[1]

My trustees whether acting as trustees or personal representatives shall have power to apply capital held on the same trusts as any land or interest in land (or which would be so held if the administration of my estate had been completed) in the improvement of such land and to apply such capital or the income of such capital on the repair or maintenance of such land.[2]

1   See para **[220.52]**, sub-para (2) for the reasons for this type of provision.
2   The restriction to capital held on the same trusts helps to ensure fairness as between beneficiaries, and is also intended to avoid the prejudice to the inheritance tax status of settled property which might arise from the possibility that it might bear expenses attributable to other settled property in the same settlement but held on different trusts. The restriction to spending capital on improvements avoids expenditure normally properly payable out of capital being paid out of income (see paras **[220.4]–[220.10]**).

[220.61]

FORM B20.12:   **Treatment of mining rent and royalties and proceeds of timber**[1]

(1)   All the rent or royalties from any mining lease or licence of land held by my trustees shall be treated as income and none shall be apportioned to capital.[2]

(2)   The net proceeds of sale of any timber which is cut and sold from any land held by my trustees shall be treated wholly as income.[3]

1   This form makes clear that mineral rents and royalties and the proceeds of sale of timber are to be treated wholly as income. Before 1 January 1997, the SLA 1925, ss 47 (mineral rents) and 66 (timber), which apportion these between capital and income, applied to land held on trust for sale by virtue of the LPA 1925, s 28(2) (subject to express provision in the trust instrument). The LPA 1925, s 28(2) was repealed by the TLATA 1996, and these provisions of the SLA 1925 do not apply to trusts of land within the meaning of the TLATA 1996 (see Part A, para **[200.51]** for this term). It is uncertain whether the non-application of these provisions means that the former rule of the general law that the whole of mineral rents and proceeds of timber are capital (see nn 2 and 3) are revived, or whether the wide power of management of land in the TLATA 1996, s 6(1) (see para **[220.49]**) has the effect that mineral rents and royalties and the sale proceeds of timber are income, or at any rate that it is within the trustees' powers to treat them as such. In this state of uncertainty, where trust property may include mining leases or saleable timber it will save argument to include provision of this kind. The other possible ways of dealing with the problem are to give the trustees a discretion to apportion some to capital, or to provide that a fixed proportion is apportioned to capital. Both these options risk treating what is really income as capital, and prejudicing the existence of an interest in possession for inheritance tax purposes or the application of the ITA 1984, s 71 (accumulation and maintenance trusts), but a discretionary power would probably not have this effect, although it would leave the problem that the trustees would have very little guidance as to how to exercise it. In *Miller v IRC* [1987] STC 108 it was held by the Court of Session that a power of the trustees to set aside income for meeting depreciation of the capital value of trust assets, or for any other reason the trustees thought advisable or necessary, was an administrative power which did not prevent the liferentrix from having an interest in possession for inheritance tax purposes. There is an express exception from the rules against excessive accumulations for the accumulation of the proceeds of timber or wood (LPA 1925, s 164(2)(iii): Part G, para **[246.42]**), but no similar provision for mineral rents, so treating the latter as capital when they were really income might be a breach of the rules against accumulations.

2   Under the general law, before statutory intervention originally by the Settled Land Act 1882, mineral rents counted as capital if the tenant for life was impeachable for waste: *Re Ridge, Hellard v Moody* (1885) 31 Ch D 504 at 508. Under the SLA 1925, s 47 if the tenant for life is impeachable for waste, three-quarters of the rents are capitalised and he is entitled to a quarter, and if he if he is not so impeachable, one-quarter is capital. This could be varied by express provision, and it has been common to exclude this provision in settled land settlements and provide that the entire rents are income. Without express provision, someone with a life interest in the proceeds of sale under a trust for sale had the same rights to income as a tenant for life impeachable for waste (*Re Ridge, Hellard v Moody*), so that the capitalisation was of three-quarters of the mineral rents.

3   Under the general law, before statutory intervention originally by the Settled Land Act 1882, the proceeds of sale of timber counted as capital if the tenant for life was impeachable for waste: *Honeywood v Honeywood* (1874) LR 18 Eq 306. Under the SLA 1925, s 66 if the tenant for life is impeachable for waste three-quarters of the net proceeds of timber are capitalised. 'Timber' in this context is oak, ash and elm of the age of 20 years or more but not so old as not to have useable timber (*Honeywood v Honeywood*), but this can be varied by local custom. As mentioned in n 1, the SLA 1925, s 66 does not apply to trusts of land within the meaning of the TLATA 1996, and there is uncertainty as to whether or not proceeds of timber should be capitalised in the absence of express provision.

[220.62]

FORM B20.13:   Exercise of powers to be subject to beneficiary's consent[1]

My trustees shall not exercise their powers (whether conferred by statute or otherwise) of sale lease licence mortgage or charge, or of effecting improvements or development, of any land comprised in [my residuary estate] without the consent of [my wife]/[any person for the time being beneficially entitled to an interest in possession in such land].

1   The TLATA 1996, s 8(2) (Part G, para **[246.93]**) expressly contemplates that exercise of the statutory powers of management of land can be made subject to consents, as the powers of

trustees for sale often were before the TLATA 1996. The kind of trust where this is most appropriate is one to provide a residence, or any other trust where the beneficiary is likely to occupy the land. It may in many circumstances be felt to be sufficient to protect the interests of the beneficiaries, however, to do no more than refrain from excluding the operation of the TLATA 1996, s 11 (duty to consult beneficiaries, see para [220.58]). It should be noted that the LPA 1925, s 28(1) was repealed by the TLATA 1996, so it is no longer the case that making sale of the land subject to consent has the effect that exercise of the trustees' powers of management is also subject to requiring that consent. It is unnecessarily burdensome for the trustees to make all exercises of their powers to be subject to consent, and this clause is confined to making the more major types of disposition or action subject to it.

Powers relating to foreign property

[220.63]

FORM B20.14:   Powers of management of foreign land

In relation to any land or immovable property outside England and Wales my trustees shall in addition to the powers conferred hereby have all the powers of an absolute owner. and a sole trustee for the time being of this my will may exercise all or any of such powers.

[220.64]

FORM B20.15:   Declaration that statutory provisions shall apply to foreign property

I declare that my trustees shall in addition to any powers authorities or discretions hereby expressly conferred on them have with respect to any property belonging to me in [*foreign country*] or elsewhere all such powers authorities and discretions as are conferred on trustees of property and personal representatives in England by statute or the general law.

[220.65]

FORM B20.16:   Power to pay foreign tax

My trustees shall have power in their absolute discretion to pay any tax in any part of the world for which they may be liable even though such tax may not be enforceable against them.

Businesses[1]

[220.66]

FORM B20.17:   Power to carry on business

My trustees shall have power to carry on any business either alone or in partnership and employ therein any capital of [my residuary estate] and they shall be fully indemnified thereout in respect of any liabilities they may incur in connection with any such business and none of my trustees shall be liable to any of the beneficiaries hereunder for any losses sustained in the course of my trustees' conduct of any such business in the absence of deliberate fraud or wrongdoing on the part of such trustee personally.

1   See also B5 at para [**205.1**] et seq, especially Forms B5.13 to B5.22 at paras [**205.70**]–[**205.79**]. Express power is always needed to carry on a business, and essential ancillary powers are powers to invest capital in the purchase of business assets, and power to incur trading liabilities and satisfy them out of the trust fund. See the Preliminary Note to B5 at para [**205.25**].

[220.67]

FORM B20.18:   Power to carry on farming business

My trustees may manage stock farm and cultivate alone or in partnership any farm or agricultural land or woodlands anywhere in the world which are comprised in [my residuary estate] and may employ any capital of [my residuary estate] held on the same trusts as such farm agricultural land or woodland is held for such purpose or for the purpose of paying or compensating outgoing tenants and shall have all the powers of a sole absolute owner in relation to such farm agricultural land or woodlands and shall be fully indemnified out of [my residuary estate] in respect of any loss arising from the exercise of these powers.

[220.68]

FORM B20.19:   Power to incorporate business

My trustees may at the expense of [my residuary estate] form or join in forming a limited or unlimited company to carry on any business or to acquire any business already carried on (alone or in partnership) by my trustees or an interest therein and may sell lease or otherwise dispose of any such business to any limited or unlimited company in consideration (partly or wholly) of shares stock or debentures of such company or for any other consideration.

Borrowing

[220.69]

FORM B20.20:   Power to borrow[1]

My trustees may borrow money with or without giving security and on such terms as to interest repayment and otherwise as my trustees may think fit for any purpose connected with the trusts affecting [my residuary estate] (including the purchase of or subscription for assets to be held as part of [my residuary estate] or any part or share thereof) and no lender from whom my trustees borrow money in purported exercise of this power shall be concerned to enquire as to the propriety amount or purpose of any such borrowing.[2]

1   In the absence of express power the only powers of trustees to borrow are the power under the TA 1925, s 16 (Part G, para [**246.14**]) to borrow on mortgage to raise money for payment or application in some way which is authorised in relation to capital money, and the powers of an absolute owner in relation to land under the TLATA 1996, s 6(1) and the TrA 2000, s 8(3) (all of which powers also apply to personal representatives). Personal representatives also have

power to borrow on the security of personal estate for the purposes of administration of the estate: AEA 1925, s 39 (Part G, para [**246.48**]). The TA 1925, s 16 does not permit borrowing to finance the purchase of further investments (*Re Suenson-Taylor's Settlement, Moores v Moores* [1974] 3 All ER 397 [1974] 1 WLR 1280), does not permit unsecured borrowing, and does not apply to settled land unless the trustees are statutory owners: TA 1925, s 16(2). It is possible, but not certain, that the powers of an an absolute owner in relation to land under the TLATA 1996, s 6(1) and the TrA 2000, s 8(3) would enable borrowing on the security of the land to finance the purchase of some other investment, but it does not authorise unsecured borrowing. Express powers of this kind are therefore desirable.

2   The TA 1925, s 17 (Part G, para [**246.15**]) gives protection of this kind to mortgagees, but not to lenders of unsecured loans.

Powers of appropriation

[220.70]
Note. The AEA 1925, s 41 (Part G, para [**246.50**]) confers extensive powers of appropriation on personal representatives, but mostly subject to obtaining the consent of the beneficiary or trustees in favour of whom the appropriation is made. There are three main reasons for making express provision for appropriation. The first is to dispense with the requirement of consent: see para [**220.74**], n 3. The second, in a case where property is to be held on trust, is to confer powers of appropriation on the trustees of the will which will be exercisable when administering the will trusts after the administration of the estate is complete (when the statutory power will have ceased to apply)— although trustees have power of appropriation under the general law, there uncertainties about the scope of it (see para [**220.71**]), and it is better to make express provision. The third reason is to authorise exercise of the power by a personal representative or trustee in his own favour. In *Re Radley-Kane, Kane v Radley-Kane* [1999] Ch 274, [1998] 3 All ER 753 it was held that a personal representative cannot as a matter of general law exercise the statutory power of appropriation in his own favour unless the assets appropriated are cash or the equivalent of cash such as stock exchange investments. There are also some tax reasons: see paras [**220.72**] and [**220.73**]. Forms B20.21 at para [**220.74**], B20.22 at para [**220.75**], B20.23 at para [**220.76**] and B20.24 at para [**220.77**] confer power of appropriation on the will trustees when acting as trustees, but Form B20.26 at para [**220.79**] does not, and it is not entirely clear whether Statutory Will Form No 6 (see Form B20.25 at para [**220.78**]) does so, but it probably does.

[220.71]
Trustees' powers under the general law. The wide powers of investment in land and other assets now conferred by the TrA 2000, ss 3 and 8 possibly mean that trustees (as opposed to personal representatives) have power under the general law to appropriate any asset to any interest, provided that it is an interest of a kind which can be satisfied by appropriation (see *Re Freeston's Charity, Sylvester v University College Oxford* [1979] 1 All ER 51, [1978] 1 WLR 741 for an example of an interest not so susceptible, namely a right to receive half the income of a fund, as contrasted with a right to the income of half a fund, which could be the subject of an appropriation). This is because it seems there is always power to appropriate an asset which is an authorised investment, and without the consent of the beneficiaries to whose interests it is appropriated: *Re*

Wragg, Wragg v Palmer [1919] 2 Ch 58 (a case concerning the power of trustees to appropriate land and private company shares to settled shares of a trust fund). The TrA 2000 renders legal estates in land and all assets other than land authorised investments (see paras **[220.12]** and **[220.17]**). Therefore, trustees have a general power to appropriate trust assets. However, it is not an entirely certain conclusion, and there are the other reasons for conferring express power to appropriate mentioned in this paragraph, see paras **[220.70]**, **[220.72]** and **[220.73]**. We therefore still recommend that express powers of appropriation are conferred in wills. Where land is held on trust in undivided shares for absolutely entitled beneficiaries of full age, the trustees of the land are given power by the TLATA 1996, s 7 (Part G, para **[246.92]** corresponding with the power formerly vested in trustees for sale by the LPA 1925, s 28(3)) to partition land with the beneficiaries' consent. This power may now be redundant, at any rate in respect of land held for a legal estate, if the view expressed here that trustees have power of appropriation under the general law anyway is correct. On appropriation, see further Vol 1, para **[29.1]** et seq.

[220.72]
Tax aspects. An appropriation by personal representatives does not give rise to any capital gains tax charge (Taxation of Chargeable Gains Act 1992, s 62(4), together with ss 64(2) and 62(3)). The requirement of a beneficiary's consent no longer makes an appropriation by personal representatives of property in satisfaction of a general legacy of money subject to stamp duty (Finance Act 1985, s 84(4), and the Stamp Duty (Exempt Instruments) Regulations 1987). However, an appropriation by trustees rather than by personal representatives with the consent of a beneficiary would probably be liable to ad valorem stamp duty because there is no specific exemption for such an appropriation, and there is authority for saying that the requirement of consent makes an appropriation subject to stamp duty, see *Jopling v IRC* [1940] 2 KB 282, [1940] 3 All ER 279, and Vol 1, para **[29.16]**. An express provision exempting trustees (and personal representatives) from obtaining the consent of beneficiaries for an appropriation or partition of land might also be wise in view of the new provisions concerning stamp duty on exchanges of interests in land introduced by the Finance Act 1994, ss 241 and 242. It is possible that these provisions would be prevented from applying on a partition of land by trustees if there is no requirement of a beneficiary's consent to such a partition.

[220.73]
Tax aspects—capital gains tax deemed disposal deferment. The presence or absence of an express power of appropriation can also be important as to whether and when there is a capital gains tax charge on beneficiaries becoming absolutely entitled. This is best illustrated by an example. Suppose that a trust fund is held on trust for such of three siblings A, B, and C as attain the age of twenty-five, if more than a one in equal shares. A is three years older than B, and B is three years older than C. When A attains 25, he becomes absolutely entitled to one third of the fund and thus there is a deemed disposal at market value of that one third by virtue of the Taxation of Chargeable Gains Act 1992, s 71 if neither of the exceptions referred to below applies. The first exception is

that if and insofar as the trust fund consists of land, when A attains 25 he will not become absolutely entitled to any of that land or assets representing it until the land is sold or there is an appropriation or partition, or C attains twenty-five (A and B already having attained that age) so that all three then become together absolutely entitled to the land. This follows from *Stephenson v Barclays Bank Trust Co* [1975] 1 All ER 625, [1975] 1 WLR 882, *Pexton v Bell* [1975] 1 All ER 498, [1975] 1 WLR 707 and *Crowe v Appleby* [1975] 3 All ER 529, [1975] 1 WLR 1539 (High Court—the CA decision is on a different point). The second exception is that where the assets are not land but there is an express power of appropriation, the Inland Revenue take the view that the effect is the same as if the assets were land, the point presumably being that (continuing the above example) when A attains 25 he cannot claim any specific assets of the trust fund because the trustees could still exercise their power of appropriation to decide which specific assets he receives in satisfaction of his share (see the Inland Revenue's *Capital Gains Manual*, para 37530). If the argument set out at para **[220.71]** that the TrA 2000 has had the effect of conferring a general power of appropriation on all trustees is correct, this Revenue practice should now be extended to all trusts including ones without an express power of appropriation. This Revenue view is in general beneficial to the taxpayer because it enables the capital gains tax charge under the TCGA 1992, s 71 to be deferred, although there are less usual situations where or it can be a disadvantage, for example where absolute entitlement when A attains twenty-five would be an occasion when holdover relief could be obtained, but the subsequent event (which is when A becomes absolutely entitled as a result of the presence of the power of appropriation) is one where holdover relief is not obtainable. In general, therefore, this is a reason for including an express power of appropriation.

[220.74]

FORM B20.21:   Power for trustees to appropriate

I declare that [notwithstanding the trust for sale hereinbefore contained][1] my trustees (whether acting as personal representatives or as trustees) may appropriate any real or personal property forming part of [my residuary estate] to or towards the share or interest whether settled or not of any person or persons in the proceeds of sale thereof under the trusts hereinbefore contained and may set apart any investments to answer any annuity hereby bequeathed and for the purposes aforesaid shall have and may at any time exercise all such powers of appropriation and other powers conferred upon personal representatives by section 41 of the Administration of Estates Act 1925[2] and with the same effect as set out in such section provided always that the power hereby conferred shall be additional to any power of appropriation or partition conferred upon my trustees by statute,[3] any such appropriation shall be valid and binding without the consent of the beneficiary or of any other person,[4] and any such appropriation shall be valid and binding notwithstanding that one of more of my trustees may be beneficially interested in the exercise of the said power.[5]

1   Trusts for sale are no longer necessary or desirable (see Part A, para **[200.55]**. Omit these words if there is no trust for sale.

2   As to the desirability of an express clause, see paras **[220.70]–[220.72]** and n 3 infra.
3   Trustees have a statutory power of partition of land (TLATA 1996, s 7) but only where the
     beneficiaries are of full age, absolutely entitled in undivided shares, and consent.
4   Dispensing with consents to appropriations may make the administration easier and in some
     situations may help to prevent such appropriations from being subject to stamp duty: see
     para **[220.72]**.
5   See para **[220.70]** for the importance of including this provision.

[220.75]

FORM B20.22:   Another power for trustees to appropriate

I declare that my trustees (whether acting as personal representatives or as
trustees) may at any time appropriate any part of the real or personal property
(including things in action) forming part of [my residuary estate] in the actual
condition or state of investment thereof at the time of appropriation in or
towards satisfaction of any share or sub-divided share in [my residuary estate] or
the proceeds of sale of [my residuary estate] whether such share be settled or not
and may for that purpose ascertain or fix the value of the property so to be
appropriated [in accordance with the powers conferred on trustees by section 22
(3) of the Trustee Act 1925] [as they shall think fit] [provided however that no
such appropriation shall be made hereunder in respect of any share or subdivided
share to which some person of full age and capacity is absolutely and
beneficially entitled in possession without the consent of such person and no
appropriation shall be made hereunder in respect of a settled share to the income
whereof some person of full age and capacity is beneficially entitled in
possession without the consent of such person but save as aforesaid no consent
of any person shall be required].[1]

Every appropriation made thereunder [with such consent (if any) as aforesaid]
shall bind all persons interested under this my will whether in the said share or
subdivided share to which the appropriation is made or in any other share or
otherwise under this my will, and every such appropriation shall be valid and
binding notwithstanding that one of more of my trustees may be beneficially
interested in the exercise of the said power.[2]

1   See para **[220.74]**, n 4.
2   See para **[220.70]** for the importance of this type of provision.

[220.76]

FORM B20.23:   Short form of power of appropriation, by reference to the statutory power

My trustees shall have all the powers of appropriation and other incidental
powers conferred on personal representatives by statute whether they are acting
as trustees or as personal representatives and although one or more of such
trustees may be beneficially interested in the exercise of such powers[1] and
without requiring any of the consents required by statute.

1   See Vol 1, para **[29.13]**.

[220.77]

FORM B20.24:   Clause allowing appropriation without the beneficiary's consent and where trustees are beneficially interested—alternative form[1]

I declare that my trustees may exercise the power of appropriation conferred upon them by section 41 of the Administration of Estates Act 1925[2] without obtaining any of the consents required by that section.

My trustees may so exercise such power of appropriation whether they are acting as personal representatives or as trustees, and even though they (or one or more of them) may be beneficially interested in such exercise.

My trustees shall wherever possible give to the persons whose consent would but for this provision be required by the said Act one month's notice of any intended appropriation but no purchaser shall be concerned to see or inquire whether such notices have been given.

1   See paras **[220.70]** and **[220.72]**.
2   See Part G, para **[246.50]**.

[220.78]

FORM B20.25:   Clause as to appropriation incorporating Statutory Will Forms 1925, Form 6

Statutory Will Forms 1925, Form No 6 is incorporated herein.[1]

1   For this form, see Part E, Form E6 at para **[238.12]**.

[220.79]

FORM B20.26:   Power of appropriation with consent of beneficiaries of full age[1]

My trustees may in extension of the power conferred on them by section 41 of the Administration of Estates Act 1925, at any time or times with the consent in writing only of all other persons for the time being entitled to share in my estate who are of full age and capacity appropriate any part of my residuary estate in its then actual condition of state of investment in or towards satisfaction of the share of any infant beneficiary in my estate. [For the purposes of this clause no consent shall be required in the case of any beneficiary or possible beneficiary whose address is not at the time of such intended appropriation known to my trustees. In all other cases my trustees shall give notice of such appropriation to all such beneficiaries of full age and capacity by sending notice thereof to the last known address of such beneficiary and if all such addresses are in Great Britain and Ireland then if no objection to the intended appropriation is received within one month of the date of posting of such notice my trustees shall assume that such consent has been given and be entitled to proceed with such appropriation without such consent in writing. If all such addresses are not in Great Britain and Ireland the last provision of this clause shall apply with the substitution of 'three months' for 'one month'.]

1   This clause is designed for use where all the gifts under the will are immediate and the desire is to distribute the estate as far as possible at the earliest date. As soon as the estate is cleared the trustees (which by the usual express definition will include the executors, so that there is no question of the power of appropriation being given both to the executors and to the trustees and it is not necessary to show that the executors have become trustees before they are entitled to exercise this power) can proceed to distribution, except in the case of the shares of minors which must be held pending the attainment of full age. However, if the appropriation is made after the executors have become trustees, with the appropriate consents, the appropriation may be subject to stamp duty, see para **[220.70]**.

[220.80]

FORM B20.27:   Power for trustees to partition and appropriate land[1]

(a)   My trustees may at any time partition any land for the time being unsold which forms part of my residuary estate among all or some of the aforesaid shares in my residuary estate and may also appropriate land to one only of such shares without partitioning or appropriating land to any other of such shares.

Provided that:

(i)   An appropriation of land to any such share as aforesaid may be made without the consent or consents of any person or persons including that of the person (if any) of full age and capacity for the time being entitled as tenant for life under the trusts aforesaid to the income of such share.

(ii)   An appropriation of land to any such share as aforesaid which has become absolutely vested in possession in a person of full age and capacity or in several persons in undivided shares may be made without the consent or consents of any person or persons.

(b)   An appropriation of land made as aforesaid shall be binding upon all persons interested in the share to which the appropriation is made and upon all persons interested in every other share in my residuary estate notwithstanding that such persons may not be in existence or may be under disability or cannot be found or ascertained at the time of such appropriation or that one or more of the trustees making the appropriation are beneficially interested in my residuary estate.

In making any such partition or appropriation my trustees may arrange that land appropriated to any share in my residuary estate shall stand charged with any sum of money whether or not by way of equality money or partition in favour of my trustees as part of my undivided or undistributed residuary estate or in favour of some other share or shares.

(c)   My trustees shall give effect to any such partition or appropriation hereunder by proper conveyance or other deeds and (if required) by executing or obtaining the execution of proper mortgages or charges and my trustees may appoint persons other than themselves to be trustees of any share in my residuary estate in the place of my trustees.

(d)   For the purpose of any such partition or appropriation my trustees may (by duly qualified agents) ascertain and fix the value of any land proposed to be or about to be partitioned or appropriated in such manner as they think proper and any valuation so made shall be binding upon all persons interested under this my will.

1   The TLATA 1996, s 7 gives to trustees of land a power to partition unsold land, but only where the land has become absolutely vested in undivided shares. Where at the time of partition the trustees for sale themselves hold any individual share directly in trust for any immediate beneficiary for his life or other interest less than an absolute interest, such share is not absolutely vested for this purpose: *Re Thomas, Thomas v Thompson* [1930] 1 Ch 194, [1929] All ER Rep 129 (a case on the LPA 1925, s 28(3), but the provisions of it material to the decision on this point were essentially the same). Where at such time the trustees hold any individual share in trust for other trustees that share is absolutely vested in the other trustees within the meaning of the subsection: *Re Gorringe and Braybons Ltd's Contract* [1934] Ch 614n, *Re Brooker, Public Trustee v Young* [1934] Ch 610. Where trustees have at any time held a share for a person absolutely that share is held absolutely within the subsection although the owner may have subsequently settled it.

Apart from statute, or special provisions, trustees having a power to invest in land can, but trustees holding land on trust for sale cannot, appropriate land to a settled share (*Re Wragg, Wragg v Palmer* [1919] 2 Ch 58). Since all trustees now have power to invest in land (see para [220.17]) and trusts for sale are not necessary and no longer implied by law where there is co-ownership (see Part A, para [200.54]), trustees of land probably can all appropriate land to a settled share in the absence of express provision to this effect in the trust instrument, except, perhaps, where there is a trust for sale. For the reasons for dispensing with any requirement of consent, see paras [220.70] and [220.72].

Inheritance tax

[220.81]

FORM B20.28:   General restriction to prevent administrative powers prejudicing inheritance tax status of beneficial trusts[1]

No power or provision herein contained shall be capable of being exercised or operating in any manner such that (if the same were capable of being so exercised or operating) the existence of such power or provision would either:

   (a)   prevent any person who would (in the absence of such power or provision) have had an interest in possession (within the meaning of Part III of the Inheritance Tax Act 1984) in any fund or part or share of a fund from having such an interest in possession as aforesaid; or

   (b)   prevent section 71 of the Inheritance Tax Act 1984 from applying to any trust to which (in the absence of such power or provision) the said section would have applied.

1   For the reason for this form, see the Note on inheritance tax at paras [220.4]–[220.9]. It has the disadvantage that when the trustees want to make some particular exercise of their powers this restriction might in some circumstances cause doubt as to whether they have power to do what they want.

Miscellaneous

[220.82]

FORM B20.29:   Power to give guarantees for loans to companies wholly or substantially owned by trustees

My trustees shall have power in their absolute discretion to give guarantees for the repayment of any loans made to companies wholly or substantially owned by them and shall be entitled to charge the whole or any part or parts of [the trust fund] in connection with such guarantees and be fully indemnified out of [the trust fund] against any personal liability to which they may become subject by reason of giving any such guarantees.

B21 Trustees and executors

1569

CONDUCT OF TRUSTEESHIP

FORMS

APPOINTMENT AND RETIREMENT OF TRUSTEES

FORMS

POWER TO CHARGE

FORMS

CROSS REFERENCES

For administration trusts, declarations concerning apportionment, incidence of inheritance tax, see B14 at para **[214.1]** et seq. For maintenance and advancement powers, powers to permit enjoyment in kind, general declarations concerning the exercise of powers, see B18 at para **[218.1]** et seq. For administrative powers and provisions, see B20 atpara **[220.1]** et seq. For disclaimer and renunciation of probate or trusteeship, see F1 at para **[239.1]** et seq.

Meaning of 'my trustees'

[221.1]

FORM B21.1: Definition of 'my trustees'

I declare that in the interpretation of this my will the expression 'my trustees' shall (where the context permits) mean and include my personal representatives and the trustees hereof whether original or substituted and if there shall be no such trustees shall (where the context permits) include the persons empowered by statute to exercise or perform any power or trust hereby or by statute conferred upon my trustees and willing or bound to exercise or perform the same.[1]

---

1   It will be remembered that in all instruments the plural includes the singular and vice versa and the word person includes a corporation (LPA 1925, s 61: Part G, para **[246.40]**). As to persons, other than actual trustees, who are empowered to act, see the AEA 1925, s 1(2); the TA 1925, s 18(2) (Part G, para **[246.16]**) and the SLA 1925, s 30(3). For a definition of 'my trustees' where the partners of a solicitors' firm are appointed, see Form B3.8 at para **[203.21]**.

[221.2]

FORM B21.2: Short definition 'my trustees'

The expression 'my trustees' herein includes my personal representatives and the trustees of this Will for the time being.

[221.3]

FORM B21.3: Powers conferred on trustees and executors

For the avoidance of doubt it is hereby declared that every power hereby or by any codicil hereto conferred on my trustees including any power of appointment or application of capital or income (but excluding any power relating to the payment or satisfaction or incidence as between persons interested in my estate of debts administration expenses taxes and general legacies) shall be exercisable both during and after the completion of the administration of my estate and whether my trustees are for the time being holding as personal representatives or as trustees the property comprised in or derived from my estate in relation to which they exercise such power.[1]

1   Where, as is usually the case, the definition of 'my trustees' includes both personal representatives and trustees, and a power is conferred on 'my trustees', it seems obvious that the power can be exercised whether 'my trustees' are for the time being personal representatives or trustees. However, the Inland Revenue have in the past tried in some cases argued that powers of appointment conferred on 'my trustees' cannot be exercised until the administration is complete (so as to argue that advantage cannot be taken of the ITA 1984, s 144 before the administration is complete—for s 144 see C3 at para **[225.83]** et seq). This provision is intended to make the position clear. Where a testator granted remuneration to 'my trustees' for services as executors and trustees, and further defined trustees as the trustees whether original substituted or otherwise, the right to remuneration was not confined to trustees who also acted as executors: *Re Chirnside, Lewis v Forrest* [1956] VLR 295. For exercise of a power before grant of probate, see Form C3.6, cl 3(2)(ii) and (iii) at para **[225.101]**.

Self-dealing

[221.4]
Note. As to the fiduciary position of trustees which prevents them in ordinary circumstances purchasing the trust property or any part of it, see *Mackreth v Fox* (1791) 4 Bro Parl Cas 258; *Thomson v Eastwood* (1877) 2 App Cas 215. For a case in which the self-dealing rule was held in the special circumstances of the case not to apply to a purchasing executor who had renounced probate see *Holder v Holder* [1968] Ch 353, [1968] 1 All ER 665. The rule extends to any transaction where a trustee's duty as trustee and his personal interest conflict, including one with a company in which the trustee has a substantial interest: see *Re Thompson's Settlement, Thompson v Thompson* [1986] Ch 99, [1985] 2 All ER 720. The rule also applies to personal representatives or trustees exercising powers relating to beneficial interests in their own favour. See para **[218.4]** for the rule as it applies to the exercise of powers of appointment and similar powers or discretions. The rule against self-dealing has also been held to apply to the widow and sole administratrix of the estate of an intestate purporting to make an appropriation of private company shares in satisfaction of her statutory legacy—the purported appropriation was held to be invalid on this ground: see *Kane v Radley-Kane* [1999] Ch 274, [1998] 3 All ER 753. Self-dealing can be authorised by the will, and authorising it should be considered where executors are being appointed who might have the greatest interest in purchasing property in the estate, such as farming partners of the deceased or co-directors or co-shareholders of a private company, or where the trustees or personal representatives are or might be persons who are also beneficially interested. Forms B21.4 to B21.8 at paras **[221.5]–[221.9]** are powers for the trustees to enter into purchases, sales or similar dealings with the trust funds. For a power for trustees to exercise beneficial powers in their own favour, see Form B18.32 at para **[218.117]**. For powers for trustees to appropriate in their own favour, see Forms B20.21 et seq at para **[220.74]** et seq.

[221.5]

FORM B21.4:   Clause giving named trustee power to purchase part of testator's estate with safeguard against improper purchase

I declare that the said A B one of the trustees of this my will shall have the power to buy any portion of my estate real or personal either by private treaty or public auction including the right to bid at any public auction notwithstanding he is a trustee of this my will and in the event of a sale by private treaty the price shall be such as may be agreed upon between the said A B and my other trustees provided that in the case of quoted securities the purchase price shall not be less than the current market price thereof at the time of the execution of the transfer and in the case of other property my trustees other than the said A B shall obtain a valuation of and a report on the property by an independent surveyor or valuer (to be paid for by the said A B) and the purchase price shall not be less than the amount of such valuation and no sale shall be made if the report shall advise against a sale for any reason whatsoever.

[221.6]

FORM B21.5:   Power to trustees to purchase the trust property—no safeguards

I authorise my son [*name*] notwithstanding that he shall be a trustee of this my will [*or* my trustees or any of them] at any time or times to purchase whether at any public auction or by private contract all or any part of the property forming my residuary estate.

[221.7]

FORM B21.6:   Power to trustees to purchase with safeguard against improper purchase

Any of my trustees may notwithstanding that he is a trustee purchase from or sell to my estate or any trust fund deriving therefrom any property provided that in the case of quoted securities the purchase price shall not be less than the current market price thereof at the time of the execution of the transfer or in the case of property of any other character my trustees shall previously have obtained a valuation and report on the proposed sale by an independent surveyor or professional valuer appointed by the trustees for the time being other than the proposed purchaser (such valuation and report to be paid for by the proposed purchaser) and that the purchase price shall not be less than the amount of such valuation and the said surveyor or valuer shall not have advised against such sale for any reason.

[221.8]

FORM B21.7:   Power to a trustee to enter into any transaction provided there is at least one other trustee

Any of my trustees may contract or otherwise deal with my trustees as vendor or purchaser or otherwise provided that there is at least one other of my trustees agreeing in writing to the contract or dealing who has no interest in such contract or dealing save as one of my trustees.

[221.9]

FORM B21.8:   Power to trustees to enter into transactions in two capacities

My trustees may in their absolute discretion enter into any agreement or effect any transaction (hereby or by law authorised) with the trustee or trustees of any settlement or will notwithstanding that my trustees or one or more of them may also be trustees or a trustee or the sole trustee of such settlement or such will and may enter into any agreement or effect any transaction (hereby or by law authorised) involving a company notwithstanding that they or any one or more of them may be in any capacity directors or a director shareholders or a shareholder of such company.

Retention of directors' remuneration etc

[221.10]

FORM B21.9:   Power for trustees to become directors and to retain remuneration[1]—short form

I declare that any one or more of my trustees may act as a director officer or other employee of [the said —— Company Limited] [any company] and may receive remuneration or any other benefit for so acting without being liable to account for the same to my estate or the persons beneficially interested therein.

1   A trustee cannot make any profit out of his trust and would in the ordinary course be liable to account for all director's fees received by him: *Re Macadam, Dallow v Codd* [1946] Ch 73, [1945] 2 All ER 664; *Re Llewellin's Will Trusts, Griffiths v Wilcox* [1949] Ch 225, [1949] 1 All ER 487. The ordinary charging clause would not give a trustee-director power to retain such remuneration: *Re Gee* [1948] Ch 284, [1948] 1 All ER 498. However, a trustee is not liable to account where his position as director, officer or employee is owed entirely to votes other than those attached to the trust assets (*Re Gee* supra).

[221.11]

FORM B21.10:   Power for trustees to become directors, retain remuneration and to hold shares as qualifying shares

My trustees or any of them may become directors officers or employees of [—— —— Company Limited] [any company] and may receive the remuneration or other benefits attaching to such office or employment without being liable to account for the same and any trustee may become qualified as a director (if the articles of the said company so allow) by holding in his own name shares belonging to my estate provided that he executes a declaration of trust thereof in favour of my trustees generally accompanied by the certificates of such shares and that he accounts to my estate for all dividends and bonuses payable in respect therof.[1]

1   If the company is governed by Table A of the Companies Act 1948, a holding as trustee is sufficient qualification unless in the articles or the qualification as fixed in general meeting (see

Table A, Part I, art 77 as contained in the Companies Act 1948, Sch 1) it is stated to the contrary: *Pulbrook v Richmond Consolidated Mining Co* (1878) 9 Ch D 610. The new Table A in the Companies (Tables A to F) Regulations 1985, SI 1985/805, does not contain the old art 77 as share qualifications for directors are now less common.

[221.12]

FORM B21.11:   Retention of benefits—fuller form including benefits from subsidiary companies

Any of my trustees may act as a director officer or employee of any company in which [my residuary estate] or any part or share thereof may be invested or as a director officer or employee of any subsidiary of any such company and any such trustee may retain any remuneration or benefit deriving from such office or employment for his own use and benefit absolutely notwithstanding that any votes or other rights incident to assets of [my residuary estate] may have been instrumental in procuring for him or continuing him in such office or employment or that his qualification for such office or employment may be constituted in whole or in part by assets comprised in [my residuary estate].

Indemnities, releases and receipts

[221.13]
Note. What are usually referred to as trustee indemnity clauses are in reality clauses which absolve trustees or executors from liability for their own negligence or from vicarious liability for the negligence or fraud of co-trustees or agents. The ills of twenty-first century civilisation, and in particular monetary and other instabilities, volatility in investment markets, and the increased popularity of professional negligence litigation, make it understandable that anyone accepting office as an executor or trustee should want protection of this kind. Indeed, anyone accepting such an office as a personal favour, and who will not be covered by professional negligence insurance when acting as trustee or personal representative, should in our opinion have the benefit of such a clause. Absolution from negligence liability seems less appropriate in the case of a professional trustee who charges for his services and is covered by insurance, and especially inappropriate in the case of a trust corporation: see, for example, the view of Millett LJ as expressed in *Armitage v Nurse* [1998] Ch 241, [1997] 2 All ER 705. It was, however, confirmed in the latter case that the liability of trustees, including professional trustees, for negligence, can be excluded. In *Wight v Olswang* (1999) Times, 18 May, CA it was held that where a settlement had two trustee exemption clauses, one protecting all trustees from liability for breach of trust and one which expressly did not apply to paid trustees, the paid trustees could not rely on the general exemption. There is also a prudential reason for a professional trustee not to exclude negligence liability. This is that if it is excluded, and there are beneficiaries who become so indignant about something the trustees have done (or not done) as to be determined to sue, those beneficiaries will be driven back onto alleging fraud or deliberate wrongdoing, which will not normally be covered by the trustee's professional negligence insurance, and depending on the facts, the negligence insurers may have no obligation to pay for the defence of the trustee against the allegations or any

interest in doing so. *Walker v Stones* [2001] QB 902, [2000] 4 All ER 412 is an example of beneficiaries making this sort of allegation where the trustees had the benefit of a clause in the settlement excluding liability for negligence—the trust fund sustained a substantial loss as a result of the trustees guaranteeing a loan as part of providing finance for a company run by the settlor (the settlor being excluded from benefit under the settlement); the trustees said that they believed it to be for the benefit of the beneficiaries; the Court of Appeal held that there was a triable issue as to whether this was a dishonest breach of trust, on the basis that it might have been so unreasonable a belief that, by any objective standard, no reasonable solicitor trustee could have thought that what he did was for the benefit of the beneficiaries. The whole area of trustee exemption clauses is currently under review: see the Trust Law Consultation Paper 'Trustee Exemption Clauses' (June 1999). A solicitor should always draw the testator's attention to any indemnity clause which it is proposed be included in the will, and should advise him upon it. In that way there cannot be any argument that testator did not know of it and approve it, so that the solicitor, if he is appointed executor and trustee, is entitled to the benefit of it. He does not have to advise the testator to take separate legal advice upon it: see *Bogg v Raper* (1998) Times, 22 April, CA.

[221.14]
Where under the power in the Trusts of Land and Appointment of Trustees Act 1996 (TLATA 1996), s 9(1) (Part G, para **[246.94]**; see also para **[220.54]** et seq), trustees of land delegate any of their functions relating to the land to a beneficiary, the TLATA 1996, s 9A (inserted by the Trustee Act 2000 (TrA 2000): Part G, para **[246.95]**), imposes a statutory duty of care on trustees when deciding to delegate the function to him, and when reviewing the delegation. It is not clear whether this liability is capable of being excluded by trustee indemnity clauses in the will or settlement: see para **[220.56]**. Trustees' liability for the acts and defaults of an agent, nominee or custodian appointed under the TrA 2000, ss 11, 16, 17 or 18, (Part G, paras **[246.126]** and **[246.131]**–**[246.133]**) is limited by the TLATA 1996, s 23 (Part G, para **[246.109]**) to cases where the trustees have failed to comply with their statutory duty of care when entering into or reviewing the arrangement (see para **[221.15]** for the statutory duty of care). The TrA 2000, s 21(3) provides that if the application of s 23 is inconsistent with the terms of the will, it does not apply. But whether this applies to the case where the trustees exercise the statutory powers, in addition to cases where they exercise express powers, is not clear. Whereas the TrA 2000, s 21(2), which provides for s 23 to apply to a case where trustees exercise express powers to appoint an agent, nominee or custodian, is expressly made subject to s 21(3), s 21(1)—which provides for s 23 to apply to a case where trustees exercise the statutory powers—is not. However, it may be possible to exclude liability for all acts or defaults of an agent, nominee or substitute appointed under the statutory powers by expressly excluding the statutory duty of care in the will: TrA 2000, Sch 1 para 7, (Part G, para **[246.156]**). If it is excluded, then it is difficult to see how the trustees can be made liable for failing to comply with it. For a form excluding the statutory duty of care in this regard, see Form B21.15 at para **[221.19]**. Where a personal representative or trustee takes advantage of the Trustee Act 1925, s 25 (on or after 1 March 2000, as

substituted by the Trustee Delegation Act 1999: see Part G, para **[246.21]**) to delegate the execution or exercise of all or any of his trusts, powers and discretions, his liability for the acts or defaults of the donee imposed by sub-s (7) probably can be excluded, since the powers of the TA 1925 apply if and so far only as a contrary intention is not expressed, and subject to the terms of the will: see the TA 1925, s 69(2), the Note at para **[221.35]** and Form B21.16 at para **[221.20]**.

[221.15]
Statutory duty of care. The TrA 2000 imposes a statutory duty of care which applies (unless expressly excluded) not only to trustees or personal representatives exercising the new powers of investment conferred by the TrA 2000, but also to trustees exercising similar powers conferred on them expressly (eg by will) or by other Acts, whether before or after the passing of the TrA 2000, and to the exercise of various other powers, set out below. This statutory duty has both subjective and objective elements, and is a duty for the trustee to exercise such care and skill as is reasonable in the circumstances, having regard in particular to any special knowledge or experience that he has or holds himself out as having (the subjective element), and if he acts in the course of a business or profession, to any special knowledge or experience that it is reasonable to expect of a person acting in the course of that kind of business or profession (the objective element): see the TrA 2000, s 1 (Part G, para **[246.116]**). In the absence of this statutory duty, a trustee always has, of course, when exercising his powers, been subject to fiduciary duties of care arising under the general law, eg a duty to invest the trust fund as an ordinary prudent man of business, or according to a higher standard if he is a professional trustee: see *Bartlett v Barclay's Bank Trust Co Ltd* [1980] Ch 515, [1980] 1 All ER 139. However, it was thought by the Law Commission that by enshrining such a duty in statute, certainty and consistency would be brought to the standard of competence and behaviour expected of trustees.

The majority of the occasions when the statutory duty of care applies are set out in the TrA 2000, Sch 1 (Part G, para **[246.156]** et seq) and are when trustees are exercising or carrying out—

(a) any power of investment, however conferred (eg by the TrA 2000, s 3 or by the will or other trust instrument), and the duties of having regard to the 'standard investment criteria' and obtaining advice, and of reviewing investments, as set out in TrA 2000, ss 4 and 5 (see Part G, paras **[246.119]** and **[246.120]**; see also **[220.12]** et seq);

(b) the power to acquire land conferred by TrA 2000, s 8 (see para **[220.17]**) or any other such power (eg one conferred by the will or other trust instrument), or any power in relation to land acquired under such a power (see para **[220.49]** et seq)—the latter category probably includes exercise of powers in relation to land acquired before 1 February 2001 under a power to do so, but clearly does not include exercise of powers in relation to land which is comprised in the testator's estate at his death and devolves on the trustees of his will;

(c) any power to appoint an agent, nominee or custodian, (however conferred, eg by the TrA 2000, ss 11, 16, 17 or 18 or by the will—see para **[220.35]** et seq and Part G, paras **[246.126]** and **[246.131]**–

[246.133]), and the duties to review such appointment (as set out in the TrA 2000, s 22: Part G, para **[246.137]**);

(d) any power to compound liabilities, compromise claims or any other powers contained in the TA 1925, s 15 (Part G, para **[246.13]**) or corresponding powers otherwise conferred;

(e) any power to insure property (however conferred, eg by the TA 1925, s 19: Part G, para **[246.17]** or by the will); and

(f) any power in relation to the valuation of reversionary property and other trust property (however conferred, eg by the TA 1925, s 22(1) or (3): Part G, para **[246.19]** or by the will).

The statutory duty of care may, however, be excluded or restricted by the will or other trust instrument (see the TrA 2000, Sch 1, para 7) and a testator may wish to exclude it, particularly if he is appointing family or friends to be his executors and trustees. See, eg Form B21.23 at para **[221.27]**. The statutory duty of care also applies in relation to delegation of land management powers to a beneficiary with an interest in possession, where it is not clear whether it may be excluded: see para **[220.56]**.

[221.16]

FORM B21.12: **General indemnity clause—proviso excluding professional and corporate trustees**

In the professed[1] administration of my estate[2] and the professed[3] execution of the trusts powers or provisions of this will or any codicil hereto none of my trustees shall be liable (whether for breach of the duty of care under the Trustee Act 2000 or otherwise) for any act or omission of his or for any act or omission of any co-personal representative or co-trustee of his or of any agent, nominee or custodian[4] employed in the administration of my estate or the execution of the said trusts powers and provisions save for any act or omission involving wilful fraud or dishonesty[5] committed by the personal representative or trustee sought to be made liable. And in particular but without prejudice to the generality of the foregoing provision none of my trustees shall be bound to take any proceedings against a co-trustee or past trustee or his personal representatives for any breach or alleged breach of trust committed or suffered by such co-trustee. [Provided that this clause shall not apply to a corporation and shall not apply to an individual authorised hereby or by law[6] to charge for acting as a personal representative or trustee [unless he has elected in writing not to charge for so acting at or before the time of his obtaining a grant of representation or (not having obtained such a grant) his being first appointed as trustee]].[7]

1 By applying to acts or defaults in the 'professed' administration of the estate and execution of the trusts, the trustees will be exonerated, save to the extent excluded by the clause, ie wilful fraud or dishonesty, for anything done by them in the 'purported' administration and execution of the trusts of the will, ie even though in fact not done in the administration or execution: see *Walker v Stones* [2000] 4 All ER 412, [2001] 2 WLR 623, CA at 440E–F and 654A–B respectively.

2 It is doubtful whether a provision of this kind can limit the rights of the creditors to make claims for eg negligence against the personal representatives. It is unclear whether such a provision can absolve trustees of land from liability under the TLATA 1996, s 9A in respect of the delegation of their functions under the TLATA 1996, s 9(1): see para **[220.56]**.

3 See n 1 supra.

4   If trustees are to be absolved from all liability for the acts or defaults of any agent, nominee or custodian appointed under the TrA 2000, the clause in Form B21.15 at para **[221.19]** should be used in addition to this clause. See para **[221.14]**.

5   In *Walker v Stones* [2000] 4 All ER 412, [2001] 2 WLR 623, CA Sir Christopher Slade considered that a clause exonerating trustees save for 'wilful fraud or dishonesty', as here, was not materially different from a clause exonerating trustees save for 'actual fraud', as was considered by the Court of Appeal in *Armitage v Nurse* [1998] Ch 241; [1997] 2 All ER 705. Millett LJ said in *Armitage v Nurse* that the words 'actual fraud' excluded constructive fraud and equitable fraud and simply connoted dishonesty. Accordingly, such a clause would exempt a trustee from liability for loss unless caused by his own dishonesty, however, indolent, imprudent, lacking in diligence, negligent or wilful he might have been, and was not void for repugnancy or on the grounds of public policy. A trustee would, however, be treated as acting dishonestly if he acted in a way which he did not honestly believe was in the interests of the beneficiaries, whether or not he stood to gain personally from his actions. Sir Christopher Slade in *Walker v Stones* at 660C qualified this, at least in the case of a solicitor-trustee, with the observation that a clause such as this would not exempt trustees from liability for breaches of trust, even if committed in the genuine belief that the course taken by them was in the interests of the beneficiaries, if such belief was so unreasonable that no reasonable solicitor trustee could have held that belief.

6   Under the TrA 2000, s 29(2) an individual who acts as trustee in a professional capacity is entitled to reasonable remuneration for his services provided on or after 1 February 2001, (whenever the will was made or the testator died: see s 33(1)) with the written agreement of his co-trustee or co-trustees if the will does not include a remuneration clause

7   It may be thought undesirable for a paid trustee to have the benefit of this indemnity, in which case provision can be made to that effect: see para **[221.13]**. Sometimes, however, a relative or friend of the testator may accept office as executor or trustee as a personal favour, but also be among the categories of person able to charge. He might prefer not to charge and have the benefit of this clause—indeed, he might be a non-practising solicitor and have no negligence insurance. For a complementary proviso to a charging clause, see Form B21.39 at para **[221.51]**.

[221.17]

FORM B21.13:   **Clause excluding the statutory duty of care[1]**

The duty of care contained in section 1 of the Trustee Act 2000 shall not apply in relation in relation to [any of] my trustees [who does not act as trustee in the course of a business or profession].[2]

1   For the statutory duty of care under the TrA 2000, s 1 and Sch 1, and its exclusion by express provision, see para **[221.15]** (Part G, paras **[246.116]** and **[246.156]**). Even though the statutory duty of care is excluded, a trustee is still, of course, subject to duties arising under the general law, eg a duty to invest the trust fund as an ordinary prudent man of business, unless he is a professional trustee when the standard of care will be higher: see *Bartlett v Barclay's Bank Trust Co Ltd* [1980] Ch 515, [1980] 1 All ER 139. Liability under the general law can also be excluded: see para **[221.13]** and Form B21.12 at para **[221.16]**.

2   See para **[221.16]**, n 7.

[221.18]

FORM B21.14:   **Indemnity to trustees acting on counsel's opinion[1]**

No trustee hereof shall be personally liable for any act or omission done or made in accordance with the written opinion of counsel [of at least [10] years call] practising at the Chancery Bar upon any question whatsoever of interpretation including questions in connection with the administration of the trusts hereof.

1   Sometimes clauses have been inserted in wills purporting to empower counsel employed by the trustees conclusively to determine the construction of a will. Such clauses try to oust the jurisdiction of the court and for this reason they are objectionable: see *Re Wynn* [1952] Ch 271, [1952] 1 All ER 341; *Re Bromson* [1958] OR 367. The insertion of a clause providing for the forfeiture of the interest of any beneficiary who disputes the decision of the trustees or of counsel advising the trustees is sometimes asked for but such a clause is not recommended. The court will always entertain bona fide proceedings in spite of any such clause and will not allow a forfeiture: *Adams v Adams* [1892] 1 Ch 369; *Re Raven, Spencer v National Association for the Prevention of Consumption and Other Forms of Tuberculosis* [1915] 1 Ch 673. It is quite a different matter to absolve the trustees from all personal liability if they act upon counsel's written opinion and this form of the clause, which has much the same result, is free from objection, though whether a trustee would be able to distribute on the strength of such an opinion if he knew of an adverse claim is open to doubt. For the High Court's power to authorise personal representatives and trustees to act on the opinion of counsel of ten years standing (or the opinion of any other person who has a ten year High Court qualification, within the meaning of the Courts and Legal Services Act 1990, s 71) without hearing argument, see the Administration of Justice Act 1985, s 48.

[221.19]

FORM B21.15:   Liability for acts of an agent, nominee or custodian appointed under the Trustee Act 2000

The duty of care of the Trustee Act 2000 shall not apply to any of my trustees when entering into any arrangements under the Trustee Act 2000 under which any person acts as agent nominee or custodian or when agreeing a term under which the agent nominee or custodian is permitted to appoint a substitute or when carrying out any duties under Section 22 of the Trustee Act 2000 and none of my trustees shall be liable for any act or default of any agent nominee or custodian appointed under the Trustee Act 2000 or of any substitute appointed by any such agent nominee or custodian[1] [Provided that this clause shall not apply to a corporation and shall not apply to an individual authorised hereby or by law to charge for acting as a personal representative or trustee [unless he has elected in writing not to charge for so acting at or before the time of his obtaining a grant of representation or (not having obtained such a grant) his being first appointed as trustee]].[2]

1   It is thought that this clause should have the effect of excluding a trustee's liability for the acts or defaults of an agent, nominee or custodian (or their substitute) appointed under the TrA 2000. See para **[221.14]**.
2   See Form B21.12, nn 6 and 7 at para **[221.16]**.

[221.20]

FORM B21.16:   Liability for attorney's acts

Notwithstanding subsection (7) of section 25 of the Trustee Act 1925 (as substituted by the Trustee Delegation Act 1999)[1] the donor of a power of attorney made pursuant to that section (as so substituted) shall not be liable for the acts or defaults of the donee.

1   The TA 1925, s 25 has been substituted by the TDA 1999, s 5(1), (2) in relation to powers of attorney created on or after 1 March 2000, and is printed as so substituted in Part G, para **[246.21]**. For the ability to exclude a trustee's liability for the acts and defaults of an attorney appointed under this section, see para **[221.14]**.

[221.21]

FORM B21.17:   No duty to intervene in the affairs of a private company[1]

My trustees shall not be under any duty to require or compel the payment of any dividend by, or interfere in or inquire into the management or conduct of the business of, any company in which [my residuary estate] may wholly or partly be invested (however extensive may be the control of such company conferred by shares or securities comprised in [my residuary estate]) or may otherwise be interested directly or indirectly[2] and in the absence of actual notice of dishonesty on the part of the directors of such company may leave the conduct of such company's affairs and the payment or non-payment of dividends wholly to its directors.

1   This form has two rather different functions. First, it gives the trustees a discretion as to whether to leave the profits of a private company in which the trustees have shares to be accumulated and reinvested inside the company instead of being distributed as dividends; without this clause they would be prima facie under a duty to obtain an income from the shares (see para [220.33]), but retention of profits by the company may have fiscal and investment advantages (albeit to the disadvantage of the income beneficiaries). Second, the clause absolves the trustees from negligent failure to intervene to prevent loss. For examples of the latter type of liability see *Re Lucking's Will Trusts, Renwick v Lucking* [1967] 3 All ER 726, [1968] 1 WLR 866 and *Bartlett v Barclays Bank Trust Co* [1980] Ch 515, [1980] 1 All ER 139. For a recent case where it was alleged that trustees had not merely failed to intervene in a company's improper affairs, but had co-operated in the improprieties, see *Walker v Stones* [2001] 2 WLR 623, CA.
2   A company in which the residuary estate may have some other direct or indirect interest would include a subsidiary or sub-subsidiary of a company in which the trustees directly hold shares. It was held in *Walker v Stones* [2001] 2 WLR 623, CA at 631A, that as a matter of construction of the trustee exoneration clause under consideration, the phrase 'any body corporate *in respect of which* the trustees shall hold shares' was wide enough to include subsidiaries or sub-subsidiaries of the company in which the trustees actually held shares.

[221.22]

FORM B21.18:   Power to life tenants of settled shares to give releases to trustees

I declare that the adoption or acceptance by any individual of any account which shall be submitted to him or her by my trustees in relation to any trust funds or property in which or in any part or share of which such individual has a life interest under this my will (of which adoption or acceptance the signature of any such individual to any such account shall be conclusive evidence) shall as against such individual and any spouse and issue of such individual operate as an absolute release and discharge to my trustees in respect of all dealings with such trust funds or property appearing in any such account.[1]

1   This form will be of use where the will contains a settlement of any legacy or a share of residue.

[221.23]

FORM B21.19:   Power to insure against liability for inheritance tax on lifetime dispositions[1]

My trustees may effect any policy or policies of insurance against any inheritance tax for which they may be or become liable for as my personal representatives whether or not there shall be any other person or persons liable for such tax and the cost of such insurance shall be paid out of my estate as a testamentary expense.

1   It is possible that there could be some lifetime dispositions of the testator which are not known to the personal representatives at the time of distribution of the estate, or that there were some dispositions to the testator which may become chargeable to inheritance tax. See Part A, paras **[200.79]** and **[200.80]** and **[200.95]**–**[200.98]**.

[221.24]

FORM B21.20:   Receipts by or on behalf of minors[1]

Whenever they have an obligation or discretion under the provisions of this will or under the general law to pay or apply income or capital to a minor or for his benefit my trustees may discharge that obligation or exercise that discretion if they so desire by paying the same to any parent or guardian of the minor or to the minor himself if of the age of 16 and their respective receipts shall be a good discharge to my trustees who shall not be obliged to see how it is used.

1   This express provision may no longer be strictly necessary for a parent of a minor to give a good receipt. In contrast to the position in the past when trustees (in the absence of an express provision to the contrary) in order to get a sufficient discharge had to retain a minor's legacy until the minor was of full age (ie 18: FLRA 1969, s 1; 6 *Halsbury's Statutes* (4th edn) (1999 Reissue) 121) and able to give a good receipt, a person with parental responsibility for a minor can now receive a legacy on the minor's behalf, and can apparently require the trustees to hand over to him or her any income or capital to which the minor is absolutely and indefeasibly entitled: see the ChA 1989, s 3(3) (Part G, para **[244.119]**; see also Vol 1, para **[9.41]**) which came into force on 14 October 1991. Trustees also have power of this kind over income— power to pay income to a parent or guardian where the TA 1925, s 31 applied (see sub-s (1)(i): Part G, para **[246.26]**), and power to obtain a good receipt for income and statutory accumulations of income from a married minor under the LPA 1925, s 21 (Part G, para **[246.39]**).

[221.25]

FORM B21.21:   Receipts on behalf of charities and unincorporated associations

I declare that if the donee of any gift under this my will or any codicil hereto shall be a charitable institution or an unincorporated association the receipt of the person who professes to be the treasurer or other proper officer for the time being of such institution or association shall be a full and sufficient discharge to my trustees.

[221.26]

FORM B21.22:   Missing beneficiaries

I declare that if any donee hereunder cannot be found within the space of three years from the date when the gift to him or her becomes payable my trustees may distribute my estate upon the footing that such donee predeceased me.

Conduct of trusteeship

[221.27]

FORM B21.23:   Clause excluding trustees' duty to consult with beneficiaries as to land[1]

Section 11(1) of the Trusts of Land and Appointment of Trustees Act 1996 (consultation with beneficiaries) shall not apply to the exercise by my trustees of their functions in relation to any land subject to the trusts of this my will.

1   For the TLATA 1996, s 11 see para **[220.58]** and Part G, para **[246.97]**.

[221.28]

FORM B21.24:   Direction as to order of names of trustees in the registers of companies to secure voting rights[1]

I direct that the name of my son [*name*] shall be placed first in the register of all registered stocks shares securities or property.

1   This clause, which is a common form where a bank or insurance company is one of several trustees, may be useful where it is desired that one of the trustees shall exercise the votes in respect of shares in a company, usually a private company. Table A, art 55 of the Companies (Tables A-F) Regulations 1985 (SI 1985/805) (replacing in identical terms, art 63 of Table A, Sch 1 to the Companies Act 1948) provides that in the case of joint holders the vote of the senior who tenders a vote, whether in person or by proxy, shall be accepted to the exclusion of the other joint holders; and for this purpose seniority shall be determined by the order in which the names stand in the register of members. The voting trustee must, however, exercise his votes in accordance with the directions of the trustees as a body, but being the first-named holder gives such trustee an added degree of control.

[221.29]

FORM B21.25:   Direction that opinion of majority of trustees is to prevail[1]

I declare that should any difference of opinion at any time exist between the trustees for the time being of this my will in relation to the commission or omission of any act or otherwise howsoever in the execution of the trusts of this my will or any codicil hereto the opinion of the majority of such trustees shall prevail and shall do so even if any one or more of such trustees may be personally interested or concerned in the matter in dispute or question provided that at least one trustee in the majority has no such personal interest.

1   Trustees other than trustees of a charity cannot without this special provision act by a majority: *Blacket v Blizard* (1829) 9 B & C 851; *Luke v South Kensington Hotel Co* (1879) 11 Ch D 121; *Re Roth, Goldberger v Roth* (1896) 74 LT 50; *Astbury v Astbury* [1898] 2 Ch 111. As to charity trustees, see *Re Whiteley, Bishop of London v Whiteley* [1910] 1 Ch 600; and the Charities Act 1993, s 82; 5 *Halsbury's Statutes* (4th edn) (1998 Reissue) 1043.

[221.30]

FORM B21.26:   Power authorising an audit

I declare that the provisions of section 22 (4) of the Trustee Act 1925[1] (relating to the audit of the accounts of the trust property) shall apply hereto with the variation that two years shall be substituted for three years in such provisions[2] [and with the addition that any apportionment between capital and income of the costs of examination and audit made by the auditor at the request of the trustees shall be binding upon the persons entitled respectively to the capital and to the income of the trust property].

1   See Part G, para **[246.19]**.
2   The trustees may allocate the cost to capital or income partly to each; in default of any direction by them, costs attributable to capital will be borne by capital, and costs attributable to income by income. It would seem advisable to ask the auditor to apportion the costs himself.

[221.31]

FORM B21.27:   Direction to employ a named solicitor[1]

It is my wish that [*name of solicitor*] shall be employed in proving this my will and in transacting any legal business in the administration of the trusts hereof.

1   This form may be included where a family member or friend is appointed executor and trustee.

[221.32]

FORM B21.28:   Nomination of trust corporation to receive notices[1]

I nominate [*trust corporation*] as the trust corporation to which notices of dealings affecting real or personal property which is subject to any trust hereunder may be given.

1   LPA 1925, s 138. This nomination is not usually required unless property is settled under the will and is then only really essential where there are numerous beneficiaries who may charge their interests and it becomes of advantage to have an effective register of such dealings.

[221.33]

FORM B21.29:   Power to vest assets in nominees[1]

My trustees may vest or register any property which or the proceeds of sale of which form part of [my residuary estate] in the name or names of any person or persons (including any one or more of my trustees) or body or bodies corporate resident in the UK or elsewhere as nominee or nominees for my trustees and remunerate such nominee or nominees[2] and agree with such nominee or nominees such terms as in their absolute discretion they think fit including (without prejudice to the generality of the foregoing) terms permitting the nominee or nominees to appoint a substitute restricting the liability of the nominee or nominees (or substitute) to my trustees or to any beneficiary hereunder and permitting the nominee or nominees (or substitute) to act in circumstances capable of giving rise to a conflict of interest [Provided always that:

[(i)   ][3]
[(ii) Section 23 of the Trustee Act 2000 (liability for nominees) shall not apply but none of my trustees shall be liable for any act or default of any nominee appointed hereunder or substitute of such nominee][4]
[(iii) the duty of care of the Trustee Act 2000 shall not apply hereto][5].

1   Personal representatives and trustees now have statutory powers to vest assets in nominees or custodians by virtue of the TrA 2000, ss 16-20 (Part G, paras **[246.131]**–**[246.135]**). However, this express power is wider than the statutory powers in that it authorises trustees to appoint one individual only of their number to be a nominee. Under TrA 2000, s 19(5)(a) trustees may only vest assets in one of their number if that one is a trust corporation, or otherwise in two or more of their number. Further, the terms expressly mentioned in this Form as terms which the trustees can agree 'in their absolute discretion' can only be agreed by trustees when making the appointment under their statutory powers if they consider it 'reasonably necessary for them to do so': TrA 2000, s 20(3). For a power to delegate investment powers, see Form B20.8 at para **[220.56]**.

2   Under the TrA 2000, s 32(2), (3) (Part G, para **[246.147]**) trustees may pay reasonable remuneration to a nominee, and reimburse him for any proper expenses.

3   Under the TrA 2000, s 22 (Part G, para **[246.137]**) trustees appointing a nominee under an express power (as well as under the statutory power) have duties to review and vary the arrangements of the appointment: TrA 2000, s 21(2) (Part G, para **[246.136]**). These duties may, however, be expressly excluded: TrA 2000, s 21(3) (Part G, para **[246.136]**). It is submitted, however, that in most cases it will be wise to retain these duties.

4   Under the TrA 2000, s 23 (Part G, para **[246.138]**) trustees appointing a nominee under an express power (as well as under the statutory power), are not liable for the acts and defaults of the nominee unless they have failed to comply with their statutory duty of care when entering into or reviewing the arrangement. This section can, however, be excluded (see TrA 2000, s 21(3): Part G, para **[246.136]**) and a wider indemnity can then be included so that trustees are exonerated from liability for all acts or defaults of the nominee even if they have not complied with the statutory duty of care. For the statutory duty of care, see note 5.

5   Under the TrA 2000, s 2 and Sch 1, para 3(1)(d), (e) (Part G, paras **[246.117]** and **[246.156]**) the statutory duty of care applies where trustees appoint a nominee under an express power. The statutory duty is to exercise such care and skill as is reasonable in the circumstances, having regard in particular to any special knowledge or experience that they have or hold themselves out as having, and if they act as trustees in the course of a business or profession, to any special knowledge or experience that it is reasonable to expect them to have: TrA 2000, s 1(1) and Sch 1, para 3(1)(d), (e) (Part G, paras **[246.116]** and **[246.156]**). It can, however, be excluded: TrA 2000, Sch 1, para 7 (Part G, para **[246.156]**).

[221.34]

FORM B21.30:   **Power to distribute on assumption that no further children**

My trustees shall have power at their absolute discretion to distribute income or capital of my estate or of any fund deriving from it on the assumption that a woman who has attained the age of 55 years will have no further children and if they exercise this power my trustees shall not be liable for the assumption turning out to be incorrect (without prejudice to any beneficiary's right to trace trust assets against any other beneficiary).[1]

1   Existing authority that trustees can distribute on the assumption that a woman of 55 is past the age of childbearing (see Vol 1, paras **[66.3]** and **[216.29]**) can no longer be relied on, because advances in medical science mean that a woman who has passed the menopause could still have a child by means of in vitro fertilisation using donated eggs, and because if this were to happen she would be treated as the mother of the child for all purposes, including gifts by will, by virtue of the HFEA 1990, ss 27 and 29 (Part G, paras **[245.85]** and **[245.87]**). It is still possible to apply to the court for liberty to distribute on the basis of evidence that a particular person having another child is impossible or very unlikely (see *Re Levy Estate Trust* [2000] CLY, para 5263 and *Re Cassidy* [1979] VR 369). There is a statutory presumption that a woman over 55 will not adopt a child: see the AA 1976, s 42(5) (Part G, para **[245.60]**). Provision as in this clause is not usually needed if the beneficial trusts, powers and provisions themselves confer powers, such as a wide power of appointment or powers of advancement over the whole of a presumptive share, which would enable a trust fund to be appointed absolutely or distributed absolutely without waiting to see if more members of a class are born.

Appointment and retirement of trustees

[221.35]

Note. Some of the forms below vary the statutory powers and provisions for the appointment of new trustees contained in the TA 1925, ss 36 and 37. A variation of the powers conferred by the TA 1925 is generally permissible since the TA 1925, s 69(2) provides that the powers conferred by the Act are in addition to powers conferred by a trust instrument and have effect subject to the terms of the instrument. However, it is also thought that a variation of provisions which are ancillary to and part of the powers, though themselves not powers since they are imperative in nature, is also permissible, see *Re Turner's Will Trusts, District Bank Ltd v Turner* [1937] Ch 15 and *London Regional Transport Pension Fund Trustee Co Ltd v Hatt* [1993] PLR 227.

[221.36]

FORM B21.31:   Power to appoint new trustees conferred by the Trustee Act 1925

I declare that the statutory power of appointing new trustees hereof shall be vested in my said wife during her life [*or* widowhood] and after her death [*or* remarriage] in such one or more of my children [*names*] as shall for the time being have attained the age of eighteen years [*or* in such person during his or her life if of full age as shall for the time being have an interest in possession in the trust property in respect whereof a new trustee is to be appointed].[1]

1   The words in these brackets will be applicable where the testator has created several separate and distinct trusts.
     A full power of appointing new trustees is in practice no longer necessary, and is omitted. The TA 1925, s 36 (Part G, para **[246.31]**), confers full powers of appointing new trustees, and (in certain circumstances) power to appoint additional trustees where no trustee is being replaced.

[221.37]

FORM B21.32:   Power to appoint separate trustees of parts of trust property[1]

My trustees shall have power to appoint a separate set of trustees for the part of the trust fund held on trusts for [the children and issue of my son] and a separate set of trustees for the part of the trust fund held on trusts for [the children and issue of my daughter] and any one or more of my trustees making such an appointment may appoint himself or herself to be one of such trustees.

1   The TA 1925, s 37(1)(b), (Part G, para **[246.32]**) authorises the appointment of separate sets of trustees for parts of trust property held on distinct trusts. This express provision would serve as a reminder. Such an appointment might be desirable where a testator has left property upon trusts for his grandchildren, where the trusts for the children of each child of his are distinct.

[221.38]

FORM B21.33:   Power to remove trustees

Any of my trustees may be removed by deed executed by [my widow] during her lifetime.

[221.39]

FORM B21.34:   Clause excluding beneficiaries' statutory right to direct retirement and appointment of trustees

Section[s]19[1] [and 20][2] of the Trusts of Land and Appointment of Trustees Act 1996 shall not apply to the trusts of this my will so that the beneficiaries shall not be entitled to direct any trustee to retire or to direct the appointment of any new trustee.

1   The TLATA 1996, s 19 provides that where no person is nominated for the purpose of appointing new trustees and the beneficiaries under the trust are of full age and capacity and between them absolutely entitled to the settled property, the beneficiaries may give a written direction to a trustee to retire from the trust or give a written direction to the trustees to appoint as a trustee or trustees the person or persons specified in the direction (Part G, para **[246.105]**). This reverses by statute the decision in *Re Brockbank, Ward v Bates* [1948] Ch 206, [1948] 1 All ER 287. The beneficiaries must act unanimously. TLATA 1996, s 19 may, however, be excluded in relation to new settlements and wills: TLATA 1996, s 21(5) (Part G, para **[246.107]**). The requirement of unanimity of the beneficiaries means that theoretically the beneficiaries have protection from each other, but exclusion could well be appropriate where trusts have been or are being created to protect beneficiaries from their own improvidence, or where one beneficiary has too much influence over another. As a practical matter settlements set up with this sort of purpose in mind are unlikely to be ones which will reach a stage where the beneficiaries become collectively entitled (because there are likely to be protective trusts or wide powers of appointment).

2   The TLATA 1996, s 20 gives power, again, to beneficiaries who are of full age and collectively entitled to the beneficial interest, where a trustee is mentally incapacitated and there is nobody with power to appoint a new trustee under the TA 1925, s 36 to direct the trustee's receiver or attorney under an enduring power to appoint a new trustee or trustees specified by the beneficiaries (Part G, para **[246.106]**). It may be excluded in relation to new wills: TLATA 1996, s 21(5) (Part G, para **[246.107]**). In the absence of such a power, an application would have to be made to the Court of Protection for the appointment of a replacement trustee under the MeHA 1983, s 96(1)(k) (Part G, para **[244.112]**). However, even if the TLATA 1996, s 20 does apply, and the beneficiaries direct the appointment of a new trustee, there is no express provision for the trustee's receiver or attorney to vest any trust property which is not subject to automatic vesting under the TA 1925, s 40 (eg stocks and shares) in the new trustee. Therefore, an application to the Court of Protection may still be required.

[221.40]

FORM B21.35:   Direction as to keeping up the number of trustees[1]

I direct that the trustees of this my will shall be never less than [three] in number and that any vacancy in the trusteeship hereof shall be filled up as soon as conveniently may be but nevertheless that the trustees hereof for the time being shall during any vacancy have the same powers authorities and discretions and may act in all respects as if there were [three] or more trustees hereof.

1   It must be remembered that not more than four executors will be allowed to take a grant, but where separate grants are taken to different parts of the estate, the number of executors is limited to four in respect of each grant and is no longer limited to four in all: see the SCA 1981, s 114(1), reversing *Re Holland's Estate* [1936] 3 All ER 13 on this point. In the case of a private trust the trustees should be not more than four. A single trustee can act for most purposes, but a single trustee cannot give a valid receipt for capital moneys on a disposition of land unless a trust corporation.

[221.41]

FORM B21.36:   Variation of statutory power to facilitate appointment of foreign trustees, and a sole trustee

The statutory power to appoint new trustees shall apply subject to the following—

(i)   Any person or persons who may be resident outside the United Kingdom may be appointed as a trustee or trustees hereof and the administration of the trusts hereof may be transferred to a place outside the United Kingdom and from and after any such transfer of the administration of the trusts hereof to a place outside the United Kingdom references in section 36 of the Trustee Act 1925 to the United Kingdom[1] shall in relation to each trustee hereof be treated as references to the territory or jurisdiction in which such trustee was resident at the time when he first became a trustee hereof.

(ii)   Any company corporation or similar incorporated body which undertakes the management and administration of trusts (whether or not a trust corporation) shall be capable of being appointed a trustee hereof and shall be entitled to payment of its normal fees and charges as are from time to time applicable.

(iii)   A a corporation or body satisfying the requirements of the last preceding sub-clause or an individual may be appointed as sole trustee hereof.

(iv)   When more than one person wishes to retire as trustees hereof at the same time and by the same instrument one person or fewer persons than the number retiring may be appointed in their place in exercise of the powers in the said section 36.[2]

(v)   Any appointment of new trustees or deed of retirement of a trustee made with the consent of the co-trustees of the retiring trustee shall be effective to discharge from all the trusts hereof the persons or person expressed therein to be ceasing to be trustees or a trustee hereof provided that after such discharge there shall be at least one individual or a corporation or body satisfying the requirements of sub-clause (ii) above acting as the trustees hereof and sections 37(1)(c) and 39(1) of the Trustee Act 1925 so far as they would prevent any such appointment of new trustees or deed of retirement from being an effective discharge as aforesaid shall be of no effect.[3]

(vi)   In this clause the expressions 'United Kingdom' and 'trust corporation' have the same meanings as in the Trustee Act 1925.[4]

1   TA 1925, s 36(1) (Part G, para **[246.31]**) provides that absence from the UK for more than twelve months is grounds for replacing a trustee.

2   This counters the effect of the decision in *Adam & Co International Trustees v Theodore Goddard* [2000] WTLR 349 that where more than one trustee wishes to retire by means of an appointment of new trustees in their place under the TA 1925, s 36 they cannot do so by the appointment of fewer trustees in their place.

3   TA 1925, ss 37(1)(c) and s 39(1) (as amended by the TLATA 1996 with effect from 1 January 1997: Part G, paras **[246.32]** and **[246.34]**) normally render an appointment of new trustees or a deed of retirement of a trustee ineffective to discharge any retiring trustees or trustee if there will not be two persons or a trust corporation as the trustees immediately afterwards. Trust corporation has a specific meaning that excludes most foreign trust corporations. Therefore, this form enables a single individual or a single non-trust corporation company to be appointed as sole trustee.

4   TA 1925, s 68(18), (20) (Part G, para **[246.36]**). For the meaning of 'trust corporation' see
    para **[221.46]**. It includes certain EC corporations with a place of business in the UK but does
    not otherwise include non-UK corporations.

Power to charge

[221.42]

NOTE – POWERS OF CHARGING AFTER THE TRUSTEE ACT 2000

Statutory and express powers for trustees to charge for their services. It was
formerly the case that generally, a solicitor or other professional person could
not charge for acting as executor or trustee unless the will authorised him to
charge for his services. However, the position has been changed by the TrA
2000 in relation to services provided on and after 1 February 2001, whatever the
date of creation of the trusts: TrA 2000, s 33(1) (Part G, para **[246.148]**). Now
TrA 2000, s 29(2) provides that in the absence of an express remuneration
clause, a trustee or personal representative acting in a professional capacity and
who is not a sole trustee is entitled to receive reasonable remuneration for any
services he provides (including services capable of being provided by a lay
trustee: s 29(4)) if each other trustee has agreed in writing that he may be
remunerated (Part G, para **[246.144]**; see also the TrA 2000, s 35: Part G,
para **[246.150]** for the application of these provisions to personal
representatives). 'Reasonable remuneration' means in relation to the provision of
services by a trustee (or personal representative), such remuneration as is
reasonable in the circumstances for the provision of those services to or on
behalf of that trust (or estate) by him (TrA 2000, s 29(3): Part G,
para **[246.144]**). Furthermore, a trust corporation (see para **[221.47]** for the
meaning of this term), including where it is a sole trustee, is also entitled to
receive reasonable remuneration (TrA 2000, s 29(1)) and special provision is
made for trustees of charitable trusts: TrA 2000, s 30 (Part G, para **[246.145]**). It
is still advisable to include an express remuneration clause in a will if it is
possible that a professional person will act as executor or trustee, because the
statutory provisions will not enable a sole executor or trustee to charge, and
where there are two or more trustees or executors, a professional person among
them will need the written agreement of his co- trustee(s) or executor(s) to do so.
Further, a trustee acting in a professional capacity for the purposes of s 29 is in
some respects quite a narrow concept: see further para **[221.46]**. Therefore, an
express remuneration clause entitling any professional or business person to
charge is also advisable in case such a person falls outside this definition—eg a
testator may appoint a business partner to be executor and trustee and wish him
to have the benefit of a charging clause in respect of carrying on or winding up
the business, or wish a professional or business person whose practice or
business is not concerned with trusts or estates, but who can lend wisdom and
experience to the trustees' deliberations, to be able to charge (and see further
para **[221.46]**).

[221.43]
**Professional trustees' charges for services capable of being provided by a
lay trustee.** In addition to the statutory power of charging described above, the

TrA 2000 makes two important changes to the law regarding trustee or personal representative remuneration under express powers of charging in wills or other trust instruments. The first is that a trustee or personal representative acting in a professional capacity (see TrA 2000, s 28(5): see Part G, para **[246.143]** and para **[221.46]** for this term) or a trust corporation (see para **[221.47]** for this term), in relation to whom there is provision in the will or other trust instrument entitling him to receive payment for services provided to or on behalf of the trust or estate, is entitled to receive payment in respect of services even if they are services which are capable of being provided by someone who is not a trust corporation or someone acting in a professional capacity: TrA 2000, s 28(1)–(3), (6) (Part G, para **[246.143]**). This is subject to any inconsistent provision made by the will or other trust instrument (TrA 2000, s 28(1)) but it applies to any services performed on or after 1 February 2001 even if the trust is created before that date: TrA 2000, s 33(1) (Part G, para **[246.148]**). Before the TrA 2000 came into force, a charging clause which conferred power to charge for professional services did not authorise charging for services which a non-professional trustee could have done unless there was express provision to that effect (*Re Chapple* (1884) 27 Ch D 584, *Clarkson v Robinson* [1900] 2 Ch 722). This change in the law means that if the only trustees or executors who might wish to charge are persons, such as solicitors or accountants, who will act in a professional capacity within the meaning of TrA 2000, s 28, or a trust corporation, the charging clause could be made more concise by leaving out provision that the persons enabled to charge by the clause may charge for things which a lay trustee could do personally (see Form B21.32 at para **[221.49]**). However, express authority to charge for what a lay trustee could do is still relevant where the persons authorised to charge include, or might turn out to include, persons who are not trust corporations and are or may be outside the definition of a trustee acting in a professional capacity in the TrA 2000, s 28(5) (Part G, para **[246.143]** and para **[221.46]** for the meaning of this), or where a new long-term charitable trust is created. The reason for the latter exception is that the statutory extension of an express power to charge for services to matters which a non-professional trustee could do only applies to a trustee of a charitable trust (who is not a trust corporation) if he is not a sole trustee and the other trustees, or a majority of them, agree to him doing so: TrA 2000, s 28(3). The more general point to bear in mind, however, is that as discussed further at para **[221.46]**, 'acting in a professional capacity' is in some respects quite a narrow concept. Accordingly, we recommend that express provision continues to be made that a trustee in a profession or business can charge for services which a non-professional non-business trustee might have performed.

[221.44]
Trustees' remuneration no longer a legacy (in some respects). The second change made by the TrA 2000 to express powers for professional trustees to charge is that it provides that a trustee's (and a personal representative's) remuneration is no longer, for certain purposes, to be regarded as a species of gift, but only in relation to the wills of testators dying on or after the commencement date of the Act, ie 1 February 2001: see TrA 2000, ss 33(2) and 35(4) (Part G, paras **[246.148]** and **[246.150]**) for this restriction on the commencement of this change in the law and the Trustee Act 2000

(Commencement) Order 2001, SI 2001/49 for the commencement date of the Act. It should also be noted that these provisions only relate to the remuneration of a trust corporation: TrA 2000, s 28(1) (for which term see para **[221.47]**), or a trustee acting in a professional capacity within the meaning of TrA 2000, s 28(5) (for which see para**[221.46]**). Thus—

(1)   It is to be regarded as remuneration, and not as a gift, for the purposes of the Wills Act 1837, s 15 (Part G, para **[244.12]**; see also Vol 1, para **[9.3]** et seq): TrA 2000, s 28(4)(a) (Part G, para **[246.143]**). Therefore, where a testator has died on or after 1 February 2001, and a solicitor or other professional person who witnessed his will (whether before, on or after that date) becomes executor or trustee of it, such executor or trustee is not deprived of the benefit of a charging clause by the operation of the Wills Act 1837, s 15 which renders void gifts to any attesting witness. Under common law, remuneration is a gift, and hence an individual who witnessed the will of a testator who died before 1 February 2001 cannot make charges for acting as executor or trustee under an express remuneration clause: see Vol 1, para **[9.11]**. It is not clear, however, whether such an individual is now entitled to remuneration under the statutory entitlement to charge in the TrA 2000, s 29(2) for services provided on or after 1 February 2001 (see para **[221.42]** for this entitlement). This entitlement depends upon there being no provision about his entitlement to remuneration in the will or in any enactment: TrA 2000, s 29(5). Since the effect of the Wills Act 1837, s 15 is to render 'utterly null and void' a remuneration clause in the will so far as regards that individual, it could be said that the will has not made any provision about his entitlement. But then should it be said that the Wills Act 1837, s 15 (ie an enactment) has made provision about his entitlement to remuneration, by denying him an entitlement so that s 29(2) cannot apply? The position is unclear.

(2)   It is to be regarded as remuneration and an administrative expense for the purposes of the AEA 1925, s 34(3) (order in which estate to be paid out: Part G, para **[246.46]**; TrA 2000, ss 28(4)(b) and 35(3)(a): Part G, paras **[246.143]** and **[246.150]**). Formerly, ie in relation to deaths before 1 February 2001, remuneration was regarded as a species of legacy which would abate along with other pecuniary or general legacies if residue was insufficient (see the AEA 1925, Sch 1, Pt II: Part G, para **[246.54]** for the order of application of the assets of a solvent estate in the absence of contrary directions). However, in relation to deaths on or after 1 February 2001, remuneration is now regarded as an administrative expense and so payable as such in priority to legacies.

(3)   It is to be regarded as an administrative expense for the purposes of any provision giving reasonable administrative expenses priority over the preferential debts listed in the Insolvency Act 1986, Sch 6: TrA 2000, s 35(3)(b). The rules regulating the administration of insolvent estates are contained in the Administration of Insolvent Estates of Deceased Persons Order 1986, SI 1986/1999, and Art 4(2) of that Order provides that reasonable funeral, testamentary and administration expenses have priority over the preferential debts listed in the Insolvency Act 1986, Sch 6 (ie debts due to the Inland Revenue; to customs and excise; social

security contributions; contributions to occupational pension schemes; remuneration of employees; and levies on coal and steel production). Therefore, in relation to deaths occurring on or after 1 February 2001, an executor's reasonable remuneration will be payable in priority to preferential debts, other debts and legacies. This means that where an estate is insolvent, a professional need not be deterred from taking a grant of probate, as he may have been in relation to a death prior to 1 February 2001, when he would not have been able to rely upon a remuneration clause in the will to charge for his services since it would have been regarded as a legacy.

[221.45]
Limits of the statutory treatment of trustees' charges as remuneration rather than gift. It should be noted that the change from treating payment to trustees for their services as a legacy, to treating it as remuneration is for the above purposes only; the rule that such payment is a legacy continues to be relevant in at least two contexts and there may be others. The first is that of a professional executor who pays himself fees, after which the grant of probate is revoked. He does not have the protection afforded to purchasers dealing in good faith: see *Gray v Richards Butler* (1996) [2001] WTLR 625 where part of the reasoning behind the decision was that the remuneration counted as a legacy. The second context is where a trustee or personal representative is entitled to charge under the express provisions of the will (or other trust instrument) but is not a trust corporation (see para **[221.47]**) or does not fall within the definition of a trustee acting in a professional capacity in the TrA 2000, s 28(5) (Part G, para **[246.143]**; see also para **[221.46]**).

[221.46]
Trustee acting in a professional capacity. All the provisions of the TrA 2000, ss 28, 29, and 35 concerning trustee and personal representative remuneration discussed at paras **[221.42]–[221.44]** only apply to a trustee acting in a professional capacity, or to a trust corporation (for the latter see para **[221.47]**). The definition of what it is to be a trustee acting in a professional capacity is in TrA 2000, s 28(5) (Part G, para **[246.143]**). To come within this definition it seems that a trustee or personal representative has to satisfy two main requirements. First, he has to be in a profession or business which consists of or includes the provision of services in connection with the management or administration of trusts generally or a particular kind of trust, or which consists of or includes the provision of services in connection with any particular aspect of the management or administration of trusts generally or a particular kind of trust (this is referred to below as 'the qualifying profession or business'). Second, he must act in the course of that profession or business to provide services to or on behalf of the trust which are services in connection with the management or administration of trusts generally or a particular kind of trust, or which are services in connection with any particular aspect of the management or administration of trusts generally or a particular kind of trust (these are referred to below as 'the qualifying services'). It seems that 'trust' here includes 'estate', by virtue of TrA 2000, s 35 (Part G, para **[246.150]**). With respect to these requirements for being a trustee acting in a professional capacity—

(1)   It is not clear whether, in order to be engaged in a qualifying profession or business, it is sufficient to be a member of a profession (such as solicitor) which includes trusts work among the possible kinds of work done by that profession, or whether the trustee must practise, or be a member of a firm which practises, in the management or administration of trusts (or one of the other categories in TrA 2000, s 28(5)). We are inclined to think the latter, but the position is not crystal clear.

(2)   It seems that the qualifying services do not have to be ones which are normally or generally provided in the course of the qualifying profession or business.

(3)   It is clear, however, that the qualifying services have to be provided in the course of the qualifying profession or business. Accordingly, some of the tasks which might be carried out by a trustee who is engaged in a qualifying profession or business might fall outside the clause. Managing the testator's business is a possible example: see *Clarkson v Robinson* [1900] 2 Ch 722 where it was held that a solicitor, an architect, and an accountant could not charge for the time they spent managing the testator's silk-mercer's business where the charging clause confined the right to charge to charging for things done in the course of the trustees' own respective businesses.

(4)   Further to the last point, it seems reasonably clear that the entitlement to charge for services capable of being provided by a lay trustee (TrA 2000, ss 28(2) and 29(4): Part G, paras **[246.143]** and **[246.144]**) is limited to things done in the course of the qualifying profession or business. Thus (for example) a stockbroker who is appointed an executor, and who is in a qualifying profession because he regularly gives investment advice to trustees, would not be able to charge under s 28(2) for attending an executors' meeting to decide on the appropriation of assets to beneficiaries, but could charge for giving investment advice to the executors. An express power of charging such as B21.38 at para **[221.50]** would enable him to charge for attending the trustees' meeting, irrespective of whether he provided services as a stockbroker to the executors.

(5)   The requirement of being in a qualifying profession or business means that a retired member of one would not fall within the statutory provisions, but it should be added that the standard charging clauses do not enable retired members of professions to be able to charge. The requirement also means that persons in professions or businesses unconnected with trusts (eg a doctor) cannot charge under the statutory power, although they could charge for time spent on the affairs of the estate or trust under the usual form of professional trustee charging clause.

(6)   The definition is not confined to individuals, and a company or other corporate body which is not a trust corporation (see para **[221.47]** for what is a trust corporation) can qualify as a trustee acting in a professional capacity, but it would have to be carrying on a qualifying business of providing trust and estate services, and a company incorporated just for the purpose of being trustee of one particular trust (for example) would not qualify.

[221.47]

Meaning of trust corporation. 'Trust corporation' has the same meaning in the TrA 2000 as in the TA 1925: TrA 2000, s 39(1) (Part G, para **[246.151]**). By virtue of the TA 1925, s 68(18) (Part G, para **[246.36]**) 'trust corporation' is confined to the Public Trustee and the corporations specified in the Public Trustee Rules 1912, r 30, as amended (Part G, para **[246.58]**), and corporations appointed by the court to be trustees. See also the Law of Property (Amendment) Act 1926 (Part G, para **[246.56]**) for certain further categories of trust corporation of small relevance to will drafting. The corporations specified in the Public Trustee Rules 1912, r 30 include certain EC corporations with a place of business in the UK but do not otherwise include non-UK corporations. Those included have to satisfy certain requirements, including requirements as to minimum capital, or be incorporated by statute or royal charter, or fall within one of the more specialised categories of, eg public authority, there set out. A corporate trustee outside the UK will thus not usually qualify as a trust corporation for the purposes of the TA 1925 or the TrA 2000, although it may qualify as a trustee acting in a professional capacity for the purposes of the TrA 2000, ss 28 and 29 if it carries on a business of administering trusts (see para **[221.46]**). For the appointment of a trust corporation as executor, see the Notes and Forms in B3 at para **[203.24]** et seq.

[221.48]

Charging by trust corporations. Prior to the coming into force of the TrA 2000, where a power of charging was inserted because a solicitor was appointed trustee it operated to allow a bank to charge its usual fees upon the bank being substituted by codicil for the solicitor: *Re Campbell's Estate* [1954] 1 All ER 448, [1954] 1 WLR 516. On the other hand, in *Re Cooper, Le-Neve Foster v National Provincial Bank* (1939) 160 LTR 453 (not reported on this point in the report at [1939] Ch 580) it was held that a standard professional trustee charging clause did not enable a trust corporation to charge, but no reasons were given and no attention was paid to the LPA 1925, s 61(b) ('person' in a document includes a corporation—see Part G, para **[246.40]**). A standard professional trustee charging clause would only enable a trust corporation to charge on a time basis for work done, however, and would probably not permit charging scale fees based on a percentage of the value of the funds irrespective of the amount of work done. If, in the circumstances of a particular case, the will and codicil cannot be so construed as to confer an entitlement to remuneration upon a trust corporation, then in relation to services performed on or after 1 February 2001, a trust corporation is entitled to reasonable remuneration under the TrA 2000, s 29: see Part G, paras **[246.144]**; see also para **[221.42]**. It is entitled to this remuneration by virtue of being a trust corporation, and does not have to satisfy any of the rules as to co-trustees' agreement (see para **[221.42]**), or as to being in a qualifying profession or business or providing qualifying services (see para **[221.46]**) which an individual (or a corporation which is not a trust corporation) has to satisfy to be entitled to charge under the TrA 2000, s 29. Reasonable remuneration means, in relation to the provision of services by a trustee, such remuneration as is reasonable in the circumstances for the provision of those services to or on behalf of that trust by that trustee and, if the trustee is a trust corporation (and not trustee of a charitable trust) and an authorised institution under the Banking Act 1987 (ie a bank), it includes in relation to the provision of banking services by that trustee, its reasonable charges for doing so: TrA 2000, s 29(3) (Part G, para [246.144]; see also para [203.27]). It seems quite possible that s 29 of the TrA 2000 would not entitle a trust corporation to charge scale fees. Trust corporations will still want express powers to charge scale fees, and will not wish to rely on the statutory power to charge. Where the court appoints a trust corporation as a trustee, it can authorise remuneration under the TA 1925, s 42 and the inherent jurisdiction of the court (see para [203.26]). There is no need to provide for the appointment or payment of the Public Trustee as the statute provides for his appointment and gives him power to charge: Public Trustee Act 1906, s 5. The Public Trustee cannot be appointed where the will expressly forbids such appointment: Public Trustee Act 1906, s 5(3), unless the court orders such appointment. For a declaration that the Public Trustee or a trust corporation shall not be appointed, see Form B3.21 at para [203.38].

[221.49]

FORM B21.37:   Power to professional trustee to charge—concise form[1]

Any of my trustees being a professional or business person may be paid reasonable remuneration for services provided by him in connection with the administration of my estate or any trust of this will or of any codicil hereto.

1   Where the only trustees or executors who might wish to charge will be trustees or personal representatives acting in a professional capacity within the meaning of the TrA 2000, s 28 (Part G, para [246.143]; see also para [221.46]), it is not necessary to provide expressly that such persons can charge for services which a non-professional trustee could provide, as this is permitted by the TrA 2000, s 28(2): see para [221.43]. This form could be used in wills for use in emergencies and simple wills giving immediate and absolute interests, but otherwise we recommend the traditional form of charging clause: see paras [221.36], n 1, [221.43] and [221.46].

[221.50]

FORM B21.38:   Power to professional trustee to charge—full form

Any of my trustees being in a profession or business may charge and be paid all usual professional and other proper charges for business transacted acts done advice given and time spent by him or his firm in connection with the administration of my estate or in connection with the trusts hereof including acts which a personal representative or trustee not being in any profession or business could have done personally.[1]

1   The express provision for a trustee to charge for acts which a lay trustee or personal representative could have done is no longer strictly necessary where the trustee will be acting in a professional capacity within the meaning of the TrA 2000, s 28(5) (Part G, para [246.143]; see also paras [221.43] and [221.46]), because the TrA 2000, s 28(2) provides that where there is an express remuneration clause, such a trustee or personal representative is entitled to receive payment for services which are capable of being provided by a lay trustee. As noted at para [221.46] the definition of a trustee acting in a professional capacity is quite narrow in scope. We therefore recommend that the traditional form of charging clause, as in this Form, continues to be used (except in the situations mentioned at para [221.49], n 1.

[221.51]

FORM B21.39: Proviso enabling professional trustee to elect not to charge[1]

. . . provided that any of my trustees being engaged in a profession or business who elects in writing not to charge for acting as my personal representative or as a trustee of this will at or before the time of his obtaining a grant of representation or (not having obtained such a grant) his being first appointed as a trustee hereof shall not be entitled as provided in the foregoing clause or by statute[2] (but shall be entitled to be relieved from liability under Clause —— above).[3]

1 This is a proviso which can be added to a professional charging clause such as Form B21.37 at para **[221.49]** or B21.38 at para **[221.50]**, where there is an indemnity clause such as Form B21.12 at para **[221.16]**, inclusive of the parts in square brackets.
2 Ie the TrA 2000, s 29(1) (see para **[221.42]**).
3 See Form B21.12 at para **[221.16]** and n 2 thereto.

[221.52]

FORM B21.40: Provision for appointment of trust corporation[1]

My trustees in exercising the power of appointment vested in them by statute may if they so desire appoint a trust corporation to be either the sole trustee hereof or to be a trustee along with another or other trustees and in the event of a trust corporation being so appointed I hereby authorise such trust corporation to charge and my trustees to pay out of my estate such fees and remuneration[2] as is agreed upon between my trustees and the said trust corporation at the time of such appointment [*or* according to the scale of fees charged by such trust corporation from time to time].[3]

1 Most trust corporations have their own form of clause and it is wiser to ask for their consent to act in advance and to incorporate their form of clause. For the meaning of trust corporation, see para **[221.17]**. As mentioned in that paragraph, certain foreign corporations of EC countries now fall within the meaning of the term. See also Form B21.36 at para **[231.41]** and for forms appointing corporations as executors see Forms B3.11 to B3.13 at paras **[203.28]–[203.31]**. Trust corporations now have a statutory power to charge under the TrA 2000, s 29 (see para **[221.42]**) but will still want an express clause so as to be certain of being able to charge scale fees (see para **[221.48]**).
2 The trust corporation will be entitled to receive payment in respect of services even if they are services which are capable of being provided by a lay trustee: TrA 2000, s 28(2): Part G, para **[246.143]**; see also para **[221.43]**.
3 For the entitlement of a trust corporation to remuneration under the TrA 2000, s 29 (Part G, para **[246.144]**) in the absence of express provision, and which is not thought to include charging scale fees, see para **[221.48]**.

B22 Testimonium and attestation clauses

PRELIMINARY NOTE

[222.1]

Care must be taken to use a recognised form of attestation clause, since if such a clause is used, a grant in common form will be obtained almost as a matter of course and no further proof of due attestation according to law will be required. The ordinary procedure for attestation is: (i) signature by the testator; (ii) the testator's signature must be written or acknowledged in the presence of two witnesses; (iii) the two witnesses then sign in the presence of the testator and of each other. That at any rate is the ordinary practice but it is not essential in law that the witnesses should sign in the presence of each other, and a witness may now sign before, and acknowledge his signature after, the testator has signed or acknowledged (See Vol 1, para **[12.1]**). The witnesses must sign or acknowledge in the presence of the testator, which means that he should be able to see the act of signing of the signature if he cares to do so. A blind person cannot witness a will. See the WA 1837, s 9, substituted by the AJA 1982, s 17 (Part G, para **[244.7]**; see also Vol 1, para **[12.15]**). In accordance with the wording of the substituted s 9, the attestation clauses which follow now state that the witnesses 'have signed our names below as witnesses' instead of the former 'have here unto subscribed our names as witnesses'.

[222.2]

To prevent disputes arising afterwards, it is usual to make certain variations in the attestation clause in certain circumstances. If there are alterations or interlineations or erasures in the will, it is an advantage though not essential to note these in the attestation clause in order to provide evidence that they were made before execution of the will. It is in law quite sufficient if the alterations etc are initialled by the testator and the witnesses at or near the place where they occur without being mentioned in the attestation clause. Where the testator is suffering from any infirmity it is usual for the attestation clause to add that the testator had the will read over to him and appeared fully to understand it. If despite the infirmity the testator can read though it might be thought that he would not be able to do so, then the fact that he read and understood the will should be noted in the clause. Where the infirmity is such that his testamentary capacity might be impugned then care must be taken to choose witnesses of such standing that there can be no doubt that their opinion as to his mental capacity is to be trusted. In any case where the will is likely to be contested on this ground, the witnesses should preferably be persons who can readily be traced if difficulties arise. A common precaution in such cases is to arrange for one witness to be a medical practitioner and the other a solicitor and to take statements as to the question of the testator's capacity from them both. It must be remembered that neither witness nor the husband or wife of a witness can take any benefit under the will. Where a testator died before 1 February 2001, a solicitor's charging clause creates such a benefit so that a solicitor will be unable to take advantage of it if he is a witness. The only exception is where such attestation is superfluous within the Wills Act 1968 (Part G, para **[243.81]**). However, in respect of deaths on or after 1 February 2001, a professional charging clause will not be regarded as such a benefit, so that a solicitor who witnessed the will of a testator dying on or after 1 February 2001, will be able to take advantage of it: TrA 2000, ss 28(4)(a) and 33(2)(a) (Part G, paras **[246.143]** and **[246.148]**; see also Vol 1, para **[9.11]**). For the particular requirements for the execution of a will on behalf of a patient see Vol 1, paras **[4.21]–[4.24]**, Form B22.14 at para **[222.16]** and the note thereto and the Mental Health Act 1983, s 97 (Part G, para **[244.113]**).

[222.3]

FORM B22.1:   Usual form of testimonium and attestation[1]

IN WITNESS whereof I have hereunto set my hand this —— day of —— 20—[2].

SIGNED by the above-named [*testator*] as his last will in the presence of us present at the same time who at his request and in his presence and in the presence of each other have signed our names below as witnesses: [*Signature of testator.*]

[*Signatures, addresses and descriptions of two witnesses*]

1   This is the full form of attestation clause. The shorter forms given in the three following forms are also accepted.

As to the formalities required for execution and attestation, see Vol 1, Chs 11 and 12. It is not necessary that the witnesses should sign in the presence of each other, but it has long been the practice for them to do so. The addresses and descriptions of the witnesses should be added to their signatures. No one who or whose spouse takes a benefit under the will can be a witness without that benefit being lost, but the fact that a person is executor or trustee does not per se prevent such person or his or her spouse from being a witness, though any legacy to which he or she would otherwise have been entitled will be forfeited. Whether remuneration under a professional charging clause is lost depends on the date of death of the testator: if he died before 1 February 2001, it is lost; if he died on or after 1 February 2001 the witness may take advantage of it, see para [222.2] and Vol 1, paras [9.3]–[9.12].

2   Wills are usually dated in the testimonium clause, but there is no objection to the date appearing at the commencement of the will when this clause may be adapted by use of the words 'the day and year first above written.' Though the words 'In witness' are commonly associated with execution as a deed, they are almost invariably used in the testimonium of a will although that document is now executed under hand. Execution as a deed might possibly be required if some foreign element is involved, but not otherwise.

[222.4]

FORM B22.2:   Short form of testimonium and attestation[1]

AS WITNESS my hand this ―― day of ―― 20 ―.

SIGNED by the testator in our presence and then by us }   [*Signature of*
in his: *testator.*]

[*Signatures, addresses and descriptions of two witnesses*]

1   This is thought to be the shortest acceptable form of attestation clause. It makes it clear that all the statutory requirements have been complied with. It was learned from the Principal Probate Registry (now the Principal Registry of the Family Division) that this form is accepted in that Registry and all District Registries, and is indeed welcomed because it enables Registrars to see at a glance that the requirements are all satisfied.

[222.5]

FORM B22.3:   Alternative form of attestation clause[1]

SIGNED by the above-named [*testator*] as his last will
in the joint presence of himself and us who at his   [*Signature of*
request and in such joint presence have signed our   *testator.*]
names below as witnesses

[*Signatures, addresses and descriptions of two witnesses*]

1   See notes to Form B22.1 at para [222.3]. One point of a shortened form is that, where wills are prepared in an emergency, it is often necessary to write down an attestation clause from memory and the shorter the clause the easier it is to memorise. There is, however, so little difference between this clause and Form B22.1 at para [222.3], that it is almost as easy to memorise the full clause as this version. Form B22.2 supra is the shortest and easiest to memorise of these attestation clauses.

[222.6]

FORM B22.4:   Further alternative form of attestation clause[1]

SIGNED by the above-named [*testator*] in our presence
and attested by us in the presence of him and each other   } [*Signature of testator.*]

[*Signatures, addresses and descriptions of two witnesses*]

1   This form was approved in *Re Selby-Bigge* [1950] 1 All ER 1009.

[222.7]

FORM B22.5:   Form where testator signs with his mark

IN WITNESS whereof I have hereunto set my hand this —— day of —— 20 —.

SIGNED by the said [*testator*] with his mark as his last
will (the same having been previously read over to him
by [*name*] [me the undersigned [*name*]] when he
seemed thoroughly to understand the same) in the   } [*Testator's mark.*]
presence of us present at the same time who at his
request in his presence and in the presence of each other
have signed our names below as witnesses
[*Signatures, addresses and descriptions of two witnesses*]

[222.8]

FORM B22.6:   Form where another signs on behalf of the testator

IN WITNESS whereof I have hereunto set my hand this —— day of —— 20—.

SIGNED by [*person signing*] with the name of the said
[*testator*] as his last will (the same having been
previously read over to him by [*name*] [me the
undersigned [*name*]] when he seemed thoroughly to   } [*Testator's name.*]
understand the same) in his presence and by his
direction and in the presence of us present at the same
time who at the request and in the presence of the said
[*testator*] and in the presence of each other have signed
our names below as witnesses
[*Signatures, addresses and descriptions of two witnesses*]

[222.9]

FORM B22.7:   Form where the testator is blind[1]

IN WITNESS whereof I have hereunto set my hand this —— day of —— 20—.

THIS will having been first read over to the said [*testator*] (who is blind) [by me the undersigned [*name*] in the presence also of me the undersigned [*name*]] [in our presence] when the said [*testator*] appeared thoroughly to understand the same and to approve the contents thereof was signed by the said [*testator*][2] as his last will in the presence of us present at the same time who at his request in his presence and in the presence of each other have signed our names below as witnesses

[*Testator's signature or name if another signs for him.*]

[*Signatures, addresses and descriptions of two witnesses*]

1 In this and the following form the clause must be so worded that so far as possible the testator's infirmity has been provided for. The essentials are to show that (i) the testator despite his infirmity understood the document, (ii) that he intended it for his will, (iii) that he signed it either with a signature or mark or authorised someone to sign it on his behalf. Appropriate words from these clauses should be inserted in any particular case with respect to the particular matters which may be in doubt. As to attestation clauses in cases of blind persons, see Non-Contentious Probate Rules 1987, r 13.
2 It is not impossible for a blind testator to sign. If, however, he is unable to sign he may make his mark, when after the word 'signed' there should be added 'by his mark'. Alternatively another may sign for him, when the clause should run as follows: 'was signed by [*name of person signing*] by his direction as his last will in the presence,' etc.

[222.10]

FORM B22.8:   Form of attestation where the testator is deaf and dumb but is able to read

SIGNED as and for his last will by the above-named [*testator*] who is deaf and dumb but is able to read he having first read over the contents hereof and signified his understanding and approval thereof in the presence of us present at the same time who at his request in his presence and in the presence of each other have signed our names below as witnesses

[*Signature of testator.*]

[*Signatures, addresses and descriptions of two witnesses*]

[222.11]

FORM B22.9:   Form of testimonium and attestation clause to a codicil

IN WITNESS whereof I have hereunto set my hand this —— day of —— 20—.

SIGNED by the said [*testator*] as a codicil to his will which bears date the—day of—in the presence of us present at the same time who at his request in his presence and in the presence of each other have signed our names below as witnesses

[*Signature of testator.*]

[*Signatures, addresses and descriptions of two witnesses*]

Part B   Clauses in wills

[222.12]

FORM B22.10:   Form of attestation where the testator acknowledges a signature which he or another has made previously

SIGNED by the said [*testator*] [*or* by *person signing*]
with the name of the said [*testator*] in his presence and
by his direction] and acknowledged by him as his last   [*Signature of
will in the presence of us present at the same time who   testator.*]
at his request in his presence and in the presence of each
other have signed our names below as witnesses

[*Signatures, addresses and descriptions of two witnesses*]

[222.13]

FORM B22.11:   Form of attestation where the testator acknowledges a signature which he has made previously—short form[1]

SIGNED by the testator and his signature acknowledged   [*Signature of
by him in our presence and our names then signed by us   testator.*]
in his presence

[*Signatures, addresses and descriptions of two witnesses*]

1   The WA 1837, s 9 (Part G, para **[244.7]**) allows the witnesses to witness the acknowledgment
     rather than the signing by the testator of his signature, provided that the signature was
     previously put there by the testator or by some other person in the testator's presence and by his
     direction. It is also possible for a witness to acknowledge his signature in some circumstances
     (see s 9(d)(ii)).

[222.14]

FORM B22.12:   Form of attestation where the will has been altered[1]

SIGNED by the above-named [*testator*] as his last will
in the presence of us present at the same time who at his
request and in his presence and in the presence of each   [*Signature of
other have signed our names below as witnesses the   testator.*]
alteration [*or* erasure *or* interlineation] in line—on
page—hereof having been made previously thereto

[*Signatures, addresses and descriptions of two witnesses*]

1   The alterations, erasures or interlineations will be initialled in the margin by the testator and the
     witnesses where they occur. As to this, see Vol 1, Ch 14. Although only one alteration is noted
     in the precedent, the clause should refer to all alterations made in the will if more than one.

[222.15]

FORM B22.13:   Attestation clause where the testator has an imperfect knowledge of English[1]

THIS will having first been read over to the said
[*testator*] (who understands the [Italian] language but
has an imperfect knowledge of and cannot read the
English language) by me the undersigned [*first witness*]
in English and having been truly interpreted to the said
[*testator*] by me the undersigned [*second witness*] who
understands both the English and [Italian] languages [*or*
both of whom the said [*witnesses*] understand both the   [*Signature of*
English and [Italian] languages] which reading and   *testator.*]
interpretation were both done in our presence when the
said [*testator*] appeared thoroughly to understand this
will and to approve the contents thereof was signed by
the said [*testator*] with his mark as his last will in the
presence of us both present at the same time who at his
request in his presence and in the presence of each other
have signed our names below as witnesses

[*Signatures, addresses and descriptions of two witnesses*]

1   As to attestation clauses in cases of illiterate persons, see Non-Contentious Probate Rules 1987,
    r 13.

[222.16]

FORM B22.14:   Forms of testimonium and attestation clause for will made on behalf of a mentally disordered person pursuant to an order of the Court of Protection[1]

A.   TESTIMONIUM CLAUSE

AS WITNESS the hand of the said [*testator*] acting by the said [*authorised person*] this [*date*]

B.   ATTESTATION CLAUSE

SIGNED by the said [*authorised person*] with the name
of the said [*testator*] and with his own name both   [*Testator*] by
signatures being made in our presence and then signed   [*Authorised*
by us in the presence of the said [*authorised person*]   *person*]
[*Signatures, addresses and descriptions of witnesses.*]

1   For the powers of the Court of Protection to order a will to be made on behalf of a patient, see
    note to Form B1.8 at para **[201.12]**. The requirements for the execution of a will on behalf of a
    patient are set out in the MeHA 1983, s 97 and are reflected in the terms of this Form. It should
    be noted that s 97 also requires that the will should be impressed with the seal of the Court of
    Protection, (Part G, para **[244.113]**). See generally Vol 1, paras **[4.21]**–**[4.24]**.

Complete wills

C1   Wills for use in emergency

[223.1]
Note. This section contains a selection of short forms which may be used or adapted for use in emergency. The advent of word processors and data banks has made it much easier than formerly to produce at speed a full form of will. But situations may still arise when this is not possible and a short will may be necessary. A short will may not be ideal but can be replaced by a fuller form of will if time allows and will undoubtedly be preferable to no will at all. For the professional adviser there is the added consideration that the failure to prepare a will for execution in a death-bed situation may expose him to a liability in negligence to the intended beneficiary for the loss caused by such failure: see *White v Jones* [1995] 2 AC 207, [1995] 1 All ER 691, HL; *Gartside v Sheffield Young and Ellis* [1983] NZLR 37, NZCA; and *Hooper v Fynmores* (2001) 5 Sol Jo LB 156, in each of which a relatively short delay in the preparation of a will by a professional draftsman was held to give rise to liability in negligence (by contrast in *X v Woolcombe Yonge* [2001] WTLR 301 a very short delay was held on the facts not to give rise to liability).

As wide powers of investment are now conferred by Parts II and III of the Trustee Act 2000 (TrA 2000) (Part G, paras **[246.118]**–**[246.125]**; see also paras **[220.11]**–**[220.39]**), none need be included. Professional executors and trustees now have power to charge under TrA 2000, ss 29 and 35 (Part G, paras **[246.144]** and **[246.150]**; see also paras **[221.42]**–**[221.48]**), but this power is not available to a sole executor or trustee and is not otherwise available unless all the co-executors or co-trustees agree in writing. Forms C1.8 at para **[223.9]** and C1.9 at para **[223.10]** accordingly contain a short-form charging power which will not be subject to these restrictions.

Part C   Complete wills

[223.2]

FORM C1.1:   Gift of entire estate to one person[1]

I [*name*] of [*address*] revoke all former testamentary dispositions and declare this to be my last will.

I give all property real and personal over which I have power to dispose by will to my [wife/husband] [*name*] absolutely and appoint [her/him] to be the sole [executrix/executor] hereof.

AS WITNESS my hand this ⸺ day of ⸺ 20⸺

SIGNED by the [testator/testatrix] in our presence and } *[Signature of*
then by us in [his/hers][2]   } *testator/testatrix]*

[Signatures, addresses and descriptions of two witnesses]

1   This form will usually be used by one spouse in favour of the other. But it can be used in any situation where one person wishes to give his or her entire estate to another person, eg a common law spouse or unmarried partner. In the latter case a will, however rudimentary in form, will be essential as the intended beneficiary will almost certainly have no rights on intestacy.

2   In the forms in this section this short form of attestation clause has been used, which is thought to be the shortest acceptable form of attestation clause. It makes it clear that all the statutory requirements have been complied with. It was learned from the Principal Probate Registry (now the Principal Registry of the Family Division) that this form is accepted in that Registry and all District Registries, and is indeed welcomed because it enables Registrars to see at a glance that the requirements are all satisfied.

[223.3]

FORM C1.2:   Gift of entire estate to children[1]

I [*name*] of [*address*] revoke all former testamentary dispositions and declare this to be my last will.

I appoint [*name*] of [*address*] and [*name*] of [*address*] to be the executors and trustees of this my will.

Subject to the payment thereout of my funeral and testamentary expenses and debts I give all my real and personal property to my trustees upon trust for such of my children as survive me and if more than one in equal shares.

AS WITNESS my hand this ⸺ day of ⸺ 20⸺

SIGNED by the [testator/testatrix] in our presence and } *[Signature of*
then by us in [his/hers][2]   } *testator/testatrix]*

[Signatures, addresses and descriptions of two witnesses]

1   This form does not contain a substitutional provision in favour of the children of a child who predeceases the testator. Such a provision is unnecessary as it is supplied by the WA 1837, s 33, as substituted by the AJA 1982 (Part G, para **[244.34]** and discussed in Vol 1, paras **[47.10]**–**[47.19]**).

[223.4]

FORM C1.3:   **Will incorporating gift of residue on discretionary charitable trusts**[1]

I [*name*] of [*address*] revoke all former testamentary dispositions and declare this to be my last will.

I appoint [*name*] of [*address*] and [*name*] of [*address*] to be the executors and trustees of this my will.

[I give the following pecuniary legacies free of inheritance tax:

(a)   to [*name*] the sum of £——
(b)   to [*name*] the sum of £——
(c)   to [*name*] the sum of £——].

Subject to the payment thereout of my funeral and testamentary expenses and debts [and the legacies hereby given] I give all property over which I have power to dispose by will to my trustees upon trust for such charitable purposes or charitable bodies as my trustees may determine and I request my trustees (but without imposing any binding trust or obligation on them) to distribute my residuary estate [amongst charities established for charitable purposes connected with——][2] [equally between the following charities namely:

(a)   [*name*]
(b)   [*name*]
(c)   [*name*].]

AS WITNESS my hand this —— day of —— 20——

SIGNED by the [testator/testatrix] in our presence and then by us in [his/hers][2]   } [*Signature of testator/testatrix*]

[*Signatures, addresses and descriptions of two witnesses*]

1   This will is intended for a childless and unmarried person who wishes to give some legacies to friends and the residue of his estate to charities of his choice but in circumstances where there is no time to confirm the existence or ascertain the correct description of such charities.
2   The first alternative enables the testator to indicate what type of charity he would like to benefit, eg charities connected with animal welfare or the relief of child poverty, rather than having to specify the charity or charities by name.

[223.5]

FORM C1.4:   **Will incorporating instructions for will**[1]

I [*name*] of [*address*] hereby revoke all former testamentary dispositions and declare this to be my last will.

I appoint [*name*] of [*address*] and [*name*] of [*address*] to be the executors and trustees of this my will.

I give all my real and personal property over which I have any power to dispose by will to my trustees upon trust to carry out the instructions attached hereto.

I declare that in giving effect to the said instructions my trustees shall have all the powers of management administration and investment of a sole beneficial owner of my estate.

AS WITNESS my hand this —— day of —— 20——

SIGNED by the [testator/testatrix] in our presence and } *[Signature of*
then by us in [his/hers][2]   } *testator/testatrix]*

[Signatures, addresses and descriptions of two witnesses]

[Annex instructions]

1   This form is intended for use only where the state of health of the testator is such that the will must be executed without delay. Where a will in this form is executed and the testator recovers sufficiently to execute a longer form of will, it would be advisable for him to do so. The efficacy of this form obviously depends on whether the instructions as taken down by the solicitor are sufficiently clear and certain in their legal consequences to be taken as the testator's dispositions.

[223.6]

FORM C1.5:   Settled gift of residue on trusts for spouse and children by reference to Statutory Will FORMS[1]

I *[name]* of *[address]* hereby revoke all former testamentary dispositions and declare this to be my last will.

1.   I appoint *[name]* of *[address]* and *[name]* of *[address]* to be the executors and trustees hereof.

2.

(a)   I bequeath to *[name]* [my gold watch and chain] [my emerald necklace] free of inheritance tax.

(b)   I bequeath the residue of my personal chattels to my [wife/husband] *[name]*.

3.   I bequeath the following pecuniary legacies free of inheritance tax:

(a)   To *[name]* the sum of £——.

(b)   To *[name]* the sum of £——.

4.   I devise and bequeath all my estate both real and personal whatsoever and wheresoever to my trustees.

5.   Form 8 of the Statutory Will Forms 1925[2] is incorporated in this my will and shall apply to all my estate [save that any income of my estate which has accrued in respect of a period wholly or partly before my death but is actually received after my death shall be deemed to have accrued after my death and shall not be apportioned] [and] [save that no sale shall be made of the dwellinghouse in which I now reside known as *[name]* during the lifetime of my [wife/husband] without [her/his] consent in writing and that until the sale thereof my trustees shall permit my [wife/husband] to occupy the same so long as [she/he] shall so desire].[3]

6.   Form 10 of the Statutory Will Forms 1925[4] is incorporated in this my will and subject as provided in clause 5 hereof shall apply to all my property.

7. Any of my trustees being a solicitor or other person engaged in any profession or business shall be entitled to charge and be paid all usual professional or other proper charges for all business transacted or acts done by him or his firm in the administration of my estate or in connection with the trusts hereof including acts which a personal representative or trustee could have done personally.

AS WITNESS my hand this —— day of —— 20——

SIGNED by the [testator/testatrix] in our presence and then by us in [his/hers][2] } [*Signature of testator/testatrix*]

[*Signatures, addresses and descriptions of two witnesses*]

1   The Statutory Will Forms (which are printed in full at paras **[238.7]**–**[238.16]**) provide a useful shorthand method of incorporating fairly elaborate beneficial and administrative provisions. The disadvantage is that the testator cannot immediately see the nature and effect of his will.
2   Form 8 of the Statutory Will Forms, the text of which is set out at para **[238.14]**, contains an elaborate administration trust which includes (in para (5)) a power to invest in 'authorised investments'. This paragraph now incorporates by implication the wide powers of investment conferred by Pts II and III of the TrA 2000 (Part G, paras **[246.118]**–**[246.125]**). No express power of investment is therefore required and none is included. (As to investment powers generally see the Preliminary Note to B20 (para **[220.11]** et seq) and Forms B20.1 to B20.9 at paras **[220.40]**–**[220.48]**. Form 8 of the Statutory Will Forms excludes the rule in *Howe v Dartmouth*, but not apportionment of income at the testator's death. If it is desired to exclude such apportionment, the first proviso should be added. The provisions of Form 8, cl (7)(c) leave the trustees free to apply or to exclude the rule in *Allhusen v Whittell*. For the rules of equitable apportionment see Vol 1, para **[38.17]** et seq, and for a discussion of methods of excluding them see the Note to B14 at para **[214.35]** et seq.
3   As to conferring rights of residence, see the Preliminary Note to B8 (para **[208.19]** et seq). The right of occupation conferred on the wife by this clause does not create a strict settlement as it has not been possible to create strict settlements after 1996: TLATA 1996, s 2 (Part G, para **[246.87]**.
4   Form 10 of the Statutory Will Forms, the text of which is set out at para **[238.16]**, confers a life interest on the testator's spouse with remainder on stirpital trusts for his issue at 21 (Form 10 of the Statutory Will Forms has not been amended so as to reduce the vesting age to 18 despite the reduction of the age of majority to 18 by the FLRA 1969, s 1).

[223.7]

FORM C1.6:   Will expressly incorporating intestacy rules[1]

I [*name*] of [*address*] hereby revoke all former testamentary dispositions and declare this to be my last will.

1.   I appoint [*name*] of [*address*] and [*name*] of [*address*] to be the executors and trustees of this my will.

2.   I give the following pecuniary legacies free of inheritance tax:

(a)   to [*name*] the sum of £——
(b)   to [*name*] the sum of £——
(c)   to [*name*] the sum of £——.

3.   Subject as aforesaid I give all my real and personal property to my trustees upon the same trusts as to the sale and administration thereof and as to the beneficial interests therein as if I had died intestate in respect thereof.[2]

4.   Any of my trustees being a solicitor or other person engaged in any profession or business shall be entitled to charge and be paid all professional or

other proper charges for all business transacted or acts done by him or his firm in the administration of my estate or in connection with the trusts hereof including acts which a personal representative or trustee could have done personally.

AS WITNESS my hand this —— day of —— 20——

SIGNED by the [testator/testatrix] in our presence and } [*Signature of*
then by us in [his/hers]² } *testator/testatrix*]

[*Signatures, addresses and descriptions of two witnesses*]

1   This form engrafts the appointment of executors and the bequest of legacies on to a disposition
     of residue by reference to the intestacy rules. If the testator recovers he would be well advised
     to execute a new will declaring express trusts of residue.
2   See the AEA 1925, ss 33, 46 and 47 (Part G, paras **[244.58]**, **[244.60]** and **[244.61]**). The spouse
     takes the 'personal chattels' (as to these, see Vol 1, para **[64.44]** and the definition in the AEA
     1925, s 55(1)(x): Part G, para **[246.52]**), a net sum (currently of £125,000 where there are
     surviving issue) with interest (at the current rate of 6 per cent per annum) from the date of death
     until payment or appropriation and a life interest in half the residue. Subject to the interests of
     the spouse the issue take the residue with stirpital substitution throughout.

[223.8]

FORM C1.7:   Adoption of intestacy rules by revocation of former wills¹

I [*name*] of [*address*] hereby revoke all former testamentary dispositions and declare that it is my intention to die intestate.

AS WITNESS my hand this —— day of —— 20——

SIGNED by the [testator/testatrix] in our presence and } [*Signature of*
then by us in [his/hers]² } *testator/testatrix*]

[*Signatures, addresses and descriptions of two witnesses*]

1   It is generally more convenient to prove a will than to obtain a grant of administration. A will in
     the form of the previous precedent is therefore preferable. But a revocation is a very short form
     which may be convenient to use in an emergency. A revocation must be executed in the
     same way as a will: see the WA 1837, s 20 (Part G, para **[244.20]**. See also Vol 1, para **[18.1]**
     et seq.

[223.9]

FORM C1.8:   Settled gift of residue on express trusts for spouse and children

I [*testator*] of [*address*] hereby revoke all former testamentary dispositions and declare this to be my last will.

    1.   I appoint [*name*] of [*address*] and [*name*] of [*address*] (hereinafter called 'my trustees' which expression shall include the trustees for the time being of this will) to be the executors and trustees hereof.

    2.   (1)   I bequeath the following items free of inheritance tax:

    (a)   to my son [*name*] my father's cuff-links
    (b)   to my daughter [*name*] my mother's engagement ring.

(2)   Subject as aforesaid I bequeath all my personal chattels within the meaning of section 55(1)(x) of the Administration of Estates Act 1925[1] to my [wife/ husband] absolutely.

3.   I bequeath:

(a) £—— to my [wife/husband] absolutely to be paid as soon as possible and in priority to all other legacies.

(b) £—— free of inheritance tax to each of my executors who shall prove my will.

4.   Subject to the payment thereout of my debts and funeral and testamentary expenses and the legacies hereby given my trustees shall hold the residue of my estate both real and personal:

(a) Upon trust to pay the income thereof to my [wife/husband] during [her/his] life [or until [she/he] shall remarry] [with power for my trustees (not being fewer than two in number) during such period to pay or apply the whole or any part of the capital thereof to [her/him] or for [her/his] benefit in such manner as they think fit[2]] and subject thereto.

(b) Upon trust as to capital and income for such of my children as shall survive me [and attain the age of [18/21/25] years] and if more than one in equal shares [provided that if any of my children shall predecease me or survive me but fail to attain a vested interest leaving a child or children surviving me or born after my death who shall attain the age of [18/21] years such last-mentioned child or children shall take and if more than equally between them the share which their parent would have taken had he or she lived to attain a vested interest].[3]

5.   In relation to my estate my trustees shall have all the powers of management and investment of a sole beneficial owner.

6.   The power of appointing trustees of my will shall be vested in my [wife/husband] during [her/his] life.

7.   Any of my trustees being a professional or business person may be paid reasonable remuneration for services provided by him as personal representative or trustee[4].

[8.   My [wife/husband] may join in exercising the power to pay or apply capital for [her/his] benefit hereby conferred notwithstanding that [she/he] is a trustee hereof.][5]

AS WITNESS my hand this —— day of —— 20——

SIGNED by the [testator/testatrix] in our presence and then by us in [his/hers][2]   }   *[Signature of testator/testatrix]*

[Signatures, addresses and descriptions of two witnesses]

---

1   See para **[246.52]** infra for the wording of this definition, and for further discussion of the meaning of 'personal chattels' see Vol 1, para **[64.44]**.

2   If the power to apply capital is included, it would be advisable to include a provision in the terms of cl 8 in case there is subsequently appointed a trustee. But such provision will not be necessary if the spouse is named as a trustee by the will itself: *Sargeant v National Westminster Bank plc* (1990) 61 P & CR 518, CA, 523; and *Edge v Pensions Ombudsman* [1998] Ch 512, 540–542.

3   If an age contingency is included in the primary gift for the children, the substitutional proviso should be added. This is because it is not clear whether the WA 1837, s 33 (Part G, para **[244.34]**) will apply where there is a class gift subject to a contingency of attaining a particular age, and anyway s 33 will not apply to the share of a child who survives the testator but fails to attain the specified age: see Vol 1, para **[47.17]**.

4   A professional executor or trustee is only entitled to charge under the powers conferred by the TrA 2000, ss 29 and 35 (Part G, paras **[246.144]** and **[246.150]**) if his co-executors or co-trustees agree in writing. A sole executor or trustee is not entitled to charge under the statutory power. An express charging provision as in cl 7 enables a professional executor or trustee to charge without obtaining the consent of his co-trustees and to charge if he is a sole executor or trustee. Under the TrA 2000, s 28(2) (Part G, para **[246.143]**) a professional trustee (and executor: see s 35) who has the benefit of an express power to charge is entitled to charge for services which are capable of being provided by a lay trustee and so a short form such as this will be adequate for the purpose.

5   See n 2 supra.

[223.10]

FORM C1.9:   Gift of estate on discretionary trusts for family[1]

I [*name*] of [*address*] revoke all former testamentary dispositions and declare this to be my last will.

1.   I appoint [*name*] of [*address*] and [*name*] of [*address*] (hereinafter called 'my trustees' which expression shall include the trustees for the time being of this will) to be the executors and trustees of this will.

2.   Subject to the payment thereout of my debts and my funeral and testamentary expenses my trustees shall hold all my estate both real and personal upon the trusts and with and subject to the powers and provisions hereinafter declared and contained.

3.   (1)   In this clause—

(a)   'the beneficiaries' means and includes
    (i)   my [wife/husband] [*name*]
    (ii)   my children and remoter issue
    (iii)   the spouse widow or widower of any of my children and remoter issue;[2]

(b)   'the trust period' means the period of 80 years immediately following my death[3] which shall be the perpetuity period applicable to the disposition effected by this will.

(2)   My trustees shall have the following powers exercisable at any time and from time to time during the trust period:

(a)   Power by deed or deeds to appoint that they shall hold the whole or any part or parts of my estate upon trust for all or such one or more of the discretionary beneficiaries and if more than one in such shares and with such trusts and powers (including trusts and powers conferring a discretion as to the disposition of capital or income) and provisions (including provisions for the accumulation of income during any period or periods permitted by law) as my trustees think fit,[4]

(b)   Power to pay or apply the whole or any part or parts of my estate to or for the advancement support or benefit of all or any one or more of the discretionary beneficiaries in such manner as my trustees think fit.[5]

(3)   Subject to any exercise of the foregoing powers my trustees shall hold my estate during the trust period upon trust to pay or apply the income thereof to or for the maintenance education support or benefit of all or any one or more of the discretionary beneficiaries for the time being living and if more than one in such shares and generally in such manner as my trustees shall think fit and shall hold the capital of my estate at the expiration of the trust period upon trust for such of my children and remoter issue then living and if more than one in equal shares per stirpes each child of mine being treated as a head of stock.

(4)   The power to appoint capital conferred by subclause (2) hereof shall be exercisable whether or not a grant of administration has been obtained and whether or not the administration of my estate is complete.[6]

(5)   The powers to appoint and apply capital and the discretion as to the distribution of income conferred by subclauses (2) and (3) hereof shall be exercisable notwithstanding that any of my trustees has a personal interest in such exercise provided that there are not fewer than two trustees and that at least one of them has no such personal interest.[7]

4.   In relation to my estate my trustees shall have all the powers of management and investment of a sole beneficial owner.[8]

5.   The power of appointing trustees of this will shall be vested in my [wife/husband] during [her/his] life.

6.   Any of my trustees being a professional or business person may be paid reasonable remuneration for services provided by him as personal representative or trustee.[9]

AS WITNESS my hand this —— day of —— 20——

SIGNED by the [testator/testatrix] in our presence and   } [*Signature of*
then by us in [his/hers][2]   *testator/testatrix*]

[*Signatures, addresses and descriptions of two witnesses*]

1   This form is intended for use by a testator who is uncertain as to the ultimate disposition of his estate and is content to leave the decision to his trustees.

2   The composition of the discretionary class will vary according to the circumstances of the individual testator.

3   This is the longest period which can be specified under the PAA 1964, s 1, the text of which appears in Part G, para **[246.59]**.

4   This is a wide power of appointment which expressly authorises the creation of discretions as to the disposition of capital and income.

5   A power to apply capital is a useful adjunct which can be exercised without any formality.

6   Although not strictly necessary, this provision may be useful in cases where a speedy appointment is required, eg an appointment within two years of the death complying with the ITA 1984, s 144 (see para **[225.83]** et seq), in view of arguments which the Revenue has been known to advance to the effect that no appointment can be made before the completion of the administration. It should be remembered that for the technical reason discussed in the note to C3.6 (para **[225.83]**) an appointment or application of capital within three months of the testator's death will not attract the operation of s 144.

7   Since family trustees may well be appointed, a provision in this form is desirable.

8   This clause confers wide powers of investment and management. For administrative powers generally see B20 at para **[220.11]**.

9   See n 4 to Form C1.8 at para **[223.9]**.

[223.11]

FORM C1.10:   Codicil reviving a former will and codicils which have been revoked[1]

I [*testator*] of [*address*] declare this to be a [[second][third]] codicil to my will dated the [*date 1*].[2]

Whereas I made my most recent will on [*date 2*] and thereby revoked my said will dated [*date 1*] [and [two] codicil—[s] [respectively] dated [*date*] [and [*date*]]].

Now I hereby revive and confirm the said will dated [*date 1*] [and the said codicil[s] thereto] and hereby revoke [the said will dated [*date 2*] and] all testamentary dispositions made by me other than the said will dated [*date 1*] [and the said codicil[s] thereto].

AS WITNESS my hand this —— day of —— 20——

SIGNED by the [testator/testatrix] in our presence and then by us in [his/hers][2]   } [*Signature of testator/testatrix*]

[*Signatures, addresses and descriptions of two witnesses*]

1   It is advisable to execute a new will in the same terms as the revoked will, but in cases of emergency and where a copy of the former will exists, it may be necessary to use this form. If the previous will was revoked by destruction animo revocandi and no copy thereof is in existence, it will not be possible to adopt this course. A new will must in such a case be executed. On revival of wills see Vol 1, para **[21.1]** et seq.
2   In the interests of clarity, in this form the date of the revoked will which is being revived is referred to as '*date 1*', and the date of the most recent will which is being revoked is referred to as '*date 2*'.

[223.12]

FORM C1.11:   Codicil reviving a will which has been revoked by marriage[1]

I [*name*] of [*address*] declare this to be a codicil to my will dated [*date*]. whereas;

(1)   By my said will I left my residuary estate to [*name*].
(2)   On [*date*] I married the said [*name*] and my said will was accordingly revoked.

Now I hereby revive and confirm my said will.

AS WITNESS my hand this —— day of —— 20——

SIGNED by the [testator/testatrix] in our presence and then by us in [his/hers][2]   } [*Signature of testator/testatrix*]

[*Signatures, addresses and descriptions of two witnesses*]

1   This will is designed for use in cases where a couple who have been living together and have made wills in favour of each other subsequently marry. The wills will be revoked by the marriage by WA 1837, s 18 (Part G, para **[244.16]**; see also Vol 1, paras **[17.5]–[17.8]**), Although it is preferable to execute a new will embodying the terms of the revoked will, this form may be used in an emergency.

[223.13]

FORM C1.12:   Codicil adding legacy and increasing the share of residue of one of the testator's children[1]

I [*testator*] of [*address*] declare this to be a codicil to my will dated the [*date*].

1.   I give a pecuniary legacy of £—— to [*name*].

2.   Whereas by my said will my residuary estate (as therein defined) is directed to be held on trust for such of my children as survive me and if more than one in equal shares NOW I hereby declare that on the division of my residuary estate my son [*name*] if surviving me shall be entitled to double the share of any other surviving child or children of mine.

3.   In all other respects I confirm my said will.

AS WITNESS my hand this —— day of —— 20——

SIGNED by the [testator/testatrix] in our presence and then by us in [his/hers][2]   } [*Signature of testator/testatrix*]

[*Signatures, addresses and descriptions of two witnesses*]

---

1   For further examples of codicils varying the terms of existing wills see Part D, para **[237.1]** et seq.

C2 Wills for married couples with young children

PRELIMINARY NOTE

[224.1]
General strategy and inheritance tax. This section contains a selection of forms for use by married couples with young children. Such couples are likely to be young or middle-aged, and the main purpose of wills for such couples is to provide for the possibility of one or other spouse meeting an early death. If this happens it is likely on average that the other spouse will survive for a long period, and it is usually more important for the surviving spouse to have the entire joint estate than to maximise inheritance tax saving on the death of the first to die by a direct gift to the children. The surviving spouse is likely to have a long period in which to make potentially exempt transfers in favour of the children as and when he or she feels able to. Accordingly, all the forms in this section provide for the entire estate or virtually the entire estate of the first to die to devolve on the surviving spouse either absolutely or for a life or widowhood interest. This means that the transfer on the death of the first to die will be exempt from inheritance tax by virtue of the exemption for gifts to spouses (see Part A, para [200.99]), but that the property of the first to die which goes to the survivor will be subject to inheritance tax on the latter's death, so far as it has not been given away by the latter by lifetime potentially exempt transfers made seven years or more before his or her death. Thus, in the forms in this section the first to die's opportunity to make tax-free non-exempt gifts up to the tax threshold is not taken; for forms which include provisions making use of the inheritance tax nil-rate band of the first to die see C3 at para [225.9] et seq. However, these reasons for not utilising the nil rate band of the first to die do not apply where both parties to the marriage die simultaneously or within a short

period of each other, eg as a result of a common accident, and survivorship conditions are therefore appropriate in wills of this type: see below.

[224.2]
Survivorship conditions. Where two persons die in circumstances rendering it uncertain which of them survived the other, the younger is generally presumed for succession purposes to have survived the older: Law of Property Act 1925 (LPA 1925), s 184 (Part G, para **[244.56]**; see also Vol 1, paras **[70.1]–[70.4]**). The rule is excluded where the older person dies intestate and the younger person is his or her spouse; in such a case the younger spouse is treated as not having survived: Administration of Estates Act 1925 (AEA 1925), s 46(3) (Part G, para **[244.60]**). In the legislation relating to inheritance tax the latter rule has been adopted and extended to all cases, so that where any two persons, whether married or not, and whether testate or intestate, die in circumstances rendering it uncertain which of them survived they are treated as having died simultaneously for the purposes of the charge to inheritance tax on death (Inheritance Tax Act 1984 (ITA 1984), s 4(2)). This means that where spouses die in circumstances rendering it uncertain which survived, neither will be treated as having survived the other for inheritance tax purposes, even if the estate of the older devolves on the younger under the older's will by virtue of the LPA 1925, s 184 (Part G, para **[244.56]**; see also para **[224.5]** and Vol 1, paras **[70.1]–[70.4]**). In these circumstances the older's estate will devolve on the younger and then under the will of the younger (or the intestacy rules as they apply to the younger), but it will not be added to the younger's estate for the purposes of the inheritance tax charge on the younger's death. The nil-rate band of each will be fully utilised, or there will be the even more favourable result, mentioned at para **[224.5]** of this Preliminary Note, of the spouse exemption applying to the estate of the first to die without that estate being charged to inheritance tax on the survivor's death.

[224.3]
However, where spouses die within a short time of each other and the order of deaths is known, and all or most of the estate of the first to die devolves on the other, the nil-rate band of the first to die will clearly be wasted. It may be possible for this to be altered retrospectively by a deed of variation (see F3, paras **[241.1]–[241.31]**), but it is also possible to reduce the risk of wasting the nil-rate band in these circumstances by the use of survivorship conditions whereby inter-spouse gifts by will are made conditional on the donee surviving the testator by a specified period. Where the period so specified does not exceed six months and the surviving spouse dies during that period, the disposition of the testator's will taking effect as a result of the spouse's death during the survivorship period is treated by the ITA 1984, s 92 as having had effect on the testator's death. The testator's estate will thus be treated for inheritance tax purposes as devolving directly on the children (or other beneficiaries to whom the estate is given if the gift to the spouse does not take effect). The transfer will be chargeable but the nil-rate band will be available to reduce the amount of tax payable. The estate of the surviving spouse will devolve separately on the children (or other beneficiaries) and will also have the benefit of the survivor's nil-rate band. Two nil-rate bands will thus be available instead of one. However, the following points should be noted:

(i)   a survivorship provision will not serve any useful purpose if the combined value of the estates does not exceed the inheritance tax threshold;

(ii) the beneficial effect of a survivorship condition will be limited if the value of the separate estate of the surviving spouse is less than the inheritance tax threshold;

(iii) a survivorship condition could be a disadvantage where a substantial amount of the estate of the first to die is the subject of non-exempt gifts in any event, the value of the separate estate of the surviving spouse is less than the inheritance tax threshold, and the estate of the first to die exceeds that threshold—ie where the property comprised in the inter-spouse gift would bear less inheritance tax as part of the surviving spouse's estate than it would as part of the first to die's estate.

[224.4]

However, where a will gives all or nearly all of the estate to the testator's spouse, the inclusion of a survivorship provision in relation to the gift to the spouse may not always serve a very useful purpose, but it will usually do no harm and may in certain circumstances save a significant amount of inheritance tax. The forms in C2 are all ones where all or nearly all the estate of the first to die goes into the inheritance tax 'estate' of the survivor (ie absolutely or for an interest in possession), and so all of them except Form C2.4 (at para **[224.66]**) contain survivorship provisions as between spouses in relation to the residuary gift and any trust of the principal residence.

For further discussion of survivorship conditions see the Note on commorientes provisions in B19 at paras **[219.1]–[219.13]** and for further forms see Forms B19.1 to B19.4 at paras **[219.14]–[219.17]**.

[224.5]

Advantages of no survivorship condition where order of deaths of spouses is uncertain. Where spouses who make wills leaving their estates to each other happen to die in a common accident and the order of their deaths is uncertain, there could be an advantage if no survivorship condition takes effect in relation to the inter-spouse gift in the will of the older of them. Although for the purposes of the inheritance tax charges on their deaths the two spouses will be treated as dying simultaneously by virtue of the ITA 1984, s 4(2) (see para **[224.2]**), the estate of the older spouse will still devolve on the younger spouse under the LPA 1925, s 184 (see para **[224.2]**) and will therefore become 'comprised in the estate of the transferor's spouse' so as to qualify for the spouse exemption under the ITA 1984, s 18 (ITA 1984, s 4(2) applies to s 4(1) but not s 18). On the other hand the younger spouse will be treated for inheritance tax purposes as not having survived the older spouse so that his or her separate estate will alone be taxable. It is not entirely clear what the Inland Revenue's attitude is to the claim that the spouse exemption is available in these circumstances. Two people dying in circumstances that the order of their deaths is unknown is an uncommon occurrence, and we have not made provision excluding the survivorship condition in the will of the older, in the event of the order of deaths being unknown, in the forms in C2. For forms of survivorship clause which do this see Forms B19.3 and B19.4 at paras **[219.16]** and **[219.17]**. See also the Note on commorientes provisions in B19 at para **[219.1]**.

[224.6]
Survivorship conditions and gifts to persons other than the testator's spouse. The use of survivorship provisions and the scope of the ITA 1984, s 92 are not confined to inter-spouse gifts. The main purpose of putting a condition of surviving the testator for a specified period in a gift to someone other than the testator's spouse is usually to control the ultimate devolution of the property in question in the event of the early death of the primary beneficiary. However, it will also mean that if the primary beneficiary dies within the survivorship period and the ITA 1984, s 92 applies, there is only one occasion of charge to inheritance tax on death in relation to the property subject to the gift instead of two, and some inheritance tax may be saved. There will not always be an inheritance tax saving as a result of the operation of the survivorship condition because one or other estate may be below the tax threshold, and where both are large enough for tax to be payable successive charges relief under the ITA 1984, s 141 will be available if there is no survivorship condition. The forms in C2 do not contain survivorship conditions in relation to gifts to persons other than the testator's spouse.

[224.7]
Guardians. Since the forms in C2 are for testators with young children, provision for the appointment of guardians is included in all cases. Under the Children Act 1989 where both parents have 'parental responsibility' (which will ordinarily be the case with married couples with young children) an appointment of guardians by one parent will not take effect during the lifetime of the other. It seems more convenient in these circumstances for the effective appointment to be made by the survivor. The forms in this section therefore provide that the appointment will not take effect if the other spouse survives. For the law relating to guardianship see Vol 1, paras **[28.1]–[28.8]**, and for the appointment of guardians see the Note in B3 at paras **[203.43]–[203.54]**, and Forms B3.26 to B3.32 at paras **[203.55]–[203.61]**.

[224.8]
Reciprocal and mutual wills. It is contemplated that most of the forms in this section will be used by both husband and wife and can be readily adapted for use by either. In this sense they are 'reciprocal', but they are not intended to be 'mutual' in the strict sense, ie executed pursuant to an agreement not to revoke them. If the parties wish to execute mutual wills in this sense, the formula used in Form B1.6 at para **[201.10]** should be adopted, but this course is not recommended. For the general law relating to mutual wills see Vol 1, paras **[2.3]–[2.9]**. If a husband and wife want to make sure in the will of the first of them to die that that person's property will go to eg the children, on the death of the survivor, then a life interest trust for the survivor, perhaps with a power to apply capital for his or her benefit, with remainder to the children, is a better arrangement than mutual wills. See eg Forms C2.3 to C2.6 at para **[224.51]** et seq and C3.2 and C3.5 at paras **[225.23]–[225.41]** and **[225.92]–[225.109]** respectively.

[224.9]
Reciprocal wills and the ultimate destination of property. Forms C2.1 and C2.2 (at paras **[224.20]–[224.50]**), in which each spouse leaves his or her estate

(or most of it) to the other absolutely, are only suitable for use where the alternative gift, which takes effect where the other has predeceased the testator or testatrix (or failed to survive the survivorship period), is to the same beneficiaries in the wills of both spouses, ie to the children of their marriage. Where one or other of them has children who are not (or not treated in law) as children of the marriage (ie he or she has illegitimate children or children of another marriage), it is not appropriate for both spouses simply to make wills which contain absolute gifts to each other with an alternative gift to 'my children', since this will mean that the children who have as a parent one of the spouses but not the other will only inherit anything if their parent survives the other spouse. If such children are intended to benefit under their parent's will, other forms (such as those in C5 at para **[227.1]** et seq) should be used. If they are not intended to take any benefit, words need to be added to the alternative gift so as to exclude them from its scope.

[224.10]
One method of excluding *illegitimate* children of one or other party to the marriage from taking under a gift is to exclude the statutory rules of construction which include illegitimate persons in words descriptive of relationship (see Part A, paras **[200.28]–[200.33]** and Vol 1, para **[72.14]**). This will not be sufficient where there are children who are intended to be excluded from the gift who are children of another marriage of one of the spouses. In Forms C2.1 (at para **[224.20]**) and C2.2 (at para **[224.35]**) where the primary gift of residue is an absolute gift to the surviving spouse, optional words are included in the alternative gift which restrict the donees of the gift to the children of the marriage (see paras **[224.28]** and **[224.43]**). If such words are included, any illegitimate children of the testator or testatrix, or children by some other marriage, will be excluded, but the gift will include legitimated children of the marriage (see the Legitimacy Act 1976, s 5(3): Part G, para **[245.48]**), adopted children of the marriage (see the Adoption Act 1976, s 39(1): Part G, para **[245.58]**) and children of the marriage born as a result of in vitro fertilisation or artificial insemination with the husband's consent (see the Human Fertilisation and Embryology Act 1990, s 28(2) and 29(1), (3): Part G, paras **[245.86]** and **[245.87]**). On these topics see also Vol 1, paras **[72.15]**–**[72.18]**, **[74.5]–[74.7]**, and **[75.1]–[75.9]** respectively.

[224.11]
This is a less significant point where the will takes the form of a life interest with remainders, because each spouse's estate will ultimately go to his own children, instead of the estate of the first to die being added to that of the survivor and going to the survivor's children. Of the life interest with remainder forms in C2, Form C2.3 (at para **[224.51]**) has, like Forms C2.1 (at para **[224.20]**) and C2.2 (at para **[224.35]**), optional words confining the trust for the children to the children of the marriage (see para **[224.58]**), but in Forms C2.4 to C2.6 (at paras **[224.66]–[224.95]**) the remainder trusts are for all the testator's children without such a restriction.

[224.12]
The possibility of divorce. In relation to deaths on or after 1 January 1996, the dissolution or annulment of a testator's marriage after he has made a will causes

his or her spouse to be deemed to have died on the date of the decree of divorce or annulment, for the purposes of any provisions of that will:

(i)   conferring a power of appointment, if it is conferred on the spouse;
(ii) appointing executors or trustees, if the spouse is so appointed;
(iii) which relate to the devolution of property which, or an interest in which, is given to the spouse.

See the Wills Act 1837 (WA 1837), s 18A(1), as amended by the Law Reform (Succession) Act 1995, s 3 (Part G, para **[244.18]** and discussed in Vol 1 (at paras **[25.7]** and **[47.2]**), in Part A (at para **[200.26]**) and below.

[224.13]
This treatment of the spouse as having died on the date of the decree has the effect not only of causing a provision in favour of the testator's spouse of any of the kinds just mentioned to fail, but also of causing any alternative provision contained in the will, which is expressed to take effect in the event of the spouse predeceasing the testator, to take effect instead. It is thus not necessary to make any express provision in wills for the possibility of s 18A applying, save that there is some uncertainty as to its effect on discretionary trusts and powers of which the testator's spouse is an object: see paras **[224.17]–[224.19]**. By contrast, the WA 1837, s 18A as originally enacted (by the AJA 1982, s 18: Part G, para **[244.17]**), which applies in relation to deaths before 1 January 1996, causes any appointment as executor, or gift by will, in favour of the testator's spouse to lapse if there has been a divorce, but does not always cause alternative gifts or other provisions which are contained in the will, and expressed to take effect in the event of the spouse predeceasing the testator, to be effective (see Vol 1, para **[47.2]**). In particular, it fails to bring into operation a gift which is expressed to take effect if the testator's spouse predeceases the testator in the alternative to an absolute gift to the spouse (*Re Sinclair* [1985] Ch 446, [1985] 1 All ER 1066).

[224.14]
In wills made before 1 January 1996, therefore, a cautious draftsman will have provided for the possibility of the testator and his spouse becoming divorced by introducing any alternative appointment of executors which is to take effect in the event of the failure of an appointment of the testator's spouse, or any alternative gift which is provided in the event of the failure of a gift to the testator's spouse, with words such as 'if my [wife/husband] shall predecease me or the foregoing [gift to/appointment of] [her/him] shall fail for any other reason' (see cls 1 and 5 of Form C2.1 at paras **[224.22]** and **[224.26]**). This is not necessary after 31 December 1995. There is no harm in retaining such wording, and its presence will mean that in the event of a disclaimer of the primary gift the alternative gift will take effect (which it would probably not otherwise do in the event of such a disclaimer—see Vol 1, para **[48.8]**). However, most draftsmen will probably prefer not to include such wording now that it is not necessary to do so in order to deal with the difficulties created by the WA 1837, s 18A as originally enacted (Part G, para **[244.17]**). Where a testator is happily married it is not appropriate when taking instructions for a

will, nor likely to improve the reputation of the legal profession, to discuss providing in it for the eventuality of a divorce.

[224.15]
For completeness we retain an example of the use of wording which refers to failure of an appointment or gift in favour of a spouse for reasons other than predeceasing the testator: see Form C2.1, cls 1 and 5 at paras **[224.22]** and **[224.26]**. We do not include such wording in the other forms in Part C which contain provisions in favour of the testator's spouse.

[224.16]
The reason why even the revised WA 1837, s 18A does not go so far as to say that a will shall have effect for *all* purposes as if the testator's spouse had died on the date of the decree of divorce or nullity is presumably that this could upset provisions for the benefit of persons other than the spouse which are contingent on, eg, the testator's spouse not surviving the testator. An example is Form C3.1, cl 2 at para **[225.12]** where both spouses make wills with the same set of pecuniary legacies which are intended to take effect only once, on the death of the survivor. If s 18A applied to the construction of this clause and there was a divorce, the legacies would have effect on both deaths.

[224.17]
The possibility of divorce—Wills Act 1837, s 18A and discretionary trusts or powers. What effect, if any, the WA 1837, s 18A, as newly amended by the Law Reform (Succession) Act 1995, s 3 in relation to deaths on or after 1 January 1996 (see Part G, para **[244.18]** for the text of it), has on discretionary trusts or powers under which the testator's spouse is a beneficiary is not obvious and requires some careful thought. The amended WA 1837, s 18A(1)(a) is not relevant because it concerns powers of appointment which are to be *exercised* by the spouse, not ones under which the spouse may benefit. The amended WA 1837, s 18A(1)(b) provides that 'any property which, or an interest in which, is devised or bequeathed to the former spouse shall pass as if the former spouse had died on the date of the decree of divorce or nullity'. It seems to us that if a will gives the testator's spouse a life interest in property with a power to pay or apply capital of that property to or for the benefit of the spouse, there is a divorce before the testator's death, and the testator predeceases his or her former spouse without changing the will, then that property will be property an interest in which (ie the life interest) is devised or bequeathed to the former spouse, s 18A(1)(b) will apply so as to cause that property to pass as if the spouse died on the date of the decree of divorce, and that will probably mean that the power to pay or apply capital, as well as the life interest, will not have effect.

[224.18]
On the other hand, if the will created a discretionary trust or power over capital or income of a fund which could be exercised in favour of the testator's spouse, without the spouse having any other beneficial interest in that fund, it is not clear that s 18A(1)(b) would have any effect where the spouse was divorced from but did not predecease the testator. This is because it is not clear that making someone a discretionary object of a trust or power relating to particular property

(and conferring no other benefit arising from that property) is to devise or bequeath to him or her an interest in that property within the meaning of s 18A(1)(b). In practice it is only in rare cases that this point will matter. If a divorced spouse turns out to be one of a class of discretionary beneficiaries under a will made before the divorce occurred, it will be open to the trustees to decide that it is not appropriate to exercise their discretion in his or her favour.

[224.19]

Despite the view expressed above about the position under the new WA 1837, s 18A(1)(b) in relation to a life interest for a spouse coupled with a power to pay or apply capital to or for him or her, we recommend that any such power is limited so as to be exercisable only over capital which is for the time being subject to the life interest, and in the forms in Part C where this type of provision is made we have mostly so provided. This eliminates any uncertainty as to the operation of s 18A(1)(b) on this type of provision, by making sure that if the life interest is rendered ineffective by s 18A(1)(b) the power will be rendered ineffective as well, and also ensures that (where there is no divorce and the spouse survives the testator) if the spouse assigns or surrenders the life interest the power will automatically be extinguished. There are various possible adverse fiscal consequences where a power to pay or apply capital to or for the benefit of the life tenant continues to be exercisable over capital in relation to which the life interest has ceased. One is that the result may be a settlement under which the former life tenant is a settlor (by virtue of settling the life interest) for income tax purposes, but is not wholly excluded from benefit (because the power to pay or apply capital continues to be exercisable) with the result that the settlement income continues to be charged to income tax as his or her income (as happened in *IRC v Cookson* [1977] 2 All ER 331, [1977] 1 WLR 962). Another is that the continued existence of the power could wreck the intended inheritance tax status of the trusts as accumulation and maintenance trusts within the ITA 1984, s 71 (see Part A, paras **[200.119]**–**[200.136]**). For a power in favour of a surviving spouse which is limited to capital of which he or she has an interest in the income, see eg Form C2.3, cl 5 at para **[224.57]**.

[224.20]

FORM C2.1: Reciprocal wills giving entire estate to spouse absolutely, with alternative gift to issue

NOTE

This form is intended to cater for the situation where the husband and wife are relatively young and their estates are not large. In such a case it will usually be appropriate for the survivor to take the estate of the first to die absolutely and for the children to take an interest only on the death of the survivor. See also the Preliminary Note on general strategy and inheritance tax at para **[224.1]**.

[224.21]

Revocation clause and declaration against mutual wills

I [*name*] of [*address*] revoke all former testamentary dispositions made by me and declare this to be my last will [And I further declare that notwithstanding that my [wife/husband] is making a will in similar terms we have agreed that our wills are not mutual wills and accordingly that each of us shall be free to revoke his or her will at any time whether before or after the death of the other and shall be free to dispose of his or her property or any property derived from the other as he or she thinks fit].[1]

1   There is no presumption that two wills in similar form are mutual wills in the technical sense, but the inclusion of the words in square brackets will remove any doubt on the point. If mutual wills are intended, then an express clause to that effect, such as Form B1.6 at para **[201.10]**, should be used instead of this clause. For the law on mutual wills see Vol 1, paras **[2.3]–[2.9]**. We recommend life interest trusts rather than mutual wills where a testator wishes to determine the destination of his property after the death of his spouse in the event of his spouse surviving him.

[224.22]

Appointment of spouse as sole executor/executrix, with alternative appointment

1.   I appoint my [wife/husband] [*name*] ('my [wife/husband]') the sole [executrix/executor] of this will but if [she/he] predeceases me or renounces probate or dies without having proved this will [or if the foregoing appointment shall fail for any other reason][1] then I appoint [*name*] of [*address*] and [*name*] of [*address*] to be the executors and trustees hereof.

1   These words allow for the possibility of the appointment ceasing to have effect as a result of a divorce, by virtue of the WA 1837, s 18A(1)(a) (Part G, para **[244.17]**) in the event of the testator's death before 1 January 1996. They are not necessary in relation to deaths on or after that date but have been included for completeness. See the Preliminary Note on the possibility of divorce at paras **[224.12]–[224.19]**.

      Although the main gift to the spouse is conditional on surviving the testator by one month, it seems preferable not to make the appointment of her or him as executor conditional on surviving that period: it could be inconvenient in some circumstances if the spouse had to wait until one month from the death before being able to take steps as executor, and the alternative appointment takes effect if the spouse dies without having proved the will. There is a slight risk that the spouse will dissipate some or all of the estate and then die within a month of the testator's death, a risk that would be more significant if the required period of survival under the survivorship condition was made longer than a month (it would be possible to have a longer period, up to six months—see the Preliminary Note at para **[224.2]**).

[224.23]

Definition of 'my trustees'

2.   In this will the expression 'my trustees' shall where the context permits mean my personal representatives for the time being and the trustees for the time being hereof.

[224.24]

Appointment of guardians[1]

3.   If my [wife/husband] shall predecease me I appoint [*name*] of [*address*] [and [*name*] of [*address*]] to be the [guardian/guardians] of my children during their respective minorities.

1   For the reasons given in the Preliminary Note at para **[224.7]**, the appointment of guardians incorporated in the forms in this section will only take effect if the other spouse dies first.

[224.25]

Primary gift of estate to spouse

4.   If my [wife/husband] shall survive me [for the period of one month][1] then subject to the payment thereout of my debts and funeral and testamentary

expenses I give devise and bequeath all my estate both real and personal [including any entailed or other property over which I shall have a general power of disposition at my death]² to [her/him] absolutely.

1   See the Preliminary Note on survivorship conditions at paras **[224.2]–[224.6]** and note that there is a possible advantage of excluding the operation of such conditions where the order of deaths of spouses is uncertain (see para **[224.5]**). The survivorship period could be any period up to six months and still take advantage of the ITA 1984, s 92 (see para **[224.3]**); if a survivorship period longer than a month is being considered, it should be remembered that it will not usually be possible to pay income or capital to the spouse before he or she has survived the period. If the survivorship condition is not wanted the words in this set of square brackets and the consequential wording in cl 5 (see para **[224.26]**, n 1) should be omitted.

2   Subject to any contrary intention expressed in the will property subject to a general testamentary power will be carried by a residuary gift under the WA 1837, s 27 (see Part G, para **[244.27]** and Vol 1, paras **[38.1]** and **[38.2]**) without express reference to the property or power. In the case of entailed property, however, the property or the instrument under which it was acquired, or entailed property generally, must be referred to: LPA 1925, s 176(1) (see Part G, para **[244.53]** and Vol 1, para **[7.1]**).

[224.26]

Alternative provisions if spouse does not survive

5.   If my [wife/husband] shall predecease me [or shall not survive me for the period aforesaid]¹ [or if the foregoing gift shall fail for any other reason]² then the following provisions shall have effect.

1   See para **[224.24]**, n 4.

2   These words catered for the possibility that the gift may lapse by reason of divorce under the WA 1837, s 18A(1)(b) (Part G, para **[244.17]**) in the event of the testator's death before 1 January 1996. They are not necessary in relation to deaths on or after that date and should be omitted in most cases. See the Preliminary Note on the possibility of divorce at paras **[224.17]–[224.19]**.

[224.27]

Administration trusts of residue

6.   (1)   I give all my property not hereby or by any codicil hereto otherwise effectively disposed of [(including any entailed or other property over which I shall have at my death a general power of disposition by will)]¹ to my trustees to hold on the trusts set out below with power at their discretion to sell all or any of it as and when they think fit.²

(2)   My trustees shall pay my funeral and testamentary expenses³ and debts and any legacies given by this will or any codicil hereto out of such property or its proceeds and shall have a discretion as to how such payments shall be borne as between capital and income.⁴

(3)   Subject as above my trustees shall hold such property and the assets from time to time representing the same (hereinafter called 'my residuary estate') on the trusts set out below and shall invest all money comprised in such property or arising from its sale in any of the investments hereby authorised with power to change such investments into any others hereby authorised.

(4)   In the administration of my estate and the execution of the trusts of this will or of any codicil to it:

(a)   my trustees shall treat all income as accruing on the date on which it becomes payable regardless of the period in respect of which it shall have accrued and shall not make any statutory apportionment of the same;⁵ and

(b)   none of the equitable rules of apportionment between capital and income shall apply in any circumstances whatever.[6]

1   Subject to any express contrary intention property subject to a general power will be carried by a residuary gift under the WA 1837, s 27 (Part G, para [244.27]), but in the case of entailed property the will must refer to the property, or the instrument under which it was acquired, or entailed property generally for the statutory power of disposition to be exercised: LPA 1925, s 176(1), (Part G, para [244.53]). Although no new entails can be created on or after 1 January 1997 (see paras [200.52] and [200.53]), entails created before that date can continue to exist and, if they do, the statutory power of disposition of them by will continues to be available.

2   For the reasons for providing a power of sale rather than a trust for sale, see para [214.1] et seq. This wording could be made even more concise, such as: 'My trustees shall have power to sell all or any of such property' or as appears in the AEA 1925, s 33(1), as amended by the TLATA 1996, Sch 2, para 5. One reason for using the slightly more elaborate wording in this form is that it follows the wording which was held in *Re Pitcairn* [1896] 2 Ch 199 to prevent the rule in *Howe v Dartmouth* from applying, (see Note at paras [214.35]–[214.37] for exclusion of the rule), although to save possible argument about the effect of this wording the express exclusion of the apportionment rules is also retained in sub-cl (4) below. Another reason is that this wording should also serve to create a mixed fund of residuary realty and personalty (see para [214.64] for the significance of this).

3   Testamentary expenses will include inheritance tax on UK free estate, including real property: ITA 1984, s 211(1) (Part G, para [246.83] and see the Preliminary Note to B14 at paras [214.55]–[214.63]). Accordingly, even if specific gifts or pecuniary legacies are intended to be free of inheritance tax, it will not be necessary to make express provision for the incidence of inheritance tax, unless (in the case of a specific gift) the gift is of property of a kind which bears its own tax, or (in the case of a pecuniary legacy) the legacy is payable out of property (usually residue) which includes property of a kind which bears its own tax. The main relevant categories of property bearing its own tax are foreign property and property which is settled property immediately before the testator's death: see the Preliminary Note to B14 at paras [214.55]–[214.63] (settled property can be disposed of under a will where it is subject to a general testamentary power of appointment or is entailed—see n 1 supra).

4   A discretion as to the apportionment between capital and income of the burden of liabilities is a middle way between the strict rule in *Allhusen v Whittell* (1867) LR 4 Eq 295 (see Vol 1, para [38.26] and para [214.43]) with its complex calculations, and a direction to pay the liabilities out of capital which can have the unsatisfactory consequences referred to at para [214.44].

5   See the Preliminary Note to B14 at paras [214.48]–[214.52] for statutory apportionment of income over time and its exclusion.

6   See Vol 1, paras [38.17]–[38.27] for the rules of equitable apportionment between capital and income, and the Preliminary Note to B14 at para [214.35] et seq for the reasons and techniques for excluding those rules. It is hoped that these words will exclude the rule in *Howe v Earl of Dartmouth* (1802) 7 Ves 137 and *Re Earl Chesterfield's Trusts* (1883) 24 Ch D 643. The power of sale in sub-cl (1) of this clause may also serve to do so (see n 2 supra). For alternative strategies, see further the Preliminary Note to B14 at para [214.38], Forms B14.4 (at para [214.13]) and B14.27 (at para [214.42]).

[224.28]

Beneficial trusts for issue

7.   My trustees shall hold my residuary estate and the income thereof upon trust for such of my children [by my [wife/husband]][1] as shall survive me and attain the age of [18/21/25/30] years[2] and if more than one in equal shares Provided that if any such child shall die before attaining a vested interest under the foregoing trust leaving a child or children living at or born after my death who shall attain the age of [18/21] years[3] [or marry under that age] then such last-mentioned child or children shall take and if more than one equally between

them the share of my residuary estate which such deceased child of mine would have taken had he or she lived to attain a vested interest.

1   These words ensure that the alternative gifts in the wills of both spouses are identical in terms of whom they benefit, in circumstances where one spouse has children who are not children of the other spouse. See, further, the Preliminary Note on reciprocal wills and the ultimate destination of property at paras **[224.9]–[224.11]** and for forms for use where one spouse has children who are not children of the marriage and wishes to benefit them by his or her will see C5 at para **[227.1]** et seq.
2   Since the children will all be lives in being for perpetuity purposes, the age contingency does not have to be restricted to 21.
3   The grandchildren will not necessarily be alive at the testator's death and it is therefore important to restrict the age contingency to 21.

[224.29]

Maintenance, accumulation and advancement[1]

8.   (1)   Section 31 of the Trustee Act 1925 (relating to accumulation and maintenance) shall apply in relation to the trusts hereby or by any codicil hereto declared as if:

(a)   in paragraph (i) of subsection (1) of the said section the words 'as the trustees think fit' were substituted for the words 'as may in all the circumstances be reasonable'; and

(b)   the proviso to the said subsection (1) were omitted.

(2)   Section 32 of the Trustee Act 1925 (relating to advancement) shall apply in relation to the said trusts as if the words 'one half of' were omitted from proviso (a) to subsection (1) thereof [provided that the powers conferred by the said section (as hereby enlarged) shall not be exercisable in favour of any minor beneficiary hereunder otherwise than so as to cause such beneficiary to become immediately entitled to or to an interest in possession in the capital thereby paid or applied within the meaning of section 71(1)(a) of the Inheritance Tax Act 1984].[2]

(3)   Whenever my trustees shall have an obligation or discretion under the provisions of this will or any codicil hereto or under the general law to apply income or capital for the benefit of a minor beneficiary they may either pay the same without liability to account to his or her parent guardian or any other adult person with whom such beneficiary may be residing or to such beneficiary himself or herself if of the age of 16 years or more and so that the receipt of such parent guardian or other person or of such minor beneficiary shall be a full and sufficient discharge to my trustees for the income or capital so applied.[3]

1   For alternative provisions relating to maintenance and advancement see Forms B18.11 to B18.23 and the text thereto at paras **[218.77]–[218.107]**.
2   The proviso is included in order to prevent the power prejudicing the application of the ITA 1984, s 71 (accumulation and maintenance trusts), but is probably unnecessary: see the Note on inheritance tax and the statutory power of advancement in B18 at para **[218.99]**. If the accumulation and maintenance trusts of income are extended so as to continue beyond the age of 18 (see eg, Forms B18.12 and B18.13 at paras **[218.78]** and **[218.79]**), then 'minor beneficiary hereunder' should be amended to eg 'beneficiary hereunder who is under the age of [*n*] years' where *n* is the highest age at which an absolute interest or an interest in possession might be attained by any of the beneficiaries.
3   A parent (with parental responsibility) and a guardian of a minor are empowered by the ChA 1989, s 3(3) (Part G, para **[244.119]**) to give a good receipt for the minor's property: see Vol 1, para **[9.41]**. The power in this subclause is wider in that it authorises the payment of income or

capital to a parent who does not have parental responsibility, any adult with whom the minor is residing, and the minor himself or herself if 16 or over.

[224.30]

Administrative powers[1]

9.   (1)   In this clause where the context so admits—

(a) the expression 'land' includes buildings and estates interests or rights of any kind in or over land; and

(b) during the administration of my estate the expression 'beneficiary' includes any person who would be a beneficiary if such administration had been completed and the expression 'beneficially interested' and references to income of any asset being payable or capable of being paid to or for the benefit of a beneficiary shall be construed accordingly.

(2)   None of the powers or provisions contained in subclause (3) below of this clause shall be capable of being exercised or operating in any manner such that if such power or provision were capable of being so exercised or so operating the existence of the same would either—

(i) prevent any person who would in the absence of such power or provision have been entitled to an interest in possession (within the meaning of Part III of the Inheritance Tax Act 1984) in any property from being entitled to such interest; or

(ii) prevent section 71 of the Inheritance Tax Act 1984 from applying to any property to which in the absence of such power or provision the said section 71 would have applied.

(3)   In the administration of my estate and the execution of the trusts hereof or of any codicil hereto my trustees shall have the following powers in addition to those conferred by law but subject to the last foregoing subclause—

(a) power to invest moneys sell assets and change investments with the unrestricted freedom of choice and powers of disposition and acquisition of a sole beneficial owner with in particular power to make unsecured loans, acquire non-income yielding assets, and purchase land anywhere in the world or chattels for any purpose including occupation or enjoyment in kind by a beneficiary under the power set out below;

(b) power to delegate all or any of their investment powers to a professional investment manager or managers whether individual or corporate and whether or not also a nominee holder of assets for my trustees (and who may be or include one or more of my trustees or the beneficiaries hereunder) upon such terms as to remuneration and otherwise (including terms authorising self-dealing or providing for the limitation of the liability of the investment manager or managers) as my trustees think fit and section 22 of the Trustee Act 2000 shall not apply;[4]

(c) power to vest or register any property in any person or persons whether individual or corporate and whether or not an investment manager to whom powers have been delegated under the foregoing power (and who may be or include one or more of my trustees or the beneficiaries hereunder) as nominee or nominees for my trustees upon such terms as to remuneration or otherwise (including terms authorising self-dealing or providing for the limitation of the liability of the nominee) as my trustees think fit and section 22 of the Trustee Act 2000 shall not apply;[5]

(d)   power to borrow money with or without giving security and on such terms as to interest and repayment and otherwise as my trustees may think fit for any purpose connected with the administration of my estate or the trusts declared herein or in any codicil hereto (including investment) And no lender from whom my trustees borrow money in purported exercise of this power shall be concerned to enquire as to the propriety amount or purpose of any such borrowing;[6]

(e)   power to lend money to a beneficiary to whom any of the income of such money is payable or to whom or for whose benefit any income of such money is capable of being paid or applied in exercise of a discretion (or who would be such a beneficiary if such money yielded income) and to do so at a full or concessionary rate of interest or interest free;[7]

(f)   all the powers of an absolute owner in relation to any land (wherever situated) held by them;[8]

(g)   power to apply capital held on the same trusts as any land (or which would be so held if the administration of my estate had been completed) in the improvement of such land and to apply such capital or the income of such capital on the repair or maintenance of such land;[9]

(h)   power to permit any beneficiary to have the beneficial occupation use or enjoyment in kind of any land or chattel or other tangible property on such terms as to repair insurance or payment of outgoings by the beneficiary or otherwise howsoever as my trustees think fit Provided that the foregoing power shall only be exercisable and such permission to occupy or enjoy in kind may only continue in the following circumstances—

    (i)   so long as any of the income of such land chattel or other tangible property is payable to such beneficiary or capable of being paid or applied to him or for his benefit in exercise of a discretion (or would be so payable or capable of being so paid or applied if such land chattel or other property yielded income);

    (ii)   in the case of land, so long as for the time being the occupation thereof by such beneficiary is compatible with any statutory rights of occupation of any other beneficiary or beneficiaries;[10]

    (i)   power to exercise all the powers of appropriation (and other incidental powers) conferred by statute on a personal representative without the necessity of obtaining any consents and notwithstanding that one or more of my trustees may be beneficially interested in the exercise of such power.[11]

1   For notes on administrative powers and the powers conferred by the general law, and for other examples of administrative powers, see B20 at para **[220.1]** et seq. For a set of administrative powers which include powers in respect of business assets see Form C11.1, cl 6 at para **[233.21]**. The TLATA 1996 and the Trustee Act 2000 (TrA 2000) have much increased the statutory powers of trustees, and many wills and will trusts could manage without any of the powers in this clause being conferred expressly, or just with the power to borrow and the power of appropriation without consent. The differences from the relevant statutory powers of the powers in this clause which overlap with statutory powers are noted in the notes below. The only power which, before 1997, was included in this clause which has been omitted because there are now statutory powers which render express provision unnecessary is the power to insure: TA 1925, s 19, as substituted by the TrA 2000, s 34 (Part G, para **[246.17]**), and para **[220.51]**.

2 This is a general restriction so as to prevent the administrative powers prejudicing the intended inheritance tax status of the beneficial trusts, either as interest in possession trusts or as accumulation and maintenance trusts within the ITA 1984, s 71. See, further, the General Preliminary Note to B20 at para **[220.5]**.

3 This power is wider than the statutory powers of investment in the TrA 2000, ss 3 and 8 (Part G, paras **[246.118]** and **[246.123]**) for these and the notes on them at paras **[220.12]**–**[220.19]**) in that it permits unsecured loans, the purchase of land outside the UK, and the purchase of interests in land (such as undivided shares) which are not legal estates. The attempt can be made to exclude the statutory obligations relating to diversification and suitability of investments, and the requirement of taking advice, but as now enacted in the TrA 2000 these cannot be excluded (although their effect can be cut down by clauses exonerating trustees from liability for negligence): TrA 2000, ss 4 and 5 (see Part G, paras **[246.119]**, **[246.120]** and **[220.37]**).

4 This is wider than the statutory power to appoint investment managers in the TrA 2000, Pt IV, ss 11–15 (see Part G, paras **[246.126]**–**[246.130]** and B20 at paras **[220.35]** and **[220.36]**) in that the detailed procedural requirements of the TrA 2000, s 15 do not apply, the trustees have a wider discretion as to restricting an investment manager's liability or permitting self-dealing by him (compare the TrA 2000, s 14(2): Part G, para **[246.129]**, under which these can only be done if it is reasonably necessary), beneficiaries can be appointed (this is forbidden in exercise of the statutory power by the TrA 2000, s 12(3)), and the duty to review the arrangement from time to time under the TrA 2000, s 22 (Part G, para **[246.137]**) does not apply. The by-passing of the TrA 2000, ss 14 and 15 is only effective if those statutory provisions apply only to the statutory powers of delegation, and do not apply to express powers to delegate investment management functions, something which is not at all clear (see para **[220.37]**). Even though trustees have an express power of this kind, unless and until there is either a definitive decision of the courts, or amending legislation, which makes it certain that ss 14 and 15 are excluded by such a power, trustees should regard themselves as bound by ss 14 and 15.

5 This is wider than the statutory power to appoint nominees in the TrA 2000, Pt IV, ss 16–20 (see Part G, paras **[246.131]**–**[246.135]** and **[220.36]**) in that the trustees have a wider discretion as to restricting a nominee's liability or permitting self-dealing by him (compare the TrA 2000, s 20(2): Part G, para **[246.135]**, under which these can only be done if it is reasonably necessary), the persons who may be appointed nominees are not confined to persons carrying on a business as nominees, a company controlled by the trustees or a solicitors' incorporated practice (compare the TrA 2000, s 19(2): Part G para **[246.134]**), and the duty to review the arrangement from time to time under the TrA 2000, s 22 (Part G, para **[246.137]**) does not apply.

6 There is no power under the general law for trustees to borrow money for the purposes of investment: see para **[220.69]**, n 1.

7 The investment power in sub-cl (a) above permits unsecured lending on a commercial basis, but express authorisation as in this subclause is needed to lend or continue to lend for the purpose of benefiting the borrower: see para **[220.32]**. A power to apply capital for the benefit of a beneficiary could in appropriate circumstances enable capital to be lent to him on beneficial terms.

8 The statutory power of management of land in similar terms in the TLATA 1996, s 6(1) (Part G, para **[246.91]**) applies only to land in England and Wales, and that in the TrA 2000, s 8(3) (Part G, para **[246.123]**) applies only to land acquired under the power in that section. As the power to acquire land in this clause is wider than the statutory power (see n 3 supra) it is appropriate to provide an express power rather than rely on the statute.

9 See para **[220.52]** for the reasons for this provision.

10 See the Note and forms concerning enjoyment in kind in B18 at para **[218.108]** and the Preliminary Note on investment powers in B20 at para **[220.30]**. For the statutory rights of occupation under the TLATA 1996, see paras **[208.5]**–**[208.18]** and the TLATA 1996, ss 12 and 13 (Part G, paras **[246.98]** and **[246.99]**). A power as in this subclause is primarily relevant to a wholly discretionary trust, and it is made subject to any statutory rights of occupation because interest in possession trusts might come to be created in exercise of a power of appointment or application. A power to permit occupation by a beneficiary of trust land is not needed in relation to land in an interest in possession trust, because the statutory rights of occupation will be sufficient provision for beneficiary occupation and anyway are likely to leave no room for permissive occupation by beneficiaries who have no rights of occupation. A clause of this kind can be included in relation to an accumulation and maintenance trust intended to be within the ITA 1984, s 71, but should always be subject an overriding restriction to prevent the power prejudicing the s 71 status of the trusts, such as the proviso at the end of

this clause. For the effect of conditions as to repair etc imposed on a beneficiary occupying or enjoying in kind trust property see the Preliminary Note to B8 at paras **[208.26]–[208.28]**.

11   For the statutory power of partition of land see the TLATA 1996, s 7 (Part G, para **[246.92]**) and for the statutory power of appropriation referred to here see the AEA 1925, s 41 (Part G, para **[246.50]**; see also Vol 1 paras **[29.17]–[29.23]** and **[220.70]**). A power of appropriation as in this subclause will be exercisable in circumstances when the power in the TLATA 1996, s 7 cannot be exercised, eg where a share of the land is still settled, and without the consent of beneficiaries. Exercise of a power of this kind which does not require the consent of beneficiaries may have stamp duty or capital gains tax advantages over one which does: see para **[220.72]**.

[224.31]

Trustee liability

10.   (1)   My trustees shall not be liable for any act or default of any investment manager or nominee employed in good faith to manage or hold assets of my estate nor for any act or default of any beneficiary having the occupation use or enjoyment of property in kind.[1]

(2)   Section 11(1) of the Trusts of Land and Appointment of Trustees Act 1996 (consultation with beneficiaries) shall not apply to the exercise by my trustees of any of their powers in relation to land subject to the trusts hereof.[2]

1   This makes it clear that the trustees are not liable for the defaults of others who may have possession or control of trust property. For a wider form of indemnity, see Form B21.12 at para **[221.16]**.

2   The requirement that trustees of land, in exercise of any function relating to land subject to the trust, consult with beneficiaries of full age beneficially entitled to an interest in possession in the land can be excluded: see the TLATA 1996, s 11 (Part G, para **[246.97]**).

[224.32]

Professional trustee charging clause

11.   Any of my trustees being a professional or business man may charge and be paid all usual professional and other proper charges for business transacted acts done advice given and time spent by him or his firm in connection with the administration of my estate or in connection with the trusts hereof including acts which a personal representative or trustee not being in any profession or business could have done personally.

[224.33]

Testimonium

IN WITNESS whereof I have hereunto set my hand this —— day of —— 20——.

[224.34]

Attestation clause

SIGNED by the above-named [testator/testatrix] as
[his/her] last will in the presence of us both present at
the same time who at [his/her] request and in   *[Signature of*
[his/her] presence and in the presence of each other   *testator/testatrix]*
have signed our names below as witnesses:

[Signatures, addresses and descriptions of two witnesses]

[224.35]

FORM C2.2:   Reciprocal wills giving entire estate to spouse absolutely with alternative gift to children in equal or variable shares, their shares being settled on them for life

NOTE

Form C2.2 is an alternative to Form C2.1, and provides for the gift to the children, which takes effect where the testator's spouse predeceases the testator or fails to survive him or her by the survivorship period, to be a settled gift under which each child is given a life interest in his or her share with remainder to his or her children, but subject to a power to pay to each child the capital of his or her share. The trusts are accumulation and maintenance trusts within the ITA 1984, s 71 if they come into operation while some or all of the children are under the age of 18, and a power to vary the children's shares while they are under the age of 18 is included (but can be omitted if preferred). The main reasons for using a form such as Form C2.2 in preference to Form C2.1 are to provide flexibility as to whether, and if so at what age, the children obtain dominion over the capital of their shares, and to enable better capital gains tax planning if a child is not to become absolutely entitled to capital immediately on the coming to an end of an accumulation and maintenance trust (when hold-over relief would be available), for which see Part A, para **[200.39]**. Form C2.2 is therefore for couples who between them have a reasonable amount of property which justifies the greater complexity and concern for capital gains tax planning which it involves. For a form with even more flexibility in the trusts for children and remoter issue see Form C2.6 at para **[224.95]** et seq.

[224.36]

Revocation clause
I [*name*] of [*address*] hereby revoke all former testamentary dispositions made by me and declare this to be my last will.[1]

1   See the note to the revocation clause in Form C2.1 at para **[224.21]**.

[224.37]

Appointment of spouse as sole executor/executrix with alternative appointment
1.   [*As in cl 1 of* Form C2.1 *at para* **[224.22]**.]

[224.38]

Definition of 'my trustees'
2.   [*As in cl 2 of* Form C2.1 *at para* **[224.23]**.]

[224.39]

Appointment of guardians
3.   [*As in cl 3 of* Form C2.1 *at para* **[224.24]**.]

[224.40]

Primary gift of estate to spouse
4.   [*As in cl 4 of* Form C2.1 *at para* **[224.25]**.]

[224.41]

Alternative provisions if spouse does not survive

5.   [*As in cl 5 of* Form C2.1 *at para* **[224.26]**.]

[224.42]

Administration trusts of estate

6.   [*As in cl 6 of* Form C2.1 *at para* **[224.27]**.]

[224.43]

Beneficial trusts for children and issue

7.   (1)   Subject to the direction for retention and settlement hereinafter contained my trustees shall hold my residuary estate upon trust for such of my children [by my [wife/husband]][1] as shall survive me and attain the age of 18 years and if more than one [in equal shares[2]]/[in such shares as my trustees shall by deed or deeds appoint and in default of appointment in equal shares provided that no appointment shall be made under the foregoing power which shall increase or diminish the share of my residuary estate of any child of mine who shall at the date of such appointment have attained the age of 18 or the share of my residuary estate in which the child or children of any deceased child of mine shall for the time being be beneficially interested under the substitutional provision contained in the next following subclause].[3]

(2)   If any child of mine [by my [wife/husband]][4] shall die before attaining a vested interest under the foregoing trust leaving a child or children surviving me or born after my death who shall attain the age of [18/21] years [or marry under that age] then such last-mentioned child or children shall take and if more than one equally between them the share of my residuary estate which such deceased child of mine would have taken had he or she lived to attain a vested interest.

(3)   My residuary estate shall carry the intermediate income of my residuary estate and section 31 of the Trustee Act 1925 (as hereinafter modified) shall apply thereto accordingly.

(4)   The provisions of section 32 of the said Act (as hereinafter modified) shall apply in relation to my residuary estate and shall apply in relation to the presumptive share of any child of mine as if such child were contingently entitled to the capital thereof notwithstanding the direction for the retention and settlement of such share hereinafter contained.[5]

1   See Form C2.1, cl 7, n 1 at para **[224.28]**.
2   If a power to vary shares is required, these words should be deleted and the second alternative employed.
3   If a power to vary shares is not required, the words in this set of square brackets should be deleted and the first alternative employed.
4   These words should be included where the gift in the preceding subclause is confined to the children of the marriage.
5   This subclause is included since it is probable, in view of the settlement of each child's share, that the statutory power would not otherwise apply in his or her favour.

[224.44]

Settlement of child's share of residue

8.   The share of my residuary estate to which any child of mine shall become entitled on attaining the age of 18 years under the last foregoing clause hereof

[(whether pursuant to or in default of appointment)]¹ shall not vest in such child but shall be retained by my trustees and held upon the following trusts:

(a)   my trustees shall hold such share (hereinafter called 'the settled share') upon trust to pay the income thereof to such child of mine (hereinafter called 'the primary beneficiary') for life;

(b)   subject as aforesaid my trustees shall hold the settled share upon trust for all or any of the children or child of the primary beneficiary who shall attain the age of [18/21] years and if more than one in equal shares;

(c)   the trust declared by paragraph (b) hereof shall carry the intermediate income of such share (so far as not disposed of under paragraph (a) hereof) and the provisions of section 31 of the Trustee Act 1925 (as hereinafter modified) shall apply thereto accordingly;

(d)   the provisions of section 32 of the said Act (as hereinafter modified) shall apply in relation to the settled share;

(e)   notwithstanding the trusts aforesaid so long as the primary beneficiary is entitled to be paid the income of all or any part of the capital of the settled share (or would be so entitled if such capital yielded income)² my trustees shall have power in their absolute discretion from time to time to pay transfer or apply the whole or any part or parts of such capital to or for the benefit of the primary beneficiary in such manner as they shall in their absolute discretion think fit;

(f)   if there shall be no child of the primary beneficiary who shall attain a vested interest under the foregoing trusts the settled share (or so much thereof as has not been applied under any of the powers aforesaid) shall as from the death or other termination of the primary beneficiary's interest therein be held on the trusts and with and subject to the powers and provisions hereinbefore declared as if the primary beneficiary had predeceased me without leaving issue.

1   If the power to vary shares is omitted from cl 7(1), the words in brackets should also be omitted.

2   The reason for restricting the power in this way is to ensure that if the principal beneficiary releases his life interest in favour of the remainderman this power automatically ceases to apply.

[224.45]

Maintenance, accumulation and advancement

9.   [*As in cl 8 of* Form C2.1 *at para* **[224.29]**.]

[224.56]

Administrative powers

10.   [*As in cl 9 of* Form C2.1 *at para* **[224.30]**.]

[224.47]

Trustee liability

11.   [*As in cl 10 of* Form C2.1 *at para* **[224.31]**.]

[224.48]

Exercise of powers¹

12.   Any power or discretion hereby or by law conferred on my trustees (including a power or discretion as to the disposition of capital or income) shall

be exercisable notwithstanding that any of my trustees has a personal interest in such exercise provided that there are not fewer than two trustees and that at least one of them has no such personal interest.

1   This clause permits a member of the family to be a trustee without disqualifying him or her from benefit under any exercise of statutory or express powers of payment or application of capital, appointment, etc. See the Note in B18 at para **[218.4]**.

[224.49]
Professional trustee charging clause
13.   [*As in cl 11 of* Form C2.1 *at para* **[224.32]**.]

[224.50]
[*Testimonium and attestation clause as in* Form C2.1 *at paras* **[224.33]** and **[224.34]**.]

[224.51]

FORM C2.3:   Reciprocal wills leaving entire estate to spouse for life with power to resort to capital and with remainder to children

NOTE

This form confines the interest of the surviving spouse to a life interest only in the property of the first to die, but gives the trustees power to pay, transfer or apply capital of the estate of the first to die to or for the benefit of the survivor. Accordingly, the property of the first to die will ultimately go to the children of the marriage so far as not so paid transferred or applied by the trustees. This contrasts with an absolute gift of the property of the first to die to the survivor, where in the absence of mutual wills (see Form B1.6 at para **[201.10]**) the survivor will of course be free to dispose of the property he or she has inherited from the first to die.

The matrimonial home will often be the couple's main or only significant asset and the purpose of putting the property of the first to die in trust for the children will be frustrated if his or her interest in the house passes to the other absolutely under a joint tenancy. *It is essential when preparing wills of this type to examine the title to the matrimonial home carefully to see how it is held*; if it is owned as joint tenants beneficially the parties must be advised to effect a severance. It is assumed for the purposes of this form that the matrimonial home is owned by the testators as tenants in common; if one of the spouses is sole owner of the matrimonial home, Form C2.5 (at para **[224.79]** et seq) would be more appropriate. Where the testators' property is small, the expense of administering trusts may be difficult to justify and Form C2.1 (at paras **[224.20]**–**[224.34]**) may be more appropriate.

[224.52]
Revocation clause
I [*name*] of [*address*] hereby revoke all former testamentary dispositions made by me and declare this to be my last will.[1]

1   If the wills are not mutual wills in the technical sense, this clause could be extended as in the revocation clause in Form C2.1 at para **[224.21]** (see also the note thereto).

Part C   Complete wills

[224.53]

Appointment of executors and trustees

1.   I appoint my [wife/husband] [*name*] ('my [wife/husband]'), [*name*] of [*address*] and [*name*] of [*address*]¹ (hereinafter called 'my trustees' which expression shall include my personal representatives for the time being and the trustees for the time being hereof) to be the executors and trustees of this will.

1   If there are two executors as well as the wife/husband, there will still be two effective appointments if there is a divorce and the appointment of the wife/husband is nullified by the WA 1837, s 18A (Part G, para **[244.18]**).

[224.54]

Appointment of guardians

2.   [*As in cl 3 of* Form C2.1 *at para* **[224.24]**.]

[224.55]

Gift of personal chattels to spouse¹

3.   I give to my [wife/husband] absolutely all my personal chattels as defined by section 55(1)(x) of the Administration of Estates Act 1925² [And I request [her/him] (but without imposing any trust or binding obligation on [her/him]) to give effect to any wishes as to the disposition of such chattels which may be contained in any memorandum that may be found amongst my papers at my death or which may have otherwise been communicated to [her/him] during my life].³

1   It is not a good idea to settle chattels, because the trouble and expense of administering them as part of a trust fund is usually out of all proportion to their value, though it may sometimes be appropriate in the case of valuable ones. Accordingly an absolute gift of these to the surviving spouse is included in this Form.
2   See Part G, para **[246.52]** for the wording of this definition, and for further discussion of the meaning of 'personal chattels' see Vol 1, para **[64.44]**.
3   If property bequeathed by a will to one person is distributed to another person in accordance with wishes expressed by the testator within two years of his death, it is treated for inheritance tax purposes as having been bequeathed by the will to that other person: ITA 1984, s 143; see also B4 at para **[204.8]**. Where it is the testator's spouse to whom the property is bequeathed in the first place, s 143 may operate disadvantageously as it will cause the property so distributed by the spouse to cease being part of an exempt gift and to become part of a chargeable one. Where this is a problem, eg where large values are involved, the spouse could wait until after two years from the testator's death to distribute in accordance with his wishes.

[224.56]

Administration trusts of residue

4.   [*As in cl 6 of* Form C2.1 *at para* **[224.27]**.]

[224.57]

Primary trust for spouse

5.   If my [wife/husband] shall survive me [for the period of one month]¹ my trustees shall hold my residuary estate upon trust to pay the income thereof to my [wife/husband] for life Provided that so long as my [wife/husband] is entitled to be paid the income of all or any part of the capital of my residuary estate (or would be so entitled if such capital yielded income)² my trustees shall

have power in their absolute discretion from time to time to pay transfer or apply the whole or any part or parts of such capital to or for the benefit of my [wife/husband] in such manner as they shall in their absolute discretion think fit.

1   See the Preliminary Note on survivorship conditions at paras **[224.2]–[224.4]** and Form C2.1, cl 4, n 1 at para **[224.25]**. If the survivorship condition is not wanted the words in this set of square brackets should be omitted.
2   There are two reasons for restricting the power to capital in which the spouse has an interest in possession: first, to ensure that the power is not exercisable if there is a divorce and the primary trust lapses and, secondly, to ensure that the power ceases to be exercisable if the spouse assigns or surrenders his or her life interest. See the Preliminary Note at paras **[224.12]–[224.19]**.

[224.58]

Remainder trusts for children and issue[1]

EITHER

[6.   Subject to the trust and to any exercise of the power aforesaid my trustees shall hold my residuary estate upon trust for such of my children [by my [wife/husband]][2] as shall survive me and attain the age of [18/21/25] years and if more than one in equal shares Provided that if any child of mine shall die in my lifetime or having survived me shall die before attaining a vested interest leaving a child or children living at or born after my death who shall attain the age of [18/21] years such last-mentioned child or children shall take if more than one equally between them the share of my residuary estate to which such deceased child of mine would have become entitled had he or she lived to attain a vested interest.]

OR

[6.   (1)   Subject to the trust and to any exercise of the power aforesaid my trustees shall hold my residuary estate and the income thereof upon trust for such of my children and remoter issue and if more than one in such shares and with such trusts powers and provisions (including trusts and powers conferring on any person or persons a discretion as to the disposition of capital or income and including provisions for the accumulation of income during any period permitted by law) as my [wife/husband] shall by any deed or deeds revocable or irrevocable or by will or codicil appoint.

(2)   Subject to and in default of any such appointment my trustees shall hold my residuary estate upon trust for such of my children [by my [wife/husband]][3] as survive me and attain the age of [18/21/25] years and if more than one in equal shares provided that:

(a)   if [any child of mine]/[any child of mine by my [wife/husband]][4] shall die in my lifetime or having survived me shall die before attaining a vested interest leaving a child or children surviving me or born after my death who shall attain the age of [18/21] years such last-mentioned child or children shall take if more than one equally between them the share of my residuary estate to which such deceased child of mine would have become entitled had he or she lived to attain a vested interest; and

(b) no person who or whose issue shall take an interest in any part or share of my residuary estate under any such appointment as aforesaid shall participate in the unappointed part without bringing into account the appointed part or share and accounting for the same accordingly.]

1   Alternative clauses are set out, the first giving the children fixed interests, the second conferring an overriding power of appointment amongst issue on the spouse. Under neither alternative are the interests of the children contingent on surviving the life tenant, so that the interest of a child who survives the testator and attains the vesting age (if any) but predeceases the life tenant will vest in his or her personal representatives as part of his or her estate on death.

2   These words will ensure that the ultimate remainders in the wills of both spouses are identical in terms of whom they benefit, in circumstances where one spouse has children who are not children of the other spouse and who are not intended to benefit. See, further, the Preliminary Note on reciprocal wills and the ultimate destination of property at paras **[224.9]–[224.11]** and for forms for use where one or both spouses have children who are not children of the marriage, and who are intended to benefit, see C5 at para **[227.1]** et seq.

3   See n 2 supra. Even if this trust is restricted in this way it is not necessary to impose the same restriction on the objects of the power in the preceding clause.

4   The second of these alternatives is appropriate where the primary trust is confined to the children of the marriage.

[224.59]

Maintenance, accumulation and advancement
7. [*As in cl 8 of* Form C2.1 *at para* **[224.29]**.]

[224.60]

Administrative powers
8. [*As in cl 9 of* Form C2.1 *at para* **[224.30]**.]

[224.61]

Trustee liability
9. [*As in cl 10 of* Form C2.1 *at para* **[224.31]**.]

[224.62]

Exercise of powers
10. [*As in cl 12 of* Form C2.2 *at para* **[224.48]**.]

[224.63]

Appointment of new trustees
[11. The power of appointing new trustees shall be vested in my [wife/husband] during [her/his] life].

[224.64]

Professional trustee charging clause
12. [*As in cl 11 of* Form C2.1 *at para* **[224.32]**.]

[224.65]

[*Testimonium and attestation clause as in* Form C2.1 *at paras* **[224.33]** and **[224.34]**.]

[224.66]

FORM C2.4:   Reciprocal wills giving spouse life interest with power of appointment amongst issue, incorporating Statutory Will Forms

NOTE

The Statutory Will Forms, the text of which appear in Part E at para **[238.1]** et seq provide a shorthand method of incorporating fairly elaborate beneficial and administrative provisions. The disadvantage is that the testator cannot immediately see the nature and effect of his will. This form is similar in effect to, but not identical with, Form C2.3 (see paras **[224.51]–[224.65]**), where the second alternative version of Form C2.3, cl 6 is used; attention is drawn to the Note at the beginning of Form C2.3 (see para **[224.51]**) and in particular the point that it is important to investigate the title to the matrimonial home and see that any joint tenancy is severed where wills of this kind are being made.

The main difference in the beneficial trusts between this form and Form C2.3 is that this form does not contain a power to pay or apply capital to or for the benefit of the surviving spouse, and a child's interest will vest on marriage if that takes place before he or she attains the vesting age. Also, the spouse's life interest is not subject to a survivorship condition (see the Preliminary Note at paras **[224.2]–[224.4]** for the merits of having such a condition in a will of this type), and in relation to the remainder trust for the children of the testator or testatrix there is no option of confining it to being a trust for the children of the marriage (see the Preliminary Note at para **[224.6]** for the significance of this point).

Although the will is shortened by the use of the Statutory Will Forms, it is necessary in order to produce a will which is reasonably in accordance with modern conditions and practice to include a fair number of express administrative and other provisions, still producing quite a long document, and it must be questioned whether use of the Statutory Will Forms is worthwhile.

[224.67]

Revocation clause

I [*name*] of [*address*] hereby revoke all former testamentary dispositions made by me and declare this to be my last will.[1]

1   If the wills are not mutual wills in the technical sense, this clause could be extended as in the revocation clause in Form C2.1 at para **[224.21]** (see the note thereto).

[224.68]

Appointment of executors and trustees

1.   [*As in cl 1 of* Form C2.3 *at para* **[224.53]**.]

[224.69]

Appointment of guardians[1]

2.   [*As in cl 3 of* Form C2.1 *at para* **[224.24]**.]

1   For the reasons given in the Preliminary Note (see para **[224.7]**), the appointment of guardians incorporated in the forms in this section will take effect only if the other spouse dies first.

[224.70]

Gift of personal chattels to spouse

3.   I give to my [wife/husband] absolutely all my personal chattels as defined by Form 2 of the Statutory Will Forms 1925[1] which is hereby incorporated in this will.

1   The text of Form 2 of the Statutory Wills Forms is set out at para **[238.8]**. It is almost exactly the same as the definition of 'personal chattels' in the AEA 1925, s 55(1)(x) (Part G, para **[246.52]**) (which is the definition used in Form C2.3, cl 3 at para **[224.55]**) and almost certainly the same in its effect. The only significant verbal difference is that the Statutory Will Forms makes an express reference to wearing apparel as included in articles of household or personal use or ornament.

[224.71]

Administration trusts of residue

4.   I give all my property not hereby or by any codicil hereto otherwise effectively disposed of to my trustees and Form 8 of the Statutory Will Forms 1925[1] shall apply thereto [provided that all income of my estate received at any time after my death shall be deemed to accrue on the date on which it is payable and shall not be apportioned to any other time or period].

1   Form 8 of the Statutory Will Forms (at para **[238.14]**) contains an elaborate administration trust but includes only a narrow power of investment. A wide power of investment is included in cl 7 of this form (see Form C2.1, cl 9(a) at para **[224.30]**) which displaces the power contained in Form 8 of the Statutory Will Forms (see Form C1.5, n 5 at para **[223.6]**). Form 8 excludes the rule in *Howe v Dartmouth*, but not time apportionment either at the testator's death or at any subsequent time. If time apportionment is to be excluded, the proviso to this clause in square brackets should be included. The provisions of Form 8, cl 7(c) leave the trustees free to apply or exclude the rule in *Allhusen v Whittell*. For a general discussion of the equitable rules of apportionment and the statutory rules of apportionment over time see Vol 1, paras **[38.17]**–**[38.25]** and B14 at paras **[214.35]**–**[214.37]**.

[224.72]

Beneficial trusts for spouse and issue

5.   Form 9 of the Statutory Will Forms 1925[1] is incorporated in this will and shall apply to so much of my estate as devolves on my trustees under clause 4 hereof as is not required for administration purposes.

1   Form 9 of the Statutory Will Forms (at para **[238.15]**) creates trusts under which the spouse takes a life interest coupled with a power to appoint among issue exercisable by deed or will with a default trust equally between all surviving children of the testator who attain 21 or marry under that age subject to hotchpot.

[224.73]

Maintenance, accumulation and advancement

6.   [*As in cl 8 of* Form C2.1 *at para* **[224.29]**.]

[224.74]

Administrative powers

7.   [*As in cl 9 of* Form C2.1 *at para* **[224.30]**.]

[224.75]

Exercise of powers

8.   [*As in cl 12 of* Form C2.2 *at para* **[224.48]**.]

[224.76]

Appointment of new trustees
9. [*As in cl 11 of* Form C2.3 *at para* **[224.63]**.]

[224.77]

Professional trustee charging clause
10. [*As in cl 11 of* Form C2.1 *at para* **[224.32]**.]

[224.78]
[*Testimonium and attestation clause as in* Form C2.1 *at paras* **[224.33]** and **[224.34]**.]

[224.79]

FORM C2.5: **Will of husband who owns matrimonial home giving wife income of residue and right of residence for life or until remarriage**

NOTE

This form caters for the situation where the matrimonial home is owned by one spouse only and assumes, as is more often the case, that that spouse is the husband. The form can, however, be readily adapted for use by a wife. The form contains alternative provisions giving the wife a full interest or an interest during widowhood only. The latter alternative may not be very effective in view of the power to advance capital to the wife and in view of the more ready acceptance nowadays of couples living together without marrying. A gift during widowhood is restored on the annulment of a second or subsequent marriage being made absolute (*Re Dewhirst, Flower v Dewhirst* [1948] Ch 198, [1948] 1 All ER 147), though not where the subsequent marriage is voidable (as distinct from void): see the Matrimonial Causes Act 1973, s 16 and see Vol 1, para **[35.8]**. A transaction carried into execution before annulment cannot be set aside, *Re Eaves, Eaves v Eaves* [1940] Ch 109, [1939] 4 All ER 260, CA. If the widowhood option is adopted, it may be desired to make a reduced provision after remarriage: see, for example, Form B16.5 at para **[216.10]**.

[224.80]

Revocation clause
I [*name*] of [*address*] hereby revoke all former testamentary dispositions made by me and declare this to be my last will.[1]

1 See n 1 to the revocation clause in Form C2.1 at para **[224.21]**.

[224.81]

Appointment of executors and trustees
1. I appoint my wife [*name*] ('my wife'), [*name*] of [*address*] and [*name*] of [*address*][1] (hereinafter together called 'my trustees' which expression shall include my personal representatives for the time being and the trustees for the time being hereof) to be the executors and trustees of this will.

1 See the note to Form C2.3, cl 1 at para **[224.53]**.

[224.82]

Appointment of guardians[1]

2.   If my wife shall not survive me I appoint [*name*] of [*address*] [and [*name*] of [*address*]] to be the [guardian/guardians] of my children during their respective minorities.

1   On this form of appointment of guardians see the Preliminary Note at para **[224.7]** and the Note in B3 at paras **[203.43]–[203.54]**; for alternative forms see Forms B3.26 to B3.32 at paras **[203.55]–[203.61]**; for the relevant law see Vol 1, para **[28.1]** et seq.

[224.83]

Gift of personal chattels to wife[1]

3.   I give to my wife all my personal chattels as defined by section 55(1)(x) of the Administration of Estates Act 1925.

1   See Form C2.3, cl 3, n 1 at para **[224.55]**.

[224.84]

Gift of pecuniary legacies

4.   I give the following pecuniary legacies free of tax:[1]

   (a)   to my wife the sum of £—— to be paid to her immediately after my death and in priority to all other legacies hereby given[2];
   (b)   to [name] the sum of £——;
   (c)   to [name] the sum of £——.

1   There is a risk with pecuniary legacies, particularly when given by a better-off testator, that they may be payable out of a residuary estate which includes property situated outside the UK, with the consequence that the legacies may be liable to bear their own inheritance tax so far as payable out of the foreign property: see the Note in B14 at para **[214.63]**. Accordingly, it is better to provide expressly for the incidence of the inheritance tax (and foreign death duties) on legacies. The expression 'free of tax' is employed here in conjunction with the definition and direction as to payment in cl 7 of this Form at para **[224.87]**.
2   In the absence of express provision a legacy will not take priority even though it is to be paid to a wife for her immediate needs: *Re Schweder's Estate, Oppenheim v Schweder* [1891] 3 Ch 44. The legacy should therefore be given priority so as to ensure that it does not abate with any other legacies which are given. The legacy should also be made payable on death so as to carry interest from that date: *Re Pollock, Pugsley v Pollock* [1943] Ch 338, [1943] 2 All ER 443.

[224.85]

Right for wife to occupy matrimonial home[1]

5.   (1)   If my wife shall survive me [for the period of one month][2] I give my freehold dwellinghouse[3] known as ——, or (if the same shall be sold or otherwise disposed of before my death) the dwellinghouse or the principal dwellinghouse (if I have more than one) which I shall own at the date of my death,[4] to my trustees free of all sums charged or otherwise secured thereon at my death (which sums shall be paid out of my residuary estate) to hold the same and the assets from time to time representing the same on trust for [my wife] during her life.

   (2)   It is a purpose of the foregoing trust to provide a home for [my wife] so long as she so desires[5] and I declare that my trustees shall not be liable for lack

of insurance repair or payment of outgoings of any home occupied by her under the foregoing trust or for not taking steps to enforce any reasonable conditions imposed by my trustees on [my wife] in relation to her occupation of any such home.[6]

(3)   My trustees may invest trust moneys and change investments with the same unrestricted freedom of choice as a sole beneficial owner, may apply the same in the purchase of any undivided share (whether in co-ownership with [my wife] or any other person) in a home to be occupied by [my wife], and may apply the same in the improvement or repair of any land or buildings for the time being subject to the foregoing trusts.[7]

(4)   All the powers of my trustees may be exercised by them in favour of or for the benefit of [my wife] even though she is one of my trustees, and at any time when she is not one of my trustees her consent shall still be required to any exercise of the trustees' powers of sale purchase or leasing in relation to any land or buildings subject to this Clause.[8]

(5)   Subject as aforesaid the said dwellinghouse and the assets representing the same shall fall into my residuary estate.

---

1   The widow is given a life or widowhood interest in residue, into which the matrimonial home would fall if this clause were omitted. However, this separate provision makes it clearer that the statutory right of occupation of a beneficiary under the TLATA 1996, s 12(1)(a) (Part G, para **[246.98]**) is to apply, and make the matrimonial home further on in the order in which assets are applied to pay debts and testamentary expenses. For rights of residence and alternative forms for providing such rights see the Preliminary Note and Forms in B8 at para **[208.1]** et seq.

2   See the Preliminary Note on survivorship conditions at paras **[224.2]–[224.4]** and the note to Form C2.1, cl 4 at para **[224.25]**. If the survivorship condition is not wanted the words in this set of square brackets should be omitted. If the survivorship condition is omitted from this clause but retained in the trusts of residue, and the wife dies after the testator but within the survivorship period, she will have a brief interest in possession in the house but not in residue. However, if the survivorship condition is omitted from the residuary trusts but retained in this clause, the effect will be the same as omitting the survivorship condition in both places, ie the wife will have a brief interest in possession in the entire estate apart from the pecuniary legacies, because the house falls into residue if the survivorship condition is not fulfilled.

3   If the testator has more than one house there could be merit in tightening the definition of the house with the words 'in which my wife and I now reside' or similar.

4   These words will create a right of residence in any house purchased in place of the matrimonial home occupied at the date of the will. Without such words the sale of the original matrimonial home prior to the testator's death would cause the gift of the right of residence to fail (although the widow would still have a life or widowhood interest in residue which would include any subsequently acquired home).

5   This should be sufficient to confer the statutory right of occupation on the beneficiary under the TLATA 1996, s 12(1)(a) (Part G, para **[246.98]**), and see the note to B8 at para **[208.5]**.

6   In the interests of economy there is no expression of wishes as to the conditions to be imposed on the beneficiary, but such could be included. See B8 at para **[208.19]**.

7   These are all thought to be applications of capital money which are not authorised by the TLATA 1996 (see Part G, para **[246.91]** and B8 at para **[208.26]**). This subclause can be omitted in whole or in part if there are provisions elsewhere in the will to the same effect which apply to this clause. It is not clear that the proceeds of sale of one property could be spent on improving another property under the powers conferred by the TLATA 1996 in the absence of express authorisation by the will. It is arguably not a power of an absolute owner in relation to the land within TLATA 1996, s 6(1), since it is something done in relation to the cash received from a sale of the land, and it is not the purchase of a legal estate in land within s 6(3).

8   TLATA 1996, s 8(2) (Part G, para **[246.93]**) enables exercise of the trustees' powers over land to be made subject to consents. The repeal by the TLATA 1996 of the LPA 1925, s 28(1) means that a requirement of consent to a sale is no longer applied by statute to other powers.

Part C   Complete wills

[224.86]

Administration trusts of residue

6.   [*As in cl 6 of* Form C2.1 *at para* **[224.27]**.]

[224.87]

Gifts made free of tax

7.   Any specific gift or pecuniary or general legacy made by this will or any codicil hereto which is expressed to be 'free of tax' shall be free from the payment of any inheritance tax or foreign tax or duty payable on or by reason of my death to which such gift or legacy would otherwise be subject and such inheritance tax or foreign tax or duty shall be paid out of my residuary estate.[1]

1   See cl 4, n 1 of this form at para **[224.84]**. Where specific gifts and pecuniary legacies are of, or wholly payable out of, free estate in the UK, the inheritance tax on them will be a testamentary expense payable out of residue without any express provision, and it is only where there is foreign property or settled property being disposed of by the will that a gift which is intended to be free of tax needs to be expressly declared to be free of tax: see further the Preliminary Note to B14 at para **[214.55]** et seq.

[224.88]

Beneficial trusts of residue

8.   My trustees shall hold my residuary estate upon the following trusts:

(a)   if my wife shall survive me [for the period of one month][1] my trustees shall pay the income of my residuary estate to my wife during her [life/widowhood];

(b)   provided that my trustees shall have power in their absolute discretion from time to time so long as my wife is entitled to be paid the income of all or any part of the capital of my residuary estate (or would be so entitled if such capital yielded income) to pay transfer or apply the whole or any part or parts of such capital[2] to her or for her benefit in such manner as they shall in their absolute discretion think fit;

(c)   subject as aforesaid my trustees shall hold my residuary estate in trust as to both capital and income in equal shares if more than one for all my children[3] who attain the age of [18/21] years [or marry under that age][4] provided that:

(i)   if any such child of mine shall have died in my lifetime whether before or after the date of this my will leaving issue living at my death who attain the age of [18/21] years or marry under that age then such issue shall take if more than one in equal shares per stirpes the share of my residuary estate which such deceased child of mine would have taken had he or she survived me and attained a vested interest but so that no issue shall take whose parent is alive at my death and so capable of taking;

(ii)   if any such child of mine shall survive me but shall die before attaining a vested interest under the foregoing trust leaving a child or children who attain the age of [18/21] years or marry under that age then such child or children shall take by substitution if more than one in equal shares the share of my residuary estate which such child of mine would have taken if he or she had attained a vested interest.[5]

1   See the Preliminary Note on survivorship conditions at paras **[224.2]–[224.4]**; and Form C2.1, cl 4, n 1 at para **[224.25]**. If the survivorship condition is not wanted the words in this set of square brackets should be omitted. If this survivorship condition is omitted, that in cl 5 supra should also be omitted: see cl 5, n 2 at para **[224.85]**.

2   There are two reasons for restricting the power to being exercisable only over capital in which the wife has an interest in possession: first, to ensure that the power is not exercisable if there is a divorce and the primary trust fails; and second, to ensure that the power ceases to be exercisable if the wife assigns or surrenders her life interest. See the Preliminary Note at paras **[224.12]–[224.19]**.

3   This trust is not confined to being in favour of the children of the marriage. See the Preliminary Note on reciprocal wills and the ultimate destination of property at paras **[224.9]–[224.11]**.

4   This form follows the rules of intestate succession and makes no difference between sons and daughters as regards marriage under 18 or 21: AEA 1925, s 47(1)(i) (Part G, para **[244.61]**). Where it is desired to make a distinction between sons and daughters, the words 'or marry under that age' should be changed to 'or being daughters attain that age or marry under that age' on each occasion where it occurs.

5   Clause 8(c) combines two different sorts of substitution, the substitution of issue remoter than children being only relevant to cases where the testator's child has predeceased the testator, since a child could not leave issue remoter than his own children if he died under the vesting age. As to substitutional provisions and inheritance tax accumulation and maintenance trusts, see Part A, para **[200.131]** and, for a slightly more comprehensive clause on the same lines, see Form B19.6 at para **[219.19]**.

[224.89]

Maintenance, accumulation and advancement

9.   [*As in cl 8 of* Form C2.1 *at para* **[224.29]**.]

[224.90]

Administrative powers

10.   [*As in cl 9 of* Form C2.1 *at para* **[224.30]**.]

[224.91]

Exercise of powers

11.   [*As in cl 12 of* Form C2.2 *at para* **[224.48]**.]

[224.92]

Appointment of new trustees

12.   [*As in cl 11 of* Form C2.3 *at para* **[224.63]**.]

[224.93]

Professional trustee charging clause

13.   [*As in cl 11 of* Form C2.1 *at para* **[224.32]**.]

[224.94]

[*Testimonium and attestation clause as* Form C2.1 *at paras* **[224.33]** and **[224.34]**.]

[224.95]

FORM C2.6:   Will of husband conferring life interest on wife with settled remainders for children and with wide overriding powers

NOTE

Like Form C2.5, this is for the wealthier spouse, again assumed to be the husband, but the form could be readily adapted for a wife. It is similar to Form

C2.5 in its provision for the testator's wife if she survives him (she is given a full life interest in residue), save that her interest is subject to the wide overriding powers in favour of other beneficiaries (mentioned further below) as well as a power to pay her capital. The remainder trusts are more elaborate, and more flexible, than those in Form C2.5, in that the shares of the testator's children, instead of vesting absolutely at a specified age as in Form C2.5, are settled on them for life, and are subject to overriding powers to appoint or apply capital amongst the testator's issue and their spouses. A will of this type gives maximum flexibility while providing essentially interest in possession trusts. It enables potentially exempt transfers to be made of the residuary estate during the widow's life in favour of the testator's issue by exercise of the trustees' powers, the shares taken by the children and the trusts affecting them can be varied by exercise of those powers, generation-skipping appointments can be made, and the vesting of capital in any of the children can be deferred indefinitely. See Part A, para **[200.39]–[200.42]** for the capital gains tax advantages of deferring vesting and of interest in possession trusts.

[224.96]

Revocation clause

I [*name*] of [*address*] hereby revoke all former testamentary dispositions made by me and declare this to be my last will.[1]

1   See n 1 to the revocation clause in Form C2.1 at para **[224.21]**.

[224.97]

Appointment of executors and trustees

1.   [*As in cl 1 of* Form C2.5 *at para* **[224.81]**.]

[224.98]

Appointment of guardians

2.   [*As in cl 2 of* Form C2.5 *at para* **[224.82]**.]

[224.99]

Gift of personal chattels to wife

3.   [*As in cl 3 of* Form C2.5 *at para* **[224.83]**.]

[224.100]

Gift of pecuniary legacies

4.   [*As in cl 4 of* Form C2.5 *at para* **[224.84]**.]

[224.101]

Right for wife to occupy matrimonial home for life[1]

5.   [*As in cl 5 of* Form C2.5 *at para* **[224.85]**, *deleting 'widowhood' in both places where it appears.*]

1   The separate provision of this clause gives the widow security of occupation, and the trustees' powers of appointment or application in cl 11 will only arise in relation to the house if it is sold

with the widow's consent. Accordingly, the widow will arguably be settlor for income tax purposes of any money or other property representing the house which is appointed or applied in favour of other beneficiaries, at any rate where she has consented to a sale in order to enable such appointment or application (although there are some indications that this may not be a point taken by the Inland Revenue). If it is preferred to avoid this risk, this clause could be omitted, and the house will be in residue subject to a trustees' power to permit the widow to reside. If the house is owned jointly or in common by the testator and his wife this clause is not appropriate and should be omitted. See Form C2.5, cl 5, n 2 at para **[224.85]** with respect to the inclusion or omission of a survivorship condition.

[224.102]

Administration trusts of residue
6.   [*As in cl 6 of* Form C2.1 *at para* **[224.27]**.]

[224.103]

Gifts made free of tax
7.   [*As in cl 7 of* Form C2.5 *at para* **[224.87]**.]

[224.104]

Beneficial trusts of residue for wife
8.   My trustees shall hold my residuary estate upon the following trusts:

(a)   if my wife shall survive me [for the period of one month][1] my trustees shall pay the income of my residuary estate to my wife during her life;

(b)   provided that my trustees shall have power in their absolute discretion from time to time so long as my wife is entitled to be paid the income of all or any part of the capital of my residuary estate (or would be so entitled if such capital yielded income)[2] to pay transfer or apply the whole or any part or parts of such capital to her or for her benefit in such manner as they shall in their absolute discretion think fit.[3]

1   See the Preliminary Note on survivorship conditions at paras **[224.2]**–**[224.4]** and Form C2.1, cl 4, n 1 at para **[224.25]**. If the survivorship condition is not wanted the words in this set of square brackets should be omitted. If this survivorship condition is omitted, that in cl 5 above should also be omitted: see Form C2.5, cl 5, n 2 at para **[224.85]**.
2   There are two reasons for restricting the power to capital in which the wife has an interest in possession: first, to ensure that the power is not exercisable if there is a divorce and the primary trust fails (see the Preliminary Note at paras **[224.12]**–**[224.19]**); and second, to ensure that the power ceases to be exercisable if the wife assigns or surrenders her life interest, although the latter is unlikely to happen if the overriding powers in cl 11 are included (any exercise of the powers in cl 11 would override the power to pay or apply in favour of the widow whether or not the latter power was restricted to property in which she has an interest in possession).
3   This power could be omitted if the overriding powers in cl 11 are included.

[224.105]

Beneficial trusts of residue for children and issue[1]
9.   (1)   Subject as aforesaid my trustees shall hold my residuary estate upon trust for such of my children[2] as shall survive me and attain the age of 18 years and if more than one in equal shares Provided that if any child of mine shall predecease me or having survived me shall fail to attain a vested interest leaving a child or children living at my death or born thereafter who shall attain the age of 21 years[3] such last-mentioned child or children shall take and if more than

one equally between them the share of my residuary estate which such deceased child of mine would have taken had he or she lived to attain a vested interest;

(2)   The foregoing trusts shall carry the intermediate income of my residuary estate and section 31 of the Trustee Act 1925 (as hereinafter modified) shall apply thereto;

(3)   Section 32 of the Trustee Act 1925 (as hereinafter modified) shall apply in relation to the said trusts and shall be exercisable for the benefit of any child of mine in relation to his or her presumptive share of my residuary estate notwithstanding the direction for the retention and settlement of such share hereinafter contained.[4]

1   The beneficial trusts contained in this clause satisfy the conditions specified in the ITA 1984, s 71(1) in relation to any child who has not attained an interest in possession. The substitutional proviso is confined to grandchildren rather than issue generally and accordingly the 25-year limit imposed by s 71(2)(a) does not apply.

2   This trust is not confined to being in favour of the children of the marriage. See the Preliminary Note on reciprocal wills and the ultimate destination of property at paras **[224.9]–[224.11]**.

3   For perpetuity reasons, the age contingency for grandchildren should not exceed 21. The age of vesting for the children is 18 because the children's interests are settled on them for life, with them becoming entitled to receive the income at 18, and a higher vesting age for them would serve little purpose.

4   See Form C2.2, cl 7(4), n 5 at para **[224.43]**. It is appropriate to include this provision even if the overriding powers in cl 11 are included: the overriding powers can only be exercised over property in which there is an interest in possession, whereas the Trustee Act 1925, s 32 as applied by this clause will be exercisable over property subject to accumulation and maintenance trusts of income during a minority.

[224.106]

Settlement of child's share of residue

10.   (1)   The share of my residuary estate to which any child of mine shall become entitled under the foregoing clause hereof shall not vest absolutely in such child but shall be retained by my trustees and held upon the following trusts:

(a)   my trustees shall hold such share upon trust to pay the income thereof to such child of mine during his or her life;

(b)   subject as aforesaid my trustees shall hold such share upon trust for such of the children of such child as shall attain the age of [18/21] years and if more than one in equal shares absolutely;

(c)   the trust declared by paragraph (b) above shall carry the intermediate income of such share and section 31 of the Trustee Act 1925 (as hereinafter modified) shall apply thereto;

(d)   section 32 of the Trustee Act 1925 (as hereinafter modified) shall apply in relation to such share;

(e)   [notwithstanding the trusts aforesaid so long as such child of mine is entitled to be paid the income of all or any part of the capital of such share (or would be so entitled if such capital yielded income)[1] my trustees shall have power in their absolute discretion from time to time to pay transfer or apply the whole or any part or parts of such capital to or for the benefit of such child in such manner as they shall in their absolute discretion think fit;[2]]

(f)   if there shall be no child of such child of mine who shall attain the age of [18/21] years such share and any other share of my residuary estate which may have accrued thereto hereunder (or so much thereof as shall not have been appointed or applied under any of the powers applicable thereto hereunder) shall go and accrue to the other shares or share of my residuary estate the trusts whereof are at the date of such accruer subsisting and capable of taking effect.

(2)   Subject as aforesaid my trustees shall hold my residuary estate and the income thereof upon trust for such of my children as shall survive me and if more than one in equal shares.

1   See Form C2.2, cl 8(e), n 2 at para **[224.44]**.
2   If the overriding powers in cl 11 are included the power contained in this paragraph will be unnecessary and may be omitted.

[224.107]

Overriding powers to appoint and apply capital[1]

[11.   (1)   In this clause the following expressions have the following meaning:

(a)   'the discretionary beneficiaries' means and includes:
  (i)   my wife [and any husband of hers];[2]
  (ii)   my children and remoter issue whether living at my death or born thereafter;
  (iii)   any spouse widow or widower of any of my said children or remoter issue (and 'widow' and 'widower' shall include a widow or widower who has remarried);
(b)   'appointable share' means any part or share of my residuary estate (up to the whole thereof) in which any beneficiary is for the time being entitled to an interest in possession within the meaning of Part III of the Inheritance Tax Act 1984 not being a part or share of my residuary estate (up to the whole thereof) which has or would (but for this present clause) have vested indefeasibly in any person under the trusts hereinbefore declared;
(c)   'the vesting day' means the day on which shall expire the period of 21 years immediately following the death of the last survivor of the following persons:
  (i)   my wife;
  (ii)   my children;
  (iii)   any grandchild of mine born in my lifetime.

(2)   Notwithstanding and in derogation of the foregoing trusts powers and provisions my trustees (being not fewer than two in number [or a trust corporation][3]) may [with the consent in writing of my wife during her life and otherwise at their discretion][4] exercise any of the following powers:

(a)   power at any time or times and from time to time before the vesting day by deed or deeds revocable or irrevocable to appoint any part or share of my residuary estate (up to the whole thereof) which is at the date of such exercise an appointable share (as hereinbefore defined) upon trust for all or such one or more exclusive of the others or other of the discretionary beneficiaries if more than one in such shares and either absolutely or at such age or time or respective ages or times and with such trusts and

powers for their respective benefit and such provisions as my trustees may think fit and my trustees may in exercise of the foregoing power:
- (i)   delegate or create powers or discretions over capital or income including powers of further delegation or powers to create further powers or discretions over capital or income;
- (ii)   create powers or trusts for the accumulation of income during any period permitted by law;
- (iii) provide for the total or partial exclusion from benefit of any person or persons or class of persons;
- (iv)   create administrative powers or provisions of whatever nature;

provided that:
- (1)   no such appointment shall invalidate any payment transfer or application of capital or income previously made or any entitlement to income which has already accrued under any of the trusts or powers herein elsewhere contained;
- (2)   every interest limited under any exercise of such power shall vest in interest (if at all) not later than the vesting day;
- (3)   any such appointment may be made in respect of income alone without any appointment of capital;
- (4)   any such revocable appointment shall (so far as then unrevoked) cease to be revocable on the vesting day;

(b)   power at any time or times and from time to time before the vesting day in their absolute discretion to pay transfer or apply any part or share of my residuary estate (up to the whole thereof) which is at the date of such payment transfer or application an appointable share (as hereinbefore defined) to or for the benefit of all or any one or more exclusive of the others or other of the discretionary beneficiaries if more than one in such shares and generally in such manner as my trustees shall think fit;

(c)   power at any time or times and from time to time before the vesting day by deed or deeds to release or restrict all or any of the powers contained in the present subclause (including this present power) either in whole or in part and in any manner they think fit.]

1   This clause confers wide powers to appoint and apply capital. To preserve the status of the trusts in favour of the testator's issue as accumulation and maintenance trusts so long as such issue have not attained an interest in possession, the powers are only exercisable in relation to 'an appointable share', ie a share of residue in which an interest in possession subsists at the date of the exercise of the power. If not required, the clause can be omitted.
2   In order to take advantage of the spouse exemption for inheritance tax it might be advantageous to include a future husband of the widow as a member of the discretionary class. However, this may well not be acceptable to the testator.
3   These words should be included if a trust corporation is to be an executor, or if there is a possibility that a trust corporation might subsequently be appointed a trustee. In either case express provision for the remuneration of a trust corporation so acting (not included in this Form) will need to be added: see eg Forms B3.11 to B3.14 (at paras **[203.28]–[203.31]**) and Form B21.35 (at para **[221.38]**). If it is desired to make it possible for a foreign corporation to be appointed as sole trustee, it will also be necessary to amend these words to '(being not fewer than two in number or a body corporate)' and to vary the statutory power of appointment of new trustees as in Form B21.40 at para **[221.52]**.
4   These words are inserted for the widow's protection, but have the disadvantage that any appointment or application of capital with the wife's consent which cuts short her income interest could make her settlor of such income for tax purposes. See also the note to cl 5 of this form at para **[224.101]**.

[224.108]

Maintenance, accumulation and advancement

12.   [*As in cl 8 of* Form C2.1 *at para* **[224.29]**.]

[224.109]

Administrative powers

13.   [*As in cl 9 of* Form C2.1 *at para* **[224.30]**.]

[224.110]

Trustee liability

14.   [*As in cl 10 of* Form C2.1 *at para* **[224.31]**.]

[224.111]

Exercise of powers

15.   [*As in cl 12 of* Form C2.2 *at para* **[224.48]**.]

[224.112]

Appointment of new trustees

16.   [*As in cl 11 of* Form C2.3 *at para* **[224.63]**.]

[224.113]

Professional trustee charging clause

17.   [*As in cl 11 of* Form C2.1 *at para* **[224.32]**.]

[224.114]

[*Testimonium and attestation clause as in* Form C2.1 *at paras* **[224.33]** and **[224.34]**.]

C3 Wills for married couples with adult children

PRELIMINARY NOTE

[225.1]
General strategy and inheritance tax. This section contains a selection of forms for use by married couples with adult children. Accordingly, trusts for their children are mostly in favour of named children, and are not contingent on attaining a specified age. Since married couples with adult children are likely to be middle-aged or elderly, some provision for tax-planning is included, principally by means of a nil-rate band legacy either direct to the children, as in Forms C3.1 and C3.2, or on discretionary trusts under which the spouse is a beneficiary, as in Forms C3.4 and C3.5. For further discussion of nil-rate band discretionary trusts see the Note in B18 at paras **[218.16]–[218.24]**. For further forms see Form B10.51 at para **[210.72]** and Form B18.2 at para **[218.32]**.

[225.2]
Form C3.3 divides residue equally between spouse and issue, and provides an element of generation-skipping by settling the son's share directly on his children, while Form C3.6 subjects residue to a two-year discretionary trust in effect leaving it to the trustees to reconcile the competing objectives of making provision for the spouse and minimising the liability of the joint estate to inheritance tax. This type of disposition relies on the Inheritance Tax Act 1984 (ITA 1984), s 144, and a Note on s 144 precedes Form C3.6 (see para **[225.83]** et seq).

[225.3]

The forms in C3 will not usually be appropriate where the estates of a married couple are small, ie together amounting to less than the inheritance tax threshold, or exceeding it by not very much. Also, a nil-rate band discretionary trust will probably not achieve its objectives if the property subject to it is the matrimonial home, lived in by the surviving spouse, as that would probably confer an interest in possession on him or her: see the Note on nil-rate band discretionary trusts in B18 at paras **[218.16]–[218.24]** and for the tax implications of rights of residence see the Preliminary Note to B8 at para **[208.30]**. A possible solution to the problem may be to set up a debt or charge scheme, see Form C3.4 at para **[225.57]** et seq. See C2, especially Form C2.1 (at para **[224.20]** et seq) for forms more appropriate to families with more modest resources, or resources comprising little more than the matrimonial home, for whom the relatively elaborate provisions of C3 are not appropriate. Special considerations arise when the estate includes business or agricultural property. These are discussed in the Preliminary Notes to C11 and C12 at paras **[233.1]** et seq and **[234.1]** et seq.

[225.4]

Survivorship conditions. See the Preliminary Note to C2 at paras **[224.2]**–**[224.6]** for a discussion of survivorship conditions (they are also discussed in B19 at paras **[219.1]–[219.13]**). Where, in the event of the testator being survived by his or her spouse, a will makes a nil-rate band non-exempt gift and leaves the remainder of the testator's estate to the spouse, there is no inheritance tax advantage in making the gift to the spouse subject to a survivorship condition, and it could be an inheritance tax disadvantage to do so if the surviving spouse's separate estate was worth less than the inheritance tax nil-rate band (see para **[224.3]**, sub-para (iii)). Accordingly survivorship conditions are not included in inter-spouse gifts in C3. Survivorship conditions in gifts to persons other than the testator's spouse are discussed in the Preliminary Note to C2 at para **[224.6]**. They are not included in the forms in C3.

[225.5]

Guardians. It is assumed for the purposes of the forms in C3 that the testators' children have grown up, and no appointment of guardians is included in any of them.

[225.6]

Reciprocal and mutual wills. The Preliminary Note to C2 on this topic (at para **[224.8]**) applies also to C3.

[225.7]

Reciprocal wills and the ultimate destination of property. See the Preliminary Note to C2 at paras **[224.9]–[224.11]**. Where a husband and wife will not have any more children, it is possible to ensure that the alternative gift or remainder trust to or for the children is in favour of the same persons, in the wills of both spouses, by naming the children. Most of the forms in C3 provide for this to be done, and where they do not there are optional words confining the gift or trust to the children of the marriage.

[225.8]
The possibility of divorce. The Preliminary Note to C2 on this topic (at paras **[224.12]–[224.19]**) applies also to C3.

[225.9]

FORM C3.1:   **Reciprocal wills giving nil-rate band legacy to children and residue to spouse with default gift to children in equal/unequal shares**

NOTE

A will in this form ensures that on the death of the first spouse to die full use is made of his or her nil-rate band (or any unused part of it) by giving a legacy of the appropriate amount direct to the children. It will not be suitable where the surviving spouse might need access to the whole estate. In such a case a discretionary legacy of the nil-rate band of which the surviving spouse is a beneficiary, as in Form C3.4 at para **[225.57]** et seq may be preferable.

[225.10]

Revocation clause[1]
I [*name*] of [*address*] hereby revoke all former testamentary dispositions made by me and declare this to be my last will.

1   There is no presumption that wills in similar form are mutual wills in the technical sense, but the matter can be put beyond doubt by incorporating an express provision to that effect: see Form B1.6 at para **[201.10]** and the revocation clause to Form C2.1 at para **[224.21]** and the note thereto.

[225.11]

Appointment of executors and trustees
1.   I appoint my [wife/husband] [*name*] ('my [wife/husband]') [*name*] of [*address*] and [*name*] of [*address*][1] (hereinafter together called 'my trustees' which expression shall include my personal representatives for the time being and the trustees for the time being hereof) to be the executors and trustees of this will.

1   If there are two executors as well as the wife/husband, there will still be two effective appointments if there is a divorce and the appointment of the wife/husband is nullified by the Wills Act 1837, s 18A (Part G, para **[243.18]**). See also the Preliminary Note to C2 at paras **[224.12]–[224.19]**.

[225.12]

Pecuniary legacies
2.   [If I survive my [wife/husband]][1] I give the following pecuniary legacies free of tax:[2]

    (a)   to [*name*] the sum of £——;
    (b)   to [*name*] the sum of £——;
    (c)   to [*name*] the sum of £——.

1   The words in square brackets should be included where these are intended to be legacies which are given once only, on the death of the second of the spouses to die. It should be noted that where the words in square brackets are not included, and the nil-rate band utilising legacy below is expressed as a specified sum of money, the latter needs to be reduced by the total amount or value of the legacies given by this clause which are not exempt legacies such as ones to the surviving spouse or to charity. For reciprocal wills containing legacies intended to take effect under only one of the wills where there is a survivorship condition in the main gift see Form C9.2 at para **[231.14]** et seq.

It should be noted that if there is a divorce, these legacies will still take effect, and only take effect, on the death of the survivor of the former spouses, if they do not change their wills.

2   See Form C2.1, cl 6, n 3 at para **[224.27]** and n 1 to cl 5 of this form at para **[225.15]**. These pecuniary legacies are declared to be 'free of tax' to take account of the risk that they may be payable out of a residuary estate which includes property of a kind which bears its own inheritance tax, such as property situated outside the UK, with the consequence that the legacies might without this declaration be liable to bear their own inheritance tax so far as payable out of that property: see the Preliminary Note to B14 at paras **[214.59]** and **[214.60]**. The expression 'free of tax' is employed here in conjunction with the definition and direction as to payment in cl 5 of this form at para **[225.15]**.

[225.13]

Gift of nil rate band legacy to children[1]

3.   (1)   If my [wife/husband] shall survive me[2] then I give to my trustees a pecuniary legacy of [£242,000 subject to payment thereout of any inheritance tax payable by reason of my death which is attributable thereto[3]]/[the maximum sum (if any) which can in the circumstances subsisting at my death be given by this clause without any liability being incurred for the payment of inheritance tax on or by reason of my death and in particular (without prejudice to the generality of the foregoing) for the purpose of determining the amount of such maximum sum the circumstances to be taken into account shall include all chargeable transfers made by me during my life (or events treated as such for inheritance tax purposes) so far as relevant for the computation of inheritance tax on my death the dispositions taking effect under this will (apart from this clause) or under any codicil hereto and any property treated as if it were part of my estate for inheritance tax purposes].

EITHER[4]

(2)   My trustees shall hold the said legacy upon trust for such of my children [*name*] [*name*] and [*name*][5] as shall survive me and if more than one in equal shares Provided that if any of my said children shall predecease me leaving a child or children surviving me who shall attain the age of [18/21/25] years[6] such last-mentioned child or children shall take and if more than one equally between them the share of the said legacy which such deceased child of mine would have taken had he or she survived me.

OR

(2)   My trustees shall hold the said legacy upon trust to divide the same into [10] equal parts and shall hold:

(a)   [5] of such parts upon trust for [my son] [*name*];

(b)   a further [3] of such parts upon trust for [my daughter] [*name*]; and
(c)   the remaining [2] of such parts upon trust for [my daughter] [*name*]⁷
Provided that:
(i)   if any of my said children shall predecease me leaving a child or children living at my death who shall attain the age of [18/21/25] years⁸ such last-mentioned child or children shall take and if more than one equally between them the share of the said legacy which such deceased child of mine would have taken had he or she survived me;
(ii)   if the trusts of any share of the said legacy shall fail because a child of mine predeceases me without leaving a child who attains a vested interest under paragraph (i) of this proviso then such share (and any share which may have accrued thereto hereunder) shall accrue to the other shares or share of the said legacy the trusts of which have not failed and if more than one [in equal shares]/[in the proportions which such shares bear to each other].

(3)   The said legacy shall carry interest at the yearly rate of 6 per cent from my death until the same shall be paid or satisfied or set apart and invested and section 31 of the Trustee Act 1925 (as hereinafter modified) shall apply thereto.⁹

---

1   Subclause (1) of this clause gives a legacy either of a fixed sum not exceeding the current inheritance tax threshold or, effectively, of a sum determined in accordance with a formula which represents the maximum sum which can be given without incurring a liability for inheritance tax. The current inheritance tax threshold (tax year 2001–2002) is £242,000, but it is likely to be subject to alteration in successive years. As matters stand, if the testator's will provides (in the event of his spouse surviving him) a non-exempt legacy of £242,000 and an exempt gift of the rest of the estate to or for the benefit of his spouse, no inheritance tax will be payable on the testator's death unless the inheritance tax threshold is reduced to less than £242,000 before the testator's death, or unless lifetime transfers fall to be taken into account or there is property treated as part of the testator's estate for inheritance tax purposes (and not exempt) such as property subject to a reservation (see Part A, para **[200.76]**) or settled property in which he had an interest in possession. Where a sum is specified for the legacy under this clause, and any other non-exempt legacies or other gifts are included which will take effect on the death of the first spouse to die, the amount of this legacy needs to be reduced by the amount or value of those legacies or other gifts.
    The alternative formula for ascertaining the amount of the legacy contained in the final set of square brackets in sub-cl (1) is intended to ensure that the amount of the discretionary legacy does not exceed the inheritance tax threshold where other non-exempt gifts are made by the will, or where there are non-exempt lifetime chargeable transfers or property treated as part of the testator's estate to be taken into account on the death. It also prevents any waste of the nil-rate band where the inheritance tax threshold is increased after the will has been made. Where the testator has business or agricultural property it may be necessary or appropriate in a gift of this kind to give a fixed sum, or, if a formula is used, to impose an upper cash limit on the gift: see the Preliminary Note to C11 at paras **[223.8]–[223.10]**.
2   This precondition is imposed to avoid unnecessary duplication of gifts (ie this one and the residuary gift) in the event of the spouse not surviving the testator. This gift should not be made conditional on the spouse surviving the testator by a survivorship period: see the Preliminary Note at para **[225.4]**.
3   Making the gift subject to inheritance tax will, in the event of this gift taking the non-exempt estate over the inheritance tax threshold (eg because of changes in the law or the testator having made lifetime gifts during the seven years preceding his death), cause the size of the chargeable estate to be less than it would be if the gift was free of inheritance tax: see B14 at para **[214.74]**.
4   The alternative forms give the legacy to the children either in equal or unequal shares, with substitutional provisions for the children of a predeceasing child. Similar alternatives are provided in the gift of residue which takes effect if the spouse does not survive the testator.

5   See the Preliminary Note on reciprocal wills and the ultimate destination of property at para **[225.7]**.
6   The grandchildren will be lives in being at the testator's death for perpetuity purposes, so that there is no risk of infringing the rule against perpetuities in specifying an age exceeding 21.
7   See the Preliminary Note on reciprocal wills and the ultimate destination of property at para **[225.7]**.
8   The grandchildren will be lives in being at the testator's death for perpetuity purposes, so that there is no risk of infringing the rule against perpetuities in specifying an age exceeding 21.
9   There is a contingency in the substitutional provision in proviso (i) to sub-cl (2) of this clause. A contingent legacy does not ordinarily carry the intermediate income, but one of the exceptions to this is where the legacy is directed to be set apart, invested and held on trust (see Vol 1, para **[32.15]**). This clause directs the trustees to hold the legacy on trust, and that may be sufficient to carry the intermediate income, but sub-cl (3) makes the position clear.

[225.14]

Administration trusts of residue

4.   (1)   I give all my property not hereby or by any codicil hereto otherwise effectively disposed of [(including any entailed or other property over which I shall have at my death a general power of disposition by will)][1] to my trustees to hold on the trusts set out below with power at their discretion to sell all or any of it as and when they think fit.[2]

(2)   My trustees shall pay my funeral and testamentary expenses[3] and debts and any legacies given by this will or any codicil hereto out of such property or its proceeds and shall have a discretion as to how such payments shall be borne as between capital and income.[4]

(3)   Subject as above my trustees shall hold such property and the assets from time to time representing the same (hereinafter called 'my residuary estate') on the trusts set out below and shall invest all money comprised in such property or arising from its sale in any of the investments hereby authorised with power to change such investments into any others hereby authorised.

(4)   In the administration of my estate and the execution of the trusts of this will or of any codicil to it:

(a)   my trustees shall treat all income as accruing on the date on which it becomes payable regardless of the period in respect of which it shall have accrued and shall not make any statutory apportionment of the same;[5] and

(b)   none of the equitable rules of apportionment between capital and income shall apply in any circumstances whatever[6].

1   See Form C2.1, cl 6, n 1 at para **[224.27]**.
2   See Form C2.1, cl 6, n 2 at para **[224.27]**.
3   See Form C2.1, cl 6, n 3 at para **[224.27]**.
4   See Form C2.1, cl 6, n 4 at para **[224.27]**.
5   See Form C2.1, cl 6, n 5 at para **[224.27]**.
6   See Form C2.1, cl 6, n 6 at para **[224.27]**.

[225.15]

Gifts made free of tax

5.   Any specific gift or pecuniary or general legacy made by this will or any codicil hereto which is expressed to be 'free of tax' shall be free from the payment of any inheritance tax or foreign tax or duty payable on or by reason of my death to which such gift or legacy would otherwise be subject and such inheritance tax or foreign tax or duty shall be paid out of my residuary estate.[1]

1   See Form C2.1, cl 6, n 3 at para **[224.27]**. Where specific gifts and pecuniary legacies are of, or wholly payable out of, free estate in the UK, the inheritance tax on them will be a testamentary expense payable out of residue without any express provision, and it is only where there is foreign property or settled property being disposed of by the will that a gift which is intended to be free of tax needs to be expressly declared to be free of tax. See also the Preliminary Note to B14 at paras **[214.59]**–**[214.60]**.

[225.16]

Beneficial trusts of residue[1]

6.   (1)   My trustees shall hold my residuary estate upon trust for my [wife/husband] if [she/he] shall survive me.

EITHER

[(2)   If my [wife/husband] fails to survive me my trustees shall hold my residuary estate upon trust for such of my children [*name*] [*name*] and [*name*][2] as shall survive me and if more than one in equal shares Provided that if any of my said children shall predecease me leaving a child or children surviving me who shall attain the age of [18/21/25] years[3] such last-mentioned child or children shall take and if more than one equally between them the share of my residuary estate which such deceased child of mine would have taken had he or she survived me.]

OR

[(2)   If my [wife/husband] fails to survive me my trustees shall hold my residuary estate upon trust to divide the same into [10] equal parts and shall hold:

(a)   [5] of such parts upon trust for [my son] [*name*];

(b)   a further [3] of such parts upon trust for [my daughter] [*name*]; and

(c)   the remaining [2] of such parts upon trust for [my daughter] [*name*];[4] provided that:

   (i)   if any of my said children predeceases me leaving a child or children living at my death who shall attain the age of [18/21/25] years[5] such last-mentioned child or children shall take and if more than one equally between them the share of my residuary estate which such deceased child of mine would have taken had he or she survived me;

   (ii)   if the trusts of any share of my residuary estate shall fail because a child of mine predeceases me without leaving a child who attains a vested interest under paragraph (i) of this proviso then such share (and any share which may have accrued thereto hereunder) shall accrue to the other shares or share of the said legacy the trusts of which have not failed and if more than one [in equal shares]/[in the proportions which such shares bear to each other].

1   Residue devolves on the other spouse, if surviving. If the other spouse does not survive the testator, residue is given to the children. In view of the nil-rate band legacy, it is not appropriate to incorporate a survivorship condition in the gift to the spouse: see the Preliminary Note on survivorship conditions at para **[225.4]**. Two alternatives are given for the trust for the children;

the alternatives correspond with the alternatives in the legacy contained in cl 3(2) of this form at para **[225.13]**.

2   See the Preliminary Note on reciprocal wills and the ultimate destination of property at para **[225.7]**.

3   The grandchildren will be lives in being at the testator's death for perpetuity purposes, so that there is no risk of infringing the rule against perpetuities in specifying an age exceeding 21.

4   See the Preliminary Note on reciprocal wills and the ultimate destination of property at para **[225.7]**.

5   The grandchildren will be lives in being at the testator's death for perpetuity purposes, so that there is no risk of infringing the rule against perpetuities in specifying an age exceeding 21.

[225.17]

Maintenance, accumulation and advancement[1]

7.   (1)   Section 31 of the Trustee Act 1925 (relating to accumulation and maintenance) shall apply in relation to the trusts hereby or by any codicil hereto declared as if:

(a)   in paragraph (i) of subsection (1) of the said section the words 'as the trustees think fit' were substituted for the words 'as may in all the circumstances be reasonable'; and

(b)   the proviso to the said subsection (1) were omitted.

(2)   Section 32 of the Trustee Act 1925 (relating to advancement) shall apply in relation to the said trusts as if the words 'one half of' were omitted from proviso (a) to subsection (1) thereof [Provided that the powers conferred by the said section (as hereby enlarged) shall not be exercisable in favour of any minor beneficiary hereunder otherwise than so as to cause such beneficiary to become immediately entitled to or to an interest in possession in the capital thereby paid or applied within the meaning of section 71(1)(*a*) of the Inheritance Tax Act 1984].[2]

(3)   Whenever my trustees shall have an obligation or discretion under the provisions of this will or any codicil hereto or under the general law to apply income or capital for the benefit of a minor beneficiary they may either pay the same without liability to account to his or her parent guardian or any other adult person with whom such beneficiary may be residing or to such beneficiary himself or herself if of the age of 16 years or more and so that the receipt of such parent guardian or other person or of such minor beneficiary shall be a full and sufficient discharge to my trustees for the income or capital so applied.[3]

1   For alternative provisions relating to maintenance and advancement see Forms B18.11 to B18.23 and the text thereto at paras **[218.77]**–**[218.107]**.

2   The proviso is included in order to prevent the power prejudicing the application of the ITA 1984, s 71 (accumulation and maintenance trusts), but is probably unnecessary: see the Note on inheritance tax and the statutory power of advancement in B18 at para **[218.99]**. If the accumulation and maintenance trusts of income are extended so as to continue beyond the age of 18 (see eg Forms B18.12 and B18.13 at paras **[218.78]** and **[218.79]**), then 'minor beneficiary hereunder' should be amended to eg 'beneficiary hereunder who is under the age of [*n*] years' where *n* is the highest age at which an absolute interest or an interest in possession might be attained by any of the beneficiaries. 25 is the maximum age compatible with the ITA 1984, s 71 applying: see Part A, paras **[200.119]** and **[200.120]**.

3   A parent (with parental responsibility) and a guardian of a minor are empowered by the ChA 1989, s 3(3) (Part G, para **[244.119]**) to give a good receipt for the minor's property: see Vol 1, para **[9.41]**. The power in this subclause is wider in that it authorises the payment of income or capital to a parent who does not have parental responsibility, any adult with whom the minor is residing, and the minor himself or herself if 16 or over.

[225.18]

Administrative powers[1]

8.   (1)   In this clause where the context so admits:

(a)   the expression 'land' includes buildings and estates interests or rights of any kind in or over land; and

(b)   during the administration of my estate the expression 'beneficiary' includes any person who would be a beneficiary if such administration had been completed and the expression 'beneficially interested' and references to income of any asset being payable or capable of being paid to or for the benefit of a beneficiary shall be construed accordingly.

(2)   None of the powers or provisions contained in subclause (3) below of this clause shall be capable of being exercised or operating in any manner such that if such power or provision were capable of being so exercised or so operating the existence of the same would either:

(i)   prevent any person who would in the absence of such power or provision have been entitled to an interest in possession (within the meaning of Part III of the Inheritance Tax Act 1984) in any property from being entitled to such interest; or

(ii)   prevent section 71 of the Inheritance Tax Act 1984 from applying to any property to which in the absence of such power or provision the said section 71 would have applied.

(3)   In the administration of my estate and the execution of the trusts hereof or of any codicil hereto my trustees shall have the following powers in addition to those conferred by law but subject to the last foregoing subclause—

(a)   power to invest moneys sell assets and change investments with the unrestricted freedom of choice and powers of disposition and acquisition of a sole beneficial owner with in particular power to make unsecured loans, acquire non-income yielding assets, and purchase land anywhere in the world or chattels for any purpose including occupation or enjoyment in kind by a beneficiary under the power set out below;

(b)   power to delegate all or any of their investment powers to a professional investment manager or managers whether individual or corporate and whether or not also a nominee holder of assets for my trustees (and who may be or include one or more of my trustees or the beneficiaries hereunder) upon such terms as to remuneration and otherwise (including terms authorising self-dealing or providing for the limitation of the liability of the investment manager or managers) as my trustees think fit and section 22 of the Trustee Act 2000 shall not apply;[4]

(c)   power to vest or register any property in any person or persons whether individual or corporate and whether or not an investment manager to whom powers have been delegated under the foregoing power (and who may be or include one or more of my trustees or the beneficiaries hereunder) as nominee or nominees for my trustees upon such terms as to remuneration or otherwise (including terms authorising self-dealing or providing for the limitation of the liability of the nominee) as my trustees think fit and section 22 of the Trustee Act 2000 shall not apply;[5]

(d) power to borrow money with or without giving security and on such terms as to interest and repayment and otherwise as my trustees may think fit for any purpose connected with the administration of my estate or the trusts declared herein or in any codicil hereto (including investment) And no lender from whom my trustees borrow money in purported exercise of this power shall be concerned to enquire as to the propriety amount or purpose of any such borrowing;[6]

(e) power to lend money to a beneficiary to whom any of the income of such money is payable or to whom or for whose benefit any income of such money is capable of being paid or applied in exercise of a discretion (or who would be such a beneficiary if such money yielded income) and to do so at a full or concessionary rate of interest or interest free;[7]

(f) all the powers of an absolute owner in relation to any land (wherever situated) held by them;[8]

(g) power to apply capital held on the same trusts as any land (or which would be so held if the administration of my estate had been completed) in the improvement of such land and to apply such capital or the income of such capital on the repair or maintenance of such land;[9]

(h) power to permit any beneficiary to have the beneficial occupation use or enjoyment in kind of any land or chattel or other tangible property on such terms as to repair insurance or payment of outgoings by the beneficiary or otherwise howsoever as my trustees think fit Provided that the foregoing power shall only be exercisable and such permission to occupy or enjoy in kind may only continue in the following circumstances—

   (i) so long as any of the income of such land chattel or other tangible property is payable to such beneficiary or capable of being paid or applied to him or for his benefit in exercise of a discretion (or would be so payable or capable of being so paid or applied if such land chattel or other property yielded income);

   (ii) in the case of land, so long as for the time being the occupation thereof by such beneficiary is compatible with any statutory rights of occupation of any other beneficiary or beneficiaries;[10]

(i) power to exercise all the powers of appropriation (and other incidental powers) conferred by statute on a personal representative without the necessity of obtaining any consents and notwithstanding that one or more of my trustees may be beneficially interested in the exercise of such power.[11]

1   See Form C2.1, cl 9, n 1 at para **[224.30]**.
2   See Form C2.1, cl 9, n 2 at para **[224.30]**.
3   See Form C2.1, cl 9, n 3 at para **[224.30]**.
4   See Form C2.1, cl 9, n 4 at para **[224.30]**.
5   See Form C2.1, cl 9, n 5 at para **[224.30]**.
6   See Form C2.1, cl 9, n 6 at para **[224.30]**.
7   See Form C2.1, cl 9, n 7 at para **[224.30]**.
8   See Form C2.1, cl 9, n 8 at para **[224.30]**.
9   See para **[220.52]** for the reasons for this provision.
10 See Form C2.1, cl 9, n 10 at para **[224.30]**.
11 See Form C2.1, cl 9, n 11 at para **[224.30]**.

[225.19]

Trustee liability

9. [(1)] My trustees shall not be liable for any act or default of any investment manager or nominee employed in good faith to manage or hold assets of my estate nor for any act or default of any beneficiary having the occupation use or enjoyment of property in kind.[1]

[(2) Section 11(1) of the Trusts of Land and Appointment of Trustees Act 1996 (consultation with beneficiaries) shall not apply to the exercise by my trustees of their functions in relation to any land subject to the trusts of this my will.][2]

1   This makes it clear that the trustees are not liable for the defaults of others who may have possession or control of trust property. In respect of the defaults of an investment manager or nominee, this indemnity may be wider than that of the Trustee Act 2000 (TrA 2000), s 23 (1) (Part G, para **[246.138]**) which only exempts a trustee from liability for such defaults if he has complied with the statutory duty of care, a standard which may be higher than that of 'good faith'. Whereas it is clear that a wider indemnity such as this can apply where trustees have exercised an express power to appoint an investment manager or nominee, it is not clear that a wider indemnity can be conferred where trustees have exercised the statutory power (see n 4 to Form C2.1, cl 9 at para **[224.30]** and the Preliminary Note to B21 at para **[221.14]**). For a wider form of indemnity, see eg Form B21.12 at para **[221.16]**.

2   The testator may wish to exclude the duties of trustees of land to consult the beneficiaries of full age and beneficially entitled to an interest in possession, and so far as consistent with the general interest of the trust to give effect to the wishes of those beneficiaries or (in the event of a dispute) the majority by value, see the TLATA 1996, s 11 (Part G, para **[246.97]** and see Preliminary Note to B20 at para **[220.58]**).

[225.20]

Professional trustee charging clause

10. Any of my trustees being a professional or business man may charge and be paid all usual professional and other proper charges for business transacted acts done advice given and time spent by him or his firm in connection with the administration of my estate or in connection with the trusts hereof including acts which a personal representative or trustee not being in any profession or business could have done personally.[1]

1   In spite of the TrA 2000, s 29(2) (Part G, para **[246.144]**) giving certain professional trustees authority to charge for their services on or after 1 February 2001, an express remuneration clause entitling any professional or business person to charge may still be advisable: see **[221.42]**.

[225.21]

Testimonium

IN WITNESS whereof I have hereunto set my hand this —— day of —— 20——.

[225.22]

Attestation clause

SIGNED by the above-named [testator/testatrix] as [his/her] last will in the presence of us both present at the same time who at [his/her] request and in [his/her] presence and in the presence of each other have signed our names below as witnesses:

[Signature of testator/testatrix]

[Signatures, addresses and descriptions of two witnesses]

[225.23]

FORM C3.2:   Reciprocal wills with nil-rate band legacy on trust for the children, residue on trust for spouse for life and then on trust for the children, son taking a life interest and daughter a protected life interest

NOTE

This form assumes a husband and wife with two adult children, a son and a daughter. On the death of the first spouse to die his or her will provides for:

(i)   a nil-rate band legacy for the children in equal shares, the son having a life interest in his share and the daughter a protected life interest in hers (but with powers to pay or apply capital of their shares to them) with remainders to their respective children;

(ii)   the settlement of residue on the surviving spouse for life with a power to pay or apply capital in the surviving spouse's favour.

[225.24]

On the death of the surviving spouse the remainder trusts of residue under the will of the first to die, and the trusts of residue under the will of the second to die, become the same as the trusts of the nil-rate band legacy for the children under the will of the first to die, ie life interest or protective trusts for the children with powers to pay or apply capital, and remainders to their children.

[225.25]

The main point of using this form in preference to, say, Form C3.1, is mainly non-fiscal; the fact that the surviving spouse is given only a life interest in the residuary estate of the first to die makes it more likely that that estate will ultimately go to the children, the settlement of the children's interests is a restraint on them squandering capital, and the protective life interest gives protection against creditors.

[225.26]

Like Form C3.1, this form is for the better-off married couple, where the surviving spouse will, after the death of the other, be able to manage without having the use of the property in the nil-rate band gift. A nil-rate band discretionary trust, like that in C3.4 (at para **[225.57]** et seq) should be used where this is not the case.

[225.27]

The matrimonial home will usually be a major item of property owned by the couple; the purpose of putting the residuary estate of the first to die in trust for the children may be frustrated if his or her interest in the house passes to the other absolutely under a joint tenancy. *It is essential when preparing wills of this type to examine the title to the matrimonial home carefully to see how it is held*; if it is owned as joint tenants beneficially the parties must be asked whether they wish the interest in the home of the first of them to die to be settled on trust under his or her will. If so, they must be advised to effect a severance, and, if not, it should be recorded that they intend the joint tenancy to continue. If similar wills are entered into by both spouses, each with the agreement of the other, then this fact may operate as a severance of the joint tenancy (see *Re Wilford's Estate* (1879) 11 Ch D 267 and *Re Hey's Estate* [1914] P 192), but if there is no clear expression of the intentions of the parties in this respect, there will be uncertainty and the possibility of litigation.

[225.28]

Revocation[1]

I [*name*] of [*address*] hereby revoke all former testamentary dispositions made by me and declare this to be my last will.

1   If the wills are not mutual wills in the technical sense, this clause could be extended as in the revocation clause in Form C2.1 at para **[224.21]**. See n 1 to that clause at para **[224.21]**, and the Preliminary Note to C2 on reciprocal and mutual wills at para **[224.8]**.

[225.29]

Appointment of executors and trustees

1.   [*As in cl 1 of* Form C3.1 *at para* **[225.11]**.]

[225.30]

Pecuniary legacies

2.   [*As in cl 2 of* Form C3.1 *at para* **[225.12]**.]

[225.31]

Gift of personal chattels to spouse[1]

3.   I give my personal chattels as defined by section 55(1)(x) of the Administration of Estates Act 1925[2] to my wife if she shall survive me and if she shall not survive me I give the same free of tax to such of my son [*name*] and my daughter [*name*] as shall survive me if both in equal shares.

1   Since residue is settled on the surviving spouse, and then on the children, a specific gift of chattels is provided. It is not a good idea to settle chattels, because the trouble and expense of administering them as part of a trust fund is usually out of all proportion to their value, though it may sometimes be appropriate in the case of valuable ones. For the reason for the inclusion of the words 'free of tax' is in case any of the chattels are outside the UK at the testator's death, and thus 'subject to tax' in the absence of a direction to the contrary. See paras **[214.59]** and **[214.60]**.

2   See Part G, para **[245.52]** for the wording of this definition, and for further discussion of the meaning of 'personal chattels' see Vol 1, para **[64.44]**.

[225.32]

Gift of nil-rate band legacy on trust for children[1]

4. (1) If my [wife/husband] shall survive me[2] then I give to my trustees a pecuniary legacy of the maximum sum (if any) which can in the circumstances subsisting at my death be given by this clause without any liability being incurred for the payment of inheritance tax on or by reason of my death and in particular (without prejudice to the generality of the foregoing) for the purpose of determining the amount of such maximum sum the circumstances to be taken into account shall include all chargeable transfers made by me during my life (or events treated as such for inheritance tax purposes) so far as relevant for the computation of inheritance tax on my death the dispositions taking effect under this will (apart from this clause) or under any codicil hereto and any property treated as if it were part of my estate for inheritance tax purposes.

(2) My trustees shall hold the said legacy upon trust to invest the same in any investments hereby authorised with power to vary the same and shall hold the same and the assets from time to time representing the same (hereinafter called the 'the trust legacy') upon trust to divide the same into two equal shares hereinafter respectively called 'my son's share' and 'my daughter's share'.

(3) My trustees shall hold my son's share upon the following trusts:

(a) my trustees shall pay the income of my son's share to my son [*name*] ('my son') during his life;

(b) provided that my trustees shall have power in their absolute discretion from time to time during my son's life to pay transfer or apply the whole or any part or parts of my son's share to him or for his benefit in such manner as they shall in their absolute discretion think fit;

(c) subject as aforesaid my son shall have power at any time by deed or deeds revocable or irrevocable or by will or codicil to appoint to any wife who may survive him as his widow (including power to appoint to a named wife contingently on her surviving him as his widow) an interest in the income of the whole or any part or parts of my son's share for the residue of her life or for any lesser period;[3]

[(d) subject as aforesaid my trustees shall hold my son's share upon such trusts for the benefit of all or such one or more exclusive of the others or other of my son's children and remoter issue if more than one in such shares and with such trusts and powers for their respective benefit (including trusts and powers conferring a discretion as to the disposition of capital or income by whomsoever exercisable) and such provisions (including provisions for the accumulation of income during any period permitted by law and administrative provisions of whatever nature) as my son may by any deed revocable or irrevocable or by will or codicil appoint;]

[(d)/(e)] subject as aforesaid my trustees shall hold my son's share upon trust for such of the children of my son as shall attain the age of [18/21] years if more than one in equal shares;

[(e)/(f)] subject as aforesaid my trustees shall hold my son's share as an accretion to my daughter's share and as one fund therewith for all purposes.

(4)   My trustees shall hold my daughter's share upon the following trusts:

(a)   my trustees shall hold my daughter's share upon protective trusts[4] for the benefit of my daughter [*name*] ('my daughter') during her life provided that none of my trustees shall be liable for paying to my daughter the income of my daughter's share accruing after the forfeiture of her protected life interest unless such trustee shall have express notice of the act thing or event giving rise to the forfeiture[5]

(b)   Provided further that my trustees shall have power in their absolute discretion from time to time during my daughter's life to pay transfer or apply the whole or any part or parts of my daughter's share to her or for her benefit in such manner as they shall in their absolute discretion think fit and whether or not any forfeiture of her foregoing protective life interest shall have occurred;

(c)   subject as aforesaid my daughter shall have power at any time by deed or deeds revocable or irrevocable or by will or codicil to appoint to any husband who may survive her as her widower (including power to appoint to a named husband contingently on him surviving her as her widower) an interest in the income of the whole or any part or parts of my daughter's share for the residue of his life or for any lesser period;[6]

[(d)   subject as aforesaid my trustees shall hold my daughter's share upon such trusts for the benefit of all or such one or more exclusive of the others or other of my daughter's children and remoter issue if more than one in such shares and with such trusts and powers for their respective benefit (including trusts and powers conferring a discretion as to the disposition of capital or income by whomsoever exercisable) and such provisions (including provisions for the accumulation of income during any period permitted by law and administrative provisions of whatever nature) as my daughter may by any deed revocable or irrevocable or by will or codicil appoint;]

[(d)/(e)]   subject as aforesaid my trustees shall hold my daughter's share upon trust for such of the children of my daughter as shall attain the age of [18/21] years if more than one in equal shares;

[(e)/(f)]   subject as aforesaid my trustees shall hold my daughter's share as an accretion to my son's share and as one fund therewith for all purposes.

(5)   The trusts hereinbefore declared of the capital of my son's share and my daughter's share shall carry the intermediate income (so far as not disposed of under any trust having priority thereto) and section 31 of the Trustee Act 1925 (as hereinafter modified) shall apply thereto.

(6)   Section 32 of the Trustee Act 1925 (as hereinafter modified) shall apply in relation to the said trusts.

---

1   See Form C3.1, cl 3, n 1 at para **[225.13]**. See Form C3.1, cl 3(1) at para **[225.13]** for the alternative specifying the amount of this legacy.

2   See Form C3.1, cl 3, n 2 at para **[225.13]**.

3   This power will enable advantage to be taken of the inheritance tax exemption for gifts to a spouse in relation to this fund.

4   The statutory protective trusts are set out in the TA 1925, s 33 (Part G, para **[246.28]**). For the inheritance tax implications of protective trusts see Part A, para **[200.20]**.

5   The proviso to this subclause will protect an innocent trustee who continues to pay income to the protected life tenant after the forfeiture of her interest unless he has express notice of the event giving rise to the forfeiture.

6   This power will enable advantage to be taken of the inheritance tax exemption for gifts to a spouse in relation to this fund.

[225.33]

Administration trusts of residue

5.   (1)   I give all my property not hereby or by any codicil hereto otherwise effectively disposed of [(including any entailed or other property over which I shall have at my death a general power of disposition by will)][1] to my trustees to hold on the trusts set out below with power at their discretion to sell all or any of it as and when they think fit[2] [provided that my trustees shall not seek to sell the freehold dwellinghouse situate at [*address*]] which is owned by my [wife/husband] and me as beneficial tenants in common in equal shares so long as my [wife/husband] shall continue to occupy the same as [her/his] only or main residence].[3]

(2)   My trustees shall pay my funeral and testamentary expenses[4] and debts and any legacies given by this will or any codicil hereto out of such property or its proceeds and shall have a discretion as to how such payments shall be borne as between capital and income.[5]

(3)   Subject as above my trustees shall hold such property and the assets from time to time representing the same (hereinafter called 'my residuary estate') on the trusts set out below and shall invest all money comprised in such property or arising from its sale in any of the investments hereby authorised with power to change such investments into any others hereby authorised.

(4)   In the administration of my estate and the execution of the trusts of this will or of any codicil to it:

(a)   my trustees shall treat all income as accruing on the date on which it becomes payable regardless of the period in respect of which it shall have accrued and shall not make any statutory apportionment of the same;[6] and

(b)   none of the equitable rules of apportionment between capital and income shall apply in any circumstances whatever.[7]

1   Subject to any express contrary intention property subject to a general power will be carried by a residuary gift under the WA 1837, s 27 (Part G, para [**244.27**]), but in the case of entailed property the will must refer to the property, or the instrument under which it was acquired, or entailed property generally for the statutory power of disposition to be exercised: LPA 1925, s 176(1) (Part G, para [**244.53**]). Although no new entails can be created on or after 1 January 1997 (see para [**200.53**]), entails created before that date can continue to exist and, if they do, the statutory power of disposition of them by will continues to be available .

2   For the reasons for providing a power of sale rather than a trust for sale see para [**214.1**] et seq. This wording could be made even more concise, such as 'My trustees shall have power to sell all or any of such property' or as appears in the AEA 1925, s 33(1), as amended by the TLATA 1996, Sch 2, para 5 (Part G, para [**244.58**]). One reason for using the slightly more elaborate wording in this form is that it follows the wording which was held in *Re Pitcairn* [1896] 2 Ch 199 to prevent the rule in *Howe v Dartmouth* from applying (see Note at paras [**214.35**]–[**214.38**] for exclusion of the rule), although to save possible argument about the effect of this wording the express exclusion of the apportionment rules is also retained in sub-cl (4) below. Another reason is that this wording should also serve to create a mixed fund of residuary realty and personalty (see paras [**210.6**] and [**214.5**] for the significance of this).

3   The proviso assumes that the matrimonial home is vested in the husband and wife as beneficial tenants in common in equal shares and, in conjunction with the TLATA 1996, s 12 (Part G, para **[246.98]**), ensures that the surviving spouse (who has a life interest in residue) has the right to continue to reside in it for so long as he or she wishes since it makes clear that the purposes of the trust include making it available for his or her occupation. See the Preliminary Note to B8 on rights of residence generally at para **[208.1]** et seq. The proviso will not be appropriate if the house is owned, and is to continue to be owned, by the husband and wife as beneficial joint tenants. Where wills of this type are being made it is important to determine how the matrimonial home is held, and for the husband and wife to decide whether they wish the interest in it of the first to die to pass to the survivor absolutely under a joint tenancy or to become settled on the survivor under the will of the first to die, and to take appropriate steps. See the Note to this form at para **[225.27]**.

4   Testamentary expenses will include inheritance tax on UK free estate, including real property: ITA 1984, s 211(1) (Part G, para **[246.83]**; see also the Note to B14 at paras **[214.55]**–**[214.63]**). Accordingly, even if specific gifts or pecuniary legacies are intended to be free of inheritance tax, it will not be necessary to make express provision for the incidence of inheritance tax unless (in the case of a specific gift) the gift is of property of a kind which bears its own tax, or (in the case of a pecuniary legacy) the legacy is payable out of property (usually residue) which includes property of a kind which bears its own tax. The main relevant categories of property bearing its own tax are foreign property and property which is settled property immediately before the testator's death: see the Note to B14 at paras **[214.55]**–**[214.63]** (settled property can be disposed of under a will where it is subject to a general testamentary power of appointment or is entailed—see n 1 to this clause).

5   A discretion as to the apportionment between capital and income of the burden of liabilities is a middle way between the strict rule in *Allhusen v Whittell* (1867) LR 4 Eq 295 (see Vol 1, para **[38.26]** and paras **[214.43]** and **[214.44]**) with its complex calculations, and a direction to pay the liabilities out of capital which can have unsatisfactory consequences.

6   See the Note to B14 at paras **[214.48]**–**[214.52]** for statutory apportionment of income over time and its exclusion.

7   See Vol 1, paras **[38.17]**–**[38.27]** for the rules of equitable apportionment between capital and income, and the Preliminary Note to B14 at para **[214.35]** et seq for the reasons and techniques for excluding those rules. It is hoped that these words will exclude the rule in *Howe v Earl of Dartmouth* (1802) 7 Ves 137 and *Re Earl Chesterfield's Trusts* (1883) 24 Ch D 643. The power of sale in sub-cl (1) of this clause may also serve to do so (see n 2 to this clause). For alternative strategies see further the Preliminary Note to B14 at para **[214.35]** et seq and Forms B14.4 at para **[214.13]** and B14.27 at para **[214.42]**.

[225.34]

Gifts made free of tax

6.   [*As in cl 5 of* Form C3.1 *at para* **[225.15]**.]

[225.35]

Beneficial trusts of residue

7.   (1)   My trustees shall hold my residuary estate upon trust to pay the income thereof to my [wife/husband] during [her/his] life.

(2)   Provided that my trustees shall have power in their absolute discretion from time to time so long as my [wife/husband] is entitled to be paid the income of all or any part of the capital of my residuary estate (or would be so entitled if such capital yielded income) to pay transfer or apply the whole or any part or parts of such capital[1] to [her/him] or for [her/his] benefit in such manner as they shall in their absolute discretion think fit.

(3)   Subject as aforesaid my trustees shall divide my residuary estate into two equal shares (hereinafter respectively called 'my son's residuary share' and 'my daughter's residuary share') and shall hold my son's residuary share upon the trusts and with and subject to the powers and provisions hereinbefore

declared in respect of my son's share of the trust legacy and shall hold my daughter's residuary share upon the trusts and with and subject to the powers and provisions hereinbefore declared in respect of my daughter's share of the trust legacy.

(4) The powers to pay transfer or apply capital of my son's residuary share to or for the benefit of my son and of my daughter's residuary share to or for the benefit of my daughter hereinbefore (by reference) declared shall be exercisable during the life of my [wife/husband] [with [her/his] written consent][2] and for this purpose my trustees shall have power during the life of my [wife/husband] to appropriate my residuary estate to or between my son's residuary share and my daughter's residuary share wholly or partially and in any manner they think fit.

1   There are two reasons for restricting the power to capital in which the spouse has an interest in possession: first, to ensure that the power is not exercisable if there is a divorce and the primary trust fails and, secondly, to ensure that the power ceases to be exercisable if the spouse assigns or surrenders his or her life interest. See the Preliminary Note to C2 at para **[224.12]–[224.19]**.

2   Including these words will give the surviving spouse protection against losing the benefit of any of the fund against his or her will. The disadvantage of including them is that the surviving spouse will be the settlor of the income for income tax purposes if the power is exercised. The latter is probably not a serious disadvantage, as this only has adverse consequences where a 'settlor' retains a possibility of benefit or where he or she settles property on his or her minor children. This form is for use where the children are adult.

[225.36]

Maintenance, accumulation and advancement

8.   [*As in cl 7 of* Form C3.1 *at para* **[225.17]**.]

[225.37]

Administrative powers

9.   [*As in cl 8(1), (2) and (3) of* Form C3.1 *at para* **[225.18]**.]

[225.38]

Trustee liability

10.   [*As in cl 9(1) of* Form C3.1 *at para* **[225.19]**.]

[225.39]

Exercise of powers[1]

11.   Any power or discretion hereby or by law conferred on my trustees shall be exercisable in favour of any person who is an object of such power or discretion notwithstanding that he or she is one of my trustees and shall be exercisable notwithstanding that any of my trustees has any other direct or indirect personal interest in the mode or result of such exercise provided that there are not fewer than two trustees and that at least one of them has no personal interest in the mode or result of exercising the same.

1   This clause permits a member of the family to be a trustee without disqualifying him or her from benefit under any exercise of statutory or express powers of payment or application of capital, appointment, etc. See the Preliminary Note to B18 at paras **[218.4]** and **[218.5]**.

[225.40]

Appointment of new trustees

[12. The power of appointing new trustees shall be vested in my [wife/husband] during [her/his] life.][1]

1   This provision will not be appropriate if the testators decide to appoint trustees who are independent of the beneficiaries. However, if it is excluded, the TLATA 1996, s 19 (Part G, para **[246.105]**) provides that where no person is nominated for the purpose of appointing new trustees and the beneficiaries under the trust are of full age and capacity and between them absolutely entitled to the settled property, the beneficiaries may give a written direction to a trustee to retire from the trust or give a written direction to the trustees to appoint as a trustee or trustees the person or persons specified in the direction. For a provision excluding the beneficiaries' statutory right to direct retirement and appointment of trustees, see Form B21.34 at para **[221.39]**.

[225.41]

Professional trustee charging clause

13.   [*As in cl 10 of* Form C3.1 *at para* **[225.20]**.]

[*Testimonium and attestation clause as in* Form C3.1 *at paras* **[225.21]** *and* **[225.22]**.]

[225.42]

FORM C3.3:   Will dividing residue between spouse and issue

NOTE

This is a form for one spouse only and makes provision for the other spouse if surviving by giving him or her the personal chattels and half the residuary estate, the balance being divided into two shares, one being settled on 'generation-skipping' (see Part A, paras **[200.91]** and **[200.92]**) trusts for the son's children and the other being settled on trusts for the benefit of the daughter and her children. It is assumed that the matrimonial home is held by the spouses on a joint tenancy, or that the other spouse owns the matrimonial home or some other residential property, or that for some other reason he or she is not in need of the testator's interest in the matrimonial home.

[225.43]

The inheritance tax efficiency of this form, in the event of the testator's spouse surviving the testator, depends on what turns out to be the taxable value of a half share of the residuary estate, and what turns out to be the extent of the inheritance tax nil-rate band at the time of the testator's death. If the taxable value of a half share of the residuary estate turns out to be less than the inheritance tax nil-rate band, some of the latter will be wasted, and if it turns out to be more, some inheritance tax will be payable on the testator's death.

[225.44]

For other forms creating accumulation and maintenance trusts for grandchildren, see Forms C8.3 and C8.4 at paras **[230.30]** and **[230.45]** et seq.

[225.45]

Revocation

I [*name*] of [*address*] hereby revoke all former testamentary dispositions made by me and declare this to be my last will.[1]

1   If the wills are not mutual wills in the technical sense, this clause could be extended as in the revocation clause in Form C2.1 at para **[224.21]**. See n 1 to that clause at para **[224.21]** and the Preliminary Note to C2 on reciprocal and mutual wills at para **[224.8]**.

[225.46]

Appointment of executors and trustees

1.   I appoint my [wife/husband] [*name*] ('my [wife/husband]'), my son [*name*] ('my son') and my daughter [*name*] ('my daughter')[1] (hereinafter together called 'my trustees' which expression shall include my personal representatives for the time being and the trustees for the time being hereof) to be the executors and trustees of this will.

1   If there are two executors as well as the wife/husband, there will still be two effective appointments if there is a divorce and the appointment of the wife/husband is nullified by the WA 1837, s 18A (added by the AJA 1982, s 18 (Part G, para **[244.17]**)). See also the Note on the possibility of divorce to C2 at paras **[224.12]**–**[224.19]**. As the spouse and the daughter get absolute interests, and the only long-term trusts will probably be for the son's children, it may be appropriate for the spouse and children to be executors.

[225.47]

Pecuniary legacies

2.   [*As in cl 2 of* Form C3.1 *at para* **[225.12]**.]

[225.48]

Gift of personal chattels to spouse[1]

3.   [*As in cl 3 of* Form C3.2 *at para* **[225.31]**.]

1   As the spouse only takes half of the residuary estate, and part of it is settled for the son's children, a specific gift of chattels is appropriate.

[225.49]

Administration trusts of residue

4.   [*As in cl 4 of* Form C3.1 *at para* **[225.14]**.]

[225.50]

Gifts made free of tax

5.   [*As in cl 5 of* Form C3.1 *at para* **[225.15]**.]

[225.51]

Beneficial trusts of residue

6.   (1)   My trustees shall hold one equal half share of my residuary estate upon trust for my [wife/husband] absolutely.[1]

(2)   Subject as aforesaid my trustees shall hold my residuary estate[2] upon trust to divide the same into two equal shares (hereinafter respectively called 'my son's children's share' and 'my daughter's share').

(3)   My trustees shall hold my son's children's share upon trust for such of the children of my son [(whenever born)][3] as shall be living on the vesting day (as hereinafter defined)[4] or shall earlier attain the age of [18/21/25] years[5] and if more than one in equal shares provided that:

(a)   if any child of my son shall predecease me or having survived me shall die before attaining a vested interest under the foregoing trust leaving a child or children surviving me or born after my death who shall be living on the vesting day or shall earlier attain the age of [18/21/25] years such last-mentioned child or children shall take if more than one equally between them the share of my son's children's share which such deceased child of my son would have taken had he or she lived to attain a vested interest therein;

(b)   if there shall be no child or grandchild of my son who shall live to attain a vested interest under the foregoing trusts my trustees shall hold my son's children's share upon trust for my son absolutely.

(5)   My trustees shall hold my daughter's share upon trust for my daughter absolutely provided that if my daughter shall predecease me my trustees shall hold my daughter's share upon trust for such of her children as shall survive me and attain the age of [18/21/25] years and if more than one in equal shares.

(6)   The foregoing trusts shall carry the intermediate income of my residuary estate and section 31 of the Trustee Act 1925 (as hereinafter modified) shall apply thereto.

(7)   Section 32 of the Trustee Act 1925 (as hereinafter modified) shall apply in relation to my residuary estate.

(8)   If the trusts of either of my son's children's share or my daughter's share shall fail or determine the same shall accrue to and be held upon the trusts affecting the other such share or such thereof as are still subsisting and capable of taking effect at the date of such accruer.

(9)   In this clause the expression 'the vesting day' means the day on which shall expire the period of 21 years immediately following the death of the last survivor of all my issue (whether children or more remote) living at my death.

(10)   I declare that if the foregoing trust for my [wife/husband] shall take effect then the half share of my residuary estate to be held in trust for [her/him] shall be ascertained by equal division of my residuary estate inclusive of any inheritance tax payable by reason of my death and attributable to my son's children's share and my daughter's children's share (which shall be borne exclusively by the latter two shares).[6]

---

1   Since the other half of the residuary estate devolves on subsequent generations, there is little point in including a survivorship condition, unless a half share of residue is likely to be worth less than the inheritance tax nil-rate band. See the Note on survivorship conditions at para **[225.4]**.

2   The gift of the residuary estate contained in this subclause will carry the wife's share if she fails to survive or the gift to her fails as a result of a divorce. See the Note on the possibility of divorce to C2.1 at paras **[224.12]–[224.19]**.

3   If included, the words in brackets will exclude the rule in *Andrews v Partington* and the class of eligible children will not be closed when the first child attains the specified age: *Re*

Edmondson's Will Trusts [1972] 1 All ER 444, [1972] 1 WLR 183, CA. However, the trustees will be able to advance the entire presumptive share of any child in exercise of the power of advancement under the TA 1925, s 32 as extended to the whole of a presumptive share under cl 7 at para **[225.52]**.

4   Since after-born children may be eligible, not all the children will necessarily be lives in being for perpetuity purposes and an ultimate vesting provision is required: see sub-cl (9) for the definition of 'the vesting day'.
5   Since an ultimate vesting provision is incorporated, any age may be specified.
6   See the Preliminary Note to B14 at para **[214.72]** for the reasons for making provision of this type in relation to residuary estates which are partially exempt from inheritance tax.

[225.52]

Maintenance, accumulation and advancement
7.   [*As in cl 7 of* Form C3.1 *at para* **[225.17]**.]

[225.53]

Administrative powers
8.   [*As in cl 8 of* Form C3.1 *at para* **[225.18]**.]

[225.54]

Trustee liability
9.   [*As in cl 9 of* Form C3.1 *at para* **[225.19]**.]

[225.55]

Exercise of powers
10.   [*As in cl 11 of* Form C3.2 *at para* **[225.39]**.]

[225.56]

Professional trustee charging clause
11.   [*As in cl 10 of* Form C3.1 *at para* **[225.20]**.]

[*Testimonium and attestation clause as in* Form C3.1 *at paras* **[225.21]** *and* **[225.22]**.]

[225.57]

FORM C3.4:   Reciprocal wills containing nil-rate band legacy on discretionary trusts with gift of residue to spouse

NOTE

For a discussion of nil-rate band discretionary trusts, see the Note in B18 at paras **[218.16]–[218.22]**. This form will be appropriate for use where the main asset of the testator's estate is likely to be the matrimonial home, or a share in it, which will be lived in by the surviving spouse. If the home (or share) is appropriated in satisfaction of the nil-rate band legacy, the spouse's continued occupation could confer an interest in possession (see Preliminary Note at para **[225.3]**), thus defeating the object of keeping property out of the survivor's estate for inheritance tax purposes. Accordingly this form contains provisions for establishing a debt or charge scheme, enabling the trustees to satisfy the nil-rate band legacy by a debt owed by the spouse or a charge on the matrimonial home or share (see Preliminary Note to B18 at paras **[218.19]–[218.22]**). In this form, the gift of residue to the spouse is an absolute gift, but if it is possible that the surviving spouse might want to change homes (eg to move to a smaller property or to be nearer to children), it is advisable for the first to die's will to give the surviving spouse a life interest in residue rather than an absolute interest (see Preliminary Note to B18 at para **[218.21]**). Form C3.5 (at para **[225.68]** et seq) is an example of such a will, with the further refinement that the spouse's life interest is a protective life interest.

[225.58]

Revocation clause

I [*name*] of [*address*] hereby revoke all former testamentary dispositions made by me and declare this to be my last will.[1]

1   There is no presumption that wills in similar form are mutual wills in the technical sense, but the matter can be put beyond doubt by incorporating an express provision to that effect: see Form B1.7 at para **[201.11]** and the revocation clause to Form C2.1 at para **[224.21]** and the note thereto.

[225.59]

Appointment of executors and trustees

1. I appoint my [wife/husband] [*name*] ('my [wife/husband]') [*name*] of [*address*] and [*name*] of [*address*][1] (hereinafter together called 'my trustees' which expression shall include my personal representatives for the time being and the trustees for the time being of the trusts of this will save for those of the trust legacy (hereafter defined)) to be the executors of this will and trustees of the trusts of this will save for those of the said trust legacy.[2]

1   If there are two executors as well as the wife/husband, there will still be two effective appointments if there is a divorce and the appointment of the wife/husband is nullified by the WA 1837, s 18A (Part G, para **[244.18]**). See also the Preliminary Note to C2 at paras **[224.12]–[224.19]**.
2   If a debt or charge scheme may be entered into, a separate set of trustees of the discretionary trusts of the nil-rate band legacy contained in cl 2 needs to be appointed (see Preliminary Note to B18 at para **[218.22]** and cl 2(2)(a) and (b) at para **[225.60]**).

[225.60]

Gift of nil-rate band legacy on discretionary trusts[1]

2. (1)   If my [wife/husband] shall survive me[2] then I give to my legacy trustees (hereafter defined) a pecuniary legacy of [£242,000 subject to payment thereout of any inheritance tax payable by reason of my death which is attributable thereto][3]/[the maximum sum (if any) which can in the circumstances subsisting at my death be given by this clause without any liability being incurred for the payment of inheritance tax on or by reason of my death and in particular (without prejudice to the generality of the foregoing) for the purpose of determining the amount of such maximum sum the circumstances to be taken into account shall include all chargeable transfers made by me during my life (or events treated as such for inheritance tax purposes) so far as relevant for the computation of inheritance tax on my death the dispositions taking effect under

this will (apart from this clause) or under any codicil hereto and any property treated as if it were part of my estate for inheritance tax purposes]

(2) In this clause the following expressions have the following meanings, namely:

(a) 'the trust legacy' means the legacy by this clause bequeathed to my legacy trustees and the assets for the time being representing the same;

(b) 'my legacy trustees' means and includes [*name*] of [*address*] and [*name*] of [*address*] or other the trustee or trustees for the time being of the trust legacy[4];

(c) 'the beneficiaries' means and includes my [wife/husband] and my children and remoter issue;[5]

(d) 'the trust period' means the period commencing on my death and expiring on the twenty first anniversary of the death of my [wife/husband];[6]

(e) 'the accumulation period' means the period commencing with my death and expiring on the twenty-first anniversary thereof.

(3) My legacy trustees shall hold the trust legacy and the income thereof upon trust for all or such one or more of the beneficiaries at such ages or times in such shares and upon such trusts for the benefit of the beneficiaries as my legacy trustees (being at least two in number [or a trust corporation][7]) may by deed or deeds revocable or irrevocable executed at any time or times during the trust period appoint and in making any such appointment my legacy trustees shall have powers as full as those which they would possess if they were an absolute beneficial owner of the trust legacy and in particular (but without prejudice to the generality of the foregoing words) my legacy trustees may in any exercise of the foregoing power as they in their absolute discretion think fit:

(a) delegate give or impose to or upon themselves or any other person or persons and in relation to any trust or disposition any discretionary powers or discretionary trusts conditions limitations restrictions or provisions including powers of further delegation or powers to create further discretionary trusts or powers;[8]

(b) create trusts or powers for the accumulation of income during the accumulation period;

(c) appoint or create administrative powers or provisions of whatever nature; Provided that:

(i) no such appointment shall invalidate any payment transfer or application of capital or income previously made under any of the trusts or powers herein elsewhere contained;

(ii) every interest limited under any exercise of such power shall vest in interest (if at all) not later than the expiration of the trust period;

(iii) any such appointment may be made in respect of income alone without any appointment of capital; and

(iv) any such revocable appointment shall (so far as then unrevoked) cease to be revocable on the expiration of the trust period.

(4) In default of and subject to any exercise of the foregoing power my legacy trustees (being at least two in number [or a trust corporation][9]) may at their discretion at any time or times during the trust period pay transfer or apply the whole or any part or parts of the trust legacy to or for the benefit of all or any

one or more of the beneficiaries for the time being living in such manner as my legacy trustees think fit.[10]

(5)   Subject to any or every exercise of the foregoing powers my legacy trustees shall during the trust period hold the trust legacy upon trust to pay or apply the income thereof to or for the maintenance education or benefit of all or any one or more of the beneficiaries for the time being living in such shares if more than one and generally in such manner as they think fit provided that my legacy trustees may during the accumulation period accumulate the whole or any part of the income of the trust legacy by investing the same and the resulting income thereof in any of the investments hereby authorised and any accumulations of income so made shall form part of the capital of the trust legacy for all purposes.

(6)   Subject to the foregoing trust and any or every exercise of the foregoing powers my legacy trustees shall hold the trust legacy and the income thereof at the expiration of the trust period in trust absolutely for such of my children and remoter issue as shall then be living in equal shares per stirpes.

(7)   Any capital or income of the trust legacy not otherwise disposed of by this clause shall be held in trust for such of my children as shall survive me if more than one in equal shares

(8)   Instead of the trust legacy being satisfied by the payment of cash or by the appropriation of property[11]:

(a)   my trustees may charge (with or without there being any personal liability of any person or persons) any property which is (or but for this clause would be) comprised in my residuary estate with payment of a sum of money equal to or less than the amount of the trust legacy to my legacy trustees and my legacy trustees shall accept such charge for such sum as the whole or a part (as the case may be) of the trust legacy; and

(b)   my trustees may require my legacy trustees to accept in satisfaction of all or part of the trust legacy a binding promise of payment (secured or unsecured) made personally by my wife or by my trustees as trustees of my residuary estate which debt shall be payable on demand and my legacy trustees shall accept such debt as the whole or a part (as the case may be) of the trust legacy.

(9)   The following shall apply in relation to the powers in the last preceding subclause:

(a)   my trustees may require to be included such terms if any as they think fit in relation to a charge under subclause (8)(a) above or a debt under subclause (8)(b) above including terms as to interest (if any) and terms linking the debt or sum charged to the index of retail prices or otherwise providing for its amount to vary with the passage of time according to a formula provided that the charge shall be enforceable by or the debt shall be payable to my legacy trustees on demand;

(b)   my legacy trustees may leave the charge or debt outstanding for as long as they think fit and refrain from exercising their rights in relation to it and waive the payment of all or any part of any interest due in respect of it and may accept any substitute debt or charge undertaken or created by any person;

(c)   my trustees may assent to the vesting of my residuary estate subject to an outstanding obligation to pay or satisfy the trust legacy and my legacy trustees may appoint new trustees in exercise of the statutory power to do so before the trust legacy has been paid or satisfied;[12]

(d)   my legacy trustees and my trustees shall not be liable if my wife is or becomes unable to pay the debt or any security is or becomes inadequate or for any other loss or disadvantage which may occur as a result of their exercising or choosing not to exercise any of the foregoing powers; and

(e)   the foregoing powers are in addition to any other powers given by this will or any codicil or by the general law and the foregoing powers may be exercised even though my trustees and my legacy trustees are the same persons or my wife is among either or both sets of trustees provided that such powers shall not be exercisable by a sole trustee who is my wife.

---

1   See Form C3.1, cl 3, n 1 at para **[225.13]**. It should be noted that it is a more practical option to provide a legacy of a fixed cash sum where the nil-rate band gift is settled on discretionary trusts than where it is not. The specified sum could be in excess of the current inheritance tax nil rate band (to allow for the possibility of the nil-rate band being increased before the testator's death), and any excess over what turns out to be the available amount of nil-rate band could be appointed absolutely to the surviving spouse within two years of the testator's death and obtain exemption as a result of the application of the ITA 1984, s 144 (see paras **[225.83]**–**[225.91]**).

2   See Form C3.1, cl 3, n 2 at para **[225.13]**.

3   See Form C3.1, cl 3, n 3 at para **[225.13]**.

4   The main reasons for having separate trustees of the legacy are where a charge scheme might be entered into, in which case the testator's spouse should not be one of the executors and trustees but could be a trustee of the legacy, or where a debt scheme might be entered into and the testator's spouse might be sole executor: see para **[218.22]** supra.

5   The definition of the discretionary class may need to be enlarged or adapted in individual cases.

6   The trust period is longer than may be needed in most cases, but gives considerable flexibility.

7   These words should be included if a trust corporation is to be an executor, or if there is a possibility that a trust corporation might subsequently be appointed a trustee. In either case express provision for the remuneration of a trust corporation so acting (not included in this form) may be added; see eg Forms B3.11 to B3.14 at paras **[203.28]**–**[203.31]** and Form B21.40 at para **[221.52]**. If express provision is not made, then the TrA 2000, s 29 authorises a trust corporation to receive reasonable remuneration (Part G, para **[246.144]**). Nonetheless, if a particular trust corporation is being appointed executor it should be ascertained whether it is content to receive only statutory remuneration or whether it requires express provision for its charges which may be in excess of those which might be authorised by statute. If it is desired to make it possible for a foreign corporation to be appointed as sole trustee, it will also be necessary to amend these words to '(being not fewer than two in number or a corporation)' and to vary the statutory power of appointment of new trustees as in Form B21.36 at para **[221.41]**.

8   These words authorise the creation of discretionary powers, eg powers to advance capital to a life tenant, which might not otherwise be valid: see Vol 1, para **[40.5]**.

9   See n 7 supra.

10 A power to apply capital, being exercisable in a less formal manner, may be useful. But it is essential that its exercise should be adequately evidenced.

11 These powers and provisions are included so as to enable a debt or charge scheme to be used as a means of avoiding the surviving spouse having an interest in possession in the trust fund subject to the trusts of this clause, where there are insufficient assets other than the matrimonial home with which to constitute that trust fund. See para **[218.19]** et seq.

12 The purpose of this is so that new trustees of the residuary estate can be appointed before a charge is entered into, in a case where the surviving spouse is one of the personal representatives or the personal representatives and the trustees of the discretionary legacy are the same persons, and to make clear that new or additional trustees of the discretionary trust legacy can be appointed before the legacy is constituted as a debt from the surviving spouse

where the surviving spouse is the sole trustee: see para **[218.22]** for the reasons for avoiding these states of affairs.

[225.61]

Administration trusts of residue

3.   (1)   [*As in cl 4(1) of* Form C3.1 *at para* **[225.14]**.]

(2)   [*As in cl 4(2) of* Form C3.1 *at para* **[225.14]**.]

(3)   [*As in cl 4(3) of* Form C3.1 *at para* **[225.14]**.]

(4)   In the administration of my estate and the execution of the trusts of this will or of any codicil to it:

(a)   my trustees and my legacy trustees shall treat all income as accruing on the date on which it becomes payable regardless of the period in respect of which it shall have accrued and shall not make any statutory apportionment of the same;[1] and

(b)   none of the equitable rules of apportionment between capital and income shall apply in any circumstances whatever.[2]

1   See Form C2.1, cl 6, n 5 at para **[224.27]**.
2   See Form C2.1, cl 6, n 6 at para **[224.27]**.

[225.62]

Beneficial trusts of residue

4.   (1)   My trustees shall hold my residuary estate upon trust for my [wife/husband] [*name*] absolutely if [she/he] shall survive me.[1]

(2)   If my [wife/husband] shall predecease me my trustees shall hold my residuary estate upon trust for such of my children [by my [wife/husband]][2] as shall survive me if more than one in equal shares, provided that if any of my [said][3] children shall predecease me leaving a child or children surviving me who shall attain the age of [18/21/25] years such last-mentioned child or children shall take if more than one equally between them the share of my residuary estate which such deceased child of mine would have taken had he or she survived me.

(3)   The foregoing trusts shall carry the intermediate income of my residuary estate and section 31 of the Trustee Act 1925 (as hereinafter modified) shall apply thereto.

(4)   Section 32 of the Trustee Act 1925 (as hereinafter modified) shall apply in relation to my residuary estate.

1   In view of the nil-rate band legacy a survivorship condition is neither necessary nor advisable. See the Preliminary Note on survivorship conditions at para **[225.4]**.
2   These words ensure that the alternative gifts for the children in the wills of both spouses are identical in terms of whom they benefit, in circumstances where one spouse has children who are not children of the other spouse. See, further, the Preliminary Note to C2 on reciprocal wills and the ultimate destination of property at paras **[224.9]**–**[224.11]**. For forms for use where one spouse has children who are not children of the marriage and wishes to benefit them by his or her will see C5 at para **[227.2]** et seq.
3   To be included if the trust is confined to the children of the marriage.

[225.63]

Maintenance, accumulation and advancement

5.   (1)   [*As in cl 7(1) of* Form C3.1 *at para* **[225.17]**.]

(2)   [*As in cl 7(1) of* Form C3.1 *at para* **[225.17]**.]

(3)   Whenever my trustees or my legacy trustees shall have an obligation or discretion under the provisions of this will or any codicil hereto, or under the general law, to apply income or capital for the benefit of a minor beneficiary, they may either pay the same without liability to account to his or her parent, guardian or any other adult person with whom such beneficiary may be residing, or to such beneficiary himself or herself if of the age of 16 years or more and so that the receipt of such parent, guardian or other person or of such minor beneficiary shall be a full and sufficient discharge to my trustees or my legacy trustees (as the case may be) for the income or capital so applied.[1]

---

1   A parent (with parental responsibility) and a guardian of a minor are empowered by the ChA 1989, s 3(3) (Part G, para **[244.119]**) to give a good receipt for the minor's property: see Vol 1, para **[9.41]**. The power in this subclause is wider, in that it authorises the payment of income or capital to a parent who does not have parental responsibility, any adult with whom the minor is residing, and the minor himself or herself if aged 16 or over.

[225.64]

Administrative powers

6.   (1)   In this clause where the context so admits:

(a)   the expression 'land' includes buildings and estates interests or rights of any kind in or over land;

(b)   during the administration of my estate the expression 'beneficiary' includes any person who would be a beneficiary if such administration had been completed and the expression 'beneficially interested' and references to income of any asset being payable or capable of being paid to or for the benefit of a beneficiary shall be construed accordingly; and

(c)   the expression 'my trustees' includes 'my legacy trustees'.

(2)   [*As in cl 8(2) of* Form C3.1 *at para* **[225.18]**.]

(3)   [*As in cl 8(3) of* Form C3.1 *at para* **[225.18]**.]

[225.65]

Trustee liability

7.   Neither my trustees nor my legacy trustees shall be liable for any act or default of any investment manager or nominee employed in good faith to manage or hold assets of my estate nor for any act or default of any beneficiary having the occupation use or enjoyment of property in kind.[1]

---

1   See Form 3.1, cl 9, n 1 at para **[225.19]**.

[225.66]

Exercise of powers

8.   Any power or discretion hereby or by law conferred on my trustees or my legacy trustees shall be exercisable in favour of any person who is an object of such power or discretion notwithstanding that he or she is one of my trustees or my legacy trustees, and shall be exercisable notwithstanding that any of my trustees or my legacy trustees has any other direct or indirect personal interest in the mode or result of such exercise.[1]

1   This clause permits a member of the family to be a trustee without disqualifying him or her from benefit under any exercise of statutory or express powers of payment or application of capital, appointment, etc. See the Preliminary Note to B18 at paras **[218.4]** and **[218.5]**.

[225.67]

Professional trustee charging clause

9.   Any of my trustees or my legacy trustees being a professional or business man may charge and be paid all usual professional and other proper charges for business transacted acts done advice given and time spent by him or his firm in connection with the administration of my estate or in connection with the trusts hereof including acts which a personal representative or trustee not being in any profession or business could have done personally.[1]

[Testimonium and attestation clause as in Form C3.1 *at paras* **[225.21]** *and* **[225.22]**.]

1   In spite of the TrA 2000, s 29(2) (Part G, para **[246.144]**) giving certain professional trustees authority to charge for their services on or after 1 February 2001 in the absence of express provision, an express remuneration clause entitling any professional or business person to charge may still be advisable: see Note to B21 at para **[221.42]**.

[225.68]

FORM C3.5:   Will giving nil-rate band legacy on discretionary trusts and settling residue on protective trusts for spouse for life, with overriding trustees' powers over capital

NOTE

This form is a variant of the preceding form and is designed to give the maximum protection to a spouse who is in danger of going bankrupt, eg because of potential Lloyd's liabilities. It is assumed that there are three grown-up children. If the husband and wife own the matrimonial home or any other property as joint tenants, a severance of the joint tenancy should be effected, since otherwise the first to die's severable share will accrue absolutely to the survivor and be wholly available to the latter's creditors. The form contains provisions (as in the previous Form C3.4) for establishing a charge scheme, enabling the trustees to satisfy the nil-rate band legacy by a charge on the matrimonial home or share (see B18 at paras **[218.19]–[218.22]**). The wife is given a protective life interest rather than an absolute interest in residue, so will be appropriate, (as would be a full life interest), if it is possible that the surviving spouse might want to change homes (see B18 at para **[218.21]**).

[225.69]

Revocation

I *[name]* of *[address]* hereby revoke all former testamentary dispositions and declare this to be my last will.

[225.70]

Appointment of executors and trustees[1]

1.   I appoint [*name*] of [*address*] and [*name*] of [*address*] (hereinafter together called 'my trustees' which expression shall include my personal representatives for the time being and the trustees for the time being of the trusts of this will save for those of the trust legacy (hereafter defined)) to be the executors of this will and trustees of the trusts of this will save for those of the trust legacy.[2]

1   It is assumed that the spouse will not be appointed an executor.
2   If a debt or charge scheme may be entered into, a separate set of trustees of the discretionary trusts of the nil-rate band legacy contained in cl 2 needs to be appointed (see B18 at para **[218.22]** and cl 2(2)(a) at para **[225.60]**).

[225.71]

Gift of chattels to spouse[1]

2.   [*As in cl 3 of* Form C3.2 *at para* **[225.31]**, *but with the gift taking effect if the spouse does not survive the testator being in favour of three children.*]

1   This clause is included because the spouse takes only a limited interest in residue. If, however, the chattels are valuable, it may not be appropriate and should be limited to household effects or omitted altogether. Reliance would have to be placed on the express power to permit a beneficiary to have the beneficial use and enjoyment of chattels contained in cl 8: see Form C3.1, cl 8(e) at para **[225.18]**.

[225.72]

Gift of nil-rate band legacy on discretionary trusts[1]

3.   [*As in cl 2 of* Form C3.4 *at para* **[225.60]**.]

1   See the notes to cl 2 of Form C3.4 at para **[225.60]**. Although the powers of sub-cl 8 et seq of cl 2 empower the trustees to require the legacy trustees to accept an unsecured promise of payment from the spouse in satisfaction of the trust legacy, since this form provides for the spouse to have a (protective) life interest in residue, rather than an absolute interest, they should satisfy the legacy by a charge on property in the residuary estate, rather than a debt owed by the spouse, since the spouse would not be providing full consideration for any such promise: see para **[218.20]**.

[225.73]

Administration trusts of residue

4.   [*As in cl 3 of* Form C3.4 *at para* **[225.61]**.]

[225.74]

Gifts made free of tax

5.   [*As in cl 5 of* Form C3.1 *at para* **[225.15]**.]

[225.75]

Beneficial trusts of residue

6.   (1)   My trustees shall hold my residuary estate upon protective trusts[1] for the benefit of my [wife/husband] during [her/his] life provided that none of my trustees shall be liable for continuing to pay the income of my residuary estate to my [wife/husband] after [she/he] has done or attempted to do or has suffered any

act or thing or an event has occurred which has caused [her/his] interest to determine unless such trustee has had actual notice of such act thing or event.[2]

(2)   Subject as aforesaid my trustees shall hold my residuary estate upon trust for such of my children [*name*] [*name*] and [*name*] as shall survive me and if more than one in equal shares provided that if any of my said children shall predecease me leaving a child or children surviving me who shall attain the age of [18/21/25] years such last-mentioned child or children shall take and if more than one equally between them the share of my residuary estate which such deceased child of mine would have taken had he or she survived me.[3]

(3)   The foregoing trusts shall carry the intermediate income of my residuary estate and section 31 of the Trustee Act 1925 (as hereinafter modified) shall apply thereto.

(4)   Section 32 of the Trustee Act 1925 (as hereinafter modified) shall apply in relation to the said trusts.

1   The statutory protective trusts are set out in the TA 1925, s 33 (Part G, para **[246.28]**). The spouse will be treated as having an interest in possession for inheritance tax purposes even if there is a forfeiture and the discretionary income trust arises: see the ITA 1984, s 88(2) and Part A, para **[200.20]**. No power to advance capital to the spouse is included in this clause in view of the wide overriding powers of appointment and application contained in cl 8.
2   The proviso is included in order to protect the trustees who may well be ignorant of the events giving rise to a forfeiture.
3   Under these remainder trusts the residuary estate will vest in the children on the death of the testator's widow or widower if they survive her or him, but the overriding powers will continue to be exercisable until they are released by the trustees or the vesting day arrives. Until either of these occurs, the children will have absolute interests subject to possible defeasance by exercise of the power, and will not be able to call for the capital. They will be entitled to the income and will have interests in possession for inheritance tax purposes. It might be preferred to have life interest trusts for the children after the widow or widower's death, as in Form C2.6, cl 10 at para **[224.106]**.

[225.76]

Overriding powers to appoint and apply capital

7.   (1)   In this clause the following expressions have the following meanings:

(a)   'the discretionary beneficiaries' means and includes:
  (i)   my [wife/husband] [and any [husband of hers]/[wife of his]];[1]
  (ii)   my children and remoter issue whether living at my death or born thereafter;
  (iii)   any spouse widow or widower of any of my said children or remoter issue (and 'widow' and 'widower' shall include a widow or widower who has remarried);[2]
(b)   'appointable share' means any part or share of my residuary estate (up to the whole thereof) in which any beneficiary is for the time being entitled to an interest in possession within the meaning of Part III of the Inheritance Tax Act 1984 or is for the time being treated for the purposes of the said Part III of the said Act[3] as entitled to an interest in possession including any part or share of my residuary estate (up to the whole thereof) which but for this present clause would have become vested absolutely in any person under the trusts hereinbefore declared;
(c)   'the vesting day' means the day on which shall expire the period of 21 years immediately following the death of my [wife/husband].

(2)   Notwithstanding and in derogation of the foregoing trusts my trustees (being not fewer than two in number [or a trust corporation][4]) may [with the consent in writing of my [wife/husband] during [her/his] life and otherwise at their discretion][5] exercise any of the following powers:

(a) power at any time or times and from time to time before the vesting day by deed or deeds revocable or irrevocable to appoint any part or share of my residuary estate (up to the whole thereof) which is at the date of such exercise an appointable share (as hereinbefore defined) upon trust for all or such one or more exclusive of the others or other of the discretionary beneficiaries if more than one in such shares and either absolutely or at such age or time or respective ages or times and with such trusts and powers for their respective benefit and such provisions as my trustees may think fit and my trustees may in exercise of the foregoing power:

    (i) delegate or create powers or discretions over capital or income including powers of further delegation or powers to create further powers or discretions over capital or income;

    (ii) create powers or trusts for the accumulation of income during any period permitted by law;

    (iii) provide for the total or partial exclusion from benefit of any person or persons or class of persons;

    (iv) create administrative powers or provisions of whatever nature;

Provided that:

    (1) no such appointment shall invalidate any payment transfer or application of capital or income previously made or any entitlement to income which has already accrued under any of the trusts or powers herein elsewhere contained;

    (2) every interest limited under any exercise of such power shall vest in interest (if at all) not later than the vesting day;

    (3) any such appointment may be made in respect of income alone without any appointment of capital;

    (4) any such revocable appointment shall (so far as then unrevoked) cease to be revocable on the vesting day;

(b) power at any time or times and from time to time before the vesting day in their absolute discretion to pay transfer or apply any part or share of my residuary estate (up to the whole thereof) which is at the date of such payment transfer or application an appointable share (as hereinbefore defined) to or for the benefit of all or any one or more exclusive of the others or other of the discretionary beneficiaries if more than one in such shares and generally in such manner as my trustees shall think fit;

(c) power at any time or times and from time to time before the vesting day by deed or deeds to release or restrict all or any of the powers contained in the present subclause (including this present power) either in whole or in part and in any manner they think fit.

1   In order to enable full advantage to be taken of the exemption from inheritance tax for inter-spouse gifts, a future spouse of the testator's spouse could be included as a discretionary beneficiary. However, this may well not be acceptable to the testator.

2   The definition of the class will need to be framed so as to fit the particular circumstances of the testator.

3   The spouse will be treated for inheritance tax purposes as having an interest in possession throughout even if her or his life interest has been forfeited and has not been reinstated under the power contained in cl 6(1)(b): see n 1 to cl 6(1) of this form at para **[225.75]**.

4   See Form C3.4, cl 2, n 7 at para **[225.60]**.

5   These words are inserted for the spouse's protection, but have the disadvantage that any appointment or application of capital with his or her consent which cuts short his or her income interest may make him or her settlor of such income for tax purposes. As it is assumed that the children are grown up, being a settlor for income tax purposes will only be a disadvantage if an appointment or application of capital is being made under which the spouse will retain a possibility of benefit.

[225.77]

Maintenance, accumulation and advancement

8.   [*As in cl 5 of* Form C3.4 *at para* **[225.63]**.]

[225.78]

Administrative powers

9.   [*As in cl 6 of* Form C3.4 *at para* **[225.64]**.]

[225.79]

Trustee liability

10.   [(1)]   [*As in cl 7 of* Form C3.4 *at para* **[225.65]**.]

[(2)   Section 11(1) of the Trusts of Land and Appointment of Trustees Act 1996 (consultation with beneficiaries) shall not apply to the exercise by my trustees or my legacy trustees of their functions in relation to any land subject to the trusts of this my will[1]]

1   See Form C3.1, cl 9, n 2 at para **[225.19]**. Section 11(1) does not apply to personal representatives (see the TLATA 1996, s 18(1): Part G, para **[246.104]**), so would not apply when the trustees are deciding in the administration of the estate how to satisfy the nil-rate band legacy. But if a charge scheme is entered into (charging the matrimonial home which will then form part of the residuary estate in which the spouse has an interest in possession) it will be relevant (unless excluded).

[225.80]

Exercise of powers

11.   [*As in cl 8 of* Form C3.4 *at para* **[225.66]**.]

[225.81]

Appointment of new trustees

12.   [*As in cl 12 of* Form C3.2 *at para* **[225.40]**.]

[225.82]

Professional trustee charging clause

13.   [*As in cl 9 of* Form C3.4 *at para* **[225.67]**.]

[*Testimonium and attestation clause as in* Form C3.1 *at paras* **[225.21]** and **[225.22]**.]

Two-year discretionary trusts (Inheritance Tax Act 1984, s 144)

[225.83]

NOTE

Section 144. The ITA 1984, s 144 provides as follows:

'(1)   This section applies where property comprised in a person's estate immediately before his death is settled by his will and, within the period of two years after his death and before any interest in possession has subsisted in the property, there occurs—

- (a)   an event on which tax would (apart from this section) be chargeable under any provision, other than section 64 or 79, of Chapter III of Part III of this Act, or
- (b)   an event on which tax would be so chargeable but for section 75 or 76 above or paragraph 16 (1) of Schedule 4 to this Act.

(2)   Where this section applies by virtue of an event within paragraph (a) of subsection (1) above, tax shall not be charged under the provision in question on that event; and in every case in which this section applies in relation to an event, this Act shall have effect as if the will had provided that on the testator's death the property should be held as it is held after the event.'

Section 144 thus applies in most cases where discretionary trusts are created by will, and an appointment or distribution is made out of the property held on those trusts within two years of the testator's death, provided that it is not made during the first three months following the death. By virtue of the ITA 1984, s 65(4) an appointment or distribution out of a discretionary trust within three months of the testator's death is not chargeable (where the trust is created by the testator's will), and accordingly s 144 does not on the face of it apply: see para **[225.85]**. Section 144 operates not only to relieve the appointment or distribution from any exit charge, but also to treat the distribution or appointment as a disposition made by the testator's will. The second of these effects is very much more important than the first, because the inheritance tax exit charge on property leaving a discretionary trust within two years of its commencement is unlikely to be very great (see the Note in B18 at paras **[218.8]**–**[218.18]**). The main importance of an appointment or distribution falling within s 144 is the exemption it may confer (eg spouse exemption, charitable exemption) on the testator's estate on death.

[225.84]
Where s 144 applies—occasions of charge on discretionary trusts. By virtue of the ITA 1984, s 144(1)(a), s 144 applies to an appointment or distribution where there would apart from s 144, be a charge under any of the provisions of the ITA 1984, Part III, apart from s 64 which imposes the ten-yearly periodic charge (see B18 at para **[218.8]**), and s 79 which imposes an inheritance tax charge in some circumstances on works of art etc comprised in a settlement where exemption from the periodic charge has been obtained and a chargeable event occurs. Part III of the ITA 1984 contains all the provisions for charging inheritance tax on settled property with no interest in possession (apart from

maintenance funds for historic buildings), including, in addition to the periodic and exit charges on ordinary discretionary trusts (see the Note to B18 at paras **[218.8]–[218.10]**), the various charging provisions which apply to property leaving some of the categories of privileged trust (see the Note to B18 at para **[218.8]**).

[225.85]
Where s 144 applies—exempt distributions. By virtue of the ITA 1984, s 144(1)(b), s 144 applies to an appointment or distribution, made within two years of a testator's death under a discretionary trust created by his will, where ITA 1984, ss 75 or 76, or Sch 4, para 16 (1) apply so as to exempt the appointment or distribution from the exit charges imposed by Part III in cases where the property appointed or distributed vests in employee trusts, charities, qualifying political parties, exempt bodies, or maintenance funds for historic buildings etc. Thus, s 144(1)(b) enables the relevant exemption to be obtained from the inheritance tax charge on the testator's estate on death where the appointment or distribution falls into one of these exempt categories, even though the appointment or distribution would not give rise to an inheritance tax charge apart from the effects of s 144. Unfortunately, subsection (1)(b) does not include s 65(4) (distributions etc within three months of the commencement of a settlement) in its list of provisions which exempt an appointment or distribution from charge, and so any appointment or distribution within three months of the testator's death will not fall within s 144. This is something of a trap for the zealous executor: see *Frankland v IRC* [1996] STC 735, and the Special Commissioner's decision *Harding (executors of Loveday) v IRC* [1997] STC (SCD) 321 in which it was held that the executors who had made an early distribution could not rely on ITA 1984, s 143 (see paras **[204.9]** and **[204.10]**) as an alternative to s 144.

[225.86]
What property s 144 can apply to. Section 144 of the ITA 1984 can apply to any property comprised in the testator's estate immediately before his death and settled by his will. It must therefore be property over which the testator had sufficient dominion to be able to settle it on trust by his will, but the reference in s 144 to property comprised in the testator's estate is not limited to his free estate as is the similar reference in s 142 (deeds of variation): see s 142(5) and the Preliminary Note to F3 at para **[242.5]**. Thus s 144 would apparently be capable of applying to settled property in which a testator had an interest in possession, and over which he had a general testamentary power of appointment in exercise of which he settled the property on discretionary trusts by his will.

[225.87]
What trusts s 144 applies to. It should be noted that the ITA 1984, s 144 only applies if there is no interest in possession between the testator's death and the time of the appointment or distribution. It would not apply, for example, to will trusts under which there was a life interest or absolute interest defeasible by exercise of a power. (In this context the ITA 1984, s 91 which deems an interest in possession in residue under a will or intestacy to commence at the testator's death for inheritance tax purposes, disregarding the period of the administration

of the estate, a provision which the Inland Revenue regards as applying to absolute interests.)

[225.88]
Advantages of testamentary discretionary trusts invoking s 144. Wills taking advantage of the ITA 1984, s 144 have become popular, and Form C3.6 is a precedent for one. It provides a useful method of allowing for changes in circumstances which might occur between the testator's will and his death. Varying the dispositions of the deceased is easier if it can be done by a distribution or appointment falling under s 144 rather than by a variation or disclaimer under s 142 (for which see Note to F3 at paras **[241.1]–[241.21]**); it will usually require the agreement of fewer people, and there is no problem where minors or unborns are benefited by the will. Also, there is no question of anyone other than the deceased being the 'settlor' for income tax or capital gains tax purposes. (For the position where there is a variation by an instrument in writing within the ITA 1984, s 142, see Note to F3 at paras **[241.11]**, **[241.17]** and **[241.19]**.) Ensuring that the testator is the settlor (and the only settlor) for capital gains tax purposes can be a particularly important point: under an instrument of variation creating a settlement, the beneficiary under the testator's will who makes the instrument will be the settlor for capital gains tax purposes, and accordingly the capital gains on the settled property will be taxed as his if he retains an interest under the trusts, and the settled property will be subject to the rules for offshore settlements with a UK domiciled settlor where it is administered abroad and the beneficiary settlor under the instrument of variation has a UK domicile, even if the testator had a foreign domicile (see Note to F3 at para **[241.17]**). Thus, a s 144 trust is a particularly good idea for a testator with a foreign domicile.

[225.89]
Disadvantages of testamentary discretionary trusts invoking s 144. The main disadvantages of this type of will are that the deceased's property can in practice only be distributed to the objects of the powers created by his will (whereas the ITA 1984, s 142 applies to an instrument whereby the deceased's property is redirected to any person, whether a beneficiary under the will or intestacy or not), it may necessitate payment of a large sum in inheritance tax before probate can be obtained (as compared with a will in favour of the testator's spouse with a view to the spouse executing a deed of variation), and strictly it may not amount to 'reasonable financial provision' within the meaning of the Inheritance (Provision for Family and Dependants) Act 1975, s 1 for the deceased's dependants (see Part G, paras **[247.1]–[247.29]** and Vol 1, para **[105.1]** et seq). As regards the first point, it will be appreciated that an appointment to a beneficiary to enable him to assign property to a non-object of the power would be a fraud on the power and void. However, it is possible to provide for a wide class of objects of the power by giving the trustees power to add persons to the class (see *Blausten v IRC* [1972] Ch 256, [1972] 1 All ER 41 and *Re Manisty's Settlement* [1974] Ch 17, [1973] 2 All ER 1203), and it seems from *Re Hay's Settlement Trusts* [1981] 3 All ER 786, [1982] 1 WLR 202 and *Re Beatty's Will Trusts* [1990] 3 All ER 844, [1990] 1 WLR 1503 that a fiduciary power conferred on trustees with no limits on the persons in whose favour it might be

exercised can be valid. A form for a *Blausten* type of power is included in Form C3.6, cl 3(1)(b) at para **[225.100]**. In *Re Beatty's Will Trusts* [1990] 3 All ER 844, [1990] 1 WLR 1503 it was held that the provision of wide discretionary trusts or powers in a will is not invalid as a delegation of the testator's power of testamentary disposition, and Form C10.2 in the 6th edition of this work, on which Form C3.6 is based, was referred to by way of example.

[225.90]
As regards the second point, attempts are sometimes made to appoint property in exercise of powers conferred by a will to the testator's widow or widower before a grant of probate is obtained. An executor's authority stems from the will, and if it is clear that the named executors are, or are among, the persons on whom a power of appointment is conferred by the will, it is difficult to see why they should not make an appointment before the grant of probate. The Inland Revenue were at one time unwilling to accept this in relation to some forms of will, but more recently have seemed to be more ready to accept the validity of such appointments. Their view is that whether there is power to make an appointment before probate, or while the estate is in the course of administration, is a question of construction of the will in each case. It is a sensible precaution to provide expressly in the will that an appointment may be made before the grant of probate and before the administration of the estate is complete. In any event an appointment should be avoided in the first three months after the death if s 144 is to be relied upon (see para **[225.85]**).

[225.91]
As regards the third point, the court will presumably make no order on a family provision application if the executors make an appointment which makes reasonable provision for the applicant, but the two-year period in which they may make an appointment or distribution which satisfies s 144 may well expire long after the six-month time limit from a grant of representation for a family provision application prescribed by the I(PFD)A 1975, s 4 (see Part G, para **[247.5]** and Vol 1, para **[105.5]**). Dependants of the deceased may feel that it is necessary to protect themselves by issuing a claim form for family provision within the six-month time limit, if no distribution or appointment has been made by that time. Where a distribution or appointment which does not make reasonable financial provision is made after the six-month time limit has expired, the court may well permit a late application under the I(PFD)A 1975.

[225.92]

FORM C3.6:   Will providing two-year discretionary trust

NOTE

This form creates a two-year discretionary trust with wide powers to appoint new trusts and to pay or apply capital, with a discretionary trust of income pending exercise of the powers or the earlier expiry of two years from the testator's death. Just before the end of the two-year period fixed trusts come into operation if there has been no exercise of the powers, and the coming into operation of these trusts in these circumstances will fall within s 144 of the ITA

1984. The fixed trusts are an absolute gift to the testator's spouse if surviving, and otherwise to the children. Different or more elaborate default trusts could be substituted, depending on what mixture of exempt and non-exempt gifts is desired, and whom the testator wishes to benefit in the event of no exercise of the powers being made. If the testator wants to have a long-term discretionary trust as the default arrangement then a form such as C6.2 (see para **[228.19]**) would be more appropriate. However, the powers in Form C3.6 would enable the trustees to create a long-term discretionary trust if they wished to do so. As well as considering what is to happen if the powers are not exercised, the testator should also leave a clear written expression of his wishes (but without imposing any trust or obligation) as to how he would like the powers exercised.

[225.93]
Joint property. When a will of this type is being made, it should be considered whether the matrimonial home, or any other property, is owned jointly by the testator and his spouse. If the testator desires to include his interest in any jointly-owned property in the property which is settled by his will on discretionary trusts, so that the ITA 1984, s 144 is capable of applying to it, or at any rate so that it is subject to the trustees' discretion before any fixed trusts come into operation, a severance of the joint tenancy should be carried out.

[225.94]
The matrimonial home. Where this, or the testator's interest in it, is included in the residuary estate subject to the discretionary trusts, and the surviving spouse is living in the home at the testator's death and continues to do so afterwards, there will be a question as to whether this gives rise to an interest in possession in the home (or the testator's interest in it) in favour of the surviving spouse from the death: see Part A, paras **[200.108]**–**[200.113]**. If the surviving spouse does have an interest in possession in it from the testator's death, it would mean that an appointment falling within the ITA 1984, s 144 could not be made of the home (or the testator's interest in it): see para **[225.87]** for the requirement that there must be no interest in possession after the death and before a s 144 appointment or distribution is made. The Inland Revenue's statement (Statement of Practice SP 10/79) that they regard an interest in possession as arising where a discretionary beneficiary is allowed to occupy trust property refers principally to an exercise of the trustees' powers so as to provide a permanent home for the beneficiary. It would be consistent with that statement not to regard an interest in possession as arising where no steps are taken to terminate the surviving spouse's existing occupation of the matrimonial home, pending the administration of the estate and a decision of the trustees on how to exercise their powers. There would be a particularly strong case for saying that there is no interest in possession in these circumstances where the home had been owned by the spouses as tenants in common, with the result that the surviving spouse's continuing occupation of the home after the testator's death could be attributed to his or her own interest in the home.

[225.95]
There is nevertheless some risk that the Inland Revenue will regard an interest in possession in the home (or the testator's interest in it) on the part of the

surviving spouse as having arisen before any appointment or distribution is made, and it is of course likely that if the home, or the testator's interest in it, is included in the property subject to the discretionary trust, the trustees will still appoint it to the surviving spouse for an absolute interest or an interest in possession. Despite these factors, it could still be desirable for the home or the testator's interest in it to be included in the property made subject to the discretionary trusts: it could be useful for the trustees to have the option of appointing the home (or interest) away from the surviving spouse and arguing the interest in possession point with the Revenue; the spouse might no longer be living in the home by the time of the testator's death, and it could be useful for the trustees to have power to decide whether the surviving spouse should have an absolute entitlement to the home (or to the testator's interest in it) or a more limited interest.

[225.96]

Chattels. A similar point to that just made concerning the matrimonial home can be made about the testator's chattels, where they are in the matrimonial home and likely to continue to be enjoyed in kind by the surviving spouse after the testator's death. However, it could save administrative difficulty, especially if the chattels are not very valuable, to include a specific gift of personal chattels to the spouse, as in Form C3.2, cl 3 at para **[225.31]**. This would also avoid questions as to which spouse owned what chattels.

[225.97]

Revocation of former wills

I [*name*] of [*address*] hereby revoke all former testamentary dispositions made by me and declare this to be my last will.

[225.98]

Appointment of executors[1]

1.   I appoint [*name*] of [*address*] and [*name*] of [*address*] (hereinafter together called 'my trustees' which expression shall where the context so admits include my personal representatives for the time being[2] and the trustees or trustee hereof for the time being) to be the executors and trustees hereof.

1   Wide powers are conferred by this form and the choice of executors must be made with care. If members of the testator's family are included, the provisions of cl 7 (exercise by trustees of powers in their own favour) must be considered carefully. See cl 7, n 2 at para **[225.108]**.
2   This makes clear that administrators will, after obtaining a grant of letters of administration, be entitled to exercise the powers of appointment and distribution if the named executors do not take a grant of probate. For the power of the named executors to exercise the powers of appointment or distribution before a grant is obtained see the provisos (ii) and (iii) to cl 3(2)(d) at para **[225.101]**.

[225.99]

Administration trusts of estate

2.   [*As in cl 4 of* Form C3.1 *at para* **[225.14]**.]

[225.100]

Definitions

3.   (1)   In this clause the following expressions shall have the following meanings, namely:

(a)   'the discretionary period' shall mean the period beginning immediately after the end of the period of three months from the day of my death and ending with the day before the second anniversary of my death;[1]

(b)   the expression 'the beneficiaries' shall mean [*here set out the class of beneficiaries. An example would be:* my [wife/husband] [*name*] the children and remoter issue of my parents [*names*] and the children and remoter issue of my [wife's/husband's] parents [*names*] the spouses and former spouses of any of the foregoing and any other person or persons who may during the discretionary period upon the nomination of my [wife/husband] or of any such children and remoter issue be appointed by my trustees at their absolute discretion by deed to be a member or members of the class of beneficiaries].[2]

---

1   The powers are only exercisable during this period, and it commences three months after the testator's death so that it is not possible to make an appointment or distribution which fails to fall within the ITA 1984, s 144 by reason of being made within three months of the testator's death (see para **[225.85]** for the non-application of s 144 to such an appointment). The period expires the day before the second anniversary of the testator's death, so that the default trust in cl 3(5) comes into operation on the second anniversary and thus commences within the two-year period from the testator's death and complies with the requirements of the ITA 1984, s 144. It is important to note that the last day for exercising the powers will be the day *before* the second anniversary of the death.

2   A power of nomination in this form is thought to be valid (cf *Blausten v IRC* [1972] Ch 256, [1972] 1 All ER 41 and *Re Manisty's Settlement* [1974] Ch 17, [1973] 2 All ER 1203), and its inclusion gives maximum flexibility to the appointments which can be made: see para **[225.89]**. It would apparently be possible to have a very wide hybrid or intermediate fiduciary power with a class of objects of virtually everyone: see *Re Hay's Settlement Trusts, Greig v McGregor* [1981] 3 All ER 786, [1982] 1 WLR 202, *Re Beatty's Will Trusts* [1990] 3 All ER 844, [1990] 1 WLR 1503, and Vol 1, para **[39.31]**. Further, in *Re Beatty's Will Trusts*, this particular form, as it appeared in the 6th edition of this work (as Form C10.2 on pp 1473–1477 of that edition), was referred to by Hoffmann J as an example of a will containing wide discretionary powers and trusts which was not, in his judgment, invalid as a delegation of the testator's powers of testamentary disposition.

[225.101]

Power of appointment

(2)   My trustees shall hold the capital and income of my residuary estate upon trust for all or such one or more of the beneficiaries at such ages or times in such shares and upon such trusts for the benefit of the beneficiaries as my trustees[1] may by irrevocable[2] deed or deeds executed at any time or times during the discretionary period[3] appoint and in making any such appointment my trustees shall have powers as full as those which they would possess if they were an absolute beneficial owner of my residuary estate and in particular (but without prejudice to the generality of the foregoing words) my trustees may in any exercise of the foregoing power as they in their absolute discretion think fit:

(a)   delegate give or impose to or upon themselves or any other person or persons and in relation to any trust or disposition any discretionary powers or discretionary trusts conditions limitations restrictions or provisions including powers of further delegation or powers to create further powers or discretions;

(b) create trusts or powers for the accumulation of income during the period of 21 years commencing on the date of my death;[4]

(c) create administrative powers or provisions of whatever nature;

(d) make provision for the burden of any testamentary expenses taxes or debts payable out of my estate as between different assets funds shares or interests in any manner and to any extent as my trustees think fit;

Provided that:

(i) no such appointment shall invalidate any payment transfer or application of capital or income previously made under any of the trusts or powers herein elsewhere contained;

(ii) the foregoing power shall be exercisable by my trustees at any time during the discretionary period[5] and any exercise thereof shall have immediate effect for all purposes notwithstanding that at the date of exercise there shall have been no grant of probate or administration in respect of the property over which the said power shall be exercised or the administration of my estate shall not have been completed in respect of such property or any other property comprised in my estate;

(iii) the persons who may exercise the foregoing power before any such grant as aforesaid are the persons hereinbefore named as my executors other than any of them who shall have died [or whose appointment as my executor shall have ceased to have effect][6] or who shall have renounced probate of my will.[7]

---

1   There should be no restrictions on the character or number of the trustees for this purpose, as it is not entirely certain that the statutory power to appoint new trustees can be exercised while the estate is in the course of administration; an alternative, where such restrictions are thought necessary, would be to have express powers to appoint new trustees of the power during the administration of the estate.

2   There seems to be little point in the trustees being able to revoke an appointment since the exercise of any power of revocation would have to be limited to the two-year period, and if s 144 applied to a revocable appointment when made (eg one appointing an interest in possession to the surviving spouse), its application to that appointment would not be altered by subsequent revocation of the appointment.

3   See n 1 to sub-cl (1)(a) of this clause at para **[225.100]**.

4   See B18 at paras **[218.72]–[218.76]** for a discussion of extended accumulation provisions in relation to accumulation and maintenance trusts.

5   See n 1 to sub-cl (1)(a) of this clause at para **[225.10]**.

6   These words could be included if the testator's spouse is a named executor. If there is a subsequent divorce the provisions appointing executors and conferring powers of appointment will have effect as if the spouse had died: WA 1837, s 18A (Part G, para **[244.18]**) and see the Preliminary Note to C2 at paras **[224.12]–[224.19]**. Section 18A would probably apply to this proviso in the absence of these words but they make the position clear.

7   This proviso is included to make clear that an appointment may be made before probate is applied for, and by whom, so that where it is decided to appoint some or all of the estate to an exempt beneficiary, such as the testator's spouse or charity, the benefit of the relevant exemption can be claimed when it comes to paying the inheritance tax due as a condition of obtaining a grant of probate.

[225.102]

Power to apply capital

(3)   In default of and subject to any exercise of the foregoing power my trustees may at their discretion at any time or times during the discretionary period[1] pay transfer or apply to or for the benefit of all or any one or more of the beneficiaries the whole or any part or parts of my residuary estate absolutely freed and discharged from the trusts powers and provisions hereof.[2]

1   See n 1 to sub-cl (1)(a) of this clause at para **[225.100]**.
2   This power is not absolutely necessary but may be administratively convenient if the trustees wish to distribute a personal chattel or capital cash for emergency maintenance, as they will be able to do so without having to execute a deed first.

[225.103]

Discretionary trust of income and power to accumulate it during the two-year period[1]

(4)   In default of and subject to any exercise of the foregoing powers the income of my residuary estate which shall become due and payable[2] at any time during the period commencing with my death and ending at the expiration of the discretionary period[3] shall be held by my trustees on trust to pay or apply the same to or for the benefit of any one or more of the beneficiaries for the time being living as my trustees may in their discretion think fit provided that my trustees shall have power at their absolute discretion to accumulate the whole or any part or parts of such income as an accretion to my residuary estate for all purposes.

1   It is essential for the application of the ITA 1984, s 144 that there should be no interest in possession before the powers in sub-cls (3) and (4) are exercised (see para **[225.87]**), and to this end a discretionary trust of income or a provision for accumulation, or both, is required.
2   These words exclude apportionment, so as to make it clear that the discretions relating to income do not affect income payable after the end of the two-year period.
3   The rather elaborate form of words is necessary in order to include the income arising in the three-month period immediately following the death, which period is excluded from the definition of the discretionary period in sub-cl (1)(a) of this clause (see n 1 at para **[225.100]**).

[225.104]

Default trusts to take effect at the end of the two-year discretionary period[1]

(5)   Subject to the foregoing trusts and any or every exercise of the foregoing powers my trustees shall hold my residuary estate and the income thereof upon the following trusts and with and subject to the following powers and provisions:

(a)   if my [wife/husband] shall survive me and be living at the expiration of the discretionary period my trustees shall hold my residuary estate and the income thereof in trust for [her/him] absolutely;[2]

(b)   if my [wife/husband] shall predecease me or die before the expiration of the discretionary period my trustees shall hold my residuary estate and the income thereof upon trust for such of my children [*name*] [*name*] and [*name*] as shall be living at the expiration of the discretionary period if more than one in equal shares provided that if any of my said children is already dead or shall die before the expiration of the discretionary period leaving a child or children living at the expiration of the discretionary period or born thereafter who shall attain the age of 21 years³ such child or children shall take if more than one equally between them the share of my residuary estate which such deceased child of mine would have taken if he or she had lived until the end of the discretionary period.

1   Care should be taken to ensure that the default trusts reflect the testator's wishes in case there should be no appointment for any reason. Different residuary trusts could be provided, such as those in Form C3.3 at para **[225.51]** or Form C3.5 at para **[225.75]**.
2   It will be apparent that s 144 permits what amounts to an extended survivorship condition, provided that there is no interest in possession during the two-year period. Contrast the ITA 1984, s 92 which applies even if there is an interest in possession during the survivorship period but which limits that period to six months: see B19 at paras **[219.1]–[219.11]** and C2 at paras **[224.2]–[224.6]**.
3   The substitutional gift is valid as it must vest if at all within 21 years of the death of the testator's deceased child who will be a life in being for perpetuity purposes.

[225.105]

Maintenance, accumulation and advancement
4.   [*As in cl 7 of* Form C3.1 *at para* **[225.17]**.]

[225.106]

Administrative powers
5.   [*As in cl 8 of* Form C3.1 *at para* **[225.18]**.]

[225.107]

Trustee liability
6.   [*As in cl 9 of* Form C3.1 *at para* **[225.19]**.]

[225.108]

Exercise of powers¹
7.   Any power or discretion hereby or by law conferred on my trustees shall be exercisable in favour of any person who is an object of such power or discretion notwithstanding that he or she is one of my trustees and shall be exercisable notwithstanding that any of my trustees has any other direct or indirect personal interest in the mode or result of such exercise [provided that there are not fewer than two trustees and that at least one of them has no personal interest in the mode or result of exercising the same].²

1   This clause permits a member of the family to be a trustee without disqualifying him or her from benefit under any exercise of the powers of appointment and payment or application of capital. See the Preliminary Note to B18 at paras **[218.4]** and **[218.5]**.
2   If all the executors are to be members of the testator's family and beneficiaries, it would be advisable to omit the words in square brackets. Even if there are some independent executors and some family members appointed as executors, it might still be better to omit these words in case the independent trustees never take office. If the proviso is omitted there is no requirement that there should be two trustees acting where a power is exercised in favour of a trustee, which might be advantageous because such a restriction could cause difficulty for exercise of the powers within two years after the testator's death (see cl 3(2), n 1 at para **[225.101]**).

If it is thought that family members cannot be relied on to act disinterestedly and without causing disputes, independent persons who are not beneficiaries should be appointed as executors, and perhaps excluded as potential objects of the power to add to the class of beneficiaries contained in cl 3(1)(b) at para **[225.100]**.

[225.109]

Professional trustee charging clause
8.   [*As in cl 10 of* Form C3.1 *at para* **[225.20]**.]

[*Testimonium and attestation clause as in* Form C3.1 *at paras* **[225.21]** and **[225.22]**.]

C4 Wills providing for someone with a disability

CROSS REFERENCES

See also Forms B11.16 (at para **[211.23]**) and B18.4 (at para **[218.34]**). For protective
trusts see Forms C3.2 (at para **[225.23]** et seq) and C3.5 (at para **[225.68]** et seq).

PRELIMINARY NOTE

[226.1]

The main factors relevant to a will providing for someone suffering from a
severe physical or mental disability will usually be the following:

(i)   the needs of the disabled person;
(ii)   where the disabled person is not capable of managing his or her own
        affairs, avoiding the necessity for the appointment of a receiver under
        the Mental Health Act 1983, so far as possible;
(iii)   minimising the adverse impact of inheritance tax, income tax and
        capital gains tax, so far as compatible with other objectives;
(iv)   trying to ensure that the benefit provided by the will does provide some
        genuine additional advantage to the disabled person, and does not
        simply cause a corresponding reduction in means-tested state benefits,
        thus leaving him or her no better off.

A discretionary trust will usually be the best solution, at any rate where the
disabled person is incapable of managing his own affairs, although it may have
income tax and capital gains tax disadvantages (see paras **[226.6]** and **[226.7]**).
In particular it will avoid the need for a receiver (at any rate as regards the trust
property and its income), and is the best that can be done to provide for the
disabled person but at the same time to avoid the trust property being taken into
account for state benefit purposes (see para **[226.2]**). Further, the testator has a
choice as to what inheritance tax charging rules will apply, ie whether the trust
fund is taxed as a fully discretionary trust under the Inheritance Tax Act 1984
(ITA 1984), Part III or as an interest in possession trust under the special
provisions of the ITA 1984, s 89 for discretionary trusts for a disabled person.
The other main possibilities are:

(i)   an interest in possession trust, which may be better from the point of
        view of income tax (see para **[226.7]**) but disadvantageous in that the

income will be taken into account in assessing means-tested benefit and a receiver might be needed to look after the income;

(ii)   a gift to the disabled person himself, where he is physically disabled but capable of managing his affairs—the main question here is the effect on state benefits, where he is in receipt of them;

(iii)   gifts of all the testator's property to other children or relatives of the testator in the hope or on the understanding that they will make provision for the disabled person when it is needed;

(iv)   a gift to a charity for the disabled in the hope or on the understanding that it will provide assistance to the disabled person—some charities for the disabled have schemes along these lines and enquiries should be made of the charities relevant to the disabled person's disability;

(v)   a discretionary charitable trust under which donations to charities which may help the disabled person can be made.

Any of (iii) to (v) will avoid the risk that the property given by the will of the testator will be taken into account as part of the disabled person's means when means-tested benefits are assessed, but of course run the risk that no benefit at all will reach the disabled person from the testator's gift. They also run the risk that family provision proceedings will be brought on behalf of the disabled person against the testator's estate.

[226.2]
State benefits. The benefits which may be available to a disabled person are many and complex, and frequently changing, and the details of them are outside the scope of this work. The main means-tested state benefit is income support, and the rules for assessing means for this purpose at the moment disregard income and capital available under a discretionary trust except so far as it is actually paid to or applied for the benefit of the disabled person. Where a disabled person has an interest in possession under a trust, the income to which he is entitled will be taken into account for these purposes. Increasingly the care of disabled persons is the responsibility of local authorities under the Community Care policy. Local authorities are entitled to take into account the resources of a person to whom they provide services in fixing the level of charge for them. There are no general rules as to whether, and, if so, how, discretionary trust income or capital will be taken into account by local authorities, but there would seem to be a better chance that the income and capital of a trust will not be taken into account, at any rate so long as not paid to or applied for the benefit of the disabled person, when it is only applicable under a discretion than when the disabled person has an entitlement under fixed trusts. However, there are many possibilities as to the type of discretionary trust. If there are wide and unrestricted powers over a substantial amount of capital exercisable in favour of the disabled person, the fund is more likely to be taken into account by the local authority (or under any future change of rules for state benefits) than if the powers over capital are more restricted (or non-existent); similarly, a fund which is tailored to the disabled person's circumstances (eg the trusts come to an end when he dies, or the trustees are directed to have regard primarily to his interests when deciding whether to exercise their powers) is more likely to be taken into account than one which is not.

[226.3]
Inheritance tax treatment of trusts for the disabled. An interest in possession trust may be preferable from an income tax point of view (see para **[226.7]**), but there is no inheritance tax disadvantage in having a discretionary trust for a disabled person. A choice of inheritance tax regime is available in relation to such a discretionary trust, ie between taxation as an interest in possession trust or taxation as a discretionary trust (the relative merits of these two options are considered at para **[226.5]**). This is because settled property subject to a discretionary trust which satisfies certain conditions in relation to a disabled person is treated for inheritance tax purposes, by virtue of the ITA 1984, s 89, as if the disabled person has an interest in possession in it (s 89(2)). Section 89 treats in this way any property which is held on trusts:

(a)   under which, during the life of a disabled person, no interest in possession subsists (s 89(1)(a)), and

(b)   which secure that not less than half the settled property which is applied during the disabled person's life is applied for his benefit (s 89(1)(b)).

[226.4]
Commentary on the ITA 1984, s 89. We have the following points concerning s 89:

(i)   A disabled person for the purposes of s 89 is someone who is incapable of administering his property or managing his affairs by reason of mental disorder within the Mental Health Act 1983 (MeHA 1983) (see (ii) infra), or who is in receipt of attendance allowance under the Social Security Contributions and Benefits Act 1992, s 64 (or the equivalent Northern Ireland legislation), or who is in receipt of a disability living allowance under the Social Security Contributions and Benefits Act 1992, s 71 (or the equivalent Northern Ireland legislation) by virtue of entitlement to the care component at the highest or middle rate (ITA 1984, s 89(4)). see further (ii) infra. Note that the latter two categories are based on *receipt* of the relevant allowance, not on being sufficiently disabled to qualify for it.

(ii)   A mental disorder within the MeHA 1983 is defined as mental illness, arrested or incomplete development of mind, psychopathic disorder, and any other disorder or disability of mind (MeHA 1983, s 1(2)). Attendance allowance (which is for persons of 65 or more), and disability living allowance (which is for persons under 65) by virtue of entitlement to the care component at the highest or middle rate, are for persons who are so severely disabled physically or mentally that they require frequent attendance in connection with bodily functions, or continual supervision to avoid substantial danger to themselves or others either by day or by night (Social Security Contributions and Benefits Act 1992, ss 64 and 72, and see *Cockburn v Chief Adjudication Officer; Secretary of State for Social Security v Fairey* [1997] 3 All ER 844, [1997] 1 WLR 799, HL). Further to the point made in (i) supra that it is *receipt* rather than qualification for these allowances which matters for the purposes of the ITA 1984, s 89, it should be noted that neither attendance allowance nor disability living allowance is payable to a person who has been living for at least 28 days in residential accommodation either provided by a local authority or in circumstances where the cost is or may be borne in whole or in part out of public or local funds, with some exceptions for persons who have been in such accommodation since 1 April 1993: Social Security (Attendance Allowance) Regulations 1991, SI 1991/2740, reg 7, and Social Security (Disability Living Allowance) Regulations 1991, SI 1991/2890, reg 9, both as subsequently amended.

(iii)   The ITA 1984, s 89 applies to property settled by will where the disabled person was disabled (within the meanings described in (i) and (ii) supra) 'when the property was transferred into settlement' (see s 89(4)), ie at the time of the testator's death. Thus where a testator makes provision in the form required by s 89 for the benefit of a person who counts as disabled (see (i) and (ii) supra) at the date of the will but who ceases to do so before the testator's death, s 89 will not apply. On the other hand where the beneficiary is a 'disabled person' within s 89 at the testator's death, and s 89 applies to funds given on trust for his benefit by the testator's will, if he subsequently ceases to count as disabled as defined in s 89, the section will nevertheless continue to apply to the funds. A person may cease to count as disabled for the purposes of s 89 because he gets better; there is also the possibility that, having fallen within the s 89 definition of 'disabled person' through receipt of attendance allowance or disability living allowance, his condition remains the same but he ceases to receive the allowance, eg because he goes into residential care provided out of public funds (see (ii) supra).

(iv)   The ITA 1984, s 89(3) provides that trusts shall not be treated as falling outside the section by reason only of the powers of advancement conferred by the TA 1925 (TA 1925), s 32 (or the Trustee Act (Northern Ireland) 1958, s 33). However, this is a reference to the statutory power as it stands, and not the statutory power as modified in any way. It would, it seems, not be compatible with the ITA 1984, s 89 for the statutory power of advancement to be made applicable to the whole of a presumptive or vested share (instead of one half as provided in the TA 1925, s 32(1), proviso (a)). Therefore, no modified statutory power of advancement which is exercisable during the disabled person's lifetime should be included. If the statutory power applies, and there are discretionary trusts of income, it is likely that the disabled person would not be someone having a 'prior life or other interest' within the TA 1925, s 32(1), proviso (c) so as to make his consent a prerequisite to any exercise of the power: see *Re Beckett's Settlement, Re Beckett, Eden v Von Stutterheim* [1940] Ch 279 and B18 at para **[218.88]**.

(v)   The ITA 1984, s 89 only applies to property if the trusts are such that during the life of the disabled person no interest in possession subsists in that property (see s 89(1)). It follows that if there is a discretionary trust of income, the entire income could in theory be applied for the benefit of persons other than the disabled person without jeopardising the application of s 89. On the other hand it seems that s 89 will not

apply to trusts under which it is possible that an interest in possession
will arise subsequently during the life of the disabled person, even if
currently there is no interest in possession. We therefore recommend
that the trusts of income exclude any interest in possession during the
disabled person's life. Unfortunately, if this is done, the trusts cannot
also comply with the similar but not identical requirements of the
Taxation of Chargeable Gains Act 1992 (TCGA 1992), Sch 1, para 1,
for a trust for a disabled person to receive a full annual allowance for
capital gains tax purposes (rather than the reduced one which normally
applies to trustees): see para **[226.6]**.

(vi)   A further point arises about the requirement of the ITA 1984, s 89(1)
that there should be no interest in possession. If it really is a
requirement that there must be no possibility of an interest in possession
arising during the life of the disabled person, it could be argued that if
s 89 is to apply there must be no powers which can be exercised so as to
create an interest in possession. A power which can be of particular
utility in trusts of this type is the power to permit the disabled person to
occupy a residence comprised in the trust fund, or to have the use of
furniture or equipment acquired by the trustees as part of the trust fund.
The exercise of such powers so as, eg, to provide the disabled person
with a permanent residence could have the effect of conferring an
interest in possession (see Part A, para **[200.110]**). Therefore, it could
be argued, if it is to be certain that a set of trusts comes within s 89, it is
necessary to avoid conferring powers of this kind. However, this would
be so inconvenient that it is in our view better to include such powers
(unless it is clear that the particular disabled person could not be
benefited by the exercise of such powers), and hope that the Inland
Revenue do not regard the existence of such powers as incompatible
with s 89 applying (we know of no published views of the Inland
Revenue concerning this point). There should be power to restrict such
powers so that they can be appropriately cut down if it becomes
apparent that the Inland Revenue do regard them as preventing s 89
from applying.

(vii)   What is said in (vi) supra applies equally to powers of appointment or
powers to pay or apply capital, which are powers which clearly enable
the creation of interests in possession unless specifically restricted so as
not to be so exercisable. There is the practical difference that it would
not usually be as inconvenient to prohibit the creation of an interest in
possession during the life of the disabled person under an exercise of a
power of appointment or a power to pay or apply capital than it would
be to prohibit the creation of an interest in possession under an exercise
of a power to permit occupation or enjoyment in kind of land or other
trust assets. However, if the Inland Revenue accept that the existence of
a power to create an interest in possession by allowing occupation or
use of trust property is compatible with the ITA 1984, s 89, then they
should also accept that the existence of a power of appointment or
payment or application of capital which enables the creation of an
interest in possession is also so compatible. We recommend the
inclusion of a power to restrict any power of appointment or power to
pay or apply capital, which can be used to bring the trusts within the

ITA 1984, s 89 should it become apparent that the Inland Revenue regard the existence of a power to create an interest in possession as incompatible with the application of s 89.

[226.5]
Relative advantages of the different inheritance tax regimes. If the ITA 1984, s 89 applies to settled property, it treats the property as subject to an interest in possession to which the relevant disabled person is beneficially entitled (s 89(2)). This will mean that there should be no occasions of inheritance tax charge during the disabled person's life, except where a payment or application of capital is made in favour of other beneficiaries and so gives rise to a deemed transfer of value by the disabled person (see Part A, para **[200.114]**). Payment of capital to the disabled person will be free of inheritance tax charge (ITA 1984, s 53(2)), and the application of capital for his direct benefit will probably be treated in the same way (although s 53(2) does not expressly include this). The periodic and exit charges applicable to discretionary trusts (see ITA 1984, Pt III, Ch III and B18 at paras **[218.8]** and **[218.9]**) will not apply. However, the deemed interest in possession also means that on the death of the disabled person the settled property will be charged to inheritance tax as part of his 'estate'. This will not be disadvantageous if, as will often be the case, his 'estate' including the trust fund is unlikely to exceed the inheritance tax threshold. For a fund substantially in excess of the inheritance tax threshold a discretionary trust not falling within the ITA 1984, s 89 would probably be more lightly taxed under the inheritance tax rules as they stand at the moment; it will bear periodic charges and exit charges under the ITA 1984, Pt III, Ch III at a modest rate (see B18 at paras **[218.8]** and **[218.9]**) and will not be taxed as part of the disabled person's estate. However, although the inheritance tax legislation taxes discretionary trusts lightly at the moment, this could change, while the privileges of trusts specifically for the disabled are more likely to remain untouched. For trusts falling within the ITA 1984, s 89 see Form B18.4 (at para **[218.34]**) and Forms C4.1 and C4.2 (at para **[226.8]** et seq). Form C4.2 (at para **[226.35]**), illustrates another reason for creating a trust within s 89 which applies where the disabled person is the testator's spouse, ie obtaining, on the testator's death, the inheritance tax exemption for gifts to spouses.

[226.6]
Capital gains tax. By the TCGA 1992, Sch 1, para 1, a trust for a person who satisfies the requirements for being a disabled person for the purposes of the ITA 1984, s 89 (there is no cross-reference but the relevant definitions in the TCGA 1992, Sch 1 are the same) has the advantage of the full amount of capital gains tax annual exemption of capital gains in any year of assessment (currently £7,500 for the tax year 2001–02), as opposed to the reduced amount usually available to trustees, where certain conditions are fulfilled. The first of these conditions, which is the same as the condition specified in the ITA 1984, s 89(1)(b), is that the trusts should secure that during the life of the disabled person not less than half the trust property which is applied is applied for his benefit. But the second condition, which provides that the trusts should also secure that during his life he is entitled to not less than half the income of the

trust property, or that no such income may be applied for the benefit of any other person, is inconsistent with the condition specified in the ITA 1984, s 89(1)(a) (ie that no interest in possession subsists throughout the life of the disabled beneficiary: see para **[226.4]**, sub-para (v)). The second limb of the second condition could be met without creating an interest in possession by providing for income to be applied for the benefit of the disabled person at the discretion of the trustees, and any not so applied to be accumulated. But since accumulation of income is only possible during limited periods, eg 21 years from the death of the testator (see the LPA 1925, s 164(1)(b): Part G, para **[246.42]**), in order to wholly satisfy the second condition the trust would have to confer an actual interest in possession on the disabled person in at least half the fund once the accumulation period had expired, since income which cannot be accumulated must be distributed to or for the benefit of somebody.

Capital gains tax on the gains of a settlement (whether discretionary or subject to an interest in possession) is charged at the income tax rate applicable to trusts under the Income and Corporation Taxes Act 1988, s 686, currently 34 per cent for the tax year 2001–02 (TCGA 1992, s 4(1AA)(a)) (see Part A, paras **[200.40]** and **[200.41]**).

[226.7]
Income tax. Income tax will, generally, be charged at 'the rate applicable to trusts' (currently 34 per cent) unless there is an actual interest in possession (see Part A, paras **[200.41]** and **[200.42]**). However, the tax on any of the income which is paid to or applied for the benefit of a beneficiary will be adjusted to that appropriate to the personal tax position of the beneficiary. For the rules specific to UK company dividend income arising to trustees of discretionary trusts, see Preliminary Note to B18 at para **[218.30]**.

[226.8]

FORM C4.1:   Reciprocal wills for husband and wife with a disabled child and other children; gift by first to die of entire estate to survivor subject to a nil-rate band discretionary trust, and a discretionary trust of residue on the death of the survivor

NOTE

When wills are being made to provide for a disabled child, there will often be uncertainty as to the future condition of the child, and there will usually be uncertainty about the future availability of and rules surrounding state benefits and local authority care, and the future incidence of taxation. Where the child is currently in the care of his parents, there is also the considerable uncertainty as to what will happen to him on the death of the second to die of his parents. Accordingly, this form for the wills of both husband and wife, leaves the decision as to what provision to make for the disabled child on the death of the second parent to die, to the executors' discretion.

[226.9]
On the death of the first to die. Under the will of the first of the spouses to die there is a nil-rate band discretionary trust under which the surviving spouse and the children, including the disabled child, are beneficiaries, and subject to that the residuary estate goes to the surviving spouse absolutely. This nil-rate band trust falls within the ordinary discretionary trust inheritance tax charging rules, and does not fall within the ITA 1984, s 89, but the powers are wide enough to enable the trustees to turn it into a s 89 trust if that turns out to be a good idea. For notes on nil-rate band discretionary trusts see B18 at paras **[218.16]–[218.18]**.

[226.10]
On the death of the survivor. Under the will of the survivor there are some pecuniary legacies and a gift of the estate on wide discretionary trusts and powers for a class which includes the disabled child and charity among the beneficiaries, with the idea that the trustees can appoint whatever seems to be the best arrangement at the time, and rely on the ITA 1984, s 144 (see C3 at paras **[225.83]–[225.91]**) where the appointment has inheritance tax implications, particularly where property is distributed to charity or a wholly charitable trust is set up in relation to part of the fund (see below). If no exercise of their powers is made by the trustees during the two years after the testator's death, the trusts of residue will continue as discretionary trusts after the end of that period. However, there are two alternatives as to the inheritance tax status of the default discretionary trusts after the end of two years from the testator's death (ie the trusts taking effect in the absence of any exercise of the trustees' powers during those two years) according to whether sub-cls (4) and (5) of cl 10 (see para **[226.28]**) are included in the will or left out. If those subclauses are included, they will bring the trusts within the ITA 1984, s 89(1)(b) (see para **[226.3]**) by restricting the powers over capital after the end of the two–year period so that at least half the capital which is applied during the disabled child's life is applied for his benefit. If the existence of powers which authorise the trustees to create interests in possession during the disabled child's life does not prevent the ITA 1984, s 89 from applying (see para **[226.4]**, sub-paras (vi) and (vii)), the inclusion of sub-cls (4) and (5) of cl 10 will mean that in default of any exercise of the trustees' powers during the two years following the testator's death s 89 will apply and the disabled child will be treated for inheritance tax purposes as entitled to an interest in possession in the whole of the residuary estate (see para **[226.5]**). If sub-cls (4) and (5) of cl 10 are not included in the will, the trusts in default of exercise of the trustees' powers within the two-year period will be subject to inheritance tax under the ordinary discretionary trust charging rules (ITA 1984, Pt III, Ch III: see B18 at paras **[218.6]–[218.15]**).

[226.11]
Scope of powers and the ITA 1984, s 89. We mention in sub-paras (vi) and (vii) of para **[226.4]** the possibility that the existence of powers which allow the trustees to create an interest or interests in possession is not compatible with the ITA 1984, s 89 applying. We also mention that this would be extremely inconvenient and that there is no indication that the Inland Revenue take this view. Accordingly the provisions in this form intended to cause s 89 to apply (ie

sub-cls (4) and (5) of cl 10 at para **[226.28]**) do not restrict the trustees' powers so as to prevent the creation of interests in possession during the life of the disabled beneficiary. However, a power to release or restrict powers is included. If during the two years following the testator's death it is clear that the Inland Revenue do regard the existence of powers to create an interest or interests in possession during the disabled beneficiary's life as incompatible with s 89, and it is desired that s 89 should apply, an appropriate restriction could be imposed.

[226.12]
After the death of the disabled child. It should also be noted that in the absence of any exercise of the trustees' powers the discretionary trusts of the surviving spouse's residuary estate will continue well beyond the death of the disabled child (see the definition of 'the trust period' in cl 8(2)(b) and the discretionary trust of income in cl 8(4) at para **[226.25]**). This means that if sub-cls (4) and (5) of cl 10 are included in the will (see para **[226.11]**), and the ITA 1984, s 89 applies during the life of the disabled child so as to treat him as having an interest in possession in the residuary estate, the inheritance tax status of the trusts from the death of the disabled child until the end of the trust period will be discretionary trusts falling within the ITA 1984, Pt III, Ch III (see B18 at paras **[218.6]**–**[218.15]**), and there will be an exit charge on property which is distributed out of the estate after the disabled child's death (in addition to the inheritance tax charge on the residuary estate as part of the disabled child's estate on his death). Under the rules as they stand at the moment this exit charge will be very small if it occurs a short time after the disabled child's death (see B18 at para **[218.11]**). However, it can be avoided altogether if an appointment is made before the disabled child's death of fixed trusts which take effect on his death. If it is found desirable to restrict the trustees' powers, either in order to get the trusts within the ITA 1984, s 89 (see para **[226.4]**, sub-paras (vi) and (vii)), or to reduce the chances of the residuary estate being taken into account for state etc benefit purposes (see para **[226.2]**), it should be done so far as possible so as to leave the trustees with flexible powers to determine what the trusts will be on or after the disabled child's death.

[226.13]
Charities as objects of the discretions. The discretionary beneficiaries under both the nil-rate band legacy trusts and the residuary trusts include charities. This means that not only are the trustees able to distribute income or capital to charities at any time , but they are also able, by virtue of the ITA 1984, s 144 (see C3 at paras **[225.83]**–**[225.91]**), to obtain inheritance tax charitable exemption on the death of the surviving spouse in relation to any of the residuary estate distributed to particular charities during the period of two years from the testator's death, or appointed during that period on permanent and irrevocable discretionary trusts which have charities as the only objects. This is also so in relation to the nil-rate band legacy under the will of the first to die, but there would be no inheritance tax advantage in obtaining exemption for part of a fund which has not borne inheritance tax in consequence of being below the tax threshold.

[226.14]
Power of advancement. Where trusts are being drafted so as to fall within the ITA 1984, s 89, or so as to be capable of doing so, it should be remembered that the statutory power of advancement, if it is declared or permitted to apply during the disabled child's life, should not be varied or modified in any way: see para **[226.4]**, sub-para (iv). There is no express provision in this form concerning the statutory power of advancement.

[226.15]
Letters of wishes. These should be left by the testators, setting out their wishes with regard to the discretionary trusts, and expressed not to create any legally binding trust or obligation. It is particularly important that they should indicate what proportion of the estate of the second of them to die they would like to go into a fund to help the disabled child and what proportion they would like to go to the other children immediately. Where the estate is likely to be fairly small it will usually be intended that the non-disabled children will only receive significant benefit after the death of the disabled child.

[226.16]
For another example of a trust falling within the ITA 1984, s 89 see Form B18.4 at para **[218.34]**.

[226.17]

Revocation clause
I [*name*] of [*address*] revoke all former testamentary dispositions made by me and declare this to be my last will.[1]

---

1   There is no presumption that wills in similar form are mutual wills in the technical sense, but in view of the close tailoring of the two wills to each other, it would be appropriate to add a declaration excluding mutual wills as in the revocation clause of Form C2.1 at para **[224.21]**.

[226.18]

Appointment of executors and trustees and definition of 'my trustees'
1.   I appoint my [wife/husband] [*name*] ('my [wife/husband]'), [*name*] of [*address*] and [*name*] of [*address*][1] (hereinafter together called 'my trustees' which expression shall where the context so admits include my personal representatives for the time being and the trustees for the time being hereof) to be the executors and trustees of this will.

---

1   If the parties are divorced before the testator's death, the appointment of the other spouse as executor or executrix will fail (WA 1837, s 18A: see Vol 1, paras **[25.7]** and **[47.2]** and Part G, para **[244.18]**). If two executors are appointed as well as the other spouse, there will still be two trustees in the event of a divorce, and of course the appointment will still be of two executors where the testator is predeceased by the other spouse. See also the Note to C2 on the possibility of divorce at paras **[224.12]**–**[224.19]**.

[226.19]

Appointment of guardians[1]

2. If my [wife/husband] shall predecease me I appoint [*name*] of [*address*] [and [*name*] of [*address*]] to be the [guardian/guardians] of my children during their respective minorities.

1 For reasons given in the Note on appointment of guardians in B3 (at paras **[203.43]–[203.54]**) it is better to provide appointments of guardians which take effect only on the death of the survivor. It should be noted that the legal status of guardians will cease in relation to a mentally disabled child when he or she attains the age of 18. This clause should be omitted if the children are all already over the age of 18.

[226.20]

Legacies to take effect on the death of the second to die

3. If I survive my [wife/husband][1] I give the following pecuniary legacies free of tax:[2]

[(a) To my son [*name*][3] the sum of £——;
(b) To my daughter [*name*][4] the sum of £——;
(c) To [*name*] of [*address*] the sum of £——.]

1 The words in square brackets should be included where these are intended to be legacies which are given once only, on the death of the second of the spouses to die. It should be noted that where the words in square brackets are not included, and the nil-rate band utilising legacy below is expressed as a specified sum of money, the latter needs to be reduced by the total amount or value of the legacies given by this clause which are not exempt legacies, such as ones to the surviving spouse or to charity. For reciprocal wills containing legacies intended to take effect under only one of the wills where there is a survivorship condition in the main gift see Form C9.2 at para **[231.14]** et seq.
    It should be noted that if there is a divorce, these legacies will still take effect, and only take effect, on the death of the survivor of the former spouses, if they do not change their wills.
2 These pecuniary legacies are declared to be 'free of tax' to take account of the risk that they may be payable out of a residuary estate which includes property of a kind which bears its own inheritance tax, such as property situated outside the UK, with the consequence that the legacies might without this declaration be liable to bear their own inheritance tax so far as payable out of that property: see the Preliminary Note to B14 at paras **[214.59]–[214.60]**. The expression 'free of tax' is employed here in conjunction with the definition and direction as to payment in cl 6 of this form at para **[226.23]**.
3 Ie one of the non-disabled children of the testator.
4 See n 3 supra.

[226.21]

Gift of nil rate band legacy on discretionary trusts[1]

4. (1) If my [wife/husband] shall survive me[2] then I give to my trustees a pecuniary legacy of [£242,000 subject to payment thereout of any inheritance tax payable by reason of my death which is attributable thereto[3]]/[the maximum sum (if any) which can in the circumstances subsisting at my death be given by this clause without any liability being incurred for the payment of inheritance tax on or by reason of my death and in particular (without prejudice to the generality of the foregoing) for the purpose of determining the amount of such maximum sum the circumstances to be taken into account shall include all chargeable transfers made by me during my life (or events treated as such for inheritance tax purposes) so far as relevant for the computation of inheritance tax on my death the dispositions taking effect under this will (apart from this clause) or

under any codicil hereto and any property treated as if it were part of my estate for inheritance tax purposes].

(2)   In this clause the following expressions have the following meanings namely:

- (a)   'the legacy beneficiaries' means and includes:
    - (i)   my [wife/husband];
    - (ii)   my children and remoter issue by my [wife/husband];[4]
    - (iii)   any spouse widow or widower of any of such children or remoter issue (and 'widow' and 'widower' shall include a widow or widower who has remarried);
    - (iv)   any institution (whether corporate or not) which is established for purposes which are exclusively charitable.[5]
- (b)   'the trust period' means the period commencing on my death and expiring on the twenty-first anniversary of the last survivor of the following persons, namely:
    - (i)   my [wife/husband];
    - (ii)   my children by my [wife/husband];[6]
- (c)   'the accumulation period' means the period commencing with my death and expiring on the twenty-first anniversary thereof.

(3)   My trustees shall hold the said legacy upon trust to invest the same in any investments hereby authorised with power to vary the same and shall hold the said legacy and the assets from time to time representing the same (hereinafter called 'the trust legacy') and the income thereof upon trust for all or such one or more of the legacy beneficiaries at such ages or times in such shares and upon such trusts for the benefit of the legacy beneficiaries as my trustees (being at least two in number or a trust corporation) may by deed or deeds revocable or irrevocable executed at any time or times during the trust period appoint and in making any such appointment my trustees shall have powers as full as those which they would possess if they were an absolute beneficial owner of the trust legacy and in particular (but without prejudice to the generality of the foregoing words) my trustees may in any exercise of the foregoing power as they in their absolute discretion think fit:

- (a)   delegate give or impose to or upon themselves or any other person or persons any discretionary powers or discretionary trusts conditions limitations restrictions or provisions including powers of further delegation or powers to create further discretionary trusts or powers;[7]
- (b)   create trusts or powers for the accumulation of income during any period permitted by law;
- (c)   create administrative powers or provisions of whatever nature;

Provided that:

- (i)   no such appointment shall invalidate any payment transfer or application of capital or income previously made under any of the trusts or powers herein elsewhere contained;
- (ii)   every interest limited under any exercise of such power shall vest in interest (if at all) not later than the expiration of the trust period;

(iii) any such appointment may be made in respect of income alone without any appointment of capital; and

(iv) any such revocable appointment shall (so far as then unrevoked) cease to be revocable on the expiration of the trust period.

(4) In default of and subject to any exercise of the foregoing power my trustees (being at least two in number or a trust corporation) may at any time or times and from time to time during the trust period in their absolute discretion pay transfer or apply the trust legacy or any part or parts thereof to or for the benefit of all or any one or more exclusive of the others or other of the legacy beneficiaries for the time being in existence if more than one in such shares and generally in such manner as my trustees think fit.[8]

(5) Subject to any exercise of the foregoing powers my trustees shall during the trust period hold the trust legacy upon trust to pay or apply the income thereof to or for the maintenance education or benefit of all or any one or more of the legacy beneficiaries for the time being living in such shares if more than one and generally in such manner as they think fit provided that my trustees may during the accumulation period accumulate the whole or any part of the income of the trust legacy by investing the same and the resulting income thereof in any of the investments hereby authorised and any accumulations of income so made shall form part of the capital of the trust legacy from which such income arose for all purposes.

(6) Subject to the foregoing trust and to any or every exercise of the foregoing powers my trustees shall hold the trust legacy and the income thereof at the expiration of the trust period in trust absolutely for such of my grandchildren and remoter issue by my [wife/husband][9] as shall then be living in equal shares per stirpes.

(7) Any capital or income of the trust legacy not otherwise disposed of by this clause shall be held in trust for such of my children by my [wife/husband] other than [name][10] as shall survive me if more than one in equal shares absolutely.

(8) After the death of my [wife/husband] my trustees shall have power during the trust period in their absolute discretion to transfer the trust legacy or any part or parts thereof to the trustees of any fund held on any discretionary or other trusts arising under the will of my [wife/husband] which are wholly or partly for the benefit of any one or more of the legacy beneficiaries (whether or not persons other than the legacy beneficiaries may also be benefited) to be held as an accretion to such fund and as one fund therewith for all purposes provided that the foregoing power shall not be exercisable unless such transfer can be effected without infringing the rule against perpetuities as it affects the trust legacy.[11]

1 Subclause (1) of this clause gives a legacy either of a fixed sum not exceeding the current inheritance tax threshold or, effectively, of a sum determined in accordance with a formula which represents the maximum sum which can be given without incurring a liability for inheritance tax. The current inheritance tax threshold (tax year 2001–02) is £242,000, but it is likely to be subject to alteration in successive years. As matters stand, if the testator's will provides (in the event of his spouse surviving him) a non-exempt legacy of £242,000 and an exempt gift of the rest of the estate to or for the benefit of his spouse, no inheritance tax will be payable on the testator's death, unless the inheritance tax threshold is reduced to less than £242,000 before the testator's death, or unless lifetime transfers fall to be taken into account or there is property treated as part of the testator's estate for inheritance tax purposes (and not

exempt), such as property subject to a reservation (see Part A, para **[200.76]**) or settled property in which he had an interest in possession. Where a sum is specified for the legacy under this clause, and any other non-exempt legacies or other gifts are included which will take effect on the death of the first spouse to die, the amount of this legacy needs to be reduced by the amount or value of those legacies or other gifts.

The alternative formula for ascertaining the amount of the legacy contained in the final set of square brackets in sub-cl (1) is intended to ensure that the amount of the discretionary legacy does not exceed the inheritance tax threshold where other non-exempt gifts are made by the will, or where there are non-exempt lifetime chargeable transfers or property treated as part of the testator's estate to be taken into account on the death. It also prevents any waste of the nil-rate band where the inheritance tax threshold is increased after the will has been made. Where the testator has business or agricultural property it may be necessary or appropriate in a gift of this kind to give a fixed sum, or, if a formula is used, to impose an upper cash limit on the gift: see the Preliminary Note to C11 at paras **[233.8]–[233.10]**.

It should be noted that it is a more practical option to provide a legacy of a fixed cash sum where the nil-rate band gift is settled on discretionary trusts than where it is not. The specified sum could be in excess of the current inheritance tax nil rate band (to allow for the possibility of the nil-rate band being increased before the testator's death), and any excess over what turns out to be the available amount of nil-rate band can be appointed absolutely to the surviving spouse within two years of the testator's death so as to obtain exemption as a result of the application of the ITA 1984, s 144 (see paras **[225.83]–[225.91]**).

2   This precondition is imposed to avoid unnecessary duplication of gifts (ie this one and the residuary gift) in the event of the spouse not surviving the testator. This gift should not be made conditional on the spouse surviving the testator by a survivorship period: see the Preliminary Note to C3 at para **[225.4]**.

3   Making the gift subject to inheritance tax will, in the event of this gift taking the non-exempt estate over the inheritance tax threshold (eg because of changes in the law or the testator having made lifetime gifts during the seven years preceding his death), cause the size of the chargeable estate to be less than it would be if the gift was free of inheritance tax: see B14 at para **[214.74]**.

4   See the Preliminary Note to C2 at paras **[224.9]–[224.11]**. There is the additional reason for including these words that it is desirable that the nil-rate band legacy in the will of the first to die is held on trusts as similar as possible to those of the residuary estate of the survivor, so that the two funds can be amalgamated after the death of the latter.

5   This definition is based on that contained in the Charities Act 1993, s 96(1). If the disabled child is being cared for by some charitable body, it may be useful to have express power to make appointments in favour of that charity.

6   See n 4 supra. That the nil-rate band legacy in the one will and the residuary estate in the other should have the same perpetuity period is particularly important if the amalgamation of the funds is to be possible. See cl 4(8) of this form, for the power to amalgamate them.

7   These words authorise the creation of discretionary trusts or powers which might not otherwise be valid: see Vol 1, para **[40.5]**.

8   A power to apply capital, being exercisable in a less formal manner, may be useful, but it is essential that its exercise should be adequately evidenced. It is an important power to include where a disabled person is a beneficiary, because it will authorise, eg payments to be made to persons or charities looking after or helping the disabled person, where such payments are beneficial to the disabled person. See the Note in B18 at para **[218.92]** et seq for the wide scope of a power to apply property for a person's benefit. The reference to a trust corporation is for the reasons given in n 1 of para **[226.32]**.

9   See n 4 supra.

10   Ie the name of the disabled child, whom it will probably be appropriate to exclude from this ultimate gift of capital.

11   In order to maximise the chances of this power being exercisable the trusts of the nil- rate band legacy and of residue are made as similar as possible.

[226.22]

Administration trusts of residue

5.   (1)   I give all my property not hereby or by any codicil hereto otherwise effectively disposed of [(including any entailed or other property over which I shall have at my death a general power of disposition by will)]¹ to my trustees to

hold on the trusts set out below with power at their discretion to sell all or any of it as and when they think fit.[2]

(2)   My trustees shall pay my funeral and testamentary expenses[3] and debts and any legacies given by this will or any codicil hereto out of such property or its proceeds and shall have a discretion as to how such payments shall be borne as between capital and income[4].

(3)   Subject as above my trustees shall hold such property and the assets from time to time representing the same (hereinafter called 'my residuary estate') on the trusts set out below and shall invest all money comprised in such property or arising from its sale in any of the investments hereby authorised with power to change such investments into any others hereby authorised.

(4)   In the administration of my estate and the execution of the trusts of this will or of any codicil to it:

(a)   my trustees shall treat all income as accruing on the date on which it becomes payable regardless of the period in respect of which it shall have accrued and shall not make any statutory apportionment of the same;[5] and

(b)   none of the equitable rules of apportionment between capital and income shall apply in any circumstances whatever[6].

1   See Form C2.1, cl 6, n 1 at para [224.27].
2   See Form C2.1, cl 6, n 2 at para [224.27].
3   See Form C2.1, cl 6, n 3 at para [224.27].
4   See Form C2.1, cl 6, n 4 at para [224.27]
5   See Form C2.1, cl 6, n 5 at para [224.27].
6   See Form C2.1, cl 6, n 6 at para [224.27].

[226.23]

Gifts made free of tax

6.   Any specific gift or pecuniary or general legacy made by this will or any codicil hereto which is expressed to be 'free of tax' shall be free from the payment of any inheritance tax or foreign tax or duty payable on or by reason of my death to which such gift or legacy would otherwise be subject and such inheritance tax or foreign tax or duty shall be paid out of my residuary estate.[1]

1   Where specific gifts and pecuniary legacies are of, or wholly payable out of, free estate in the UK, the inheritance tax on them will be a testamentary expense payable out of residue without any express provision, and it is only where there is foreign property or settled property being disposed of by the will that a gift which is intended to be free of tax needs to be expressly declared to be free of tax. See also the Note to B14 at paras [214.59]–[214.60].

[226.24]

Primary trust of residue in favour of spouse if surviving

7.   If my [wife/husband] shall survive me[1] my trustees shall hold my residuary estate and the income thereof upon trust for [her/him] absolutely.

1   Residue devolves on the other spouse, if surviving. If the other spouse does not survive the testator, residue is given to the children, see cl 8 at para [226.25]. In view of the nil-rate band legacy, it is not appropriate to incorporate a survivorship condition in the gift to the spouse: see the Note on survivorship conditions in C3 at para [225.4].

[226.25]

Alternative gift of residue on discretionary trusts for children and issue

8.   (1)   If my [wife/husband] shall fail to survive me[1] my trustees shall hold my residuary estate and the income thereof upon the trusts and with and subject to the powers and provisions hereinafter in this clause declared and contained.

(2)   In this clause the following expressions have the following meanings namely:

(a)   'the residuary beneficiaries' means and includes:[2]
   (i)   my children and remoter issue by my [wife/husband];[3]
   (ii)   any spouse widow or widower of any of such children or remoter issue (and 'widow' and 'widower' shall include a widow or widower who has remarried);[4]
   (iii)   any institution (whether corporate or not) which is established for purposes which are exclusively charitable;[5]
(b)   'the trust period' means the period commencing on the day of my death and expiring on the twenty-first anniversary of the death of the last survivor of my children by my [wife/husband];[6]
(c)   'the accumulation period' means the period commencing with my death and expiring on the twenty-first anniversary thereof;
(d)   'the relevant day' means the day falling two years less one day after my death.

(3)   Subject as provided in clause 10 below[7] my trustees (being not less than two in number or a trust corporation except as hereinafter provided)[8] may at any time or times and from time to time during the trust period exercise either or both of the following powers namely:

(a)   power at any time or times and from time to time by deed or deeds revocable or irrevocable to appoint the whole or any part or parts of my residuary estate upon trust for all or such one or more exclusive of the others or other of the residuary beneficiaries if more than one in such shares and either absolutely or at such age or time or respective ages or times and with such trusts and powers for their respective benefit and such provisions as my trustees may think fit and in making any such appointment my trustees shall have powers as full as those which they would possess if they were an absolute beneficial owner of my residuary estate and in particular (but without prejudice to the generality of the foregoing words) my trustees may in any exercise of the foregoing power as they in their absolute discretion think fit:
   (i)   to delegate give or impose to or upon themselves or any other person or persons any discretionary powers or discretionary trusts conditions limitations restrictions or provisions including powers of further delegation or powers to create further discretionary trusts or powers;
   (ii)   create powers or trusts for the accumulation of income during any period permitted by law;
   (iii)   create administrative powers or provisions of whatever nature;
Provided that:

(i)   no such appointment shall invalidate any payment transfer or application of capital or income previously made under any of the trusts or powers herein elsewhere contained;

(ii)   every interest limited under any exercise of such power shall vest in interest (if at all) not later than the expiration of the trust period;

(iii)   any such appointment may be made in respect of income alone without any appointment of capital;

(iv)   any such revocable appointment shall (so far as then unrevoked) cease to be revocable on the expiration of the trust period;

(v)   in any appointment made before the relevant day (but not in any appointment made thereafter) my trustees may make provision for the burden of any testamentary expenses taxes or debts payable out of my estate as between different assets funds shares or interests in such manner and to such extent as my trustees think fit;

(vi)   any appointment made in favour of or for the benefit of a charity or charities (or charity generally) made or attempted to be made before the expiry of the period of three months from the day of my death shall be void and of no effect;[9]

(vii)   the foregoing power of appointment may be exercised notwithstanding that there shall have been no grant of probate or administration in respect of the property over which the said power shall be exercised or that the administration of my estate shall not have been completed in respect of such property or any other property comprised in my estate and so long as no such grant as aforesaid has been obtained the persons who may exercise the foregoing power are the persons hereinbefore named as my executors other than any of them who shall have died or whose appointment as my executor shall have ceased to have effect or who shall have renounced probate of my will;

(viii) the foregoing power of appointment may be exercised before the relevant day by a sole trustee who is not a trust corporation;[10]

(b) power (subject to any or every exercise of the foregoing power) at any time or times and from time to time in their absolute discretion to pay transfer or apply my residuary estate or any part or parts thereof to or for the benefit of all or any one or more exclusive of the others or other of the residuary beneficiaries for the time being in existence if more than one in such shares and generally in such manner as my trustees shall think fit provided that the foregoing power of payment transfer or application of capital may be exercised before the relevant day by a sole trustee who is not a trust corporation.[11]

(4)   In default of and subject to any or every exercise of the foregoing powers my trustees shall hold my residuary estate during the trust period upon trust to pay or apply the income thereof to or for the maintenance education or benefit of all or any one or more of the residuary beneficiaries and if more than one in such shares and in such manner generally as my trustees think fit provided that during the accumulation period my trustees may accumulate all or any part or parts of such income by investing the same and the resulting income thereof in any investments hereby authorised and so that any accumulations so made shall form part of the capital of my residuary estate from which such income arose for all purposes.

(5)   Subject as aforesaid my trustees shall hold my residuary estate and the income thereof at the expiration of the trust period upon trust for such of my grandchildren and remoter issue by my [wife/husband] as shall be then living in equal shares per stirpes.

(6)   Any capital or income of my residuary estate not otherwise disposed of by this clause shall be held in trust for such of my children by my [wife/husband] other than [*name*][12] as shall survive me and if more than one in equal shares.

1   Residue devolves on the other spouse, if surviving. If the other spouse does not survive the testator, residue is given to the children. In view of the nil-rate band legacy, it is not appropriate to incorporate a survivorship condition in the gift to the spouse: see the Preliminary Note on survivorship conditions in C3 at para **[225.4]**.

2   For a wider class, including power to add to it, see Form C3.6, cl 3(1)(b) at para **[225.100]**.

3   See cl 4(2), n 4 at para **[226.21]**.

4   Instructions must be taken on the composition of the class, but it may be useful on tax-planning grounds to be able to appoint interests in favour of spouses.

5   See cl 4(2), n 5 at para **[226.21]**. See also the Note to this form at para **[226.13]**.

6   Since the trusts are principally for the benefit of the disabled child, a common law perpetuity period based on lives (including that of the disabled child) seems appropriate. See cl 4, nn 4 and 6 at para **[226.21]** on the restriction of the relevant lives to those of the children of the marriage.

7   Clause 10 contains a power to release and restrict powers (cl 10(2) at para **[226.27]**) and an optional restriction intended to bring the ITA 1984, s 89 into operation (cl 10(4) and (5) at para **[226.27]**).

8   See proviso (viii) to sub-cl (3)(a) and sub-cl (3)(b) of this clause, for the modification of this provision during the two years following the testator's death. For the appointment of a trust corporation see cl 14 at para **[226.32]** and the note thereto.

9   This is included to prevent an appointment intended to obtain the exemption for a gift to charity on the testator's death by the application of the ITA 1984, s 144, failing to do so by being made within the first three months after the testator's death: see C3 at para **[225.85]** for this hazard of the ITA 1984, s 144. The spouse exemption is not relevant because these trusts only take effect if the testator's spouse has predeceased him.

10   If it were required that there should be two trustees during the two years after the testator's death, difficulty could arise if the number of trustees was reduced to one and the administration of the estate was not complete, as it is not clear that the statutory power to appoint new trustees could be exercised in such circumstances.

11   See cl 4(4), n 8 at para **[226.21]** and, for the reasons for the proviso, see n 10 supra.

12   Ie the name of the disabled child, whom it will probably be appropriate to exclude from this ultimate gift of capital.

[226.26]

Administrative powers[1]

9.   (1)   In this clause where the context so admits:

(a)   the expression 'land' includes buildings and estates interests or rights of any kind in or over land; and

(b)   during the administration of my estate the expression 'beneficiary' includes any person who would be a beneficiary if such administration had been completed and the expression 'beneficially interested' and references to income of any asset being payable or capable of being paid to or for the benefit of a beneficiary shall be construed accordingly.

(2)   None of the powers or provisions contained in subclause (3) below of this clause shall be capable of being exercised or operating in any manner such that if such power or provision were capable of being so exercised or so operating the existence of the same would either:

(i)   prevent any person who would in the absence of such power or provision have been entitled to an interest in possession (within the meaning of Part III of the Inheritance Tax Act 1984) in any property from being entitled to such interest; or

(ii)   prevent section 71 of the Inheritance Tax Act 1984 from applying to any property to which in the absence of such power or provision the said section 71 would have applied.[2]

(3)   In the administration of my estate and the execution of the trusts hereof or of any codicil hereto my trustees shall (subject to clause 10 below) have the following powers in addition to those conferred by law but subject to the last foregoing subclause:

(a)   power to invest moneys sell assets and change investments with the unrestricted freedom of choice and powers of disposition and acquisition of a sole beneficial owner with in particular power to make unsecured loans, acquire non-income yielding assets, and purchase land anywhere in the world or chattels for any purpose including occupation or enjoyment in kind by a beneficiary under the power set out below;[3]

(b)   power to delegate all or any of their investment powers to a professional investment manager or managers whether individual or corporate and whether or not also a nominee holder of assets for my trustees (and who may be or include one or more of my trustees or the beneficiaries hereunder) upon such terms as to remuneration and otherwise (including terms authorising self-dealing or providing for the limitation of the liability of the investment manager or managers) as my trustees think fit and section 22 of the Trustee Act 2000 shall not apply;[4]

(c)   power to vest or register any property in any person or persons whether individual or corporate and whether or not an investment manager to whom powers have been delegated under the foregoing power (and who may be or include one or more of my trustees or the beneficiaries hereunder) as nominee or nominees for my trustees upon such terms as to remuneration or otherwise (including terms authorising self-dealing or providing for the limitation of the liability of the nominee) as my trustees think fit and section 22 of the Trustee Act 2000 shall not apply;[5]

(d)   power to borrow money with or without giving security and on such terms as to interest and repayment and otherwise as my trustees may think fit for any purpose connected with the administration of my estate or the trusts declared herein or in any codicil hereto (including investment) and no lender from whom my trustees borrow money in purported exercise of this power shall be concerned to enquire as to the propriety amount or purpose of any such borrowing;[6]

(e)   power to lend money to a beneficiary to whom any of the income of such money is payable or to whom or for whose benefit any income of such money is capable of being paid or applied in exercise of a discretion (or who would be such a beneficiary if such money yielded income) and to do so at a full or concessionary rate of interest or interest free;[7]

(f)   all the powers of an absolute owner in relation to any land (wherever situated) held by them;[8]

(g) power to apply capital held on the same trusts as any land (or which would be so held if the administration of my estate had been completed) in the improvement or adaptation of such land and to apply such capital or the income of such capital on the repair or maintenance of such land;[9]

(h) power to permit any beneficiary to have the beneficial occupation use or enjoyment in kind of any land or chattel or other tangible property on such terms as to repair insurance or payment of outgoings by the beneficiary or any other person or persons or otherwise howsoever as my trustees think fit including power for the benefit of a beneficiary to permit any other person or persons (whether beneficiaries or not) to occupy use or enjoy any of the types of asset aforesaid together with such beneficiary or otherwise. Provided that the foregoing power shall only be exercisable and such permission to occupy or enjoy in kind may only continue in the following circumstances:

   (i) so long as any of the income of such land chattel or other tangible property is payable to such beneficiary or capable of being paid or applied to him or for his benefit in exercise of a discretion (or would be so payable or capable of being so paid or applied if such land chattel or other property yielded income);

   (ii) in the case of land, so long as for the time being the occupation thereof is compatible with any statutory rights of occupation of any other beneficiary or beneficiaries;[10]

(i) power to exercise all the powers of appropriation (and other incidental powers) conferred by statute on a personal representative without the necessity of obtaining any consents and notwithstanding that one or more of my trustees may be beneficially interested in the exercise of such power.[11]

1 See Form C2.1, cl 9, n 1 at para **[224.30]**.
2 See Form C2.1, cl 9, n 2 at para **[224.30]**. This proviso is not needed so long as the trusts are discretionary, but it is included in case trusts of either of these kinds are created by the trustees in exercise of any of their powers.
3 See Form C2.1, cl 9, n 3 at para **[224.30]**.
4 See Form C2.1, cl 9, n 4 at para **[224.30]**.
5 See Form C2.1, cl 9, n 5 at para **[224.30]**.
6 See Form C2.1, cl 9, n 6 at para **[224.30]**.
7 See Form C2.1, cl 9, n 7 at para **[224.30]**.
8 See Form C2.1, cl 9, n 8 at para **[224.30]**.
9 See para **[220.52]** for the reasons for this provision.
10 See Form C2.1, cl 9, n 10 at para **[224.30]**. Express provision for occupation etc by persons other than a beneficiary is added to this subclause to make it clear that the trustees may, eg provide a residence for a disabled beneficiary and someone who is looking after him. It is not entirely clear whether permitting such a person to reside with a beneficiary would give that person an interest in possession.
11 See Form C2.1, cl 9, n 11 at para **[224.30]**.

[226.27]

Exercise and release of powers

10. (1) In this clause:

   (a) the expression 'the relevant day' has the same meaning as in clause 8 above of this will;

(b)   the expression 'the trust period' has in relation to the trust legacy the same meaning as in clause 4 above of this will and has in relation to my residuary estate the same meaning as in clause 8 above of this will.

(2)   My trustees shall have power at any time or times and from time to time during the trust period by deed or deeds to release or restrict all or any of the powers hereinbefore contained (whether dispositive or administrative) or this present power either in whole or in part and in any manner they think fit Provided that except in the case of any exercise of the foregoing power in respect of my residuary estate before the relevant day the trustees shall be at least two in number or a trust corporation.[1]

(3)   Any power or discretion hereby or by law conferred on my trustees (including a power or discretion as to the disposition of capital or income) shall be exercisable notwithstanding that any of my trustees has a personal interest in such exercise [Provided that except in the case of any exercise of a power over my residuary estate before the relevant day[2] there are not fewer than two trustees and at least one of my trustees has no such personal interest].[3]

1   This power could be used to convert the trusts of the trust legacy into discretionary trusts falling within the ITA 1984, s 89 (see para **[226.4]**, sub-paras (vi) and (vii)), and also those of the residuary estate if sub-cls (4) and (5) of this clause are not included in the will. It could also be used to narrow the trustees' powers over capital if it is found that extensive powers over capital exercisable in favour of the disabled child are having an adverse effect on state benefits or local authority provision for him or her, or to restrict their powers so that they cannot create an interest or interests in possession during the disabled child's life if that turns out to be necessary for the Inland Revenue to accept that the ITA 1984, s 89 applies (see para **[226.4]**, sub-paras (vi) and (vii)), and it is desired that s 89 should apply.
2   This restriction is only imposed after the initial two-year period from the testator's death because it could cause difficulty for exercise of the powers during the initial period.
3   The words in square brackets should be omitted if the executors and trustees will or might all be members of the testator's family.

[226.28]

Restriction for the purposes of the ITA 1984, s 89

[(4)   If my [son/daughter] [*name of disabled child*] shall be living after the relevant day none of the powers hereinbefore contained shall be exercisable after the relevant day during the life of my said [son/daughter] so as to cause the aggregate amount or value of the capital of my residuary estate which shall for the time being have been applied (within the meaning of section 89(1)(b) of the Inheritance Tax Act 1984) otherwise than for the benefit of my said [son/daughter] to exceed the aggregate amount or value of such capital which shall for the time being have been applied (within the meaning aforesaid) for the benefit of my said [son/daughter] to the intent that section 89 of the Inheritance Tax Act 1984 shall apply to my residuary estate after the relevant day during the life of my said [son/daughter].[1]

(5)   Provided that my trustees may by any deed or deeds executed before the relevant day declare that the foregoing subclause (4) of this clause shall not apply to the whole or any part or share of my residuary estate which may be specified in such deed and the operation of the foregoing subclause (4) shall be excluded or restricted accordingly.[2]]

1   This and the next subclause, if included, will restrict the exercise of the trustees' powers after the expiry of two years from the surviving spouse's death in a way which will convert the trusts

into 'disabled trusts' within the ITA 1984, s 89, provided that the disabled child is disabled within the meaning of s 89 at the testator's death (see para **[226.4]**, sub-paras (i) and (ii)), and provided that the existence of powers under which the trustees could create an interest in possession during the disabled child's life is compatible with s 89 (see para **[226.4]**, sub-paras (vi) and (vii) and cl 10(2), n 1 at para **[226.27]**). Since the restriction will come into effect no more than two years after the death, its doing so will not constitute a chargeable event and the disabled trusts will be deemed to have been a provision of the testator's will: ITA 1984, s 144 (see C3 at paras **[225.83]**–**[225.91]**). The restriction applies to the powers in cl 9 as well as those in cl 8, as there are various powers in cl 9 which could be characterised as powers to apply capital, such as the power to permit enjoyment in kind in cl 9(h) and the power to lend in cl 9(e).

2   Subclause (5) enables the executors by deed executed within two years of the death to exclude the operation of sub-cl (4) in relation to the whole or any part of residue. If sub-cls (4) and (5) are omitted, or they are included but the power in sub-cl (5) is exercised, the residuary estate or the part to which the exercise of the power relates will continue to be held on full discretionary trusts without any restriction on the powers of appointment or application and will be subject to inheritance tax periodic and exit charges under the ITA 1984, Pt III, Ch III (see B18 at paras **[218.8]** and **[218.9]**).

[226.29]

Receipts on behalf of charitable institutions

11.   The receipt of any person who professes to be the treasurer or other proper officer for the time being of any institution (whether corporate or not) shall be a sufficient discharge to my trustees in respect of any money or other asset which becomes payable or transferable to such institution under any exercise of any power or discretion herein contained.

[226.30]

Trustee indemnity

12.   (1)   My trustees shall not be liable for any act or default of any investment manager or nominee employed in good faith to manage or hold assets of my estate nor for any act or default of any person having the occupation use or enjoyment of property in kind nor for any depreciation wear and tear or damage to any such property while in the possession of any such person.[1]

[(2)   Section 11(1) of the Trusts of Land and Appointment of Trustees Act 1996 (consultation with beneficiaries) shall not apply to the exercise by my trustees of their functions in relation to any land subject to the trusts of this my will].[2]

1   This makes it clear that the trustees are not liable for the defaults of others who may have possession or control of trust property, nor for the depreciation of property (such as chattels made available to a disabled beneficiary) which remain trust assets but are being enjoyed in kind. In respect of the defaults of an investment manager or nominee, this indemnity may be wider than that of the TrA 2000, s 23(1) (Part G, para **[246.138]**) which only exempts a trustee from liability for such defaults if he has complied with the statutory duty of care, a standard which may be higher than that of 'good faith'. Whereas it is clear that a wider indemnity such as this can apply where trustees have exercised an express power to appoint an investment manager or nominee, it is not clear that a wider indemnity can be conferred where trustees have exercised the statutory power (see n 4 to cl 8 at para **[225.18]** and Preliminary Note to B21 at para **[221.14]**). For a wider form of indemnity, see eg Form B21.12 at para **[221.16]**.

2   The TLATA 1996, s 11(1) which obliges trustees of land to consult beneficiaries of full age and beneficially entitled to an interest in possession, and so far as consistent with the general interest of the trust to give effect to the wishes of those beneficiaries or (in the event of a

dispute) the majority by value, will not be relevant so long as the trusts are discretionary, but it may become so in the event that interest in possession trusts are created by the trustees in exercise of any of their powers. In that case the testator may wish to exclude it (Part G, para [246.97] and see Preliminary Note to B20 at para [220.58]).

[226.31]

Professional trustee charging clause

13.   Any of my trustees being a professional or business man may charge and be paid all usual professional and other proper charges for business transacted acts done advice given and time spent by him or his firm in connection with the administration of my estate or in connection with the trusts hereof including acts which a personal representative or trustee not being in any profession or business could have done personally[1].

1   In spite of the TrA 2000, s 29(2) (Part G, para [246.144]) giving certain professional trustees authority to charge for their services on or after 1 February 2001, an express remuneration clause entitling any professional or business person to charge may still be advisable: see B21 at para [221.35].

[226.32]

Appointment of a trust corporation

14.   A trust corporation (within the meaning of the Trustee Act 1925) may be appointed a trustee hereof (whether as a sole trustee or jointly with another trustee or trustees) and may charge for so acting in accordance with its published scale of charges at the time of its appointment or on such other basis as may be agreed between the trust corporation and the persons making the appointment.[1]

1   It may become necessary for a trust corporation to take on the trusteeship if suitable family members die or do not want to act. Further, it may be possible and appropriate to appoint a trust corporation which is connected with a charity for persons with the relevant disability. If express provision is not made for a corporate trustee's remuneration, then the TrA 2000, s 29 authorises it to receive reasonable remuneration (Part G, para [246.144]). Nonetheless, an express charging clause such as this may be desirable since a particular trust corporation might not be prepared to act in return for the statutory remuneration.

[226.33]

Testimonium

IN WITNESS whereof I have hereunto set my hand this —— day of ——20——
—.

[226.34]

Attestation clause

SIGNED by the above-named [testator/testatrix] as   } *[Signature of*
[his/her] last will in the presence of us both present at   } *testator/testatrix]*
the same time who at [his/her] request and in [his/her]   }
presence and in the presence of each other have signed   }
our names below as witnesses: }

[Signatures, addresses and descriptions of two witnesses]

[226.35]

FORM C4.2:   Will providing for spouse suffering from mental disorder

NOTE

This form incorporates a nil-rate band legacy on discretionary trusts under which the mentally disabled spouse is a beneficiary, and settles residue on trusts for the benefit of the spouse which by virtue of the ITA 1984, s 89 will be treated as conferring an interest in possession on the spouse. The estate is thus made fully available for the upkeep of the spouse while making use of the nil-rate band available on the testator's death, and making sure that the inheritance tax exemption for inter-spouse transfers applies to the remainder of the estate.

[226.36]

Revocation clause
I [*name*] of [*address*] revoke all former testamentary dispositions made by me and declare this to be my last will.

[226.37]

Appointment of executors and trustees and definition of 'my trustees'
1.   I appoint [*name*] of [*address*] and [*name*] of [*address*] (hereinafter together called 'my trustees' which expression shall where the context so admits include my personal representatives for the time being and the trustees for the time being hereof) to be the executors and trustees of this will.

[226.38]

Bequest of personal chattels[1]
2.   (1)   I give the following items free of tax:[2]

[(a) To my son [*name*] my father's signet ring;
(b)   to my daughter [*name*] my mother's engagement ring;]

(2)   If my [wife/husband] [*name*] ('my [wife/husband]') shall survive me then subject as aforesaid I give all my personal chattels as defined by section 55(1)(x) of the Administration of Estates Act 1925[3] to my trustees upon trust as follows:

(a)   my trustees shall have power during the life of my [wife/husband] to distribute the said chattels among the legacy beneficiaries (as defined in clause 3 below) or any one or more of them and in such manner as my trustees think fit;
(b)   my trustees shall have power during the life of my [wife/husband] to sell any of the said chattels and to dispose of any thereof which are of little value to any person and in any manner (including power to dispose of the same for no consideration) as they think fit;
(c)   subject to and in default of any distribution sale or disposal as aforesaid my trustees shall hold the said chattels on trust for my [wife/husband] during [her/his] life;
(d)   subject as aforesaid my trustees shall hold the said chattels or their proceeds of sale as part of my residuary estate.[4]

1   If the testator's spouse survives the testator, it is not appropriate for the chattels to go to the spouse absolutely (because of the spouse's mental incapacity), nor is it appropriate for them to fall into the residuary estate as there are no powers to distribute the capital of the latter to persons other than the spouse (contrast the extensive powers over residue in Form C4.1 at para **[226.25]**).

2   See Form C3.1, cl 2, n 2 at para **[225.12]**. The words 'free of tax' would only be of significance if the items given were outside the UK at the testator's death.

3   See Part G, para **[246.52]** for the wording of this definition, and for further discussion of the meaning of 'personal chattels' see Vol 1, para **[64.44]**.

4   With a disposition in this form, if the testator's spouse survives the testator, the inheritance tax spouse exemption will apply to the chattels on the testator's death, and that will not be affected by subsequent distribution to other persons: neither of the ITA 1984, s 143 (see B4 at paras **[204.9]** and **[204.10]**) or s 144 (see C3 at paras **[225.83]**–**[225.91]**) will apply. A wider class of objects of the discretion could be introduced as in sub-cls (4) and (5) of Form B4.11 at para **[204.25]**.

If it is preferred to have a non-exempt gift of chattels, at any rate so far as they do not fall into the residuary estate, a short-term discretionary trust such as that in Form B4.11 at para **[204.25]** could be used; if it is used, and the amount of the legacy given by cl 3 is calculated by reference to a formula rather than a specified amount, Form B4.11 should perhaps be varied so that the trustees can add chattels to the residuary estate before the period of two years from death has ended, so that the size of the non-exempt estate apart from cl 3, and thus the size of the nil-rate band legacy given by cl 3, can be ascertained at an early date.

[226.39]

Gift of nil-rate band legacy on discretionary trusts

3.   (1)   [*As in cl 4(1) of* Form C4.1 *at para* **[226.21]**.]

(2)   In this clause the following expressions have the following meanings, namely:

(a)   'the legacy beneficiaries' means and includes:

    (i)   my [wife/husband];

    (ii)   my children and remoter issue;

    (iii)   any spouse widow or widower of any of such children or remoter issue (and 'widow' and 'widower' shall include a widow or widower who has remarried);

    (iv)   any institution (whether corporate or not) which is established for purposes which are exclusively charitable;[1]

(b)   'the trust period' means the period commencing on my death and expiring on the twenty-first anniversary of the last survivor of the following persons, namely:

    (i)   my [wife/husband];

    (ii)   my children;

(c)   'the accumulation period' means the period commencing with my death and expiring on the twenty-first anniversary thereof.

(3)   [*As in cl 4(3) of* Form C4.1 *at para* **[226.21]**.]

(4)   [*As in cl 4(4) of* Form C4.1 *at para* **[226.21]**.]

(5)   [*As in cl 4(5) of* Form C4.1 *at para* **[226.21]**.]

(6)   Subject to the foregoing trust and any or every exercise of the foregoing powers my trustees shall hold the trust legacy and the income thereof at the expiration of the trust period in trust absolutely for such of my grandchildren and remoter issue as shall then be living in equal shares per stirpes.

(7)   Any capital or income of the trust legacy not otherwise disposed of by this clause shall be held in trust for such of my children as shall survive me if more than one in equal shares absolutely.

1   This definition is based on that contained in the CA 1993, s 96(1). If the spouse is being cared for by some charitable body, it may be useful to have express power to make appointments in favour of that charity.

[226.40]

Administration trusts of residue
4.   [*As in cl 5 of* Form C4.1 *at para* **[226.22]**.]

[226.41]

Gifts made free of tax
5.   [*As in cl 6 of* Form C4.1 *at para* **[226.23]**.]

[226.42]

Beneficial trusts of residue for spouse[1]
6.   During the life of my [wife/husband] my trustees shall hold my residuary estate and the income thereof upon the trusts following:

[EITHER]

[(a) My trustees shall apply the income of my residuary estate for the maintenance or otherwise for the benefit of my [wife/husband] in such manner as they shall think fit [Provided that during the period commencing on my death and expiring on the twenty-first anniversary thereof or on the earlier death of my [wife/husband] my trustees may accumulate the whole or any part of such income by investing the same and the resulting income thereof in any of the investments hereby authorised and the accumulations so made shall form part of the capital of my residuary estate for all purposes;]]

[OR]

[(a) My trustees shall pay or apply the income of my residuary estate to or for the maintenance of any one or more of the following persons namely my [wife/husband] and children and remoter issue[2] and if more than one in such shares and generally in such manner as my trustees think fit [Provided that during the period commencing on my death and expiring on the twenty-first anniversary thereof or on the earlier death of my [wife/husband] my trustees may accumulate the whole or any part of such income by investing the same and the resulting income thereof in any of the investments hereby authorised and the accumulations so made shall form part of the capital of my residuary estate for all purposes;]]

(b)   Notwithstanding the foregoing trust my trustees (being not fewer than two in number or a trust corporation) may at any time or times and from time to time during the life of my [wife/husband] apply the whole or any part or parts of my residuary estate for [her/his] maintenance support or benefit in such manner as they think fit.

1   This clause contains alternative forms of provision for the benefit of the mentally disabled spouse in sub-cl (a), the first requiring the trustees to apply all the trust income for her or his benefit subject to an optional power to accumulate during the 21-year period following the testator's death (or during the spouse's life if shorter), and the second creating a discretionary trust of income for the testator's spouse and the children and remoter issue (subject a gain to an optional power to accumulate income). Whichever is selected is followed by a power in sub-cl (b), which enables the trustees to resort to capital for the spouse's maintenance.

    The first version of sub-cl (a) would probably give rise to an actual interest in possession for inheritance tax purposes if the proviso permitting accumulation of income were omitted, but with that proviso included it would probably not fall within the ITA 1984, s 89 because of the possibility of the trusts giving rise to an interest in possession during the spouse's life (see para **[226.4]**, sub-para (v)). It is thought that the second form of sub-cl (a) would (together with sub-cl (b)) be treated for inheritance tax purposes as giving rise to a deemed interest in possession under the ITA 1984, s 89(1) and (2). It is thought that the first form of sub-cl (a) would qualify the trust for the full capital gains tax annual allowance: see in particular the TCGA 1992, Sch 1, para 1(1)(b) and para **[226.6]**. On the other hand, the first version of sub-cl (a) could result in the whole of the income being taken into account as the spouse's in any means test for benefit purposes. See for the social security and fiscal implications of disabled trusts the Preliminary Note at para **[226.2]** et seq.

2   It may be advantageous to add spouses, widows and widowers of the children and remoter issue.

[226.43]

Remainder trusts for children and issue

7.   (1)   Subject as aforesaid my trustees shall hold my residuary estate and the income thereof upon trust for such of my children as shall survive me and if more than one in equal shares absolutely.

(2)   Provided that if any of my children shall predecease me leaving a child or children me surviving who shall attain the age of [18/21/25] years such last-mentioned child or children shall take and if more than one equally between them the share of my residuary estate which such deceased child of mine would have taken had he or she survived me.

(3)   Section 32 of the Trustee Act 1925 (relating to advancement) shall apply in relation to the foregoing trusts in this clause contained without modification during the life of my [wife/husband] but after the death of my [wife/husband] the said section 32 shall apply to the said trusts as if the words 'one half of' were omitted from proviso (a) to subsection (1) thereof.[1]

1   The ITA 1984, s 89 is not prevented from applying to settled property by reason of the statutory power of advancement applying to it during the disabled person's life, provided that it is not subject to modification: see the ITA 1984, s 89(3).

[226.44]

Administrative powers

8.   [*As in cl 9 of* Form C4.1 *at para* **[226.26]**, *amending '(subject to cl 10 below)' in the second line of cl 9(3) to '(subject to cl 9 below)'.*]

[226.45]

Exercise and release of powers

9.   (1)   My trustees (being not fewer than two in number or a trust corporation) shall have power at any time or times and from time to time during the life of my [wife/husband] by deed or deeds to release or restrict all or any of the powers hereinbefore contained (whether dispositive or administrative) or this present power either in whole or in part and in any manner they think fit.[1]

(2)   Any power or discretion hereby or by law conferred on my trustees (including a power or discretion as to the disposition of capital or income) shall be exercisable notwithstanding that any of my trustees has a personal interest in such exercise [provided that at least one of my trustees has no such personal interest].[2]

(3)   None of the powers hereinbefore contained shall be exercisable while my [wife/husband] is living so as to cause the aggregate amount or value of the capital of my residuary estate which shall for the time being have been applied (within the meaning of section 89(1)(b) of the Inheritance Tax Act 1984) other than for the benefit of my [wife/husband] to exceed the aggregate amount or value of such capital which shall for the time being have been applied (within the meaning aforesaid) for the benefit of my [wife/husband] to the intent that section 89 of the Inheritance Tax Act 1984 shall apply to my residuary estate during the life of my [wife/husband].][3]

1   The main reason for including such a power is in case any of the powers turn out to be regarded by the Inland Revenue as incompatible with the ITA 1984, s 89. For the main concern of this kind, see para **[226.4]**, sub-paras (vi) and (vii). It could also be useful where the first alternative cl 6(a) at para **[226.42]**, including the proviso permitting accumulation of income, has been included in the will, and it is found that the Inland Revenue will not accept that the ITA 1984, s 89 applies, but would accept that there would be an interest in possession if the power to accumulate were released; if the release were effected during the two years after the testator's death the spouse exemption might be obtained on the testator's death by virtue of the ITA 1984, s 144 (see C3 at paras **[225.83]**–**[225.91]**).

2   The words in square brackets should be omitted if the executors and trustees will or might all be members of the testator's family.

3   The purpose of this subclause is to make sure that the condition as to powers over capital in the ITA 1984, s 89(1)(b) is satisfied. Although the main dispositive power over capital in this form, ie cl 6(b) at para **[226.42]** can only be applied in favour of the spouse, it is possible that some of the administrative powers in cl 8 could be exercised so as to apply capital for other beneficiaries.

[226.46]

Receipts on behalf of charitable institutions

10.   [*As in cl 11 of* Form C4.1 *at para* **[226.29]**.]

[226.47]

Trustee indemnity

11.   [*As in cl 12 of* Form C4.1 *at para* **[226.30]**.]

[226.48]

Professional trustee charging clause

12.   [*As in cl 13 of* Form C4.1 *at para* **[226.31]**.]

[226.49]

Appointment of a trust corporation
13.   [*As in cl 14 of* Form C4.1 *at para* **[226.32]**.]

[*Testimonium and attestation clause as in* Form C4.1 *at paras* **[226.33]** and **[226.34]**.]

C5   Wills where there is more than one family

PRELIMINARY NOTE

[227.1]
This section contains forms for use by married couples where one or both of the
spouses have children by someone other than his or her present spouse. The
forms in this section do not contain any provision for a former spouse; it is
assumed that any former spouse is either dead, or has been divorced with a clean
break financial settlement and with an order having been made by the court
under the Inheritance (Provision for Family and Dependants) Act 1975
(I(PFD)A 1975), s 15 (Part G, para **[247.16]**) that the former spouse shall not be
entitled on the death of the testator to make a claim under that Act.

Wills for married couples where one or both has children by someone other
than the other spouse frequently have in common with wills for childless
couples (for which see C9 at para **[231.1]** et seq) that each wants to benefit the
other if he or she is the first to die, but wants to benefit different ultimate
beneficiaries from those the other wants to benefit after the death of the survivor.
Reciprocal wills and the ultimate destination of property is discussed in the
Preliminary Note to C2 at para **[224.9]** et seq and in the Preliminary Note to C9
at para **[231.7]** et seq. Forms C5.1 and C5.2 (at paras **[227.2]** and **[227.21]**) deal
with this problem by providing a life interest in residue for the surviving spouse,
with remainders to named children of the testator. Form C5.3 (at para **[227.35]**)
adopts the strategy of the first to die leaving his or her estate to the other, and the
survivor leaving his or her estate to the children and stepchildren in proportions
intended to reflect the relative assets of each of the spouses (for an alternative

approach see Form C9.6 at para **[231.62]**). Where both spouses have the same wishes as to the ultimate destination of their property, there may well be forms in C2 (at para **[224.1]** et seq and C3 (at para **[225.1]** et seq) which will be readily capable of adaptation for their use.

On the use of conditions as to surviving the testator by a particular period see the Preliminary Notes to C2 and C3 at paras **[224.2]** et seq and **[225.4]**. In each form in C5 there is either such a condition or a substantial non-exempt legacy.

For wills for unmarried couples see C6 at para **[228.1]** et seq, for wills for childless couples see C9 at para **[231.1]**, and for a will of someone who is separated and may divorce see Form C6.3 at para **[228.33]** et seq.

[227.2]

FORM C5.1:   Will of twice-married testator who has adult children from his first marriage and minor children from his second and who owns the matrimonial home; nil-rate band discretionary trust, and gift of matrimonial home and residue on trust for second wife for life with remainder to all the testator's children

NOTE

This is not one of a pair of wills. It is assumed that the husband is well-off, and wealthier than his wife, and that she will leave her estate exclusively to her children. This form can, however, be readily adapted for the converse situation. It is assumed that the testator wishes to provide support for his wife, and the children of the second marriage while minors, but wishes to ensure, so far as practical, that the capital goes ultimately to all his children including the children of the first marriage. It is also assumed that relations between his present wife and the children of his previous marriage are not especially warm, and that he feels that it is unlikely that any capital which he gives to his wife absolutely will be passed on by her to those children.

[227.3]
The will includes a nil-rate band discretionary legacy, under which the income can be used to support the wife but the capital goes to the children, and the house and residue are given to the wife for life with remainders to the children. There is an optional power to pay or apply part of the capital of residue to or for the benefit of the wife. As there is a nil-rate band legacy there is no survivorship condition in relation to the gift of a life interest in residue to the wife: see the Preliminary Note to C3 at para **[225.1]**.

It will be important for the testator to leave a letter of wishes. If there is a power to pay capital to or for the benefit of the wife it will be particularly important for him to indicate the circumstances in which he wants it to be exercised.

[227.4]

Revocation clause
I [*name*] of [*address*] hereby revoke all former testamentary dispositions made by me and declare this to be my last will.

[227.5]

Appointment of executors and trustees

1.   I appoint [*name*] of [*address*] and [*name*] of [*address*][1] (hereinafter together called 'my trustees' which expression shall include my personal representatives for the time being and the trustees for the time being hereof) to be the executors and trustees of this will.

1   It is assumed that the testator's wife is not appointed an executor or trustee. The choice of executors and trustees will have to be made carefully, as they may have to keep a balance between the widow and the children, especially the children of the first marriage.

[227.6]

Appointment of guardians[1]

2.   If my wife [*name*] ('my wife') shall predecease me I appoint [*name*] of [*address*] [and [*name*] of [*address*]] to be the [guardian/guardians] of the children of our marriage during their respective minorities.

1   This form assumes that the children of the second marriage are under 18. For the reasons given in the Preliminary Note to C2 at para **[224.1]**, the appointment will take effect only if the wife dies first. It is assumed that her will has a corresponding provision so that if she survives the testator but dies while the children are still minors the same persons will be appointed guardians.

[227.7]

Gift of chattels[1]

3.   (1)   I give free of tax[2] the following items:

(a)   to my son [*name*] [my guns and fishing tackle];
(b)   to my daughter [*name*] [my mother's engagement ring];
(c)   to my son [*name*] [my gold watch].

(2)   Subject as aforesaid I give all my personal chattels as defined by section 55(1)(x) of the Administration of Estates Act 1925[3] to my wife if she shall survive me [and I request her (but without imposing any trust or binding obligation on her) to give effect to any wishes as to the disposition of such chattels which may be contained in any memorandum that may be found amongst my papers at my death or which may have otherwise been communicated to her during my life].[4]

1   It is not usually appropriate or practical to settle chattels, because the trouble and expense of administering them is usually out of all proportion their value, unless they are exceptionally valuable ones. Accordingly, as the residuary estate is settled on trust for the testator's wife for life, this absolute gift of chattels is included. For alternative forms see B4, at paras **[204.15]**–**[204.34]**.
2   See Form C8.1, cl 3, n 2 at para **[230.6]**.
3   See Part G, para **[246.52]** for the wording of this definition, and for further discussion of the meaning of 'personal chattels' see Vol 1, para **[64.44]**.
4   If property bequeathed by a will to one person is distributed to another person in accordance with wishes expressed by the testator within two years of his death, it is treated for inheritance tax purposes as having been bequeathed by the will to that other person: Inheritance Tax Act 1984 (ITA 1984), s 143, and see B4 at paras **[204.9]** and **[204.10]**. Where it is the testator's spouse to whom the property is bequeathed in the first place, s 143 will operate disadvantageously as it will cause the property so distributed by the spouse to cease being part of an exempt gift and to become part of a chargeable one. Where this is a problem, eg where large values are involved, the spouse could wait until after two years from the testator's death to distribute in accordance with his wishes.

[227.8]

Gift of legacies

4.   I give free of tax[1] the following legacies:

   (a)   to [*name*] the sum of £——;
   (b)   to [*name*] the sum of £——;
   (c)   to [*name*] the sum of £——.

1   See Form C3.1, cl 2, n 2 at para **[225.12]**.

[227.9]

Gift of nil-rate band legacy on discretionary trusts[1]

5.   (1)   If my [wife/husband] shall survive me[2] then I give to my trustees a pecuniary legacy of [£242,000 subject to payment thereout of any inheritance tax payable by reason of my death which is attributable thereto[3]]/[the maximum sum (if any) which can in the circumstances subsisting at my death be given by this clause without any liability being incurred for the payment of inheritance tax on or by reason of my death and in particular (without prejudice to the generality of the foregoing) for the purpose of determining the amount of such maximum sum the circumstances to be taken into account shall include all chargeable transfers made by me during my life (or events treated as such for inheritance tax purposes) so far as relevant for the computation of inheritance tax on my death the dispositions taking effect under this will (apart from this clause) or under any codicil hereto and any property treated as if it were part of my estate for inheritance tax purposes].

   (2)   In this clause the following expressions have the following meanings, namely:

   (a)   'the income beneficiaries' means my wife and my children and remoter issue;
   (b)   'the capital beneficiaries' means my children and remoter issue;
   (c)   'the trust period' means the period commencing on my death and expiring on the twenty-first anniversary of the death of my wife;[4]
   (d)   'the accumulation period' means the period commencing with my death and expiring on the twenty-first anniversary thereof.

   (3)   My trustees shall hold the said legacy upon trust to invest the same in any investments hereby authorised with power to vary the same and shall hold the said legacy and the assets from time to time representing the same (hereinafter called 'the trust legacy') and the income thereof upon trust for all or such one or more of the capital beneficiaries at such ages or times in such shares and upon such trusts for the benefit of the beneficiaries as my trustees (being at least two in number [or a trust corporation][5]) may by deed or deeds revocable or irrevocable executed at any time or times during the trust period appoint and in making any such appointment my trustees shall have powers as full as those which they would possess if they were an absolute beneficial owner of the trust legacy and in particular (but without prejudice to the generality of the foregoing words) my trustees may in any exercise of the foregoing power as they in their absolute discretion think fit:

   (a)   delegate give or impose to or upon themselves or any other person or persons and in relation to any trust or disposition any discretionary powers or discretionary trusts conditions limitations restrictions or provisions including powers of further delegation or powers to create further discretionary trusts or powers;[6]

(b) create trusts or powers for the accumulation of income during any period permitted by law;

(c) create administrative powers or provisions of whatever nature;

Provided that:

(i) no such appointment shall invalidate any payment transfer or application of capital or income previously made under any of the trusts or powers herein elsewhere contained;

(ii) every interest limited under any exercise of such power shall vest in interest (if at all) not later than the expiration of the trust period;

(iii) any such appointment may be made in respect of income alone without any appointment of capital; and

(iv) any such revocable appointment shall (so far as then unrevoked) cease to be revocable on the expiration of the trust period.

(4) In default of and subject to any exercise of the foregoing power my trustees (being at least two in number [or a trust corporation][7]) may at their discretion at any time or times during the trust period pay transfer or apply to or for the benefit of all or any one or more of the capital beneficiaries for the time being living the whole or any part or parts of the trust legacy in any manner they in their absolute discretion think fit.[8]

(5) Subject to any or every exercise of the foregoing powers my trustees shall during the trust period hold the trust legacy upon trust to pay or apply the income thereof to or for the maintenance education or benefit of all or any one or more of the income beneficiaries for the time being living in such shares if more than one and generally in such manner as they think fit provided that my trustees may during the accumulation period accumulate the whole or any part of the income of the trust legacy by investing the same and the resulting income thereof in any of the investments hereby authorised and any accumulations of income so made shall form part of the capital of the trust legacy from which such income arose for all purposes [provided that my trustees shall have power during the trust period to pay or apply such accumulations of income as if they were income of the current year].[9]

(6) Subject to the foregoing trust and any or every exercise of the foregoing powers my trustees shall hold the trust legacy and the income thereof at the expiration of the trust period in trust absolutely for such of my children and remoter issue as shall then be living in equal shares per stirpes so that no child or issue of mine shall take a share if his or her parent is living at the expiration of the trust period and so capable of taking.

(7) Any capital or income of the trust legacy not otherwise disposed of by this clause shall be held in trust for such of my children as shall survive me if more than one in equal shares absolutely.

1 For a discussion of nil rate band discretionary trusts, see B18 at paras **[218.16]**–**[218.30]**.
  As regards the amount of, or formula for, the legacy given by this clause, see Form C3.1, cl 3, n 1 at para **[225.13]**. It is not practical in this case to provide a discretionary legacy of a cash amount in excess of the nil-rate band, with the idea that the trustees can appoint the excess over the nil-rate band to the widow within two years of the testator's death and obtain exemption for

it by virtue of the ITA 1984, s 144 because the widow is not an object of the powers over capital.

The trusts of this legacy are such that the widow is an object of the discretionary trust of income, but capital can only be appointed, paid or applied for the benefit of the children and remoter issue. If the testator dies while the children of the second marriage are still minors the capital can be used to pay for their education or support, which will relieve the widow of expense she would otherwise incur.

If the testator prefers the trusts to include powers to appoint, pay or apply capital in favour of the widow, Form C3.4, cl 2 at para [225.60] could be substituted.

2   This precondition is imposed to avoid unnecessary duplication of gifts (ie this one and the residuary gift), and to avoid difficulties as to the effect where the amount of the legacy is determined by a formula, in the event of the spouse not surviving the testator. This gift should not be made conditional on the spouse surviving the testator by a survivorship period: see the Preliminary Note to C3 at para [225.1] et seq.

3   See Form C3.1, cl 3, n 3 at para [225.13].

4   The trust period is longer than may be needed in most cases, but gives considerable flexibility. In particular, if both parents were to die while the children of the second marriage were still minors, the whole of this fund would continue to be available for their support at the discretion of the trustees.

5   These words in square brackets should be included if a trust corporation is to be an executor, or there is a possibility that a trust corporation might subsequently be appointed a trustee. In either case express provision for the remuneration of a trust corporation so acting (not included in this form) should be added: see, eg Forms B3.11 to B3.14 at paras [203.28]–[203.31], Form B21.40 [221.52] and Form C4.1, cl 1 at para [226.18].

6   These words authorise the creation of discretionary powers which might not otherwise be valid: see Vol 1, para [40.5].

7   See n 5 supra.

8   Such a power to apply capital could be used to apply cash for the benefit of the children of the second marriage quickly and informally, eg paying fees for education or direct to the educational institution. However, it is essential that its exercise should be adequately evidenced.

9   The addition of these words will enable accumulated income to be paid or applied for the benefit of the wife; if they are omitted, any income which has been accumulated will form part of capital for all purposes and be unavailable for the wife.

[227.10]

Right of residence to wife[1]

6.   (1)   If my wife shall survive me I give my freehold dwellinghouse known as ———, or (if the same shall be sold or otherwise disposed of before my death) the dwellinghouse or the principal dwellinghouse (if I have more than one) which I shall own at the date of my death, to my trustees free of all sums charged or otherwise secured thereon at my death (which sums shall be paid out of my residuary estate) to hold the same and the assets from time to time representing the same on trust for [my wife] during her life.

(2)   It is a purpose of the foregoing trust to provide a home for [my wife] so long as she so desires[2] and I declare that my trustees shall not be liable for lack of insurance repair or payment of outgoings of any home occupied by her under the foregoing trust or for not taking steps to enforce any reasonable conditions imposed by my trustees on [my wife] in relation to her occupation of any such home.[3]

(3)   All the powers of my trustees may be exercised by them in favour of or for the benefit of [my wife] even though she is one of my trustees, and at any time when she is not one of my trustees her consent shall still be required to any exercise of the trustees' powers of sale purchase or leasing in relation to any land or buildings subject to this Clause.[4]

(4)   Subject as aforesaid the said dwellinghouse and the assets representing the same shall fall into my residuary estate.

1   This clause providing the wife with a life interest in the matrimonial home, and so a statutory right of occupation under the TLATA 1996, s 12(1) (Part G, para **[246.98]**), may not be strictly necessary since the wife has a life interest in residue. However, by making the matrimonial home the subject of a specific gift it is much further on in the order in which assets are applied to pay debts and testamentary expenses. Further, it enables express provision to be made for sale and other dispositions to be subject to the wife's consent (see sub-cl (4)), and the purpose of the trust can be set out as including occupation of the house (see sub-cl (2)), with the consequence that the precondition of the statutory right of occupation in s 12(1)(a) is satisfied. Under this clause, if the house is sold and the beneficiary goes to live with a relative or in rented accommodation, she will be entitled to the income of the proceeds of sale as invested.
2   This should be sufficient to confer the statutory right of occupation on the beneficiary under the TLATA 1996, s 12(1)(a) (Part G, para **[246.98]**).
3   The trustees have power under the TLATA 1996, s 13(3) (Part 'G, para **[246.99]**) to impose reasonable conditions on an occupying beneficiary. A will probably cannot determine in advance what conditions it will be reasonable to impose (see para **[208.18]**), but there is nothing to prevent the trustees being absolved from liability for the beneficiary's failing to observe the conditions.
4   The TLATA 1996, s 8(2) (Part G, para **[246.93]**) enables exercise of the trustees' powers over land to be made subject to consents. The repeal of the LPA 1925, s 28(1) means that a requirement of consent to a sale is no longer applied by statute to other powers.

[227.11]
Administration trusts of residue
7.   (1)   I give all my property not hereby or by any codicil hereto otherwise effectively disposed of [(including any entailed or other property over which I shall have at my death a general power of disposition by will)][1] to my trustees to hold on the trusts set out below with power at their discretion to sell all or any of it as and when they think fit.[2]

(2)   My trustees shall pay my funeral and testamentary expenses[3] and debts and any legacies given by this will or any codicil hereto out of such property or its proceeds and shall have a discretion as to how such payments shall be borne as between capital and income.[4]

(3)   Subject as above my trustees shall hold such property and the assets from time to time representing the same (hereinafter called 'my residuary estate') on the trusts set out below and shall invest all money comprised in such property or arising from its sale in any of the investments hereby authorised with power to change such investments into any others hereby authorised.

(4)   In the administration of my estate and the execution of the trusts of this will or of any codicil to it:

(a)   my trustees shall treat all income as accruing on the date on which it becomes payable regardless of the period in respect of which it shall have accrued and shall not make any statutory apportionment of the same;[5] and
(b)   none of the equitable rules of apportionment between capital and income shall apply in any circumstances whatever.[6]

1   See Form C2.1, cl 6, n 1 at para **[224.27]**.
2   See Form C2.1, cl 6, n 2 at para **[224.27]**.
3   See Form C2.1, cl 6, n 3 at para **[224.27]**.
4   See Form C2.1, cl 6, n 4 at para **[224.27]**.
5   See Form C2.1, cl 6, n 5 at para **[224.27]**.
6   See Form C2.1, cl 6, n 6 at para **[224.27]**.

[227.12]

Gifts made free of tax

8.   Any specific gift or pecuniary or general legacy made by this will or any codicil hereto which is expressed to be 'free of tax' shall be free from the payment of any inheritance tax or foreign tax or duty payable on or by reason of my death to which such gift or legacy would otherwise be subject and such inheritance tax or foreign tax or duty shall be paid out of my residuary estate.[1]

1   See Form C3.1, cl 5, n 1 at para **[225.15]**.

[227.13]

Beneficial trusts of residue

9.   (1)   My trustees shall hold my residuary estate upon trust to pay the income thereof to my wife during her life.

[(2)   Notwithstanding the foregoing trust my trustees (being not fewer than two in number [or a trust corporation][1] may at any time and from time to time during the life of my wife pay transfer or apply any part or parts not exceeding in the aggregate [one quarter]/[one half][2] of my residuary estate to or for the benefit of my wife in such manner as they think fit provided that the foregoing power shall only be exercisable over capital of which the income is for the time being payable to my wife (or would be payable if such capital yielded income).][3]

(3)   Subject as aforesaid my trustees shall hold my residuary estate and the income thereof upon trust for such of my children as shall survive me and in the case of those who are then under the age of [18/21/25] years as shall attain that age and if more than one in equal shares provided that if any child of mine shall predecease me or having survived me shall fail to attain the age of [18/21/25] years leaving a child or children surviving me or born after my death who shall attain the age of [18/21] years such last mentioned child or children shall take if more than one equally between them the share of my residuary estate which such deceased child of mine would have taken had he or she lived to attain a vested interest.[4]

1   See n 3 to cl 5(3) of this form at para **[227.9]**.
2   One of these should be deleted, or both deleted and some other fraction substituted.
3   There are two reasons for restricting the exercise of the power to capital in which the widow has an interest in possession: first, to ensure that the power is not exercisable if there is a divorce and the life interest given by the previous subclause lapses (see the Preliminary Note to C2, at para **[224.12]** et seq); and second, to ensure that the power ceases to be exercisable if the wife assigns or surrenders her life interest.
   This entire clause can be omitted if the testator does not wish there to be any power to pay the widow capital. On the other hand, if he wants this power to apply to the whole of the residuary estate, a provision such as cl 7(2) of Form C3.2 at para **[225.35]** could be substituted.
4   A substitutional proviso is included as it is unclear whether the saving provisions contained in the WA 1837, s 33 apply where there is a class gift subject to an age contingency, and in any case s 33 will not apply to the share of a child of the testator who survives him and dies before attaining the vesting age: see Vol 1, para **[47.14]** et seq. For the text of s 33 see Part G, para **[244.34]**.

[227.14]

Maintenance, accumulation and advancement[1]

10.   (1)   Section 31 of the Trustee Act 1925 (relating to accumulation and maintenance) shall apply in relation to the trusts hereby or by any codicil hereto declared as if:

(a) in paragraph (i) of subsection (1) of the said section the words 'as the trustees think fit' were substituted for the words 'as may in all the circumstances be reasonable'; and

(b) the proviso to the said subsection (1) were omitted.

(2) Section 32 of the Trustee Act 1925 (relating to advancement) shall apply in relation to the said trusts as if the words 'one half of' were omitted from proviso (a) to subsection (1) thereof [provided that the powers conferred by the said section (as hereby enlarged) shall not be exercisable in favour of any minor beneficiary hereunder otherwise than so as to cause such beneficiary to become immediately entitled to or to an interest in possession in the capital thereby paid or applied within the meaning of section 71(1)(a) of the Inheritance Tax Act 1984].[2]

(3) Whenever my trustees shall have an obligation or discretion under the provisions of this will or any codicil hereto or under the general law to apply income or capital for the benefit of a minor beneficiary they may either pay the same without liability to account to his or her parent guardian or any other adult person with whom such beneficiary may be residing or to such beneficiary himself or herself if of the age of 16 years or more and so that the receipt of such parent guardian or other person or of such minor beneficiary shall be a full and sufficient discharge to my trustees for the income or capital so applied.[3]

1   For alternative provisions see the forms in B18 at paras **[218.77]–[218.107]**.
2   The proviso is included in order to prevent the power prejudicing the application of the ITA 1984, s 71 (accumulation and maintenance trusts), but is probably unnecessary: see the Note on inheritance tax and the statutory power of advancement in B18 at para **[218.85]**. If the accumulation and maintenance trusts of income are extended so as to continue beyond the age of 18 (see eg Forms B18.12 and B18.13 at paras **[218.78]–[218.79]**), then 'minor beneficiary hereunder' should be amended to eg 'beneficiary hereunder who is under the age of [*n*] years' where *n* is the highest age at which an absolute interest or an interest in possession might be attained by any of the beneficiaries. 25 is the maximum age compatible with the ITA 1984, s 71: see Part A, paras **[200.119]** and **[200.120]**.
3   A parent (with parental responsibility) and a guardian of a minor are empowered by the ChA 1989, s 3(3) (Part G, para **[244.119]**) to give a good receipt for the minor's property: see Vol 1, para **[9.41]**. The power in this subclause is wider in that it authorises the payment of income or capital to a parent who does not have parental responsibility, any adult with whom the minor is residing, and the minor himself or herself if 16 or over.

[227.15]

Administrative powers[1]

11.   (1)   In this clause where the context so admits:

(a) the expression 'land' includes buildings and estates, interests or rights of any kind in or over land; and

(b) during the administration of my estate the expression 'beneficiary' includes any person who would be a beneficiary if such administration had been completed, and the expression 'beneficially interested' and references to income of any asset being payable or capable of being paid to or for the benefit of a beneficiary shall be construed accordingly.

(2)   None of the powers or provisions contained in subclause (3) below of this clause shall be capable of being exercised or operating in any manner such

that if such power or provision were capable of being so exercised or so operating the existence of the same would either:

(i) prevent any person who would in the absence of such power or provision have been entitled to an interest in possession (within the meaning of Part III of the Inheritance Tax Act 1984) in any property from being entitled to such interest; or

(ii) prevent section 71 of the Inheritance Tax Act 1984 from applying to any property to which in the absence of such power or provision the said section 71 would have applied.[2]

(3) In the administration of my estate and the execution of the trusts hereof or of any codicil hereto my trustees shall (subject to clause 10 below) have the following powers in addition to those conferred by law but subject to the last foregoing subclause:

(a) power to invest moneys sell assets and change investments with the unrestricted freedom of choice and powers of disposition and acquisition of a sole beneficial owner with in particular power to make unsecured loans, acquire non-income yielding assets, and purchase land anywhere in the world or chattels for any purpose including occupation or enjoyment in kind by a beneficiary under the power set out below;[3]

(b) power to delegate all or any of their investment powers to a professional investment manager or managers whether individual or corporate and whether or not also a nominee holder of assets for my trustees (and who may be or include one or more of my trustees or the beneficiaries hereunder) upon such terms as to remuneration and otherwise (including terms authorising self-dealing or providing for the limitation of the liability of the investment manager or managers) as my trustees think fit and section 22 of the Trustee Act 2000 shall not apply;[4]

(c) power to vest or register any property in any person or persons whether individual or corporate and whether or not an investment manager to whom powers have been delegated under the foregoing power (and who may be or include one or more of my trustees or the beneficiaries hereunder) as nominee or nominees for my trustees upon such terms as to remuneration or otherwise (including terms authorising self-dealing or providing for the limitation of the liability of the nominee) as my trustees think fit and section 22 of the Trustee Act 2000 shall not apply;[5]

(d) power to borrow money with or without giving security and on such terms as to interest and repayment and otherwise as my trustees may think fit for any purpose connected with the administration of my estate or the trusts declared herein or in any codicil hereto (including investment) and no lender from whom my trustees borrow money in purported exercise of this power shall be concerned to enquire as to the propriety amount or purpose of any such borrowing;[6]

(e) power to lend money to a beneficiary to whom any of the income of such money is payable or to whom or for whose benefit any income of such money is capable of being paid or applied in exercise of a discretion (or who would be such a beneficiary if such money yielded income) and to do so at a full or concessionary rate of interest or interest free;[7]

(f) all the powers of an absolute owner in relation to any land (wherever situated) held by them;[8]

(g) power to apply capital held on the same trusts as any land (or which would be so held if the administration of my estate had been completed) in the improvement or adaptation of such land and to apply such capital or the income of such capital on the repair or maintenance of such land;[9]

(h) power to permit any beneficiary to have the beneficial occupation use or enjoyment in kind of any land or chattel or other tangible property on such terms as to repair insurance or payment of outgoings by the beneficiary or any other person or persons or otherwise howsoever as my trustees think fit including power for the benefit of a beneficiary to permit any other person or persons (whether beneficiaries or not) to occupy use or enjoy any of the types of asset aforesaid together with such beneficiary or otherwise. Provided that the foregoing power shall only be exercisable and such permission to occupy or enjoy in kind may only continue in the following circumstances:

    (i) so long as any of the income of such land chattel or other tangible property is payable to such beneficiary or capable of being paid or applied to him or for his benefit in exercise of a discretion (or would be so payable or capable of being so paid or applied if such land chattel or other property yielded income);

    (ii) in the case of land, so long as for the time being the occupation thereof is compatible with any statutory rights of occupation of any other beneficiary or beneficiaries;[10]

(i) power to exercise all the powers of appropriation (and other incidental powers) conferred by statute on a personal representative without the necessity of obtaining any consents and notwithstanding that one or more of my trustees may be beneficially interested in the exercise of such power.[11]

---

1 See Form C2.1, cl 9, n 1 at para **[224.30]**.
2 See Form C2.1, cl 9, n 2 at para **[224.30]**. This proviso is not needed so long as the trusts are discretionary, but it is included in case trusts of either of these kinds are created by the trustees in exercise of any of their powers.
3 See Form C2.1, cl 9, n 3 at para **[224.30]**.
4 See Form C2.1, cl 9, n 4 at para **[224.30]**.
5 See Form C2.1, cl 9, n 5 at para **[224.30]**.
6 See Form C2.1, cl 9, n 6 at para **[224.30]**.
7 See Form C2.1, cl 9, n 7 at para **[224.30]**. If a power to pay or apply capital is included in relation to a beneficiary, it will enable loans to be made to or for the benefit of that beneficiary (as an application of capital for his or her benefit), and a separate power to lend of this type is probably unnecessary. However, it is a useful power to include if, in relation to a particular beneficiary such as the testator's spouse, the testator does not wish there to be a power to pay or apply capital at all, or wants such power to be restricted to less than the entire fund.
8 See Form C2.1, cl 9, n 8 at para **[224.30]**.
9 See para **[220.52]** for the reasons for this provision.
10 See Form C2.1, cl 9, n 10 at para **[224.30]**. Express provision for occupation etc by persons other than a beneficiary are added to this subclause to make it clear that the trustees may eg, provide a residence for a disabled beneficiary and someone who is looking after him. It is not entirely clear whether permitting such a person to reside with a beneficiary would give that person an interest in possession.
11 See Form C2.1, cl 9, n 11 at para **[224.30]**.

[227.16]

Trustee indemnity

12. My trustees shall not be liable for any act or default of any investment manager or nominee employed in good faith to manage or hold assets of my estate nor for any act or default of any beneficiary having the occupation use or enjoyment of property in kind.[1]

1 This makes it clear that the trustees are not liable for the defaults of others who may have possession or control of trust property. In respect of the defaults of an investment manager or nominee, this indemnity may be wider than that of the TrA 2000, s 23(1) (see Part G, para **[246.138]**) which only exempts a trustee from liability for such defaults if he has complied with the statutory duty of care, a standard which may be higher than that of 'good faith'. Whereas it is clear that a wider indemnity such as this can apply where trustees have exercised an express power to appoint an investment manager or nominee, it is not clear that a wider indemnity can be conferred where trustees have exercised the statutory power (see Preliminary Note to B21 at para **[221.14]**). For a wider form of indemnity see eg Form B21.12 at para **[221.16]**.

[227.17]

Exercise of powers[1]

13. Any power or discretion hereby or by law conferred on my trustees shall be exercisable in favour of any person who is an object of such power or discretion notwithstanding that he or she is one of my trustees and shall be exercisable notwithstanding that any of my trustees has any other direct or indirect personal interest in the mode or result of such exercise provided that there are not fewer than two trustees and that at least one of them has no personal interest in the mode or result of exercising the same.

1 This clause permits a member of the family to be a trustee without disqualifying him or her from benefit under any exercise of statutory or express powers of payment or application of capital, appointment etc. See the Preliminary Note to B18 at paras **[218.4]** and **[218.5]**.

[227.18]

Professional trustee charging clause

14. Any of my trustees being a professional or business man may charge and be paid all usual professional and other proper charges for business transacted acts done advice given and time spent by him or his firm in connection with the administration of my estate or in connection with the trusts hereof including acts which a personal representative or trustee not being in any profession or business could have done personally[1].

1 In spite of the TrA 2000, s 29(2) (Part G, para **[246.144]**) giving certain professional trustees authority to charge for their services on or after 1 February 2001, an express remuneration clause entitling any professional or business person to charge may still be advisable: see Preliminary Note to B21 at para **[221.42]** et seq.

[227.19]

Testimonium

IN WITNESS whereof I have hereunto set my hand this —— day of —— 20— —.

[227.20]

Attestation clause

SIGNED by the above-named testator as his last will in the presence of us both present at the same time who at his request and in his presence and in the presence of each other have signed our names below as witnesses: } [*Signature of testator*]

[*Signatures, addresses and descriptions of two witnesses*]

[227.21]

FORM C5.2: Reciprocal wills of spouses both having adult children by previous marriages (but none by their own), the first to die making a nil-rate band gift to his or her own children and giving the survivor a life interest in residue with remainder to his or her own children, and the survivor leaving his or her estate to his or her own children

NOTE

This form is for use by both spouses. It is assumed that they both have children of their own, but that there are no children of their marriage, and that none are likely to be born. On the death of the first to die a nil-rate band legacy goes direct to his or her children, and the surviving spouse is given a life interest only in residue with the capital passing to the testator's own children on the survivor's death. On the death of the survivor his or her own estate goes to his or her own children. *Where testators want an arrangement of this sort, the draftsman must find out whether they own the matrimonial home, or any other property of significant value, as joint tenants, and advise them to effect a severance if they do.* If the matrimonial home is owned, or an interest as tenant in common in it is owned, by the first of the spouses to die, the survivor will have a life interest in whatever interest in it was owned by the first to die, by virtue of that interest being comprised in the latter's residuary estate. This is on the assumption, of course, that it is not required to satisfy the nil-rate band legacy. If there is a possibility that it will be so required, the testators might wish to incorporate provisions in their wills for the establishment of a debt or charge scheme: see Preliminary Note to B18 at paras **[218.19]**–**[218.22]**, Form B18.2 at para **[218.32]**, Form C3.4 at para **[225.57]** et seq and Form C3.5 at para **[225.68]** et seq. But if the matrimonial home does fall into residue, it should be possible for the survivor to occupy the home by virtue of the statutory right of occupation under the TLATA 1996: see Preliminary Note to B8 at para **[208.5]** et seq. As in Form C5.1, there is a power to pay or apply at least some of the capital of residue to or for the benefit of the surviving spouse, which can be omitted if that is preferred. As there is a nil-rate band legacy there is no condition of survivorship for a period after the testator's death in relation to the gift of a life interest in residue to the survivor: see the Preliminary Note to C3 at para **[225.4]**.

It will be important for the testators to leave letters of wishes. If there is a power to pay capital to or for the benefit of the survivor it will be particularly important for them to indicate the circumstances in which they want it to be exercised.

[227.22]

Revocation clause

I [*name*] of [*address*] hereby revoke all former testamentary dispositions made by me and declare this to be my last will.[1]

1   There is no presumption that wills in similar form are mutual wills in the technical sense, but it could save argument to add a declaration excluding mutual wills as in the revocation clause of Form C2.1 at para **[224.21]**.

[227.23]

Appointment of executors and trustees[1]

1.   I appoint [my [wife/husband] [*name*] ('my wife/husband')[2] my son [*name*] and my daughter [*name*]] (hereinafter together called 'my trustees' which expression shall where the context so admits include my personal representatives for the time being and the trustees for the time being hereof) to be the executors and trustees of this will.

1   The identity of the trustees will be of particular importance if a power to advance capital to the surviving spouse is included: see cl 5(2) of this form at para **[227.27]** and the notes thereto.
2   If the parties are divorced before the testator's death, the appointment of the other spouse as executor or executrix will fail (WA 1837, s 18A: see Vol 1, paras **[25.7]**, **[47.2]** and **[47.3]**, and Part G, para **[244.18]**). If two executors are appointed as well as the other spouse, there will still be two trustees in the event of a divorce, and of course the appointment will still be of two executors where the testator is predeceased by the other spouse. See also the Preliminary Note to C2 on the possibility of divorce at paras **[224.12]**–**[224.19]**.

[227.24]

Gift of chattels to spouse[1]

2.   I give to my [wife/husband] absolutely all my personal chattels as defined by section 55(1)(x) of the Administration of Estates Act 1925[2] if [she/he] shall survive me [and I request [her/him] (but without imposing any trust or binding obligation on her) to give effect to any wishes as to the disposition of such chattels which may be contained in any memorandum that may be found amongst my papers at my death or which may have otherwise been communicated to [her/him] during my life].[3]

1   See Form C5.1, cl 3, n 1 at para **[227.7]**.
2   See Part G, para **[246.52]** for the wording of this definition, and for further discussion of the meaning of 'personal chattels' see Vol 1, para **[64.44]**.
3   See Form C5.1, cl 3, n 4 at para **[227.7]**.

[227.25]

Gift of nil rate band legacy to children[1]

3.   (1) If my [wife/husband] shall survive me[2] then I give a legacy of [£242,000 subject to payment thereout of any inheritance tax payable by reason of my death which is attributable thereto[3]]/[the sum hereinafter specified] to such of my children [*name*] [*name*] and [*name*] as survive me and if more than one in equal shares provided that if any of my said children shall predecease me

leaving issue living at my death who shall attain the age of [18/21/25] years such issue shall take and if more than one in equal shares per stirpes the share of the legacy hereby given which such deceased child of mine would have taken had he or she lived to attain a vested interest.

[(2)   The amount of the legacy hereby given shall be the maximum sum (if any) which can in the circumstances subsisting at my death be given by this clause without any liability being incurred for the payment of inheritance tax on or by reason of my death. And in particular (without prejudice to the generality of the foregoing) for the purpose of determining the amount of such maximum sum the circumstances to be taken into account shall include all chargeable transfers made by me during my life (or events treated as such for inheritance tax purposes) so far as relevant for the computation of inheritance tax on my death the dispositions taking effect under this will (apart from this clause) or under any codicil hereto and any property treated as if it were part of my estate for inheritance tax purposes].[4]

[(3)/(2)]   The legacy hereby given shall carry interest at the yearly rate of [6 per cent] from my death until paid or satisfied and section 31 of the Trustee Act 1925 (as hereinafter modified) shall apply thereto.[5]

[[4)/(3)]   Section 32 of the Trustee Act 1925 (as hereinafter modified) shall apply in relation to the foregoing trusts.

1   A legacy in favour of the children either of a fixed sum or a sum calculated in accordance with the formula contained in sub-cl (2) can be included if the estate is of sufficient value and the testator wishes to make full use of the inheritance tax nil-rate band to make inheritance tax-free non-exempt gifts. If the surviving spouse might need access to the income or capital of the legacy, a discretionary legacy such as that contained in Form C3.4, cl 2, (at para **[225.60]**), or Form C5.1, cl 4, (at para **[227.8]**) (which has more restricted powers to benefit the surviving spouse) could be substituted. For nil-rate band gifts see paras **[225.1]**–**[225.3]** and for nil-rate band discretionary trusts see the Note in B18 at paras **[218.16]**–**[218.22]**.
     As regards the amount of the legacy, or the formula used to determine the amount, see Form C3.1, cl 3, n 1 at para **[225.13]** and Form C3.4, cl 2, n 1 at para **[225.60]**.
     A nil-rate band legacy for the children will not be appropriate if the estate is small.
2   This precondition is imposed to avoid unnecessary duplication of gifts (ie this one and the residuary gift), and to avoid difficulties as to the effect where the amount of the legacy is determined by a formula, in the event of the spouse not surviving the testator. This gift should not be made conditional on the spouse surviving the testator by a survivorship period: see the Preliminary Note to C3 at para **[225.4]**.
3   Making the gift subject to inheritance tax will, in the event of this gift taking the non-exempt estate over the inheritance tax threshold (eg because of changes in the law or the testator having making lifetime gifts during the seven years preceding his death), cause the size of the chargeable estate to be less than it would be if the gift was free of inheritance tax: see B14 at para **[214.74]**.
4   See Form C3.1, cl 3, n 1 at para **[225.13]**. This subclause should be omitted altogether if a fixed sum is given by sub-cl (1).
5   There is a contingency in the substitutional proviso to sub-cl (1) of this clause. A contingent legacy does not ordinarily carry the intermediate income, a factor which might have the unwelcome inheritance tax consequence that the surviving spouse has an interest in possession in the capital out of which the legacy is payable from the testator's death until the time when the legacy becomes payable. Subclause (3) is introduced to ensure that the legacy does carry the intermediate income.

[227.26]

Administration trusts of residue

4.   [*As in cl 7 of* Form C5.1 *at para* **[227.11]**.]

[227.27]

Beneficial trusts of residue

5.   (1)   My trustees shall stand possessed of my residuary estate upon trust to pay the income thereof to my [wife/husband] during [her/his] life.

   [(2)   Notwithstanding the foregoing trust my trustees (being not fewer than two in number [or a trust corporation]¹) may at any time and from time to time during the life of my [wife/husband] pay transfer or apply [the whole or any part or parts of my residuary estate]/[any part or parts of my residuary estate not exceeding in the aggregate [one quarter]/[one half]² thereof]³ to or for the benefit of my [wife/husband] in such manner as they think fit provided that the foregoing power shall only be exercisable over capital of which the income is for the time being payable to my [wife/husband] (or would be payable if such capital yielded income).]⁴

   [(3)/(2)]   Subject as aforesaid my trustees shall stand possessed of my residuary estate upon trust for such of my children [*name*] [*name*] and [*name*] as shall survive me and if more than one in equal shares provided that if any of my said children shall predecease me leaving issue living at my death who shall attain the age of [18/21/25] years such issue shall take and if more than one in equal shares per stirpes the share of my residuary estate which such deceased child of mine would have taken had he or she lived to attain a vested interest.

   [(4)/(3)]   The trusts aforesaid shall carry the intermediate income of my residuary estate and section 31 of the Trustee Act 1925 (as hereinafter modified) shall apply thereto.

   [(5)/(4)]   Section 32 of the Trustee Act 1925 (as hereinafter modified) shall apply in relation to the foregoing trusts.

1   See Form C5.1, cl 5(3), n 5 at para **[227.9]**.
2   One of these should be deleted, or both deleted and some other fraction substituted.
3   The testators may wish to restrict the power to only a part of the residuary estate, in which case the second of these alternatives in square brackets should be used and the first alternative omitted. If they are content for the whole of residue to be subject to the power, the first alternative should be included and the second alternative should be omitted.
4   There are two reasons for restricting the exercise of the power to capital in which the widow has an interest in possession: first, to ensure that the power is not exercisable if there is a divorce and the life interest given by the previous subclause lapses (see the Preliminary Note to C2 at para **[224.12]** et seq); and second, to ensure that the power ceases to be exercisable if the wife assigns or surrenders her life interest.
      The entire subclause can be omitted if the testators do not wish there to be any power to pay the survivor capital. If it is included it will be a power to direct capital to the surviving spouse and away from the children of the first to die, and careful thought will need to be given to the identity of the trustees.

[227.28]

Maintenance, accumulation and advancement

6.   [*As in cl 10 of* Form C5.1 *at para* **[227.14]**.]

[227.29]

Administrative powers

7.   [*As in cl 11 of* Form C5.1 *at para* **[227.15]**.]

[227.30]

Trustee indemnity

8.   [(1)]   [*As in cl 12 of* Form C5.1 *at para* **[227.16]**.]

   [(2)   Section 11(1) of the Trusts of Land and Appointment of Trustees Act 1996 (consultation with beneficiaries) shall not apply to the exercise by my trustees of their functions in relation to any land subject to the trusts of this my will.[1]]

1   The testator may or may not wish to exclude the TLATA 1996, s 11(1) which obliges trustees of land to consult beneficiaries of full age and beneficially entitled to an interest in possession, and so far as consistent with the general interest of the trust, to give effect to the wishes of those beneficiaries, or (in the event of a dispute) the majority by value (see Part G, para **[246.97]** and the Note to B20 at para **[220.58]**).

[227.31]

Exercise of powers

9.   [*As in cl 13 of* Form C5.1 *at para* **[227.17]**.]

[227.32]

Professional trustee charging clause

10.   [*As in cl 14 of* Form C5.1 *at para* **[227.18]**.]

[227.33]

Appointment of new trustees

[11.   The power of appointing trustees hereof shall be vested in my [wife/husband] during [her/his] life.][1]

1   This provision will not be appropriate if the testators decide to appoint trustees who are independent of the beneficiaries, for example, where relations between the present spouse and the children of the previous marriage are not good, so that the presence of independent trustees might reduce the possibility of friction. However, if it is excluded, the TLATA 1996, s 19 (Part G, para **[246.105]**) provides that where no person is nominated for the purpose of appointing new trustees and the beneficiaries under the trust are of full age and capacity and between them absolutely entitled to the settled property, the beneficiaries may give a written direction to a trustee to retire from the trust, or give a written direction to the trustees to appoint as a trustee or trustees the person or persons specified in the direction. For a provision excluding the beneficiaries' statutory right to direct retirement and appointment of trustees, see Form B21.36 at para **[221.41]**.

[227.34]

Attestation clause

SIGNED by the above-named [testator/testatrix] as [his/her] last will in the presence of us both present at the same time who at [his/her] request and in [his/her] presence and in the presence of each other have signed our names below as witnesses: *[Signature of testator/testatrix]*

[*Signatures, addresses and descriptions of two witnesses*]

[227.35]

FORM C5.3: Reciprocal wills of spouses both having adult children by previous marriages (but none by their own), the first to die giving the survivor his or her estate absolutely and the survivor dividing his or her estate between children and stepchildren

NOTE

This is again a form for reciprocal wills, in which the entire estate of the first to die goes to the surviving spouse absolutely. On the death of the surviving spouse his or her estate is divided between the respective families of the two spouses in specified proportions, which may be equal or unequal. This form has the merit of administrative convenience, but should not be used unless the two spouses have complete confidence that the survivor will honour the arrangement and not cut out the children of the first to die. Even where this is not the case, it may be necessary to use this form where a couple have insufficient assets to justify the expense and complexity of life interest trusts such as those in Forms C5.1 or C5.2.

[227.36]

The proportions in which the estate of the survivor will be divided between the two families will require careful thought. What is envisaged is that the spouses should work out and agree the value of what each of them owns, and then agree to express what each of them owns as a percentage of their combined assets. The latter percentages would then be used to divide up the residuary estate of the survivor between the two families. It is assumed in this form that one spouse owns 63 per cent of the total of their assets and the other 37 per cent: see cl 3(2) and (3) of this form at para **[227.41]**. Other percentages can be substituted where indicated in cl 3(2). It may be appropriate to use this form even if it is decided that the spouses' combined assets should be shared equally between the two families, as it will ensure that each family gets half of the assets irrespective of what happens. If the trust was simply for the children of both spouses in equal shares, with substitution of issue, the ultimate division of the couple's assets between the two families would vary according to how many children each spouse had, or whether or not any of those children died without issue before the death of the survivor of the two spouses.

[227.37]

Where there is jointly-owned property, it is not absolutely essential for making the proposed testamentary dispositions that a severance of any joint tenancy should take place (compare, eg Form C5.2 at para **[227.21]** et seq). Whether property passes from the first to die to the survivor under the will of the first to die, or under the right of accruer under a joint tenancy, the survivor will get an absolute interest, and the effect is the same subject to one point. If the will imposes a condition that the survivor only takes residue if he or she survives the first to die by a specified period (see cl 3(1) of this form at para **[227.41]**), and the survivor dies within the survivorship period, there obviously will be a difference between the effect of property being owned jointly and property being owned as tenants in common. The difference is not so much relevant to the ultimate destination of their property, because under both wills the dispositions of residue will be the same, as to the inheritance tax position. There could be waste of the first to die's nil-rate band in these circumstances if substantial property passes to the survivor under a joint tenancy.

[227.38]

Revocation clause

I [*name*] of [*address*] hereby revoke all former testamentary dispositions made by me and declare this to be my last will.[1]

1   If the spouses wish to ensure that the survivor has to abide by the arrangement, the wills could take effect as mutual wills in which case an express declaration to that effect would have to be included, though this course is not recommended: see the Preliminary Note to C2 at para **[224.8]**. For a declaration creating mutual wills see Form B1.6 at para **[201.10]**.
   If there is no intention to create mutual wills, a declaration excluding mutual wills could be added as in the revocation clause of Form C2.1 at para **[224.21]**. There is no presumption that wills in similar form are mutual wills in the technical sense, but in the absence of an express declaration there is more scope for argument or even litigation on the point.

[227.39]

Appointment of spouse as sole executor/executrix, with alternative appointment

1.   (1)   I appoint my [wife/husband] [*name*] ('my [wife/husband]') the sole [executrix/executor] of this will but if [she/he] predeceases me or renounces probate or dies without having proved this will[1] then I appoint [*name*] of [*address*] and [*name*] of [*address*] to be the executors and trustees hereof.

   (2)   In this will the expression 'my trustees' shall where the context permits mean my personal representatives for the time being and the trustees for the time being hereof.

1   In the event of a divorce this alternative appointment will have effect as if the testator's husband or wife died on the date of the decree: WA 1837, s 18A (Part G, para **[244.18]**) and the Preliminary Note to C2 at para **[224.12]** et seq.
   Although the main gift to the spouse is conditional on surviving the testator by one month, it seems preferable not to make the appointment of her or him as executor conditional on surviving that period: it could be inconvenient in some circumstances if the spouse had to wait until one month from the death before being able to take steps as executor, and the alternative appointment takes effect if the spouse dies without having proved the will. There is a slight risk that the spouse will dissipate some or all of the estate and then die within a month of the testator's death, a risk that would be more significant if the required period of survival under the survivorship condition was made longer than a month (it would be possible to have a longer period: up to six months: see the Preliminary Note to C2 at para **[224.2]** et seq).

[227.40]

Administration trusts of residue

2.   [*As in cl 7 of* Form C5.1 *at para* **[227.11]**.]

[227.41]

Beneficial trusts of residue

3.   (1)   If my [wife/husband] shall survive me [for the period of one month][1] my trustees shall hold my residuary estate upon trust for my [wife/husband]

absolutely [*In the will of the older spouse*: Provided that if I and my [husband/wife] shall die in circumstances where it cannot be known which of us survived the other then the foregoing survival condition shall not apply and the foregoing gift shall take effect].[2]

(2)   If my [wife/husband] shall die without attaining a vested interest under the foregoing trust my trustees shall hold my residuary estate and the income thereof upon trust to divide the same into two shares as follows:

(a)   a [63] per cent share of my residuary estate (hereinafter called 'the first share'); and

(b)   a [37] per cent share of my residuary estate (hereinafter called 'the second share').

(3)   My trustees shall hold the first share upon trust for such of my [children/stepchildren] [*name*] [*name*] and [*name*][3] as shall survive me if more than one in equal shares and shall hold the second share upon trust for such of my [stepchildren/children] [*name*] and [*name*][4] as shall survive me if more than one in equal shares Provided that:

(a)   if any of my said children or stepchildren shall predecease me leaving issue living at my death who shall attain the age of [18/21/25] years such issue shall take and if more than one in equal shares per stirpes the share of my residuary estate which such deceased child or stepchild of mine would have taken had he or she survived me but so that no issue shall take whose parent (being such issue as aforesaid) survives me and attains the said age;

(b)   if the foregoing trusts for the benefit of my said stepchildren shall fail or determine then the share of my residuary estate hereinbefore directed to be held on trust for my said stepchildren shall devolve as if it formed part of my [wife's/husband's] estate and [she/he] had died intestate immediately after my death.[5]

---

1   See the Preliminary Note to C2 on survivorship conditions at para **[224.2]** et seq. The survivorship period could be any period up to six months and still take advantage of the ITA 1984, s 92 (see para **[224.3]**); if a survivorship period longer than a month is being considered, it should be remembered that it will not usually be possible to pay income or capital to the spouse before he or she has survived the period. If the survivorship condition is not wanted the words in this set of square brackets and the proviso (see n 2 infra) should be omitted. There is not much point in having a survivorship condition if most of the assets of the testator are owned as joint tenants.

2   For the reasons for including this proviso see the Preliminary Note to C2 at para **[224.2]**. *It must only be included in the will of the older of the two spouses.* If the survivorship condition is omitted then this proviso should also be omitted.

3   The names at this point will be the same in both wills, but the description will be 'children' in one will and 'stepchildren' in the other. Care should be taken to get the names and descriptions the right way round, and the testators should be given drafts of their wills and asked specifically to confirm that the descriptions (ie 'children' or 'stepchildren') are correctly matched with the names in each will, and that the first share and second share are respectively given to the right families.

4   The names at this point will be the same in both wills, but the description will be 'stepchildren' in one will and 'children' in the other. See also the previous note.

5   Proviso (b) is designed to ensure that if the trusts of the stepchildren's share fail, the share will nevertheless go to their side of the family.

[227.42]

Maintenance, accumulation and advancement
4.   [*As in cl 10 of* Form C5.1 *at para* **[227.14]**.]

[227.43]

Administrative powers
5.   [*As in cl 11 of* Form C5.1 *at para* **[227.15]**.]

[227.44]

Trustee indemnity
6.   [*As in cl 12 of* Form C5.1 *at para* **[227.16]**.]

[227.45]

Professional trustee charging clause
7.   [*As in cl 14 of* Form C5.1 *at para* **[227.18]**.]

[*Testimonium and attestation clause, as in* Form C5.2 *at para* **[227.34]**.]

[227.46]

FORM C5.4:   Will of married man with adult children making provision for an illegitimate child who is a minor by means of a settled legacy

NOTE

It is assumed in this form that the illegitimate child is living with his or her mother, and that the testator is not living with them.

[227.47]

Revocation clause
I [*name*] of [*address*] hereby revoke all former testamentary dispositions made by me and declare this to be my last will.

[227.48]

Appointment of executors and trustees
1.   [*As in cl 1 of* Form C5.1 *at para* **[227.5]**.]

[227.49]

Appointment of guardians[1]
2.   [If [*name of mother of illegitimate child*] predeceases me I appoint [*name*] of [*address*] [and [*name*] of [*address*]] to be the [guardian/guardians] of my [son/daughter] [*name of illegitimate child*] during [his/her] minority.]

1   The testator will not have power to appoint a guardian of the child unless both parents have entered into an agreement in the prescribed form conferring parental responsibility on the testator (see Vol 1, para **[28.2]**), which is perhaps not very likely to have happened in a case of this kind. If there is no parental responsibility agreement, it remains possible that the mother might appoint the testator to be the guardian of the child in the event of her death, and then predecease the testator (while the child is still under 18). If the testator becomes a guardian of

the child in this way, he will then acquire parental responsibility and have power to appoint a successor to himself as guardian (see Vol 1, para **[28.2]**). It seems reasonably clear that the acquisition by the father of parental responsibility under a parental responsibility agreement will not retrospectively validate the appointment of a guardian by a will made by him at a time when he did not have parental responsibility (see Vol 1, para **[28.4]**), but it is not quite so clear that, if he becomes guardian of the child after the death of the child's mother, an appointment of a guardian to succeed him which was made before he became such guardian will not be valid, although it seems likely that this is the case. For the law relating to guardians generally, see Vol 1, para **[28.1]** et seq and B3 at para **[203.43]** et seq.

[227.50]

Settled legacy for illegitimate child[1]

3.   (1)   I give free of tax[2] a pecuniary legacy of £—— to [*name*] of [*address*] and [*name*] of [*address*].

(2)   In this clause 'the legacy fund trustees' means and includes the said named persons or other the trustees or trustee for the time being of the legacy fund as hereinafter defined and pending the payment or transfer of the legacy fund as hereinafter defined shall also include my trustees.

(3)   The said legacy shall carry interest from the date of my death at the rate of [6] per cent per annum until paid set aside or satisfied by appropriation.

(4)   The legacy fund trustees shall hold the said legacy upon trust to invest the same in any investments hereby authorised with power to vary the same and shall hold the said legacy and the investments from time to time representing the same (in this clause together called 'the legacy fund') and the income thereof upon the trusts set out below.

(5)   The legacy fund trustees shall hold the legacy fund and the income thereof upon trust for my [son/daughter] [*name of illegitimate child*] (hereinafter called 'the beneficiary') absolutely if [he/she] shall attain the age of 25 years provided that if [he/she] shall die before the said age of 25 years leaving a child or children [him/her] surviving who shall attain the age of 21 years such child or children shall take the legacy fund absolutely and if more than one equally between them.[3]

(6)   The foregoing trusts shall carry the intermediate income of the legacy fund and section 31 of the Trustee Act 1925 (as hereinafter modified) shall apply thereto [provided that for all the purposes of the said section the age of majority shall in the case of the beneficiary be deemed to be the age of [21/25] years and so that in the said section the expressions infancy minority and infant and all references to the age of 18 years shall be construed accordingly].[4]

(7)   Section 32 of the Trustee Act 1925 (as hereinafter modified shall apply to the foregoing trusts.

(8)   Subject as aforesaid the legacy fund shall [fall into my residuary estate].

(9)   The following provisions shall have effect with regard to the legacy fund trustees:

(a)   if the said [*name of trustee appointed in subclause (1)*] shall die in my lifetime or shall refuse or be unable to act as a legacy fund trustee then I appoint [*name*] of [*address*] to be such a trustee in his place;

(b)   if the said [*name of other trustee appointed in subclause (1)*] shall die in my lifetime or shall refuse or be unable to act as an original legacy fund trustee then I appoint [*name*] of [*address*] to be such a trustee in his place;

(c) if one of the persons appointed by name as an original trustee of the legacy fund in subclause (1) of this clause and the person appointed in his or her place under the foregoing provisions of this subclause shall both die in my lifetime or refuse or be unable to act as such a trustee then any other person appointed by name as an original trustee of the legacy fund by subclause (1) of this clause or the foregoing provisions of this subclause (as the case may be) may nominate additional trustees of the legacy fund;

(d) if all the persons hereinbefore appointed by name as original trustees shall die in my lifetime or shall refuse or be unable to act as such trustees then [*name*] of [*address*] [or failing [him/her] my trustees] may nominate additional trustees of the legacy fund;

(e) subject as aforesaid the power of appointing new trustees of the legacy fund [shall be vested in [the said] [*name*] of [*address*] during [his/her] life and otherwise] shall be the statutory power.[5]

1 In deciding what the amount of the legacy should be the testator needs to consider the level of support he is currently providing for the child, and what level of provision will be sufficient to avoid a claim being made under the Inheritance (Provision for Family and Dependants) Act 1975. He may need to make codicils from time to time to increase the legacy for inflation or to take account of changed circumstances. It could be tied to the inheritance tax threshold, as in Form C5.2, cl 3(2) at para [**227.25**], but that could work capriciously and would not be a level of provision fixed by reference to the child's circumstances.

2 See Form C3.1, cl 2, n 2 at para [**225.12**].

3 An alternative would be to provide a life interest with power to pay or apply capital to or for the benefit of the child; Form C2.2, cls 7 and 8 at paras [**224.43**] and [**224.44**] could be adapted for this purpose.

4 Advantage may be taken of the 21-year accumulation period following the testator's death which is sanctioned by the LPA 1925, s 164(1)(b) (Part G, para [**246.42**] to extend the provisions for maintenance and accumulation contained in the TA 1925, s 31 to at least the age of 21. In cases where the illegitimate child is already over 4 when the will is made, he or she will attain the age of 25 during the 21-year accumulation period from the testator's death, and the operation of the accumulation and maintenance trusts can be further extended to the age of 25 (an extension beyond the age of 25 would prevent ITA 1984, s 71 from applying to the trusts: see Part A, para [**200.119**]). For further discussion of the extension of accumulation and maintenance trusts in this way, and alternative forms for doing so, see B18 at paras [**218.72**]–[**218.79**].

5 The reason for these rather elaborate provisions is that the executors and the testator's immediate family may not be the most appropriate people to decide who should be trustees of this fund if the nominated persons do not take office. Further, the testator may not wish the child's mother to have too much influence on the trusteeship or administration of this fund. Accordingly, this subclause provides for alternative trustees to be nominated, and for someone to be nominated to decide who should be trustees in the absence of any of the named persons taking office. These provisions are mostly concerned with who will be the trustees in the first place; once the separate trustees are constituted they will appoint their own successors under the statutory power, unless someone is nominated to exercise it in sub-cl (9)(e).

[227.51]

Administration trusts of residue
4. [*As in cl 7 of* Form C5.1 *at para* [**227.11**].]

[227.52]

Gifts made free of tax
5. [*As in cl 8 of* Form C5.1 *at para* [**227.12**].]

[227.53]

Beneficial trusts of residue

6.   (1)   My trustees shall hold my residuary estate upon trust for my wife [*name*] absolutely if she shall survive me.[1]

(2)   If my wife shall predecease me my trustees shall hold my residuary estate upon trust for such of my children [*name*] [*name*] and [*name*][2] as shall survive me if more than one in equal shares Provided that if any of my said children shall predecease me leaving a child or children surviving me who shall attain the age of [18/21/25] years such last-mentioned child or children shall take if more than one in equal shares the share of my residuary estate which such deceased child of mine would have taken had he or she survived me.

(3)   The foregoing trusts shall carry the intermediate income of my residuary estate and section 31 of the Trustee Act 1925 (as hereinafter modified) shall apply thereto.

(4)   Section 32 of the Trustee Act 1925 (as hereinafter modified) shall apply to the foregoing trusts.

1   If the legacy in cl 3 at para **[227.50]** is sufficiently substantial to use up all of the testator's inheritance tax nil-rate band, a condition of survival for a period is not needed. See the Preliminary Note to C2 at para **[224.2]** et seq and the Preliminary Note to C3 at para **[225.4]**. If the legacy is less than the nil-rate band, then a survivorship condition (as in, eg Form C5.3, cl 3(1) at para **[227.41]**), could be added, or a nil-rate band 'formula' legacy in favour of his wife and/or legitimate children (as in Form C5.1, cl 5 at para **[227.9]** or Form C5.2, cl 3 at para **[227.25]**) could be included.
2   Ie the children of the marriage.

[227.54]

Maintenance, accumulation and advancement

7.   [*As in cl 10 of* Form C5.1 *at para* **[227.14]**.]

[227.55]

Administrative powers

8.   [*As in cl 11 of* Form C5.1 *at para* **[227.15]**.]

[227.56]

Trustee indemnity

9.   [*As in cl 12 of* Form C5.1 *at para* **[227.16]**.]

[227.57]

Exercise of powers

10.   [*As in cl 13 of* Form C5.1 *at para* **[227.17]**.]

[227.58]

Professional trustee charging clause

11.   [*As in cl 14 of* Form C5.1 *at para* **[227.18]**.]

[*Testimonium and attestation clause, as in* Form C5.1 *at paras* **[227.19]** *and* **[227.20]**.]

C6   Wills for unmarried couples with children

PRELIMINARY NOTE

[228.1]
Special reasons for unmarried couples making wills. It is especially important
for an unmarried couple (whether or not they have children) to make wills
providing for each other, because if one of them dies intestate the other will not
inherit any of his or her estate; by contrast, illegitimate children inherit on the
death of one of their parents intestate in the same way as legitimate ones (see
Vol 1, para **[72.14]**). It is also important, so long as an unmarried couple have
one or more minor children in respect of which there is no agreement between
the parents (or court order) giving the father parental responsibility, that the
mother should appoint the father as guardian of the minor children in the event
of her death: see B3 at para **[203.43]** et seq and Vol 1, para **[28.2]**.

[228.2]
Special factors relating to unmarried couples' wills. When it comes to the
preparation of wills for an unmarried couple, it should be remembered that the
wills will be revoked by their subsequent marriage unless the wills are made in
expectation of marriage (see Vol 1, paras **[17.5]**–**[17.8]** and Form C6.1 at para
[228.5] et seq), but that if the relationship breaks up, any wills which they have
made in favour of each other will continue in full force unless revoked (contrast
the lapse by divorce of a gift to a spouse, for which see the Preliminary Note to
C2 at para **[224.12]** et seq). The principal fiscal difference between their
situation and that of a married couple is that in the case of an unmarried couple
there is no exemption from inheritance tax for gifts between them (see Part A,
para **[200.99]** et seq for this exemption for gifts between spouses). This means
that nil-rate band using-up strategies of the kinds illustrated in Forms C3.1,
C3.2, C3.4, and C3.5 at paras **[225.9]**–**[225.41]** and **[225.57]**–**[225.82]**, are not
relevant, and, more generally, that it makes no difference to the inheritance tax
charge on the death of the first to die how much or how little of the estate of the
first to die is given to (or settled on interest in possession trusts for) the survivor.
Thus a long-term discretionary trust of residue (see Form C6.2 at paras
[228.19]–**[228.32]**), or a substantial proportion of residue going direct to the

children (as in Form C3.3 at paras **[225.42]–[225.56]**, suitably adapted), are possibilities worth considering for inclusion in the will of the first to die.

[228.3]
Unmarried couples and lifetime gifts. One possible inheritance tax planning strategy for an unmarried couple where the poorer of them, in the event of him or her surviving the richer, will need to be provided for by the latter, is to try to make up for the lack of a general exemption for gifts between them by lifetime potentially exempt transfers from the richer of them to the poorer. These will be free of inheritance tax if the transferor survives them by seven years (see Part A, paras **[200.70]–[200.75]**), although as the couple are living together careful thought needs to be given to how to avoid making gifts with reservation of benefit (see Part A, para **[200.76]**), and it may not always be practical to do so. Lifetime transfers have most to recommend them where the richer of the two is quite a lot older than the other, or there are other good reasons for thinking that the richer will die first, but, before such transfers are made, thought should always be given to the consequences if, contrary to expectations, the richer of the two outlives the other. It may be worth considering insurance against such an eventuality or against the inheritance tax on the lifetime transfers. Another important factor is the likelihood of the couple marrying; lifetime potentially exempt transfers could be very advantageous if the couple never marry, but if they do marry it could turn out that it would have been better to have left making transfers between them until after the marriage, when such transfers are wholly exempt. A couple's marriage will not cause the inheritance tax exemption for transfers between spouses to apply retrospectively to transfers made between them before their marriage.

[228.4]
Forms of will for use by unmarried couples with children. Despite the lack of the exemption for gifts to spouses, unmarried couples will often make the same dispositions in their wills as they would make if they were married, and for many unmarried couples with children there will be a form in C2 at para **[224.1]** et seq, or C3 at para **[225.1]** et seq (omitting, in the case of forms in C3, the nil-rate band legacies) which will be suitable if adapted appropriately.

Form C6 contains some further forms with features specific to unmarried couples. As mentioned above, it is only a will made in expectation of marriage that is not revoked by marriage (see Vol 1, paras **[17.5]–[17.8]**); accordingly, Form C6.1 at paras **[228.5]–[228.18]** provides an example of a will made in expectation of marriage which is intended to operate both before and after the marriage. However, if the parties do in fact marry, it would be wise for them to review their wills.

As mentioned above, wills creating a discretionary trust, of all or most of the estate, are an option worth considering by the better-off unmarried couple, because the absence of spouse exemption (see above) means that a discretionary trust arising under the will of the first to die does not make any difference to the inheritance tax charge on his or her death. For further aspects of this, see the Note to Form C6.2 at paras **[228.19]** and **[228.20]** and see Form C6.2 at paras **[228.21]–[228.32]** for an example of this type of will.

Finally, Form C6.3 at paras **[228.33]**–**[228.43]** is an example of a will for a situation where one partner (assumed in this form to be the man) has a spouse (by whom he has children) from whom he is separated, and whom he intends to divorce. It will be a sensible precaution for him to make a temporary will benefiting the new partner in case of death before a financial settlement is agreed and the divorce is finalised, to prevent the spouse becoming entitled to all his estate under the intestacy rules (or a previous will). He should also sever any beneficial joint tenancy of property he holds jointly with the wife.

[228.5]

FORM C6.1:   Reciprocal wills of couple living together who have young children and who are planning to marry

NOTE

Wills in this form are intended to make continuing provision for the other partner and the children whether or not the marriage takes place. However, if the parties do in fact marry, it would be wise for them to review their wills.

[228.6]

Revocation

I [*name*] of [*address*] hereby revoke all former testamentary dispositions made by me and declare this to be my last will.[1]

> 1   There is no presumption that wills in similar form are mutual wills in the technical sense, but the matter can be put beyond doubt by incorporating an express provision to that effect: see Form B1.7 at para **[201.11]** for a precedent, and the revocation clause to Form C2.1 and the note thereto at para **[224.21]**.

[228.7]

Expectation of marriage

1.   I declare that I make this will in the expectation of marrying [*name of intended spouse*] and that it shall not be revoked by reason of the said marriage[1] and I further declare that this will shall take effect whether or not the said marriage takes place.[2]

> 1   Marriage will revoke a will unless the will is made in expectation of marriage: see the WA 1837, s 18 (Part G, para **[244.16]**) and see generally Vol 1, paras **[17.5]**–**[17.8]**. The expectation must be of marriage to a particular person not marriage in general.
> 2   This further declaration makes it plain that the will is to have immediate effect and is to govern the devolution of the estate whether or not the marriage takes place.

[228.8]

Appointment of guardians[1]

[*In the will of the woman:*
2.   (1)   If I die without having been married to [*name of the man*] and he shall survive me then I appoint him to be the guardian of any child or children of ours who are minors at the date of my death.

(2)   If the said [*name of the man*] shall predecease me then (whether or not he and I shall have been married) I appoint [*name*] of [*address*] [and [*name*] of

[*address*]] to be the [guardian/guardians] of any child or children of ours who are minors at the date of my death.]
[*In the will of the man*:
2.   If the said [*name of the woman*] shall predecease me I appoint [*name*] of [*address*] [and [*name*] of [*address*]] to be the [guardian/guardians] of any child or children of ours who are minors at the date of my death.]

1   These clauses are appropriate for an unmarried couple where there is no parental responsibility agreement (or court order) conferring on the man parental responsibility for their children. In these circumstances only the woman has such parental responsibility, and it is important that she should appoint the man to be the guardian of their children in the event of her death (see Vol 1, para **[28.2]** and B3 at para **[203.43]** et seq). It is our opinion that an appointment of a guardian by the man which is made before he acquires parental responsibility will not be validated by him subsequently acquiring such responsibility, but it is probably worthwhile for him to attempt to make such an appointment in case we are wrong about this, and because even if we are right it will be an expression of wishes which the court can consider when appointing a guardian in the absence of a valid appointment by the mother.

   If the man does have parental responsibility for the children at the time of making wills based on this Form then these clauses will not be appropriate, and the man and woman should each make an appointment of a guardian or guardians which takes effect only if the other does not survive him or her, such as Form B3.26 at para **[203.55]**, or Form C2.1, cl 3 at para **[224.24]**. They should also both make fresh appointments of the latter type if the man subsequently acquires parental responsibility for the children—as a result of marriage to the woman or a parental responsibility agreement or court order—after they have made appointments of guardians as in these clauses of this form.

[228.9]

Gift of estate to intended spouse
3.   If the said [*name of intended spouse*] shall survive me [by the period of [one] month][1] then subject to the payment thereout of my funeral and testamentary expenses and my debts I give all my estate both real and personal (including all entailed or other property over which I have a power of disposition by will at the time of my death)[2] to [her/him] in fee simple and absolutely and appoint [her/him] the sole [executrix/executor] hereof.

1   The words in square brackets will ensure that if the parties die in a common accident or within the period of one month of each other the estates of both will devolve directly on the children. If the period does not exceed six months, the gifts to the children under each will either will actually have taken effect, or will be treated (by the Inheritance Tax Act 1984 (ITA 1984), s 92) for inheritance tax purposes as having taken effect, on the testator's death. The overall inheritance tax effect will be different according to whether the marriage has taken place before the deaths: see the Preliminary Note to C2 at paras **[224.1]**–**[224.6]**.
2   Subject to any contrary intention expressed in the will property subject to a general testamentary power will be carried by a residuary gift under the WA 1837, s 27 (Part G, para **[244.27]**) without express reference to the property or power. In the case of entailed property, however, the property or the instrument under which the entailed interest arises or entailed property generally must be referred to: LPA 1925, s 176(1) (Part G, para **[244.53]**). Although no new entails can be created on or after 1 January 1997 (see para **[200.53]**), entails created before that date can continue to exist and, if they do, the statutory power of disposition of them by will continues to be available.

[228.10]

Alternative provisions
4.   If the said [*name of intended spouse*] predeceases me [or does not survive me for the period aforesaid][1] then the following provisions of this will shall take effect.

1   If the contingency of survival for a specified period is omitted from cl 3 the words in square
brackets in this clause should also be omitted: see para **[228.9]**, n 1.
　　If the couple marry and then divorce this gift will fail and the alternative gift to the children
will have effect: see the WA 1837, s 18A(1)(b) (Part G, para **[244.18]**). See the section in the
Preliminary Note to C2 on the possibility of divorce at para **[224.12]** et seq. Note that if the
couple marry and then divorce the gift will lapse; if they never marry and separate the gift will
remain effective.

[228.11]

Appointment of executors and trustees

5.   I appoint [*name*] of [*address*] [and] [*name*] of [*address*] [and [*name*] of
[*address*]] (hereinafter together called 'my trustees' which expression shall
include my personal representatives for the time being and the trustees for the
time being hereof) to be the executors and trustees hereof.

[228.12]

Administration trusts of residue

6.   (1)   I give all my property not hereby or by any codicil hereto otherwise
effectively disposed of [(including any entailed or other property over which I
shall have at my death a general power of disposition by will)][1] to my trustees to
hold on the trusts set out below with power at their discretion to sell all or any of
it as and when they think fit.[2]

(2)   My trustees shall pay my funeral and testamentary expenses[3] and debts
and any legacies given by this will or any codicil hereto out of such property or
its proceeds and shall have a discretion as to how such payments shall be borne
as between capital and income.[4]

(3)   Subject as above my trustees shall hold such property and the assets
from time to time representing the same (hereinafter called 'my residuary
estate') on the trusts set out below and shall invest all money comprised in such
property or arising from its sale in any of the investments hereby authorised with
power to change such investments into any others hereby authorised.

(4)   In the administration of my estate and the execution of the trusts of this
will or of any codicil to it:

(a)   my trustees shall treat all income as accruing on the date on which it
becomes payable regardless of the period in respect of which it shall
have accrued and shall not make any statutory apportionment of the
same;[5] and

(b)   none of the equitable rules of apportionment between capital and income
shall apply in any circumstances whatever.[6]

1   See Form C2.1, cl 6, n 1 at para **[224.27]**.
2   See Form C2.1, cl 6, n 2 at para **[224.27]**.
3   See Form C2.1, cl 6, n 3 at para **[224.27]**.
4   See Form C2.1, cl 6, n 4 at para **[224.27]**.
5   See Form C2.1, cl 6, n 5 at para **[224.27]**.
6   See Form C2.1, cl 6, n 6 at para **[224.27]**.

[228.13]

Beneficial trusts of residue

7.   (1)   My trustees shall hold my residuary estate upon trust for such of my
children by the said [*name of intended spouse*] as survive me and attain the age

of [18/21/25] years[1] and if more than one in equal shares provided that if any such child of mine shall predecease me or having survived me shall die before attaining the age aforesaid leaving a child or children living at or born after my death who shall attain the age of [18/21] years[2] such last-mentioned child or children shall take if more than one equally between them the share of my residuary estate to which such deceased child of mine would have become entitled had he or she lived to attain a vested interest.

(2)   The foregoing trusts shall carry the intermediate income of my residuary estate and section 31 of the Trustee Act 1925 (as hereinafter modified) shall apply thereto accordingly.

(3)   Section 32 of the Trustee Act 1925 (as hereinafter modified) shall apply in relation to my residuary estate.

[(4)   Subject as aforesaid my trustees shall hold my residuary estate and the income thereof [for [*name*] absolutely]/[for such charitable purposes as my trustees may declare]].

1   Since the children will all be lives in being for perpetuity purposes the age contingency does not have to be restricted to 21.
2   The grandchildren will not necessarily be alive at the testator's death, and it is therefore advisable to restrict the age contingency to not more than 21.

[228.14]

Maintenance, accumulation and advancement

8.   (1)   Section 31 of the Trustee Act 1925 (relating to accumulation and maintenance) shall apply in relation to the trusts hereby or by any codicil hereto declared as if:

(a)   in paragraph (i) of subsection (1) of the said section the words 'as the trustees think fit' were substituted for the words 'as may in all the circumstances be reasonable'; and

(b)   the proviso to the said subsection (1) were omitted.

(2)   Section 32 of the Trustee Act 1925 (relating to advancement) shall apply in relation to the said trusts as if the words 'one half of' were omitted from proviso (a) to subsection (1) thereof [provided that the powers conferred by the said section (as hereby enlarged) shall not be exercisable in favour of any minor beneficiary hereunder otherwise than so as to cause such beneficiary to become immediately entitled to or to an interest in possession in the capital thereby paid or applied within the meaning of section 71(1)(a) of the Inheritance Tax Act 1984].[1]

(3)   Whenever my trustees shall have an obligation or discretion under the provisions of this will or any codicil hereto or under the general law to apply income or capital for the benefit of a minor beneficiary they may either pay the same without liability to account to his or her parent guardian or any other adult person with whom such beneficiary may be residing or to such beneficiary himself or herself if of the age of 16 years or more and so that the receipt of such parent guardian or other person or of such minor beneficiary shall be a full and sufficient discharge to my trustees for the income or capital so applied.[2]

1   The proviso is included in order to prevent the power prejudicing the application of the ITA 1984, s 71 (accumulation and maintenance trusts), but is probably unnecessary: see the Note on

inheritance tax and the statutory power of advancement in B18 at para **[218.99]**. If the accumulation and maintenance trusts of income are extended so as to continue beyond the age of 18 (see eg Forms B18.12 and B18.13 at paras **[218.78]** and **[218.79]**), then 'minor beneficiary hereunder' should be amended to eg 'beneficiary hereunder who is under the age of [*n*] years' where *n* is the highest age at which an absolute interest or an interest in possession might be attained by any of the beneficiaries.

2   See Form C3.1, cl 7(3), n 3 at para **[225.17]**.

[228.15]

Administrative powers[1]

9.   (1)   In this clause where the context so admits:

(a)   the expression 'land' includes buildings and estates interests or rights of any kind in or over land; and

(b)   during the administration of my estate the expression 'beneficiary' includes any person who would be a beneficiary if such administration had been completed and the expression 'beneficially interested' and references to income of any asset being payable or capable of being paid to or for the benefit of a beneficiary shall be construed accordingly.

(2)   None of the powers or provisions contained in subclause (3) below of this clause shall be capable of being exercised or operating in any manner such that if such power or provision were capable of being so exercised or so operating the existence of the same would either:

(i)   prevent any person who would in the absence of such power or provision have been entitled to an interest in possession (within the meaning of Part III of the Inheritance Tax Act 1984) in any property from being entitled to such interest; or

(ii)   prevent section 71 of the Inheritance Tax Act 1984 from applying to any property to which in the absence of such power or provision the said section 71 would have applied.

(3)   In the administration of my estate and the execution of the trusts hereof or of any codicil hereto my trustees shall (subject to clause 10 below) have the following powers in addition to those conferred by law but subject to the last foregoing subclause:

(a)   power to invest moneys sell assets and change investments with the unrestricted freedom of choice and powers of disposition and acquisition of a sole beneficial owner with in particular power to make unsecured loans, acquire non-income yielding assets, and purchase land anywhere in the world or chattels for any purpose including occupation or enjoyment in kind by a beneficiary under the power set out below;

(b)   power to delegate all or any of their investment powers to a professional investment manager or managers whether individual or corporate and whether or not also a nominee holder of assets for my trustees (and who may be or include one or more of my trustees or the beneficiaries hereunder) upon such terms as to remuneration and otherwise (including terms authorising self-dealing or providing for the limitation of the liability of the investment manager or managers) as my trustees think fit and section 22 of the Trustee Act 2000 shall not apply;[4]

(c) power to vest or register any property in any person or persons whether individual or corporate and whether or not an investment manager to whom powers have been delegated under the foregoing power (and who may be or include one or more of my trustees or the beneficiaries hereunder) as nominee or nominees for my trustees upon such terms as to remuneration or otherwise (including terms authorising self-dealing or providing for the limitation of the liability of the nominee) as my trustees think fit and section 22 of the Trustee Act 2000 shall not apply;[5]

(d) power to borrow money with or without giving security and on such terms as to interest and repayment and otherwise as my trustees may think fit for any purpose connected with the administration of my estate or the trusts declared herein or in any codicil hereto (including investment) and no lender from whom my trustees borrow money in purported exercise of this power shall be concerned to enquire as to the propriety amount or purpose of any such borrowing;[6]

(e) power to lend money to a beneficiary to whom any of the income of such money is payable or to whom or for whose benefit any income of such money is capable of being paid or applied in exercise of a discretion (or who would be such a beneficiary if such money yielded income) and to do so at a full or concessionary rate of interest or interest free;[7]

(f) all the powers of an absolute owner in relation to any land (wherever situated) held by them;[8]

(g) power to apply capital held on the same trusts as any land (or which would be so held if the administration of my estate had been completed) in the improvement or adaptation of such land and to apply such capital or the income of such capital on the repair or maintenance of such land;[9]

(h) power to permit any beneficiary to have the beneficial occupation use or enjoyment in kind of any land or chattel or other tangible property on such terms as to repair insurance or payment of outgoings by the beneficiary or any other person or persons or otherwise howsoever as my trustees think fit including power for the benefit of a beneficiary to permit any other person or persons (whether beneficiaries or not) to occupy use or enjoy any of the types of asset aforesaid together with such beneficiary or otherwise[2] , provided that the foregoing power shall only be exercisable and such permission to occupy or enjoy in kind may only continue in the following circumstances:

    (i) so long as any of the income of such land chattel or other tangible property is payable to such beneficiary or capable of being paid or applied to him or for his benefit in exercise of a discretion (or would be so payable or capable of being so paid or applied if such land chattel or other property yielded income);

    (ii) in the case of land, so long as for the time being the occupation thereof is compatible with any statutory rights of occupation of any other beneficiary or beneficiaries;[10]

(i) power to exercise all the powers of appropriation (and other incidental powers) conferred by statute on a personal representative without the necessity of obtaining any consents and notwithstanding that one or more of my trustees may be beneficially interested in the exercise of such power.[11]

1   See Form C2.1, cl 9, n 1 at para **[224.30]**.
2   See Form C2.1, cl 9, n 2 at para **[224.30]**. This proviso is not needed so long as the trusts are discretionary, but it is included in case trusts of either of these kinds are created by the trustees in exercise of any of their powers.
3   See Form C2.1, cl 9, n 3 at para **[224.30]**.
4   See Form C2.1, cl 9, n 4 at para **[224.30]**.
5   See Form C2.1, cl 9, n 5 at para **[224.30]**.
6   See Form C2.1, cl 9, n 6 at para **[224.30]**.
7   See Form C2.1, cl 9, n 7 at para **[224.30]**. If a power to pay or apply capital is included in relation to a beneficiary, it will enable loans to be made to or for the benefit of that beneficiary (as an application of capital for his or her benefit), and a separate power to lend of this type is probably unnecessary. However, it is a useful power to include if, in relation to a particular beneficiary such as the testator's spouse, the testator does not wish there to be a power to pay or apply capital at all, or wants such power to be restricted to less than the entire fund.
8   See Form C2.1, cl 9, n 8 at para **[224.30]**.
9   See para **[220.52]** for the reasons for this provision.
10 See Form C2.1, cl 9, n 10 at para **[224.30]**. Express provision for occupation etc by persons other than a beneficiary are added to this subclause to make it clear that the trustees may, eg provide a residence for a disabled beneficiary and someone who is looking after him. It is not entirely clear whether permitting such a person to reside with a beneficiary would give that person an interest in possession.
11 See Form C2.1, cl 9, n 11 at para **[224.30]**.

[228.16]

Trustee indemnity

10.   [(1) My trustees shall not be liable for any act or default of any investment manager or nominee employed in good faith to manage or hold assets of my estate nor for any act or default of any beneficiary having the occupation use or enjoyment of property in kind.[1]

[[(2)   Section 11(1) of the Trusts of Land and Appointment of Trustees Act 1996 (consultation with beneficiaries) shall not apply to the exercise by my trustees of their functions in relation to any land subject to the trusts of this my will].[2]

1   This makes it clear that the trustees are not liable for the defaults of others who may have possession or control of trust property. In respect of the defaults of an investment manager or nominee, this indemnity may be wider than that of the TrA 2000, s 23(1) (Part G, para **[246.138]**) which only exempts a trustee from liability for such defaults if he has complied with the statutory duty of care, a standard which may be higher than that of 'good faith'. Whereas it is clear that a wider indemnity such as this can apply where trustees have exercised an express power to appoint an investment manager or nominee, it is not clear that a wider indemnity can be conferred where trustees have exercised the statutory power (see Preliminary Note to B21 at paras **[221.13]** and **[221.14]**). For a wider form of indemnity see Form B21.12 at para **[221.16]**.
2   The Trusts of Land and Appointment of Trustees Act 1996 (TLATA 1996), s 11(1) which obliges trustees of land to consult beneficiaries of full age and beneficially entitled to an interest in possession, and so far as consistent with the general interest of the trust, to give effect to the wishes of those beneficiaries or (in the event of a dispute) the majority by value (Part G, para **[246.97]**; see also para **[220.58]**) will only be relevant in the circumstances contemplated by this form on the death of the survivor when children might become entitled to interests in possession in residue which might include land. It would probably be convenient for it to be excluded.

[228.17]

Professional trustee charging clause

11.   Any of my trustees being a professional or business man may charge and be paid all usual professional and other proper charges for business transacted

acts done and advice given by him or his firm in connection with the administration of my estate or in connection with the trusts hereof including acts which a personal representative or trustee not being in any profession or business could have done personally[1].

---

1   In spite of the TrA 2000, s 29(2) (Part G, para **[246.144]**) giving certain professional trustees authority to charge for their services on or after 1 February 2001, an express remuneration clause entitling any professional or business person to charge may still be advisable: see Preliminary Note to B21 at para **[221.35]**.

[228.18]

Testimonium and attestation clause

IN WITNESS whereof I have hereunto set my hand this —— day of —— 20——

SIGNED by the above-named [testator/testatrix] as [his/her] last will in the presence of us both present at the same time who at [his/her] request and in [his/her] presence and in the presence of each other have signed our names below as witnesses:

    [Signature of testator/testatrix]

[Signatures, addresses and descriptions of two witnesses]

[228.19]

FORM C6.2:   Reciprocal wills of couple living together who have children, leaving residue on discretionary trusts

NOTE

Where a couple are unmarried there is no spouse exemption, and the inheritance tax on the death of the first to die is the same whether his will creates a discretionary trust or gives an absolute interest or interest in possession to the survivor. A discretionary trust can thus be an appropriate option and this form provides an example of one. The main point of a discretionary trust would be to give greater flexibility and to avoid what in some circumstances might be a heavy inheritance tax charge arising on the survivor's death in respect of property given to the survivor absolutely or for an interest in possession from the estate of the first to die. At the same time inheritance tax on discretionary trusts is not too onerous a burden at the moment and for a fund of a size not exceeding the inheritance tax threshold it can be nil (see B18 at paras **[218.6]**–**[218.18]**).

A discretionary trust would enable some or all of the income to be paid to the survivor without the latter having an interest in possession in the property subject to the trust, and thus without that property being treated as part of his estate for inheritance tax purposes, and would enable income to be paid directly for the benefit of a child and treated as the child's for income tax purposes. The rate of capital gains tax on property subject to a discretionary trust is a flat rate (currently 34 per cent): see B18 at paras **[218.26]** and **[218.27]**.

However, tangible property, such as personal chattels or a dwellinghouse used as a residence, are not suitable items for inclusion in a discretionary trust because the actual enjoyment of such items may constitute an interest in possession for inheritance tax purposes: see Part A, paras **[200.108]–[200.114]**. Accordingly in this form these are given absolutely to the survivor. This form is thus principally of interest where the couple have stock exchange investments etc of a significant value. If the major asset of either estate is a dwellinghouse, however, a discretionary trust strategy could still be used, but with the incorporation of provisions for the establishment of a debt or charge scheme; see Preliminary Note to B18 at paras **[218.19]–[218.22]**, Form B18.2 at para **[218.32]**, Form C3.4 at para **[225.57]** et seq and Form C3.5 at para **[225.68]** et seq.

[228.20]

In the case of an unmarried couple creating discretionary wills which might continue as discretionary trusts in the medium to long term, it is important that there should be no other settled gifts in the will without carefully weighing the consequences. Any other property which is settled will be taken into account as a 'related settlement' when it comes to calculating the inheritance tax exit or periodic charges on the discretionary trust property (see B18 at para **[218.14]**), while property given absolutely by the will is not taken into account in this way. This difficulty can be avoided by the will adding property to a lifetime settlement made by the testator, but this is not always a practical course of action.

  If it turns out after the death of the first to die that some other arrangement would be better, the trustees can, by virtue of the ITA 1984, s 144, make an appointment or distribution within two years of the death (but more than three months after) which is treated for inheritance tax purposes as a disposition by the will (see C3 at paras **[225.83]–[225.91]**).

  The provision of a discretionary trust is made with the will of the first to die principally in mind. However, the same discretionary trust arises on both deaths, with the difference that on the death of the survivor it will apply to the whole estate, since the gifts of chattels and the residence to the other partner will have lapsed as a result of the other partner's previous death. It is of course likely that continuing discretionary trusts will not be wanted in relation to the estate of the survivor after his death, but a discretionary trust gives greater flexibility, and again a distribution of the estate can be made within two years of death (but more than three months after) which is treated for inheritance tax as made by the will, in reliance on the ITA 1984, s 144 (see C3 at paras **[225.83]–[225.91]**).

[228.21]

Revocation clause[1]

I [*name*] of [*address*] hereby revoke all former testamentary dispositions made by me and declare this to be my last will.

1   There is no presumption that wills in similar form are mutual wills in the technical sense, but the matter can be put beyond doubt by incorporating an express provision to that effect: see Form B1.7 at para **[201.11]** for a precedent; see also the revocation clause to Form C2.1 at para **[224.21]**.

[228.22]

Appointment of executors and trustees

1.   [*As in cl 5 of* Form C6.1 *at para* **[228.11]**.]

[228.23]

Appointment of guardians[1]
[*In the will of the woman:*
2.   (1)   If [*name of the man*] shall survive me then I appoint him to be the guardian of any child or children of mine who are minors at the date of my death.
     (2)   If the said [*name of the man*] shall predecease me I appoint [*name*] of [*address*] [and [*name*] of [*address*]] to be the [guardian/guardians] of any child or children of mine who are minors at the date of my death.]
[*In the will of the man*:
2.   If the said [*name of the woman*] shall predecease me I appoint [*name*] of [*address*] [and [*name*] of [*address*]] to be the [guardian/guardians] of any child or children of mine who are minors at the date of my death.]

1   See Form C6.1, cl 2, n 1 at para **[228.8]**. Like Form C6.1, cl 2 this clause is appropriate where the father does not have parental responsibility for the children. This clause differs from that in C6.1 in two respects: no provision is made for the possibility of marriage, and each partner makes an appointment in respect of his or her children whether or not they are also children of the other partner.

[228.24]

Gift of chattels to partner[1]
3.   I give free of tax[2] all my personal chattels as defined by section 55(1)(x) of the Administration of Estates Act 1925[3] to [*name of partner*] absolutely.

1   It is not a good idea to settle personal chattels because the trouble and expense of administering them as part of a trust fund is usually out of all proportion to their value, though it may sometimes be appropriate in the case of valuable chattels. A couple living together will anyway normally want the chattels owned by the first to die to go to the survivor. In relation to Form C6.2 there is also the point that the tax-planning objectives of a discretionary trust will probably not be furthered by including chattels in the property subject to the discretionary trust, because enjoyment in kind of chattels might well give rise to an interest in possession: see the Note at para **[228.19]**.
2   These words are only included in case any of the chattels might be outside the UK at the time of the testator's death. Property outside the UK bears its own inheritance tax in the absence of express provision to the contrary: see the Preliminary Note to B14 at para **[214.60]**. See also cl 6 of this form at para **[228.27]** for the definition of 'free of tax'.
3   See Part G, para **[246.52]** for the wording of this definition, and for further discussion of the meaning of 'personal chattels' see Vol 1, para **[64.44]**.

[228.25]

Gift of interest in dwellinghouse to partner[1]
4.   I give [free of tax][2] [and] [free of all sums charged or otherwise secured thereon at my death (which sums shall be paid out of my residuary estate)] all my interest in the dwellinghouse known as [*address*] in which I currently reside or in any other dwellinghouse purchased in substitution therefor in which I may be residing at the time of my death to [*name of partner*] absolutely.

1   It is not advisable to settle a dwellinghouse on discretionary trusts as the occupant will probably be treated as having an interest in possession: see the Note at para **[228.19]**. By this clause the house is given to the partner outright. If the dwellinghouse is owned by the couple as joint tenants it will not be essential for the joint tenancy to be severed, since the joint tenancy will have the same effect as this clause, but this clause will be redundant, although it could still be included in case a severance occurs between the making of the will and the death.

If the testators would prefer to confer a life interest only (which would carry the statutory right of occupation of the TLATA 1996, s 12(1), see para **[208.5]**), it is important to consider the point that if the survivor is given a life interest in the house, the house will be taken into account in calculating inheritance tax exit and periodic charges on the discretionary trust fund, which would not happen if the house were given absolutely: see B18 at paras **[218.6]–[218.18]**. If it is nevertheless decided to put up with this disadvantage, or to get round it by adding property by the will to a discretionary lifetime settlement made by the same settlor, a life interest could be created by use of, eg Form B8.5 at para **[208.41]**, or Form C2.5, cl 5 at para **[224.85]**, in which case it would be essential to sever any joint tenancy of the house.

2   The inheritance tax on land in the UK is a testamentary expense, and strictly speaking these words are only needed if the residence is outside the UK or might be replaced by one which is. If the parties are already living outside the UK there are special factors to consider, such as foreign laws of succession: see further C14 at para **[236.1]** et seq. See cl 6 of this form at para **[228.27]** for the definition of 'free of tax'. However, where there are specific gifts or pecuniary legacies elsewhere in the will which are declared to be 'free of tax', it would be a good idea to include those words here as well, even if the residence is in the UK, to avoid any suggestion that, because of the absence of the words have when they are included elsewhere, this gift is intended to be subject to tax.

[228.26]

Administration trusts of residue

5.   [*As in cl 6 of* Form C6.1 *at para* **[228.12]**.]

[228.27]

Gifts made free of tax

6.   Any specific gift or pecuniary or general legacy made by this will or any codicil hereto which is expressed to be 'free of tax' shall be free from the payment of any inheritance tax or foreign tax or duty payable on or by reason of my death to which such gift or legacy would otherwise be subject and such inheritance tax or foreign tax or duty shall be paid out of my residuary estate.[1]

1   See Form C3.1, cl 5, n 1 at para **[225.15]**. Where specific gifts and pecuniary legacies are of, or wholly payable out of, free estate in the UK, the inheritance tax on them will be a testamentary expense payable out of residue without any express provision, and it is only where there is foreign property or settled property being disposed of by the will that a gift which is intended to be free of tax needs to be expressly declared to be free of tax. See also the Preliminary Note to B14 at para **[214.55]** et seq.

[228.28]

Discretionary trusts of residue[1]

7.   (1)   In this clause the following expressions have the following meanings namely:

(a)   'the beneficiaries' means and includes:
   (i)   the said [*name of partner*];
   (ii)   my children and remoter issue whenever born;
   [(iii)   the children and remoter issue whenever born of [*name of partner*]];[2]
   (iv)   the spouses widows and widowers of any of the said children or remoter issue (and 'widow' and 'widower' shall include a widow or widower who has remarried);
   (v)   any other person or persons or charitable institution or institutions (whether corporate or not) who may be added to the class of beneficiaries under the power for that purpose hereinafter contained; and

   (vi)   any other persons who become beneficiaries under subclause (2) below of this clause;

(b)   'the trust period' means the period of 80 years immediately following my death (which period shall be the perpetuity period applicable hereto);[3]

(c)   'the accumulation period' means the period commencing with my death and expiring on the twenty-first anniversary thereof; and

(d)   'the relevant day' means the day falling two years less one day after my death.[4]

(2)   If at any time during the trust period the said [*name of partner*] shall have died and there shall be no living child or remoter issue of mine then the beneficiaries shall also include:

(a)   the children and remoter issue of each of my grandparents;

(b)   the children and remoter issue of each of the grandparents of the said [*name of partner*]; and

(c)   any institution (whether corporate or not) which is established for purposes which are exclusively charitable.[5]

(3)   My trustees (being not less than two in number or a trust corporation except as hereinafter provided)[6] may at any time or times and from time to time during the trust period exercise any of the following powers, namely:

(a)   power at any time or times and from time to time by deed or deeds[7] revocable or irrevocable to appoint the whole or any part or parts of my residuary estate upon trust for all or such one or more exclusive of the others or other of the beneficiaries if more than one in such shares and either absolutely or at such age or time or respective ages or times and with such trusts and powers for their respective benefit and such provisions as my trustees may think fit and in making any such appointment my trustees shall have powers as full as those which they would possess if they were an absolute beneficial owner of my residuary estate and in particular (but without prejudice to the generality of the foregoing words) my trustees may in any exercise of the foregoing power as they in their absolute discretion think fit:

   (i)   delegate give or impose to or upon themselves or any other person or persons any discretionary powers or discretionary trusts conditions limitations restrictions or provisions including powers of further delegation or powers to create further discretionary trusts or powers;[8]

   (ii)   create powers or trusts for the accumulation of income during any period permitted by law;

   (iii)   create administrative powers or provisions of whatever nature;
   Provided that:

   (i)   no such appointment shall invalidate any payment transfer or application of capital or income previously made under any of the trusts or powers herein elsewhere contained;

   (ii)   every interest limited under any exercise of such power shall vest in interest (if at all) not later than the expiration of the trust period;

   (iii)   any such appointment may be made in respect of income alone without any appointment of capital;

(iv)   any such revocable appointment shall (so far as then unrevoked) cease to be revocable on the expiration of the trust period;

(v)   any such appointment may make provision for the burden of any testamentary expenses taxes or debts payable out of my estate as between different assets funds shares or interests in such manner and to such extent as my trustees think fit;

(vi)   the foregoing power of appointment may be exercised notwithstanding that there shall have been no grant of probate or administration in respect of the property over which the said power shall be exercised or that the administration of my estate shall not have been completed in respect of such property or any other property comprised in my estate and so long as no such grant as aforesaid has been obtained the persons who may exercise the foregoing power are the persons hereinbefore named as my executors other than any of them who shall have died or whose appointment as my executor shall have ceased to have effect or who shall have renounced probate of my will;[9]

(vii)   the foregoing power of appointment may be exercised before the relevant day by a sole trustee who is not a trust corporation;[10]

(b)   power (subject to any or every exercise of the foregoing power) at any time or times and from time to time in their absolute discretion to pay transfer or apply my residuary estate or any part or parts thereof to or for the benefit of all or any one or more exclusive of the others or other of the beneficiaries for the time being in existence if more than one in such shares and generally in such manner as my trustees shall think fit provided that the foregoing power of payment transfer or application of capital may be exercised before the relevant day by a sole trustee who is not a trust corporation;[11]

(c)   power at any time or times and from time to time to appoint at their absolute discretion by deed any person or persons or charitable institution or institutions (whether corporate or not) to be a member or members of the class of beneficiaries upon the nomination of the said [*name of partner*] or of any children or remoter issue of mine [or of [*name of partner*]][12] who are for the time being over the age of 16 years; provided that:

(i)   the foregoing power may be exercised before the relevant day by a sole trustee who is not a trust corporation; and

(ii)   proviso (vi) (exercise of power before probate or completion of the administration of my estate) to the power of appointment in subclause (3)(a) above shall apply to this power as if the references in it to the said power of appointment were references to this power and as if references to property comprised in my residuary estate were references to the whole of my residuary estate;[13]

(d)   power at any time or times and from time to time by deed or deeds to release or restrict all or any of the foregoing powers or this present power either in whole or in part and in any manner they think fit provided that the foregoing power may be exercised before the relevant day by a sole trustee who is not a trust corporation.

(4)   In default of and subject to any or every exercise of the foregoing powers my trustees shall hold my residuary estate during the trust period upon

trust to pay or apply the income thereof to or for the maintenance education or benefit of all or any one or more of the beneficiaries and if more than one in such shares and in such manner generally as my trustees think fit; provided that during the accumulation period[14] my trustees may accumulate all or any part or parts of such income by investing the same and the resulting income thereof in any investments hereby authorised and so that any accumulations so made shall form part of the capital of my residuary estate (or the part thereof from which such income arose) for all purposes.

(5)   Subject as aforesaid my trustees shall hold my residuary estate and the income thereof at the expiration of the trust period upon trust for such of my grandchildren and remoter issue as shall be then living in equal shares per stirpes.

(6)   Any capital or income of my residuary estate not otherwise disposed of by this clause shall be held in trust for such of my children as shall survive me and if more than one in equal shares.

1   Because it may be important to be able to make appointments or distributions within two years of death falling within the ITA 1984, s 144 (see C3 at paras **[225.83]–[225.91]**), various provisions are included to facilitate such appointments. However, in contrast with Form C3.6, cl 3 at paras **[225.100]–[225.104]** (which is formulated with s 144 in mind), in this form the discretionary trusts and powers continue for a full perpetuity period and do not cease at the end of two years from the testator's death. Also, again in contrast with Form C3.6, cl 3 at paras **[225.100]–[225.104]**, there is no safety mechanism to prevent an appointment or distribution being made within three months of death: see C3 at para **[225.83]** for the point that an appointment or distribution made within that period does not fall within s 144.

2   This should be included where either partner has children by someone other than the current partner.

3   80 years is the maximum fixed period of years permissible under the PAA 1964, s 1 (Part G, para **[246.59]**). The disadvantage of adopting an 80-year period for these trusts is that when it comes to making an appointment, eg a life interest with remainders, an old-style perpetuity period of a life in being plus 21 years cannot be used, and express perpetuity restrictions will often have to be imposed to make sure that the interests which are appointed vest within the perpetuity period. The discretionary trusts and powers continue throughout the perpetuity period: see n 1 to this clause infra.

4   This definition relates to some short-term measures to make it easier for appointments within the ITA 1984, s 144 to be made.

5   If the primary beneficiaries die out, this will enables the trustees to distribute the estate to more distant relations or charity, and avoids an intestacy, or the class of beneficiaries being reduced to consisting only of the widows and widowers of issue.

6   See proviso (vii) to sub-cl (3)(a) and sub-cls (3)(b), (c) and (d) of this clause at para **[228.28]** for the modification of this provision during the two years following the testator's death, so as to make it easier for appointments within the ITA 1984, s 144 to be made.

7   For precedents of appointments see the forms in F4 at paras **[242.7]–[242.16]**.

8   These words authorise the creation of discretionary trusts or powers which might not otherwise be valid: see Vol 1, para **[40.5]**.

9   This is included so as to make it easier to make an appointment within the ITA 1984, s 144 at an early stage. The main reason for such a provision, ie to make exempt appointments before applying for a grant of probate (see C3 at paras **[225.83]–[225.91]**), is not likely to apply in relation to wills in this form, however, because of the lack of a spouse exemption.

10   This is included with the ITA 1984, s 144 (see C3 at paras **[225.83]–[225.91]**) in mind. If it were required that there should be two trustees during the two years after the testator's death, difficulty could arise if the number of trustees were reduced to one and the administration of the estate was not complete, as it is not clear that the statutory power to appoint new trustees could be exercised in such circumstances.

11   For the reasons for the proviso, see n 10 supra. A power to apply capital is a useful alternative to a power of appointment, because fewer formalities are needed for its exercise, and because it permits a wide range of applications for a person's benefit such as lending him money, paying

his debts, etc: see B18 at paras **[218.92]–[218.97]** for the scope of a power of this type. It is important that the exercise of such a power should be adequately evidenced.

12   To be included where either partner has children by someone other than the current partner.

13   See Form C3.6, cl 3(1)(b), n 2 at para **[225.100]**. In wills of this type for unmarried couples with children, it is a particularly good idea to include a power to add to the class of beneficiaries such as this subclause, as it will be a means of adding, eg unmarried partners of the testator's issue, or children of uncertain paternity, to the class of beneficiaries. The power to add charities would enable transfers to charity to be made so as to obtain inheritance tax charitable gift exemption on the testator's death where the transfer fell within the ITA 1984, s 144 (for which see C3 at paras **[225.83]–[225.91]**), and the second proviso enables charity to be added to the class of beneficiaries before probate is obtained. For the purpose of the first proviso see sub-cl 3(a)(vii), n 10 supra.

14   Accumulation for the period of 21 years following the death of the testator is a permitted period under the LPA 1925, s 164(1)(b) (Part G, para **[246.42]**).

[228.29]

Administrative powers

8.   [*As in cl 9 of* Form C6.1 *at para* **[228.15]**.]

[228.30]

Trustee indemnity

9.   [*As in cl 10(1) of* Form C6.1 *at para* **[228.16]**.]

[228.31]

Exercise of powers[1]

10.   Any power or discretion hereby or by law conferred on my trustees shall be exercisable in favour of any person who is an object of such power or discretion notwithstanding that he or she is one of my trustees and shall be exercisable notwithstanding that any of my trustees has any other direct or indirect personal interest in the mode or result of such exercise [provided that there are not fewer than two trustees and at least one of them has no personal interest in the mode or result of exercising the same].[2]

1   This clause permits a member of the family to be a trustee without disqualifying him or her from benefit under any exercise of statutory or express powers of payment or application of capital, appointment, etc. See the Preliminary Note to B18 at paras **[218.4]** and **[218.5]**.

2   If all the executors are to be members of the testator's family and beneficiaries, it would be advisable to omit these words in square brackets. Even if there are some independent executors and some family members as executors, it might still be better to omit these words in case the independent trustees never take office. It should also be noted that this clause does not impose a requirement that there should be two trustees acting where a power is exercised in favour of a trustee (compare Form C3.2, cl 11 at para **[225.39]**), because such a restriction could cause difficulty in exercising the powers within two years after the testator's death (see cl 7, n 1 at para **[228.28]**).

If it is thought that family members cannot be relied on to act disinterestedly and without causing disputes, independent persons who are not beneficiaries should be appointed as executors, and perhaps excluded as potential objects of the power to add to the class of beneficiaries contained in cl 7(3)(c) at para **[228.28]**.

[228.32]

Professional trustee charging clause

11.   [*As in cl 11 of* Form C6.1 *at para* **[228.17]**.]

[*Testimonium and attestation clause as in* Form C6.1 *at para* **[228.18]**.]

[228.33]

FORM C6.3:   Will of man separated (but not judicially separated) from wife and living with another woman, where divorce proceedings are contemplated

NOTE

This will is intended as a temporary measure pending divorce proceedings. It is assumed that the testator is separated from his wife and children, and is living with another woman whom he wishes to benefit so far as practicable by his will. It is assumed that the wife and children are living in the former matrimonial home, and that the testator and his wife own that home as tenants in common, the testator having taken steps to sever any joint tenancy. This will should be reviewed as and when the divorce takes place and the financial arrangements are settled. The provision for the wife is confined to a right to occupy the former matrimonial home. Such provision will lapse on the dissolution of the marriage—the Wills Act 1837, s 18A (Part G, para **[244.18]**)—if it is not superseded by the financial settlement on divorce, which may well bring about some alteration of the ownership of the matrimonial home in the wife's or children's favour.

[228.34]

Revocation clause
I [*name*] of [*address*] hereby revoke all former testamentary dispositions made by me and declare this to be my last will.

[228.35]

Appointment of executors and trustees
1.   [*As in cl 5 of* Form C6.1 *at para* **[228.11]**.]

[228.36]

Appointment of guardians¹
2.   If my wife [*name*] ('my wife') shall predecease me I appoint [*name*] of [*address*] [and [*name*] of [*address*]] to be the [guardian/guardians] of any child or children of ours who are minors at the date of my death.

1   For appointments of guardians where both parents are living and have parental responsibility, see the Note in B3 at para **[203.43]** et seq and the Preliminary Note to C2 at para **[224.7]**.

[228.37]

Gift of interest in dwellinghouse on trusts permitting wife to occupy dwellinghouse for life or during widowhood¹
3.   (1)   I give to my trustees all my interest in the dwellinghouse situate at [*address*] which is now occupied by my wife and which is vested in us both as beneficial tenants in common in equal shares to hold the same upon the trusts hereinafter declared.
    (2)   So long as my wife [shall not remarry and] shall desire to occupy the said dwellinghouse my trustees shall not seek to bring about a sale of the same

or take any step to prevent my wife from having the beneficial use and occupation thereof.

(3)   Subject as aforesaid[2] my trustees shall hold the said interest and the assets for the time being representing the same (hereinafter called 'the trust fund') upon trust for such of my children as shall survive me and attain the age of 25 years and if more than one in equal shares; provided that if any of my children shall not live to attain a vested interest under the foregoing trust leaving a child or children living at or born after my death who shall attain the age of 21 years such last-mentioned child or children shall take and if more than one equally between them the share of the trust fund which his her or their parent would have taken had he or she lived to attain a vested interest.

(4)   The foregoing trusts shall carry the intermediate income of the trust fund and section 31 of the Trustee Act 1925 (as hereinafter modified) shall apply thereto.

(5)   Section 32 of the Trustee Act 1925 (as hereinafter modified) shall apply in relation to the said trusts.

[(6)   I declare that I have made no further provision for my wife on the grounds that if she survives me as my widow she will become entitled to a widow's pension and that she is otherwise adequately provided for].[3]

1   This gift confers a residence right on the wife which will lapse on divorce. It will create a trust of an undivided share in land, which will be a trust of land within the TLATA 1996 (see the LPA 1925, s 205(1)(ix), as amended by the TLATA 1996, s 23(2) and Sch 4: Part G, para **[246.44A]**). It is assumed that the testator has severed any joint tenancy to which the matrimonial home is subject. See the Note to this form at para **[228.33]**.
2   The gift in favour of the children will be accelerated on the dissolution of the marriage: see the WA 1837, s 18A (Part G, para **[244.18]**).
3   A declaration in this form may possibly be useful in the event that the husband dies before the marriage is dissolved and the wife makes a claim under the I(PFD)A 1975 (Part G, para **[247.1]** et seq and discussed in Vol 1 at para **[105.1]** et seq).

[228.38]

Administration trusts of residue
4.   [*As in cl 6 of* Form C6.1 *at para* **[228.12]**.]

[228.39]

Beneficial trusts of residue
5.   (1)   My trustees shall hold my residuary estate and the income thereof upon trust for [*name of partner*] if she survives me absolutely.

(2)   If the said [*name of partner*] shall not survive me then my trustees shall hold my residuary estate upon trust for such of my children as shall survive me and attain the age of 25 years and if more than one in equal shares provided that if any of my children shall not live to attain a vested interest under the foregoing trust leaving a child or children living at or born after my death who shall attain the age of [18/21] years such last-mentioned child or children shall take and if more than one equally between then the share of my residuary estate which his her or their parent would have taken had he or she lived to attain a vested interest.

(3)   The foregoing trust shall carry the intermediate income of my residuary estate and section 31 of the Trustee Act 1925 (as hereinafter modified) shall apply thereto.

(4)   Section 32 of the Trustee Act 1925 (as hereinafter modified) shall apply in relation to the said trusts.

[228.40]

Maintenance, accumulation and advancement
6.   [*As in cl 8 of* Form C6.1 *at para* **[228.14]**.]

[228.41]

Administrative powers
7.   [*As in cl 9 of* Form C6.1 *at para* **[228.15]**.]

[228.42]

Trustee indemnity
8.   [*As in cl 10(1) of* Form C6.1 *at para* **[228.16]**.]

[228.43]

Professional trustee charging clause
9.   [*As in cl 11 of* Form C6.1 *at para* **[228.17]**.]

[*Testimonium and attestation clause as in* Form C6.1 *at para* **[228.18]**.]

C7 Wills for sole parents with young children

PRELIMINARY NOTE

[229.1]
This section is intended to cater for the needs of a sole parent with young children. The parent, usually the mother, may be single for one of a variety of reasons, but whatever the reason there will be no spouse or partner to provide for. Very often the sole parent will not have much to leave and making a will may not seem important. But a sole parent with young children would be wise to make a will, if only to appoint a guardian, and all the forms in the section contain provision for such an appointment. For a discussion of the law relating to guardianship see Vol 1, para **[28.1]** et seq and the Note to Forms B3.26 to B3.32 at paras **[203.43]–[203.54]**.

The forms in this section contain a few alternative beneficial dispositions of the parent's estate. In Forms C7.1 (at paras **[229.2]–[229.12]**) and C7.3 (at paras **[229.26]–[229.36]**) the entire estate is left on contingent trusts for the child or children at 25 with substitutional trusts in favour of his, her or their children, whereas in Form C7.4 (at paras **[229.37]–[229.50]**) the entire estate is settled on the children for life with power to apply capital for their benefit and with remainder in favour of their children. Where the estate is small, the cost and trouble of administering trusts during a minority may be disproportionately great, and a possible solution would be to give the estate to the guardian if he or she accepts office as in Form C7.2 (at paras **[229.13]–[229.25]**). This might be a suitable course where the guardian is a close relative and the child would effectively become a member of the guardian's family. Where the estate is large or includes business or agricultural property or foreign property, the forms in this section may not be suitable and the forms in C11, C12 or C13 (at paras **[233.1]–[235.39]**) should be consulted.

Although Forms C7.3 to C7.5 are entitled wills for a widow or widower, they are suitable for other sole parents.

[229.2]

FORM C7.1:   Will of mother giving entire estate to her minor child[1]

NOTE

This form is intended for a single mother with one child only.

[229.3]

Revocation clause
I [*name*] of [*address*] hereby revoke all former testamentary dispositions made by me and declare this to be my last will.

[229.4]

Appointment of executors and trustees
1.   I appoint [*name*] of [*address*] and [*name*] of [*address*] (hereinafter together called 'my trustees' which expression shall include my personal representatives for the time being and the trustees for the time being hereof) to be the executors and trustees of this will.

[229.5]

Appointment of guardians[1]
2.   I appoint [the said [*name*] and the said [*name*]]/[[*name*] of [*address*] [and [*name*] of [*address*]]] to be the [guardian/guardians] of my [son/daughter] [*name*] during [his/her] minority.

1   One of the main reasons for a sole parent with young children to make a will is to appoint a guardian or guardians. It may be possible or appropriate to appoint the same persons as executors and guardians. As to the appointment of guardians see Note to Forms B3.26 to B3.32 at paras **[203.43]–[203.54]** and the more general discussion of the law in Vol 1 at para **[28.1]** et seq.

[229.6]

Administration trusts of residue
3.   (1)   I give all my property not hereby or by any codicil hereto otherwise effectively disposed of [(including any entailed or other property over which I shall have at my death a general power of disposition by will)][1] to my trustees to hold on the trusts set out below with power at their discretion to sell all or any of it as and when they think fit.[2]

(2)   My trustees shall pay my funeral and testamentary expenses[3] and debts and any legacies given by this will or any codicil hereto out of such property or its proceeds and shall have a discretion as to how such payments shall be borne as between capital and income[4].

(3)   Subject as above my trustees shall hold such property and the assets from time to time representing the same (hereinafter called 'my residuary estate') on the trusts set out below and shall invest all money comprised in such property or arising from its sale in any of the investments hereby authorised with power to change such investments into any others hereby authorised.

(4)   In the administration of my estate and the execution of the trusts of this will or of any codicil to it:

(a) my trustees shall treat all income as accruing on the date on which it becomes payable regardless of the period in respect of which it shall have accrued and shall not make any statutory apportionment of the same;[5] and

(b) none of the equitable rules of apportionment between capital and income shall apply in any circumstances whatever.[6]

1   See para [**224.27**], n 1.
2   See para [**224.27**], n 2.
3   See para [**224.27**], n 3.
4   See para [**224.27**], n 4.
5   See para [**224.27**], n 5.
6   See para [**224.27**], n 6.

[229.7]

Beneficial trusts of estate

4.   (1)   My trustees shall hold my residuary estate upon trust for my said [son/daughter] if [he/she] shall attain the age of 25 years[1] absolutely provided that if [he/she] shall die before attaining the said age leaving a child or children [him/her] surviving who attain the age of 21 years[2] such last mentioned child or children shall take my residuary estate and if more than one in equal shares.

(2)   The foregoing trusts shall carry the intermediate income of my residuary estate and section 31 of the Trustee Act 1925 (as hereinafter modified) shall apply thereto provided that in relation to my said [son/daughter] the said section shall take effect for all purposes as if the age of majority were the age of [21/25] years[3] and so that all references in the said section to 'infancy' 'minority' and 'infant' and all references therein to the age of 18 years shall be construed accordingly.

(3)   Section 32 of the Trustee Act 1925 (as hereinafter modified) shall apply in relation to my residuary estate.

(4)   My trustees may exercise their powers to apply income or capital for the benefit of my said [son/daughter] by paying or transferring the same to [his/her] guardian for the time being.[4]

(5)   Subject as aforesaid my trustees shall hold my residuary estate upon trust for such of my brothers and sisters [*name*] [*name*] [*name*] and [*name*] as survive me and if more than one in equal shares.

1   Since the child will be a life in being for perpetuity purposes, the age contingency does not have to be restricted to any particular age.
2   The grandchildren will not necessarily be lives in being and the age contingency is therefore restricted to 21.
3   It is possible to extend the statutory provisions for maintenance and accumulation to any age which will be attained during the period of 21 years following the testator's death (LPA 1925, s 164(1)(b): Part G, para [**246.42**]); accordingly, these provisions may be extended to the age of 21 in relation to a beneficiary who will be living at the testator's death, and to the age of 25 where the beneficiary has attained the age of four: see the note on extended accumulation and maintenance provisions in B18 at paras [**218.72**]–[**218.76**]. The age at which accumulation and maintenance trusts of income cease should not be greater than 25 where (as will usually be the case) it is desired that the ITA 1984, s 71 should apply: see Part A, para [**200.119**] et seq.
4   It is not strictly necessary to include a power to pay income or capital to a guardian in view of the ChA 1989, s 3(3) (Part G, para [**244.119**]) which authorises any person with 'parental responsibility' in respect of a child to receive or recover property which the child is entitled to receive or recover, but it does no harm to include an express power.

[229.8]

Maintenance, accumulation and advancement[1]

5. (1)   Section 31 of the Trustee Act 1925 (relating to accumulation and maintenance) shall apply in relation to the trusts hereby or by any codicil hereto declared as if:

(a)   in paragraph (i) of subsection (1) of the said section the words 'as the trustees think fit' were substituted for the words 'as may in all the circumstances be reasonable'; and

(b)   the proviso to the said subsection (1) were omitted.

(2)   Section 32 of the Trustee Act 1925 (relating to advancement) shall apply in relation to the said trusts as if the words 'one half of' were omitted from proviso (a) to subsection (1) thereof [Provided that the powers conferred by the said section (as hereby enlarged) shall not be exercisable in favour of any beneficiary hereunder who is under the age of [21/25][2] years otherwise than so as to cause such beneficiary to become immediately entitled to or to an interest in possession in the capital thereby paid or applied within the meaning of section 71(1)(a) of the Inheritance Tax Act 1984].[3]

(3)   Whenever my trustees shall have an obligation or discretion under the provisions of this will or any codicil hereto or under the general law to apply income or capital for the benefit of a minor beneficiary they may either pay the same without liability to account to his or her parent guardian or any other adult person with whom such beneficiary may be residing or to such beneficiary himself or herself if of the age of 16 years or more and so that the receipt of such parent guardian or other person or of such minor beneficiary shall be a full and sufficient discharge to my trustees for the income or capital so applied.[4]

1   For alternative provisions relating to maintenance and advancement see Forms B18.11 to B18.21 and the notes thereto at paras **[218.77]**–**[218.105]**.

2   Ie the maximum age to which accumulation and maintenance trusts of income are extended by the beneficial trusts of residue (see cl 4(2) of this form at para **[229.7]** and see n 3 to that clause).

3   The proviso is included in order to prevent the power prejudicing the application of the Inheritance Tax Act 1984 (ITA 1984), s 71 (accumulation and maintenance trusts), but is probably unnecessary: see the Note on inheritance tax and the statutory power of advancement in B18 at paras **[218.99]**–**[218.102]**.

4   A parent (with parental responsibility) and a guardian of a minor are empowered by the ChA 1989, s 3(3) (Part G, para **[244.119]**) to give a good receipt for the minor's property: see Vol 1, para **[9.42]**. The power in this subclause is wider in that it authorises the payment of income or capital to a parent who does not have parental responsibility, any adult with whom the minor is residing, and the minor himself or herself if 16 or over.

[229.9]

Administrative powers[1]

6. (1)   In this clause where the context so admits:

(a)   the expression 'land' includes buildings and estates interests or rights of any kind in or over land; and

(b)   during the administration of my estate the expression 'beneficiary' includes any person who would be a beneficiary if such administration had been completed and the expression 'beneficially interested' and references to income of any asset being payable or capable of being paid to or for the benefit of a beneficiary shall be construed accordingly.

(2)   None of the powers or provisions contained in subclause (3) below of this clause shall be capable of being exercised or operating in any manner such that if such power or provision were capable of being so exercised or so operating the existence of the same would either:

(i)   prevent any person who would in the absence of such power or provision have been entitled to an interest in possession (within the meaning of Part III of the Inheritance Tax Act 1984) in any property from being entitled to such interest; or

(ii)   prevent section 71 of the Inheritance Tax Act 1984 from applying to any property to which in the absence of such power or provision the said section 71 would have applied.[2]

(3)   In the administration of my estate and the execution of the trusts hereof or of any codicil hereto my trustees shall have the following powers in addition to those conferred by law but subject to the last foregoing subclause:

(a)   power to invest moneys sell assets and change investments with the unrestricted freedom of choice and powers of disposition and acquisition of a sole beneficial owner with in particular power to make unsecured loans, acquire non-income yielding assets, and purchase land anywhere in the world or chattels for any purpose including occupation or enjoyment in kind by a beneficiary under the power set out below;[3]

(b)   power to delegate all or any of their investment powers to a professional investment manager or managers whether individual or corporate and whether or not also a nominee holder of assets for my trustees (and who may be or include one or more of my trustees or the beneficiaries hereunder) upon such terms as to remuneration and otherwise (including terms authorising self-dealing or providing for the limitation of the liability of the investment manager or managers) as my trustees think fit and section 22 of the Trustee Act 2000 shall not apply;[4]

(c)   power to vest or register any property in any person or persons whether individual or corporate and whether or not an investment manager to whom powers have been delegated under the foregoing power (and who may be or include one or more of my trustees or the beneficiaries hereunder) as nominee or nominees for my trustees upon such terms as to remuneration or otherwise (including terms authorising self-dealing or providing for the limitation of the liability of the nominee) as my trustees think fit and section 22 of the Trustee Act 2000 shall not apply;[5]

(d)   power to borrow money with or without giving security and on such terms as to interest and repayment and otherwise as my trustees may think fit for any purpose connected with the administration of my estate or the trusts declared herein or in any codicil hereto (including investment) And no lender from whom my trustees borrow money in purported exercise of this power shall be concerned to enquire as to the propriety amount or purpose of any such borrowing;[6]

(e)   power to lend money to a beneficiary to whom any of the income of such money is payable or to whom or for whose benefit any income of such money is capable of being paid or applied in exercise of a discretion (or who would be such a beneficiary if such money yielded income) and to do so at a full or concessionary rate of interest or interest free;[7]

(f) all the powers of an absolute owner in relation to any land (wherever situated) held by them;[8]

(g) power to apply capital held on the same trusts as any land (or which would be so held if the administration of my estate had been completed) in the improvement of such land and to apply such capital or the income of such capital on the repair or maintenance of such land;[9]

(h) power to permit any beneficiary to have the beneficial occupation use or enjoyment in kind of any land or chattel or other tangible property on such terms as to repair insurance or payment of outgoings by the beneficiary or otherwise howsoever as my trustees think fit Provided that the foregoing power shall only be exercisable and such permission to occupy or enjoy in kind may only continue in the following circumstances:

    (i) so long as any of the income of such land chattel or other tangible property is payable to such beneficiary or capable of being paid or applied to him or for his benefit in exercise of a discretion (or would be so payable or capable of being so paid or applied if such land chattel or other property yielded income);

    (ii) in the case of land, so long as for the time being the occupation thereof by such beneficiary is compatible with any statutory rights of occupation of any other beneficiary or beneficiaries;[10]

(i) power to exercise all the powers of appropriation (and other incidental powers) conferred by statute on a personal representative without the necessity of obtaining any consents and notwithstanding that one or more of my trustees may be beneficially interested in the exercise of such power.[11]

1 See para **[224.30]**, n 1.
2 See para **[224.30]**, n 2.
3 See para **[224.30]**, n 3.
4 See para **[224.30]**, n 4.
5 See para **[224.30]**, n 5.
6 See para **[224.30]**, n 6.
7 See para **[224.30]**, n 7.
8 See para **[224.30]**, n 8.
9 See para **[224.30]**, n 9.
10 See para **[224.30]**, n 10.
11 See para **[224.30]**, n 11.

[229.10]

Trustee liability

7. (1) My trustees shall not be liable for any act or default of any investment manager or nominee employed in good faith to manage or hold assets of my estate nor for any act or default of any beneficiary having the occupation use or enjoyment of property in kind.[1]

(2) Section 11(1) of the Trusts of Land and Appointment of Trustees Act 1996 (consultation with beneficiaries) shall not apply to the exercise by my trustees of any of their powers in relation to land subject to the trusts hereof.[2]

1   This makes it clear that the trustees are not liable for the defaults of others who may have possession or control of trust property. For a wider form of indemnity, see eg Form B21.12 at para **[221.16]**.
2   The requirement that trustees of land in exercise of any function relating to land subject to the trust consult with beneficiaries of full age beneficially entitled to an interest in possession in the land can be excluded: TLATA 1996, s 11 (Part G, para **[246.97]**).

[229.11]

Professional trustee charging clause
8.   Any of my trustees being a professional or business man may charge and be paid all usual professional and other proper charges for business transacted acts done advice given and time spent by him or his firm in connection with the administration of my estate or in connection with the trusts hereof including acts which a personal representative or trustee not being in any profession or business could have done personally.

[229.12]

Testimonium and attestation clause

IN WITNESS whereof I have hereunto set my hand this —— day of —— 20——.

SIGNED by the above-named testatrix as her last will in the presence of us both present at the same time who at her request and in her presence and in the presence of each other have signed our names below as witnesses: *[Signature of testatrix]*
[Signatures, addresses and descriptions of two witnesses]

[229.13]

FORM C7.2:   Will of mother appointing sister sole executrix and guardian of children and giving entire estate to her if accepting office, with alternative gift to children

NOTE

This form gives the entire estate to the guardian beneficially and is unlikely to be suitable unless the estate is relatively small: see the Preliminary Note to this section at para **[229.1]** et seq. A will in this form will need to be kept under review especially as the children approach the age of majority.

[229.14]

Revocation clause
I *[name]* of *[address]* hereby revoke all former testamentary dispositions made by me and declare this to be my last will.

[229.15]

Appointment of guardian[1]

1. If my children or any of them are minors at the time of my death I appoint my sister [*name*] of [*address*] to be the guardian of my children during their respective minorities.

1   See Form C7.1, cl 2, n 1 at para **[229.5]**.

[229.16]

Gift of estate to guardian and appointment of guardian as sole executrix

2. If my children or any of them are minors at the time of my death and my said sister is willing to act as guardian then I appoint my said sister sole executrix of this will and subject to the payment thereout of any funeral and testamentary expenses and debts I give all of my estate both real and personal to my said sister absolutely [with the request (but not so as to impose on her any trust or obligation) that she apply the same and the income thereof for the benefit of my children].[1]

1   If included, the words in square brackets will impose on the sister only a moral obligation to apply the estate for the benefit of the deceased's children. To impose a legal obligation to do so would frustrate the purpose of the precedent which is to allow the guardian (in this form the sister of the testatrix) to treat the estate as her own and to avoid the need to administer a separate trust fund.

[229.17]

Alternative provisions[1]

3. If my said sister shall predecease me or having survived me shall decline to accept office as guardian of such of my children as are minors at the time of my death or if at my death none of my children are minors then the following provisions shall have effect.

1   Alternative beneficial provisions similar to those contained in Form C7.1 are included in case the primary gift fails.

[229.18]

Appointment of executors and trustees

4. [*As in cl 1 of* Form C7.1 *at para* **[229.4]**.]

[229.19]

Appointment of guardians

5. I appoint [*name*] of [*address*] [and [*name*] of [*address*]] to be the [guardian/guardians] of my children during their respective minorities.

[229.20]

Administration trusts of estate

6. [*As in cl 3 of* Form C7.1 *at para* **[229.6]**.]

[229.21]

Beneficial trusts of estate

7.　(1)　My trustees shall hold my residuary estate upon trust for such of my children as shall survive me and attain the age of [21/25] years[1] and if more than one in equal shares provided that if any of my children shall predecease me leaving a child or children living at my death who shall attain the age of 21 years[2] such last-mentioned child or children shall take and if more than one equally between them the share of my residuary estate which such deceased child of mine would have taken had he or she survived me.

(2)　The foregoing trusts shall carry the intermediate income of my residuary estate and section 31 of the Trustee Act 1925 (as hereinafter modified) shall apply thereto provided that in relation to my children the said section shall take effect for all purposes as if the age of majority were the age of [21/25][3] years and so that all references in the said section to 'infancy' 'minority' and 'infant' and all references therein to the age of 18 years shall be construed accordingly.

(3)　Section 32 of the Trustee Act 1925 (as hereinafter modified) shall apply in relation to my residuary estate.

(4)　My trustees may exercise their powers to apply income or capital for the benefit of any of my said children by paying or transferring the same to [his/her] guardian for the time being.[4]

(5)　Subject as aforesaid my trustees shall hold my residuary estate upon trust for such of my brothers and sisters [*name*] [*name*] [*name*] and [*name*] as survive me if more than one in equal shares.

1　See Form C7.1, cl 4(1), n 1 at para **[229.7]**.
2　See Form C7.1, cl 4(1), n 2 at para **[229.7]**.
3　See Form C7.1, cl 4(2), n 3 at para **[229.7]**.
4　See Form C7.1, cl 4(4), n 4 at para **[229.7]**.

[229.22]

Maintenance, accumulation and advancement

8.　[*As in cl 5 of* Form C7.1 *at para* **[229.8]**.][1]

1　If the proviso to Form C7.1, cl 5(2) is incorporated in this form, the age referred to in it should be that which is selected as the highest age to which accumulation and maintenance trusts of income can continue by virtue of cl 7(2) of this form.

[229.23]

Administrative powers

9.　[*As in cl 6 of* Form C7.1 *at para* **[229.9]**.]

[229.24]

Trustee liability

10.　[*As in cl 7 of* Form C7.1 *at para* **[229.10]**.]

[229.25]

Professional trustee charging clause

11.　[*As in cl 8 of* Form C7.1 *at para* **[229.11]**.]

[*Testimonium and attestation clause as in* Form C7.1 *at para* **[229.12]**.]

[229.26]

FORM C7.3:   **Will of widow or widower in favour of children**

NOTE

This form in effect reproduces the alternative provisions contained in cls 3 to 9 of Form C7.2 (at paras **[229.17]–[229.23]**).

[229.27]

Revocation clause
I [*name*] of [*address*] hereby revoke all former testamentary dispositions made by me and declare this to be my last will.

[229.28]

Appointment of executors and trustees
1.   [*As in cl 1 of* Form C7.1 *at para* **[229.4]**.]

[229.29]

Appointment of guardians
2.   [*As in cl 5 of* Form C7.2 *at para* **[229.19]**.]

[229.30]

Administration trusts of estate
3.   [*As in cl 3 of* Form C7.1 *at para* **[229.6]**.]

[229.31]

Beneficial trusts of residue
4.   [*As in cl 7 of* Form C7.2 *at para* **[229.21]**.]

[229.32]

Maintenance, accumulation and advancement
5.   [*As in cl 5 of* Form C7.1 *at para* **[229.8]**.]

[229.33]

Administrative powers
6.   [*As in cl 6 of* Form C7.1 *at para* **[229.9]**.]

[229.34]

Trustee liability
7.   [*As in cl 7 of* Form C7.1 *at para* **[229.10]**.]

[229.35]

Professional trustee charging clause
8.   [*As in cl 8 of* Form C7.1 *at para* **[229.11]**.]

[229.36]

Testimonium and attestation clause

IN WITNESS whereof I have hereunto set my hand this —— day of —— 20——.

SIGNED by the above-named [testator/testatrix] as [his/her] last will in the presence of us both present at the same time who at [his/her] request and in [his/her] presence and in the presence of each other have signed our names below as witnesses: } *[Signature of testator/testatrix]*

[Signatures, addresses and descriptions of two witnesses]

[229.37]

FORM C7.4:   Will of widow or widower settling residue on children equally for life with remainder to their children

NOTE

This form is an alternative to Form C7.3 in that the interest of each child instead of being a contingent interest in capital is settled on the child for life, with a power to pay capital to him or for his benefit. This provides flexibility as to whether, and if so at what age, the children obtain control of the capital of their shares, and enables better capital gains tax planning if a child is not to become absolutely entitled to capital immediately on the coming to an end of an accumulation and maintenance trust (when hold-over relief would be available) (see Part A, para **[200.39]**).

[229.38]

Revocation clause

I [*name*] of [*address*] hereby revoke all former testamentary dispositions made by me and declare this to be my last will.

[229.39]

Appointment of executors and trustees

1.   [*As in cl 1 of* Form C7.1 *at para* **[229.4]**.]

[229.40]

Appointment of guardians

2.   [*As in cl 5 of* Form C7.2 *at para* **[229.19]**.]

[229.41]

Pecuniary legacies

3.   I give free of tax[1] the following pecuniary legacies:

   (a)   to [*name*] of [*address*] the sum of ——;
   (b)   to [*name*] of [*address*] the sum of ——;

(c)   to [*name*] of [*address*] the sum of ——.

1   See Form C3.1, cl 2, n 2 at para **[225.12]**. These words are included in case there is foreign or settled property comprised in residue. See cl 6 of this form for the definition of 'free of tax'.

[229.42]

Specific bequests

4.   I make the following specific bequests free of tax:[1]

(a)   to [my son] [*name*] [my/my late husband's] gold watch;
(b)   to [my daughter] [*name*] [my/my late wife's] jewellery;
(c)   to [my son] [*name*] [my/my late husband's] gold cuff-links.

1   These words are only included in case any of the chattels might be outside the UK at the time of the testator's death. Property outside the UK bears its own inheritance tax in the absence of express provision to the contrary: see the Note to B14 at para **[214.63]**. See cl 6 of this form for the definition of 'free of tax'.

[229.43]

Administration trusts of residue

5.   [*As in cl 3 of* Form C7.1 *at para* **[229.6]**.]

[229.44]

Gifts made free of tax

6.   Any specific gift or pecuniary or general legacy made by this will or any codicil hereto which is expressed to be 'free of tax' shall be free from the payment of any inheritance tax or foreign tax or duty payable on or by reason of my death to which such gift or legacy would otherwise be subject and such inheritance tax or foreign tax or duty shall be paid out of my residuary estate.[1]

1   See the note to Form C3.1, cl 5 at para **[225.15]**. Where specific gifts and pecuniary legacies are of, or wholly payable out of, free estate in the UK, the inheritance tax on them will be a testamentary expense payable out of residue without any express provision, and it is only where foreign property or settled property is being disposed of by the will that a gift which is intended to be free of tax needs to be expressly declared to be free of tax. See also the Preliminary Note to B14 at para **[214.63]**.

[229.45]

Beneficial trusts of residue for children and issue[1]

7.   (1)   My trustees shall hold my residuary estate upon trust for such of my children as shall survive me and attain the age of 18 years and if more than one in equal shares provided that if any child of mine shall predecease me or having survived me shall fail to attain a vested interest under the foregoing trust leaving a child or children living at my death or born thereafter who shall attain the age of 21 years[2] such last-mentioned child or children shall take absolutely and if more than one equally between them the share of my residuary estate which such deceased child of mine would (subject to clause 8 below) have taken had he or she lived to attain a vested interest.

(2)   The foregoing trusts shall carry the intermediate income of my residuary estate and section 31 of the Trustee Act 1925 (as hereinafter modified) shall apply thereto.

(3)   Section 32 of the Trustee Act 1925 (as hereinafter modified) shall apply in relation to the foregoing trusts and shall be exercisable for the benefit of any child of mine in relation to his or her presumptive share of my residuary estate notwithstanding the direction for the retention and settlement of such share hereinafter contained.[3]

1   The beneficial trusts contained in this clause satisfy the conditions specified in the ITA 1984, s 71(1) in relation to any child who has not attained an interest in possession. The substitutional proviso is confined to grandchildren rather than issue generally and accordingly the 25-year limit imposed by s 71(2)(a) does not apply.
2   For perpetuity reasons, the age contingency for grandchildren should not exceed 21. The age of vesting for the children is 18 because the children's interests are settled on them for life, with them becoming entitled to receive the income at 18, and a higher vesting age for them would serve little purpose.
3   This subclause is included since it is probable, in view of the settlement of each child's share, that the statutory power would not otherwise apply in his or her favour. The power to pay or apply capital in cl 8(e) will not apply to a share of the residuary estate until a child has an interest in possession in it.

[229.46]

Settlement of child's share of residue[1]
8.   (1)   The share of my residuary estate to which any child of mine shall become entitled under the last foregoing clause hereof shall not vest absolutely in such child but shall be retained by my trustees and held upon the following trusts:

(a)   my trustees shall hold such share upon trust to pay the income thereof to such child of mine during his or her life;
(b)   subject as aforesaid my trustees shall hold such share upon trust for such of the children of such child as shall attain the age of [18/21] years and if more than one in equal shares absolutely;
(c)   the trust declared by paragraph (b) above shall carry the intermediate income of such share and section 31 of the Trustee Act 1925 (as hereinafter modified) shall apply thereto;
(d)   section 32 of the Trustee Act 1925 (as hereinafter modified) shall apply in relation to such share;
(e)   notwithstanding the trusts aforesaid so long as such child of mine is entitled to be paid the income of all or any part of the capital of such share (or would be so entitled if such capital yielded income)[2] my trustees shall have power in their absolute discretion from time to time to pay transfer or apply the whole or any part or parts of such capital to or for the benefit of such child in such manner as they shall in their absolute discretion think fit;
(f)   if there shall be no child of such child of mine who shall attain the age of [18/21] years such share and any other share of my residuary estate which may have accrued thereto hereunder (or so much thereof as shall not have been paid or applied under any of the powers applicable thereto hereunder) shall go and accrue to the other shares or share of my residuary estate the trusts of which are at the date of such accruer subsisting and capable of taking effect.

(2)   Subject as aforesaid my trustees shall hold my residuary estate upon trust for such of my children as shall survive me and if more than one in equal shares.

1   See the note at the beginning of this form at para **[229.37]**.
2   See Form C2.2, cl 8(e), n 2 at para **[224.44]**.

[229.47]

Maintenance, accumulation and advancement
9.   (1)   [*As in cl 5(1) of* Form C7.1 *at para* **[229.8]**.]
    (2)   Section 32 of the Trustee Act 1925 (relating to advancement) shall apply in relation to the said trusts as if the words 'one half of' were omitted from proviso (a) to subsection (1) thereof [provided that the powers conferred by the said section (as hereby enlarged) shall not be exercisable in favour of any minor beneficiary hereunder otherwise than so as to cause such beneficiary to become immediately entitled to or to an interest in possession in the capital thereby paid or applied within the meaning of section 71(1)(a) of the Inheritance Tax Act 1984].[1]
    (3)   [*As in cl 5(3) of* Form C7.1 *at para* **[229.8]**.]

1   The proviso is included in order to prevent the power prejudicing the application of the ITA 1984, s 71 (accumulation and maintenance trusts), but is probably unnecessary: see the Note on inheritance tax and the statutory power of advancement in B18 at paras **[218.99]**–**[218.102]**. If the accumulation and maintenance trusts of income are extended so as to continue beyond the age of 18 (see eg Forms B18.12 and B18.13 at paras **[218.78]** and **[218.79]** and Form C7.1, cl 4(2) at para **[229.7]**), then Form C7.1, cl 5(2) at para **[229.8]** should be used instead of cl 9(2).

[229.48]

Administrative powers
10.   [*As in cl 6 of* Form C7.1 *at para* **[229.9]**.]

[229.49]

Trustee liability
11.   [*As in cl 7 of* Form C7.1 *at para* **[229.10]**.]

[229.49]

Exercise of powers[1]
12.   Any power or discretion hereby or by law conferred on my trustees (including a power or discretion as to the disposition of capital or income) shall be exercisable notwithstanding that any of my trustees has a personal interest in such exercise provided that at least one of them has no such personal interest.

1   This clause permits a member of the family to be a trustee without disqualifying him or her from benefit under any exercise of statutory or express powers of payment or application of capital. See the Preliminary Note to B18 at para **[218.4]**.

[229.50]

Professional trustee charging clause
13.   [*As in cl 8 of* Form C7.1 *at para* **[229.11]**.]

[*Testimonium and attestation clause as in* Form C7.3 *at para* **[229.36]**.]

[229.51]

FORM C7.5:   Will of widow or widower in favour of children with the principal intention of providing a residence for them until the youngest attains a specified age

NOTE

The principal feature of this precedent is the clause giving residence rights to the children. Quite what are the inheritance tax implications of a trust under which the members of a fluctuating class have the right to reside in a particular property is unclear (see note to Form B8.6 at para **[208.42]**). However, the potential inheritance tax difficulties will not be significant unless the house is very valuable and in any event such difficulties will usually be outweighed by the personal and family advantages in providing a home for the children. For rights of residence generally see the Preliminary Note to B8 at para **[208.1]** et seq; and for the inheritance tax implications see further, Part A, para **[200.107]**.

[229.52]

Revocation clause

I [*name*] of [*address*] hereby revoke all former testamentary dispositions made by me and declare this to be my last will.

[229.53]

Appointment of executors and trustees

1.   [*As in cl 1 of* Form C7.1 *at para* **[229.4]**.]

[229.54]

Appointment of guardians[1]

2.   [*As in cl 5 of* Form C7.2 *at para* **[229.19]**.]

1   Where there are no other suitable guardians, the oldest child, if of age, might be considered as a possible guardian for his younger siblings. As to the appointment of guardians, see Note to Forms B3.26 to B3.32 at paras **[203.43]**–**[203.54]** and the more general discussion of the law in Vol 1 at para **[28.1]** et seq.

[229.55]

Pecuniary legacies

3.   [*As in cl 3 of* Form C7.4 *at para* **[229.41]**.]

[229.56]

Specific bequests

4.   [*As in cl 4 of* Form C7.4 *at para* **[229.42]**.]

[229.57]

Rights of residence

5.   (1)   I give to my trustees [free of all sums charged thereon or otherwise secured thereon at my death (which sums shall be paid out of my residuary estate)] [and] [free of tax][1] my freehold dwellinghouse known as [*name*] and

situate at [*address*] [or any other dwellinghouse owned by me at my death and occupied by me as my residence][2] [and the contents thereof][3] upon trust for the purpose of providing a home for my children until my youngest child for the time being living has attained the age of [18/21/25] years;[4] I wish my trustees not to sell the said dwellinghouse while any of my children are under the said age and I wish them to sell the same as soon as no living child of mine is under the said age and [any child of mine]/[a majority of my children] shall in writing request them to do so].[5]

(2) While the said dwellinghouse shall remain unsold my trustees shall permit my children or any of them to reside therein and may permit any guardian of a child of mine or any other person to reside therein if in the opinion of my trustees such residence by such guardian or other person will be for the benefit of a child of mine.

(3) Any person permitted to reside in the said dwellinghouse under the foregoing trust or power shall do so on such terms as to the payment of rates taxes and other outgoings and the repair and insurance of the said dwellinghouse as my trustees shall think fit.[6]

(4) Subject as aforesaid my said dwellinghouse [and the contents thereof] and the net proceeds of sale thereof [respectively] shall fall into and form part of my residuary estate hereinafter defined.[7]

[(5) My trustees shall not be under any obligation to make an inventory of any chattels devolving under this clause nor to see to the repair or insurance of the same].[8]

[(6) Section 11(1) of the Trusts of Land and Appointment of Trustees Act 1996 (consultation with beneficiaries) shall not apply to the exercise by my trustees of their power of sale of the said dwellinghouse at any time when no living child of mine is under the said age.][9]

---

1   The inheritance tax on land in the UK is a testamentary expense (see B14 at para **[214.55]**), and strictly speaking these words are only needed if the residence is outside the UK or might be replaced by one which is. If the testator is already living outside the UK there are special factors to consider, such as foreign laws of succession: see further C14 at para **[236.5]**. See cl 7 of this form at para **[229.59]** for the definition of 'free of tax'.

       Where there are specific gifts or pecuniary legacies elsewhere in the will which are declared to be 'free of tax', it would be a good idea to include those words here as well, even if the residence is in the UK, to avoid any suggestion that, because of the absence of those words here when they are included elsewhere, this gift is intended to be subject to tax.

2   These ensure that the gift of the rights of residence will not be adeemed if the original dwellinghouse is sold and replaced by another.

3   Settlements of chattels are not usually to be recommended (see Preliminary Note to B4 at para **[204.2]** et seq), but may be convenient in a case such as this where the household effects will be required by the occupants. If the contents are settled on the same trusts as the house a provision in the terms of sub-cl (5) below should be included. If not, sub-cl (5) and the words in square brackets in sub-cl (4) should be omitted.

4   The intention that the house should not be sold while the youngest child is under the specified age is expressed in precatory terms rather than as a binding direction in order to avoid the risk of creating a strict settlement of the dwellinghouse.

5   If included, the proviso will ensure that a child or a majority of the children will be entitled to have the property sold once the youngest child has attained the specified age.

6   The trustees will be able to apply income or capital of the residuary estate held on trust for children residing in the house, in exercise of their powers under the TA 1925, ss 31 and 32 as modified, to pay outgoings on the property on behalf those children.

7   If the contents of the house are not included in the gift, the words in both sets of square brackets in this clause should be omitted.

8   See n 3 supra. If the contents of the house are not included in the gift, this subclause should be omitted.

9   This subclause should be included if the wish is expressed in sub-cl (1) that there should be a sale at the request of any child, but will not be necessary unless cl 11, sub-cl 2 of this form is not included (see para **[229.63]**).

[229.58]

Administration trusts of residue

6.   [*As in cl 3 of* Form C7.1 *at para* **[229.6]**.]

[229.59]

Gifts made free of tax

7.   [*As in cl 6 of* Form C7.4 *at para* **[229.44]**.]

[229.60]

Beneficial trusts of residue

8.   [*As in cl 7 of* Form C7.2 *at para* **[229.21]**.]

[229.61]

Maintenance, accumulation and advancement[1]

9.   [*As in cl 5 of* Form C7.1 *at para* **[229.8]**.]

1   If the proviso to Form C7.1, cl 5(2) is incorporated in this form, the age referred to in it should be that which is selected as the highest age to which accumulation and maintenance trusts of income can continue by virtue of Form C7.2, cl 7(2) at para **[229.21]** (incorporated by reference into this form).

[229.62]

Administrative powers

10.   [*As in cl 6 of* Form C7.1 *at para* **[229.9]**.]

[229.63]

Trustee liability

11.   [*As in cl 7 of* Form C7.1 *at para* **[229.10]**.]

[229.64]

Professional trustee charging clause

12.   [*As in cl 8 of* Form C7.1 *at para* **[229.11]**.]

[*Testimonium and attestation clause as in* Form C7.3 *at para* **[229.36]**.]

C8 Wills for sole parents with adult children

PRELIMINARY NOTE

[230.1]
These forms are entitled forms for widows or widowers, but they are suitable for other sole parents. The forms in C7 for sole parents with young children concentrate on providing for the children, but where a sole parent's children are grown up there are wider possibilities as to the form which testamentary dispositions may take. In particular, there is the possibility of making 'generation skipping' provision for grandchildren, which has the advantages set out in Part A, para **[200.91]**. The most usual form of a trust for grandchildren is an accumulation and maintenance trust: for discussion of the inheritance tax aspects of this type of trust see Part A, paras **[200.119]**–**[200.136]** and for further discussion of the taxation and other aspects of it see the Note to Form C8.4 at paras **[230.45]**–**[230.52]**.

[230.2]

FORM C8.1:   Will of widow or widower leaving residue to children absolutely

NOTE

This form incorporates an absolute gift of residue to the testator's surviving children with a substitutional proviso in favour of the issue of any predeceasing child.

[230.3]

Revocation clause

I [*name*] of [*address*] hereby revoke all former testamentary dispositions made by me and declare this to be my last will.

[230.4]

Appointment of executors and trustees

1.   I appoint my son [*name*] my daughter [*name*] and my son [*name*] (hereinafter together called 'my trustees' which expression shall include my personal representatives for the time being and the trustees for the time being hereof) to be the executors and trustees of this will.

[230.5]

Pecuniary legacies

2.   I give free of tax[1] the following pecuniary legacies:

    (a)   to [*name*] of [*address*] the sum of £——;
    (b)   to [*name*] of [*address*] the sum of £——;
    (c)   to [*name*] of [*address*] the sum of £——.

1   Although the inheritance tax on legacies or specific gifts of UK property is a testamentary expense, it is preferable to include an express direction that a pecuniary legacy is free of tax in case residue includes foreign property or settled property; if it does include such property, a proportion of the legacies, corresponding to the proportion of residue which made up of foreign or settled property, would probably have to bear inheritance in the absence of a direction to the contrary. See, further, the Note to B14 at para **[214.63]**. For the definition of 'free of tax' see cl 5 of this form at para **[230.8]**.

[230.6]

Gifts of chattels[1]

3.   (1)   I make the following specific bequests free of tax:[2]

    (a)   to [my son] [*name*] [my/my late husband's] gold watch;
    (b)   to [my daughter] [*name*] [my/my late wife's] jewellery;
    (c)   to [my son] [*name*] [my/my late husband's] gold cuff-links.

(2)   Subject as aforesaid I give all my personal chattels as defined by section 55(1)(x) of the Administration of Estates Act 1925[3] free of tax[4] to such of my said children [*name*] [*name*] and [*name*] as shall survive me if more than one in equal shares [And I request them (but without imposing any trust or binding obligation) to give effect to any wishes as to the disposition of such chattels which may be contained in any memorandum that may be found amongst my papers at my death or which may have otherwise been communicated to her during my life].[5]

1   Gifts are made of specific items, and the remainder of the personal chattels are left to the children who survive the testator. Where all three children of the testator survive him or her, the latter gift will have the same effect as if the chattels had been left to fall into residue, but if a child predeceases the testator the chattels will go to the surviving children. This may introduce an element of unfairness as between families, but it avoids chattels being included in the deceased child's issue's share of residue, which may well have to be retained and managed by the trustees until the deceased child's issue attain the vesting age. It also means that the chattels

are at the disposal of persons who are of full age who can (if they an agree among themselves) give away items to relatives and friends of the testator.

2   This is included in case any of the chattels are outside the UK at the testator's death, and thus 'subject to tax' in the absence of a direction to the contrary. See the Note to B14 at para **[214.71]** and the definition of 'free of tax' in cl 5 of this form at para **[230.8]**.

3   See Part G, para **[246.52]** for the wording of this definition, and for further discussion of the meaning of 'personal chattels' see Vol 1, para **[64.44]**.

4   See the note to the last preceding subclause at para **[230.5]**.

5   If property bequeathed by a will to one person is distributed to another person in accordance with wishes expressed by the testator within two years of his death, it is treated for inheritance tax purposes as having been bequeathed by the will to that other person: Inheritance Tax Act 1984 (ITA 1984), s 143; see also B4 at para **[204.6]**.

[230.7]

Administration trusts of residue

4.   (1)   I give all my property not hereby or by any codicil hereto otherwise effectively disposed of [(including any entailed or other property over which I shall have at my death a general power of disposition by will)][1] to my trustees to hold on the trusts set out below with power at their discretion to sell all or any of it as and when they think fit.[2]

(2)   My trustees shall pay my funeral and testamentary expenses[3] and debts and any legacies given by this will or any codicil hereto out of such property or its proceeds and shall have a discretion as to how such payments shall be borne as between capital and income.[4]

(3)   Subject as above my trustees shall hold such property and the assets from time to time representing the same (hereinafter called 'my residuary estate') on the trusts set out below and shall invest all money comprised in such property or arising from its sale in any of the investments hereby authorised with power to change such investments into any others hereby authorised.

(4)   In the administration of my estate and the execution of the trusts of this will or of any codicil to it:

(a)   my trustees shall treat all income as accruing on the date on which it becomes payable regardless of the period in respect of which it shall have accrued and shall not make any statutory apportionment of the same;[5] and

(b)   none of the equitable rules of apportionment between capital and income shall apply in any circumstances whatever.[6]

1   Subject to any express contrary intention, property subject to a general power will be carried by a residuary gift under the WA 1837, s 27 (Part G, para **[244.27]**), but in the case of entailed property the will must refer to the property, or the instrument under which it was acquired, or entailed property generally for the statutory power of disposition to be exercised: LPA 1925, s 176(1), (Part G, para **[244.53]**). Although no new entails can be created on or after 1 January 1997 (see paras **[200.52]** and **[200.53]**), entails created before that date can continue to exist and, if they do, the statutory power of disposition of them by will continues to be available .

2   For the reasons for providing a power of sale rather than a trust for sale, see para **[214.1]** et seq. This wording could be made even more concise, such as 'My trustees shall have power to sell all or any of such property' or as appears in the AEA 1925, s 33(1), as amended by the TLATA 1996, Sch 2, para 5 (Part G, para **[244.58]**). One reason for using the slightly more elaborate wording in this form is that it follows the wording which was held in *Re Pitcairn* [1896] 2 Ch 199 to prevent the rule in *Howe v Dartmouth* from applying, (see Note at paras **[214.35]**–**[214.37]** for exclusion of the rule), although to save possible argument about the effect of this wording the express exclusion of the apportionment rules is also retained in sub-cl (4). Another

reason is that this wording should also serve to create a mixed fund of residuary realty and personalty (see para **[214.64]** for the significance of this).

3   Testamentary expenses will include inheritance tax on UK free estate, including real property: ITA 1984, s 211(1) (Part G, para **[246.83]**; see also the Note to B14 at paras **[214.55]**–**[214.63]**). Accordingly, even if specific gifts or pecuniary legacies are intended to be free of inheritance tax, it will not be necessary to make express provision for the incidence of inheritance tax unless (in the case of a specific gift) the gift is of property of a kind which bears its own tax, or (in the case of a pecuniary legacy) the legacy is payable out of property (usually residue) which includes property of a kind which bears its own tax. The main relevant categories of property bearing its own tax are foreign property and property which is settled property immediately before the testator's death: see the Note to B14 at paras **[214.55]**–**[214.63]** (settled property can be disposed of under a will where it is subject to a general testamentary power of appointment or is entailed—see n 1 supra).

4   A discretion as to the apportionment between capital and income of the burden of liabilities is a middle way between the strict rule in *Allhusen v Whittell* (1867) LR 4 Eq 295 (see Vol 1, para **[38.26]** and para **[214.43]**) with its complex calculations, and a direction to pay the liabilities out of capital which can have the unsatisfactory consequences referred to at para **[214.44]**.

5   See the Note to B14 at paras **[214.48]**–**[214.52]** for statutory apportionment of income over time and its exclusion.

6   See Vol 1, paras **[38.17]**–**[38.27]**, for the rules of equitable apportionment between capital and income, and the Note to B14 at para **[214.35]** et seq for the reasons and techniques for excluding those rules. It is hoped that these words will exclude the rule in *Howe v Earl of Dartmouth* (1802) 7 Ves 137 and *Re Earl Chesterfield's Trusts* (1883) 24 Ch D 643. The power of sale in sub-cl (1) of this clause may also serve to do so (see n 2 supra). For alternative strategies see further the Note to B14 at para **[214.38]** and Forms B14.4 at para **[214.13]** and B14.27 at para **[214.42]**.

[230.8]

Gifts made free of tax

5.   Any specific gift or pecuniary or general legacy made by this will or any codicil hereto which is expressed to be 'free of tax' shall be free from the payment of any inheritance tax or foreign tax or duty payable on or by reason of my death to which such gift or legacy would otherwise be subject and such inheritance tax or foreign tax or duty shall be paid out of my residuary estate.[1]

1   See the note to Form C3.1, cl 5 at para **[224.15]** and the note to cl 2 of this form at para **[230.5]** and cl 3 of this form at para **[230.6]**. Where specific gifts and pecuniary legacies are of, or wholly payable out of, free estate in the UK, the inheritance tax on them will be a testamentary expense payable out of residue without any express provision, and it is only where a specific gift or pecuniary legacy is of foreign or settled property, or wholly or partly payable out of such property, and intended to be free of tax, that it needs to be expressly declared to be free of tax. See also the Note to B14 at para **[214.55]**.

[230.9]

Beneficial trusts of residue

6.   (1)   My trustees shall hold my residuary estate upon trust for such of my children [*name*] [*name*] and [*name*][1] as shall survive me and if more than one in equal shares.

(2)   Provided that if any of my said children shall predecease me leaving issue me surviving who shall attain the age of [18/21/25/30] years[2] such issue shall take through all degrees according to their stocks the share of my residuary estate which such deceased child of mine would have taken had he or she survived me and so that no issue shall take whose parent (being such issue as aforesaid) survives me and attains the said age.[3]

(3)   The trusts declared by the foregoing sub-clause shall carry the intermediate income of my residuary estate and section 31 of the Trustee Act 1925 (as hereinafter modified) shall apply thereto.

(4)   Section 32 of the Trustee Act 1925 (as hereinafter modified) shall apply in relation to the said trusts.

(5)   Subject as aforesaid my trustees shall hold my residuary estate and the income thereof upon trust for [such of my nephews and nieces [*name*] [*name*] [*name*] and [*name*]] as shall survive me if more than one in equal shares provided that if any of my said [nephews and nieces] shall predecease me leaving issue me surviving who shall attain the age of [18/21/25/30] years[4] such issue shall take through all degrees according to their stocks the share of my residuary estate which such deceased [nephew or niece] of mine would have taken had he or she survived me and so that no issue shall take whose parent (being such issue as aforesaid) survives me and attains the said age.[5]

(6)   Subject as aforesaid my trustees shall hold my residuary estate and the income thereof upon trust for [such charitable purposes or institutions (whether corporate or not) having exclusively charitable purposes and in such proportions as they think fit].

1   Identifying the children who are intended to take by name will have the effect of excluding any other children, eg illegitimate children, who might otherwise be able to claim an interest.
2   Since the eligible issue are all ascertained at the testator's death, they will all be lives in being for perpetuity purposes and the vesting age for their interests need not therefore be limited to 21.
3   The wording of the substitutional proviso is based on the wording of the statutory trusts contained in the AEA 1925, s 47(1)(i) (Part G, para **[244.61]**). A substitutional proviso which is limited to children may be more appropriate to the testator's family circumstances, in which case Form C4.2, cl 7(2) at para **[226.43]** may be adopted instead.
4   See n 2 supra.
5   See n 3 supra.

[230.10]

Maintenance, accumulation and advancement[1]

7.   (1)   Section 31 of the Trustee Act 1925 (relating to accumulation and maintenance) shall apply in relation to the trusts hereby or by any codicil hereto declared as if:

(a)   in paragraph (i) of subsection (1) of the said section the words 'as the trustees think fit' were substituted for the words 'as may in all the circumstances be reasonable'; and
(b)   the proviso to the said subsection (1) were omitted.

(2)   Section 32 of the Trustee Act 1925 (relating to advancement) shall apply in relation to the said trusts as if the words 'one half of' were omitted from proviso (a) to subsection (1) thereof [provided that the powers conferred by the said section (as hereby enlarged) shall not be exercisable in favour of any minor beneficiary hereunder otherwise than so as to cause such beneficiary to become immediately entitled to or to an interest in possession in the capital thereby paid or applied within the meaning of section 71(1)(a) of the Inheritance Tax Act 1984].[2]

(3)   Whenever my trustees shall have an obligation or discretion under the provisions of this will or any codicil hereto or under the general law to apply

income or capital for the benefit of a minor beneficiary they may either pay the same without liability to account to his or her parent guardian or any other adult person with whom such beneficiary may be residing or to such beneficiary himself or herself if of the age of 16 years or more and so that the receipt of such parent guardian or other person or of such minor beneficiary shall be a full and sufficient discharge to my trustees for the income or capital so applied.[3]

1   For alternative provisions relating to maintenance and advancement see Forms B18.11 to B18.23 and the notes thereto at paras **[218.77]–[218.107]**.
2   The proviso is included in order to prevent the power prejudicing the application of the ITA 1984, s 71 (accumulation and maintenance trusts), but is probably unnecessary: see the Note on inheritance tax and the statutory power of advancement in B18 at paras **[218.85]–[218.102]**. If the accumulation and maintenance trusts of income are extended so as to continue beyond the age of 18 (see eg, Forms B18.12 and B18.13 at paras **[218.78]–[218.79]**), then 'minor beneficiary hereunder' should be amended to eg 'beneficiary hereunder who is under the age of [*n*] years' where *n* is the highest age at which an absolute interest or an interest in possession might be attained by any of the beneficiaries.
3   A parent (with parental responsibility) and a guardian of a minor are empowered by the ChA 1989, s 3(3) (Part G, para **[244.119]**) to give a good receipt for the minor's property: see Vol 1, para **[9.42]**. The power in this subclause is wider in that it authorises the payment of income or capital to a parent who does not have parental responsibility, any adult with whom the minor is residing, and the minor himself or herself if 16 or over.

[230.11]

Administrative powers[1]

8.   (1)   In this clause where the context so admits:

(a)   the expression 'land' includes buildings and estates interests or rights of any kind in or over land; and

(b)   during the administration of my estate the expression 'beneficiary' includes any person who would be a beneficiary if such administration had been completed and the expression 'beneficially interested' and references to income of any asset being payable or capable of being paid to or for the benefit of a beneficiary shall be construed accordingly.

(2)   None of the powers or provisions contained in subclause (3) below of this clause shall be capable of being exercised or operating in any manner such that if such power or provision were capable of being so exercised or so operating the existence of the same would either:

(i)   prevent any person who would in the absence of such power or provision have been entitled to an interest in possession (within the meaning of Part III of the Inheritance Tax Act 1984) in any property from being entitled to such interest; or

(ii)   prevent section 71 of the Inheritance Tax Act 1984 from applying to any property to which in the absence of such power or provision the said section 71 would have applied.[2]

(3)   In the administration of my estate and the execution of the trusts hereof or of any codicil hereto my trustees shall have the following powers in addition to those conferred by law but subject to the last foregoing subclause:

(a)   power to invest moneys sell assets and change investments with the unrestricted freedom of choice and powers of disposition and acquisition of a sole beneficial owner with in particular power to make unsecured loans, acquire non-income yielding assets, and purchase land anywhere in the world or chattels for any purpose including occupation or enjoyment in kind by a beneficiary under the power set out below;[3]

(b) power to delegate all or any of their investment powers to a professional investment manager or managers whether individual or corporate and whether or not also a nominee holder of assets for my trustees (and who may be or include one or more of my trustees or the beneficiaries hereunder) upon such terms as to remuneration and otherwise (including terms authorising self-dealing or providing for the limitation of the liability of the investment manager or managers) as my trustees think fit and section 22 of the Trustee Act 2000 shall not apply;[4]

(c) power to vest or register any property in any person or persons whether individual or corporate and whether or not an investment manager to whom powers have been delegated under the foregoing power (and who may be or include one or more of my trustees or the beneficiaries hereunder) as nominee or nominees for my trustees upon such terms as to remuneration or otherwise (including terms authorising self-dealing or providing for the limitation of the liability of the nominee) as my trustees think fit and section 22 of the Trustee Act 2000 shall not apply;[5]

(d) power to borrow money with or without giving security and on such terms as to interest and repayment and otherwise as my trustees may think fit for any purpose connected with the administration of my estate or the trusts declared herein or in any codicil hereto (including investment) and no lender from whom my trustees borrow money in purported exercise of this power shall be concerned to enquire as to the propriety amount or purpose of any such borrowing;[6]

(e) power to lend money to a beneficiary to whom any of the income of such money is payable or to whom or for whose benefit any income of such money is capable of being paid or applied in exercise of a discretion (or who would be such a beneficiary if such money yielded income) and to do so at a full or concessionary rate of interest or interest free;[7]

(f) all the powers of an absolute owner in relation to any land (wherever situated) held by them;[8]

(g) power to apply capital held on the same trusts as any land (or which would be so held if the administration of my estate had been completed) in the improvement of such land and to apply such capital or the income of such capital on the repair or maintenance of such land;[9]

(h) power to permit any beneficiary to have the beneficial occupation use or enjoyment in kind of any land or chattel or other tangible property on such terms as to repair insurance or payment of outgoings by the beneficiary or otherwise howsoever as my trustees think fit Provided that the foregoing power shall only be exercisable and such permission to occupy or enjoy in kind may only continue in the following circumstances:

(i) so long as any of the income of such land chattel or other tangible property is payable to such beneficiary or capable of being paid or applied to him or for his benefit in exercise of a discretion (or would be so payable or capable of being so paid or applied if such land chattel or other property yielded income);

    (ii)   in the case of land, so long as for the time being the occupation thereof by such beneficiary is compatible with any statutory rights of occupation of any other beneficiary or beneficiaries;[10]

  (i)   power to exercise all the powers of appropriation (and other incidental powers) conferred by statute on a personal representative without the necessity of obtaining any consents and notwithstanding that one or more of my trustees may be beneficially interested in the exercise of such power.[11]

1   For notes on administrative powers and the powers conferred by the general law, and for other examples of administrative powers, see B20 at para **[220.1]** et seq. For a set of administrative powers which include powers in respect of business assets see Form C11.1, cl 6 at para **[233.21]**. The TLATA 1996 and the Trustee Act 2000 (TrA 2000) have much increased the statutory powers of trustees, and many wills and will trusts could manage without any of the powers in this clause being conferred expressly, or just with the power to borrow and the power of appropriation without consent. The differences to the relevant statutory powers of the powers in this clause that overlap with statutory powers are set out in the notes below. The only power which before 1997 was included in this clause that has been omitted because there are now statutory powers which render express provision unnecessary is the power to insure: see the Trustee Act 1925 (TA 1925), s 19, as substituted by the TrA 2000, s 34 (Part G, para **[246.17]**; see also B20 at para **[220.51]**).

2   This is a general restriction so as to prevent the administrative powers prejudicing the intended inheritance tax status of the beneficial trusts, either as interest in possession trusts or as accumulation and maintenance trusts within the ITA 1984, s 71. See further the General Preliminary Note to B20 at para **[220.5]** et seq.

3   This power is wider than the statutory powers of investment in the TrA 2000, ss 3 and 8 (Part G, paras **[246.118]** and **[246.123]** and the notes on them at paras **[220.12]**–**[220.19]**) in that it permits unsecured loans, the purchase of land outside the UK, and the purchase of interests in land (such as undivided shares) which are not legal estates. The attempt can be made to exclude the statutory obligations relating to diversification and suitability of investments, and the requirement of taking advice, but, as now enacted in the TrA 2000, these cannot be excluded (although their effect can be cut down by clauses exonerating trustees from liability for negligence): see the TrA 2000, ss 4 and 5 (Part G, paras **[246.119]** and **[246.120]**; see also para **[220.37]**.

4   This is wider than the statutory power to appoint investment managers in the TrA 2000, Pt IV, ss 11–15 (Part G, paras **[246.126]**–**[246.130]**; see also paras **[220.35]** and **[220.36]**), in that the detailed procedural requirements of the TrA 2000, s 15 do not apply; the trustees have a wider discretion as to restricting an investment manager's liability or permitting self-dealing by him (compare the TrA 2000, s 14(2): Part G, para **[246.129]**, under which these can only be done if it is reasonably necessary); beneficiaries can be appointed (this is forbidden in exercise of the statutory power by the TrA 2000, s 12(3)); and the duty to review the arrangement from time to time under the TrA 2000, s 22 (Part G, para **[246.137]**) does not apply. The by-passing of the TrA 2000, ss 14 and 15 is only effective if those statutory provisions apply only to the statutory powers of delegation, and do not apply to express powers to delegate investment management functions – something which is not at all clear (see para **[220.37]**). Even though trustees have an express power of this kind, unless and until there is either a definitive decision of the courts, or amending legislation, which makes it certain that ss 14 and 15 are excluded by such a power, trustees should regard themselves as bound by ss 14 and 15.

5   This is wider than the statutory power to appoint nominees in the TrA 2000, Pt IV, ss 16–20 (Part G, **[246.131]**–**[246.135]**; see also para **[220.36]**), in that the trustees have a wider discretion as to restricting a nominee's liability or permitting self-dealing by him (compare TrA 2000, s 20(2): Part G, para **[246.135]**, under which these can only be done if it is reasonably necessary); the persons who may be appointed nominees are not confined to persons carrying on a business as nominees, a company controlled by the trustees, or a solicitors' incorporated practice (compare the TrA, 2000, s 19(2): Part G, para **[246.134]**); and the duty to review the arrangement from time to time under the TrA 2000, s 22 (Part G, para **[246.137]**) does not apply.

6   There is no power under the general law for trustees to borrow money for the purposes of investment: see para **[220.69]**, n 1.

7   The investment power in sub-cl (a) above permits unsecured lending on a commercial basis, but express authorisation as in this subclause is needed to lend or continue to lend for the purpose

of benefiting the borrower: see para **[220.32]**. A power to apply capital for the benefit of a beneficiary could in appropriate circumstances enable capital to be lent to him on beneficial terms.

8   The statutory power of management of land expressed in similar terms in the TLATA 1996, s 6(1) (Part G, para **[246.91]**) applies only to land in England and Wales, and that in the TrA 2000, s 8(3) applies only to land acquired under the power in that section. As the power to acquire land in this clause is wider than the statutory power (see n 3 supra), it is appropriate to provide an express power rather than rely on the statute.

9   See para **[220.52]** for the reasons for this provision.

10   See the Note and forms concerning enjoyment in kind in B18 at para **[218.108]** and the Preliminary Note on investment powers in B20 at para **[220.30]**. For the statutory rights of occupation under the TLATA 1996, see paras **[208.5]**–**[208.18]** and the TLATA, ss 12 and 13: (Part G, paras **[246.98]** and **[246.99]**). A power as in this subclause is primarily relevant to a wholly discretionary trust, and it is made subject to any statutory rights of occupation because interest in possession trusts might come to be created in exercise of a power of appointment or application. A power to permit occupation by a beneficiary of trust land is not needed in relation to land in an interest in possession trust, because the statutory rights of occupation will be sufficient provision for beneficiary occupation and anyway are likely to leave no room for permissive occupation by beneficiaries who have no rights of occupation. A clause of this kind can be included in relation to an accumulation and maintenance trust intended to be within the ITA 1984, s 71, but should always be subject an overriding restriction to prevent the power prejudicing the s 71 status of the trusts, such as the proviso at the end of this clause. For the effect of conditions as to repair etc imposed on a beneficiary occupying or enjoying in kind trust property, see the Preliminary Note to B8 at paras **[208.26]**–**[208.28]**.

11   For the statutory power of partition of land, see the TLATA 1996, s 7 (Part G, para **[246.92]**) and for the statutory power of appropriation referred to here see the AEA 1925, s 41 (Part G, para **[246.50]**; see also Vol 1, paras **[29.17]**–**[29.23]** and B20 at para **[220.70]**. A power of appropriation as in this subclause will be exercisable in circumstances when the power in the TLATA 1996, s 7 cannot be exercised, eg where a share of the land is still settled, and without the consent of beneficiaries. Exercise of a power of this kind which does not require the consent of beneficiaries may have stamp duty or capital gains tax advantages over one which does: see para **[220.72]**.

[230.12]

Trustee liability

9,   (1)   My trustees shall not be liable for any act or default of any investment manager or nominee employed in good faith to manage or hold assets of my estate nor for any act or default of any beneficiary having the occupation use or enjoyment of property in kind.[1]

(2)   Section 11(1) of the Trusts of Land and Appointment of Trustees Act 1996 (consultation with beneficiaries) shall not apply to the exercise by my trustees of any of their powers in relation to land subject to the trusts hereof.[2]

1   This makes it clear that the trustees are not liable for the defaults of others who may have possession or control of trust property. For a wider form of indemnity, see eg Form B21.12 at para **[221.16]**.

2   The requirement that trustees of land, in exercise of any function relating to land subject to the trust, consult with beneficiaries of full age beneficially entitled to an interest in possession in the land can be excluded: TLATA 1996, s 11 (Part G, para **[246.97]**).

[230.13]

Receipts on behalf of charitable institutions

10.   The receipt of the person who professes to be the treasurer or other proper officer for the time being of any institution (whether corporate or not) shall be a sufficient discharge to my trustees in respect of any money or other asset which

becomes payable or transferable to such institution under any exercise of any power or discretion herein contained.

[230.14]

Professional trustee charging clause

11.   Any of my trustees being a professional or business man may charge and be paid all usual professional and other proper charges for business transacted acts done advice given and time spent by him or his firm in connection with the administration of my estate or in connection with the trusts hereof including acts which a personal representative or trustee not being in any profession or business could have done personally.

[230.15]

Testimonium and attestation clause

IN WITNESS whereof I have hereunto set my hand this —— day of —— 20——

SIGNED by the above-named [testator/testatrix] as [his/her] last will in the presence of us both present at the same time who at [his/her] request and in [his/her] presence and in the presence of each other have signed our names below as witnesses:

    [Signature of testator/testatrix]

[*Signatures, addresses and descriptions of two witnesses*]

[230.16]

FORM C8.2:   Will of widow or widower dividing residue between son and daughter, son's share being settled on protective trusts for his benefit and daughter's share being either given to her absolutely or settled on trusts for her benefit

NOTE

In this form it is assumed that the son is in financial difficulty, eg because he is a Lloyd's name, or that he is otherwise in need of financial protection. His share of residue is settled on trusts for his benefit under which he takes a protected life interest with power for the trustees to reinstate his interest after forfeiture. It is considered that trusts in this Form are trusts 'to the like effect' as those contained in the TA 1925, s 33 (Part G, para **[246.28]**), but there has not yet been an expression of opinion on this by the Revenue. If they are trusts to the like effect as those in the TA 1925, s 33 the son will be treated as having an interest in possession in his share for inheritance tax purposes even if he has forfeited his life interest: see the ITA 1984, s 88 and Part A, para **[200.116]**. Power is also included for the trustees to apply capital for the son's benefit, something which the Revenue have said they regard as not preventing a predecessor of the ITA 1984, s 88 from applying (see Part A, para **[200.116]**). There are also powers to appoint a life interest to a widow and a power to appoint capital among issue, exercisable by the trustees rather than the son, because of the possibility of the son becoming bankrupt.

[230.17]

As regards the daughter's share this form includes two options. Under the first she takes the share absolutely if surviving with a substitutional proviso for her children (or for her issue generally). Under the second her share is settled on conventional trusts giving her a life interest, a power to appoint a life interest to a widower, a power of appointment amongst her issue and a default trust for her children (with substitution of issue). A power for the trustees to apply capital for her benefit is also included, and if she has no issue at or after attaining the age of 50 she has a general power to appoint her share by deed. If she dies at any time without issue she has a general testamentary power of appointment.

[230.18]

Revocation clause

I [*name*] of [*address*] hereby revoke all former testamentary dispositions made by me and declare this to be my last will.

[230.19]

Appointment of executors and trustees

1.   I appoint [my son [*name*]]¹ [and] my daughter [*name*] [and [*name*] of [*address*]]² (hereinafter together called 'my trustees' which expression shall include my personal representatives for the time being and the trustees for the time being hereof) to be the executors and trustees of this will.

1   Clause 9 of this form allows a trustee to exercise powers for his or her own benefit in certain circumstances. However, if there is a real risk that the son may become bankrupt, it would be better not to appoint him as an executor. It will in particular be an embarrassment if he has to join in any exercise of discretions or powers under which income or capital is diverted away from his trustee in bankruptcy.

2   If the son and daughter are appointed executors, it may be sensible to appoint a third, independent executor to act as a mediator should any disputes arise, and it will be useful to have a third appointee in case the son decides not to prove the will, eg because he has become bankrupt. There is also the point that exercise of powers in favour of the son and/or daughter will require an independent trustee also making the exercise: see cl 9 of this form at para **[230.27]**. If the son is not appointed an executor then another executor in addition to the daughter will of course be needed.

[230.20]

Pecuniary legacies

2.   I give free of tax¹ the following pecuniary legacies:

   (a)   to the Vicar and Churchwardens of [*name*] Church, [*location*], the sum of £—— [as an addition to the church restoration fund];

   (b)   to the —— Golf Club the sum of £—— for the general purposes of the Club and the receipt of the person professing to be the treasurer or other proper officer of the Club shall be a full and sufficient discharge to my trustees;

   (c)   to my friend [*name*] of [*address*] the sum of £——.

1   See the note to Form C8.1, cl 2 at para **[230.5]**.

[230.21]

Gift of chattels[1]

3.   I give free of tax[2] all my personal chattels as defined by section 55(1)(x) of the Administration of Estates Act 1925[3] to [such of my son and my daughter as shall survive me and if both in equal shares] [my daughter absolutely and I request her (but without imposing any trust or binding obligation upon her) to give effect to any wishes of mine as to the disposition of such chattels which may be contained in any memorandum which may be found amongst my papers at my death or which may have otherwise been communicated to her during my life].

1   A gift of chattels to the daughter with a request to distribute in accordance with the testator's known wishes is included as an alternative to a simple gift of chattels to the son and daughter equally in case there is a real danger of the son going bankrupt. A gift conferring power on the trustees to distribute the chattels amongst members of the family may be preferred in which case Form B4.11 at para **[204.25]** could be used.

2   See Form C8.1, cl 3, n 2 at para **[230.6]**.

3   See Form C8.1, cl 3, n 3 at para **[230.6]**.

[230.22]

Administration trusts of residue

4.   [*As in cl 4 of* Form C8.1 *at para* **[230.7]**.]

[230.23]

Gifts made free of tax

5.   [*As in cl 5 of* Form C8.1 *at para* **[230.8]**.]

[230.24]

Beneficial trusts of residue[1]

6.   (1)   My trustees shall hold my residuary estate upon trust to divide the same into two equal half shares (hereinafter respectively called 'my son's share' and 'my daughter's share').

(2)   My trustees shall hold my son's share upon the following trusts:

(a)   my trustees shall hold the income of my son's share upon protective trusts for my son's benefit during his life provided that:

(i)   none of my trustees shall be liable for paying to my son the income of my son's share accruing after the forfeiture of his protected life interest unless such trustee shall have express notice of the act thing or event giving rise to the forfeiture; and

(ii)   if and as often as my son shall do or attempt to do or suffer any act or thing or any event shall occur which causes his interest to determine my trustees may in writing reinstate his protective life interest and my son shall thereupon become entitled to a protected life interest in the income of my residuary estate accruing thereafter as if no forfeiture had occurred (but without prejudice to any forfeiture by reason of any act thing or event occurring after such reinstatement);[2]

(b)   subject as aforesaid my trustees shall have power at any time during the life of my son by deed or deeds revocable during his life or irrevocable to appoint to any wife who may survive my son as his widow (including power to appoint to a named wife contingently on her surviving him as his widow) an interest in the income of the whole or any part or parts of my son's share for the residue of her life or for any less period and in exercise of the foregoing power may appoint a protective trust of such income for the benefit of such widow for such period within the meaning of section 33 of the Trustee Act 1925;[3]

(c) subject as aforesaid my trustees shall hold my son's share upon trust for all or such one or more exclusive of the others or other of his children and remoter issue and if more than one in such shares and upon and with such trusts powers and provisions (including trusts and powers conferring a discretion on any person or persons as to the distribution of capital or income and including provisions relating to the accumulation of income during any period permitted by law and administrative provisions of whatever nature) as my trustees shall during the life of my son by deed or deeds revocable during the life of my son or irrevocable in their absolute discretion appoint;

(d) subject as aforesaid my trustees shall hold my son's share upon trust for such of his children as shall attain the age of [18/21] years and if more than one in equal shares;

(e) the foregoing trust shall carry the intermediate income of my son's share (so far as not disposed of under any trust or power having priority thereto) and section 31 of the Trustee Act 1925 (as hereinafter modified) shall apply thereto;

(f) section 32 of the Trustee Act 1925 (as hereinafter modified) shall apply in relation to the said trusts;

(g) notwithstanding the foregoing trusts powers and provisions my trustees may at any time or times and from time to time during my son's life pay transfer or apply the whole or any part or parts of the capital of my son's share to or for the benefit of my son in such manner as they think fit and whether or not any forfeiture of his foregoing protective life interest shall have occurred;

(h) if my son shall have no child who shall attain a vested interest under the foregoing trust of capital my son's share (or so much thereof as has not been paid transferred or applied under any of the powers aforesaid) shall accrue to and be held on the trusts applicable to my daughter's share and as one fund therewith for all purposes;

(i) my trustees shall have power at any time or times during the life of my son by deed to release or restrict the future exercise of any of their foregoing powers in any manner whatsoever.

EITHER

[(3) My trustees shall hold my daughter's share upon the following trusts:

(a) my trustees shall hold my daughter's share upon trust for my daughter if surviving me absolutely;

(b) if my daughter shall not survive me then my trustees shall hold my daughter's share upon trust absolutely for [such of the children of my daughter as shall survive me and attain the age of [18/21/25] years and if more than one in equal shares]/[such of the issue of my daughter who shall survive me and attain the age of [18/21/25] years and if more than one in equal shares through all degrees according to their stocks (each child of my daughter being for this purpose a head of stock) and so that no issue shall take whose parent survives me and attains the said age and is accordingly capable of taking];

(c)   if my daughter shall predecease me without leaving any issue who shall attain a vested interest under the foregoing trust my daughter's share shall accrue to and be held on the trusts applicable to my son's share and as one fund therewith for all purposes.]

OR

[(3) My trustees shall hold my daughter's share upon the following trusts:

(a)   my trustees shall hold my daughter's share upon trust to pay the income thereof to my daughter during her life;

(b)   subject as aforesaid my daughter shall have power at any time by deed or deeds revocable or irrevocable or by will or codicil to appoint to any husband who may survive her as her widower (including power to appoint to a named husband contingently on him surviving her as her widower) an interest in the income of the whole or any part or parts of my daughter's share for the residue of his life or for any less period;[4]

(c)   subject as aforesaid my trustees shall hold my daughter's share upon trust for all or such one or more exclusive of the others or other of her children and remoter issue and if more than one in such shares and upon and with such trusts powers and provisions (including trusts and powers conferring a discretion on any person or persons as to the distribution of capital or income and including provisions relating to the accumulation of income during any period permitted by law and administrative provisions of whatever nature) as my daughter shall by deed or deeds revocable or irrevocable or by will or codicil appoint;

(d)   subject to and in default of any appointment under the foregoing power my trustees shall hold my daughter's share upon trust for such of my daughter's children as shall attain the age of [18/21] years and if more than one in equal shares provided that if any of my daughter's children shall predecease me or be living at or after my death but die under the said age of [18/21] years leaving issue who shall be living at or after my death such issue shall take through all degrees according to their stocks the share of my residuary estate which such deceased child of my daughter would have taken had he or she survived to attain a vested interest and so that no issue shall take whose parent (being such issue as aforesaid) attains a vested interest under the foregoing trusts;[5]

(e)   the foregoing trusts shall carry the intermediate income of my daughter's share and section 31 of the Trustee Act 1925 (as hereinafter modified) shall apply thereto;

(f)   section 32 of the Trustee Act 1925 (as hereinafter modified) shall apply in relation to the foregoing trusts;

(g)   subject to the trusts and to any exercise of the powers aforesaid my trustees shall hold my daughter's share upon trust for such persons or purposes as she shall by will or codicil appoint;

(h) notwithstanding the foregoing trusts powers and provisions my trustees may at any time or times and from time to time during my daughter's life pay transfer or apply the whole or any part or parts of the capital of my daughter's share to or for the benefit of my daughter in such manner as they think fit;

(i) notwithstanding the foregoing trusts powers and provisions if at any time after my daughter shall have attained the age of 50 years there shall be no issue of hers living and no issue of hers shall have died after having attained a vested interest in my daughter's share under the foregoing trusts then my daughter shall have power to appoint by deed the whole or any part or parts of my daughter's share upon such trusts for such persons (including herself) or purposes as she shall think fit.]⁶

1   This clause contains the beneficial trusts outlined in the Note to this form at paras **[230.16]** and **[230.17]**.
2   The first proviso to this subclause will protect an innocent trustee who continues to pay income to the protected life tenant after the forfeiture of his interest unless he has express notice of the event giving rise to the forfeiture. The second proviso enables the trustees to restore the beneficiary to a full protected life interest. It is not entirely clear whether the Inland Revenue accept that a protective trust with a power of reinstatement of this type falls within the ITA 1984, s 88: see Part A, para **[200.116]**.
3   This power will enable advantage to be taken of the inheritance tax exemption for gifts to a spouse in relation to this share, and will allow a protective trust to be appointed. For the inheritance tax treatment of protective trusts see the Note to this form at para **[230.16]** and Part A, para **[200.116]**.
4   See n 3 supra.
5   The substitutional proviso is not very likely to be relevant. The reason for including it is that without it the daughter would, in the event of her children dying under the vesting age leaving issue, be able to appoint the fund to persons other than her issue in exercise of the testamentary general power in sub-cl (g) below.
6   The main reason for providing that if the daughter attains 50 and has no issue, she becomes entitled to a general power over the fund, as in this subclause, rather than to an absolutely vested interest, is capital gains tax: she can choose the moment of becoming absolutely entitled to the fund, or put it off indefinitely if she does not need to have absolute ownership of it. Becoming absolutely entitled is an occasion of capital gains tax charge, with hold-over relief now available in only limited circumstances: see Part A, para **[200.39]**.
    Ultimate trusts, as in Form C8.1, cl 6(5) and (6) at para **[230.9]**, could be added after this subclause.

[230.25]

Maintenance, accumulation and advancement
7.   [*As in cl 7 of* Form C8.1 *at para* **[230.10]**.]

[230.26]

Administrative powers
8.   [*As in cl 8 of* Form C8.1 *at para* **[230.11]**.]

[230.27]

Exercise of powers¹
9.   Any power or discretion hereby or by law conferred on my trustees (including a power or discretion as to the disposition of capital or income) shall be exercisable notwithstanding that any of my trustees has a personal interest in

such exercise provided that there are not fewer than two trustees and that at least one of them has no such personal interest.

1   This clause permits a member of the family to be a trustee without disqualifying him or her from benefit under any exercise of statutory or express powers of payment or application of capital, appointment, etc. See the Note to B18 at para **[218.4]**.

[230.28]

Trustee liability
10.   [*As in cl 9 of* Form C8.1 *at para* **[230.12]**.]

[230.29]

Professional trustee charging clause
11.   [*As in cl 11 of* Form C8.1 *at para* **[230.14]**.]

[*Testimonium and attestation clause as in* Form C8.1 *at para* **[230.15]**.]

[230.30]

FORM C8.3:   **Will of widow or widower leaving one share of residue on trust for the children absolutely and the other share on accumulation and maintenance trusts for the grandchildren**

NOTE

In this Form part of residue is given to the testator's children, but the Form also contains an element of 'generation skipping' by providing for the remainder of residue to be settled on immediate accumulation and maintenance trusts for the benefit of the testator's grandchildren (for 'generation skipping' dispositions see Part A, para **[200.89]**). Such trusts will qualify as accumulation and maintenance trusts within the ITA 1984, s 71 only if a grandchild is actually living at the testator's death: ITA 1984, s 71(7); see also Part A and the Note to Form C8.4 at paras **[230.45]**–**[230.52]**.

On accumulation and maintenance trusts generally see Part A, paras **[200.119]**–**[200.136]** and the Note to Form C8.4 at paras **[230.49]**–**[230.52]**.

[230.31]

Revocation clause
I [*name*] of [*address*] hereby revoke all former testamentary dispositions made by me and declare this to be my last will.

[230.32]

Appointment of executors and trustees
1.   [*As cl 1 of* Form C8.1 *at para* **[230.4]**, *or cl 1 of* Form C8.2 *at para* **[230.19]**.][1]

1   The main long-term function of the trustees will be to administer the fund for the grandchildren. It will often be appropriate for the children to be these trustees, as in Form C8.1, cl 1, but if they are likely to disagree with each other it will be better to appoint an independent executor trustee as well, as in Form C8.2, cl 1, or to appoint wholly independent executors and trustees.

[230.33]

Pecuniary legacies
2.   [*As in cl 2 of* Form C8.1 *at para* **[230.5]**.]

[230.34]

Gifts of chattels
3.   [*As in cl 3 of* Form C8.1 *at para* **[230.6]**.]

[230.35]

Administration trusts of residue
4.   [*As in cl 4 of* Form C8.1 *at para* **[230.7]**.]

[230.36]

Gifts made free of tax
5.   [*As in cl 5 of* Form C8.1 *at para* **[230.8]**.]

[230.37]

Beneficial trusts of residue[1]
6.   (1)   My trustees shall hold [a two thirds share]/[one equal half share][2] of my residuary estate (hereinafter called 'my children's fund') upon trust for such of my children as shall survive me and if more than one in equal shares absolutely provided that if any of my children shall predecease me leaving a child or children surviving me who shall attain the age of [18/21/25/30] years such last-mentioned child or children shall take absolutely and if more than one equally between them the share of my children's fund which such deceased child of mine would have taken had he or she survived me.

(2)   My trustees shall hold the balance[3] of my residuary estate (hereinafter called 'my grandchildren's fund') upon trust for such of my grandchildren (whether living at my death or [whenever][4] born thereafter) as shall attain the age of 18 years and if more than one in equal shares [per stirpes each child of mine being for this purpose a head of stock].[5]

(3)   The trusts declared by subclauses (1) and (2) hereof shall carry the intermediate income of my residuary estate and section 31 of the Trustee Act 1925 (as hereinafter modified) shall apply thereto.

(4)   Section 32 of the Trustee Act 1925 (as hereinafter modified) shall apply in relation to the said trusts and shall apply in relation to my grandchildren's fund as if each of my grandchildren were entitled to a contingent interest in capital notwithstanding the direction for retention and settlement hereinafter contained.

1   See Form C8.4, cls 7 and 8 at paras **[230.60]** and **[230.61]** for more elaborate accumulation and maintenance trusts.
2   One share of the residuary estate is given to the children equally with a substitutional proviso in favour of the children of any child of the testator who predeceases him.
3   The proportion of the residuary estate represented by the grandchildren's fund is not specified and will depend on the extent of the share given to the children by cl 6(1).
4   This will keep the class open indefinitely, instead of it being closed when the first grandchild to do so attains a vested interest: see Vol 1, para **[66.20]**.
5   Without these words the grandchildren will share equally, so that a grandchild who is part of a family of three siblings will get the same share as a grandchild who is an only child; if these

words are included each family will be treated equally, so that a family of three will together receive a share equal to that taken by an only child.

[230.38]

Settlement of grandchildren's shares of grandchildren's fund[1]

7.   (1)   The share of my grandchildren's fund to which any grandchild of mine shall become entitled on attaining the age of 18 years shall not vest in such grandchild absolutely but shall be retained by my trustees and held upon the following trusts (such share and such grandchild being hereinafter respectively referred to as 'the share' and 'the grandchild'):

(a)   my trustees shall hold the share upon trust to pay the income thereof to the grandchild during his or her life;

(b)   subject as aforesaid my trustees shall hold the share upon trust for such of the children of the grandchild as shall attain the age of [18/21/25] years or be living on the earlier occurrence of the vesting day[2] and if more than one in equal shares;

(c)   the foregoing trust shall carry the intermediate income of the share and section 31 of the Trustee Act 1925 (as hereinafter modified) shall apply thereto;

(d)   section 32 of the Trustee Act 1925 (as hereinafter modified) shall apply in relation to the share;

(e)   if the foregoing trusts of the share shall fail or determine (otherwise than by absolute vesting) before the vesting day then subject as aforesaid the share shall accrue to and be held as one fund with the other share or shares of the grandchildren's fund the trusts of which shall be for the time being subsisting and capable of taking effect (if more than one in equal proportions);

(f)   notwithstanding the trusts aforesaid my trustees may at any time or times and from time to time during the grandchild's life and before the vesting day pay transfer or apply the whole or any part or parts of the share to or for the benefit of the grandchild in such manner as they think fit.

(2)   In this clause the expression 'the vesting day' means the twenty-first anniversary of the death of the last survivor of such of my children and remoter issue as shall be living at my death.

1   The grandchildren's shares of the grandchildren's fund are settled by this and the preceding clause on fixed trusts for their benefit. If more flexible trusts are required, Form C2.6, cls 10 and 11 at paras **[224.106]** and **[224.107]** or Form C8.4, cl 8 at para **[230.61]** could readily be adapted for the purpose.

2   This expression is defined in cl 7(2). This perpetuity restriction is needed because the trust is for the children of persons who may be born after the testator's death.

[230.39]

Maintenance, accumulation and advancement

8.   [*As in cl 7 of* Form C8.1 *at para* **[230.10]**.]

[230.40]

Administrative powers

9.   [*As in cl 8 of* Form C8.1 *at para* **[230.11]**.]

[230.41]

Trustee liability
10.   [*As in cl 9 of* Form C8.1 *at para* **[230.12]**.]

[230.42]

Exercise of powers
11.   [*As in cl 9 of* Form C8.2 *at para* **[230.27]**.]

[230.43]

Professional trustee charging clause
12.   [*As in cl 11 of* Form C8.1 *at para* **[230.14]**.]

[230.44]

[*Testimonium and attestation clause as in* Form C8.1 *at para* **[230.15]**.]

[230.45]

FORM C8.4:   Will of grandparent incorporating fixed or flexible accumulation and maintenance trusts of residue for grandchildren

NOTE

This form is primarily for a testator who has one or more grandchildren, with or without a hope or expectation that more may be born, and who wishes to make a 'generation skipping' disposition in their favour of his entire estate, apart from chattels (for generation skipping dispositions see Part A, para **[200.88]**). It could also be used by a testator who does not currently have any grandchildren, but whose family circumstances are such that some might be born before the testator's death (see further para **[230.50]** concerning use of this form where there might not be any grandchildren at the testator's death). The form which the generation skipping disposition takes is an accumulation and maintenance trust falling within the ITA 1984, s 71, including an optional power to vary the shares of the grandchildren before they attain interests in possession, and provision for settlement of their shares on life interest trusts with powers to pay them capital and overriding powers of appointment. The opportunities for flexibility in an accumulation and maintenance trust are limited, because of the requirement that fixed interests vest in the beneficiaries no later than attaining the age of 25, but there is some scope for varying the shares which they will ultimately take while they are under the vesting age, and it is also possible to provide flexible powers to override the interest in possession trusts after they have attained the vesting age.

[230.46]
Accumulation and maintenance trusts within the ITA 1984, s 71 (see Part A, para **[200.119]** et seq) are often a suitable choice where a trust for a class of minors which may continue for some time is desired. The inheritance tax advantages of these in comparison with discretionary trusts are now less significant than they were formerly because the reduction of inheritance tax rates has diminished inheritance tax on discretionary trusts, but, where trusts may continue for some time, accumulation and maintenance trusts have the

advantage that if there is a change of government it is more likely that accumulation and maintenance trusts will retain their privileged position than that discretionary trusts will continue to be so lightly taxed. Even under the present inheritance tax regime a discretionary trust fund which together with any lifetime gifts made by the testator in the seven years before his death exceeded the nil-rate band would certainly be subject to an inheritance tax charge at least every ten years, while a trust fund subject to accumulation and maintenance trusts would probably not pay any inheritance tax before the beneficiaries attained vested interests, and thereafter the assets devolving on each beneficiary would be unlikely to bear inheritance tax before his or her death.

The inheritance tax advantages of an accumulation and maintenance trust over an interest in possession trust are also not as great as they used to be, but an interest in possession trust for minors is a curious and artificial device with administrative difficulties (income has to be held on trust absolutely for minor beneficiaries or their estates if they die), and a flexible interest in possession trust would become less attractive if immediate inheritance tax charges on the lifetime termination of an interest in possession were reintroduced with a resultant inheritance tax charge on the diminution of a beneficiary's share.

[230.47]
The capital gains tax rate for an accumulation and maintenance trust (which is the same as for a discretionary trust or an interest in possession trust) is a flat rate (currently 34 per cent): TCGA 1992, s 4; see also Part A, para **[200.39]**.

[230.48]
Trusts which are capable of early termination or of continuing for some time are advantageous since they give flexibility as to when the trust will terminate. The restrictions on hold-over relief introduced by the Finance Act 1989, s 124 and Sch 14 mean that hold-over relief can now only be obtained on an absolute distribution to a 'beneficiary' before he has attained an interest in possession (see now the Taxation of Chargeable Gains Act 1992, s 260(2)(d)), but that once the beneficiary has attained an interest in possession hold-over relief will not be available on an absolute distribution to him unless it is of appropriate business or agricultural property (see the Taxation of Chargeable Gains Act 1992, s 165 and Sch 7, para 1).

Such trusts also have the advantage that the individual beneficiaries do not automatically become entitled to capital at any age, and can be protected against any tendency they may develop to dissipate capital. The vesting of the right to income can be postponed beyond the age of 18 up to the age of 25, within the constraints of the 21-year accumulation period; it can be postponed to 25 only if the beneficiary is over the age of four at the testator's death, but can be extended beyond 18 to some extent in relation to any beneficiary born before the expiry of three years from the testator's death (see further B18 at para **[218.72]**).

[230.49]
The form which follows is an accumulation and maintenance trust for grandchildren providing (if desired) a measure of flexibility as to the shares they take at the specified age and an extension of the accumulation and maintenance trusts of income to the maximum possible age in whole years. The statutory power of advancement is made to apply to the whole of a grandchild's

presumptive share while he is under the specified age. Each grandchild's share is retained and settled on trusts giving the grandchild a life interest but with powers for the trustees to appoint or apply the capital of a share which is for the time being subject to an interest in possession. The form could be adapted for a trust for some other class of minors where members of it may be born after the testator's death, eg nephews and nieces. It should be remembered that a class consisting entirely of persons with a common grandparent will have the advantage that the ITA 1984, s 71 will not automatically cease to apply after 25 years (see Part A, para **[200.119]** et seq). The form could also be adapted for a class consisting of the testator's own children, but it would not need the class-closing provisions because the testator's own children must necessarily be living or en ventre sa mère at his death and therefore lives in being for perpetuity purposes. Form C2.2 at paras **[224.35]–[224.50]** contains accumulation and maintenance trusts for the testator's children with a degree of flexibility, though not as much as in this form.

[230.50]

It should be emphasised that accumulation and maintenance trusts should only be included in a will if it is reasonably certain that there will be one or more 'beneficiaries' under the trust living at the testator's death (see further below). If there is serious doubt as to whether there will be grandchildren in existence at the testator's death, it would be better to provide a full discretionary trust, such as Form C3.6 at para **[225.92]** et seq, under which accumulation and maintenance trusts such as in Form C8.4 can be appointed for the grandchildren or the funds can be distributed to, eg, the testator's children, according to what seems best at the time. If the distribution or appointment is within two years of the testator's death it will be free of inheritance tax by virtue of the ITA 1984, s 144 (see the Notes to Form C3.6 at paras **[225.83]–[225.91]**).

The importance of there being a good chance that there will be grandchildren (or great-grandchildren) in existence at the time of the testator's death is that the ITA 1984, s 71 is capable of applying only when there is or has been a living beneficiary (and, in the case of a will trust, living after the death of the testator), although once there has been a living beneficiary future born children can be counted as 'beneficiaries' for the purposes of s 71: ITA 1984, s 71(7); see also Part A, paras **[200.132]** and **[200.133]**. Thus if a testator made a will as in Form C8.4 and there were to be no grandchild or great-grandchild of his living at his death, s 71 would only start to apply to the residuary estate at the birth of the first grandchild to be born after his death before the closing day (if any). Until this happened the ordinary discretionary trust charging rules (see B18 at para **[218.8]**) would apply if there were no interest in possession (as under cl 7(4) of this form—see further infra), with an 'exit charge' being imposed when the first grandchild was born and s 71 started to apply. Alternatively, the interest in possession rules (see Part A, para **[200.108]** et seq) would apply during this period if there were an interest or interests in possession under the trusts taking effect on failure of the accumulation and maintenance trusts, with a lifetime transfer of value deemed to be made by the person or persons entitled to the interest in possession on the birth of the first grandchild (which could be potentially exempt): see Part A, para **[200.108]** et seq and para **[200.138]**.

[230.51]

On the other hand, if there has been a grandchild (or great-grandchild) in existence after the testator's death, but the grandchildren (and/or great-grandchildren) have then died out, the ITA 1984, s 71 can continue to apply so long as there is no interest in possession and more grandchildren could come into existence. This means that in these circumstances there will be no inheritance tax charge on further grandchildren coming into existence while s 71 continues to apply, but that if the trusts fail without any further grandchild coming into existence there will be quite a significant inheritance tax charge under s 71(3) on s 71 ceasing to apply, the tax rates in relation to such a charge now being higher than under the ordinary discretionary trust charging rules. By contrast if s 71 had ceased to apply on the death of a grandchild (or great-grandchild) there would have been no inheritance tax charge on the section ceasing to apply (see s 71(4)(a)).

Under the trusts contained in Form C8.4 there is provision for accumulation during any period during the 21 years from the testator's death in which there are no living grandchildren or great-grandchildren: see cl 7(4) at para **[230.60]**. As just described, this will cause s 71 to continue to apply after grandchildren (or great-grandchildren) have been in existence after the testator's death but then died, but incurs the risk of a fairly heavy inheritance tax charge under s 71(3) if that has happened and no more of them come into existence before the closing date. If cl 7(4) were not included there would probably be interests in possession under the ultimate trust in cl 9 while there were no grandchildren (or great-grandchildren).

[230.52]

Clause 7(4) of this form can be omitted, in which case interests in possession for the testator's children under the trust in cl 9 (if the children are all over 18) will arise while there is no grandchild or great-grandchild in existence. Thus if cl 7(4) is omitted and there is a grandchild or great-grandchild in existence after the testator's death, and then they all die out, s 71 will cease to apply at the death of the last of them to die (as it cannot apply to property in which there is an interest in possession; see s 71(1)(b)), and there will be no charge under s 71(3).

Another possibility would be for cl 7(4) of this Form to be restricted so that it only operates if there is no living grandchild at the testator's death, and then only operates from the testator's death until the birth of the first grandchild to come into existence after the testator's death or the failure of the trusts (ie so that it cannot operate after grandchildren have been born and then died out). If the subclause was limited in this way, the termination of accumulation under this subclause by the birth, after the testator's death, of the first grandchild or the complete failure of the trusts would give rise to an inheritance tax charge under the ordinary discretionary trust charging rules (see B18 at para **[218.8]**), but there would be no risk taken of a charge arising under the more onerous provisions of the ITA 1984, s 71(3).

[230.53]

Revocation clause

I [*name*] of [*address*] hereby revoke all former testamentary provisions made by me and declare this to be my last will.

[230.54]

Appointment of executors and trustees
1.   [*As in cl 1 of* Form C8.1 *at para* **[230.4]**.]

[230.55]

Pecuniary legacies
2.   [*As in cl 2 of* Form C8.1 *at para* **[230.5]**.]

[230.56]

Gifts of chattels
3.   [*As in cl 3 of* Form C8.1 *at para* **[230.6]**.]

[230.57]

Administration trusts of residue
4.   [*As in cl 4 of* Form C8.1 *at para* **[230.7]**.]

[230.58]

Gifts made free of tax
5.   [*As in cl 5 of* Form C8.1 *at para* **[230.8]**.]

[230.59]

Interpretation
6.   In this and the following clauses of this will the following expressions have the following meanings:

(a)   'the vesting day' means the day on which shall expire the period of 80 years immediately following my death which period shall be the perpetuity period applicable to the disposition hereby made;

(b)   'the specified age'[1] means in relation to any grandchild of mine the age of 18 years save that in relation to any grandchild of mine born during my lifetime or within the period of two years immediately following my death 'the specified age' means the lesser of the following two ages, namely:

   (i)   the age such grandchild will attain (if he or she so long lives) on the anniversary of his or her birth falling during the last year of the period of 21 years immediately following my death; or

   (ii)   the age of 25 years;

(c)   'the closing day'[2] means the first of the following days to occur, namely:

   (i)   the twenty-first anniversary of my death; or

   (ii)   such earlier day (not being earlier than the date on which this present power is exercised) as my trustees may by deed declare to be the closing day;

(d)   'the primary beneficiaries'[3] means my grandchildren born during my lifetime or after my death[4] not later than the closing day and 'primary beneficiary' has a corresponding meaning;

(e)   'the discretionary beneficiaries' means [my children and remoter issue and the spouses and former spouses of the same];[5] and

(f)   'interest in possession' has the same meaning as in Part III of the Inheritance Tax Act 1984.

1   The definition of 'the specified age' in cl 6(b) should be read with the definitions of 'the closing day' and 'the primary beneficiaries' in cls 6(c) and 6(d) and with the trusts declared by cls 7 and 8. The two conditions which need to be satisfied in order that trusts may qualify as 'accumulation and maintenance trusts' are (a) that the beneficiaries will 'on or before attaining a specified age not exceeding 25' become entitled to the settled property or an interest in possession in it and (b) that in the meantime no interest in possession subsists in the settled property and the income falls to be 'accumulated so far as not applied for the maintenance, education or benefit of a beneficiary': ITA 1984, s 71(1). The formula for ascertaining 'the specified period' is designed to defer the vesting of interests in possession for as long as possible consistently with the condition specified in s 71(1)(a) but not so as to infringe the rules against excessive accumulation. See further B18 at para **[218.69]**.

2   See preceding note. The class of eligible grandchildren automatically closes on the 21st anniversary of the testator's death and can be closed at any time prior thereto at the discretion of the trustees. This discretion can be used to close the class early, in order to prevent the birth of further grandchildren causing the partial termination of interests in possession to which the existing grandchildren may have become entitled. For authority that an express class closing date is effective to exclude the rule in *Andrews v Partington*, see *Re Tom's Settlement, Rose v Evans* [1987] 1 All ER 1081, [1987] 1 WLR 1021 and Vol 1, para **[66.12]**.

3   See n 2 supra.

4   For the trusts of residue to qualify as accumulation and maintenance trusts at the testator's death, it is essential that a member of the class should actually be living at that time: ITA 1984, s 71(7), and see the Note to this form at paras **[230.49]–[230.52]**.

5   This definition is for the purposes of the power of appointment in cl 8(a). The class could be widened to include eg issue of the testator's siblings or charity. Inclusion of spouses of the grandchildren will enable the appointment of trusts taking advantage of the inheritance tax exemption for gifts to spouses. For other or wider classes of objects of powers of appointment, including powers to add to the class, see, eg Form C3.6, cl 3(1)(b) at para **[225.101]**, Form C4.1, cl 8(2)(a) at para **[226.25]** and Form C6.2, cl 7(1)(a), (2) and (3)(c) at para **[228.28]**.

[230.60]

Residue: primary beneficial trusts for grandchildren

7.   (1)   My trustees shall hold my residuary estate upon trust for such of the primary beneficiaries as shall have attained or shall attain the specified age[1] and if more than one [in such shares as my trustees (not being fewer than two in number or being a trust corporation) shall (subject to the restrictions hereafter in this present clause contained) by any deed or deeds revocable or irrevocable appoint and in default of and subject to any such appointment][2] in equal shares provided that if any of the primary beneficiaries shall predecease me or shall die after my death without having attained the specified age leaving a child or children him or her surviving and living at my death or born thereafter who shall attain the age of 25 years[3] such child or children shall take absolutely and if more than one equally between them the share of my residuary estate which such deceased primary beneficiary would have taken [(whether pursuant to or in default of appointment)][4] if he or she had lived to attain a vested interest [and provided further that no appointment made pursuant to the foregoing power and no revocation of any such appointment shall affect (whether by increasing or diminishing the same) the share of any primary beneficiary who shall at or before the date of such appointment or revocation have attained the specified age or the share (devolving on his or her child or children) of any primary beneficiary who shall at or before the said date have predeceased me or died under the specified age].[5]

(2)   The foregoing trusts shall carry the intermediate income of my residuary estate and section 31 of the Trustee Act 1925 (as hereinafter modified) shall accordingly apply thereto save that in relation to each of the primary beneficiaries the said section (as hereinafter modified) shall take effect in all respects as if the age of majority were the specified age (and so that the expressions 'infancy' 'minority' and 'infant' and all references to the age of eighteen years in the said section 31 shall be construed accordingly)[6] To the intent that each of the primary beneficiaries shall on attaining the specified age become entitled to an interest in possession[7] in his or her share in accordance with the trusts hereinafter contained.

(3)   The powers (relating to the payment or application of capital) conferred by section 32 of the Trustee Act 1925 (as hereinafter modified) shall apply to the foregoing trusts and shall be exercisable for the benefit of any of the primary beneficiaries who shall for the time being be under the specified age in all respects as if (notwithstanding the trusts of the share of such primary beneficiary hereinafter declared) such primary beneficiary were entitled to the capital of his or her share contingently on attaining the specified age provided that the said powers shall not be exercisable for the benefit of a child of a primary beneficiary while such primary beneficiary shall be living and under the specified age.

(4)   If and so long as prior to the closing day there shall be no primary beneficiary and no child of a primary beneficiary for the time being living and no child of a primary beneficiary shall have died after attaining a vested interest under the foregoing trusts then subject as aforesaid my trustees shall accumulate the income of my residuary estate by investing the same and the resulting income thereof in any of the investments hereby authorised and shall hold the accumulations of income so made as part of the capital of my residuary estate for all purposes.[8]

---

1   The interests of grandchildren and great-grandchildren under sub-cl (1) must vest, if at all, within the perpetuity period of 80 years from the death of the testator because of the combination of the closing date and the ages of vesting. Express perpetuity restrictions as in cl 8(c) are not necessary here, but if this form is adapted and there is the slightest doubt as to whether interests will vest within the perpetuity period, or no perpetuity period of a fixed number of years is provided, such a restriction should be included (it can do no harm even where it is not strictly needed).

2   Clause 6 contains the initial trust for the division of the fund between the eligible grandchildren. Power is conferred on the trustees to vary the shares of the grandchildren subject to the restrictions contained in the second proviso to sub-cl (1), which are designed to preserve the fiscal status of the trusts. The power of variation can be omitted, if desired, by deleting the words in the first set of square brackets and in two other places in this subclause (see nn 4 and 5 to this subclause), and also deleting the words in square brackets near the beginning of cl 8 at para **[230.61]** (see n 2 at para **[230.61]**).

3   See n 1 supra.

4   See n 2 supra. This part in square brackets is to be omitted if the power to vary shares is omitted.

5   See n 2 supra. This part in square brackets is to be omitted if the power to vary shares is omitted.

6   This modification is designed to defer the vesting of interests in possession for as long as is consistent with the conditions governing accumulation and maintenance trusts and the rules against excessive accumulation. See cl 6(b), n 1 at **[230.59]** and see further B18 at para **[218.69]**.

7   See cl 6(f) at para **[230.59]**.

8   See the Note to this form at paras **[230.45]**–**[230.52]** and cl 6(d), n 4 at para **[230.59]**. If at any time before 'the closing day' there should be no beneficiary living, income is to be

accumulated. Since 'the closing day' cannot fall more than 21 years after the testator's death (see cl 6(c)), the direction for accumulation is not excessive. For the disadvantages of this provision, and the alternative possibilities, see the Note at paras **[230.50]**–**[230.52]**.

[230.61]

Settlement of grandchildren's shares[1]

8.   The share of my residuary estate to which a primary beneficiary shall become entitled [(whether pursuant to or in default of appointment)][2] under the last foregoing clause hereof (hereinafter in this clause called 'the settled share' which expression shall include all accretions thereto) shall not vest absolutely in such primary beneficiary but shall be retained by my trustees and shall thereafter be held upon the following trusts and with and subject to the following powers and provisions:

  (a)   my trustees shall hold the settled share and the income thereof upon trust for all or such one or more exclusive of the other or others of the discretionary beneficiaries[3] at such age or time or respective ages or times if more than one in such shares and with such trusts powers and provisions for their respective benefit (including trusts or powers conferring a discretion as to the disposition of capital or income or providing for the accumulation of income within the period of 21 years from the date of my death or administrative powers or provisions of whatever nature) as my trustees (not being fewer than two in number or being a trust corporation) shall at their absolute discretion after such primary beneficiary shall have attained the specified age during the life of such primary beneficiary and before the vesting day by deed or deeds revocable or irrevocable appoint[4] provided that:

   (i)   no appointment under the foregoing power shall be capable of taking effect while such primary beneficiary is living until the expiration of one month from the date of his or her attaining the specified age (or one month from my death if later);

   (ii)   any revocable appointment made under the foregoing power shall become irrevocable (so far as then unrevoked) on the death of such primary beneficiary or on the earlier occurrence of the vesting day;

   (iii)   the foregoing power shall not be capable of being exercised so as to prejudice or affect the entitlement of such primary beneficiary to any income which shall have arisen before such exercise or (if later) the occasion on which such exercise takes effect;

   (iv)   the foregoing power shall not be capable of being exercised so as to prejudice or affect any payment transfer or application of capital which shall be made before such exercise of the foregoing power or (if later) the occasion when such exercise takes effect;

   (v)   any appointment under the foregoing power may be made in respect of income alone without any appointment of capital; and

   (vi)   my trustees (not being fewer than two in number or being a trust corporation) shall have power at any time or times by deed to release or restrict the future exercise of the foregoing power in any manner whatsoever;

  (b)   subject to any or every exercise of the foregoing power my trustees shall stand possessed of the settled share upon trust to pay the income thereof to such primary beneficiary during his or her life to the intent that such primary beneficiary shall immediately upon attaining the specified age or my death (if later) become entitled to an interest in possession[5] in the settled share;

(c)   subject as aforesaid my trustees shall hold the settled share upon trust for such of the children of such primary beneficiary as shall attain the age of 25 years or be living on the earlier occurrence of the vesting day and if more than one in equal shares absolutely;

(d)   the trust in paragraph (c) of this subclause contained shall carry the intermediate income of the settled share (so far as not disposed of under any trust or power having priority thereto) and section 31 of the Trustee Act 1925 (as hereinafter modified) shall apply thereto accordingly;

(e)   section 32 of the Trustee Act 1925 (as hereinafter modified) shall apply in relation to the foregoing trusts;

(f)   in the event that there shall be no child of such primary beneficiary who shall attain the age of 25 years or be living on the earlier occurrence of the vesting day the settled share and any other share of my residuary estate which may have accrued thereto hereunder (or so much thereof respectively as shall not have been appointed or applied under any of the powers applicable thereto hereunder) shall go and accrue to the other shares or share of my residuary estate the trusts whereof are for the time being subsisting and capable of taking effect and if more than one equally between them and so that any such accruing share shall thereafter devolve as one fund with such other shares or share;

(g)   notwithstanding the foregoing trusts my trustees (not being fewer than two in number or being a trust corporation) shall have power at any time or times and from time to time before the vesting day so long as such primary beneficiary shall be living to raise the whole or any part or parts of the settled share in which for the time being such primary beneficiary has an interest in possession and pay transfer or apply the same to or for the advancement support or benefit of such primary beneficiary in such manner as they shall think fit.

1   Clause 8 settles each grandchild's share on conventional trusts for the grandchild for life, and subject thereto on trust for his or her children at 25 with an accruer provision. An overriding power of appointment, exercisable in favour of a wide class, and power to apply capital for the grandchild's benefit, are conferred on the trustees. It should be noted that this clause does not apply to the shares taken by substitution by great-grandchildren. If the discretionary beneficiaries include spouses of the grandchildren, appointments can be made taking advantage of the inheritance tax exemption for gifts to spouses.

2   See cl 7(1), n 2 at para **[230.60]**. The words in square brackets are to be omitted if there is no power to vary shares included in cl 7(1).

3   See cl 6(e) at para **[230.59]**.

4   The main purpose of having a power of appointment as well as a power to apply capital is that the power of appointment can be used to create new trusts (eg for the primary beneficiary's children) without creating a new settlement; the creation of a new settlement could give rise to a capital gains tax charge and general hold-over relief has been abolished. The provisos to the power are included largely for the purpose of preventing the power from prejudicing the existence of an interest in possession.

5   See cl 6(f) at para **[230.59]**.

[230.62]

Ultimate trust of residue

9.   Subject to the foregoing trusts and to any or every exercise of the powers hereby or by law conferred my trustees shall hold my residuary estate and the income thereof upon trust for [such of my children as shall be living at my death and if more than one in equal shares absolutely and if no child of mine is living at my death for such charitable purposes as my trustees may determine].[1]

1   Other ultimate gifts may be preferred. See eg Form C8.1, cl 6(5) and (6) at para **[230.9]**.

[230.63]

Maintenance, accumulation and advancement

10.   (1)   [*As in cl 7(1) of* Form C8.1 *at para* **[230.10]**.]

(2)   Section 32 of the Trustee Act 1925 (relating to advancement) shall apply in relation to the said trusts as if the words 'one half of' were omitted from proviso (a) to subsection (1) thereof [provided that:

(a)   the powers conferred by the said section (as hereby enlarged) shall not be exercisable in favour of any primary beneficiary hereunder who is under the specified age otherwise than so as to cause such primary beneficiary to become immediately entitled to or to an interest in possession in the capital thereby paid or applied within the meaning of section 71(1)(a) of the Inheritance Tax Act 1984; and

(b)   the powers conferred by the said section (as hereby enlarged) shall not be exercisable in favour of any minor beneficiary hereunder otherwise than so as to cause such beneficiary to become immediately entitled to or to an interest in possession in the capital thereby paid or applied within the meaning aforesaid].[1]

1   See Form C8.1, cl 7, n 2 at para **[230.10]**. This proviso has been adapted on the lines recommended in that note to allow for the fact that in this form, in relation to 'the primary beneficiaries', the accumulation and maintenance trusts can continue to 'the specified age' (see cl 6(b) of this form at para **[230.59]**), which can be higher than 18.

[230.64]

(3)   [*As in cl 7(3) of* Form C8.1 *at para* **[230.10]**.]

[230.65]

Administrative powers

11.   [*As in cl 8 of* Form C8.1 *at para* **[230.11]**.]

[230.66]

Exercise of powers

12.   [*As in cl 9 of* Form C8.2 *at para* **[230.27]**.]

[230.67]

Trustee liability

13.   [*As in cl 9 of* Form C8.1 *at para* **[230.12]**.]

[230.68]

Receipts on behalf of charitable institutions
14.   [*As in cl 10 of* Form C8.1 *at para* **[230.13]**.]

[230.69]

Professional trustee charging clause
15.   [*As in cl 11 of* Form C8.1 *at para* **[230.14]**.]

[*Testimonium and attestation clause as in* Form C8.1 *at para* **[230.15]**.]

[230.70]

FORM C8.5:   Will of widow leaving her house to a daughter who is looking after her and residue to children equally

Revocation clause
I [*name*] of [*address*] hereby revoke all former testamentary dispositions made by me and declare this to be my last will.

[230.71]

Appointment of executors and trustees
1.   [*As in cl 1 of* Form C8.1 *at para* **[230.4]**.]

[230.72]

Gift of personal chattels to daughter
2.   I give all my personal chattels (as defined by section 55(1)(x) of the Administration of Estates Act 1925)[1] to my daughter [*name*] free of tax[2] [and I request her (but without imposing any trust or binding obligation on her) to give effect to my wishes as to the disposition of such chattels which may be contained in any memorandum that may be found amongst my papers at my death or which may otherwise have been communicated to her during my life].[3]

1   See Form C8.1, cl 3, n 3 at para **[230.6]** and Part G, para **[246.52]**.
2   See Form C8.1, cl 3, n 2 at para **[230.6]**.
3   See Form C8.1, cl 3, n 5 at para **[230.6]**.

[230.73]

Gift of dwellinghouse or its value to daughter[1]
3.   (1)   I give my freehold dwellinghouse known as [*address*] or (if it is sold during my lifetime) any other dwellinghouse which I may own at my death and which was purchased for use by me as my principal residence[2] to my said daughter [*name*] [free of all sums charged thereon or otherwise secured thereon at my death (which sums shall be paid out of my residuary estate)] [and] [free of tax].[3]
    (2)   If the foregoing gift shall fail by reason of the sale during my lifetime of the last dwellinghouse owned by me and used or intended to be used by me as my principal residence then I give to my said daughter free of tax[4] a pecuniary legacy equal in value to the net proceeds of such dwellinghouse.

1   This clause contains a gift not only of the dwellinghouse owned by the testatrix at the date of the will but of any dwellinghouse substituted for it and caters for the possibility of the testatrix having no home, eg because she has gone into a nursing home and has sold her house, by giving the daughter a legacy in lieu.

2   This form of words should ensure that the daughter takes any house purchased as a substitute residence even though it has ceased to be used as such by the testatrix, eg because she has gone into a home.

3   The inheritance tax on land in the UK is a testamentary expense (see B14 at para **[214.55]**) and strictly speaking, these words are only needed if the residence is outside the UK or might be replaced by one which is. If the testator is already living outside the UK there are special factors to consider, such as foreign laws of succession: see further C14 at paras **[236.1]–[236.8]**. See Form C8.1, cl 5 at para **[230.8]** incorporated as cl 5 of this form, for the definition of 'free of tax'.

    Where there are specific gifts or pecuniary legacies elsewhere in the will which are declared to be 'free of tax', it would be a good idea to include those words here as well, even if the residence is in the UK, to avoid any suggestion that, because of the absence of those words here when they are included elsewhere, this gift is intended to be subject to tax.

4   There are stronger reasons for including these words in relation to a pecuniary legacy than there are for land: see the note to Form C8.1, cl 2 at para **[230.5]**.

[230.74]

Administration trusts of residue

4.   [*As in cl 4 of* Form C8.1 *at para* **[230.7]**.]

[230.75]

Gifts made free of tax

5.   [*As in cl 5 of* Form C8.1 *at para* **[230.8]**.]

[230.76]

Beneficial trusts of residue

6.   (1)   My trustees shall hold my residuary estate upon trust for such of my children as survive me and if more than one in equal shares provided that if any of my children shall predecease me leaving a child or children living at my death who shall attain the age of [18/21/25] years[1] such last-mentioned child or children shall take and if more than one equally between them the share of my residuary estate which such deceased child of mine would have taken had he or she survived me.

    (2)   The trusts declared by the proviso to the foregoing subclause shall carry the intermediate income of any share of my residuary estate to which such proviso relates and section 31 of the Trustee Act 1925 (as hereinafter modified) shall apply thereto.

    (3)   Section 32 of the Trustee Act 1925 (as hereinafter modified) shall apply in relation to the said trusts.

1   The children will all be lives in being for perpetuity purposes so any age contingency may be included.

[230.77]

Maintenance, accumulation and advancement

7.   [*As in cl 7 of* Form C8.1 *at para* **[230.10]**.]

[230.78]

Administrative powers
8.   [*As in cl 8 of* Form C8.1 *at para* **[230.11]**.]

[230.79]

Trustee liability
9.   [*As in cl 9 of* Form C8.1 *at para* **[230.12]**.]

[230.80]

Professional trustee charging clause
10.   [*As in cl 11 of* Form C8.1 *at para* **[230.14]**.]

[*Testimonium and attestation clause as in* Form C8.1 *at para* **[230.15]**.]

[230.81]

FORM C8.6:   Will of widow or widower settling residue on trusts for children with progressive powers to pay them capital at different ages

NOTE

In this form residue is settled in equal shares on the children for life with remainders over in favour of their children, the trustees being given power to apply each child's share for the benefit of such child which is initially fairly restricted but which increases in scope as the child gets older and which finally authorises the application of the entire share. If the testator or testatrix would prefer to include an unrestricted power, Form C2.2, cl 8(e) (at para **[224.44]**) could be substituted for cl 7(g) of this form.

[230.82]

Revocation clause
I [*name*] of [*address*] hereby revoke all former testamentary dispositions made by me and declare this to be my last will.

[230.83]

Appointment of executors and trustees
1.   [*As in cl 1 of* Form C8.1 *at para* **[230.4]**.]

[230.84]

Pecuniary legacies
2.   [*As in cl 2 of* Form C8.1 *at para* **[230.5]**.]

[230.85]

Specific bequests
3.   [*As in cl 3 of* Form C8.1 *at para* **[230.6]**.]

[230.86]

Administration trusts of residue
4.   [*As in cl 4 of* Form C8.1 *at para* **[230.7]**.]

[230.87]

Gifts made free of tax

5.   [*As in cl 5 of* Form C8.1 *at para* **[230.8]**.]

[230.88]

Beneficial trusts of residue for children and issue

6.   (1)   Subject to the direction for retention and settlement hereinafter contained my trustees shall hold my residuary estate upon trust for such of my children as shall survive me and if more than one in equal shares provided that if any of my children shall predecease me leaving a child or children surviving me who shall attain the age of [18/21/25] years such last-mentioned child or children shall take and if more than one equally between them the share of my residuary estate which such deceased child of mine would have taken had he or she survived me.

(2)   The trusts declared by the proviso to the foregoing subclause shall carry the intermediate income of any share of my residuary estate to which such proviso relates and section 31 of the Trustee Act 1925 (as hereinafter modified) shall apply thereto.

(3)   Section 32 of the Trustee Act 1925 (as hereinafter modified) shall apply in relation to any such share and shall be exercisable for the benefit of any child of mine in relation to his or her presumptive share of my residuary estate notwithstanding the direction for the retention and settlement of such share hereinafter contained.[1]

1   This subclause is included since it is probable, in view of the settlement of each child's share, that the statutory power would not otherwise apply in his or her favour.

[230.89]

Settlement of child's share of residue

7.   The share of my residuary estate to which any child of mine who survives me shall become entitled under the last foregoing clause hereof shall not vest in such child absolutely but shall be retained by my trustees and held upon the following trusts:

(a)   my trustees shall hold such share upon trust to pay the income thereof to such child during his or her life;

(b)   subject as aforesaid such child shall have power at any time by deed or deeds revocable or irrevocable or by will or codicil to appoint to any spouse who may survive him or her as his or her widow or widower (including power to appoint to a named spouse contingently on such named spouse surviving him or her as his or her widow or widower) an interest in the income of the whole or any part or parts of such share for the residue of such spouse's life or for any less period;[1]

(c)   subject as aforesaid my trustees shall hold such share upon trust for such of the children of such child of mine as shall attain the age of [18/21] years and if more than one in equal shares;

(d)   the trust declared by paragraph (c) above shall carry the intermediate income of such share and section 31 of the Trustee Act 1925 (as hereinafter modified) shall apply thereto;

(e) section 32 of the Trustee Act 1925 (as hereinafter modified) shall apply in relation to such share;

(f) if there shall be no child of such child of mine who shall attain a vested interest in such share then such share and any other share of my residuary estate as may have accrued thereunder (or so much thereof as shall not have been applied under any of the powers applicable thereto hereunder) shall accrue to the other shares or share of my residuary estate the trusts whereof are at the date of such accruer subsisting and capable of taking effect;

(g) notwithstanding the trusts aforesaid my trustees may from time to time pay transfer or apply to or for the benefit of such child of mine:

(i) if such child shall have attained the age of [25] years any part or parts of the capital of such share not exceeding in the aggregate one quarter thereof;

(ii) if such child shall have attained the age of [30] years any part or parts of the capital of such share not exceeding in the aggregate one half thereof;

(iii) if such child shall have attained the age of [35] years any part or parts of the capital of such share not exceeding in the aggregate three quarters thereof; and

(iv) if such child shall have attained the age of [40] years the whole or any part or parts of the capital of such share.

1   This power will enable advantage to be taken of the inheritance tax exemption for gifts to a spouse in relation to the share.

[230.90]

Maintenance, accumulation and advancement

8.   [*As in cl 7 of* Form C8.1 *at para* **[230.10]**.]

[230.91]

Administrative powers

9.   [*As in cl 8 of* Form C8.1 *at para* **[230.11]**.]

[230.92]

Exercise of powers

10.   [*As in cl 9 of* Form C8.2 *at para* **[230.27]**.]

[230.93]

Trustee liability

11.   [*As in cl 9 of* Form C8.1 *at para* **[230.12]**.]

[230.94]

Professional trustee charging clause

12.   [*As in cl 11 of* Form C8.1 *at para* **[230.14]**.]

[*Testimonium and attestation clause as in* Form C8.1 *at para* **[230.15]**.]

C9   Wills for members of childless households

PRELIMINARY NOTE

[231.1]

The wills in C9 are not only for childless married couples, but for any two or more childless persons living together where each wishes to provide for the other or others on his or her death. Except in the case of married couples it is essential that such persons should make wills, because they will not (except possibly where they are siblings) benefit from each other's estates under the intestacy rules. The Forms in C9, apart from Form C9.5 (which is for three unmarried sisters), are for couples, but could be adapted for use by more than two persons.

When a couple are making wills, they may be only concerned with securing the position of the survivor after one of them has died, and thus may be content with a simple disposition of each to the other if surviving, leaving it entirely to the survivor to dispose of the joint estate. Such couples are catered for by Form C9.1 at para **[231.10]**. The obvious drawback to wills in this form is that the second of them to die, if he or she never gets round to making a further will, will die intestate, and where the testators are not blood relatives it will be only the relatives of the second to die who benefit from the combined estates, to the exclusion of the relatives of the first to die.

[231.2]
Gifts to take effect after the deaths of both. It is more common for each testator to want to make, in addition to a primary gift in favour of the other, an alternative disposition to take effect if the other predeceases him. This presents a problem where each of them has a different destination for his property in the event of the other not surviving him. If each testator makes a will leaving all his estate to the other if surviving, with an alternative gift to his own ultimate beneficiaries, one of the two sets of beneficiaries will inherit the combined estates of the two of them, with the other set of beneficiaries receiving nothing, and which set of beneficiaries inherits which will depend on which of the two testators dies first.

One solution, adopted in Form C9.2 (at para **[231.14]**), is for each spouse or partner to give his entire estate to the other if surviving and for the survivor to leave the combined estates on trust for the ultimate beneficiaries intended by both testators, either equally between the two sets of beneficiaries or, where the estates of the two testators differ significantly in value and they so wish, in unequal proportions. A variant of this solution, embodied in Form C9.3 (at para **[231.30]**), is for the survivor to leave a cash legacy equal in value to the estate of the first to die to the latter's chosen ultimate beneficiaries. Where the shares are proportional, as in Form C9.2, both sets of beneficiaries will share in any increase or decrease in the combined estates in the period between the death of the first to die and the death of the survivor, whereas if there is a legacy equal to the first to die's estate, as in Form C9.3, the ultimate beneficiaries chosen by the first to die will receive no increase for inflation in the period after the death of the first to die, but will have priority for what they are given over the ultimate beneficiaries chosen by the second to die if the combined estates come to be diminished by, eg, the second to die spending large amounts of capital. Either arrangement can cause unfairness if substantial lifetime gifts are made, although this is perhaps less likely to happen where the arrangement is a legacy to the beneficiaries of the first to die as in Form C9.3.

The solutions adopted in Forms C9.2 and C9.3 have the drawback that unless the wills are mutual wills in the technical sense (a course which is not recommended), the survivor will be free to change his or her will to the detriment of the chosen beneficiaries of the first to die. Many couples will have sufficient confidence in each other to take this risk, but if they are not content with such an arrangement the settlement of the first to die's estate on trust during the life of the survivor should be considered. A form of trust which could be used is Form C9.4 (at para **[231.42]**), where each spouse or partner settles his estate on the other for life (with or without a power to apply capital) instead of giving it outright, and provides specifically in his will for the ultimate destination of his separate estate. Another possibility, which might be more efficient from an inheritance tax point of view where the testators are not a married couple, is a discretionary trust: see Form C6.2 and the Note thereto at para **[228.19]** et seq.

[231.3]
The definition of the persons who take on the second death. The Forms in C9 all assume that the class of nephews and nieces or other persons who take on the death of the surviving testator are already a closed class. If it is desired to benefit a class which might include persons born after the death of the testator it is

important that it is not defined as 'the children of X who survive me' but, eg, 'the children of X who shall be living at or born after my death'. See, eg Form C10.1, cl 6(3) at para **[232.9]**.

[231.4]
Other provisions. Forms C9.5 and C9.6 (at paras **[231.53]** and **[231.62]**) are for households consisting of childless unmarried sisters. Form C9.5 contains a gift of residue by each sister to the survivors or survivor, and failing them to charity. Here it is assumed that they all wish to benefit the same charity when the last survivor of them dies, or else that they do not mind if it is the charity nominated by the last to die which scoops the pool. Where this is not the case Form C9.2 or Form C9.3 should be adopted. Form C9.6 contains a gift by one sister of a right of residence to the other, with the residue of her estate immediately, and the residence on the death of the other sister, being divided between charity and named nephews and nieces.

[231.5]
Inheritance tax. Members of childless households are less likely to be concerned about inheritance tax saving than testators with children, and the forms in this section contain no devices designed to achieve any saving of inheritance tax apart from some survivorship contingencies (for which see below). The main feature which might be added to wills for childless married couples is a non-exempt gift in the will of the first to die so as to make use of the latter's nil-rate band, and the main inheritance tax-saving step which might be taken in other cases is to provide a discretionary trust of the estate of the first to die. If it is desired to take such inheritance tax-saving steps, reference should be made to the Preliminary Note and forms in C3 at paras **[225.1]**–**[225.8]** if the testators are a married couple, and to Form C6.2 and the Note thereto at para **[228.19]** et seq, if the testators are not married to each other.

[231.6]
Survivorship contingencies. In Forms C9.2, C9.3, and C9.5, which are all reciprocal wills, the primary gift made by each testator in favour of the other or others is contingent on the other or others surviving the testator by one month. This is principally in case they all die in a common accident. The purpose and effect of including such a provision are different according to whether the testators are a married couple or not: see the Preliminary Note to C2 at para **[224.6]**.

[231.7]
Reciprocal wills, survivorship conditions, and gifts intended to take effect only once. Care needs to be taken where a couple make reciprocal wills under which each gives his entire estate to the other if surviving him by a specified period, with an alternative gift if the other does not survive by that period, and there is also any pecuniary legacy or specific gift which appears in both wills but which is intended to take effect only once. Care has to be taken to prevent any such legacy taking effect under both wills, and to see that any such pecuniary legacy or specific gift will be effective, in the event of the testators dying within

the survivorship period of each other. The considerations relevant to pecuniary legacies are rather different from those relevant to specific gifts.

If such a pecuniary legacy is, like the alternative residuary gift, included in both wills and in both wills directed to take effect in the event of the failure of the other spouse to survive the testator by the survivorship period, that legacy will take effect under both wills if they die within the survivorship period of each other. The simplest way of dealing with this problem is to provide in both wills that the legacy takes effect only in the event of the testator surviving the other spouse (ie without reference to any survivorship period), and examples of pecuniary legacies of this type are included in Form C9.2, cl 2 at para **[231.17]**.

In relation to pecuniary legacies of this type, ie ones which are in both wills but intended to take effect once only, there is one circumstance where it could be appropriate to make special provision for the eventuality of the testators dying within the survivorship period of each other. This is where the estate of one of the testators by itself might, in the event of that testator dying within the survivorship period after the other's death (when that testator will not inherit the other's estate), be insufficient to pay all such legacies as well as make any other legacies or specific gifts which would take effect in the same event. In Form C9.2, cl 2 (at para **[231.17]**) an optional alternative is included under which these legacies take effect under the will of the wealthier testator, even if he dies first, where the testators die within the survivorship period of each other.

[231.8]
The position is rather different in the case of specific gifts. There is not a potential problem of duplication of a gift which is intended to have effect only once if it is a gift of specific property. If the testators die within the survivorship period of each other the property will either be owned in its entirety by one of them, in which case a gift of it in the other's will cannot have any effect, or it will be shared between the testators, in which case both shares will be intended to be given. It will usually be a workable arrangement if such a specific gift is worded so as to take effect in the same circumstances as the alternative gift of residue, ie in the event of the other testator predeceasing or failing to survive by the survivorship period. The main thing to avoid is any inappropriate duplication-avoiding formulae related to deaths within the survivorship period of the kinds sometimes found in precedents for pecuniary legacies.

If the specific gift is of property held by the testators as joint tenants, it is particularly important for the gift to take effect under the will of the second to die in all circumstances, including cases where the testators die within the survivorship period of each other; the first to die's interest in the property will accrue to the survivor even if the first to die's will does not take effect in favour of the survivor by reason of the latter surviving the first to die by less than the survivorship period.

Where the subject matter of the gift is or might be held by the testators as tenants in common, the gift should take effect under both wills in the event of the death of the testators within the survivorship period of each other, and should be of the entire property (in case one testator inherits the other's share) and of the testator's interest in it (in case neither inherits the other's share because they die within the survivorship period of each other): see Form C9.2, cl 6 at para **[231.21]** for an example. Where a property is held by them as joint tenants there is always a possibility that the joint tenancy might be severed before they die.

If the property is wholly owned by one testator it is also important that the gift should be worded so as to operate under that testator's will if he is the first to die and the other does not survive him by the survivorship period. The formula in Form C9.2, cl 6 at para **[231.21]** would be effective in this respect.

[231.9]

Gifts to nephews and nieces. Wills of childless persons often contain gifts in favour of collateral relatives such as nephews and nieces or cousins. These terms frequently give rise to difficulty. General descriptions by relationship will prima facie include persons related by the half blood as well as the whole blood but not those related by affinity only. The term nephews and nieces will not prima facie include great nephews or great nieces and the term cousins is prima facie confined to first cousins: see generally Vol 1, para **[71.5]**. The safest course is to describe the intended beneficiaries by name or as the children of named persons: see *Re Daoust, Dobell v Dobell* [1944] 1 All ER 443. Where they are named it is also a good idea to give their addresses, as it is quite possible for there to be more than one person with the same name in the same family. Naming the (legitimate) nephews and nieces is also a discreet way of excluding illegitimate ones if that is what the testator wishes; if they are referred to as the children of named persons, or as the nephews and nieces of either or both of the testators, illegitimate ones will be included (see Part A, para **[200.28]** and Vol 1, para **[72.1]** et seq).

See also the note on the definition of the persons who take on the second death at para **[231.2]** of this Preliminary Note.

[231.10]

FORM C9.1:   Reciprocal wills for a childless couple, each giving his or her entire estate to the other absolutely

NOTE

This form is only slightly more elaborate than the emergency will in favour of single individual in Form C1.1 at para **[223.2]**. The obvious disadvantage of a will in this form is that a new will will be needed if the legatee predeceases the testator or if the parties are a married couple and get divorced. A will containing an alternative gift (such as Form C9.2) is usually preferable particularly if the will is one of a pair of reciprocal wills and the joint estate will otherwise go in different directions depending on which one of them survives.

The form is very short but as executor and universal legatee the beneficiary has all the powers necessary to administer the estate and no express powers need be included. The form will not be suitable where the beneficiary is not of full age because a minor, though he may be appointed an executor, will not be granted probate: Supreme Court Act 1981, s 118. Furthermore a minor beneficiary, if unmarried, would not take any freehold property comprised in the estate absolutely but would be treated as having an entailed interest in it: AEA 1925, s 51(3) (Part G, para **[244.66]**).

[231.11]

Revocation clause

I [*name*] of [*address*] revoke all former dispositions made by me and declare this to be my last will.

[231.12]

Gift of entire estate to spouse partner or other person and appointment of spouse as sole executor

Subject to the payment thereout of my funeral and testamentary expenses[1] and debts I give all my estate both real and personal (including any entailed or other property over which I have a general power of disposition by will)[2] to [my [wife/husband] [*name*]] [*name of partner or the other person*] absolutely and appoint [her/him] sole [executrix/executor] hereof.

1   This will include inheritance tax payable in respect of the estate, though where the parties are married the gift will be exempt.
2   Subject to any contrary intention expressed in the will property subject to a general testamentary power will be carried by a residuary gift under the Wills Act 1837 (WA 1837), s 27 (Part G, para **[244.27]**; see also Vol 1, paras **[38.1]** and **[38.2]**) without express reference to the property or power. In the case of entailed property, however, the property or the instrument under which it was acquired, or entailed property generally, must be referred to: LPA 1925, s 176(1) (Part G, para **[244.53]**; see also Vol 1, para **[7.1]**).

[231.13]

AS WITNESS my hand this ⸺ day of ⸺ 20⸺

SIGNED by the [testator/testatrix] in our presence and
then by us in [his/hers][1]   } [*Signature of testator/testatrix*]

[*Signatures, addresses and descriptions of two witnesses*]

1   This is a short form of testimonium which is acceptable to the Probate Registry: see Form C1.1, n 2 at para **[223.2]**.

[231.14]

FORM C9.2:   Reciprocal wills for husband and wife, each giving his or her entire estate to the other contingently on surviving him or her by a specified period, and providing in the alternative pecuniary legacies, a specific gift and a gift of residue in favour of the nephews and nieces of both spouses in equal or other specified proportions

NOTE

This form is intended for use by a childless married couple who wish the survivor to have the entire estate of both, but who each have their own relatives whom they ultimately wish to benefit after the death of both. If each has property exceeding the inheritance tax nil-rate threshold in value, the nil-rate band of the first to die will be lost. If this is a matter of concern, a legacy of an amount equal to the nil- rate band and settled on trusts under which the survivor is eligible to benefit could be used. Form C3.4 (at para **[225.60]**), cl 2 of which contains a legacy of this description, could readily be adapted for use in such a case.

This form divides up the survivor's residue between the two families, while Form C9.3 provides a legacy (on the survivor's death) equal to the value of the first to die's estate in favour of the latter's relatives. For discussion of the relative merits of the two forms see the Preliminary Note at para **[231.2]**. For further points on gifts as in this form, see the Note to Form C5.3 at paras **[227.35]–[227.45]**.

This form could also be used for a couple who are not married to each other. The name of the other person should be substituted for 'my [wife/husband]' throughout.

[231.15]

Revocation clause

I [*name*] of [*address*] revoke all former testamentary dispositions made by me and declare this to be my last will.

[231.16]

Appointment of executors and trustees

1.   (1)   I appoint my [wife/husband] [*name*] ('my [wife/husband]') the sole [executrix/executor] of this will but if [she/he] predeceases me or renounces probate or dies without having proved this will[1] then I appoint [*name*] of [*address*] and [*name*] of [*address*] to be the executors and trustees hereof.

(2)   In this will the expression 'my trustees' shall where the context permits mean my personal representatives for the time being and the trustees for the time being hereof.

---

1   If there is a divorce the spouse will be deemed to have died and the alternative appointment will take effect, by virtue of the WA 1837, s 18A(1)(a) (Part G, para **[244.18]**). See the Preliminary Note to C2 on the possibility of divorce at paras **[224.12]–[224.19]**. See also the note to cl 1 of Form C2.1 at para **[224.22]** on the reasons for not making the appointment of the spouse as executor conditional on surviving the testator by the survivorship period which is provided in the primary gift in cl 3.

[231.17]

Pecuniary legacies to take effect only on one death[1]

EITHER

[2.   If my [wife/husband] shall predecease me then I give the following pecuniary legacies free of tax:[2]

(a)   to [*name*] the sum of ——;
(b)   to [*name*] the sum of ——;
(c)   to [*name*] the sum of ——].

OR

[2.   [*In the will of the less well-off testator*: If I survive my [wife/husband] by the period of one month]/[*In the will of the wealthier testator*: if my [wife/husband] shall predecease me or fail to survive me for the period of [one month][3]] then I give the following pecuniary legacies free of tax:

(a)   to [*name*] the sum of ——;
(b)   to [*name*] the sum of ——;
(c)   to [*name*] the sum of ——].

1   For the reasons behind these alternative provisions see the Preliminary Note at para **[231.7]**. Both alternatives are worded so that the legacies in this clause take effect under only one of the two wills. The only difference between them is that if the testators die within the specified survivorship period of each other (one month in this form), under the first alternative the legacies take effect under the will of the second to die, while under the second alternative the legacies take effect under the will of the wealthier of the two testators.
2   Although the inheritance tax on legacies or specific gifts of UK property is a testamentary expense, it is preferable to include an express direction that a pecuniary legacy is free of tax in case residue includes foreign property or settled property; if it does include such property, a proportion of the legacies, corresponding to the proportion of residue which made up of foreign or settled property, would probably have to bear inheritance tax in the absence of a direction to the contrary. See further the Note to B14 at para **[214.55]** et seq. For the definition of 'free of tax', see cl 8 of this form at para **[231.23]**.
3   This period should be the same as the period by which the other spouse has to survive the testator in order to become entitled to the testator's residuary estate under cl 3 of this form at para **[231.18]**.

[231.18]

Gift of residue to spouse as universal legatee
3. If my [wife/husband] shall survive me for the period of [one month][1] then subject to the payment thereout of my funeral and testamentary expenses and debts and any legacies given hereby or by any codicil hereto I give all my estate both real and personal not otherwise disposed of hereby (including any entailed or other property over which I have a general power of disposition by will)[2] to [her/ him] absolutely and I declare that clauses 10 to 13 below hereof shall apply.[3]

1   For the inheritance tax and other implications of such survivorship conditions see the Preliminary Note to C2 at para **[224.6]** and for the length of the survivorship period see Form C2.1, cl 4, n 1 at para **[224.25]**.
?   See Form C9.1, n 2 at para **[231.12]**.
3   An error which can easily creep into wills of this type is that all the ancillary administrative and other provisions have effect only in the event of the alternative gift taking effect. This declaration is one way round this problem.

[231.19]

Alternative provisions
4. If [my [wife/husband]] shall fail to survive me for the period aforesaid[1] then the following provisions shall have effect.

1   See cl 3, n 1 at para **[231.18]**.

[231.20]

Discretionary trust of chattels[1]
5. (1) I give all my personal chattels as defined by section 55(1)(x) of the Administration of Estates Act 1925[2] to my trustees free of tax.[3]
    (2) My trustees may during the period of twelve months following the grant of probate to my will distribute the said chattels amongst any one or more of the children and remoter issue of my grandparents and the grandparents of my [wife/husband] and the spouses and former spouses of the foregoing[4] in such

manner as they think fit And I request my trustees in making such distribution (but without imposing any binding trust or obligation on them) to have regard to any memorandum of wishes I may leave with my papers at my death or any wishes I may have communicated to any of them during my life.

(3)   My trustees may delegate the exercise of their foregoing power as regards all or any of my personal chattels to such person or persons and to such extent and in such manner as they think fit.

(4)   Subject as aforesaid my trustees shall hold my personal chattels upon trust to divide the same between such of my nephews and nieces and the nephews and nieces of [my wife/husband] namely [*names of nephews and nieces of both spouses*][5] as survive me as nearly as may be in equal shares according to value provided that my trustees shall not be obliged to obtain a valuation of the said chattels specifically for the foregoing purpose and may act on their own estimate of the value thereof or on any probate valuation obtained for the purposes of determining the inheritance tax arising on my death.

1   A large class of beneficiaries may be interested in residue, some of whom may be minors who take under the substitution clause. Dividing up chattels among residuary beneficiaries can cause difficulties, and there may be persons other than the residuary beneficiaries to whom it would be appropriate to distribute some of the chattels. A discretionary power to distribute the chattels as in this clause could therefore have much to recommend it. Where professional executors are appointed, or at any rate ones who are independent of the residuary beneficiaries, a trust in this form may serve to ensure that the distribution of chattels to persons other than the residuary beneficiaries is given serious consideration (it will also help to ensure that this is done if the testator also leaves a memorandum of wishes). The main alternative would be to make an absolute gift to some or all of the nephews and nieces, coupled with a precatory request, as in Form C8.1, cl 3(2) at para **[230.6]** or Form C8.2, cl 3 at para **[230.21]**.
       The inheritance tax consequence of the use of a simple trustees' discretionary power over chattels as in this clause is not entirely clear. It is thought that the nephews and nieces who survive the testator will have interests in possession in all the chattels before any distribution to other beneficiaries takes place, and that neither s 143 (see B4 at para **[204.8]**) nor s 144 (see C3 at para **[225.83]** et seq) of the Inheritance Tax Act 1984 (ITA 1984) will apply. This will mean that distributions under the power in cl 5(2) will be treated for inheritance tax as gifts by the nephews and nieces rather than gifts by the testator, though they will usually be potentially exempt (see Part A, paras **[200.71]** and **[200.96]**). If substantial values could be involved, it would be preferable to provide a notional discretionary trust of income so that the ITA 1984, s 144 could apply to distributions, as in Form B4.11 at para **[204.24]**.
2   See Part G, para **[246.52]** for the wording of this definition, and for further discussion of the meaning of 'personal chattels' see Vol 1, para **[64.44]**.
3   This is included in case any of the chattels are outside the UK at the testator's death, and thus 'subject to tax' in the absence of a direction to the contrary. See the Note to B14 at para **[214.63]** and the definition of 'free of tax' in cl 8 of this form at para **[231.23]**.
4   This class may need broadening further. An alternative would be a power to add beneficiaries as in Form C3.6, cl 3(1)(b) at para **[225.100]**.
5   It is advisable to give the names and addresses of the nephews and nieces or otherwise identify them: see the Preliminary Note to this section at para **[231.9]**.

[231.21]

Specific devise of house to nephew of wife[1]

6.   I give to my [wife's][2] nephew [*name*] of [*address*] free of tax[3] and free of all sums charged thereon or otherwise secured thereon at my death (which sums shall be paid out of my residuary estate) the freehold dwellinghouse and grounds situate at [*address*] if in my ownership at my death or all or any the estate or interest therein or in the proceeds of sale thereof to which I may be entitled at my death in fee simple or absolutely.

1   See the Preliminary Note at para **[231.2]**. This is a gift of the named property to the named nephew to take effect on the deaths of both testators, whether the property is owned by one of them or both and, if both, whether it is owned by them as tenants in common or joint tenants. It should be noted that this gift will be adeemed if the house is sold by one or both of the testators before the gift can take effect (see cl 3 of Form C8.5 at para **[230.73]** for a gift which makes provision for such an eventuality).

2   This word will be included in the husband's will only. What is contemplated here is a gift in both wills to the same person.

3   If the property is in the UK the gift would be free of inheritance tax under the general law (see the Note to B14 at para **[214.55]** et seq). The main reason for putting these words here is prevent it being argued, in the absence of these words, that because other gifts in the will are declared to be free of tax this gift is not intended to be.

[231.22]

Administration trusts of residue

7.   (1)   I give all my property not hereby or by any codicil hereto otherwise effectively disposed of [(including any entailed or other property over which I shall have at my death a general power of disposition by will)][1] to my trustees to hold on the trusts set out below with power at their discretion to sell all or any of it as and when they think fit.[2]

(2)   My trustees shall pay my funeral and testamentary expenses[3] and debts and any legacies given by this will or any codicil hereto out of such property or its proceeds and shall have a discretion as to how such payments shall be borne as between capital and income[4].

(3)   Subject as above my trustees shall hold such property and the assets from time to time representing the same (hereinafter called 'my residuary estate') on the trusts set out below and shall invest all money comprised in such property or arising from its sale in any of the investments hereby authorised with power to change such investments into any others hereby authorised.

(4)   In the administration of my estate and the execution of the trusts of this will or of any codicil to it:

(a)   my trustees shall treat all income as accruing on the date on which it becomes payable regardless of the period in respect of which it shall have accrued and shall not make any statutory apportionment of the same;[5] and

(b)   none of the equitable rules of apportionment between capital and income shall apply in any circumstances whatever.[6]

1   See para **[230.7]**, n 1.
2   See para **[230.7]**, n 2.
3   See para **[230.7]**, n 3.
4   See para **[230.7]**, n 4.
5   See para **[230.7]**, n 5.
6   See para **[230.7]**, n 6.

[231.23]

Gifts made free of tax

8.   Any specific gift or pecuniary or general legacy made by this will or any codicil hereto which is expressed to be 'free of tax' shall be free from the payment of any inheritance tax or foreign tax or duty payable on or by reason of my death to which such gift or legacy would otherwise be subject and such inheritance tax or foreign tax or duty shall be paid out of my residuary estate.[1]

1   Where specific gifts and pecuniary legacies are of, or wholly payable out of, free estate in the UK, the inheritance tax on them will be a testamentary expense payable out of residue without any express provision, and it is only where foreign property or settled property is being disposed of by the will that a gift which is intended to be free of tax needs to be expressly declared to be free of tax. See also the Note to B14 at para **[214.55]** et seq. See cls 2, 5, and 6 of this form for clauses which direct gifts to be free of tax.

[231.24]

Beneficial trusts of residue

EITHER[1]

[9.   (1)   My trustees shall hold my residuary estate upon trust for such of my nephews and nieces and the nephews and nieces of [my wife/husband] namely [*names of nephews and nieces of both spouses*][2] as shall survive me and if more than one in equal shares provided that if any of the said nephews or nieces shall predecease me leaving a child or children living at my death who shall attain the age of [18/21/25][3] years such child or children shall take if more than one equally between them the share of my residuary estate which such deceased nephew or niece would have taken had he or she survived me.

(2)   The foregoing trusts shall carry the intermediate income of my residuary estate and section 31 of the Trustee Act 1925 (as hereinafter modified) shall apply thereto.

(3)   Section 32 of the Trustee Act 1925 (as hereinafter modified) shall apply in relation to my residuary estate.]

OR[4]

[9.   (1)   My trustees shall hold my residuary estate upon trust to divide the same into two shares as follows—

(a)   a [70] per cent share (hereinafter called 'the first share'); and
(b)   a [30] per cent share (hereinafter called 'the second share').

(2)   My trustees shall hold the first share upon trust for such of [my nephews and nieces]/[the nephews and nieces of my husband] namely [*name*] [*name*] [*name*] and [*name*][5] as shall survive me and if more than one in equal shares and shall hold the second share upon trust for such of [the nephews and nieces of my wife]/[my nephews and nieces] namely [*name*] [*name*] and [*name*][6] as shall survive me and if more than one in equal shares provided that—

(a)   if any of such nephews and nieces of myself or my [wife/husband] shall predecease me leaving issue living at my death who attain the age of [18/21/25][7] years such issue shall take and if more than one in equal shares per stirpes the share of my residuary estate which such deceased nephew or niece would have taken had he or she survived me but so that no such issue shall take whose parent (being such issue as aforesaid) survives me and attains the said age;

(b)   if the foregoing trusts for the benefit of the nephews and nieces of my [wife/husband] shall fail or determine then the share of my residuary estate hereinbefore directed to be held on trust for them shall devolve as

1831

if it formed part of my [wife's/husband's] estate and [she/he] had died intestate immediately after my death.[8]

(3)   The foregoing trusts shall carry the intermediate income of my residuary estate and section 31 of the Trustee Act 1925 (as hereinafter modified) shall apply thereto.

(4)   Section 32 of the Trustee Act 1925 (as hereinafter modified) shall apply in relation to my residuary estate.]

1   The first alternative for cl 9 divides residue equally between the nephews and nieces of both parties. It should be noted that it produces equality between *beneficiaries*, not necessarily equality between *families*. If it is desired to have half or other specified proportion of the combined estates going to one spouse's relations and the balance to the other's, irrespective of the number of the relations of each who survive to attain an interest, then the second alternative cl 9 should be used with the 'first share' and 'second share' both set at the appropriate proportions.

2   It is advisable to give the names and addresses of the nephews and nieces or otherwise identify them: see the Preliminary Note to this section at para **[231.9]**.

3   The nephews and nieces will all be lives in being for perpetuity purposes, so any age contingency may be specified; it is not necessary to confine it to 21.

4   The second alternative cl 9 divides residue in specified proportions between the two sides of the family. It is phrased so as to require the minimum of alteration when adapting a draft prepared for one spouse for use by the other spouse. This alternative for cl 9 can be used where the two sides of the family are to receive unequal shares of the combined estates (eg where the parties' respective estates are of significantly different value), and where it is desired that each side of the family should receive half of the combined estates irrespective of the number of beneficiaries on each side of the family (see also n 2 supra). If there are substantial legacies taking effect in favour of any of the residuary beneficiaries, or a specific gift of a house to a nephew as in cl 6, these should not be forgotten in the calculations of the proportions which should go to each testator's relatives.

It should be noted that if the testators die within the survivorship period of each other, both estates are divided between the two families in the agreed proportions instead of the estate of each going to his or her own relatives exclusively. This is likely to be fairer, because the testators may make lifetime gifts to each other or share heavy expenditure unequally after the wills have been made, and it will clearly be fairer if there are any assets held by the testators as joint tenants, since these will end up wholly in the estate of the survivor even if he dies within the survivorship period following the other's death.

5   It is advisable to give the names and addresses of the nephews and nieces or otherwise identify them with precision: see the Preliminary Note at para **[231.9]**.

The names at this point will be the same in both wills, but the description will be 'my nephews and nieces' in the husband's will and 'the nephews and nieces of my husband' in the wife's. Care should be taken to get the names and descriptions the right way round, and the testators should be given drafts of their wills and asked specifically to confirm that the descriptions are correctly matched with the names in each will, and that the first share and second share are respectively given to the right families. There may be only nephews or only nieces in one or other category, in which case the description should be amended accordingly.

6   The names at this point will be the same in both wills, but the description will be 'the nephews and nieces of my wife' in the husband's will and 'my nephews and nieces' in the wife's will. See also the previous note.

7   See n 3 supra.

8   Proviso (b) is designed to ensure that if the trusts of the share intended for the other spouse's nephews and nieces, that share will nevertheless go to their side of the family.

[231.25]

Maintenance, accumulation and advancement

10.   (1)   Section 31 of the Trustee Act 1925 (relating to accumulation and maintenance) shall apply in relation to the trusts hereby or by any codicil hereto declared as if:

(a) in paragraph (i) of subsection (1) of the said section the words 'as the trustees think fit' were substituted for the words 'as may in all the circumstances be reasonable'; and

(b) the proviso to the said subsection (1) were omitted.

(2) Section 32 of the Trustee Act 1925 (relating to advancement) shall apply in relation to the said trusts as if the words 'one half of' were omitted from proviso (a) to subsection (1) thereof [provided that the powers conferred by the said section (as hereby enlarged) shall not be exercisable in favour of any minor beneficiary hereunder otherwise than so as to cause such beneficiary to become immediately entitled to or to an interest in possession in the capital thereby paid or applied within the meaning of section 71(1)(a) of the Inheritance Tax Act 1984].[1]

(3) Whenever my trustees shall have an obligation or discretion under the provisions of this will or any codicil hereto or under the general law to apply income or capital for the benefit of a minor beneficiary they may either pay the same without liability to account to his or her parent guardian or any other adult person with whom such beneficiary may be residing or to such beneficiary himself or herself if of the age of 16 years or more and so that the receipt of such parent guardian or other person or of such minor beneficiary shall be a full and sufficient discharge to my trustees for the income or capital so applied.[2]

---

1   The proviso is included in order to prevent the power prejudicing the application of the ITA 1984, s 71 (accumulation and maintenance trusts), but is probably unnecessary: see the Note on inheritance tax and the statutory power of advancement in B18 at para **[218.74]**. If the accumulation and maintenance trusts of income are extended so as to continue beyond the age of 18 (see eg Forms B18.12 and B18.13 at paras **[218.78]** and **[218.79]**), then 'minor beneficiary hereunder' should be amended to eg 'beneficiary hereunder who is under the age of [*n*] years' where *n* is the highest age at which an absolute interest or an interest in possession might be attained by any of the beneficiaries. 25 is the maximum age compatible with the ITA 1984, s 71 applying: see Part A, para **[200.119]**.

2   A parent (with parental responsibility) and a guardian of a minor are empowered by the ChA 1989, s 3(3) (Part G, para **[244.119]**) to give a good receipt for the minor's property: see Vol 1, para **[9.42]**. The power in this subclause is wider in that it authorises the payment of income or capital to a parent who does not have parental responsibility, any adult with whom the minor is residing, and the minor himself or herself if 16 or over.

[231.26]

Administrative powers[1]

11. (1) In this clause where the context so admits:

(a) the expression 'land' includes buildings and estates interests or rights of any kind in or over land; and

(b) during the administration of my estate the expression 'beneficiary' includes any person who would be a beneficiary if such administration had been completed and the expression 'beneficially interested' and references to income of any asset being payable or capable of being paid to or for the benefit of a beneficiary shall be construed accordingly.

(2) None of the powers or provisions contained in subclause (3) below of this clause shall be capable of being exercised or operating in any manner such that if such power or provision were capable of being so exercised or so operating the existence of the same would either:

   (i)   prevent any person who would in the absence of such power or provision have been entitled to an interest in possession (within the meaning of Part III of the Inheritance Tax Act 1984) in any property from being entitled to such interest; or

  (ii)   prevent section 71 of the Inheritance Tax Act 1984 from applying to any property to which in the absence of such power or provision the said section 71 would have applied.[2]

(3)   In the administration of my estate and the execution of the trusts hereof or of any codicil hereto my trustees shall have the following powers in addition to those conferred by law but subject to the last foregoing subclause:

  (a) power to invest moneys sell assets and change investments with the unrestricted freedom of choice and powers of disposition and acquisition of a sole beneficial owner with in particular power to make unsecured loans, acquire non-income yielding assets, and purchase land anywhere in the world or chattels for any purpose including occupation or enjoyment in kind by a beneficiary under the power set out below;[3]

  (b) power to delegate all or any of their investment powers to a professional investment manager or managers whether individual or corporate and whether or not also a nominee holder of assets for my trustees (and who may be or include one or more of my trustees or the beneficiaries hereunder) upon such terms as to remuneration and otherwise (including terms authorising self-dealing or providing for the limitation of the liability of the investment manager or managers) as my trustees think fit and section 22 of the Trustee Act 2000 shall not apply;[4]

  (c) power to vest or register any property in any person or persons whether individual or corporate and whether or not an investment manager to whom powers have been delegated under the foregoing power (and who may be or include one or more of my trustees or the beneficiaries hereunder) as nominee or nominees for my trustees upon such terms as to remuneration or otherwise (including terms authorising self-dealing or providing for the limitation of the liability of the nominee) as my trustees think fit and section 22 of the Trustee Act 2000 shall not apply;[5]

  (d) power to borrow money with or without giving security and on such terms as to interest and repayment and otherwise as my trustees may think fit for any purpose connected with the administration of my estate or the trusts declared herein or in any codicil hereto (including investment) and no lender from whom my trustees borrow money in purported exercise of this power shall be concerned to enquire as to the propriety amount or purpose of any such borrowing;[6]

  (e) power to lend money to a beneficiary to whom any of the income of such money is payable or to whom or for whose benefit any income of such money is capable of being paid or applied in exercise of a discretion (or who would be such a beneficiary if such money yielded income) and to do so at a full or concessionary rate of interest or interest free;[7]

  (f) all the powers of an absolute owner in relation to any land (wherever situated) held by them;[8]

  (g) power to apply capital held on the same trusts as any land (or which would be so held if the administration of my estate had been completed) in the improvement of such land and to apply such capital or the income of such capital on the repair or maintenance of such land;[9]

(h) power to permit any beneficiary to have the beneficial occupation use or enjoyment in kind of any land or chattel or other tangible property on such terms as to repair insurance or payment of outgoings by the beneficiary or otherwise howsoever as my trustees think fit Provided that the foregoing power shall only be exercisable and such permission to occupy or enjoy in kind may only continue in the following circumstances:

(i) so long as any of the income of such land chattel or other tangible property is payable to such beneficiary or capable of being paid or applied to him or for his benefit in exercise of a discretion (or would be so payable or capable of being so paid or applied if such land chattel or other property yielded income);

(ii) in the case of land, so long as for the time being the occupation thereof by such beneficiary is compatible with any statutory rights of occupation of any other beneficiary or beneficiaries;[10]

(i) power to exercise all the powers of appropriation (and other incidental powers) conferred by statute on a personal representative without the necessity of obtaining any consents and notwithstanding that one or more of my trustees may be beneficially interested in the exercise of such power.[11]

1   See para **[230.11]**, n 1.
2   See para **[230.11]**, n 2.
3   See para **[230.11]**, n 3.
4   See para **[230.11]**, n 4.
5   See para **[230.11]**, n 5.
6   See para **[230.11]**, n 6.
7   See para **[230.11]**, n 7.
8   See para **[230.11]**, n 8.
9   See para **[230.11]**, n 9.
10 See para **[230.11]**, n 10.
11 See para **[230.11]**, n 11.

[231.27]

Trustee liability

12. (1) My trustees shall not be liable for any act or default of any investment manager or nominee employed in good faith to manage or hold assets of my estate nor for any act or default of any beneficiary having the occupation use or enjoyment of property in kind.[1]

(2) Section 11(1) of the Trusts of Land and Appointment of Trustees Act 1996 (consultation with beneficiaries) shall not apply to the exercise by my trustees of any of their powers in relation to land subject to the trusts hereof.[2]

1   This makes it clear that the trustees are not liable for the defaults of others who may have possession or control of trust property. For a wider form of indemnity, see eg Form B21.12 at para **[221.16]**.
2   The requirement that trustees of land in exercise of any function relating to land subject to the trust consult with beneficiaries of full age beneficially entitled to an interest in possession in the land can be excluded: TLATA 1996, s 11 (Part G, para **[246.97]**)

[231.28]

Professional trustee charging clause

13.   Any of my trustees being a professional or business man may charge and be paid all usual professional and other proper charges for business transacted acts done advice given and time spent by him or his firm in connection with the administration of my estate or in connection with the trusts hereof including acts which a personal representative or trustee not being in any profession or business could have done personally.

[231.29]

Testimonium and attestation clause

IN WITNESS whereof I have hereunto set my hand this —— day of —— 20— ——

SIGNED by the above-named testator as his last will in the presence of us both present at the same time who at his request and in his presence and in the presence of each other have signed our names below as witnesses: } *[Signature of testator]*

[Signatures, addresses and descriptions of two witnesses]

[231.30]

FORM C9.3:   Reciprocal wills for childless couple, the first to die giving entire estate to the survivor, and the survivor giving a legacy equal in value to the estate of the first to die to the latter's relatives and leaving residue to the survivor's own relatives

NOTE

In this form the relatives of the first to die benefit from a legacy equal in value to his or her estate rather than participating in a share of residue as in the preceding form. This device has the disadvantage that inflation may erode the benefit received by this class especially if the survivor survives the first to die by a long period. By contrast Form C9.2 divides the survivor's residue between the two families. For discussion of the relative merits of the two forms see the Preliminary Note at para **[231.2]**.

This form could also be used for a couple who are not married to each other. The name of the other person should be substituted for 'my [wife/husband]' throughout. There is also a modification which could be made to cl 4(1), noted in n 3 to that subclause at para **[231.35]**.

[231.31]

Revocation clause

I *[name]* of *[address]* hereby revoke all former testamentary dispositions made by me and declare this to be my last will.

[231.32]

Gift of entire estate to spouse and appointment of spouse as sole executor

1. If my [wife/husband] shall survive me for the period of one month[1] then subject to the payment thereout of my funeral and testamentary expenses[2] and debts I give all my estate both real and personal (including all entailed or other property over which I have at my death a general power of disposition by will)[3] to my [wife/husband] and appoint [her/him] to be the sole [executrix/executor] hereof and I declare that clauses 6 to 9 below hereof shall apply.[4]

1   For the inheritance tax and other implications of such survivorship conditions see the Preliminary Note to C2 at paras **[224.2]–[224.6]** and for the length of the survivorship period see Form C2.1, cl 4, n 1 at para **[224.25]**. It would not be appropriate to have a survivorship period longer than a month in this form because the appointment of the spouse as executor is dependent on survival by the specified period as well as the primary gift to the spouse.
2   See Form C9.1, n 1 at para **[231.12]**.
3   See Form C9.1, n 2 at para **[231.12]**.
4   See Form C9.2, cl 3, n 3 at para **[231.18]**.

[231.33]

Alternative provisions

2. If my [wife/husband] shall fail to survive me for the period aforesaid then the following provisions shall have effect.

[231.34]

Appointment of executors and trustees

3. I appoint [*name*] of [*address*] and [*name*] of [*address*] (hereinafter together called 'my trustees' which expression shall include my personal representatives for the time being and the trustees for the time being hereof) to be the executors and trustees of this will.

[231.35]

Gift to other spouse's beneficiaries of legacy equal in value to his or her estate

4. (1) If any property shall have devolved upon me under my [wife's/husband's] will[1] or from my [wife/husband] under any relevant joint tenancy (as defined below) I give to my trustees subject to and charged with a rateable proportion of any inheritance payable in respect of my death[2] a pecuniary legacy (hereinafter called 'the trust legacy') of such sum as shall be equal to the value (as at the date of the death of my [wife/husband]) of all such property as aforesaid[3] such legacy to carry interest at the rate of six per cent per annum from the date of my death until paid or satisfied by appropriation.

(2) For the foregoing purposes a relevant joint tenancy is one which has come to an end before my death and the value of property devolving upon me from my [wife/husband] under a relevant joint tenancy shall be the value immediately before [her/his] death of [her/his] severable share of the property subject to such joint tenancy or (where there were other joint tenants in addition to the two of us) the proportion of such value as corresponds to the proportion of such severable share which shall have accrued to me on [her/his] death.

(3) In calculating the amount of the sum aforesaid my trustees may rely on such valuations (whether agreed for probate purposes or not) or other estimates of value as they may in their absolute discretion think fit and so that any

calculation so made shall not be open to challenge to any person beneficially interested hereunder.

(4) My trustees shall hold the trust legacy upon trust for such of my [wife's/husband's] nephews and nieces [*name*] [*name*] [*name*] and [*name*]⁴ as shall survive me and if more than one in equal shares absolutely Provided that if any of my [wife's/husband's] said nephews and nieces shall predecease me leaving issue who shall survive me and attain the age of [18/21/25] years⁵ such issue shall take and if more than one in equal shares per stirpes the share of the trust legacy which such deceased would have taken had he or she survived me but so that no such issue shall take whose parent (being such issue as aforesaid) survives me and attains the said age.

(5) The foregoing trusts shall carry the intermediate income of the trust legacy and section 31 of the Trustee Act 1925 (as hereinafter modified) shall apply thereto.

(6) Section 32 of the Trustee Act 1925 (as hereinafter modified) shall apply in relation to the trust legacy.

1   If either spouse will be exercising a testamentary power of appointment in favour of the other spouse, words should be added to make clear whether or not the property appointed is to be included in this value.

2   Prima facie the inheritance tax attributable to a legacy is a testamentary expense payable out of residue (ITA 1984, s 211: Part G, para **[246.83]**; see also B14 at para **[214.55]** et seq), but it will in most cases be fairer for this legacy to bear its due proportion of the tax payable in respect of the entire joint estate on the survivor's death. Although the beneficiaries of the legacy would have borne less inheritance tax if the first to die's property had been left to them direct, it seems even more unfair that the testator's relations should have to bear all the inheritance tax on this legacy.

3   If this Form is used for persons who are not married to each other, there should be express wording to make it clear that the value to be taken into account is after deduction of any inheritance tax payable on the first to die's death, eg '(after deduction of any inheritance tax or foreign death duties arising from the death of [*name of other person*] and borne by me)'.

4   As to the desirability of identifying nephews and nieces (or other relatives) see the Preliminary Note to this section at para **[231.9]**.

5   See Form C9.2, cl 9, n 3 at para **[231.24]**.

[231.36]

Administration trusts of residue

5. [*As in cl 7 of* Form C9.2 *at para* **[231.22]**.]

[231.37]

Beneficial trusts of residue

6. (1) My trustees shall hold my residuary estate upon trust for such of my nephews and nieces [*name*] [*name*] [*name*] and [*name*]¹ as shall survive me and if more than one in equal shares absolutely provided that if any of my said nephews or nieces shall predecease me leaving issue who shall survive me and attain the age of [18/21/25] years² such issue shall take and if more than one in equal shares per stirpes the share of my residuary estate which such deceased nephew or niece could have taken had he or she survived me but so that no such issue shall take whose parent (being such issue as aforesaid) survives me and attains the said age.

(2)   The foregoing trusts shall carry the intermediate income of my residuary estate and section 31 of the Trustee Act 1925 (as hereinafter modified) shall apply thereto.

(3)   Section 32 of the Trustee Act 1925 (as hereinafter modified) shall apply in relation to my residuary estate.

1   See para **[231.35]**, n 1.
2   See para **[231.35]**, n 2.

[231.38]

Maintenance, accumulation and advancement
7.   [*As in cl 10 of* Form C9.2 *at para* **[231.25]**.]

[231.39]

Administrative powers
8.   [*As in cl 11 of* Form C9.2 *at para* **[231.26]**.]

[231.40]

Trustee liability
9.   [*As in cl 12 of* Form C9.2 *at para* **[231.27]**.]

[231.41]

Professional trustee charging clause
10.   [*As in cl 13 of* Form C9.2 *at para* **[231.28]**.]

[*Testimonium and attestation clauses as in* Form C9.2 *at para* **[231.29]**.]

[231.42]

FORM C9.4:   Reciprocal wills for couple each giving the other a life interest in residue with legacies payable on the death of the survivor and different ultimate trusts of their respective estates

NOTE

This form deals with the problem outlined in the Preliminary Note of childless couples wishing to provide for each other while ensuring that their respective estates ultimately pass to their own relatives by settling residue on the survivor for life rather than making an outright gift of it. It is drafted for married couples but may be adapted for others.

The matrimonial home will usually be a major item of property owned by the couple; the purpose of putting the residuary estate of the first to die in trust for his or her relatives may be frustrated if his or her interest in the house passes to the other absolutely under a joint tenancy. *It is essential when preparing wills of this type to examine the title to the matrimonial home carefully to see how it is held*; if it is owned by the testators as joint tenants beneficially the parties must be asked whether they wish the interest in the home of the first of them to die to be settled on trust under his or her will. If so, they must be advised to effect a severance, and, if not, a careful record should be made and retained of their intention that the joint tenancy should continue.

If a will of this type is being made for a married couple who are concerned about the utilisation of the nil-rate band of the first to die, Form C3.2, cl 4 at para **[225.32]**, or Form C3.4, cl 2 at para **[225.60]** could be adapted for the purpose.

[231.43]

Revocation clause

I [*name*] of [*address*] hereby revoke all former testamentary dispositions made by me and declare this to be my last will.

[231.44]

Appointment of executors and trustees[1]

1.   I appoint my [wife/husband] [*name*] [*name*] of [*address*] and [*name*] of [*address*][2] (hereinafter called 'my trustees' which expression shall include my personal representatives for the time being and the trustees for the time being hereof) to be the executors and trustees of this will.

1   The choice of executors and trustees will be especially important if a power to advance the capital of residue to the survivor is included.
2   If there are two executors as well as the wife/husband, there will still be two effective appointments if there is a divorce and the appointment of the wife/husband is nullified by the WA 1837, s 18A (added by the LR(S)A 1995, s 3: Part G, para **[244.18]**). See also the Preliminary Note on the possibility of divorce to C2 at paras **[224.12]–[224.19]**.

[231.45]

Gift of personal chattels[1]

2.   I give to my [wife/husband] absolutely all my personal chattels as defined by section 55(1)(x) of the Administration of Estates Act 1925.[2]

1   As residue is settled on the survivor for life, and settling chattels is something to be avoided, an outright gift to the survivor of the personal chattels is included. However, one consequence is that all the combined chattels will fall into the residuary estate of the survivor, and go to the latter's relations, unless they are willing to give some of them to the first to die's relatives. It may be preferred to provide a discretionary trust or power arising under the will of the second to die with the relations of both testators made objects of the discretion. Forms which could be used are Form B4.11 at para **[204.25]** and Form C9.2, cl 5 at para **[231.20]**.
2   See Part G, para **[246.52]**. See also Vol 1, para **[64.44]** for discussion of the meaning of the term.

[231.46]

Administration trusts of residue

3.   [*As in cl 7 of* Form C9.2 *at para* **[231.22]**.]

[231.47]

Beneficial trusts of residue

4.   (1)   My trustees shall hold my residuary estate upon trust to pay the income thereof to my [wife/husband] during [her/his] life [provided that so long as my [wife/husband] is entitled to be paid the income of all or any part of the capital of my residuary estate (or would be so entitled if it yielded income)[1] my trustees shall have power from time to time to pay transfer or apply the whole or

any part or parts of such capital to or for the support or benefit of my [wife/husband] as they shall in their absolute discretion think fit].[2]

(2)   Subject to the trust [and to any exercise of the power] aforesaid my trustees shall hold my residuary estate upon trust on the later to occur of my death or the death of my [wife/husband] to pay to the following persons [if then living][3] pecuniary legacies free of all inheritance tax and foreign death duties payable on or by reason of my death or the death of my [wife/husband][4] (and with interest thereon at the yearly rate of 6 per cent from the later to occur of my death or the death of my [wife/husband]) of the amounts hereinafter respectively mentioned namely:

(a)   to [*name*] of [*address*] the sum of ——;
(b)   to [*name*] of [address] the sum of ——;
(c)   to [the Vicar and Churchwardens of the Parish of ——] the sum of £—
        — for such charitable purposes in the said Parish as they think fit.

(3)   Subject as aforesaid my trustees shall hold my residuary estate and the income thereof upon trust for such of my nephews and nieces [*name*] [*name*] [*name*] and [*name*][5] as shall survive me and if more than one in equal shares absolutely provided that if any of my said nephews or nieces shall predecease me leaving a child or children surviving me who shall attain the age of [18/21] years such child or children shall take and if more than one equally between them the share of my residuary estate which such deceased nephew or niece would have taken had he or she lived to attain a vested interest.

1   For the reasons for limiting the power in this way see the Preliminary Note to C2 at paras **[224.17]–[224.19]**.
2   For a provision of this type which limits the amount which can be paid or applied to or for the benefit of the beneficiary see Form C5.2, cl 5(2) at para **[227.27]**.
3   If the provisions of cl 4(1) fail by reason of divorce, the remainder trusts will have effect as if the spouse had died on the date of the decree: see the WA 1837, s 18A (Part G, para **[244.18]**) and the Preliminary Note to C2 at paras **[224.17]–[224.19]**.
4   If the testator's spouse survives the testator, the legacies are likely to be subject to a rateable share of the inheritance tax arising on the spouse's death in the absence of an express direction to the contrary: see *Foster's Inheritance Tax*, K2.03.
5   As to the desirability of identifying nephews and nieces (or other relatives) see the Preliminary Note to this section at para **[231.9]**. The persons named at this point will be different persons in each will, and persons other than nephews and nieces can readily be substituted.

[231.48]

Maintenance, accumulation and advancement
5.   [*As in cl 10 of* Form C9.2 *at para* **[231.25]**.]

[231.49]

Administrative powers
6.   [*As in cl 11 of* Form C9.2 *at para* **[231.26]**.]

[231.50]

Exercise of powers[1]
7.   Any power or discretion hereby or by law conferred on my trustees (including a power or discretion as to the disposition of capital or income) shall be exercisable notwithstanding that any of my trustees has a personal interest in

such exercise provided that there are not fewer than two trustees and that at least one of them has no such personal interest.

1   This clause will make it clear that the other spouse, if he or she is a trustee, may join in exercising the power to pay or apply capital (see cl 4(1) at para **[231.46]**) in his or her favour. See the Preliminary Note to B18 at para **[218.4]** on this subject.

[231.51]

Trustee liability
8.   [*As in cl 12 of* Form C9.2 *at para* **[231.27]**.]

[231.52]

Professional trustee charging clause
9.   [*As in cl 13 of* Form C9.2 *at para* **[231.28]**.]

[*Testimonium and attestation clauses as in* Form C9.2 *at para* **[231.29]**.]

[231.53]

FORM C9.5:   Reciprocal wills for unmarried sisters leaving residue to survivor(s) with alternative gift to charity

NOTE

This form assumes a household of unmarried sisters but could be adopted for use by brothers or other relatives or friends living together. It also assumes that there are three members of such household who all make wills in similar form. Subject to the gift of legacies residue devolves on the surviving sisters or sister and the death of the last survivor goes to charity. As mentioned in the Preliminary Note, there is not much scope for tax-planning where the primary concern of the members of the household is to provide for each other, but an optional survival contingency is included in the residuary trusts.

[231.54]

Revocation clause and declaration against mutual wills
I [*name*] of [*address*] revoke all former testamentary dispositions made by me and declare this to be my last will [and I further declare that notwithstanding that my sisters [*name*] and [*name*] are making wills in similar terms we have agreed that our wills are not mutual wills and accordingly that each of us shall be free to revoke her will at any time whether before or after the death of either of the others and shall be free to dispose of her property or any property derived from either of the others as she thinks fit].[1]

1   There is no presumption that two wills in similar form are mutual wills in the technical sense, but the inclusion of the words in square brackets will remove any doubt on the point. If mutual wills are intended, then an express clause to that effect, such as Form B1.6 at para **[201.10]** should be used instead of this clause. For the law on mutual wills see Vol 1, paras **[2.3]**–**[2.9]**. We recommend life interest trusts rather than mutual wills where a testator wishes to determine the destination of his property after the death of a primary beneficiary or beneficiaries.

[231.55]

Directions as to burial
1.   I desire that my body may be buried in the family vault in the churchyard of the Church of —— in the Parish of ——.

[231.56]

Appointment of executors
2.   I appoint [my sisters [*name*] and [*name*]] and [*name*] of [*address*] (hereinafter together called 'my trustees' which expression shall include my personal representatives for the time being and the trustees for the time being hereof) to be the executors and trustees of this will.

[231.57]

Pecuniary legacies
3.   I give free of tax¹ the following pecuniary legacies—

   (a)   to [my god-daughter [*name*]] the sum of £——;
   (b)   to [my cousin [*name*]] the sum of £——;
   (c)   to my friend [*name*] the sum of £——;
   (d)   to [the Vicar and Churchwardens of the Parish of ——] the sum of £—— to be applied for such charitable purposes in the said Parish as they think fit.

1   See Form C9.2, cl 2, n 2 at para **[231.17]**.

[231.58]

Administration trusts of residue
4.   [*As in cl 7 of* Form C9.2 *at para* **[231.22]**.]

[231.59]

Gifts made free of tax
5.   [*As in cl 8 of* Form C9.2 *at para* **[231.23]**.]

[231.60]

Beneficial trusts of residue
6.   My trustees shall stand possessed of my residuary estate—

   (a)   upon trust for such of my said sisters as shall survive me [for the period of one month]¹ and if both in equal shares absolutely;
   (b)   in default of and subject to the foregoing trust upon trust for [*name of charity*] absolutely and I declare that the receipt of any person professing to be the treasurer or other proper officer of the said charity shall be a full and sufficient discharge to my trustees.

1   For the utility of survivorship conditions in gifts in favour of persons other than the testator's spouse, see the Preliminary Note to C2 at para **[224.6]**.

[231.61]

Professional trustee charging clause
7.   [*As in cl 13 of* Form C9.2 *at para* **[231.28]**.]

[*Testimonium and attestation clause as in* Form C9.2 *at para* **[231.29]**.]

[231.62]

FORM C9.6:   Will of unmarried and childless testatrix giving her unmarried and childless sister a right of residence in her house and dividing residue between her nephews and nieces and charity

NOTE

The provision provided by this will for the unmarried sister is limited to a right of residence in the house. For alternative possibilities see Form C9.5 at paras **[231.53]**–**[231.61]** and Form C10.5 at paras **[232.52]**–**[232.63]**.

[231.63]

Revocation
I [*name*] of [*address*] hereby revoke all former testamentary dispositions made by me and declare this to be my last will.

[231.64]

Appointment of executors and trustees
1.   [*As in cl 3 of* Form C9.3 *at paras* **[231.34]**.]

[231.65]

Gift of chattels to sister
2.   I give [free of tax][1] all my personal chattels as defined by section 55(1)(x) of the Administration of Estates Act 1925 to my sister [*name*] absolutely.

---

1   Inheritance tax on specifically given property is prima facie a testamentary expense payable out of residue unless the property is situate out of the United Kingdom: ITA 1984, s 211(1) (Part G, para **[246.83]**; see also B14 at para **[214.55]** et seq). However, the inclusion of the words 'free of tax' (ie free of inheritance tax: see the definition in cl 6) will do no harm and will exclude the tax charge in respect of any property which happens to be situate out of the jurisdiction at the death.

[231.66]

Pecuniary legacies
3.   [*As in cl 3 of* Form C9.5 *at para* **[231.57]**.]

[231.67]

Right of residence to sister[1]
4.   (1)   I give my freehold dwellinghouse known as ———, or (if the same shall be sold or otherwise disposed of before my death) the dwellinghouse or the principal dwellinghouse (if I have more than one) which I shall own at the date of my death, to my trustees free of all sums charged or otherwise secured thereon at my death (which sums shall be paid out of my residuary estate) to

hold the same and any dwellinghouse acquired in substitution therefor (as provided below) upon trust to provide a residence for my sister [*name*] so long as she wishes to reside there subject as provided below.

(2)   My trustees shall not exercise their power to sell the said or any substitute dwellinghouse or their power to purchase any substitute dwellinghouse or exercise any of their other powers[2] over any such dwellinghouse without the consent in writing of my sister so long as her interest continues and (if for the time being a dwellinghouse is held subject to the provisions of this Clause) so long as she shall perform and observe any conditions reasonably imposed by my trustees in relation to her residence in any such dwellinghouse.[3]

(3)   I wish my trustees to impose as a condition in relation to my sister's residence in any such dwellinghouse that she should keep the same fully insured in the name of my trustees, keep the same in good repair, observe and perform the lessee's covenants (if the dwellinghouse is leasehold), and pay all taxes and other outgoings in respect thereof[4] and my trustees shall not be liable for lack of insurance repair or payment of outgoings or for not taking steps to enforce any reasonable conditions imposed in relation to my sister's residence in any such dwellinghouse.[5]

(4)   On the death of my sister or (subject to subclause (5) below) in the event of her giving up residence, such dwellinghouse and any property representing it shall fall into my residuary estate.

(5)   For the purposes of this clause:

(a)   no involuntary ceasing by my sister to reside in a dwellinghouse subject to this clause shall be treated as ceasing to reside therein unless my sister shall have been out of residence continuously for six months and shall not have expressed in writing to my trustees her intention to take up residence again;[6]

(b)   references to a dwellinghouse include a flat and an interest in a dwellinghouse.

(6)   All the powers of my trustees may be exercised by them in favour of or for the benefit of my sister even though she may be one of my trustees.

---

1   This is a simple form which permits the sister to reside only in the property held at the testator's death. For a more elaborate form which enables a replacement property to be purchased for her to live in, see Form B8.5 at para **[208.41]**. For a discussion of rights of residence see the Preliminary Note to B8 at para **[208.1]** et seq.

2   This is no longer statutorily implied from the requirement of consent to a sale as a result of the repeal of the LPA 1925, s 28(1): see Part A, para **[200.60]**. The TLATA 1996, s 8(2) (Part G, para **[246.93]**) provides that exercise of the trustees' powers may be subject to consents (see Part A, para **[200.60]** and para **[208.19]**).

3   Subclause (2) could be omitted, since so long as the beneficiary is in residence the trustees cannot sell the property without first applying to the court under the TLATA 1996, s 14 (Part G, para **[246.100]**) and making the requirement of her consent end if she does not fulfil the conditions of her occupation does not help the trustees much if she is still in occupation.

4   See para **[208.26]** for the reasons for making this an expression of wishes rather than a direction that the beneficiary's occupation shall be subject to these burdens.

5   Although it is thought that the will cannot predetermine what obligations an occupying beneficiary will be subject to (see para **[208.26]**) there is nothing to prevent the trustees being absolved from liability for want of repair etc which it is contemplated will be the beneficiary's responsibility.

6   The idea here is to protect the beneficiary against precipitate sale if she is hospitalised after an accident or illness, but if she is hospitalised and is mentally incapacitated she will not be able to express an intention to return and the trustees will be free to sell the property after six months. This paragraph may be omitted if preferred.

[231.68]

Administration trusts of residue
5.   [*As in cl 7 of* Form C9.2 *at para* **[231.22]**.]

[231.69]

Gifts made free of tax
6.   [*As in cl 8 of* Form C9.2 *at para* **[231.23]**.]

[231.70]

Division of residue
7.   (1)   My trustees shall hold my residuary estate upon trust to divide the same into [two equal shares]/[two shares of one third and two thirds] (hereinafter respectively called 'the charity share' and 'the family share').
    (2)   The foregoing shares shall be determined by division of my residuary estate in the foregoing proportions before making any deduction for the inheritance tax payable by reason of my death and attributable to the family share and such inheritance tax shall then be borne by the family share as so determined.[1]

1   For the reasons for making provision of this sort, see paras **[200.138]** et seq and **[214.69]**.

[231.71]

Trusts of charity share
8.   My trustees shall hold the charity share and the income thereof upon trust for such institution or institutions (whether corporate or not) having exclusively charitable purposes connected with the relief of poverty or for such exclusively charitable purposes connected with the relief of poverty as my trustees shall in their absolute discretion determine.

[231.72]

Trusts of family share
9.   (1)   My trustees shall hold the family share and the income thereof upon trust for such of my nephews and nieces [*name*] [*name*] [*name*] and [*name*][1] as shall survive me and if more than one in equal shares absolutely provided that if any of my said nephews or nieces shall predecease me leaving a child or children surviving me who shall attain the age of [18/21] years such child or children shall taken and if more than one equally between them the share of my residuary estate which such deceased nephew or niece would have taken had he or she lived to attain a vested interest.

1   It is advisable to give the names and addresses of them or otherwise identify them fully: see the Preliminary Note at para **[231.9]**.

[231.73]

Maintenance, accumulation and advancement
10.   [*As in cl 10 of* Form C9.2 *at para* **[231.25]**.]

[231.74]

Administrative powers
11.   [*As in cl 11 of* Form C9.2 *at para* **[231.26]**.]

[231.75]

Trustee liability
12.   [*As in cl 12 of* Form C9.2 *at para* **[231.27]**.]

[231.76]

Professional trustee charging clause
13.   [*As in cl 13 of* Form C9.2 *at para* **[231.28]**.]

[*Testimonium and attestation clause as in* Form C9.2 *at para* **[231.29]**.]

C10 Wills for childless individuals

PRELIMINARY NOTE

[232.1]
The forms in this section provide a selection of alternative dispositions for childless individuals. These forms are in many respects similar to those in C7 and C8 for sole parents. One significant difference, however, is that in the case of wills of parents in favour of their own children, the class will necessarily close on the parent's death. In the case of an uncle or aunt, especially one who is relatively young, this is not necessarily so and, unless special provision is made, after-born nephews and nieces may be excluded from benefit. If the estate is substantial and includes landed estates, reference should be made to Form C13.2 at para **[235.18]** et seq.

One tax planning possibility to bear in mind is generation skipping. Gifts direct to the youngest available generation could save significant amounts of inheritance tax in the long run (see Part A, paras **[200.88]** and **[200.91]**). Form C10.1 is an example of a will which gives each sibling's share direct to his or her children if he or she has any at the testator's death. If it is desired to create an accumulation and maintenance trust for the youngest available generation, Form C8.4 at paras **[230.45]**–**[230.69]** could be adapted.

Where it is desired to assist older generations, particularly where it is desired to benefit the elderly, a discretionary trust could save inheritance tax. Form C10.2 at paras **[232.15]**–**[232.26]** is an example of this strategy.

[232.2]

FORM C10.1:   Will of young person dividing his or her estate equally between his or her siblings but making a gift of the share of a sibling with living children direct to such children

NOTE

The idea of this form is to include the maximum amount of generation skipping (for which see Part A, para **[200.91]**), according to the circumstances at the testator's death. The residuary estate is divided into shares according to the number of siblings then living, or then dead leaving issue. The share of any sibling of whom there are issue living at the testator's death goes direct to that issue, whether or not the sibling is still living.

[232.3]

Revocation clause

I [*name*] of [*address*] hereby revoke all former testamentary dispositions made by me and declare this to be my last will.

[232.4]

Appointment of executors and trustees

1.   I appoint [*name*] of [*address*] and [*name*] of [*address*] (hereinafter together called 'my trustees' which expression shall include my personal representatives for the time being and the trustees for the time being hereof) to be the executors and trustees of this will.

[232.5]

Gift of personal chattels

2.   I give free of tax[1] all my personal chattels as defined by section 55(1)(x) of the Administration of Estates Act 1925[2] to my [brother/sister] [*name*] absolutely and I request [him/her] (but without imposing any trust or binding obligation on [him/her]) to give effect to any wishes of mine as to the disposition of such chattels which may be contained in any memorandum which may be found amongst my papers at my death or which may have been otherwise communicated to [him/her] during my life.[3]

1   This is included in case any of the chattels are outside the UK at the testator's death, and thus subject to tax in the absence of a direction to the contrary. See the Note to B14 at para **[214.55]** and the definition of 'free of tax' in cl 5 of this form at para **[232.8]**.
2   See Part G, para **[246.52]** and Vol 1, para **[64.44]**.
3   A distribution in accordance with the testator's wishes within two years of the testator's death will be treated for inheritance tax purposes as a direct gift by the testator's will (Inheritance Tax Act 1984 (ITA 1984), s 143): see B4 at paras **[204.6]–[204.9]**.

[232.6]

Pecuniary legacies

3.   (1)   I give free of tax[1] pecuniary legacies of £—— to each of my godchildren [*name*] [*name*] and [*name*].[2]
      (2)   I give the following charitable legacies:[3]

(a)   to [*name of charity*] the sum of £——;
(b)   to [*name of charity*] the sum of £——;
(c)   to [*name of charity*] the sum of £——;

And I declare that the receipt of the person professing to be the treasurer or other proper officer of any of the said charities shall be a full and sufficient discharge to my trustees for the legacy hereby given to such charity.[4]

1   Although the inheritance tax on legacies or specific gifts of UK property is a testamentary expense, it is preferable to include an express direction that a pecuniary legacy is free of tax in case residue includes foreign property or settled property; if it does include such property, a proportion of the legacies, corresponding to the proportion of residue which made up of foreign or settled property, would probably have to bear inheritance in the absence of a direction to the contrary. See further the Note to B14 at para [214.55] et seq. For the definition of 'free of tax' see cl 5 of this form at para [232.8].
2   It is essential to identify godchildren by name.
3   Gifts for charitable purposes are exempt from inheritance tax and it is not therefore necessary to incorporate the 'free of tax' formula.
4   If there is the slightest doubt as to whether any of these charitable donees are correctly described or still exist, a discretionary charitable trust to operate in case of difficulty, such as Form C10.6, cl 4 at para [232.68] could be added.

[232.7]

Administration trusts of residue

4.   (1)   I give all my property not hereby or by any codicil hereto otherwise effectively disposed of [(including any entailed or other property over which I shall have at my death a general power of disposition by will)][1] to my trustees to hold on the trusts set out below with power at their discretion to sell all or any of it as and when they think fit.[2]

(2)   My trustees shall pay my funeral and testamentary expenses[3] and debts and any legacies given by this will or any codicil hereto out of such property or its proceeds and shall have a discretion as to how such payments shall be borne as between capital and income.[4]

(3)   Subject as above my trustees shall hold such property and the assets from time to time representing the same (hereinafter called 'my residuary estate') on the trusts set out below and shall invest all money comprised in such property or arising from its sale in any of the investments hereby authorised with power to change such investments into any others hereby authorised.

(4)   In the administration of my estate and the execution of the trusts of this will or of any codicil to it:

(a)   my trustees shall treat all income as accruing on the date on which it becomes payable regardless of the period in respect of which it shall have accrued and shall not make any statutory apportionment of the same;[5] and

(b)   none of the equitable rules of apportionment between capital and income shall apply in any circumstances whatever.[6]

1   See para [230.7], n 1.
2   See para [230.7], n 2.
3   See para [230.7], n 3.
4   See para [230.7], n 4.
5   See para [230.7], n 5.
6   See para [230.7], n 6.

[232.8]

Gifts made free of tax

5.   Any specific gift or pecuniary or general legacy made by this will or any codicil hereto which is expressed to be 'free of tax' shall be free from the payment of any inheritance tax or foreign tax or duty payable on or by reason of my death to which such gift or legacy would otherwise be subject and such inheritance tax or foreign tax or duty shall be paid out of my residuary estate.[1]

1   See Form C3.1, cl 5, n 1 at para **[225.15]**.

[232.9]

Beneficial trusts of residue

6.   (1)   My trustees shall hold my residuary estate upon trust to divide the same into such number of equal shares as shall be equal to the number of such of my brothers and sisters as shall be living at the date of my death or shall have predeceased me (whether before or after the date of this will)[1] leaving children or grandchildren living at my death.

(2)   In the case of any of my brothers or sisters who shall be living at the date of my death but who shall have no children or grandchildren then living my trustees shall hold one such equal share of my residuary estate upon trust for such brother or sister absolutely.

(3)   In the case of any of my brothers and sisters who shall have children or grandchildren living at the date of my death (and whether or not such brother or sister shall himself or herself then be living) my trustees shall hold one such equal share of my residuary estate upon the following trusts:

(a)   my trustees shall hold such share upon trust for such of the children of such brother or sister (whether living at the date of my death or born thereafter at any time before any of such children shall attain a vested interest hereunder)[2] as shall attain the age of [18/21/25/30] years [or be living at the expiration of the trust period[3] (if earlier)][4] and if more than one in equal shares;

(b)   Provided that if any child of such brother or sister of mine shall predecease me or otherwise fail to attain a vested interest in such share[5] leaving a child or children living at my death or born thereafter during the trust period who shall attain the age of [18/21/25/30] years or be living at the expiration of the trust period (if earlier) such last-mentioned child or children shall take and if more than equally between them the share of such share of my residuary estate which his her or their parent would have taken had he or she lived to attain a vested interest;

(c)   the foregoing trusts shall carry the intermediate income of such share and section 31 of the Trustee Act 1925 (as hereinafter modified) shall apply thereto;

(d)   section 32 of the Trustee Act 1925 (as hereinafter modified) shall apply in relation to such share;

(e)   subject as aforesaid my trustees shall hold such share upon trust for such brother or sister of mine if living at the date of my death absolutely and if such brother or sister shall have predeceased me such share shall devolve in all respects as if he or she had predeceased me without leaving any child or grandchild living at my death.

(4)   The expression 'the trust period' means the period expiring on the twenty-first anniversary of the death of the last survivor of such of my brothers and sisters and their respective children and grandchildren as are living at my death.

1   If any brother or sister is dead at the date of the will, it is likely that any issue of his or hers who may be living at the testator's death will be eligible under the trusts declared by sub-cl (3), but it is advisable to include the words in brackets so as to make this absolutely clear: cf *Re Earle's Settlement Trusts, Reiss v Norrie* [1971] 2 All ER 1188, [1971] 1 WLR 1118 and see generally Vol 1, paras **[68.3]–[68.9]**.
2   The words in brackets will let in a nephew or niece who is born after the death of the testator but before any brother or sister of his attains a vested interest.
3   Defined in sub-cl (4).
4   The words in square brackets will not be necessary if the age contingency does not exceed 21.
5   The latter alternative contemplates a subsequently born child who fails to attain the vesting age.

[232.10]

Maintenance, accumulation and advancement[1]

7.   (1)   Section 31 of the Trustee Act 1925 (relating to accumulation and maintenance) shall apply in relation to the trusts hereby or by any codicil hereto declared as if:

(a)   in paragraph (i) of subsection (1) of the said section the words 'as the trustees think fit' were substituted for the words 'as may in all the circumstances be reasonable'; and

(b)   the proviso to the said subsection (1) were omitted.

(2)   Section 32 of the Trustee Act 1925 (relating to advancement) shall apply in relation to the said trusts as if the words 'one half of' were omitted from proviso (a) to subsection (1) thereof [Provided that the powers conferred by the said section (as hereby enlarged) shall not be exercisable in favour of any minor beneficiary hereunder otherwise than so as to cause such beneficiary to become immediately entitled to or to an interest in possession in the capital thereby paid or applied within the meaning of section 71(1)(a) of the Inheritance Tax Act 1984].[2]

(3)   Whenever my trustees shall have an obligation or discretion under the provisions of this will or any codicil hereto or under the general law to apply income or capital for the benefit of a minor beneficiary they may either pay the same without liability to account to his or her parent guardian or any other adult person with whom such beneficiary may be residing or to such beneficiary himself or herself if of the age of 16 years or more and so that the receipt of such parent guardian or other person or of such minor beneficiary shall be a full and sufficient discharge to my trustees for the income or capital so applied.[3]

1   For alternative provisions see the forms in B18 at para **[218.77]** et seq.
2   The proviso is included in order to prevent the power prejudicing the application of the ITA 1984, s 71 (accumulation and maintenance trusts), but is probably unnecessary: see the Note on inheritance tax and the statutory power of advancement in B18 at paras **[218.99]–[218.102]**. If the accumulation and maintenance trusts of income are extended so as to continue beyond the age of 18 (see eg, Forms B18.12 and B18.13 at paras **[218.78]** and **[218.79]**), then 'minor beneficiary hereunder' should be amended to eg 'beneficiary hereunder who is under the age of [*n*] years' where *n* is the highest age at which an absolute interest or an interest in possession might be attained by any of the beneficiaries. 25 is the maximum age compatible with the ITA 1984, s 71 applying: see Part A, para **[200.119]**.

3   A parent (with parental responsibility) and a guardian of a minor are empowered by the ChA 1989, s 3(3) (Part G, para **[244.119]**) to give a good receipt for the minor's property: see Vol 1, para **[9.42]**. The power in this subclause is wider in that it authorises the payment of income or capital to a parent who does not have parental responsibility, any adult with whom the minor is residing, and the minor himself or herself if 16 or over.

[232.11]

Administrative powers[1]

8.   (1)   In this clause where the context so admits:

   (a)   the expression 'land' includes buildings and estates interests or rights of any kind in or over land; and

   (b)   during the administration of my estate the expression 'beneficiary' includes any person who would be a beneficiary if such administration had been completed and the expression 'beneficially interested' and references to income of any asset being payable or capable of being paid to or for the benefit of a beneficiary shall be construed accordingly.

   (2)   None of the powers or provisions contained in subclause (3) below of this clause shall be capable of being exercised or operating in any manner such that if such power or provision were capable of being so exercised or so operating the existence of the same would either:

   (i)   prevent any person who would in the absence of such power or provision have been entitled to an interest in possession (within the meaning of Part III of the Inheritance Tax Act 1984) in any property from being entitled to such interest; or

   (ii)   prevent section 71 of the Inheritance Tax Act 1984 from applying to any property to which in the absence of such power or provision the said section 71 would have applied.[2]

   (3)   In the administration of my estate and the execution of the trusts hereof or of any codicil hereto my trustees shall have the following powers in addition to those conferred by law but subject to the last foregoing subclause—

   (a)   power to invest moneys sell assets and change investments with the unrestricted freedom of choice and powers of disposition and acquisition of a sole beneficial owner with in particular power to make unsecured loans, acquire non-income yielding assets, and purchase land anywhere in the world or chattels for any purpose including occupation or enjoyment in kind by a beneficiary under the power set out below;[3]

   (b)   power to delegate all or any of their investment powers to a professional investment manager or managers whether individual or corporate and whether or not also a nominee holder of assets for my trustees (and who may be or include one or more of my trustees or the beneficiaries hereunder) upon such terms as to remuneration and otherwise (including terms authorising self-dealing or providing for the limitation of the liability of the investment manager or managers) as my trustees think fit and section 22 of the Trustee Act 2000 shall not apply;[4]

   (c)   power to vest or register any property in any person or persons whether individual or corporate and whether or not an investment manager to whom powers have been delegated under the foregoing power (and who may be or include one or more of my trustees or the beneficiaries hereunder) as nominee or nominees for my trustees upon such terms as to remuneration or otherwise (including terms authorising self-dealing or providing for the limitation of the liability of the nominee) as my trustees think fit and section 22 of the Trustee Act 2000 shall not apply;[5]

(d)   power to borrow money with or without giving security and on such terms as to interest and repayment and otherwise as my trustees may think fit for any purpose connected with the administration of my estate or the trusts declared herein or in any codicil hereto (including investment) And no lender from whom my trustees borrow money in purported exercise of this power shall be concerned to enquire as to the propriety amount or purpose of any such borrowing;[6]

(e)   power to lend money to a beneficiary to whom any of the income of such money is payable or to whom or for whose benefit any income of such money is capable of being paid or applied in exercise of a discretion (or who would be such a beneficiary if such money yielded income) and to do so at a full or concessionary rate of interest or interest free;[7]

(f)   all the powers of an absolute owner in relation to any land (wherever situated) held by them;[8]

(g)   power to apply capital held on the same trusts as any land (or which would be so held if the administration of my estate had been completed) in the improvement of such land and to apply such capital or the income of such capital on the repair or maintenance of such land;[9]

(h)   power to permit any beneficiary to have the beneficial occupation use or enjoyment in kind of any land or chattel or other tangible property on such terms as to repair insurance or payment of outgoings by the beneficiary or otherwise howsoever as my trustees think fit Provided that the foregoing power shall only be exercisable and such permission to occupy or enjoy in kind may only continue in the following circumstances:

   (i)   so long as any of the income of such land chattel or other tangible property is payable to such beneficiary or capable of being paid or applied to him or for his benefit in exercise of a discretion (or would be so payable or capable of being so paid or applied if such land chattel or other property yielded income);

   (ii)   in the case of land, so long as for the time being the occupation thereof by such beneficiary is compatible with any statutory rights of occupation of any other beneficiary or beneficiaries;[10]

(i)   power to exercise all the powers of appropriation (and other incidental powers) conferred by statute on a personal representative without the necessity of obtaining any consents and notwithstanding that one or more of my trustees may be beneficially interested in the exercise of such power.[11]

1   See para **[230.11]**, n 1.
2   See para **[230.11]**, n 2.
3   See para **[230.11]**, n 3.
4   See para **[230.11]**, n 4.
5   See para **[230.11]**, n 5.
6   See para **[230.11]**, n 6.
7   See para **[230.11]**, n 7.
8   See para **[230.11]**, n 8.

9   See para **[230.11]**, n 9.
10   See para **[230.11]**, n 10.
11   See para **[230.11]**, n 11.

[232.12]

Trustee liability
9.   (1)   My trustees shall not be liable for any act or default of any investment manager or nominee employed in good faith to manage or hold assets of my estate nor for any act or default of any beneficiary having the occupation use or enjoyment of property in kind.[1]

(2)   Section 11(1) of the Trusts of Land and Appointment of Trustees Act 1996 (consultation with beneficiaries) shall not apply to the exercise by my trustees of any of their powers in relation to land subject to the trusts hereof.[2]

1   This makes it clear that the trustees are not liable for the defaults of others who may have possession or control of trust property. For a wider form of indemnity, see eg Form B21.12 at para **[221.16]**.
2   The requirement that trustees of land in exercise of any function relating to land subject to the trust consult with beneficiaries of full age beneficially entitled to an interest in possession in the land can be excluded: TLATA 1996, s 11 (Part G, para **[246.97]**).

[232.13]

Professional trustee charging clause
10.   Any of my trustees being a professional or business man may charge and be paid all usual professional and other proper charges for business transacted acts done advice given and time spent by him or his firm in connection with the administration of my estate or in connection with the trusts hereof including acts which a personal representative or trustee not being in any profession or business could have done personally.

[232.14]

Testimonium and attestation clause
IN WITNESS whereof I have hereunto set my hand this —— day of —— 20—

SIGNED by the above-named testator as his last will in the presence of us both present at the same time who at his request and in his presence and in the presence of each other have signed our names below as witnesses   *[Signature of testator]*

[Signatures, addresses and descriptions of two witnesses]

[232.15]

FORM C10.2:   Will of young person creating discretionary trust of residue for his or her parents and brothers and sisters and their issue

NOTE

For the taxation of property comprised in a discretionary trust see B18 at paras **[218.6]**–**[218.15]** and **[218.26]**–**[218.30]**. The reason for creating a discretionary trust of most of the estate as in this Form is that it enables income to be received by beneficiaries without the capital being treated as part of their 'estates' for inheritance tax purposes. Accordingly, the death of any of the beneficiaries will not give rise to an inheritance tax charge on the trust fund. It is particularly worth considering where those who are intended to receive benefit include the testator's parents, grandparents, or any other persons with a moderate or short expectation of life. For other points on the use of discretionary trusts in this way, see the Note to Form C6.2 at paras **[228.19]** and **[228.20]**.

If during the two years following the testator's death some other arrangement seems to the trustees to be better, they can make an appointment which is treated for inheritance tax purposes as a disposition made by the testator's will by virtue of the ITA 1984, s 144 (see the Note on s 144 in C3 at paras **[225.83]**–**[225.91]**). Section 144 applying is not likely to make a lot of difference unless the testator has a very substantial taxable estate, or the taxation of discretionary trusts becomes much heavier, or there might be substantial discretionary distributions to charity which would make the testator's estate exempt from inheritance tax on his death if s 144 applied. The possibility of the testator getting married, and thus the possibility of there being distributions to the testator's widow or widower which would be exempt if s 144 applied, is not relevant since a will made in this form will be revoked by the testator's marriage (WA 1837, s 18(1), as amended: Part G, para **[244.16]**). As matters stand at the moment, a distribution within a short period after the testator's death out of a discretionary trust created by his will is unlikely to be subject to very much inheritance tax under the ordinary inheritance tax charging rules for discretionary trusts (see B18 at para **[218.8]**), and the main advantage of s 144 applying is usually that spouse or charitable exemption is obtained in relation to the testator's death.

If it might be important to be able to take advantage of the ITA 1984, s 144 (eg because charity is an object of the power of appointment), it would be possible to add features to the provisos to the power of appointment making it easier for an appointment within s 144 to be made within the two years following the testator's death, such as appear in provisos (v) to (vii) of Form C6.2, cl 7(3)(a) at para **[228.28]** (and see also Form C3.6, cl 7 at para **[225.108]** and n 2 thereto). The only provision of this sort in the form as it stands is the provision in the opening words of cl 6(3) that the powers there referred to may be exercised before or after the grant of probate or the completion of the administration of the estate.

[232.16]

Revocation clause
I [*name*] of [*address*] hereby revoke all former testamentary dispositions made by me and declare this to be my last will.

[232.17]

Appointment of executors and trustees
1.   [*As in cl 1 of* Form C10.1 *at para* **[232.4]**.]

[232.18]

Gift of personal chattels
2.   [*As in cl 2 of* Form C10.1 *at para* **[232.5]**.]

[232.19]

Pecuniary legacies

3.   [*As in cl 3 of* Form C10.1 *at para* **[232.6]**.]

[232.20]

Administration trusts of residue

4.   [*As in cl 4 of* Form C10.1 *at para* **[232.7]**.]

[232.21]

Gifts made free of tax

5.   [*As in cl 5 of* Form C10.1 *at para* **[232.8]**.]

[232.22]

Discretionary trusts of residue

6.   (1)   My trustees shall hold my residuary estate and the income thereof upon the trusts and with and subject to the powers and provisions hereinafter declared and contained.

(2)   In this clause the following expressions have the following meanings, namely:

(a)   'the residuary beneficiaries' means and includes:[1]
  (i)   my parents [*name*] and [*name*] [and my grandparents [*names of surviving grandparents*]];
  (ii)   my brothers and sisters [*name*] [*name*] [*name*] [*name*] and [*name*] and their respective children and remoter issue;
  (iii) any spouse widow or widower of any of my said brothers and sisters or their respective children or remoter issue (including any widow or widower who has remarried);

(b)   'the trust period' means the period commencing on the day of my death and expiring on [the twenty-first anniversary of the death of the last survivor of the residuary beneficiaries living at the date of my death]/[the eightieth anniversary thereof (and so that the perpetuity period applicable to the disposition hereby created shall be the period of 80 years from my death)];[2]

(c)   'the accumulation period' means the period commencing with my death and expiring on the twenty-first anniversary thereof.

(3)   Subject as hereinafter provided my trustees (being not fewer than two in number or being a trust corporation)[3] may at any time or times and from time to time during the trust period (and whether before or after the grant of probate and regardless of whether the administration of my estate is complete) exercise either or both of the following powers namely:

(a)   power at any time or times and from time to time by deed or deeds revocable or irrevocable to appoint the whole or any part or parts of my residuary estate upon trust for all or such one or more exclusive of the others or other of the residuary beneficiaries if more than one in such shares and either absolutely or at such age or time or respective ages or times and with such trusts and powers for their respective benefit and such provisions as my trustees think fit and in making any such appointment my trustees shall have powers as full as those which they would possess if they were an absolute beneficial owner of my residuary estate and in particular (but without prejudice to the generality of the foregoing words) my trustees may in any exercise of the foregoing power:

    (i)   delegate give or impose to or upon themselves or any other person or persons any discretionary powers or discretionary trusts conditions limitations restrictions or provisions including powers of further delegation or powers of further creation of discretionary trusts or powers;

    (ii)   create powers or trusts for the accumulation of income during any period permitted by law;

    (iii)   create administrative powers or provisions of whatever nature;

Provided that:

    (i)   no such appointment shall invalidate any payment transfer or application of capital or income previously made under any of the trusts or powers herein elsewhere contained;

    (ii)   every interest limited under any exercise of such power shall vest in interest (if at all) not later than the expiration of the trust period;

    (iii)   any such appointment may be made in respect of income alone without any appointment of capital; and

    (iv)   any such revocable appointment shall (so far as then unrevoked) cease to be revocable on the expiration of the trust period;

(b)   power (subject to any or every exercise of the foregoing power) at any time or times and from time to time in their absolute discretion to pay transfer or apply my residuary estate or any part or parts thereof to or for the benefit of all or any one or more exclusive of the others or other of the residuary beneficiaries for the time being in existence if more than one in such shares and generally in such manner as my trustees think fit.

(4)   In default of and subject to any or every exercise of the foregoing powers my trustees shall hold my residuary estate during the trust period upon trust to pay or apply the income thereof to or for the maintenance education or benefit of all or any one or more of the residuary beneficiaries and if more than one in such shares and in such manner generally as my trustees think fit provided that during the accumulation period my trustees may accumulate all or any part or parts of such income by investing the same and the resulting income thereof in any investments hereby authorised and so that any accumulations so made shall form part of the capital of my residuary estate (or the part thereof from which such income arose) for all purposes.

(5)   Subject as aforesaid my trustees shall hold my residuary estate and the income thereof at the expiration of the trust period upon trust for such of the residuary beneficiaries as shall be then living in equal shares per capita.

(6)   Any capital or income of my residuary estate not otherwise disposed of by this clause shall be held in trust for such of my brothers and sisters as shall survive me and if more than one in equal shares.

---

1   For an alternative definition, including power to add people to the class, see Form C3.6, cl 3(1)(b) at para **[225.100]** or Form C6.2, cl 7(1)(a) and (3)(c) at para **[228.28]**.

2   A common law perpetuity period and an 80-year period are included as alternatives. An 80-year period has the advantage that there is no difficulty in deciding when the period comes to an end, but the disadvantage that an appointment of, eg a life interest with remainders over, will need express perpetuity restrictions which it might not have needed if a common law period had been chosen.

3   For more elaborate provisions permitting the exercise of powers by a sole trustee during the two-year period following the death see Form C4.1, cl 8 at para **[226.25]**, see also the Note to this form at para **[232.15]**.

[232.23]

Administrative powers
7.   [*As in cl 8 of* Form C10.1 *at para* **[232.11]**.]

[232.24]

Trustee liability
8.   [*As in cl 9 of* Form C10.1 *at para* **[232.12]**.]

[232.25]

Exercise of powers[1]
9.   Any power or discretion hereby or by law conferred on my trustees (including a power or discretion as to the disposition of capital or income) shall be exercisable notwithstanding that any of my trustees has a personal interest in such exercise provided that there are not fewer than two trustees and that at least one of them has no such personal interest.

1   This clause enables a family member who may be an object of, eg a power of appointment or a power to apply capital, to be a trustee without being thereby disqualified from benefiting under an exercise of the power. See B18 at para **[218.4]**.

[232.26]

Professional trustee charging clause
10.   [*As in cl 10 of* Form C10.1 *at para* **[232.13]**.]

[*Testimonium and attestation clause as in* Form C10.1 *at para* **[232.14]**.]

[232.27]

FORM C10.3:   Will of older person in favour of brothers and sisters, with substitution of issue of those who predecease the testator

NOTE

This form contains a gift of residue to surviving brothers and sisters absolutely with a substitutional gift in favour of the issue of any deceased brother or sister. The form could readily be adapted so as to skip a generation by substituting references to nephews and nieces for references to brothers and sisters.

[232.28]

Revocation clause
I [*name*] of [*address*] hereby revoke all former testamentary dispositions made by me and declare this to be my last will.

[232.29]

Appointment of executors and trustees
1.   [*As in cl 1 of* Form C10.1 *at para* **[232.4]**.]

[232.30]

Gift of personal chattels
2.   [*As in cl 2 of* Form C10.1 *at para* **[232.5]**.]

[232.31]

Pecuniary legacies
3.   [*As in cl 3 of* Form C10.1 *at para* **[232.6]**.]

[232.32]

Administration trusts of residue
4.   [*As in cl 4 of* Form C10.1 *at para* **[232.7]**.]

[232.33]

Gifts made free of tax
5.   [*As in cl 5 of* Form C10.1 *at para* **[232.8]**.]

[232.34]

Beneficial trusts of residue
6.   My trustees shall hold my residuary estate and the income thereof upon trust for such of my brothers and sisters [*name*] [*name*] [*name*] and [*name*] as shall be living at my death and if more than in equal shares absolutely Provided that if any brother or sister of mine shall have predeceased me leaving issue surviving me who shall attain the age of [18/21/25] years such issue shall take and if more than one in equal shares per stirpes the share of my residuary estate which such deceased brother or sister of mine would have taken had he or she survived me and so that no issue shall take whose parent is living at my death and attains a vested interest.

[232.35]

Maintenance, accumulation and advancement
7.   [*As in cl 7 of* Form C10.1 *at para* **[232.10]**.]

[232.36]

Administrative powers
8.   [*As in cl 8 of* Form C10.1 *at para* **[232.11]**.]

[232.37]

Trustee liability
9.   [*As in cl 9 of* Form C10.1 *at para* **[232.12]**.]

[232.38]

Professional trustee charging clause
10.   [*As in cl 10 of* Form C10.1 *at para* **[232.13]**.]

[*Testimonium and attestation clause as in* Form C10.1 *at para* **[232.14]**.]

[232.39]

FORM C10.4:   Will of older childless person settling residue in equal shares on brothers and sisters (or nephews and nieces) for life with remainders for their children

NOTE

This form is a variant of the preceding form and differs in that the interests of the brothers and sisters (or nephews and nieces) are settled on them for life with power (if desired) to advance the capital of each beneficiary's share to or for the benefit of such beneficiary. If any of the brothers and sisters (or nephews and nieces) have children an element of generation skipping might be considered appropriate, in which case Form C10.1 at paras **[232.4]**–**[232.14]** could be used or adapted.

[232.40]

Revocation clause
I [*name*] of [*address*] hereby revoke all former testamentary dispositions made by me and declare this to be my last will.

[232.41]

Appointment of executors and trustees
1.   [*As in cl 1 of* Form C10.1 *at para* **[232.4]**.]

[232.42]

Gift of personal chattels
2.   [*As in cl 2 of* Form C10.1 *at para* **[232.5]**.]

[232.43]

Pecuniary legacies
3.   [*As in cl 3 of* Form C10.1 *at para* **[232.6]**.]

[232.44]

Administration trusts of residue
4.   [*As in cl 4 of* Form C10.1 *at para* **[232.7]**.]

[232.45]

Gifts made free of tax
5.   [*As in cl 5 of* Form C10.1 *at para* **[232.8]**.]

[232.46]

Beneficial trusts of residue

6. (1) Subject as hereinafter provided my trustees shall hold my residuary estate upon trust for such of my [brothers and sisters]/ [nephews and nieces] [*name*] [*name*] [*name*] [*name*] and [*name*][1] (hereinafter together called 'the beneficiaries') as shall survive me and if more than one in equal shares provided that if any of the beneficiaries shall predecease me leaving issue living at my death such issue shall take absolutely[2] and if more than one in equal shares per stirpes the share of my residuary estate to which such deceased beneficiary would have become entitled had he or she survived me and so that no such issue shall take whose parent is living at my death and attains a vested interest.

(2) The share of my residuary estate to which any of the beneficiaries shall become entitled under the foregoing subclause hereof on surviving me shall not vest in such beneficiary absolutely but shall be retained by my trustees and held on the following trusts:

(a) my trustees shall hold such share upon trust to pay the income thereof to such beneficiary during his or her life [provided that my trustees (being not fewer than two in number or being a trust corporation) may at any time or times and from time to time during the life of such beneficiary pay transfer or apply the whole or any part or parts of such share to or for the advancement support or benefit of such beneficiary in such manner as they think fit];

(b) subject as aforesaid my trustees shall hold such share upon trust for such one or more of the children and remoter issue of such beneficiary and if more than one in such shares and with such trusts powers and provisions (including trusts and powers conferring on my trustees or any other person or persons a discretion as to the disposition of capital or income or provisions for the accumulation of income during any period permitted by law or administrative powers) as such beneficiary shall by deed or deeds revocable or irrevocable or by will or codicil appoint;

(c) subject as aforesaid my trustees shall hold such share upon trust for such of the children of such beneficiary as shall attain the age of [18/21] years and if more than one in equal shares provided that no such child who or whose issue shall take any part of such share by virtue of any appointment under the foregoing power shall be entitled to participate in the unappointed part of such share without bringing the part so appointed into hotchpot and accounting for the same accordingly (except to the extent that there is a contrary direction in such appointment);

(d) the foregoing trusts shall carry the intermediate income of such share and section 31 of the Trustee Act 1925 (as hereinafter modified) shall apply thereto;

(e) section 32 of the Trustee Act 1925 (as hereinafter modified) shall apply in relation to such share;

(f) subject as aforesaid such share and the income thereof shall be held in trust for such beneficiary absolutely.

---

1   It is advisable to name the beneficiaries and give their addresses rather than describe them merely by relationship especially in the case of nephews and nieces or cousins: see the Preliminary Note to C9 at para **[231.9]** and Vol 1, para **[71.5]**.

2   It should be noted that the interests of substituted issue are not settled under cl 6(2).

[232.47]

Maintenance, accumulation and advancement
7.   [*As in cl 7 of* Form C10.1 *at para* **[232.10]**.]

[232.48]

Administrative powers
8.   [*As in cl 8 of* Form C10.1 *at para* **[232.11]**.]

[232.49]

Trustee liability
9.   [*As in cl 9 of* Form C10.1 *at para* **[232.12]**.]

[232.50]

Exercise of powers
10.   [*As in cl 9 of* Form C10.2 *at para* **[232.25]**.]

[232.51]

Professional trustee charging clause
11.   [*As in cl 10 of* Form C10.1 *at para* **[232.13]**.]

[*Testimonium and attestation clause as in* Form C10.1 *at para* **[232.14]**.]

[232.52]

FORM C10.5:   Will of unmarried childless person in favour of unmarried sister for life with remainders over to brothers and sisters or their issue

Revocation clause
I [*name*] of [*address*] hereby revoke all former testamentary dispositions made by me and declare this to be my last will.

[232.53]

Appointment of executors and trustees
1.   [*As in cl 1 of* Form C10.1 *at para* **[232.4]**.]

[232.54]

Gift of personal chattels
2.   I give free of tax[1] all my personal chattels as defined by section 55(1)(x) of the Administration of Estates Act 1925[2] to my sister [*name of unmarried sister*] absolutely.

1   See Form C10.1, cl 2, n 1 at para **[232.5]**.
2   See Part G, para **[246.52]** and Vol 1, para **[64.44]**.

[232.55]

Pecuniary legacies
3.   I give free of tax[1] to each of the children living at my death of my brothers and sisters [*name*] [*name*] and [*name*][2] a pecuniary legacy of £——.

1   See Form C10.1, cl 3, n 1 at para **[232.6]**.
2   The names here are intended of course to be those of the brothers and sisters, not those of their children. Illegitimate children are not excluded.

[232.56]

Administration trusts of residue
4.   [*As in cl 4 of* Form C10.1 *at para* **[232.7]**.]

[232.57]

Gifts made free of tax
5.   [*As in cl 5 of* Form C10.1 *at para* **[232.8]**.]

[232.58]

Beneficial trusts of residue
6.   (1)   My trustees shall hold my residuary estate upon trust to pay the income thereof to my said sister [*name of unmarried sister*] during her life [provided that my trustees (being not fewer than two in number or being a trust corporation) may at any time or times and from time to time during the life of my said sister pay transfer or apply the capital of the whole or any part or parts of my residuary estate to or for the support or benefit of my said sister in such manner as they think fit].[1]

(2)   Subject as aforesaid my trustees shall hold my residuary estate and the income thereof upon trust in equal shares for such of my brothers and sisters [*name*] [*name*] and [*name*][2] as shall be living at the later to occur of my death and the death of my said sister [*name of unmarried sister given the life interest under subclause (1)*] and the issue who shall attain the age of [18/21] years of such of my said brothers and sisters as shall be dead at the date hereof or shall predecease me or my said sister [*name of unmarried sister given the life interest under subclause (1)*] such issue to take if more than one in equal shares per stirpes the share which such deceased brother or sister of mine would have taken had he or she had lived to attain a vested interest and so that no issue shall take whose parent lives to attain a vested interest.[3]

(3)   The foregoing trusts shall carry the intermediate income of such share and section 31 of the Trustee Act 1925 (as hereinafter modified) shall apply thereto.

(4)   Section 32 of the Trustee Act 1925 (as hereinafter modified) shall apply in relation to the foregoing trusts.

1   For a power of this type which is limited to being exercisable only over part of the capital see Form C5.1, cl 9(2) at para **[227.13]**.
2   The names here will not include the unmarried sister who gets a life interest under the preceding subclause.
3   It is assumed that the unmarried sister who is given a life interest has no children. If she did have any children this clause would need modifying to enable them to be capable of benefiting under it.

[232.59]

Maintenance, accumulation and advancement
7.   [*As in cl 7 of* Form C10.1 *at para* **[232.10]**.]

[232.60]

Administrative powers

8.   [*As in cl 8 of* Form C10.1 *at para* **[232.11]**.]

[232.61]

Trustee liability

9.   [*As in cl 9 of* Form C10.1 *at para* **[232.12]**.]

[232.62]

Exercise of powers

10.   [*As in cl 9 of* Form C10.2 *at para* **[232.25]**.]

[232.63]

Professional trustee charging clause

11.   [*As in cl 10 of* Form C10.1 *at para* **[232.13]**.]

[*Testimonium and attestation clause as in* Form C10.1 *at para* **[232.14]**.]

[232.64]

FORM C10.6:   Will of childless individual giving charitable and other legacies, with a specific gift of a house and residue given on trust for nephews and nieces for life with remainders for their children

Revocation clause

I [*name*] of [*address*] hereby revoke all former testamentary dispositions made by me and declare this to be my last will.

[232.65]

Appointment of executors and trustees

1.   [*As in cl 1 of* Form C10.1 *at para* **[232.4]**.]

[232.66]

Gift of personal chattels to brother or sister

2.   [*As in cl 3 of* Form C10.1 *at para* **[232.6]**.]

[232.67]

Pecuniary legacies

3.   I give the following pecuniary legacies free of tax:[1]

   (a)   to each of my trustees [except [*name of professional trustee*]] who shall prove my will and act in the trusts thereof the sum of £——;[2]

   (b)   to my brother [*name*] the sum of £—— and I direct that the same shall be paid to him as soon as possible after my death[3] and in priority to all other legacies hereby given;

   (c)   to each of the children of my brother [*name*] who shall be living at the date of my death and shall attain the age of [18/21] years the sum of £—

> — with interest thereon from the date of my death at the rate of [6] per cent per annum;[4]

(d) to my god-daughter [*name*] the sum of £—— and I declare that the receipt of the said [*name*] if of the age of 16 years or more shall be a full and sufficient discharge to my trustees for the same;[5]

(e) to my chauffeur and handyman [*name*] if in service at my death[6] the sum of £—— in addition to any sums then owing to him for wages or otherwise [and if he shall then have left my service I give to him the sum of £——];

(f) to my friend [*name*] the sum of £—— and without imposing any trust or obligation upon him I desire that he may employ the same in the furtherance of the research project on which we have worked together for so many years;

(g) to the Management Committee of —— Hospital the sum of £—— to be applied in the provision of additional comforts for the in-patients of the said Hospital the receipt of the treasurer for the time being of the said hospital to be a sufficient discharge for such sum;[7]

(h) to the Vicar for the time being of the Parish of —— the sum of £—— to be applied by him in such manner as he may think best for the relief of the poor of the said Parish the receipt of the Vicar to be a sufficient discharge to my trustees for the said sum and so that my trustees are not to be bound to see to the application thereof;[8]

(i) to the Governing Body of —— School the sum of £—— for the purpose of [building] [enlarging] [equipping] [providing] [fives courts] [a swimming bath] [a gymnasium] [playing fields] with power for the said governors to purchase thereout land for the purpose aforesaid and the receipt of the Chairman of the said Governing Body or other proper officer thereof for the said sum shall be a sufficient discharge to my trustees and so that my trustees shall not be bound to see to the application thereof.

1   See Form C10.1, cl 3, n 1 at para [232.6].

2   As to this clause, see *Re Sharman's Will Trusts, Public Trustee v Sharman* [1942] Ch 311, [1942] 2 All ER 74, and *Re Parry, Dalton v Cooke* [1969] 2 All ER 512, [1969] 1 WLR 614, and see also Vol 1, paras [30.14]–[30.18] and B10 at paras [210.51]–[210.53]. This paragraph will provide legacies only for the executors who prove the will. A testator may wish to exclude a professional trustee from this clause if cl 14 is included.

3   The foregoing words providing for early payment would give the legacy no priority over other legacies without the words which follow (*Re Schweder's Estate, Oppenheim v Schweder* [1891] 3 Ch 44) and it would otherwise be liable to abate with other legacies. If executors have any doubt about the assets being sufficient, they must either withhold payment or obtain some security for repayment of any amount overpaid.

4   A contingent legacy does not ordinarily carry interest and in the absence of a specific direction will only carry interest from the end of the executor's year. See Vol 1, para [32.1] et seq.

5   *Re Denekin, Peters v Tanchereau* (1895) 72 LT 220 shows that it is not sufficient to direct payment to a minor, and that the clause must go on to provide that the receipt of the minor shall be a sufficient discharge to the executors or trustees. Despite the specific provision for payment to the legatee while under 18 a trustee still has a discretion to withhold payment until the age of eighteen is attained: *Re Somech, Westminster Bank Ltd v Phillips* [1957] Ch 165, [1956] 3 All ER 523 (where the trustee surrendered his discretion to the court and an order for immediate payment was made). However, it seems that, while the legatee is a minor, a parent or guardian of the legatee with parental responsibility could insist on being paid the legacy: ChA 1989, s 3(3) (Part G, para [244.119]); see also Vol 1, para [9.42].

6   As to the importance of these words, see *Re Sharland, Kemp v Rozey* [1896] 1 Ch 517. Testators should be reminded of the law relating to redundancy payments (now embodied in Pt VI of the Employment Protection (Consolidation) Act 1978). For a form which adjusts the servant's legacy by reference to the amount of any redundancy payment to which he may be entitled see Form B10.46 at para **[210.63]**.

7   Since the introduction of the National Health Service, gifts to the Hospital itself have in general been discontinued, but there are a number of ways in which a charitable testator can help patients, nurses and medical research. See Form B12.23 at para **[212.25]**.

8   This gift is obviously charitable. As to what gifts for parish work and such like are charitable, see Vol 1, para **[102.16]**.

[232.68]

Provision against lapse of charitable gifts

4. If any institution society or body of persons (incorporated or unincorporated) or holder of an office which or who is intended to be the legatee under any legacy given by me herein or in any codicil hereto shall be found never to have existed or to have ceased to exist or to have been amalgamated with another institution society body of persons or office or changed its name or constitution before my death then such legacy shall be paid transferred or applied to such charitable institutions societies or bodies of persons established in the United Kingdom or for such charitable purposes in the said United Kingdom and if more than one in such shares as my trustees in their absolute discretion think fit and I express the wish without imposing any trust or obligation that in carrying out the foregoing trust my trustees should seek to benefit a charity or charities with objects as close as possible with those of the institution society body of persons or office-holder intended to receive the original legacy.

[232.69]

Gift of house and contents

5. I give [free of tax][1] my property situate at [*address*] and my furniture and effects of household use or ornament therein or belonging thereto (save and except such of the same as may be otherwise specifically disposed of by this will or any codicil hereto) to my brother [*name*] absolutely.[2]

1   Inheritance tax on land in the UK which is specifically given is now a testamentary expense payable out of residue: ITA 1984, s 211 (Part G, para **[246.83]**); see also B14 at para **[214.55]** et seq. But if the 'free of tax' formula is being used elsewhere, it may be prudent to employ it here also, to avoid any suggestion that its absence here means that this gift was intended to be subject to inheritance tax.

2   This gift will be subject to any sums charged on the property: AEA 1925, s 35 (Part G, para **[246.47]**).

[232.70]

Administration trusts of residue

6. [*As in cl 4 of* Form C10.1 *at para* **[232.7]**.]

[232.71]

Gifts made free of tax

7. [*As in cl 5 of* Form C10.1 *at para* **[232.8]**.]

[232.72]

Beneficial trusts of residue

8.   (1)   My trustees shall hold my residuary estate upon trust for such of my nephews and nieces (being children of my brothers [*name*] [*name*] and [*name*]) as shall be living at or born after my death (before any of such nephews and nieces shall attain a vested interest hereunder)[1] and shall attain the age of [18/21] years and if more than one in equal shares Provided that if any of my said nephews and nieces is now dead or shall predecease me or die before attaining a vested interest hereunder leaving a child or children living at or born after my death such child or children shall take absolutely if more than one equally between them the share of my residuary estate which such deceased nephew or niece of mine would have become interested in had he or she lived to attain a vested interest.

(2)   The foregoing trusts shall carry the intermediate income of my residuary estate and section 31 of the Trustee Act 1925 (as hereinafter modified) shall apply thereto.

(3)   Section 32 of the Trustee Act 1925 (as hereinafter modified) shall apply in relation to the said trusts and shall apply in relation to the presumptive share of any such nephew or niece of mine notwithstanding the direction for retention and settlement hereinafter contained.

1   The class of nephews and nieces who may take under this trust will close on the first of them to attain the vesting age doing so, or on the testator's death if by that time there is at least one nephew or niece who has attained the vesting age and survives him.

[232.73]

Settlement of shares

9.   The share of my residuary estate to which any nephew or niece of mine shall become entitled under the last foregoing clause hereof shall not vest in such nephew or niece absolutely but shall be retained by my trustees and held upon the trusts following namely (such nephew or niece hereinafter being referred to as 'the beneficiary'):

   (a)   my trustees shall hold such share upon trust to pay the income thereof to the beneficiary during his or her life;
   (b)   provided that my trustees shall have power in their absolute discretion from time to time during the beneficiary's life and before the vesting day to pay transfer or apply the whole or any part or parts of such share to him or for his benefit in such manner as they shall in their absolute discretion think fit;
   (c)   subject as aforesaid the beneficiary shall have power at any time before the vesting day by deed or deeds revocable or irrevocable or by will or codicil to appoint to any spouse who may survive him or her as his or her widow or widower in the event of his or her death before the vesting day (including power to appoint to a named spouse contingently on such named spouse surviving him or her as his or her widow or widower in such event) an interest in the income of the whole or any part or parts of such share for the residue of such spouse's life or for any less period;[1]
   (d)   subject as aforesaid if the beneficiary shall die before the vesting day my trustees shall hold such share upon trust as to both capital and income for

all or such one or more exclusively of the others or other of the children and remoter issue of the beneficiary at such time or times and if more than one in such shares and with such trusts powers and provisions (including trusts and powers conferring on any person or persons a discretion as to the disposition of capital or income or provisions for the accumulation of income during any period permitted by law or administrative powers of whatever description) as the beneficiary shall before the vesting day by deed or deeds revocable or irrevocable or by will or codicil appoint;

(e) subject as aforesaid my trustees shall hold such share upon trust as to both capital and income for all or any the children or child of the beneficiary who shall attain the age of [18/21] years [or marry under that age] before the vesting day or shall be living (but under the said age [and unmarried]) on the vesting day and if more than one in equal shares [provided that no child of the beneficiary who or whose issue shall take any part of such share by virtue of any appointment under the foregoing power shall be entitled to participate in the unappointed part of such share without bringing the part so appointed into hotchpot and accounting for the same accordingly (except to the extent that there is a contrary direction in such appointment)];

(f) the trust declared by paragraph (e) above shall carry the intermediate income of such share and section 31 of the Trustee Act 1925 (as hereinafter modified) shall apply thereto;

(g) section 32 of the Trustee Act 1925 (as hereinafter modified) shall apply in relation to such share;

(h) subject as aforesaid if the beneficiary shall die before the vesting day my trustees shall hold such share upon trust as to both capital and income for such persons or purposes as the beneficiary shall by will or codicil appoint and subject to any such appointment;

(i) subject as aforesaid my trustees shall hold such share upon trust for the next of kin of the beneficiary living at his or her death or the earlier occurrence of the vesting day ascertained as if the beneficiary had died intestate without having married;

(j) in this clause 'the vesting day' means the day on which shall expire 21 years less three days after the death of the last survivor of such of my said nephews and nieces as shall be living at my death.

1   This power will enable advantage to be taken of the inheritance tax exemption for gifts to a spouse in relation to the share.

[232.74]

Maintenance, accumulation and advancement
10.   [*As in cl 7 of* Form C10.1 *at para* **[232.10]**.]

[232.75]

Administrative powers
11.   [*As in cl 8 of* Form C10.1 *at para* **[232.11]**.]

Part C   Complete wills

[232.76]

Trustee liability
12.   [*As in cl 9 of* Form C10.1 *at para* **[232.12]**.]

[232.77]

Exercise of powers
13.   [*As in cl 9 of* Form C10.2 *at para* **[232.25]**.]

[232.78]

Professional trustee charging clause
14.   [*As in cl 10 of* Form C10.1 *at para* **[232.13]**.]

[232.79]

[*Testimonium and attestation clause as in* Form C10.1 *at para* **[232.14]**.]

C11 Wills disposing of business property

PRELIMINARY NOTE

[233.1]
Notes on business property, inheritance tax business relief, payment of inheritance tax on business property by instalments, and the implications of these for testamentary dispositions, are to be found in the Preliminary Note to B5 at paras **[205.1]–[205.57]**, and clauses disposing of business property and ancillary provisions are to be found in B5 at paras **[205.58]–[205.79]**. For testamentary options see B9 at para **[209.1]** et seq; for trustees' powers in relation to business property see B5 at paras **[205.70]–[205.79]**, B20 at paras **[220.66]–[220.68]** and B21 at para **[221.1]** et seq; for agricultural property, including notes on inheritance tax agricultural relief, see C12 at para **[234.1]** et seq. For wills in favour of spouses and children see the Preliminary Notes to C2 and C3 at paras **[224.1]–[224.19]** and **[225.1]–[225.8]**.

This Preliminary Note is concerned with the inheritance tax implications of the pattern of disposition in a will as a whole in cases where the testator has business property or agricultural property, and with certain other practical problems which can arise in wills where the testator has property of either kind (agricultural property is included because many of the points relating to business property are equally relevant to it).

Allocation of business and agricultural relief between the exempt and non-exempt parts of an estate

[233.2]
Where the testator has made exempt gifts by will to, eg his spouse or charity, and the remainder of the estate is not exempt, and the testator owns assets which qualify for business or agricultural relief, the amount of advantage gained from the relief depends on the form taken by his testamentary dispositions.

Business relief and agricultural relief operate to reduce the value transferred by a transfer of value, ie, in the case of an estate on death, the value of the estate before any exempt parts are deducted to determine the extent of the chargeable transfer. Where an estate is partially exempt the transfer of value then has to be allocated between exempt and non-exempt gifts under the sometimes rather difficult rules in the Inheritance Tax Act 1984 (ITA 1984), Part II, Ch III (ss 36–42: see Part A, paras **[200.138]–[200.145]** and *Foster's Inheritance Tax*, D2.31–43). As part of these rules, the ITA 1984, s 39A determines the allocation of any business or agricultural relief between exempt and non-exempt gifts for the purposes of determining the extent of the chargeable part of the transfer of value. Section 39A has at first sight an appearance of complexity (for a detailed account see *Foster's Inheritance Tax*, D2.40), but its effect can be summarised fairly simply in two propositions.

[233.3]
Summary of the effect of the Inheritance Tax Act 1984, s 39A.

(1) Any 'specific gifts of relevant business property or agricultural property' are treated as reduced by any business or agricultural relief relating to that property: ITA 1984, s 39A(2). This is so whether the specific gift of the business or agricultural property is exempt or non-exempt; if it is non-exempt, all the business or agricultural relief relating to the property given by it will go to reduce the chargeable part of the estate, and if it is exempt the relief will reduce the exempt part of the estate and so will confer no tax saving.

(2) If available business or agricultural relief does not go to reduce the value of a specific gift of business or agricultural property as described under (1) above (in most cases this is where the business or agricultural property falls into the residuary estate), it is apportioned rateably between the exempt and non-exempt gifts, other than any specific gifts which have been reduced as described under (1) above: ITA 1984, s 39A (3), (4).

Thus, when an estate is partially exempt, any available business or agricultural relief is likely to be most fully utilised by making non-exempt specific gifts of the business or agricultural property, and to be least or not at all utilised by making exempt specific gifts of it. In between lie cases where such property falls into residue. Where it is desirable or necessary for the surviving spouse to have the benefit of property on which there will be business or agricultural relief, a discretionary trust could be considered, as in Form C11.1 at para **[233.13]** et seq. Other possible ways of utilising the relief while arranging for the surviving spouse to benefit from or obtain the business or agricultural property are considered at para **[233.7]**.

[233.4]
Gifts charged on business or agricultural property. A gift, typically a pecuniary legacy, which is payable out of business or agricultural property will not be treated as a specific gift of business or agricultural property, and will have allocated to it only a rateable part of any relief not attributed to specific gifts of business or agricultural property where the estate is partially exempt: ITA 1984, s 39A(6). Charging pecuniary or general legacies on specifically given business or agricultural property will therefore in these circumstances have the effect of reducing the benefit of the business or agricultural relief, and should be avoided so far as possible in a will where there are substantial exempt gifts.

[233.5]
Business or agricultural relief and specific gifts of other sorts of property. The ITA 1984, s 39A contains no provision treating a specific gift of property which is not business or agricultural property as having a value unreduced by business or agricultural relief. Accordingly, if there is any business or agricultural relief on property comprised in residue, for the purposes of the partial exemption rules an apportioned part of the relief will go to reduce the value of a specific gift of property (exempt or non-exempt) which does not itself attract either relief. This may cause uncertainty as to the tax payable by the donee where a subject to tax gift is made of such property in such circumstances: Form B14.36 at para **[214.79]** and Form C11.3, cl 4 at para **[233.42]** are examples of clauses which deal with this point.

[233.6]
What is a specific gift for the purposes of the Inheritance Tax Act 1984, s 39A. As stated above, a testator's estate will get maximum benefit from business relief or agricultural relief if there is a specific gift to a non-exempt beneficiary *of* 'relevant business property' (ie property qualifying for business relief) or *of* 'agricultural property' (see para **[234.2]** for the meaning of this expression). 'Specific gift' is defined in the ITA 1984, s 42(1) (which applies to s 39A, among other sections of the Act) to mean any gift other than a gift of residue or a share of residue, but this does not determine what is a specific gift *of* a particular kind of property. The only other provision with any relevance to its meaning is s 39A(6) mentioned at para **[233.4]**—gifts payable out of business or agricultural property are not for the purposes of s 39A specific gifts of that property.

It is our view that a specific gift will only qualify as a specific gift of relevant business property or agricultural property for the purposes of the ITA 1984, s 39A(2) if the property comprised in the gift and going to the beneficiary, considered in isolation from the rest of the estate, is relevant business property or agricultural property. If this is correct, the following points should be noted—

(1)   When a business is carried on by the testator as sole proprietor and the business as a whole qualifies for business relief on his death as 'a business' (see B5 at para **[205.22]**), a specific gift of an individual asset of that business by itself will on this view not be a specific gift of relevant business property (see B5 at para **[205.23]** for the distinction between a business and individual business assets). Whether business relief is available in respect of a business on a testator's death depends on the circumstances immediately before his death, not on the dispositions made by his will, and so it is thought that the business relief attributable to this individual asset comprised in a specific gift will not be lost completely in a case such as this, but will be divided rateably between the exempt and non-exempt parts of the estate instead of being concentrated on the specific gift.

(2)   A similar point would arise in relation to a specific gift of a farm building or farm house, where the farm land itself was the subject of another gift. As stated in the Preliminary Note to C12 at paras **[234.2]** and **[234.3]**, buildings and farmhouses only qualify as agricultural property if they are combined with agricultural land and are of a character appropriate to it: ITA 1984, s 115(2). Again, it is thought that a farm house or building given by a specific gift which did not also include the farm land would still qualify for agricultural relief on the testator's death, but that the relief attributable to the farmhouse would be apportioned rateably between the non-exempt and exempt parts of the estate because the house by itself is not 'agricultural property' for the purposes of the ITA 1984, s 39A(2).

(3)   In the rare cases of controlling holdings of unquoted voting securities qualifying for 100 per cent business relief or controlling holdings of quoted shares or securities qualifying for 50 per cent business relief (ITA 1984, ss 104(1) and 105(1)(b) and (cc)), the type of problem described above does not seem to arise where, for example, a testator makes a specific gift of part only of his holding. Shares or securities in either category qualify for the relief even if they do not by themselves give control, provided that they contribute to the testator's control of the company together with other shares or securities owned by him: see the ITA 1984, s 105(1)(b) and (cc).

(4)   There is also a question as to whether a gift of relevant business property or agricultural property to one person, subject to a testamentary option for another to purchase it, is a specific gift of that property for the purposes of the ITA 1984, s 39A. It might be argued that it is not a gift of such property to the person to whom the primary gift is made, because he may end up with cash instead of the property, and that the option holder is not the recipient of a *gift* of such property (or not wholly—it depends on the price) and anyway might not exercise the option and receive the business (or agricultural) property. Such an arrangement is at its most provocative to the Revenue where the property entitled to relief is given to a non-exempt beneficiary subject to an option given to the testator's spouse to purchase it. However, whether or not it is an exempt beneficiary who is given the option is not strictly relevant to the legal merits of the argument. The attitude of the Inland Revenue to this point

is not known, and in the absence of a clear indication that the Revenue accept such arrangements as specific gifts of the business or agricultural property within the ITA 1984, s 39A(2) they are better avoided if possible; see para **[233.7]** for alternatives.

[233.7]
Where the testator's spouse is intended to benefit from or inherit the business (or agricultural) property. Where the testator wants his spouse to be able to benefit from business or agricultural property after his death, but not necessarily to own it, a discretionary trust of the property such as in Form C11.1 at para **[233.13]** et seq would be a way of taking advantage of the business or agricultural relief on the property on his death and keeping the property out of the taxable estate of the spouse, while enabling the spouse to benefit from the income. This is not an approach to adopt where the property is, eg agricultural land which it is intended that the trustees will permit the spouse to occupy or use in carrying on the spouse's own business, because that might have the effect of conferring an interest in possession on the spouse and thus including the property in the spouse's taxable estate (see *Foster's Inheritance Tax*, E1.47 and Part A, para **[200.110]**).

Where it is necessary or desirable for the testator's spouse to have after the testator's death an absolute interest or an interest in possession in business or agricultural property of the testator (being property entitled to business or agricultural relief), there may still be ways in which advantage could be taken of that relief in the event of the spouse surviving the testator. For example, the property could be the subject-matter of a specific gift to the testator's son, with the idea that the son would sell it to, or exchange it for other assets with, the spouse after the testator's death. Where there is doubt whether the potential non-exempt beneficiary will sell or exchange the property back to the spouse, a testamentary option is not recommended, for the reasons given at para **[233.6]**, sub-para (4), but there are other possibilities.

One possibility is to create an interest in possession trust for the *non-exempt* beneficiary of the business or agricultural property, or a discretionary trust of it, so structured that the trustees can sell the business or agricultural assets back to the spouse. See Form C11.1 at para **[233.13]** et seq. Such arrangements have the disadvantage that the spouse will not he able to have the testator's period of ownership taken into account for the purpose of business relief on his or her death under the ITA 1984, ss 108(b) or 109 (see B5 at para **[205.11]**), and any right to pay any inheritance tax on the property by instalments will cease on its sale to the surviving spouse (but the rate of relief may be 100 per cent with the result that there is no inheritance tax).

A further possibility is the grant to the spouse by inter vivos agreement of an option to purchase the property, combined with a non-exempt specific gift by will of that property. The existence at the testator's death of an (unexercised) option to purchase a property does not by itself affect the availability of business or agricultural relief in to relation to that property: see B5 at para **[205.28]**. Consideration would need to be given to the tax consequences of the creation of the option, however. It should also be remembered that where the option is created after the date of the will its exercise after the testator's death could cause the gift to be adeemed under the rule in *Lawes v Bennett* (1785) 1 Cox Eq Cas

167: see Vol 1, para **[41.20]** and the second alternative cl 2(2) of Form C11.3 at para **[233.40]** for a form of words excluding ademption in these circumstances.

Nil-rate band gifts and business (or agricultural) property

[233.8]
Nil-rate band gifts are gifts intended to use up some or all of the testator's nil-rate band on a non-exempt gift, in a will which is otherwise in favour of the testator's spouse. For discussion of these see Part A, para **[200.101]** and for nil-rate band discretionary trusts see the Note in B18 at para **[218.16]** et seq. Examples of nil-rate band gifts without a business element are to be found in, eg Forms B10.51 at para **[210.72]**, B18.2 at para **[218.32]**, C3.1 at paras **[225.9]**–**[225.22]** and C3.4 at paras **[225.57]**–**[225.67]**. Where there is business or agricultural property entitled to inheritance tax business or agricultural relief there are some additional factors to take into account.

[233.9]
100 per cent relief property and 'formula' nil-rate band gifts. Where the testator has a significant amount of property entitled to 100 per cent business or agricultural relief, and a nil-rate band legacy is given to non-exempt beneficiaries by reference to a formula such as 'the maximum sum I can give without any inheritance tax being payable on my death', such a gift could operate to pass too much to the non-exempt beneficiaries. If after deduction of the relief the total transfer of value on death was less than the amount of the nil-rate band at death, the whole estate might pass under the nil-rate band gift leaving the surviving spouse with nothing except a claim under the Inheritance (Provision for Family and Dependants) Act 1975 (see Vol 1, para **[105.9]**).

Consider this example: T dies in the tax year 2001–02 leaving business property, to which 100 per cent relief applies, and of which the market value is £500,000, and other assets worth £242,000. He had made no lifetime chargeable transfers. His will gives a legacy to the children of the maximum sum he can give without any inheritance tax being payable on his death, with residue going to his spouse. The transfer of value on his death after business relief is £242,000. However, the legacy determined by the formula is £742,000, not £242,000. He can give a legacy of this amount without inheritance tax being payable because if his will gave a legacy of £742,000 it would be treated as abated to £242,000 for the purposes of inheritance tax on his death by virtue of the ITA 1984, s 37(2).

Where there is a risk of something like this happening, it may be advisable to set an upper limit of actual value on the amount to pass under the nil-rate band gift, as in Form C11.1, cl 2(1)(b) at para **[233.17]**. Where the nil-rate band legacy is to be held on a discretionary trust under which the spouse will be a beneficiary, the consequences of the legacy being of the entire estate will not be as serious for the surviving spouse as they would be if the legacy was given absolutely to, eg the children, but the testator may still want some of the estate to vest in his spouse absolutely, in which case a limit on the size of the legacy will still be appropriate.

Where a testator has business or agricultural property, and intends to leave his residuary estate to his spouse, it will be an excellent arrangement from a tax planning point of view to make a non-exempt specific gift of some or all of that property (see para **[233.3]** for the advantages of such gifts), and also to provide a non-exempt top up legacy (defined by a formula) so as to use, or use the rest of, the nil-rate band (see Form C11.1, cl 2 at para **[233.17]**). The specific gift may have no taxable value because it gets 100 per cent relief (in which case the legacy will be the full amount of the available nil-rate band), or it may use up some or all of the nil-rate band because, for example it gets only 50 per cent relief or it is not wholly entitled to relief (see further B5 at para **[205.51]**). A consequence of this combination of specific gift and formula legacy, if the specific gift turns out to use up some of the nil-rate band, is that in order to determine the amount of the legacy it will be necessary to determine the value of the business or agricultural property comprised in the specific gift. This makes administrative difficulties for the executors where the specific gift is of assets which are very difficult to value, such as private company shares, particularly as it can take a long time for the Revenue to express an opinion on the value of such property.

[233.10]
Non-exempt specific gifts of business or agricultural property. As described at para **[233.3]**, where there is an exempt gift of residue, the maximum use is made of business or agricultural relief by making a specific gift or gifts of the property qualifying for the relief(s) to non-exempt beneficiaries (which may be combined with a top up 'formula' pecuniary legacy, as in Form C11.1, cl 2 at para **[233.17]**, so as to use up the rest of the available nil-rate band). Where a non-exempt specific gift of business or agricultural property is made in this way, there may be a possibility that the taxable value of the specifically given property will exceed the available amount of nil-rate band, eg because the nil-rate available on death comes to be diminished by lifetime gifts, or because the business or agricultural property does not turn out to be entitled to as much relief or at as high a rate as expected. Possible ways of dealing with this or minimising its consequences are:

(1) Making the specific gift subject to inheritance tax. This reduces considerably the adverse effect of the taxable value of the property turning out to exceed the nil-rate band, because it prevents grossing up of the non-exempt specific gift(s): see B5 at para **[205.52]** et seq, and eg Form B5.1 at para **[205.58]**, Form C11.1, cl 2 at para **[233.17]** and Form C11.3, cl 2 at para **[233.40]**.

(2) Trying to limit the gift to such part of the business or agricultural assets as qualifies for business relief. It is questionable whether it is always possible to do this, and whether it is possible depends on the type of asset and the nature of the exclusionary provision involved. For example, where some of the testator's shares in a particular company have been owned for two years and some not, it should be possible to make a gift of only the shares which have been owned for two years (see Form B5.9 at para **[205.66]** and Form C11.2, cl 2 at para **[233.29]**). Where an asset is an 'excepted asset' (see B5 at para **[205.9]** for the meaning of this term) it should be possible to exclude it from a gift of a sole trader's business

(see Form B5.4 at para **[205.61]**) or possibly from a gift of a partnership share in a business. On the other hand, if the assets owned by the testator are company shares, and the company owns 'excepted assets', it is difficult to see how the gift could be of that part of the company shares which is not attributable to the excepted assets, as the shares do not constitute a proprietary interest in particular assets of the company.

(3) Imposing an upper limit in monetary terms on the value of the specific gift, either by reference to its taxable value (ie as reduced by business or agricultural relief) or its actual value. A problem about this is that it makes difficulties for the executors, because they have to decide on the value to attribute to assets which may be very difficult to value, such as private company shares, and it can take a long time for the Revenue to express an opinion on the value of the property in question.

Other factors relevant to wills of spouses

[233.11]
In some cases business or agricultural property owned by one party to a marriage is likely to qualify for agricultural or business relief on the death of the current owner of it, but is likely to cease to qualify for the relief after his or her death, eg because it relates to a business which is personal to the current owner, or the executors may have to sell it, or it is a partnership share subject to an option for the surviving partners to buy it. It is obviously a good idea in such circumstances for the current owner to make a non-exempt gift of the property in the event of him or her predeceasing his or her spouse. If the other spouse might not have enough to live on without it, a discretionary trust with the spouse as an object is a possible solution: see Form C11.1 at para **[233.15]**.

On the other hand, where the other spouse would, if given the property, continue to hold it in such a way that it would continue to qualify for the relief (bearing in mind that the succession provisions—see B5 at para **[205.11]**—will probably apply) there is less disadvantage in leaving it to the other spouse. There is also the point that leaving the property to the other spouse will enable there to be a tax-free uplift in the capital gains tax base value on the spouse's death, which will not occur if the property is settled by will on discretionary trusts. Private company shares are perhaps the type of property most likely to continue to qualify for business relief in the hands of the current owner's spouse. If there are no good reasons for creating a trust by will of business or agricultural property, an advantage of making an absolute gift, or creating a trust where all the beneficiaries are ascertained and of full age, is that it is easier for the beneficiaries to make a deed of variation to, eg, maximise the use of the nil-rate band.

Where only one or some of the testator's children will carry on a business

[233.12]
Where there is a clear successor or successors, typically a child or children of the testator, who will carry on the testator's business after his death and to whom the testator wishes to leave his business assets (whether directly owned or owned as a partnership interest or company shares), there are often other

children or other relations with a claim on the testator who will not do so. There can then be a serious problem of what provision to make for the ones who will not carry on the business, if the testator does not have significant assets apart from his business assets. This problem is often at its most acute for farmers, particularly where there are no or hardly any assets apart from the farm and farming business, and where the child or children who want to carry on the farming will not be able to make a living if they have to pay a significant amount to acquire the farm and farming business. There is no easy solution to this, and to avoid over-burdening those who inherit the business it will often be necessary for the provision to be unequal. The rules for allocation of business relief where some of the estate is exempt (see paras **[233.2]–[233.7]**) can also render disadvantageous the making of cash provision for one set of beneficiaries out of a gift of business or agricultural property to another set of them (see para **[233.4]**). Ways in which provision for those do not inherit the business assets may be made in appropriate cases are:

(1)   Provision for the intended recipient(s) of the business or agricultural assets to buy them in easy or interest-free payments in instalments, the payments going into a trust fund for the other beneficiaries: see B9 at para **[209.1]** et seq for options, and Form C12.1 at para **[234.17]** for a will on these lines. Dispositions in this form may affect the availability of the business or agricultural relief where the estate is partially exempt (see para **[233.6]**, sub-para (4)).

(2)   Provision for the business or agricultural assets to go to the intended recipients subject to payment of legacies to the other beneficiaries. This can be by way of a charge of legacies on specific gifts, or a residuary gift of the business or agricultural assets subject to legacies (as in Form C12.2 at para **[234.31]** et seq). Easy terms for payment of the legacies can be included, as in Form C12.2, cl 4(3) at para **[234.36]**. It should be remembered that charging a legacy on a specific gift of business or agricultural assets will affect the availability of the business or agricultural relief where the estate is partially exempt (see para **[233.4]**).

(3)   A gift of residue in equal shares among all the beneficiaries, with those who will work in the business being given an option to purchase the business or agricultural property with the purchase money being set off so far as possible against their shares of residue (see Form C12.1 at para **[234.17]** et seq).

(4)   A specific gift of the business or agricultural property to the beneficiaries who will work in the business, with all the testator's other assets going to the other beneficiaries unless they exceed the value of the business assets, in which case there is an equal division. A possible way of doing this is through a hotchpot clause, as in Form C11.3 at para **[233.36]** et seq (and for a similar provision see B5.8 at para **[205.65]**).

(5)   Where what the testator owns is shares in a private company they can be divided up among the different beneficiaries if the beneficiary or beneficiaries who are going to run the business are safely installed as directors and managers. This is better from a business relief point of view than charging legacies on the shares in favour of the beneficiaries who are not working in the business, but could lead to the beneficiaries running the business to lose control and be ousted, and could be of little

benefit to the beneficiaries who do not work in the business if the shares never pay dividends. In the case of a company which owns agricultural property this course of action could prevent agricultural relief on subsequent deaths (see the Preliminary Note to C12 at para **[234.6]**).

(6)   Another possibility for private company shares is a discretionary trust of the shares with those working in the business and those who are not as beneficiaries (see Form C11.1 at para **[233.15]** et seq), thus keeping the holding together for relief purposes and preventing either faction from using their votes as shareholders against the interests of the other, but possibly creating a difficult task for the trustees of mediating between the conflicting interests.

[233.13]

FORM C11.1:   Will settling private company shares entitled to business relief and 'top up' legacy on a nil-rate band discretionary trust, with residue given to wife with alternative gift to issue

NOTE

The main point of this form is to make a specific gift of the testator's unquoted shareholding in a trading company on discretionary trusts. It is assumed that the shareholding is entitled to 100 per cent business relief (see the Preliminary Note to B5 at para **[205.5]** et seq for the conditions for this). Even if there is thought to be 100 per cent relief, some inheritance tax may turn out to be payable on the shares: see B5 at para **[205.51]** for circumstances in which this might occur.

There are a number of possible reasons for making a disposition in this form, as follow—

(1)   If the testator's spouse survives the testator, it can be used to make a non-exempt gift of the shares, but one from which the surviving spouse can benefit, so as not to waste the business relief by making an exempt gift of the shares to the spouse (see para **[233.7]**). This is a particularly good idea where it is likely that, if the shares were given to the spouse, business relief would not be available on the spouse's death, eg because they are subject to an option for other shareholders to buy them on the testator's death, the business is personal to the testator, or the shares will have to be sold after the testator's death to raise cash (see para **[233.11]**).

(2)   If the testator's spouse survives the testator, to make a non-exempt gift of the shares where it is intended that the spouse will purchase some or all of the shares from the trustees. The business relief will thus be used to put funds in the hands of non-exempt beneficiaries, but the spouse can obtain the shares. This may be desirable because the spouse works in the business and/or has his or her own shares in it. It should be noted that it is not necessary for this purpose that the trust should be a discretionary trust; any trust, other than one which gives the surviving spouse an interest in possession or an absolute interest, will do. What is most important is that there should be no obstacles to the surviving spouse being able to buy the shares, such as him or her being a trustee without any specific authorisation to buy trust property (see cl 8(1) of this form at para **[233.23]** for such authorisation).

(3)   Where some (or only one) of the testator's children work in the business, and the testator wants to enable the other children to benefit while keeping the holding together and to some extent under the control or influence those (or the one) who work in the business. The latter would be executors and trustees, but there could be a difficult problem as to whether the children who do not work in the business should also be represented among the executors or trustees.

[233.14]
One further point about creating a discretionary trust of this sort in cases where the testator's spouse survives the testator is that if the shares do turn out to be subject to more inheritance tax than expected the liability can be reduced by making an appointment falling within the ITA 1984, s 144 (see C3 at para **[225.83]** et seq) of some or all of the shares to the surviving spouse within two years of the testator's death, so as to increase the amount of the testator's estate to which the exemption for gifts to spouses applies.

A further feature of this form, (at para **[233.17]**, cl 2(1)(b)), is a 'top up' legacy, so as to make maximum use of the testator's nil-rate band as well as the business relief, if the testator's spouse survives the testator and the taxable value of the shares is less than the amount of nil-rate band available on the testator's death. For further discussion of this type of disposition see the Preliminary Note at para **[233.9]** and the Note on nil-rate band discretionary trusts in B18 at para **[218.16]** et seq. The legacy is defined by a formula so as to be the maximum which can be given without an inheritance tax charge arising on the testator's death. It is intended to ensure that the amount of the discretionary trust fund does not exceed the inheritance tax threshold where other non-exempt gifts are made by the will, or where there are non-exempt lifetime chargeable transfers or other property treated as part of the testator's estate which have to be taken into account in determining the inheritance tax charge on the testator's estate on death. It also prevents any waste of the nil-rate band where the inheritance tax threshold is increased after the will has been made. However, in view of the presence of business relief it may be necessary or appropriate to impose an upper cash limit on the gift to prevent the entire estate going into the discretionary trust: see the Preliminary Note at para **[233.9]** and the words in square brackets in cl 2(1)(b) of this form at para **[233.17]** which are commented on in n 4 to that paragraph.

FORM

[233.15]

Revocation clause
I [*name*] of [*address*] hereby revoke all former testamentary dispositions made by me and declare this to be my last will.

[233.16]

Appointment of executors and trustees
1.   I appoint my wife [*name*] ('my wife') [*name*] of [*address*] and [*name*] of [*address*]¹ (hereinafter together called 'my trustees' which expression shall include my personal representatives for the time being and the trustees for the time being hereof) to be the executors and trustees of this will.

1   If there are two executors as well as the wife, there will still be two effective appointments if there is a divorce and the appointment of the wife is nullified by the Wills Act 1837 (WA 1837), s 18A (added by the AJA 1982, s 18: Part G, para **[244.17]**). See also the Preliminary Note to C2 on the possibility of divorce at para **[224.12]** et seq.

[233.17]

Gift of shares and nil-rate band legacy on discretionary trusts[1]

2.   (1)   [If my wife shall survive me and the trust for her of my residuary estate hereinafter contained shall take effect][2] I give to my trustees the following—

(a)   all the [25p] ordinary shares in [Will Williams & Company Limited] (hereinafter called 'the company') which I shall own at my death subject to payment thereout of any inheritance tax payable by reason of my death which is attributable thereto (after allowing for any reduction in value for inheritance tax purposes which is attributed thereto);[3] and

(b)   the maximum sum (if any) [not exceeding £——][4] which can in the circumstances subsisting at my death be given by virtue of this subclause (b) without any liability being incurred for the payment of inheritance tax on or by reason of my death; and in particular (without prejudice to the generality of the foregoing) for the purpose of determining the amount of such maximum sum the circumstances to be taken into account shall include all chargeable transfers made by me during my life (or events treated as such for inheritance tax purposes) so far as relevant for the computation of inheritance tax on my death the dispositions taking effect under this will (apart from this subclause) or under any codicil hereto and any property treated as if it were part of my estate for inheritance tax purposes[5] [provided that the foregoing gift of a sum of money contained in this subclause (b) shall not have effect if my wife shall predecease me or the trust for her of my residuary estate hereinafter contained shall fail for any other reason].[6]

(2)   In this clause the following expressions have the following meanings namely:

(a)   'the relevant beneficiaries' means and includes my wife my children and remoter issue (whether living at my death or born thereafter) and the spouses widows and widowers (including widows and widowers who have remarried) of my children and remoter issue;[7]

(b)   'the trust period' means the period commencing on my death and expiring on the twenty-first anniversary of the death of the last survivor of my wife and my children and remoter issue who shall be living at my death;

(c)   'the accumulation period' means the period commencing with my death and expiring on the twenty first anniversary thereof.

(3)   My trustees may at their absolute discretion sell or retain the said shares for as long as they think fit and shall invest the said legacy (if any) and the proceeds of sale of the said shares when and if sold in any investments hereby authorised with power to vary the same and shall hold the said shares and the said legacy and the assets from time to time representing the same (hereinafter called 'the trust fund') and the income thereof upon the trusts and with and subject to the powers and provisions hereinafter declared and contained.

(4)   My trustees shall hold the trust fund and the income thereof upon trust for all or such one or more of the relevant beneficiaries at such ages or times in such shares and upon such trusts for the benefit of the relevant beneficiaries as my trustees (being at least two in number or a trust corporation) may by deed or deeds revocable or irrevocable executed at any time or times during the trust period appoint and in making any such appointment my trustees shall have powers as full as those which they would possess if they were an absolute beneficial owner of the trust fund and in particular (but without prejudice to the generality of the foregoing words) my trustees may in any exercise of the foregoing power as they in their absolute discretion think fit:

(a)   delegate give or impose to or upon themselves or any other person or persons and in relation to any trust or disposition any discretionary powers or discretionary trusts including powers of further delegation or powers to create further discretionary trusts or powers;[8]

(b)   create trusts or powers for the accumulation of income during any period permitted by law;

(c)   create administrative powers or provisions of whatever nature;

Provided that:

(i)   no such appointment shall invalidate any payment transfer or application of capital or income previously made under any of the trusts or powers herein elsewhere contained;

(ii)   every interest limited under any exercise of such power shall vest in interest (if at all) not later than the expiration of the trust period;

(iii) any such appointment may be made in respect of income alone without any appointment of capital; and

(iv) any such revocable appointment shall (so far as then unrevoked) cease to be revocable at the expiration of the trust period.

(5)   In default of and subject to any exercise of the foregoing power my trustees (being at least two in number or a trust corporation) may at their discretion at any time or times during the trust period pay transfer or apply the whole or any part or parts of the trust fund to or for the benefit of all or any one or more exclusive of the others or other of the relevant beneficiaries for the time being living if more than one in such shares and generally in such manner as my trustees shall think fit.[9]

(6)   Subject to any or every exercise of the foregoing powers my trustees shall during the trust period hold the trust fund upon trust to pay or apply the income thereof to or for the maintenance education or benefit of all or any one or more of the relevant beneficiaries for the time being living in such shares if more than one and generally in such manner as they think fit provided that my trustees may during the accumulation period accumulate the whole or any part of the income of the trust fund by investing the same and the resulting income thereof in any of the investments hereby authorised and any accumulations of income so made shall form part of the capital of the trust fund (or the part thereof from which such income arose) for all purposes.

(7)   Subject to the foregoing trust and to any or every exercise of the foregoing powers my trustees shall hold the trust fund and the income thereof at the expiration of the trust period in trust absolutely for such of my children and remoter issue as shall then be living in equal shares per stirpes.

(8)   Any capital or income of the trust fund not otherwise disposed of by this clause shall be held in trust for such of my children as shall survive me if more than one in equal shares absolutely.

1   See the Note to this form at paras **[233.13]** and **[233.14]**.

2   Where the main or only objective of the discretionary trust is to make use of the business relief on the shares and the testator's nil-rate band if the testator's spouse survives the testator and becomes entitled to the residuary estate (see the Note to this form at para **[233.13]**), it is appropriate to impose this precondition. However, where an objective of the discretionary trust is to keep the holding together irrespective of whether the spouse becomes entitled to residue (see the Note to this form at para **[233.13]**), these words should be omitted at this point and instead the proviso to sub-cl (1)(b) should be included (see n 6 infra).

3   Making the gift subject to inheritance tax will, in the event of the testator's spouse surviving the testator and the gift of the shares giving rise to an inheritance tax charge (see B5 at para **[205.51]** for possible reasons why this should happen), cause the size of the chargeable estate to be less than it would be if the gift was free of inheritance tax: see B14 at para **[214.74]**. Without these words the gift of the shares will be free of inheritance tax if they are located in the UK: see B14 at para **[214.55]** et seq.

Where this gift is to take effect even if the testator's spouse does not survive the testator (see the last preceding note), it may be preferable for this gift to be free of inheritance tax in those circumstances, which can be achieved by making the direction that the gift is subject to tax contingent on the spouse surviving the testator and becoming entitled to the residuary estate.

4   If the shares given by sub-cl (a) are entitled to 100 per cent business relief (see B5 at para **[205.29]** et seq for 100 per cent relief on shares), and the testator has made no lifetime gifts within the seven years preceding his death, and there is no property outside his free estate which is taxable as part of his estate on his death, this legacy will be equal at least to the nil-rate band (£242,000 for transfers in 2001–02). Further, for reasons given in the Preliminary Note at para **[233.9]**, if there are other assets of the estate qualifying for business or agricultural relief then the cash legacy could exceed the nil-rate band or even, in an extreme case, use up the entire estate. In either case the testator might prefer to limit the amount of this legacy, as in these words in square brackets, so that his spouse gets some assets absolutely under the gift of residue.

However, the spouse is not excluded from benefit where the trusts of the legacy are, as in this form, discretionary trusts under which the spouse is a beneficiary. If the testator does not mind the possibility that the benefit to his spouse under the will might be solely that of being an object of a discretionary trust, he can take maximum advantage of the inheritance tax reliefs if no upper limit is imposed on the legacy. It is much more important to impose an upper limit of this kind where the trusts of the legacy are such that the spouse is excluded from benefit, as in Form C11.2, cl 2 at para **[233.29]**.

5   See the Preliminary Note at para **[233.9]** and the Note to this form at para **[233.14]**.

6   See n 2 supra. This proviso should be included if the condition as to the wife's survival is omitted from the opening words of this sub-cl (1) so that the discretionary trust of the shares takes effect even if the spouse predeceases the testator (for reasons given in the Note to this form at para **[233.13]**, sub-para (3)).

7   The definition of the discretionary class may need to be enlarged or adapted in individual cases. For wider classes, and power to add to the class of beneficiaries, see Form C3.6. cl 3(1)(b) at para **[225.100]**, Form C4.1, cl 8(2)(a) at para **[226.25]**, Form C6.2, cls 7(1)(a), (2) and (3)(c) at para **[228.28]** and Form C8.4, cl 6(e) at para **[230.59]**.

8   These words authorise the creation of discretionary trusts and powers which otherwise might not be within the scope of the power: see Vol 1, para **[40.5]**.

9   A power to apply capital, being exercisable in a less formal manner, may be useful. But it is essential that its exercise should be adequately evidenced.

[233.18]

Administration trusts of residue

3.   (1)   I give all my property not hereby or by any codicil hereto otherwise effectively disposed of [(including any entailed or other property over which I shall have at my death a general power of disposition by will)][1] to my trustees to

hold on the trusts set out below with power at their discretion to sell all or any of it as and when they think fit.[2]

(2)   My trustees shall pay my funeral and testamentary expenses[3] and debts and any legacies given by this will or any codicil hereto out of such property or its proceeds and shall have a discretion as to how such payments shall be borne as between capital and income.[4]

(3)   Subject as above my trustees shall hold such property and the assets from time to time representing the same (hereinafter called 'my residuary estate') on the trusts set out below and shall invest all money comprised in such property or arising from its sale in any of the investments hereby authorised with power to change such investments into any others hereby authorised.

(4)   In the administration of my estate and the execution of the trusts of this will or of any codicil to it:

(a)   my trustees shall treat all income as accruing on the date on which it becomes payable regardless of the period in respect of which it shall have accrued and shall not make any statutory apportionment of the same;[5] and

(b)   none of the equitable rules of apportionment between capital and income shall apply in any circumstances whatever.[6]

1   See para **[230.7]**, n 1.
2   See para **[230.7]**, n 2.
3   See para **[230.7]**, n 3.
4   See para **[230.7]**, n 4.
5   See para **[230.7]**, n 5.
6   See para **[230.7]**, n 6.

[233.19]

Beneficial trusts of residue

4.   (1)   My trustees shall hold my residuary estate upon trust for my wife absolutely if she shall survive me.[1]

(2)   If my wife shall predecease me my trustees shall hold my residuary estate upon trust for such of my children [by my wife][2] as shall survive me if more than one in equal shares provided that if any of my children [by my wife][3] shall predecease me leaving a child or children surviving me who shall attain the age of [18/21/25] years such last-mentioned child or children shall take if more than one the share of my residuary estate which such deceased child of mine would have taken had he or she survived me.

(3)   The foregoing trusts shall carry the intermediate income of my residuary estate and section 31 of the Trustee Act 1925 (as hereinafter modified) shall apply thereto.

(4)   Section 32 of the Trustee Act 1925 (as hereinafter modified) shall apply in relation to my residuary estate.

1   In view of the nil-rate band legacy a condition of survival for a survivorship period would not serve any useful purpose (see the Preliminary Notes to C2 at para **[224.2]** et seq and to C3 at para **[225.4]**), unless the testator's spouse's will leaves his or her property to different beneficiaries from those who take under the testator's will, or there is a cash limit on the amount of the legacy (for which see n 4 to cl 2(1)(b) of this form at para **[233.17]** and the wording to which it relates).

A cash limit on the amount of the nil-rate band legacy means that if the testator's spouse survives the testator the testator's nil-rate band and available business and agricultural relief will not be used to full advantage if the legacy would exceed the cash limit if it were not imposed. Accordingly, if a cash limit is imposed, it might be preferred to include a survivorship condition, as in, eg Form C2.1, cl 4 at para **[224.25]**, particularly where the spouse's own assets are likely to be sufficient to use up his or her own nil-rate band (see further the Preliminary Note to C2 at para **[224.3]**, sub-para (iii) for the latter point). If a survivorship condition is added to this gift, appropriate amendment should be made of the references to the spouse surviving or predeceasing the testator in the opening words of cl 2(1) (para **[233.17]**), the proviso to cl 2(1)(b) and the opening words of cl 4(2).

2   These words are for inclusion where the testator has children other than children of the marriage who are not intended to benefit. An alternative, for where there will not be any more children of the marriage, is to make the gift to named children. See further the Preliminary Note to C2 on reciprocal wills and the ultimate destination of property at para **[224.9]** et seq. For forms for use where one spouse has children who are not children of the marriage and wishes to benefit them by his or her will see C5 at para **[227.1]** et seq.

3   To be included if the trust is confined to the children of the marriage. See n 2 supra.

[233.20]

Maintenance, accumulation and advancement[1]

5.   (1)   Section 31 of the Trustee Act 1925 (relating to accumulation and maintenance) shall apply in relation to the trusts hereby or by any codicil hereto declared as if:

   (a)   in paragraph (i) of subsection (1) of the said section the words 'as the trustees think fit' were substituted for the words 'as may in all the circumstances be reasonable'; and

   (b)   the proviso to the said subsection (1) were omitted.

   (2)   Section 32 of the Trustee Act 1925 (relating to advancement) shall apply in relation to the said trusts as if the words 'one half of' were omitted from proviso (a) to subsection (1) thereof [provided that the powers conferred by the said section (as hereby enlarged) shall not be exercisable in favour of any minor beneficiary hereunder otherwise than so as to cause such beneficiary to become immediately entitled to or to an interest in possession in the capital thereby paid or applied within the meaning of section 71(1)(a) of the Inheritance Tax Act 1984][2]

   (3)   Whenever my trustees shall have an obligation or discretion under the provisions of this will or any codicil hereto or under the general law to apply income or capital for the benefit of a minor beneficiary they may either pay the same without liability to account to his or her parent guardian or any other adult person with whom such beneficiary may be residing or to such beneficiary himself or herself if of the age of 16 years or more and so that the receipt of such parent guardian or other person or of such minor beneficiary shall be a full and sufficient discharge to my trustees for the income or capital so applied.[3]

1   For alternative provisions relating to maintenance and advancement see Forms B18.11 to B18.23 and the notes thereto at paras **[218.41]**–**[218.107]**.

2   The proviso is included in order to prevent the power prejudicing the application of the ITA 1984, s 71 (accumulation and maintenance trusts), but is probably unnecessary: see the Note on inheritance tax and the statutory power of advancement in B18 at para **[218.99]**. If the accumulation and maintenance trusts of income are extended so as to continue beyond the age of 18 (see eg Forms B18.12 and B18.13 at paras **[218.78]** and **[218.79]**), then 'minor beneficiary hereunder' should be amended to eg 'beneficiary hereunder who is under the age of [*n*] years' where *n* is the highest age at which an absolute interest or an interest in possession might be attained by any of the beneficiaries. 25 is the maximum age compatible with the ITA 1984, s 71 applying: see Part A, para **[200.19]**.

3   A parent (with parental responsibility) and a guardian of a minor are empowered by the ChA 1989, s 3(3) (Part G, para **[244.119]**) to give a good receipt for the minor's property: see Vol 1, para **[9.42]**.The power in this subclause is wider in that it authorises the payment of income or capital to a parent who does not have parental responsibility, any adult with whom the minor is residing, and the minor himself or herself if 16 or over.

[233.21]

Administrative powers[1]

6.   (1)   In this clause where the context so admits—

(a)   the expression 'land' includes buildings and estates interests or rights of any kind in or over land; and

(b)   during the administration of my estate the expression 'beneficiary' includes any person who would be a beneficiary if such administration had been completed and the expression 'beneficially interested' and references to income of any asset being payable or capable of being paid to or for the benefit of a beneficiary shall be construed accordingly.

(2)   None of the powers or provisions contained in subclause (3) below of this clause shall be capable of being exercised or operating in any manner such that if such power or provision were capable of being so exercised or so operating the existence of the same would either—

(i)   prevent any person who would in the absence of such power or provision have been entitled to an interest in possession (within the meaning of Part III of the Inheritance Tax Act 1984) in any property from being entitled to such interest; or

(ii)   prevent section 71 of the Inheritance Tax Act 1984 from applying to any property to which in the absence of such power or provision the said section 71 would have applied.[2]

(3)   In the administration of my estate and the execution of the trusts hereof or of any codicil hereto my trustees shall have the following powers in addition to those conferred by law but subject to the last foregoing subclause—

(a)   power to invest moneys sell assets and change investments with the unrestricted freedom of choice and powers of disposition and acquisition of a sole beneficial owner with in particular power to make unsecured loans, acquire non-income yielding assets, and purchase land anywhere in the world or chattels for any purpose including occupation or enjoyment in kind by a beneficiary under the power set out below;[3]

(b)   power to delegate all or any of their investment powers to a professional investment manager or managers whether individual or corporate and whether or not also a nominee holder of assets for my trustees (and who may be or include one or more of my trustees or the beneficiaries hereunder) upon such terms as to remuneration and otherwise (including terms authorising self-dealing or providing for the limitation of the liability of the investment manager or managers) as my trustees think fit and section 22 of the Trustee Act 2000 shall not apply;[4]

(c)   power to vest or register any property in any person or persons whether individual or corporate and whether or not an investment manager to whom powers have been delegated under the foregoing power (and who may be or include one or more of my trustees or the beneficiaries hereunder) as nominee or nominees for my trustees upon such terms as to remuneration or otherwise (including terms authorising self-dealing or providing for the limitation of the liability of the nominee) as my trustees think fit and section 22 of the Trustee Act 2000 shall not apply;[5]

(d)   power to borrow money with or without giving security and on such terms as to interest and repayment and otherwise as my trustees may think fit for any purpose connected with the administration of my estate or the trusts declared herein or in any codicil hereto (including investment) And no lender from whom my trustees borrow money in purported exercise of this power shall be concerned to enquire as to the propriety amount or purpose of any such borrowing;[6]

(e)   power to lend money to a beneficiary to whom any of the income of such money is payable or to whom or for whose benefit any income of such money is capable of being paid or applied in exercise of a discretion (or who would be such a beneficiary if such money yielded income) and to do so at a full or concessionary rate of interest or interest free;[7]

(f)   without prejudice to the generality of subclause (a) above power in connection with the sale of any assets (in particular the sale of any business or any private company shares) to give any warranty indemnity guarantee undertaking or other agreement or covenant whatever or to enter into any type of agreement they think fit;

(g)   power to give guarantees or otherwise assist or finance any company or corporate body in which shares are held by my trustees or any beneficiary;

(h)   power to carry on any business whether alone or in partnership or any other form of joint venture with others and to employ in it any capital held on the same trusts as the assets of the business or the partnership share (as the case may be) and to appoint any person (including any one or more of my trustees) manager servant or agent to act in any such business at a salary or otherwise;

(i)   power to incorporate any company or other corporation in any part of the world with limited or unlimited liability for any purpose including the acquisition of any business or other assets subject to any of the trusts hereof (or of any codicil hereto) or the carrying on of any trade or business and any consideration for the acquisition of any such assets by any company incorporated under this subclause may consist wholly or partly of shares or securities (including unsecured loan stock) allotted to my trustees;[8]

(j)   all the powers of an absolute owner in relation to any land (wherever situated) held by them;[9]

(k)   power to apply capital held on the same trusts as any land (or which would be so held if the administration of my estate had been completed) in the improvement of such land and to apply such capital or the income of such capital on the repair or maintenance of such land;[10]

(l)   power to permit any beneficiary to have the beneficial occupation use or enjoyment in kind of any land or chattel or other tangible property on such terms as to repair insurance or payment of outgoings by the beneficiary or otherwise howsoever as my trustees think fit Provided that the foregoing power shall only be exercisable and such permission to occupy or enjoy in kind may only continue in the following circumstances—

(i) so long as any of the income of such land chattel or other tangible property is payable to such beneficiary or capable of being paid or applied to him or for his benefit in exercise of a discretion (or would be so payable or capable of being so paid or applied if such land chattel or other property yielded income),

(ii) in the case of land, so long as for the time being the occupation thereof by such beneficiary is compatible with any statutory rights of occupation of any other beneficiary or beneficiaries;[11]

(m) power to exercise all the powers of appropriation (and other incidental powers) conferred by statute on a personal representative without the necessity of obtaining any consents and notwithstanding that one or more of my trustees may be beneficially interested in the exercise of such power.[12]

1   See para **[230.11]**, n 1.
2   See para **[230.11]**, n 2.
3   See para **[230.11]**, n 3.
4   See para **[230.11]**, n 4.
5   See para **[230.11]**, n 5.
6   See para **[230.11]**, n 6.
7   See para **[230.11]**, n 7.
8   The powers in sub-cls (f) to (i) are specific to business property of various kinds. Where the testator does not have a business owned personally and is not a partner in a business, and not likely to acquire a business or partnership interest before his death, his business interests all being held through companies, sub-cls (h) and (i) could be omitted.
9   See para **[230.11]**, n 8.
10   See para **[230.11]**, n 9.
11   See para **[230.11]**, n 10.
12   See para **[230.11]**, n 11.

[233.22]

Exercise of powers[1]

7. Any power or discretion hereby or by law conferred on my trustees (including a power or discretion as to the disposition of capital or income) shall be exercisable notwithstanding that any of my trustees has a personal interest in such exercise provided that there are not fewer than two trustees and that at least one of them has no such personal interest.

1   This clause permits a member of the family to be a trustee without disqualifying him or her from benefit under any exercise of statutory or express powers of payment or application of capital, appointment, etc. See the Preliminary Note to B18 at para **[218.4]**.

[233.23]

Trustee self-dealing, indemnity and similar provisions

8. (1) Any of my trustees in his personal capacity or in a fiduciary capacity other than as one of my trustees may enter into any transaction (including a sale purchase lease loan or partnership) with my trustees provided that there is at least one other of my trustees agreeing in writing to the transaction who has no interest therein save as one of my trustees.[1]

(2)   None of my trustees nor any officer or employee of any of my trustees shall be accountable for any remuneration or other benefit gained as an officer employee agent or adviser of any company body or firm notwithstanding that his situation or office may have been obtained or may be held or retained in right or by means or by reason of his position as one of my trustees or of any shares stock property rights or powers whatsoever held by my trustees.[2]

(3)   In the professed administration of my estate and the professed execution of the trusts powers or provisions of this will or any codicil hereto none of my trustees (nor any officer or employee of any of my trustees) shall be liable (whether for breach of the duty of care under the Trustee Act 2000 or otherwise) for any act or omission of his or for any act or omission of any co-personal representative or co-trustee of his or of any agent adviser manager delegate nominee or other person employed in the administration of my estate or the execution of any of the said trusts powers and provisions save for any act or omission involving wilful fraud or dishonesty committed by the personal representative or trustee sought to be made liable.[3]

(4)   Without prejudice to the generality of the foregoing none of my trustees shall be liable for leaving the conduct of the business and affairs (including the payment and non-payment of dividends) of any company or corporation whose securities are subject to the trusts hereof or of any codicil hereto to the directors or other governing body thereof (whether or not such securities give control of the company or corporation) unless my trustees have express notice of some act of dishonesty or other misconduct on the part of such directors or governing body.

(5)   My trustees shall be fully indemnified out of the assets they hold on the trusts hereof or of any codicil hereto against any liability they may incur in exercise of any of the powers hereby or by any codicil hereto or by law conferred.[4]

[(6)   My trustees shall not be liable for any act or default of any investment manager or nominee employed in good faith to manage or hold assets of my estate nor for any act or default of any beneficiary having the occupation use or enjoyment of property in kind nor for any loss which may be incurred by reason of the carrying on of a business in exercise of the foregoing power to do so.][5]

(7)   Section 11(1) of the Trusts of Land and Appointment of Trustees Act 1996 (consultation with beneficiaries) shall not apply to the exercise by my trustees of any of their powers in relation to land subject to the trusts hereof.[6]

---

1   See para **[221.4]**. A power to purchase trust property or otherwise deal with the trustees is often a convenient power to have where business property or private company shares form part of the estate, because it is often necessary or appropriate to appoint executors and/or trustees who are involved in the business, and who are the most likely purchasers if the business assets or company shares have to be sold. It is particularly relevant if it is intended that the surviving spouse will purchase some or all of the shares. It could also be particularly relevant if the trustees wish to continue with a business which the deceased carried on in partnership where one of the trustees is also one of the partners.

2   Without a provision of this kind a trustee or employee of a trustee who owed his position in a company to the exercise or non-exercise of votes attached to shares held by the trustees would be accountable for his remuneration to the trust fund: see the note to Form B21.9 at para **[221.10]**. This is not so where his position is owed entirely to votes other than those attached to the trust assets (*Re Gee* [1948] Ch 284, [1948] 1 All ER 498). A provision of this kind should be included if the will disposes of private company shares, particularly where persons connected with the company are appointed executors or might subsequently become trustees.

3   This is a wide form of indemnity, and may not be appropriate where a professional executor and trustee, charging for his services, is being appointed. It also needs to be fully explained where the draftsman of the will is also going to be a professional executor, and have the benefit of such a clause. Where the executors will include both professional and non-professional executors, it may be appropriate for this clause to be included but not to apply to a corporate or professional executor: see the proviso to Form B21.12 at para **[221.16]**. If this is omitted or restricted to non-professional executors, the more limited indemnity in sub-cl (6) could be included. For the duty of care under the TrA 2000 see para **[221.15]** and the TrA 2000, s 1 and Sch 1 at Part G, paras **[246.116]** and **[246.156]**.

4   This is implicit anyway in the powers concerned, which are principally the powers to give guarantees, and warranties on sale of shares or business assets, to carry on a business, and to borrow (cl 6(d), (f), (g), and (h)).

5   This makes it clear that the trustees are not liable for the defaults of others who may have possession or control of trust property or for carrying on a business in good faith. This clause should be omitted if sub-cl (3) is included and applies to all trustees: see n 3 supra.

6   The requirement that trustees of land in exercise of any function relating to land subject to the trust consult with beneficiaries of full age beneficially entitled to an interest in possession in the land can be excluded: see the TLATA 1996, s 11 (Part G, para **[246.97]**)

[233.24]

Professional trustee charging clause

9.   Any of my trustees being a professional or business man may charge and be paid all usual professional and other proper charges for business transacted acts done advice given and time spent by him or his firm in connection with the administration of my estate or in connection with the trusts hereof including acts which a personal representative or trustee not being in any profession or business could have done personally.

[233.25]

Testimonium and attestation clause

IN WITNESS whereof I have hereunto set my hand this —— day of —— 20—
—.

SIGNED by the above-named testator as his last will in
the presence of us both present at the same time who at   *[Signature of*
his request and in his presence and in the presence of   *testator]*
each other have signed our names below as witnesses:

[Signatures, addresses and descriptions of two witnesses]

[233.26]

FORM C11.2:   Reciprocal wills for husband and wife who have recently acquired share capital of private trading company, the first to die making nil-rate band gift to the children and otherwise leaving estate to the survivor

NOTE

It is assumed that the testators are husband and wife making wills shortly after acquiring part of the voting ordinary share capital of a private trading company. It is also assumed that the shares do not already qualify for business relief as replacement property within the ITA 1984, s 107 or under the succession provisions of the ITA 1984, ss 108 and 109 (see B5 at para **[205.11]**), but that the shares will qualify fully for inheritance tax business relief after they have been owned by the testators for two years.

This form illustrates making a non-exempt gift of such shares which only takes effect in relation to those which qualify for business relief by the time of the testator's death (see B5 at para **[205.31]** and also Forms B5.9 and B5.10 at paras **[205.66]** and **[205.67]**).

As there is a nil-rate band gift in cl 2, taking effect on the death of the first to die, it will not be appropriate to make the gift in cl 2 or the residuary gift to the surviving spouse conditional on the wife/husband surviving the testator for a specific period (see further the Preliminary Note to C2 at para **[224.2]** et seq). It is possible that the company will change its name or be taken over, or shares with a different par value substituted, or more shares of the same type acquired by either testator (including by a bonus or rights issue), or some of the shares sold by either of them before the testator's death. It is not practicable to try to make provision for the numerous possibilities of this kind, and the testators will have to be warned (preferably in writing) that they must have their wills reviewed if there is a takeover, capital reconstruction, bonus or rights issue, change of name of the company, acquisition by either of them of more shares, or sale or other disposal by either of them of any of the shares, etc.

It is assumed that the testators' children are grown up. For notes on reciprocal wills for married couples with children, see the Preliminary Notes to C2 at paras **[224.8]–[224.11]** and C3 at para **[225.7]**.

[233.27]

Revocation clause

I [*name*] of [*address*] hereby revoke all former testamentary dispositions made by me and declare this to be my last will.

[233.28]

Appointment of executors and trustees

1.   I appoint my [wife/husband] [*name*] ('my [wife/husband]') [*name*] of [*address*] and [*name*] of [*address*][1] (hereinafter together called 'my trustees' which expression shall include my personal representatives for the time being and the trustees for the time being hereof) to be the executors and trustees of this will.

---

1   If there are two executors as well as the wife/husband, there will still be two effective appointments if there is a divorce and the appointment of the wife/husband is nullified by the WA 1837, s 18A (added by the AJA 1982, s 18): Part G, para **[244.17]**. See also the Preliminary Note to C2 on the possibility of divorce at paras **[224.12]–[224.19]**.

[233.29]

Nil-rate band gift to children including private company shares[1]

2.   (1)   In this clause 'the relevant shares' means the [25p] ordinary shares in [Will Williams & Company Limited] owned by me at the date of this my will.

(2)   If my [wife/husband] shall survive me[2] and if by the time of my death I shall have owned the relevant shares for a continuous period of two years[3] then I give [all]/[100][4] of the relevant shares subject to payment thereout of any inheritance tax payable by reason of my death which is attributable thereto (after

allowing for any reduction in value for inheritance tax purposes which is attributed thereto)[5] to my trustees to hold the same on the trusts set out below.

(3) If my [wife/husband] shall survive me[6] I further give to my trustees to hold on the trusts set out below the maximum sum (if any) [not exceeding £——][7] which can in the circumstances subsisting at my death be given by virtue of this subclause (in addition to any relevant shares given by the last preceding subclause) without any liability being incurred for the payment of inheritance tax on or by reason of my death; and in particular (without prejudice to the generality of the foregoing) for the purpose of determining the amount of such maximum sum the circumstances to be taken into account shall include all chargeable transfers made by me during my life (or events treated as such for inheritance tax purposes) so far as relevant for the computation of inheritance tax on my death the dispositions taking effect under this will (apart from this subclause) or under any codicil hereto and any property treated as if it were part of my estate for inheritance tax purposes.[8]

(4) My trustees may at their absolute discretion sell or retain the said shares for as long as they think fit and shall invest the said legacy (if any) and the proceeds of sale of the said shares when and if sold in any investments hereby authorised with power to vary the same and shall hold the said shares and the said legacy and the assets from time to time representing the same (hereinafter called 'the trust fund') and the income thereof upon the trusts and with and subject to the powers and provisions hereinafter declared and contained.

(5) My trustees shall hold the trust fund and the income thereof upon trust for such of my children [*name*] [*name*] and [*name*][9] as shall survive me and if more than one in equal shares provided that if any of my said children shall predecease me leaving a child or children surviving me who shall attain the age of [18/21/25] years[10] such last-mentioned child or children shall take and if more than one equally between them the share of the trust fund which such deceased child of mine would have taken had he or she survived me.

(6) The foregoing trusts shall carry the intermediate income of the trust fund and section 31 of the Trustee Act 1925 (as hereinafter modified) shall apply thereto.

(7) Section 32 of the Trustee Act 1925 (as hereinafter modified) shall apply in relation to the trust fund.

1 See the Note above, for the importance of reviewing the terms of this gift if more of the same shares are acquired, or there is any relevant change in the company or its share capital. It may be preferred to have a discretionary trust of the property given by this clause, such as in Form C11.1, cl 2 at para **[233.17]**.
2 The objective of this gift is to make use of the business relief on the shares and the testator's nil-rate band if the testator's spouse survives the testator (see the Note to this form at para **[233.26]**), and this precondition is imposed to avoid unnecessary duplication of gifts (ie this one and the residuary gift) in the event of the spouse not surviving the testator. If the residuary gift to the spouse fails through divorce, there will be such duplication, but the trusts taking effect will be the same.
3 If the shares do not qualify for business relief by the time of the testator's death it is better for them to pass to the surviving spouse under the exempt residuary gift in the hope that the combined period of ownership of the testator and surviving spouse (taken into account together under the ITA 1984, s 108) will be sufficient for business relief to apply on the death of the spouse.
4 Delete one alternative, and if 'all' is deleted, amend the number of shares as appropriate. It is a matter for decision how much of the holding should be the subject of a non-exempt gift on the first death, and how much of it should go to the surviving spouse, depending on factors such as whether the shares may be entitled to business relief in the hands of the surviving spouse, what

other resources the surviving spouse will have, and whether he or she will be working for the company (see also para **[233.11]**). If there is business or agricultural relief applicable which depends on control of the company (see paras **[205.5]**, **[205.6]** and **[234.6]** for the categories of relief depending on control) and the spouses between them have control of it, that will favour giving sufficient to the surviving spouse for him or her to maintain control.

5   Making the gift subject to inheritance tax will, in the event of the gift of the shares giving rise to an inheritance tax charge (see B5 at para **[205.51]** for possible reasons why this should happen), cause the size of the chargeable estate to be less than it would be if the gift was free of inheritance tax: see B14 at para **[214.74]**. Without these words the gift of the shares will be free of inheritance tax if they are located in the UK: see B14 at para **[214.59]**.

6   See n 2 supra.

7   See C11.1, cl 2(1)(b), n 4 at para **[233.17]**. Note that in relation to this form there is a stronger case for a cash limit than there is in relation to the corresponding clause in Form C11.1, because under the trusts of this clause the shares and legacy go to the children absolutely, to the complete exclusion of the surviving spouse from benefit.

8   See the Preliminary Note at para **[233.9]** and the Note to Form C11.1 at para **[233.14]**.

9   See the Preliminary Note to C2 on reciprocal wills and the ultimate destination of property at paras **[224.8]–[224.10]**.

10   The grandchildren will be lives in being at the testator's death for perpetuity purposes, so that there is no risk of infringing the rule against perpetuities in specifying an age exceeding 21.

[233.30]

Administration trusts of residue

3.   [*As in cl 3 of* Form C11.1 *at para* **[233.18]**.]

[233.31]

Beneficial trusts of residue

4.   (1)   My trustees shall hold my residuary estate upon trust for my [wife/husband] absolutely if [she/he] shall survive me.[1]

(2)   If my [wife/husband] shall predecease me my trustees shall hold my residuary estate upon trust for such of my children [*name*] [*name*] and [*name*][2] as shall survive me if more than one in equal shares provided that if any of my said children shall predecease me leaving a child or children surviving me who shall attain the age of [18/21/25] years such last-mentioned child or children shall take if more than one the share of my residuary estate which such deceased child of mine would have taken had he or she survived me.

(3)   The foregoing trusts shall carry the intermediate income of my residuary estate and section 31 of the Trustee Act 1925 (as hereinafter modified) shall apply thereto.

(4)   Section 32 of the Trustee Act 1925 (as hereinafter modified) shall apply in relation to my residuary estate.

1   See Form C11.1, cl 4(1), n 1 at para **[233.19]**.

2   See the Preliminary Note to C2 on reciprocal wills and the ultimate destination of property at paras **[224.9]–[224.10]**.

[233.32]

Maintenance, accumulation and advancement

5.   [*As in cl 5 of* Form C11.1 *at para* **[233.20]**.]

[233.33]

Administrative powers

6.   [*As in cl 6 of* Form C11.1 *at para* **[233.21]**.]

[233.34]

Trustee self-dealing, indemnity, and similar provisions
7. [*As in cl 8 of* Form C11.1 *at para* **[233.23]**.]

[233.35]

Professional trustee charging clause
8. [*As in cl 9 of* Form C11.1 *at para* **[233.24]**.]

[*Testimonium and attestation clause as in* Form C11.1 *at para* **[233.25]**.]

[233.36]

FORM C11.3: Will giving business carried on as sole trader or in partnership to sons, and legacies to daughters, with residue to wife for life with remainder to children with substitution clause and hotchpot of specific gifts

NOTE

This form illustrates a possible solution to the problem which may arise where some of the testator's children are interested in carrying on the testator's business after his death and others are not (discussed in the Preliminary Note at para **[233.12]**): the business is specifically given to those who are interested in running it, but they have to bring it into hotchpot against their shares of residue. For other possibilities, see Form C11.1 at paras **[233.13]**–**[233.25]** and Forms C12.1 and C12.2 at paras **[234.17]**–**[234.44]**. This is a complicated form, not to be used without careful reflection on its consequences.

This form assumes that the testator has two sons who are interested in carrying on the business and a wife and two daughters who are not. The wife, if surviving, is given a life interest in residue, which will not include the business, which is the subject of an immediate gift to the sons (or the survivor of them if only one is living at the testator's death) whether or not the gift to the wife takes effect; there are alternative clauses, one for a sole proprietor's business, the other for a partnership share. To counterbalance the gift to the sons the daughters are given legacies in the event of the wife surviving and taking her life interest, so as to give them an immediate gift of whatever it is thought might be spared from what is needed for the wife's support.

When residue comes to be divided there is hotchpot of the specific gift to the sons and the legacies to the daughters (if any) at their value at the testator's death. The aim is that the estate other than the business goes to the daughters if its value is less than the value of the business, and if it is equal to or more than the value of the business the estate is ultimately divided in equal shares. It should be noted that, even where the widow's life interest takes effect, the interests of the children in residue vest on the testator's death, so that if one dies after the testator and before the testator's widow his or her share of residue will fall into his or her estate, and that the hotchpot is at the values at the testator's death. It would involve an unacceptable increase in the complexity of an already complicated form to provide otherwise on either of these points, but to compensate there is a power of appointment which enables alteration of the interests in residue during the widow's life if the trustees can agree on it (the

1895

suggested trustees are a son a daughter and the widow). This is a form for a united family, but there is an expression of wishes as to how the power of appointment should be exercised in cl 8 (at para **[233.46]**) in the hope that it will promote agreement.

[233.37]

The hope is that in the event of the wife's life interest taking effect the specific gifts will be within the inheritance tax nil-rate band (assuming that the gift of the business property to the sons will obtain 100 per cent business relief), but they are made subject to inheritance tax in case any inheritance tax is payable, so as to avoid the adverse consequences of grossing up (see B5 at para **[205.52]** et seq and B14 at para **[214.74]**).

Where, as in this form, a will gives a life interest to the testator's spouse, it is essential to find out whether the testator and his spouse own property (in particular a residence) jointly, and if so to obtain instructions as to whether the testator's interest in that property is to be included in the property passing under his will and becoming subject to the trusts of his residuary estate. If his interest in the property is to be included in the residuary estate it is then necessary to advise the testator to sever the joint tenancy (see further the Note to Form C3.2 at para **[225.27]**).

It is also essential to make sure exactly what the testator does own; for example, it is possible for him to talk of his business, when investigation might show that what he owned was shares in a private company which owned the business. A misdescription of this kind in the will could cause the gift to fail, as it did in *Re Lewis's Will Trusts* [1984] 3 All ER 930, [1985] 1 WLR 102, where a gift by will of a farm and farming business was ineffective because what the testator owned was shares in a company which owned the farm and business.

If the testator's business or the business in which he is a partner is transferred to a company after the will is made, with the testator receiving company shares in place of his interest in the business or partnership share, a new gift by will or codicil of the company shares will be needed in substitution for the gift of the business or partnership share, as the latter is most unlikely to have effect as a gift of the company shares.

[233.38]

Revocation clause
I [*name*] of [*address*] hereby revoke all former testamentary dispositions made by me and declare this to be my last will.

[233.39]

Appointment of executors and trustees
1.   (1)   Subject to subclause (2) below I appoint my wife [*name*] ('my wife') my son [*name*] and my daughter [*name*][1] to be the executors and trustees of this will.

(2)   If the gift in clause 2 below hereof takes effect I appoint my said son [*name*] and my son [*name*] to be the executors of the property comprised in such gift.[2]

(3)   In this will the expression 'my trustees' shall where the context so admits mean and include my general personal representatives for the time being

the trustees for the time being hereof and the executors of the said property comprised in the said gift in clause 2 hereof for the time being.

1   If there are two executors as well as the wife, there will still be two effective appointments if there is a divorce and the appointment of the wife is nullified by the WA 1837, s 18A (added by the AJA 1982 s 18): Part G, para **[244.17]**. See also the Preliminary Note to C2 on the possibility of divorce at paras **[224.12]–[224.19]**.

2   It may be inconvenient administratively to appoint the legatees of business property as special executors of it and this course should not be adopted where the legatees are not under the terms of the bequest entitled to the debts due to the business, or where the testator's estate may, apart the business, be insufficient to pay his debts. On the other hand the legatees of a business who are also appointed executors for the purposes of the business are thereby enabled to sue in their own names for the debts due to the business, and the general executors of the will are relieved from trouble and responsibility with regard to the business. It may also be convenient to appoint special executors of a business where a testator's business is to be carried on after his death as part of the testator's residuary estate, and the business is extensive. Appointment of special executors is particularly appropriate where the persons appointed are already working in the business.

There may be up to four executors in respect of any part of a testator's estate: Supreme Court Act 1981, s 114(1), reversing the effect of the decision in *Re Holland's Estate* [1936] 3 All ER 13 that the limit of four executors imposed by the corresponding previous legislation related to the totality of a testator's estate.

It should be remembered that the Public Trustee may not carry on a business for more than a year, and he should never be appointed trustee of any estate which includes the carrying on of a business, and the same considerations in effect apply to the appointment of a bank or other trust corporation.

If the appointment in sub-cl (2) takes effect the general executors will not be entitled to probate of the property of which there are separate executors (*Re Wakeham's Goods* (1872) LR 2 P & D 395). The general executors alone can make a good title to the land not included in that property: *Re Cohen's Executors and LCC* [1902] 1 Ch 187.

[233.40]

Gift of business property to sons

EITHER[1]

[2.   I give to such of my said sons [*name*] and [*name*] as shall be living at my death if both in equal shares absolutely the goodwill of my business[2] of a [description of business] carried on by me at [location] and all the [equipment plant stock-in-trade][3] vehicles and all other assets of any kind employed or used in carrying on the same at my death and all book debts then owing to me in respect of such business together with the then balances (if any) to the credit of the current [and business reserve] accounts of the said business at the [*name*] Branch of [*name*] Bank plc[4] and the benefit of all contracts relating thereto but subject to taking over all my liabilities in connection with the said business existing at my death and indemnifying the rest of my estate against the same and subject as follows:

   (a)   [the foregoing gift shall include the freehold or such other estate or interest I may have at my death in the premises in which the said business is carried on but subject to any mortgage charge or other liability on or of such premises subsisting at my death[5] *or where the premises are leasehold* [the foregoing gift shall include the lease or tenancy of the premises on which the said business is carried on but subject to accepting the covenants liabilities and obligations thereunder and keeping my estate indemnified against all liability under the said lease or tenancy whether or not such liability has arisen in my lifetime or arises from acts or omissions done or occurring during my lifetime];

(b)   if there is any inheritance tax payable on my estate by reason of my death which is attributable to the foregoing gift (after allowing for any reduction in value for inheritance tax purposes which is attributed thereto) then the foregoing gift shall be subject to such inheritance tax and it shall be borne by my said sons or the survivor of them in exoneration of the rest of my estate.][6]

OR[7]

[2.   (1)   I give to such of my said sons [*name*] and [*name*] as shall be living at my death if both in equal shares all my share and interest of and in the capital goodwill stock-in-trade plant machinery and other assets of the firm of [*name*] carrying on business as [*description of business*] subject to:

(a)   payment thereout of any inheritance tax payable by reason of my death which is attributable thereto (after allowing for any reduction in value for inheritance tax purposes which is attributed thereto);[8] and

(b)   my said sons or the survivor of them indemnifying my general estate from all debts and liabilities of the said firm and accounting to my general estate for any sum due or owing to me at my death from the said firm by way of profit.[9]

(2)   If there shall be any exercise after my death of any option granted during my lifetime to which my said share and interest shall after my death be subject the foregoing gift shall take effect in relation to the consideration received for such share and interest and shall not be adeemed thereby.][10]

---

1   The first alternative is a gift of a sole trader's business, and the second a gift of a partnership share. See the Note at para [233.37] for the consequences of subsequent incorporation of the business.

2   The word 'business' has no definite legal meaning. In its narrowest sense it may pass the mere right to carry on the business as the testator's successor and to use his trade name; in its widest sense it may include everything enumerated in this clause: see generally Vol 1, para [64.7]. The draftsman should consider in each case which of the things enumerated in this clause are intended to pass and specify them. It is important to state whether the gift of the business is subject to trade liabilities (see *Re Timberlake, Archer v Timberlake* (1919) 63 Sol Jo 286).

3   The list may need amendment depending on the kind of business.

4   Banking arrangements vary, and the conscientious will-draftsmen should enquire into those of his client's business and get instructions on what bank balances to include in the gift.

5   A bequest of a business prima facie passes all the testator's interest in all the assets of the business, including the business premises: *Re Rhagg, Easten v Boyd* [1938] Ch 828, [1938] 3 All ER 314, and under the AEA 1925, s 35 (Part G, para [246.47]) a gift is subject to any mortgages or charges on the property in the absence of the expression of a contrary intent. However, to avoid doubt and possible dispute, we recommend that express provision is made about the business premises, and charges on it where relevant. There may need to be amendment where the business is carried on on part only of premises owned or leased by the testator, and the donee of the business is not intended to receive the whole of the premises. There will be an avoidable loss of business relief where liabilities which are not incurred for the purposes of the business are charged on the business premises or other business assets: see the Preliminary Note to B5 at paras [205.10] and [205.24].

6   There should be no inheritance tax on the gift because of 100 per cent business relief (see B5 at para **[205.22]**), but see the Preliminary Note to B5 at para **[205.51]** for the circumstances in which inheritance tax may be paid on such property. The advantage of including this subclause is that, if the residuary gift is exempt and there is any inheritance tax payable on this gift, the amount of inheritance tax payable on this gift will be much reduced if this gift is subject to tax rather than free of it: see B14 at para **[214.74]**.

   If a possible reason for inheritance tax being payable on this gift is the presence of excepted assets (see the Preliminary Note to B5 at para **[205.9]**) it would be possible to exclude these from the gift: see Form B5.4 at para **[205.61]** for an example.

7   This alternative is for a gift of a partnership share. See the Note to this form at para **[233.37]**, for the consequences of subsequent incorporation of the partnership business.

8   See n 6 to the first alternative cl 2 supra.

9   Alternatively undrawn profit could be included in the gift.

10 The gift could be adeemed under the rule in *Lawes v Bennett* (1785) 1 Cox Eq Cas 167 by exercise after the death of the testator of an option granted by lifetime disposition after the will was made (eg to the testator's partners), unless express provision is made to the contrary: see Vol 1, para **[41.20]**. An option granted but not exercised during the testator's life would not prevent there being business relief on the partnership share, although an automatic sale provision would probably exclude the relief: see the Preliminary Note to B5 at para **[205.28]** and also the Preliminary Note at para **[233.7]**. This clause is not intended to prevent ademption by exercise of an option before the testator's death, something which would of course prevent there being any business relief on the business property on his death even if the contract created by the exercise of the option had not been completed at the time of his death: ITA 1984, s 113; see also B5 at para **[205.14]**.

[233.41]

Gift of personal chattels to spouse or children[1]

3.   I give my personal chattels as defined by section $55(1)(x)$ of the Administration of Estates Act 1925[2] to my wife if she shall survive me and if she shall not survive me I give the same to such of my children [*name*] [*name*] [*name*] and [*name*] as shall survive me if more than one in equal shares.[3]

1   Since residue is settled on the surviving spouse, and then on the children, a specific gift of chattels is provided. It is not a good idea to settle chattels, because the trouble and expense of administering them as part of a trust fund is usually out of all proportion to their value, though it may sometimes be appropriate in the case of valuable ones.

2   See Part G, para **[246.52]** for the wording of this definition, and for further discussion of the meaning of 'personal chattels' see Vol 1, para **[64.44]**.

3   The gift to the children will be free of inheritance tax provided that all the chattels are in the UK: see B14 at paras **[214.59]**, **[214.60]** and **[214.63]**. If any might have a foreign location this gift to the children could be declared to be free of tax as in Form C3.2, cls 3 and 6 at paras **[225.31]** and **[225.34]**.

[233.42]

Legacies to daughters if trust for widow takes effect

4.   If the trust for my wife for life of my residuary estate hereinafter contained takes effect I give to each of my daughters [*name*] and [*name*] if she shall survive me the sum of [£25,000] subject to payment thereout of any inheritance tax payable in respect thereof by reason of my death[1] [and I declare that if the value of the legacy or legacies given by this clause is treated as reduced by virtue of section 39A of the Inheritance Tax Act 1984 the inheritance tax attributable to the foregoing legacy or legacies and borne thereby shall be the inheritance tax attributable to such legacy or legacies as so reduced].[2]

1   These legacies are made subject to inheritance tax to prevent grossing up of the gifts when the tax charge on death is calculated: see n 6 to the first alternative cl 2 at para **[233.40]**.

2   For a discussion of the ITA 1984, s 39A see the Preliminary Note at para **[233.2]** et seq and for the reasons for a provision of this kind see B14 at para **[214.73]**. This is to be included if there is or might be property with business or agricultural relief comprised in residue; the business property subject to the gift in cl 2 is not relevant because the relief relating to it will be allocated wholly to that gift.

[233.43]

Exclusion of Wills Act 1837, s 33 in relation to specific gifts and pecuniary legacies

5.   Section 33 of the Wills Act 1837 (as substituted by section 19 of the Administration of Justice Act 1982) shall not apply to the foregoing gifts and pecuniary legacies.[1]

1   For the WA 1837, s 33, as substituted by the AJA 1982, s 19: see Part G, para **[244.34]** and Vol 1, para **[47.14]** et seq. Section 33 would provide substitution of issue for a child who predeceases the testator, and is excluded because the specific gifts are intended for surviving children only, with the trusts of residue having a substitution clause and hotchpot provisions, and in the case of the gift of chattels because it would be impractical to administer a trust for minors of a share of chattels. See n 1 to para **[233.41]**.

[233.44]

Administration trusts of residue

6.   [*As in cl 3 of* Form C11.1 *at para* **[233.18]**.]

[233.45]

Beneficial trusts of residue

7.   (1)   My trustees shall hold my residuary estate upon trust to pay the income thereof to my wife during her life.

(2)   Provided that my trustees shall have power in their absolute discretion from time to time so long as my wife is entitled to be paid the income of all or any part of the capital of my residuary estate (or would be so entitled if such capital yielded income) to pay transfer or apply the whole or any part or parts of such capital[1] to her or for her benefit in such manner as they shall in their absolute discretion think fit.

(3)   Subject as aforesaid my trustees shall hold my residuary estate upon such trusts for the benefit of all or such one or more exclusive of the others or other of my children and remoter issue if more than one in such shares and with such trusts and powers for their respective benefit (including trusts and powers conferring a discretion as to the disposition of capital and income by whomsoever exercisable) and such provisions (including provisions for the accumulation of income during any period permitted by law and administrative provisions of whatever nature) as my trustees may during the life of my wife by any deed revocable during the life of my wife or irrevocable appoint provided that my trustees may at any time or times and from time to time during the life of my wife by deed or deeds release or restrict the foregoing power either in whole or in part and in any manner they think fit.[2]

(4)   Subject as aforesaid my trustees shall hold my residuary estate upon trust for such of my children [*name*] [*name*] [*name*] and [*name*] as shall survive me if more than one in the shares set out below Provided that if any of my said children shall predecease me leaving a child or children surviving me who shall attain the age of [18/21/25] years[3] such last-mentioned child or children shall

take and if more than one equally between them the share of my residuary estate which such deceased child of mine would have taken had he or she survived me.

(5)   The shares referred to in the last foregoing subclause shall be equal shares provided that—

(a)   any child of mine who is or has been entitled to a gift under clause 2 or 3 above shall bring the same into hotchpot as part of his or her share (net of inheritance tax) of my residuary estate and account for the same accordingly;[4]

(b)   the value or amount of any gift brought into hotchpot as aforesaid shall be the net value or amount thereof (after deduction of any inheritance tax or other liabilities to which it is subject) at my death[5] and for this purpose my trustees may as soon as practical after my death (whether or not my wife's foregoing life interest takes effect) at the expense of my residuary estate obtain a professional valuation of whatever is taken by either of my said sons under clause 2 above and any such valuation shall be binding on all parties;[6] and

(c)   for the avoidance of doubt I declare that if any gift to a child of mine directed to be brought into hotchpot as aforesaid exceeds the value of what would be that child's share if the property comprised in such gift formed part of my residuary estate then he or she shall not be under any obligation to make any repayment or transfer of any part of such gift to my residuary estate or to the other persons interested in my residuary estate and my residuary estate shall be divided among the other persons interested as if that child of mine was not entitled to a share thereof.[7]

(6)   The foregoing trusts shall carry the intermediate income of my residuary estate and section 31 of the Trustee Act 1925 (as hereinafter modified) shall apply thereto.

(7)   Section 32 of the Trustee Act 1925 (as hereinafter modified) shall apply in relation to my residuary estate.

1   There are two reasons for restricting the power to capital in which the wife has an interest in possession: first, to ensure that the power is not exercisable if there is a divorce and the primary trust lapses (see the Preliminary Note to C2 on the possibility of divorce at paras **[224.12]**–**[224.19]**); and, second, to ensure that the power ceases to be exercisable if the wife assigns or surrenders her life interest (for an example of the possible importance of the latter point see *IRC v Cookson* [1977] 2 All ER 331, [1977] 1 WLR 962).

2   This enables account to be taken of events occurring during the widow's life, such as the death of children of the testator, high inflation, or a major increase in the value of the business given to the sons. See cl 8 at para **[233.46]** for an expression of wishes as to how this power should be exercised, and the Note at para **[233.36]**.

3   The grandchildren will be lives in being at the testator's death for perpetuity purposes, so that there is no risk of infringing the rule against perpetuities in specifying an age exceeding 21.

4   It should be noted that the specific gifts do not have substitution clauses, and the testator's children's interests vest on the testator's death both under the specific gifts and the trusts of residue, so that these hotchpot provisions do not need to refer to the position of substituted beneficiaries. There is no hotchpot of interests appointed under the power of appointment.

5   This could clearly be very unfair, particularly if the testator's wife's life interest has taken effect and there has been significant inflation since the testator's death. However, it is not practical to make provision for all the things which might happen between the testator's and the wife's death; instead the arrangements can be varied by exercise of the power of appointment if the trustees can agree during the testator's widow's lifetime on how they should be varied.

6   It is not advisable to provide for the value to be that agreed with the Inland Revenue for probate purposes because if the business property given by cl 2 is subject to 100 per cent business relief,

or it is not but the gifts in cls 2 and 3 are clearly within the testator's nil-rate band, the Inland Revenue will not wish to engage in negotiations over the value.

7   This is implicit in a direction for hotchpot, but this is not always readily appreciated and it can save disappointment and argument if it is spelt out expressly.

[233.46]

Expression of wishes concerning power of appointment

8.   I express the wish without imposing any trust or obligation that my trustees shall exercise their foregoing power of appointment over the capital of my residuary estate as follows—

(a)   in the event of the death of any child of mine after my death but before my wife's death so as to substitute the issue of that child if any and otherwise so as to extinguish that child's interest; and

(b)   so as to maintain so far as possible equality of benefit among my children—

   (i)   if there is any significant increase or decrease after my death in the value of the property given to my sons under clause 2 above not attributable to the efforts or defaults (respectively) of my sons or either of them;

   (ii)   if there are high levels of inflation between my death and that of my wife;

   (iii)   if a substantial proportion of my residuary estate is paid or applied to or for the benefit of my wife; or

   (iv)   if there are any other events or circumstances which might produce an unfair distribution of my residuary estate between my sons and daughters in the absence of any exercise of the said power of appointment.

[233.47]

Maintenance, accumulation and advancement

9.   [*As in cl 5 of* Form C11.1 *at para* **[233.20]**.]

[233.48]

Administrative powers

10.   [*As in cl 6 of* Form C11.1 *at para* **[233.21]**.]

[233.49]

Exercise of powers

11.   [*As in cl 7 of* Form C11.1 *at para* **[233.22]**.]

[233.50]

Trustee self-dealing, indemnity, and similar provisions

12.   [*As in cl 8 of* Form C11.1 *at para* **[233.23]**.]

[233.51]

Professional trustee charging clause

13.   [*As in cl 9 of* Form C11.1 *at para* **[233.24]**.]

[*Testimonium and attestation clause as in* Form C11.1 *at para* **[233.25]**.]

C12 Wills disposing of farms and farming businesses

PRELIMINARY NOTE

Inheritance tax agricultural relief

[234.1]
Relief from inheritance tax is available under the Inheritance Tax Act 1984 (ITA 1984), Part V, Chapter II, in relation to agricultural property in certain circumstances. For a full discussion of the qualifying conditions the reader is referred to *Foster's Inheritance Tax*, Division G3. An outline of the relief and some notes of points particularly relevant to will-making are provided here. The rules for agricultural relief have many features in common with business relief, as a result of a revision of the agricultural relief rules by the Finance Act 1981 so as to bring them in line with the business relief rules so far as possible. Any agricultural property which is also an asset of a business is likely to satisfy the qualifying conditions for business relief as well, but where both reliefs would confer a reduction in taxable value it is agricultural relief which applies: ITA 1984, s 114(1). A brief comparison of the scope of the two reliefs—when they overlap, when they do not—appears at para **[234.8]**.

For notes on business relief see the Preliminary Note to B5 at para **[205.1]** et seq, and for notes on business and agricultural relief in relation to partially exempt estates, nil-rate band gifts, and gifts to spouses see the Preliminary Note to C11 at para **[233.1]** et seq. For testamentary options see B9 at para **[209.1]** et seq.

[234.2]
Meaning of agricultural property. This is defined by ITA 1984, s 115(2) as agricultural land or pasture and as including woodland and any building used in

connection with the intensive rearing of livestock or fish if such woodland or building is occupied with agricultural land or pasture and such occupation is ancillary to that of the land or pasture; the definition also includes such cottages, farm buildings and farmhouses and land occupied with them as are of a character appropriate to the property. Other assets which are included expressly or as a matter of Revenue practice are stud farms (ITA 1984, s 115(4)), milk quota when given or devolving on death with the land, ponds, land used for short-rotation coppice (ITA 1984, as amended by Finance Act 1995, s 145), set aside land, and land in a wildlife habitat scheme (ITA 1984, as amended by the Finance Act 1997, s 124C). In order to qualify for relief, agricultural property must be situated in the UK, the Channel Islands or the Isle of Man (ITA 1984, s 115(5)).

[234.3]
The inclusion of houses and buildings. The Interpretation Act 1978 defines 'land' to include buildings so far as no contrary intention is expressed, and it applies to ITA 1984. However, it has been held that the express reference in the ITA 1984, s 115(2) to cottages, farm buildings and farmhouses of a character appropriate to the property excludes the general definition from applying, so that a house used for agricultural purposes but not owned together with agricultural land did not qualify for relief (see *Starke v IRC* [1995] STC 689).

The inclusion of farmhouses is an important aspect of the relief; it enables a farmhouse which was occupied by the deceased (or by the transferor in the case of a lifetime transfer) as his residence to qualify for agricultural relief when it could never qualify for business relief, and such a house can represent a significant part of the value of agricultural property. The following points should be borne in mind:

(1)   Severance of the agricultural land from the house, eg by making a lifetime gift of the farmland without the house, is to be avoided where possible because it will cause the relief to cease to be available in relation to the house.

(2)   If the amount of agricultural land is perhaps on the low side in relation to the house for the house to qualify for the relief, buying some extra adjacent land could be a worthwhile investment (it would still have to be occupied for two years or owned for seven years before it counted—see below).

(3)   When it comes to making a will, a non-exempt gift of the farmhouse and an exempt gift of the farmland is not a good idea because the house by itself is not agricultural property—a non-exempt gift of the land and an exempt gift of the house would be better, and a non-exempt gift of both even better (from an inheritance tax point of view). See the Preliminary Note to C11 at paras **[233.2]–[233.6]**.

(4)   The farmhouse will not qualify for the relief unless it is occupied by someone engaged in agriculture for the required period (see para **[234.4]**). In *Harrold v IRC* [1996] STC (SCD) 195, the Special Commissioners held that the relief did not apply to a farmhouse which was unoccupied and awaiting renovation.

(5)   The relief is restricted to the agricultural value (see para **[234.7]**). Houses which are restricted to agricultural use (for planning purposes) often sell

at a discount from the value they would have without the restriction. The Inland Revenue have taken to arguing that part of the value of any farmhouse which is not so restricted, typically a third of its value, is not entitled to the relief.

[234.4]

Conditions for relief. The principal condition for relief is that the property shall have been *either* (a) occupied by the deceased (or the transferor in the case of a lifetime transfer) for the purposes of agriculture throughout the period of two years ending with the date of the deceased's death (or the transfer)—it is immaterial whether the property is *owned* throughout the entirety of this period provided that it is owned on the death—*or* (b) owned by him throughout the period of seven years ending with that date *and* occupied throughout that period (whether by the transferor or another) for the purposes of agriculture (see ITA 1984, s 117). If there has been replacement of one agricultural property by another the period of ownership or occupation of both can be taken into account (ITA 1984, s 118). If a cottage on a farm is occupied by an employee working on a farm which was farmed (alone or in partnership) by the deceased (or the transferor under a lifetime transfer) that will be regarded as having been occupied by the deceased (or transferor), and by concession the same treatment is given to a cottage occupied by a retired agricultural employee or his or her widow or widower with statutory protection or a contractual equivalent (see *Foster's Inheritance Tax*, G3.11). It was held by the Special Commissioners in *Wheatley (Wheatley's Executors) v IRC* [1998] STC (SCD) 60 that use of a field for grazing by a horse kept for recreational riding was not occupation for an agricultural purpose (see also para **[234.3]** concerning the occupation requirement in relation to farmhouses).

[234.5]

Succession provisions. Section 120(1) of the ITA 1984 provides (a) that in computing the period of two or seven years a transferor who succeeds to the property on the death of another person is deemed to have owned it and, if he subsequently occupies it, to have occupied it since the death of such other person and (b) that where that other person was his spouse he is deemed to have occupied it for the purpose of agriculture for any period for which it was so occupied by his spouse and to have owned it for any period for which his spouse owned it. Thus if the testator has not occupied or owned his agricultural property (including any it replaced) for long enough to qualify for relief on his death he should give it to his spouse by will, who will be able to carry on where he leaves off in building up a sufficient period of ownership or occupation, and be able to qualify for agricultural relief in relation to the property once the combined period of occupation or ownership by the testator and the testator's spouse is sufficient. Inheritance of the property by the spouse could be made to be contingent on the property not having been owned or occupied long enough to qualify for agricultural relief; compare Form B5.9 (at para **[205.66]**), which is a specific gift of shares contingent on them having been owned long enough to qualify for business relief—such a gift could be a non-exempt gift on failure of which the property subject to it falls into the residuary estate, and be combined with a gift of the residuary estate to the spouse.

The Inland Revenue regard the succession provisions in the ITA 1984, s 120 as applying not only where agricultural property is specifically given, but also where it devolves under a residuary gift. They regard the ITA 1984, s 91, which deems an interest in possession in a residuary estate to commence at the deceased's death (overriding the rule that strictly speaking no trust arises until the administration is complete), as applying to absolute gifts: see B5 at para **[205.12]**.

As already mentioned, a person's spouse, after succeeding to an agricultural property of that person, will only be able to count periods of occupation or ownership by him or her under the ITA 1984, s 120(1)(b) where the spouse succeeded to the property on the *death* of the person and not where the spouse succeeded to the property on an inter vivos transfer. However, the ITA 1984, s 121 provides an additional measure of relief in cases of successive transfers of agricultural property. Under this section where the property was eligible for relief on the earlier transfer (or would have been so eligible had the legislation been in force), relief will usually be available on the subsequent transfer, regardless of the length of the subsequent transferor's period of occupation or ownership, provided that either the earlier or the subsequent transfer was a transfer on death, and that at the time of the subsequent transfer the second transferor or the first transferor's personal representatives are in occupation of the property. The relief afforded by s 121 is general in its operation and is not confined to transfers as between spouses. It does mean, however, that where a person has acquired qualifying agricultural property from his spouse by way of inter vivos transfer and still owns and occupies such property at his death, agricultural relief will be available on his death, even though the requirements of ss 117 and 120 have not been satisfied, provided that at the time of the inter vivos transfer the transferor spouse had owned or occupied the property for long enough to qualify for the relief.

[234.6]
Farming companies. Shares in a farming company of which the testator had control and in which agricultural land is vested can also qualify for agricultural relief to the extent that the value of the shares is attributable to the land: see the ITA 1984, s 122 and 123 and *Foster's Inheritance Tax*, G3.31–G3.35. If the testator's shareholding is not a controlling one it can qualify for business relief if the company is carrying on a farming business: see B5 at paras **[205.5]–[205.14]** and **[205.29]–[205.31]**.

[234.7]
The relief conferred. When it applies, agricultural relief (like business relief) operates by providing a percentage reduction of the taxable value of the property concerned, but the reduction relates only to the agricultural value, so that if and to the extent that the property has development or hope value it will not get agricultural relief (but might get business relief). The Inland Revenue have also taken to arguing that part of the value of many farmhouses is non-agricultural and does not qualify for the relief: see para **[234.3]**. There are two rates of agricultural relief, 100 per cent and 50 per cent. The 100 per cent relief is available under the ITA 1984, s 116(2)(a) in cases where the interest of the transferor in the property carries the right to vacant possession or the right to

obtain it within twelve months. The latter words cover the common situation of land being occupied for less than twelve months under a seasonal grazing licence, and by concession the Inland Revenue will treat them as applying to land where there is a right to vacant possession within 24 months, eg because the land is let for a term certain of more than one year and less than two, or a valid notice to quit has been served which takes more than twelve months to expire (see *Foster's Inheritance Tax*, G3.04).

An important extension to relief at the rate of 100 per cent took effect from 1 September 1995 (ITA 1984, s 116(1)(c), added by Finance Act 1995, s 146): tenanted agricultural land, where the tenancy is granted on or after 1 September 1995, also qualifies for 100 per cent relief. This coincides with the date from which security of tenure under the Agricultural Holdings Act 1986 (AHA 1986) ceases to apply to most kinds of tenancy of agricultural land (Agricultural Tenancies Act 1995, s 4), and is part of a government policy of encouraging new lettings of agricultural land. It should be noted that it helps on the *rate* of relief but not on the qualifying conditions; anyone buying agricultural land with a view to letting it will still have to own it for seven years or occupy it for two years before qualifying for any agricultural relief. This 100 per cent relief has been extended to certain cases of tenanted land where, broadly, on or after 1 September 1995 a new tenancy was in the process of coming into existence when the taxpayer died (ITA 1984, s 116(5A) to (5E), inserted by Finance Act 1996, s 185).

100 per cent agricultural relief is also available for tenanted land in cases where: (i) the transferor has been entitled to his interest since before 10 March 1981; (ii) the interest then qualified for agricultural relief under the now superseded provisions of Finance Act 1975, Sch 8 (as to which see *Foster's Inheritance Tax*, G2); and (iii) the transferor's interest has not at any time since then carried with it the right to vacant possession or to obtain it within twelve months and the transferor has not deliberately failed to obtain such a right: ITA 1984, s 116(2)(b) and (3).

Section 116(2) of the ITA 1984 provides that the 50 per cent relief is to apply in all other cases, ie land let on a tenancy granted before 1 September 1995 where the transitional relief just mentioned, for land entitled to relief under the superseded provisions of the Finance Act 1975, Sch 8, does not apply. It may be possible to cause land to become potentially entitled to 100 per cent relief where it is let on a pre–1 September 1995 tenancy by negotiating a surrender of the tenancy and a grant to the tenant of a new tenancy on or after that date: see *Foster's Inheritance Tax*, G3.04. Where land is tenanted but the value of the land for inheritance tax purposes comes out at something close to a vacant possession value, eg where the tenancy is vested in a company wholly owned by the freeholder, or the tenancy is vested in a partnership consisting of the freeholder and his spouse (the spouse's interest being 'related property' within the ITA 1984, s 161), the Inland Revenue will by concession allow 100 per cent relief: see *Foster's Inheritance Tax*, G3.04.

[234.8]
Comparison of agricultural relief and business relief. Where agricultural property is an asset of a business or a farming company, or is used by a partnership or company in which the owner of the land is a partner or

shareholder, it will often satisfy the conditions for business relief as well as those for agricultural relief. Where there is such an overlap it is the agricultural relief which prevails; if agricultural relief gives a reduction in value, business relief is excluded from also reducing that value by the ITA 1984, s 114(1).

Agricultural property in relation to which agricultural relief may apply where business relief would not apply includes: agricultural land which is not farmed by the owner of it, agricultural land owned by a company controlled by an individual where the company does not farm the land, farmhouses, and land farmed by but not owned by a company where the owner of the land does not control the company. Where someone owns agricultural land personally and it is farmed by a partnership in which he is a partner or a company which he controls, it can qualify for agricultural relief at the rate of 100 per cent, while it could only ever qualify for business relief at the rate of 50 per cent.

Agricultural property in relation to which business relief may apply where agricultural relief would not apply includes: a non-controlling shareholding in a farming company, development value in land forming part of the assets of a farming business or farming company, agricultural property which has not been owned or occupied long enough for agricultural relief where it was a replacement of a non-farming business property and the combined period of ownership of both properties is sufficient for business relief, and agricultural property outside the UK, the Channel Islands and the Isle of Man, which forms part of the assets of a farming business or farming company.

[234.9]

Agricultural relief and partially exempt estates. Like business relief agricultural relief operates so as to reduce the value transferred by the transfer on death before exemptions are taken into account. Section 39A of the ITA 1984, introduced by Finance Act 1986, s 105, applies where there is agricultural relief on assets comprised in a partially exempt estate (see the Preliminary Note to C11 at paras **[233.2]–[233.7]**). Accordingly, where a farmer owning qualifying agricultural property wishes to make provision for a wife and children, he would be well-advised to consider making a specific gift of agricultural property to the children and the balance of the estate to the spouse. This is likely to be considerably cheaper in fiscal terms than the other way round: see the Preliminary Note to C11 at paras **[233.6]–[233.10]**. On the other hand, as mentioned at para **[234.5]**, if agricultural property does not qualify for relief because it has not been owned or occupied by the transferor for either of the periods mentioned in the ITA 1984, s 117, a gift of the property to the testator's spouse could enable the spouse to take advantage of the testator's period of ownership or occupation.

[234.10]

Debts charged on agricultural property. If agricultural property is subject to mortgages or other charges, they will reduce the 'agricultural value' of the property and therefore the amount of the relief: ITA 1984, s 162(4). It would be of obvious advantage if loans for the purposes of the farming business or any other purposes could be charged or primarily charged on assets other than property qualifying for relief.

Other aspects

[234.11]
Business relief and farming businesses. Agricultural relief is available for land and buildings, and does not apply at all to the other assets of a farming business such as live and dead stock, farm machinery, etc. These may qualify for business relief: see B5 at para **[205.6]** et seq for an outline of the conditions for this relief to apply.

[234.12]
Tenant farmers. Where a testator farms agricultural land under an AHA 1986 protected tenancy, he may have the right to designate a successor by will under the AHA 1986, Part IV unless he is a successor himself. These succession provisions, originally introduced in 1976, were abolished in relation to protected tenancies granted on or after 12 July 1984 subject to the limited exceptions referred to in the AHA 1986, s 34(1). But tenants farming under tenancies granted prior to that date continue to be able to designate successors and Form C12.3 contains a clause at para **[234.48]** exercising this right. There are advantages in designating a son or daughter rather than a spouse because only two successions are allowed, and business relief is likely to be wasted if the farming business is given to the spouse. However, the testator's spouse may in practice be the only person who could take over.

[234.13]
Farming partnerships with agricultural tenancies. Situations arise in which a testator who owns agricultural land farms the land in partnership with one or more other persons under a tenancy granted to the partners. (The grant of an agricultural tenancy for full consideration is not a transfer of value: ITA 1984, s 16.) The existence of the tenancy is likely to reduce the value of the freehold very considerably. But if the only other partner (and co-tenant) is his spouse, no reduction in value will be achieved for inheritance tax purposes by virtue of the related property provisions contained in the ITA 1984, s 161: see in particular s 161(2)(a). However, the Revenue will by concession allow 100 per cent agricultural relief on the property (if all the conditions for the relief are met) if the valuation comes out close to vacant possession value.

[234.14]
Woodlands. Woodlands which are not ancillary to agricultural land and which do not therefore qualify for agricultural relief may qualify for the separate relief which is available under the ITA 1984, Part V, Chapter III for woodlands which have been beneficially owned for five years or acquired by gift: see generally *Foster's Inheritance Tax*, G4. The relief takes the form of a deferment of the charge to inheritance tax on death until the woodlands are sold or given away by inter vivos transfer other than to the donor's spouse. This relief resembles the conditional exemption for works of art etc under the ITA 1984, ss 30–34 but it is not strictly an exemption within the meaning of the Act, but a right to elect to have the woodlands left out of account in determining the chargeable transfer made on death: see ss 126(1)(a) and 130(1)(a). Since anyone who inherits woodlands which qualify for this relief will himself be qualified for the relief on his death however soon it may occur (see s 125(1)), there are less strong reasons

than in the case of business assets or agricultural property for testators avoiding gifts of woodlands which qualify for relief to their spouses. It is advisable for specific gifts of woodlands to be made subject to the inheritance tax attributable thereto and payable on the testator's death for the reasons given in B14 at para **[214.67]**.

[234.15]
Where only one or some of the testator's children will carry on with farming. The problem of passing on business/farming assets to the child or children who want to carry on with the business or farming while making fair provision for the other children is discussed in the Preliminary Note to C11 at para **[233.12]**. Forms C12.1 and C12.2 at paras **[234.17]** et seq and **[234.31]** et seq illustrate two of the possibilities there mentioned.

One further possibility peculiar to farming is that either accidentally or deliberately the child or children who want to carry on with farming may already have an agricultural tenancy with security of tenure under the AHA 1986, or be partners in a partnership which does. Where the testator is the owner of the freehold and is a member of the partnership, the partners other than the testator may have security of tenure as against him or his successors in title: see *Sykes v Land* (1984) 271 Estates Gazette 1264, and *Featherstone v Staples* [1986] 2 All ER 461, [1986] 1 WLR 861. Where the child or children carrying on the farming have such security of tenure the testator can leave his estate in equal shares among his children without disturbing the child's or children's possession of the farm. It should be noted that tenancies granted on or after 1 September 1995 will not in general have security of tenure (Agricultural Tenancies Act 1995, s 4). If someone who has already acquired an agricultural tenancy over the testator's land then becomes an executor of the testator, he will be under no obligation to the other beneficiaries to sell his tenancy along with the freehold to enable a better price to be obtained: *Sergeant v National Westminster Bank* (1988) 59 P & CR 182.

[234.16]
Checking the nature of the assets. In *Re Lewis's Will Trusts* [1984] 3 All ER 930, [1985] 1 WLR 102, the deceased had made a gift by will of a farm and farming business when what he owned was shares in a private company which owned the farm and business. The gift in the will was held to be ineffective. It is essential to check exactly what the form of the testator's ownership of the farm and farming business is. There are numerous possibilities, including companies and partnerships, and if there is a company or partnership the farmland may be owned by the company or partnership, or by the testator personally, or by him and others personally in a joint tenancy or tenancy in common.

[234.17]

FORM C12.1:   **Will of widower giving estate equally between his children, one son being given an option to purchase the farming assets**

NOTE

This form illustrates one possible solution to the problem of one or some of the testator's children wanting to carry on with the farming business and others not (see the Preliminary Note to C11 at para **[233.12]**). It is assumed that the testator is a widower with two sons ('AB' and 'EF') and a daughter ('CD'), of whom only the son AB has taken up farming and wishes to take over the testator's farmland and farming business. The residuary estate is given in equal shares, but AB is given an option to purchase the farming assets. There is some help given to him in the terms of the option, in particular the price could be directed to be less than market value, and the trustees are empowered to accept payment by instalments carrying low or no interest.

It has been mentioned in the Preliminary Note to C11 at para **[233.6]** that a testamentary option to purchase business or agricultural property might have adverse consequences for the allocation of any available business or agricultural relief where the estate is partially exempt. This problem does not arise where, as here, there are no exempt gifts.

For testamentary options see also B9 at para **[209.1]** et seq.

[234.18]

Revocation clause

I [*name*] of [*address*] hereby revoke all former testamentary dispositions made by me and declare this to be my last will.

[234.19]

Appointment of executors and trustees

1.   I appoint my son AB ('AB') my daughter CD ('CD') and my son EF ('EF') (hereinafter together called 'my trustees' which expression shall include my personal representatives for the time being and the trustees for the time being hereof) to be the executors and trustees of this will.

[234.20]

Gifts of chattels[1]

2.   (1)   I make the following specific bequests free of tax:[2]

   (a)   to AB my shot gun;
   (b)   to CD my late wife's jewellery;
   (c)   to EF the motor car I shall have at my death (and if I have more than one at my death he may select one of them).

(2)   Subject as aforesaid I give all my personal chattels as defined by Section 55(1)(x) of the Administration of Estates Act 1925[3] free of tax[4] to such of AB CD and EF as shall survive me if more than one in equal shares [and I request them (but without imposing any trust or binding obligation) to give effect to any wishes as to the disposition of such chattels which may be contained in any memorandum that may be found amongst my papers at my death or which may have otherwise been communicated to them during my life][5] provided that section 33 of the Wills Act 1837 (as substituted by section 19 of the Administration of Justice Act 1982) shall not apply to the foregoing gift.[6]

---

1   Gifts are made of specific items, and the remainder of the personal chattels are left to the children who survive the testator. Where all three children of the testator survive him or her, the latter gift will have the same effect as if the chattels had been left to fall into residue, but if a child predeceases the testator the chattels will go to the surviving children. This may introduce an element of unfairness as between families, but it avoids chattels passing to the deceased

child's issue', which may well have to be retained and managed by the trustees until such issue attain their majority. It also means that the chattels are at the disposal of persons who are of full age who can (if they an agree among themselves) give away items to relatives and friends of the testator.

2   This is included in case any of the chattels are outside the UK at the testator's death, and thus 'subject to tax' in the absence of a direction to the contrary. See the Preliminary Note to B14 at paras **[214.55]–[214.60]** and the definition of 'free of tax' in cl 5 of this form at para **[234.23]**. If there is no risk of this the words 'free of tax' can be omitted and so can cl 5.

3   See Part G, para **[246.52]** for the wording of this definition, and for further discussion of the meaning of 'personal chattels' see Vol 1, para **[64.44]**.

4   See n 2 to this clause supra.

5   If property bequeathed by a will to one person is distributed to another person within two years of the testator's death, in accordance with wishes expressed by the testator, it is treated for inheritance tax purposes as having been bequeathed by the will to that other person: ITA 1984, s 143, and see B4 at paras **[204.9]** and **[204.10]**.

6   See Part G, para **[244.34]** for this provision, and Vol 1, paras **[47.14]–[47.19]**. Section 33 would provide substitution of issue for a child who predeceases the testator, and is excluded because it would be impractical to administer a trust for minors of a share of chattels. See also n 1 to this clause.

[234.21]

Option for one of the sons to purchase farming assets[1]

3.   (1)   In this clause references to my trustees in relation to any time when AB is one of my trustees are references to my trustees other than AB and in relation to any time when there has been no grant of probate to this will are references to such of CD and EF as shall be living.

(2)   In this clause 'my farming assets' means and includes such of the following as I may own at my death:

(a)   any farm land farm buildings interests in farm land (or in the proceeds of sale thereof) equipment livestock milk quota growing or harvested crops and other assets of any farming business I may be carrying on at my death (other than any motor car hereinbefore specifically given and other than cash or bank accounts);[2]

(b)   any assets of the foregoing types owned by me at my death which are of a kind which could be used in a farming business but which at my death are not in such use including any such assets which may be leased or licensed to AB or any other person;

(c)   any shares in any company carrying on a farming business or any interest in any partnership carrying a farming business as may be owned by me at my death.[3]

(3)   AB shall have an option to purchase my farming assets as set out below.

(4)   As soon as practical after my death my trustees shall serve a written notice on AB notifying him of this option and specifying the assets to which it relates. My trustees shall have power to require AB to acquire my farming assets subject to such liabilities of any farming business which shall have been carried on by me or partnership in which I shall have been a partner or such incumbrances or charges to which my farming assets are subject as may be specified in such notice. My trustees shall make available to AB or his agents or advisers all documents of title books of account or other documents in their possession relevant to the decision whether to exercise the option.

(5)   To exercise such option AB must serve a notice of exercise of it on my trustees within two months after service on AB of my trustees' said notice. If no

notice as aforesaid by my trustees has been served on AB within 18 months of my death AB may serve a notice on my trustees exercising the option without the service of a notice by my trustees on him. AB's said option shall finally cease to be exercisable if no notice of exercise is served on my trustees by AB within two years of my death. A contract to sell and purchase binding on both parties shall arise on service of such notice by AB, subject to the right of rescission on the part of AB set out below and subject to the terms set out below. If land or an interest in land or in the proceeds of sale of land is included in the assets subject to the option the Standard Conditions of Sale in force at the date hereof shall apply so far as consistent with the terms set out herein.

(6)   The option price shall be [[70] per cent of the net amount. The net amount shall be][4] the price which my farming assets might reasonably be expected to fetch if sold in the open market[5] [(with vacant possession in the case of any land)][6] at the date of AB's notice exercising the option less the value of such (if any) liabilities or incumbrances as AB's purchase may be subject to (as required by my trustees as provided above).

(7)   After service of such notice by AB he and my trustees shall endeavour to agree the amount of the option price. My trustees shall have power to obtain such valuation or other relevant advice as they think fit at the expense of my residuary estate.

(8)   If AB and my trustees are unable to agree the option price within two months of the service of such notice either AB or my trustees may at any time after expiry of that period of two months require (by notice served on the other) a reference to an expert (not acting as an arbitrator) to determine the price to be paid.

(9)   Such expert shall in default of agreement be appointed by the President of the Royal Institution of Chartered Surveyors. The decision of such expert shall be final, and the costs of his determination and the procedure adopted for his determination shall be at his discretion (but such costs shall be borne equally between AB and my trustees if no determination as to costs is made by such expert and there is no rescission by AB under the next following subclause).

(10)   If the purchase price is determined by an expert as provided above then AB shall be entitled to rescind the agreement to purchase created by the option notice by a written notice served on my trustees within 21 days of AB first knowing the determination of such expert. In the event of such rescission by AB he shall pay or refund to the trustees any reasonable costs they shall have incurred in consequence of his service of the option notice including costs of advice in relation thereto and the costs of the said determination of the price by an expert.

(11)   Completion of the said purchase by AB (if there shall be no rescission by AB as aforesaid) shall if the purchase price is fixed by agreement be 21 days after such agreement is reached and otherwise shall be 42 days after the price determined by such expert first becomes known to AB provided that the foregoing periods shall run from the date of first grant of probate or administration to my estate if that occurs after such agreement or determination.

(12)   My farming assets shall be transferred or conveyed to AB free from incumbrances save in so far as the purchase is subject to such of the same as are specified in my trustees' said notice. The title to my farming assets deduced by my trustees shall not be open to objection by AB save in respect of matters

which he did not know of and could not have known of from documents or information in his or his agents' possession before exercise of the option. On completion AB shall give my trustees a covenant of indemnity against all liabilities or sums charged on my farming assets to which the purchase is subject. AB and my trustees shall bear their own respective costs of such transfers or other assurances of property or covenants as may be required for completion as aforesaid.

(13)   AB may require his share of my residuary estate (as defined below) to be offset against the purchase price. If the net value of my residuary estate has not been ascertained at the completion date and AB so requires completion shall be on the basis of my trustees' best estimate of AB's share of my residuary estate subject to further payment by my trustees or repayment by AB when AB's share of my residuary estate comes to be finally ascertained.

(14)   My trustees shall have power to agree any terms they think fit for the purchase price to remain outstanding in whole or in part or to be paid in instalments after such completion provided that AB shall agree to complete payment of the purchase price within 10 years of my death and my trustees may renounce their vendor's lien accept any security they think fit (or no security at all)[7] and shall not be obliged to charge interest at a full market rate or at all on outstanding purchase money or any money which may become repayable when AB's share of my residuary estate is ascertained and shall not be liable for any default of AB or any other adverse consequences of leaving purchase money outstanding.[8]

(15)   I express the wish that unless a sale is necessary for carrying out their duties under the administration trusts in clause 4 below my trustees shall postpone the sale of my farming assets at least until the expiry of two years from my death but no purchaser shall be concerned with the terms of this clause or whether the foregoing circumstances for a sale within two years of my death have arisen. Pending the exercise of AB's said option or the sale of my farming assets in the absence of such option being exercised my trustees may exercise their power hereinafter contained[9] to carry on any farming business comprised in my estate and/or may engage AB to carry on such business or join in carrying on such business on whatever terms they think fit.

(16)   Time shall be of the essence of the time limits set out above for exercise of the option to purchase and right of rescission and either AB or my trustees may make time of the essence for completion of the purchase arising from any exercise of the foregoing option after the date for completion set out above has passed by service of at least 14 days' notice to that effect on the other party.

(17)   The foregoing rights of AB shall be personal to him and shall not be exercisable by any personal representative or assign of AB or other successor in title of AB provided that if AB having during his lifetime served an effective notice of exercise of the foregoing option shall die before the same shall have been completed his personal representatives shall be obliged and entitled in relation thereto to the same extent as AB would have been if still living.

(18)   Section 196 of the Law of Property Act 1925 shall apply to the service of all the foregoing notices.

[(19)   Any inheritance tax attributable to the benefit of the foregoing option to AB (making due allowance for any reduction in value for inheritance tax purposes which is attributed thereto) shall be borne by AB in exoneration of my residuary estate.]¹⁰

1 The basic division of the estate is in equal shares under the trusts of residue, but the son AB who wishes to carry on the farming business is given an option to acquire the farming assets under this clause, which can be on terms which have an element of bounty towards him. The option price could be a concessionary one, and provision is made for payment by instalments. His share of residue can be offset against the purchase price. For further discussion and examples of option clauses see B9 at para **[209.1]** et seq.
2 There is not much point in the option holder paying cash to purchase cash.
3 Not all these categories will be appropriate and it may often be found that some of them can be omitted. However, it may be preferred to retain them all in case the testator changes his trading arrangements, or retires from active farming but retains ownership of some of the assets, before he dies.
4 This could be some other proportion or could be omitted completely so that he has to pay the full market price. The testator needs to consider how deserving AB is of a discount, how necessary a discount might be to enable him to acquire the assets, and how unfair to the other children such a discount will be. The reason for starting a new sentence in this way where the price is a reduced one is to make clear that the assets are valued and the liabilities are deducted before applying the percentage, as opposed to applying the percentage to the value and then deducting the liabilities in full.
5 It would be unsafe to provide that this should be the value agreed with the Revenue for inheritance tax purposes because if there is 100 per cent agricultural relief and/or business relief the Revenue will not wish to agree a value for the farming assets.
6 If the person given the option is already farming the land, and there is any possibility that there might be an agricultural tenancy, it will be important (to save argument) that the basis of valuation is made clear. A tenanted valuation could alternatively be specified, but if this is done it will be important (if done by reference to a hypothetical tenancy) to specify what sort of tenancy should be assumed and when it should be assumed to have been granted. Agricultural tenancies granted on or after 1 September 1995 will in general not have security of tenure under the AHA 1986: see the Agricultural Tenancies Act 1995, s 4.
7 If the purchase money is charged on the agricultural assets it will reduce the agricultural relief in the event of AB's death: see the Preliminary Note at para **[234.10]**. A vendor's lien for unpaid purchase money would constitute such a charge, and express waiver would be needed for there not to be such a lien while the purchase money remained outstanding.
8 This is needed in case there are minors interested in a share of residue by virtue of the substitution clause, or not all the persons beneficially interested in residue are executors (for without this subclause the other beneficiaries if of full age could always agree to such terms). If the value at the testator's death is less than the sale price there may be a capital gains tax charge, and if so the tax may be payable in full without any deferment even if the payment of the purchase price is in part deferred. However, if the option price is less than the market value it will be arguable that AB takes as 'legatee', with the result that there is no capital gains tax charge on the exercise of the option by virtue of the Taxation of Chargeable Gains Act 1992, s 62(4).
9 See cl 6(3)(h) of Form C11.1 at para **[233.21]**, incorporated in this form by reference in cl 8 at para **[234.26]**.
10 Assuming the farming assets are in the UK, any inheritance tax attributable to the farming assets will be payable out of residue in the absence of a contrary direction (see B14 at paras **[214.55]–[214.60]**). There will be no inheritance tax on the farming assets if they wholly qualify for 100 per cent agricultural relief, but if there is or might be some tax on these assets, and the option terms are beneficial to the option holder, the testator may want him to bear the tax attributable to that benefit. See the Preliminary Note to B9 at paras **[209.1]–[209.5]** for further discussion of testamentary options and their taxation and other aspects.

[234.22]

Administration trusts of residue

4. (1) I give all my property not hereby or by any codicil hereto otherwise effectively disposed of [(including any entailed or other property over which I shall have at my death a general power of disposition by will)]¹ to my trustees to

hold on the trusts set out below with power at their discretion to sell all or any of it as and when they think fit.[2]

(2)   My trustees shall pay my funeral and testamentary expenses[3] and debts and any legacies given by this will or any codicil hereto out of such property or its proceeds and shall have a discretion as to how such payments shall be borne as between capital and income.[4]

(3)   Subject as above my trustees shall hold such property and the assets from time to time representing the same (hereinafter called 'my residuary estate') on the trusts set out below and shall invest all money comprised in such property or arising from its sale in any of the investments hereby authorised with power to change such investments into any others hereby authorised.

(4)   In the administration of my estate and the execution of the trusts of this will or of any codicil to it:

(a)   my trustees shall treat all income as accruing on the date on which it becomes payable regardless of the period in respect of which it shall have accrued and shall not make any statutory apportionment of the same;[5] and

(b)   none of the equitable rules of apportionment between capital and income shall apply in any circumstances whatever.[6]

1   See n 1 to cl 4 of Form C8.1 at para **[230.7]**.
2   See n 2 to cl 4 of Form C8.1 at para **[230.7]**.
3   See n 3 to cl 4 of Form C8.1 at para **[230.7]**.
4   See n 4 to cl 4 of Form C8.1 at para **[230.7]**.
5   See B14 at paras **[214.48]**–**[214.52]** for statutory apportionment of income over time and its exclusion.
6   See n 6 to cl 4 of Form C8.1 at para **[230.7]**.

[234.23]

Gifts made free of tax

5.   Any specific gift or pecuniary or general legacy made by this will or any codicil hereto which is expressed to be 'free of tax' shall be free from the payment of any inheritance tax or foreign tax or duty payable on or by reason of my death to which such gift or legacy would otherwise be subject and such inheritance tax or foreign tax or duty shall be paid out of my residuary estate.[1]

1   See n 3 to cl 4 of Form C8.1 at para **[230.7]** and n 2 to cl 2 of this form at para **[234.20]**. Where specific gifts and pecuniary legacies are of, or wholly payable out of, free estate in the UK, the inheritance tax on them will be a testamentary expense payable out of residue without any express provision, and it is only where a specific gift or pecuniary legacy is foreign or settled property, or wholly or partly payable out of such property, and intended to be free of tax, that it needs to be expressly declared to be free of tax. See also B14 at paras **[214.55]**–**[214.60]**.

[234.24]

Beneficial trusts of residue

6.   (1)   My trustees shall hold my residuary estate upon trust for such of my children AB CD and EF as shall survive me and if more than one in equal shares.

(2)   Provided that if any of my said children shall predecease me leaving issue surviving me who shall attain the age of 18 years[1] such issue shall take through all degrees according to their stocks the share of my residuary estate which such deceased child of mine would have taken had he or she survived me

and so that no issue shall take whose parent (being such issue as aforesaid) survives me and attains the said age.[2]

(3) The trusts declared by the foregoing subclause shall carry the intermediate income of my residuary estate and section 31 of the Trustee Act 1925 (as hereinafter modified) shall apply thereto.

(4) Section 32 of the Trustee Act 1925 (as hereinafter modified) shall apply in relation to the said trusts.

1   Since the eligible issue are all ascertained at the testator's death, they will all be lives in being for perpetuity purposes and the vesting age for their interests need not therefore be limited to 18. However, the requirement in relation to all substituted issue that they be living at the testator's death means that where, for example, a child of the testator predeceases him, leaving a child who survives the testator but dies under the vesting age leaving a child of his who was born after the death of the testator, the latter will not take a share. The greater the age of vesting, the greater is the risk of this happening.

2   The wording of the substitutional proviso is based on the wording of the statutory trusts contained in the AEA 1925, s 47(1)(i) (Part G, para **[244.61]**). A substitutional proviso which is limited to children may be more appropriate to the testator's family circumstances in which case cl 7(2) of Form C4.2 at para **[226.43]** may be adopted instead.

[234.25]

Maintenance advancement and accumulation
7.   [*As in cl 5 of* Form C11.1 *at para* **[233.20]**.]

[234.26]

Administrative powers[1]
8.   [*As in cl 6 of* Form C11.1 *at para* **[233.21]**.]

1   The powers in cl 6 of Form C11.1 include power to carry on a business (see sub-cl (3)(h)), which would enable the executors to carry on the farming business.

[234.27]

Exercise of powers
9.   [*As in cl 7 of* Form C11.1 *at para* **[233.22]**.]

[234.28]

Trustee self-dealing, indemnity, and similar provisions
10.   [*As in cl 8 of* Form C11.1 *at para* **[233.23]**.]

[234.29]

Professional trustee charging clause
11.   [*As in cl 9 of* Form C11.1 *at para* **[233.24]**.]

[234.30]

Testimonium and attestation clause
SIGNED by the above-named testator as his last will in the presence of us both present at the same time who at his request and in his presence and in the presence of each other have signed our names below as witnesses: } [*Signature of testator*]

[*Signatures, addresses and descriptions of two witnesses*]

[234.31]

FORM C12.2:   Will of farmer leaving legacies to his daughters, a right of residence in a farm cottage to his wife, and residue to his son if farming at his death, with residue given to the children in equal shares if he is not

NOTE

This form illustrates another possible solution to the problem of one or some of the testator's children wanting to carry on with the farming business and others not (see the Preliminary Note to C11 at para **[233.12]**). It is assumed that the testator has a wife, a son, and two daughters, and that the son works on the farm (in partnership with the testator or otherwise) but the daughters do not. If the son is working on the farm at the testator's death he is given the residuary estate, which will include the farming assets owned by the testator apart from the cottage for the wife mentioned further below, and the daughters are given legacies, which will in practice be paid by the son and which he can be given time to pay. One of the farm cottages is given to the trustees to be held on trust as a residence for the testator's wife, which after her death or ceasing to reside falls into residue. Although this involves some waste of agricultural relief, it is thought that, because the cottage taken by itself is not agricultural property, the agricultural relief attributable to the cottage will be spread rateably between the exempt and non-exempt parts of the estate rather than concentrated entirely on the cottage: see the Preliminary Note to C11 at paras **[233.2]**–**[233.6]**. The hope is that the wife may have sufficient savings and pension entitlement for her support after the testator's death, and, if not, that the son will take her into partnership in the farming business and pay her some income from the farm profits. Although the cottage will form part of the wife's estate on death (if she has not by then given up residence) and will not qualify for agricultural relief on her death, her estate may be within the nil-rate band or may not much exceed it.

[234.32]

Revocation clause
I [*name*] of [*address*] hereby revoke all former testamentary dispositions made by me and declare this to be my last will.

[234.33]

Appointment of executors and trustees
1.   I appoint my wife [*name*] ('my wife') my son [*name*] and my daughters [*name*] and [*name*] (hereinafter together called 'my trustees' which expression shall include my personal representatives for the time being and the trustees for the time being hereof) to be the executors and trustees of this will.

[234.34]

Gifts of chattels
2.   (1)   If my wife shall survive me I give her absolutely all my personal chattels as defined by section 55(1)(x) of the Administration of Estates Act 1925.[1]

(2)   If my wife shall predecease me I give all my personal chattels as defined as aforesaid free of tax[2] to such of my said children as shall survive me if more than one in equal shares provided that section 33 of the Wills Act 1837 (as substituted by section 19 of the Administration of Justice Act 1982) shall not apply to the foregoing gift.[3]

(3)   I request my wife or children who become entitled to my personal chattels under either of the foregoing gifts (but without imposing any trust or binding obligation) to give effect to any wishes as to the disposition of such chattels which may be contained in any memorandum that may be found amongst my papers at my death or which may have otherwise been communicated to her or them during my life.[4]

1   See Part G, para **[246.52]** for the wording of this definition, and for further discussion of the meaning of 'personal chattels' see Vol 1, para **[64.44]**.

2   This is included in case any of the chattels are outside the UK at the testator's death, and thus 'subject to tax' in the absence of a direction to the contrary. See B14 at paras **[214.55]**–**[214.60]** and the definition of 'free of tax' as incorporated by reference in cl 6 of this form at para **[234.38]**. If there is no risk of this the words 'free of tax' can be omitted and so can cl 6.

3   See Part G, para **[244.34]** for this provision, and Vol 1, paras **[47.14]**–**[47.19]**. Section 33 would provide substitution of issue for a child who predeceases the testator, and is excluded because it would be impractical to administer a trust for minors of a share of chattels.

4   If property bequeathed by a will to one person is distributed to another person within two years of the testator's death in accordance with wishes expressed by the testator, it is treated for inheritance tax purposes as having been bequeathed by the will to that other person: ITA 1984, s 143; see also B4 at paras **[204.9]**–**[204.10]**.

[234.35]

Right of residence for wife[1]

3.   (1)   I give — Cottage [*address*] to my trustees free of all sums charged thereon or otherwise secured thereon at my death (which sums shall be paid out of my residuary estate)[2] to hold the same upon trust to provide a residence for my wife so long as she wishes to reside there.

(2)   I declare that my trustees shall not be liable for lack of insurance repair or payment of outgoings or for not taking any steps to enforce any reasonable conditions[3] imposed by my trustees on my wife in relation to her occupation of my said cottage .

(3)   On the death of my wife or in the event of her ceasing to reside in my said cottage my trustees shall hold the said cottage as part of my residuary estate as hereinafter defined.

(4)   For the purposes of this clause no involuntary ceasing by my wife to reside in the said cottage shall be treated as ceasing to reside therein unless my wife shall have been out of residence continuously for six months and shall not have expressed in writing to my trustees her intention to take up residence again.

1   See the Note to this form at para **[234.31]**. This is a simple form of residence trust which permits the wife to reside only in the specified property held at the testator's death. In the event of her death or earlier ceasing to reside, it will fall into residue. For a more elaborate form which enables a replacement property to be purchased for her to live in, see Forms B8.1 and B8.2 at paras **[208.37]** and **[208.38]**. For a discussion of rights of residence see the Preliminary Note to B8 at paras **[208.1]**–**[208.36]**. The gift should be exempt from inheritance tax on the basis that the widow has an interest in possession under these trusts. If her right to reside ceases during her lifetime so that the property falls into residue, her interest in possession in the same will terminate and she will be deemed to make a potentially exempt transfer. If her right continues until her death, the property will be treated as part of her estate for inheritance tax

purposes transfer (see Part A, para **[200.114]** for the inheritance tax consequences of an interest in possession).

2   Where property specifically given is charged with the payment of money, then in the absence of a contrary intention expressed in the will, the property is primarily liable for the payment of the moneys so charged as between the persons claiming through the deceased: AEA 1925, s 35 (Part G, para **[246.47]**).

3   By virtue of the TLATA 1996, s 13(3), (5) (Part G, para **[246.99]**), the trustees will be able to impose reasonable conditions on the wife's occupation, eg that she pay outgoings or assume other obligations such as insurance and repair.

[234.36]

Pecuniary legacies for daughters

4.   (1)   If the gift of the whole of my residuary estate in favour of my son set out below shall take effect I give to each of my said daughters who shall survive me free of tax[1] the sum of [£50,000].

(2)   Provided that if either of my said daughters shall predecease me leaving a child or children surviving me who shall attain the age of [18/21/25] years[2] such last-mentioned child or children shall take and if more than one equally between them the legacy which such deceased daughter of mine would have taken had she survived me.

(3)   My trustees shall have power to assent to the vesting of the assets comprised in my residuary estate (as defined below) in my son before the foregoing legacies are paid or satisfied in full or at all and whether or not they have so assented my trustees may agree with my son any terms they think fit for deferment of the payment of the said legacies for up to [10] years from my death and my trustees may accept any security they think fit (or no security at all)[3] shall not be obliged to require interest to be paid at a full market rate or at all on any outstanding legacies and shall not be liable for any default of AB or any other adverse consequences of leaving payment of such legacies outstanding.[4]

1   The pecuniary legacies are declared to be 'free of tax' in case the residuary estate out of which they are payable includes property of a kind which bears its own tax, such as foreign property or settled property, with the consequence that without this express provision the legacies might, at least to some extent, have to bear their own tax. See B14 at paras **[214.55]–[214.60]**. The definition of 'free of tax' will be in cl 6 of this form. There is no inheritance tax advantage in making the legacies subject to tax because residue is not exempt (contrast cl 4 of Form C11.3 at para **[233.42]**).

2   The grandchildren will be lives in being at the testator's death for perpetuity purposes, so that there is no risk of infringing the rule against perpetuities in specifying an age exceeding 21.

3   If the legacies are charged on the agricultural assets it will reduce the agricultural relief in the event of the son's death: see para **[234.10]**.

4   These powers are conferred expressly in case there are minors interested in one or both of the legacies or the daughters may not be willing to leave the legacies outstanding unless obliged to do so. If the farmland is subjected to a charge to secure the payment of the legacies in regular instalments over a fixed period there is a risk that this will cause the farmland to be settled property for inheritance tax purposes (ITA 1984, s 43(2)(c)) and that, if no interest is paid on the legacies, it might be argued that the son then has an interest in possession in the entire property which is partially terminated on the payment of any instalment of the legacies (see Part A, para **[200.114]** for the inheritance tax consequences of the termination of an interest in possession). It will be better either to have a personal covenant, or a charge for payment of a single sum on a particular date.

[234.37]

Administration trusts of residue

5.   [*As in cl 4 of* Form C12.1 *at para* **[234.22]**.]

[234.38]

Gifts made free of tax

6.   [*As in cl 5 of* Form C12.1 *at para* **[234.23]**.]

[234.39]

Beneficial trusts of residue

7.   (1)   If my son shall survive me and shall at my death be employed in agricultural work or engaged in a farming business on any land comprised in my residuary estate my trustees shall hold my residuary estate on trust for my son [*name*] absolutely if he shall survive me.

(2)   Subject as aforesaid my trustees shall hold my residuary estate upon trust for such of my son and my said daughters as shall survive me if more than one in equal shares provided that if any of my said son or daughters shall predecease me leaving a child or children surviving me who shall attain the age of [18/21/25] years[1] such last-mentioned child or children shall take and if more than one equally between them the share of my residuary estate which such deceased son or daughter of mine would have taken had he or she survived me.

1   Since the grandchildren will all be lives in being for perpetuity periods, the age contingency does not have to be limited to 21.

[234.40]

Maintenance advancement and accumulation

8.   [*As in cl 5 of* Form C11.1 *at para* **[233.20]**.]

[234.41]

Administrative powers[1]

9.   [*As in cl 6 of* Form C11.1 *at para* **[233.21]**.]

1   The powers in cl 6 of Form C11.1 include power to carry on a business (see sub-cl (3)(h)), which would enable the executors to carry on the farming business.

[234.42]

Exercise of powers

10.   [*As in cl 7 of* Form C11.1 *at para* **[233.22]**.]

[234.43]

Trustee self-dealing, indemnity, and similar provisions

11.   [*As in cl 8 of* Form C11.1 *at para* **[233.23]**.]

[234.44]

Professional trustee charging clause

12.   [*As in cl 9 of* Form C11.1 *at para* **[233.24]**.]

[*Testimonium and attestation clause as in* Form C12.1 *at para* **[234.30]**.]

[234.45]

FORM C12.3:   Will of tenant farmer leaving his farming business either to his wife or his son with residue held on trust for wife for life with remainders to children with substitution of issue

Revocation clause

I [*name*] of [*address*] hereby revoke all former testamentary dispositions made by me and declare this to be my last will.

[234.46]

Appointment of executors and trustees

1.   [*As in cl 1 of* Form C12.2 *at para* **[234.33]**.]

[234.47]

Gifts of chattels

2.   [*As in cl 2 of* Form C12.2 *at para* **[234.34]**.]

[234.48]

Bequest of farming business and nomination of successor to tenancy[1]

EITHER

[3.   (1)   I give to my wife my tenancy of —— Farm [*address*] and the assets of the farming business carried on by me thereat including live and dead stock agricultural equipment book debts growing crops milk quota and the money (if any) standing to the credit of my farm current [and business reserve] account[s] but [excluding any motor car and] subject to all debts and liabilities of my said business at my death [and for the purposes of Part IV of the Agricultural Holdings Act 1986 I designate my wife as the person whom I desire to succeed me as tenant of the said holding.[2]]

(2)   If my wife shall predecease me or the foregoing gift to her shall fail for any other reason then I give [and designate] as provided in the last preceding subclause in favour of my son [*name*] in place of my wife and as if the last foregoing subclause were written out again with references to my said son substituted for references to my wife.

(3)   If the foregoing gift to my son [*name*] takes effect and there is any inheritance tax payable on my estate by reason of my death which is attributable to the foregoing gift (after allowing for any reduction in value for inheritance tax purposes which is attributed thereto) then such gift shall be subject to such inheritance tax and it shall be borne by my said son in exoneration of the rest of my estate.[3]]

OR

[3.   (1)   I give to my son [*name*] my tenancy of —— Farm [address] and the assets of the farming business carried on by me thereat including live and dead stock agricultural equipment book debts growing crops milk quota and the money (if any) standing to the credit of my farm current [and business reserve] account[s] but [excluding any motor car and] subject to all debts and liabilities of my said business at my death [and for the purposes of Part IV of the Agricultural Holdings Act 1986 I designate my said son as the person whom I desire to succeed me as tenant of the said holding.[4]]

(2) If there is any inheritance tax payable on my estate by reason of my death which is attributable to the foregoing gift to my said son (after allowing for any reduction in value for inheritance tax purposes which is attributed thereto) then the foregoing gift shall be subject to such inheritance tax and it shall be borne by my said son in exoneration of the rest of my estate.[5]]

1   This provides two alternatives: (i) a gift of the farming business to the testator's wife and designation of her as tenant (with alternative gift and nomination in favour of the son) or (ii) a gift of the business to and designation as successor of the son. There may be practical reasons why it is necessary for the farming business to go to the wife, but where it is practical there are two good reasons for the gift and designation being in favour of the son: (a) there can only be two successions to the agricultural tenancy; and (b) the business relief on the farming business (and agricultural relief on the tenancy if it has a value) will be wasted if the business is given to the wife (see the Preliminary Note to C11 at para [233.3]).
2   Where a testator farms agricultural land under an AHA 1986 protected tenancy granted before 12 July 1984 (or after that date in exceptional cases referred to in s 34(1)), he may have the right to designate a successor by will. To be effective a designation of a successor must specifically mention the holding, and must exclusively designate one person; different persons may be designated to be the successor in different circumstances, so long as the result is the designation of one person in the events which happen: AHA 1986, s 40(1) and (2). There will normally only be a right to succession to the tenancy if it was granted before 12 July 1984.
3   There should be no inheritance tax on the gift because of 100 per cent business relief (see B5 at paras [205.22]–[205.28]), but for the circumstances in which tax may be paid on such property see B5 at para [205.51]. Making this gift subject to tax rather than free of it will have the effect, if the residuary gift is exempt and there is any inheritance tax payable on this gift, that the amount of inheritance tax payable will be much reduced: see B14 at para [214.74]. It would also be possible to exclude 'excepted assets' from the gift: see the Preliminary Note to B5 at para [205.9], on excepted assets, and Form B5.4 at para [205.61], for an example.
     Another reason for making the gift subject to tax, even where the residuary gift is not exempt, is that it enables the administration of residue to be completed more quickly, since the inheritance tax on the gift is likely to be payable by instalments (see the Preliminary Note to B5 at paras [205.17]–[205.20]) and part of residue might have to be retained for some time to pay the tax if it is payable out of residue.
4   See n 1 and 2 supra.
5   See n 3 supra.

[234.49]

Administration trusts of residue
4.   [*As in cl 4 of* Form C12.1 *at para* **[234.22]**.]

[234.50]

Gifts made free of tax
5.   [*As in cl 5 of* Form C12.1 *at para* **[234.23]**.]

[234.51]

Beneficial trusts of residue
6.   (1) My trustees shall hold my residuary estate upon trust to pay the income thereof to my wife during her life.

(2) Provided that my trustees shall have power in their absolute discretion from time to time so long as my wife is entitled to be paid the income of all or any part of the capital of my residuary estate (or would be so entitled if such

capital yielded income) to pay transfer or apply the whole or any part or parts of such capital[1] to her or for her benefit in such manner as they shall in their absolute discretion think fit.

(3)   Subject as aforesaid my trustees shall hold my residuary estate upon trust for such of my children [*name*] [*name*] and [*name*] as shall be living at the death of the survivor of myself and my wife if more than one in equal shares Provided that if any of my said children shall die before the death of the survivor of myself and my wife leaving issue living at the death of the survivor of myself and wife who attain the age of 21 years such issue shall take and if more than one in equal shares per stirpes the share of my residuary estate which such deceased child of mine would have taken had he or she survived to attain a vested interest but so that no such issue shall take whose parent (being such issue as aforesaid) is living at the death of the survivor of myself and my wife and attains the said age.[2]

(4)   The foregoing trusts of capital shall carry the intermediate income and section 31 of the Trustee Act 1925 (as hereinafter modified) shall apply thereto.

(5)   Section 32 of the Trustee Act 1925 (as hereinafter modified) shall apply in relation to the foregoing trusts of capital.

1   There are two reasons for restricting the power to capital in which the spouse has an interest in possession: first, to ensure that the power is not exercisable if there is a divorce and the primary trust lapses and, secondly, to ensure that the power ceases to be exercisable if the spouse assigns or surrenders his or her life interest. See C2 on the possibility and effects of divorce at paras **[224.12]–[224.19]**.

2   In most remainder trusts of this type in the complete forms in Part C the interests of the primary class of beneficiaries vest on the death of the testator, and are not contingent on surviving the life tenant. This clause is an exception. Early vesting has the advantage that it makes it easier for the parties to rearrange or break the trusts, if they so desire, but the disadvantage that the estate of a child who predeceases the life tenant will take his or her share, which may thus pass to that child's widow or widower rather than to his or her issue. The inflexibility of the interests being contingent on surviving the life tenant is mitigated to some extent in this clause by the presence of a wide power of advancement.

[234.52]

Maintenance, accumulation and advancement
7.   [*As in cl 5 of* Form C11.1 *at para* **[233.20]**.]

[234.53]

Administrative powers
8.   [*As in cl 6 of* Form C11.1 *at para* **[233.21]**.]

[234.54]

Exercise of powers
9.   [*As in cl 7 of* Form C11.1 *at para* **[233.22]**.]

[234.55]

Trustee self-dealing, indemnity, and similar provisions
10.   [*As in cl 8 of* Form C11.1 *at para* **[233.23]**.]

[234.56]

Professional trustee charging clause
11.   [*As in cl 9 of* Form C11.1 *at para* **[233.24]**.]

[*Testimonium and attestation clause as in* Form C12.1 *at para* **[234.30]**.]

C13   Wills for owners of substantial property

PRELIMINARY NOTE

[235.1]
The two forms in this section are very different in character and both contain
unusual features. The principal features of the first form are the gift of family
company shares on trusts for the benefit of the employees and the settlement of
residue on charitable trusts. The implications of these gifts are more fully
explained in the Note preceding the form and in the footnotes to it. The principal
feature of the second form is the inclusion of a settled gift of a landed estate with
a maintenance fund for the restoration and upkeep of the mansion house and its
contents. Formerly a strict settlement would have been an appropriate vehicle,
but strict settlements can no longer be created: see Part A, para **[200.52]**;
entailed interests have suffered the same fate: see Part A, para **[200.53]**. No form
for a strict settlement is therefore included in this edition but Form C13.2 is
intended to fulfil the same function.

[235.2]

**FORM C13.1:   Will of owner of substantial property with no immediate
family containing specific gift of controlling shareholding in family
company on trusts for the employees and leaving residue on charitable
trusts**

NOTE

The particular features of this form are (i) a specific gift of private company
shares on trusts for the benefit of the company's employees and (ii) a gift of
residue on charitable trusts. A detailed account of the law relating to employee
trusts is beyond the scope of this work and reference should be made to *Foster's
Inheritance Tax*, E6.31. The position briefly is that where settled property is held
on discretionary trusts (whether indefinite or for a fixed period) for the benefit of
all or most of the persons employed by or holding office with a body carrying on
a trade or undertaking and their dependants (and whether or not those trusts also
permit the settled property to be applied for charitable purposes), then such

property is exempt from the periodic and exit charges applicable under the code for discretionary trusts contained in the the Inheritance Tax Act 1984 (ITA 1984), Part III, Ch III, and an interest in possession in any part not exceeding five per cent of the settled property will be disregarded: see the ITA 1984, ss 58(1)(b) and 86(1), (2), (3)(a) and (4)(b). Additionally, if an individual settles shares in a company on employee trusts within s 86, then provided that the class of beneficiaries includes all or most of the persons employed by or holding office with the company and the shares comprised in the gift represent more than half the ordinary shares in the company and yield more than half the votes on all questions affecting the company as a whole, the initial gift will also be exempt: ITA 1984, s 28. However, for this section to apply no part of the settled property should be capable of being applied for the benefit of any person who is at the date of the gift or has at any time thereafter or within the period of ten years immediately preceding the gift been a 'participator' in the company (or in any close company which settles property on the trusts by a disposition which is not a transfer of value by reason of s 13): s 28(4). (For this purpose a 'participator' is a person who is entitled to or entitled to acquire not less than five per cent of or of any class of the company's issued share capital or who is entitled on a winding up to not less than five per cent of its assets: s 28(5).) The specific gift of private company shares contained in this form is intended for use by a testator who not only wishes to make provision for the company employees but who has a controlling shareholding and is therefore in a position to do so by way of exempt transfer.

As the law stands, the gift of a controlling holding in a company (not being an investment company) would also attract 100 per cent business property relief under the ITA 1984, ss 104(1)(a) and 105(1)(b) and (3). But it should be noted that by virtue of s 112 this relief (unlike the exemption under s 28) does not extend to the value of 'excepted assets' (as to which see the Preliminary Note to B5 at para **[205.9]**) and that the relief may quite possibly be reduced by a future government, whereas the exception for employee trusts is less likely to be affected.

The form also contains a charitable gift of residue which confers power on the trustees to form a new charitable company or trust and to transfer the assets comprised in residue to such new body.

[235.3]

Revocation clause

I [name] of [address] hereby revoke all former testamentary dispositions made by me and declare this to be my last will.

[235.4]

Appointment of executors and trustees

1. I appoint [name] of [address] [name] of [address] and [name] of [address] (hereinafter together called 'my trustees' which expression shall include my personal representatives for the time being and the trustees for the time being hereof) to be the executors and trustees of this will.

[235.5]

Pecuniary legacies

2. I give the following pecuniary legacies free of tax[1]—

(a) to [*name*] the sum of £——;
(b) to [*name*] the sum of £——;
(c) to [*name*] the sum of £——.

1   Inheritance tax on assets situate in the UK, whether real or personal, is a testamentary expense and accordingly payable out of residue without express provision: ITA 1984, s 211 (Part G, para **[246.83]** and see the Preliminary Note to B14 at paras **[214.55]**–**[214.58]**). The legacies are expressly declared to be 'free of tax' (a formula defined in cl 7 at para **[235.10]** in order to cater for the risk that residue includes property which bears its own tax, eg foreign property, in which event the legacies would be liable to contribute to the tax on such property unless expressly exonerated from it: see the notes to cls 6(1) and 7 at paras **[235.9]** and **[235.10]** and to Form C8.1, cl 4 at para **[230.7]**.

[235.6]

Specific gifts
3.   I make the following specific gifts free of tax[1]—

(a) to [*name*] all my vintage cars;
(b) to [*name*] my guns and fishing tackle;
(c) to [*name*] all my books and papers;
(d) to [*name*] my sailing boat known as [*name of boat*].

1   See the preceding note. In the ordinary case a specific gift of personal chattels will devolve free of tax. The 'free of tax' formula is included in case any personal chattels, eg the sailing boat, happens to be situate out of the UK (eg the Channel Islands which are not part of the UK) at the testator's death and also to exclude any argument that the use of the 'free of tax' formula elsewhere in the will and its absence in the specific gift of the personal chattels implies that the chattels bear their own tax: cf *Re Phuler's Will Trusts* [1964] 2 All ER 948, [1965] 1 WLR 68.

[235.7]

Gift of company shares to separate trustees on employee trusts
4.   (1)   I give free of tax[1] to [*name*] [and] [*name*] [and [*name*]][2] all my shares in my family company known as [*name of company*][3] to hold on the trusts and with and subject to the powers and provisions hereinafter declared and contained.

(2)   In this clause the following expressions have the following meanings—

(a) 'the company' means the said [*name of company*];
(b) 'the company fund trustees' means the said [*name*] [and] the said [*name*] [and the said [*name*]] and the [survivors or] survivor of them or other the trustees or trustee for the time being of the company fund;[4]
(c) 'the company fund' means the shares in the company hereby given to the company fund trustees and the assets from time to time representing the same;
(d) 'excluded person' means any person referred to in paragraphs (a) to (d) of subsection (4) of section 28 of the Inheritance Tax Act 1984 on the footing that—
   (i)   the company referred to in paragraph (a) of the said subsection is the company as hereinbefore defined,
   (ii) the settlement referred to in paragraph (b) of the said subsection is the disposition on trust contained in this present clause,
   (iii) the transfer of value referred to in paragraph (c) of the said subsection is that which is deemed to occur immediately before my death for inheritance tax purposes, and

      (iv)   the said paragraphs shall be construed and applied subject to and in accordance with all other statutory provisions to which they are subject or which contain definitions relevant to their interpretation.[5]

 (e)   'the employees'[6] means and includes all persons who at any time after my death have either held office with or been employed (in whatever capacity) by the company (whether or not such person continues to hold office with or be employed by the company) and 'employee' means any one of the employees;

 (f)   'dependants'[7] means in relation to any employee or deceased employee—

      (i)   the spouse widow or widower of such employee,

      (ii)   any child of such employee during his or her minority,

      (iii)   any other person whom the company fund trustees may consider to be a dependant of such employee;

 (g)   'the beneficiaries'[8] means and includes—

      (i)   the employees,

      (ii)   the dependants of any employee or deceased employee;

   Provided that no excluded person shall be a beneficiary and any person who becomes an excluded person shall forthwith cease to be a beneficiary;

 (h)   'the trust period' means the period of 80 years immediately following my death which shall be the perpetuity period applicable to the disposition made hereby;[9]

 (i)   'the accumulation period' means the period of 21 years immediately following my death.[10]

   (3)   During the trust period the company fund trustees shall pay or apply the income of the company fund to or for the maintenance education support or benefit of all or such one or more exclusively of the others or other of the beneficiaries for the time being in existence and if more than one in such shares and generally in such manner [or for such charitable purposes generally][11] as the company fund trustees shall in their absolute discretion think fit Provided that during the accumulation period the company fund trustees may accumulate the whole or any part or parts of the income of the company fund by investing the same and the resulting income thereof in any of the investments hereby authorised and any accumulations so made shall form part of the capital of the company fund for all purposes.

   (4)   Notwithstanding the trust aforesaid the company fund trustees may at any time or times and from time to time during the trust period pay or apply the whole or any part or parts of the capital of the company fund to or for the advancement or benefit of all or any one or more exclusively of the others or other of the beneficiaries for the time being in existence and if more than one in such shares and in such manner generally [or for such charitable purposes generally][12] as the company fund trustees may in their absolute discretion think fit.

   (5)   Subject to the trusts and to any exercise of the powers aforesaid the company fund trustees shall hold the company fund and the income thereof upon trust for such charitable purposes generally[13] as they may in their absolute discretion think fit.

(6)   The administrative powers and provisions contained in clause 9 hereof shall apply in relation to the company fund and the income thereof as if references therein to 'my trustees' were references to 'the company fund trustees'.

1   See the notes to cls 2 and 3 at paras **[235.5]** and **[235.6]**. If the shares in the company confer control, the gift should be exempt from inheritance tax: see the Note to this form at para **[235.2]**.
2   It may be convenient to appoint separate trustees of the company fund.
3   If the shares in the company confer control, the gift should be exempt for inheritance tax: see the Note to this form at para **[235.2]**.
4   See n 2 supra.
5   The excluded categories are essentially participators in the company entitled to five per cent or more of the share capital. It is not very satisfactory to use referential drafting of this kind, but the elaboration of the statutory provisions is such that it is not practical to attempt to reproduce them in full: see the ITA 1984, ss 13(5), 28(4) to (7), and 102 and the Income and Corporation Taxes Act 1988, ss 414 to 417.
6   The definitions of 'the employees' and 'the beneficiaries' are based on the provisions of the ITA 1984, ss 86(1) and (3)(a) and 28(1), (4) and (5).
7   The definition of 'dependants' is based on the ITA 1984, s 86(1)(b).
8   See nn 6 and 7 supra.
9   This is the maximum fixed period of years permitted by the PAA 1964, s 1 (Part G, para **[246.59]**).
10   The 21-year accumulation period is available under the LPA 1925, s 164(1)(b) (Part G, para **[246.42]**) and is the only suitable period.
11   It is permissible to include charitable objects without prejudicing the exempt status of the trusts: see the ITA 1984, s 86(3) and the Note to this form at para **[235.2]**. If a power to benefit charity is not required the words in square brackets should be omitted.
12   See n 11 supra.
13   See n 11 supra. A trust for charitable purposes is a convenient ultimate trust.

[235.8]

Gift of family seat
5.   I give free of tax[1] the mansion house and grounds known as [*name of house*] and situate in the Parish of [ ] in the County of [ ] and the contents thereof to my nephew [*name*] in fee simple and absolutely.

1   See n 3 to cls 2 and 3 of this form at paras **[235.5]** and **[235.6]**.

[235.9]

Administration trusts of residue[1]
6.   (1)   I give all my property not hereby or by any codicil hereto otherwise effectively disposed of [(including any entailed or other property over which I shall have at my death a general power of disposition by will)] to my trustees to hold on the trusts set out below with power at their discretion to sell all or any of it as and when they think fit.

(2)   My trustees shall pay my funeral and testamentary expenses and debts and any legacies given by this will or any codicil hereto out of such property or its proceeds and shall have a discretion as to how such payments shall be borne as between capital and income.

(3)   Subject as above my trustees shall hold such property and the assets from time to time representing the same (hereinafter called 'my residuary estate') on the trusts set out below and shall invest all money comprised in such

property or arising from its sale in any of the investments hereby authorised with power to change such investments into any others hereby authorised.

(4)   In the administration of my estate and the execution of the trusts of this will or of any codicil to it:

(a)   my trustees shall treat all income as accruing on the date on which it becomes payable regardless of the period in respect of which it shall have accrued and shall not make any statutory apportionment of the same; and

(b)   none of the equitable rules of apportionment between capital and income shall apply in any circumstances whatever.

1   See the notes to the administration trusts contained in Form C8.1, cl 4 at para **[230.7]**.

[235.10]

Gifts made free of tax

7.   Any specific gift or pecuniary or general legacy made by this will or any codicil hereto which is expressed to be 'free of tax' shall be free from the payment of any inheritance tax or foreign tax or duty payable on or by reason of my death to which such gift or legacy would otherwise be subject and such inheritance tax or foreign tax or duty shall be paid out of my residuary estate.[1]

1   See the notes to cls 2 and 3 of this form at paras **[235.5]** and **[235.6]**. Where specific gifts and pecuniary legacies consist of, or are wholly payable out of, free estate in the UK, the inheritance tax on them will be a testamentary expense payable out of residue without any express provision, and it is only where foreign property or settled property is being disposed of by the will that a gift which is intended to be free of tax needs to be expressly declared to be free of tax. See also the Preliminary Note to B14 at para **[214.60]**.

[235.11]

Charitable trusts of residue

8.   (1)   The charity hereby constituted shall be known as '[*name of charity*]'.

(2)   In this clause the following expressions have the following meanings namely—

(a)   'charitable purposes' means purposes which are exclusively charitable;

(b)   'charity' means any institution (whether corporate or unincorporated) established for charitable purposes and 'charities' has a corresponding meaning.

(3)   My trustees shall hold my residuary estate upon trust to apply the income thereof[1] for such charitable purposes connected with [*here state nature of desired charitable purposes: eg* the relief of poverty *or* the promotion of research for the public benefit into the causes and treatment of diabetes][2] [and for such charitable purposes generally][3] as my trustees may from time to time determine provided that my trustees may at any time or times during the accumulation period accumulate the whole or any part or parts of the income of my residuary estate by investing the same and the resulting income thereof in any of the investments hereby authorised and any accumulations so made shall form part of the capital of my residuary estate for all purposes.[4]

[(4)   My trustees may at any time and from time to time resort to the whole or any part or parts of the capital of my residuary estate and apply the same as if it were income.][5]

(5)   In the administration of the charity hereby constituted my trustees shall have the following powers (in addition to those conferred by clause 9 below)—

(a)   power either themselves to apply the income [or capital]⁶ for the purposes hereby declared or for that purpose to pay the same to any other charity or charities having similar objects;

(b)   power to do all such things as may in the opinion of my trustees be conducive to the promotion of the charitable objects hereby declared;

(c)   power by deed to extend restrict vary or modify the trusts powers and provisions relating to my residuary estate in any manner whatever provided that the foregoing power shall not be exercisable so as to cause or permit any of my residuary estate or the income thereof to be payable or applicable otherwise than for charitable purposes;

(d)   power to create a new charitable body (whether corporate or unincorporated) having exclusively charitable objects identical with or similar to the objects hereby declared and to confer on such body such administrative and other powers as my trustees think fit and as shall be consistent with charitable status and to transfer to such body the whole or any part of my residuary estate for the promotion of its objects.

1   The primary (and only) trust is to apply the income of residue for charitable purposes, but power is conferred by cl 8(4) to resort to capital. A perpetual income trust for charitable purposes is valid: *Re Levy* [1960] Ch 346, [1960] 1 All ER 42. If the testator wishes to create such a trust, the power to resort to capital should be omitted.

2   Care should be taken to ensure that the charitable purposes are adequately described.

3   It is wise to include charitable purposes generally in case the specific purposes are defectively described or there is some development which makes it desirable to modify the original purposes.

4   The proviso confers a power to accumulate income for 21 years. The restrictions on accumulating income apply to charitable trusts as well as to private trusts.

   The exemption from income tax for charity income is only available in relation to income of the appropriate kind which is 'applied' for charitable purposes: see the Income and Corporation Taxes Act 1988, s 505. It is therefore preferable, where trustees accumulate income of funds held on charitable trusts, that they should do so with some specific charitable objective in view. It is probable that income which is accumulated as a general accretion to the funds of a charity counts as 'applied' for charitable purposes and qualifies for this exemption, but it is not absolutely certain: see *IRC v Helen Slater Charitable Trust Ltd* [1982] Ch 49, [1981] 3 All ER 98.

5   See n 1 supra.

6   If sub-cl (4) is not included, the words in square brackets should be omitted.

[235.12]

Administrative powers[1]

9.   (1)   In this clause where the context so admits:

(a)   the expression 'land' includes buildings and estates interests or rights of any kind in or over land; and

(b)   during the administration of my estate the expression 'beneficiary' includes any person who would be a beneficiary if such administration had been completed and the expression 'beneficially interested' and references to income of any asset being payable or capable of being paid to or for the benefit of a beneficiary shall be construed accordingly.

(2)   None of the powers or provisions contained in subclause (3) below of this clause shall be capable of being exercised or operating in any manner such that if such power or provision were capable of being so exercised or so operating the existence of the same would either:

(i)   prevent any person who would in the absence of such power or provision have been entitled to an interest in possession (within the meaning of Part III of the Inheritance Tax Act 1984) in any property from being entitled to such interest; or

(ii)   prevent section 71 of the Inheritance Tax Act 1984 from applying to any property to which in the absence of such power or provision the said section 71 would have applied.

(3)   In the administration of my estate and the execution of the trusts hereof or of any codicil hereto my trustees shall have the following powers in addition to those conferred by law but subject to the last foregoing subclause:

(a)   power to invest moneys sell assets and change investments with the unrestricted freedom of choice and powers of disposition and acquisition of a sole beneficial owner with in particular power to make unsecured loans, acquire non-income yielding assets, and purchase land anywhere in the world or chattels for any purpose including occupation or enjoyment in kind by a beneficiary under the power set out below;

(b)   power to delegate all or any of their investment powers to a professional investment manager or managers whether individual or corporate and whether or not also a nominee holder of assets for my trustees (and who may be or include one or more of my trustees or the beneficiaries hereunder) upon such terms as to remuneration and otherwise (including terms authorising self-dealing or providing for the limitation of the liability of the investment manager or managers) as my trustees think fit and section 22 of the Trustee Act 2000 shall not apply;

(c)   power to vest or register any property in any person or persons whether individual or corporate and whether or not an investment manager to whom powers have been delegated under the foregoing power (and who may be or include one or more of my trustees or the beneficiaries hereunder) as nominee or nominees for my trustees upon such terms as to remuneration or otherwise (including terms authorising self-dealing or providing for the limitation of the liability of the nominee) as my trustees think fit and section 22 of the Trustee Act 2000 shall not apply;

(d)   power to borrow money with or without giving security and on such terms as to interest and repayment and otherwise as my trustees may think fit for any purpose connected with the administration of my estate or the trusts declared herein or in any codicil hereto (including investment) and no lender from whom my trustees borrow money in purported exercise of this power shall be concerned to enquire as to the propriety amount or purpose of any such borrowing;

(e)   power to lend money to a beneficiary to whom any of the income of such money is payable or to whom or for whose benefit any income of such money is capable of being paid or applied in exercise of a discretion (or who would be such a beneficiary if such money yielded income) and to do so at a full or concessionary rate of interest or interest free;

(f)   all the powers of an absolute owner in relation to any land (wherever situated) held by them;

(g)   power to apply capital held on the same trusts as any land (or which would be so held if the administration of my estate had been completed) in the improvement of such land and to apply such capital or the income of such capital on the repair or maintenance of such land;

(h)   power to permit any beneficiary to have the beneficial occupation use or enjoyment in kind of any land or chattel or other tangible property on such terms as to repair insurance or payment of outgoings by the beneficiary or otherwise howsoever as my trustees think fit Provided that the foregoing power shall only be exercisable and such permission to occupy or enjoy in kind may only continue in the following circumstances:

    (i)   so long as any of the income of such land chattel or other tangible property is payable to such beneficiary or capable of being paid or applied to him or for his benefit in exercise of a discretion (or would be so payable or capable of being so paid or applied if such land chattel or other property yielded income),

    (ii)   in the case of land, so long as for the time being the occupation thereof by such beneficiary is compatible with any statutory rights of occupation of any other beneficiary or beneficiaries;

(i)   power to exercise all the powers of appropriation (and other incidental powers) conferred by statute on a personal representative without the necessity of obtaining any consents and notwithstanding that one or more of my trustees may be beneficially interested in the exercise of such power.[1]

1   See the notes to the administrative powers contained in Form C8.1, cl 8 at para **[230.11]**.

[235.13]

Trustee liability

10.   (1) My trustees shall not be liable for any act or default of any investment manager or nominee employed in good faith to manage or hold assets of my estate nor for any act or default of any beneficiary having the occupation use or enjoyment of property in kind.[1]

(2)   Section 11(1) of the Trusts of Land and Appointment of Trustees Act 1996 (consultation with beneficiaries) shall not apply to the exercise by my trustees of any of their powers in relation to land subject to the trusts hereof.[2]

1   This makes it clear that the trustees are not liable for the defaults of others who may have possession or control of trust property. For a wider form of indemnity, see eg Form B21.12 at para **[221.16]**.

2   The requirement that trustees of land in exercise of any function relating to land subject to the trust consult with beneficiaries of full age beneficially entitled to an interest in possession in the land can be excluded: see the Trusts of Land and Appointment of Trustees Act 1996 (TLATA 1996), s 11(2)(a) (Part G, para **[246.97]**).

[235.14]

Receipts on behalf of charitable institutions

11.   The receipt of the person who professes to be the treasurer or other proper officer of any institution shall be a sufficient discharge to my trustees in respect of any money or property payable or transferable thereto.

[235.15]

Professional trustee charging clause

12.   Any of my trustees being a professional or business man may charge and be paid all usual professional and other proper charges for business transacted acts done advice given and time spent by him or his firm in connection with the administration of my estate or in connection with the trusts hereof including acts which a personal representative or trustee not being in any profession or business could have done personally.

[235.16]

Testimonium

IN WITNESS whereof I have hereunto set my hand this —— day of —— 20——
——

[235.17]

Attestation clause

SIGNED by the above-named [testator/testatrix] as
[his/her] last will in the presence of us both present at
the same time who at [his/her] request and in [his/her]   } *[Signature of*
presence and in the presence of each other have signed   *testator/testatrix]*
our names below as witnesses:

[Signatures, addresses and descriptions of witnesses]

[235.18]

FORM C13.2:   Will of a bachelor landowner settling the principal family estate together with a share of residue on one nephew and his issue , creating a maintenance fund for the upkeep of the mansion house and settled chattels and settling substantial legacies on two nieces and their issue

NOTE

This form replaces Form C13.2 of the previous edition, which contained a precedent for a devise of land in strict settlement with remainders in tail. Strict settlements and entailed interests can no longer be created: see Part A, paras **[200.52]** and **[200.53]**. This form contains instead a settled devise of a landed estate on rather simpler trusts. The name and arms clause has been retained in modified form. A novel feature is the inclusion of a gift of a substantial legacy on trusts for the maintenance, repair and preservation of the mansion house and contents. This gift will constitute an exempt transfer for inheritance tax purposes but only if the mansion house and chattels qualify for conditional exemption and the appropriate undertakings are given. Substantial settled legacies for the benefit of the testator's nieces and their issue are included as before.

Revocation clause

I [*name*] of [*address*] hereby revoke all former testamentary dispositions made by me and declare this to be my last will.

[235.19]

Appointment of executors and trustees

I appoint [*name*] of [*address*] [*name*] of [*address*] and [*name*] of [*address*] to be executors and trustees of this will

[235.20]

Interpretation clause

2.   (1)   I declare that in the interpretation of this will the following words and expressions have the following meanings, namely—

(a)   'my trustees' means and includes my personal representatives for the time being and the trustees or trustee for the time being hereof whether original or substituted and if there shall at any time be no such trustees shall (where the context permits) include the persons empowered by statute to exercise or perform any power or trust hereby or by statute conferred upon my trustees and willing or bound to exercise or perform the same;

(b)   'the mansion house' means the mansion house at present occupied by me known as ——— together with the outbuildings and appurtenances thereto belonging;

(c)   'the settled chattels' means the pictures items of furniture objets d'art and other chattels located at the mansion house which are listed in an inventory prepared by Messrs ——— and dated ———;

(d)   'the principal estate' means and includes:

(i)   the mansion house,

(ii)   the settled chattels,

(iii)   my agricultural estate known as the ——— estate situate at ——— — in the County of ——— together with all other real and leasehold property and other interests in land in the said County to which I may be entitled at the time of my death,

(iv)   the share of my residuary estate hereinafter bequeathed to my trustees as part of the principal estate, and

(v)   the assets from time to time representing the premises respectively;[1]

(e)   'the maintenance fund' means the sum of [£2,000,000] hereinafter bequeathed for the maintenance repair and preservation of the heritage property and the investments for the time being representing the same;

(f)   'the [W] trust fund' shall mean the sum of [£500,000] hereinafter settled on my niece [MW] and her issue and the investments for the time being representing the same;

(g)   'the [L] trust fund' shall mean the like sum of [£500,000] hereinafter settled on my niece [VL] and her issue and the investments for the time being representing the same;

(h)   'younger children' or 'younger child' in relation to any person shall mean and include all daughters (including an eldest or elder daughter) of such person who shall live to attain the age [18/21] years or previously marry and also every son (except an eldest or only son) who shall live to attain the age of [18/21] years including any son who being originally a younger son shall after attaining the age of [18/21] years become an eldest son or only son by the death of an elder brother but (except for the purposes of any power of maintenance or advancement hereinafter contained or conferred upon my trustees by statute) shall not include any child who being male shall die under the age of [18/21] years or being female shall die under that age a spinster.

[(2) This will shall be read and construed as if section 15 of the Family Law Reform Act 1969 [the Children Act 1975/the Legitimacy Act 1976/the Adoption Act 1976], the Family Law Reform Act 1987 and the Human Fertilisation and Embryology Act 1990 had not been enacted.][2]

1 The clauses disposing of the principal estate are only appropriate to land in England and Wales.
2 References to children and issue will now, in the absence of a contrary intention, be read as including references to illegitimate, adopted and legitimated persons by virtue of the enactments mentioned in this paragraph: (Part G, paras **[245.39]**, **[245.48]**, **[245.60]**, **[245.72]** and **[245.77]** and Vol 1, paras **[72.10]**–**[72.18]** and **[74.3]**–**[74.7]**). In a will of this type the testator may desire to exclude the statutory rules of construction (or some of them) in which case this paragraph should be included and adapted as appropriate.

[235.21]

Pecuniary legacies
3. I give the following pecuniary legacies free of tax[1]—

(a) to [*name*] the sum of £——;
(b) to [*name*] the sum of £——;
(c) to [*name*] the sum of £——.

1 See notes to cls 2 and 7 of Form C13.1 at paras **[235.5]** and **[235.10]**.

[235.22]

Bequest of legacy on trust
4. I bequeath to my trustees free of tax[1] the sum of [£500,000] with interest thereon from the date of my death until the appropriation thereof or of investments thereto at the rate of [six] per cent per annum[2] upon trust to invest the said sum in or upon any of the investments hereinafter authorised and to hold such investments and the investments for the time being representing the same (hereinafter called 'the [W] trust fund') upon the following trusts, namely—

(a) the income of the [W] trust fund and the said interest payable from the date of my death shall be held [upon trust to pay the same to]/[upon protective trusts for the benefit of] my niece [MW] wife of [JW] during her life;
(b) after the death of the said [MW] the [W] trust fund shall be held in trust for such one or more of the children and remoter issue of the said [MW] upon with and subject to such trusts powers and provisions (including trusts and powers conferring a discretion as to the disposition of capital and income or provisions for the accumulation of income during any period permitted by law) as the said [MW] may by deed or deeds with or without power of revocation and new appointment or by will or codicil appoint;
(c) in default of any such appointment and subject to any partial appointment the [W] trust fund shall be held in trust for all the children

or any the child of the said [MW] who being male have attained or shall attain the age of [18/21] years or being female have attained or shall attain that age or have married or shall previously marry as tenants in common equally provided always that no child of the said [MW] shall take any part or share of and in the [W] trust fund in default of appointment without bringing into hotchpot any part or share therein which may have been appointed to him or her or to his or her issue;

(d)   in default of any child or remoter issue of the said [MW] living to attain a vested interest in the whole of the [W] trust fund the same shall upon her decease be held in trust for such person or persons as she shall by will or codicil appoint and in default of any such appointment and subject to any partial appointment;[3]

(e)   in trust for her next of kin[4] living at her death [*alternatively* for the persons or person who would have been her statutory next-of-kin if she had died intestate possessed thereof domiciled in England and a spinster [and without a parent] and (if more than one) in the same shares as those in which they would have been entitled to her estate];

(f)   provided nevertheless that notwithstanding and in priority to the preceding trusts it shall be lawful for the said [MW] by will or codicil to appoint that the income of [any part not exceeding [two-thirds] of] the [W] trust fund shall be paid to any husband who may survive her during his life or for any less period or determinable upon the happening of any event;

(g)   the foregoing trusts shall carry the intermediate income of the [W] trust fund and the provisions of section 31 of the Trustee Act 1925 (as hereinafter modified) shall apply thereto;

(h)   section 32 of the Trustee Act 1925 (as hereinafter modified) shall apply in relation to the [W] trust fund.

1   See notes to cls 2 and 7 of Form C13.1 at paras **[235.5]** and **[235.10]**. Where a legacy given free of inheritance tax is settled, the freedom from the tax should extend only to tax payable upon or by reason of the death of the testator himself. Otherwise there is a danger that future taxes (eg inheritance tax payable on the deaths of the tenants for life) may be thrown upon residue, a result which would render the administration of the residue impossibly difficult (see such cases as *Re Stoddart, Bird v Grainger* [1916] 2 Ch 444; *Re Eve, Hall v Eve* [1917] 1 Ch 562; *Re Kennedy, Corbould v Kennedy* [1917] 1 Ch 9).

2   This is the rate of interest currently payable in respect of legacies in an administration by the court: CPR Sch 1, RSC Ord 44, r 10.

3   For a clause allowing the fund to be paid to a female tenant for life who is past the age of childbearing, where the trusts are similar to these, see Form B16.24 at para **[216.29]** and for a form enabling her to take over the trust fund in these circumstances, see the second alternative cl 6(3) of Form C8.2 at para **[230.24]**.

4   See Vol 1, para **[77.1]** and see the AEA 1925, ss 46 to 50, (Part G, paras **[244.60]**–**[244.65]**).

[235.23]

Bequest of legacy on trusts by reference to prior legacy

5.   I bequeath free of tax[1] to my trustees the further sum of [£500,000] with interest thereon at the rate of [six] per cent per annum[2] from the date of my death until the appropriation thereof or of investments thereto upon trust to invest the same upon any of the investments hereinafter authorised and to hold such

investments and the investments for the time being representing the same (hereinafter called 'the [L] trust fund') and the said interest upon with and subject to similar trusts powers and provisions as are hereinbefore contained in relation to the [W] trust fund but substituting throughout the name of my niece [VL] for that of my said niece [MW] and the expression the [L] trust fund for the expression the [W] trust fund.

1   See Form C13.1, cl 2, n 1 at para **[235.5]**.
2   See n 2 to cl 4 of this form at para **[235.22]**.

[235.24]

Settled devise of principal estate
6.   I devise and bequeath the principal estate [free of tax]/[subject to payment thereout of any inheritance tax attributable thereto (making due allowance for any reduction in value for inheritance tax purposes which is attributed thereto)]¹ unto my trustees upon the following trusts—

(a)   upon trust for my nephew [JE the elder] the son of my late sister [SE] during his life with remainder;
(b)   upon trust for [JE the younger] his only son living at the date of this my will during his life with remainder;
(c)   upon trust for the first son of the said [JE the younger] to attain the age of 21 years absolutely with remainder;
(d)   upon trust for the first daughter of the said [JE the younger] to attain the age of 21 years absolutely with remainder;
(e)   upon trust for the first future-born son of the said [JE the elder] to attain the age of 21 years absolutely with remainder;
(f)   upon trust for [ME] the only daughter living at the date of this my will of the said [JE the elder] during her life with remainder;
(g)   upon trust for the first son of the said [ME] to attain the age of 21 years absolutely with remainder;
(h)   upon trust for the first daughter of the said [ME] to attain the age of 21 years absolutely with remainder;
(i)   upon trust for the first future-born daughter of the said [JE the elder] to attain the age of 21 years absolutely with remainder;
(j)   upon trust for my own right heirs absolutely.²

1   This gift will be free of inheritance tax unless the contrary is stated: see the Preliminary Note to B14 at paras **[214.55]**–**[214.58]**, although if it is intended to be free of tax it will be advisable to say so specifically at this point because other gifts are expressed to be free of tax, and the absence of any direction as to the burden of inheritance tax in relation to this gift might give rise to doubt as to what was intended in this respect. If it is a substantial agricultural estate, in hand or let on tenancies commencing after 31 August 1995, it may be wholly entitled to 100 per cent agricultural relief: see the Preliminary Note to C12 at paras **[234.1]**–**[234.10]**.
   However, there may be a likelihood or a risk that this gift will not be wholly free from inheritance tax, and, if so, it may be appropriate to make it bear its own inheritance tax. The inheritance tax would be likely to be payable by instalments, and by interest-free instalments in relation to land on which there is a agricultural relief (see the Preliminary Note to B5 at paras **[205.17]**–**[205.20]**). It would enable the administration of the residuary estate to be speeded up if the executors did not have to retain any of it against the payment of the instalments of inheritance tax on this estate. A share of the residuary estate is added to this gift which might be used to pay the tax.

2   It is assumed in the above clause that at the date of the will there are living only two children, ie one son and one daughter of the testator's nephew. For the effect of a gift to a person's right heirs, see Vol 1, para **[78.1]** et seq.

[235.25]

Clause cutting down absolute interests to life interests
7.   I declare that every child of the said [JE the elder] or of the said [JE the younger] or of the said [ME] who shall be hereafter born[1] in my lifetime shall instead of taking an absolute interest in the principal estate under the foregoing trusts take a life interest only therein with remainder to his or her first and other sons successively absolutely with remainder upon trust for his or her first and other daughters successively absolutely.

1   A child en ventre sa mère at the testator's death and born afterwards would not, it seems, come within this clause: see *Villar v Gilbey* [1907] AC 139, HL.

[235.26]

Consultation and consents of, and delegation to, beneficiaries of the principal estate[1]
8.   If and so long as there is a person who is for the time being entitled to a life interest in possession in the principal estate under the foregoing trusts who has attained the age of 21 years—
   (1)   My trustees shall be under an obligation to consult such person as to their exercise of their functions in relation to any land comprised in the principal estate but subject as aforesaid section 11(1) of the Trusts of Land and Appointment of Trustees Act 1996[2] shall not apply in relation to such land or any other land comprised in my estate or any fund deriving therefrom and I request that so far as they may lawfully do so my trustees do delegate their functions in relation to the principal estate to such person;[3] and
   (2)   My trustees shall not exercise their powers (whether conferred by statute or otherwise) of sale lease licence mortgage or charge, or of effecting improvements or development, of any land comprised in the principal estate without the consent of such person.[4]

1   This provision is designed to put an adult life tenant in possession of the principal estate in a position as analogous to that of a tenant for life under a strict settlement as can be achieved under the TLATA 1996, see para **[220.54]**.
2   See the TLATA 1996, s 11 (Part G, para **[246.97]**); see also para **[220.55]**.
3   For the statutory power of delegation of management of land to a beneficiary with an interest in possession, under the TLATA 1996, s 9, see paras **[220.56]** and **[220.57]**. It is reasonably clear from the wording of the power that the trustees cannot be put under a duty to delegate, and an expression of wishes of this kind is the appropriate provision to make.
4   See note to Form B20.13 at para **[220.62]**.

[235.27]

Name and arms clause
9.   Provided nevertheless that every person who under the trusts aforesaid (including the divesting limitations in this clause contained) shall become entitled in possession to the principal estate as tenant for life or contingently on attaining 21 years or absolutely and shall not then use[1] the name and arms of [*testator's family name*] shall within one year thereafter (or if a minor within one year after attaining majority) endeavour to procure the Royal Licence to take

such name either alone or suffixed (but not prefixed) to his or her previous surname and to use such arms either alone or quartered with his or her own arms and if such application be successful shall thenceforth use such name and arms for all purposes and in default of compliance with this condition[2] the trusts hereinbefore declared in favour of such person shall determine and become void as if such person (being a person entitled to a life interest or contingently on attaining 21 years) were then dead or (being a person otherwise entitled to an absolute interest) had died before attaining the age of 21 years provided always that if such person be under such trusts only tenant for life then during the rest of his of her life the principal estate shall be held by my trustees upon trust to receive the rents and profits thereof for the benefit of the person or persons who under the trusts following the said trust for such tenant for life hereinbefore contained would for the time being be entitled to the possession of the principal estate but for the trust for such tenant for life.

1   As to using a name, see *Re Drax, Dunsany v Sawbridge* (1906) 75 LJ Ch 317. See also as to disuse of a name, Vol 1, para **[35.43]** and the cases there cited. As to the effect of a 'name and arms' clause without a gift over, see *Re Evans's Contract* [1920] 2 Ch 469, and see generally, Vol 1, paras **[35.39]–[35.44]**. For an alternative precedent see Form B6.18 at para **[206.27]**.

2   If the clause goes on to prohibit disuse, it may be void for uncertainty: *Re Lewis' Will Trust, Whitelaw v Beaumont* [1951] 2 TLR 1032; *Re Bouverie, Bouverie v Marshall* [1952] Ch 400, [1952] 1 All ER 408; *Re Wood's Will Trusts, Wood v Donnelly* [1952] Ch 406, [1952] 1 All ER 740, but the present tendency is to hold such a clause certain; see *Re Howard's Will Trusts, Levin v Bradley* [1961] Ch 507, [1961] 2 All ER 413, and *Re Neeld, Carpenter v Inigo-Jones* [1962] Ch 643, [1962] 2 All ER 335, where all the authorities are considered, and see also *Re Neeld, Inigo-Jones v Inigo-Jones (No 3)* [1969] 2 All ER 1025, [1969] 1 WLR 988.

[235.28]

Gift of maintenance fund

10.   (1)   In this clause the following expressions have the following meanings, namely—

(a)   'the heritage trustees' means such persons as my trustees may appoint and the Inland Revenue may approve pursuant to paragraph 2(1)(b) of Schedule 4;[1]

(b)   'the maintenance fund' means the fund so defined in subclause (2) hereof;

(c)   'the vesting day' means the day on which the principal estate shall vest in a beneficiary absolutely under the trusts declared by clause 6 hereof;

(d)   'the heritage period' means the period commencing on my death and expiring on the later to occur of the following two events:
   (i)   the sixth anniversary of the day immediately following my death,[2] and
   (ii)   the vesting day[3];

(e)   'the Act' means the Inheritance Tax Act 1984;

(f)   'Schedule 3' and 'Schedule 4' mean Schedule 3 and Schedule 4 respectively to the Act;

(g)   'the heritage property' means so much of the mansion house and the settled chattels as shall for the time being from time to time during the heritage period be qualifying property[4] within the meaning of paragraph 3(2) of Schedule 4;

(h) 'the heritage bodies' means and includes:
   (i)   the bodies mentioned in Schedule 3,[5] and
   (ii) any body established for exclusively charitable purposes which is a
         qualifying charity within the meaning of paragraph 3(4) of
         Schedule 4.[6]

(2)   For the purpose of maintaining repairing and preserving the heritage
property I bequeath to the heritage trustees free of tax[7] the sum of [£2,000,000]
with interest thereon from the date of my death until the appropriation thereof or
of investments thereto at the rate of [six] per cent per annum[8] upon trust to
invest the said sum in or upon any of the investments hereinafter authorised and
to hold such investments and the investments for the time being representing the
same (hereinafter called 'the maintenance fund') upon the trusts hereinafter
declared and contained And for the purpose aforesaid my trustees shall as soon
as reasonably possible after my death and in any event within two years of my
death[9] apply to the Inland Revenue[10] for a direction under paragraph 1 of
Schedule 4 in relation to the bequest hereby made Provided that if no such
direction shall be given the bequest made by this clause shall be null and void
and the said sum of [£2,000,000] shall be deemed to have devolved on my death
free of tax[11] as part of my principal estate.

(3)   The heritage trustees shall stand possessed of the maintenance fund and the
income thereof upon the trusts and with and subject to the powers and provisions
following:

(a) the heritage trustees shall stand possessed of the maintenance fund upon
    trust during the heritage period to apply all or so much of the income
    thereof (including all income thereof accruing after my death) as may be
    required for the maintenance repair or preservation of or making
    provision for public access to the heritage property (by whomsoever the
    same may from time to time be owned and on whatever trusts the same
    may from time to time be held) or for defraying the expenses of the
    heritage trustees in relation to the maintenance fund;

(b) if at any time or times during the heritage period the income of the
    maintenance fund or some part thereof for any reason cannot be applied
    in accordance with paragraph (a) hereof the heritage trustees shall pay
    the same to all or any one or more of the heritage bodies and if more than
    one in such shares as the heritage trustees in their absolute discretion
    shall think fit;

(c) notwithstanding the foregoing trusts the heritage trustees shall have
    power during the accumulation period to accumulate the whole or any
    part or parts of the income of the maintenance fund by investing the
    same and the resulting income thereof in any of the investments hereby
    authorised and so that all such accumulations of income shall be held as
    a separate fund which shall be applied (as to both capital and income) at
    any time or times and from time to time during the heritage period and in
    any event not later than the expiration of the heritage period as if the
    same were income of the maintenance fund applicable under paragraphs
    (a) and (b) hereof;[12]

(d) notwithstanding the trusts and any exercise of the power aforesaid the
    trustees shall have power at any time or times and from time to time
    during the heritage period to raise any sum or sums [not exceeding in the

aggregate the sum of £[500,000]] out of the capital of the maintenance fund (not for this purpose including any accumulations of income) and apply the same for any of the purposes for which income is applicable under paragraph (a) hereof;

Provided always that the heritage trustees shall have power by deed to modify the foregoing trusts to such extent as may be necessary to secure the approval of the Inland Revenue pursuant to paragraph 2(1)(a)(i) of Schedule 4.[13]

(4)   For so long after the sixth anniversary of the day immediately following my death as the vesting day has not occurred the heritage trustees shall have power by deed or deeds to declare that as from the date of any such deed all or any part of the maintenance fund shall cease to be held on the trusts and with and subject to the powers set out in subclause (2) above and so that thereafter during the remainder of the heritage period the maintenance fund or such part thereof shall be held upon the trusts and with and subject to the powers and provisions applicable to the principal estate and as one fund therewith for all purposes.[14]

(5)   Subject as aforesaid the heritage trustees shall hold the maintenance fund upon the trusts and with and subject to the powers and provisions as are hereinbefore declared of and concerning the principal estate and as one fund therewith for all purposes.

(6)   The powers conferred on my trustees by this clause may be exercised before as well as after obtaining a grant of probate of this will and notwithstanding that the administration of my estate is not complete.[15]

1   The trustees must be approved by the Inland Revenue and must include a trust corporation, a solicitor, an accountant or a member of such professional body as they may allow in the case of the property concerned: ITA 1984, Sch 4, para 2(1)(b).
      The legislation refers to the Treasury but the Treasury's functions under Schedule 4 were transferred to the Revenue by the Finance Act 1985, s 95.
2   The minimum duration required for the trusts a maintenance fund is six years: ITA 1984, Sch 4, para 3(1)(a).
3   The heritage period is defined so as to last for six years or until the principal estate vests in a beneficiary absolutely under cl 6, whichever is the longer. During this period the maintenance fund will not be form part of the taxable estate of a beneficiary unless the power conferred by sub-cl (3) is exercised.
4   Property is qualifying property if designated under the ITA 1984, s 31 and if the requisite undertaking is given under s 30 (if conditional exemption is claimed) or under Sch 4, para 3(3) (if not).
5   The bodies mentioned in ITA 1984, Sch 3 are national heritage bodies such as the National Gallery and the British Museum.
6   A charity is a qualifying charity if it exists wholly or mainly for maintaining, repairing or preserving heritage property: ITA 1984, Sch 4, para 3(4).
7   This 'free of tax' formula is not strictly necessary as the gift will qualify as an exempt transfer under ITA 1984, s 27 if the Revenue give a direction: ITA 1984, Sch 4, para 1.
8   This is the rate of interest currently payable on legacies in an administration by the court: CPR Sch 1, RSC Ord 44, r 10.
9   The claim should ordinarily be made within 2 years: ITA 1984, s 27(1A).
10 See n 1 supra.
11 See Form C13.1, cl 2, n 1 at para **[235.5]**.
12 Although income accruing during the heritage period may be accumulated, it must be applied for heritage purposes: ITA 1984, Sch 4, para 3(1)(c).
13 This power is inserted in case the Revenue insist on a modification of the trusts as a condition of giving a direction pursuant to the ITA 1984, Sch 4, para 1.
14 This power enables the heritage trustees to determine the trusts after the minimum six-year period. The exercise of the power will trigger a tax charge under the ITA 1984, Sch 4, Pt II.

15 The trustees probably are probably entitled to exercise their powers before the grant of probate and before the administration is complete, but this provision removes any doubt on the point.

[235.29]

Contingent interests to carry intermediate income

11. I declare that whenever any beneficiary is entitled under the trusts of this my will to an interest in any portion or any fund or share of a fund contingently on attaining the age of [18/21] years or (in the case of females) previous marriage such portion or fund or share therein as the case may be shall carry the intermediate income except so far as such income or any part thereof is under the provisions hereof expressly otherwise disposed of and section 31 of the Trustee Act 1925 (as hereinafter modified) shall apply.[1]

1 It is advisable to include an express provision to this effect as general legacies do not as a rule carry the intermediate income under the LPA 1925, s 175 (Part G, para **[244.52]**). This could have adverse inheritance tax consequences.

[235.30]

Administration trusts of residue

12. [*As in cl 6 of* Form C13.1 *at para* **[235.9]**.]

[235.31]

Gifts made free of tax

13. [*As in cl 7 of* Form C13.1 *at para* **[235.10]**.]

[235.32]

Beneficial trusts of residue

14. My trustees shall hold my residuary estate—

(a) as to a 40 per cent share thereof as part of the principal estate settled by this my will;

(b) as to a further 30 per cent share thereof upon trust to add the same to the [W] trust fund as an accretion thereto;

(c) as to the remaining 30 per cent share thereof upon trust to add the same to the [L] trust fund as an accretion thereto.

[235.33]

Maintenance accumulation and advancement

15. (1) Section 31 of the Trustee Act 1925 (relating to accumulation and maintenance) shall apply in relation to the trusts hereby or by any codicil hereto declared as if:

(a) in paragraph (i) of subsection (1) of the said section the words 'as the trustees think fit' were substituted for the words 'as may in all the circumstances be reasonable'; and

(b) the proviso to the said subsection (1) were omitted.

(2)   Section 32 of the Trustee Act 1925 (relating to advancement) shall apply in relation to the said trusts as if the words 'one half of' were omitted from proviso (a) to subsection(1) thereof.

[Provided that the powers conferred by the said section (as hereby enlarged) shall not be exercisable in favour of any minor beneficiary hereunder otherwise than so as to cause such beneficiary to become immediately entitled to or to an interest in possession in the capital thereby paid or applied within the meaning of section 71(1)(a) of the Inheritance Tax Act 1984].[1]

(3)   Whenever my trustees shall have an obligation or discretion under the provisions of this will or any codicil hereto or under the general law to apply income or capital for the benefit of a minor beneficiary they may either pay the same without liability to account to his or her parent guardian or any other adult person with whom such beneficiary may be residing or to such beneficiary himself or herself if of the age of 16 years or more and so that the receipt of such parent guardian or other person or of such minor beneficiary shall be a full and sufficient discharge to my trustees for the income or capital so applied.[2]

1   The proviso is included in order to prevent the power prejudicing the application of the ITA 1984, s 71 (accumulation and maintenance trusts), but is probably unnecessary: see the Note on inheritance tax and the statutory power of advancement in B18 at para **[218.99]**. If accumulation and maintenance trusts of income are extended so as to continue beyond the age of 18 (see, eg Forms B18.12 and B18.13 at paras **[218.78]** and **[218.79]**), then 'minor beneficiary hereunder' should be amended to eg 'beneficiary hereunder who is under the age of [*n*] years' where *n* is the highest age at which an absolute interest or an interest in possession might be attained by any of the beneficiaries. 25 is the maximum age compatible with the ITA 1984, s 71 applying: see Part A, paras **[200.119]**–**[200.136]**. One particular disadvantage of including this proviso in the present context is that it will prevent the power being used to advance with the consent of the life tenant a fund of capital on accumulation and maintenance trusts for minor beneficiaries interested in remainder (because of the requirement that they take an absolute interest or an interest in possession).

2   A parent (with parental responsibility) and a guardian of a minor are empowered by the ChA 1989, s 3(3) (Part G, para **[244.119]**) to give a good receipt for the minor's property: see Vol 1, para **[9.42]**. The power in this subclause is wider in that it authorises the payment of income or capital to a parent who does not have parental responsibility, any adult with whom the minor is residing, and the minor himself or herself if 16 or over.

[235.34]

Administrative powers

16.   [*As in cl 9 of* Form C13.1 *at para* **[235.12]**.]

[235.35]

Timber and mineral rents[1]

17.   (1)   All the rent or royalties from any mining lease or licence of land held by my trustees shall be treated as income and none shall be apportioned to capital.

(2)   The net proceeds of sale of any timber which is cut and sold from any land held by my trustees shall be treated wholly as income.

1   See Form B20.12 at para **[220.61]** and the notes thereto.

[235.36]

Trustee liability

17.   [*As in cl 10(1) of* Form C13.1 *at para* **[235.13]**.]

[235.37]

Professional trustee charging clause

18.   [*As in cl 12 of* Form C13.1 *at para* **[235.15]**.]

[*Testimonium and attestation clause as in* Form C13.1 *at paras* **[235.16]** and **[235.17]**.]

C14 Wills with a foreign element

PRELIMINARY NOTE

[236.1]
Domicile. The forms in this work are for use by testators who have an English
domicile. Catering for the needs of testators with a foreign domicile is a
specialised topic and gives rise to fiscal and other considerations on which
specialist advice, including the advice of foreign lawyers, will usually be
required. However, some of the general considerations affecting testators with a
foreign domicile are mentioned below, even though forms for wills with a
foreign proper law, which are normally appropriate for testators with a foreign
domicile, are outside the scope of this work. Domicile is itself a rather technical
topic. For a discussion of the concept generally, see Vol 1, paras **[23.2]–[23.5]**,
and for a more extended discussion reference should be made to *Cheshire and
North's Private International Law* (13th edn), pp 139 et seq and Dicey and
Morris, *The Conflict of Laws* (13th edn), Vol 1, pp 107 et seq. Recent proposals
on the part of the Government to introduce legislation reforming and simplifying
the law of domicile have been shelved for the time being.

[236.2]
Fiscal domicile. The basic territorial scope of inheritance tax, subject to a
number of qualifications and exceptions, is that it is imposed on the worldwide
estate of someone who has a UK domicile, and on the UK property only of

someone who has a non-UK domicile (see, further, *Foster's Inheritance Tax*, J1.01). Even if someone has an actual domicile outside the UK, he will be treated as having a UK domicile for inheritance tax purposes if he has been domiciled in the UK within the preceding three years or has been resident in the UK for 17 out of the preceding 20 years of assessment ending with the year of assessment in which the relevant time falls: Inheritance Tax Act 1984 (ITA 1984), s 267, and see *Foster's Inheritance Tax*, J2.06. The position as to fiscal domicile and charges to inheritance tax (or foreign taxes of a similar sort) on the death or a transfer of value by someone with foreign domicile, nationality or residence, or who has property in a foreign country, can also be affected by one or more double taxation agreements which can, for example, define a 'treaty domicile'. See further *Foster's Inheritance Tax*, Division J5.

[236.3]
Persons with a foreign domicile. As mentioned above, forms which cater for testators who do not have a UK domicile are outside the scope of this work, but we would mention the following general points. Property situated outside the UK is 'excluded property' for inheritance tax purposes if an individual domiciled outside the UK (and not deemed to be domiciled in the UK under the ITA 1984, s 267: see para **[236.2]**) is beneficially entitled to it: ITA 1984, s 6(1). Settled property situated outside the UK which was settled by a settlor or testator who was not domiciled in the UK (or deemed to be so: see above) at the date of the settlement or death is also 'excluded property': s 48(3). Broadly speaking 'excluded property' escapes inheritance tax altogether and settled property which is 'excluded property' will escape tax regardless of the domicile and residence of the beneficiaries. It would therefore be quite possible for an individual who is not domiciled in the UK (and not deemed to be so domiciled under the ITA 1984, s 267: see para **[236.2]**), even if he lives in the UK, to make a will leaving his foreign estate on discretionary trusts for beneficiaries who live in the UK which avoid future inheritance tax charges. So long as the property remains situated outside the UK it will escape the periodic and exit charges which would otherwise apply (see B18 at paras **[218.8]–[218.15]** for these). A testator with a non-UK actual and fiscal domicile, at any rate if he has substantial property outside the UK, will usually be advised to make appropriate arrangements, either by way of inter vivos settlement or by will, which are governed by foreign law rather than to incorporate such arrangements in his English will. (If he were to make a will in English form it might possibly prejudice his status as a non-UK domiciliary.) A non UK-domiciled testator may of course own property in the UK which will be liable to inheritance tax in the normal way and may wish to make a will in English form disposing of such property. If so, he should use a commencement, such as that contained in Form B1.4 at para **[201.8]**, limiting the operation of his English will to his UK assets.

[236.4]
Spouses with different domiciles. Since the abolition of the wife's dependent domicile by the Domicile and Matrimonial Proceedings Act 1973, s 1 spouses have been able to have different domiciles from each other. If a case arises where one spouse has a UK domicile and the other has a foreign domicile, the unlimited inheritance tax exemption for inter-spouse transfers will apply only to

transfers by the non-domiciled spouse to the UK-domiciled spouse. Transfers by the UK-domiciled spouse to the non-domiciled spouse will be exempt only up to a limit of £55,000: ITA 1984, s 18(2). Lifetime transfers under which the non-domiciled spouse takes an absolute interest or an interest in possession will qualify as potentially exempt transfers and will fall out of charge if the donor spouse survives the transfer by seven years. The present amount of the limit on the spouse exemption for a transfer by someone with a UK domicile to his foreign domiciled spouse has been in force without increase with effect from 9 March 1982. There is sometimes a relevant double taxation convention which provides for a more generous exemption in some circumstances: see eg the Convention with the USA of 19 October 1978 (SI 1979/1454), art 8(4).

[236.5]
Foreign property of UK domiciliaries. This section contains forms for use by individuals who are domiciled and resident in England but who own property situate abroad. In all such cases, especially where the foreign property is of substantial value or includes land, advice should be sought from local lawyers. One possible problem is that the local law may impose restrictions on an individual's freedom to dispose of his property which would be given effect to under English conflict of laws rules, at any rate in the case of immovable property, and there may also be local fiscal considerations to be taken into account. The forms in this section must be regarded as tentative solutions which may well have to be adapted to the local law and practice.

Form C14.1 may be appropriate for use in cases where the testator owns substantial assets in a foreign jurisdiction and where it may be convenient to have a separate administration of those assets. The form provides for the appointment of a separate set of local executors to administer the foreign assets and remit the proceeds to the English executors. In such cases it may be more convenient for the testator to execute a separate will governed by the local law dealing exclusively with such assets. If so, an English will confined to his property in the UK or a will dealing with all his property except that situate in one or more particular jurisdictions may be preferred, in which case a commencement provision such as Form B1.4 at para **[201.8]** may be appropriate. However, before this is done the possible inheritance tax problem described at para **[236.8]** should be considered. The beneficial trusts of residue in Form C14.1 have no specific foreign element and others may be preferred: for alternatives see the forms in C2 and C3 at paras **[224.20]** et seq and **[225.9]** et seq.

Forms C14.2 and C14.3 are intended for use by couples who own a foreign holiday home which they wish to give to one of their children on the death of the survivor. As mentioned above, where foreign property is owned, especially immovable property, it will be prudent to take the advice of local lawyers as to the manner and extent to which it may be disposed of on death. It is possible, for example, that the local law has forced heirship rules which may be recognised and enforced by English law in relation to immovables in that territory which a deceased person with an English domicile owns at his death. It may also turn out to be desirable to make wills in appropriate foreign form dealing with the foreign property. Form C14.2 contemplates a situation where it is intended to make such a will. It contains a specific free of tax gift of the foreign property by the survivor of the couple which is designed to take effect pending the execution of the intended foreign wills. (Unless the donee is to pay the inheritance tax attributable to the property, the gift requires to be expressed to be free of tax: see para **[236.6]**.) The execution of the foreign wills will revoke the specific gift. In that event Form C14.2 provides for the donee to be given a tax-free legacy of a sum equal to the inheritance tax and any foreign taxes attributable to the foreign property. Form C14.3 closely corresponds with Form C14.2, the difference being that in relation to C14.3 it is assumed that the foreign wills have already been executed. C14.3 therefore contains no specific free of tax gift of the foreign property, but simply a legacy equal to the inheritance tax and local taxes on it.

[236.6]
Incidence of inheritance tax on foreign property and of foreign taxes of a similar nature. Inheritance tax on foreign property in a deceased person's estate is not a testamentary expense but is (in the absence of express directions to the contrary) payable out of the property to which it relates: see the Preliminary Note to B14 at paras **[214.59]** and **[214.60]**. A specific gift of foreign property will also be subject to any foreign estate or inheritance taxes payable in respect of that property, in the absence of an express direction to the contrary: *Re Matthews's Will Trusts, Bristow v Matthews* [1961] 3 All ER 869, [1961] 1 WLR 1415. However, although it seems that a pecuniary legacy payable out of a residuary estate which includes foreign property will (in the absence of an express contrary direction) bear inheritance tax so far as the legacy is to be regarded as paid out of the foreign property (see the Preliminary Note to B14 at para **[214.64]**), it also seems that such a legacy will not also (in the absence of an express contrary direction) bear any of any foreign estate taxes or duties which might be payable in respect of the foreign property (see *Peter v Stirling* (1878) 10 Ch D 279). It is important to make express 'free of tax' provision in relation to any specific gift of foreign property, or any pecuniary legacy payable out of a residuary estate which may include foreign property, if that is the testator's intention.

[236.7]
Inheritance tax and foreign liabilities and expenses. If a person has any liabilities to foreign resident persons, those liabilities will, for the purposes of inheritance tax, be regarded as deducted so far as possible from property outside the UK, unless they are payable in the UK or charged on property in the UK: ITA 1984, s 162(5). It is also Inland Revenue practice to deduct debts in a particular country primarily from property in that country. These are points to remember when estimating the inheritance tax on death likely to be attributable to particular foreign assets, or when advising on directions as to the incidence of inheritance tax. They can also be important in the case of a foreign domiciled testator with some property in the UK and some outside it, as they could affect the extent to which liabilities can be deducted from the taxable estate in the UK.

The expense of administering or realising assets outside the UK which are comprised in the estate of a deceased person can be deducted from their value for the purposes of the inheritance tax charge on them on that person's death, up to a limit of five per cent of their value, if the expense can be shown to be attributable to the situation of the property: ITA 1984, s 173.

[236.8]
Testators with a UK domicile and substantial foreign assets. If a person is domiciled in the UK and owns assets which may be subject to inheritance tax on his death and of which a high or significant proportion are foreign property, he should if possible make a single will disposing of all his property to the same beneficiaries and appoint either a single set of executors or foreign executors who will remit the net foreign assets to the UK executors (as in Form C14.1, cl 5 at para **[236.15]**). If there were separate wills and executors of the UK and foreign property, the UK executors might not be able to obtain probate without paying more inheritance tax on his worldwide estate than the total value of his UK estate, and without any certainty that they could recover any of this tax out of his foreign estate. The same point applies to a foreign-domiciled testator living in the UK, because he might by the time of his death have resided in the UK long enough to have a deemed UK domicile for inheritance tax purposes (see para **[236.2]**).

[236.9]

FORM C14.1:   Will of English-domiciled testator/testatrix owning property in England and in foreign country, appointing separate executors to administer foreign property with direction to remit the proceeds of the foreign estate to the English executors

NOTE

This form caters for the English-domiciled testator/testatrix whose dependants live in England but who owns property of significant value in a foreign jurisdiction as well as property in England (or elsewhere in the UK). It may well be difficult for English executors to exercise effective control and supervision over the administration of the foreign estate. This form caters for this difficulty by providing for the appointment of separate local executors to administer the foreign estate and remit the proceeds to the English executors. Such a device would normally be appropriate when the foreign estate is situate in a common law jurisdiction which recognises the office of executor, but it may not be suitable in other cases. The advice of lawyers practising in the particular jurisdiction should be taken. In the case of federal states, eg the United States, Canada and Australia, the relevant jurisdiction may be an individual state or province rather than the federal state itself.
    In this form the gifts to the testator's children are in favour of all his children without being confined to children of the marriage or named children. See the Preliminary Note to C2 at para **[224.10]** for the significance of this point.

[236.10]

Revocation clause and declaration of domicile
I [*name*] of [*address*] hereby revoke all former dispositions made by me and declare this to be my last will And I further declare that my domicile is English[1] and that my will is to be construed and to take effect according to English law[2] [and that all sums of money herein mentioned are stated and payable in sterling].[3]

1   A declaration by a testator to the above effect may be useful when, owing to the testator's birth or residence or the nature and location of his business interests, a reasonable doubt may arise as to his true domicile. Domicile is not, however, a mere question of intention, and such a declaration, if contradicted or unsupported by the actual facts, is inoperative: *Re Steer* (1858) 3 H & N 594; *Brunel v Brunel* (1871) LR 12 Eq 298; *Doucet v Geoghegan* (1878) 9 Ch D 441; *Bradford v Young* (1885) 29 Ch D 617; *Winans v A-G* [1904] AC 287; *Re Liddell-Grainger's Will Trusts, Dormer v Liddell-Grainger* [1936] 3 All ER 173. As to domicile generally see *Cheshire and North's Private International Law* (13th edn), pp 139 et seq and Dicey and Morris, *The Conflict of Laws* (13th edn), Vol 1, pp 107 et seq, especially at pp 119–120 with regard to the effect of declarations of this sort.

2   The general rule is that in the absence of any contrary indication the construction of a will of movables is governed by the law of the testator's domicile (*Re Cunnington, Healing v Webb* [1924] 1 Ch 68); it seems that the construction of a will of immovable property is also prima facie governed by the law of the domicile but subject to the constraints imposed by the local law: Dicey & Morris, *The Conflict of Laws* (13th edn), Vol 2, pp 1040–1041. This declaration resolves any possible doubt on this point in favour of English law. It should be noted, however, that the operation of such a declaration is confined to construction. The material or essential validity of any disposition of immovable property, eg the application of forced heirship rules, will depend on the local law: Dicey & Morris, Vol 2, pp 1039–1040.

3   References to currency in a will are prima facie to be construed in accordance with the law of the domicile: Dicey & Morris, *The Conflict of Laws* (13th edn), Vol 2, pp 1042–1045. Even so, difficulties can arise where a legacy expressed in 'pounds' is given to a beneficiary resident in a foreign jurisdiction that also denotes its money in 'pounds'. It is safer to make the position clear if legacies to non-residents are to be included.

[236.11]

Appointment of English executors and trustees

1.   (1)   I appoint my [wife/husband] [*name*] my solicitor [*name*] of [*address*] and my friend [*name*] of [*address*] to be the executors of this will for the purpose of administering and dealing with all my movable and immovable property[1] which is situate anywhere in the world at the time of my death except [*foreign country*][2] and for the purpose of receiving from my foreign trustees hereinafter appointed and administering the proceeds of property and any unsold property situate in [*foreign country*] which my foreign trustees are hereby directed to transfer to them and to be the trustees of this will for the purpose of executing the trusts hereby declared.[3]

(2)   I declare that in this will the expression 'my trustees' shall mean and include my [wife/husband] and the said [*name*] and the said [*name*] and my personal representatives for the time being for the purposes of administering all such property as aforesaid and the trustees for the time being of this will.

1   It is better to use the private international law terms, viz movable and immovable, to distinguish between the property to be administered by the English executors and the property to be administered by the foreign executors.

2   It is contemplated in this form that the foreign executors will be appointed to administer property situate in a particular foreign jurisdiction rather than foreign property generally.

3   It is contemplated that the English executors alone will become trustees of the trusts declared by the will.

[236.12]

Appointment of foreign executors

2.   (1)   I appoint [*name*] of [*address*] and [*name*] of [*address*][1] to be the executors of this will for the purpose of administering all my movable and immovable property which is situate in [*foreign country*] at the time of my death.[2]

(2)   I declare that in this will the expression 'my foreign trustees' shall mean and include the said [*name*] and the said [*name*] and my personal representatives for the time being for the purpose of administering all such foreign property as aforesaid.

1   It is contemplated that individuals will be appointed as executors to administer the foreign property. It may be possible to appoint a corporate trustee, eg a trust corporation or a locally incorporated trust company. This will depend on the local law. Although a trust corporation can take a grant of probate in England and Wales (see the Supreme Court Act 1981, s 115), this may not be the case in the foreign jurisdiction. For cases on the remuneration of foreign corporate trustees see *Re Sandys' Will Trusts, Sandys v Kirton* [1947] 2 All 302, CA, and *Re Northcote's Will Trusts, Northcote v Northcote* [1949] 1 All ER 442.

2   See n 2 to cl 1 of this form at para **[236.11]**.

[236.13]

Gift of personal chattels to spouse

3.   (1)   I give to my [wife/husband] all my personal chattels as defined by section 55(1)(x) of the Administration of Estates Act 1925[1] not otherwise effectually disposed of hereby or by any codicil hereto.

(2)   If my [wife/husband] does not survive me then I give the said chattels free of tax[2] to such of my children as shall survive me and if more than one in equal shares according to value and in the event of any dispute as to the value or distribution of such chattels the decision of my trustees shall be final and I declare that section 33 of the Wills Act 1837 shall not apply to the foregoing gift.[3]

1   See Part G, para **[246.52]** for the wording of this definition, and for further discussion of the meaning of 'personal chattels' see Vol 1, para **[64.44]**.

2   The words 'free of tax' are included in case any of the chattels are outside the UK at the testator's death, and thus subject to tax in the absence of a direction to the contrary. See the Preliminary Note to B14 at para **[214.63]** and the definition of 'free of tax' in cl 7 of this form at para **[236.17]**.

3   See Part G, para **[244.34]** for this provision, and Vol 1, paras **[47.10]–[47.19]**. Section 33 would provide substitution of issue for a child who predeceases the testator, and is excluded because it would be impractical to administer a trust for minors of a share of chattels.

[236.14]

Gift of legacies

4.   I give the following pecuniary legacies free of tax:[1]

(a)   to [*name*] the sum of £——;
(b)   to [*name*] the sum of £——;
(c)   to [*name*] the sum of £——.

1   These pecuniary legacies are declared to be 'free of tax' to take account of the real possibility that they may be payable out of a residuary estate which includes property situated outside the UK, with the consequence that the legacies might without this declaration be liable to bear their own inheritance tax so far as payable out of that property: see the Preliminary Note to B14 at para **[214.64]**. The expression 'free of tax' is employed here in conjunction with the definition and direction as to payment in cl 7 of this form at para **[236.17]**.

[236.15]

Gift of foreign property to foreign trustees with direction to convert and transmit proceeds to English trustees

5.   (1)   I give to my foreign trustees all my movable and immovable property[1] which is situate in [*foreign country*] at the time of my death (hereinafter called my 'foreign estate') to administer the same in accordance with this clause.

(2)   My foreign trustees shall hold so much of my foreign estate as shall not consist of money upon trust to sell the same with full power to postpone the sale thereof without being responsible for loss and to pay out of the moneys to arise from such sale and any ready moneys comprised in my foreign estate all taxes and duties due in respect of my foreign estate in [*foreign country*] all debts due to persons resident in [*foreign country*] and all expenses of the realisation and administration of my foreign estate.²

(3)   I declare that in the administration of my foreign estate my foreign trustees shall have and may exercise all such powers of administration (including powers of charging) as are conferred on my trustees by this will or the general law and that all such other administrative provisions as are applicable hereunder or under the general law in relation to the residue of my estate shall apply in relation to my foreign estate.

(4)   My foreign trustees shall hold the residue of all such moneys as aforesaid and all parts of my foreign estate for the time being unsold and the net income thereof (after deducting therefrom all liabilities properly payable thereout whether on account of taxes duties or otherwise) upon trust to transfer the same to my trustees to hold the same as hereinafter provided.

1   See n 1 to cl 1(1) of this form at para **[236.11]**.
2   For the limited right to deduct such expenses for inheritance tax purposes, see the Preliminary Note at para **[236.7]**.

[236.16]

Administration trusts of residue¹

6.   (1)   I give all my property not hereby or by any codicil hereto otherwise effectively disposed of [((including any entailed or other property over which I shall have at my death a general power of disposition by will)]¹ to my trustees to hold on the trusts set out below with power at their discretion to sell all or any of it as and when they think fit.²

(2)   My trustees shall pay my funeral and testamentary expenses³ and debts and any legacies given by this will or any codicil hereto out of such property or its proceeds and shall have a discretion as to how such payments shall be borne as between capital and income.⁴

(3)   Subject as above my trustees shall hold such property and the assets from time to time representing the same (hereinafter called 'my residuary estate') on the trusts set out below and shall invest all money comprised in such property or arising from its sale in any of the investments hereby authorised with power to change such investments into any others hereby authorised.

(4)   In the administration of my estate and the execution of the trusts of this will or of any codicil to it:

(a)   my trustees shall treat all income as accruing on the date on which it becomes payable regardless of the period in respect of which it shall have accrued and shall not make any statutory apportionment of the same;⁵ and

(b)   none of the equitable rules of apportionment between capital and income shall apply in any circumstances whatever.⁶

1   See para **[230.7]**, n 1.
2   See para **[230.7]**, n 2.
3   See para **[230.7]**, n 3.

4   See para **[230.7]**, n 4.
5   See para **[230.7]**, n 5.
6   See para **[230.7]**, n 6.

[236.17]

Gifts made free of tax

7.   Any specific gift or pecuniary or general legacy made or given by this will or any codicil hereto which is expressed to be 'free of tax' shall be free from the payment of any inheritance tax or foreign tax or duty payable on or by reason of my death to which such gift or legacy would otherwise be subject and such inheritance tax or foreign tax or duty shall be paid out of my residuary estate.[1]

1   Testamentary expenses will include inheritance tax on UK free estate, including real property, but not on foreign property of any description: ITA 1984, s 211(1) (Part G, para **[246.83]** and see the Preliminary Note to B14 at paras **[214.59]** and **[214.60]**). Accordingly, it is essential that any specific gift of foreign property and any pecuniary legacies should be expressly declared to be free of tax if that is the intention. In this form chattels are given 'free of tax' (the term is defined in cl 7) in case any of them are situated abroad, and pecuniary legacies are given 'free of tax' because residue is likely to include foreign property. See generally the Preliminary Note to B14 at para **[214.71]**. See the Preliminary Note at para **[236.6]** for the incidence of foreign estate tax or duty.

[236.18]

Beneficial trusts of residue

8.   My trustees shall hold my residuary estate:

(a)   upon trust to pay the income thereof to my [wife/husband] during [her/his] life;

(b)   Provided that my trustees shall have power in their absolute discretion from time to time so long as my [wife/husband] is entitled to be paid the income of all or any part of the capital of my residuary estate (or would be so entitled if such capital yielded income) to pay transfer or apply the whole or any part or parts of such capital[1] to [her/him] or for [her/his] benefit in such manner as they shall in their absolute discretion think fit;

(c)   subject as aforesaid upon trust as to both capital and income for all or such one or more exclusively of the others or other of my children or remoter issue at such times and if more than one in such shares and with such trusts and powers (including trusts and powers conferring a power or discretion on my trustees or any other person or persons as to the disposition of capital or income) and such provisions (including provisions for the accumulation of income during any period permitted by law and including administrative provisions of whatever nature) and generally in such manner as my [wife/husband] shall by deed revocable or irrevocable or by will or codicil appoint;

(d)   subject as aforesaid upon trust for such of my children[2] as survive me if more than one in equal shares;

(e)   Provided always that if any child of mine dies (or has already died) in my lifetime leaving a child or children living at my death who attain the age of [25/21/18] years such child or children shall take if more than one equally between them the share which his her or their parent would have taken had such parent survived me;

(f)   Provided further that no child of mine who or whose children shall take by virtue of any such appointment as aforesaid shall unless my [wife/husband] so directs share in the unappointed part of my residuary estate without bringing the part appointed into hotchpot and accounting therefor;

(g) subject as aforesaid upon trust for the children of my deceased brother [*name*] living at my death and the children then living of any then deceased child of my said brother who whether children or children of children attain the age of [25/21/18] years in equal shares if more than one but so that the children of any then deceased child of my said brother shall take (if more than one equally between them) only the share which their parent would have taken had such parent lived to attain a vested interest; and

(h) subject as aforesaid upon the trusts upon which the same would be held at my death if I had died possessed thereof intestate domiciled in England and Wales and without having married or had issue.[3]

1   There are two reasons for restricting the power to capital in which the spouse has an interest in possession: first, to ensure that the power is not exercisable if there is a divorce and the primary trust fails; and second, to ensure that the power ceases to be exercisable if the spouse assigns or surrenders his or her life interest. See the Preliminary Note to C2 at paras **[224.12]–[224.19]**.

2   See the Note to this form at para **[236.9]**.

3   In some cases it may be appropriate to ascertain the class of next-of-kin at some other time, eg the death of the spouse if surviving, so as to confine the gift to the kin then living. There is no objection to so doing: see *Hutchinson v National Refuges for Homeless and Destitute Children* [1920] AC 795, [1920] All ER Rep 701.

[236.19]

Maintenance, accumulation and advancement[1]

9. (1) Section 31 of the Trustee Act 1925 (relating to accumulation and maintenance) shall apply in relation to the trusts hereby or by any codicil hereto declared as if:

(a) in paragraph (i) of subsection (1) of the said section the words 'as the trustees think fit' were substituted for the words 'as may in all the circumstances be reasonable'; and

(b) the proviso to the said subsection (1) were omitted.

(2) Section 32 of the Trustee Act 1925 (relating to advancement) shall apply in relation to the said trusts as if the words 'one half of' were omitted from proviso (a) to subsection (1) thereof [provided that the powers conferred by the said section (as hereby enlarged) shall not be exercisable in favour of any minor beneficiary hereunder otherwise than so as to cause such beneficiary to become immediately entitled to or to an interest in possession in the capital thereby paid or applied within the meaning of section 71(1)(a) of the Inheritance Tax Act 1984].[2]

(3) Whenever my trustees shall have an obligation or discretion under the provisions of this will or any codicil hereto or under the general law to apply income or capital for the benefit of a minor beneficiary they may either pay the same without liability to account to his or her parent guardian or any other adult person with whom such beneficiary may be residing or to such beneficiary himself or herself if of the age of 16 years or more and so that the receipt of such parent guardian or other person or of such minor beneficiary shall be a full and sufficient discharge to my trustees for the income or capital so applied.[3]

1   For alternative provisions relating to maintenance and advancement see Forms B18.11 to
     B18.23 and the notes thereto at paras **[218.77]–[218.84]** and **[218.103]–[218.107]**.
2   The proviso is included in order to prevent the power prejudicing the application of the ITA
     1984, s 71 (accumulation and maintenance trusts), but is probably unnecessary: see the Note on
     inheritance tax and the statutory power of advancement in B18 at para **[218.99]**. See also Form
     C11.1, cl 5(2), n 2 at para **[233.20]**. For the reasons there given this proviso could be
     particularly restrictive for the purposes of the present form, ie where the power of advancement
     applies to the trusts in remainder upon a life interest.
3   A parent (with parental responsibility) and a guardian of a minor are empowered by the ChA
     1989, s 3(3) (Part G, **[244.119]**) to give a good receipt for the minor's property: see Vol 1,
     para **[9.42]**. The power in this subclause is wider in that it authorises the payment of income or
     capital to a parent who does not have parental responsibility, any adult with whom the minor is
     residing, and the minor himself or herself if 16 or over.

[236.20]

Administrative powers[1]
10.   (1)   In this clause where the context so admits:

(a)   the expression 'land' includes buildings and estates interests or rights of
       any kind in or over land; and
(b)   during the administration of my estate the expression 'beneficiary'
       includes any person who would be a beneficiary if such administration
       had been completed and the expression 'beneficially interested' and
       references to income of any asset being payable or capable of being paid
       to or for the benefit of a beneficiary shall be construed accordingly.

(2)   None of the powers or provisions contained in subclause (3) below of
this clause shall be capable of being exercised or operating in any manner such
that if such power or provision were capable of being so exercised or so
operating the existence of the same would either:

(i)   prevent any person who would in the absence of such power or provision
        have been entitled to an interest in possession (within the meaning of
        Part III of the Inheritance Tax Act 1984) in any property from being
        entitled to such interest; or
(ii)   prevent section 71 of the Inheritance Tax Act 1984 from applying to any
        property to which in the absence of such power or provision the said
        section 71 would have applied.

(3)   In the administration of my estate and the execution of the trusts hereof
or of any codicil hereto my trustees shall have the following powers in addition
to those conferred by law but subject to the last foregoing subclause:

(a)   power to invest moneys sell assets and change investments with the
       unrestricted freedom of choice and powers of disposition and acquisition
       of a sole beneficial owner with in particular power to make unsecured
       loans, acquire non-income yielding assets, and purchase land anywhere
       in the world or chattels for any purpose including occupation or
       enjoyment in kind by a beneficiary under the power set out below;
(b)   power to delegate all or any of their investment powers to a professional
       investment manager or managers whether individual or corporate and
       whether or not also a nominee holder of assets for my trustees (and who
       may be or include one or more of my trustees or the beneficiaries
       hereunder) upon such terms as to remuneration and otherwise (including

terms authorising self-dealing or providing for the limitation of the liability of the investment manager or managers) as my trustees think fit and section 22 of the Trustee Act 2000 shall not apply;[4]

(c)   power to vest or register any property in any person or persons whether individual or corporate and whether or not an investment manager to whom powers have been delegated under the foregoing power (and who may be or include one or more of my trustees or the beneficiaries hereunder) as nominee or nominees for my trustees upon such terms as to remuneration or otherwise (including terms authorising self-dealing or providing for the limitation of the liability of the nominee) as my trustees think fit and section 22 of the Trustee Act 2000 shall not apply;[5]

(d)   power to borrow money with or without giving security and on such terms as to interest and repayment and otherwise as my trustees may think fit for any purpose connected with the administration of my estate or the trusts declared herein or in any codicil hereto (including investment) and no lender from whom my trustees borrow money in purported exercise of this power shall be concerned to enquire as to the propriety amount or purpose of any such borrowing;[6]

(e)   power to lend money to a beneficiary to whom any of the income of such money is payable or to whom or for whose benefit any income of such money is capable of being paid or applied in exercise of a discretion (or who would be such a beneficiary if such money yielded income) and to do so at a full or concessionary rate of interest or interest free;[7]

(f)   all the powers of an absolute owner in relation to any land (wherever situated) held by them;[8]

(g)   power to apply capital held on the same trusts as any land (or which would be so held if the administration of my estate had been completed) in the improvement of such land and to apply such capital or the income of such capital on the repair or maintenance of such land;[9]

(h)   power to permit any beneficiary to have the beneficial occupation use or enjoyment in kind of any land or chattel or other tangible property on such terms as to repair insurance or payment of outgoings by the beneficiary or otherwise howsoever as my trustees think fit Provided that the foregoing power shall only be exercisable and such permission to occupy or enjoy in kind may only continue in the following circumstances:

(i)   so long as any of the income of such land chattel or other tangible property is payable to such beneficiary or capable of being paid or applied to him or for his benefit in exercise of a discretion (or would be so payable or capable of being so paid or applied if such land chattel or other property yielded income),

(ii)   in the case of land, so long as for the time being the occupation thereof by such beneficiary is compatible with any statutory rights of occupation of any other beneficiary or beneficiaries;[10]

(i)   power to exercise all the powers of appropriation (and other incidental powers) conferred by statute on a personal representative without the necessity of obtaining any consents and notwithstanding that one or more of my trustees may be beneficially interested in the exercise of such power.[11]

1   See para **[230.11]**, n 1.
2   See para **[230.11]**, n 2.
3   See para **[230.11]**, n 3.
4   See para **[230.11]**, n 4.
5   See para **[230.11]**, n 5.
6   See para **[230.11]**, n 6.
7   See para **[230.11]**, n 7.
8   See para **[230.11]**, n 8.
9   See para **[230.11]**, n 9.
10 See para **[230.11]**, n 10.
11 See para **[230.11]**, n 11.

[236.21]

Trustee liability

11.   (1)   My trustees shall not be liable for any act or default of any investment manager or nominee employed in good faith to manage or hold assets of my estate nor for any act or default of any beneficiary having the occupation use or enjoyment of property in kind.[1]

(2)   Section 11(1) of the Trusts of Land and Appointment of Trustees Act 1996 (consultation with beneficiaries) shall not apply to the exercise by my trustees of any of their powers in relation to land subject to the trusts hereof.[2]

1   This makes it clear that the trustees are not liable for the defaults of others who may have possession or control of trust property. For a wider form of indemnity, see eg Form B21.12 at para **[221.16]**.
2   The requirement that trustees of land in exercise of any function relating to land subject to the trust consult with beneficiaries of full age beneficially entitled to an interest in possession in the land can be excluded: see the TLATA 1996, s 11(2)(a) (Part G, para **[246.97]**).

[236.22]

Professional trustee charging clause

12.   Any of my trustees being a professional or business man may charge and be paid all usual professional and other proper charges for business transacted acts done advice given and time spent by him or his firm in connection with the administration of my estate or in connection with the trusts hereof including acts which a personal representative or trustee not being in any profession or business could have done personally.

[236.23]

Testimonium and attestation clause

IN WITNESS whereof I have hereunto set my hand this —— day of —— 20—
—.

SIGNED by the above-named [testator/testatrix]as [his/her] last will in the presence of us both present at the same time who at [his/her] request and in [his/her] presence and in the presence of each other have signed our names below as witnesses:

[Signature of testator/testatrix]

[Signatures, addresses and descriptions of witnesses]

[236.24]

FORM C14.2:   Reciprocal wills of English-domiciled couple who own foreign holiday home and who intend to execute foreign wills giving the home to their son on the death of the survivor, leaving their estates to each other with the survivor making a tax-free gift of holiday home to the son (with a tax-free legacy equal to the amount of the inheritance tax on the home in the event that the foreign wills are executed), giving the daughter a compensating legacy and leaving residue to the son and daughter equally

NOTE

The ownership of foreign holiday homes is becoming increasingly common. This form is intended to cater for a couple who own such a home and intend that it should devolve on the death of the survivor on one of their children. Clients in the position of such a couple should be advised to take the advice of a local lawyer with a view to making wills in local form. (It is particularly important in the case of immovable property to establish whether there are any relevant forced heirship rules under the local law and whether English law would give effect to them where the property is owned by an English domiciliary.) This form contemplates that local wills will in due course be made revoking and replacing the specific gift of the house, but provides in the meantime for a specific free of tax gift of the holiday home to the son. (Foreign property prima facie bears its own inheritance tax, and for most purposes also bears any foreign estate or inheritance taxes on it: see the Preliminary Note at para **[236.6]**.) The free of tax gift of the home will be revoked by the foreign wills when they are made and the form provides in that event for the gift to the son of a tax-free legacy of the amount of the inheritance tax and any local taxes which would otherwise be payable by him.

[236.25]

Revocation clause

I [*name*] of [*address*] hereby revoke all former testamentary dispositions made by me and declare this to be my last will.

[236.26]

Gift of estate to spouse and appointment of spouse as sole executrix/executor

1.   If my [wife/husband] shall survive me [by the period of one month][1] then subject to the payment thereout of my funeral and testamentary expenses and debts I give all my estate of whatever nature and wherever situate to my [wife/husband] [*name*] and appoint [her/him] to be the sole [executrix/executor] hereof.

1   See generally the Preliminary Note to C2 at paras **[224.1]–[224.6]** for the significance of these words.

[236.27]

Alternative provisions

2.   If my [wife/husband] shall fail to survive me [by the period aforesaid][1] then the following provisions of this will shall have effect.

1   See para **[236.26]**, n 1.

[236.28]

Appointment of executors and trustees

3.   I appoint my son [*name*] my daughter [*name*] and [*name*] of [*address*] (hereinafter together called 'my trustees' which expression shall include my personal representatives for the time being and the trustees for the time being hereof) to be the executors and trustees of this will.

[236.29]

Gift of chattels to son and daughter

4.   I give free of tax[1] all my personal chattels (as defined by section 55(1)(x) of the Administration of Estates Act 1925)[2] not otherwise effectually disposed of hereby or by any codicil hereto or by any other will of mine to my said son and my said daughter in equal shares and I declare that section 33 of the Wills Act 1837 shall not apply to the foregoing gift.[3]

1   See Form C14.1, cl 3, n 2 at para **[236.13]**. The testator may have chattels outside the UK which do not form part of the contents of the holiday home and thus are not comprised in the specific gift of those contents to the son.
2   See Part G, para **[246.52]** for the wording of this definition, and for further discussion of the meaning of 'personal chattels', see Vol 1, para **[64.44]**.
3   See Form C14.1, cl 3, n 3 at para **[236.13]**.

[236.30]

Gift of legacy to daughter

5.   If a gift to my said son of the holiday home referred to below is effectually made by this will or by any further will of mine then I give to my said daughter a pecuniary legacy of £—— free of tax.[1]

1   See Form C14.1, cl 4, n 1 at para **[236.14]** as regards the 'free of tax' provision. As the legacy is intended to make up for the daughter not getting the holiday home, it is made contingent on the gift to the son taking effect.

[236.31]

Specific gift of foreign holiday home and legacy of the inheritance tax on it to son

6.   (1)   I give to my said son free of tax[1] all my interest in the family holiday home at [*address*] and the contents thereof[2] (hereinafter collectively called 'my foreign property').

(2)   Whereas I intend to make a will in foreign form giving my foreign property to my said [wife/husband] if [she/he] survives me [by the period of one month][3] and if [she/he] fails to survive me [by the said period] to my said son Now I declare that if I make such a will and the same (or any will in foreign form subsequently executed by me and containing the like gift of my foreign property) is a valid and subsisting will at the date of my death (and if my said [wife/husband] fails to survive me [by the said period]) then I give to my said son free of tax[4] a pecuniary legacy of an amount equal to the inheritance tax and any local taxes or duties payable in respect of my foreign property on or by reason of my death.[5]

1   A specific gift of foreign property prima facie bears its own inheritance tax and any foreign duties: see the Preliminary Note at para **[236.6]**. The 'free of tax' formula will exonerate the gift from all these liabilities: see Form C14.1, cl 7 at para **[236.17]** which is incorporated as cl 8 of this form.
2   For the effect of the gift of the contents of a property, see Vol 1, para **[63.1]**, n 1.

3   See n 1 to cl 1 of this form at para **[236.26]**.
4   See Form C14.1, cl 4, n 1 at para **[236.14]**.
5   If foreign wills are executed in the form contemplated, the son will receive the home under those wills and the inheritance tax and any local duties to which the property will be subject are given to him in the form of a tax free legacy. It is intended that whether cl 6(1) or cl 6(2) operates, the son will receive the home free of tax.

[236.32]

Administration trusts of residue
7.   [*As in cl 6 of* Form C14.1 *at para* **[236.16]**.]

[236.33]

Gifts made free of tax
8.   [*As in cl 7 of* Form C14.1 *at para* **[236.17]**.]

[236.34]

Beneficial trusts of residue
9.   (1)   My trustees shall hold my residuary estate upon trust for my said son and my said daughter in equal shares.

(2)   Provided that if either of my said son or my said daughter shall predecease me leaving a child or children me surviving who shall attain the age of [25/21/18] years[1] such child or children shall take if more than one equally between them the share of my residuary estate which his her or their parent would have taken had he or she survived me.

(3)   The trusts declared by the foregoing subclause hereof shall carry the intermediate income of my residuary estate and section 31 of the Trustee Act 1925 (as hereinafter modified) shall apply thereto.

(4)   Section 32 of the Trustee Act 1925 (as hereinafter modified) shall apply in relation to the said trusts.

1   The grandchildren will be lives in being for perpetuity purposes, so any age may safely be chosen.

[236.35]

Maintenance, accumulation and advancement
10.   [*As in cl 9 of* Form C14.1 *at para* **[236.19]**.]

[236.36]

Administrative powers
11.   [*As in cl 10 of* Form C14.1 *at para* **[236.20]**.]

[236.37]

Trustee liability
12.   [*As in cl 11 of* Form C14.1 *at para* **[236.21]**.]

[236.38]

Professional trustee charging clause
13.   [*As in cl 12 of* Form C14.1 *at para* **[236.22]**.]

[*Testimonium and attestation clause as in* Form C14.1 *at para* **[236.23]**.]

[236.39]

FORM C14.3:   Reciprocal wills of English-domiciled couple who own foreign holiday home and who have already executed foreign wills giving the home to their son on the death of the survivor, leaving their estates to each other with the survivor leaving a tax-free legacy to the son equal to the amount of the inheritance tax on the holiday home, giving the daughter a compensating legacy and leaving residue to the son and daughter equally

NOTE

The form corresponds closely with Form C14.2, the difference being that this form is intended for use after foreign wills making gifts of the foreign holiday home (and its contents) have been executed. It is assumed that there is no relevant restriction on the power to dispose of the property under the local law, and that the wills made under the local law are ones whereby the husband and wife each gives his or her interest in the property (and contents) to the other, subject to the same survivorship condition (if any) as in this will, and in the alternative gives it to their son if the gift to the other does not take effect. This form is thus for wills which do not deal with the foreign holiday home and no specific gift of the holiday home is included, but the will of the survivor gives a tax-free legacy to the son of an amount equal to the inheritance tax and any local taxes payable in respect of the holiday home if the gift of it in the foreign will to the son takes effect.

The holiday home is excluded from this will only to the extent that it is effectually disposed of under the foreign will, and so if the foreign will fails for some reason, this will will be effective to dispose of it.

[236.40]

Revocation clause

I [*name*] of [*address*] hereby revoke all former testamentary dispositions made by me save for my will made according to the law of [*name of foreign country*] dated [*date*] (hereinafter called 'my foreign will') and declare this to be my last will in respect of all movable and immovable property of mine which is situate anywhere in the world at the time of my death except for the property disposed of by my foreign will.

[236.41]

Gift of estate to spouse and appointment of spouse as sole executrix/executor

1.   If my [wife/husband] shall survive me [by the period of one month][1] then subject to the payment thereout of my funeral and testamentary expenses and debts I give all my estate of whatever nature and wherever situate other than property effectually disposed of by any other will of mine to my [wife/husband] [*name*] and appoint [her/him] to be the sole [executrix/executor] hereof.

1   See generally the Preliminary Note to C2 at paras **[224.1]**–**[224.6]** for the significance of these words.

[236.42]

Alternative provisions

2.   [*As in cl 2 of* Form C14.2 *at para* **[236.27]**.]

[236.43]

Appointment of executors and trustees
3.   I appoint my son [*name*] my daughter [*name*] and [*name*] of [*address*] (hereinafter together called 'my trustees' which expression shall include the executors or trustees for the time being of this will and any personal representatives of mine for the time being under letters of administration with this will annexed)[1] to be the executors and trustees of this will.

1   This definition is intended to exclude anyone who is a personal representative in respect of the foreign property. If the holiday home is in a civil law jurisdiction there may not be any personal representatives in respect of it.

[236.44]

Specific gift of chattels to son and daughter
4.   [*As in cl 4 of* Form C14.2 *at para* **[236.29]**.]

[236.45]

Gift of legacy to daughter
5.   If a gift to my said son of the holiday home referred to below is effectually made by my foreign will or by a further will of mine then I give to my said daughter a pecuniary legacy of £—— free of tax.[1]

1   See Form C14.1, cl 4, n 1 at para **[236.14]** on the significance of the 'free of tax' provision. As the legacy is supposed to make up for the daughter not getting the holiday home, it is made contingent on the gift of the holiday home to the son taking effect.

[236.46]

Gift to son of legacy equal to tax on foreign property[1]
6.   Whereas by my foreign will I have given my interest in the family holiday home at [*address*] and the contents thereof (hereinafter together called 'my foreign property') to my said [wife/husband] if [she/he] survives me [by the period of one month] and if [she/he] fails to survive me [by the said period] to my said son Now I declare that if my foreign will (or any will in foreign form subsequently executed by me and containing the like gift of my foreign property) shall be a valid and subsisting will at the date of my death (and if my said [wife/husband] fails to survive me [by the said period]) then I give to my said son free of tax[2] a pecuniary legacy of an amount equal to the inheritance tax and any taxes or duties payable in [*name of foreign country*] in respect of my foreign property on or by reason of my death.

1   This clause in effect reproduces the alternative gift contained in Form C14.2, cl 6(2) at para **[236.31]**.
2   See Form C14.1, cl 4, n 1 at para **[236.14]**.

[236.47]

Administration trusts of residue
7.   [*As in cl 6 of* Form C14.1 *at para* **[236.16]**.]

[236.48]

Gifts made free of tax
8.   [*As in cl 7 of* Form C14.1 *at para* **[236.17]**.]

Part C   Complete wills

[236.49]

Beneficial trusts of residue
9.   [*As in cl 8 of* Form C14.1 *at para* **[236.18]**.]

[236.50]

Maintenance accumulation and advancement
10.   [*As in cl 9 of* Form C14.1 *at para* **[236.19]**.]

[236.51]

Administrative powers
11.   [*As in cl 10 of* Form C14.1 *at para* **[236.20]**.]

[236.52]

Trustee liability
12.   [*As in cl 11 of* Form C14.1 *at para* **[236.21]**.]

[236.53]

Professional trustee charging clause
13.   [*As in cl 12 of* Form C14.1 *at para* **[236.22]**.]

[*Testimonium and attestation clause as in* Form C14.1 *at para* **[236.23]**.]

PART D

Codicils

D   Codicils

CORRECTING ERRORS

FORMS

REVIVAL AND REPUBLICATION

FORM

REVOCATION

FORM

PRELIMINARY NOTE

[237.1]
A codicil is a useful device for making changes to a will, such as a change of executors, or a change of the amount of a legacy. Great care should be taken, however, when drafting a codicil to ensure that it alters the will only to the required extent and that it does not affect other parts of the will. It should also be considered whether there are any consequential changes which need to be made to, eg the administration trusts of residue or the administrative provisions in the will, as a result of the main changes being made by the codicil. If a substantial amendment is to be made it may in most cases be preferable to execute a new will, and this will particularly be so if a significant reduction in the benefit given to a beneficiary is being made, as the beneficiary will be far less likely to find out what the testator's disposition in his favour was before the change was made if a completely new will is made.

[237.2]
Changes in the law since the date of a will may necessitate or make desirable changes to the provisions of the will. The Trusts of Land and Appointment of Trustees Act 1996 (TLATA 1996) (see Part G, para **[246.85]** et seq) and the Trustee Act 2000 (TrA 2000) (see Part G, para **[246.115]** et seq) in particular are two recent statutes making changes in the law which will have a bearing on a great many wills. It may be possible to incorporate such changes in a codicil, although again great care has to be taken to ensure that nothing is overlooked, and it may be preferable to make a new will. Also, some changes mean that

there is an opportunity to simplify the provisions of many wills—eg as a result of the TLATA 1996 trusts for sale may not need to be created, (see paras **[200.55]** and **[214.1]** et seq), or administrative powers or provisions as to occupation by beneficiaries could be excluded as they are adequately covered by the statutory provisions (see paras **[208.18]**, **[208.19]**, **[220.49]** et seq). Therefore, a new, simpler, will may well be preferable to a codicil in such circumstances.

[237.3]
However, certain changes made by the TLATA 1996 could be dealt with by codicil, eg:

(a) No new Settled Land Act 1925 (SLA 1925) settlements can be created on or after 1 January 1997 (see para **[200.52]**), so SLA 1925 forms which may have been used in a pre-1997 will should be revised. See Form D14 at para **[237.21]**.

(b) Entailed interests cannot be created after the commencement of the TLATA 1996 and any entailed interest purportedly granted thereafter will take effect as an absolute interest (see para **[200.53]**). Therefore, where an entail is purportedly created, it should be replaced with new trust provisions. See Form D14 at para **[237.21]**.

(c) Trustees of land now have all the powers of an absolute owner under TLATA 1996, s 6(1). If it was intended that the trustees' powers over land should be more restricted, express restriction should be made (see TLATA 1996, s 8(1)). See Form D14 at para **[237.21]**.

(d) The Law of Property Act 1925, s 28(1) has been repealed by the TLATA 1996 (see para **[200.60]**) so that a requirement of consent to a sale is no longer applied by statute to other powers. Therefore, a testator may wish to provide expressly for the requirement of consent to the exercise of some or all of the trustees' powers in respect of land, (see the TLATA 1996, s 8(2), which enables the exercise of the trustees' powers over land to be made subject to consents). Revision of the will is probably not required simply to maintain as effective an express requirement of a beneficiary's consent to exercise of one of the trustees' administrative powers. See Form D14 at para **[237.21]**.

(e) Beneficiaries under a trust who are of full age and collectively entitled to the whole beneficial interest have powers under the TLATA 1996, ss 19 and 20, to direct the retirement of trustees and appoint new trustees (see para **[221.39]**). These powers may be excluded (see TLATA 1996, s 21(5)), and a testator may indeed wish to exclude them in a trust created to protect the beneficiaries from their own improvidence. See Form D14 at para **[237.21]**.

(f) The doctrine of conversion is abolished by the TLATA 1996, s 3, in relation to trusts for sale, whether made before or after the commencement of the Act, with the consequence that land held on trust for sale is no longer regarded as personalty. (There is an exception for trusts for sale created by the wills of testators dying before the commencement of the Act: see para **[200.54]**). Therefore, in the rare case of a will which relies on the doctrine of conversion under a trust for sale for a particular disposition to be effective according to the testator's intention (eg which contains a gift of all personalty which is intended to include an undivided share of land), a revision of the will should be made.

(g) Statutory trusts for co-owners under the Law of Property Act 1925, ss 34 (tenants in common) and 36 (joint tenants), and of intestates' estates under the Administration of Estates Act 1925, s 33, cease to be trusts for sale and become trusts of land without any duty to sell (but with a power of sale) by virtue of the amendments to those sections made by the TLATA 1996, Sch 2 (see paras **[246.39I]** and **[246.39K]**). Therefore, where there is a specific gift of an undivided share in land phrased as a bequest of personalty, eg: 'I bequeath my interest in the proceeds of sale of Blackacre to X', and Blackacre is no longer held upon trust for sale, a simple affirmatory codicil should be made.

[237.4]

The principal changes brought about by the TrA 2000 are the introduction of a standard duty of care which will apply to trustees in the exercise of many of their powers, the creation of a new wider statutory power of investment to replace the limited power under the Trustee Investments Act 1961, new powers to appoint agents, nominees and custodians; to insure trust property; and to pay professional trustees (see paras **[220.12]**, **[220.36]**, **[220.51]**, **[221.15]** and **[221.42]**). The new powers generally apply to trusts whenever created, however, as under the present law the new powers will only apply to the extent that the will permits. Therefore, a testator who has already made his will might conceivably wish to exclude or restrict some of the new powers. This could be achieved by codicil. See, for example Form D15 at para **[237.22]**.

[237.5]

Each codicil which follows contains a confirmation of the will which it is altering, so far as that will is not altered by it. The confirmation of a will may influence the construction of the will, as in *Re Clarke, Sheldon v Redrup* [1942] Ch 434, [1942] 2 All ER 294, and see also Vol 1, paras **[20.4]** (effect of confirmation of wills by codicils) and **[22.3]** (effect of republication of wills). Before adding into a codicil a confirmation of the will, it is as well to go through the will and make sure that there are no gifts of which the donees have died or otherwise become incapable of taking under the provisions of the will.

[237.6]

New statutory rules affecting wills or the interpretation of them sometimes apply according to the date of death of the testator, and sometimes according to the date of making the will. Two important statutory provisions which only apply to wills made after they came into force are the Family Law Reform Act 1969 (FLRA 1969), s 15 and the Family Law Reform Act 1987 (FLRA 1987), s 1, extending the rights of illegitimate persons so that, among other things, a gift to a person or persons defined by relationship to someone else is presumed to include illegitimate persons (see Vol 1, paras **[72.10]–[72.14]**, and Part A, paras **[200.28]–[200.32]**, and the statutes are set out in Part G, paras **[245.37]** et seq and **[245.69]** et seq). However, each of these statutory provisions also provides that the subsequent confirmation of a will which was made before the statute came into force, by a codicil made after it came into force, does not have the effect of treating the will as made after it came into force (FLRA 1969, s 15(8): Part G, para **[245.39]** and FLRA 1987, s 19(7): Part G, para **[245.72]**). As a result, the confirmation of a will made before the FLRA 1987 came into force (on 4 April 1988), by a codicil made on or after 4 April 1988, will not by itself cause the construction of the will to be governed by the 1987 Act; if the will was made after 1969 it will continue to be governed by the FLRA 1969 (see FLRA 1987, Sch 3, para 9: Part G, para **[245.80]**), although the practical consequences of this are quite likely to be the same as they would be if the will was governed by the FLRA 1987, and if it was made before 1970 it will continue to be governed by the common law rules whereby illegitimate persons were presumed to be excluded in the absence of words to the contrary. To avoid possible uncertainties of construction where a codicil is being made to a pre-4 April 1988 will, particularly where it is a pre-1 January 1970 will, it is recommended that express provision should be made either excluding the statutory rule or rules introduced since the will was made, or else making them applicable (see further Part A, para **[200.30]**): see cl 3 of Form D1 at para **[237.8]** for an example.

[237.6A]
The TLATA 1996, s 11 imposes a duty on trustees of land in the exercise of any function relating to the land subject to the trust 'so far as practicable' to consult the beneficiaries of full age and beneficially entitled to an interest in possession, and so far as consistent with the general interest of the trust, to give effect to the wishes of those beneficiaries or (in the event of a dispute) the majority by value: see para **[220.58]**. Section 11 will apply to any trust created on or after 1 January 1997 unless expressly excluded (see s 11(2)(a): Part G, para **[246.97]**), but it does not apply to a will made before 1 January 1997 of a person who dies on or after that date (s 11(2)(b)). However, confirmation of a pre-1997 will by a codicil made on or after 1 January 1997 could have the effect of causing s 11 to apply. Exclusion of s 11 should therefore be considered in such a codicil.

[237.7]
The statutory rules of construction relating to adopted persons which have had effect from 1 January 1976 (they were introduced by the Children Act 1975 and consolidated into the Adoption Act 1976 as from 1 January 1988) apply to the will of a person dying on or after 1 January 1976 regardless of the date of execution of the will, so that a confirmation of a codicil can make no difference (see Vol 1, para **[75.4]** and the AA 1976, s 46(3): Part G, para **[245.64]**). The position is the same as regards the rules of construction relating to legitimated children contained in the Legitimacy Act 1976 (see Vol 1, para **[72.16]** and the Legitimacy Act 1976, s 10(3): Part G, para **[245.51]**). The Human Fertilisation and Embryology Act 1990 (HFEA 1990), ss 27 to 29, which came into force on 1 August 1991 and makes provision for who is to be treated as father and mother of a child produced by means (such as artificial insemination or in vitro fertilisation) regulated by the Act, seems to apply to dispositions made before or after the Act so that a post-Act confirmation of a pre-Act instrument will not bring these provisions into play; they will already apply (see Vol 1, para **[74.6]** and the HFEA 1990, s 29(3): Part G, para **[245.87]**). For the law relating to codicils generally, see Vol 1, para **[20.1]** et seq.

Changes in circumstances or wishes

[237.8]

FORM D1:   Codicil appointing an executor and trustee in substitution for an executor and trustee who has died; revocation of a gift of a one-fifth share of residue to a son by name, where such son has died without children, and gift of such share of residue to other children of testator

I [*testator*] of [*address*] declare this to be a [first] codicil to my will which is dated the —— day of ——.

WHEREAS

Recitals
(1)   By my said will I have appointed my son [*name*] to be an executor and trustee thereof together with my brother [*name*].
   (2)   By my said will I have directed my trustees to stand possessed of one-fifth of my residuary estate in trust for my said son absolutely.
   (3)   My said son died on —— without leaving any issue him surviving.

Revocation of appointment of son and appointment of a substitute
1.   Now I hereby appoint my friend [*name*] of [*address*] to be executor and trustee thereof in place of my said son and I declare that my said.will shall have effect as if the name of the said [*new trustee*] were substituted therein as an executor and trustee thereof for the name of my said son and I bequeath to the said [*new trustee*] a legacy of £—— if he accepts the office of [executor and] trustee.[1]
   2.   I hereby revoke the bequest to my said son of the said one-fifth share of my residuary estate and I direct my trustees to hold the same in trust for my children other than my said son as an accretion to their respective shares therein and upon the trusts in my said will declared of such shares and in the proportions which such respective shares bear to each other.[2]

Confirmation of will
3.   In all other respects I hereby confirm my said will[3] [and I hereby declare that [for the purposes of construing my said will and this codicil Family Law Reform Act 1987 shall apply] [my said will and this codicil shall be construed as if section 15(1) of the Family Law Reform Act 1969 and the Family Law Reform Act 1987 had not been enacted][4] [and I further declare that section 11(1) of the Trusts of Land and Appointment of Trustees Act 1996 (consultation with beneficiaries) shall not apply to the exercise by my trustees of any of their functions in relation to any land subject to the trusts of my said will].[5]

Testimonium and attestation clause
IN WITNESS whereof I have hereunto set my hand this —— day of —— 20——

SIGNED by the above-named [testator/testatrix] as a
codicil to [his/her] will dated [date] in the presence of us   } *[Signature of*
both present at the same time who at [his/her] request   *testator/testatrix]*
and in [his/her] presence and in the presence of each
other have signed our names below as witnesses:

[*Signatures, addresses and descriptions of two witnesses*]

1   What amounts to acceptance of the trusteeship is largely a question of fact, see *Re Sharman's Will Trusts, Public Trustee v Sharman* [1942] Ch 311, [1942] 2 All ER 74 and *Re Parry, Dalton v Cooke* [1969] 2 All ER 512, [1969] 1 WLR 614, and see generally Vol 1, para **[25.12]**. A distinction has been drawn between duties as an executor and those as a trustee and, as the duties as executor are commonly more arduous, it is usual to give a legacy conditionally on acceptance of the office executor as well as that of trustee.

2   When an executor-beneficiary has died and a new executor is appointed by codicil, care should be taken that the substitution does not affect beneficial interests. It is dangerous merely to substitute the name of the new executor for that of the old (*Re Freeman, Hope v Freeman* [1910] 1 Ch 681; *Re Percival, Boote v Dutton* (1888) 59 LT 21; *Re Mellor, Dodgson v Ashworth* (1912) 28 TLR 473. See also *Re Wilkins, Wilkins v Wilkins* [1920] 2 Ch 63. See further as to revocation of gifts, *Re Yates, Singleton v Povah* (1922) 128 LT 619. *Re Joseph, Pain v Joseph* [1908] 2 Ch 507; *Re Backhouse, Salmon v Backhouse* [1916] 1 Ch 65; *Choa Eng Wan v Choa Giang Tee* [1923] AC 469). The substitution of a new trustee by a codicil has been held to operate as a substitution of the new trustee as devisee in trust: *Re Turner* (1860) 2 De GF & J 527.

   A gift of property by codicil which is itself void for perpetuity will not revoke a gift of the same property in the will unless there is an express revocation provision to that effect: *Ward v Van der Loeff, Burnyeat v Van der Loeff* [1924] AC 653. Where the gift in the will is revoked the revocation will stand despite the invalidity of the gift in the codicil unless there is a contrary intention: see *Quinn v Butler* (1868) LR 6 Eq 225 at 227. A clause in the codicil which is ambiguous will not operate to revoke a gift in the will: *Re Wray, Wray v Wray* [1951] Ch 425, [1951] 1 All ER 375.

3   For the effect of this confirmation, see Preliminary Note at para **[237.5]**.
4   See Preliminary Note at para **[237.6]** and Part A, para **[200.30]**. One of these alternatives must be omitted.
5   See Preliminary Note at para **[237.6A]**.

[237.9]

FORM D2:   Codicil revoking settlement of a one-third share of testator's residuary estate on his sister, and giving such one-third share to a niece on the same trusts by reference

I [*testator*] of [*address*] declare this to be a [first] codicil to my will which is dated the —— day of ——.

   Whereas by my said will I have bequeathed a one-third share of my residuary estate upon certain trusts therein declared for my sister [*name*] and her children issue general appointees and next-of-kin. Now I hereby revoke such bequest and declare that my trustees shall stand possessed of such one-third share of my residuary estate upon trusts and with and subject to powers and provisions in favour of my niece [*name*] her children issue general appointees and next-of-kin similar in all respects to the trusts powers and provisions by my said will declared in favour of my said sister as if the name of my said niece were throughout my said will substituted for the name of my said sister in respect of the said share of residue. In all other respects I confirm my said will.[1]

IN WITNESS ETC.

[*Testimonium and attestation clause as in* Form D1 *at para* **[237.8]**.]

1   See Preliminary Note at paras **[237.5]**–**[237.6A]** and cl 3 of Form D1 at para **[237.8]**.

[237.10]

FORM D3:   Codicil on a gift or advance being made to a child

I [*testator*] of [*address*] declare this to be a [first] codicil to my will which is dated the —— day of ——.

WHEREAS

Recitals
(1)   By my said will my residuary estate (as therein defined) is to be held for my children in equal shares.
    (2)   On —— last I gave to my son [*name*] a sum of £—— upon condition that it was an advance of part of his share of my said residuary estate.[1]

Duty to account
1.   Now I hereby declare in distributing my residuary estate my trustees shall so distribute it that my said son [*name*] receives £—— [*the amount of the advance*] less than each of my other children sharing therein.

Interest
2.   I direct that the said sum of £—— shall not carry interest.[2]

Confirmation
3.   In all other respects I hereby confirm my said will.[3]

[*Testimonium and attestation clause as in* Form D1 *at para* **[237.8]**.]

1   It is always wise, if possible, for a testator to declare by will or codicil whether a lifetime gift is to adeem a testamentary gift or not, so as to avoid disputes: see, for example, *Re Cameron* [1999] Ch 386, [1999] 2 All ER 924.
2   The advance would normally carry interest from the date of death. As to accounting for hotchpot generally, see Vol 1, paras **[100.1]**–**[100.5]**.
3   See Preliminary Note at paras **[237.5]**–**[237.6A]** and cl 3 of Form D1 at para **[237.8]**.

[237.11]

FORM D4:   Codicil directing sums given to daughters on marriage to be brought into hotchpot

I [*testator*] of [*address*] declare this to be a [second] codicil to my will which is dated the —— day of ——.

Direction that sums given to daughters on marriage to be brought into hotchpot
1.   Whereas by my said will I have given the proceeds of sale of my residuary estate to my trustees upon trust for the benefit of all my children who shall be living at my death in equal shares to hold the same upon the trusts declared therein and whereas on the marriage of each of my two daughters [*name*] and [*name*] I transferred to each of them on such marriage a sum of £10,000. Now I hereby declare that in ascertaining the amount of the settled shares of my children in my residuary estate, the said two sums of £10,000 so transferred as aforesaid shall be brought into hotchpot as part of the respective settled shares of my said two daughters in my residuary estate.[1]

Confirmation of will and earlier codicil

2.   In all other respects I confirm my said will [and a first codicil thereto bearing date the —— day of ——].²

[*Testimonium and attestation clause as in* Form D1 *at para* **[237.8]**.]

1   It is always wise, if possible, for a testator to declare by will or codicil whether a lifetime gift is to adeem a testamentary gift or not, so as to avoid disputes: see, for example, *Re Cameron* [1999] Ch 386, [1999] 2 All ER 924. Interest on advances brought into hotchpot is charged at the rate of 4 per cent (*Re Wills, Dulverton v Macleod* [1939] Ch 705, [1939] 2 All ER 775).

2   See Preliminary Note at paras **[237.5]–[237.6A]** and cl 3 of Form D1 at para **[237.8]**.

[237.12]

FORM D5:   Codicil altering the trusts of a settled share

I [*testator*] of [*address*] declare this to be a [first] codicil to my will which is dated the —— day of ——.

Recital of absolute legacy and one-third share of residuary estate to brother

Whereas by my said will I have bequeathed to my brother [*name*] absolutely a legacy or sum of £—— and I have directed my trustees to stand possessed of a one-third share of my residuary estate upon certain trusts therein declared for (in effect) my said brother his wife and children issue and appointees.

Revocation of legacy

1.   I hereby revoke the said bequest of £—— to my said brother.

Revocation of one-third share

2.   I hereby revoke the said bequest of such one-third share of my residuary estate and all the trusts thereof declared in my said will.

Re-settlement of one-third share

3.   I direct my trustees to stand possessed of such one-third share of my residuary estate upon trust [*here set out the new trusts.*]

Confirmation

4.   I confirm my said will as modified by this codicil.¹

[*Testimonium and attestation clause as in* Form D1 *at para* **[237.8]**.]

1   See Preliminary Note at paras **[237.5]–[237.6A]** and cl 3 of Form D1 at para **[237.8]**.

[237.13]

FORM D6:   Codicil on the occasion of testator's second marriage, reviving his will, substituting the name of his second wife for that of his first, and including any children by his second wife in the gift of residue contained in his will¹

I [*testator*] of [*address*] declare this to be a [first] codicil to my will which is dated the —— day of ——.

WHEREAS

Recitals

(1)   Since the date of my said will my wife [*name*] died on the —— day of —
— and on the —— day of —— I married [*name*].

(2)   By my said will I have directed my trustees to stand possessed of my
residuary estate in trust for my late wife [*name*] for life and after her death in
trust for my children and issue as therein mentioned.

Substitution of second wife for deceased wife and declaration that children by second marriage shall take

1.   Now I hereby declare that the gift of my residuary estate in my said will
contained shall have effect as if the name of my wife [*name*] had been
substituted therein for the name of my late wife [*name*]. I further declare that the
expression 'child children and issue' where used in my said will shall mean and
include as well any child children and issue of mine by my present marriage as
any child children and issue of mine by my said first marriage.

Revival of will

2.   In all other respects I confirm and revive[2] my said will and declare that my
said will as modified by this codicil shall operate and take effect as if it had been
made since my marriage with my said wife [*name*].[3]

[*Testimonium and attestation clause as in* Form D1 *at para* **[237.8]**.]

1   This form is inserted as an example of a codicil reviving a revoked will. The better (and more
    tactful) course in the circumstances is for the testator to make a new will altogether; but cases
    may arise where the form is convenient as a temporary expedient.
2   Wills Act 1837 (WA 1837), s 22 (Part G, para **[244.22]**).
3   See Preliminary Note at paras **[237.5]**–**[237.6A]** and cl 3 of Form D1 at para **[237.8]**.

[237.14]

FORM D7:   **Codicil where specifically devised realty has been sold after the
execution of the will**[1]

I [*testator*] of [*address*] declare this to be a [first] [*or as the case may be*] codicil
to my will which is dated the —— day of ——.

WHEREAS

Devise of freehold

1.   By my said will dated —— I have devised a freehold property known as —
— and situated —— to my son —— in fee simple.

Conveyance by way of sale

2.   The said property was on —— conveyed by way of sale to a purchaser for
the sum of £——.

Bequest of legacy

3.   Now I hereby bequeath to my said son in place of the said devise which has
been adeemed a legacy of the said sum of £—— [free of inheritance tax and
foreign death duties].[2]

4.   I confirm my said will as modified by this codicil.[3]

[*Testimonium and attestation clause as in* Form D1 *at para* **[237.8]**.]

1   As to ademption on sale of property specifically devised, see Vol 1, para **[41.5]**.
2   These words are appropriate where the testator's residuary estate will or may include property of a kind which bears its own tax: see the Preliminary Note to B14 at para **[214.71]**.
3   See Preliminary Note at paras **[237.5]**–**[237.6A]** and cl 3 of Form D1 at para **[237.8]**.

[237.15]

FORM D8:   **Codicil after divorce**[1]

I [*testator*] of [*address*] declare this to be a [first] codicil to my will which is dated the —— day of ——.

WHEREAS

(1)   By my said will dated the —— day of —— I made certain gifts to my then wife [*name*] and also gave my residuary estate upon trust for my said wife during her life and upon her death for my children as therein stated.

(2)   By a decree absolute of divorce pronounced by the Family Division of the High Court of Justice on the —— day of —— the marriage between myself and my said wife was dissolved.

(3)   By virtue of section 18A of the Wills Act 1837 my residuary estate and the other property given to my said former wife now devolve under my said will as if she died on the date of the said decree absolute.

Now I hereby direct that the gift in my said will to my said former wife of [my half share of the property known as [*address*]] shall continue to have effect [free of inheritance tax][2] despite the said dissolution of our marriage and I also bequeath the sum of £—— to [*name*] [free of inheritance tax].

I confirm my said will as modified by the said section 18A of the Wills Act 1837 and as further modified by this codicil.[3]

[*Testimonium and attestation clause as in* Form D1 *at para* **[237.8]**.]

1   For WA 1837, s 18A, as amended by Law Reform (Succession) Act 1995, s 3 in relation to deaths on or after 1 January 1996, see Part G, para **[244.18]**, and the discussion of it in Vol 1, para **[47.2]** and the Preliminary Note to C2 at paras **[224.12]**–**[224.19]**. Section 18A only applies to a will made before a divorce, and so a codicil made after a divorce to a will made before it could nullify the effect of s 18A by republishing the will (see Vol 1, paras **[20.4]** and **[22.3]**). Such a codicil should therefore make clear whether s 18A is to continue to apply or not. If the will contained an appointment of the wife as an executor a reference to that appointment and the effect of s 18A on it should be added to the recitals.
2   The gift to the former spouse will not be exempt from inheritance tax. It may be appropriate to make it subject to tax as in Form B6.30 at para **[206.39]**.
3   See Preliminary Note at paras **[237.5]**–**[237.6A]**, n 1 supra and cl 3 of Form D1 at para **[237.8]**.

[237.16]

FORM D9:   **Codicil reducing benefits owing to reduction of estate**

I [*testator*] of [*address*] declare this to be a [first] codicil to my will which is dated the —— day of ——.

Recital of value

1.   Whereas I now know that the total value of my estate will be less than anticipated at the time when my said will was executed.

Revocation of legacies

2.   Now I hereby revoke all pecuniary legacies given by my said will except that given to my wife for her immediate needs.

Reduction of settled legacy

3.   I also revoke the settled legacy of £5000 settled on my daughter [and in its place I give my trustees a sum of £2000 to be subject to the same provisions in all respects as the said settled legacy of £5000 was by my said will].

    4.   I hereby confirm my said will in all other respects.[1]

[Testimonium and attestation clause as in Form D1 *at para* **[237.8]**.*]*

1   See Preliminary Note at paras **[237.5]**–**[237.6A]** and cl 3 of Form D1 at para **[237.8]**.

[237.17]

FORM D10:   Codicil increasing an annuity[1]

I *[testator]* of *[address]* declare this to be a [first] codicil to my will dated the —— day of ——.

Recital

Whereas by my said will dated the —— day of —— I have directed my trustees to pay an annuity of the gross sum of £—— to [annuitant] on the days and out of the fund therein mentioned.

Increase

Now I hereby direct my trustees to increase the said annuity by the sum of £—— so that at the times and out of the fund mentioned in my said will my trustees shall pay to the said *[annuitant]* a total yearly gross sum of £—— being the said annuity mentioned in my will increased as above stated.

    Except as modified by this codicil [and the codicils dated ——] I hereby confirm my said will.[2]

[Testimonium and attestation clause as in Form D1 *at para* **[237.8]**.*]*

1   As to annuities generally and their fiscal disadvantages, see para **[211.1]** et seq.
2   See Preliminary Note at paras **[237.5]**–**[237.6A]** and cl 3 of Form D1 at para **[237.8]**.

[237.18]

FORM D11:   Codicil altering legacies

I *[testator]* of *[address]* declare this to be a [first] codicil to my will which is dated the —— day of ——.

Increase in amount of legacy

1.   Whereas by my said will I have bequeathed to *[name]* absolutely a legacy of £——. Now I hereby declare that the said legacy to the said *[name]* shall be increased to £——.

Revocation of legacy

2.   And whereas by my said will I have bequeathed to [*name*] absolutely a legacy of £——. Now I hereby revoke the said legacy of £—— to the said [*name*].

Substitution of one charity for another in respect of a legacy

3.   And whereas by my said will I have bequeathed to [*name of charity*] a legacy of £——. Now I hereby revoke the said legacy of £—— to the said [*name of charity*] and I give to [*name and address of substituted charity*] a legacy of £—— and I declare that the receipt of the person who professes to be the treasurer or other proper officer for the time being of the said [*name of substituted charity*] shall be a sufficient discharge to my trustees in respect of such legacy.

Confirmation

4.   In all other respects I hereby confirm my said will.[1]

[*Testimonium and attestation clause as in* Form D1 *at para* **[237.8]**.]

1   See Preliminary Note at paras **[237.5]**–**[237.6A]** and cl 3 of Form D1 at para **[237.8]**.

[237.19]

FORM D12:   Codicil imposing protective trusts on share of a child who might become insolvent

I [*testator*] of [*address*] declare this to be a [first] codicil to my will which is dated the —— day of ——.

Recital of life interest for son

Whereas by my said will I have directed my trustees to stand possessed of a one-half share of my residuary estate to pay the income thereof to my son [*name*] for his life and subject thereto to hold the said one-half share of my residuary estate on the trusts declared in clauses —— to —— of my said will.

Imposition of protective trusts on son's life interest

1.   Now I hereby revoke the said life interest for my said son in the said one-half share of my residuary estate and declare that my trustees shall stand possessed of the said one-half share of my residuary estate to hold the income thereof on protective trusts as defined by section 33 of the Trustee Act 1925 for the benefit of my said son for the period of his life provided always that my trustees shall have the following powers:

   (i)   power at any time while my said son shall be living and before a trust in accordance with section 33(1)(ii) of the Trustee Act 1925 shall have come into existence to declare by any deed that my son shall henceforth be entitled absolutely to the income from the said one-half share of my residuary estate for his life; and

   (ii)   power at any time or times while my said son shall be living to pay or apply all or any of the capital of the said one-half share of my residuary estate to or for the benefit of my said son.

2.   Subject thereto my trustees shall hold the said one-half share of my residuary estate on the trusts declared in clauses —— to —— of my said will.

Protection for trustees against liability for payment of income to son after forfeiture without notice of it

3.   My trustees shall not be liable for paying any income of the said one-half share of my residuary estate to my son or permitting him to receive such income after the failure or determination during his life of his right to receive such income if or whenever they shall do so without having had express notice of the act or event causing such failure or determination.

Confirmation

4.   In all other respects I hereby confirm my said will.[1]

[*Testimonium and attestation clause as in* Form D1 *at para* **[237.8]**.]

1   See Preliminary Note at paras **[237.5]**–**[237.6A]** and cl 3 of Form D1 at para **[237.8]**.

[237.20]

FORM D13:   Codicil appointing a guardian, the testator having acquired parental responsibility for his illegitimate children since making his will

I [*testator*] of [*address*] declare this to be a [first] codicil to my will which is dated the —— day of ——.
   1.   Since my said will was made I and [*name of the mother of the children*] have made a parental responsibility agreement dated [*date*] by which I have parental responsibility for our children [*name*] and [*name*] and the said agreement was registered with the Principal Registry of the Family Division of the High Court on [*date*].[1]
   2.   If the said [*name of the mother of the children*] dies before me I appoint [*name*] to be the guardian of such of our said children as shall be under the age of 18 years at my death.

Confirmation

3.   In all other respects I hereby confirm my said will.[2]

[*Testimonium and attestation clause as in* Form D1 *at para* **[237.8]**.]

1   For the appointment of guardians see B3 at paras **[203.43]**–**[203.54]** and Vol 1, para **[28.1]** et seq. As stated there, it is thought that a parent can only make an appointment of a guardian of a child at a time when he or she has parental responsibility for the child, and the father of an illegitimate child only acquires parental responsibility for the child if there is a parental responsibility agreement between him and the mother (and in the prescribed form and duly registered with the Family Division), or he marries the mother, or the mother dies appointing him the guardian.
2   See Preliminary Note at paras **[237.5]**–**[237.6A]** and cl 3 of Form D1 at para **[237.8]**.

Changes in the law

[237.21]

FORM D14:   Codicil making revisions consequent upon the Trusts of Land and Appointment of Trustees Act 1996[1]

I [*testator*] of [*address*] declare this to be a [first] codicil to my will dated the —— — day of ——.

Where a Settled Land Act 1925 settlement was purportedly created by the will[2]

1.   Whereas by clause [*clause*] of my said will dated the —— day of —— I have given my property known as Blackacre to my wife for her life and appointed X and Y to be the trustees for the purposes of the Settled Land Act 1925. Now I hereby revoke the said clause [*clause*] and declare that my said will shall be read and construed as if it contained the following clause:[2]

'I give Blackacre to [my wife and X][3]/[X and Y]/[*otherwise*][4] to hold it on trust for my wife for life'

Where an entailed interest was purportedly created by the will[5]

1.   Whereas by clause [*clause*] of my said will dated the —— day of —— I have purported to create an entailed interest of my property known as Blackacre. Now I hereby revoke the said clause [*clause*] and declare that my said will shall be read and construed as if it contained the following clause:

'I give Blackacre [set out the new gift and trusts of Blackacre]'

Where a testator wishes to restrict the powers of trustees of land[6]

1.   Whereas under Section 6 of the Trusts of Land and Appointment of Trustees Act 1996 trustees of land have in relation to the land subject to the trust all the powers of an absolute owner including certain powers there expressly set out. Now I hereby declare that the trustees of this my will shall have only those powers in relation to land subject to the trusts of this my will as are set out [expressly in my will]/[below]:

Where a testator wishes to impose a requirement of consent to the exercise of powers over land[7]

1.   Whereas by clause [*clause*] of my said will dated the —— day of —— I have given my property known as Blackacre to my trustees upon to sell the same with the consent of my wife. Now I hereby declare that my wife's consent shall be required to any exercise of any of the trustees' powers over or in relation to Blackacre.

Where a testator wishes to restrict beneficiaries' powers in relation to the retirement and appointment of trustees of land[8]

1.   I hereby declare that Section[s] [19] [and] [20] of the Trusts of Land and Appointment of Trustees Act 1996 shall not apply to the trusts created by my said will.

2.   Except as modified by this codicil [and the codicils dated ——] I hereby confirm my said will.[9]

[Testimonium and attestation clause as in Form D1 *at para* **[237.8]**.]

1   The TLATA 1996 came into force on 1 January 1997, and made fundamental changes to the law relating to land held upon trust. See Preliminary Note at paras **[237.2]** and **[237.3]**.
2   No new SLA 1925 settlements can be created on or after 1 January 1997, so SLA 1925 forms which may have been used in a pre-1997 will should be revised. See Preliminary Note at para **[237.3]**, sub-para (a).
3   A testator may have wished to create a settlement under the SLA 1925 because he wished the land to be vested in the tenant for life and to have the powers of disposition of a tenant for life. Therefore, he may now wish to make the tenant for life one of the trustees.
4   It may be that X and/or Y were willing to be SLA 1925 trustees but would not want the greater burden of being trustees of land under the 1996 Act.

5   Entailed interests cannot be created on or after 1 January 1997 and any entailed interest purportedly granted thereafter will take effect as an absolute interest. See Preliminary Note at para **[237.3]**, sub-para (b).

6   Trustees of land now have all the powers of an absolute owner under s 6(1) of the Act. A testator may wish to restrict these powers. See Preliminary Note at para **[237.3]**, sub-para (c).

7   See Preliminary Note at para **[237.3]**, sub-para (d).

8   Beneficiaries under a trust who are of full age and collectively entitled to the whole beneficial interest have powers under the TLATA 1996, ss 19 and 20, to direct the retirement and appointment of trustees . A testator may wish to exclude or restrict them. See Preliminary Note at para **[237.3]**, sub-para (e).

9   See Preliminary Note at paras **[237.5]–[237.6A]** and cl 3 of Form D1 at para **[237.8]**.

[237.22]

FORM D15:   Codicil excluding or restricting provisions of the trustee act 2000[1]

I [*testator*] of [*address*] declare this to be a [first] codicil to my will dated the —— — day of ——.

   1.   I hereby declare that the duty of care of the Trustee Act 2000 shall not apply to [any of] my trustees [who does not act as trustee in the course of a business or profession].[2]

   2.   I hereby declare that the general power of investment of the Trustee Act 2000 shall not apply to the trusts of this my will and trustees shall have only those powers of investment as are set out [expressly in my will]/[below].[3]

   3.   Except as modified by this codicil [and the codicils dated ——] I hereby confirm my said will.[4]

[*Testimonium and attestation clause as in* Form D1 *at para* **[237.8]**.]

1   The TrA 2000 came into force on 1 February 2000, and confers many new powers upon trustees. See Preliminary Note at para **[237.2]** et seq.

2   TrA 2000, s 1, confers a duty of care on a trustee when exercising certain statutory or express powers, namely a duty to exercise such care and skill as is reasonable in the circumstances, having regard in particular to any special knowledge or experience that he has or holds himself out as having, and if he acts in the course of a business or profession, to any special knowledge or experience that it is reasonable to expect a person acting in the course of that kind of business or profession. The duty may, however, be excluded or restricted (see Sch 1, para 7) and a testator may wish to exclude it, particularly if he is appointing family or friends to be his executors and trustees. Even though the statutory duty of care is excluded, a trustee is still, of course, subject to duties arising under the general law, eg a duty to invest the trust fund as an ordinary prudent man of business, unless he is a professional trustee, when the standard of care will be higher; see *Bartlett v Barclay's Bank Trust Co Ltd* [1980] Ch 515, [1980] 1 All ER 139.

3   TrA 2000, ss 3 to 5, confer a general power of investment upon trustees namely, a power to make any kind of investment that they could make if they were absolutely entitled to the assets of the trust, having regard to the suitability of a particular investment to the trust, and the need for appropriate diversification and upon taking advice, unless they reasonably conclude that in all the circumstances it is unnecessary or inappropriate to do so. The power may, however, be excluded or restricted; see s 6(1)(b).

4   See Preliminary Note at paras [237.5]–[237.6A] and cl 3 of Form D1 at para **[237.8]**.

[237.23]

FORM D16:   Codicil varying appointment of guardian[1]

I [*testator*] of [*address*] declare this to be a [first] codicil to my will which is dated the —— day of ——.

Recital of previous appointment

1.   Whereas by my said will I have appointed my wife [*name*] and my brother [*name*] to be guardians of my minor children.

Revocation and reappointment

2.   I hereby revoke the said appointment of guardians and I hereby appoint my said brother [*name*] to be guardian of my minor children in the event of my said wife predeceasing me.

Confirmation

3.   In all other respects I hereby confirm my said will.[2]

[*Testimonium and attestation clause as in* Form D1 *at para* **[237.8]**.]

1   ChA 1988, s 5(8) provides that if one of two parents with parental responsibility for minor children dies leaving the other surviving, an appointment of a guardian made by the will of the first to die will not take effect until the death of the other parent, see Vol 1, para **[28.2]**. This codicil appoints a guardian only in the event of the testator being predeceased by his spouse, so if the spouse survives she will have a free hand to appoint a guardian in the event of her death leaving infant children. For various forms of appointments of guardians, see Forms B3.27 to B3.32 at paras **[203.56]**–**[203.61]** and see also the Note on appointment of guardians in B3 at paras **[203.43]**–**[203.54]**.

2   See Preliminary Note at paras **[237.5]**–**[237.6A]** and cl 3 of Form D1 at para **[237.8]**.

[237.24]

FORM D17:   Codicil imposing, on the shares of beneficiaries under an accumulation and maintenance trust, life interests with powers to pay or apply capital[1]

I [*testator*] of [*address*] declare this to be a [first] codicil to my will which is dated the —— day of ——.

Recital of accumulation and maintenance trusts of will

Whereas by my said will I have given the proceeds of sale of my residuary estate to my trustees upon trust for all my children who shall be living at my death and who shall attain the age of 25 years if more than one in equal shares absolutely.

Imposition of life interests with power to pay or apply capital

1.   Now I hereby declare that on the attainment of the age of 25 by each and every child of mine who shall attain that age my trustees shall retain the share ('the Share') of my residuary estate to which such child ('the Child') would become entitled under the trusts of my said will to hold the same upon trust to pay the income of the Share to the Child during his or her life provided that my trustees shall have power at any time or times to pay transfer or apply the whole or any part or parts of the capital of the Share to or for the benefit of the Child in such manner as my trustees shall in their absolute discretion think fit and subject to the foregoing trust and to any or every exercise of the foregoing power my trustees shall hold the Share and the income thereof in trust for such of the children of the Child as shall attain the age of 21 years if more than one in equal shares absolutely.

Confirmation
2.   In all other respects I hereby confirm my said will.[2]

[Testimonium and attestation clause as in Form D1 *at para* **[237.8]**.]

1   On a beneficiary becoming entitled to capital absolutely as against trustees there is generally a disposal for capital gains tax purposes under the Taxation of Chargeable Gains Act 1992 (TCGA 1992), s 71. Since 14 March 1989 there has been hold-over relief in only a limited number of circumstances (see Part A, para **[200.39]** et seq) A testator who made his will before the abolition of general hold-over relief may wish to alter it to prevent beneficiaries becoming absolutely entitled to capital upon the attainment of a given age if they will already have interests in possession when they attain that given age, and prefer to give them life interests with trustees having a power to pay or apply capital. This gives much greater flexibility, and enables, for example, the postponement of any capital gains tax charge under the TCGA 1992, s 71 indefinitely, or until a convenient time such as when trust assets come to be sold, when distributing the proceeds of such sale to the beneficiary will cause there to be no capital gains tax charge over and above that which is caused by the sale. (Hold-over relief is available where a beneficiary under accumulation and maintenance trusts becomes absolutely entitled to capital without having previously had an interest in possession in the capital: see TCGA 1992, s 260(2)(*d*)).
2   See Preliminary Note at paras **[237.5]**–**[237.6A]** and cl 3 of Form D1 at para **[237.8]**.

[237.25]

FORM D18:   Codicil increasing the amount of a legacy to the current inheritance tax nil-rate band[1]

I *[testator]* of *[address]* declare this to be a [first] codicil to my will which is dated the —— day of ——.

Recital of legacy
Whereas by my said will I have bequeathed to *[name]* a legacy of £—— which was the upper limit of the nil-rate inheritance tax band at the date of my said will and that upper limit has since increased to £——.

Increase of legacy
1.   Now I hereby increase the said legacy of £—— to the said *[name]* to the said sum of £——.

Confirmation
2.   In all other respects I hereby confirm my said will.[2]

[Testimonium and attestation clause as in Form D1 *at para* **[237.8]**.]

1   For nil-rate band legacies see Part A, para **[200.101]**, the Preliminary Note to B18 at para **[218.16]** et seq and Form B10.51 at para **[210.72]**.
2   See Preliminary Note at paras **[237.5]**–**[237.6A]** and cl 3 of Form D1 at para **[237.8]**.

[237.26]

FORM D19:   Codicil imposing an actual value limit on a formula nil-rate band legacy to the testator's children[1]

I *[testator]* of *[address]* declare this to be a [first] codicil to my will which is dated the —— day of ——.

Recital of nil-rate band legacy

Whereas by clause —— of my said will I have bequeathed to my children in equal shares a legacy equivalent to the maximum sum of money which can in the circumstances subsisting at my death be given by the said clause without any liability being incurred for the payment of inheritance tax on or by reason of my death.

Limit on legacy

1.   Now I hereby declare that in the event that the said maximum sum of money exceeds the sum of £—— the said legacy to my children shall be the said sum of £——.

Confirmation

2.   In all other respects I hereby confirm my said will[2].

[*Testimonium and attestation clause as in* Form D1 *at para* **[237.8]**.]

1   A testator whose estate will include property with the benefit of business or agricultural property relief may wish to place a limit on a nil-rate legacy because the availability of such relief may cause the nil-rate legacy to exceed the upper limit of the nil-rate inheritance tax band at the date of the testator's death. See the Preliminary Note to C11 at paras **[233.8]**–**[233.10]**. A limit may be particularly desirable where the bulk of the testator's estate comprises business property with the benefit of 100 per cent relief because then a nil-rate legacy without a limit might include most of the estate.

2   See Preliminary Note at paras **[237.5]**–**[237.6A]** and cl 3 of Form D1 at para **[237.8]**.

Correcting errors

[237.27]

FORM D20:   Codicil correcting a clerical error in a will

I [*testator*] of [*address*] declare this to be a [first] codicil to my will dated the —— —— day of ——.

Whereas in my said will at line —— on page ——there are written the words [*set out wrong word or words in will with the remainder of the phrase or sentence in which they occur*] now I hereby declare that the words —— in that passage in my said will should be —— and that the passage should read [*set out quoted passage in its correct form*] and that my said will shall be read and construed as if the words —— had been written in the place of the words —— as aforesaid and in all other respects I confirm my said will.[1]

[*Testimonium and attestation clause as in* Form D1 *at para* **[237.8]**.]

1   See Preliminary Note at paras **[237.5]**–**[237.6A]** and cl 3 of Form D1 at para **[237.8]**.

[237.28]

FORM D21:   Codicil to render valid alterations made in will[1]

I [*testator*] of [*address*] declare this to be [the second] codicil to my will dated the —— day of ——.

Whereas in my said will at

line —— on page ——;

line —— on page ——

certain words are crossed out and other words have been substituted by interlineations and such alterations were not initialled in the margin or elsewhere on the said will by myself and the attesting witnesses nor were such alterations noted in the attestation clause.

Now I hereby declare that the said alterations were made prior to the execution of my said will and that my said will shall at all times be read and construed subject to the said alterations and as if the said substituted words were the original words written in my said will and I hereby confirm my said will.[2]

[Testimonium and attestation clause as in Form D1 *at para* **[237.8]**.]

1   There is a presumption that alterations made in a will are made after execution and are invalid. The usual practice where alterations are necessary is for the testator and the witnesses to initial such alterations in the margin in which case the above presumption will be negatived and the will construed as altered: see Vol 1, paras **[14.3]**–**[14.14]**. This initialling must of course be done at the time of execution. If it has been omitted then the better plan is to execute a codicil in the above form. This form can be adapted to validate alterations made after execution by merely altering the recital of the facts. The general effect of a codicil upon alterations in a will is considered with the relevant cases in Vol 1, para **[14.9]**.
2   See Preliminary Note at paras **[237.5]**–**[237.6A]** and cl 3 of Form D1 at para **[237.8]**.

Revival and republication

[237.29]

FORM D22:   Codicil reviving a former will and codicils thereto which have been revoked[1]

I *[testator]* of *[address]* declare this to be [a third] codicil to my will dated the ——.

Whereas I made my last will on the —— and thereby revoked my said will dated —— and [two] codicil[s] [respectively] dated the —— [and the ——].

Now I hereby revive and confirm the said will dated —— [and the said codicil[s] thereto] and hereby revoke [the said will dated —— and] all testamentary dispositions made by me other than the said will dated —— [and the said dated codicil[s] thereto].

[Testimonium and attestation clause as in Form D1 *at para* **[237.8]**.]

1   It is advisable to execute a new will in the same terms as the revoked will, but in cases of emergency and where a copy of the former will exists it may be necessary to use this form. If the previous will was revoked by destruction animo revocandi and no copy thereof is in existence, it will not be possible to adopt this course. A new will must in such a case be executed. See Vol 1, para **[21.3]**. See also Form D6 at para **[237.13]**.

Revocation

[237.30]

FORM D23:   Revocation of a will[1]

I [*testator*] of [*address*] hereby revoke my will dated —— and all other testamentary dispositions made by me and hereby declare that it is my intention to die intestate.

[*Testimonium and attestation clause as in* Form D1 *at para* **[237.8]**.]

1   This revocation will seldom be required as the testator will normally execute a new will. While the intestacy provisions may accord with the testator's testamentary wishes, it must be remembered that it is generally more convenient to prove a will than to obtain a grant of administration. A revocation must be executed in the same way as a will. See WA 1837, s 20 (Part G, para **[244.20]**) and see generally Vol 1, paras **[18.8]**–**[18.16]** et seq.

PART E

Statutory Will Forms 1925

E   Statutory Will Forms 1925

PRELIMINARY NOTE

[238.1]
Section 179 of the Law of Property Act 1925 (see Part G, para **[244.55]**) provides that the Lord Chancellor may from time to time prescribe and publish forms to which a testator may refer in his will, and give directions as to the manner in which they may be referred to, but, unless so referred to, such forms shall not be deemed to be incorporated in a will.

[238.2]
The Order printed below was made under the provisions of the section in 1925 and has not since been modified or replaced. It will be observed that the forms can be incorporated with or without modification.

[238.3]
Forms C1.5 (at para **[223.6]**) and C2.4 (at para **[224.66]**) incorporated a number of the forms. Certain of these forms were successfully incorporated in a will in Queensland: *Re Staple* [1954] QWN 54.

[238.4]

The Statutory Will Forms Order 1925 (SR & O 1925 No 780)

1.   The forms hereinafter contained may be cited as the Statutory Will Forms 1925, and are divided into two groups called Part I and Part II respectively.

2.   The forms in Part I may be incorporated in a will by a general reference to that part, and the forms in Part I and Part II or any of them may be incorporated in a will in manner indicated in the Schedule hereto in any other manner indicating an intention to incorporate them and in the case of forms in Part II also indicating what property or disposition is to be affected thereby.

3.—(1)   In any form when incorporated in a will—

(i)   The provisions thereof shall have effect subject to the express provisions of the will;

(ii)   'Disposition' means a devise, bequest, and a testamentary appointment, whether in exercise of a general or special power includes a disposition under the statutory power to dispose of entailed interests by will; 'dispose of' has a corresponding meaning; and references to a testator's property include property which he disposes of in exercise of a power;

(iii)   'The trustees' mean the trustees appointed by the testator either generally or for a specific purpose, as the case may require, and the persons who by appointment by the court or otherwise become the trustees, and include his personal representatives, when acting as his trustees;

(iv)   'Authorised investments' mean investments authorised by the will creating the trust, for the investment of any money subject to the trusts of the will, or by the law.

(v)   Other words and expressions have the same meanings as in the Law of Property Act 1925.

The Schedule is as follows:

Incorporation of all the Forms in Part I
All the forms contained in Part I of the Statutory Will Forms 1925, are incorporated in my will [subject to the following modifications, namely*   ].

*   Here insert the modifications (if any).

Incorporation of specified Forms from Part I
The following forms contained in Part I of the Statutory Will Forms 1925, shall be incorporated in my will:

[*Specify those of the following forms which it is desired to incorporate.*]

Form 1   (*Confirmation of settlements*).

Form 2   (*Meaning of 'personal chattels'*).

Form 3   (*Inventories and provisions respecting chattels*).

Form 4   (*Legacies to charities*).

Form 5   (*Directions respecting annuities*).

Form 6   (*Power of appropriation*).

[subject to the following modifications, namely*   ].

*   Here insert the modifications (if any).

Incorporation of specified Forms from Part II

Form 7: *Trusts of a Settled Legacy*
Form 7 of the Statutory Will Forms 1925, is incorporated in my will, and shall apply to the following legacies*

[subject to the following modifications].

*   Here insert the legacies of money or investments to be settled.

Here insert the modifications (if any).

Form 8: *Administration Trusts*
Form 8 of the Statutory Will Forms 1925, is incorporated in my will, and shall apply to*

[subject to the following modifications   ].

*   Here insert description of property to be held upon administration trusts.

Here insert the modifications (if any).

Form 9: *Trusts for Spouse for life with power to appoint to issue and gift over to them*
Form 9 of the Statutory Will Forms 1925, is incorporated in my will, and shall apply to*

[subject to the following modifications   ].

*   Here insert description of property to be held on trusts for spouse for life with power to appoint to issue and gift over to them.

Here insert the modifications (if any).

Form 10: *Trusts for Spouse and issue without a power of appointment*
Form 10 of the Statutory Will Forms 1925, is incorporated in my will, and shall apply to*

[subject to the following modifications   ].

*   Here insert description of property to be held on trusts for spouse and issue without power of appointment.

Here insert the modifications (if any).

[238.5]
The Statutory Forms are set out below. As appears from para 2 of the Order (at para **[238.4]**), all the forms in Part I may be incorporated in a will, eg by using the words 'All the forms contained in the Statutory Will Forms 1925 are incorporated in my will' or some only may be incorporated thus 'Form I of the Statutory Will Forms 1925 is incorporated in this my will'. It may be desired to refer in general terms to the nature of the form. The forms in Part II (at paras **[238.7]–[238.16]**) can be used only by specific reference and the property to which the form applies must be identified. For forms of will incorporating some of the statutory forms see Form C1.5 at para **[223.6]** and Form C2.4 at para **[224.66]**.

[238.6]
It should be noted that the statutory forms have not been amended to take account of the Family Law Reform Act 1969 (FLRA 1969), the Inheritance Tax

Act 1984 (ITA 1984), or the Trusts of Land and Appointment of Trustees Act 1996 (TLATA 1996). Accordingly while reference to persons of 'full age' in Form 3 are now to be construed as references to persons who have attained the age of 18 years, the express references to the age of 21 years contained in the beneficial trusts set out in Forms 9 and 10 remain unchanged. The administration trusts set out in Form 8 continue to refer to 'duties' but this term is deemed to include a reference to inheritance tax: see ITA 1984, Sch 6, para 1 and Finance Act 1986, s 100(1)(b). Further, a trust for sale and conversion as appears in Form E8 at para **[238.14]** is in general no longer necessary in administration trusts as a result of the TLATA 1996: see para **[214.1]** et seq.

Forms which may be applied either generally or by specific reference

[238.7]

Form E1:   Statutory Will Forms 1925, Form 1: Confirmation of settlements

I confirm every settlement of property made by me which is subsisting at my death, and subject to any express provision to the contrary in my will, the provisions made by my will for the benefit of persons beneficially interested under such settlements, shall be in addition to, and not in satisfaction of, those made, or covenanted to be made by me in such settlement.

[238.8]

Form E2:   Statutory Will Forms 1925, Form 2: Meaning of 'personal chattels'

(1)   'Personal chattels' shall mean 'carriages, horses, stable furniture and effects (not used for business purposes), motor cars and accessories (not used for business purposes), garden effects, domestic animals, plate, plate articles, linen, china, glass, books, pictures, prints, furniture, jewellery, articles of household or personal use or ornament (including wearing apparel), also musical and scientific instruments and apparatus, wines, liquors and consumable stores, but shall not include any chattels used at my death for business purposes, nor money or securities for money.'[1]

(2)   But a general disposition of personal chattels shall take effect subject to any specific disposition.

---

1   This differs slightly from the definition of personal chattels in the AEA 1925, s 55(1)(x); (Part G, para **[246.52]**); see also B4 at paras **[204.2]** and **[204.3]** and Vol 1, para **[64.44]**.

[238.9]

Form E3:   Statutory Will Forms 1925, Form 3: Inventories and provisions respecting chattels[1]

(1)   An inventory of chattels given by my will, otherwise than by way of absolute gift, shall be made in duplicate, one part shall be retained by the

trustees and the other part shall be delivered to the person of full age[2] for the time being entitled to the use or possession of the chattels, in this clause called the 'usufructuary'.

(2)   A receipt shall be signed by the usufructuary, at the foot of the inventory retained by the trustees.

(3)   The inventory delivered to the usufructuary shall, if he so requires, be signed at the foot thereof by the trustees.

(4)   On any change of the right to the use or possession of the chattels a new receipt shall be signed by the usufructuary at the foot of the inventory retained by the trustees.

(5)   Where, by reason of the exercise of any power to sell, exchange, purchase, alter the fashion of, or otherwise deal with the chattels, or of any destruction or loss of any chattel, the inventories become inaccurate, the inventories shall be altered and re-signed, or new inventories shall, if convenient, be made and signed.

(6)   The trustees may, at their discretion, exclude from an inventory, any chattels which, by reason of their trifling value or wearing out nature, they may consider ought to be so excluded.

(7)   Where the chattels have been delivered to the usufructuary and a receipt is given therefor, the trustees, so long as the usufructuary remains entitled to the use of the chattels, shall not be liable in any way—

(a)   for any authorised disposition thereof or dealing therewith,
(b)   to see the insurance (so far as the same are capable of being insured), repair, or safe custody of the chattels,

unless and until required, in writing, to insure the chattels or to take any proceedings in reference thereto, by some person beneficially interested in the chattels or by his guardian, committee or receiver, and unless also due provision be made, to the satisfaction of the trustees, for the payment of the costs of insurance or of any proceedings required to be taken.

(8)   Where there is no person of full age[2] and capacity entitled to the use of the chattels, the trustees may, during the period of disability make such arrangements for the safe custody, repair, insurance and use of the chattels as, having regard to the circumstances of the case, they may in their absolute discretion, think expedient.

1   Compare Forms B4.1 and B4.2 at paras **[204.15]** and **[204.16]**.
2   The age of majority is 18 years: FLRA 1969, s 1 (Part G, para **[246.74]**).

[238.10]

Form E4:   Statutory Will Forms 1925, Form 4: Legacies to charities

The receipt of the treasurer or other proper officer of a charitable benevolent or philanthropic institution, society or body of persons (corporate or incorporate), to which a legacy is given by my will shall be a complete discharge to my personal representatives.

[238.11]

Form E5: Statutory Will Forms 1925, Form 5: Directions\respecting annuities[1]

The following provisions shall have effect in regard to any annuities or annuity given by my will—

(1) The trustees may, and (if so requested by or on behalf of any person beneficially interested in the property affected), shall, as soon as may be after any annuity commences to accrue, set apart in their names or under their control authorised investments, to provide a fund, the income whereof will be sufficient, in the opinion of the trustees, to produce an annual sum equal to the amount of the annuities for the time being payable under my will.

(2) The income or, if necessary, the capital of the fund so appropriated, shall be applied in payment of every subsisting annuity.

(3) Until a fund shall be so appropriated, my residuary estate shall stand charged with the payment of every subsisting annuity, but, after appropriation, the said estate shall be thereby discharged therefrom.

(4) The appropriated fund, or, where more than one annuity is bequeathed, such parts thereof as, in the opinion of the trustees, may not be required to answer any subsisting annuity, shall, on the cesser of an annuity, fall into my residuary personal estate.

(5) Accordingly, as each annuity ceases, the trustees may treat as part of my residuary personal estate, the whole or a corresponding part of the appropriated fund, as the case may require, retaining only such part thereof (if any) as may, from time to time, in their opinion, be sufficient to produce, by the income thereof, an annual sum equal to the amount of any subsisting annuities.

(6) Any surplus income of the appropriated fund shall be applied in the same manner as the income of my residuary personal estate.

(7) The trustees may, at their discretion, vary any of the investments for the time being representing the appropriated fund for other authorised investments.

(8) In this clause 'annuity' includes any periodic payment (not being a rentcharge) for life or other terminable interest.

1   For the disadvantages of gifts of annuities, see the Preliminary Note to B11 at para **[211.1]** et seq. For a direction to set apart separate funds for each annuity, see Form B11.8 at para **[211.15]**.

[238.12]

Form E6: Statutory Will Forms 1925, Form 6: Power of appropriation

(1)   The power of appropriation conferred by the Administration of Estates Act 1925[1], shall be exercisable by the trustees, without any of the consents made requisite by that Act.[2]

(2)   So far as practicable, the trustees shall give one month's notice, at least, of an intended appropriation, to the persons whose consent would, but for this

clause, be required under that Act; but a purchaser shall not be concerned to see or inquire whether any such notices have been given.

(3)   In this clause 'trustees' includes my personal representatives

1   See TLATA 1996, s 41.
2   The main purpose of this qualification is to facilitate the administration. It may also avoid an appropriation amounting to a sale but with the abolition of the ad valorem charge to stamp duty on appropriation by the Finance Act 1985, s 84(4), this factor is less significant: see the Note preceding Form B20.21 at para **[220.70]**.

Forms which may only be applied by specific reference

[238.13]

Form E7:   Statutory Will Forms 1925, Form 7: Trusts of a settled legacy

Any legacy of money or investments to which this clause is applied shall be subject to the following provisions:

(1)   The trustees shall stand possessed of the legacy upon trust to invest the same in their names or under their control in any authorised investments, with power, at the like discretion, to vary the investments thereof for others of a like nature.

(2)   The trustees shall stand possessed of the legacy, and of the investments representing the same and all statutory accumulations, if any, of income thereof, hereinafter included in the description of such legacy upon trust to pay the income thereof to the legatee during the life of the legatee.

(3)   After the death of the legatee, the capital and income of the legacy shall be held—

In trust for all or any one or more exclusively of the other or others, of the issue[1] of the legatee, whether children or remoter descendants, at such time, and if more than one in such shares, with such provisions for maintenance, education, advancement, and otherwise, at the discretion of any person or persons, and with such gifts over, and generally in such manner, for the benefit of such issue, or some or one of them, as the legatee shall, by deed, revocable or irrevocable, or by will appoint; but so that, under any appointment, a child shall not, otherwise than by way of advancement, take a vested interest, except upon attaining the age of twenty-one years or upon marriage.

And in default of and until and subject to any such appointment—

In trust for all or any the children or child[1] of the legatee, who attain the age of twenty-one years, or marry under that age, and if more than one in equal shares.

(4)   Any child of the legatee, who, or whose issue, takes any part of the legacy under any appointment by the legatee, shall not, in the absence of any direction by the legatee to the contrary, take any share in the unappointed part without bringing the share or shares appointed to him or his issue into hotchpot and accounting for the same accordingly.

(5)   If the legatee shall not have any child who, under the trusts in default of appointment hereinbefore contained, attains a vested interest in the

legacy, then, subject to the trusts and powers hereinbefore expressed in favour of the legatee and his issue, the legacy and the income thereof and all statutory accumulations, if any, of income shall fall into and form part of my residuary personal estate.

(6) The legatee may, notwithstanding any of the trusts hereinbefore expressed concerning his legacy, from time to time or at any time by deed, revocable or irrevocable, or by will, appoint to or for the benefit of any spouse who may survive the legatee, during the residue of the life of such spouse or for any less period (and subject or not to any conditions, and with such gifts over, and discretionary or other trusts for the benefit of the spouse and issue of the legatee, as the legatee may think fit), all or any part of the annual income of the legacy of the legatee, or of so much thereof as shall not before the death of the legatee, have been paid or applied under any power affecting the same.

And, upon any such appointment, the trusts and powers limited to take effect after the death of the legatee, shall take effect subject to the interest limited by any such appointment:

Provided that the power last aforesaid, to appoint by deed, shall not be exercisable by a woman while under coverture.

1   Unless excluded, the statutory rules of construction, whereby references to children and issue include references to illegitimate, legitimated and adopted persons (Part G, Section 2, para [245.1]), will apply. For a form in which the statutory rules are excluded see Form C13.2, cl 2(f) at para [235.18].

[238.14]

Form E8:   Statutory Will Forms 1925, Form 8: Administration trusts

Any property disposed of by my will (otherwise than in exercise of a special power) to which this clause is applied shall be subject to the following provisions:

(1) The property shall be held—
   (a) as to the real property, if any, including chattels real, upon trust to sell the same[1], and
   (b) as to the personal property, if any, upon trust to call in, sell, and convert into money such part thereof as may not consist of money.
(2) The trustees shall have power to postpone such sale and conversion for such a period as they, without being liable to account, may think proper.
(3) A reversionary interest shall not be sold, until it falls into possession, unless the trustees see special reason for sale.
(4) The trustees shall out of the net money to arise from the sale and conversion of the property (after payment of costs) and out of any ready money of mine, included in the disposition, pay or provide for—
   (a) my funeral and testamentary expenses;
   (b) my debts, except charges on other property of mine so far as those charges are discharged out of the property primarily charged therewith under the Administration of Estates Act 1925;[2]

(c)   the duties,[3] payable out of capital on my death, and not charged on or primarily payable out of other property;[4]

(d)   any other liabilities properly payable out of the property, or the proceeds of sale thereof;

(e)   the legacies (including money directed to be paid by my will), and annuities, bequeathed by me, but so that all legacies and annuities, and the duty[3] on all legacies and annuities bequeathed free of duty[3] shall be paid primarily out of personal property, if any, included in the disposition.

(5)   The trustees may invest, in their names or under their control, the residue of the said money, or so much thereof as may not have been distributed, in any authorised investments, with power, at their discretion, to vary such investments for others of a like nature.

(6)   The income (including net rents and profits of real property and chattels real, after payment of rates, taxes, rent, costs of insurance and of repairs and other outgoings properly attributable to income) of so much of the property as is not required for the administration purposes aforesaid shall, however the property is invested, as from my death, be treated and applied as income; and for that purpose any necessary apportionment may be made between capital and income.[5]

(7)   Provided that

(a)   statutory accumulations of income made during a minority[6], or pending a contingency, or accumulations made under an express trust for accumulation, may be added to capital;

(b)   income may be applied in effecting and maintaining a leasehold sinking fund policy, or may be set aside and invested for providing a fund to answer any liabilities which in the opinion of the trustees ought to be borne by income;

(c)   the trustees may in their discretion adjust, in such manner as they shall think fit, having regard to the circumstances of the case, the incidence, as between capital and income, of the payments made in due course of administration.[7]

---

1   A trust for sale and conversion is in general no longer necessary in administration trusts as a result of the TLATA 1996, see paras **[214.1]** et seq. The inclusion of such a trust in this form might be a reason for not using it or expressly varying it.

2   See Administration of Estates Act 1925, s 35 (Part G, para **[246.47]**).

3   References in this clause to death duties are construed as including a reference to inheritance tax: see the ITA 1984, Sch 6, para 1 and the FA 1986, s 100(1)(b).

4   It was held in *Re Previté, Sturges v Previté* [1931] 1 Ch 447 that cl (4)(c) of this form did not alter the incidence of estate duty. It is thought that the incidence of inheritance tax is similarly unaffected. Note the incidence of inheritance tax is not in some respects the same as the incidence of estate duty in that realty is not now prima facie subject to its own tax: see the Preliminary Note to B14 at paras **[214.55]** et seq.

5   Clause (6) excludes the rule in *Howe v Earl of Dartmouth* as to which see Vol 1, para **[38.17]** et seq and see also the Preliminary Note to B14 at paras **[214.37]** and **[214.38]**.

6   See Trustee Act 1925, s 31(2) (Part G, para **[246.26]**).

7   Clause (7)(c) does not expressly exclude the rule in *Allhusen v Whittell* (as to which see Vol 1, para **[38.25]** and the Preliminary Note to B14 at para **[214.43]**), but gives the trustees power to disregard it.

[238.15]

Form E9:   Statutory Will Forms 1925, Form 9: Trusts for spouse for life, with power to appoint to issue and gift over to them

Any property disposed of by my will (otherwise than in exercise of a special power) to which this clause is applied[1] shall be subject to the following provisions:

(1)   The property (including the investments for the time being representing the same) shall be held upon trust to pay the income thereof to my spouse for life.

(2)   After the death of my spouse, the capital and income of the property shall be held—

    (i)   In trust for all or any one or more, exclusively of the other or others, of my issue, whether children or remoter descendants,[2] at such time, and if more than one in such shares, with such provisions for maintenance, education, advancement and otherwise, at the discretion of any person or persons, and with such gifts over, and generally in such manner, for the benefit of such issue, or some or one of them, as my spouse shall, by deed, revocable or irrevocable, or by will, appoint; but so that, under any appointment, a child shall not, otherwise than by way of advancement, take a vested interest, except upon attaining the age of twenty-one years or upon marriage.

    (ii)   And in default of and until and subject to any such appointment in trust, in equal shares if more than one, for all or any of my children or child[2] who survive me and attain the age of twenty-one years[3] or marry under that age, and for all or any of the issue[2] living at my death who attain the age of twenty-one years[3] or marry under that age or any child of mine who predeceases me, such issue to take through all degrees, according to their stocks, in equal shares if more than one, the share or shares which his or their parent would have taken if living at my death and so that no issue shall take whose parent is living at my death and so capable of taking.

(3)   Any person who, or whose issue, takes any part of the property, under any appointment by my spouse, shall not, in the absence of any direction by my spouse to the contrary, take any share in the unappointed part, without bringing the shares appointed to such person or his issue into hotchpot, and accounting for the same accordingly.

1   These provisions will commonly be applied to residue.
2   See para **[238.13]**, n 1.
3   The reference to 21 years in this and the following form are unaffected by the FLRA 1969.

[238.16]

Form E10:   Statutory Will Forms 1925, Form 10: Trusts for spouse and issue, without a power of appointment

Any property disposed of by my will (otherwise than in exercise of a special power) to which this clause is applied shall be subject to the following provisions:

(1)   The property (including the investments for the time being representing the same) shall be held upon trust to pay the income thereof to my spouse for life.

(2)   After the death of my spouse the capital and income of the property shall be held in trust, in equal shares if more than one, for all or any of my children or child,[1] who survive me and attain the age of twenty-one years[2] or marry under that age, and for all or any of the issue[1] living at my death, who attain the age of twenty-one years[1] or marry under that age, of any child of mine who predeceases me, such issue to take through all degrees, according to their stocks, in equal shares, if more than one, the share or shares which his or their parent would have taken if living at my death; and so that no issue shall take whose parent is living at my death and so capable of taking.

1   See para **[238.13]**, n 1.
2   See para **[238.15]**, n 3.

Non-testamentary instruments

F1 Renunciation of probate and disclaimer of trusteeships

PRELIMINARY NOTE

[239.1]

An executor appointed by the will of a deceased person who has not intermeddled with the estate may either reserve his position, in which case powers will be reserved to him to prove the will at a later stage if he so wishes, or he may renounce probate. The renunciation should be in writing and should be filed in court. A renunciation can be withdrawn but, if it has been filed, not without the leave of the court. See generally as to renunciation Vol 1, para **[25.13]**.

A renunciation of probate by an executor who is also appointed a trustee is not conclusive evidence that the trusteeship is renounced as well (see Vol 1, para **[27.4]**, n 8). He should therefore expressly disclaim the trusteeship, and a separate document is convenient because a renunciation of probate has to be filed with the court. A deed of disclaimer of the trusteeship will also be appropriate where someone appointed trustee but not executor wishes to disclaim. Where someone appointed a sole executor is willing to be executor but not trustee, he should take out probate and appoint new trustees in his place, when the administration is complete, under the statutory power in Trustee Act 1925 (TA 1925), s 36 (Part G, para **[246.31]**). See Form F1.4 at para **[239.5]**. If none of the named executors proves the will or accepts office as trustee of it the administrators will become trustees of the will on completion of the administration and among all the other usual powers of trustees will be able to appoint new trustees under the statutory power: see *Re Cockburn's Will Trusts, Cockburn v Lewis* [1957] Ch 438, [1957] 2 All ER 522.

Section 50 of the Administration of Justice Act 1985 confers jurisdiction on the High Court to appoint a new personal representative in substitution of some or all of the existing ones, or, if there are two or more of them, terminate the appointment of one or more, but not all, of the personal representatives. The Court is not empowered to increase the number of personal representatives. Application can be made by a personal representative or a beneficiary, and so an application under this section is a means whereby a personal representative can apply to be relieved of his office after he has obtained a grant. A personal representative who is substituted under this section is an executor (except for the purposes of any chain of representation) if he is appointed to act together with executors, and otherwise is an administrator.

[239.2]

FORM F1.1:   Renunciation of probate[1]

In the High Court of Justice.

Family Division.

The Principal [*or* The —— District] Probate Registry.

In the Estate of [*deceased's* [*name*], deceased.

WHEREAS [*deceased's* [*name*] late of [*deceased's last address*], deceased, died on the —— day of ——, 20—, at ——, having made and duly executed his last will and testament bearing date the —— day of ——, 20—, and thereof appointed the undersigned A B his sole executor; now I the said A B do hereby declare that I have not intermeddled in the estate of the said deceased and will not hereafter intermeddle therein with intent to defraud creditors, and I hereby renounce all my right and title to the probate and execution of the said will [and to letters of administration (with the said will annexed) of the estate of the said deceased[2]].

[*Signature of A B*]

Signed by the said A B this

    —— day of ——, 20—, in

    the presence of[3] ——,

    Signature of Witness ——,

    Address ——.

1   The renunciation is not effective until it is filed in the Registry: *Re Morant's Goods* (1874) LR 3 P & D 151. An executor cannot renounce until the testator is dead: *Re Fenton's Goods* (1825) 3 Add 35. Until that time the proper course is for the testator to execute a codicil revoking the appointment and, if necessary, making another appointment in its place. The executor need not renounce. He can if he wishes just stand aside and then if he is cited to come in and prove the will and simply refrains from doing so, his rights as executor wholly cease: AEA 1925, s 5(ii). The renunciation being filed in the appropriate Registry, it is sometimes executed in duplicate and the duplicate endorsed by the solicitor acting in the matter as follows: 'The instrument of renunciation of probate of which this is a duplicate was duly filed in the —— Registry of the Family Division on ——.' This, however, is not absolutely essential, since the grant will record the renunciation. If the disclaiming executor also intends to disclaim the office of trustee, Form F1.2 at para **[239.3]** or Form F1.3 at para **[239.4]**, should be used. As to probate generally see *Tristram and Coote's Probate Practice* (28th edn), and for renunciation of probate see Non-Contentious Probate Rules 1987, r 37 and Vol 1, para **[25.13]**.

2   This should be added if the executor might be entitled to a grant of administration in some other character under r 20 of the Non-Contentious Probate Rules 1987.

3   One disinterested witness is sufficient.

[239.3]

FORM F1.2:   Deed of disclaimer of the trusteeship of a will by an executor and trustee who has renounced probate[1]

THIS DEED OF DISCLAIMER is made the —— day of —— by [*disclaiming trustee*] of etc.

WHEREAS

(1)   By his will dated —— [*testator*] late of etc (hereinafter called 'the testator') deceased devised and bequeathed all his real and personal property unto [*disclaiming trustee*] and [*other trustees*] upon certain trusts therein mentioned and appointed the said [*disclaiming trustee*] and [*other trustees*] executors of his said will.

(2)   The testator died on —— and his said will was on —— proved by the said [*other trustees*] alone in the [Principal] [—— District] [Registry of the Family Division] the said [*disclaiming trustee*] having renounced probate thereof [or having by an instrument dated —— duly renounced probate thereof which renunciation was duly filed in the said Registry].

(3)   The said [*disclaiming trustee*] is desirous of disclaiming the trusts reposed in him by the said will.

NOW THIS DEED WITNESSES that the said [*disclaiming trustee*] hereby disclaims all the estate and interest in the real and personal estate of the testator devised and bequeathed to him by the said will as a trustee jointly with the said [*other trustees*] and the trusts and powers thereby reposed in him jointly with the said [*other trustees*].

[*If the disclaiming trustee is or may become entitled to a beneficial interest, add:* Provided that the disclaimer aforesaid shall not operate to disclaim or release any beneficial interest whether vested or contingent to which the said [*disclaiming trustee*] now is or may hereafter become entitled under the trusts or provisions of the said will [or any legacy thereby given to him for his own benefit] but any legacy or remuneration for acting in the trusts thereof is hereby disclaimed.[2]

IN WITNESS ETC

[*Signature of and execution as a deed by disclaiming trustee.*][3]

1   As to disclaimer, see Vol 1, para [27.4]. Where a disclaimer is in writing it may be by deed: see LPA 1925, s 52(2)(b), and Vol 1, para [27.4], n 2. Owing to the difficulty of proving a disclaimer by conduct, this deed should be executed in every case where the trustee does not intend to act in the trusts. In any ordinary case, the shorter form given in the next following precedent is quite sufficient.
2   The trustee would be disentitled to this benefit in any event if he did not act in the trusts. However, difficult questions sometimes arise as to whether a trustee has acted: see *Re Sharman's Will Trusts, Public Trustee v Sharman* [1942] Ch 311, [1942] 2 All ER 74.
3   For execution of an instrument as a deed, see the Law of Property (Miscellaneous Provisions) Act, 1989, s 1 and Form F3.5 at para [241.26].

[239.4]

FORM F1.3:   Deed of disclaimer of the trusteeship of a will—short form[1]

BY THIS DEED made the —— day of —— I [*disclaiming trustee*] of etc hereby disclaim all the estate and interest in the real and personal estate of [*testator*] late of etc devolving upon me as [executor and] trustee of the will of the said [testator] deceased dated —— and the trusts and powers thereby reposed in me either solely or jointly with other persons [Provided that this disclaimer shall not operate to disclaim or release any beneficial interest to which I now am or may become entitled under the said will other than a benefit given to me for acting in the said trusts][2].

IN WITNESS ETC

[Signature of and execution as a deed by disclaiming trustee.][3]

1   This short form is sufficient in practically every case. See notes to the immediately preceding precedent. It must be remembered that where a person is appointed executor and trustee, the taking out of probate is prima facie evidence of the acceptance of the trusts, and this is still more so where the trusts are engrafted on to the executorship without specifically appointing the executor a trustee. In such cases, therefore, where a person has taken a grant (probably for the convenience of the estate) but does not intend to act in the trusts, he should either execute a disclaimer in this form or, better still, as soon as he has concluded the duties of the executorship secure the appointment of another trustee in his place. He cannot, of course, secure the appointment of anyone to perform the duties of executor without the concurrence of the court, but once those duties of clearing the estate are concluded, he is free to secure the appointment of a new trustee: see Vol 1, paras **[25.13]** and **[27.4]**. A trustee who has acted in the trusts cannot disclaim: *Re Sharman's Will Trusts, Public Trustee v Sharman* [1942] Ch 311, [1942] 2 All ER 74; he must secure the appointment of another trustee in his place.
2   See para **[239.3]**, n 2.
3   For execution of an instrument as a deed, see the Law of Property (Miscellaneous Provisions) Act 1989, s 1 and Form F3.5 at para **[241.26]**.

[239.5]

FORM F1.4:   Appointment of new trustees by disclaiming trustee who has proved testator's will[1]

THIS DEED OF APPOINTMENT OF NEW TRUSTEE is made the ―― day of ―― BETWEEN *[disclaiming trustee]* of etc (hereinafter called 'the appointor') of the one part and *[new trustees]* of etc (hereinafter called 'the new trustees') of the other part.

WHEREAS

(1)   By his will dated ―― *[testator]* late of ―― (hereinafter called 'the testator') appointed the appointor to be the sole executor and trustee thereof and devised and bequeathed his property as therein mentioned and inter alia bequeathed an annuity of £―― per annum to the appointor in consideration of his acting as trustee of his will.

(2)   The testator died on ―― and the appointor on ―― obtained a grant of probate thereof in the ―― Probate Registry.

(3)   The appointor though he has fulfilled the duties of executor of the said will desires to be discharged from the trusts thereof.

(4)   The appointor has paid the funeral and testamentary expenses of the testator and discharged all taxes and duties for which he is accountable.[2]

(5)   The new trustees are willing to act as the trustees of the said will in place of the appointor.

NOW THIS DEED WITNESSES as follows:

1.   The appointor in exercise of the power given by the Trustee Act 1925 and every other power hereunto enabling him hereby appoints the new trustees to be

the trustees of the said will in place of the appointor for all the purposes for which the appointor was appointed trustee thereof.

2.   The appointor hereby disclaims all that the annuity of £—— per annum [*or* the legacy of £——] bequeathed to him as trustee of the said will.[3]

IN WITNESS ETC

[Signatures of and execution as a deed by all parties.][4]

1   This is an appointment by a trustee refusing to act within the meaning of the TA 1925, s 36(1) (Part G, para **[246.31]**). The sole executor and trustee may be willing to take the grant to avoid delay in securing payment of policy moneys or to avoid the difficulty of securing an administrators' bond. He should in general appoint two new trustees.

2   It is thought that new trustees of a will can be appointed even though the administration is incomplete and no part of the estate has vested in the personal representative as trustee, though it would be unusual for an appointment to be made in such circumstances. In the case of land a written assent is necessary to vest title in the trustees: *Re King's Will Trusts, Assheton v Boyne* [1964] Ch 542, [1964] 1 All ER 833.

3   It may be advisable to add a clause of this nature to make the position clear. If an annuity is given it will be reasonably clear that such gift was given to the disclaiming trustee as trustee and not as executor. In the case of a legacy it may well be if the amount is relatively small that the disclaiming party is entitled to it for acting in the executorship and it may not need to be disclaimed. These doubts may be resolved by the party disclaiming as in this second clause, but if he intends to claim a legacy as executor this clause should be omitted. At one time it was thought necessary to add a clause disclaiming the trusts and the trust property, but the appointment acts as a discharge of the trustee and the property either passes under the TA 1925, s 40 (Part G, para **[246.35]**), or under an assent by the personal representatives. It is not thought that this deed operates to divest a personal representative of property which he still holds as such and, despite the execution of this deed, all proving executors should also execute the usual assent.

4   For execution of an instrument as a deed, see the Law of Property (Miscellaneous Provisions) Act 1989, s 1 and Form F3.5 at para **[241.26]**.

F2   Executors and trustees

[240.1]

FORM F2.1:   Notice to the Public Trustee of death of a testator who has appointed the Public Trustee as an executor of his will[1]

[*Address and date.*]

[*Testator*] *deceased.*

To the PUBLIC TRUSTEE,
81 Chancery Lane,
London, WC2A 1DD

DEAR SIR,

I regret to inform you that the above-named formerly of etc died on ——. By his will dated —— (*or* by a codicil dated —— to his will dated ——) he appointed the Public Trustee and myself to be the executors and trustees thereof and I enclose a copy of the said will [and codicil[s]].

The solicitors who acted for the deceased in his lifetime are Messrs —— of [*address*] who have agreed, subject to your approval, to act in the administration and to look to the estate and not to the executors personally for their costs.

The funeral arrangements are being made by [*name*] in accordance with the wishes expressed by the deceased in his lifetime and I shall be glad to learn that this meets with your approval.

I enclose a short statement showing the assets and liabilities of the estate so far as they are known to me. So far as I can estimate the gross value of the estate is about £——.

I shall be glad to learn that the Public Trustee will join with me in proving the will.

[*Signature of co-executor.*]

1   It is the duty of any person appointed co-executor with the Public Trustee, and not renouncing, to give the Public Trustee notice in writing of such appointment as soon as practicable after the same comes to his knowledge: Public Trustee Rules 1912, rr 8(3), 1, 6(c). See Forms B3.15 to B3.21 at paras **[203.32]–[203.38]**, for will clauses concerning the appointment of the Public Trustee.

[240.2]

FORM F2.2:   Notice to the Public Trustee of death of a testator who has appointed the Public Trustee as a trustee or as custodian trustee under his will[1]

[*Address and date.*]

[*Name of testator*] Will Trust.

To the PUBLIC TRUSTEE,
81 Chancery Lane,
London, WC2A 1DD

DEAR SIR,

I regret to inform you that the above-named formerly of etc died on ——.

I enclose a copy of his will dated —— [and of the —— codicil[s] thereto [respectively] dated ——].

It will be observed that under the will [and codicils] —— and —— are appointed as executors and that the Public Trustee is appointed as sole [*or* custodian] trustee thereof [*or* as trustee thereof jointly with [*names*]] [*or* that by clause —— of the will [*or* by the —— codicil] a legacy of £—— is bequeathed to the Public Trustee upon the trusts thereby declared].

I am acting for the executors of the will who are proposing to prove the same in due course and the estate is likely to comprise [*nature of assets*] to the value of about £—— [and the trust legacy is likely to be available in due course].

[*Where the Public Trustee is concerned with residue, add:* A copy of the Inland Revenue account will be supplied as soon as it has been agreed with the authorities and in due course a copy of the executors' accounts.]

I shall be glad to learn that the Public Trustee sees no difficulty in agreeing to act as [custodian] trustee [*or* trustee of the said legacy] in due course and to furnish any further information desired.

[*Signature of solicitor.*]

1   It is the duty of any person appointed co-trustee with the Public Trustee, and not disclaiming, to give the Public Trustee notice in writing of such appointment as soon as practicable after the same comes to his knowledge: Non-Contentious Probate Rules 1987, r 8(3). The notice may be given by the executors or one of them, but will commonly be given by their solicitor. No appointment is binding on the Public Trustee until he has sealed a formal consent to act: Public Trustee Rules 1912, rr 8(2), 10, and *Re Shaw, Public Trustee v Little* (1914) 110 LT 924. See Forms B3.15 to B3.21 at paras **[203.32]–[203.38]**, for will clauses concerning the appointment of the Public Trustee.

[240.3]

FORM F2.3:   Words to be included in executors' oath where partners in a solicitors' firm have been appointed executors[1]

I.   WHERE THERE WERE PARTNERS AT THE DATE OTHER THAN THOSE WHO ARE APPLYING.

That at the date of death of the said deceased there were [*state number*] partners in the firm of [*name*] of [*address*] [*add if it be the case[2]* the firm which had at that date succeeded to and at that date carried on the practice of [*name and address of firm stated in appointment clause in will*]] namely myself/ourselves and [*states names of other partners and if any has since died or renounced recite details*]. That I am/we are the surviving [*or* [*state number*] of the] executor[s] named in the said will.

II.   WHERE THERE WERE NO PARTNERS AT THE DATE OTHER THAN THOSE (OR THE ONE) APPLYING.

That at the date of death of the said deceased I was the sole principal of [*or* we were the only partners in] the firm of [*name*] of [*address*] [*add if it be the case[2]* the firm which had at that date succeeded to and at that date carried on the practice of [*name and address of firm stated in the appointment clause in will*]] and as such I am/we are the [sole] executor[s] named in the said will.

1   See B3 at paras **[203.14]–[203.20]** and Form B3.8 at para **[203.21]** generally for the appointment of partners in a solicitors' firm to be executors and trustees of a will. Where one or more partners apply for probate and power is to be reserved to other partners in the firm who have been appointed executors by reference to their being partners in that firm and not by their names, notice of the application need not be given to the partners to whom power is to be reserved; see the Non-Contentions Probate Rules 1987, r 27(1A), as amended by S1 1991/1876 as from 14 October 1991.

2   If the Oath states that the firm named in the appointment clause has been succeeded by another which carries on its practice, this must be established to the satisfaction of the district judge or registrar.

[240.4]

FORM F2.4:   Application for an advance from a bank by executors and undertaking to repay[1]

To —— Bank Plc.

   [*Date*]

   [*Branch*]

As executors of the will of [*testator*] deceased, which will we intend to prove at once, we have to request that you will advance to us the sum of £—— for payment of inheritance tax and expenses; and in consideration of your so doing we hereby undertake that the sum shall be so applied, and that we will duly obtain a grant of probate of the said will and forthwith produce the same to you for registration in your books and we hereby undertake to repay such advance out of the first moneys received on account of the estate of the deceased, and we hereby charge with such payment any cash and securities in your hands belonging to the deceased. The net value of the estate of the deceased is at present estimated to be £——.

1   An immediate necessity is the obtaining of sufficient funds for the payment of the inheritance tax in order to obtain a grant of probate. Such funds are often supplied by a bank and this form of undertaking is usually required. An advance is usually given as soon as the bank are satisfied as to the solvency of the estate. Even if the estate proves insolvent, administration expenses have priority: Article 4(2) of the Administration of Insolvent Estates of Deceased Persons Order 1986 (SI 1986/1999), made under the Insolvency Act 1986, s 421. Executors can give a security of this nature before probate, though there would be a difficulty in suing upon it so as to bind the estate before probate was granted. It would be better from the purely legal aspect of this matter to make the personal representatives personally liable, but that is not always practicable and in any event is asking them to undertake a liability which they should not be asked to undertake.

[240.5]

FORM F2.5: Declaration of trust of property devised or bequeathed by will on a secret trust[1]

THIS DECLARATION OF TRUST is made the —— day of —— BY [*declarants*] of etc (hereinafter called 'the declarants').

WHEREAS:

(1)   [*Testator*] of etc has by his will intended to be executed shortly after the execution hereof devised [and bequeathed] certain property to the declarants for their own absolute use and benefit.

(2)   The declarants as they hereby acknowledge are not to hold the said property for their own absolute use and benefit but upon the trusts hereinafter declared.

(3)   The said property is specified in the schedule hereto.

NOW IT IS HEREBY DECLARED that if and when the said will shall become effective in law and the said property shall be vested in the declarants such property shall be held by the declarants upon the following trusts:

[SET OUT TRUSTS.]

[SCHEDULE.]

IN WITNESS ETC

[Signatures and execution as a deed by declarants.][2]

1   Stamp £5. It is immaterial whether this is executed under hand or as a deed. It attracts a £5 stamp in either case as a declaration of trust and is not liable to any exemption under the Stamp Duty (Exempt Instruments) Regulations 1987. This declaration must be in existence at the time when the will is executed and the declaration cannot contain any provision for the alteration or revision of the trusts: see *Re Jones* [1942] Ch 328, [1942] 1 All ER 642. For secret trusts see, further, Vol 1,Ch 36.
2   For execution of an instrument as a deed, see the Law of Property (Miscellaneous Provisions) Act 1989, s 1 and Form F3.5 at para **[241.26]**.

F3 Disclaimers and variations of beneficial interests

PRELIMINARY NOTE

[241.1]
Disclaimers and variations have become important because the legislation relating to inheritance tax allows the dispositions taking effect on a person's death to be re-arranged by the beneficiaries within two years of the death, without tax being charged on the re-arrangement but with the re-arrangement being treated for inheritance tax purposes as if effected by the deceased. There is a similar but more limited provision relating to capital gains tax. The relevant provisions are now embodied in the Inheritance Tax Act 1984 (ITA 1984), s 142 and Taxation of Chargeable Gains Act 1992 (TCGA 1992), s 62(6)–(10). See also *Foster's Inheritance Tax*, D4.1123. Also, the ITA 1984, s 17(*a*) provides that a variation or disclaimer to which s 142(1) applies is not a transfer of value for inheritance tax purposes, ie the making of such a variation or disclaimer cannot be charged to inheritance tax as the making of a lifetime disposition by the beneficiary or beneficiaries who make the variation or disclaimer.

[241.2]
Persons for whose benefit dispositions may be varied. It will be apparent that whether an instrument varying a deceased person's dispositions comes within the ITA 1984, s 142 does not depend at all on who benefits from the variation. It can benefit absolutely anybody, and there is no requirement of any connection with the deceased.

[241.3]

Notice of election. Since the effect of the ITA 1984, s 142 is to treat a disposition made by a beneficiary as one made by the deceased, it can result in additional inheritance tax becoming payable where an exempt beneficiary, such as the deceased's wife, assigns her interest. The personal representatives might not have enough assets left in their possession with which to pay the extra tax, and anyway s 142 not applying could be more advantageous in some circumstances (such as where the deceased has fully utilised his available nil-rate inheritance tax band and the wife makes a substantial gift out of the deceased's assets). Section 142(2) therefore provides that for the section to apply to an instrument varying the deceased's dispositions there must be an election by written notice given within six months of the instrument by the persons who made it, and by the personal representatives if additional tax will be chargeable, though the latter may only decline to join in if they have insufficient estate assets left to pay the extra tax. Therefore, if it is desired that some dispositions should be made to which s 142 applies, and some to which it does not, they should be made by separate instruments. It should also be noted that s 142(2) does not apply to *disclaimers* within s 142(1), and that the application of s 142 to disclaimers is thus automatic (unless they are made orally—in which case s 142 does not apply at all). Where the deceased's surviving spouse makes an instrument of variation under which he or she assigns (to a non-exempt beneficiary) a specific gift or legacy which does not bear its own inheritance tax, the persons interested in residue, out of which any extra tax will be paid, cannot, it seems, prevent an election under s 142(2) being made. An election under s 142(2), once made, cannot be revoked.

If an instrument of variation contains a notice of election the Inland Revenue will accept as sufficient notice of election the receipt by the Capital Taxes Office within the six-month period of a copy of the instrument. A relevant notice of election or a copy of the deed containing one must be sent to the relevant Inspector of Taxes as well as the Capital Taxes Office if there is a capital gains tax election (see para **[241.17]**) as well as an inheritance tax one. The Inland Revenue take the view that notices of election must refer to the relevant statutory provisions. The Inland Revenue have power under ITA 1984, s 142(2) to extend the time for giving notice of election beyond the six-month period, but it is their policy only to do so where there has been some genuine difficulty, such as inaccessibility or serious illness of a necessary signatory, and not where there has been failure to make the election through forgetfulness or oversight.

For an example of a notice of election in a deed of variation see cl 3 of Form F3.5 at para **[241.26]**.

[241.4]

Receipt of benefit before the instrument is executed. The fact that a person has received a benefit under some interest in a deceased person's estate does not prevent him from transferring that interest to someone else by an instrument within the ITA 1984, s 142. This is emphasised by the words in s 142(4) after the semi-colon. It should be remembered, however, that as a matter of ordinary law a purported *disclaimer* will be ineffective if any benefit has been accepted under the gift purportedly disclaimed (see para **[241.16]**).

A separate but related problem is whether a person who is transferring by written instrument to another person some interest in a deceased person's estate must transfer also any benefit received by him or due to him, by virtue of that interest, during or in respect of the period between the death and the making of the instrument, for that instrument to fall within the ITA 1984, s 142. In many cases this is strictly impossible (for example, where the benefit received was the occupation of a house) but there is no reason why the transferor should not assign income due but unpaid, or account for income already received, to the transferee (for the income tax consequences of doing so—see para **[241.19]**). It seems reasonably clear from the wording of s 142(1) that an instrument does not have to have retrospective effect in this manner to be within the section. There is specific provision in s 142(4) for variations which terminate an interest in possession (see para **[241.8]**).

[241.5]
Meaning of 'estate' for the purposes of section 142. Section 142(1) is expressly confined to variations or disclaimers relating to the property comprised in a deceased person's estate immediately before his death, which at first glance means the aggregate of all property to which that person was beneficially entitled other than excluded property (see ITA 1984, s 5(1)). However, s 142(5) gives a special meaning to 'estate' for the purposes of s 142(1), by providing that it includes excluded property. It also provides that it does not include property in which the deceased had an interest in possession immediately before his death. This means that the only relieving provision where someone wishes not to receive an interest in settled property which falls into possession on the death of a life tenant is s 93 of the ITA 1984, which applies only to a disclaimer made otherwise than for a consideration in money or money's worth.

It should also be noted that s 142 can apply to assets passing on a person's death, other than property which was settled property immediately before the death, which do not pass under that person's will, such as nominated savings bank accounts and interests in joint tenancies. For a form of variation of the disposition of a deceased's interest under a joint tenancy, see Form F3.5 at para **[241.26]**.

[241.6]
Form of instrument. Section 142 can only apply to a written instrument. Such instruments can take the form of disclaimers (provided that the requirements for a valid disclaimer are present, as to which see para **[241.16]**) or dispositions by assignment or conveyance. It is usual to call the latter 'deeds of variation'. Special provision will, however, be often needed where an assignment or conveyance is to operate as from the death of the deceased. Forms F3.4 to F3.10 at paras **[241.25]–[241.31]**, are intended to operate in this manner. The Inland Revenue take the view that an instrument of variation must identify the disposition of the deceased which is being varied, then vary the destination of that disposition as laid down by the terms of the will or the intestacy rules.

In practice instruments of variation are made by deed, to make sure that the variation is binding on the maker or makers of it, and are often expressed to vary the terms of the will or intestacy rules, as in the examples in Forms F3.4 to F3.10 at paras **[241.25]–[241.31]**.

[241.7]
Consideration. Section 142(3) of the ITA 1984 provides that s 142(1) does not apply to a variation or disclaimer made for any consideration in money or money's worth, other than consideration consisting of the making in respect of another of the deceased's dispositions of a variation or disclaimer to which s 142(1) applies. One particular point to watch in relation to this provision is that if the donee under an instrument of variation agrees to pay the costs of the instrument that could be consideration which takes the instrument outside s 142(1). For further points relating to this provision see paras **[241.13]** and **[241.14]**.

[241.8]
Interests in possession. Section 142(4) of the ITA 1984 provides that where a variation within s 142(1) results in property being held in trust for a person which ends not more than two years after the deceased's death, the ITA 1984 applies as if the disposition of the property that takes effect at the end of the period had had effect from the beginning of the period. It will be recalled that although a residuary estate will not strictly speaking be held on the trusts applicable to it under the testator's will until the administration of the estate is complete (*Stamp Duties Comr (Queensland) v Livingston* [1965] AC 694, [1964] 3 All ER 692), ITA 1984, s 91 has the effect that, during the administration of the estate, any interest in possession which would subsist if the administration were complete is treated as subsisting for inheritance tax purposes, and, consequently, that if there is an event which would be the coming to an end of an interest in possession in residue if the administration were complete it is treated as the termination of an interest in possession for inheritance tax purposes. Section 142(4) can thus be relevant even where there is a variation relating to an interest in possession in unadministered residue.

An example of the operation of ITA 1984, s 142(4) would be where the deceased's will gives his son a life interest in his residuary estate with effect from the deceased's death, and the son makes a deed of variation whereby his interest in possession terminates and the capital comes to be held on trust for the deceased's widow (either absolutely or for an interest in possession). Provided that the son's interest terminates by virtue of the deed of variation within two years from the deceased's death (and the other requirements of s 142 are satisfied), the variation will be treated as having effect from the deceased's death as well as not being itself a transfer of value by the son. This means that the property subject to the interest will be exempt from inheritance tax on the deceased's death as going to the deceased's spouse (see Part A, para **[200.99]** et seq), even if the son retains the income which accrued before the deed took effect.

However, s 142(4) contains a possible hazard for the unwary, and there is a limit on its scope—

(a) The possible hazard is that if a deed of variation creates a short-term interest in possession with the intention that the capital subject to that interest in possession will be treated by virtue of s 142 as if it were subject to the short-term interest in possession from the deceased's death, s 142(4) would have the effect of frustrating that intention if the short-term interest terminates within two years of the deceased's death because then the disposition taking effect on the termination of the interest in possession would be deemed to have had effect from the death of the deceased. A short-term interest created under an instrument of variation should thus be made to end more than two years after the deceased's death. For an example of this type of variation see Form F3.7 at para **[241.28]**. However, where a deed of variation creates an interest in possession, and the owner of it dies within two years of the deceased, it seems that the Revenue do not regard s 142 (4) as applying to treat the disposition taking effect on his death as having had effect from the death of the deceased: see *Foster's Inheritance Tax*, D4.14.

(b) The limit on the scope of s 142(4) is that it provides that it does not affect the application of the ITA 1984 in relation to any distribution or application of property occurring before the termination of an interest in possession by virtue of a variation to which s 142(1) applies. This seems to mean, as regards property formerly subject to an interest in possession under the will and distributed in exercise of a power before the instrument of variation is made, that an instrument of variation cannot have a retrospective effect under s 142 (eg converting an exempt part of the deceased's estate on death to a non-exempt part or vice versa, or altering the inheritance tax treatment of the distribution) in relation that property: see further, *Foster's Inheritance Tax*, D4.14. The short point is that substantial discretionary distributions of capital subject to an interest in possession under a will should so far as possible be avoided until any proposals for an instrument of variation have been decided upon.

[241.9]

Consequences of s 142 applying. These have already been mentioned in general terms in the first paragraph of this Preliminary Note at para **[241.1]**. Two particular consequences of the provision in s 142(1) that ITA 1984 applies as if a variation within s 142(1) was made by the deceased are worth noting. One is that if a variation within s 142 creates a settlement, the settlor of it for inheritance tax purposes will be the deceased rather than the maker of the variation. This could be significant for the application of the rules for charging inheritance tax on discretionary trusts (see the Note on these in B18 at para **[218.6]** et seq), or the application of the excluded property rules where the deceased had a non-UK domicile for inheritance tax purposes (see the Preliminary Note to C14 at para **[236.1]** et seq). Unfortunately, for both income tax and capital gains tax purposes it is the maker of the variation, not the deceased, who will be the settlor.

The second point is that it seems reasonably clear that the gift with reservation rules (see Part A, para **[200.76]**) apply as if the gift arising under an instrument of variation within s 142 is one made by the deceased and not by the maker of the instrument, ie in effect, the gift with reservation rules will not apply. Although the gift with reservation rules are contained in the Finance Act 1986, s 102 and Sch 20, those provisions are 'construed as one with' the ITA 1984 (Finance Act 1986, s 114(5)). This means that an instrument of variation can eg create a discretionary trust under which the maker of the instrument is a beneficiary, and still be inheritance tax effective: see Form F3.9 at para **[241.30]**.

[241.10]
Variations made before a grant of probate. If a variation of a deceased person's dispositions is decided on which will reduce or eliminate the inheritance tax liability of his estate on his death, it will be an advantage if it can be put into effect before the grant of probate, so that the lesser amount consequent on the variation having been made is what is payable on account when applying for the grant. An instrument of variation may be made before there is a grant of representation and before the estate has been administered; although the right of a beneficiary who is interested in the unadministered estate of a deceased person does not amount to an equitable interest, he has a right to have the estate duly administered which he can make a disposition of: *Re Leigh's Will Trusts, Handyside v Durbridge* [1970] Ch 277, [1969] 3 All ER 432. The Inland Revenue accept that instruments of variation may validly be made before the grant of probate and their guidance note on Inland Revenue Accounts (January 1994—see *Foster's Inheritance Tax*, X3.53) says that such an instrument should state who are the proposed personal representatives and recite that they intend to apply for a grant at a (named) Probate Registry shortly. A copy of the deed and the notice of election (if a separate one has been executed) must be submitted with the Account when applying for the grant if the inheritance tax to be paid as a condition of probate is to be assessed on the basis that the variation has been made.

[241.11]
Necessary parties. Problems sometimes arise as to who are the necessary parties to an instrument of variation, typically where minors have beneficial interests in the estate, or there are beneficiaries who refuse to join in the variation, or are far away or difficult to contact. Section 142(1) requires that a variation of a disposition must be made by all those who benefit under the disposition. These might include not only persons with absolutely vested interests in the property whose disposition it is sought to vary, but also those with contingent interests, or those who are merely objects of a discretionary power over such property. On the other hand, where there is an absolute gift coupled with an expression of a wish which does not create a legal obligation that the donee should distribute the property in a particular way, only the donee would be a necessary party to a variation of the disposition. The personal representatives are not a necessary party (unless they are also beneficiaries relevant to the variation), although it is usual to include them, and they are a necessary party to the election that s 142(1) applies if it involves additional inheritance tax being payable (see para **[241.3]**). It is also important that the personal representatives should have notice of any instrument of variation to which they have not been parties, so that they know who to pay or distribute assets of the estate to.

Who are necessary parties to an instrument of variation is thus a matter of construction of the will in relation to the result which it is desired to achieve, and they are not necessarily everybody interested under the will. For example, if there are numerous pecuniary legacies in the will which it is not intended to cut down or alter in any way, the persons entitled to those legacies will not be needed as parties, or it may be possible to alter a life interest without altering remainder trusts under which minors are interested (for an example, see Form F3.9 at para **[241.30]**). The donees under a variation, or the trustees where the variation takes the form of creating or varying a trust, would usually be named as parties to the instrument, but the importance of their executing the instrument would usually be confined to showing that they accept the benefit conferred by it, unless they are also making some variation of dispositions in their favour under the same estate.

If there is the problem for a proposed deed of variation that the desired objectives cannot be attained without the variation of interests which are or might become vested in minors or unborn or unascertained persons, a possible solution is to apply for a variation of the trusts under the Variation of Trusts Act 1958. The Inland Revenue accept that an arrangement approved under that Act can be an instrument of variation within s 142. This is only a course to pursue where substantial amounts of tax are at stake, and if it is to be pursued proceedings need to be instituted promptly in order to get a court hearing date before two years have elapsed from the deceased's death.

For the appropriate parties to 'double death' variations see para **[241.14]**.

[241.12]
Subject to tax or free of tax. When framing a variation, careful consideration should be given to whether the dispositions which are to take effect as a result of the variation, and which will be deemed to have been made by the deceased, will be free of inheritance tax or subject to inheritance tax on the deceased's death. This is particularly important where the result of the variation is that part of the estate will be exempt from inheritance tax and part will not, because if the non-exempt part of the estate exceeds the deceased's available nil-rate inheritance tax band at the time of his death so that inheritance tax will be payable, more inheritance tax may be payable if non-residuary gifts to non-exempt persons are free of tax on the deceased's death than if they are subject to tax: see the Preliminary Note to B14 at para **[214.74]**. When drafting a variation by which a deceased person is deemed to have made non-residuary gifts to non-exempt persons these non-residuary gifts should be expressly made either free of tax or subject to tax on the testator's death (see, for example, cl 1 of Form F3.6 at para **[241.27]**). If no such direction is included, they will usually be free of tax: see the Preliminary Note to B14 at paras **[214.55]**–**[214.60]**.

[241.13]
Tax avoidance. A common type of variation is one which results in an amount equal to the value of the testator's available nil-rate inheritance tax band passing to non-exempt beneficiaries, and the rest of the estate passing to the surviving spouse in order to obtain the spouse exemption. If the testator's estate includes property with the benefit of business or agricultural property relief, this can often be advantageously passed to non-exempt beneficiaries. In all cases where an estate containing such property is being varied, careful consideration should be given as to whether and how the dispositions of such property are to be varied. For the relevant considerations, see the Preliminary Notes to B5 at **[205.1]** et seq and to C11 at **[233.1]** et seq. There is also discussion of agricultural relief in the Preliminary Note to C12 at **[234.1]** et seq.

When formulating and drafting a variation to take advantage of s 142(1), one must take care that the Revenue will not be able to invoke s 142(3) (extraneous consideration—see para **[241.7]**) or the doctrine of *W T Ramsay Ltd v IRC* [1982] AC 300, [1981] 1 All ER 865, under which a step taken in a pre-ordained series of transactions and having no purpose other than tax avoidance can be disregarded. It is sometimes the case that on a testator's death a part, at least, of his estate passes to his children triggering an inheritance tax charge. If his children entered into a deed of variation redirecting property they received under the will to the testator's widow so as to obtain the surviving spouse exemption on the testator's death, but upon the understanding that the widow later passed the property back to the children by a potentially exempt transfer, the Revenue could contend either that extraneous consideration prohibited by s 142(3) had been provided for the variation, or else that the whole arrangement, ie the deed and the later transfer of property, is vitiated by an application of the *Ramsay* doctrine. It seems that the Revenue does consider that *Ramsay* can apply in an inheritance tax context, and in a case where property is redirected by instrument of variation to the testator's spouse they may enquire whether before the variation there was any discussion between the parties as to how the property redirected to the spouse should be dealt with and whether the spouse has made or is contemplating any transfers of the property redirected to her: see *Foster's Inheritance Tax*, D4.15.

However, the decision of the House of Lords in *Fitzwilliam v IRC* [1993] 3 All ER 184, [1993] 1 WLR 1189, that *Ramsay* did not apply in the particular circumstances of that case, may have paved the way for the contention that the *Ramsay* doctrine cannot apply where each step in a series of transactions has its own tax consequences. So where, for example, by virtue of a deed of variation a widow takes an interest in possession in property which is to terminate some time after the date of the deed of variation (and after the expiry of the period of two years from the testator's death) when absolute remainder trusts for the children are to take effect, it is arguable that *Ramsay* cannot apply to prevent, first, the spouse exemption from being available in respect of the property on the testator's death, and secondly, to prevent the widow from being treated as making a potentially exempt transfer on the termination of her interest in possession, because while the widow is entitled to the interest in possession there are income tax and potential inheritance tax consequences which make it impossible to ignore her brief entitlement and it is only if one can ignore such an entitlement that *Ramsay* can have any application. Form F3.7 (at para **[241.28]**), is an example of a variation conferring a short-term interest in possession on a surviving spouse. The interest in possession should terminate under the terms of the deed after the expiry of two years after the testator's death for reasons given at para **[241.8]**. But it should be noted that the Revenue are known not to approve of such variations: see *Foster's Inheritance Tax*, D4.15.

[241.14]
Double death variations. Where two spouses die within two years of each other, and the estate, or part of the estate, of the first spouse to die (the husband, say) has passed to the surviving spouse (the wife) without his available nil-rate inheritance tax band being fully utilised, but the wife's chargeable estate (enhanced by her husband's estate) exceeds her available inheritance tax nil-rate band, the personal representatives and beneficiaries of the wife's estate may consider executing a deed of variation within two years of the husband's death, redirecting property up to the value of the husband's available unused inheritance tax nil-rate band away from the wife's estate and into a non-exempt gift. In this way the husband's available nil-rate inheritance tax band is fully

utilised, and the wife's estate is reduced for inheritance tax purposes, thereby reducing the amount of inheritance tax payable.

The Revenue accept that such a variation can fall within the ITA 1984, s 142(1) if an appropriate election is made, even where no significant change of substance is made to the ultimate destination of the property subject to the instrument of variation. For it to be effective it must be made by the personal representatives of the second to die, but with the consent of the beneficiaries under the estate of the second to die (or at any rate those whose interests under the second estate are affected). The Revenue will accept the written consent of such beneficiaries in a separate document (*Inland Revenue Tax Bulletin*, Issue 15 (February 1995); *Variation of inheritances following a death*—see *Foster's Inheritance Tax*, X6.63).

One important point to watch in relation to double death variations is the prohibition of extraneous consideration in s 142(3) (see para **[241.7]**). If a double death variation was to involve an exchange of beneficial interests under one estate for beneficial interests under the other, the arrangement would fall foul of s 142(3); the latter only permits exchanges of interests under the same estate to fall within s 142(1).

It seems that the Revenue will regard the variation as ineffective if it purports to vary a life interest of the surviving spouse in the first to die's estate: see Inland Revenue Capital Taxes *IHT Newsletter* December 2001, p 5. It also seems, from the same source, that they will accept a disclaimer by the life tenant's personal representatives as effective where it is possible as a matter of general law for them to disclaim it.

Form F3.8 (at para **[241.29]**), is an example of a 'double death' variation.

[241.15]
Multiple variations. It was held in *Russell v IRC* [1988] 2 All ER 405, [1988] 1 WLR 834 that it is not possible in relation to an instrument of variation within s 142 to vary the dispositions of it in such a way as to have s 142 apply to such a variation of a variation. Thus if there is a mistake in an instrument of variation a further variation of it cannot be used as a remedy, although it may be possible (if there is appropriate evidence) to apply to the court for rectification of it (see *Foster's Inheritance Tax*, C1.34). On the other hand, it is possible to have more than one instrument of variation within s 142 relating to the same estate if each instrument affects different assets.

[241.16]
Disclaimers. If a disclaimer is contemplated the following points should be borne in mind:

(i) The law relating to disclaimers is technical and obscure. While some of its salient features are noted below, reference should be made to *Ing on Bona Vacantia* at pp 207 et seq and *Halsbury's Laws of England*, 4th edn Reissue, Vol 50, paras **[390]**–**[392]** at pp 284–286, for a fuller treatment. See also Vol 1, para **[46.1]** et seq.

(ii) The disclaimer does not strictly speaking operate as a disposition of property. As was said in an old case, a man 'cannot have an estate put into him in spite of his teeth'. Thus a disclaimer will not divest a gift in favour of the disclaiming beneficiary, but will prevent it from vesting in him. Acceptance of a gift or any part of it is inconsistent with an intention to renounce or disclaim it. The right to disclaim a gift is therefore extinguished as soon as any benefit has been received thereunder: see eg *Re Wimperis, Wicken v Wilson* [1914] 1 Ch 502. While it is usually possible to disclaim one testamentary gift without disclaiming another, this will not be permissible where such right is impliedly excluded. This will often be the case where gifts of onerous property and unencumbered property are made to the same person. Nor is it permissible to disclaim part only of a single gift. In *Re Joel, Rogerson v Joel* [1943] Ch 311, [1943] 2 All ER 263, CA, a gift of a leasehold house 'together with its contents' was in fact held to be a single gift and the legatee was accordingly held not to be entitled to disclaim the onerous leasehold whilst accepting the contents of the house.

(iii) Since, as we have already seen, disclaimers operate not to divest a gift but to prevent it from vesting, there is no requirement of form. A disclaimer even of an interest in land may thus be effected by informal writing, by conduct or even orally. But to be effective for the purposes of s 142 of the ITA 1984 the disclaimer must be in writing. In general a disclaimer may also be retracted where nobody has altered his position on the faith of it. This right is not thought to be available where the disclaimer is by deed: see *Ing*, supra at pp 209–210. In the interests of certainty it seems preferable for a disclaimer to be effected by deed.

(iv) It has sometimes been argued that it is not possible to disclaim an interest arising under an intestacy on the grounds that such interest is conferred by statute: see eg Sir William Goodhart QC's article 'Disclaimer of Interests on Intestacy?' in 40 *Conveyancer* at p 292. This would be an inconvenient restriction and, as Sir William himself points out, is inconsistent with the actual decision of Walton J in *Re Scott, Widdows v Friends of the Clergy Corpn* [1975] 2 All ER 1033, [1975] 1 WLR 1260, though the point was not in fact argued in that case.

(v) It is essential to give careful thought to what dispositions will take effect on a disclaimer being made. For example, sometimes a disclaimer of a life interest will accelerate the remainder interests, and sometimes it will give rise to a partial intestacy, depending on the nature of the remainder trusts; see Vol 1, para **[48.4]** et seq. *Re Scott* discusses the effect of a disclaimer of certain interests arising under the intestacy rules, but the difficult problem as to the effect of a disclaimer by a child of a deceased intestate of his interest in that intestate's estate where that child himself has issue seems now to have been answered by the Court of Appeal in *Re DWS* [2001] Ch 568, [2001] 1 All ER 97, a case concerned with the effect on intestate succession of the forfeiture rule disqualifying a murderer from benefiting from his intestate victim's estate. Aldous LJ held that the Administration of Estates Act 1925, s 47(1)(I) was unambiguous and should be given its literal meaning that no issue could take if the parent was living at the death of the intestate; that if a surviving parent was prevented from taking by disclaimer or disqualification, the intestate's estate should pass not to the surviving parent's child, but to others. The Court was divided upon who should take, however, the majority holding in favour of the collateral relations within the Administration of Estates Act 1925, s 47(1)(v), but Sedley LJ preferring the estate to pass bona vacantia.

[241.17]
Capital gains tax. The TCGA 1992, s 62(6) to (10) contains provisions for capital gains tax which are for the most part identical with the ITA 1984, s 142, though with some necessary differences arising from differences in the nature of the tax and one important difference of substance. These subsections apply to property of which the deceased was competent to dispose by will, other than under a power of appointment or the statutory power to dispose of entailed property, but with the express addition of any severable share under a joint tenancy (see sub-s (10)); it seems to us that this covers the same kinds of property as the differently worded provisions of ITA 1984, s 142. Again an election by notice in writing is needed for the section to apply to a disposition varying the deceased's dispositions, though not for a disclaimer, but in no circumstances do the personal representatives have to join in (see s 62(7)).

The important difference between the TCGA 1992, s 62(6) and the ITA 1984, s 142(1), however, is that whereas the result of an election that the latter should apply is that the variation is treated as made by the deceased for all inheritance tax purposes, the result of the corresponding capital gains tax election is that the variation is treated as made by the deceased only for the purposes of the TCGA 1992, s 62, a section containing general provisions relevant to death (see *Marshall v Kerr* [1995] 1 AC 148, [1994] 3 All ER 106, HL). So the consequences of a capital gains tax election are only that the variation is not a disposal for capital gains tax purposes and the persons who have assets transferred to them pursuant to the variation will receive them 'as legatees' within the TCGA 1992, s 62(4), so that the acquisition value of the assets in their hands is that of the personal representatives. For all other capital gains tax purposes, such as identifying the settlor of a settlement for the purposes of charging capital gains tax on a settlor with an interest in a settlement under the TCGA 1992, s 77, or identifying the settlor of a settlement of foreign property, the person who made the variation will be the settlor and not the deceased.

Where a variation is entered into before the administration of an estate is complete, or before it is complete in respect of any property which is to be the subject of the variation, an election in accordance with the TCGA 1992, s 62(7) should always be made because the subject-matter of the variation is not strictly any specific asset of the estate but a chose in action, namely a right to have the estate duly administered, for which a beneficiary has no capital gains tax acquisition cost: *Re Leigh's Will Trusts, Handyside v Durbridge* [1970] Ch 277, [1969] 3 All ER 432 and *Marshall v Kerr* [1995] 1 AC 148, [1994] 3 All ER 106, HL. Therefore, an election would seem to be essential to prevent the variation from being a disposal for capital gains tax purposes.

[241.18]
Stamp duty. An instrument within the ITA 1984, s 142 other than a disclaimer used to attract ad valorem stamp duty as a voluntary disposition to the extent of the bounty passing thereunder: cf *Thorn v IRC* [1976] 2 All ER 622, [1976] 1 WLR 915. The charge to ad valorem stamp duty on voluntary dispositions has now been abolished as has the charge to ad valorem duty on instruments varying the dispositions of the estate of a deceased person where such instruments would formerly have attracted duty as conveyances on sale, provided that such instruments are executed within two years of the death: Finance Act 1985,

ss 82(1) and 84(1). But the fixed £5 duty and the need for adjudication are avoided if the instrument is certified to be an instrument falling within category L or category M of the Schedule to the Stamp Duty (Exempt Instruments) Regulations 1987. As a disclaimer operates to prevent the vesting of property in the disclaiming beneficiary, it is not thought that it constituted a 'voluntary disposition' for stamp duty purposes. Accordingly a disclaimer by deed has never attracted more than nominal duty.

[241.19]
Income tax. There is no income tax provision corresponding to the ITA 1984, s 142, and an instrument within s 142 will not be treated as a disposition by the deceased for the purposes of income tax. The main implication of this is that where an instrument of variation settles property on trust it will be a settlement of which the maker of the instrument is the settlor for income tax purposes. Accordingly, if the maker of the instrument retains a beneficial interest (eg he is a beneficiary under a discretionary trust), the income of the relevant property will be subject to income tax as his income under the Income and Corporation Taxes Act 1988, s 660A and, even if he is not a beneficiary, if his minor children are beneficiaries income which is applied for them will be taxed as his under s 660B of the same Act.

However, it is thought that the Inland Revenue view is that a disclaimer does not constitute a 'settlement' for income tax purposes. Thus if it is possible for a beneficiary under a deceased person's estate to achieve a desired result by a disclaimer rather than an instrument of variation, and that desired result would have adverse consequences under the provisions for charging income tax on settlors of settlements (for example, a parent wants to dispose of a life interest in favour of his minor children who are interested in remainder), a disclaimer would have the advantage that he would not be treated as the settlor.

For instruments of variation made after 5 April 1995 there is a change in income tax law which enables an instrument of variation to have some retrospective effect for income tax purposes, if the instrument relates to a residuary estate which is still in the course of administration when the instrument is made. Where this is the case, and there is any income of that residuary estate which has already accrued to the personal representatives before the date of the transfer, and which has not been distributed by them to any beneficiaries, then the Income and Corporation Taxes Act 1988, ss 695 to 701 (as amended by Finance Act 1995, Sch 18) have the effect that someone with an interest (absolute or limited) in a residuary estate still in the course of administration is able to transfer the right to such income so that the income is charged to income tax as the income of the person to whom the income is transferred. The essential scheme is, broadly, that any income of the estate which is distributed to a beneficiary while the estate is being administered is taxed as the income of that beneficiary, and any income which is still undistributed at the point when the administration is completed is taxed as the income of the person who is then entitled to it. These new rules can apply in relation to the estate of a person who died before 6 April 1995, if the administration of his estate had not been completed before that date. Accordingly, it can now be worthwhile from an income tax point of view to include in an instrument of variation, which disposes of the present or future right to income or capital of a residuary estate in the course of administration, a disposition of the right to undistributed income of the residuary estate which has accrued before the variation, if the personal income tax rates of the recipient of the income will be lower than those of the maker of the instrument.

[241.20]
Family provision claims. A provision with an effect similar to the ITA 1984, s 142, is s 146 of the same Act, which treats an order made under the Inheritance (Provision for Family and Dependants) Act 1975, including the terms of a compromise scheduled to an order staying or dismissing proceedings under that Act, as dispositions made by the deceased. But s 29A of the ITA 1984 reduces the exemption available on death where an exempt beneficiary settles a claim under the Inheritance (Provision for Family and Dependants) Act 1975 against the estate out of his or her own resources. Thus, if the deceased's widow takes the whole estate under his will but settles a claim by the deceased's mistress out of the widow's personal assets, the exempt part of the deceased's estate will be appropriately reduced. For a more detailed treatment of the ITA 1984, ss 146 and 29A, see *Foster's Inheritance Tax*, D4.41–D4.47.

[241.21]
Other events deemed to be dispositions by the deceased. For distributions of personalty in accordance with the deceased's wishes within two years of his death which are treated as dispositions by the deceased by virtue of the ITA 1984, s 143, see B4 at paras **[204.9]** and **[204.10]**. For distributions out of discretionary trusts created by will within two years of the deceased's death which are treated as dispositions by the deceased see C3 at para **[225.83]** et seq, the Preliminary Note to F4 at paras **[242.4]–[242.6]** and Form F4.1 at para **[242.7]**.

[241.22]

FORM F3.1: Disclaimer by devisee of a gift under a will—short form[1]

BY THIS DEED I the undersigned [*name of devisee*] of etc hereby disclaim all benefit under the devise in my favour contained in the will of [*testator*] dated —— —— and proved in the —— Registry of the Family Division on —— by —— the executors named therein and also disclaim all estate and interest in the property the subject of the said devise.

IN WITNESS WHEREOF I have executed these presents as my deed this —— day of ——

SIGNED and delivered as a deed by the said [*name*] in the presence of— }   [*Signature of party*]

[*Signature, address and description of witness*]

[*Signature of and execution as a deed by the party disclaiming*][2]

1   Although a disclaimer may be effected informally, a deed is preferable: see para **[241.16]**, sub-para (iii). Devisees occasionally wish to disclaim property subject to onerous charges, covenants, or conditions. Forms F3.1 and F3.2 are alternatives. The shorter one is quite sufficient in the case of a specific devisee who is only once referred to in the will. The longer form may be required where it is necessary to set out the particular devise disclaimed in order to make the position clear. It must be remembered that there may be cases of related gifts where one cannot be disclaimed and the other accepted. See further Vol 1, para **[46.1]** et seq and **[241.16]**, sub-para (ii).

2   The requirements of the Law of Property (Miscellaneous Provisions) Act 1989, s 1, for the making of a deed are that it is clear on its face that it is intended by the parties to it to be a deed, that it is signed by each party in the presence of a witness who attests the signature (two witnesses if someone signs for a party), and that it is delivered as a deed by each party or someone authorised to do so on his behalf. Sealing is not necessary.

[241.23]

FORM F3.2:   Disclaimer—longer form[1]

THIS DEED OF DISCLAIMER is made the —— day of —— BY [*devisee*] of etc (hereinafter called 'the devisee').

WHEREAS by his will (hereinafter called 'the will') dated —— [testator] late of —— appointed —— (hereinafter called 'the executors') to be the executors thereof and thereby (inter alia) devised unto the devisee [set out devise].

AND WHEREAS the said [testator] died on —— and the executors duly proved the will on —— in the —— Registry of the Family Division.

AND WHEREAS the devisee has duly notified the executors that he does not intend to accept the said devise and is desirous of disclaiming all interest thereunder.

AND WHEREAS the executors have made no assent in respect of the said devise nor has the devisee in any way entered into possession of the property devised or done any act or thing that might be or amount to an acceptance of the said devise.

NOW THIS DEED WITNESSES that the devisee hereby disclaims the said devise in his favour contained in the will and all benefit thereunder and further disclaims all estate and interest in the property thereby devised to him [provided that nothing herein contained shall in any way affect his acceptance of and the right to receive all other gifts and benefits under the will nor his acceptance of his appointment as trustee thereby made].[2]

IN WITNESS ETC[3]

1   Although a disclaimer may be effected informally, a deed is preferable: see para **[241.16]**, sub-para (iii). Devisees occasionally wish to disclaim property subject to onerous charges, covenants, or conditions. Forms F3.1 and F3.2 are alternatives. The shorter one is quite sufficient in the case of a specific devisee who is only once referred to in the will. The longer form may be required where it is necessary to set out the particular devise disclaimed in order to make the position clear. It must be remembered that there may be cases of related gifts where one cannot be disclaimed and the other accepted. See further Vol 1, para **[46.1]** et seq and **[241.16]**, sub-para (ii).

2   As to when one gift cannot be disclaimed if another is accepted, see Vol 1, para **[46.3]**.

3   For execution, see Form F3.1 at para **[241.22]**.

[241.24]

FORM F3.3:   Disclaimer of a life interest

THIS DEED OF DISCLAIMER[1] is made the [*date*] BETWEEN [*name*] of [*address*] (hereinafter called 'the Widow') of the one part and [*name*] of [*address*] and [*name*] of [*address*] (hereinafter called 'the Trustees') of the other part.

WHEREAS:

(A)   By his last Will dated the [*date*] [*name*] late of [*address*] (hereinafter called 'the Testator') appointed the Trustees to be the executors and trustees thereof and left his estate Upon Trust for the Widow for life with remainder Upon Trust for the Testator's children [*name*] and [*name*] in equal shares absolutely.

(B)   The Testator died on the [*date*][2] survived by the Widow and his said children [and on the [*date*] his said Will was duly proved by the Trustees].[3]

(C)   The Widow has not received any benefit from the estate of the Testator[4] and desires to disclaim all her said life interest therein.

NOW THIS DEED made in pursuance of the said desire WITNESSES that the WIDOW HEREBY IRREVOCABLY DISCLAIMS AND RENOUNCES all right title or interest to or in the estate of the Testator and the income thereof or any part thereof respectively to which she is or may be entitled under the Testator's said Will or otherwise.[5]

IN WITNESS whereof the parties hereto have executed these presents as their deed the day and year first above written.[6]

SIGNED and delivered as a deed by the said [*name*]
in the presence of—   [*Signature of party*]

[*Signature, address and description of witness*]

[*The foregoing from 'SIGNED' to be repeated for each party to the deed*]

---

1   Although a disclaimer may be affected informally, a deed is preferable: see para **[241.16]**, sub-para (iii).
2   The death must not be more than two years before the disclaimer if advantage is to be taken of the ITA 1984, s 142(1).
3   It is not essential that the will of the testator should have been proved or that his estate should have been administered: see paras **[241.10]** and **[241.25]**, n 3.
4   It is essential if a disclaimer is to be effective that no benefit should have been received by the person disclaiming: see para **[241.16]**, sub-para (ii).
5   It is sometimes necessary (though not in this case) that the disclaimer should operate not only on the interest conferred by the will but also on any interest that the widow would take on an intestacy. See para **[241.16]**, sub-para (v).
6   The requirements of the Law of Property (Miscellaneous Provisions) Act 1989, s 1, for the making of a deed are that it is clear on its face that it is intended by the parties to it to be a deed, that it is signed by each party in the presence of a witness who attests the signature (two witnesses if someone signs for a party), and that it is delivered as a deed by each party or someone authorised to do so on his behalf. Sealing is not necessary.

[241.25]

FORM F3.4: Deed of variation of dispositions effected by a will

THIS DEED OF VARIATION is made the [*date*] BETWEEN [*name*] of [*address*] (hereinafter called 'the Widow') of the first part [*name*] of [*address*] (hereinafter called 'the Son') of the second part and [*name*] of [*address*] and [*name*] of [*address*] (hereinafter together called 'the Trustees') of the third part.

WHEREAS:

(A)   By his last Will (hereinafter called 'the Will') dated [*date*] [*name*] late of [*address*] (hereinafter called 'the Testator') appointed the Trustees to be the executors and trustees thereof and after bequeathing his personal chattels to the Widow absolutely left his residuary estate (subject to the payment thereout of his funeral and testamentary expenses and debts) Upon Trust to pay the income thereof to the Widow during her life and after her death Upon Trust as to both capital and income for the Son absolutely.

(B)   The Testator died on the [*date*][1] [and on the [*date*] the Will was duly proved by the Trustees][2].

(C)   The Son has two children only (hereinafter called 'the Children') namely [*name*] and [*name*].

(D)   The Widow and the Son desire to vary the trusts of the Will for the benefit of the Children in manner hereinafter appearing.

NOW THIS DEED WITNESSES as follows:

1.   IT IS HEREBY AGREED AND DECLARED by way of variation of the disposition of the Testator's residuary estate effected by the Will that the Will shall be construed and take effect and be deemed to have taken effect as from the death of the Testator[3] as if in lieu of the trusts therein declared of the Testator's said residuary estate it had contained a direction that (subject to the payment thereout of his funeral and testamentary expenses and debts) the said residuary estate and the income thereof should be held IN TRUST for the Children in equal shares absolutely.[4]

2.   The parties hereto hereby give notice to the Board of Inland Revenue in accordance with section 142(2) of the Inheritance Tax Act 1984 and section 62(7) of the Taxation of Chargeable Gains Act 1992 that they elect that the provisions of section 142(1) thereof and section 62(6) thereof respectively shall apply to the variation made by this deed To the intent that such variation shall be treated as if it was made by the Deceased for the purposes of inheritance tax and capital gains tax.[5]

3.   The parties hereto hereby certify that this instrument falls within category M in the Schedule to the Stamp Duty (Exempt Instruments) Regulations 1987.[6]

IN WITNESS ETC[7]

---

1   The death must have occurred within the two years immediately preceding the deed to take advantage of the ITA 1984, s 142(1): see para **[241.1]**.

2   It is not essential that the will should have been proved or the estate administered. Although the right of a beneficiary who is interested in the unadministered estate of a deceased person does not amount to an equitable interest, he has the right to have the estate duly administered and this right is transmissible: *Re Leigh's Will Trusts, Handyside v Durbridge* [1970] Ch 277, [1969] 3 All ER 432. Accordingly persons interested in unadministered estate can deal with their interests by way of deed of variation. However, in such a case an election that the TCGA 1992, s 62(6) should apply should always be made, see Preliminary Note at para **[241.7]**. See the Preliminary Note at para **[241.10]** for Inland Revenue practice on variations made before a grant of probate.

3   These words are designed to ensure that the variation is retrospective and that all intervening interests are eliminated. But it is probably not essential for intervening interests to be eliminated: see para **[241.4]**. However, it could be effective for income tax purposes: see para **[241.19]**.

4   The substituted trusts are of a very simple nature, but more elaborate trusts may be substituted.

5   The Inland Revenue will accept a copy of the deed containing this clause as an effective notice of election. A copy must be sent to the relevant Inspector of Taxes, as well as the Capital Taxes Office, if there is a capital gains tax election as well as an inheritance tax one. The notice of election must be given within six months after the date of the deed. For further points on the notice of election see the Preliminary Note at para **[241.3]**.

6   See the Preliminary Note at para **[241.18]**.

7   For execution, see Form F3.3 at para **[241.24]**.

[241.26]

FORM F3.5:   Deed of variation of disposition of property held by deceased and spouse on a joint tenancy

THIS DEED OF VARIATION is made the [*date*] BETWEEN [*name*] of [*address*] (hereinafter called 'the Widow') of the one part and [*name*] of [*address*] (hereinafter called 'the Daughter') of the other part.

WHEREAS:

(A)   Immediately prior to the death on the [*date*][1] of [*name*] late of [*address*] (hereinafter called 'the Deceased') the Deceased and the Widow held the property (hereinafter called 'the Property') known as —— upon trust [to sell the same to hold the net proceeds of sale thereof][2] for themselves as beneficial joint tenants.

(B)   Following the death of the Deceased the Widow is absolutely entitled to the Property by right of survivorship.

(C)   The Widow desires to vary the disposition of the Deceased's severable share in the Property [(or the net proceeds of sale thereof)][3] effected by right of survivorship so as to benefit the Daughter in the manner hereinafter appearing.

NOW THIS DEED WITNESSES as follows:

1.   The Widow and the Daughter hereby agree and declare by way of variation of the disposition of the Deceased's severable share in the Property [(or the net proceeds of sale thereof)][4] which took effect on the Deceased's death by right of survivorship as follows—

(1)   That it shall be deemed that the beneficial joint tenancy of the Deceased and the Widow in the Property [(or the net proceeds of sale thereof)][5] had been severed immediately prior to the death of the Deceased so that immediately prior to the death of the Deceased he and the Widow held the Property upon trust [to sell the same to hold the net proceeds of sale thereof][6] for themselves as beneficial tenants in common in equal shares.

(2)   That the Deceased's deemed one-half share of the Property [(or the net proceeds of sale thereof)][7] as aforesaid shall be deemed to have been given to the Daughter absolutely by a will made by the Deceased (subject to the payment of any inheritance tax attributable thereto on or by reason of his death)[8] and the Widow shall henceforth hold the Property upon trust [to sell the same to hold the net proceeds of sale thereof][9] for herself and the Daughter as beneficial tenants in common in equal shares.[10]

2.   The parties hereto hereby certify that this instrument falls within category M in the Schedule to the Stamp Duty (Exempt Instruments) Regulations 1987.[11]

[3.   The parties hereto hereby give notice to the Board of Inland Revenue in accordance with section 142(2) of the Inheritance Tax Act 1984 and section 62(7) of the Taxation of Chargeable Gains Act 1992 that they elect that the provisions of section 142(1) thereof and section 62(6) thereof respectively shall apply to the variation made by this deed To the intent that such variation shall be treated as if it was made by the Deceased for the purposes of inheritance tax and capital gains tax.[12]]

IN WITNESS[13]

1   The deed must be made within two years of the death if an election is to be made for ITA 1984, s 142(1) to apply: see the Preliminary Note at paras **[241.1]–[241.3]**.
2   These words will not be appropriate if the joint tenancy was not under a trust for sale at the Deceased's death, and should be omitted if it was not. The TLATA 1996 has the effect that it will not have been under a trust for sale if the Deceased died on or after 1 January 1997 and there was no express trust for sale in the disposition creating the joint tenancy.
3   See n 2 supra.
4   See n 2 supra.
5   See n 2 supra.
6   See n 2 supra.
7   See n 2 supra.
8   A deceased's severable share of joint property bears its own tax on the deceased's death (see para **[214.60]**, sub-para (2)), but we would suggest that in the case of a variation of a deceased's severable share of joint property the variation should always be made expressly subject to its bearing any inheritance tax payable on or by reason of the death of the deceased to avoid any doubt as to where the burden should fall. Although it would not seem necessary for a deceased's personal representatives to be a party to a variation of a severable share of joint property since it at no time vests in them, they are necessary parties to any election that the ITA 1984, s 142(1) should apply to the variation where the variation results in additional tax being payable (ITA 1984, s 142(2)(b)). They will be liable for this additional tax (ITA 1984, s 200(1)), even if the ultimate burden of it will fall on the donee (see the Preliminary Note to B14 at para **[214.60]**, sub-para (2)).
9   If the parties wish that the Widow should hold the property upon trust for sale (whether it was so held at the time of the Deceased's death or not) these words should be included. Although held upon trust for sale, a power to postpone sale will be implied: see TLATA 1996, s 4(1) (Part G, para **[246.89]**). Otherwise, the words can be omitted and the Property will be held on a trust of land, with the Widow having wide powers to manage it, including power to sell it.
10   If the Deceased's estate apart from this severable share under the joint tenancy is or may be insolvent, it should be made clear that the deed is conferring an interest in the property on the Daughter or other donee under the deed, and not upon the Deceased's creditors. It was held in *Re Palmer (a debtor)* [1994] Ch 316, [1994] 3 All ER 835, CA that a deceased person's unsevered interest under a joint tenancy is not part of his estate available for creditors, where the estate goes into insolvent administration. This has now been reversed by the Insolvency Act 1986, s 421A, which enables an application to be made to the court for a surviving joint tenant to provide compensation to creditors of the deceased.
11   See the Preliminary Note at para **[241.18]**.

12   The Inland Revenue will accept a copy of the deed containing this clause as an effective notice
    of election. A copy must be sent to the relevant Inspector of Taxes as well as the Capital Taxes
    Office if there is a capital gains tax election as well as an inheritance tax one. The notice of
    election must be given within six months after the date of the deed. If the personal
    representatives are necessary parties to the election (see n 2 supra), it will be better to have a
    separate notice of election and omit this clause from the deed. For further points on the notice of
    election see the Preliminary Note at para **[241.3]**.
13   For execution, see Form F3.3 at para **[241.24]**.

[241.27]

FORM F3.6:   Deed of variation creating a nil-rate band non-exempt legacy where entire estate given to the deceased's widow[1]

THIS DEED OF VARIATION is made the [*date*] BETWEEN [*name*] of [*address*] (hereinafter called 'the Widow') of the first part [*name*] of [*address*] and [*name*] of [*address*] (hereinafter called 'the Children') of the second part and [*name*] of [*address*] and [*name*] of [*address*] (hereinafter together called 'the Trustees') of the third part.

WHEREAS:

(A)   By his last Will (hereinafter called 'the Will') dated [*date*] [*name*] late of [*address*] (hereinafter called 'the Testator') appointed the Trustees the executors and trustees thereof.

(B)   The Testator died on [*date*][2] [and on the [*date*] the Will was proved by the Trustees in the —— Probate Registry].[3]

(C)   By Clause —— of the Will the Testator gave his residuary estate (therein defined and hereinafter called 'the Residuary Estate') to the Trustees to hold the same upon trust for the Widow absolutely.

(D)   The Widow desires to vary the disposition of the Residuary Estate effected by the Will so as to benefit the Children in the manner hereinafter appearing.

NOW THIS DEED WITNESSES as follows:

1.   By way of variation of the above-recited disposition of the Residuary Estate of the Testator effected by the Will the Widow the Children and the Trustees hereby agree and declare that the Will shall have effect and the estate of the Testator shall be administered as if the Testator had given by the Will a pecuniary legacy of [£234,000][4] to the Children in equal shares absolutely subject to payment thereout of any inheritance tax payable in respect of the Testator's death and attributable thereto.[5]

2.   Subject as aforesaid the provisions of the Will shall continue to have effect.

3.   The parties hereto hereby certify that this instrument falls within category M in the Schedule to the Stamp Duty (Exempt Instruments) Regulations 1987.[6]

4.   The parties hereto hereby give notice to the Board of Inland Revenue in accordance with section 142(2) of the Inheritance Tax Act 1984 and section 62(7) of the Taxation of Chargeable Gains Act 1992 that they elect that the provisions of section 142(1) thereof and section 62(6) thereof respectively shall apply to the variation made by this deed To the Intent that the variation made

hereby shall be treated as if it was made by the Testator for the purposes of inheritance tax and capital gains tax.[7]

IN WITNESS ETC[8]

1   This is perhaps one of the commonest types of deed of variation. It makes use of the deceased's nil-rate band where it is wholly or largely unused as a result of all or most of the estate being given to his widow. For nil-rate band gifts see Part A, para **[200.101]** and for nil-rate band discretionary trusts see the Note in B18 at para **[218.16]**–**[218.18]**.

2   The deed must be made within two years of the death if an election is to be made for the ITA 1984, s 142(1) to apply: see the Preliminary Note at paras **[241.1]** and **[241.3]**.

3   An instrument of variation can be made before probate is granted: see the Preliminary Note at para **[241.1]**.

4   This is the inheritance tax threshold in relation to a death after 5 April 2000. The legacy should be reduced from the amount of the nil-rate band at the deceased's death by any lifetime transfers of value made in the seven years before the deceased's death which are chargeable, by any non-exempt specific gifts or pecuniary legacies contained in the will, and by any other property which is chargeable to inheritance tax as part of the deceased's estate on death. A formula can be used if there is uncertainty about the correct amount of the legacy: see cl 1 of Form F3.8 at para **[241.29]**.

5   These words are worth including if there is the slightest doubt as to whether there might be an inheritance tax liability, and do no harm if there is not. See the Preliminary Note at para **[241.12]** and the Preliminary Note to B14 at para **[214.74]**.

6   See the Preliminary Note at para **[241.18]**.

7   A copy of the deed containing the notice of election must be sent to the Capital Taxes Office and the Inspector of Taxes within six months of the date of the deed. See also the Preliminary Note at para **[241.3]**.

8   For execution, see Form F3.3 at para **[241.24]**.

[241.28]

FORM F3.7:   Deed of variation conferring a short-term interest in possession on a surviving spouse[1]

THIS DEED OF VARIATION is made the [*date*] BETWEEN [*name*] of [*address*] and [*name*] of [*address*] (hereinafter together called 'the Children') of the first part [*name*] of [*address*] (hereinafter called 'the Widow') of the second part and [*name*] of [*address*] and [*name*] of [*address*] (hereinafter together called 'the Trustees') of the third part.

WHEREAS:

(A)   By his last Will (hereinafter called 'the Will') dated [*date*] [*name*] late of [*address*] (hereinafter called 'the Testator') appointed the Trustees executors and trustees thereof.

(B)   The Testator died on the [*date*][2] [and on the [*date*] the Will was duly proved by the Trustees].[3]

(C)   By Clause —— of the Will the Testator gave his residuary estate (therein defined and hereinafter called 'the Residuary Estate') to the Trustees to hold the same upon trust for the Children in equal shares absolutely.

(D)   The Children desire to vary the disposition of the Residuary Estate effected by Clause —— of the Will in the manner hereinafter appearing.

NOW THIS DEED made in pursuance of the said desire and by way of variation of the disposition of the Residuary Estate effected by Clause —— of the Will WITNESSES as follows:

1.   The parties hereto hereby agree and declare that the Will shall have effect and be deemed to have had effect as from the death of the Testator and the Testator's estate shall be administered as if in lieu of the above-recited direction to the Trustees to hold the Residuary Estate upon trust for the Children in equal shares absolutely the Will had contained—

(1)   a legacy to the Children in equal shares absolutely of [£234,000][4] and a direction that any inheritance tax attributable to such legacy by reason of the death of the Testator should be borne by the Children in equal shares absolutely in exoneration of the Residuary Estate of the Testator;[5] and

(2)   a direction to the Trustees to hold the Residuary Estate (subject to the above-mentioned legacy) upon trust to pay the income thereof to the Widow for the period of her life or for a period expiring on the [date][6] (whichever shall be the shorter period) and subject thereto to hold the Residuary Estate (subject to the above-mentioned legacy) and the income thereof upon trust for the Children in equal shares absolutely.

2.   [*Stamp duty certificate as cl 3 of* Form F3.6 *at para* **[241.27]**.]
3.   [*Election as cl 4 of* Form F3.6 *at para* **[241.27]**.]

IN WITNESS ETC[7]

1   This form is designed to pass a testator's estate to non-exempt persons, but channelled through the estate of the surviving spouse by giving him or her a short-term interest in possession so that the spouse exemption may be claimed on the testator's death. Upon the termination of the interest in possession, when the remainder trusts for non-exempt persons take effect, the surviving spouse should be treated as making a potentially exempt transfer which should escape a charge to inheritance tax if the surviving spouse survives it for seven years. See Preliminary Note at para **[241.13]**.
2   The deed must be made within two years of the death if an election is to be made for the ITA 1984, s 142(1) to apply: see the Preliminary Note at paras **[241.1]** and **[241.3]**.
3   An instrument of variation can be made before probate is granted: see the Preliminary Note at para **[241.10]**.
4   See n 4 to cl 1 of Form F3.6 at para **[241.27]**.
5   See n 5 to cl 1 of Form F3.6 at para **[241.27]**.
6   This date should be after the date of the deed of variation and after the expiry of the two-year period from the death of the testator, see Preliminary Note at para **[241.13]**.
7   For execution, see Form F3.3 at para **[241.24]**.

[241.29]

FORM F3.8:   Deed of variation where spouses have died within two years of each other varying the disposition of the estate of the first to die[1]

THIS DEED OF VARIATION is made the [*date*] BETWEEN [*name*] of [*address*] and [*name*] of [*address*] (hereinafter together called 'the Wife's Administrators') of the first part [*name*] of [*address*] [*name*] of [*address*] and [*name*] of [*address*] (hereinafter together called 'the Children') of the second part and [*name*] of [*address*] and [*name*] of [*address*] (hereinafter together called 'the Husband's Executors') of the third part.

WHEREAS:

(A)   By his last Will (hereinafter called 'the Husband's Will') dated *[date]* *[name]* late of *[address]* (hereinafter called 'the Husband') appointed the Husband's Executors executors and trustees thereof and left his whole estate (subject to the payment thereout of his funeral and testamentary expenses and debts) to his widow *[name]* (hereinafter called 'the Wife').

(B)   The Husband died on the *[date]*[2] [and on the *[date]* the Husband's Will was duly proved by the Husband's Executors].[3]

(C)   The Wife died intestate on the *[date]* survived by her three children namely the Children who have all attained the age of 18 and on the *[date]* the Wife's Administrators were granted letters of administration to the Wife's estate.[4]

(D)   Under the law relating to intestacy the Wife's residuary estate (as defined in section 33 of the Administration of Estates Act 1925) is held upon trust for the Children in equal shares absolutely.

(E)   The parties hereto desire to vary the disposition of the estate of the Husband effected by the Husband's Will in the manner hereinafter appearing.

NOW THIS DEED WITNESSES as follows:

1.   The parties hereto hereby agree and declare by way of variation of the disposition of the estate of the Husband effected by the Husband's Will that the Husband's Will shall have effect and be deemed to have had effect as from the death of the Husband and the Husband's estate shall be administered as if the Husband's Will had contained a legacy to the Children in equal shares absolutely of the maximum sum of money which could in the circumstances subsisting at his death have been given by the Husband's Will to them without any liability being incurred for the payment of inheritance tax on or by reason of his death.[5]

2.   Subject as aforesaid the Husband's Will shall continue to have effect.

3.   [*Stamp duty certificate as cl 3 of* Form F3.6 *at para* **[241.27]**.]

4.   The parties hereto hereby give notice to the Board of Inland Revenue in accordance with section 142(2) of the Inheritance Tax Act 1984 and section 62(7) of the Taxation of Chargeable Gains Act 1992 that they elect that the provisions of section 142(1) thereof and section 62(6) thereof respectively shall apply to the variation made by this deed To the Intent that the variation made hereby shall be treated as if it was made by the Husband for the purposes of inheritance tax and capital gains tax.[6]

IN WITNESS ETC[7]

1   This form is for use where two spouses have died within two years of each other, the first spouse to die not having fully utilised his available nil rate inheritance tax band: see Preliminary Note at para **[241.14]**. The variation must be made by the personal representatives of the second to die with the consent of the beneficiaries interested in the second to die's estate: see the Preliminary Note at para **[241.14]**. In this form the beneficiaries are actual parties to the deed, but the Inland Revenue will accept their consent being put in a separate instrument.
2   The deed must be made within two years of the husband's death if an election is to be made for ITA 1984, s 142(1) to apply: see the Preliminary Note at paras **[241.1]** and **[241.3]**.
3   An instrument of variation can be made before probate is granted: see the Preliminary Note at para **[241.10]**.

4   It is arguable that the deed must be made after letters of administration to the wife's estate have been obtained, because the benefit of the disposition by the husband which is being varied is vested in the wife's estate, not the persons beneficially interested in it, and there are no personal representatives before a grant is obtained. If the wife had left a will which appointed executors, the named executors could arguably make the deed before obtaining a grant, but we recommend that a grant is obtained in respect of the second estate before making the deed, wherever possible, even where executors have been appointed.

5   Instead of using this general formula to pass to the children the maximum sum which could be passed to them without incurring any liability for inheritance tax, a specific sum could be included. If it is possible that the specific sum might exceed the inheritance tax threshold, a direction that the legacy should be subject to tax should reduce the amount of tax payable. See cl 1 of Form F3.6 at para **[241.27]** for such a legacy and direction, and the Preliminary Note at para **[241.12]**.

6   A copy of the deed containing the notice of election must be sent to the Capital Taxes Office and the Inspector of Taxes within six months of the date of the deed. See also the Preliminary Note at para **[241.3]**.

7   For execution, see Form F3.3 at para **[241.24]**.

[241.30]

FORM F3.9   Deed of variation of trusts of a will settling a life interest on discretionary trusts without disturbing remainders[1]

THIS DEED OF VARIATION is made the [*date*] BETWEEN [*name*] of [*address*] (hereinafter called 'the Life Tenant') of the one part and [*name*] of [*address*] and [*name*] of [*address*] (hereinafter together called 'the Trustees') of the other part.

WHEREAS:

(A)   By his last Will (hereinafter called 'the Will') dated [*date*] [*name*] late of [*address*] (hereinafter called 'the Testator') appointed the Trustees executors and trustees thereof.

(B)   The Testator died on the [*date*][2] [and on the [*date*] the Will was duly proved by the Trustees].[3]

(C)   By Clause —— of the Will the Testator gave his residuary estate (therein defined and hereinafter called 'the Residuary Estate') to the Trustees to hold the same upon trust to pay the income thereof to the Life Tenant for his life and subject thereto upon trust for such of the children of the Life Tenant who should attain the age of 21 and be living at his death in equal shares absolutely with a substitutional trust for the children of any such child who should die before attaining a vested interest.

(D)   The Life Tenant desires to vary the disposition of the Residuary Estate effected by Clause —— of the Will for the benefit of his children and remoter issue (who together with the Life Tenant are hereinafter called 'the Beneficiàaries')[4] in the manner hereinafter appearing.

NOW THIS DEED WITNESSES as follows:

1.   By way of variation of the above-recited disposition of the Residuary Estate of the Testator made by Clause —— of the Will the Life Tenant HEREBY ASSIGNS his life interest in the Residuary Estate (which life interest shall include the net income of the Residuary Estate which shall have arisen between the Testator's death and the date of this Deed)[5] unto the Trustees to hold the same as follows—

(1)   The Trustees shall hold the income of the Residuary Estate arisen or arising during the life of the Life Tenant upon trust to pay or apply the same to or for the benefit of all or such one or more exclusively of the others or other of the Beneficiaries and if more than one in such shares and in such manner generally as the Trustees shall in their absolute discretion think fit Provided that until the expiration of the period of 21 years from the death of the Testator or until the death of the Life Tenant if sooner[6] the Trustees shall have power to accumulate the whole or any part of such income by investing the same and the resulting income thereof in any manner authorised by the Will so that any accumulations shall be held as an accretion to the Residuary Estate but subject to a power exercisable by the Trustees at any time during the life of the Life Tenant to pay or apply any such accumulations or any part thereof as if they were income of the Residuary Estate arising in the then current year.

(2)   Notwithstanding the foregoing the Trustees shall have power by any deed or deeds revocable or irrevocable from time to time during the life of the Life Tenant to appoint that all or any part or parts of the income of the Residuary Estate during the remainder of the life of Life Tenant or any less period shall be held upon with and subject to such trusts powers and provisions (including discretionary trusts or powers) in favour or for the benefit of all or such one or more exclusively of the others or other of the Beneficiaries if more than one in such shares and in such manner generally as the Trustees shall in their absolute discretion think fit Provided that no exercise of the said power shall invalidate any prior payment application or accumulation of income hereunder.[7]

2.   Nothing herein shall effect the devolution under the Will of the Residuary Estate on and following the death of the Life Tenant.

3.   [*Stamp duty certificate as cl 3 of* Form F3.6 *at para* **[241.27]**.]

4.   [*Election as cl 4 of* Form F3.6 *at para* **[241.27]**.]

IN WITNESS ETC[8]

---

1   It can happen that a will leaves property upon trust for a life tenant for life, with remainder to individuals who are minors or whose identity cannot be finally ascertained until the death of the life tenant. This form allows a life tenant to remove property from his estate for inheritance tax purpose by settling his life interest on discretionary trusts, with the remainder trusts taking effect on his death being unaffected. For the inheritance tax charging regime for settlements without an interest in possession see B18 at para **[218.6]** et seq. If the life tenant is elderly or infirm, check that he or she was not at the testator's death in receipt of attendance allowance or otherwise qualified under the ITA 1984, s 89(4) as the principal beneficiary under a disabled trust for inheritance tax purposes (see para **[226.3]** et seq). If so, the trusts might fall within the ITA 1984, s 89 so that he or she is treated as retaining an interest in possession. This could be avoided by a variation which amends the powers over capital in such a way that s 89 does not apply, but if the remaindermen are minors or unborns this may only be achievable by applying to the court under the Variation of Trusts Act 1958.

   Note also that the Revenue will apparently not regard a variation varying or disposing of a life interest as effective for inheritance tax purposes if the deed of variation is made after the life tenant's death: see Inland Revenue Capital Taxes *IHT Newsletter* December 2001, p 5 (but a disclaimer by the life tenant's personal representatives could in their view be effective).

2   The deed must be made within two years of the death if an election is to be made for ITA 1984, s 142(1) to apply: see the Preliminary Note at paras **[241.1]** and **[241.3]**.

3   An instrument of variation can be made before probate is granted: see the Preliminary Note at para **[241.10]**.

4   If the life tenant is to be an object of the discretionary trust, provided that an election is made that ITA 1984, s 142(1) should apply to the variation, the life tenant's assignment should not be a gift subject to a reservation: see the Preliminary Note at para **[241.9]**.

   An election that the TCGA 1992, s 62(6) should apply would not, however, have the result that the deceased is treated as the settlor of the life tenant's life interest for all capital gains tax purposes (see Preliminary Note at para **[241.17]**). So by being an object of the discretionary trust, any chargeable gains in respect of any accumulations of income will be taxed as the life tenant's as such accumulations would be property originating from him: see TCGA 1992, ss 77 and 79(2). However, it is thought that the capital of the residuary estate would not be property originating from the life tenant for the purposes of these provisions, and therefore that chargeable gains in respect of it would be chargeable at the rate applicable to trusts and not at the life tenant's rates: see Part A, para **[200.39]** for the rates of capital gains tax on settled property. For income tax purposes the income would be treated as the life tenant's by reason of his being an object of the trust and the person who settled the income on the discretionary trusts: see Preliminary Note at para **[241.19]**.

5   If the deed is made before the administration is compete, this would be effective to transfer any undistributed income, for income tax purposes, from the life tenant to the discretionary trusts: see the Preliminary Note at para **[241.19]**.

6   Since the variation is to be deemed to have been made by the deceased for inheritance tax purposes, it may be wise to limit accumulation to a period which the deceased could have chosen in his will, and which is also not longer than a period which the life tenant could have chosen for a lifetime disposition. A period of not longer than 21 years from the deceased's death could have been chosen by the deceased (see the LPA 1925, s 164(1)(b) (Part G, para **[246.42]**)), which allows accumulation for a period of 21 years from death, and is also within a period which the life tenant could have chosen for a lifetime disposition (see the PAA 1964, s 13(1)(a) (Part G, para **[246.71]**), which allows accumulation for a period of 21 years from the date of the disposition).

7   This power would permit the trustees to appoint an interest in possession to any of the beneficiaries. This might be desirable if, for example, the inheritance tax charging regime for settlements without an interest in possession should change and become less favourable.

8   For execution, see Form F3.3 at para **[241.24]**.

[241.31]

FORM F3.10:   Deed of variation of trusts of a will settling a life interest on the same trusts as contingent remainders from time to time[1]

THIS DEED OF VARIATION is made the *[date]* BETWEEN *[name]* of *[address]* (hereinafter called 'the Life Tenant') of the one part and *[name]* of *[address]* and *[name]* of *[address]* (hereinafter together called 'the Trustees') of the other part.

WHEREAS:

   (A)   By his last Will (hereinafter called 'the Will') dated *[date]* *[name]* late of *[address]* (hereinafter called 'the Testator') appointed the Trustees executors and trustees thereof.

   (B)   The Testator died on the *[date]*[2] [and on the *[date]* the Will was duly proved by the Trustees].[3]

   (C)   By Clause —— of the Will the Testator gave his residuary estate (therein defined and hereinafter called 'the Residuary Estate') to the Trustees to hold the same upon trust to pay the income thereof to the Life Tenant for his life and subject thereto to hold the capital and income thereof upon trust for such of the children of the Life Tenant who should attain the age of 21 and be living at the Life Tenant's death if more than one in equal shares provided that if any child of the Life Tenant should predecease the Life Tenant leaving issue who should attain the age of 21 such issue should take in equal shares per stirpes the share their parent would have become entitled to if surviving the Life Tenant.

(D)   The Life Tenant desires to vary the disposition of the Residuary Estate effected by the Will in the manner hereinafter appearing.

NOW THIS DEED WITNESSES as follows:

1.   By way of variation of the above-recited disposition of the Residuary Estate of the Testator made by Clause —— of the Will the Life Tenant HEREBY ASSIGNS his life interest in the Residuary Estate (which life interest shall include the net income of the Residuary Estate which shall have accrued between the Testator's death and the date of this Deed)[4] unto the Trustees to hold each instalment of the income of the Residuary Estate which shall arise or shall have arisen during the Life Tenant's life upon the trusts which would apply thereto under the Will if the Life Tenant had died immediately before such instalment arose.

2.   Nothing herein shall affect the devolution under the Will of the Residuary Estate on and following the death of the Life Tenant.

3.   [*Stamp duty certificate as cl 3 of* Form F3.6 *at para* **[241.27]**.]

4.   [*Election as cl 4 of* Form F3.6 *at para* **[241.27]**.]

IN WITNESS ETC[5]

> 1 Where the remainder trusts after a life interest are contingent on surviving the life tenant, particularly where the class of remainderman might include future born persons, it presents a problem for the termination of the life interest and acceleration of the remainders. This deed includes a formula for settling the life interest on the same trusts as the remainder from time to time. Once the deed is executed the trustees will have to retain the trust fund until the death of the life tenant, unless (i) they have a power of advancement exercisable over the whole of each presumptive share, or (ii) a scheme of distribution can be agreed with all the potential remaindermen who are in existence (and who are all of full age) and it is clear that no more persons entitled to an interest will be born, or (iii) an order of the court is obtained authorising distribution or varying the trusts under the Variation of Trusts Act 1958 in a way which allows a distribution to be made. Note that the Revenue will apparently not regard a variation varying or disposing of a life interest as effective for inheritance tax purposes if the deed of variation is made after the life tenant's death: see Inland Revenue Capital Taxes *IHT Newsletter* December 2001, p 5 (but a disclaimer by the life tenant's personal representatives could in their view be effective).
>
> 2   The deed must be made within two years of the death if an election is to be made for ITA 1984, s 142(1) to apply: see the Preliminary Note at paras **[241.1]** and **[241.2]**.
>
> 3   An instrument of variation can be made before probate is granted: see the Preliminary Note at para **[241.10]**.
>
> 4   See the Preliminary Note at para **[241.19]** for the income tax consequences of disposing of the right to undistributed income of an unadministered estate.
>
> 5   For execution, see Form F3.3 at para **[241.24]**.

F4   Exercises of dispositive powers created by wills

PRELIMINARY NOTE

[242.1]
When exercising a special power of appointment, care must be taken that the exercise is authorised by the terms of the power. For example, it can only be exercised for the benefit of the named objects of the power; trusts and powers should not be delegated (by eg the appointment of discretionary trusts and dispositive powers) unless the power authorises such delegation; the interests which it creates must vest within the perpetuity period applicable to the instrument creating the power; and excessive accumulations must not be directed. If the power requires, as powers of appointment usually do, an appointment by deed then a deed is necessary for the appointment to be valid. For some observations on these points in relation to exercises of special powers of appointment by will (which will apply with any necessary modifications to appointments made by an inter vivos instrument), see B13 at **[213.1]** et seq (and for a fuller treatment of the exercise of special powers of appointment, see Vol 1, paras **[39.1]** and **[40.1]** et seq).

One obvious, though important, difference between the exercise of a dispositive power by will or codicil, and the exercise of such a power by an inter vivos instrument such as a deed, is that an appointment by deed takes effect immediately following the execution of the deed whereas an appointment by will only takes effect upon the death of the appointor. Accordingly, an exercise by will can be revoked or altered at any time before the death of the appointor and before the appointment has taken effect. An appointment by deed, however, will have effect according to its terms unless and until it is made expressly revocable and is in fact revoked.

Some examples of the exercise of powers of advancement are also provided here (in Forms F4.5 and F4.6 at paras **[242.13]**–**[242.15]**). By powers of advancement we mean the statutory power of advancement (Trustee Act 1925, s 32: Part G, para **[246.27]**), or express powers in the same essential form, ie powers to pay or apply capital to or for the benefit of one or more persons, or the like. Such a power is, like a power of appointment, subject to the rule against perpetuities in such a way that interests created in exercise of the power need to vest within a perpetuity period calculated from the creation of the power (*Pilkington v IRC* [1964] AC 612, [1962] 3 All ER 622), but the rules as to what may be done in exercise of such a power may be more liberal and rather different from those surrounding a power of appointment: see B18 at para **[218.85]** et seq. Also, it is usually the case that a power of advancement is not subject to the formal requirements for its exercise to which a power of appointment is commonly subject.

[242.2]
Inheritance tax consequences of an appointment or advance. Where an interest in possession in any property is brought to an end by an appointment or advance the inheritance tax consequences are as described for lifetime gifts in Part A, para **[200.70]**. Generally, a potentially exempt transfer of that property is deemed to be made by the person formerly entitled to the interest in possession if the appointment or advance causes another person or persons to acquire absolute interests or interests in possession in the property or creates an accumulation and maintenance trust of it; an immediately chargeable transfer is deemed to be made by that person if the appointment or advance creates discretionary trusts; and there is no inheritance tax charge if the person formerly entitled to the interest in possession becomes entitled to the property absolutely or to another interest in possession in it.

If the appointment or advance is of property held on discretionary trusts, and has the effect that the property ceases to be subject to discretionary trusts, the consequence will usually be an exit charge as described in B18 at paras **[218.8]**–**[218.14]**. There is, however, the special case of appointments or advances made within two years of a testator's death out of a discretionary trust created by his will, which do not give rise to an exit charge: see the note on s 144 of the Inheritance Tax Act 1984 (ITA 1984) at para **[242.4]**.

[242.3]
Capital gains tax on appointments or advances. If an appointment or advance results in someone becoming absolutely entitled to any property that will be an occasion of deemed disposal for capital gains tax purposes: Taxation of Chargeable Gains Act 1992 (TCGA 1992), s 71(1). If property continues to be held on trust after the appointment or advance it will be such an occasion of deemed disposal only if the property becomes comprised in a new or different settlement from that in which it was comprised before the appointment or advance: see further B18 at paras **[218.26]**, **[218.100]**–**[218.102]** and the notes to Form F4.3 at para **[242.9]** and Form F4.6 at para **[242.15]**. However, in either case, there may be no deemed disposal if the estate is still in the course of administration at the time of the appointment or advance, see para **[242.5]**.

Even where there is a deemed disposal for capital gains tax purposes, there may be hold-over relief where the property is business or agricultural property (TCGA 1992, s 165), or the appointment or advance is an occasion of immediate inheritance tax charge (TCGA 1992, s 260). The most likely circumstances to arise in which the latter type of hold-over relief is available are those where the appointment or advance terminates an interest in possession so that it is followed by discretionary trusts, or where the appointment or advance is of property subject to a discretionary trust and it is an occasion of exit charge. See also Part A, para **[200.39]** and B18 at para **[218.26]**.

[242.4]
Inheritance Tax Act 1984, s 144. Many wills these days contain discretionary trusts drafted with ITA 1984, s 144 in mind. The general effect of this section is that where property settled by will is within two years of the testator's death, but not sooner than three months after his death, and before an interest in possession has subsisted in the property, appointed or distributed to someone either absolutely or upon interest in possession trusts, there is no inheritance tax 'exit charge' on this event, and the will is treated for inheritance tax purposes as if it had provided that on the testator's death the property should be held as it is held after the appointment: see C3 at para **[225.83]** et seq for a fuller discussion. Accordingly, an appointment of property to a spouse will mean that the appointed property has the benefit of the spouse exemption upon the testator's death.

Although the requirement that an appointment should not be made less than three months after the testator's death does not expressly appear in s 144, it is a requirement because s 144 only applies where there would, apart from the section, be an exit charge under the ITA 1984, s 65, but there can be no such exit charge in the first three months of a settlement: ITA 1984, ss 65(4), 83 and 144(1)(a). This is confirmed by *Frankland v IRC* [1996] STC 735 and the Special Commissioner's decision *Harding (executors of Loveday) v IRC* [1997] STC (SCD) 321.

When making an appointment to come within s 144, and where part of the estate following the appointment will be exempt from inheritance tax and part will not be exempt, and an appointment of specific property or a specified sum of cash is being made to a non-exempt beneficiary, it will often be advisable to make the appointment expressly subject to inheritance tax payable in respect of the testator's death, particularly where the purpose of the exercise is to appoint property equal to the inheritance tax nil-rate band to non-exempt beneficiaries with the rest of the estate going to the testator's surviving spouse. If in such a case the non-exempt part of the estate turns out to exceed the inheritance tax threshold, less inheritance tax will be payable on the estate if such appointments to non-exempt persons are subject to inheritance tax in respect of the testator's death than if they are free of tax: see the Preliminary Note to B14 at para **[214.74]**. If no express direction as to inheritance tax is included, a specific gift will usually be free of tax: see Preliminary Note to B14 at para **[214.55]** et seq.

[242.5]
Capital gains tax and s 144 appointments. If an absolute appointment is made to which ITA 1984, s 144 applies, there will be a deemed disposal by the trustees of the appointed assets at their market value under the TCGA 1992, s 71, and hold-over relief will not be available (because the appointment will not be a chargeable transfer for inheritance tax purposes—see TCGA 1992, s 260) unless the assets are business or agricultural property which qualify for it under s 165 of the 1992 Act. Therefore a chargeable gain may accrue, the acquisition cost of the appointed assets being their market value as at the testator's death. Such gain will be chargeable to tax at the rate applicable to trusts under the TCGA 1992, s 5; see Part A, para **[200.38]**. However, if the appointment is

made while the estate is still in the course of administration it is arguable that for capital gains tax purposes the appointees take the appointed assets as 'legatees' within the TCGA 1992, s 62(4), being persons who take under the will, with the consequence that no chargeable gain should accrue and the appointees will take the appointed assets with the personal representatives' acquisition cost for capital gains tax purposes, ie the market value of the assets at the date of death of the testator (TCGA 1992, ss 62 (4) and 64 (2)). This seems to be accepted by the Revenue, see *Foster's Inheritance Tax*, D4.35. If an appointment within s 144 results in the property continuing to be held on trust and as property comprised in the same settlement, it is not an occasion of capital gains tax disposal.

[242.6]
Stamp duty. No stamp duty is payable on an instrument exercising a power of appointment or advancement.

[242.7]

FORM F4.1 **Appointment from discretionary trust within two years of testator's death**[1]

THIS DEED OF APPOINTMENT is made the [*date*] BY [*name*] of [*address*] and [*name*] of [*address*] (hereinafter together called 'the Trustees').

WHEREAS:

(A)   By his last Will (hereinafter called 'the Will') dated [*date*] [*name*] late of [*address*] (hereinafter called 'the Testator') appointed the Trustees to be the executors and trustees thereof.

(B)   The Testator died on the [*date*][2] and on the [*date*] the Will was duly proved by the Trustees.[3]

(C)   By Clause —— of the Will the Testator directed the Trustees to hold the capital and income of his residuary estate (hereinafter called 'the residuary estate') upon trust for all or such one or more of the beneficiaries (defined in the Will and hereinafter called 'the beneficiaries') at such ages or times in such shares and upon such trusts for the benefit of the beneficiaries as the Trustees should by irrevocable deed or deeds executed at any time or times during the discretionary period (as defined in the Will) appoint.

(D)   The discretionary period was defined by Clause —— of the Will to mean the period beginning immediately after the end of the period of three months from the day of the Testator's death and ending with the day before the second anniversary of his death.

(E)   The beneficiaries as defined in the Will include [*name*] who is the widow of the Testator and [*name*] and [*name*] who are the children of the Testator.

(F)   The Trustees desire to exercise their above-mentioned power of appointment for the benefit of the said [*name*] [*name*] and [*name*] in the manner hereinafter appearing.

NOW THIS DEED WITNESSETH that the Trustees in exercise of their above mentioned power of appointment and each and every other power them enabling HEREBY IRREVOCABLY APPOINT that the residuary estate shall be held upon the following trusts:

(1)   upon trust as to [£234,000] for the said children of the Testator [*name*] and [*name*] in equal shares absolutely [Provided that any inheritance tax attributable thereto and payable in respect of the death of the Testator should be borne by the said [*name*] and [*name*] in equal shares absolutely];[4] and

(2)   subject as aforesaid upon trust for the said widow of the Testator [*name*] absolutely.

IN WITNESS whereof the Trustees have executed these presents as their deed the day and year first above written.[5]

SIGNED and delivered as a deed by the said [*name*]   [*Signature of trustee*]
in the presence of—

[*Signature, address and description of witness*]

[*The foregoing from 'SIGNED' to be repeated for each trustee*]

1   This form is designed to take advantage of ITA 1984, s 144. For a form of will which envisages such an appointment, see Form C3.6 at para **[225.92]** et seq, and for notes on s 144 see C3 at para **[225.83]** et seq and the Preliminary Note at paras **[242.4]** and **[242.5]** on the capital gains tax consequences of an absolute appointment. The recitals of the terms of the will in this form are based on Form C3.6.
      Provided that the appointment fulfils the conditions of s 144, there will be no exit charge under the ITA 1984, s 65 on the appointment and the appointment will be treated as having effect from the deceased's death.
2   To take advantage of the ITA 1984, s 144, the appointment must be made not more than two years after the testator's death, but not within the first three months after his death: see the Preliminary Note at para **[242.4]**.
3   Whether or not the power of appointment may be exercised before the will has been proved, or before the executors have become trustees will depend upon the terms of the will. The Revenue once took the view that executors could not exercise a power of appointment until the property which was to be appointed was vested in them as trustees, but they now seem to accept that a power may be exercised by executors if on the true construction of the will they have authority to exercise it in that capacity, for example, where a will expressly confers the power on them in their capacity as executors as well as trustees, or appoints the individuals who actually exercise the power as executors and trustees, referring to them in the will as 'my trustees' with the power being given to 'my trustees'.
4   So as to avoid inheritance tax in respect of the death of the testator, the sum appointed should not be more than the maximum which non-exempt persons can take without any liability being incurred for inheritance tax on or by reason of the testator's death, taking into account the testator's lifetime chargeable transfers, property treated as his for inheritance tax purposes at the time of his death and the dispositions taking effect under his will and under the deed of appointment. In case this appointment should happen to push the testator's chargeable estate above the inheritance tax threshold, for example, on its subsequently being discovered that the testator had made a lifetime chargeable transfer, a direction that any inheritance tax should be borne by the appointees should result in less inheritance tax being payable than if the legacy was free of tax: see the Preliminary Note at para **[242.4]**.
5   The requirements of the Law of Property (Miscellaneous Provisions) Act 1989, s 1, for the making of a deed are that it is clear on its face that it is intended by the parties to it to be a deed, that it is signed by each party in the presence of a witness who attests the signature (two witnesses if someone signs for a party), and that it is delivered as a deed by each party or someone authorised to do so on his behalf. Sealing is not necessary.

[242.8]

FORM F4.2:   Appointment from discretionary trust of money to beneficiaries who are sui juris[1]

THIS DEED OF APPOINTMENT is made the ⸺ day of ⸺ BY [*names and addresses of trustees*] (hereinafter called 'the Trustees') and is SUPPLEMENTAL To the Will (hereinafter called 'the Will') dated ⸺ of [*name of testator*] who died on ⸺ and whose said will was on ⸺ duly proved by [*names of executors*] the executors therein named

WHEREAS:

(1)   The property now subject to the trusts of the will includes the sum of [*amount*] in cash

(2)   The trustees desire by this deed to exercise the power of appointment given them by Clause [*insert number of relevant clause*] of the Will

NOW THIS DEED WITNESSETH that the Trustees in exercise of their said power of appointment under the will hereby irrevocably appoint the said sum of [amount] upon the following trusts:

(a)   As to [*amount*] thereof upon trust as to both capital and income for [*beneficiary*] absolutely

(b)   As to [*amount*] thereof upon trust as to both capital and income for [*beneficiary*] absolutely

(c)   Etc, etc.

IN WITNESS][2]

1   This form is for use in the simplest case – where the trust property has already been converted into cash and it is being appointed absolutely to beneficiaries who are all sui juris. There may be an exit charge for inheritance tax purposes under ITA 1984, s 65, see paras **[218.8]–[218.14]** (assuming the appointment does not come within ITA 1984, s 144), but there will be no capital gains tax charge because the appointed property is cash.

2   For execution, see Form F4.1 at para **[242.7]**.

[242.9]

FORM F4.3   Appointment from discretionary trust of investments upon trusts

NOTE

This form pre-supposes that the trust property is still in the form of investments and that these are being appointed in specie amongst beneficiaries some of whom are not yet of age. So far as adult beneficiaries are concerned, the effect of the appointment is that they become absolutely entitled to the investments appointed to them so that there will be an exit charge under ITA 1984, s 65 (see paras **[218.8]–[218.14]**), unless the appointment comes within ITA 1984, s 144 (see para **[242.4]**) and a deemed disposal by the trustees for capital gains tax purposes under the TCGA 1992 (see para **[242.3]**), unless, perhaps, the estate is stll in the course of administration (see para **[242.3]**). The investments can be transferred to them by the trustees in exchange for formal receipts, although if there is an election for capital gains tax hold-over relief under the TCGA 1992, s 260 (which allows hold-over relief in cases where the occasion of the disposal is also a chargeable transfer, and it seems that an exit charge is a chargeable transfer for these purposes) the trustees may need to retain some assets for six years in case a capital gains tax charge arises under the TCGA 1992, s 168, on the emigration of an appointee, for which the trustees are liable (see especially sub-ss (7) and (8)). The appointments to infant beneficiaries which are contingent on their attaining a specified age will (unless they come within the ITA 1984, s 144, see para **[242.4]**) trigger an exit charge if the property so appointed becomes subject to accumulation and maintenance trusts within the ITA 1984, s 71. Whether or not there is a deemed disposal by the trustees of the property in question under the TCGA 1992, s 71, depends upon whether the trust property moves to a new and separate settlement. If the power which is exercised does not authorise the trustees to remove the property from the original settlement, there will be no deemed disposal. If it does so authorise them, an Inland Revenue Statement of Practice, SP 7/84, 11 October 1984, states that there will be no deemed disposal where the appointed trusts are non-exhaustive or revocable, and that it is unlikely that a deemed disposal will occur when the duties with regard to the appointed assets fall to the trustees of the original settlement in their capacity as such. The trusts of this appointment are neither non-exhaustive nor revocable, however, and the trustees of the appointed assets are the trustees of the will, so that it is probable that no disposal can be deemed to have been made.

[242.10]

THIS DEED OF APPOINTMENT [*continue as in* Form F4.2 *at para* **[242.8]**.

WHEREAS:

(1)   The property now subject to the trusts of the Will consists of the investments [and cash] set out in the schedule hereto
(2)   The trustees desire by this deed to exercise the power of appointment given them by Clause [*insert number of relevant clause*] of the Will.

NOW THIS DEED WITNESSETH as follows:
1.   The Trustees in exercise of their said power of appointment under the Will hereby irrevocably appoint the property set out in the said Schedule upon the following trusts:

(a)
    (i)   As to the property set out in the first part of the schedule upon trust as to both capital and income for [*adult beneficiary*] absolutely
    (ii)   As to the property set out in the second part of the schedule upon trust as to both capital and income for [*infant beneficiary*] if he attains the age of [18]/[21] years absolutely.
    (iii)   Etc, etc.

(b)   Provided that if any of the persons named in paragraphs [*set out the numbers of those paragraphs which appoint contingent interests*] of subclause (a) of this Clause dies before attaining a vested interest but leaving a child or children living at his death then such child or children shall take absolutely and if more than one in equal shares so much of the trust property as that person would have taken had he attained a vested interest

(c)   Provided also that if at any time the trusts declared by any of those same paragraphs read in conjunction with subclause (b) of this Clause shall fail then from the date of failure that share (and any part of the trust property which may have already accrued to it under this provision) shall accrue to the other share or shares (and equally if more than one) the trusts of which shall not at that date have failed and be held upon the trusts from time to time affecting such other share or shares.

2.   The administrative provisions of the will which are contained in Clauses [*set out here relevant clauses*] thereof shall apply to the trusts declared by this deed [save only for the following modifications [*set out any modifications which may be desired*].

3.   All income of the said property shall be treated as accruing on the date on which it becomes payable regardless of the period in respect of which it shall have accrued and shall not be subject to statutory apportionment.[1]

IN WITNESS[2]

THE SCHEDULE

[*The schedule is to contain all the trust property and is to be divided into parts, the first part listing the property appointed to the first-named beneficiary, and so on*]

1   For statutory apportionment over time and its exclusion see B14 at para **[214.35]** et seq.
2   For execution, see Form F4.1 at para **[242.7]**.

[242.11]

FORM F4.4:   Appointment of accumulation and maintenance trusts terminating an interest in possession

NOTE

This appointment terminates an individual's interest in possession in trust property and appoints accumulation and maintenance trusts within the ITA 1984, s 71 so that the life tenant will be treated as having made a potentially exempt transfer: ITA 1984, s 3A (1)(c), (3) and (6) and s 52. For the trusts to take effect immediately as ones within s 71 there must be at least one member of the relevant class of 'beneficiaries' (in this form the Testator's grandchildren) already in existence: see Part A, para **[200.122]**. It is assumed that the will provides life interest trusts subject to an overriding power of appointment, such as in Form C2.6 at para **[224.95]** et seq with the inclusion of cl 11 of it. The recitals of the terms of the will in this form are based on Form C2.6, on the basis that the requirement of the testator's widow's consent to an appointment (which is an option in square brackets in cl 11(2) of Form C2.6 at para **[224.107]**) has not been included. The appointed trusts are not exhaustive (the trust property

2047

would become held on the trusts of the will in the event of no beneficiary of the appointed trusts attaining a vested interest), the trustees of the appointed trusts are expressed to be the trustees of the will, and the administrative powers and provisions of the will will continue to apply, so the appointment should not be the occasion of a deemed disposal by the trustees under the TCGA 1992, s 71, because the Inland Revenue Statement of Practice SP 7/84, 11 October 1984 states that when present these factors prevent there being a deemed disposal on the exercise of a power, (see Note to Form F4.3 at para **[242.9]**).

[242.12]

THIS DEED OF APPOINTMENT is made the [*date*] BY [*name*] of [*address*] and [*name*] of [*address*] (hereinafter together called 'the Trustees' which expression shall where the context so admits include the trustee or trustees for the time being of the Will hereinafter mentioned).

WHEREAS:

(A) This deed is supplemental to the Will (hereinafter called 'the Will') dated the [*date*] of [*name*] (hereinafter called 'the Testator') who died on the [*date*] and which was duly proved by [*names of executors*] the executors named therein on the [*date*] in the [*name*] Probate Registry.

(B) By Clauses —— to —— of the Will the trustees of the Will were directed to hold the Testator's residuary estate (hereinafter called 'the residuary estate') upon trust to pay the income therefrom to the Testator's widow [*name*] (hereinafter called 'the Life Tenant') and subject thereto upon certain trusts and subject to certain powers for the benefit of the Testator's children and remoter issue.

(C) By Clause —— of the Will 'appointable share' was defined as any part or share of the residuary estate (up to the whole thereof) in which any beneficiary is for the time being entitled to an interest in possession within the meaning of Part III of the Inheritance Tax Act 1984 not being a part or share which has or would (but for that Clause) have vested indefeasibly in any person under the trusts thereinbefore declared and it is apprehended that by virtue of the Life Tenant's said life interest the whole of the residuary estate is an appointable share within the said definition.

(D) By Clause —— of the Will 'the vesting day' was defined to mean the day on which shall expire the period of 21 years immediately following the death of the last survivor of the Life Tenant the Testator's children and any grandchild of the Testator born in the Testator's lifetime.

(E) By Clause —— of the Will notwithstanding and in derogation of the above-recited trusts and powers the Trustees (being not fewer than two in number or a trust corporation) have power at any time or times and from time to time before the vesting day by any deed or deeds revocable or irrevocable to appoint any part or share of the residuary estate (up to the whole thereof) which is at the date of such exercise an appointable share (as defined in the Will as aforesaid) upon trust for all or such one or more exclusive of the others or other of the discretionary beneficiaries (as defined in the Will and hereinafter called 'the discretionary beneficiaries') if more than one in such shares and either absolutely or at such age or time or respective ages or times and with such trusts and powers for their respective benefit and such provisions as the Trustees think fit and the Trustees may in exercise of the foregoing power (inter alia) delegate or create powers or discretions over capital or income or appoint administrative powers or provisions but subject to a proviso that (inter alia) every interest limited under any exercise of the foregoing power shall vest in interest (if at all) not later than the vesting day.

(F)   The Trustees are the present trustees of the Will and the residuary estate now consists of the assets specified in the Schedule hereto.

(G)   The discretionary beneficiaries include the grandchildren and remoter issue of the Testator living at his death or born thereafter.

(H)   There are now living [two] grandchildren of the Testator namely [*name*] of [*address*] who was born on the [*date*] and [*name*] of [*address*] who was born on the [*date*].[1]

(I)   The Trustees desire to exercise their above-mentioned power of appointment for the benefit of the grandchildren and remoter issue of the Testator in the manner hereinafter appearing.

NOW THIS DEED WITNESSETH as follows:

1.   The Trustees in exercise of their above mentioned power of appointment and each and every other power them enabling HEREBY IRREVOCABLY APPOINT that the residuary estate and the income thereof shall henceforth be held upon the following trusts (to the intent and so that the interest of the Life Tenant shall cease) and with and subject to the following powers:

(1)   The Trustees shall hold the residuary estate Upon Trust for such of the grandchildren of the Testator as shall attain the age of twenty-one years if more than one in equal shares absolutely Provided always that if any of such grandchildren shall die without having attained the age of twenty-one years leaving a child or children him or her surviving who shall attain the age of twenty-one years or be living on the earlier occurrence of the vesting day such child or children shall take if more than one equally between them the share of the residuary estate which their parent would have taken if he or she had lived to attain the age of twenty-one years.

(2)   The foregoing trusts shall carry the intermediate income of the residuary estate and section 31 of the Trustee Act 1925 (relating to maintenance and accumulation) shall accordingly apply thereto as if the proviso to subsection (1) thereof had been omitted therefrom.

(3)   The powers in section 32 of the Trustee Act 1925 (relating to the payment or application of capital) shall apply to the foregoing trusts as if the words 'one-half of' were omitted from proviso (a) to subsection (1) thereof [Provided that the said powers shall not be exercisable otherwise than so as to cause the person for whose benefit the same shall be exercised to become immediately entitled to or to an interest in possession (within the meaning of Part III of the Inheritance Tax Act 1984) in the capital thereby paid or applied].[2]

(4)   In this clause 'the vesting day' has the same meaning as in clause —— of the Will.

2.   For the avoidance of doubt it is hereby declared that the powers and provisions of Clauses —— to —— of the Will shall continue to apply to the residuary estate.[3]

3.   Without prejudice to and subject always to the Life Tenant's entitlement to income prior to this appointment all income of the residuary estate shall be treated as accruing on the date on which it becomes payable regardless of the period in respect of which it shall have accrued and shall not be subject to statutory apportionment.[4]

IN WITNESS ETC[5]

THE SCHEDULE

[List of assets comprised in Trust Fund]

1   If the trusts are to be accumulation and maintenance trusts within the ITA 1984, s 71 from the making of the appointment there must be at least one grandchild already in existence: see Part A, para **[200.122]**.

2   The proviso is included in order to prevent the power prejudicing the application of the ITA 1984, s 71 (accumulation and maintenance trusts), but is probably unnecessary: see the Note on inheritance tax and the statutory power of advancement in B18 at para **[218.99]**.

3   The administrative powers of the will will continue to apply. The power of appointment recited is, however, wide enough for further administrative provisions to be included in the appointment.

4   If the will does not exclude statutory apportionment of income, it may be convenient to exclude it in the appointment. However, if apportionment is not excluded by the will, it will not be possible to exclude apportionment so as to deprive the Life Tenant of any income payable after the appointment, but apportionable to the period prior to the making of the appointment. For statutory apportionment of income over time and its exclusion see the Preliminary Note to B14 at para **[214.35]** et seq.

5   For execution, see Form F4.1 at para **[242.7]**.

[242.13]

FORM F4.5:   Exercise of power of advancement

NOTE

This is a form of resolution (not executed as a deed) whereby trustees resolve to exercise the statutory power of advancement by transferring less than half of a beneficiary's presumptive share in a trust fund to that beneficiary. By transferring less than half of the beneficiary's presumptive share, in this case only a quarter of his share, the statutory power is not exhausted, and the trustees may later exercise their power with respect to the balance of a half share , see *Marquess of Abergavenny's Estate Act Trusts* [1981] 2 All ER 643, [1981] 1 WLR 843. Whether the beneficiary has an interest in possession in the advanced assets at the time of the advance (for example under the Trustee Act 1925, s 31(1)(ii)) or they are held on accumulation and maintenance trusts under the ITA 1984, s 71, the advance will not trigger an inheritance tax charge: ITA 1984, ss 53(2) and 71(4)(a). The trustees will be deemed to have disposed of the advanced assets at their market value under the TCGA 1992, s 71, so that a capital gains tax charge may be triggered, although if the advanced assets are held on accumulation and maintenance trusts at the time of the advance, hold-over relief will be available: TCGA 1992, s 260(2)(d).

[242.14]

THIS RESOLUTION is made the [*date*] BY [*name*] of [*address*] and [*name*] of [*address*] (hereinafter together called 'the Trustees').

WHEREAS:

(A)   This resolution is supplemental to the Will (hereinafter called 'the Will') dated [*date*] of [*name*] (hereinafter called 'the Testator') who died on the [*date*] and which was duly proved by [*names of executors*] the executors named therein.

(B)   The Trustees are the present trustees of the Will.

(C)   The Trust Fund which is defined in Clause —— of the Will is held by the Trustees upon trust for such of the children of the Testator as should attain the age of twenty-five years if more than one in equal shares absolutely.

(D)   There are three children of the Testator who are now living none of whom has attained the age of twenty-five.

(E)   The power conferred by section 32 of the Trustee Act 1925 (relating to the payment or application of capital) applies to the trusts of the Will.

(F)   The Trustees desire to exercise the said statutory power for the benefit of the eldest child of the Testator [*name*] who has attained the age of eighteen in the manner hereinafter appearing.

NOW the Trustees in exercise of the power conferred on them by section 32 of the Trustee Act 1925 HEREBY RESOLVE to transfer[1] from the Trust Fund to the said [*name*] for his own use and benefit absolutely the assets listed in the Schedule to this Resolution which assets represent one-quarter of the presumptive share in the Trust Fund of the said [*name*].

[*Signatures of trustees*]

THE SCHEDULE

[*List of assets being transferred*]

---

1   Although the statutory power is to 'pay or apply any capital money subject to a trust' it seems that the power is properly exercised if trust property is transferred in specie: see B18 at para **[218.97]**.

   If the resolution is in this form the advance may only become irrevocably effective at the point when the assets are transferred to the beneficiary. If it is important that the advance should take effect from the making of the resolution, it is recommended that the resolution is by deed and declares that the trustees hold the assets on trust for the beneficiary: see Form F4.6 at para **[242.15]**.

[242.15]

FORM F4.6:   Exercise of power of advancement for the benefit of someone by creating a trust for his minor children

NOTE

A power which may be exercised for the 'benefit' of a beneficiary, may be properly exercised in favour of, for example, his minor children to his own exclusion so long as the exercise can be said to be for his benefit, for example, where the beneficiary himself is well provided for and he has a moral and legal obligation to maintain the children: see *Re Hampden Settlement Trusts* [1977] TR 177 and B18 at paras **[218.92]–[218.96]**. Assuming that prior to the advance the beneficiary has an interest in possession in the fund which is being advanced, he will be treated as making a potentially exempt transfer on the advance: see para **[242.2]**. The trusts of the advance are not exhaustive, the trustees of the trusts of the advance are expressed to be the trustees of the will, and the administrative powers and provisions of the will will continue to apply, so that the advance should not be the occasion of a deemed disposal by the trustees under the TCGA 1992, s 71: see the Inland Revenue Statement of Practice SP 7/84, 11 October 1984, which contemplates that these factors when present in relation to an 'advanced' fund prevent there being a deemed disposal on the exercise of a power (see the Note to Form 4.3 at para **[242.9]**), notwithstanding that there has been some doubt as to whether an advance onto new trusts can ever be made without a new and separate settlement being created. See also B18 at paras **[218.100]–[218.102]**.

[242.16]

THIS DEED is made the [*date*] BY [*name*] of [*address*] and [*name*] of [*address*] (hereinafter together called 'the Trustees' which term shall where the context so admits include the trustee or trustees for the time being of the Will hereinafter mentioned).

WHEREAS:

(A)   This Deed is supplemental to the Will (hereinafter called 'the Will') dated the [*date*] of [*name*] who died on the [*date*] and which was duly proved by [*names of executors*] the executors named therein.

(B)   The Trustees are the present trustees of the Will.

(C)   The Trust Fund which is defined in Clause —— of the Will comprises the property set out in the Schedule hereto and in accordance with Clause —— of the Will is held by the Trustees upon trust for [*name*] contingently upon his attaining the age of ——.

(D)   By Clause —— of the Will the power in section 32 of the Trustee Act 1925 (relating to the payment or application of capital) is modified so as to apply to the whole of the presumptive share of a beneficiary in the Trust Fund.

(E)   The Trustees desire to exercise the above-mentioned power for the benefit of the said [*name*] in the manner hereinafter appearing.

NOW THIS DEED WITNESSETH as follows:

1.   The Trustees in exercise of the above mentioned power HEREBY DECLARE that they shall henceforth hold the Trust Fund and the income thereof as follows—

(1)   upon trust for such of the children of the said [*name*] as shall attain the age of twenty-one if more than one in equal shares absolutely;

(2)   the foregoing trust shall carry the intermediate income of the Trust Fund and section 31 of the Trustee Act 1925 (relating to maintenance and accumulation) shall accordingly apply thereto as if the proviso to subsection (1) thereof had been omitted therefrom;

(3)   the powers in section 32 of the Trustee Act 1925 (relating to the payment or application of capital) shall apply to the foregoing trusts as if the words 'one-half of' were omitted from proviso (a) to subsection (1) thereof [Provided that the said powers shall not be exercisable otherwise than so as to cause the person for whose benefit the same shall be exercised to become immediately entitled to or to an interest in possession (within the meaning of Part III of the Inheritance Tax Act 1984) in the capital thereby paid or applied].[1]

2.   For the avoidance of doubt it is hereby declared that the powers and provisions of Clauses —— to —— of the Will shall continue to apply to the Trust Fund and that in the event of the failure of the foregoing trusts the Trust Fund shall be held upon the trusts of the Will.

3.   Without prejudice to and subject always to any entitlement to income prior to this advance all income of the Trust Fund shall be treated as accruing on the date on which it becomes payable regardless of the period in respect of which it shall have accrued and shall not be subject to statutory apportionment.[2]

IN WITNESS ETC.[3]

THE SCHEDULE

[List of assets in the Trust Fund]

1   The proviso is included in order to prevent the power prejudicing the application of the ITA 1984, s 71 (accumulation and maintenance trusts), but is probably unnecessary: see the Note on inheritance tax and the statutory power of advancement in B18 at para **[218.99]**.

2   If the will does not exclude statutory apportionment of income, it may be convenient to exclude it in the advance. However, if apportionment is not excluded by the will, it will not be possible to exclude apportionment so as to deprive of income anyone entitled to income immediately prior to the appointment. Therefore, any income payable after the advance, but apportionable to the period prior to the making of the advance, will still be apportioned. For statutory apportionment over time and its exclusion see the Preliminary Note to B14 at para **[214.35]** et seq.

3   For execution, see Form F4.1 at para **[242.7]**.

F5 Miscellaneous documents giving effect to legacies

PRELIMINARY NOTE

[243.1]
This section contains various forms for giving effect to the dispositions contained in a will. Form F5.1 can be used or adapted where executors exercise a power of appropriation (which could be that conferred by the Administration of Estates Act 1925 (AEA 1925), s 41 (Part G, para **[246.50]**) or by the will) and wish to have written evidence of it, particularly of the consents of the beneficiaries if their consents are required (as under the statutory power, or perhaps if the executor is also a beneficiary in whose favour an appropriation is to be made: see *Kane v Radley-Kane* [1999] Ch 274, [1998] 3 All ER 753). Form F5.2 is a general form of assent, and Forms F5.3 and F5.4 are forms to put into effect a nil-rate band debt or charge scheme, as described at paras **[218.19]**–**[218.22]** and to be used in conjunction with Form B18.2 at para **[218.32]**, Form C3.4 at para **[225.57]** et seq, or Form C3.5 at para **[225.68]** et seq.

[243.2]

FORM F5.1:   Resolution of appropriation[1]

IN THE MATTER of the trusts of the Will ('the Will') dated [*date*] of [*name*] ('the Testator') who died on [*date*] which was proved on [*date*] by [*names of executors*] in the [*name*] Registry.

(1)   We, the said [*names of executors*], have paid and discharged all of the Testator's debts, funeral and testamentary expenses and the specific and pecuniary legacies given by the Will.

(2)   The property remaining in our hands which comprises the residuary estate of the Testator is described in the Schedule hereto.

(3)   Under clause + of the Will the said residuary estate is to be divided into [equal one third shares to be paid as to one share to [*name of beneficiary*] one share to [*name of beneficiary*] and one share to [*names of trustees*] as trustees on the trusts set out in clause + of the Will].

(4)   By virtue of [section 41 of the Administration of Estates Act 1925]/[clause + of the Will] we have power to appropriate any part or parts of the said residuary estate in or towards satisfaction of any share of the same given by the Will.

(5)   [We have ascertained and fixed the values of the respective parts of the said residuary estate, for which purpose we have employed a duly qualified valuer namely [*name*] to value the freehold property known as and situate at [*address*], and] [t]/[T]he values of the property described in Part 1, Part 2 and Part 3 of the Schedule [are equal at the date hereof].[2]

[(6)   The said [*name of beneficiary*] [*name of beneficiary*] and [*names of trustees*] have consented to an appropriation of the property described in Part 1 of the Schedule hereto to [*name of beneficiary*], an appropriation of the property described in Part 2 of the Schedule hereto to [*name of beneficiary*], and an appropriation of the property described in Part 3 of the Schedule hereto to [*names of trustees*] in full and final satisfaction of their entitlements to the residuary estate].[3]

[(6)]/[(7)]   We hereby resolve to appropriate the property described in Part 1 of the Schedule hereto to [*name of beneficiary*], the property described in Part 2 of the Schedule hereto to [*name of beneficiary*], and the property described in Part 3 of the Schedule hereto to [*names of trustees*] in full and final satisfaction of their entitlements to the residuary estate.

THE SCHEDULE

PART 1

Property appropriated to [*name of beneficiary*]

[*Description of property*]

PART 2

Property appropriated to [*name of beneficiary*]

[*Description of property*]

PART 3

Property appropriated to [*name of trustees*]

[*Description of property*]

[*Signatures of executors, and, if they are consenting, the beneficiaries and trustees*]

[*Date*]

1   Under the AEA 1925, s 41 (Part G, para [**246.50**]) personal representatives have power to appropriate any part of a testator's estate in or towards satisfaction of any legacy, subject to a number of provisos including the requirement of the consent of a beneficiary in whose favour the appropriation is made, and the requirement that a duly qualified valuer value property where necessary. However, an express power of appropriation is commonly conferred on executors removing the requirement of the beneficiaries' consents, (see for example sub-cl (3)(i) at para [**224.30**]). This may have stamp duty or capital gains tax advantages over one where consents are required: see paras [**220.72**] and [**220.73**]. For appropriation generally, see Vol. 1, para [**29.1**] et seq.

2   The value of property to be appropriated should be taken as at the date of appropriation, unless the will specifies some other date: see *Re Charteris, Charteris v Biddulph* [1917] 2 Ch 379 at 386.

3   If the consents of beneficiaries are required (as under the statutory power of appropriation, or perhaps if the executor is also a beneficiary in whose favour an appropriation is to be made: see

Kane v Radley-Kane [1999] Ch) 274, [1998] 3 All ER 753, this clause should be included. Under the statutory power the trustees of a settled legacy may consent to an appropriation in satisfaction of that legacy provided that they are not also the executors: see the AEA 1925, s 41(1)(ii)(b) (Part G, para **[246.50]**). If the consents of such persons are required this may have stamp duty or capital gains tax disadvantages: see paras **[220.72]** and **[220.73]**.

[243.3]

FORM F5.2:   Assent[1]

IN THE MATTER of the Will ('the Will') dated [*date*] of [*name*] ('the Testator') who died on [*date*] which was proved on [*date*] by [*names of executors*] in the [*name*] Registry

We, [*names of executors*], as executors of the Will HEREBY ASSENT to the vesting in [*name of beneficiary*] of the property described in the Schedule hereto in [full and final]/[partial] satisfaction of the beneficial entitlement of the said [*name of beneficiary*] under the Will.

OR

We, [*names of executors*], as executors of the Will HEREBY ASSENT to the vesting in ourselves, as trustees of the trusts of the Will, of the property described in the Schedule hereto.[2]

THE SCHEDULE

[*Description of property*]

[*Signatures of executors*]

[*Date*]

1   It is only the assent of a legal estate in land which is required to be in writing (see the AEA 1925, s 36(4)); however, executors may wish to make a written assent in respect of other forms of property, particularly if it is not capable of physical delivery, eg an undivided share in land. If the assent is in respect of registered land, Land Registry Forms should be used: ie Form AS1 where the whole of the title is subject to the assent (prescribed under the Land Registration Rules 1925, SI 1925/1092, r 98(1)(b), as amended), or Form 56 where only part of a registered title is subject to the assent (prescribed under the Land Registration Rules 1925, SI 1925/1092, r 98(2)(b), as amended). Form AS1 can also be used where the land to be assented is unregistered: an assent induces compulsory first registration, see the Land Registration Act 1925, s 123, as substituted by the Land Registration Act 1997, s 1.

2   This alternative form will be suitable where the executors have also been appointed trustees of trusts contained in the will, and upon the completion of the administration of the estate, or completion in respect only of a specific asset, wish to evidence the change in the capacity in which they hold the estate or asset from that of executors to that of trustees. This might be particularly desirable if there are powers they wish to exercise which are vested in them specifically as trustees rather than as executors. Even after such an assent, however, they are not discharged from any of their remaining duties as executors: see *Re Timmis, Nixon v Smith* [1902] 1 Ch 176 at 183. Where land is to be held subject to the trusts of the will, it appears that the executors must assent to its vesting in them as trustees in accordance with the AEA 1925, s 36(4): see *Re King's Will Trusts, Assheton v Boyne* [1964] Ch 542 (although the case of *Re Cockburn's Will Trusts, Cockburn v Lewis* [1957] Ch 438 which accepted that an assent was not necessary to pass the legal estate in such circumstances was not cited). In the case of registered land, the appropriate Land Registry forms should be used (see n 1 supra).

[243.4]

FORM F5.3:   Deed of promise to give effect to a nil-rate band debt scheme[1]

THIS DEED is made the [*date*] BETWEEN (1) [*name of surviving spouse*] of [*address*] ('the Promisor') (2) [*name of executor*] of [*address*] and [*name of executor*] of [*address*] ('the Executors') and (3) [*name of Legacy Trustee*] of [*address*] and [*name of Legacy Trustee*] of [*address*] ('the Legacy Trustees')[2]

SUPPLEMENTAL to the will ('the Will') dated [*date*] of [*name of testator*] ('the Testator') who died on [*date*] and which was proved by the Executors on [*date*] in the [*name*] Registry

WHEREAS—

(A)   By clause + of the Will the Testator gave to the Legacy Trustees a pecuniary legacy determined according to a formula ('the Trust Legacy') to hold the same upon the trusts there set out.

(B)   In the events which have happened the amount of the Trust Legacy is [£242,000].[3]

(C)   By clause + of the Will the Executors were given power instead of satisfying the Trust Legacy by the payment of cash or the appropriation of property to require the Legacy Trustees to accept a binding promise of payment made personally by the Promisor which shall be repayable on demand.[4]

(D)   The Executors have decided to satisfy the Trust Legacy by exercising such power to require the Legacy Trustees to accept a binding promise of payment made personally by the Promisor and the Promisor has agreed to make such promise.

NOW THIS DEED WITNESSETH:

1.   The Promisor promises to pay on demand[5] to the Legacy Trustees the sum of [£242,000].

2.   The Legacy Trustees declare that they hold the foregoing debt and all moneys payable thereunder upon the trusts declared by the Will in respect of the Trust Legacy.

IN WITNESS whereof the parties hereto have executed these presents as their deed the day and year first above written.[6]

SIGNED and delivered as a deed by the said [*name*] in the presence of—   }   [*Signature*]

[*Signature, address and description of witness*]

[*The foregoing from 'SIGNED' to be repeated for each party*]

---

1   This form is for use where a testator has given residue to his spouse absolutely, made a nil-rate band gift onto discretionary trusts in his will, made provision for his executors to require the trustees of those trusts to accept a promise of payment from the surviving spouse in satisfaction of the gift, as in Forms B18.2 or C3.4 at paras **[218.32]** and **[225.57]** et seq, and the executors and surviving spouse have agreed to satisfy the gift in this way. For an explanation of the scheme, see paras **[218.19]–[218.22]**.

2   The Legacy Trustees will have been appointed by the will and should include at least one person who is not the surviving spouse: see para **[218.22]**, sub-para (3).

3   Insert the amount of the legacy ascertained in accordance with the terms of the will.

4   It is important that the loan is repayable on demand so as to assist the argument that an interest
    in possession is not created: see paras **[218.19]** and **[218.20]**.
5   See n 4 supra.
6   The requirements of the Law of Property (Miscellaneous Provisions) Act 1989, s 1 for the
    making of a deed are that it is clear on its face that it is intended by the parties to it to be a deed,
    that it is signed by each party in the presence of a witness who attests the signature (two
    witnesses if someone signs for a party), and that it is delivered as a deed by each party or
    someone authorised to do so on his behalf. Sealing is not necessary.

[243.5]

FORM F5.4:   **Deed of charge to give effect to a nil-rate band charge scheme**[1]

THIS DEED is made the [*date*] BETWEEN (1) [*name of executor*] of [*address*] and [*name of executor*] of [*address*] ('the Executors')[2] and (2) [*name of Legacy Trustee*] of [*address*] and [*name of Legacy Trustee*] of [*address*] ('the Legacy Trustees')

SUPPLEMENTAL to the will ('the Will') dated [*date*] of [*name*] ('the Testator') who died on [*date*] and which was proved by the Executors on [*date*] in the [*name*] Registry

WHEREAS—

(A)   By clause + of the Will the Testator gave to the Legacy Trustees a pecuniary legacy determined according to a formula ('the Trust Legacy') to hold the same upon the trusts there set out.

(B)   In the events which have happened the amount of the Trust Legacy is [£242,000].[3]

(C)   By clause + of the Will the Executors were given power instead of satisfying the Trust Legacy by the payment of cash or the appropriation of property to charge property comprised in the Testator's residuary estate (or but for clause + would be comprised) with payment of a sum of money equal to or less than the amount of the Trust Legacy.

(D)   There is comprised in the Testator's residuary estate (or but for clause + would be comprised) [a one-half beneficial share in the property known as [*description*] ('the Beneficial Share')].

(E)   The Executors have decided to satisfy the Trust Legacy by exercising such power to charge [the Beneficial Share] with payment of the sum of [£242,000] enforceable on demand.[4]

NOW THIS DEED WITNESSETH:

1.   The Executors HEREBY CHARGE [the Beneficial Share] with payment to the Legacy Trustees of the sum of [£242,000] enforceable on demand.[5]

2.   The Legacy Trustees declare that they hold the foregoing charge and all moneys received thereunder upon the trusts declared by the Will in respect of the Trust Legacy.

IN WITNESS whereof the parties hereto have executed these presents as their deed the day and year first above written.[6]

SIGNED and delivered as a deed by the said [*name*] in the presence of—   } [*Signature*]

[Signature, address and description of witness]

[The foregoing from 'SIGNED' to be repeated for each party]

1   This form is for use where a testator has made a nil-rate band gift onto discretionary trusts in his will, made provision for his executors to charge property comprised in his estate with payment of a sum of money in satisfaction of the gift, as in Forms B18.2, C3.4, or C3.5 at paras **[218.32]**, **[225.57]** et seq and **[225.68]** et seq, and the executors have decided to satisfy the gift in this way. For an explanation of the scheme, see paras **[218.19]**–**[218.22]** and for reasons for using the charge scheme rather than the debt scheme (as in Form F5.3 at para **[243.4]**), see also para **[218.21]**.

2   The surviving spouse should not be one of the executors, and the executors and legacy trustees should not be exactly the same persons, see para **[218.22]**, sub-paras (4) and (5).

3   Insert the amount of the legacy ascertained in accordance with the terms of the will.

4   It is important that the charge is enforceable on demand so as to assist the argument that an interest in possession is not created, see paras **[218.19]**–**[218.20]**.

5   See n 4 supra.

6   The requirements of the Law of Property (Miscellaneous Provisions) Act 1989, s 1 for the making of a deed are that it is clear on its face that it is intended by the parties to it to be a deed, that it is signed by each party in the presence of a witness who attests the signature (two witnesses if someone signs for a party), and that it is delivered as a deed by each party or someone authorised to do so on his behalf. Sealing is not necessary.

PART G

Statutes

CONTENTS

Section 1
WILLS AND INTESTACY

Section 2
PROPERTY RIGHTS OF ADOPTED, LEGITIMATED AND
ILLEGITIMATE CHILDREN

Section 3
MISCELLANEOUS PROVISIONS RELEVANT TO THE DRAFTING OF WILLS

Section 4
FAMILY PROVISION AND RELIEF FROM FORFEITURE

INHERITANCE (PROVISION FOR FAMILY AND DEPENDANTS) ACT 1975

Wills and intestacy

[244.1]
Note. This section contains the Acts of Parliament currently in force concerning wills and intestacy. The only repealed provisions which are included are the more recently repealed provisions of the Wills Act 1837 (WA 1837), the Wills Act Amendment Act 1852, the Wills Act 1861, and the Law of Property Act 1925, s 177.

WILLS ACT 1837

(7 Will 4 & 1 Vict c 26)   [3 July 1837]

[244.2]
Note. The provisions here printed are as amended by the Statute Law Revision (No 2) Act 1888. Further amendments are noted to the specific provisions concerned. Sections 9, 18 and 33 were substituted, and s 18A was inserted, by the Administration of Justice Act 1982 (AJA 1982), ss 17 to 19 (see paras **[244.93]–[244.95]** et seq). Sections 9 and 33 continue to apply, as originally enacted, to wills of *testators dying before 1 January 1983*, whereas s 18, as originally enacted, continues to apply to *wills made before 1 January 1983*, irrespective of the date of the tesator's death. Section 18A applies as respects wills made by persons dying on or after 1 January 1983 and is itself substantively amended by the Law Reform (Succession) Act 1995 (LR(S)A 1995 (see paras **[244.129]–[244.134]**) as respects wills made by persons dying on or after 1 January 1996.

[244.3]
1. Meaning of certain words in this Act. . . . the words and expressions herein-after mentioned, which in their ordinary signification have a more confined or a different meaning, shall in this Act, except where the nature of the provision or the context of the Act shall exclude such construction, be interpreted as follows; (that is to say,) the word 'will' shall extend to a testament, and to a codicil, and to an appointment by will or by writing in the nature of a will in exercise of a power, [and also to an appointment by will of a guardian of a child], . . . and to any other testamentary disposition; and the words 'real estate' shall extend to manors, advowsons, messuages, lands, tithes, rents, and hereditaments, . . . whether corporeal, incorporeal, or personal, . . . and to any estate, right, or interest (other than a chattel interest) therein; and the words 'personal estate' shall extend to leasehold estates and other chattels real, and also to monies, shares of government and other funds, securities for money

(not being real estates), debts, choses in action, rights, credits, goods, and all other property whatsoever which by law devolves upon the executor or administrator, and to any share or interest therein; and every word importing the singular number only shall extend and be applied to several persons or things as well as one person or thing; and every word importing the masculine gender only shall extend and be applied to a female as well as a male.[1]

1   Section 1 is printed above in the form currently in force. The omitted words were repealed by the Statute Law Revision Act 1893, the Statute Law (Repeals) Act 1969 (SL(R)A 1969) and the Trusts of Land and Appointment of Trustees Act 1996 (TLATA 1996), s 25(2), Sch 4. The words in square brackets were substituted by the Children Act 1989, s 108(5), Sch 13, para 1 with effect from 11 October 1991 by the Children Act (Commencement and Transitional Provisions) Order 1991 (SI 1991/828).

*   *   *   *   *

[244.4]
3.   All property may be disposed of by will. . . . it shall be lawful for every person to devise, bequeath, or dispose of, by his will executed in manner hereinafter required, all real estate and all personal estate which he shall be entitled to, either at law or in equity, at the time of his death, and which, if not so devised, bequeathed, or disposed of, would devolve [*upon the heir at law or customary heir of him, or, if he became entitled by descent, of his ancestor, or*] upon his executor or administrator; and . . . the power hereby given shall extend [*to all real estate of the nature of customary freehold or tenant right, or customary or copyhold, notwithstanding that the testator may not have surrendered the same to the use of his will, or notwithstanding that, being entitled as heir, devisee, or otherwise to be admitted thereto, he shall not have been admitted thereto or notwithstanding that the same, in consequence of the want of a custom to devise or surrender to the use of a will or otherwise, could not at law have been disposed of by will if this Act had not been made or notwithstanding that the same, in consequence of there being a custom that a will or a surrender to the use of a will should continue in force for a limited time only, or any other special custom, could not have been disposed of by will according to the power contained in this Act, if this Act had not been made; and also to estates pur autre vie, whether there shall or shall not by any special occupant thereof, and whether the same shall be freehold, customary freehold, tenant right, customary or copyhold, or of any other tenure, and whether the same shall be a corporeal or an incorporeal hereditament; and also*] to all contingent, executory or other future interests in any real or personal estate, whether the testator may or may not be ascertained as the person or one of the persons in whom the same respectively may become vested, and whether he may be entitled thereto under the instrument by which the same respectively were created, or under any disposition thereof by deed or will; and also to all rights of entry for conditions broken, and other rights of entry; and also to such of the same estates, interests, and rights respectively, and other real and personal estate, as the testator may be entitled to at the time of his death, notwithstanding that he may become entitled to the same subsequently to the execution of his will.[1]

1   The words in brackets were repealed by the SL(R)A 1969, s 1, Sch, Pt III.

*   *   *   *   *

[244.5]

7. No will of a person under age valid. . . . no will made by any person under the age of [eighteen years] shall be valid.[1]

1   In relation to wills made before the Family Law Reform Act 1969 (FLRA 1969), s 3(1) came into force on 1 January 1970, the age was 21 years.

*   *   *   *   *

Deaths before 1 January 1983

(see note at para **[244.2]***)*

[244.6]

9. *Every will shall be in writing, and signed or acknowledged by the testator in the presence of two witnesses at one time, who shall attest the will.* . . . *no will shall be valid unless it shall be in writing and executed in manner hereinafter mentioned; (that is to say), it shall be signed at the foot or end thereof by the testator, or by some other person in his presence and by his direction;[1] and such signature shall be made or acknowledged by the testator in the presence of two or more witnesses present at the same time, and such witnesses shall attest and shall subscribe the will in the presence of the testator, but no form of attestation shall be necessary.[2]*

1   Explained and extended by the Wills Act Amendment Act 1852 (paras **[244.37]**–**[244.40]**).

2   Section 9, as here printed, continues to apply to the will of a testator who died before 1 January 1983. See the Mental Health Act 1983, ss 96 and 97 (paras **[244.112]** and **[244.113]**) for the court's power to direct the execution of a will or codicil on behalf of a person incapable of managing his own affairs.

Deaths on or after 1 January 1983

[244.7]

9. Signing and attestation of wills. No will shall be valid unless—

(a) it is in writing, and signed by the testator, or by some other person in his presence and by his direction; and

(b) it appears that the testator intended by his signature to give effect to the will; and

(c) the signature is made or acknowledged by the testator in the presence of two or more witnesses present at the same time; and

(d) each witness either—

    (i) attests and signs the will; or

    (ii) acknowledges his signature,

    in the presence of the testator (but not necessarily in the presence of any other witness),

but no form of attestation shall be necessary.[1]

1   This section was substituted by the WA 1837, s 17, in relation to the will of a testator who died on or after 1 January 1983.

[244.8]
10. Appointments by will to be executed like other wills, and to be valid, although other required solemnities are not observed. . . . no appointment made by will, in exercise of any power, shall be valid, unless the same be executed in manner hereinbefore required; and every will executed in manner hereinbefore required shall, so far as respects the execution and attestation thereof, be a valid execution of a power of appointment by will, notwithstanding it shall have been expressly required that a will made in exercise of such power should be executed with some additional or other form of execution or solemnity.

[244.9]
11. Saving as to wills of soldiers and mariners. Provided always, . . . that any soldier being in actual military service, or any mariner or seaman being at sea, may dispose of his personal estate as he might have done before the passing of this Act.[1]

1   Explained and extended by the Wills (Soldiers and Sailors) Act 1918 (paras **[244.46]**–**[244.50]**).

[244.10]
13. Publication not to be requisite. . . . every will executed in manner hereinbefore required shall be valid without any other publication thereof.

[244.11]
14. Will not to be void on account of incompetency of attesting witness. . . . if any person who shall attest the execution of a will shall at the time of the execution thereof or at any time afterwards be incompetent to be admitted a witness to prove the execution thereof, such will shall not on that account be invalid.

[244.12]
15. Gifts to an attesting witness to be void. . . . if any person shall attest the execution of any will to whom or to whose wife or husband any beneficial devise, legacy, estate, interest, gift, or appointment, of or affecting any real or personal estate (other than and except charges and directions for the payment of any debt or debts), shall be thereby given or made, such devise, legacy, estate, interest, gift or appointment shall, so far only as concerns such person attesting the execution of such will, or the wife or husband of such person, or any person claiming under such person or wife or husband, be utterly null and void, and such person so attesting shall be admitted as a witness to prove the execution of such will, or to prove the validity or invalidity thereof, notwithstanding such devise, legacy, estate, interest, gift, or appointment mentioned in such will.[1]

1   The attestation of a will by a person to whom, or to whose spouse, there is given or made any such disposition as is described in s 15 is to be disregarded if the will is also attested by at least two 'independent' witnesses: see the Wills Act 1968 (paras **[244.82]** and **[244.83]**). Section 15 will no longer apply to a charging clause in the will of a testator dying after 1 February 2001 as the right of an executor or trustee to payment in respect of services is treated as remuneration and not as a gift: TrA 2000, ss 28(4) and 35(1), paras **[246.143]** and **[246.150]**.

[244.13]
16. Creditor attesting to be admitted a witness. . . . . in case by any will any real or personal estate shall be charged with any debt or debts, and any creditor, or the wife or husband of any creditor, whose debt is so charged, shall attest the execution of such will, such creditor, notwithstanding such charge, shall be admitted a witness to prove the execution of such will, or to prove the validity or invalidity thereof.

[244.14]
17. Executor to be admitted a witness. . . . . no person shall, on account of his being an executor of a will, be incompetent to be admitted a witness to prove the execution of such will, or a witness to prove the validity or invalidity thereof.

Wills made before 1 January 1983

[244.15]
18. *Will to be revoked by marriage.* . . . *every will made by a man or woman shall be revoked by his or her marriage (except a will made in exercise of a power of appointment, when the real or personal estate thereby appointed would not in default of such appointment pass to his or her heir, customary heir, executor, or administrator, or the person entitled as his or her next of kin, under the Statute of Distributions).*[1]

1 The Law of Property Act 1925, s 177 (para **[244.54]**) excepts from this provision a will made on or after 1 January 1926 and, by virtue of the WA 1837, before 1 January 1983, which is *expressed* to be made in contemplation of a particular marriage. For wills made on or after 1 January 1983, see s 18, as substituted by the AJA 1982, s 18(1): para **[244.16]**.

Wills made on or after 1 January 1983

[244.16]
18. Wills to be revoked by marriage, except in certain cases.—(1) Subject to subsections (2) to (4) below, a will shall be revoked by the testator's marriage.
(2) A disposition in a will in exercise of a power of appointment shall take effect notwithstanding the testator's subsequent marriage unless the property so appointed would in default of appointment pass to his personal representatives.
(3) Where it appears from a will that at the time it was made the testator was expecting to be married to a particular person and that he intended that the will should not be revoked by the marriage, the will shall not be revoked by his marriage to that person.
(4) Where it appears from a will that at the time it was made the testator was expecting to be married to a particular person and that he intended that a disposition in the will should not be revoked by his marriage to that person,—

(a) that disposition shall take effect notwithstanding the marriage; and
(b) any other disposition in the will shall take effect also, unless it appears from the will that the testator intended the disposition to be revoked by the marriage.[1]

1 See para **[244.15]**, n 1 supra.

Deaths on or after 1 January 1983 and before 1 January 1996

[244.17]
18A.   Effect of dissolution or annulment of marriage on wills.—(1)
Where, after a testator has made a will, a decree of a court [of civil jurisdiction
in England and Wales] dissolves or annuls his marriage [or his marriage is
dissolved or annulled and the divorce or annulment is entitled to recognition in
England and Wales by virtue of Part II of the Family Law Act 1986],—

(a) the will shall take effect as if any appointment of the former spouse as an
executor or as the executor and trustee of the will were omitted; and
(b) any devise or bequest to the former spouse shall lapse,

except in so far as a contrary intention appears by the will.[1]
(2) Subsection (1)(b) above is without prejudice to any right of the former
spouse to apply for financial provision under the Inheritance (Provision for
Family and Dependants) Act 1975.
(3) Where—

(a) by the terms of a will an interest in remainder is subject to a life interest;
and
(b) the life interest lapses by virtue of subsection (1)(b) above,

the interest in remainder shall be treated as if it had not been subject to the life
interest and, if it was contingent upon the termination of the life interest, as if it
had not been so contingent.[2]

1   As originally enacted the opening words of s 18A(1) read:
'Where, after a testator has made a will, a decree of a court dissolves or annuls his marriage
or declares it void,—'.
The words in square brackets were added or substituted by the Family Law Act 1986, s 53 with
effect from 4 April 1988 (SI 1988/375).
2   This section was inserted by the AJA 1982, s 18(2), in relation to the wills (whenever made) of
persons dying on or after 1 January 1983. It was substantially amended for deaths on or after 1
January 1996, as set out below.

Deaths on or after 1 January 1996

[244.18]
18A.   Effect of dissolution or annulment of marriage on wills.—(1)
Where, after a testator has made a will, a decree of a court of civil jurisdiction in
England and Wales dissolves or annuls his marriage or his marriage is dissolved
or annulled and the divorce or annulment is entitled to recognition in England
and Wales by virtue of Part II of the Family Law Act 1986,—

(a) provisions of the will appointing executors or trustees or conferring a
power of appointment, if they appoint or confer the power on the former
spouse, shall take effect as if the former spouse had died on the date on
which the marriage is dissolved or annulled, and
(b) any property which, or an interest in which, is devised or bequeathed to
the former spouse shall pass as if the former spouse had died on that
date,

except in so far as a contrary intention appears by the will.

(2) Subsection (1)(b) above is without prejudice to any right of the former spouse to apply for financial provision under the Inheritance (Provision for Family and Dependants) Act 1975.[1]

1   Paragraphs (a) and (b) of s 18A(1) were substituted by the LR(S)A 1995, s 3, as respects a will made by a person dying on or after 1 January 1996 (regardless of the date of the will and the date of the dissolution or annulment) and s 18A(3) was repealed by s 5 of, and the Schedule to, the 1995 Act, as respects a will of a person dying on or after the same date.

[244.19]
19.   No will to be revoked by presumption. . . . no will shall be revoked by any presumption of an intention on the ground of an alteration in circumstances.

[244.20]
20.   No will to be revoked otherwise than as aforesaid or by another will or codicil, or by destruction thereof. . . . no will or codicil, or any part thereof, shall be revoked otherwise than as aforesaid, or by another will or codicil executed in manner herein-before required, or by some writing declaring an intention to revoke the same and executed in the manner in which a will is herein-before required to be executed, or by the burning, tearing, or otherwise destroying the same by the testator, or by some person in his presence and by his direction, with the intention of revoking the same.

[244.21]
21.   No alteration in a will after execution except in certain cases, shall have any effect unless executed as a will. . . . no obliteration, interlineation, or other alteration made in any will after the execution thereof shall be valid or have any effect, except so far as the words or effect of the will before such alteration shall not be apparent, unless such alteration shall be executed in like manner as herein-before is required for the execution of the will; but the will, with such alteration as part thereof, shall be deemed to be duly executed if the signature of the testator and the subscription of the witnesses be made in the margin or on some other part of the will opposite or near to such alteration, or at the foot or end of or opposite to a memorandum referring to such alteration, and written at the end or some other part of the will.

[244.22]
22.   No revoked will shall be revived otherwise than by re-execution or a codicil, etc. . . . no will or codicil, or any part thereof, which shall be in any manner revoked, shall be revived otherwise than by the re-execution thereof or by a codicil executed in manner herein-before required and showing an intention to revive the same; and when any will or codicil which shall be partly revoked, and afterwards wholly revoked, shall be revived, such revival shall not extend to so much thereof as shall have been revoked before the revocation of the whole thereof, unless an intention to the contrary shall be shown.

[244.23]
23.   A devise not to be rendered inoperative by any subsequent conveyance or act. . . . no conveyance or other act made or done subsequently to the execution of a will of or relating to any real or personal estate therein comprised, except an act by which such will shall be revoked as aforesaid, shall prevent the

operation of the will with respect to such estate or interest in such real or personal estate as the testator shall have power to dispose of by will at the time of his death.

[244.24]
24.   A will shall be construed to speak from the death of the testator. . . . every will shall be construed, with reference to the real estate and personal estate comprised in it, to speak and take effect as if it had been executed immediately before the death of the testator, unless a contrary intention shall appear by the will.

[244.25]
25.   A residuary devise shall include estates comprised in lapsed and void devises. . . . unless a contrary intention shall appear by the will, such real estate or interest therein as shall be comprised or intended to be comprised in any devise in such will contained, which shall fail or be void by reason of the death of the devisee in the lifetime of the testator, or by reason of such devise being contrary to law or otherwise incapable of taking effect shall be included in the residuary devise (if any) contained in such will.

[244.26]
26.   A general devise of the testator's lands shall include copyhold and leasehold as well as freehold lands. . . . a devise of the land of the testator, or of the land of the testator in any place or in the occupation of any person mentioned in his will, or otherwise described in a general manner, and any other general devise which would describe a [*customary, copyhold, or*] leasehold estate if the testator had no freehold estate which could be described by it, shall be construed to include the [*customary, copyhold, and*] leasehold estates of the testator, or his [*customary, copyhold, and*] leasehold estates, or any of them, to which such description shall extend, as the case may be, as well as freehold estates, unless a contrary intention shall appear by the will.[1]

1   Words in brackets repealed by the SL(R)A 1969, s 1, Sch, Pt III.

[244.27]
27.   A general gift shall include estates over which the testator has a general power of appointment. . . . a general devise of the real estate of the testator, or of the real estate of the testator in any place or in the occupation of any person mentioned in his will, or otherwise described in a general manner, shall be construed to include any real estate, or any real estate to which such description shall extend (as the case may be), which he may have power to appoint in any manner he may think proper, and shall operate as an execution of such power, unless a contrary intention shall appear by the will; and in like manner a bequest of the personal estate of the testator, or any bequest of personal property described in a general manner, shall be construed to include any personal estate, or any personal estate to which such description shall extend (as the case may be), which he may have power to appoint in any manner he may think proper, and shall operate as an execution of such power, unless a contrary intention shall appear by the will.

[244.28]
28. A devise without any words of limitation shall be construed to pass the fee. . . . where any real estate shall be devised to any person without any words of limitation, such devise shall be construed to pass the fee simple, or other the whole estate or interest which the testator had power to dispose of by will in such real estate, unless a contrary intention shall appear by the will.

[244.29]
29. The words 'die without issue', or 'die without leaving issue', shall be construed to mean die without issue living at the death. . . . in any devise or bequest of real or personal estate the words 'die without issue,' or 'die without leaving issue,' or 'have no issue,' or any other words which may import either a want or failure of issue of any person in his lifetime or at the time of his death, or an indefinite failure of his issue, shall be construed to mean a want or failure of issue in the lifetime or at the time of the death of such person, and not an indefinite failure of his issue, unless a contrary intention shall appear by the will, by reason of such person having a prior estate tail, or of a preceding gift, being, without any implication arising from such words, a limitation of an estate tail to such person or issue, or otherwise: Provided, that this Act shall not extend to cases where such words as aforesaid import if no issue described in a preceding gift shall be born, or if there shall be no issue who shall live to attain the age or otherwise answer the description required for obtaining a vested estate by a preceding gift to such issue.

[244.30]
30. No devise to trustees or executors, except for a term or a presentation to a church, shall pass a chattel interest. . . . where any real estate (other than or not being a presentation to a church) shall be devised to any trustee or executor, such devise shall be construed to pass the fee simple or other the whole estate or interest which the testator had power to dispose of by will in such real estate, unless a definite term of years, absolute or determinable, or an estate of freehold, shall thereby be given to him expressly or by implication.

[244.31]
31. Trustees under an unlimited devise, where the trust may endure beyond the life of a person beneficially entitled for life, shall take the fee. . . . where any real estate shall be devised to a trustee, without any express limitation of the estate to be taken by such trustee, and the beneficial interest in such real estate, or in the surplus rents and profits thereof, shall not be given to any person for life, or such beneficial interest shall be given to any person for life, but the purposes of the trust may continue beyond the life of such person, such devise shall be construed to vest in such trustee the fee simple, or other the whole legal estate which the testator had power to dispose of by will in such real estate, and not an estate determinable when the purposes of the trust shall be satisfied.

[244.32]
32. Devises of estates tail shall not lapse. . . . where any person to whom any real estate shall be devised for an estate tail or an estate in quasi entail shall die in the lifetime of the testator leaving issue who would be inheritable under such entail, and any such issue shall be living at the time of the death of the testator,

such devise shall not lapse, but shall take effect as if the death of such person had happened immediately after the death of the testator, unless a contrary intention shall appear by the will.[1]

> 1   An entailed interest cannot be created by an instrument coming into operation on or after 1 January 1997, the commencement date of the TLATA 1996; the grant of such an interest by an instrument coming into operation after that date will take effect as the grant of an absolute interest: s 2(6) and Sch 1, para 5. The 1996 Act also repealed the WA 1837, s 32: s 25(2) and Sch 4. The joint effect of these provisions is that the gift of an entailed interest in a will made before 1997 by a testator who dies after 1996 will lapse.

Deaths before 1 January 1983

[244.33]
33.   Gifts to children or other issue who leave issue living at the testator's death shall not lapse. *Where any person being a child or other issue of the testator to whom any real or personal estate shall be devised or bequeathed for any estate or interest not determinable at or before the death of such person shall die in the lifetime of the testator leaving issue, and any such issue of such person shall be living at the time of the death of the testator, such devise or bequest shall not lapse, but shall take effect as if the death of such person had happened immediately after the death of the testator, unless a contrary intention shall appear by the will.*[1]

> 1   Section 33, as here printed, applies in relation to the wills of persons dying before 1 January 1983. In the case of deaths on or after 1 January 1970, the definitions of 'child' and 'issue' are extended so as to include illegitimate children and remoter descendants by the FLRA 1969, s 16, (para **[245.40]**), and, by virtue of the Adoption Act 1976, s 39 (para **[245.58]**), replacing the Children Act 1975, Sch 1, para 3(1), include adopted children and issue in relation to deaths occurring on or after 1 January 1976.

Deaths on or after 1 January 1983

[244.34]
33.   Gifts to children or other issue who leave issue living at the testator's death shall not lapse.—(1)   Where—

(a)   a will contains a devise or bequest to a child or remoter descendant of the testator; and
(b)   the intended beneficiary dies before the testator, leaving issue; and
(c)   issue of the intended beneficiary are living at the testator's death,

then, unless a contrary intention appears by the will, the devise or bequest shall take effect as a devise or bequest to the issue living at the testator's death.
(2)   Where—

(a)   a will contains a devise or bequest to a class of persons consisting of children or remoter descendants of the testator; and
(b)   a member of the class dies before the testator, leaving issue; and
(c)   issue of that member are living at the testator's death,

then, unless a contrary intention appears by the will, the devise or bequest shall take effect as if the class included the issue of its deceased member living at the testator's death.

(3)   Issue shall take under this section through all degrees, according to their stock, in equal shares if more than one, any gift or share which their parent would have taken and so that no issue shall take whose parent is living at the testator's death and so capable of taking.

(4)   For the purposes of this section—

(a)   the illegitimacy of any person is to be disregarded; and

(b)   a person conceived before the testator's death and born living thereafter is to be taken to have been living at the testator's death.[1]

1   Section 33, as printed here, was substituted by the AJA 1982, s 19 in relation to the wills of persons dying on or after 1 January 1983. By virtue of the FLRA 1969, s 16 (para **[245.40]**), replaced as regards deaths on or after 4 April 1988 by The Family Law Reform Act 1987 (FLRA 1987), ss 1 and 18 (paras **[245.70]** and **[245.71]**) the definitions of 'child' and 'issue' include illegitimate children and issue and by virtue of the Adoption Act 1976, s 39 (para **[245.58]**) also include adopted children and issue.

[244.35]
34.   Act not to extend to wills made before 1838, nor to estates pur autre vie of persons who die before 1838. . . . this Act shall not extend to any will made before the first day of January one thousand eight hundred and thirty-eight; and every will re-executed or republished, or revived by any codicil, shall for the purposes of this Act be deemed to have been made at the time at which the same shall be so re-executed, republished or revived; and this Act shall not extend to any estate pur autre vie of any person who shall die before the first day of January one thousand eight hundred and thirty-eight.

[244.36]
35.   Act not to extend to Scotland. . . . this Act shall not extend to Scotland.

WILLS ACT AMENDMENT ACT 1852

(15 & 16 Vict c 24)   [17 June 1852]

Lord St Leonards' Act

[244.37]
Note. Although the whole of this Act was repealed by the AJA 1982, s 75 and Sch 9, Pt I, its provisions continue to apply to wills of *testators dying before 1 January 1983.*

[244.38]
1.   *Position of the testator's signature.* *Where by the Wills Act, 1837, it is enacted, that no will shall be valid unless it shall be signed at the foot or end thereof by the testator, or by some other person in his presence, and by his direction: Every will shall, so far only as regards the position of the signature of the testator, or of the person signing for him as aforesaid, be deemed to be valid within the said enactment, as explained by this Act, if the signature shall be so placed at or after, or following, or under, or beside, or opposite to the end of the will, that it shall be apparent on the face of the will that the testator intended to give effect by such his signature to the writing signed as his will; and . . . no*

such will shall be effected by the circumstance that the signature shall not follow or be immediately after the foot or end of the will, or by the circumstance that a blank space shall intervene between the concluding word of the will and the signature, or by the circumstance that the signature shall be placed among the words of the testimonium clause or of the clause of attestation, or shall follow or be after or under the clause of attestation, either with or without a blank space intervening, or shall follow or be after, or under, or beside the names or one of the names of the subscribing witnesses, or by the circumstance that the signature shall be on a side or page or other portion of the paper or papers containing the will whereon no clause or paragraph or disposing part of the will shall be written above the signature, or by the circumstance that there shall appear to be sufficient space on or at the bottom of the preceding side or page or other portion of the same paper on which the will is written to contain the signature; and the enumeration of the above circumstances shall not restrict the generality of the above enactment; but no signature under the said Act or this Act shall be operative to give effect to any disposition or direction which is underneath or which follows it, nor shall it give effect to any disposition or direction inserted after the signature shall be made.[1]

1   The omitted word was repealed by the Statute Law Revision Act 1893.

[244.39]
2.   *Act to extend to certain wills already made*. *The provisions of this Act shall extend and be applied to every will already made, where administration or probate has not already been granted or ordered by a court of competent jurisdiction in consequence of the defective execution of such will, or where the property, not being within the jurisdiction of the ecclesiastical courts, has not been possessed or enjoyed by some person or persons claiming to be entitled thereto in consequence of the defective execution of such will, or the right thereto shall not have been decided to be in some other person or persons than the persons claiming under the will, by a court of competent jurisdiction, in consequence of the defective execution of such will.*

[244.40]
3.   *Interpretation of 'will'*. *The word 'will' shall in the construction of this Act be interpreted in like manner as the same is directed to be interpreted under the provisions in this behalf contained in the Wills Act 1837.*

WILLS ACT 1861[1]

(24 & 25 Vict c 114)

Lord Kingsdown's Act

[244.41]
1.   *Wills of personalty made by British subjects out of the United Kingdom to be admitted, if made according to the forms required by the law of the place where made, or the law of the domicile, or domicile of origin*. *Every will and other testamentary instrument made out of the United Kingdom by a British subject (whatever may be the domicile of such person at the time of making the*

same or at the time of his or her death) shall as regards personal estate be held to be well executed for the purpose of being admitted in England and Ireland^2 to probate, and in Scotland to confirmation, if the same be made according to the forms required either by the law of the place where the same was made, or by the law of the place where such person was domiciled when the same was made, or by the laws then in force in that part of Her Majesty's dominions where he had his domicile of origin.

1   The Wills Act 1861 is repealed with effect from 1 January 1964 (Wills Act 1963, s 7(3)) but the repeal does not invalidate a will executed before that date (Wills Act 1963, s 7(4)). See now the Wills Act 1963 (paras **[244.75]–[244.80]**) which applies to the wills (whenever made) of persons dying on or after 1 January 1964.

2   The expression 'Ireland' used in this Act now excludes the Republic of Ireland (see Art 2 of the Irish Free State (Consequential Adaptation of Enactments) Order 1923).

[244.42]
2.   *Wills of personalty made in the United Kingdom to be admitted, if made according to the forms required by the law of the place where made.* *Every will and other testamentary instrument made within the United Kingdom by any British subject (whatever may be the domicile of such person at the time of making the same or at the time of his or her death) shall as regards personal estate be held to be well executed, and shall be admitted in England and Ireland^1 to probate, and in Scotland to confirmation, if the same be executed according to the forms required by the laws for the time being in force in that part of the United Kingdom where the same is made.*

1   The expression 'Ireland' used in this Act now excludes the Republic of Ireland (see Art 2 of the Irish Free State (Consequential Adaptation of Enactments) Order 1923).

[244.43]
3.   *Change of domicile not to invalidate will.* No *will or other testamentary instrument shall be held to be revoked or to have become invalid, nor shall the construction thereof be altered, by reason of any subsequent change of domicile of the person making the same.*

[244.44]
4.   *Nothing in this Act to invalidate wills of personalty otherwise valid.* *Nothing in this Act contained shall invalidate any will or other testamentary instrument as regards personal estate which would have been valid if this Act had not been passed, except as such will or other testamentary instrument may be revoked or altered by any subsequent will or testamentary instrument made valid by this Act.*

[244.45]
5.   *Application of Act.* *This Act shall extend only to wills and other testamentary instruments made by persons who die after the passing of this Act.*^{1}

1   The Act is repealed with effect from 1 January 1964: see n 1 to s 1 at para **[244.41]**.

WILLS (SOLDIERS AND SAILORS) ACT 1918

(7 & 8 Geo 5 c 58)   [6 February 1918]

[244.46]
1.   Explanation of s 11 of Wills Act 1837. In order to remove doubts as to the construction of the Wills Act 1837, it is hereby declared and enacted that section eleven of that Act authorises and always has authorised any soldier being in actual military service, or any mariner or seaman being at sea, to dispose of his personal estate as he might have done before the passing of that Act, though under the age of [eighteen years[1]].

1   In relation to wills made before the FLRA 1969, s 3(1) came into force on 1 January 1970, the age was 21 years.

[244.47]
2.   Extension of s 11 of Wills Act 1837. Section 11 of the Wills Act 1837 shall extend to any member of His Majesty's naval or marine forces not only when he is at sea but also when he is so circumstanced that if he were a soldier he would be in actual military service within the meaning of that section.

[244.48]
3.   Validity of testamentary dispositions of real property made by soldiers and sailors.—(1)   A testamentary disposition of any real estate in England or Ireland made by a person to whom section eleven of the Wills Act 1837, applies, and who dies after the passing of this Act, shall, notwithstanding that the person making the disposition was at the time of making it under [eighteen years[1]] of age or that the disposition has not been made in such manner or form as was at the passing of this Act required by law, be valid in any case where the person making the disposition was of such age and the disposition has been made in such manner and form that if the disposition had been a disposition of personal estate made by such a person domiciled in England or Ireland it would have been valid.

(2)   [*Repealed by the Succession (Scotland) Act 1964, s 34(2) and Sch 3.*]

1   In relation to wills made before the FLRA 1969, s 3(1) came into force on 1 January 1970, the age was 21 years.

[244.49]
4.   Power to appoint testamentary guardians. Where any person dies after the passing of this Act having made a will which is, or which, if it had been a disposition of property, would have been rendered valid by section eleven of the Wills Act 1837, any appointment contained in that will of any person as guardian of the infant children of the testator shall be of full force and effect.

[244.50]
5.   Short title and interpretation.

$$*\quad\quad*\quad\quad*\quad\quad*\quad\quad*$$

(2)   For the purposes of section eleven of the Wills Act 1837 and this Act the expression 'soldier' includes a member of the Air Force, and references in this

Act to the said section eleven include a reference to that section as explained and extended by this Act.

LAW OF PROPERTY ACT 1925

(15 & 16 Geo 5 c 20)   [9 April 1925]

[244.51]
Note. This Act came into force on 1 January 1926 (s 209(2) (repealed)).

*   *   *   *   *

PART X

WILLS

[244.52]
175. Contingent and future testamentary gifts to carry the intermediate income.—(1)   A contingent or future specific devise or bequest of property, whether real or personal, and a contingent residuary devise of freehold land, and a specific or residuary devise of freehold land to trustees upon trust for persons whose interests are contingent or executory shall, subject to the statutory provisions relating to accumulations, carry the intermediate income of that property from the death of the testator, except so far as such income, or any part thereof, may be otherwise expressly disposed of.
(2)   This section applies only to wills coming into operation after the commencement of this Act.

[244.53]
176. Power for tenant in tail in possession to dispose of property by specific devise or bequest.—(1)   A tenant in tail of full age shall have power to dispose by will, by means of a devise or bequest referring specifically either to the property or to the instrument under which it was acquired or to entailed property generally—

(a)   of all property of which he is tenant in tail in possession at his death; and
(b)   of money (including the proceeds of property directed to be sold) subject to be invested in the purchase of property, of which if it had been so invested he would have been tenant in tail in possession at his death;

in like manner as if, after barring the entail, he had been tenant in fee simple or absolute owner thereof for an equitable interest at his death, but, subject to and in default of any such disposition by will, such property shall devolve in the same manner as if this section had not been passed.
(2)   This section applies to entailed interests authorised to be created by this Act as well as to estates tail created before the commencement of this Act, but does not extend to a tenant in tail who is by statute restrained from barring or defeating his estate tail, whether the land or property in respect whereof he is so restrained was purchased with money provided by Parliament in consideration of public services or not, or to a tenant in tail after possibility of issue extinct,

and does not render any interest which is not disposed of by the will of the tenant in tail liable for his debts or other liabilities.

(3)   In this section 'tenant in tail' includes an owner of a base fee in possession who has power to enlarge the base fee into a fee-simple without the concurrence of any other person.

(4)   This section only applies to wills executed after the commencement of this Act, or confirmed or republished by codicil executed after such commencement.[1]

1   Note that it has not been possible to create entailed interests since 31 December 1996: TLATA 1996, s 2(6), Sch 1, para 5 (paras **[246.87]** and **[246.114]**). But this section continues to apply to entailed interests created before 1 January 1997.

Wills made before 1 January 1983

[244.54]
177.   Wills in contemplation of marriage.—*(1)   A will expressed to be made in contemplation of a marriage shall, notwithstanding anything in section eighteen of the Wills Act 1837, or any other statutory provision or rule of law to the contrary, not be revoked by the solemnisation of the marriage contemplated.*
(2)   This section only applies to wills made after the commencement of this Act.[1]

1   Note that s 177 was repealed, with effect from 1 January 1983, by the AJA 1982, s 75, which further substituted replacement provisions in the WA 1837, s 18 (see para **[244.16]**). Section 177, however, continues to apply to wills made before 1 January 1983 (see s 73(7) of the 1982 Act, para **[244.105]**).

*   *   *   *   *

[244.55]
179.   Prescribed forms for reference in wills. The Lord Chancellor may from time to time prescribe and publish forms to which a testator may refer in his will, and give directions as to the manner in which they may be referred to, but, unless so referred to, such forms shall not be deemed to be incorporated in a will.[1]

1   The Statutory Will Forms prescribed pursuant to this section are printed in Part E, para **[238.7]** et seq.

PART XI

Miscellaneous

*   *   *   *   *

[244.56]
184.   Presumption of survivorship in regard to claims to property. In all cases where, after the commencement of this Act, two or more persons have died in circumstances rendering it uncertain which of them survived the other or others,

such deaths shall (subject to any order of the court), for all purposes affecting the title to property, be presumed to have occurred in order of seniority, and accordingly the younger shall be deemed to have survived the elder.[1]

1   Where an intestate and his or her spouse die on or after 1 January 1953, in circumstances rendering it uncertain which of them survived the other, and the spouse would, by virtue of this section, be deemed to be the survivor, the AEA 1925, s 46, is nevertheless to have effect, as respects the intestate, as if the spouse had not survived him or her (AEA 1925, s 46(3), added in relation to deaths after 1952 by the Intestates' Estates Act 1952 (see para [244.60])).

*   *   *   *   *

ADMINISTRATION OF ESTATES ACT 1925

(15 & 16 Geo 5 c 23)   [9 April 1925]

[244.57]
Note. This Act came into force on 1 January 1926 (s 58(2) (repealed)).

*   *   *   *   *

PART III

ADMINISTRATION OF ASSETS

[244.58]
33.   Trust for sale.—[(1)   On the death of a person intestate as to any real or personal estate, that estate shall be held in trust by his personal representatives with the power to sell it.][1]
(2)   [The personal representatives shall pay out of

(a)   the ready money of the deceased (so far as not disposed of by his will, if any); and
(b)   any net money arising from disposing of any other part of his estate (after payment of costs),

all][2] such funeral, testamentary and administration expenses, debts and other liabilities as are properly payable thereout having regard to the rules of administration contained in this Part of this Act, and out of the residue of the said money the personal representative shall set aside a fund sufficient to provide for any pecuniary legacies bequeathed by the will (if any) of the deceased.
(3)   During the minority of any beneficiary or the subsistence of any life interest and pending the distribution of the whole or any part of the estate of the deceased, the personal representatives may invest the residue of the said money, or so much thereof as may not have been distributed, [under the Trustee Act 2000][3].
(4)   The residue of the said money and any investments for the time being representing the same, [and any part of the estate of the deceased which remains][4] unsold and is not required for the administration purposes aforesaid, is in this Act referred to as the residuary estate of the intestate.

(5)   The income (including net rents and profits of real estate and chattels real after payment of rates, taxes, rent, costs of insurance, repairs and other outgoings properly attributable to income) of so much of the real and personal estate of the deceased as may not be disposed of by his will, if any, or may not be required for the administration purposes aforesaid, may, however such estate is invested, as from the death of the deceased, be treated and applied as income, and for that purpose any necessary apportionment may be made between tenant for life and remainderman.

(6)   Nothing in this section affects the rights of any creditor of the deceased or the rights of the Crown in respect of death duties.

(7)   Where the deceased leaves a will, this section has effect subject to the provisions contained in the will.

1   Sub-s (1): substituted with retrospective effect by the TLATA 1996, s 5, Sch 2, para 5(2), (6).
2   Sub-s (2): words in square brackets substituted with retrospective effect by the TLATA 1996, s 5, Sch 2, para 5(3), (4), (6).
3   Sub-s (3): words in square brackets substituted by the TrA 2000, s 40(1), Sch 2, para 27.
4   Sub-s (4): words in square brackets substituted with retrospective effect by the TLATA 1996, s 5, Sch 2, para 5(3), (4), (6).

*   *   *   *   *

PART IV

DISTRIBUTION OF RESIDUARY ESTATE

*   *   *   *   *

[244.59]
Note to sections 46 to 49. Sections 46 to 49 of this Act were extensively amended in relation to deaths occurring on or after 1 January 1953 by the Intestates' Estates Act 1952.

They were further amended in relation to deaths on or after 1 January 1967 by the Family Provision Act 1966 (FPA 1966), s 1, and further minor amendments were made by the Administration of Justice Act 1977 (AJA 1977), s 28.

Further amendments as respects intestates dying on or after 1 January 1996 were effected by the Law Reform (Succession) Act 1995, s 1 (see para **[244.129]**) and are noted to the provisions concerned.

In relation to the estates of persons dying on or after 1 January 1970 and before 4 April 1988 Part IV of the AEA 1925 takes effect subject to the FLRA 1969, s 14 (para **[245.38]**) and in relation to deaths on or after 4 April 1988 subject to the FLRA 1987, ss 1 and 18 (paras **[245.70]** and **[245.71]**).

Only the provisions currently applicable are printed here. They apply to deaths on or after 1 January 1953.

[244.60]
46.   Succession to real and personal estate on intestacy.—(1)   The residuary estate of an intestate shall be distributed in the manner or be held on the trusts mentioned in this section, namely:—

2092

(i)   If the intestate leaves a husband or wife, then in accordance with the following Table:

TABLE

If the intestate—
(1) leaves—
    (a) no issue, and
    (b) no parent, or brother or
        sister of the whole blood,
        or issue of a brother or
        sister of the whole blood

the residuary estate shall be held in trust for the surviving husband or wife absolutely.

(2) leaves issue (whether or not persons mentioned in subparagraph (b) above also survive)

the surviving husband or wife shall take the personal chattels absolutely and, in addition, the residuary estate of the intestate (other than the personal chattels) shall stand charged with the payment of a [fixed net sum],[1] free of death duties and costs, to the surviving husband or wife with interest thereon from the date of the death . . . [at such rate as the Lord Chancellor may specify by order][2] until paid or appropriated, and, subject to providing for that sum and the interest thereon, the residuary estate (other than the personal chattels) shall be held—

(a) as to one half upon trust for the surviving husband or wife during his or her life, and, subject to such life interest, on the statutory trusts for the issue of the intestate, and

(b) as to the other half, on the statutory trusts for the issue of the intestate.

(3) leaves one or more of the following, that is to say, a parent, a brother or sister of the whole blood, or issue of a brother or sister of the whole blood, but leaves no issue

the surviving husband or wife shall take the personal chattels absolutely and, in addition, the residuary estate of the intestate (other than the personal chattels) shall stand charged with the payment of a [fixed net sum],[3] free of death duties and costs, to the surviving husband or wife with interest thereon from the date of the death... [at such rate as the Lord Chancellor may specify by order][4] until paid or appropriated, and, subject to providing for that sum and the interest thereon, the residuary estate (other than the personal chattels) shall be held—

(a) as to one half in trust for the surviving husband or wife absolutely, and

(b) as to the other half—

    (i) where the intestate leaves one parent or both parents (whether or not brothers or sisters of the intestate or their issue also survive) in trust for the parent absolutely or, as the case may be, for the two parents in equal shares absolutely

    (ii) where the intestate leaves no parent, on the statutory trusts for the brothers and sisters of the whole blood of the intestate.

[The fixed net sums referred to in paragraphs (2) and (3) of this Table shall be of the amounts provided by or under section 1 of the Family Provision Act 1966]

  (ii) If the intestate leaves issue but no husband or wife the residuary estate of the intestate shall be held on the statutory trusts for the issue of the intestate;

  (iii) If the intestate leaves no husband or wife and no issue but both parents, then the residuary estate of the intestate shall be held in trust for the father and mother in equal shares absolutely;

  (iv) If the intestate leaves no husband or wife and no issue but one parent, then the residuary estate of the intestate shall be held in trust for the surviving father or mother absolutely;

  (v) If the intestate leaves no husband or wife and no issue and no parent, then the residuary estate of the intestate shall be held in trust for the following persons living at the death of the intestate, and in the following order and manner, namely:—

First, on the statutory trusts for the brothers and sisters of the whole blood of the intestate; but if no person takes an absolutely vested interest under such trusts; then

Secondly, on the statutory trusts for the brothers and sisters of the halfblood of the intestate, but if no person takes an absolutely vested interest under such trusts; then

Thirdly, for the grandparents of the intestate and, if more than one survive the intestate, in equal shares; but if there is no member of this class; then

Fourthly, on the statutory trusts of the uncles and aunts of the intestate (being brothers or sisters of the whole blood of a parent of the intestate); but if no person takes an absolutely vested interest under such trusts; then

Fifthly, on the statutory trusts for the uncles and aunts of the intestate (being brothers or sisters of the half blood of a parent of the intestate);

  (vi) In default of any person taking an absolute interest under the foregoing provisions, the residuary estate of the intestate shall belong to the Crown or to the Duchy of Lancaster or to the Duke of Cornwall for the time being, as the case may be, as bona vacantia, and in lieu of any right to escheat.

The Crown or the said Duchy or the said Duke may (without prejudice to the powers reserved by section nine of the Civil List Act 1910, or any other powers), out of the whole or any part of the property devolving on them respectively, provide, in accordance with the existing practice, for dependants, whether kindred or not, of the intestate, and other persons for whom the intestate might reasonably have been expected to make provision.

(1A) The power to make orders under subsection (1) above shall be exercisable by statutory instrument subject to annulment in pursuance of a resolution of either House of Parliament; and any such order may be varied or revoked by a subsequent order made under the power.[5]

(2) A husband and wife shall for all purposes of distribution or division under the foregoing provisions of this section be treated as two persons.

(2A) Where the intestate's husband or wife survived the intestate but died before the end of the period of 28 days beginning with the day on which the intestate died, this section shall have effect as respects the intestate as if the husband or wife had not survived the intestate.[6]

(3) Where the intestate and the intestate's husband or wife have died in circumstances rendering it uncertain which of them survived the other and the intestate's husband or wife is by virtue of section one hundred and eighty-four of the Law of Property Act 1925 deemed to have survived the intestate, this section shall, nevertheless, have effect as respects the intestate as if the husband or wife had not survived the intestate.

(4) The interest payable on the [fixed net sum][7] payable to a surviving husband or wife shall be primarily payable out of income.

1   Words in square brackets substituted by the Family Provisions Act 1966, s 1(2), in relation to persons dying on or after 1 January 1967, for the words 'net sum of five thousand pounds'. The Lord Chancellor has power under s 1(3), (4) to vary this fixed net sum by statutory instrument. This 'fixed net sum' was £8,750 where the date of death was prior to 1 July 1972 (FPA 1966, s 1(1)) but is £15,000 where the death occurred on or after that date and before 15 March 1977 (Family Provision (Intestate Succession) Order 1977, SI 1977/415); £40,000 where the death occurred on or after 1 March 1981 (Family Provision (Intestate Succession) Order 1981, SI 1981/255); £75,000 where the death occurred on or after 1 June 1987 (Family Provision (Intestate Succession) Order 1987, SI 1987/799); and £125,000 where the death occurred on or after 1 December 1993 (Family Provision (Intestate Succession) Order 1993, SI 1993/2906).

2   Words omitted were repealed by the Statute Law (Repeals) Act 1981. Words in square brackets substituted by the AJA 1977, s 28(1) for the rate of per cent per annum. The rate of interest was 7 per cent per annum from 15 September 1977 to 30 September 1983 and from 1 October 1983 is 6 per cent per annum: see the Intestate Succession (Interest and Capitalisation) Order 1977 (SI 1977/1491), art 2, as amended by SI 1983/1374 (para **[244.90]**).

3   Words in square brackets substituted by the FPA 1966, s 1(2), in relation to persons dying on or after 1 January 1967, for the words 'net sum of twenty thousand pounds'. The Lord Chancellor has power under s 1(3), (4) to vary this fixed net sum by statutory instrument. This fixed net sum was £30,000 where the death occurred before 1 July 1972, £40,000 for deaths on or after that date and before 15 March 1977, £55,000 for deaths on or after the latter date and before 1 March 1981, and is £85,000 for deaths on or after 1 March 1981 and before 1 June 1987, £125,000 for deaths on or after 1 June 1987 and before 1 December 1993, and is £200,000 for deaths on or after 1 December 1993. The relevant statutory instruments are the same as those relating to the other fixed net sum; see note 2.

4   The words omitted were repealed by the SL(R)A 1981. See n 2 for the rates of interest.
5   Sub-s (1A): inserted by the AJA 1977, s 28(1).
6   Sub-s (2A): inserted by the LR(S)A 1995, s 1(1), as respects an intestate dying on or after 1
    January 1996.
7   Words in square brackets substituted by the FPA 1966, s 1(2), in relation to persons dying on or
    after 1 January 1967, for the words 'net sum of five thousand pounds or, as the case may be,
    twenty thousand pounds'. As to the fixed net sum, see n 2 supra.

[244.61]
**47.   Statutory trusts in favour of issue and other classes of relatives of
intestate.**—(1)   Where under this Part of this Act the residuary estate of an
intestate, or any part thereof, is directed to be held on the statutory trusts for the
issue of the intestate, the same shall be held upon the following trusts,
namely:—

   (i)   In trust, in equal shares if more than one, for all or any of the children or
         child of the intestate, living at the death of the intestate, who attain the
         age of [eighteen] years[1] or marry under that age, and for all or any of the
         issue living at the death of the intestate who attain the age of [eighteen]
         years[1] or marry under that age of any child of the intestate who
         predeceases the intestate, such issue to take through all degrees,
         according to their stocks, in equal shares if more than one, the share
         which their parent would have taken if living at the death of the intestate,
         and so that no issue shall take whose parent is living at the death of the
         intestate and so capable of taking;
  (ii)   The statutory power of advancement, and the statutory provisions which
         relate to maintenance and accumulation of surplus income, shall apply,
         but when an infant marries such infant shall be entitled to give valid
         receipts for the income of the infant's share or interest;
 (iii)   *Where the property held on the statutory trusts for issue is divisible into
         shares, then any money or property which, by way of advancement or on
         the marriage of a child of the intestate, has been paid to such child by
         the intestate or settled by the intestate for the benefit of such child
         (including any life or less interest and including property covenanted to
         be paid or settled) shall, subject to any contrary intention expressed or
         appearing from the circumstances of the case, be taken as being so paid
         or settled in or towards satisfaction of the share of such child or the
         share which such child would have taken if living at the death of the
         intestate, and shall be brought into account, at a valuation (the value to
         be reckoned as at the death of the intestate), in accordance with the
         requirements of the personal representatives;*[2]
  (iv)   The personal representatives may permit any infant contingently
         interested to have the use and enjoyment of any personal chattels in such
         manner and subject to such conditions (if any) as the personal
         representatives may consider reasonable, and without being liable to
         account for any consequential loss.

(2)   If the trusts in favour of the issue of the intestate fail by reason of no child
or other issue attaining an absolutely vested interest—

   (a)   the residuary estate of the intestate and the income thereof and all
         statutory accumulations, if any, of the income thereof, or so much

thereof as may not have been paid or applied under any power affecting the same, shall go, devolve and be held under the provisions of this Part of this Act as if the intestate had died without leaving issue living at the death of the intestate;

(b) references in this Part of this Act to the intestate 'leaving no issue' shall be construed as 'leaving no issue who attain an absolutely vested interest';

(c) references in this Part of this Act to the intestate 'leaving issue' or 'leaving a child or other issue' shall be construed as 'leaving issue who attain an absolutely vested interest.'

(3) Where under this Part of this Act the residuary estate of an intestate or any part thereof is directed to be held on the statutory trusts for any class of relatives of the intestate, other than issue of the intestate, the same shall be held on trusts corresponding to the statutory trusts for the issue of the intestate (other than the provision for bringing any money or property into account) as if such trusts (other than as aforesaid) were repeated with the substitution of references to the members or member of that class for references to the children or child of the intestate.

(4) References in paragraph (i) of subsection (1) of the last foregoing section to the intestate leaving, or not leaving, a member of the class consisting of brothers or sisters of the whole blood of the intestate and issue of brothers or sisters of the whole blood of the intestate shall be construed as references to the intestate leaving, or not leaving, a member of that class who attains an absolutely vested interest.

(5) [*Repealed by the Family Provision Act 1966, ss 9, 10, Sch 2.*]

---

1   In relation to intestates dying before the FLRA 1969, s 3(2) came into force on 1 January 1970, the age was 21 years.

2   Sub-s (1)(iii): repealed by the LR(S)A 1995, ss 1(2)(a), 5, Sch, as respects intestates dying on or after 1 January 1996.

[244.62]
47A.   Right of surviving spouse to have his own life interest redeemed.—
(1)   Where a surviving husband or wife is entitled to a life interest in part of the residuary estate, and so elects, the personal representative shall purchase or redeem the life interest by paying the capital value thereof to the tenant for life, or the persons deriving title under the tenant for life, and the costs of the transaction; and thereupon the residuary estate of the intestate may be dealt with and distributed free from the life interest.

(2)   [*Repealed by the Administration of Justice Act 1977, s 32, Sch 5, Pt VI.*][1]

(3)   An election under this section shall only be exercisable if at the time of the election the whole of the said part of the residuary estate consists of property in possession, but, for the purposes of this section, a life interest in property partly in possession and partly not in possession shall be treated as consisting of two separate life interests in those respective parts of the property.

(3A)   The capital value shall be reckoned in such manner as the Lord Chancellor may by order direct, and an order under this subsection may include transitional provisions.

(3B)   The power to make orders under subsection (3A) above shall be exercisable by statutory instrument subject to annulment in pursuance of a resolution of either House of Parliament; and any such order may be varied or revoked by a subsequent order made under the power,[2]

(4)   [*Repealed by the Administration of Justice Act 1977, s 32, Sch 5, Pt VI.*]

(5)   An election under this section shall be exercisable only within the period of twelve months from the date on which representation with respect to the estate of the intestate is first taken out:

Provided that if the surviving husband or wife satisfies the court that the limitation to the said period of twelve months will operate unfairly—

(a)   in consequence of the representation first taken out being probate of a will subsequently revoked on the ground that the will was invalid, or

(b)   in consequence of a question whether a person had an interest in the estate, or as to the nature of an interest in the estate, not having been determined at the time when representation was first taken out, or

(c)   in consequence of some other circumstances affecting the administration or distribution of the estate,

the court may extend the said period.

(6)   An election under this section shall be exercisable, except where the tenant for life is the sole personal representative, by notifying the personal representative (or, where there are two or more personal representatives of whom one is the tenant for life, all of them except the tenant for life) in writing; and a notification in writing under this subsection shall not be revocable except with the consent of the personal representative.

(7)   Where the tenant for life is the sole personal representative an election under this section shall not be effective unless written notice thereof is given to the [Senior Registrar of the Family Division of the High Court][3] within the period within which it must be made; and provision may be made by probate rules for keeping a record of such notices and making that record available to the public.

In this subsection the expression 'probate rules' means rules [of court made under section 127 of the Supreme Court Act 1981].[4]

(8)   An election under this section by a tenant for life who is an infant shall be as valid and binding as it would be if the tenant for life were of age; but the personal representative shall, instead of paying the capital value of the life interest to the tenant for life, deal with it in the same manner as with any other part of the residuary estate to which the tenant for life is absolutely entitled.

(9)   In considering for the purposes of the foregoing provisions of this section the question when representation was first taken out, a grant limited to settled land or to trust property shall be left out of account and a grant limited to real estate or to personal estate shall be left out of account unless a grant limited to the remainder of the estate has previously been made or is made at the same time.

---

1   Rules (having effect as from 15 September 1977), replacing those formerly enacted by s 47A(2) to calculate the capital value of a life interest in favour of a surviving spouse in the residuary estate are prescribed by the Intestate Succession (Interest and Capitalisation) Order 1977, (SI 1977/1491), art 3 (para **[244.91]**).

2   Sub-ss (3A), (3B): inserted by the AJA 1977, s 28(3).

3   Words in brackets substituted by the AJA 1970, s 1, Sch 2 and the SCA 1981, s 152(1), Sch 5.

4   Words in brackets substituted by the SCA 1981, s 152(1), Sch 5.

[244.63]
48. Powers of personal representative in respect of interests of surviving spouse.—(1) [*Repealed by the Intestates' Estates Act 1952, s 2(a).*]
(2) The personal representatives may raise—

(a) [the fixed net sum]¹ or any part thereof and the interest thereon payable to the surviving husband or wife of the intestate on the security of the whole or any part of the residuary estate of the intestate (other than the personal chattels), so far as that estate may be sufficient for the purpose of the said sum and interest may not have been satisfied by an appropriation under the statutory power available in that behalf; and

(b) in like manner the capital sum, if any, required for the purchase or redemption of the life interest of the surviving husband or wife of the intestate, or any part thereof not satisfied by the application for that purpose of any part of the residuary estate of the intestate;

and in either case the amount, if any, properly required for the payment of the costs of the transaction.

1   Words in square brackets substituted by the FPA 1966, s 1(2), in relation to persons dying on or after 1 January 1967, for the words 'the net sum of five thousand, or as the case may be, twenty thousand pounds'. As to the fixed net sum, see nn 1 and 3 to para **[244.60]**.

[244.64]
49. Application to cases of partial intestacy.—(1) Where any person dies leaving a will effectively disposing of part of his property, this Part of this Act shall have effect as respects the part of his property not so disposed of subject to the provisions contained in the will and subject to the following modifications:—

(aa) where the deceased leaves a husband or wife who acquires any beneficial interests under the will of the deceased (other than personal chattels specifically bequeathed) the references in this Part of this Act to [the fixed net sum] payable to a surviving husband or wife, and to interest on that sum, shall be taken as references to the said sum diminished by the value at the date of death of the said beneficial interests, and to interest on that sum as so diminished, and accordingly, where the said value exceeds the said sum, this Part of this Act shall have effect as if references to the said sum and interest thereon, were omitted;

(a) the requirements of section forty-seven of this Act as to bringing property into account shall apply to any beneficial interests acquired by any issue of the deceased under the will of the deceased, but not to beneficial interests so acquired by any other persons;

(b) the personal representative shall, subject to his rights and powers for the purposes of administration, be a trustee for the persons entitled under this Part of this Act in respect of the part of the estate not expressly disposed of unless it appears by the will that the personal representative is intended to take such part beneficially.

(2) References in the foregoing provisions of this section to beneficial interests acquired under a will shall be construed as including a reference to a beneficial

interest acquired by virtue of the exercise by the will of a general power of appointment (including the statutory power to dispose of entailed interests), but not of a special power of appointment.

(3) For the purposes of paragraph (aa) in the foregoing provisions of this section the personal representative shall employ a duly qualified valuer in any case where such employment may be necessary.[1]

(4) The references in subsection (3) of section forty-seven A of this Act to property are references to property comprised in the residuary estate and, accordingly, where a will of the deceased creates a life interest in property in possession, and the remaining interest in that property forms part of the residuary estate, the said references are references to that remaining interest (which, until the life interest determines, is property not in possession).

---

1 Words in square brackets substituted by the FPA 1966, s 1(2), in relation to persons dying on or after 1 January 1967, for the words 'the net sum of five thousand pounds or twenty thousand pounds'. As to the fixed net sum, see nn 1 and 3 to para **[244.60]**; sub-ss (1)(aa), (a), (2), (3) were repealed by the LR(S)A 1995, ss 1(2)(b), 5, Sch, as respects intestates dying on or after 1 January 1996: see paras **[244.129]**, **[244.132]** and **[244.134]**.

[244.65]
50. Construction of documents.—(1) References to any Statutes of Distribution in an instrument inter vivos made or in a will coming into operation after the commencement of this Act; shall be construed as references to this Part of this Act; and references in such an instrument or will to statutory next of kin shall be construed, unless the context otherwise requires, as referring to the persons who would take beneficially on an intestacy under the foregoing provisions of this Part of this Act.[1]

(2) Trusts declared in an instrument inter vivos made, or in a will coming into operation, before the commencement of this Act by reference to the Statutes of Distribution, shall, unless the contrary thereby appears, be construed as referring to the enactments (other than the Intestates' Estates Act 1890) relating to the distribution of effects of intestates which were in force immediately before the commencement of this Act.

[(3) In subsection (1) of this section the reference to this Part of this Act, or the foregoing provisions of this Part of this Act, shall in relation to an instrument inter vivos made, or a will or codicil coming into operation, after the coming into force of section 18 of the Family Law Reform Act 1987 (but not in relation to instruments inter vivos made or wills or codicils coming into operation earlier) be construed as including references to that section.][2]

---

1 Sub-s (1): modified by the Intestates Estates Act 1952, s 6(2) (para **[244.72]**) and the LR(S)A 1995, s 1(4) (para **[244.129]**).
2 Sub-s (3): added by the FLRA 1987; in relation to deaths on or after 4 April 1988; cf the FLRA 1987, ss 18(3), 33(1), Sch 2 (paras **[245.71]**, **[245.77]** and **[245.79]**).

[244.66]
51. Savings.—(1) Nothing in this Part of this Act affects the right of any person to take beneficially, by purchase, as heir either general or special.

(2) The foregoing provisions of this Part of this Act do not apply to any beneficial interest in real estate (not including chattels real) to which a [person

of unsound mind] or defective living and of full age at the commencement of this Act, and unable, by reason of his incapacity, to make a will, who thereafter dies intestate in respect of such interest without having recovered his testamentary capacity, was entitled at his death, and any such beneficial interest (not being an interest ceasing on his death) shall, without prejudice to any will of the deceased, devolve in accordance with the general law in force before the commencement of this Act applicable to freehold land, and that law shall, notwithstanding any repeal, apply to the case.

For the purposes of this subsection, a [person of unsound mind] or defective who dies intestate as respects any beneficial interest in real estate shall not be deemed to have recovered his testamentary capacity unless his . . . receiver has been discharged.[1]

(3)   Where an infant dies after the commencement of this Act without having been married [and without issue], and independently of this subsection he would, at his death, have been equitably entitled under a [trust or] settlement (including a will) to a vested estate in fee simple or absolute interest in freehold land, or in any property . . . to devolve therewith or as freehold land, such infant shall be deemed to have had [a life interest], and the [trust or] settlement shall be construed accordingly.[2]

(4)   [*Repealed by the Trusts of Land and Appointment of Trustees Act 1996, s 25(2), Sch 4.*]

---

1   Sub-s (2): words in square brackets substituted by the Mental Treatment Act 1930, s 20(5); words omitted repealed by the Mental Health Act 1959, s 149(2), Sch 8.
2   Sub-s (3): first, second and final words in square brackets added, third words in square brackets substituted and words omitted repealed by the TLATA 1996, s 25(1), (2), Sch 3, para 6(4), Sch 4.

[244.67]
52.   Interpretation of Part IV. In this Part of this Act 'real and personal estate' means every beneficial interest (including rights of entry and reverter) of the intestate in real and personal estate which (otherwise than in right of a power of appointment or of the testamentary power conferred by statute to dispose of entailed interests) he could, if of full age and capacity, have disposed of by his will [and references (however expressed) to any relationship between two persons shall be construed in accordance with section 1 of the Family Law Reform Act 1987].[1]

---

1   For s 55 of this Act (general definitions) see para **[246.52]**. The words in brackets were added by the FLRA 1987, s 33(1), Sch 2, para 4.

*   *   *   *   *

[244.68]
54.   Application of Act. Save as otherwise expressly provided,this Act does not apply in any case where the death occurred before the commencement of this Act.

*   *   *   *   *

INTESTATES' ESTATES ACT 1952

(15 & 16 Geo 6 & 1 Eliz 2 c 64)   [30 October 1952]

[244.69]
Note. The provisions of this Act printed below confer a right on the surviving spouse of an intestate to have the matrimonial home appropriated in or towards satisfaction of his or her share of the intestate's estate.

PART I

AMENDMENTS OF LAW OF INTESTATE SUCCESSION

[244.70]
1.   Succession to estate of intestate leaving a surviving spouse.—(1) . . . the Administration of Estates Act 1925 (hereafter in this Part of this Act referred to as 'the principal Act') . . .

*   *   *   *   *

[244.71]
5.   Rights of surviving spouse as respects the matrimonial home. The Second Schedule to this Act shall have effect for enabling the surviving husband or wife of a person dying intestate after the commencement of this Act to acquire the matrimonial home.

[244.72]
6.   Interpretation and construction.—(1) In this Part of this Act the expression 'intestate' has the meaning assigned to it by section fifty-five of the principal Act.
(2)   The references in subsection (1) of section fifty of the principal Act (which relates to the construction of documents) to Part IV of that Act, or to the foregoing provisions of that Part, shall in relation to an instrument inter vivos made or a will coming into operation, after the commencement of this Act, but not in relation to instruments inter vivos made or wills coming into operation earlier, be construed as including references to this Part of this Act and the Schedules to be read therewith.

*   *   *   *   *

PART III

GENERAL

*   *   *   *   *

[244.73]
9.   Short title and commencement.—(1) This Act may be cited as the Intestates' Estates Act 1952.

(2)   This Act shall come into operation on the first day of January, nineteen hundred and fifty-three.

*   *   *   *   *

SECOND SCHEDULE

Section 5

RIGHTS OF SURVIVING SPOUSE AS RESPECTS THE MATRIMONIAL HOME

[244.74]
1.—(1)   Subject to the provisions of this Schedule, where the residuary estate of the intestate comprises an interest in a dwelling-house in which the surviving husband or wife was resident at the time of the intestate's death, the surviving husband or wife may require the personal representative in exercise of the power conferred by section forty-one of the principal Act (and with due regard to the requirements of that section as to valuation) to appropriate the said interest in the dwelling-house in or towards satisfaction of any absolute interest of the surviving husband or wife in the real and personal estate of the intestate.
(2)   The right conferred by this paragraph shall not be exercisable where the interest is—

(a)   a tenancy which at the date of the death of the intestate was a tenancy which would determine within the period of two years from that date; or
(b)   a tenancy which the landlord by notice given after that date could determine within the remainder of that period.[1]

(3)   Nothing in subsection (5) of section forty-one of the principal Act (which requires the personal representative, in making an appropriation to any person under that section, to have regard to the rights of others) shall prevent the personal representative from giving effect to the right conferred by this paragraph.
(4)   The reference in this paragraph to an absolute interest in the real and personal estate of the intestate includes a reference to the capital value of a life interest which the surviving husband or wife has under this Act elected to have redeemed.
(5)   Where a part of a building was, at the date of the death of the intestate, occupied as a separate dwelling, that dwelling shall for the purposes of this Schedule be treated as a dwelling-house.
2.   Where—

(a)   the dwelling-house forms part of a building and an interest in the whole of the building is comprised in the residuary estate; or
(b)   the dwelling-house is held with agricultural land and an interest in the agricultural land is comprised in the residuary estate; or
(c)   the whole or part of the dwelling-house was at the time of the intestate's death used as a hotel or lodging house; or

(d) a part of the dwelling-house was at the time of the intestate's death used for purposes other than domestic purposes,

the right conferred by paragraph 1 of this Schedule shall not be exercisable unless the court, on being satisifed that the exercise of that right is not likely to diminish the value of assets in the residuary estate (other than the said interest in the dwelling-house) or make them more difficult to dispose of, so orders.

3.—(1) The right conferred by paragraph 1 of this Schedule—

(a) shall not be exercisable after the expiration of twelve months from the first taking out of representation with respect to the intestate's estate;

(b) shall not be exercisable after the death of the surviving husband or wife;

(c) shall be exercisable, except where the surviving husband or wife is the sole personal representative, by notifying the personal representative (or, where there are two or more personal representatives of whom one is the surviving husband or wife, all of them except the surviving husband or wife) in writing.

(2) A notification in writing under paragraph (c) of the foregoing sub-paragraph shall not be revocable except with the consent of the personal representative; but the surviving husband or wife may require the personal representative to have the said interest in the dwelling-house valued in accordance with section forty-one of the principal Act and to inform him or her of the result of that valuation before he or she decides whether to exercise the right.

(3) Subsection (9) of the section forty-seven A added to the principal Act by section two of this Act shall apply for the purposes of the construction of the reference in this paragraph to the first taking out of representation, and the proviso to subsection (5) of that section shall apply for the purpose of enabling the surviving husband or wife to apply for an extension of the period of twelve months mentioned in this paragraph.

4.—(1) During the period of twelve months mentioned in paragraph 3 of this Schedule the personal representative shall not without the written consent of the surviving husband or wife sell or otherwise dispose of the said interest in the dwelling-house except in the course of administration owing to want of other assets.

(2) An application to the court under paragraph 2 of this Schedule may be made by the personal representative as well as by the surviving husband or wife, and if, on an application under that paragraph, the court does not order that the right conferred by paragraph 1 of this Schedule shall be exercisable by the surviving husband or wife, the court may authorise the personal representative to dispose of the said interest in the dwelling-house within the said period of twelve months.

(3) Where the court under sub-paragraph (3) of paragraph 3 of this Schedule extends the said period of twelve months, the court may direct that this paragraph shall apply in relation to the extended period as it applied in relation to the original period of twelve months.

(4) This paragraph shall not apply where the surviving husband or wife is the sole personal representative or one of two or more personal representatives.

(5)   Nothing in this paragraph shall confer any right on the surviving husband or wife as against a purchaser from the personal representative.

5.—(1)   Where the surviving husband or wife is one of two or more personal representatives, the rule that a trustee may not be a purchaser of trust property shall not prevent the surviving husband or wife from purchasing out of the estate of the intestate an interest in a dwelling-house in which the surviving husband or wife was resident at the time of the intestate's death.

(2)   The power of appropriation under section forty-one of the principal Act shall include power to appropriate an interest in a dwelling-house in which the surviving husband or wife was resident at the time of the intestate's death partly in satisfaction of an interest of the surviving husband or wife in the real and personal estate of the intestate and partly in return for a payment of money by the surviving husband or wife to the personal representative.

6.—(1)   Where the surviving husband or wife is a person of unsound mind or a defective, a requirement or consent under this Schedule may be made or given on his or her behalf by the committee or receiver, if any, or, where there is no committee or receiver, by the court.

(2)   A requirement or consent made or given under this Schedule by a surviving husband or wife who is an infant shall be as valid and binding as it would be if he or she were of age, and, as respects an appropriation in pursuance of paragraph 1 of this Schedule, the provisions of section forty-one of the principal Act as to obtaining the consent of the infant's parent or guardian, or of the court on behalf of the infant, shall not apply.

7.—(1)   Except where the context otherwise requires, references in this Schedule to a dwelling-house include references to any garden or portion of ground attached to and usually occupied with the dwelling-house or otherwise required for the amenity or convenience of the dwelling-house.

(2)   This Schedule shall be construed as one with Part IV of the principal Act.

1   For an exception to this sub-paragraph where the tenancy could give rise to a right to enfranchise, see the Leasehold Reform Act 1967, s 7(8).

*   *   *   *   *

WILLS ACT 1963

(1963 c 44)   [31 July 1963]

[244.75]
1.   General rule as to formal validity. A will shall be treated as properly executed if its execution conformed to the internal law in force in the territory where it was executed, or in the territory where, at the time of its execution or of the testator's death, he was domiciled or had his habitual residence, or in a state of which, at either of those times, he was a national.

[244.76]
2.   Additional rules.—(1)   Without prejudice to the preceding section, the following shall be treated as properly executed—

(a)   a will executed on board a vessel or aircraft of any description, if the execution of the will conformed to the internal law in force in the territory with which, having regard to its registration (if any) and other relevant circumstances, the vessel or aircraft may be taken to have been most closely connected;

(b)   a will so far as it disposes of immovable property, if its execution conformed to the internal law in force in the territory where the property was situated;

(c)   a will so far as it revokes a will which under this Act would be treated as properly executed or revokes a provision which under this Act would be treated as comprised in a properly executed will, if the execution of the later will conformed to any law by reference to which the revoked will or provision would be so treated;

(d)   a will so far as it exercises a power of appointment, if the execution of the will conformed to the law governing the essential validity of the power.

(2)   A will so far as it exercises a power of appointment shall not be treated as improperly executed by reason only that its execution was not in accordance with any formal requirements contained in the instrument creating the power.

[244.77]
3.   Certain requirements to be treated as formal. Where (whether in pursuance of this Act or not) a law in force outside the United Kingdom falls to be applied in relation to a will, any requirement of that law whereby special formalities are to be observed by testators answering a particular description, or witnesses to the execution of a will are to possess certain qualifications, shall be treated, notwithstanding any rule of that law to the contrary, as a formal requirement only.

[244.78]
4.   Construction of wills. The construction of a will shall not be altered by reason of any change in the testator's domicile after the execution of the will.

[244.79]
5.   [*Repealed and replaced by the Succession (Scotland) Act 1964, s 34(2), Sch 3.*]

[244.80]
6.   Interpretation.   (1)   In this Act—
    'internal law' in relation to any territory or state means the law which would apply in a case where no question of the law in force in any other territory or state arose;
    'state' means a territory or group of territories having its own law of nationality;
    'will' includes any testamentary instrument or act, and 'testator' shall be construed accordingly.

(2) Where under this Act the internal law in force in any territory or state is to be applied in the case of a will, but there are in force in that territory or state two or more systems of internal law relating to the formal validity of wills, the system to be applied shall be ascertained as follows—

    (a) if there is in force throughout the territory or state a rule indicating which of those systems can properly be applied in the case in question, that rule shall be followed; or

    (b) if there is no such rule, the system shall be that with which the testator was most closely connected at the relevant time, and for this purpose the relevant time is the time of the testator's death where the matter is to be determined by reference to circumstances prevailing at his death, and the time of execution of the will in any other case.

(3) In determining for the purposes of this Act whether or not the execution of a will conformed to a particular law, regard shall be had to the formal requirements of that law at the time of execution, but this shall not prevent account being taken of an alteration of law affecting wills executed at that time if the alteration enables the will to be treated as properly executed.

[244.81]
7. Short title, commencement, repeal and extent.—(1) This Act may be cited as the Wills Act 1963.
(2) This Act shall come into operation on 1 January 1964.
(3) The Wills Act 1861 is hereby repealed.
(4) This Act shall not apply to a will of a testator who died before the time of the commencement of this Act and shall apply to a will of a testator who dies after that time whether the will was executed before or after that time, but so that the repeal of the Wills Act 1861 shall not invalidate a will executed before that time.
(5) It is hereby declared that this Act extends to Northern Ireland [*Remaining words repealed by the Northern Ireland Constitution Act 1973, s 41(1), Sch 6.*]

WILLS ACT 1968

(1968 c 28)   [30 May 1968]

[244.82]
1. Restriction of operation of Wills Act 1837, s 15.—(1) For the purposes of section 15 of the Wills Act 1837 (avoidance of gifts to attesting witnesses and their spouses) the attestation of a will by a person to whom or to whose spouse there is given or made any such disposition as is described in that section shall be disregarded if the will is duly executed without his attestation and without that of any other such person.
(2) This section applies to the will of any person dying after the passing of this Act, whether executed before or after the passing of this Act.

[244.83]
2.   Short title and extent.—(1)   This Act may be cited as the Wills Act 1968.
(2)   This Act does not extend to Scotland or Northern Ireland.

FAMILY LAW REFORM ACT 1969

(1969 c 46)   [25 July 1969]

[244.84]
Note. This Act, which was brought into force on 1 January 1970, reduced the age of majority from 21 to 18 years. The Act also made provision (since repealed) increasing the property rights of illegitimate children: see paras **[245.38]–[245.41]**.

PART I

REDUCTION OF AGE OF MAJORITY AND RELATED PROVISIONS

*   *   *   *   *

[244.85]
3.   Provisions relating to wills and intestacy.—(1)   [*Amends the Wills Act 1837, s 7,* (para **[244.5]**) *and the Wills (Soldiers and Sailors Act) 1918, ss 1, 3(1)* (paras **[244.46]** and **[244.48]**).]
(2)   [*Amends   the   Administration   of   Estates   Act   1925,   s 47(1)(i)* (para **[244.61]**).]
(3)   Any will which –

   (a)   has been made, whether before or after the coming into force of this section, by a person under the age of eighteen; and
   (b)   is valid by virtue of section 11 of the said Act of 1837 and the said Act of 1918,

may be revoked by that person notwithstanding that he is still under that age whether or not the circumstances are then such that he would be entitled to make a valid will under those provisions.
(4)   In this section 'will' has the same meaning as in the said Act of 1837 and 'intestate' has the same meaning as the said Act of 1925.

*   *   *   *   *

MATRIMONIAL CAUSES ACT 1973

(1973 c 18)   [23 May 1973]

[244.86]
Note. Section 18(2) of the Matrimonial Causes Act 1973, which deprives the husband or wife of an intestate of any interest in the intestate's estate under the intestacy rules when the parties were judicially separated at the time of the death, replaces the corresponding provisions contained in the Matrimonial

Proceedings and Property Act 1970, s 40(1), in relation to deaths on or after 1 August 1970, the commencement date of the earlier Act.

PART I

DIVORCE, NULLITY AND OTHER MATRIMONIAL SUITS

*   *   *   *   *

Other matrimonial suits

*   *   *   *   *

[244.87]
18.   Effects of judicial separation

*   *   *   *   *

(2)   If while a decree of judicial separation is in force and the separation is continuing either of the parties to the marriage dies intestate as respects all or any of his or her real or personal property, the property as respects which he or she died intestate shall devolve as if the other party to the marriage had then been dead.

*   *   *   *   *

INTESTATE SUCCESSION (INTEREST AND
CAPITALISATION) ORDER 1977, SI 1977/1491

[244.88]
Note. This Order was made on 4 September 1977 by the Lord Chancellor under the AEA 1925, s 46(1)(i) (as substituted by the Intestates' Estates Act 1952, s 1, and as amended by the AJA 1977, s 28(1)) and s 47A(3A) of the 1925 Act (as inserted by the AJA 1977, s 28(3)). The Order came into force on 15 September 1977: see article 1(1). The Order is printed below as amended by the Intestate Succession (Interest and Capitalisation) Order 1983, SI 1983/1374.

Article 2 of the Order originally increased the rate of interest payable on the statutory legacy until paid or appropriated to 7 per cent pa (from 4 per cent pa or, in the case of persons dying before 1 January 1953, 8 per cent, pa). Article 2 was amended by the 1983 Order so as to reduce the rate to 6 per cent per annum with effect from 1 October 1983.

Article 3 and the Schedule sets out the formula for calculating the value of the life interest of the surviving spouse of an intestate who elects to capitalise his or her life interest.

[244.89]
1. Citation and Interpretation.—(1) This Order may be cited as the Intestate Succession (Interest and Capitalisation) Order 1977 and shall come into operation on 15th September 1977.
(2) The Interpretation Act 1889 shall apply to the interpretation of this Order as it applies to the interpretation of an Act of Parliament.

[244.90]
2. Interest on Statutory Legacy. For the purposes of section 46(1)(i) of the Administration of Estates Act 1925, as it applies both in respect of persons dying before 1953 and in respect of persons dying after 1952, the specified rate of interest shall be [6] per cent per annum.[1]

1   The figure in square brackets was substituted by SI 1983/1374 with effect from 1 October 1983: see para **[244.88]** supra.

[244.91]
3. Capitalisation of Life Interests.—(1) Where after the coming into operation of this Order an election is exercised in accordance with subsection (6) or (7) of section 47A of the Administration of Estates Act 1925, the capital value of the life interest of the surviving spouse shall be reckoned in accordance with the following provisions of this article.
(2) There shall be ascertained, by reference to the index compiled by the Financial Times, The Institute of Actuaries and the Faculty of Actuaries, the average gross redemption yield on medium coupon fifteen-year Government Stocks at the date on which the election was exercised or, if the index was not compiled on that date, by reference to the index on the last date before that date on which it was compiled; and the column which corresponds to that yield in whichever of the Tables set out in the Schedule hereto is applicable to the sex of the surviving spouse shall be the appropriate column for the purposes of paragraph (3) of this article.
(3) The capital value for the purposes of paragraph (1) of this article is the produce of the part of the residuary estate (whether or not yielding income) in respect of which the election was exercised and the multiplier shown in the appropriate column opposite the age which the surviving spouse had attained at the date on which the election was exercised.

SCHEDULE

TABLE 1

Multiplier to be applied to the part of the residuary estate in respect of which the election is exercised to obtain the capital value of the life interest of a surviving husband when the average gross redemption yield on medium coupon fifteen-year Government Stocks is at the rate shown

Age Last Birthday of Husband	Less than 8.50%	8.50% or between 8.50% and 9.50%	9.50% or between 9.50% and 10.50%	10.50% or between 10.50% and 11.50%	11.50% or between 11.50% and 12.50%	12.50% or between 12.50% and 13.50%	13.50% or between 13.50% and 14.50%	14.50% or between 14.50% and 15.50%	15.50% or more
16	0.882	0.897	0.908	0.917	0.923	0.927	0.931	0.934	0.936
17	0.879	0.895	0.906	0.915	0.921	0.926	0.930	0.933	0.935
18	0.876	0.892	0.904	0.913	0.920	0.925	0.929	0.932	0.934
19	0.873	0.890	0.902	0.911	0.918	0.923	0.928	0.931	0.933
20	0.870	0.887	0.900	0.909	0.917	0.922	0.926	0.930	0.933
21	0.866	0.884	0.897	0.907	0.915	0.921	0.925	0.929	0.932
22	0.863	0.881	0.895	0.905	0.913	0.919	0.924	0.928	0.931
23	0.859	0.878	0.892	0.903	0.911	0.918	0.923	0.927	0.930
24	0.855	0.875	0.890	0.901	0.909	0.916	0.921	0.925	0.929
25	0.852	0.872	0.887	0.898	0.907	0.914	0.920	0.924	0.928
26	0.847	0.868	0.884	0.896	0.905	0.912	0.918	0.923	0.926
27	0.843	0.864	0.880	0.893	0.903	0.910	0.916	0.921	0.925
28	0.838	0.860	0.877	0.890	0.900	0.908	0.914	0.919	0.923
29	0.834	0.856	0.873	0.887	0.897	0.905	0.912	0.917	0.922
30	0.828	0.851	0.869	0.883	0.894	0.903	0.910	0.915	0.920
31	0.823	0.847	0.865	0.879	0.891	0.900	0.907	0.913	0.918
32	0.818	0.842	0.861	0.876	0.887	0.897	0.904	0.911	0.916
33	0.812	0.837	0.856	0.871	0.884	0.893	0.901	0.908	0.913
34	0.806	0.831	0.851	0.867	0.880	0.890	0.898	0.905	0.911
35	0.799	0.825	0.846	0.862	0.875	0.886	0.895	0.902	0.908
36	0.792	0.819	0.840	0.857	0.871	0.882	0.891	0.899	0.905
37	0.785	0.813	0.834	0.852	0.866	0.878	0.887	0.895	0.902
38	0.778	0.806	0.828	0.846	0.861	0.873	0.883	0.891	0.898
39	0.771	0.799	0.822	0.840	0.856	0.868	0.879	0.887	0.894
40	0.763	0.792	0.815	0.834	0.850	0.863	0.874	0.883	0.890

TABLE 1—*(Contd)*

Age Last Birthday of Husband	Less than 8.50%	8.50% or between 8.50% and 9.50%	9.50% or between 9.50% and 10.50%	10.50% or between 10.50% and 11.50%	11.50% or between 11.50% and 12.50%	12.50% or between 12.50% and 13.50%	13.50% or between 13.50% and 14.50%	14.50% or between 14.50% and 15.50%	15.50% or more
41	0.755	0.784	0.808	0.828	0.844	0.857	0.869	0.878	0.886
42	0.746	0.776	0.801	0.821	0.838	0.852	0.863	0.873	0.881
43	0.737	0.768	0.793	0.814	0.831	0.845	0.857	0.868	0.876
44	0.728	0.759	0.785	0.806	0.824	0.839	0.851	0.862	0.871
45	0.719	0.750	0.776	0.798	0.816	0.832	0.845	0.856	0.866
46	0.709	0.741	0.768	0.790	0.809	0.825	0.838	0.850	0.860
47	0.699	0.731	0.758	0.781	0.801	0.817	0.831	0.843	0.853
48	0.688	0.721	0.749	0.772	0.792	0.809	0.823	0.836	0.847
49	0.678	0.711	0.739	0.763	0.783	0.800	0.815	0.828	0.839
50	0.566	0.700	0.729	0.753	0.774	0.791	0.807	0.820	0.832
51	0.655	0.689	0.718	0.743	0.764	0.782	0.798	0.812	0.824
52	0.643	0.678	0.707	0.732	0.754	0.772	0.789	0.803	0.815
53	0.631	0.666	0.695	0.721	0.743	0.762	0.779	0.794	0.807
54	0.619	0.654	0.684	0.710	0.732	0.752	0.769	0.784	0.797
55	0.606	0.641	0.671	0.698	0.721	0.741	0.758	0.774	0.787
56	0.594	0.628	0.659	0.685	0.709	0.729	0.747	0.763	0.777
57	0.580	0.615	0.646	0.673	0.696	0.717	0.735	0.752	0.766
58	0.567	0.602	0.633	0.660	0.683	0.705	0.723	0.740	0.755
59	0.553	0.588	0.619	0.646	0.670	0.692	0.711	0.728	0.743
60	0.539	0.574	0.605	0.632	0.657	0.678	0.698	0.715	0.731
61	0.525	0.560	0.590	0.618	0.642	0.664	0.684	0.702	0.718
62	0.510	0.545	0.576	0.603	0.628	0.650	0.670	0.688	0.704
63	C.496	0.530	0.561	0.588	0.613	0.636	0.656	0.674	0.691
64	0.481	0.515	0.546	0.573	0.598	0.621	0.641	0.659	0.676
65	0.466	0.500	0.530	0.558	0.583	0.605	0.626	0.644	0.661
66	0.451	0.485	0.515	0.542	0.567	0.590	0.610	0.629	0.646
67	0.436	0.469	0.499	0.526	0.551	0.574	0.594	0.613	0.631
68	0.421	0.454	0.483	0.510	0.535	0.557	0.578	0.597	0.615
69	0.407	0.438	0.467	0.494	0.518	0.541	0.562	0.581	0.598
70	0.392	0.423	0.452	0.478	0.502	0.524	0.545	0.564	0.582

TABLE 1—(Contd)

Age Last Birthday of Husband	Less than 8.50%	8.50% or between 8.50% and 9.50%	9.50% or between 9.50% and 10.50%	10.50% or between 10.50% and 11.50%	11.50% or between 11.50% and 12.50%	12.50% or between 12.50% and 13.50%	13.50% or between 13.50% and 14.50%	14.50% or between 14.50% and 15.50%	15.50% or more
71	0.377	0.407	0.436	0.462	0.485	0.508	0.528	0.547	0.565
72	0.362	0.392	0.420	0.445	0.469	0.491	0.511	0.530	0.548
73	0.348	0.377	0.404	0.429	0.452	0.474	0.494	0.513	0.531
74	0.333	0.362	0.388	0.413	0.436	0.457	0.477	0.496	0.513
75	0.319	0.347	0.373	0.397	0.419	0.441	0.460	0.479	0.496
76	0.305	0.332	0.357	0.381	0.403	0.424	0.443	0.461	0.479
77	0.292	0.318	0.342	0.365	0.387	0.407	0.426	0.444	0.461
78	0.278	0.304	0.328	0.350	0.371	0.391	0.410	0.427	0.444
79	0.265	0.290	0.313	0.335	0.355	0.375	0.393	0.410	0.427
80	0.253	0.277	0.299	0.320	0.340	0.359	0.377	0.394	0.410
81	0.241	0.264	0.285	0.306	0.325	0.343	0.361	0.377	0.393
82	0.229	0.251	0.272	0.292	0.310	0.328	0.345	0.361	0.377
83	0.218	0.239	0.259	0.278	0.296	0.313	0.330	0.346	0.361
84	0.207	0.227	0.246	0.265	0.282	0.299	0.315	0.331	0.345
85	0.196	0.216	0.234	0.252	0.269	0.285	0.301	0.316	0.330
86	0.186	0.205	0.223	0.240	0.256	0.272	0.287	0.302	0.315
87	0.177	0.195	0.212	0.228	0.244	0.259	0.274	0.288	0.301
88	0.168	0.185	0.201	0.217	0.232	0.247	0.261	0.275	0.288
89	0.159	0.176	0.191	0.207	0.221	0.235	0.249	0.262	0.275
90	0.151	0.167	0.182	0.197	0.211	0.224	0.237	0.250	0.262
91	0.144	0.159	0.173	0.187	0.201	0.214	0.227	0.239	0.251
92	0.137	0.151	0.165	0.179	0.192	0.205	0.217	0.229	0.240
93	0.130	0.144	0.158	0.171	0.183	0.196	0.208	0.219	0.230
94	0.124	0.138	0.151	0.163	0.175	0.187	0.199	0.210	0.221
95	0.119	0.132	0.144	0.156	0.168	0.179	0.190	0.201	0.212
96	0.113	0.126	0.138	0.149	0.161	0.172	0.182	0.193	0.203
97	0.108	0.120	0.132	0.143	0.154	0.164	0.175	0.185	0.195
98	0.103	0.115	0.126	0.137	0.147	0.157	0.167	0.177	0.187
99	0.098	0.109	0.119	0.130	0.140	0.150	0.159	0.169	0.178
100 and over	0.093	0.103	0.112	0.123	0.133	0.143	0.151	0.161	0.169

TABLE 2

Multiplier to be applied to the part or the residuary estate in respect of which the election is exercised to obtain the capital value of the life interest of a surviving wife, when the average gross redemption yield on medium coupon fifteen-year Government Stocks is at the rate shown.

Age Last Birthday of Wife	Less than 8.59%	8.50% or between 8.50% and 9.50%	9.50% or between 9.50% and 10.50%	10.50% or between 10.50% and 11.50%	11.50% or between 11.50% and 12.50%	12.50% or between 12.50% and 13.50%	13.50% or between 13.50% and 14.50%	14.50% or between 14.50% and 15.50%	15.50% or more
16	0.892	0.905	0.915	0.922	0.927	0.930	0.933	0.936	0.937
17	0.889	0.903	0.913	0.920	0.925	0.929	0.933	0.935	0.937
18	0.887	0.901	0.911	0.919	0.924	0.929	0.932	0.934	0.936
19	0.884	0.899	0.910	0.917	0.923	0.928	0.931	0.934	0.936
20	0.882	0.897	0.908	0.916	0.922	0.927	0.930	0.933	0.935
21	0.879	0.895	0.906	0.915	0.921	0.926	0.929	0.932	0.934
22	0.877	0.893	0.904	0.913	0.920	0.925	0.928	0.931	0.934
23	0.874	0.890	0.902	0.911	0.918	0.923	0.927	0.931	0.933
24	0.871	0.888	0.900	0.910	0.917	0.922	0.926	0.930	0.932
25	0.868	0.885	0.898	0.908	0.915	0.921	0.925	0.929	0.932
26	0.864	0.882	0.896	0.906	0.914	0.920	0.924	0.928	0.931
27	0.861	0.879	0.893	0.904	0.912	0.918	0.923	0.927	0.930
28	0.857	0.876	0.891	0.901	0.910	0.916	0.921	0.925	0.929
29	0.853	0.873	0.888	0.899	0.908	0.915	0.920	0.924	0.928
30	0.849	0.869	0.885	0.896	0.906	0.913	0.918	0.923	0.926
31	0.845	0.866	0.882	0.894	0.903	0.911	0.916	0.921	0.925
32	0.840	0.862	0.878	0.891	0.901	0.908	0.914	0.919	0.923
33	0.836	0.858	0.875	0.888	0.898	0.906	0.912	0.918	0.922
34	0.831	0.853	0.871	0.884	0.895	0.903	0.910	0.916	0.920
35	0.826	0.849	0.867	0.881	0.892	0.901	0.908	0.913	0.918
36	0.820	0.844	0.863	0.877	0.889	0.898	0.905	0.911	0.916
37	0.815	0.839	0.858	0.873	0.885	0.895	0.902	0.909	0.914
38	0.809	0.834	0.853	0.869	0.881	0.891	0.899	0.906	0.911
39	0.803	0.828	0.848	0.864	0.877	0.888	0.896	0.903	0.909
40	0.796	0.822	0.843	0.860	0.873	0.884	0.893	0.900	0.906
41	0.790	0.816	0.838	0.855	0.869	0.880	0.889	0.897	0.903
42	0.783	0.810	0.832	0.850	0.864	0.876	0.885	0.893	0.900

TABLE 2—(Contd)

Age Last Birthday of Wife	Less than 8.50%	8.50% or between 8.50% and 9.50%	9.50% or between 9.50% and 10.50%	10.50% or between 10.50% and 11.50%	11.50% or between 11.50% and 12.50%	12.50% or between 12.50% and 13.50%	13.50% or between 13.50% and 14.50%	14.50% or between 14.50% and 15.50%	15.50% or more
43	0.775	0.803	0.826	0.844	0.859	0.871	0.881	0.889	0.896
44	0.768	0.796	0.820	0.838	0.854	0.866	0.877	0.885	0.893
45	0.760	0.789	0.813	0.832	0.848	0.861	0.872	0.881	0.889
46	0.752	0.782	0.806	0.826	0.842	0.856	0.867	0.876	0.885
47	0.744	0.774	0.799	0.819	0.836	0.850	0.862	0.872	0.880
48	0.735	0.766	0.791	0.812	0.829	0.844	0.856	0.866	0.875
49	0.726	0.757	0.783	0.804	0.822	0.837	0.850	0.861	0.870
50	0.716	0.748	0.775	0.797	0.815	0.831	0.844	0.855	0.865
51	0.707	0.739	0.766	0.788	0.807	0.823	0.837	0.849	0.859
52	0.697	0.729	0.757	0.780	0.799	0.816	0.830	0.842	0.853
53	0.686	0.719	0.747	0.771	0.791	0.808	0.822	0.835	0.846
54	0.676	0.709	0.737	0.761	0.782	0.799	0.814	0.827	0.839
55	0.664	0.698	0.727	0.751	0.772	0.790	0.806	0.820	0.831
56	0.653	0.687	0.716	0.741	0.763	0.781	0.797	0.811	0.823
57	0.641	0.676	0.705	0.730	0.752	0.771	0.788	0.802	0.815
58	0.629	0.664	0.693	0.719	0.741	0.761	0.778	0.793	0.806
59	0.616	0.651	0.681	0.707	0.730	0.750	0.767	0.783	0.796
60	0.603	0.638	0.669	0.695	0.718	0.739	0.757	0.772	0.786
61	0.590	0.625	0.656	0.683	0.706	0.727	0.745	0.761	0.776
62	0.577	0.612	0.643	0.670	0.693	0.715	0.733	0.750	0.764
63	0.563	0.598	0.629	0.656	0.680	0.702	0.721	0.738	0.753
64	0.549	0.584	0.615	0.642	0.667	0.688	0.708	0.725	0.740
65	0.534	0.569	0.600	0.628	0.653	0.674	0.694	0.712	0.728
66	0.520	0.555	0.586	0.613	0.638	0.660	0.680	0.698	0.714
67	0.505	0.540	0.570	0.598	0.623	0.645	0.666	0.684	0.700
68	0.490	0.524	0.555	0.583	0.608	0.630	0.651	0.669	0.686
69	0.475	0.509	0.539	0.567	0.592	0.615	0.635	0.654	0.671
70	0.459	0.493	0.523	0.551	0.576	0.599	0.619	0.638	0.655
71	0.444	0.477	0.507	0.535	0.560	0.582	0.603	0.622	0.640

TABLE 2—*(Contd)*

Age Last Birthday of Wife	Less than 8.50%	8.50% or between 8.50% and 9.50%	9.50% or between 9.50% and 10.50%	10.50% or between 10.50% and 11.50%	11.50% or between 11.50% and 12.50%	12.50% or between 12.50% and 13.50%	13.50% or between 13.50% and 14.50%	14.50% or between 14.50% and 15.50%	15.50% or more
72	0.428	0.461	0.491	0.518	0.543	0.566	0.586	0.606	0.623
73	0.413	0.445	0.475	0.501	0.526	0.549	0.570	0.589	0.606
74	0.398	0.429	0.458	0.485	0.509	0.532	0.552	0.572	0.589
75	0.382	0.413	0.442	0.468	0.492	0.514	0.535	0.554	0.572
76	0.367	0.397	0.425	0.451	0.475	0.497	0.517	0.536	0.554
77	0.352	0.381	0.408	0.434	0.457	0.479	0.499	0.518	0.536
78	0.337	0.365	0.392	0.417	0.440	0.461	0.482	0.500	0.518
79	0.322	0.350	0.376	0.400	0.423	0.444	0.464	0.482	0.500
80	0.307	0.334	0.360	0.383	0.406	0.426	0.446	0.464	0.482
81	0.293	0.319	0.344	0.367	0.389	0.409	0.428	0.446	0.463
82	0.279	0.304	0.328	0.351	0.372	0.392	0.410	0.428	0.445
83	0.265	0.290	0.313	0.335	0.355	0.375	0.393	0.410	0.427
84	0.252	0.276	0.298	0.319	0.339	0.358	0.376	0.393	0.409
85	0.239	0.262	0.284	0.304	0.323	0.342	0.359	0.376	0.392
86	0.227	0.249	0.269	0.289	0.308	0.326	0.343	0.359	0.374
87	0.215	0.236	0.256	0.275	0.293	0.310	0.327	0.342	0.357
88	0.204	0.224	0.243	0.261	0.279	0.295	0.311	0.327	0.341
89	0.193	0.212	0.230	0.248	0.265	0.281	0.296	0.311	0.325
90	0.182	0.201	0.218	0.235	0.251	0.267	0.282	0.296	0.310
91	0.173	0.190	0.207	0.223	0.239	0.254	0.268	0.282	0.296
92	0.164	0.180	0.197	0.212	0.227	0.242	0.256	0.269	0.282
93	0.155	0.171	0.187	0.202	0.216	0.230	0.243	0.256	0.269
94	0.147	0.162	0.177	0.192	0.205	0.219	0.232	0.244	0.256
95	0.139	0.154	0.168	0.182	0.195	0.208	0.221	0.233	0.244
96	0.132	0.146	0.159	0.173	0.185	0.198	0.210	0.222	0.233
97	0.125	0.138	0.151	0.164	0.176	0.188	0.199	0.211	0.222
98	0.118	0.130	0.143	0.155	0.167	0.178	0.189	0.200	0.210
99	0.110	0.122	0.134	0.146	0.157	0.168	0.178	0.189	0.199
100 and over	0.102	0.114	0.125	0.137	0.147	0.158	0.167	0.178	0.188

ADMINISTRATION OF JUSTICE ACT 1982

(1982 c 53)   [28 October 1982]

[244.92]
Note. Part IV of the AJA 1982 effects the most significant changes to the law of wills since the enactment of the WA 1837. With effect from 1 January 1983 the WA 1837, ss 9, 18 and 33 (relating to the signing and attestation of wills, the revocation of wills by marriage and the saving of gifts to children and other issue who predecease a testator in favour of the surviving issue of such children or issue) were replaced (see paras **[244.7]**, **[244.16]** and **[244.34]**) and a new s 18A (effect of dissolution or annulment of marriage on wills) introduced, which has itself since been replaced (see paras **[244.17]** and **[244.18]**). Provision is also made by Part IV for the rectification of the wills of testators dying on or after 1 January 1983 and for the admissibility of extrinsic evidence, including evidence of intention, in the interpretation of the wills of testators dying on or after that date. Part IV also makes provision, not yet implemented, for the registration and deposit of wills and for the recognition of international wills by adopting the Annex to the Convention on International Wills (set out in the AJA 1982, Sch 2).

PART IV

WILLS

*   *   *   *   *

Amendments of Wills Act 1837

[244.93]
17.   Relaxation of formal requirements for making wills. (*[For text, see the Wills Act 1837, s 9 (as substituted) at para* **[244.7]**.*]*)

[244.94]
18.   Effect of marriage or its termination on wills. (*[For text, see the Wills Act 1837, ss 18 (as substituted) and 18A at paras* **[244.16]** *and* **[244.17]**.*]*)

[244.95]
19.   Gifts to children etc who predecease testator. (*[For text, see the Wills Act 1837, s 33 (as substituted) at para* **[244.34]**.*]*)

Rectification and interpretation of wills

[244.96]
20.   Rectification.—(1)   If a court is satisfied that a will is so expressed that it fails to carry out the testator's intentions, in consequence—

  (a)   of a clerical error; or
  (b)   of a failure to understand his instructions,

it may order that the will shall be rectified so as to carry out his intentions.

(2)   An application for an order under this section shall not, except with the permission of the court, be made after the end of the period of six months from the date on which representation with respect to the estate of the deceased is first taken out.

(3)   The provisions of this section shall not render the personal representatives of a deceased person liable for having distributed any part of the estate of the deceased, after the end of the period of six months from the date on which representation with respect to the estate of the deceased is first taken out, on the ground that they ought to have taken into account the possibility that the court might permit the making of an application for an order under this section after the end of that period; but this subsection shall not prejudice any power to recover, by reason of the making of an order under this section, any part of the estate so distributed.

(4)   In considering for the purposes of this section when representation with respect to the estate of a deceased person was first taken out, a grant limited to settled land or to trust property shall be left out of account, and a grant limited to real estate or to personal estate shall be left out of account unless a grant limited to the remainder of the estate has previously been made or is made at the same time.

[244.97]
21.   Interpretation of wills—general rules as to evidence.—(1)   This section applies to a will—

 (a)   in so far as any part of it is meaningless;
 (b)   in so far as the language used in any part of it is ambiguous on the face of it;
 (c)   in so far as evidence, other than evidence of the testator's intention, shows that the language used in any part of it is ambiguous in the light of surrounding circumstances.

(2)   In so far as this section applies to a will extrinsic evidence, including evidence of the testator's intention, may be admitted to assist in its interpretation.

[244.98]
22.   Presumption as to effect of gifts to spouses. Except where a contrary intention is shown it shall be presumed that if a testator devises or bequeaths property to his spouse in terms which in themselves would give an absolute interest to the spouse, but by the same instrument purports to give his issue an interest in the same property, the gift to the spouse is absolute notwithstanding the purported gift to the issue.

Registration of wills

[244.99]
23.   Deposit and registration of wills of living persons.[1]—(1)   The following, namely—

(a) the Principal Registry of the Family Division of the High Court of Justice;

*   *   *   *   *

shall be registering authorities for the purposes of this section.

(2) Each registering authority shall provide and maintain safe and convenient depositories for the custody of the wills of living persons.

(3) Any person may deposit his will in such a depository in accordance with regulations under section 25 below and on payment of the prescribed fee.

(4) It shall be the duty of a registering authority to register in accordance with regulations under section 25 below—

(a) any will deposited in a depository maintained by the authority; and
(b) any other will whose registration is requested under Article 6 of the Registration Convention.

(5) A will deposited in a depository provided—

(a) under section 172 of the Supreme Court of Judicature (Consolidation) Act 1925 or section 126 of the Supreme Court Act 1981; or
(b) under Article 27 of the Administration of Estates (Northern Ireland) Order 1979,

shall be treated for the purposes of this section as if it had been deposited under this section.

(6) In this section 'prescribed' means—

(a) in the application of this section to England and Wales, prescribed by an order under section 130 of the Supreme Court Act 1981;

*   *   *   *   *

1   No statutory instrument under s 76(5), (6) (para **[244.106]**) bringing this section into force has yet been made.

[244.100]
24. Designation of Principal Registry as national body under Registration Convention.[1]—(1) The Principal Registry of the Family Division of the High Court of Justice shall be the national body for the purposes of the Registration Convention, and shall accordingly have the functions assigned to the national body by the Registration Convention including, without prejudice to the general application of the Convention to the Principal Registry by virtue of this section, the functions—

(a) of arranging for the registration of wills in other Contracting States as provided for in Article 6 of the Convention;
(b) of receiving and answering requests for information arising from the national bodies of other Contracting States.

(2) In this Part of this Act 'the Registration Convention' means the Convention on the Establishment of a Scheme of Registration of Wills concluded at Basle on 16th May 1972.

1   No statutory instrument under s 76(5), (6) (para **[244.106]**) bringing this section into force has yet been made.

[244.101]
25. Regulations as to deposit and registration of wills etc.[1]—(1)
Regulations may make provision—

   (a) as to the conditions for the deposit of a will;
   (b) as to the manner of and procedure for—
       (i)   the deposit and registration of a will; and
       (ii)   the withdrawal of a will which has been deposited; and
       (iii) the cancellation of the registration of a will; and

   (c) as to the manner in which the Principal Registry of the Family Division
is to perform its functions as the national body under the Registration
Convention.

(2) Regulations under this section may contain such incidental or
supplementary provisions as the authority making the regulations considers
appropriate.
(3) Any such regulations are to be made—

   (a) for England and Wales, by the President of the Family Division of the
High Court of Justice, with the concurrence of the Lord Chancellor;

*   *   *   *   *

(4) Regulations made by virtue of subsection (1)(c) above shall be made by the
Lord Chancellor.
(5) Subject to subsection (6) below, regulations under this section shall be
made by statutory instrument and shall be laid before Parliament after being
made.

*   *   *   *   *

(7) The Statutory Instruments Act 1946 shall apply to a statutory instrument
containing regulations made in accordance with subsection (3)(a) . . . above as if
the regulations had been made by a Minister of the Crown.
(8) Any regulations made under section 172 of the Supreme Court of
Judicature (Consolidation) Act 1925 or section 126 of the Supreme Court Act
1981 shall have effect for the purposes of this Part of this Act as they have effect
for the purposes of the enactment under which they were made.

1   No statutory instrument under s 76(5), (6) (para **[244.106]**) bringing this section into force has
    yet been made.

[244.102]
26.   (*Fees as to registration in Scotland.*)

[244.103]
27. The form of an international will.[1]—(1)   The Annex to the Convention
on International Wills shall have the force of law in the United Kingdom.
(2)   The Annex is set out in Schedule 2 to this Act.
(3)   In this Part of this Act—

'international will' means a will made in accordance with the requirements of the Annex, as set out in Schedule 2 to this Act; and

'the Convention on International Wills' means the Convention providing a Uniform Law on the Form of an International Will concluded at Washington on 26th October 1973.

1   Section 75 effects repeals of previous legislation. No statutory instrument under s 76(5), (6) (para [**244.106**]) bringing this section into force has yet been made.

[244.104]
28. International wills—procedure.[1]—(1)   The persons authorised to act in the United Kingdom in connection with international wills are—

(a)   solicitors, and
(b)   notaries public.

(2)   A person who is authorised under section 6(1) of the Commissioners for Oaths Act 1889 to do notarial acts in any foreign country or place is authorised to act there in connection with international wills.

(3)   An international will certified by virtue of subsection (1) or (2) above may be deposited in a depository provided under section 23 above.

(4)   Section 23 above shall accordingly have effect in relation to such international wills.

(5)   Subject to subsection (6) below, regulations under section 25 above shall have effect in relation to such international wills as they have effect in relation to wills deposited under section 23 above.

(6)   Without prejudice to the generality of section 25 above, regulations under that section may make special provision with regard to such international wills.

(7)   In section 10 of the Consular Relations Act 1968 (by virtue of which diplomatic agents and consular officials may administer oaths and do notarial acts in certain cases)—

(a)   at the end of subsection (1)(b) there shall be added the words 'or (c) in connection with an international will.'; and
(b)   at the end of subsection (4) there shall be added the words 'and 'international will' has the meaning assigned to it by section 27 of the Administration of Justice Act 1982'.

1   No statutory instrument under s 76(5), (6) (para [**244.106**]) bringing this section into force has yet been made.

*   *   *   *   *

PART IX

GENERAL AND SUPPLEMENTARY

[244.105]
73. Transitional provisions and savings.

*   *   *   *   *

(6)   Nothing in the following provisions of this Act—

    (a)   section 17;

    (b)   section 18(2);

    (c)   sections 19 to 22;

    (d)   section 75,[1] so far as it relates—

        (i)   to the Wills Act Amendment Act 1852; and

        (ii)   to the Family Law Reform Act 1969,

affects the will of a testator who dies before the commencement of the provision in question.

(7)   Neither section 18(1) above nor the repeal by this Act of section 177 of the Law of Property Act 1925 affects a will made before the commencement of section 18(1) above.

1   Section 75 effects repeals of previous legislation.

*   *   *   *   *

[244.106]
76.   Commencement.

*   *   *   *   *

(5)   The provisions of this Act specified in subsection (6) below shall come into operation on such day as the Lord Chancellor and the Secretary of State may by order jointly appoint.

(6)   The provisions of this Act mentioned in subsection (5) above are—

    (a)   sections 23 to 25;

    (b)   sections 27 and 28;

    (c)   section 75, so far as it relates—

        (i)   to section 126 of the Supreme Court Act 1981;[1] and

        (ii)   to Article 27 of the Administration of Estates (Northern Ireland) Order 1979.

(7)   Any order under this section shall be made by statutory instrument.

(8)   Any such order may appoint different days for different provisions and for different purposes.

*   *   *   *   *

(11)   Subject to the foregoing provisions of this section, this Act shall come into operation on 1st January 1983.

1   The SCA 1981, s 126 contains the existing provisions for deposit of wills, which will be repealed by s 75, Sch 9, Pt 1, when a commencement order under s 76 is made bringing ss 23 to 25 of the AJA 1982 into force.

[244.107]
77.   Extent.—(1)   Subject to subsection (6) below, the following provisions of this Act—

*   *   *   *   *

(c)   sections 17 to 22;

*   *   *   *   *

extend to England and Wales only.

*   *   *   *   *

(5)   The repeal of the Wills Act Amendment Act 1852 by section 75 above does not extend to Northern Ireland.

(6)   Subject to subsection (5) above, where any enactment repealed or amended or instrument revoked by this Act extends to any part of the United Kingdom, the repeal, amendment or revocation extends to that part.

[244.108]
78.   Citation. This Act may be cited as the Administration of Justice Act 1982.

*   *   *   *   *

SCHEDULE 2[1]

Section 27

THE ANNEX TO THE CONVENTION ON INTERNATIONAL WILLS

Uniform Law on the Form of an International Will

[244.109]

ARTICLE 1

1.   A will shall be valid as regards form, irrespective particularly of the place where it is made, of the location of the assets and of the nationality, domicile or residence of the testator, if it is made in the form of an international will complying with the provisions set out in Articles 2 to 5 hereinafter.

2.   The invalidity of the will as an international will shall not affect its formal validity as a will of another kind.

1   No statutory instrument under s 76(5), (6) (para **[244.106]**) bringing s 27, and thus this Schedule, into force has yet been made.

ARTICLE 2

This law shall not apply to the form of testamentary dispositions made by two or more persons in one instrument.

ARTICLE 3

1.   The will shall be made in writing.
2.   It need not be written by the testator himself.
3.   It may be written in any language, by hand or by any other means.

ARTICLE 4

1.   The testator shall declare in the presence of two witnesses and of a person authorized to act in connection with international wills that the document is his will and that he knows the contents thereof.
2.   The testator need not inform the witnesses, or the authorized person, of the contents of the will.

ARTICLE 5

1.   In the presence of the witnesses and of the authorized person, the testator shall sign the will or, if he has previously signed it, shall acknowledge his signature.
2.   When the testator is unable to sign, he shall indicate the reason therefor to the authorized person who shall make note of this on the will. Moreover, the testator may be authorized by the law under which the authorized person was designated to direct another person to sign on his behalf.
3.   The witnesses and the authorized person shall there and then attest the will by signing in the presence of the testator.

ARTICLE 6

1.   The signatures shall be placed at the end of the will.
2.   If the will consists of several sheets, each sheet shall be signed by the testator or, if he is unable to sign, by the person signing on his behalf or, if there is no such person, by the authorized person. In addition, each sheet shall be numbered.

ARTICLE 7

1.   The date of the will shall be the date of its signature by the authorized person.
2.   This date shall be noted at the end of the will by the authorized person.

ARTICLE 8

In the absence of any mandatory rule pertaining to the safekeeping of the will, the authorized person shall ask the testator whether he wishes to make a declaration concerning the safekeeping of his will. If so and at the express request of the testator the place where he intends to have his will kept shall be mentioned in the certificate provided for in Article 9.

ARTICLE 9

The authorized person shall attach to the will a certificate in the form prescribed in Article 10 establishing that the obligations of this law have been complied with.

ARTICLE 10

The certificate drawn up by the authorized person shall be in the following form or in a substantially similar form:

CERTIFICATE

(Convention of October 26th, 1973)
1. I, ... (name, address and capacity), a person authorized to act in connection with international wills
2. Certify that on .... (date) at ....
.... (place)
3. (testator) .... (name, address, date and place of birth)
in my presence and that of the witnesses
4. (a) .... (name, address, date and place of birth)
(b) .... (name, address, date and place of birth
has declared that the attached document is his will and that he knows the contents thereof.
5. I furthermore certify that:
6. (a) in my presence and in that of the witnesses
   (1) the testator has signed the will or has acknowledged his signature previously affixed.
  *(2) following a declaration of the testator stating that he was unable to sign his will for the following reason
     ....
    —I have mentioned this declaration on the will
    *—the signature has been affixed by .... (name, address)
7. (b) the witnesses and I have signed the will;
8. *(c) each page of the will has been signed by and numbered:
9. (d) I have satisfied myself as to the identity of the testator and of the witnesses as designated above;
10. (e) the witnesses met the conditions requisite to act as such according to the law under which I am acting;
11. *(f) the testator has requested me to include the following statement concerning the safekeeping of his will:
    ....
    ....
12. PLACE
13. DATE
14. SIGNATURE and, if necessary, SEAL

*To be completed if appropriate.

ARTICLE 11

The authorised person shall keep a copy of the certificate and deliver another to the testator.

ARTICLE 12

In the absence of evidence to the contrary, the certificate of the authorised person shall be conclusive of the formal validity of the instrument as a will under this Law.

ARTICLE 13

The absence or irregularity of a certificate shall not affect the formal validity of a will under this Law.

ARTICLE 14

The international will shall be subject to the ordinary rules of revocation of wills.

ARTICLE 15

In interpreting and applying the provisions of this law, regard shall be had to its international origin and to the need for uniformity in its interpretation.

*   *   *   *   *

MENTAL HEALTH ACT 1983

(1983 c 20)   [9 May 1983]

[244.110]
Note. Part VII of this Act gives the court power to authorise a person to make a will on behalf of a patient and makes provision for the manner in which such will is to be executed. The court is also empowered on directing any disposal of a patient's property under Part VII to give consequential directions which may affect the devolution of the patient's estate on his death.

*   *   *   *   *

PART VII

MANAGEMENT OF PROPERTY AND AFFAIRS OF PATIENTS

*   *   *   *   *

[244.111]
95.   General functions of the judge with respect to property and affairs of patient.—(1)   The judge may, with respect to the property and affairs of a patient, do or secure the doing of all such things as appear necessary or expedient—

   (a)   for the maintenance or other benefit of the patient,
   (b)   for the maintenance or other benefit of members of the patient's family,
   (c)   for making provision for other persons or purposes for whom or which the patient might be expected to provide if he were not mentally disordered, or
   (d)   otherwise for administering the patient's affairs.

(2)   In the exercise of the powers conferred by this section regard shall be had first of all to the requirements of the patient, and the rules of law which restricted the enforcement by a creditor of rights against property under the control of the judge in lunacy shall apply to property under the control of the judge; but, subject to the foregoing provisions of this subsection, the judge shall, in administering a patient's affairs, have regard to the interests of creditors and also to the desirability of making provision for obligations of the patient notwithstanding that they may not be legally enforceable.

[244.112]
96. Powers of the judge as to patient's property and affairs.—(1) Without prejudice to the generality of section 95 above, the judge shall have power to make such orders and give such directions and authorities as he thinks fit for the purposes of that section and in particular may for those purposes make orders or give directions or authorities for—

(a)   the control (with or without the transfer or vesting of property or the payment into or lodgment in the Supreme Court of money or securities) and management of any property of the patient;

(b)   the sale, exchange, charging of other disposition of or dealing with any property of the patient;

(c)   the acquisition of any property in the name or on behalf of the patient;

(d)   the settlement of any property of the patient, or the gift of any property of the patient to any such persons or for any such purposes as are mentioned in paragraphs (b) and (c) of section 95(1) above;

(e)   the execution for the patient of a will making any provision (whether by way of disposing of property or exercising a power or otherwise) which could be made by a will executed by the patient if he were not mentally disordered;

(f)   the carrying on by a suitable person of any profession, trade or business of the patient;

(g)   the dissolution of a partnership of which the patient is a member;

(h)   the carrying out of any contract entered into by the patient;

(i)   the conduct of legal proceedings in the name of the patient or on his behalf;

(j)   the reimbursement out of the property of the patient, with or without interest, of money applied by any person either in payment of the patient's debts (whether legally enforceable or not) or for the maintenance or other benefit of the patient or members of his family or in making provision for other persons or purposes for whom or which he might be expected to provide if he were not mentally disordered;

(k)   the exercise of any power (including a power to consent) vested in the patient, whether beneficially, or as guardian or trustee, or otherwise.

(2)   If under subsection (1) above provision is made for the settlement of any property of a patient, or the exercise of a power vested in a patient of appointing trustees or retiring from a trust, the judge may also make as respects the property settled or trust property such consequential vesting or other orders as the case may require, including (in the case of the exercise of such a power) any order which could have been made in such a case under Part IV of the Trustee Act 1925.

(3)   Where under this section a settlement has been made of any property of a patient, and the Lord Chancellor or a nominated judge is satisfied, at any time before the death of the patient, that any material fact was not disclosed when the settlement was made, or that there has been any substantial change in circumstances, he may by order vary the settlement in such manner as he thinks fit, and give any consequential directions.

(4)   The power of the judge to make or give an order, direction or authority for the execution of a will for a patient—

(a)   shall not be exercisable at any time when the patient is a minor, and
(b)   shall not be exercised unless the judge has reason to believe that the patient is incapable of making a valid will for himself.

(5)   The powers of a patient as patron of a benefice shall be exercisable by the Lord Chancellor only.

[244.113]
97.   Supplementary provisions as to wills executed under s 96.—(1) Where under section 96(1) above the judge makes or gives an order, direction or authority requiring or authorising a person (in this section referred to as 'the authorised person') to execute a will for a patient, any will executed in pursuance of that order, direction or authority shall be expressed to be signed by the patient acting by the authorised person, and shall be—

(a)   signed by the authorised person with the name of the patient, and with his own name, in the presence of two or more witnesses present at the same time, and
(b)   attested and subscribed by those witnesses in the presence of the authorised person, and
(c)   sealed with the official seal of the Court of Protection.

(2)   The Wills Act 1837 shall have effect in relation to any such will as if it were signed by the patient by his own hand, except that in relation to any such will—

(a)   section 9 of that Act (which makes provision as to the signing and attestation of wills) shall not apply, and
(b)   in the subsequent provisions of that Act any reference to execution in the manner required by the previous provisions of that Act shall be construed as a reference to execution in the manner required by subsection (1) above.

(3)   Subject to the following provisions of this section, any such will executed in accordance with subsection (1) above shall have the same effect for all purposes as if the patient were capable of making a valid will and the will had been executed by him in the manner required by the Wills Act 1837.

(4)   So much of subsection (3) above as provides for such a will to have effect as if the patient were capable of making a valid will—

(a)   shall not have effect in relation to such a will in so far as it disposes of any immovable property, other than immovable property in England and Wales, and
(b)   where at the time when such a will is executed the patient is domiciled in Scotland or Northern Ireland or in a country or territory outside the

United Kingdom, shall not have effect in relation to that will in so far as it relates to any other property or matter, except any property or matter in respect of which, under the law of his domicile, any question of his testamentary capacity would fall to be determined in accordance with the law of England and Wales.

[244.114]
98. Judge's powers in cases of emergency. Where it is represented to the judge, and he has reason to believe, that a person may be incapable, by reason of mental disorder, of managing and administering his property and affairs, and the judge is of the opinion that it is necessary to make immediate provision for any of the matters referred to in section 95 above, then pending the determination of the question whether that person is so incapable the judge may exercise in relation to the property and affairs of that person any of the powers conferred on him in relation to the property and affairs of a patient by this Part of this Act so far as is requisite for enabling that provision to be made.

* * * * *

[244.115]
101. Preservation of interests in patient's property.—(1) Where any property of a person has been disposed of under this Part of this Act, and under his will or his intestacy, or by any gift perfected or nomination taking effect on his death, any other person would have taken an interest in the property but for the disposal—

(a) he shall take the same interest, if and so far as circumstances allow, in any property belonging to the estate of the deceased which represents the property disposed of; and

(b) if the property disposed of was real property any property representing it shall so long as it remains part of his estate be treated as if it were part of his estate.

(2) The judge, in ordering, directing or authorising under this Part of this Act any disposal of property which apart from this section would result in the conversion of personal property into real property, may direct that the property representing the property disposed of shall, so long as it remains the property of the patient or forms part of his estate, be treated as if it were personal property.

(3) References in subsections (1) and (2) above to the disposal of property are refences to—

(a) the sale, exchange,charging or other dealing (otherwise than by will) with property other than money,

(b) the removal of property from one place to another,

(c) the application of money in acquiring property, or

(d) the transfer of money from one account to another;

and references to property representing property disposed of shall be construed accordingly and as including the result of successive disposals.

(4) The judge may give such directions as appear to him necessary or expedient for the purpose of facilitating the operation of subsection (1) above,

including the carrying of money to a separate account and the transfer of property other than money.

* * * * *

PART X

MISCELLANEOUS AND SUPPLEMENTARY

* * * * *

Supplemental

* * * * *

[244.116]
149. Short title, commencement . . .—(1) This Act may be cited as the Mental Health Act 1983.
(2) . . . this Act shall come into force on 30 September 1983.

* * * * *

CHILDREN ACT 1989

(1989 c 41)   [16 November 1989]

[244.117]
Note. The Children Act 1989 (ChA 1989) effects a comprehensive reform of the law relating to children, including their guardianship. The powers to appoint guardians are now contained in s 5 of the ChA 1989. A parent with 'parental responsibility' (a term defined by s 3) has power under s 5(3) to appoint an individual to be the child's guardian after his or her death and a guardian is given the like power by s 5(4). The power may be exercised by will or any other writing, subject to the requirement that it be dated and either signed by the person making the appointment or signed at his direction before witnesses; see s 5(5). Sections 2 to 4 prescribe the circumstances in which a parent is deemed to have the parental responsibility which is a prerequisite to the exercise of the power to appoint guardians. Section 6 sets out the circumstances in which the appointment of a guardian may be revoked or disclaimed. One additional important feature of the ChA 1989 is that s 3(3) extends to a parent with parental responsibility the right to call for and deal with all property belonging to his minor child, a right which was formerly available under the Guardianship Act 1973, s 7 only to a guardian.
    The provisions printed below were brought into force on 14 October 1991 (SI 1991/828). For a more detailed account of these provisions, and for their practical implications for will drafting, see Vol 1, para **[28.1]** et seq and para **[203.43]** et seq.

PART I

INTRODUCTORY

*   *   *   *   *

[244.118]
2. Parental responsibility for children.—(1) Where a child's father and mother were married to each other at the time of his birth, they shall each have parental responsibility for the child.
(2) Where a child's father and mother were not married to each other at the time of his birth—

   (a) the mother shall have parental responsibility for the child;
   (b) the father shall not have parental responsibility for the child, unless he acquires it in accordance with the provisions of this Act.

(3) References in this Act to a child whose father and mother were, or (as the case may be) were not, married to each other at the time of his birth must be read with section 1 of the Family Law Reform Act 1987 (which extends their meaning).
(4) The rule of law that a father is the natural guardian of his legitimate child is abolished.
(5) More than one person may have parental responsibility for the same child at the same time.
(6) A person who has parental responsibility for a child at any time shall not cease to have that responsibility solely because some other person subsequently acquires parental responsibility for the child.
(7) Where more than one person has parental responsibility for a child, each of them may act alone and without the other (or others) in meeting that responsibility; but nothing in this Part shall be taken to affect the operation of any enactment which requires the consent of more than one person in a matter affecting the child.
(8) The fact that a person has parental responsibility for a child shall not entitle him to act in any way which would be incompatible with any order made with respect to the child under this Act.
(9) A person who has parental responsibility for a child may not surrender or transfer any part of that responsibility to another but may arrange for some or all of it to be met by one or more persons acting on his behalf.
(10) The person with whom any such arrangement is made may himself be a person who already has parental responsibility for the child concerned.
(11) The making of any such arrangement shall not affect any liability of the person making it which may arise from any failure to meet any part of his parental responsibility for the child concerned.

[244.119]
3. Meaning of 'parental responsibility'.—(1) In this Act 'parental responsibility' means all the rights, duties, powers, responsibilities and authority which by law a parent of a child has in relation to the child and his property.
(2) It also includes the rights, powers and duties which a guardian of the child's estate (appointed, before the commencement of section 5, to act generally) would have had in relation to the child and his property.

(3)   The rights referred to in subsection (2) include, in particular, the right of the guardian to receive or recover in his own name, for the benefit of the child, property of whatever description and wherever situated which the child is entitled to receive or recover.

(4)   The fact that a person has, or does not have, parental responsibility for a child shall not affect—

   (a)   any obligation which he may have in relation to the child (such as a statutory duty to maintain the child); or
   (b)   any rights which, in the event of the child's death, he (or any other person) may have in relation to the child's property.

(5)   A person who—

   (a)   does not have parental responsibility for a particular child; but
   (b)   has care of the child,

may (subject to the provisions of this Act) do what is reasonable in all the circumstances of the case for the purpose of safeguarding or promoting the child's welfare.

[244.120]
4.   Acquisition of parental responsibility by father.—(1)   Where a child's father and mother were not married to each other at the time of his birth—

   (a)   the court may, on the application of the father, order that he shall have parental responsibility for the child; or
   (b)   the father and mother may by agreement ('a parental responsibility agreement') provide for the father to have parental responsibility for the child.

(2)   No parental responsibility agreement shall have effect for the purposes of this Act unless—

   (a)   it is made in the form prescribed by regulations made by the Lord Chancellor; and
   (b)   where regulations are made by the Lord Chancellor prescribing the manner in which such agreements must be recorded, it is recorded in the prescribed manner.

(3)   Subject to section 12(4), an order under subsection (1)(a), or a parental responsibility agreement, may only be brought to an end by an order of the court made on the application—

   (a)   of any person who has parental responsibility for the child; or
   (b)   with leave of the court, of the child himself.

(4)   The court may only grant leave under subsection (3)(b) if it is satisfied that the child has sufficient understanding to make the proposed application.

[244.121]
5.   Appointment of guardians.—(1)   Where an application with respect to a child is made to the court by any individual, the court may by order appoint that individual to be the child's guardian if—

(a) the child has no parent with parental responsibility for him; or

(b) a residence order has been made with respect to the child in favour of a parent or guardian of his who has died while the order was in force.

(2) The power conferred by subsection (1) may also be exercised in any family proceedings if the court considers that the order should be made even though no application has been made for it.

(3) A parent who has parental responsibility for his child may appoint another individual to be the child's guardian in the event of his death.

(4) A guardian of a child may appoint another individual to take his place as the child's guardian in the event of his death.

(5) An appointment under subsection (3) or (4) shall not have effect unless it is made in writing, is dated and is signed by the person making the appointment or—

(a) in the case of an appointment made by a will which is not signed by the testator, is signed at the direction of the testator in accordance with the requirements of section 9 of the Wills Act 1837; or

(b) in any other case, is signed at the direction of the person making the appointment, in his presence and in the presence of two witnesses who each attest the signature.

(6) A person appointed as a child's guardian under this section shall have parental responsibility for the child concerned.

(7) Where—

(a) on the death of any person making an appointment under subsection (3) or (4), the child concerned has no parent with parental responsibility for him; or

(b) immediately before the death of any person making such an appointment, a residence order in his favour was in force with respect to the child,

the appointment shall take effect on the death of that person.

(8) Where, on the death of any person making an appointment under subsection (3) or (4)—

(a) the child concerned has a parent with parental responsibility for him; and

(b) subsection (7)(b) does not apply,

the appointment shall take effect when the child no longer has a parent who has parental responsibility for him.

(9) Subsections (1) and (7) do not apply if the residence order referred to in paragraph (b) of those subsections was also made in favour of a surviving parent of the child.

(10) Nothing in this section shall be taken to prevent an appointment under subsection (3) or (4) being made by two or more persons acting jointly.

(11) Subject to any provision made by rules of court, no court shall exercise the High Court's inherent jurisdiction to appoint a guardian of the estate of any child.

(12) Where rules of court are made under subsection (11) they may prescribe the circumstances in which, and conditions subject to which, an appointment of such a guardian may be made.

(13) A guardian of a child may only be appointed in accordance with the provisions of this section.

[244.122]
6. Guardians: revocation and disclaimer.—(1) An appointment under section 5(3) or (4) revokes an earlier such appointment (including one made in an unrevoked will or codicil) made by the same person in respect of the same child, unless it is clear (whether as the result of an express provision in the later appointment or by any necessary implication) that the purpose of the later appointment is to appoint an additional guardian.
(2) An appointment under section 5(3) or (4) (including one made in an unrevoked will or codicil) is revoked if the person who made the appointment revokes it by a written and dated instrument which is signed—

   (a) by him; or
   (b) at his direction, in his presence and in the presence of two witnesses who each attest the signature.

(3) An appointment under section 5(3) or (4) (other than one made in a will or codicil) is revoked if, with the intention of revoking the appointment, the person who made it—

   (a) destroys the instrument by which it was made; or
   (b) has some other person destroy that instrument in his presence.

[(3A) An appointment under section 5(3) or (4) (including one made in an unrevoked will or codicil) is revoked if the person appointed is the spouse of the person who made the appointment and either—

   (a) a decree of a court of civil jurisdiction in England and Wales dissolves or annuls the marriage, or
   (b) the marriage is dissolved or annulled and the divorce or annulment is entitled to recognition in England and Wales by virtue of Part II of the Family Law Act 1986,

unless a contrary intention appears by the appointment.][1]
(4) For the avoidance of doubt, an appointment under section 5(3) or (4) made in a will or codicil is revoked if the will or codicil is revoked.
(5) A person who is appointed as a guardian under section 5(3) or (4) may disclaim his appointment by an instrument in writing signed by him and made within a reasonable time of his first knowing that the appointment has taken effect.
(6) Where regulations are made by the Lord Chancellor prescribing the manner in which such disclaimers must be recorded, no such disclaimer shall have effect unless it is recorded in the prescribed manner.
(7) Any appointment of a guardian under section 5 may be brought to an end at any time by order of the court—

   (a) on the application of any person who has parental responsibility for the child;
   (b) on the application of the child concerned, with leave of the court; or
   (c) in any family proceedings, if the court considers that it should be brought to an end even though no application has been made.

1   Sub-s (3A): inserted by the LR(S)A 1995, s 4(1). Section 4(2) of that Act (para **[244.131]**) provides that the new subsection is to have effect as regards an appointment made by any person dying on or after 1 January 1996 (regardless of the date of the appointment or the date of the dissolution or annulment).

*   *   *   *   *

PART II

ORDERS WITH RESPECT TO CHILDREN IN FAMILY PROCEEDINGS

General

[244.123]
8.   Residence, contact and other orders with respect to children.—(1)   In this Act—

*   *   *   *   *

'a residence order' means an order settling the arrangements to be made as to the person with whom a child is to live; . . .

*   *   *   *   *

PART XII

MISCELLANEOUS AND GENERAL

*   *   *   *   *

General

*   *   *   *   *

[244.124]
105.   Interpretation.—(1)   In this Act—

*   *   *   *   *

'child' means . . . a person under the age of eighteen;

*   *   *   *   *

'guardian of a child' means a guardian (other than a guardian of the estate of a child) appointed in accordance with the provisions of section 5;

*   *   *   *   *

'prescribed' means prescribed by regulations made under this Act;

*   *   *   *   *

'residence order' has the meaning given by section 8(1);

*   *   *   *   *

(2)   References in this Act to a child whose father and mother were, or (as the case may be) were not, married to each other at the time of his birth must be read with section 1 of the Family Law Reform Act 1987 (which extends the meaning of such references).

*   *   *   *   *

[244.125]
108.   Short title, commencement, extent etc.—(1)   This Act may be cited as the Children Act 1989.
(2)   Sections 89 and 96(3) to (7), and paragraph 35 of Schedule 12, shall come into force on the passing of this Act and paragraph 36 of Schedule 12 shall come into force at the end of the period of two months beginning with the day on which this Act is passed but otherwise this Act shall come into force on such date as may be appointed by order made by the Lord Chancellor or the Secretary of State, or by both acting jointly.
(3)   Different dates may be appointed for different provisions of this Act and in relation to different cases.
(4)   The minor amendments set out in Schedule 12 shall have effect.
(5)   The consequential amendments set out in Schedule 13 shall have effect.
(6)   The transitional provisions and savings set out in Schedule 14 shall have effect.
(7)   The repeals set out in Schedule 15 shall have effect.
(8)   An order under subsection (2) may make such transitional provisions or savings as appear to the person making the order to be necessary or expedient in connection with the provisions brought into force by the order, including—

   (a)   provisions adding to or modifying the provisions of Schedule 14; and
   (b)   such adaptations—
         (i)   of the provisions brought into force by the order; and
         (ii)   of any provisions of this Act then in force,

as appear to him necessary or expedient in consequence of the partial operation of this Act.
(9)   The Lord Chancellor may by order make such amendments or repeals, in such enactments as may be specified in the order, as appear to him to be necessary or expedient in consequence of any provision of this Act.
(10)   This Act shall, in its application to the Isles of Scilly, have effect subject to such exceptions, adaptations and modifications as the Secretary of State may by order prescribe.
(11)   (*Applies to Scotland only.*)
(12)   (*Applies to Northern Ireland only.*)

SCHEDULE 13

Section 108(5)

CONSEQUENTIAL AMENDMENTS

The Wills Act 1837 (c 26)

1.   ([*Amends the Wills Act 1837, s 1: see para* **[244.3]**.])

*   *   *   *   *

2136

SCHEDULE 14

Section 108(6)

*   *   *   *   *

CUSTODY ORDERS, ETC

*   *   *   *   *

THE FAMILY LAW REFORM ACT 1987 (C 42)

Conversion of orders under section 4

[244.126]
4. Where, immediately before the day on which Parts I and II come into force, there was in force an order under section 4(1) of the Family Law Reform Act 1987 (order giving father parental rights and duties in relation to a child), then, on and after that day, the order shall be deemed to be an order under section 4 of this Act giving the father parental responsibility for the child.

Orders to which paragraphs 6 to 11 apply

5.—(1)   In paragraphs 6 to 11 'an existing order' means any order which—

  (a)   is in force immediately before the commencement of Parts I and II;
  (b)   was made under any enactment mentioned in sub-paragraph (2);
  (c)   determines all or any of the following—
    (i)   who is to have custody of a child;
    (ii)   who is to have care and control of a child;
    (iii)   who is to have access to a child;
    (iv)   any matter with respect to a child's education or upbringing; and
  (d)   is not an order of a kind mentioned in paragraph 15(1).

(2)   The enactments are—

  (a)   the Domestic Proceedings and Magistrates' Courts Act 1978;
  (b)   the Children Act 1975;
  (c)   the Matrimonial Causes Act 1973;
  (d)   the Guardianship of Minors Acts 1971 and 1973;
  (e)   the Matrimonial Causes Act 1965;
  (f)   the Matrimonial Proceedings (Magistrates' Courts) Act 1960.

(3)   For the purposes of this paragraph and paragraphs 6 to 11 'custody' includes legal custody and joint as well as sole custody but does not include access.

2137

Parental responsibility of parents

6.—(1)   Where—

(a)   a child's father and mother were married to each other at the time of his birth; and
(b)   there is an existing order with respect to the child,

each parent shall have parental responsibility for the child in accordance with section 2 as modified by sub-paragraph (3).

(2)   Where—

(a)   a child's father and mother were not married to each other at the time of his birth; and
(b)   there is an existing order with respect to the child,

section 2 shall apply as modified by sub-paragraphs (3) and (4).

(3)   The modification is that for section 2(8) there shall be substituted—

'(8)The fact that a person has parental responsibility for a child does not entitle him to act in a way which would be incompatible with any existing order or any order made under this Act with respect to the child'.

(4)   The modifications are that—

(a)   for the purposes of section 2(2), where the father has custody or care and control of the child by virtue of any existing order, the court shall be deemed to have made (at the commencement of that section) an order under section 4(1) giving him parental responsibility for the child; and
(b)   where by virtue of paragraph (a) a court is deemed to have made an order under section 4(1) in favour of a father who has care and control of a child by virtue of an existing order, the court shall not bring the order under section 4(1) to an end at any time while he has care and control of the child by virtue of the order.

*   *   *   *   *

GUARDIANS

Existing guardians to be guardians under this Act

[244.127]
12.—(1)   Any appointment of a person as guardian of a child which—

(a)   was made—
  (i)   under sections 3 to 5 of the Guardianship of Minors Act 1971;
  (ii)   under section 38(3) of the Sexual Offences Act 1956; or
  (iii)   under the High Court's inherent jurisdiction with respect to children; and
(b)   has taken effect before the commencement of section 5,

shall (subject to sub-paragraph (2)) be deemed, on and after the commencement of section 5, to be an appointment made and having effect under that section.

(2)   Where an appointment of a person as guardian of a child has effect under section 5 by virtue of sub-paragraph (1)(a)(ii), the appointment shall not have effect for a period which is longer than any period specified in the order.

Appointment of guardian not yet in effect

13.   Any appointment of a person to be a guardian of a child—

(a)   which was made as mentioned in paragraph 12(1)(a)(i); but

(b)   which, immediately before the commencement of section 5, had not taken effect,

shall take effect in accordance with section 5 (as modified, where it applies, by paragraph 8(2)).

Persons deemed to be appointed as guardians under existing wills

14.   For the purposes of the Wills Act 1837 and of this Act any disposition by will and testament or devise of the custody and tuition of any child, made before the commencement of section 5 and paragraph 1 of Schedule 13, shall be deemed to be an appointment by will of a guardian of the child.

*   *   *   *   *

SCHEDULE 15

Section 108(7)

Repeals

[244.128]
Note. This Schedule repeals a large number of legislative provisions, including all the extant provisions of the Guardianship of Minors Act 1971 and the Children Act 1975.

LAW REFORM (SUCCESSION) ACT 1995

(1995 c 41)   [8 November 1995]

Distribution of estates

[244.129]
1.   Intestacy and partial intestacy.—(1)   (*[Inserts the Administration of Estates Act 1925, s 46(2A): see para* **[244.60]**.*]*)

(2)   [*Repeals the Administration of Estates Act 1925, ss 47(1)(iii), 49(1)(aa), (a), 49(2), (3): see paras* **[244.61]** *and* **[244.64]**.]

(3)   Subsections (1) and (2) above have effect as respects an intestate dying on or after 1st January 1996.

(4)   In section 50 of the 1925 Act (construction of documents), the references in subsection (1) to Part IV of that Act and to the foregoing provisions of that Part shall, in relation to an instrument inter vivos made or a will or codicil

coming into operation on or after 1st January 1996 (but not in relation to instruments inter vivos made or wills or codicils coming into operation earlier), be construed as including references to this section.

(5)   In this section 'intestate' shall be construed in accordance with section 55(1)(vi) of the 1925 Act.

*   *   *   *   *

Effect of dissolution or annulment of marriage

[244.130]
3.   Effect of dissolution or annulment of marriage on will.—(1)   (*[Amends the Wills Act 1837, s 18A(1): see para* **[244.18]**.])
(2)   Subsection (1) above has effect as respects a will made by a person dying on or after 1st January 1996 (regardless of the date of the will and the date of the dissolution or annulment).

[244.131]
4.   Effect of dissolution or annulment of marriage on appointment of guardian.—(1)   (*[Amends the Children Act 1989, s 6: see para* **[244.122]**.])
(2)   Subsection (1) above has effect as respects an appointment made by a person dying on or after 1st January 1996 (regardless of the date of the appointment and the date of the dissolution or annulment).

Supplemental

[244.132]
5.   Repeals. The enactments mentioned in the Schedule to this Act are repealed in accordance with that Schedule.

[244.133]
6.   Citation and extent.—(1)   This Act may be cited as the Law Reform (Succession) Act 1995.
(2)   This Act extends to England and Wales only.

SCHEDULE

Section 5

REPEALS

[244.134]
(*[This Schedule repeals (inter alia) the Wills Act 1837, s 18A(3): see para* **[244.18]**, *as respects the wills of persons dying on or after 1 January 1996 and the Administration of Estates Act 1925, ss 47(1)(iii), 49(1)(aa), (a), (2), (3): see paras* **[244.61]** *and* **[244.64]**, *as respects intestates (as defined by s 1(5), above) dying on or after that date.*])

SECTION 2

Property rights of adopted, legitimated and illegitimate children

[245.1]

Note. This Section reproduces in chronological order all the statutory provisions which have governed and now govern the property rights of adopted, legitimated, and illegitimate children under dispositions of property and the rules of intestate succession. They also of course govern the rights of such children's parents and other relatives. We have omitted the Adoption of Children Act 1949, the relevant provisions of which were replaced retrospectively from the same commencement date by the Adoption Act 1950, and the provisions of the Children Act 1975 concerning the effects of legitimation and adoption which were replaced, again with retrospective effect from the same commencement date, by the Legitimacy Act 1976 (LA 1976) and the Adoption Act 1976 (AA 1976).

The main effect of these statutes has been to reverse the common law presumptions as to the meaning of words descriptive of relationship in dispositions of property, such as wills or settlements (for these presumptions see Vol 1, paras **[72.1]**–**[72.9]** and **[75.1]**) and to enlarge the categories of issue who can take under the intestacy rules. With one exception, each change in the law has only applied to dispositions made after the change in the law has taken effect, and so the repealed statutes included here continue to be relevant to dispositions made when they were in force. The exception is to be found in the Human Fertilisation and Embryology Act 1990 (HFEA 1990), s 29(3) at para **[245.87]**.

At common law references to children were presumed to be references to legitimate children, ie children born in lawful wedlock, and references to other relationships were likewise confined to persons who were legitimate and who claimed descent or kinship exclusively through persons who were legitimate. Not only were illegitimate persons excluded but also persons who were adopted or legitimated. Statute has made progressive inroads on the austerity of the common law rule. As regards adopted and legitimated children this process culminated in the Children Act 1975 which provided that in relation to instruments made on or after 1 January 1976 (including the wills whenever made of persons dying on or after that date) references to children (or persons related in any other way) were to be deemed in the absence of a contrary intention to include references to adopted and legitimated children (or persons who were adopted or legitimated and claimed descent or kinship through adopted or legitimated persons) and to be deemed to do so whether the adoption or legitimation occurred before or after the date of the instrument or death. The relevant provisions of the Children Act 1975 are not reproduced in this section as they were replaced (with effect from the same commencement date) by the identical provisions of the LA 1976 and the AA 1976.

As regards illegitimate persons the process of development culminated in the comprehensive provisions contained in the Family Law Reform Act 1987 (FLRA 1987) which provides that in relation to instruments made on or after the commencement of the Act (which in the case of wills means wills actually made and not merely confirmed by codicil on or after that time) references to children (or other relatives) are to be deemed to include illegitimate children (or persons claiming kinship through illegitimate persons). This Act (which replaced the more limited provisions of the Family Law Reform Act 1969 (FLRA 1969) was brought into force on 4 April 1988. (For the background to the Act see the Law Commission's Second Report on Illegitimacy, October 1986 (Law Com No 157, Cmnd 9913).)

Mention should also be made of the HFEA 1990 which makes special provision in relation to persons born as a result of artificial insemination, in vitro fertilization or other artificial means.

In relation to older instruments, however, the superseded rules of construction may still be relevant. This section therefore reproduces all the relevant statutory provisions.

For an account of the law governing the property rights of adopted, legitimated and illegimate children see Vol 1, paras **[72.1]** and **[75.1]** et seq.

ADOPTION OF CHILDREN ACT 1926

(16 & 17 Geo 5 c 29)   [4 August 1926]

[245.2]
Note. Before the passing of this Act adoption had never been recognised by the law, though agreements may have been made which for many purposes placed a stranger in loco parentis. But an adoption order under the Act did not affect rights of succession on an intestacy or the construction of references to children and issue in wills or other dispositions of property.

[245.3]
1. *Power to make adoption orders.*—*(1) Upon an application in the prescribed manner by any person desirous of being authorised to adopt an infant who has never been married, the Court may, subject to the provisions of this Act, make an order (in this Act referred to as 'an adoption order') authorising the applicant to adopt that infant.*
(2) A person so authorised to adopt the infant and an infant authorised to be adopted are in this Act referred to as an 'adopter' and an 'adopted child' respectively, and 'infant' means a person under the age of twenty-one.

*   *   *   *   *

[245.4]
5. Effect of adoption order.

*   *   *   *   *

(2)   An adoption order shall not deprive the adopted child of any right to or interest in property to which, but for the order, the child would have been entitled under any intestacy or disposition, whether occurring or made before or after the making of the adoption order, or confer on the adopted child any right to or interest in property as a child of the adopter, and the expressions 'child,' 'children' and 'issue' where used in any disposition whether made before or after the making of an adoption order, shall not, unless the contrary intention appears, include an adopted child or children or the issue of an adopted child.[1]

*   *   *   *   *

(4)   For the purposes of this section 'disposition' means an assurance of any interest in property by any instrument whether inter vivos or by will including codicil.

1   Sub-s (2): repealed with effect from 1 January 1950 by the Adoption of Children Act 1949, ss 10(5), 16(3).

*   *   *   *   *

[245.5]
12.   *Short title, commencement and extent.*—*(1)*   *This Act may be cited as the Adoption of Children Act 1926.*
(2)   This Act shall come into operation on the first day of January, nineteen hundred and twenty-seven.
(3)   This Act shall not apply to Scotland or Northern Ireland.

LEGITIMACY ACT 1926

(16 & 17 Geo 5 c 60)   [15 December 1926]

[245.6]
Note. This Act, which came into force on 1 January 1927, recognised, for the first time in English law, the principle of legitimation by the subsequent marriage of the illegitimate child's parents. Legitimation by subsequent marriage was expressly excluded by this Act in cases where either parent was married to a third person at the date of the child's birth. This bar was removed by the Legitimacy Act 1959, s 1 (para **[245.32]**) with effect from 29 October 1959. The Legitimacy Act 1926, unlike the Adoption of Children Act 1926 (paras **[245.2]**–**[245.5]**) provided for legitimation to confer property rights on legitimated children by deeming the legitimated child to have been born legitimate, but only in relation to intestacies or dispositions (including wills) taking effect after the date of legitimation. These provisions were replaced for most purposes by the FLRA 1969, s 15(4) (para **[245.39]**) and wholly replaced by the Children Act 1975, which was itself replaced by identical provisions in the LA 1976 (paras **[245.43]**–**[245.54]**) and the AA 1976 (paras **[245.55]**–**[245.68]**) in relation to dispositions on or after 1 January 1976.

[245.7]
1.   *Legitimation by subsequent marriage of parents.*—*(1)*   *Subject to the provisions of this section, where the parents of an illegitimate person marry or*

have married one another, whether before or after the commencement of this Act, the marriage shall, if the father of the illegitimate person was or is at the date of the marriage domiciled in England or Wales, render that person, if living, legitimate from the commencement of this Act, or from the date of the marriage, whichever last happens.[1]

(2) Nothing in this Act shall operate to legitimate a person whose father or mother was married to a third person when the illegitimate person was born.[2]

(3) The legitimation of a person under this Act does not enable him or his spouse, children or remoter issue to take any interest in real or personal property save as is hereinafter in this Act expressly provided.[3]

1   Sub-s (1): repealed by the LA 1976, Sch 2.
2   Sub-s (2): repealed with effect from 29 October 1959 by the Legitimacy Act 1959, ss 1(1), 6(3), paras **[245.32]** and **[245.34]**.
3   Sub-s (3): repealed with effect from 1 January 1976 by the Children Act 1975, ss 108(1)(b), (4)(d), Sch 2, Pt II.

*   *   *   *   *

[245.8]
3. Rights of legitimated persons, etc, to take interests in property.—
(1) Subject to the provisions of this Act, a legitimated person and his spouse, children or more remote issue shall be entitled to take any interest—

    (a) in the estate of an intestate dying after the date of legitimation;
    (b) under any disposition coming into operation after the date of legitimation;
    (c) by descent under an entailed interest created after the date of legitimation;

in like manner is if the legitimated person had been born legitimate.

(2) Where the right to any property, real or personal, depends on the relative seniority of the children of any person, and those children include one or more legitimated persons, the legitimated person or persons shall rank as if he or they had been born on the day when he or they became legitimated by virtue of this Act, and if more than one such legitimated person became legitimated at the same time, they shall rank as between themselves in order of seniority.

(3) Where property real or personal or any interest therein is limited in such a way that, if this Act had not been passed, it would (subject or not to any preceding limitations or charges) have devolved (as nearly as the law permits) along with a dignity or title of honour, then nothing in this Act shall operate to sever the property or any interest therein from such dignity, but the same shall go and devolve (without prejudice to the preceding limitations or charges aforesaid) in like manner as if this Act had not been passed. This subsection applies, whether or not there is any express reference to the dignity or title of honour and notwithstanding that in some events the property, or some interest therein, may become severed therefrom.

(4) This section applies only if and so far as a contrary intention is not expressed in the disposition, and shall have effect subject to the terms of the disposition and to the provisions therein contained.[1]

1   This section was repealed with effect from 1 January 1976 by the Children Act 1975, s 108(1)(b), (4)(d), Sch 2, Pt II.

[245.9]

4. *Succession on intestacy of legitimated persons and their issue.* *Where a legitimated person or a child or remoter issue of a legitimated person dies intestate in respect of all or any of his real or personal property, the same persons shall be entitled to take the same interests therein as they would have been entitled to take if the legitimated person had been born legitimate.*[1]

1   This section was repealed with effect from 1 January 1976 by the Children Act 1975, s 108(1)(b), (4)(d), Sch 2, Pt II.

[245.10]

5. *Application to illegitimate person dying before marriage of parents.* *Where an illegitimate person dies after the commencement of this Act and before the marriage of his parents leaving any spouse, children or remoter issue living at the date of such marriage, then, if that person would, if living at the time of the marriage of his parents, have become a legitimated person, the provisions of this Act with respect to the taking of interests in property by, or in succession to, the spouse, children and remoter issue of a legitimated person (including those relating to the rate of death duties) shall apply as if such person as aforesaid had been a legitimated person and the date of the marriage of his parents had been the date of legitimation.*[1]

1   This section was repealed with effect from 1 January 1976 by the Children Act 1975, s 108(1)(b), (4)(d), Sch 2, Pt II.

*   *   *   *   *

[245.11]

8. *Provisions as to persons legitimated by extraneous law.* — *(1)   Where the parents of an illegitimate person marry or have married one another, whether before or after the commencement of this Act, and the father of the illegitimate person was or is, at the time of the marriage, domiciled in a country, other than England or Wales, by the law of which the illegitimate person became legitimated by virtue of such subsequent marriage, that person, if living, shall in England and Wales be recognised as having been so legitimated from the commencement of this Act or from the date of the marriage, whichever last happens, notwithstanding that his father was not at the time of the birth of such person domiciled in a country in which legitimation by subsequent marriage was permitted by law.*

(2)   All the provisions of this Act relating to legitimated persons and to the taking of interests in property by or in succession to a legitimated person and the spouse, children and remoter issue of a legitimated person (including those relating to the rate of death duties) shall apply in the case of a person recognised as having been legitimated under this section, or who would, had he survived the marriage of his parents, have been so recognised; and, accordingly, this Act shall have effect as if references therein to a legitimated person included a person so recognised as having been legitimated.

(3)   For the purposes of this section, the expression 'country' includes Scotland and any other part of His Majesty's Dominions, as well as a foreign country.[1]

1   This section was repealed with effect from 22 August 1976 by the LA 1976, s 11, Sch 2.

[245.12]

9. *Right of illegitimate child and mother of illegitimate child to succeed on intestacy of the other.*—(1) *Where, after the commencement of this Act, the mother of an illegitimate child, such child not being a legitimated person, dies intestate as respects all or any of her real or personal property, and does not leave any legitimate issue her surviving, the illegitimate child, or, if he is dead, his issue, shall be entitled to take any interest therein to which he or such issue would have been entitled if he had been born legitimate.*

(2) Where, after the commencement of this Act, an illegitimate child, not being a legitimated person, dies intestate in respect of all or any of his real or personal property, his mother if surviving shall be entitled to take any interest therein to which she would have been entitled if the child had been born legitimate and she had been the only surviving parent.

(3) This section does not apply to or affect the right of any person to take by purchase or descent any entailed interest in real or personal property. [1]

1   This section was repealed with effect from 1 January 1970 by the FLRA 1969, s 14(7) (para **[245.38]**).

[245.13]

10. *Savings.*—(1) *Nothing in this Act shall affect the succession to any dignity or title of honour or render any person capable of succeeding to or transmitting a right to succeed to any such dignity or title.*

(2) Nothing in this Act shall affect the operation or construction of any disposition coming into operation before the commencement of this Act, or affect any rights under the intestacy of a person dying before the commencement of this Act. [1]

1   This section was repealed with effect from 1 January 1976 by the Children Act 1975, s 108(1)(b), (4)(d), Sch 2, Pt II.

[245.14]

11. *Interpretation.* For the purposes of this Act, unless the context otherwise requires:—

The expression 'legitimated person' means a person legitimated by this Act;

The expression 'date of legitimation' means the date of the marriage leading to the legitimation, or where the marriage occurred before the commencement of this Act, the commencement of this Act;

The expression 'disposition' means an assurance of any interest in property by any instrument whether inter vivos or by will;

The expression 'intestate' has the same meaning as in the Administration of Estates Act, 1925, and 'will' includes 'codicil';

The expression 'entailed interest [1] *' has the same meaning as in the Law of Property Act 1925.* [2]

1   See the LPA 1925, s 130(2).
2   This section was repealed with effect from 1 January 1976 by the Children Act 1975, s 108(1)(b), (4)(d), Sch 2, Pt II.

[245.15]

12. *Short title and commencement.*—(1) *This Act may be cited as the Legitimacy Act 1926.*

(2) This Act shall come into operation on the first day of January, nineteen hundred and twenty-seven.

(3) The provisions of this Act shall, save as therein otherwise expressly provided, extend only to England and Wales.[1]

1   This section was repealed with effect from 1 January 1976 by the Children Act 1975, s 108(1)(b), (4)(d), Sch 2, Pt II.

*   *   *   *   *

ADOPTION ACT 1950

(14 Geo 6 c 26)   [28 July 1950]

[245.16]
Note. This Act came into force on 1 October 1950 but with retrospective effect from 1 January 1950, replacing the similar provisions of the Adoption of Children Act 1949 from the commencement date of that Act. The Act of 1950 gave an adopted child the same rights of succession as a lawful child of the adopter on the death intestate of any person on or after 1 January 1950, provided that the adoption order was made before the death. The Act also reversed the common law rule of construction in relation to dispositions taking effect on or after 1 January 1950 by providing that an adopted child was to be treated as a lawful child of the adopter, provided again that the adoption order was made before the disposition. The Act provided that in the case of a will the date of the disposition was the date on which the will was made, not the date of the testator's death and, further, that a will was not to be treated as made at a later date by reason only of its having been confirmed by a codicil. These provisions were replaced in respect of deaths on or after 1 April 1959 by the very similar provisions contained in the Adoption Act 1958 (paras **[245.24]–[245.30]**).

PART I

ADOPTION ORDERS

Making of adoption orders

[245.17]
1.   Power to make adoption orders.—*(1)   Subject to the provisions of this Act, the court may, upon an application made in the prescribed manner by a person domiciled in England or Scotland, make an order (in this Act referred to as an adoption order) authorising the applicant to adopt an infant.*

*   *   *   *   *

Effects of adoption orders

*   *   *   *   *

[245.18]

**13.   *English intestacies, wills and settlements.*—*(1)   Where, at any time after the making of an adoption order, the adopter or the adopted person or any other person dies intestate in respect of any real or personal property (other than property subject to an entailed interest under a disposition made before the date of the adoption order), that property shall devolve in all respects as if the adopted person were the child of the adopter born in lawful wedlock and were not the child of any other person.*

(2)   In any disposition of real or personal property made, whether by instrument inter vivos or by will (including codicil), after the date of an adoption order—

   (a)   *any reference (whether express or implied) to the child or children of the adopter shall, unless the contrary intention appears, be construed as, or as including, a reference to the adopted person;*

   (b)   *any reference (whether express or implied) to the child or children of the adopted person's natural parents or either of them shall, unless the contrary intention appears, be construed as not being, or as not including, a reference to the adopted person; and*

   (c)   *any reference (whether express or implied) to a person related to the adopted person in any degree shall, unless the contrary intention appears, be construed as a reference to the person who would be related to him in that degree if he were the child of the adopter born in lawful wedlock and were not the child of any other person.*

(3)   Where under any disposition any real or personal property or any interest in such property is limited (whether subject to any preceding limitation or charge or not) in such a way that would, apart from this section, devolve (as nearly as the law permits) along with a dignity or title of honour, then, whether or not the disposition contains an express reference to the dignity or title of honour, and whether or not the property or some interest in the property may in some event become severed therefrom, nothing in this section shall operate to sever the property or any interest therein from the dignity, but the property or interest shall devolve in all respects as if this section had not been enacted.

*   *   *   *   *

[245.19]

**14.   *Provisions supplementary to s 13.*—*(1)   For the purposes of the application of the Administration of Estates Act 1925, to the devolution of any property in accordance with the provisions of the last foregoing section, and for the purposes of the construction of any such disposition as is mentioned in that section, an adopted person shall be deemed to be related to any other person being the child or adopted child of the adopter or (in the case of a joint adoption) of either of the adopters—*

   (a)   *where he or she was adopted by two spouses jointly, and that other person is the child or adopted child of both of them, as brother or sister of the whole blood;*

   (b)   *in any other case, as brother or sister of the half-blood.*

(2) Notwithstanding any rule of law, a disposition made by will or codicil executed before the date of an adoption order shall not be treated for the purposes of the last foregoing section as made after that date by reason only that the will or codicil is confirmed by a codicil executed after that date.

(3) Notwithstanding anything in the last foregoing section, trustees or personal representatives may convey or distribute any real or personal property to or among the persons entitled thereto without having ascertained that no adoption order has been made by virtue of which any person is or may be entitled to any interest therein, and shall not be liable to any such person of whose claim they have not had notice at the time of the conveyance or distribution; but nothing in this subsection shall prejudice the right of any such person to follow the property, or any property representing it, into the hands of any person, other than a purchaser, who may have received it.

(4) Where an adoption order is made in respect of a person who has been previously adopted, the previous adoption shall be disregarded for the purposes of the last foregoing section in relation to the devolution of any property on the death of a person dying intestate after the date of the subsequent adoption order and in relation to any disposition of property made after that date.

*　　*　　*　　*　　*

PART IV

MISCELLANEOUS AND GENERAL

*　　*　　*　　*　　*

[245.20]
45. *Interpretation.*—(1) *In this Act, unless the context otherwise requires, the following expressions have the meanings hereby respectively assigned to them, that is to say—*

*　　*　　*　　*　　*

'adoption order' has the meaning assigned to it by section one of this Act,

*　　*　　*　　*　　*

[245.21]
46. . . . *transitional provisions.*

*　　*　　*　　*　　*

(2) Without prejudice to the application of section thirty-eight of the Interpretation Act, 1889 (which relates to the effect of repeals), the provisions of the Fifth Schedule to this Act shall have effect in relation to the enactments repealed by this section.

*　　*　　*　　*　　*

[245.22]
47. *Short title . . . and commencement.*—(1) *This Act may be cited as the Adoption Act 1950.*

*   *   *   *   *

(3) This Act shall come into force on the first day of October, nineteen hundred and fifty.

*   *   *   *   *

FIFTH SCHEDULE

Section 46

TRANSITIONAL PROVISIONS

*   *   *   *   *

[245.23]
4. *Sections thirteen to fifteen of this Act shall apply in relation to an adoption order made under the Adoption of Children Act 1926 . . . as if it were an adoption order within the meaning of those sections respectively:*
Provided that nothing in section thirteen of this Act shall affect the devolution of any property on the intestacy of a person who died before the first day of January, nineteen hundred and fifty, or any disposition made before that date.

*   *   *   *   *

ADOPTION ACT 1958

(7 Eliz 2 c 5)   [18 December 1958]

[245.24]
Note. This Act contains very similar provisions governing the rights of adopted children under the intestacy rules and under wills and settlements as the Adoption Act 1950 (paras **[245.16]–[245.23]**). The one significant difference is that a disposition by will is treated as made on the testator's death not on the date of the will. A person adopted after the execution of the will but before the testator's death was therefore eligible to take under this Act, though not under the former Act. Sections 16 and 17 of the Act came into force on 1 April 1959 and were repealed as respects things done or events occurring (eg deaths) after 31 December 1975, by the Children Act 1975, s 108, Sch 4, Pt I. Succession rights of adopted persons were regulated by the Children Act 1975, Sch 1. Those provisions were re-enacted by the AA 1976, and are contained in Part IV of that Act (paras **[245.57]–[245.64]**) which was brought into force on 1 January 1988 (SI 1987/1242).

PART I

ADOPTION ORDERS

Making of adoption orders

[245.25]
1.   *Power to make adoption orders.* *—(1)   Subject to the provisions of this Act, the court may, upon an application made in the prescribed manner by a person domiciled in England or Scotland, make an order (in this Act referred to as an adoption order) authorising the applicant to adopt an infant.*

*   *   *   *   *

Effects of adoption orders

*   *   *   *   *

[245.26]
16.   *English intestacies, wills and settlements.* *—(1)   Where, at any time after the making of an adoption order, the adopter or the adopted person or any other person dies intestate in respect of any real or personal property (other than property subject to an entailed interest under a disposition to which subsection (2) of this section does not apply), that property shall devolve in all respects as if the adopted person were the child of the adopter born in lawful wedlock and were not the child of any other person.*
(2)   In any disposition of real or personal property made, whether by instrument inter vivos or by will (including codicil) after the date of an adoption order—

(a)   *any reference (whether express or implied) to the child or children of the adopter shall, unless the contrary intention appears, be construed as, or as including a reference to the adopted person;*
(b)   *any reference (whether express or implied) to the child or children of the adopted person's natural parents or either of them shall, unless the contrary intention appears, be construed as not being, or as not including, a reference to the adopted person; and*
(c)   *any reference (whether express or implied) to a person related to the adopted person in any degree shall, unless the contrary intention appears, be construed as a reference to the person who would be related to him in that degree if he were the child of the adopter born in lawful wedlock and were not the child of any other person.*

(3)   Where under any disposition any real or personal property or any interest in such property is limited (whether subject to any preceding limitation or charge or not) in such a way that it would, apart from this section, devolve (as

2151

nearly as the law permits) along with a dignity or title of honour, then, whether or not the disposition contains an express reference to the dignity or title of honour, and whether or not the property or some interest in the property may in some event become severed therefrom, nothing in this section shall operate to sever the property or any interest therein from the dignity, but the property or interest shall devolve in all respects as if this section had not been enacted.[1]

1   The repeal of ss 16, 17 by the Children Act 1975, s 108, Sch 4, Pt I, has effect subject to the AA 1976, s 73, Sch 2, para 6(2) (see para **[245.68]**).

*   *   *   *   *

[245.27]
17. *Provisions supplementary to s 16.*—*(1) For the purposes of the application of the Administration of Estates Act 1925, to the devolution of any property in accordance with the provisions of the last foregoing section, and for the purposes of the construction of any such disposition as is mentioned in that section, an adopted person shall be deemed to be related to any other person being the child or adopted child of the adopter or (in the case of a joint adoption) of either of the adopters—*

(a) *where he or she was adopted by two spouses jointly, and that other person is the child or adopted child of both of them, as brother or sister of the whole blood;*
(b) *in any other case, as brother or sister of the half-blood.*

(2) For the purposes of subsection (2) of the last foregoing section, a disposition made by will or codicil shall be treated as made on the date of the death of the testator.
(3) Notwithstanding anything in the last foregoing section, trustees or personal representatives may convey or distribute any real or personal property to or among the persons entitled thereto without having ascertained that no adoption order has been made by virtue of which any person is or may be entitled to any interest therein, and shall not be liable to any such person of whose claim they have not had notice at the time of the conveyance or distribution; but nothing in this subsection shall prejudice the right of any such person to follow the property, or any property representing it, into the hands of any person, other than a purchaser, who may have received it.[1]
(4) Where an adoption order is made in respect of a person who has been previously adopted, the previous adoption shall be disregarded for the purposes of the last foregoing section in relation to the devolution of any property on the death of a person dying intestate after the date of the subsequent adoption order, and in relation to any disposition of property made, or taking effect on the death of a person dying, after that date.[2]

1   Section 17(3) was extended to adoption orders made in the Isle of Man or any of the Channel Islands by the Adoption Act 1964, s 1(1).
2   The repeal of ss 16, 17 by the Children Act 1975, s 108, Sch 4, Pt I, has effect subject to the AA 1976, s 73, Sch 2, para 6(2) (see para **[245.68]**).

*   *   *   *   *

PART V

MISCELLANEOUS AND GENERAL

*   *   *   *   *

[245.28]
59. *Transitional provisions . . .*—*(1)* This Act has effect subject to the transitional provisions set out in the Fifth Schedule to this Act.*

*   *   *   *   *

[245.29]
60. *Short title, extent and commencement.*—*(1)* This Act may be cited as the Adoption Act 1958.*

*   *   *   *   *

(3) This Act comes into force on the first day of April, nineteen hundred and fifty-nine.

FIFTH SCHEDULE

Section 59

TRANSITIONAL PROVISIONS

*   *   *   *   *

[245.30]
4.—*(1) Subject to the following provisions of this paragraph, sections sixteen to eighteen of this Act apply in relation to an adoption order made under the Adoption Act, 1950, or any enactment repealed by that Act, . . . as they apply in relation to an adoption order within the meaning of those sections respectively.*
(2) Nothing in sub-paragraph (1) of this paragraph affects the devolution of any property on the intestacy of a person who died before the first day of January, nineteen hundred and fifty, or any disposition made before that date.
(3) Subsection (2) of the said section seventeen does not apply in relation to a disposition made by will or codicil executed before the commencement of this Act unless the will or codicil is confirmed by codicil executed after the commencement of this Act.
(4) Notwithstanding any rule of law, a disposition made by will or codicil executed before the date of an adoption order (within the meaning of section thirteen of the Adoption Act, 1950) shall not be treated for the purposes of section sixteen of this Act as made after that date by reason only that, before the commencement of this Act, the will or codicil was confirmed by a codicil executed after that date.

*   *   *   *   *

LEGITIMACY ACT 1959

(7 & 8 Eliz 2 c 73)   [29 July 1959]

[245.31]
Note. The Legitimacy Act 1926, s 1 (para **[245.7]**) established the principle of legitimation by subsequent marriage save in cases where either parent was married to a third person at the date of the illegitimate child's birth. This Act removed that bar. It also extended the principle of legitimacy to cases where the parents or either of them reasonably believed that they were validly married either at the time of conception or by virtue of any subsequent ceremony. These provisions came into force on 29 October 1959 and were repealed by the LA 1976 (paras **[245.43]–[245.54]**).

[245.32]
1.   *Amendment of Legitimacy Act 1926.*—(*1*)   *Subsection (2) of section one of the Legitimacy Act, 1926 (which excludes the operation of that Act in the case of an illegitimate person whose father or mother was married to a third person at the time of the birth) is hereby repealed.*
(2)   In relation to an illegitimate person to whom it applies by virtue of this section, the Legitimacy Act 1926, shall have effect as if for references to the commencement of that Act there were substituted references to the commencement of this Act.[1]

1   This section was repealed by the LA 1976, Sch 2.

[245.33]
2.   *Legitimacy of children of certain void marriages.*—(*1*)   *Subject to the provisions of this section, the child of a void marriage, whether born before or after the commencement of this Act, shall be treated as the legitimate child of his parents if at the time of the act of intercourse resulting in the birth (or at the time of the celebration of the marriage if later) both or either of the parties reasonably believed that the marriage was valid.*
(2)   This section applies, and applies only, where the father of the child was domiciled in England at the time of the birth or, if he died before the birth, was so domiciled immediately before his death.
(3)   This section, so far as it affects the succession to a dignity or title of honour, or the devolution of property settled therewith, applies only to children born after the commencement of this Act.
(4)   This section does not affect any rights under the intestacy of a person who died before the commencement of this Act, and does not (except so far as may be necessary to avoid the severance from a dignity or title of honour of property settled therewith) affect the operation or construction of any disposition coming into operation before the commencement of this Act.
(5)   In this section the following expressions have the meanings hereby assigned to them, that is to say—
'void marriage' means a marriage, not being voidable only, in respect of which the High Court has or had jurisdiction to grant a decree of nullity, or would have had such jurisdiction if the parties were domiciled in England;
'disposition' has the same meaning as in the Legitimacy Act 1926;

and any reference in this section to property settled with a dignity or title of honour is a reference to any real or personal property, or any interest in such property, which is limited by any disposition (whether subject to a preceding limitation or charge or not) in such a way as to devolve with the dignity or title as nearly as the law permits, whether or not the disposition contains an express reference to the dignity or title and whether or not the property or some interest in the property may in some event become severed from it.[1]

1   Sub-ss (1) to (5): repealed by the LA 1976, Sch 2.

*   *   *   *   *

[245.34]
6.   Extent, short title, commencement, and saving.—*(1)   This Act shall not apply to Scotland or Northern Ireland.*
(2)   This Act may be cited as the Legitimacy Act 1959.
(3)   This Act shall come into force on the expiration of three months beginning with the day on which it is passed.
(4)   It is hereby declared that nothing in this Act affects the Succession to the Throne.[1]

1   Sub-s (4): repealed by the LA 1976, Sch 2.

ADOPTION ACT 1960

(8 & 9 Eliz 2 c 59)   [29 July 1960]

[245.35]
Note. This Act catered for the rather odd situation which arose where an illegitimate child who had been adopted by his natural parents was subsequently legitimated. It will be remembered that under the Legitimacy Act 1926 (paras **[245.6]**–**[245.15]**) an illegitimate child was not legitimated by the subsequent marriage of his parents if at the time of his birth either of his parents was married to a third person. The only step that the parents could take to regularise the position was to adopt the child. However, this bar to legitimation was abolished by the Legitimacy Act 1959, s 1 (para **[245.32]**). The Adoption Act 1960 provided that in a case of this sort any interested party may apply to revoke the adoption order but expressly provided that such revocation should not affect the rights acquired by the child under the Adoption Act 1958 (paras **[245.24]**–**[245.30]**) before the revocation of the adoption order. The latter provision was repealed as from 1 January 1976, and the former as from 1 January 1988.

[245.36]
1.   Further provision for revocation of adoption orders in cases of legitimation.—*(1)   Where any person legitimated by virtue of section one of the Legitimacy Act 1959, had been adopted by his father and mother before the commencement of that Act, the court by which the adoption order was made may, on the application of any of the parties concerned, revoke that order.*[1]

(2)   The revocation of an adoption order under this section, or under section twenty-six of the Adoption Act 1958, shall not affect the operation of sections sixteen and seventeen of that Act in relation to an intestacy which occurred, or a dispotion which was made, before the revocation.[2]

1   Sub-s (1): repealed with effect from 1 January 1988 by the AA 1976, s 73(3), Sch 4 (SI 1987/1242).
2   Sub-s (2): repealed with effect from 1 January 1976 by the Children Act 1975, s 108, Sch 4, Pt I.

*   *   *   *   *

FAMILY LAW REFORM ACT 1969

(1969 c 46)   [25 July 1969]

[245.37]
Note. Pt II of this Act, which came into force on 1 January 1970, conferred rights of succession on illegitimate children on deaths intestate on or after that date. In relation to dispositions of property made on or after that date, the Act reversed the common law presumptions as to the construction of references to children, issue and other expressions descriptive of relationship. In this context, dispositions by will were treated as made at the date of the will and not on the testator's death and a will was not treated as made at a later date merely because it is confirmed by a codicil. (Compare the similar provisions contained in the Adoption Act 1950, s 14(2) at para **[245.19]**.) These provisions were replaced as from 4 April 1988 by the more comprehensive provisions contained in the FLRA 1987, ss 1 and 18 to 20 at paras **[245.70]** and **[245.71]**–**[245.73]**.

*   *   *   *   *

PART II

PROPERTY RIGHTS OF ILLEGITIMATE CHILDREN

[245.38]
**14.   *Right of illegitimate child to succeed on intestacy of parents, and of parents to succeed on intestacy of illegitimate child.*—*(1)   Where either parent of an illegitimate child dies intestate as respects all or any of his or her real or personal property, the illegitimate child or, if he is dead, his issue, shall be entitled to take any interest therein to which he or such issue would have been entitled if he had been born legitimate.*
(2)   Where an illegitimate child dies intestate in respect of all or any of his real or personal property, each of his parents, if surviving, shall be entitled to take any interest therein to which that parent would have been entitled if the child had been born legitimate.
(3)   In accordance with the foregoing provisions of this section, Part IV of the Administration of Estates Act 1925 (which deals with the distribution of the estate of an intestate) shall have effect as if—

2156

(a) *any reference to the issue of the intestate included a reference to any illegitimate child of his and to the issue of any such child;*

(b) *any reference to the child or children of the intestate included a reference to any illegitimate child or children of his; and*

(c) *in relation to an intestate who is an illegitimate child, any reference to the parent, parents, father or mother of the intestate were a reference to his natural parent, parents, father or mother.*

(4) For the purposes of subsection (2) of this section and of the provisions amended by subsection (3)(c) thereof, an illegitimate child shall be presumed not to have been survived by his father unless the contrary is shown.

(5) This section does not apply to or affect the right of any person to take any entailed interest in real or personal property.

(6) The reference in section 50 (1) of the said Act of 1925 (which relates to the construction of documents) to Part IV of that Act, or to the foregoing provisions of that Part, shall in relation to an instrument inter vivos made, or a will or codicil coming into operation, after the coming into force of this section (but not in relation to instruments inter vivos made or wills or codicils coming into operation earlier) be construed as including references to this section.

(7) Section 9 of the Legitimacy Act 1926 (under which an illegitimate child and his issue are entitled to succeed on the intestacy of his mother if she leaves no legitimate issue, and the mother of an illegitimate child is entitled to succeed on his intestacy as if she were the only surviving parent) is hereby repealed.

(8) In this section 'illegitimate child' does not include an illegitimate child who is—

(a) *a legitimated person within the meaning of the said Act of 1926 or a person recognised by virtue of that Act or at common law as having been legitimated; or*

(b) *an adopted person under an adoption order made in any part of the United Kingdom, the Isle of Man or the Channel Islands or under an overseas adoption as defined in section 4(3) of the Adoption Act 1968.*

(9) This section does not affect any rights under the intestacy of a person dying before the coming into force of this section.[1]

1   Sub-s (8): repealed by the Children Act 1975, s 108(1)(b), (4)(d), Sch 4, Pt II, as from 1 January 1976 and the remainder of s 14 was repealed as from 4 April 1988 by the FLRA 1987, s 33(2), (4), Sch 3, paras 8 to 10 and Sch 4.

[245.39]
15. Presumption that in dispositions of property references to children and other relatives include references to, and to persons related through, illegitimate children.— *(1) In any disposition made after the coming into force of this section—*

(a) *any reference (whether express or implied) to the child or children of any person shall, unless the contrary intention appears, be construed as, or as including, a reference to any illegitimate child of that person; and*

(b) *any reference (whether express or implied) to a person or persons related in some other manner to any person shall, unless the contrary intention appears, be construed as, or as including, a reference to anyone who would be so related if he, or some other person through whom the relationship is deduced, had been born legitimate.*

(2)   The foregoing subsection apples only where the reference in question is to a person who is to benefit or to be capable of benefiting under the disposition or, for the purpose of designating such a person, to someone else to or through whom that person is related; but that subsection does not affect the construction of the word 'heir' or 'heirs' or of any expression which is used to create an entailed interest in real or personal property.

(3)   In relation to any disposition made after the coming into force of this section, section 33 of the Trustee Act 1925 (which specifies the trusts implied by a direction that income is to be held on protective trusts for the benefit of any person) shall have effect as if—

(a)   *the reference to the children or more remote issue of the principal beneficiary included a reference to any illegitimate child of the principal beneficiary and to anyone who would rank as such issue if he, or some other person through whom he is descended from the principal beneficiary, had been born legitimate; and*

(b)   *the reference to the issue of the principal beneficiary included a reference to anyone who would rank as such issue if he, or some other person through whom he is descended from the principal beneficiary, had been born legitimate.*

(4)   In this section references to an illegitimate child include references to an illegitimate child who is or becomes a legitimated person within the meaning of the Legitimacy Act 1926 or a person recognised by virtue of that Act or at common law as having been legitimated; and in section 3 of that Act—

(a)   *subsection (1)(b) (which relates to the effect of dispositions where a person has been legitimated) shall not apply to a disposition made after the coming into force of this section except as respects any interest in relation to which the disposition refers only to persons who are, or whose relationship is deduced through, legitimate persons; and*

(b)   *subsection (2) (which provides that, where the right to any property depends on the relative seniority of the children of any person, legitimated persons shall rank as if born on the date of legitimation) shall not apply in relation to any right conferred by a disposition made after the coming into force of this section unless the terms of the disposition are such that the children whose relative seniority is in question cannot include any illegitimate children who are not either legitimated persons within the meaning of that Act or persons recognised by virtue of that Act as having been legitimated.*

(5)   Where under any disposition any real or personal property or any interest in such property is limited (whether subject to any preceding limitation or charge or not) in such a way that it would, apart from this section, devolve (as nearly as the law permits) along with a dignity or title of honour, then, whether or not the disposition contains an express reference to the dignity or title of honour, and whether or not the property or some interest in the property may in some event become severed therefrom, nothing in this section shall operate to sever the property or any interest therein from the dignity or title, but the property or interest shall devolve in all respects as if this section had not been enacted.

(6)   This section is without prejudice to sections 16 and 17 of the Adoption Act 1958 (which relate to the construction of dispositions in cases of adoption).

(7)   There is hereby abolished, as respects dispositions made after the coming into force of this section, any rule of law that a disposition in favour of illegitimate children not in being when the disposition takes effect is void as contrary to public policy.

(8)   In this section 'disposition' means a disposition, including an oral disposition, of real or personal property whether inter vivos or by will or codicil; and, notwithstanding any rule of law, a disposition made by will or codicil executed before the date on which this section comes into force shall not be treated for the purposes of this section as made on or after that date by reason only that the will or codicil is confirmed by a codicil executed on or after that date.[1]

1   Sub-ss (4) to (6): repealed by the Children Act 1975, s 108(1)(b), (4)(d), Sch 4, Pt II, as from 1 January 1976; and the remainder of s 15 was repealed as from 4 April 1988 by the FLRA 1987. Section 15 continues to apply to wills made on or after 1 January 1970 and before 4 April 1988.

[245.40]
16.   *Meaning of 'child' and 'issue' in s 33 of Wills Act 1837.*—*(1)   In relation to a testator who dies after the coming into force of this section, section 33 of the Wills Act 1837 (gift to children or other issue of testator not to lapse if they predecease him but themselves leave issue) shall have effect as if—*

(a)   *the reference to a child or other issue of the testator (that is, the intended beneficiary) included a reference to any illegitimate child of the testator and to anyone who would rank as such issue if he, or some other person through whom he is descended from the testator, had been born legitimate; and*

(b)   *the reference to the issue of the intended beneficiary included a reference to anyone who would rank as such issue if he, or some other person through whom he is descended from the intended beneficiary, had been born legitimate.*

(2)   In this section 'illegitimate child' includes an illegitimate child who is a legitimated person within the meaning of the Legitimacy Act 1926 or a person recognised by virtue of that Act or at common law as having been legitimated.[1]

1   Sub-s (2): repealed by the LA 1976, ss 11, Sch 2. Sub-s (1): repealed by the FLRA 1987.

[245.41]
17.   *Protection of trustees and personal representatives.* Notwithstanding the *foregoing provisions of this Part of this Act, trustees or personal representatives may convey or distribute any real or personal property to or among the persons entitled thereto without having ascertained that there is no person who is or may be entitled to any interest therein by virtue of—*

(a)   *section 14 of this Act so far as it confers any interest on illegitimate children or their issue or on the father of an illegitimate child; or*

(b)   *section 15 or 16 of this Act,*

and shall not be liable to any such person of whose claim they have not had notice at the time of the conveyance or distribution; but nothing in this section shall prejudice the right of any such person to follow the property, or any property representing it, into the hands of any person, other than a purchaser, who may have received it.[1]

1   Repealed by the FLRA 1987, s 20 (para **[245.73]**).

*   *   *   *   *

PART IV

MISCELLANEOUS AND GENERAL

[245.42]
28.   Short title, interpretation, commencement and extent.—*(1)   This Act may be cited as the Family Law Reform Act 1969.*
(2)   Except where the context otherwise requires, any reference in this Act to any enactment shall be construed as a reference to that enactment as amended, extended or applied by or under any other enactment, including this Act.
(3)   This Act shall come into force on such date as the Lord Chancellor may appoint by order made by statutory instrument, and different dates may be appointed for the coming into force of different provisions.[1]

1   Pt II of the Act was brought into force on 1 January 1970 (Family Law Reform Act (Commencement No 1) Order 1969, SI 1969/1140).

*   *   *   *   *

LEGITIMACY ACT 1976

(1976 c 31)   [22 July 1976]

[245.43]
Note. This Act currently governs the property rights of legitimated children. In effect, the Act protects the rights of legitimated children by treating them as if they had been born legitimate. The rules of construction reflecting this policy are contained in s 5 (para **[245.48]**) and apply to instruments made on or after 1 January 1976, replacing the corresponding rules introduced by the Children Act 1975 from the same commencement date. The new rules apply to a will made before 1 January 1976 if the testator dies on or after that date and apply whether the legitimation takes place before or after the death. The relevant provisions of the Act are printed below, as amended by the AA 1976 and the FLRA 1987.

[245.44]
1.   Legitimacy of children of certain void marriages.—(1)   The child of a void marriage, whenever born, shall, subject to subsection (2) below and Schedule 1 to this Act, be treated as the legitimate child of his parents if at the time of [the insemination resulting in the birth or, where there was no such act of

insemination, the child's conception (or at the time of the celebration of the marriage if later) both or either of the parties reasonably believed that the marriage was valid.

(2)   This section only applies where the father of the child was domiciled in England and Wales at the time of the birth, or, if he died before the birth, was so domiciled immediately before his death.

[(3)   It is hereby declared for the avoidance of doubt that subsection (1) above applies notwithstanding that the belief that the marriage was valid was due to a mistake as to law.

(4)   In relation to a child born after the coming into force of section 28 of the Family Law Reform Act 1987, it shall be presumed for the purposes of subsection (1) above, unless the contrary is shown, that one of the parties to the void marriage reasonably believed at the time of the insemination resulting in the birth or, where there was no such insemination, the child's conception (or at the time of the celebration of the marriage if later) that the marriage was valid.][1]

1   The words in square brackets in sub-s (1) were substituted, and sub-ss (3) and (4) were added, by the FLRA 1987, s 28, with effect from 4 April 1988 (SI 1988/425).

[245.45]
2.   Legitimation by subsequent marriage of parents. Subject to the following provisions of this Act, where the parents of an illegitimate person marry one another, the marriage shall, if the father of the illegitimate person is at the date of marriage domiciled in England and Wales, render that person, if living, legitimate from the date of the marriage.

[245.46]
3.   Legitimation by extraneous law. Subject to the following provisions of this Act, where the parents of an illegitimate person marry one another and the father of the illegitimate person is not at the time of the marriage domiciled in England and Wales but is domiciled in a country by the law of which the illegitimate person became legitimated by virtue of such subsequent marriage, that person, if living, shall in England and Wales be recognised as having been so legitimated from the date of the marriage notwithstanding that, at the time of his birth, his father was domiciled in a country the law of which did not permit legitimation by subsequent marriage.

[245.47]
4.   Legitimation of adopted child.—(1)   [Section 39 of the Adoption Act 1976][1] does not prevent an adopted child being legitimated under section 2 or 3 above if either natural parent is the sole adoptive parent.

(2)   Where an adopted child (with a sole adoptive parent) is legitimated—

   (a)   [subsection (2) of the said section 39][1] shall not apply after the legitimation to the natural relationship with the other natural parent, and
   (b)   revocation of the adoption order in consequence of the legitimation shall not affect [section 39, 41 or 42 of the Adoption Act 1976][1] as it applies to any instrument made before the date of legitimation.

1   The words in square brackets in this section were substituted by the AA 1976, s 73(2), Sch 3, para 23 for reference to corresponding provisions of the Children Act 1975, as from 1 January 1988 (SI 1987/1242).

[245.48]
5.   Rights of legitimated persons and others to take interests in property.—
(1)   Subject to any contrary indication, the rules of construction contained in this section apply to any instrument other than an existing instrument, so far as the instrument contains a disposition of property.
(2)   For the purposes of this section, provisions of the law of intestate succession applicable to the estate of a deceased person shall be treated as if contained in an instrument executed by him (while of full capacity) immediately before his death.
(3)   A legitimated person, and any other person, shall be entitled to take any interest as if the legitimated person had been born legitimate.
(4)   A disposition which depends on the date of birth of a child or children of the parent or parents shall be construed as if—

(a)   a legitimated child had been born on the date of legitimation,
(b)   two or more legitimated children legitimated on the same date had been born on that date in the order of their actual births,

but this does not affect any reference to the age of a child.
(5)   Examples of phrases in wills on which subsection (4) above can operate are—

1.   Children of A 'living at my death or born afterwards'.
2.   Children of A 'living at my death or born afterwards before any one of such children for the time being in existence attains a vested interest, and who attain the age of 21 years'.
3.   As in example 1 or 2, but referring to grandchildren of A, instead of children of A.
4.   A for life 'until he has a child' and then to his child or children.

Note. Subsection (4) above will not affect the reference to the age of 21 years in example 2.
(6)   If an illegitimate person or a person adopted by one of his natural parents dies, or has died before the commencement of this Act, and—

(a)   after his death his parents marry or have married; and
(b)   the deceased would, if living at the time of the marriage, have become a legitimated person,

this section shall apply for the construction of the instrument so far as it relates to the taking of interests by, or in succession to, his spouse, children and remoter issue as if he had been legitimated by virtue of the marriage.
(7)   In this section 'instrument' includes a private Act settling property, but not any other enactment.

[245.49]
6.   Dispositions depending on date of birth.—(1)   Where a disposition depends on the date of birth of a child who was born illegitimate and who is legitimated (or, if deceased, is treated as legitimated), section 5(4) above does not affect entitlement under Part II of the Family Law Reform Act 1969 (illegitimate children).
(2)   Where a disposition depends on the date of birth of an adopted child who is legitimated (or, if deceased, is treated as legitimated) section 5(4) above does not affect entitlement by virtue of [Section 42(2) of the Adoption Act 1976].[1]

(3)   This section applies for example where—

   (a)   a testator dies in 1976 bequeathing a legacy to his eldest grandchild living at a specified time,

   (b)   his daughter has an illegitimate child in 1977 who is the first grandchild,

   (c)   his married son has a child in 1978,

   (d)   subsequently the illegitimate child is legitimated.

and in all those cases the daughter's child remains the eldest grandchild of the testator throughout.

1   The words in square brackets in sub-s (2) were substituted by the AA 1976, s 73(2), Sch 3, para 24 for a reference to the corresponding provisions of the Children Act 1975, as from 1 January 1988 (SI 1987/1242).

[245.50]

7.   Protection of trustees and personal representatives.—(1)   A trustee or personal representative is not under a duty, by virtue of the law relating to trusts or the administration of estates, to enquire, before conveying or distributing any property, whether any person is illegitimate or has been adopted by one of his natural parents, and could be legitimated (or if deceased be treated as legitimated), if that fact could affect entitlement to the property.

(2)   A trustee or personal representative shall not be liable to any person by reason of a conveyance or distribution of the property made without regard to any such fact if he has not received notice of the fact before the conveyance or distribution.

(3)   This section does not prejudice the right of a person to follow the property, or any property representing it, into the hands of another person, other than a purchaser, who has received it.

*   *   *   *   *

[245.51]

10.   Interpretation.—(1)   In this Act, except where the context otherwise requires—

   'disposition' includes the conferring of a power of appointment and any other disposition of an interest in or right over property;

   'existing', in relation to an instrument, means one made before 1st January 1976;

   'legitimated person' means a person legitimated or recognised as legitimated—

      (a)   under section 2 or 3 above;

      (b)   under section 1 or 8 of the Legitimacy Act 1926; or

      (c)   except in section 8, by legitimation (whether or not by virtue of the subsequent marriage of his parents) recognised by the law of England and Wales and effected under the law of any other country;

   and cognate expressions shall be construed accordingly;

   'power of appointment' includes any discretionary power to transfer a beneficial interest in property without the furnishing of valuable consideration;

'void marriage' means a marriage, not being voidable only, in respect of which the High Court has or had jurisdiction to grant a decree of nullity, or would have or would have had such jurisdiction if the parties were domiciled in England and Wales.

(2)   For the purposes of this Act 'legitimated person' includes, where the context admits, a person legitimated, or recognised as legitimated, before the passing of the Children Act 1975.

(3)   For the purpose of this Act, except where the context otherwise requires—

(a)   the death of the testator is the date at which a will or codicil is to be regarded as made;

(b)   an oral disposition of property shall be deemed to be contained in an instrument made when the disposition was made.

(4)   It is hereby declared that references in this Act to dispositions of property include references to a disposition by the creation of an entailed interest.

(5)   Except in so far as the context otherwise requires, any reference in this Act to an enactment shall be construed as a reference to that enactment as amended by or under any other enactment, including this Act.

[245.52]
11.   Savings, amendments and repeals.—(1)   Schedule 1 to this Act, which contains savings and amendments to enactments consequential upon the provisions of this Act, shall have effect.

*   *   *   *   *

[245.53]
12.   Short title, commencement and extent.—(1)   This Act may be cited as the Legitimacy Act 1976.

(2)   This Act shall come into force at the end of the period of one month beginning with the date on which it is passed.

(3)   This Act does not extend to Scotland or to Northern Ireland.

SCHEDULE 1

Section 11

SAVINGS

[245.54]
1.—(1)   Notwithstanding the repeal by this Act of sections 1 and 8 of the Legitimacy Act 1926 persons legitimated or recognised as legitimated under that Act shall continue to be legitimated or recognised as legitimated by virtue of section 1 or, as the case may be, section 8 of that Act.

(2)   In any enactment whether passed before or after this Act references to persons legitimated or recognised as legitimated under section 1 or section 8 of the Legitimacy Act 1926 or under section 2 or section 3 of this Act shall be construed as including references to persons legitimated or recognised as

legitimated under section 2 or section 3 of this Act or under section 1 or section 8 of the said Act of 1926 respectively.

2.—(1) The enactments repealed by Part II of Schedule 4 to the Children Act 1975 (which are superseded by section 5 of this Act) shall, notwithstanding those repeals, continue to have effect as respects existing instruments.

In this sub-paragraph 'instrument' has the same meaning as in section 5 of this Act.

(2) Subject to paragraph 3(b) below, nothing in this Act or in the Legitimacy Act 1926 (in so far as the effect of that Act is preserved by sub-paragraph (1) above) shall affect the operation or construction of any disposition coming into operation before 1st January 1927 or affect any rights under the intestacy of a person dying before that date.

(3) Sub-paragraph (2) above shall apply in relation to a person to whom the said Act of 1926 applied by virtue of section 1(1) of the Legitimacy Act 1959 with the substitution for '1st January 1927' of '29th October 1959'.

3. Section 1 does not—

(a) affect any rights under the intestacy of a person who dies before 29th October 1959, or

(b) affect the operation or construction of any disposition coming into operation before 29th October 1959 except so far as may be necessary to avoid the severance from a dignity or title of honour of property limited (expressly or not) to devolve (as nearly as the law permits) along with the dignity or title of honour.

4.—(1) Section 1 of this Act, so far as it affects the succession to a dignity or title of honour, or the devolution of property limited as aforesaid, only applies to children born after 28th October 1959.

(2) Apart from section 1, nothing in this Act shall affect the succession to any dignity or title of honour or render any person capable of succeeding to or transmitting a right to succeed to any such dignity or title.

(3) Apart from section 1, nothing in this Act shall affect the devolution of any property limited (expressly or not) to devolve (as nearly as the law permits) along with any dignity or title of honour.

This sub-paragraph applies only if and so far as a contrary intention is not expressed in the instrument, and shall have effect subject to the instrument.

5. It is hereby declared that nothing in this Act affects the Succession to the Throne.

ADOPTION ACT 1976

(1976 c 36)   [22 July 1976]

[245.55]

Note. This Act currently governs the property rights of adopted children. In effect, the Act protects the rights of adopted children by treating them as if they were the legitimate children of their adoptive parents. The rules of construction embodying this policy are set out in ss 39 to 46 (paras **[245.58]**–**[245.64]**). These rules were brought into force as from 1 January 1988 (SI 1987/1242), replacing the corresponding provisions of the Children Act 1975 with effect from the same commencement date. These rules apply to a will made before 1 January 1976 if the testator dies on or after that date and apply whether the adoption takes place before or after the death.

* * * * *

PART II

ADOPTION ORDERS

The making of adoption orders

[245.56]
12. Adoption orders.—(1) An adoption order is an order [giving parental responsibility for a child to]¹ the adopters, made on their application by an authorised court.

1   The words in square brackets were substituted by the ChA 1989, s 88(1), Sch 10, Pt I, para 3.

* * * * *

PART IV

STATUS OF ADOPTED CHILDREN

[245.57]
38. Meaning of 'adoption' in Part IV.—(1) In this Part 'adoption' means adoption—

(a) by an adoption order;
(b) by an order made under the Children Act 1975, the Adoption Act 1958, the Adoption Act 1950 or any enactment repealed by the Adoption Act 1950;
(c) by an order made in Scotland, Northern Ireland, the Isle of Man or in any of the Channel Islands;
(d) which is an overseas adoption; or
(e) which is an adoption recognised by the law of England and Wales and effected under the law of any other country,

and cognate expressions shall be construed accordingly.
(2)   The definition of adoption includes, where the context admits, an adoption effected before the passing of the Children Act 1975, and the date of an adoption effected by an order is the date of the making of the order.

[245.58]
39. Status conferred by adoption.—(1) An adopted child shall be treated in law—

(a)   where the adopters are a married couple, as if he had been born as a child of the marriage (whether or not he was in fact born after the marriage was solemnized);

(b)   in any other case, as if he had been born to the adopter in wedlock (but not as a child of any actual marriage of the adopter).

(2)   An adopted child shall, subject to subsection (3), be treated in law as if he were not the child of any person other than the adopters or adopter.

(3)   In the case of a child adopted by one of its natural parents as sole adoptive parent, subsection (2) has no effect as respects entitlement to property depending on relationship to that parent, or as respects anything else depending on that relationship.

(4)   It is hereby declared that this section prevents an adopted child from being illegitimate.

(5)   This section has effect—

(a)   in the case of an adoption before 1 January 1976, from that date, and

(b)   in the case of any other adoption, from the date of the adoption.

(6)   Subject to the provisions of this Part, this section—

(a)   applies for the construction of enactments or instruments passed or made before the adoption or later, and so applies subject to any contrary indication; and

(b)   has effect as respects things done, or events occurring, after the adoption, or after 31st December 1975, whichever is the later.

*   *   *   *   *

[245.59]
41.   Adoptive relatives. A relationship existing by virtue of section 39 may be referred to as an adoptive relationship, and—

(a)   a male adopter may be referred to as the adoptive father;

(b)   a female adopter may be referred to as the adoptive mother;

(c)   any other relative of any degree under an adoptive relationship may be referred to as an adoptive relative of that degree,

but this section does not prevent the term 'parent', or any other term not qualified by the word 'adoptive' being treated as including an adoptive relative.

[245.60]
42.   Rules of construction for instruments concerning property.—(1) Subject to any contrary indication, the rules of construction contained in this section apply to any instrument, other than an existing instrument, so far as it contains a disposition of property.

(2)   In applying section 39(1) to a disposition which depends on the date of birth of a child or children of the adoptive parent or parents, the disposition shall be construed as if—

(a)   the adopted child had been born on the date of adoption,

(b)   two or more children adopted on the same date had been born on that date in the order of their actual births.

but this does not affect any reference to the age of a child.

(3)   Examples of phrases in wills on which subsection (2) can operate—

1. Children of A 'living at my death or born afterwards'.
2. Children of A 'living at my death or born afterwards before any one of such children for the time being in existence attains a vested interest and who attain the age of 21 years'.
3. As in example 1 or 2, but referring to grandchildren of A instead of children of A.
4. A for life 'until he has a child', and then to his child or children.

Note. Subsection (2) will not affect the reference to the age of 21 years in example 2.

(4)   Section 39(2) does not prejudice any interest vested in possession in the adopted child before the adoption, or any interest expectant (whether immediately or not) upon an interest so vested.[1]

(5)   Where it is necessary to determine for the purposes of a disposition of property effected by an instrument whether a woman can have a child, it shall be presumed that once a woman has attained the age of 55 years she will not adopt a child after execution of the instrument, and, notwithstanding section 39, if she does so that child shall not be treated as her child or as the child of her spouse (if any) for the purposes of the instrument.

(6)   In this section, 'instrument' includes a private Act settling property, but not any other enactment.

---

1   In *Staffordshire County Council v B* [1998] 1 FLR 261, [1998] Fam Law 8, Ch D it was held that a child's contingent remainder interest expectant upon his biological mother's life interest was an interest expectant upon an interest vested in possession within this subsection and so was preserved following his adoption.

[245.61]

43.   Dispositions depending on date of birth.—(1)   Where a disposition depends on the date of birth of a child who was born illegitimate and who is adopted by one of the natural parents as sole adoptive parent, section 42(2) does not affect entitlement under Part II of the Family Law Reform Act 1969 (illegitimate children).

(2)   Subsection (1) applies for example where—

(a)   a testator dies in 1976 bequeathing a legacy to his eldest grandchild living at a specified time,
(b)   his daughter has an illegitimate child in 1977 who is the first grandchild,
(c)   his married son has a child in 1978,
(d)   subsequently the illegitimate child is adopted by the mother as sole adoptive parent,

and in all those cases the daughter's child remains the eldest grandchild of the testator throughout.

[245.62]

44.   Property devolving with peerages etc.—(1)   An adoption does not affect the descent of any peerage or dignity or title of honour.

(2)   An adoption shall not affect the devolution of any property limited (expressly or not) to devolve (as nearly as the law permits) along with any peerage or dignity or title of honour.

(3)   Subsection (2) applies only if and so far as a contrary intention is not expressed in the instrument, and shall have effect subject to the terms of the instrument.

[245.63]
45.   Protection of trustees and personal representatives.—(1)   A trustee or personal representative is not under a duty, by virtue of the law relating to trusts or the administration of estates, to enquire, before conveying or distributing any property, whether any adoption has been effected or revoked if that fact could affect entitlement to the property.

(2)   A trustee or personal representative shall not be liable to any person by reason of a conveyance or distribution of the property made without regard to any such fact if he has not received notice of the fact before the conveyance or distribution.

(3)   This section does not prejudice the right of a person to follow the property, or any property representing it, into the hands of another person, other than a purchaser, who has received it.

[245.64]
46.   Meaning of 'disposition'.—(1)   In this Part, unless the context otherwise requires,

'disposition' includes the conferring of a power of appointment and any other disposition of an interest in or right over property;

'power of appointment' includes any discretionary power to transfer a beneficial interest in property without the furnishing of valuable consideration.

(2)   This Part applies to an oral disposition as if contained in an instrument made when the disposition was made.

(3)   For the purposes of this Part, the death of the testator is the date at which a will or codicil is to be regarded as made.

(4)   For the purposes of this Part, provisions of the law of intestate succession applicable to the estate of a deceased person shall be treated as if contained in an instrument executed by him (while of full capacity) immediately before his death.

(5)   It is hereby declared that references in this Part to dispositions of property include references to a disposition by the creation of an entailed interest.

*   *   *   *   *

PART VI

MISCELLANEOUS AND SUPPLEMENTAL

*   *   *   *   *

[245.65]
72.   Interpretation.—(1)   In this Act, unless the context otherwise requires—

*   *   *   *   *

['adoption order'—
(a)   means an order under section 12(1) . . .]¹

*   *   *   *   *

'existing', in relation to an enactment or other instrument, means one passed or made at any time before 1st January 1976;

1   This definition was substituted by the ChA 1989, s 88(1), Sch 10, Pt I, para 30.

[245.66]
73. Transitional provisions . . .—(1)   The transitional provisions contained in Schedule 2 shall have effect.

*   *   *   *   *

[245.67]
74. Short title commencement and extent.—(1)   This Act may be cited as the Adoption Act 1976.
(2)   This Act shall come into force on such date as the Secretary of State may by order appoint and different dates may be appointed for different provisions.¹
[(3)   This Act extends to England and Wales only.]²

1   The foregoing provisions were brought into force on 1 January 1988: see para **[245.55]**.
2   Sub-s (3): substituted for the original sub-ss (3) and (4) by the ChA 1989, s 88(1), Sch 10, Pt I, para 31.

*   *   *   *   *

SCHEDULE 2

Section 73

Transitional Provisions and Savings

*   *   *   *   *

Rights relating to property

[245.68]
6.—(1)   Section 39—

(a)   does not apply to an existing instrument or enactment in so far as it contains a disposition of property, and
(b)   does not apply to any public general Act in its application to any disposition of property in an existing instrument or enactment.

(2)   Sections 16 and 17 of the Adoption Act 1958, and provisions containing references to those sections shall continue to apply in relation to dispositions of property effected by existing instruments notwithstanding the repeal of those sections, and such provisions, by the Children Act 1975.
(3)   Section 46 shall apply in relation to this paragraph as if it were contained in Part IV.

*   *   *   *   *

FAMILY LAW REFORM ACT 1987

(1987 c 42)   [15 May 1987]

[245.69]

Note. This Act implements a number of Law Commission recommendations for the removal of the legal disadvantages attaching to illegitimacy. The general principle established by s 1 is embodied in the rule of construction set out in sub-s (1) thereof that both in the 1987 Act itself and in all enactments passed and instruments made after the coming into force of the section, references to any relationship between two persons shall, in the absence of a contrary intention, be construed without regard to whether or not the parents of either of them have or had been married to each other at any time. Subsections (2) and (3) exclude the primary rule of construction in relation to any person who is treated as legitimate by statute or who is legitimated or adopted or is otherwise treated in law as legitimate. This qualification of the primary rule of construction preserves the rights of these categories of person, who are otherwise catered for under the general law or under existing legislation (ie the LA 1976 and the AA 1976). Section 1 was brought into force on 4 April 1988 by the Family Law Reform Act 1987 (Commencement No 1) Order 1988 (SI 1988/425).

Part II of the 1987 Act amended, inter alia, the Guardianship of Minors Act 1971, ss 3 and 4; as from 1 April 1989 (SI 1989/382). These provisions were themselves replaced by the ChA 1989, ss 5 and 6, as from 14 October 1991 (ss 5(1) to (10), (13) and 6) and 1 February 1992 (s 5(11), (12)) (SI 1991/828, as amended by SI 1991/1990), which are the provisions currently in force (see paras **[244.121]**–**[244.122]**).

Part III of the 1987 Act is concerned with property rights. Section 18 (which replaced the more limited provisions of the Family Law Reform Act 1969, s 14) expressly extends the general principle established by s 1 to the rules of intestate succession as they apply to the estates of persons dying after the coming into force of that section. Section 18(2) provides that for the purposes of the intestacy rules an illegitimate person (not being a person treated as legitimate or a legitimated or adopted person) is to be presumed not to have been survived by his father or any person related to him only through his father, unless the contrary is shown. (Compare the more limited presumption contained in s 14(4) of the 1969 Act: para **[245.38]**). Section 19 (which replaced s 15 of the 1969 Act: para **[245.39]**) makes more detailed provision for the application of the general principle to inter vivos dispositions and wills and codicils made on or after the date on which that section comes into force. It should be noted that s 19(7) (like s 15(8) of the 1969 Act) provides that a will or codicil made before that date is not to be treated as made on or after that date by reason only that it is confirmed by a codicil made on or after that date. However, the 1987 Act differs from the 1969 Act in the following respects:—

(i)   Unlike s 15 of the 1969 Act, it applies to words creating an entailed interest unless a contrary intention appears (see s 19(2) of the 1987 Act, and compare s 15(2) of the 1969 Act). However, like s 15 of the 1969 Act, it does not apply to property limited to devolve with a dignity or title of honour (s 19(4) of the 1987 Act, s 15(5) of the 1969 Act).

(ii)   Section 15(1) of the 1969 Act would not have applied if the only illegitimacy causing difficulty was that of the person from whom the relationship had to be traced, eg 'the uncles of R', where R, but not his father, mother or uncles, was illegitimate. The 1987 Act (see in particular s 1(1)) applies to such a case. However, in this type of case the common law presumption that words of relationship were confined to legitimate relations would usually have been displaced because the gift could only have any meaning if the presumption were to be displaced.

(iii) Section 15 of the 1969 Act only applied to references to a relationship where it had the effect of benefiting or rendering capable of benefit someone who was either himself illegitimate or claimed to be related through a person who was illegitimate (s 15(2)); there is no such restriction in the 1987 Act. Thus the descendants of a named monarch for the purposes of a royal lives perpetuity period, in a post-3 April 1988 disposition, will include illegitimate descendants if no contrary intention is shown. To avoid the risk of uncertainty in such a perpetuity period the 1987 Act should be excluded in relation to it. Another example to which the 1987 Act applies but s 15 of the 1969 Act would not have so applied is 'issue' in the precondition of a conditional gift such as 'If X shall predecease me leaving issue', where the gift does not confer any benefit on the issue of X (see eg Form B19.11 at para **[219.24]**).

(iv) Unlike s 15 of the 1969 Act, the general principle embodied in s 1 of the 1987 Act applies in relation to the construction of statutes and statutory instruments passed or made after the coming into force of the section. (See also the corresponding provision added to the Interpretion Act 1978, Sch 1.) Previously specific provision was often made in statutes to cater for illegitimate children. This will no longer be necessary.

Section 20 repeals (without replacing) s 17 of the 1969 Act (para **[245.41]**) which enabled personal representatives and trustees to distribute property without having ascertained whether or not illegitimate persons were entitled to the property or a share of it under ss 14, 15 or 16 of the 1969 Act (paras **[245.38]**–**[245.40]**). It should be noted the repeal takes effect in relation to all distributions made after the date on which s 20 of the 1987 Act comes into force, including distributions out of the estates of persons dying before that date and of trust property settled before that date. In all such cases personal representatives and trustees will need to protect themselves by giving notice by advertisement pursuant to the Trustee Act 1925 (TA 1925), s 27 (para **[246.23]**); see *Re Aldhous* [1955] 2 All ER 80, [1955] 1 WLR 459. The provisions of Pt III of the 1987 Act were bought into force on 4 April 1988 at the same time as s 1 (SI 1988/425).

The 1987 Act also effects certain minor and consequential amendments to other statutory provisions, in particular the TA 1925, s 33 and the AEA 1925, s 50: see paras **[246.28]** and **[244.65]**.

PART I

GENERAL PRINCIPLE

[245.70]
1. General principle.—(1) In this Act and enactments passed and instruments made after the coming into force of this section, references

(however expressed) to any relationship between two persons shall, unless the contrary intention appears, be construed without regard to whether or not the father and mother of either of them, or the father and mother of any person through whom the relationship is deduced, have or had been married to each other at any time.

(2) In this Act and enactments passed after the coming into force of this section, unless the contrary intention appears—

    (a) references to a person whose father and mother were married to each other at the time of his birth include; and

    (b) references to a person whose father and mother were not married to each other at the time of his birth do not include,

references to any person to whom subsection (3) below applies, and cognate references shall be construed accordingly.

(3) This subsection applies to any person who—

    (a) is treated as legitimate by virtue of section 1 of the Legitimacy Act 1976;

    (b) is a legitimated person within the meaning of section 10 of that Act;

    (c) is an adopted child within the meaning of Part IV of the Adoption Act 1976; or

    (d) is otherwise treated in law as legitimate.

(4) For the purpose of construing references falling within subsection (2) above, the time of a person's birth shall be taken to include any time during the period beginning with—

    (a) the insemination resulting in his birth; or

    (b) where there was no such insemination, his conception,

and (in either case) ending with his birth.

* * * * *

PART III

PROPERTY RIGHTS

[245.71]

18. Succession on intestacy.—(1) In Part IV of the Administration of Estates Act 1925 (which deals with the distribution of the estate of an intestate), references (however expressed) to any relationship between two persons shall be construed in accordance with section 1 above.

(2) For the purposes of subsection (1) above and that Part of that Act, a person whose father and mother were not married to each other at the time of his birth shall be presumed not to have been survived by his father, or by any person related to him only through his father, unless the contrary is shown.

(3) In section 50(1) of that Act (which relates to the construction of documents), the reference to Part IV of that Act, or to the foregoing provisions of that Part, shall in relation to an instrument inter vivos made, or a will or codicil coming into operation, after the coming into force of this section (but not

in relation to instruments inter vivos made or wills or codicils coming into operation earlier) be construed as including references to this section.

(4) This section does not affect any rights under the intestacy of a person dying before the coming into force of this section.

[245.72]
19. Dispositions of property.—(1) In the following dispositions, namely—

    (a) dispositions inter vivos made on or after the date on which this section comes into force; and

    (b) dispositions by will or codicil where the will or codicil is made on or after that date,

references (whether express or implied) to any relationship between two persons shall be construed in accordance with section 1 above.

(2) It is hereby declared that the use, without more, of the word 'heir' or 'heirs' or any expression which is used to create an entailed interest in real or personal property does not show a contrary intention for the purposes of section 1 as applied by subsection (1) above.

(3) In relation to the dispositions mentioned in subsection (1) above, section 33 of the Trustee Act 1925 (which specifies the trust implied by a direction that income is to be held on protective trusts for the benefit of any person) shall have effect as if any reference (however expressed) to any relationship between two persons were construed in accordance with section 1 above.

(4) Where under any disposition of real or personal property, any interest in such property is limited (whether subject to any preceding limitation or charge or not) in such a way that it would, apart from this section, devolve (as nearly as the law permits) along with a dignity or title of honour, then—

    (a) whether or not the disposition contains an express reference to the dignity or title of honour; and

    (b) whether or not the property or some interest in the property may in some event become severed from it,

nothing in this section shall operate to sever the property or any interest in it from the dignity or title, but the property or interest shall devolve in all respects as if this section had not been enacted.

(5) This section is without prejudice to section 42 of the Adoption Act 1976 (construction of dispositions in cases of adoption).

(6) In this section 'disposition' means a disposition, including an oral disposition, of real or personal property whether inter vivos or by will or codicil.

(7) Notwithstanding any rule of law, a disposition made by will or codicil executed before the date on which this section comes into force shall not be treated for the purposes of this section as made on or after that date by reason only that the will or codicil is confirmed by a codicil executed on or after that date.

[245.73]
20. No special protection for trustees and personal representatives. Section 17 of the Family Law Reform Act 1969 (which enables trustees and personal representatives to distribute property without having ascertained that no person whose parents were not married to each other at the time of his birth, or who

claims through such a person, is or may be entitled to an interest in the property) shall cease to have effect.

*   *   *   *   *

PART VI

MISCELLANEOUS AND SUPPLEMENTAL

Miscellaneous

[245.74]
27. Artificial insemination.—(1)   Where after the coming into force of this section a child is born in England and Wales as the result of the artificial insemination of a woman who—

(a)   was at the time of the insemination a party to a marriage (being a marriage which had not at that time been dissolved or annulled); and

(b)   was artificially inseminated with the semen of some person other than the other party to that marriage,

then, unless it is proved to the satisfaction of any court by which the matter has to be determined that the other party to that marriage did not consent to the insemination, the child shall be treated in law as the child of the parties to that marriage and shall not be treated as the child of any person other than the parties to that marriage.

(2)   Any reference in this section to a marriage includes a reference to a void marriage if at the time of the insemination resulting in the birth of the child both or either of the parties reasonably believed that the marriage was valid; and for the purposes of this section it shall be presumed, unless the contrary is shown, that one of the parties so believed at that time that the marriage was valid.

(3)   Nothing in this section shall affect the succession to any dignity or title of honour or render any person capable of succeeding to or transmitting a right to succeed to any such dignity or title.[1]

1   Note that this section ceased to have effect in relation to children carried by women as a result of their artificial insemination after the commencement of the HFEA 1990, ss 27 to 29 (paras **[245.85]**–**[245.87]**); see s 49(4) of the 1990 Act (para **[245.91]**). These provisions of the 1990 Act commenced on 1 August 1991 (SI 1991/1400 1990).

[245.75]
28. Children of void marriages. . . .[1]

1   Note that this section amends the LA 1976, s 1, the text of which (as amended) appears at para **[245.44]**.

*   *   *   *   *

Supplemental

[245.76]
30. Orders applying section 1 to other enactments.—(1)   The Lord Chancellor may by order make provision for the construction in accordance with

2175

section 1 above of such enactments passed before the coming into force of that section as may be specified in the order.

(2)   An order under this section shall so amend the enactments to which it relates as to secure that (so far as practicable) they continue to have the same effect notwithstanding the making of the order.

(3)   An order under this section shall be made by statutory instrument which shall be subject to annulment in pursuance of a resolution of either House of Parliament.

*   *   *   *   *

[245.77]
33.   Amendments, transitional provisions, savings and repeals.—(1)   The enactments mentioned in Schedule 2 to this Act shall have effect subject to the amendments there specified, being minor amendments and amendments consequential on the provisions of this Act.

(2)   The transitional provisions and savings in Schedule 3 to this Act shall have effect.

(3)   The inclusion in this Act of any express saving or amendment shall not be taken as prejudicing the operation of sections 16 and 17 of the Interpretation Act 1978 (which relate to the effect of repeals).

(4)   The enactments mentioned in Schedule 4 to this Act are hereby repealed to the extent specified in the third column of that Schedule.

[245.78]
34.   Short title, commencement and extent.—(1)   This Act may be cited as the Family Law Reform Act 1987.

(2)   This Act shall come into force on such day as the Lord Chancellor may by order made by statutory instrument appoint; and different days may be so appointed for different provisions or different purposes.

(3)   Without prejudice to the transitional provisions contained in Schedule 3 to this Act, an order under subsection (2) above may make such further transitional provisions as appear to the Lord Chancellor to be necessary or expedient in connection with the provisions brought into force by the order, including—

   (a)   such adaptations of the provisions so brought into force; and
   (b)   such adaptations of any provisions of this Act then in force,

as appear to him necessary or expedient in consequence of the partial operation of this Act.

*   *   *   *   *

SCHEDULE 2

Section 33(1)

MINOR AND CONSEQUENTIAL AMENDMENTS

[245.79]
Note. Relevant amendments are contained in paras 2, 3 which amend the TA 1925, s 33, and the AEA 1925, s 50 which are printed (as amended) at paras **[246.28]** and **[244.65]**.

SCHEDULE 3

Section 33(2)

TRANSITIONAL PROVISIONS AND SAVINGS

*   *   *   *   *

Property rights

[245.80]
8. The repeal by this Act of section 14 of the Family Law Reform Act 1969 shall not affect any rights arising under the intestacy of a person dying before the coming into force of the repeal.
9. The repeal by this Act of section 15 of the Family Law Reform Act 1969 shall not affect, or affect the operation of section 33 of the Trustee Act 1925 in relation to—

(a) any disposition inter vivos made before the date on which the repeal comes into force; or
(b) any disposition by will or codicil executed before that date.

10. The repeal by this Act of section 17 of the Family Law Reform Act 1969 shall not affect the liability of trustees or personal representatives in respect of any conveyance or distribution made before the coming into force of the repeal.

*   *   *   *   *

SCHEDULE 4

Section 33(4)

REPEALS

[245.81]
Note. The provisions repealed include the whole of the Legitimacy Act 1959 and certain provisions of the FLRA 1969. So far as relevant, the repeals are referred to in the notes to each of these statutes.

HUMAN FERTILISATION AND EMBRYOLOGY ACT 1990

(1990 c 37)   [1 November 1990]

[245.82]
Note. This Act introduces a new system of control for the treatment of infertility and for research involving human embryos. It also contains provisions identifying the persons who are to be treated in law as the father (if any) and mother of persons coming into existence as a consequence of artificial insemination or other techniques to deal with infertility that are regulated by the Act (ss 27 and 28). These provisions will affect the construction of wills and

other dispositions (even if made before the commencement of the relevant provision), and the operation of the intestacy rules (s 29(3)). There is also provision (s 30) for the courts to make orders, inter alia applying the adoption legislation, in cases of surrogate motherhood. Sections 1, 2, 27 to 29 came into force on 1 August 1991 (SI 1991/1400), and the ancillary provisions in ss 47 to 49 came into force on or before that date. Section 30 was brought into force on dates in 1994 (SI 1994/1776).

Principal terms used

[245.83]
1.   Meaning of 'embryo', 'gamete' and associated expressions.—(1)   In this Act, except where otherwise stated—

  (a)   embryo means a live human embryo where fertilisation is complete, and
  (b)   references to an embryo include an egg in the process of fertilisation,

and, for this purpose, fertilisation is not complete until the appearance of a two cell zygote.
(2)   This Act, so far as it governs bringing about the creation of an embryo, applies only to bringing about the creation of an embryo outside the human body; and in this Act—

  (a)   references to embryos the creation of which was brought about *in vitro* (in their application to those where fertilisation is complete) are to those where fertilisation began outside the human body whether or not it was completed there, and
  (b)   references to embryos taken from a woman do not include embryos whose creation was brought about *in vitro*.

(3)   This Act, so far as it governs the keeping or use of an embryo, applies only to keeping or using an embryo outside the human body.
(4)   References in this Act to gametes, eggs or sperm, except where otherwise stated, are to live human gametes, eggs or sperm but references below in this Act to gametes or eggs do not include eggs in the process of fertilisation.

[245.84]
2.   Other terms.

*   *   *   *   *

(3)   For the purposes of this Act, a woman is not to be treated as carrying a child until the embryo has become implanted.

*   *   *   *   *

Status

[245.85]
27.   Meaning of 'mother'.—(1)   The woman who is carrying or has carried a child as a result of the placing in her of an embryo or of sperm and eggs, and no other woman, is to be treated as the mother of the child.

(2)   Subsection (1) above does not apply to any child to the extent that the child is treated by virtue of adoption as not being the child of any person other than the adopter or adopters.

(3)   Subsection (1) above applies whether the woman was in the United Kingdom or elsewhere at the time of the placing in her of the embryo or the sperm and eggs.

[245.86]

28.   Meaning of 'father'.—(1)   This section applies in the case of a child who is being or has been carried by a woman as the result of the placing in her of an embryo or of sperm and eggs or her artificial insemination.

(2)   If—

   (a)   at the time of the placing in her of the embryo or the sperm and eggs or of her insemination, the woman was a party to a marriage, and
   (b)   the creation of the embryo carried by her was not brought about with the sperm of the other party to the marriage,

then, subject to subsection (5) below, the other party to the marriage shall be treated as the father of the child unless it is shown that he did not consent to the placing in her of the embryo or the sperm and eggs or to her insemination (as the case may be).

(3)   If no man is treated, by virtue of subsection (2) above, as the father of the child but—

   (a)   the embryo or the sperm and eggs were placed in the woman, or she was artificially inseminated, in the course of treatment services provided for her and a man together by a person to whom a licence applies, and
   (b)   the creation of the embryo carried by her was not brought about with the sperm of that man,

then, subject to subsection (5) below, that man shall be treated as the father of the child.

(4)   Where a person is treated as the father of the child by virtue of subsection (2) or (3) above, no other person is to be treated as the father of the child.

(5)   Subsections (2) and (3) above do not apply—

   (a)   in relation to England and Wales and Northern Ireland, to any child who, by virtue of the rules of common law, is treated as the legitimate child of the parties to a marriage,
   (b)   (*applies to Scotland only*), or
   (c)   to any child to the extent that the child is treated by virtue of adoption as not being the child of any person other than the adopter or adopters.

(6)   Where—

   (a)   the sperm of a man who had given such consent as is required by paragraph 5 of Schedule 3 to this Act was used for a purpose for which such consent was required, or
   (b)   the sperm of a man, or any embryo the creation of which was brought about with his sperm, was used after his death,

he is not to be treated as the father of the child.

(7) The references in subsection (2) above to the parties to a marriage at the time there referred to—

    (a) are to the parties to a marriage subsisting at that time, unless a judicial separation was then in force, but

    (b) include the parties to a void marriage if either or both of them reasonably believed at that time that the marriage was valid; and for the purposes of this subsection it shall be presumed, unless the contrary is shown, that one of them reasonably believed at that time that the marriage was valid.

(8) This section applies whether the woman was in the United Kingdom or elsewhere at the time of the placing in her of the embryo or the sperm and eggs or her artificial insemination.

(9) In subsection (7)(a) above, 'judicial separation' includes a legal separation obtained in a country outside the British Islands and recognised in the United Kingdom.

[245.87]
29. Effect of sections 27 and 28.—(1) Where by virtue of section 27 or 28 of this Act a person is to be treated as the mother or father of a child, that person is to be treated in law as the mother or, as the case may be, father of the child for all purposes.

(2) Where by virtue of section 27 or 28 of this Act a person is not to be treated as the mother or father of a child, that person is to be treated in law as not being the mother or, as the case may be, father of the child for any purpose.

(3) Where subsection (1) or (2) above has effect, references to any relationship between two people in any enactment, deed or other instrument or document (whenever passed or made) are to be read accordingly.

(4) In relation to England and Wales and Northern Ireland, nothing in the provisions of section 27(1) or 28(2) to (4), read with this section, affects—

    (a) the succession to any dignity or title of honour or renders any person capable of succeeding to or transmitting a right to succeed to any such dignity or title, or

    (b) the devolution of any property limited (expressly or not) to devolve (as nearly as the law permits) along with any dignity or title of honour.

(5) *(Applies to Scotland only.)*

[245.88]
30. Parental orders in favour of gamete donors.—(1) The court may make an order providing for a child to be treated in law as the child of the parties to a marriage (referred to in this section as 'the husband' and 'the wife') if—

    (a) the child has been carried by a woman other than the wife as the result of the placing in her of an embryo or sperm and eggs or her artificial insemination,

    (b) the gametes of the husband or the wife, or both, were used to bring about the creation of the embryo, and

    (c) the conditions in subsections (2) to (7) below are satisfied.

(2) The husband and the wife must apply for the order within six months of the birth of the child or, in the case of a child born before the coming into force of this Act, within six months of such coming into force.

(3) At the time of the application and of the making of the order—

    (a) the child's home must be with the husband and the wife, and

    (b) the husband or the wife, of both of them, must be domiciled in a part of the United Kingdom or in the Channel Islands or the Isle of Man.

(4) At the time of the making of the order both the husband and the wife must have attained the age of eighteen.

(5) The court must be satisfied that both the father of the child (including a person who is the father by virtue of section 28 of this Act), where he is not the husband, and the woman who carried the child have freely, and with full understanding of what is involved, agreed unconditionally to the making of the order.

(6) Subsection (5) above does not require the agreement of a person who cannot be found or is incapable of giving agreement and the agreement of the woman who carried the child is ineffective for the purposes of that subsection if given by her less than six weeks after the child's birth.

(7) The court must be satisfied that no money or other benefit (other than for expenses reasonably incurred) has been given or received by the husband or the wife for or in consideration of—

    (a) the making of the order,

    (b) any agreement required by subsection (5) above,

    (c) the handing over of the child to the husband and the wife, or

    (d) the making of any arrangements with a view to the making of the order, unless authorised by the court.

(8) For the purposes of an application under this section—

    (a) in relation to England and Wales, section 92(7) to (10) of, and Part I of Schedule 11 to, the Children Act 1989 (jurisdiction of courts) shall apply for the purposes of this section to determine the meaning of 'the court' as they apply for the purposes of that Act and proceedings on the application shall be 'family proceedings' for the purposes of that Act,

    (b) *(applies to Scotland only)*, and

    (c) in relation to Northern Ireland, 'the court' means the High Court or any county court within whose division the child is.

(9) Regulations may provide—

    (a) for any provision of the enactments about adoption to have effect, with such modifications (if any) as may be specified in the regulations, in relation to orders under this section, and applications for such orders, as it has effect in relation to adoption, and applications for adoption orders, and

    (b) for references in any enactment to adoption, an adopted child or an adoptive relationship to be read (respectively) as references to the effect of an order under this section, a child to whom such an order applies and a relationship arising by virtue of the enactments about adoption, as applied by the regulations, and for similar expressions in connection with adoption to be read accordingly,

and the regulations may include such incidental or supplemental provision as appears to the Secretary of State necessary or desirable in consequence of any provision made by virtue of paragraph (a) or (b) above.

(10)   In this section 'the enactments about adoption' means the Adoption Act 1976, the Adoption (Scotland) Act 1978 and the Adoption (Northern Ireland) Order 1987.

(11)   Subsection (1)(a) above applies whether the woman was in the United Kingdom or elsewhere at the time of the placing in her of the embryo or the sperm and eggs or her artificial insemination.

*   *   *   *   *

Miscellaneous and General

*   *   *   *   *

[245.89]
47.   Index   The expressions listed in the left-hand column below are respectively defined or (as the case may be) are to be interpreted in accordance with the provisions of this Act listed in the right-hand column in relation to those expressions.

Expression	Relevant provision
Carry, in relation to a child	Section 2(3)
. . . . . .	. . . . . .
Embryo	Section 1
Gametes, eggs or sperm	Section 1
. . . . . .	. . . . . .

[245.90]
48.   Northern Ireland.—(1)   This Act (except section 37) extends to Northern Ireland.

(2)   Subject to any Order made after the passing of this Act by virtue of subsection (1)(a) of section 3 of the Northern Ireland Constitution Act 1973, the activities governed by this Act shall not be transferred matters for the purposes of that Act, but shall for the purposes of subsection (2) of that section be treated as specified in Schedule 3 to that Act.

[245.91]
49.   Short title, commencement, etc.—(1)   This Act may be cited as the Human Fertilisation and Embryology Act 1990.

(2)   This Act shall come into force on such day as the Secretary of State may by order made by statutory instrument appoint and different days may be appointed for different provisions and for different purposes.

(3)   Sections 27 to 29 of this Act shall have effect only in relation to children carried by women as a result of the placing in them of embryos or of sperm and eggs, or of their artificial insemination (as the case may be), after the commencement of those sections.

(4)   Section 27 of the Family Law Reform Act 1987 (artificial insemination) does not have effect in relation to children carried by women as the result of their artificial insemination after the commencement of sections 27 to 29 of this Act.

*   *   *   *   *

(6)   An order under this section may make such transitional provision as the Secretary of State considers necessary or desirable and, in particular, may provide that where activities are carried on under the supervision of a particular individual, being activities which are carried on under the supervision of that individual at the commencement of sections 3 and 4 of this Act, those activities are to be treated, during such period as may be specified in or determined in accordance with the order, as authorised by a licence (having, in addition to the conditions required by this Act, such conditions as may be so specified or determined) under which that individual is the person responsible.

(7)   Her Majesty may by Order in Council direct that any of the provisions of this Act shall extend, with such exceptions, adaptations and modifications (if any) as may be specified in the Order, to any of the Channel Islands.

*   *   *   *   *

Miscellaneous provisions relevant to the drafting of wills

[246.1]
Note. This section does not contain a comprehensive collection of conveyancing statutes, but a selection of statutes which a will draftsman may often have to consider. It includes statutes relating to beneficial interests, administrative powers conferred on personal representatives and trustees and powers to appoint new trustees and trustees' investment powers.

APPORTIONMENT ACT 1870

(33 & 34 Vict c 35)   [1 August 1870]

[246.2]
1. Short title. This Act may be cited for all purposes as 'The Apportionment Act, 1870.'

[246.3]
2. Rents, etc to be apportionable in respect of time. . . . . All rents, annuities, dividends, and other periodical payments in the nature of income (whether reserved or made payable under an instrument in writing or otherwise) shall, like interest on money lent, be considered as accruing from day to day, and shall be apportionable in respect of time accordingly.[1]

1   The words omitted from this section were repealed by the Statute Law Revision (No 2) Act 1893.

[246.4]
3. Apportioned part of rent, etc to be payable when the next entire portion shall have become due. The apportioned part of any such rent, annuity, dividend, or other payment shall be payable or recoverable in the case of a continuing rent, annuity, or other such payment when the entire portion of which such apportioned part shall form part shall become due and payable, and not before, and in the case of a rent, annuity, or other such payment determined by re-entry, death, or otherwise when the next entire portion of the same would have been payable if the same had not so determined, and not before.

[246.5]
4. Persons shall have the same remedies for recovering apportioned parts as for entire portions—Proviso as to rents reserved in certain cases. All persons and their respective heirs, executors, administrators, and assigns, and also the executors, administrators, and assigns respectively of persons whose

interests determine with their own deaths, shall have such or the same remedies at law and in equity for recovering such apportioned parts as aforesaid when payable (allowing proportionate parts of all just allowances) as they respectively would have had for recovering such entire portions as aforesaid if entitled thereto respectively; provided that persons liable to pay rents reserved out of or charged on lands or other hereditaments of any tenure, and the same lands or other hereditaments, shall not be resorted to for any such apportioned part forming part of an entire or continuing rent as aforesaid specifically, but the entire or continuing rent, including such apportioned part, shall be recovered and received by the heir or other person who, if the rent had not been apportionable under this Act, or otherwise, would have been entitled to such entire or continuing rent, and such apportioned part shall be recoverable from such heir or other person by the executors or other parties entitled under this Act to the same by action at law or suit in equity.

[246.6]
5. Interpretation. In the construction of this Act—
The word 'rents' includes rent service, rentcharge, and rent seck, and also tithes and all periodical payments or renderings in lieu of or in the nature of rent or tithe.
The word 'annuities' includes salaries and pensions.
The word 'dividends' includes (besides dividends strictly so called) all payments made by the name of dividend, bonus, or otherwise out of the revenue of trading or other public companies, divisible between all or any of the members of such respective companies, whether such payments shall be usually made or declared, at any fixed times or otherwise; and all such divisible revenue shall, for the purposes of this Act, be deemed to have accrued by equal daily increment during and within the period for or in respect of which the payment of the same revenue shall be declared or expressed to be made, but the said word 'dividend' does not include payments in the nature of a return or reimbursement of capital.

[246.7]
6. Act not to apply to policies of assurance. Nothing in this Act contained shall render apportionable any annual sums made payable in policies of assurance of any description.

[246.8]
7. Nor where stipulation made to the contrary. The provisions of this Act shall not extend to any case in which it is or shall be expressly stipulated that no apportionment shall take place.

TRUSTEE ACT 1925

(15 & 16 Geo 5 c 19)   [9 April 1925]

[246.9]
Note. The Trustee Act 1925 (TA 1925) came into force on 1 January 1926. The Act is printed as amended by the Trustee Investments Act 1961, the Statute Law

Revision Act 1963, the Law of Property (Amendment) Act 1926 (LP(Λ)A 1926), the Powers of Attorney Act 1971 (PAA 1971), the Statute Law (Repeals) Act 1978, the Trusts of Land and Appointment of Trustees Act 1996 (TLATA 1996) and, more recently, by the Trustee Act 2000 (TrA 2000) which repealed the whole of Part I of the TA 1925 (relating to investments), so far as not already repealed. Other amendments are noted to the provisions concerned.

PART II

GENERAL POWERS OF TRUSTEES AND PERSONAL REPRESENTATIVES

General Powers

[246.10]
12.   Power of trustees for sale to sell by auction, etc.—(1)   Where [a trustee has a duty or power to sell property],[1] he may sell or concur with any other person in selling all or any part of the property, either subject to prior charges or not, and either together or in lots, by public auction or by private contract, subject to any such conditions respecting title or evidence of title or other matter as the trustee thinks fit, with power to vary any contract for sale, and to buy in at any auction, or to rescind any contract for sale and to re-sell, without being answerable for any loss.
(2)   A [duty][1] or power to sell or dispose of land includes a [duty][1] or power to sell or dispose of part thereof, whether the division is horizontal, vertical, or made in any other way.
(3)   This section does not enable an express power to sell settled land to be exercised where the power is not vested in the tenant for life or statutory owner.

1   Sub-ss (1), (2): words in square brackets substituted by the TLATA 1996, s 25(1), Sch 3, para 3(2).

[246.11]
13.   Power to sell subject to depreciatory conditions.—(1)   No sale made by a trustee shall be impeached by any beneficiary upon the ground that any of the conditions subject to which the sale was made may have been unnecessarily depreciatory, unless it also appears that the consideration for the sale was thereby rendered inadequate.
(2)   No sale made by a trustee shall, after the execution of the conveyance, be impeached as against the purchaser upon the ground that any of the conditions subject to which the sale was made may have been unnecessarily depreciatory, unless it appears that the purchaser was acting in collusion with the trustee at the time when the contract for sale was made.
(3)   No purchaser, upon any sale made by a trustee, shall be at liberty to make any objection against the title upon any of the grounds aforesaid.
(4)   This section applies to sales made before or after the commencement of this Act.

[246.12]
14.   Power of trustees to give receipts.—(1)   The receipt in writing of a trustee for any money, securities, [investments][1] or other personal property or

effects payable, transferable, or deliverable to him under any trust or power shall be a sufficient discharge to the person paying, transferring, or delivering the same and shall effectually exonerate him from seeing to the application or being answerable for any loss or misapplication thereof.

(2)   This section does not, except where the trustee is a trust corporation, enable a sole trustee to give a valid receipt for—

[(a)   proceeds of sale or other capital money arising under a trust of land;]²
  (b)   capital money arising under the Settled Land Act 1925³.

(3)   This section applies notwithstanding anything to the contrary in the instrument, if any, creating the trust.

1   Word in square brackets added by the TrA 2000, s 40, Sch 2, para 19.
2   Sub-s (2): para (a) substituted by the TLATA 1996, s 25(1), Sch 3, para 3(3).
3   Although it has not been possible to create settlements under the Settled Land Act 1925 (SLA 1925) since 1 January 1997, this reform is without prejudice to existing strict settlements: TLATA 1996, s 2 (para **[246.87]**). Sub-s (2)(b) therefore continues to apply in relation to such settlements.

[246.13]
15.   Power to compound liabilities. A personal representative, or two or more trustees acting together, or, subject to the restrictions imposed in regard to receipts by a sole trustee not being a trust corporation, a sole acting trustee where by the instrument, if any, creating the trust, or by statute, a sole trustee is authorised to execute the trusts and powers reposed in him, may, if and as he or they think fit—

(a)   accept any property, real or personal, before the time at which it is made transferable or payable; or
(b)   sever and apportion any blended trust funds or property; or
(c)   pay or allow any debt or claim on any evidence that he or they think sufficient; or
(d)   accept any composition or any security, real or personal, for any debt or for any property, real or personal, claimed; or
(e)   allow any time of payment of any debt; or
(f)   compromise, compound, abandon, submit to arbitration, or otherwise settle any debt, account, claim, or thing whatever relating to the testator's or intestate's estate or to the trust;

and for any of these purposes may enter into, give, execute, and do such agreements, instruments of composition or arrangement, releases, and other things as to him or them seem expedient, without being responsible for any loss occasioned by any act or thing so done by him or them [if he has or they have discharged the duty of care set out in section 1(1) of the Trustee Act 2000].¹

1   Words in square brackets substituted by the TrA 2000, s 40, Sch 2, para 20.

[246.14]
16.   Power to raise money by sale, mortgage, etc.—(1)   Where trustees are authorised by the instrument, if any, creating the trust or by law to pay or apply capital money subject to the trust for any purpose or in any manner, they shall have and shall be deemed always to have had power to raise the money required

by sale, conversion, calling in, or mortgage of all or any part of the trust property for the time being in possession.

(2)   This section applies notwithstanding anything to the contrary contained in the instrument, if any, creating the trust, but does not apply to trustees of property held for charitable purposes, or to trustees of a settlement for the purposes of the Settled Land Act 1925, not being also the statutory owners.

[246.15]
17.   Protection to purchasers and mortgagees dealing with trustees. No purchaser or mortgagee, paying or advancing money on a sale or mortgage purporting to be made under any trust or power vested in trustees, shall be concerned to see that such money is wanted, or that no more than is wanted is raised, or otherwise as to the application thereof.

[246.16]
18.   Devolution of powers or trusts.—(1)   Where a power or trust is given to or imposed on two or more trustees jointly, the same may be exercised or performed by the survivors or survivor of them for the time being.

(2)   Until the appointment of new trustees, the personal representatives or representative for the time being of a sole trustee, or, where there were two or more trustees of the last surviving or continuing trustee, shall be capable of exercising or performing any power or trust which was given to, or capable of being exercised by, the sole or last surviving or continuing trustee, or the other trustees or trustee for the time being of the trust.

(3)   This section takes effect subject to the restrictions imposed in regard to receipts by a sole trustee, not being a trust corporation.

(4)   In this section 'personal representative' does not include an executor who has renounced or has not proved.

[246.17]
19.   Power to insure.—[(1)   A trustee may—

(a)   insure any property which is subject to the trust against risks of loss or damage due to any event, and
(b)   pay the premiums out of the trust funds.

(2)   In the case of property held on a bare trust, the power to insure is subject to any direction given by the beneficiary or each of the beneficiaries—

(a)   that any property specified in the direction is not to be insured;
(b)   that any property specified in the direction is not to be insured except on such conditions as may be so specified.

(3)   Property is held on a bare trust if it is held on trust for—

(a)   a beneficiary who is of full age and capacity and absolutely entitled to the property subject to the trust, or
(b)   beneficiaries each of whom is of full age and capacity and who (taken together) are absolutely entitled to the property subject to the trust.

(4)   If a direction under subsection (2) of this section is given, the power to insure, so far as it is subject to the direction, ceases to be a delegable function for the purposes of section 11 of the Trustee Act 2000 (power to employ agents).

(5) In this section 'trust funds' means any income or capital funds of the trust.]¹

1   This section was substituted by the TrA 2000, s 34(1) as from 1 February 2001. Note that the substitution applies to trusts whether created before or after its commencement.

[246.18]
20. Application of insurance money where policy kept up under any trust, power or obligation.—(1) Money receivable by trustees or any beneficiary under a policy of insurance against the loss or damage of any property subject to a trust or to a settlement within the meaning of the Settled Land Act 1925 ...¹ shall, where the policy has been kept up under any trust in that behalf or under any power statutory or otherwise, or in performance of any covenant or of any obligation statutory or otherwise, or by a tenant for life impeachable for waste, be capital money for the purposes of the trust or settlement, as the case may be.
(2) If any such money is receivable by any person, other than the trustees of the trust or settlement, that person shall use his best endeavours to recover and receive the money, and shall pay the net residue thereof, after discharging any costs of recovering and receiving it, to the trustees of the trust or settlement, or, if there are no trustees capable of giving a discharge therefor, into court.
(3) Any such money—

(a) if it was receivable in respect of settled land within the meaning of the Settled Land Act 1925, or any building or works thereon, shall be deemed to be capital money arising under that Act from the settled land, and shall be invested or applied by the trustees, or, if in court, under the direction of the court, accordingly;

(b) if it was receivable in respect of personal chattels settled as heirlooms within the meaning of the Settled Land Act, 1925, shall be deemed to be capital money arising under that Act; and shall be applicable by the trustees, or, if in court, under the direction of the court, in like manner as provided by that Act with respect to money arising by sale of chattels as heirlooms as aforesaid;

(c) if it was receivable in respect of [land subject to a trust of land or personal property held on trust for sale],² shall be held upon the trusts and subject to the powers and provisions applicable to money arising by a sale under such trust;

(d) in any other case, shall be held upon trusts corresponding as nearly as may be with the trusts affecting the property in respect of which it was payable.

(4) Such money, or any part thereof, may also be applied by the trustees, or, if in court, under the direction of the court, in rebuilding, reinstating, replacing, or replacing the property loss or damaged, but any such application by the trustees shall be subject to the consent of any person whose consent is required by the instrument, if any, creating the trust to the investment of money subject to the trust, and, in the case of money which is deemed to be capital money arising under the Settled Land Act 1925, be subject to the provisions of that Act with respect to the application of capital money by the trustees of the settlement.
(5) Nothing contained in this section prejudices or affects the right of any person to require any such money or any part thereof to be applied in rebuilding

reinstating, or repairing the property lost or damaged, or the rights of any mortgagee, lessor, or lessee, whether under any statute or otherwise.

(6) This section applies to policies effected either before or after the commencement of this Act, but only to money received after such commencement.

1   Sub-s (1): words omitted repealed by the TrA 2000, ss 34(2), 40(3), Sch 4, Pt II.
2   Sub-s (3): in para (c) words in square brackets substituted by the TLATA 1996, s 25(1), Sch 3, para 3(5).

[246.18A]

21. [*Repealed by the Trustee Act 2000, s 40(1), (3), Sch 2, Pt II, para 21, Sch 4, Pt II.*]

[246.19]

22. Reversionary interests, valuations, and audit.—(1)   Where the trust property includes any share or interest in property not vested in the trustees, or the proceeds of the sale of any such property, or any other thing in action, the trustees on the same falling into possession, or becoming payable or transferable may—

(a)   agree or ascertain the amount or value thereof or any part thereof in such manner as they may think fit;

(b)   accept in or towards satisfaction thereof, at the market or current value, or upon any valuation or estimate of value which they may think fit, any authorised investments;

(c)   allow any deductions for duties, costs, charges and expenses which they may think proper or reasonable;

(d)   execute any release in respect of the premises so as effectually to discharge all accountable parties from all liability in respect of any matters coming within the scope of such release;

without being responsible in any such case for any loss occasioned by any act or thing so done by them [if they have discharged the duty of care set out in section 1(1) of the Trustee Act 2000]. [1]

(2)   The trustees shall not be under any obligation and shall not be chargeable with any breach of trust by reason of any omission—

(a)   to place any distringas notice or apply for any stop or other like order upon any securities or other property out of or on which such share or interest or other thing in action as aforesaid is derived, payable or charged; or

(b)   to take any proceedings on account of any act, default, or neglect on the part of the persons in whom such securities or other property or any of them or any part thereof are for the time being, or had at any time been, vested;

unless and until required in writing so to do by some person, or the guardian of some person, beneficially interested under the trust, and unless also due provision is made to their satisfaction for payment of the costs of any proceedings required to be taken:

Provided that nothing in this subsection shall relieve the trustees of the obligation to get in and obtain payment or transfer of such share or interest or other thing in action on the same falling into possession.

(3)   Trustees may, for the purpose of giving effect to the trust, or any of the provisions of the instrument, if any, creating the trust or of any statute, from time to time (by duly qualified agents) ascertain and fix the value of any trust property in such manner as they think proper, and any valuation so made . . . shall be binding upon all persons interested under the trust [if the trustees have discharged the duty of care set out in section 1(1) of the Trustee Act 2000].[2]

(4)   Trustees may, in their absolute discretion, from time to time, but not more than once in every three years unless the nature of the trust or any special dealings with the trust property make a more frequent exercise of the right reasonable, cause the accounts of the trust property to be examined or audited by an independent accountant, and shall, for that purpose, produce such vouchers and give such information to him as he may require, and the costs of such examination or audit, including the fee of the auditor, shall be paid out of the capital or income of the trust property, or partly in one way and partly in the other as the trustees, in their absolute discretion, think fit, but, in default of any direction by the trustees to the contrary in any special case, costs attributable to capital shall be borne by capital and those attributable to income by income.

1   Words in square brackets in sub-s (1) substituted by the TrA 2000, s 40(1), Sch 2, para 22.
2   Sub-s (3): amended by the TrA 2000, s 40(1), Sch 2, Pt II, para 22.

[246.19A]
23.   [*Repealed by the Trustee Act 2000, s 40(1), (3), Sch 2, Pt II, para 23, Sch 4, Pt II.*]

[246.20]
24.   Power to concur with others. Where an undivided share in [any]¹ property, is subject to a trust, or forms part of the estate of a testator or intestate, the trustees or personal representatives may (without prejudice to the [trust]¹ affecting the entirety of the land and the powers of the [trustees]¹ in reference thereto), execute or exercise any [duty or]¹ power vested in them in relation to such share in conjunction with the persons entitled to or having power in that behalf over the other share or shares, and notwithstanding that any one or more of the trustees or personal representatives may be entitled to or interested in any such other share, either in his or their own right or in a fiduciary capacity.

1   Words in square brackets substituted by the TLATA 1996, s 25(1), Sch 3, para 3(6).

[246.21]
[25.   Delegation of trustee's functions by power of attorney.]—[(1) Notwithstanding any rule of law or equity to the contrary, a trustee may, by power of attorney, delegate the execution or exercise of all or any of the trusts, powers and discretions vested in him as trustee either alone or jointly with any other person or persons.

(2)   A delegation under this section—

  (a)   commences as provided by the instrument creating the power or, if the instrument makes no provision as to the commencement of the delegation, with the date of the execution of the instrument by the donor; and

(b) continues for a period of twelve months or any shorter period provided by the instrument creating the power.

(3)   The persons who may be donees of a power of attorney under this section include a trust corporation.

(4)   Before or within seven days after giving a power of attorney under this section the donor shall give written notice of it (specifying the date on which the power comes into operation and its duration, the donee of the power, the reason why the power is given and, where some only are delegated, the trusts, powers and discretions delegated) to—

(a) each person (other than himself), if any, who under any instrument creating the trust has power (whether alone or jointly) to appoint a new trustee; and

(b) each of the other trustees, if any;

but failure to comply with this subsection shall not, in favour of a person dealing with the donee of the power, invalidate any act done or instrument executed by the donee.

(5)   A power of attorney given under this section by a single donor—

(a) in the form set out in subsection (6) of this section; or

(b) in a form to the like effect but expressed to be made under this subsection,

shall operate to delegate to the person identified in the form as the single donee of the power the execution and exercise of all the trusts, powers and discretions vested in the donor as trustee (either alone or jointly with any other person or persons) under the single trust so identified.

(6)   The form referred to in subsection (5) of this section is as follows—

'THIS GENERAL TRUSTEE POWER OF ATTORNEY is made on [date] by [name of one donor] of [address of donor] as trustee of [name or details of one trust].

I appoint [name of one donee] of [address of donee] to be my attorney [if desired, the date on which the delegation commences or the period for which it continues (or both)] in accordance with section 25(5) of the Trustee Act 1925.

[To be executed as a deed]'.

(7)   The donor of a power of attorney given under this section shall be liable for the acts or defaults of the donee in the same manner as if they were the acts or defaults of the donor.

(8)   For the purpose of executing or exercising the trusts or powers delegated to him, the donee may exercise any of the powers conferred on the donor as trustee by statute or by the instrument creating the trust, including power, for the purpose of the transfer of any inscribed stock, himself to delegate to an attorney power to transfer, but not including the power of delegation conferred by this section.

(9)   The fact that it appears from any power of attorney given under this section, or from any evidence required for the purposes of any such power of

attorney or otherwise, that in dealing with any stock the donee of the power is acting in the execution of a trust shall not be deemed for any purpose to affect any person in whose books the stock is inscribed or registered with any notice of the trust.

(10) This section applies to a personal representative, tenant for life and statutory owner as it applies to a trustee except that subsection (4) shall apply as if it required the notice there mentioned to be given—

(a) in the case of a personal representative, to each of the other personal representatives, if any, except any executor who has renounced probate;

(b) in the case of a tenant for life, to the trustees of the settlement and to each person, if any, who together with the person giving the notice constitutes the tenant for life; and

(c) in the case of a statutory owner, to each of the persons, if any, who together with the person giving the notice constitute the statutory owner and, in the case of a statutory owner by virtue of section 23(1)(a) of the Settled Land Act 1925, to the trustees of the settlement.]¹

1 This section was substituted by the Trustee Delegation Act 1999, s 5(1), (2). Note that this section applies to powers of attorney created *after* 1 March 2000.

Indemnities

[246.22]
26. Protection against liability in respect of rents and covenants.—(1) Where a personal representative or trustee liable as such for—

(a) any rent, covenant, or agreement reserved by or contained in any lease; or

(b) any rent, covenant or agreement payable under or contained in any grant made in consideration of a rentcharge; or

(c) any indemnity given in respect of any rent, covenant or agreement referred to in either of the foregoing paragraphs;

satisfies all liabilities under the lease or grant [which may have accrued and been claimed] up to the date of the conveyance hereinafter mentioned, and, where necessary, sets apart a sufficient fund to answer any future claim that may be made in respect of any fixed and ascertained sum which the lessee or grantee agreed to lay out on the property demised or granted, although the period for laying out the same may not have arrived, then and in any such case the personal representative or trustee may convey the property demised or granted to a purchaser, legatee, devisee, or other person entitled to call for a conveyance thereof and thereafter—

(i) he may distribute the residuary real and personal estate of the deceased testator or intestate, or, as the case may be, the trust estate (other than the fund, if any, set apart as aforesaid) to or amongst the persons entitled thereto, without appropriating any part, or any further part, as the case may be, of the estate of the deceased or of the trust estate to meet any future liability under the said lease or grant;

(ii) notwithstanding such distribution, he shall not be personally liable in respect of any subsequent claim under the said lease or grant.

[(1A)   Where a personal representative or trustee has as such entered into, or may as such be required to enter into, an authorised guarantee agreement with respect to any lease comprised in the estate of a deceased testator or intestate or a trust estate (and, in a case where he has entered into such an agreement, he has satisfied all liabilities under it which may have accrued and been claimed up to the date of distribution)—

(a) he may distribute the residuary real and personal estate of the deceased testator or intestate, or the trust estate, to or amongst the persons entitled thereto—

(i)   without appropriating any part of the estate of the deceased, or the trust estate, to meet any future liability (or as the case may be, any liability) under any such agreement, and

(ii)   notwithstanding any potential liability of his to enter into any such agreement; and

(b) notwithstanding such distribution, he shall not be personally liable in respect of any subsequent claim (or, as the case may be, any claim) under any such agreement.

In this subsection 'authorised guarantee agreement' has the same meaning as in the Landlord and Tenant (Covenants) Act 1955.][1]

(2)   This section operates without prejudice to the right of the lessor or grantor, or the persons deriving title under the lessor or grantor, to follow the assets of the deceased or the trust property into the hands of the persons amongst whom the same may have been respectively distributed, and applies notwithstanding anything to the contrary in the will or other instrument, if any, creating the trust.

(3)   In this section 'lease' includes an underlease and an agreement for a lease or underlease and any instrument giving any such indemnity as aforesaid or varying the liabilities under the lease; 'grant' applies to a grant whether the rent is created by limitation, grant, reservation, or otherwise, and includes an agreement for a grant and any instrument giving any such indemnity as aforesaid or varying the liabilities under the grant; 'lessee' and 'grantee' include persons respectively deriving title under them.

---

1   Sub-s (1A): inserted by the Landlord and Tenant (Covenants) Act 1995, s 30(1), Sch 1, para 1, and brought into force on 1 January 1996 by the Landlord and Tenant (Covenants) Act 1995 (Commencement) Order 1995, SI 1995/2963.

[246.23]
27. Protection by means of advertisements.—(1) With a view to the conveyance to or distribution among the persons entitled to any real or personal property, the trustees of a settlement [, trustees of land, trustees for sale of personal property][1] or personal representatives, may give notice by advertisement in the Gazette, and in a newspaper circulating in the district in which the land is situated and such other like notices, including notices elsewhere than in England and Wales, as would, in any special case, have been directed by a court of competent jurisdiction in an action for administration, of their intention to make such conveyance or distribution as aforesaid, and requiring any person interested to send to the trustees or personal representatives

within the time, not being less than two months, fixed in the notice or, where more than one notice is given, in the last of the notices, particulars of his claim in respect of the property or any part thereof to which the notice relates.

(2)   At the expiration of the time fixed by the notice the trustees or personal representatives may convey or distribute the property or any part thereof to which the notice relates, to or among the persons entitled thereto, having regard only to the claims, whether formal or not, of which the trustees or personal representatives then had notice and shall not, as respects the property so conveyed or distributed, be liable to any person of whose claim the trustees or personal representatives have not had notice at the time of conveyance or distribution; but nothing in this section—

(a)   prejudices the right of any person to follow the property, or any property representing the same, into the hands of any person, other than a purchaser, who may have received it; or

(b)   frees the trustees or personal representatives from any obligation to make searches or obtain official certificates of search similar to those which an intending purchaser would be advised to make or obtain.

(3)   This section applies notwithstanding anything to the contrary in the will or other instrument, if any, creating the trust.

1   Sub-s (1): words in square brackets substituted by the TLATA 1996, s 25(1), Sch 3, para 3(7).

[246.24]
28.   Protection in regard to notice. A trustee or personal representative acting for the purposes of more than one trust or estate shall not, in the absence of fraud, be affected by notice of any instrument, matter, fact or thing in relation to any particular trust or estate if he has obtained notice thereof merely by reason of his acting or having acted for the purposes of another trust or estate.

[246.25]
29. [*Repealed by the Powers of Attorney Act 1971, s 11(2), (4), Sch 2.*]

[246.25A]
30. [*Repealed by the Trustee Act 2000, s 40(1), (3), Sch 2, Pt II, para 24, Sch 4, Pt II.*]

Maintenance, Advancement and Protective Trusts

[246.26]
31.   Power to apply income for maintenance and to accumulate surplus income during a minority.—(1)   Where any property is held by trustees in trust for any person for any interest whatsoever, whether vested or contingent, then, subject to any prior interests or charges affecting that property—

(i)   during the infancy of any such person, if his interest so long continues, the trustees may, at their sole discretion, pay to his parent or guardian, if any, or otherwise apply for or towards his maintenance, education, or benefit, the whole or such part, if any, of the income of that property as may, in all the circumstances, be reasonable, whether or not there is—

   (a)   any other fund applicable to the same purpose; or
   (b)   any person bound by law to provide for his maintenance or education; and

(ii)   if such person on attaining the age of [eighteen years][1] has not a vested interest in such income, the trustees shall thenceforth pay the income of that property and of any accretion thereto under subsection (2) of this section to him, until he either attains a vested interest therein or dies, or until failure of his interest:

Provided that, in deciding whether the whole or any part of the income of the property is during a minority to be paid or applied for the purposes aforesaid, the trustees shall have regard to the age of the infant and his requirements and generally to the circumstances of the case, and in particular to what other income, if any, is applicable for the same purposes; and where trustees have notice that the income of more than one fund is applicable for those purposes, then, so far as practicable, unless the entire income of the funds is paid or applied as aforesaid or the court otherwise directs, a proportionate part only of the income of each fund shall be so paid or applied.

(2)   During the infancy of any such person, if his interest so long continues, the trustees shall accumulate all the residue of that income [by investing it, and any profits from so investing it][1] from time to time in authorised investments, and shall hold those accumulations as follows—

(i)   If any such person—
   (a)   attains the age of [eighteen years],[2] or marries under that age, and his interest in such income during his infancy or until his marriage is a vested interest; or
   (b)   on attaining the age of [eighteen years][2] or on marriage under that age becomes entitled to the property from which such income arose in fee simple, absolute or determinable, or absolutely, or for an entailed interest;

   the trustees shall hold the accumulations in trust for such person absolutely, but without prejudice to any provision with respect thereto contained in any settlement by him made under any statutory powers during his infancy, and so that the receipt of such person after marriage, and though still an infant, shall be a good discharge; and

(ii)   In any other case the trustees shall, notwithstanding that such person had a vested interest in such income, hold the accumulations as an accretion to the capital of the property from which such accumulations arose, and as one fund with such capital for all purposes, and so that, if such property is settled land, such accumulations shall be held upon the same trusts as if the same were capital money arising therefrom;

but the trustees may, at any time during the infancy of such person if his interest so long continues, apply those accumulations, or any part thereof, as if they were income arising in the then current year.

(3)   This section applies in the case of a contingent interest only if the limitation or trust carries the intermediate income of the property, but it applies to a future or contingent legacy by the parent of, or a person standing in loco parentis to, the legatee, if and for such period as, under the general law, the

legacy carries interest for the maintenance of the legatee, and in any such case as last aforesaid the rate of interest shall (if the income available is sufficient, and subject to any rules of court to the contrary) be five pounds per centum per annum.

(4)   This section applies to a vested annuity in like manner as if the annuity were the income of property held by trustees in trust to pay the income thereof to the annuitant for the same period for which the annuity is payable, save that in any case accumulations made during the infancy of the annuitant shall be held in trust for the annuitant or his personal representatives absolutely.

(5)   This section does not apply where the instrument, if any, under which the interest arises came into operation before the commencement of this Act.

1   Words substituted by the TrA 2000, s 40(1), Sch 2, para 25.
2   The word 'eighteen' was substituted (twice) by the FLRA, s 1(3), Sch 1, Pt I, for the words 'twenty-one years' but by virtue of s 1(4) of the FLRA 1969 and Sch 3, para 5(1) thereto, the amendment does not affect this section in its application to interests under instruments made before 1970 or, in its application by virtue of the AEA 1925, s 47(1)(ii), to the estate of an intestate dying before 1970 and, by virtue of s 1(4) of, and Sch 3, para 9 to the FLRA 1969, the amendment does not affect the construction of any statutory provision where it is incorporated in and has effect as part of any deed, will or other instrument not otherwise affected by s 1 of the FLRA 1969.

[246.27]

32.   Power of advancement.—(1)   Trustees may at any time or times pay or apply any capital money subject to a trust, for the advancement or benefit, in such manner as they may, in their absolute discretion, think fit, of any person entitled to the capital of the trust property or of any share thereof, whether absolutely or contingently on his attaining any specified age or on the occurrence of any other event, or subject to a gift over on his death under any specified age or on the occurrence of any other event, and whether in possession or in remainder or reversion, and such payment or application may be made notwithstanding that the interest of such person is liable to be defeated by the exercise of a power of appointment or revocation, or to be diminished by the increase of the class to which he belongs—

Provided that—

(a)   the money so paid or applied for the advancement or benefit of any person shall not exceed altogether in amount one-half of the presumptive or vested share or interest of that person in the trust property; and

(b)   if that person is or becomes absolutely and indefeasibly entitled to a share in the trust property the money so paid or applied shall be brought into account as part of such share; and

(c)   no such payment or application shall be made so as to prejudice any person entitled to any prior life or other interest, whether vested or contingent, in the money paid or applied unless such person is in existence and of full age and consents in writing to such payment or application.

[(2)   This section does not apply to capital money arising under the Settled Land Act 1925.][1]

(3)   This section does not apply to trusts constituted or created before the commencement of this Act.

1   Sub-s (2): substituted by the TLATA 1996, s 25(1), Sch 3, para 3(8).

[246.28]

33.   Protective trusts.—(1)   Where any income, including an annuity or other periodical income payment, is directed to be held on protective trusts for the benefit of any person (in this section called 'the principal beneficiary') for the period of his life or for any less period, then, during that period (in this section called the 'trust period') the said income shall, without prejudice to any prior interest, be held on the following trusts, namely:—

(i)   Upon trust for the principal beneficiary during the trust period or until he, whether before or after the termination of any prior interest, does or attempts to do or suffers any act or thing, or until any event happens, other than an advance under any statutory or express power, whereby, if the said income were payable during the trust period to the principal beneficiary absolutely during that period, he would be deprived of the right to receive the same or any part thereof, in any of which cases, as well as on the termination of the trust period, whichever first happens, this trust of the said income shall fail or determine;

(ii)   If the trust aforesaid fails or determines during the subsistence of the trust period, then, during the residue of that period, the said income shall be held upon trust for the application thereof for the maintenance or support, or otherwise for the benefit, of all or any one or more exclusively of the other or others of the following persons (that is to say)—

(a)   the principal beneficiary and his or her wife or husband, if any, and his or her children or more remote issue, if any; or

(b)   if there is no wife or husband or issue of the principal beneficiary in existence, the principal beneficiary and the persons who would, if he were actually dead, be entitled to the trust property or the income thereof or to the annuity fund, if any, or arrears of the annuity, as the case may be;

as the trustees in their absolute discretion, without being liable to account for the exercise of such discretion, think fit.

(2)   This section does not apply to trusts coming into operation before the commencement of this Act, and has effect subject to any variation of the implied trusts aforesaid contained in the instrument creating the trust.

(3)   Nothing in this section operates to validate any trust which would, if contained in the instrument creating the trust, be liable to be set aside.

[(4)   In relation to the dispositions mentioned in section 19(1) of the Family Law Reform Act 1987, this section shall have effect as if any reference (however expressed) to any relationship between two persons were construed in accordance with section 1 of that Act.][1]

1   Sub-s (4): added by the Family Law Reform Act 1987, s 33(1), Sch 2, as from 4 April 1988.

PART III

APPOINTMENT AND DISCHARGE OF TRUSTEES

[246.29]

34.   Limitation   of   the   number   of   trustees.—(1)   Where,   at   the commencement of this Act, there are more than four trustees of a settlement of land, or more than four trustees holding land on trust for sale, no new trustees shall (except where as a result of the appointment the number is reduced to four or less) be capable of being appointed until the number is reduced to less than four, and thereafter the number shall not be increased beyond four.

(2) In the case of settlements and dispositions [creating trusts of land][1] made or coming into operation after the commencement of this Act—

 (a) the number of trustees thereof shall not in any case exceed four, and where more than four persons are named as such trustees, the four first named (who are able and willing to act) shall alone be the trustees, and the other persons named shall not be trustees unless appointed on the occurrence of a vacancy;
 (b) the number of the trustees shall not be increased beyond four.

(3) This section only applies to settlements and dispositions of land, and the restrictions imposed on the number of trustees do not apply—

 (a) in the case of land vested in trustees for charitable, ecclesiastical, or public purposes; or
 (b) where the net proceeds of the sale of the land are held for like purposes; or
 (c) to the trustees of a term of years absolute limited by a settlement on trusts for raising money, or of a like term created under the statutory remedies relating to annual sums charged on land.

1   Sub-s (2): words in square brackets substituted by the TLATA 1996, s 25(1), Sch 3, para 3(9).

[246.30]
35. Appointments of trustees of settlements and [trustees of land].[1]—[(1) Appointments of new trustees of land and of new trustees of any trust of the proceeds of sale of the land shall, subject to any order of the court, be effected by separate instruments, but in such manner as to secure that the same persons become trustees of land and trustees of the trust of the proceeds of sale.][1]

(2) Where new trustees of a settlement are appointed, a memorandum of the names and addresses of the persons who are for the time being the trustees thereof for the purposes of the Settled Land Act 1925, shall be endorsed on or annexed to the last or only principal vesting instrument by or on behalf of the trustees of the settlement, and such vesting instrument shall, for that purpose, be produced by the person having the possession thereof of the trustees of the settlement when so required.

[(3) Where new trustees of land are appointed, a memorandum of the persons who are for the time being the trustees of the land shall be endorsed on or annexed to the conveyance by which the land was vested in trustees of land; and that conveyance shall be produced to the persons who are for the time being the trustees of the land by the person in possession of it in order for that to be done when the trustees require its production.][1]

(4) This section applies only to settlements and dispositions of land.

1   Sub-ss (1), (3) and words in square brackets in heading substituted by the TLATA 1996, s 25(1), Sch 3, para 3(10)(a), (b), (c).

[246.31]
36. Power of appointing new or additional trustees.—(1) Where a trustee, either original or substituted, and whether appointed by a court or otherwise, is

dead, or remains out of the United Kingdom for more than twelve months, or desires to be discharged from all or any of the trusts or powers reposed in or conferred on him, or refuses or is unfit to act therein, or is incapable of acting therein, or is an infant, then, subject to the restrictions imposed by this Act on the number of trustees—

(a) the person or persons nominated for the purpose of appointing new trustees by the instrument, if any, creating the trust; or

(b) if there is no such person, or no such person able and willing to act, then the surviving or continuing trustees or trustee for the time being, or the personal representatives of the last surviving or continuing trustee;

may, by writing, appoint one or more other persons (whether or not being the persons exercising the power) to be a trustee or trustees in the place of the trustee so deceased remaining out of the United Kingdom, desiring to be discharged, refusing, or being unfit or being incapable, or being an infant, as aforesaid.

(2) Where a trustee has been removed under a power contained in the instrument creating the trust, a new trustee or new trustees may be appointed in the place of the trustee who is removed, as if he were dead, or, in the case of a corporation, as if the corporation desired to be discharged from the trust, and the provisions of this section shall apply accordingly, but subject to the restrictions imposed by this Act on the number of trustees.

(3) Where a corporation being a trustee is or has been dissolved, either before or after the commencement of this Act, then, for the purposes of this section and of any enactment replaced thereby, the corporation shall be deemed to be and to have been from the date of the dissolution incapable of acting in the trusts or powers reposed in or conferred on the corporation.

(4) The power of appointment given by subsection (1) of this section or any similar previous enactment to the personal representatives of a last surviving or continuing trustee shall be and shall be deemed always to have been exercisable by the executors for the time being (whether original or by representation) of such surviving or continuing trustee who have proved the will of their testator or by the administrators for the time being of such trustee without the concurrence of any executor who has renounced or has not proved.

(5) But a sole or last surviving executor intending to renounce, or all the executors where they all intend to renounce, shall have and shall be deemed always to have had power, at any time before renouncing probate, to exercise the power of appointment given by this section, or by any similar previous enactment, if willing to act for that purpose and without thereby accepting the office of executor.

[(6) Where, in the case of any trust, there are not more than three trustees—][1]

(a) the person or persons nominated for the purpose of appointing new trustees by the instrument, if any, creating the trust; or

(b) if there is no such person, or no such person able and willing to act, then the trustee or trustees for the time being;

may, by writing appoint another person or other persons to be an additional trustee or additional trustees, but it shall not be obligatory to appoint any additional trustee, unless the instrument, if any, creating the trust, or any statutory enactment provides to the contrary, nor shall the number of trustees be increased beyond four by virtue of any such appointment.

[(6A) A person who is either—

(a) both a trustee and attorney for the other trustee (if one other), or for both of the other trustees (if two others), under a registered power; or
(b) attorney under a registered power for the trustee (if one) or for both or each of the trustees (if two or three),

may, if subsection (6B) of this section is satisfied in relation to him, make an appointment under subsection (6)(b) of this section on behalf of the trustee or trustees.

(6B) This subsection is satisfied in relation to an attorney under a registered power for one or more trustees if (as attorney under the power)—

(a) he intends to exercise any function of the trustee or trustees by virtue of section 1(1) of the Trustee Delegation Act 1999; or
(b) he intends to exercise any function of the trustee or trustees in relation to any land, capital proceeds of a conveyance of land or income from land by virtue of its delegation to him under section 25 of this Act or the instrument (if any) creating the trust.

(6C) In subsections (6A) and (6B) of this section 'registered power' means a power of attorney created by an instrument which is for the time being registered under section 6 of the Enduring Powers of Attorney Act 1985.

(6D) Subsection (6A) of this section—

(a) applies only if and so far as a contrary intention is not expressed in the instrument creating the power of attorney (or, where more than one, any of them) or the instrument (if any) creating the trust; and
(b) has effect subject to the terms of those instruments.][2]

(7) Every new trustee appointed under this section as well before as after all the trust property becomes by law, or by assurance, or otherwise, vested in him, shall have the same powers, authorities, and discretions, and may in all respects act as if he had been originally appointed a trustee by the instrument, if any, creating the trust.

(8) The provisions of this section relating to a trustee who is dead include the case of a person nominated trustee in a will but dying before the testator, and those relative to a continuing trustee include a refusing or retiring trustee, if willing to act in the execution of the provisions of this section.

[(9) Where a trustee is incapable, by reason of mental disorder within the meaning of [the Mental Health Act 1983], of exercising his functions as trustee and is also entitled in possession to some beneficial interest in the trust property, no appointment of a new trustee in his place shall be made by virtue of paragraph (b) of subsection (1) of this section unless leave to make the appointment has been given by the authority having jurisdiction under [Part VII of the Mental Health Act 1983].][3]

1 Sub-s (6): words in square brackets substituted by the TLATA 1996, s 25(1), Sch 3, para 3(11).
2 Sub-ss (6A)–(6D): inserted by the Trustee Delegation Act 1999, s 8. Note that this applies to powers of attorney created *after* 1 March 2000.
3 Sub-s (9): substituted by the Mental Health Act 1959, s 149(1), Sch 7, Pt I; words in square brackets therein substituted by the Mental Health Act 1983 (MeHA 1983), s 148, Sch 4, para 4.

[246.32]
37.   Supplemental provisions as to appointment of trustees.—(1)   On the
appointment of a trustee for the whole or any part of trust property—

(a)   the number of trustees may, subject to the restrictions imposed by this
Act on the number of trustees, be increased; and

(b)   a separate set of trustees, not exceeding four, may be appointed for any
part of the trust property held on trusts distinct from those relating to any
other part or parts of the trust property, notwithstanding that no new
trustees or trustee are or is to be appointed for other parts of the trust
property, and any existing trustee may be appointed or remain one of
such separate set of trustees, or, if only one trustee was originally
appointed, then, save as hereinafter provided, one separate trustee may
be so appointed; and

(c)   it shall not be obligatory, save as hereinafter provided, to appoint more
than one new trustee where only one trustee was originally appointed, or
to fill up the original number of trustees where more than two trustees
were originally appointed, but, except where only one trustee was
originally appointed, and a sole trustee when appointed will be able to
give valid receipts for all capital money, a trustee shall not be discharged
from his trust unless there will be either a trust corporation or at least two
[persons][1] to act as trustees to perform the trust; and

(d)   any assurance or thing requisite for vesting the trust property, or any part
thereof, in a sole trustee, or jointly in the persons who are the trustees,
shall be executed or done.

(2)   Nothing in this Act shall authorise the appointment of a sole trustee, not
being a trust corporation, where the trustee, when appointed, would not be able
to give valid receipts for all capital money arising under the trust.

1   Sub-s (1): in para (c) word in square brackets substituted by the TLATA 1996, s 25(1), Sch 3,
para 3(12).

[246.33]
38.   Evidence as to a vacancy in a trust.—(1)   A statement, contained in any
instrument coming into operation after the commencement of this Act by which
a new trustee is appointed for any purpose connected with land, to the effect that
a trustee has remained out of the United Kingdom for more than twelve months
or refuses or is unfit to act, or is incapable of acting, or that he is not entitled to a
beneficial interest in the trust property in possession, shall, in favour of a
purchaser of a legal estate, be conclusive evidence of the matter stated.
(2)   In favour of such purchaser any appointment of a new trustee depending on
that statement, and any vesting declaration, express or implied, consequent on
the appointment, shall be valid.

[246.34]
39.   Retirement of trustee without a new appointment.—(1)   Where a
trustee is desirous of being discharged from the trust, and after his discharge
there will be either a trust corporation or at least two [persons][1] to act as trustees
to perform the trust, then, if such trustee as aforesaid by deed declares that he is
desirous of being discharged from the trust, and if his co-trustees and such other
person, if any, as is empowered to appoint trustees, by deed consent to the

discharge of the trustee, and to the vesting in the co-trustees alone of the trust property, the trustee desirous of being discharged shall be deemed to have retired from the trust, and shall, by the deed, be discharged therefrom under this Act, without any new trustee being appointed in his place.

(2) Any assurance or thing requisite for vesting the trust property in the continuing trustees alone shall be excecuted or done.

1   Sub-s (1): word in square brackets substituted by the TLATA 1996, s 25(1), Sch 3, para 3(13).

[246.35]
40.   Vesting of trust property in new or continuing trustees.—(1)   Where by a deed a new trustee is appointed to perform any trust, then—

(a)   if the deed contains a declaration by the appointor to the effect that any estate or interest in any land subject to the trust, or in any chattel so subject, or right to recover or receive any debt or other thing in action so subject, shall vest in the persons who by virtue of the deed become or are the trustees for performing the trust, the deed shall operate, without any conveyance or assignment, to vest in those persons as joint tenants and for the purposes of the trust the estate interest or right to which the declaration relates; and

(b)   if the deed is made after the commencement of this Act and does not contain such a declaration, the deed shall, subject to any express provision to the contrary therein contained, operate as if it had contained such a declaration by the appointor extending to all the estates interests and rights with respect to which a declaration could have been made.

(2)   Where by a deed a retiring trustee is discharged under [section 39 of this Act or section 19 of the Trusts of Land and Appointment of Trustees Act 1996]¹ without a new trustee being appointed, then—

(a)   if the deed contains such a declaration as aforesaid by the retiring and continuing trustees, and by the other person, if any, empowered to appoint trustees, the deed shall, without any conveyance or assignment, operate to vest in the continuing trustees alone, as joint tenants, and for the purposes of the trust, the estate, interest, or right to which the declaration relates; and

(b)   if the deed is made after the commencement of this Act and does not contain such a declaration, the deed shall, subject to any express provision to the contrary therein contained, operate as if it had contained such a declaration by such persons as aforesaid extending to all the estates, interests and rights with respect to which a declaration could have been made.

(3)   An express vesting declaration, whether made before or after the commencement of this Act, shall, notwithstanding that the estate, interest or right to be vested is not expressly referred to, and provided that the other statutory requirements were or are complied with, operate and be deemed always to have operated (but without prejudice to any express provision to the contrary contained in the deed of appointment or discharge) to vest in the persons respectively referred to in subsections (1) and (2) of this section, as the case may require, such estates, interests and rights as are capable of being and ought to be vested in those persons.

(4) This section does not extend—

(a) to land conveyed by way of mortgage for securing money subject to the trust, except land conveyed on trust for securing debentures or debenture stock;

(b) to land held under a lease which contains any covenant, condition or agreement against assignment or disposing of the land without licence or consent, unless, prior to the execution of the deed containing expressly or impliedly the vesting declaration, the requisite licence or consent has been obtained, or unless, by virtue of any statute or rule of law, the vesting declaration, express or implied, would not operate as a breach of covenant or give rise to a forfeiture;

(c) to any share, stock, annuity or property which is only transferable in books kept by a company or other body, or in manner directed by or under an Act of Parliament.

In this subsection lease includes an underlease and an agreement for a lease or underlease.

(5) For purposes of registration of the deed in any registry, the person or persons making the declaration expressly or impliedly, shall be deemed the conveying party or parties, and the conveyance shall be deemed to be made by him or them under a power conferred by this Act.

(6) This section applies to deeds of appointment or discharge executed on or after the first day of January, eighteen hundred and eighty-two.

1   Sub-s (2): words in square brackets substituted by the TLATA 1996, s 25(1), Sch 3, para 3(14).

[246.36]
68. Definitions.—(1) In this Act, unless the context otherwise requires, the following expressions have the meanings hereby assigned to them respectively, that is to say:—

(1) 'Authorised investments' mean investments authorised by the instrument, if any, creating the trust for the investment of money subject to the trust, or by law;

*   *   *   *   *

(11) 'Property' includes real and personal property, and any estate share and interest in any property, real or personal, and any debt, and any thing in action, and any other right or interest, whether in possession or not;

(12) 'Rights' include estates and interests;

(13) 'Securities' include stocks, funds, and shares; . . . and 'securities payable to bearer' include securities transferable by delivery or by delivery and endorsement;[1]

*   *   *   *   *

(17) 'Trust' does not include the duties incident to an estate conveyed by way of mortgage, but with this exception the expressions 'trust' and 'trustee' extend to implied and constructive trusts, and to cases where the trustee has a beneficial interest in the trust property, and to the duties incident to the office of a personal representative, and 'trustee' where the context

admits, includes a personal representative, and 'new trustee' includes an additional trustee;

(18) 'Trust corporation' means the Public Trustee or a corporation either appointed by the court in any particular case to be a trustee, or entitled by rules made under subsection (3) of section four of the Public Trustee Act 1906, to act as custodian trustee;[2]

* * * * *

(20) 'United Kingdom' means Great Britain and Northern Ireland.

1   The words omitted from para (13) were repealed by the Administration of Justice Act 1965, s 17(1), Sch 1.
2   The relevant rule is r 30 of the Public Trustee Rules 1912 (para **[246.58]**). The definition is enlarged so as to include the Treasury Solicitor, the Official Solicitor, trustees in bankruptcy and certain charitable corporations by the LP(A)A 1926, s 3(1), para **[246.56]** and is further enlarged by the Charities Act 1993 (CA 1993), s 35 (para **[246.84]**) so as to include certain corporations appointed by the Charity Commission.

* * * * *

[246.37]
69. Application of Act.—(1)   This Act, except where otherwise expressly provided, applies to trusts including, so far as this Act applies thereto, executorships and administratorships constituted or created either before or after the commencement of this Act.
(2)   The powers conferred by this Act on trustees are in addition to the powers conferred by the instrument, if any, creating the trust, but those powers, unless otherwise stated, apply if and so far only as a contrary intention is not expressed in the instrument, if any, creating the trust, and have effect subject to the terms of that instrument.

* * * * *

LAW OF PROPERTY ACT 1925

(15 & 16 Geo 5 c 20)   [9 April 1925]

[246.38]
Note. This Act came into force on 1 January 1926.

PART I

GENERAL PRINCIPLES AS TO LEGAL ESTATES, EQUITABLE INTERESTS AND POWERS

* * * * *

Infants and Lunatics

* * * * *

[246.39]
21.   Receipts by married infants. A married infant shall have power to give valid receipts for all income (including statutory accumulations of income made during the minority) to which the infant may be entitled in like manner as if the infant were of full age.

*   *   *   *   *

[246.39A]
[Section 23 (duration of trusts for sale) and the heading to it repealed by the Trusts of Land and Appointment of Trustees Act 1996, s 25(2), Sch 4: see now s 16 of the 1996 Act at para **[246.102]**.*]*

Trusts of land[1]

[246.39B]
24.   Appointment of trustees of land.—(1)   The persons having power to appoint new trustees of land shall be bound to appoint the same persons (if any) who are for the time being trustees of any trust of the proceeds of sale of the land.
(2)   A purchaser shall not be concerned to see that subsection (1) of this section has been complied with.
(3)   This section applies whether the trust of land and the trust of proceeds of sale are created, or arise, before or after the commencement of this Act.[1]

1   The heading and the entire section were substituted by the TLATA 1996, s 25(1), Sch 3, para 4(7).

[246.39C]
[Sections 25 (power to postpone sale) and 26 (consents to the execution of a trust for sale) repealed by Trusts of Land and Appointment of Trustees Act 1996, s 25(2), Sch 4: see now ss 4 and 10 respectively of the 1996 Act at paras **[246.89]** *and* **[246.96]**.*]*

[246.39D]
27.   Purchaser not to be concerned with the trusts of the proceeds of sale which are to be paid to two or more trustees or to a trust corporation.—[(1) A purchaser of a legal estate from trustees of land shall not be concerned with the trusts affecting the land, the net income of the land or the proceeds of sale of the land whether or not those trusts are declared by the same instrument as that by which the trust of land is created.][1]
(2)   Notwithstanding anything to the contrary in the instrument (if any) creating a [trust][2] of land or in [any trust affecting the net proceeds of sale of the land if it is sold],[2] the proceeds of sale or other capital money shall not be paid to or applied by the direction of fewer than two persons as [trustees],[2] except where the trustee is a trust corporation, but this subsection does not affect the right of a sole personal representative as such to give valid receipts for, or direct the application of, proceeds of sale or other capital money, nor, except where capital money arises on the transaction, render it necessary to have more than one trustee.

1   Sub-s (1): substituted by the TLATA 1996, s 25(1), Sch 3, para 4(8)(a).
2   Sub-s (2): words in square brackets substituted by the TLATA 1996, s 25(1), Sch 3, para 4(8)(b).

[246.39E]
[Sections 28 (powers of management, &c. conferred on trustees of sale), 29 (delegation of powers of management by trustees for sale), and 30 (powers of court where trustees for sale refuse to exercise powers) repealed by the Trusts of Land and Appointment of Trustees Act 1996, s 25(2), Sch 4: see now ss 6 and 7, 9 and 14 and 15 of the 1996 Act respectively at paras [246.91], [246.92], [246.94], [246.100] and [246.101].]

[246.39F]
31. [Trust]¹ of mortgaged property where right of redemption is barred.—(1)   Where any property, vested in trustees by way of security, becomes, by virtue of the statutes of limitation, or of an order for foreclosure or otherwise, discharged from the right of redemption, it shall be held by them [in trust—

    (a)   to apply the income from the property in the same manner as interest paid on the mortgage debt would have been applicable; and
    (b)   if the property is sold, to apply the net proceeds of sale, after payment of costs and expenses, in the same manner as repayment of the mortgage debt would have been applicable.]¹

[(2)   Subsection (1) of this section]² operates without prejudice to any rule of law relating to the apportionment of capital and income between tenant for life and remainderman.
(3)   . . .³
[(4)   Where—

    (a)   the mortgage money is capital money for the purposes of the Settled Land Act 1925;
    (b)   land other than any forming the whole or part of the property mentioned in subsection (1) of this section is, or is deemed to be, subject to the settlement; and
    (c)   the tenant for life or statutory owner requires the trustees to execute with respect to land forming the whole or part of that property a vesting deed such as would have been required in relation to the land if it had been acquired on a purchase with capital money,

the trustees shall execute such a vesting deed.]⁴
(5)   This section applies whether the right of redemption was discharged before or after the first day of January, nineteen hundred and twelve, but has effect without prejudice to any dealings or arrangements made before that date.

1   Words in square brackets in section heading and in sub-s (1) substituted by the TLATA 1996, s 5(1), Sch 2, para 1(2), (6).
2   Sub-s (2): words in square brackets substituted by the TLATA 1996, s 5(1), Sch 2, para 1(3).
3   Sub-s (3): repealed by the TLATA 1996, ss 5(1), 25(2), Sch 3, para 1(4), Sch 4.
4   Sub-s (4): substituted by the TLATA 1996, s 5(1), Sch 2, para 1(5).

[246.39G]
[Section 32 (implied trust for sale in personalty settlements) repealed in relation to land purchased on or after 1 January 1997 whether trust or will came into operation before or after that date by Trusts of Land and Appointment of Trustees Act 1996, ss 5(1), 25(2), Sch 2, para 2(1), (2), Sch 4.]

[246.39H]
33.   Application of Part I to personal representatives. The provisions of this Part of this Act relating to [trustees of land][1] apply to personal representatives holding [land in trust],[1] but without prejudice to their rights and powers for purposes of administration.

1   Words in square brackets substituted by the TLATA 1996, s 25(1), Sch 3, para 4(9).

Undivided Shares and Joint Ownership

[246.39I]
34.   Effect of future dispositions to tenants in common.—(1)   An undivided share in land shall not be capable of being created except as provided by the Settled Land Act 1925 or as hereinafter mentioned.
(2)   Where, after the commencement of this Act, land is expressed to be conveyed to any persons in undivided shares and those persons are of full age, the conveyance shall (notwithstanding anything to the contrary in this Act) operate as if the land had been expressed to be conveyed to the grantees, or, if there are more than four grantees, to the four first named in the conveyance, as joint tenants [in trust for the persons interested in the land][1]:
    Provided that, where the conveyance is made by way of mortgage the land shall vest in the grantees or such four of them as aforesaid for a term of years absolute (as provided by this Act) as joint tenants subject to cesser on redemption in like manner as if the mortgage money had belonged to them on a joint account, but without prejudice to the beneficial interests in the mortgage money and interest.
(3)   A devise bequest or testamentary appointment, coming into operation after the commencement of this Act, of land to two or more persons in undivided shares shall operate as a devise bequest or appointment of the land to . . .[2] the personal representatives of the testator, and . . .[2] (but without prejudice to the rights and powers of the personal representatives for purposes of administration) [in trust for the persons interested in the land].[2]
[(3A)   In subsections (2) and (3) of this section references to the persons interested in the land include persons interested as trustees or personal representatives (as well as persons beneficially interested).][3]
(4)   . . .[4]

1   Sub-s (2): words in square brackets substituted with retrospective effect by the TLATA 1996, s 5(1), Sch 2, para 3(2), (6).
2   Sub-s (3): words omitted repealed and words in square brackets substituted, in each case with retrospective effect, by the TLATA 1996, ss 591), 25(2), Sch 2, para 3(3), (6), Sch 4.
3   Sub-s (3A): inserted with retrospective effect by the TLATA 1996, s 5(1), Sch 2, para 3(4), (6).
4   Sub-s (4): repealed with retrospective effect by the TLATA 1996, ss 5(1), 25(2), Sch 2, para 3(5), (6), Sch 4.

[246.39J]

[*Section 35 (meaning of the statutory trusts) repealed by Trusts of Land and Appointment of Trustees Act 1996, s 25(2), Sch 4.*]

[246.39K]

36. Joint tenancies.—(1) Where a legal estate (not being settled land) is beneficially limited to or held in trust for any persons as joint tenants, the same shall be held [in trust],[1] in like manner as if the persons beneficially entitled were tenants in common, but not so as to sever their joint tenancy in equity.

(2) No severance of a joint tenancy of a legal estate, so as to create a tenancy in common in land, shall be permissible, whether by operation of law or otherwise, but this subsection does not affect the right of a joint tenant to release his interest to the other joint tenants, or the right to sever a joint tenancy in an equitable interest whether or not the legal estate is vested in the joint tenants:

Provided that, where a legal estate (not being settled land) is vested in joint tenants beneficially, and any tenant desires to sever the joint tenancy in equity, he shall give to the other joint tenants a notice in writing of such desire or do such other acts or things as would, in the case of personal estate, have been effectual to sever the tenancy in equity, and thereupon [the land shall be held in trust on terms][2] which would have been requisite for giving effect to the beneficial interests if there had been an actual severance.

Nothing in this Act affects the right of a survivor of joint tenants, who is solely and beneficially interested, to deal with his legal estate as if it were not held [in trust].[2]

(3) Without prejudice to the right of a joint tenant to release his interest to the other joint tenants no severance of a mortgage term or trust estate, so as to create a tenancy in common, shall be permissible.

1   Sub-s (1): words in square brackets substituted with retrospective effect by the TLATA 1996, s 5(1), Sch 2, para 4(2), (4).
2   Sub-s (2): words in square brackets substituted with retrospective effect by the TLATA 1996, s 5, Sch 2, para 4(3), (4).

*   *   *   *   *

PART II

CONTRACTS, CONVEYANCES AND OTHER INSTRUMENTS

*   *   *   *   *

Conveyances and other Instruments

*   *   *   *   *

[246.40]

61. Construction of expressions used in deeds and other instruments. In all deeds, contracts, wills, orders and other instruments executed, made or coming into operation after the commencement of this Act, unless the context otherwise requires—

(a)   'Month' means calendar month;
(b)   'Person' includes a corporation;
(c)   The singular includes the plural and vice versa;
(d)   The masculine includes the feminine and vice versa.

*   *   *   *   *

PART VII

PERPETUITIES AND ACCUMULATIONS

Perpetuities

*   *   *   *   *

[246.41]
163.   *Validation of certain gifts void for remoteness.* [1]—*(1)   Where in a will, settlement or other instrument the absolute vesting either of capital or income of property, or the ascertainment of a beneficiary or class of beneficiaries, is made to depend on the attainment by the beneficiary or members of the class of an age exceeding twenty-one years, and thereby the gift to that beneficiary or class or any member thereof, or any gift over, remainder, executory limitation, or trust arising on the total or partial failure of the original gift, is, or but for this section would be, rendered void for remoteness, the will, settlement, or other instrument shall take effect for the purposes of such gift, gift over, remainder, executory limitation, or trust as if the absolute vesting or ascertainment aforesaid had been made to depend on the beneficiary or member of the class attaining the age of twenty-one years, and that age shall be substituted for the age stated in the will, settlement, or other instrument.*
(2)   This section applies to any instrument executed after the commencement of this Act and to any testamentary appointment (whether made in exercise of a general or special power), devise, or bequest contained in the will of a person dying after such commencement, whether the will is made before or after such commencement.
(3)   This section applies without prejudice to any provision whereby the absolute vesting or ascertainment is also made to depend on the marriage of any person, or any other event which may occur before the age stated in the will, settlement, or other instrument is attained.

1   This section was repealed by the PAA 1964, s 4(6) (para **[246.62]**) but only as regards instruments taking effect after the commencement of the 1964 Act, ie 16 July 1964 (see s 15(5) of the 1964 Act at para **[246.73]**).

Accumulations

[246.42]
164.   General restrictions on accumulation of income.—(1)   No person may by any instrument or otherwise settle or dispose of any property in such manner that the income thereof shall, save as hereinafter mentioned, be wholly

or partially accumulated for any longer period than one of the following, namely:—

(a) the life of the grantor or settlor; or

(b) a term of twenty-one years from the death of the grantor, settlor or testator; or

(c) the duration of the minority or respective minorities of any person or persons living or en ventre sa mere at the death of the grantor, settlor or testator; or

(d) the duration of the minority or respective minorities only of any person or persons who under the limitations of the instrument directing the accumulations would, for the time being, if of full age, be entitled to the income directed to be accumulated.

In every case where any accumulation is directed otherwise than as aforesaid, the direction shall (save as hereinafter mentioned) be void; and the income of the property directed to be accumulated shall, so long as the same is directed to be accumulated contrary to this section, go to and be received by the person or persons who would have been entitled thereto if such accumulation had not been directed.

(2) This section does not extend to any provision—

(i) for payment of the debts of any grantor, settlor, testator or other person;

(ii) for raising portions for—

(a) any child, children or remoter issue of any grantor, settlor or testator; or

(b) any child, children or remoter issue of a person taking any interest under any settlement or other disposition directing the accumulations or to whom any interest is thereby limited;

(iii) respecting the accumulation of the produce of timber or wood;

and accordingly such provisions may be made as if no statutory restrictions on accumulation of income had been imposed.

(3) The restrictions imposed by this section apply to instruments made on or after the twenty-eighth day of July, eighteen hundred, but in the case of wills only where the testator was living and of testamentary capacity after the end of one year from that date.[1]

---

1   This section has been amended by the PAA 1964, s 13 (para **[246.71]**) which specifies two further periods of lawful accumulation.

[246.43]

165. Qualification of restrictions on accumulation. Where accumulations of surplus income are made during a minority under any statutory power or under the general law, the period for which such accumulations are made is not (whether the trust was created or the accumulations were made before or after the commencement of this Act) to be taken into account in determining the periods for which accumulations are permitted to be made by the last preceding section, and accordingly an express trust for accumulation for any other permitted period shall not be deemed to have been invalidated or become invalid, by reason of accumulations also having been made as aforesaid during such minority.

[246.44]
166.   Restriction on accumulation for the purchase of land.—(1) No person may settle or dispose of any property in such manner that the income thereof shall be wholly or partially accumulated for the purchase of land only, for any longer period than the duration of the minority or respective minorities of any person or persons who, under the limitations of the instrument directing the accumulation, would for the time being, if of full age, be entitled to the income so directed to be accumulated.

(2)   This section does not, nor do the enactments which it replaces, apply to accumulations to be held as capital money for the purposes of the Settled Land Act 1925 or the enactments replaced by that Act, whether or not the accumulations are primarily liable to be laid out in the purchase of land.

(3)   This section applies to settlements and dispositions made after the twenty-seventh day of June eighteen hundred and ninety-two.

*   *   *   *   *

PART XII

CONSTRUCTION, JURISDICTION, AND GENERAL PROVISIONS

*   *   *   *   *

[246.44A]
205.   General definitions.—(1) In this Act unless the context otherwise requires, the following expressions have the meanings hereby assigned to them respectively, that is to say:—

*   *   *   *   *

   (ix) 'Land' includes land of any tenure, and mines and minerals, whether or not held apart from the surface, buildings or parts of buildings (whether the division is horizontal, vertical or made in any other way) and other corporeal hereditaments; also a manor, an advowson, and a rent and other incorporeal hereditaments, and an easement, right, privilege, or benefit in, over, or derived from land; [but not an undivided share in land][1]; and 'mines and minerals' include any strata or seam of minerals or substances in or under any land, and powers of working and getting the same [but not an undivided share thereof][1]; and 'manor' includes a lordship, and reputed manor or lordship; and 'hereditament' means any real property which on an intestacy occurring before the commencement of this Act might have devolved upon an heir;

*   *   *   *   *

---

1   The words in square brackets were repealed by the TLATA 1996, s 25(2), Sch 4, presumably on the basis that with the abolition of the doctrine of conversion in relation to land held on trust for sale by s 3 of that Act (para **[246.88]**), undivided shares in land constitute real property.

ADMINISTRATION OF ESTATES ACT 1925

(15 & 16 Geo 5 c 23)   [9 April 1925]

[246.45]
Note. This Act came into force on 1 January 1926.

*   *   *   *   *

[246.46]
34. Administration of assets.—*(1) Where the estate of a deceased person is insolvent, his real and personal estate shall be administered in accordance with the rules set out in Part I. of the First Schedule to this Act.*[1]
(2) . . .[2]
(3)   Where the estate of a deceased person is solvent his real and personal estate shall, subject to rules of court and the provisions hereinafter contained as to charges on property of the deceased, and to the provisions, if any, contained in his will, be applicable towards the discharge of the funeral, testamentary and administration expenses, debts and liabilities payable thereout in the order mentioned in Part II of the First Schedule to this Act.

1   Sub-s (1): repealed by the Insolvency Act 1985, s 235(3), Sch 10, Pt III with effect from 29 December 1986. It is replaced by rules under the Insolvency Act 1986, s 421; see the Administration of Insolvent Estates of Deceased Persons Order 1986, SI 1986/1999.
2   Sub-s (2): repealed with savings by the Administration of Estates Act 1971, s 12(2), (4), (6), Sch 2, Pt II.

[246.47]
35. Charges on property of deceased to be paid primarily out of the property charged.—(1)   Where a person dies possessed of, or entitled to, or, under a general power of appointment (including the statutory power to dispose of entailed interests) by his will disposes of, an interest in property, which at the time of his death is charged with the payment of money, whether by way of legal mortgage, equitable charge or otherwise (including a lien for unpaid purchase money), and the deceased has not by will deed or other document signified a contrary or other intention, the interest so charged, shall as between the different persons claiming through the deceased, be primarily liable for the payment of the charge; and every part of the said interest, according to its value, shall bear a proportionate part of the charge on the whole thereof.
(2)   Such contrary or other intention shall not be deemed to be signified—

   (a)   by a general direction for the payment of debts or of all the debts of the testator out of his personal estate, or his residuary real and personal estate, or his residuary real estate; or
   (b)   by a charge of debts upon any such estate;

unless such intention is further signified by words expressly or by necessary implication referring to all or some part of the charge.
(3)   Nothing in this section affects the right of a person entitled to the charge to obtain payment or satisfaction thereof either out of the other assets of the deceased or otherwise.

*   *   *   *   *

[246.48]
39. Powers of management.—(1) In dealing with the real and personal estate of the deceased his personal representatives shall, for purposes of administration, or during a minority of any beneficiary or the subsistence of any life interest, or until the period of distribution arrives, have—

(i) the same powers and discretions, including power to raise money by mortgage or charge (whether or not by deposit of documents), as a personal representative had before the commencement of this Act, with respect to personal estate vested in him, and such power of raising money by mortgage may in the case of land be exercised by way of legal mortgage; and

(ii) all the powers, discretions and duties conferred or imposed by law on trustees holding land upon an effectual trust for sale (including power to overreach equitable interests and powers as if the same affected the proceeds of sale); and

(iii) all the powers conferred by statute on trustees for sale, and so that every contract entered into by a personal representative shall be binding on and be enforceable against and by the personal representative for the time being of the deceased, and may be carried into effect, or be varied or rescinded by him, and, in the case of a contract entered into by a predecessor, as if it had been entered into by himself.

(2) Nothing in this section shall affect the right of any person to require an assent or conveyance to be made.

(3) This section applies whether the testator or intestate died before or after the commencement of this Act.

[246.49]
40. Powers of personal representative for raising money, etc.—(1) For giving effect to beneficial interests the personal representative may limit or demise land for a term of years absolute, with or without impeachment for waste, to trustees on usual trusts for raising or securing any principal sum and the interest thereon for which the land, or any part thereof, is liable, and may limit or grant a rentcharge for giving effect to an annual or periodical sum for which the land or the income thereof or any part thereof is liable.

(2) This section applies whether the testator or intestate died before or after the commencement of this Act.

[246.50]
41. Powers of personal representative as to appropriation.—(1) The personal representative may appropriate any part of the real or personal estate, including things in action, of the deceased in the actual condition or state of investment thereof at the time of appropriation in or towards satisfaction of any legacy bequeathed by the deceased, or of any other interest or share in his property, whether settled or not, as to the personal representative may seem just and reasonable, according to the respective rights of the persons interested in the property of the deceased:

Provided that—

(i) an appropriation shall not be made under this section so as to affect prejudicially any specific devise or bequest;

(ii) an appropriation of property, whether or not being an investment authorised by law or by the will, if any, of the deceased for the investment of money subject to the trust, shall not (save as hereinafter mentioned) be made under this section except with the following consents:—

    (a)   when made for the benefit of a person absolutely and beneficially entitled in possession, the consent of that person;

    (b)   when made in respect of any settled legacy share or interest, the consent of either the trustee thereof, if any (not being also the personal representative), or the person who may for the time being be entitled to the income:

    If the person whose consent is so required as aforesaid is an infant or [is incapable by reason of mental disorder within the meaning of [the Mental Health Act 1983], of managing and administering his property and affairs]¹ the consent shall be given on his behalf by his parents or parent, testamentary or other guardian . . . or receiver, or if, in the case of an infant, there is no such parent or guardian, by the court on the application of his next friend;

(iii) no consent (save of such trustee as aforesaid) shall be required on behalf of a person who may come into existence after the time of appropriation, or who cannot be found or ascertained at that time;

(iv) if no [receiver is acting for a person suffering from mental disorder]¹ then, if the appropriation is of an investment authorised by law or by the will, if any, of the deceased for the investment of money subject to the trust, no consent shall be required on behalf of the [said person]¹

(v) if, independently of the personal representative, there is no trustee of a settled legacy share or interest, and no person of full age and capacity entitled to the income thereof, no consent shall be required to an appropriation in respect of such legacy share or interest, provided that the appropriation is of an investment authorised as aforesaid.

[(1A)   The county court has jurisdiction under proviso (ii) to subsection (1) of this section where the estate in respect of which the application is made does not exceed in amount or value the county court limit.]²

(2)   Any property duly appropriated under the powers conferred by this section shall thereafter be treated as an authorised investment, and may be retained or dealt with accordingly.

(3)   For the purposes of such appropriation, the personal representative may ascertain and fix the value of the respective parts of the real and personal estate and the liabilities of the deceased as he may think fit, and shall for that purpose employ a duly qualified valuer in any case where such employment may be necessary; and may make any conveyance (including an assent) which may be requisite for giving effect to the appropriation.

(4)   An appropriation made pursuant to this section shall bind all persons interested in the property of the deceased whose consent is not hereby made requisite.

(5)   The personal representative shall, in making the appropriation, have regard to the rights of any person who may thereafter come into existence, or who

cannot be found or ascertained at the time of appropriation, and of any other person whose consent is not required by this section.

(6)   This section does not prejudice any other power of appropriation conferred by law or by the will (if any) of the deceased, and takes effect with any extended powers conferred by the will (if any) of the deceased, and where an appropriation is made under this section, in respect of a settled legacy, share or interest, the property appropriated shall remain subject to all trusts for sale and powers of leasing, disposition, and management or varying investments which would have been applicable thereto or to the legacy, share or interest in respect of which the appropriation is made, if no such appropriation had been made.

(7)   If after any real estate has been appropriated in purported exercise of the powers conferred by this section, the person to whom it was conveyed disposes of it or any interest therein, then, in favour of a purchaser, the appropriation shall be deemed to have been made in accordance with the requirements of this section and after all requisite consents, if any, had been given.

(8)   In this section, a settled legacy, share or interest includes any legacy, share or interest to which a person is not absolutely entitled in possession at the date of the appropriation, also an annuity, and 'purchaser' means a purchaser for money or money's worth.

(9)   This section applies whether the deceased died intestate or not, and whether before or after the commencement of this Act, and extends to property over which a testator exercises a general power of appointment, including the statutory power to dispose of entailed interests, and authorises the setting apart of a fund to answer an annuity by means of the income of that fund or otherwise.

1   The words in the first (outer) pair of square brackets in sub-s (1)(ii) together with the words in square brackets in sub-s (1)(iv), were substituted, and the words omitted from sub-s (1)(ii) were repealed, by the MHA 1959, s 149(1), Sch 7, Pt I. The words in the second (inner) pair of square brackets in sub-s (1)(ii) were further substituted by the MeHA 1983, s 148, Sch 4, para 7.

2   Sub-s (1A): inserted by the CCA 1984, s 148(1), Sch 2, Pt III, para 13.

[246.51]
42.   Power to appoint trustees of infants' property.—(1)   Where an infant is absolutely entitled under the will or on the intestacy of a person dying before or after the commencement of this Act (in this subsection called 'the deceased') to a devise or legacy, or to the residue of the estate of the deceased, or any share therein, and such devise, legacy, residue or share is not under the will, if any, of the deceased, devised or bequeathed to trustees for the infant, the personal representatives of the deceased may appoint a trust corporation or two or more individuals not exceeding four (whether or not including the personal representatives or one or more of the personal representatives), to be the trustee or trustees of such devise, legacy, residue or share for the infant, and to be trustees of any land devised or any land being or forming part of such residue or share for the purposes of the Settled Land Act 1925, and of the statutory provisions relating to the management of land during a minority, and may execute or do any assurance or thing requisite for vesting such devise, legacy, residue or share in the trustee or trustees so appointed.

On such appointment the personal representatives, as such, shall be discharged from all further liability in respect of such devise, legacy, residue, or share, and the same may be retained in its existing condition or state of investment, or may be converted into money, and such money may be invested in any authorised investment.

(2) Where a personal representative has before the commencement of this Act retained or sold any such devise, legacy, residue or share, and invested the same or the proceeds thereof in any investments in which he was authorised to invest money subject to the trust, then, subject to any order of the court made before such commencement, he shall not be deemed to have incurred any liability on that account, or by reason of not having paid or transferred the money or property into court.

*   *   *   *   *

[246.52]
55. Definitions. In this Act, unless the context otherwise requires, the following expressions have the meanings hereby assigned to them respectively, that is to say—
(1)—

(i)   'Administration' means, with reference to the real and personal estate of a deceased person, letters of administration whether general or limited, or with the will annexed or otherwise;

(ii)   'Administrator' means a person to whom administration is granted;

(iii)   'Conveyance includes a mortgage, charge by way of legal mortgage, lease, assent, vesting, declaration, vesting instrument, disclaimer, release and every other assurance of property or of an interest therein by any instrument, except a will, and convey has a corresponding meaning, and disposition includes a conveyance also a devise bequest and an appointment of property contained in a will, and dispose of has a corresponding meaning;

[(iiiA)   'the County Court limit', in relation to any enactment contained in this Act, means the amount for the time being specified by an Order in Council under section 145 of the County Courts Act 1984 as the county court limit for the purposes of that enactment (or, where no such Order in Council has been made, the corresponding limit specified by Order in Council under section 192 of the County Courts Act 1959);][1]

(iv)   'the Court' means the High Court and also the county court, where that court has jurisdiction . . .;[2]

(v)   'Income' includes rents and profits;

(vi)   'Intestate' includes a person who leaves a will but dies intestate as to some beneficial interest in his real or personal estate;

[(via)   'Land' has the same meaning as in the Law of Property Act 1925;][3]

(vii)   'Legal estates' mean the estates charges and interests in or over land (subsisting or created at law) which are by statute authorised to subsist or to be created at law; and equitable interests mean all other interests and charges in or over land . . . ;[4]

(viii)   '[Person of unsound mind]' includes a [person of unsound mind] whether so found or not, and in relation to a [person of unsound mind] not so found; . . . and defective includes every person affected by the provisions of section one hundred and sixteen of the Lunacy

Act 1890, as extended by section sixty-four of the Mental Deficiency Act 1913, and for whose benefit a receiver has been appointed;[5]

(ix)   'Pecuniary legacy' includes an annuity, a general legacy, a demonstrative legacy so far as it is not discharged out of the designated property, and any other general direction by a testator for the payment of money, including all death duties free from which any devise, bequest, or payment is made to take effect;

(x)   'Personal chattels' mean carriages, horses, stable furniture and effects (not used for business purposes), motor cars and accessories (not used for business purposes), garden effects, domestic animals, plate, plated articles, linen, china, glass, books, pictures, prints, furniture, jewellery, articles of household or personal use or ornament, musical and scientific instruments and apparatus, wines, liquors and consumable stores, but do not include any chattels used at the death of the intestate for business purposes nor money or securities for money;

(xi)   'Personal representative' means the executor, original or by representation, or administrator for the time being of a deceased person, and as regards any liability for the payment of death duties includes any person who takes possession of or intermeddles with the property of a deceased person without the authority of the personal representatives or the court, and executor includes a person deemed to be appointed executor as respects settled land;

(xii)   'Possession' includes the receipt of rents and profits or the right to receive the same, if any;

(xiii)   'Prescribed' means prescribed by rules of court . . . ;[6]

(xiv)   'Probate' means the probate of a will;

(xv)   [*Repealed by the Law of Property (Miscellaneous Provisions) Act 1994, s 21(2), Sch 2.*]

(xvi)   *(Repealed by the Supreme Court Act 1981, s 152(4), Sch 7.)*

(xvii)   'Property' includes a thing in action and any interest in real or personal property;

(xviii)   'Purchaser' means a lessee, mortgagee, or other person who in good faith acquires an interest in property for valuable consideration, also an intending purchaser and valuable consideration includes marriage, but does not include a nominal consideration in money;

(xix)   'Real estate' save as provided in Part IV of this Act means real estate, including chattels real, which by virtue of Part I of this Act devolves on the personal representative of a deceased person;

(xx)   'Representation means the probate of a will and administration, and the expression taking out representation refers to the obtaining of the probate of a will or of the grant of administration;

(xxi)   'Rent' includes a rent service or a rentcharge, or other rent, toll, duty, or annual or periodical payment in money or moneys worth, issuing out of or charged upon land, but does not include mortgage interest; and rentcharge includes a fee farm rent;

(xxii)   [*Repealed by the Supreme Court Act 1981, s 152(4), Sch 7.*]

(xxiii)   'Securities' include stocks, funds, or shares;

(xxiv) 'Tenant for life', 'statutory owner', . . .⁷ 'settled land', 'settlement', 'trustees of the settlement', 'term of years absolute', 'death duties', and 'legal mortgage', have the same meanings as in the Settled Land Act 1925, and 'entailed interest' and 'charge by way of legal mortgage' have the same meanings as in the Law of Property Act 1925;

(xxv) 'Treasury solicitor' means the solicitor for the affairs of His Majesty's Treasury, and includes the solicitor for the affairs of the Duchy of Lancaster;

(xxvi) 'Trust corporation' means the public trustee or a corporation either appointed by the court in any particular case to be a trustee or entitled by rules made under subsection (3) of section four of the Public Trustee Act 1906, to act as custodian trustee;⁸

(xxvii) [*Repealed by the Trusts of Land and Appointment of Trustees Act 1996, s 25(2), Sch 4.*]

(xxviii) 'Will' includes codicil.

(2) References to a child or issue living at the death of any person include child or issue en ventre sa mère at the death.

(3) References to the estate of a deceased person include property over which the deceased exercises a general power of appointment (including the statutory power to dispose of entailed interests) by his will.

1   Paragraph (iiiA): inserted by the County Courts Act 1984, s 148(1), Sch 2, Pt III, para 15.
2   The remainder of para (iv) was repealed by the Courts Act 1971, s 56(4), Sch 11, Pt II.
3   Paragraph (via): added by the TLATA 1996, s 25(1), Sch 3, para 6(5).
4   The words omitted in para (vii) were repealed by the TLATA 1996, s 25(2), Sch 4.
5   The words in square brackets in para (viii) were substituted by the Mental Treatment Act 1930, s 20(5), as saved by the MeHA 1983, s 148, Sch 5, para 29, and the words omitted were repealed by the MHA 1959, s 149(2), Sch 8, Pt I.
6   The words omitted from para (xiii) were repealed by the SCA 1981, s 152(4), Sch 7.
7   The word omitted from para (xxiv) were repealed by the TLATA 1996, s 25(2), Sch 4.
8   Para (xxvi): see the Public Trustee Rules 1912, r 30: para **[246.58]**. The definition is enlarged so as to include the Treasury Solicitor, the Official Solicitor, trustees in bankruptcy and certain charitable corporations by the LP(A)A 1926 (para **[246.56]**) and is further enlarged by the CA 1993, s 35 (para **[246.84]**) so as to include certain corporations appointed by the Charity Commission.

*   *   *   *   *

FIRST SCHEDULE

Section 34

PART 1

RULES AS TO PAYMENT OF DEBTS WHERE THE ESTATE IS INSOLVENT

[246.53]
1. *The funeral, testamentary, and administration expenses have priority.*
2. *Subject as aforesaid, the same rules shall prevail and be observed as to the respective rights of secured and unsecured creditors and as to debts, and liabilities provable and as to the valuation of annuities and future and contingent liabilities respectively, and as to the priorities of debts and liabilities*

as may be in force for the time being under the law of bankruptcy with respect to the assets of persons adjudged bankrupt.[1]

1   Pt I was repealed as from 29 December 1986 by the Insolvency Act 1985, s 253(3), Sch 10, Pt III. It is replaced by rules under the Insolvency Act 1986, s 421; see the Administration of Insolvent Estates of Deceased Persons Order 1986, SI 1986/1999.

PART II

ORDER OF APPLICATION OF ASSETS WHERE THE ESTATE IS SOLVENT

[246.54]
1.   Property of the deceased undisposed of by will, subject to the retention thereout of a fund sufficient to meet any pecuniary legacies.
2.   Property of the deceased not specifically devised or bequeathed but included (either by a specific or general description) in a residuary gift, subject to the retention out of such property of a fund sufficient to meet any pecuniary legacies, so far as not provided for as aforesaid.
3.   Property of the deceased specifically appropriated or devised or bequeathed (either by a specific or general description) for the payment of debts.
4.   Property of the deceased charged with, or devised or bequeathed (either by a specific or general description) subject to a charge for the payment of debts.
5.   The fund, if any, retained to meet pecuniary legacies.
6.   Property specifically devised or bequeathed, rateably according to value.
7.   Property appointed by will under a general power, including the statutory power to dispose of entailed interests, rateable according to value.
8.   The following provisions shall also apply—

(a)   The order of application may be varied by the will of the deceased.
(b) . . .[1]

1   Paragraph 8(b) (saving for liability of land for its own death duty) was repealed by the Finance (No 2) Act 1983, s 16(4), Sch 2, Pt II, in relation to deaths on or after 26 July 1983, on the introduction of the rules for the incidence of tax now contained in the ITA 1984, s 211: para **[246.83]**.

LAW OF PROPERTY (AMENDMENT) ACT 1926

(16 & 17 Geo 5 c 11)   [16 June 1926]

[246.55]
Note. Section 3 of this Act, which enlarges the definition of 'trust corporation' contained in the 1925 property legislation, is printed below, as amended by the Supreme Court Act 1981, s 152(1), Sch 5. The definition was further enlarged by the CA 1993, s 35 (para **[246.84]**) so as to include certain corporations appointed by the Charity Commission.

*   *   *   *   *

[246.56]
3.   Meaning of 'trust corporation'.—(1)   For the purposes of the Law of Property Act 1925, the Settled Land Act 1925, the Trustee Act 1925, the Administration of Estates Act 1925, and the [Supreme Court Act 1981], the

expression 'Trust Corporation' includes the Treasury Solicitor, the Official Solicitor and any person holding any other official position prescribed by the Lord Chancellor, and, in relation to the property of a bankrupt and property subject to a deed of arrangement, includes the trustee in bankruptcy and the trustee under the deed respectively, and, in relation to charitable ecclesiastical and public trusts, also includes any local or public authority so prescribed, and any other corporation constituted under the laws of the United Kingdom or any part thereof which satisfies the Lord Chancellor that it undertakes the administration of any such trusts without remuneration, or that by its constitution it is required to apply the whole of its net income after payment of outgoings for charitable, ecclesiastical or public purposes, and is prohibited from distributing, directly or indirectly, any part thereof by way of profits amongst any of its members, and is authorised by him to act in relation to such trusts as a trust corporation.

(2)   For the purposes of this provision, the expression 'Treasury Solicitor' means the solicitor for the affairs of His Majesty's Treasury, and includes the solicitor for the affairs of the Duchy of Lancaster.

*   *   *   *   *

PUBLIC TRUSTEE RULES 1912, SI 1912/348

[246.57]
Note. Rule 30 of the Public Trustee Rules 1912, SR & O 1912/348, is included as an appendix to the definition of 'trust corporation' contained in the Trustee Act 1925, s 68(18) and the AEA 1925, s 55(1)(xxvi), paras **[246.36]** and **[246.52]**, (and reproduced in the Settled Land Act 1925, s 117(1)(xxx) and in the Law of Property Act 1925, s 205(1)(xxviii)). The rule is printed here, as substituted by SI 1975/1189 and as further amended by SI 1976/ 836, SI 1981/358, SI 1984/109, SI 1985/132, SI 1987/1891 and SI 1994/2519. See also the extension of the definition of 'trust corporation' contained in the LP(A)A 1926, s 3 (para **[246.56]**). This latter extension is further extended by the CA 1993, s 35 (para **[246.84]**) so as to include certain corporation appointed by the Charity Commission.

*   *   *   *   *

[246.58]
30.—(1)   The following corporations shall be entitled to act as custodian trustees:—

(a)   the Treasury Solicitor;
(b)   any corporation which:—
   (i)   is constituted under the law of the United Kingdom or of any part thereof, or under the law of any other Member State of the European Economic Community or of any part thereof;
   (ii)   is empowered by its constitution to undertake trust business (which for the purpose of this rule means the business of acting as trustee under wills and settlements and as executor and administrator) in England and Wales;

2221

(iii)   has one or more places of business in the United Kingdom; and
(iv)   is—

a company incorporated by special Act of Parliament or Royal Charter, or

a company registered (with or without limited liability) in the United Kingdom under the Companies Act 1948[1] or under the Companies Act (Northern Ireland) 1960 or in another Member State of the European Economic Community and having a capital (in stock or shares) for the time being issued of not less than £250,000 (or its equivalent in the currency of the State where the company is registered), of which not less than £100,000 (or its equivalent) has been paid up in cash, or

a company which is registered without limited liability in the United Kingdom under the Companies Act 1948[1] or the Companies Act (Northern Ireland) 1960 or in another Member State of the European Economic Community and of which one of the members is a company within any of the classes defined in this sub-paragraph;

(c)   any corporation which is incorporated by special Act or Royal Charter or under the Charitable Trustees Incorporation Act 1872 which is empowered by its constitution to act as a trustee for any charitable purposes, but only in relation to trusts in which its constitution empowers it to act;

(d)   any corporation which is constituted under the law of the United Kingdom or of any part thereof and having its place of business there, and which is either:

(i)   established for the purpose of undertaking trust business for the benefit of Her Majesty's Navy, Army, Air Force or Civil Service or of any unit, department, member or association of members thereof, and having among its directors or members any persons appointed or nominated by the Defence Council or any Department of State or any one or more of those Departments, or

(ii)   authorised by the Lord Chancellor to act in relation to any charitable, ecclesiastical or public trusts as a trust corporation, but only in connection with any such trust as is so authorised;

(e)   —

(i)   any Regional Health Authority, District Health Authority or special health authority, but only in relation to any trust which the authority is authorised to accept or hold by virtue of section 90 of the National Health Service Act 1977;

(ii)   any preserved Board as defined by section 15(6) of the National Health Service Reorganisation Act 1973, but only in relation to any trust which the Board is authorised to accept or hold by virtue of an order made under that section;

(f)   the British Gas Corporation, or any subsidiary of the British Gas Corporation, but only in relation to a pension scheme or pension fund established or maintained by the Corporation by virtue of section 36 of the Gas Act 1972;

(g)   the London Transport Executive, but only in relation to a pension scheme or pension fund—

(i) which is established or administered by the Executive by virtue of section 6 of the Transport (London) Act 1969, or

(ii) in relation to which rights, liabilities and functions have been transferred to the Executive by an order under section 74 of the Transport Act 1962 as applied by section 18 of the Transport (London) Act 1969;

(h) any of the following, namely:—

(i) the Greater London Council,

(ii) the corporation of any London borough (acting by the council),

(iii) a county council, district council, parish council or community council,

(iv) the Council of the Isles of Scilly,

(v) the Common Council of the City of London,

but only in relation to charitable or public trusts (and not trusts for an ecclesiastical charity or for a charity for the relief of poverty) for the benefit of the inhabitants of the area of the local authority concerned and its neighbourhood, or any part of that area.

(i) any of the following, namely:—

(i) a metropolitan district council or a non-metropolitan county council,

(ii) the corporation of any London borough (acting by the council),

(iii) the Common Council of the City of London,

(iv) the Council of the Isles of Scilly,

but only in relation to any trust under which property devolves for the sole benefit of a person who occupies residential accommodation provided under section 21(1)(a) of the National Assistance Act 1948 by the local authority concerned or is in the care of that authority; and a corporation acting as a custodian trustee by virtue of this paragraph in relation to any trust shall be entitled to continue so to act in relation to that trust until a new custodian trustee is appointed, notwithstanding that the person concerned ceases to occupy such accommodation or to be in the care of that authority, as the case may be.

(j) the National Coal Board or any subsidiary of the National Coal Board, but only in relation to a scheme or arrangements established under regulations made under section 37 of the Coal Industry Nationalisation Act 1946.

(k) any corporation acting as trustee of the trusts of any pension scheme or pension fund established or maintained by the British Broadcasting Corporation, but only in relation to those trusts.

(l) any corporation appointed by the Secretary of State as a trustee of any scheme having effect by virtue of regulations made under section 37 of the Coal Industry Nationalisation Act 1946 for purposes relating to

pensions, gratuities or other like benefits and in relation to which provision is, or has been, made by regulations made under paragraph 2(1) of Schedule 5 to the Coal Industry Act 1994 for the scheme to continue in force notwithstanding the repeal by the Coal Industry Act 1994 of section 37 of the Coal Industry Nationalisation Act 1946 and of the enactments modifying that section, but only in relation to such a scheme.

(2)   In this rule 'subsidiary' has the same meaning as in section 154 of the Companies Act 1948.[1]

---

1   References in sub-rr (1)(b) and (2) to the Companies Act 1948 will now operate as references to the Companies Act 1985, s 736, which re-enacts s 154 of the 1948 Act; see the Interpretation Act 1978, s 17(2) (para **[246.80]**).

*   *   *   *   *

PERPETUITIES AND ACCUMULATIONS ACT 1964

(1964 c 55)   [16 July 1964]

Perpetuities

[246.59]
1.   Power to specify perpetuity period.—(1)   Subject to section 9(2) of this Act and subsection (2) below, where the instrument by which any disposition is made so provides, the perpetuity period applicable to the disposition under the rule against perpetuities, instead of being of any other duration, shall be of a duration equal to such number of years not exceeding eighty as is specified in that behalf in the instrument.
(2)   Subsection (1) above shall not have effect where the disposition is made in exercise of a special power of appointment, but where a period is specified under that subsection in the instrument creating such a power the period shall apply in relation to any disposition under the power as it applies in relation to the power itself.

[246.60]
2.   Presumptions and evidence as to future parenthood.—(1)   Where in any proceedings there arises on the rule against perpetuities a question which turns on the ability of a person to have a child at some future time, then—

(a)   subject to paragraph (b) below, it shall be presumed that a male can have a child at the age of fourteen years or over, but not under that age, and that a female can have a child at the age of twelve years or over, but not under that age or over the age of fifty-five years; but

(b)   in the case of a living person evidence may be given to show that he or she will or will not be able to have a child at the time in question.

(2)   Where any such question is decided by treating a person as unable to have a child at a particular time, and he or she does so, the High Court may make such order as it thinks fit for placing the persons interested in the property comprised in the disposition, so far as may be just, in the position they would have held if the question had not been so decided.
(3)   Subject to subsection (2) above, where any such question is decided in relation to a disposition by treating a person as able or unable to have a child at a particular time, then he or she shall be so treated for the purpose of any question which may arise on the rule against perpetuities in relation to the same disposition in any subsequent proceedings.

(4)   In the foregoing provisions of this section references to having a child are references to begetting or giving birth to a child, but those provisions (except subsection (1)(b)) shall apply in relation to the possibility that a person will at any time have a child by adoption, legitimation or other means as they apply to his or her ability at that time to beget or give birth to a child.

[246.61]
3.   Uncertainty as to remoteness.—(1)   Where, apart from the provisions of this section and sections 4 and 5 of this Act, a disposition would be void on the ground that the interest disposed of might not become vested until too remote a time, the disposition shall be treated, until such time (if any) as it becomes established that the vesting must occur, if at all, after the end of the perpetuity period, as if the disposition were not subject to the rule against perpetuities; and its becoming so established shall not affect the validity of anything previously done in relation to the interest disposed of by way of advancement, application of intermediate income or otherwise.

(2)   Where, apart from the said provisions, a disposition consisting of the conferring of a general power of appointment would be void on the ground that the power might not become exercisable until too remote a time, the disposition shall be treated, until such time (if any) as it becomes established that the power will not be exercisable within the perpetuity period, as if the disposition were not subject to the rule against perpetuities.

(3)   Where, apart from the said provisions, a disposition consisting of the conferring of any power, option or other right would be void on the ground that the right might be exercised at too remote a time, the disposition shall be treated as regards any exercise of the right within the perpetuity period as if it were not subject to the rule against perpetuities and, subject to the said provisions, shall be treated as void for remoteness only if, and so far as, the right is not fully exercised within that period.

(4)   Where this section applies to a disposition and the duration of the perpetuity period is not determined by virtue of section 1 or 9(2) of this Act, it shall be determined as follows:—

(a)   where any persons falling within subsection (5) below are individuals in being and ascertainable at the commencement of the perpetuity period the duration of the period shall be determined by reference to their lives and no others, but so that the lives of any description of persons falling within paragraph (b) or (c) of that subsection shall be disregarded if the number of persons of that description is such as to render it impracticable to ascertain the date of death of the survivor;

(b)   where there are no lives under paragraph (a) above the period shall be twenty-one years.

(5)   The said persons are as follows:—

(a)   the person by whom the disposition was made;
(b)   a person to whom or in whose favour the disposition was made, that is to say—

(i)   in the case of a disposition to a class of persons, any member or potential member of the class;

(ii)   in the case of an individual disposition to a person taking only on certain conditions being satisfied, any person as to whom some of the conditions are satisfied and the remainder may in time be satisfied;

(iii) in the case of a special power of appointment exercisable in favour of members of a class, any member or potential member of the class;

(iv)   in the case of a special power of appointment exercisable in favour of one person only, that person or, where the object of the power is ascertainable only on certain conditions being satisfied, any person as to whom some of the conditions are satisfied and the remainder may in time be satisfied;

(v)   in the case of any power, option or other right, the person on whom the right is conferred;

(c)   a person having a child or grandchild within sub-paragraphs (i) to (iv) of paragraph (b) above, or any of whose children or grandchildren, if subsequently born, would by virtue of his or her descent fall within those sub-paragraphs;

(d)   any person on the failure or determination of whose prior interest the disposition is limited to take effect.

[246.62]
4. Reduction of age and exclusion of class members to avoid remoteness.—(1)   Where a disposition is limited by reference to the attainment by any person or persons of a specified age exceeding twenty-one years, and it is apparent at the time the disposition is made or becomes apparent at a subsequent time—

(a)   that the disposition would, apart from this section, be void for remoteness, but

(b)   that it would not be so void if the specified age had been twenty-one years,

the disposition shall be treated for all purposes as if, instead of being limited by reference to the age in fact specified, it had been limited by reference to the age nearest to that age which would, if specified instead, have prevented the disposition from being so void.

(2)   Where in the case of any disposition different ages exceeding twenty-one years are specified in relation to different persons—

(a)   the reference in paragraph (b) of subsection (1) above to the specified age shall be construed as a reference to all the specified ages, and

(b)   that subsection shall operate to reduce each such age so far as is necessary to save the disposition from being void for remoteness.

(3)   Where the inclusion of any persons, being potential members of a class or unborn persons who at birth would become members or potential members of the class, prevents the foregoing provisions of this section from operating to save a disposition from being void for remoteness, those persons shall thenceforth be deemed for all the purposes of the disposition to be excluded from the class, and the said provisions shall thereupon have effect accordingly.

(4)   Where in the case of a disposition to which subsection (3) above does not apply, it is apparent at the time the disposition is made or becomes apparent at a subsequent time that, apart from this subsection, the inclusion of any persons,

being potential members of a class or unborn persons who at birth would become members or potential members of the class, would cause the disposition to be treated as void for remoteness, those persons shall, unless their exclusion would exhaust the class, thenceforth be deemed for all the purposes of the disposition to be excluded from the class.

(5)   Where this section has effect in relation to a disposition to which section 3 above applies, the operation of this section shall not affect the validity of anything previously done in relation to the interest disposed of by way of advancement, application of intermediate income or otherwise.

(6)   Section 163 of the Law of Property Act 1925 (which saves a disposition from remoteness arising out of a condition requiring the attainment of an age exceeding twenty-one years) is hereby repealed.

[(7)   For the avoidance of doubt is is hereby declared that a question arising under section 3 of this Act or subsection (1)(a) above of whether a disposition would be void apart from this section is to be determined as if subsection (6) above had been a separate section of this Act.]^1

---

1   Sub-s (7): added by the Children Act 1975, s 108, Sch 3, para 43, and preserved from the general repeal of that Act by the ChA 1989, s 108(6), Sch 14, para 38.

[246.63]
5.   Condition relating to death of surviving spouse. Where a disposition is limited by reference to the time of death of the survivor of a person in being at the commencement of the perpetuity period and any spouse of that person, and that time has not arrived at the end of the perpetuity period, the disposition shall be treated for all purposes, where to do so would save it from being void for remoteness, as if it had instead been limited by reference to the time immediately before the end of that period.

[246.64]
6.   Saving and acceleration of expectant interests. A disposition shall not be treated as void for remoteness by reason only that the interest disposed of is ulterior to and dependent upon an interest under a disposition which is so void, and the vesting of an interest shall not be prevented from being accelerated on the failure of a prior interest by reason only that the failure arises because of remoteness.

[246.65]
7.   Powers of appointment. For the purposes of the rule against perpetuities, a power of appointment shall be treated as a special power unless—

(a)   in the instrument creating the power it is expressed to be exercisable by one person only, and

(b)   it could, at all times during its currency when that person is of full age and capacity, be exercised by him so as immediately to transfer to himself the whole of the interest governed by the power without the consent of any other person or compliance with any other condition, not being a formal condition relating only to the mode of exercise of the power:

Provided that for the purpose of determining whether a disposition made under a power of appointment exercisable by will only is void for remoteness, the power shall be treated as a general power where it would have fallen to be so treated if exercisable by deed.

[246.66]

8. Administrative powers of trustees.—(1) The rule against perpetuities shall not operate to invalidate a power conferred on trustees or other persons to sell, lease, exchange or otherwise dispose of any property for full consideration, or to do any other act in the administration (as opposed to the distribution) of any property, and shall not prevent the payment to trustees or other persons of reasonable remuneration for their services.

(2) Subsection (1) above shall apply for the purpose of enabling a power to be exercised at any time after the commencement of this Act notwithstanding that the power is conferred by an instrument which took effect before that commencement.

[246.67]

9. Options relating to land.—(1) The rule against perpetuities shall not apply to a disposition consisting of the conferring of an option to acquire for valuable consideration an interest reversionary (whether directly or indirectly) on the term of a lease if—

(a) the option is exercisable only by the lessee or his successors in title, and

(b) it ceases to be exercisable at or before the expiration of one year following the determination of the lease.

This subsection shall apply in relation to an agreement for a lease as it applies in relation to a lease, and 'lessee' shall be construed accordingly.

(2) In the case of a disposition consisting of the conferring of an option to acquire for valuable consideration any interest in land, the perpetuity period under the rule against perpetuities shall be twenty-one years, and section 1 of this Act shall not apply:

Provided that this subsection shall not apply to a right of pre-emption conferred on a public or local authority in respect of land used or to be used for religious purposes where the right becomes exercisable only if the land ceases to be used for such purposes.

[246.68]

10. Avoidance of contractual and other rights in cases of remoteness. Where a disposition inter vivos would fall to be treated as void for remoteness if the rights and duties thereunder were capable of transmission to persons other than the original parties and had been so transmitted, it shall be treated as void as between the person by whom it was made and the person to whom or in whose favour it was made or any successor of his, and no remedy shall lie in contract or otherwise for giving effect to it or making restitution for its lack of effect.

[246.69]

11. Rights for enforcement of rentcharges.—(1) The rule against perpetuities shall not apply to any powers or remedies for recovering or compelling the payment of an annual sum to which section 121 or 122 of the Law of Property Act 1925 applies, or otherwise becoming exercisable or enforceable on the breach of any condition or other requirement relating to that sum.

(2) [*Repeals in part the Law of Property Act 1925, s 121(6).*]

[246.70]

12. Possibilities of reverter, conditions subsequent, exceptions and reservations.—(1) In the case of—

(a) a possibility of reverter on the determination of a determinable fee simple, or

(b) a possibility of a resulting trust on the determination of any other determinable interest in property.

the rule against perpetuities shall apply in relation to the provision causing the interest to be determinable as it would apply if that provision were expressed in the form of a condition subsequent giving rise, on breach thereof, to a right of re-entry or an equivalent right in the case of property other than land, and where the provision falls to be treated as void for remoteness the determinable interest shall become an absolute interest.

(2) Where a disposition is subject to any such provision, or to any such condition subsequent, or to any exception or reservation, the disposition shall be treated for the purposes of this Act as including a separate disposition of any rights arising by virtue of the provision, condition subsequent, exception or reservation.

Accumulations

[246.71]
13. Amendment of s 164 of Law of Property Act 1925.—(1) The periods for which accumulations of income under a settlement or other disposition are permitted by section 164 of the Law of Property Act 1925 shall include—

(a) a term of twenty-one years from the date of the making of the disposition and

(b) the duration of the minority or respective minorities of any person or persons in being at that date.

(2) It is hereby declared that the restrictions imposed by the said section 164 apply in relation to a power to accumulate income whether or not there is a duty to exercise that power, and that they apply whether or not the power to accumulate extends to income produced by the investment of income previously accumulated.

[246.72]
14. Right to stop accumulations. Section 2 above shall apply to any question as to the right of beneficiaries to put an end to accmulations of income under any disposition as it applies to questions arising on the rule against perpetuities.

Supplemental

[246.73]
15. Short title, interpretation and extent.—(1) This Act may be cited as the Perpetuities and Accumulations Act 1964.

(2) In this Act—

'disposition' includes the conferring of a power of appointment and any other disposition of an interest in or right over property, and references to the interest disposed of shall be construed accordingly;

'in being' means living or en ventre sa mere;

'power of appointment' includes any discretionary power to transfer a beneficial interest in property without the furnishing of valuable consideration;

'will' includes a codicil;

and for the purposes of this Act a disposition contained in a will shall be deemed to be made at the death of the testator.

(3)   For the purposes of this Act a person shall be treated as a member of a class if in his case all the conditions identifying a member of the class are satisfied, and shall be treated as a potential member if in his case some only of those conditions are satisfied but there is a possibility that the remainder will in time be satisfied.

(4)   Nothing in this Act shall affect the operation of the rule of law rendering void for remoteness certain dispositions under which property is limited to be applied for purposes other than the benefit of any person or class of persons in cases where the property may be so applied after the end of the perpetuity period.

(5)   The foregoing sections of this Act shall apply (except as provided in section 8(2) above) only in relation to instruments taking effect after the commencement of this Act, and in the case of an instrument made in the exercise of a special power of appointment shall apply only where the instrument creating the power takes effect after that commencement;

Provided that section 7 above shall apply in all cases for construing the foregoing reference to a special power of appointment.

(6)   This Act shall apply in relation to a disposition made otherwise than by an instrument as if the disposition had been contained in an instrument taking effect when the disposition was made.

(7)   This Act binds the Crown.

*   *   *   *   *

FAMILY LAW REFORM ACT 1969

(1969 c 46)   [25 July 1969]

PART I

REDUCTION OF AGE OF MAJORITY AND RELATED PROVISIONS

[246.74]
1.   Reduction of age of majority from 21 to 18.—(1)   As from the date on which this section comes into force a person shall attain full age on attaining the age of eighteen instead of on attaining the age of twenty-one; and a person shall attain full age on that date if he has then already attained the age of eighteen but not the age of twenty-one.

(2)   The foregoing subsection applies for the purposes of any rule of law, and, in the absence of a definition or of any contrary intention, for the construction of 'full age', 'infant', 'infancy', 'minor', 'minority' and similar expressions in—

   (a)   any statutory provision, whether passed or made before, on or after the date on which this section comes into force; and
   (b)   any deed, will or other instrument of whatever nature (not being a statutory provision) made on or after that date.

(3)   In the statutory provisions specified in Schedule 1 to this Act for any reference to the age of twenty-one years there shall be substituted a reference to the age of eighteen years; but the amendment by this subsection of the

provisions specified in Part II of that Schedule shall be without prejudice to any power of amending or revoking those provisions.

(4)   This section does not affect the construction of any such expression as is referred to in subsection (2) of this section in any of the statutory provisions described in Schedule 2 to this Act, and the transitional provisions and savings contained in Schedule 3 to this Act shall have effect in relation to this section.

(5)   The Lord Chancellor may by order made by statutory instrument amend any provision in any local enactment passed on or before the date on which this section comes into force (not being a provision described in paragraph 2 of Schedule 2 to this Act) by substituting a reference to the age of eighteen years for any reference therein to the age of twenty-one years; and any statutory instrument containing an order under this subsection shall be subject to annulment in pursuance of a resolution of either House of Parliament.

(6)   In this section 'statutory provision' means any enactment (including, except where the context otherwise requires, this Act) and any order, rule, regulation, byelaw or other instrument made in the exercise of a power conferred by any enactment.

(7)   Notwithstanding any rule of law, a will or codicil executed before the date on which this section comes into force shall not be treated for the purposes of this section as made on or after that date by reason only that the will or codicil is confirmed by a codicil executed on or after that date.

*   *   *   *   *

SCHEDULE 1

Section 1(3)

STATUTORY PROVISIONS AMENDED BY SUBSTITUTING 18 FOR 21 YEARS

PART I

Enactments

[246.75]

	Short title	Sections	Subject matter
	...	...	...
c 19	The Trustee Act 1925	Section 31(1)(ii), (2)(i)(a) and (b)	Power to apply income for maintenance and to accumulate surplus income during a minority.

*   *   *   *   *

SCHEDULE 3

Section 1(4)

TRANSITIONAL PROVISIONS AND SAVINGS

Interpretation

[246.76]
1.—(1)   In this Schedule 'the principal section' means section 1 of this Act and 'the commencement date' means the date on which that section comes into force.
(2)   Subsection (7) of the principal section shall apply for the purposes of this Schedule as it applies for the purposes of that section.

*   *   *   *   *

Power of trustees to apply income for maintenance of minor

[246.77]
5.—(1)   The principal section shall not affect section 31 of the Trustee Act 1925—

   (a)   in its application to any interest under an instrument made before the commencement date; or
   (b)   in its application, by virtue of section 47(1)(ii) of the Administration of Estates Act 1925, to the estate of an intestate (within the meaning of that Act) dying before that date.

(2)   In any case in which (whether by virtue of this paragraph or paragraph 9 of this Schedule) trustees have power under subsection (1)(i) of the said section 31 to pay income to the parent or guardian of any person who has attained the age eighteen, or to apply it for or towards the maintenance, education or or benefit of any such person, they shall also have power to pay it to that person himself.

*   *   *   *   *

Accumulation periods

[246.78]
7.   The change, by virtue of the principal section, in the construction of—

   (a)   sections 164 to 166 of the Law of Property Act 1925;
   (b)   section 13(1) of the Perpetuities and Accumulations Act 1964,

(which lay down permissible periods for the accumulation of income under settlements and other dispositions) shall not invalidate any direction for accumulation in a settlement or other disposition made by a deed, will or other instrument which was made before the commencement date.

*   *   *   *   *

Statutory provisions incorporated in deeds, wills etc

[264.79]
9.   The principal section shall not affect the construction of any statutory provision where it is incorporated in and has effect as part of any deed, will or other instrument the construction of which is not affected by that section.

INTERPRETATION ACT 1978

(1978 c 30)   [20 July 1978]

Interpretation and construction

[246.79A]
5.   Definitions. In any Act, unless the contrary intention appears, words and expressions listed in Schedule 1 to this Act are to be construed according to that Schedule.

*   *   *   *   *

[246.80]
17.   Repeal and re-enactment—. . . (2)   Where an Act repeals and re-enacts, with or without modification, a previous enactment then, unless the contrary intention appears,—

   (a)   any reference in any other enactment to the enactment so repealed shall be construed as a reference to the provision re-enacted;

*   *   *   *   *

[246.81]
23.   Application to other instruments—. . . (3) . . . and in the application to section 17(2)(a) to Acts passed or subordinate legislation made after the commencement of this Act, the reference to any other enactment includes any deed or other instrument or document.

*   *   *   *   *

SCHEDULE 1

Section 5

WORDS AND EXPRESSIONS DEFINED

*   *   *   *   *

Definitions

*   *   *   *   *

[246.81A]

'Land' includes buildings and other structures, land covered with water, and any estate, interest, easement, servitude or right in or over land.

* * * * *

INHERITANCE TAX ACT 1984

(1984 c 51)   [31 July 1984]

[246.82]

Note. The original short title of this Act was the Capital Transfer Act 1984. The alternative title was provided by the Finance Act 1986, s 100(1)(a) as from 25 July 1986.

[246.83]

211.   Burden of tax on death.—(1)   Where personal representatives are liable for tax on the value transferred by a chargeable transfer made on death, the tax shall be treated as part of the general testamentary and administration expenses of the estate, but only so far as it is attributable to the value of property in the United Kingdom which—

(a)   vests in the deceased's personal representatives, and
(b)   was not immediately before the death comprised in a settlement.

(2)   Subsection (1) above shall have effect subject to any contrary intention shown by the deceased in his will.
(3)   Where any amount of tax paid by personal representatives on the value transferred by a chargeable transfer made on death does not fall to be borne as part of the general testamentary and administration expenses of the estate, that amount shall, where occasion requires, be repaid to them by the person in whom the property to the value of which the tax is attributable is vested.
(4)   References in this section to tax include references to interest on tax.

CHARITIES ACT 1993

(1993 c 10)   [27 May 1993]

PART IV

APPLICATION OF PROPERTY CY-PRÈS AND ASSISTANCE AND SUPERVISION OF CHARITIES BY COURT AND COMMISSIONERS

* * * * *

Meaning of 'trust corporation'

[246.84]

35.   Application of provisions to trust corporations appointed under s 16 or 18.—(1)   In the definition of 'trust corporation' contained in the following provisions—

(a)   section 117(xxx) of the Settled Land Act 1925,

(b)   section 68(18) of the Trustee Act 1925,

(c)   section 205(xxviii) of the law of Property Act 1925,

(d)   section 55(xxvi) of the Administration of Estates Act 1925, and

(e)   secion 128 of the Supreme Court Act 1981,

the reference to a corporation appointed by the court in any particular case to be a trustee includes a reference to a corporation appointed by the Commissioners under this Act to be a trustee.

(2)   This section shall be deemed always to have had effect; but the reference to section 128 of the Supreme Court Act 1981 shall in relation to any time before 1 January 1982, be construed as a reference to section 175(1) of the Supreme Court of Judicature (Consolidation) Act 1925.[1]

1   Section 175(1) of the Supreme Court (Consolidation) Act 1925 was repealed by the Supreme Court Act 1981, s 152(4), Sch 7 and replaced by s 128 of that Act.

TRUSTS OF LAND AND APPOINTMENT OF TRUSTEES ACT 1996

(1996 c 47)   [24 July 1996]

[246.85]
Note. The TLATA 1996, which came into force on 1 January 1997, makes fundamental changes to the law relating to land held on trust and also effects limited, though significant, changes to the law relating to the appointment and retirement of trustees whether of realty or personalty. The most significant change contained in Part I of the Act (concerning land held on trust) is the introduction of a single system governing land held on trust (the so-called 'trust of land') replacing strict settlements and trusts for sale. The SLA 1925 ceases to apply to newly created trusts, though it continues to apply to existing strict settlements (and strict settlements which derive from existing strict settlements). (Entailed interests have suffered the same fate as strict settlements and can no longer be created either in realty or personalty.) All other forms of trust in relation to land, whether created before or after the coming into force of the Act and whether or not such trusts import a trust for sale, fall within the Act's provisions. It is still possible to create a trust for sale but the doctrine of conversion is abolished in relation to express trusts for sale of land and it now makes no practical difference whether or not land is subjected to a trust for sale.

The Act confers wide administrative powers on trustees of land but imposes a positive (though excludable) duty to consult beneficiaries so far as practicable as to the exercise of their functions in relation to land. The Act confers on beneficiaries with interests in possession rights to occupy land held in trust subject to certain restrictions. The Act confers on the court a wider jurisdiction than it possessed under the Law of Property Act 1925, s 30 (which is repealed) to regulate the exercise by trustees of their functions in relation to land. Part I of the Act applies with appropriate modifications to personal representatives. Part II concerns the appointment and retirement of trustees. This Part gives power to beneficiaries who are sui juris and between them absolutely entitled to property which is held on a trust under which no person is nominated for the purpose of appointing new trustees, to give a unanimous written direction to a trustee to retire, or to the trustees (or the personal representatives of the last surviving trustee) to appoint the person or persons specified in such direction as a new trustee or new trustees. (This provision reverses *Re Brockbank, Ward v Bates* [1948] Ch 206, [1948] 1 All ER 287. A similar power is conferred where a trustee is incapable.

PART I

TRUSTS OF LAND

Introductory

[246.86]
1.   Meaning of 'trust of land'.—(1)   In this Act—

   (a)   'trust of land' means (subject to subsection (3)) any trust of property which consists of or includes land, and

   (b)   'trustees of land' means trustees of a trust of land.

(2)   The reference in subsection (1)(a) to a trust—

   (a)   is to any description of trust (whether express, implied, resulting or constructive), including a trust for sale and a bare trust, and

   (b)   includes a trust created, or arising, before the commencement of this Act.

(3)   The reference to land in subsection (1)(a) does not include land which (despite section 2) is settled land or which is land to which the Universities and College Estates Act 1925 applies.

Settlements and trusts for sale as trusts of land

[246.87]
2.   Trusts in place of settlements.—(1)   No settlement created after the commencement of this Act is a settlement for the purposes of the Settled Land Act 1925; and no settlement shall be deemed to be made under that Act after that commencement.

(2)   Subsection (1) does not apply to a settlement created on the occasion of an alteration in any interest in, or of a person becoming entitled under, a settlement which—

   (a)   is in existence at the commencement of this Act, or

   (b)   derives from a settlement within paragraph (a) or this paragraph.

(3)   But a settlement created as mentioned in subsection (2) is not a settlement for the purposes of the Settled Land Act 1925 if provision to the effect that it is not is made in the instrument, or any of the instruments, by which it is created.

(4)   Where at any time after the commencement of this Act there is in the case of any settlement which is a settlement for the purposes of the Settled Land Act 1925 no relevant property which is, or is deemed to be, subject to the settlement,

the settlement permanently ceases at that time to be a settlement for the purposes of that Act.

In this subsection 'relevant property' means land and personal chattels to which section 67(1) of the Settled Land Act 1925 (heirlooms) applies.

(5) No land held on charitable, ecclesiastical or public trusts shall be or be deemed to be settled land after the commencement of this Act, even if it was or was deemed to be settled land before that commencement.

(6) Schedule 1 has effect to make provision consequential on this section (including provision to impose a trust in circumstances in which, apart from this section, there would be a settlement for the purposes of the Settled Land Act 1925 (and there would not otherwise be a trust)).

[246.88]
3. Abolition of doctrine of conversion.—(1) Where land is held by trustees subject to a trust for sale, the land is not to be regarded as personal property; and where personal property is subject to a trust for sale in order that the trustees may acquire land, the personal property is not to be regarded as land.

(2) Subsection (1) does not apply to a trust created by a will if the testator died before the commencement of this Act.

(3) Subject to that, subsection (1) applies to a trust whether it is created, or arises, before or after that commencement.

[246.89]
4. Express trusts for sale as trusts of land.—(1) In the case of every trust for sale of land created by a disposition there is to be implied, despite any provision to the contrary made by the disposition, a power for the trustees to postpone sale of the land; and the trustees are not liable in any way for postponing sale of the land, in the exercise of their discretion, for an indefinite period.

(2) Subsection (1) applies to a trust whether it is created, or arises, before or after the commencement of this Act.

(3) Subsection (1) does not affect any liability incurred by trustees before that commencement.

[246.90]
5. Implied trusts for sale as trusts of land.—(1) Schedule 2 has effect in relation to statutory provisions which impose a trust for sale of land in certain circumstances so that in those circumstances there is instead a trust of the land (without a duty to sell).

(2) Section 1 of the Settled Land Act 1925 does not apply to land held on any trust arising by virtue of that Schedule (so that any such land is subject to a trust of land).

Functions of trustees of land

[246.91]
6. General powers of trustees.—(1) For the purpose of exercising their functions as trustees, the trustees of land have in relation to the land subject to the trust all the powers of an absolute owner.

(2)   Where in the case of any land subject to a trust of land each of the beneficiaries interested in the land is a person of full age and capacity who is absolutely entitled to the land, the powers conferred on the trustees by subsection (1) include the power to convey the land to the beneficiaries even though they have not required the trustees to do so; and where land is conveyed by virtue of this subsection—

    (a)   the beneficiaries shall do whatever is necessary to secure that it vests in them, and

    (b)   if they fail to do so, the court may make an order requiring them to do so.

(3)   The trustees of land have power to [acquire land under the power conferred by section 8 of the Trustee Act 2000].

(4)   . . .

(5)   In exercising the powers conferred by this section trustees shall have regard to the rights of the beneficiaries.

(6)   The powers conferred by this section shall not be exercised in contravention of, or of any order made in pursuance of, any other enactment or any rule of law or equity.

(7)   The reference in subsection (6) to an order includes an order of any court or of the Charity Commissioners.

(8)   Where any enactment other than this section confers on trustees authority to act subject to any restriction, limitation or condition, trustees of land may not exercise the powers conferred by this section to do any act which they are prevented from doing under the other enactment by reason of the restriction, limitation or condition.

[(9)   The duty of care under section 1 of the Trustee Act 2000 applies to trustees of land when exercising the powers conferred by this section.]¹

1   Sub-ss (3) and (4) amended, and sub-s (9) inserted by the TrA 2000, Sch 2, Pt II, para 45.

[246.92]

7.   Partition by trustees.—(1)   The trustees of land may, where beneficiaries of full age are absolutely entitled in undivided shares to land subject to the trust, partition the land, or any part of it, and provide (by way of mortgage or otherwise) for the payment of any equality money.

(2)   The trustees shall give effect to any such partition by conveying the partitioned land in severalty (whether or not subject to any legal mortgage created for raising equality money), either absolutely or in trust, in accordance with the rights of those beneficiaries.

(3)   Before exercising their powers under subsection (2) the trustees shall obtain the consent of each of those beneficiaries.

(4)   Where a share in the land is affected by an incumbrance, the trustees may either give effect to it or provide for its discharge from the property allotted to that share as they think fit.

(5)   If a share in the land is absolutely vested in a minor, subsections (1) to (4) apply as if he were of full age, except that the trustees may act on his behalf and retain land or other property representing his share in trust for him.

[246.93]

8.   Exclusion and restriction of powers.—(1)   Sections 6 and 7 do not apply in the case of a trust of land created by a disposition in so far as provision to the effect that they do not apply is made by the disposition.

(2) If the disposition creating such a trust makes provision requiring any consent to be obtained to the exercise of any power conferred by section 6 or 7, the power may not be exercised without that consent.

(3) Subsection (1) does not apply in the case of charitable, ecclesiastical or public trusts.

(4) Subsections (1) and (2) have effect subject to any enactment which prohibits or restricts the effect of provision of the description mentioned in them.

[246.94]

9. Delegation by trustees.—(1) The trustees of land may, by power of attorney, delegate to any beneficiary or beneficiaries of full age and beneficially entitled to an interest in possession in land subject to the trust any of their functions as trustees which relate to the land.

(2) Where trustees purport to delegate to a person by a power of attorney under subsection (1) functions relating to any land and another person in good faith deals with him in relation to the land, he shall be presumed in favour of that other person to have been a person to whom the functions could be delegated unless that other person has knowledge at the time of the transaction that he was not such a person.

And it shall be conclusively presumed in favour of any purchaser whose interest depends on the validity of that transaction that that other person dealt in good faith and did not have such knowledge if that other person makes a statutory declaration to that effect before or within three months after the completion of the purchase.

(3) A power of attorney under subsection (1) shall be given by all the trustees jointly and (unless expressed to be irrevocable and to be given by way of security) may be revoked by any one or more of them; and such a power is revoked by the appointment as a trustee of a person other than those by whom it is given (though not by any of those persons dying or otherwise ceasing to be a trustee).

(4) Where a beneficiary to whom functions are delegated by a power of attorney under subsection (1) ceases to be a person beneficially entitled to an interest in possession in land subject to the trust—

    (a)   if the functions are delegated to him alone, the power is revoked;

    (b)   if the functions are delegated to him and to other beneficiaries to be exercised by them jointly (but not separately), the power is revoked if each of the other beneficiaries ceases to be so entitled (but otherwise functions exercisable in accordance with the power are so exercisable by the remaining beneficiary or beneficiaries); and

    (c)   if the functions are delegated to him and to other beneficiaries to be exercised by them separately (or either separately or jointly), the power is revoked in so far as it relates to him.

(5) A delegation under subsection (1) may be for any period or indefinite.

(6) A power of attorney under subsection (1) cannot be an enduring power within the meaning of the Enduring Powers of Attorney Act 1985.

(7) Beneficiaries to whom functions have been delegated under subsection (1) are, in relation to the exercise of the functions, in the same position as trustees (with the same duties and liabilities); but such beneficiaries shall not be regarded as trustees for any other purposes (including, in particular, the purposes of any

enactment permitting the delegation of functions by trustees or imposing requirements relating to the payment of capital money).

(8) . . .

(9)   Neither this section nor the repeal by this Act of section 29 of the Law of Property Act 1925 (which is superseded by this section) affects the operation after the commencement of this Act of any delegation effected before that commencement.[1]

1   Sub-s (8): amended by the TrA 2000, Sch 2, Pt II, para 46.

[246.95]
9A.   Duties of trustees in connection with delegation etc.—(1)   The duty of care under section 1 of the Trustee Act 2000 applies to trustees of land in deciding whether to delegate any of their functions under section 9.

(2)   Subsection (3) applies if the trustees of land—

   (a)   delegate any of their functions under section 9, and
   (b)   the delegation is not irrevocable.

(3)   While the delegation continues, the trustees—

   (a)   must keep the delegation under review,
   (b)   if circumstances make it appropriate to do so, must consider whether there is a need to exercise any power of intervention that they have, and
   (c)   if they consider that there is a need to exercise such a power, must do so.

(4)   'Power of intervention' includes—

   (a)   a power to give directions to the beneficiary;
   (b)   a power to revoke the delegation.

(5)   The duty of care under section 1 of the 2000 Act applies to trustees in carrying out any duty under subsection (3).

(6)   A trustee of land is not liable for any act or default of the beneficiary, or beneficiaries, unless the trustee fails to comply with the duty of care in deciding to delegate any of the trustees' functions under section 9 or in carrying out any duty under subsection (3).

(7)   Neither this section nor the repeal of section 9(8) by the Trustee Act 2000 affects the operation after the commencement of this section of any delegation effected before that commencement.[1]

1   This section was inserted by the TrA 2000, s 40(1), Sch 2, para 47.

Consents and consultation

[246.96]
10.   Consents.—(1)   If a disposition creating a trust of land requires the consent of more than two persons to the exercise by the trustees of any function relating to the land, the consent of any two of them to the exercise of the function is sufficient in favour of a purchaser.

(2)   Subsection (1) does not apply to the exercise of a function by trustees of land held on charitable, ecclesiastical or public trusts.

(3)   Where at any time a person whose consent is expressed by a disposition creating a trust of land to be required to the exercise by the trustees of any function relating to the land is not of full age—

(a)   his consent is not, in favour of a purchaser, required to the exercise of the function, but
(b)   the trustees shall obtain the consent of a parent who has parental responsibility for him (within the meaning of the Children Act 1989) or of a guardian of his.

[246.97]
11.   Consultation with beneficiaries.—(1)   The trustees of land shall in the exercise of any function relating to land subject to the trust—

(a)   so far as practicable, consult the beneficiaries of full age and beneficially entitled to an interest in possession in the land, and
(b)   so far as consistent with the general interest of the trust, give effect to the wishes of those beneficiaries, or (in case of dispute) of the majority (according to the value of their combined interests).

(2)   Subsection (1) does not apply—

(a)   in relation to a trust created by a disposition in so far as provision that it does not apply is made by the disposition,
(b)   in relation to a trust created or arising under a will made before the commencement of this Act, or
(c)   in relation to the exercise of the power mentioned in section 6(2).

(3)   Subsection (1) does not apply to a trust created before the commencement of this Act by a disposition, or a trust created after that commencement by reference to such a trust, unless provision to the effect that it is to apply is made by a deed executed—

(a)   in a case in which the trust was created by one person and he is of full capacity, by that person, or
(b)   in a case in which the trust was created by more than one person, by such of the persons who created the trust as are alive and of full capacity.

(4)   A deed executed for the purposes of subsection (3) is irrevocable.

Right of beneficiaries to occupy trust land

[246.98]
12.   The right to occupy.—(1)   A beneficiary who is beneficially entitled to an interest in possession in land subject to a trust of land is entitled by reason of his interest to occupy the land at any time if at that time—

(a)   the purposes of the trust include making the land available for his occupation (or for the occupation of beneficiaries of a class of which he is a member or of beneficiaries in general), or
(b)   the land is held by the trustees so as to be so available.

(2)   Subsection (1) does not confer on a beneficiary a right to occupy land if it is either unavailable or unsuitable for occupation by him.
(3)   This section is subject to section 13.

[246.99]
13. Exclusion and restriction of right to occupy.—(1) Where two or more beneficiaries are (or apart from this subsection would be) entitled under section 12 to occupy land, the trustees of land may exclude or restrict the entitlement of any one or more (but not all) of them.
(2) Trustees may not under subsection (1)—

(a) unreasonably exclude any beneficiary's entitlement to occupy land, or
(b) restrict any such entitlement to an unreasonable extent.

(3) The trustees of land may from time to time impose reasonable conditions on any beneficiary in relation to his occupation of land by reason of his entitlement under section 12.
(4) The matters to which trustees are to have regard in exercising the powers conferred by this section include—

(a) the intentions of the person or persons (if any) who created the trust,
(b) the purposes for which the land is held, and
(c) the circumstances and wishes of each of the beneficiaries who is (or apart from any previous exercise by the trustees of those powers would be) entitled to occupy the land under section 12.

(5) The conditions which may be imposed on a beneficiary under subsection (3) include, in particular, conditions requiring him—

(a) to pay any outgoings or expenses in respect of the land, or
(b) to assume any other obligation in relation to the land or to any activity which is or is proposed to be conducted there.

(6) Where the entitlement of any beneficiary to occupy land under section 12 has been excluded or restricted, the conditions which may be imposed on any other beneficiary under subsection (3) include, in particular, conditions requiring him to—

(a) make payments by way of compensation to the beneficiary whose entitlement has been excluded or restricted, or
(b) forgo any payment or other benefit to which he would otherwise be entitled under the trust so as to benefit that beneficiary.

(7) The powers conferred on trustees by this section may not be exercised—

(a) so as prevent any person who is in occupation of land (whether or not by reason of an entitlement under section 12) from continuing to occupy the land, or
(b) in a manner likely to result in any such person ceasing to occupy the land,

unless he consents or the court has given approval.
(8) The matters to which the court is to have regard in determining whether to give approval under subsection (7) include the matters mentioned in subsection (4)(a) to (c).

Powers of court

[246.100]

14. Applications for order.—(1) Any person who is a trustee of land or has an interest in a property subject to a trust of land may make an application to the court for an order under this section.

(2) On an application for an order under this section the court may make any such order—

(a) relating to the exercise by the trustees of any of their functions (including an order relieving them of any obligation to obtain the consent of, or to consult, any person in connection with the exercise of any of their functions), or

(b) declaring the nature or extent of a person's interest in property subject to the trust,

as the court thinks fit.

(3) The court may not under this section make any order as to the appointment or removal of trustees.

(4) The powers conferred on the court by this section are exercisable on an application whether it is made before or after the commencement of this Act.

[246.101]

15. Matters relevant in determining applications.—(1) The matters to which the court is to have regard in determining an application for an order under section 14 include—

(a) the intentions of the person or persons (if any) who created the trust,

(b) the purposes for which the property subject to the trust is held,

(c) the welfare of any minor who occupies or might reasonably be expected to occupy any land subject to the trust as his home, and

(d) the interests of any secured creditor of any beneficiary.

(2) In the case of an application relating to the exercise in relation to any land of the powers conferred on the trustees by section 13, the matters to which the court is to have regard also include the circumstances and wishes of each of the beneficiaries who is (or apart from any previous exercise by the trustees of those powers would be) entitled to occupy the land under section 12.

(3) In the case of any other application, other than one relating to the exercise of the power mentioned in section 6(2), the matters to which the court is to have regard also include the circumstances and wishes of any beneficiaries of full age and entitled to an interest in possession in property subject to the trust or (in case of dispute) of the majority (according to the value of their combined interests).

(4) This section does not apply to an application if section 335A of the Insolvency Act 1986 (which is inserted by Schedule 3 and relates to applications by a trustee of a bankrupt) applies to it.

Purchaser protection

[246.102]

16. Protection of purchasers.—(1) A purchaser of land which is or has been subject to a trust need not be concerned to see that any requirement imposed on the trustees by section 6(5), 7(3) or 11(1) has been complied with.

(2)   Where—

(a)   trustees of land who convey land which (immediately before it is conveyed) is subject to the trust contravene section 6(6) or (8), but

(b)   the purchaser of the land from the trustees has no actual notice of the contravention,

the contravention does not invalidate the conveyance.

(3)   Where the powers of trustees of land are limited by virtue of section 8—

(a)   the trustees shall take all reasonable steps to bring the limitation to the notice of any purchaser of the land from them, but

(b)   the limitation does not invalidate any conveyance by the trustees to a purchaser who has no actual notice of the limitation.

(4)   Where trustees of land convey land which (immediately before it is conveyed) is subject to the trust to persons believed by them to be beneficiaries absolutely entitled to the land under the trust and of full age and capacity—

(a)   the trustees shall execute a deed declaring that they are discharged from the trust in relation to that land, and

(b)   if they fail to do so, the court may make an order requiring them to do so.

(5)   A purchaser of land to which a deed under subsection (4) relates is entitled to assume that, as from the date of the deed, the land is not subject to the trust unless he has actual notice that the trustees were mistaken in their belief that the land was conveyed to beneficiaries absolutely entitled to the land under the trust and of full age and capacity.

(6)   Subsections (2) and (3) do not apply to land held on charitable, ecclesiastical or public trusts.

(7)   This section does not apply to registered land.

Supplementary

[246.103]

17.   Application of provisions to trusts of proceeds of sale.—(1)   [*Repealed by the Trustee Act 2000, Sch 2, Pt II, para 48.*]

(2)   Section 14 applies in relation to a trust of proceeds of sale of land and trustees of such a trust as in relation to a trust of land and trustees of land.

(3)   In this section 'trust of proceeds of sale of land' means (subject to subsection (5)) any trust of property (other than a trust of land) which consists of or includes—

(a)   any proceeds of a disposition of land held in trust (including settled land), or

(b)   any property representing any such proceeds.

(4)   The references in subsection (3) to a trust—

(a)   are to any description of trust (whether express, implied, resulting or constructive), including a trust for sale and a bare trust, and

(b)   include a trust created, or arising, before the commencement of this Act.

(5) A trust which (despite section 2) is a settlement for the purposes of the Settled Land Act 1925 cannot be a trust of proceeds of sale of land.

(6) In subsection (3)—

(a) 'disposition' includes any disposition made, or coming into operation, before the commencement of this Act, and

(b) the reference to settled land includes personal chattels to which section 67(1) of the Settled Land Act 1925 (heirlooms) applies.

[246.104]

18. Application of Part to personal representatives.—(1) The provisions of this Part relating to trustees, other than sections 10, 11 and 14, apply to personal representatives, but with appropriate modifications and without prejudice to the functions of personal representatives for the purposes of administration.

(2) The appropriate modifications include—

(a) the substitution of references to persons interested in the due administration of the estate for references to beneficiaries, and

(b) the substitution of references to the will for references to the disposition creating the trust.

(3) Section 3(1) does not apply to personal representatives if the death occurs before the commencement of this Act.

PART II

APPOINTMENT AND RETIREMENT OF TRUSTEES

[246.105]

19. Appointment and retirement of trustee at instance of beneficiaries.—

(1) This section applies in the case of a trust where—

(a) there is no person nominated for the purpose of appointing new trustees by the instrument, if any, creating the trust, and

(b) the beneficiaries under the trust are of full age and capacity and (taken together) are absolutely entitled to the property subject to the trust.

(2) The beneficiaries may give a direction or directions of either or both of the following descriptions—

(a) a written direction to a trustee or trustees to retire from the trust, and

(b) a written direction to the trustees or trustee for the time being (or, if there are none, to the personal representative of the last person who was a trustee) to appoint by writing to be a trustee or trustees the person or persons specified in the direction.

(3) Where—

(a) a trustee has been given a direction under subsection (2)(a),

(b) reasonable arrangements have been made for the protection of any rights of his in connection with the trust,

(c) after he has retired there will be either a trust corporation or at least two persons to act as trustees to perform the trust, and

(d) either another person is to be appointed to be a new trustee on his retirement (whether in compliance with a direction under subsection (2)(b) or otherwise) or the continuing trustees by deed consent to his retirement,

he shall make a deed declaring his retirement and shall be deemed to have retired and be discharged from the trust.

(4) Where a trustee retires under subsection (3) he and the continuing trustees (together with any new trustee) shall (subject to any arrangements for the protection of his rights) do anything necessary to vest the trust property in the continuing trustees (or the continuing and new trustees).

(5) This section has effect subject to the restrictions imposed by the Trustee Act 1925 on the number of trustees.

[246.106]

20. Appointment of substitute for incapable trustee.—(1) This section applies where—

(a) a trustee is incapable by reason of mental disorder of exercising his functions as trustee,

(b) there is no person who is both entitled and willing and able to appoint a trustee in place of him under section 36(1) of the Trustee Act 1925, and

(c) the beneficiaries under the trust are of full age and capacity and (taken together) are absolutely entitled to the property subject to the trust.

(2) The beneficiaries may give to—

(a) a receiver of the trustee,

(b) an attorney acting for him under the authority of a power of attorney created by an instrument which is registered under section 6 of the Enduring Powers of Attorney Act 1985, or

(c) a person authorised for the purpose by the authority having jurisdiction under Part VII of the Mental Health Act 1983,

a written direction to appoint by writing the person or persons specified in the direction to be a trustee or trustees in place of the incapable trustee.

[246.107]

21. Supplementary.—(1) For the purposes of section 19 or 20 a direction is given by beneficiaries if—

(a) a single direction is jointly given by all of them, or

(b) (subject to subsection (2)) a direction is given by each of them (whether solely or jointly with one or more, but not all, of the others),

and none of them by writing withdraws the direction given by him before it has been complied with.

(2) Where more than one direction is given each must specify for appointment or retirement the same person or persons.

(3) Subsection (7) of section 36 of the Trustee Act 1925 (powers of trustees appointed under that section) applies to a trustee appointed under section 19 or 20 as if he were appointed under that section.

(4)   A direction under section 19 or 20 must not specify a person or persons for appointment if the appointment of that person or those persons would be in contravention of section 35(1) of the Trustee Act 1925 or section 24(1) of the Law of Property Act 1925 (requirements as to identity of trustees).

(5)   Sections 19 and 20 do not apply in relation to a trust created by a disposition in so far as provision that they do not apply is made by the disposition.

(6)   Sections 19 and 20 do not apply in relation to a trust created before the commencement of this Act by a disposition in so far as provision to the effect that they do not apply is made by a deed executed—

   (a)   in a case in which the trust was created by one person and he is of full capacity, by that person, or
   (b)   in a case in which the trust was created by more than one person, by such of the persons who created the trust as are alive and of full capacity.

(7)   A deed executed for the purposes of subsection (6) is irrevocable.

(8)   Where a deed is executed for the purposes of subsection (6)—

   (a)   it does not affect anything done before its execution to comply with a direction under section 19 or 20, but
   (b)   a direction under section 19 or 20 which has been given but not complied with before its execution shall cease to have effect.

PART III

SUPPLEMENTARY

[246.108]
22.   Meaning of 'beneficiary'.—(1)   In this Act 'beneficiary', in relation to a trust, means any person who under the trust has an interest in property subject to the trust (including a person who has such an interest as a trustee or a personal representative).

(2)   In this Act references to a beneficiary who is beneficially entitled do not include a beneficiary who has an interest in property subject to the trust only by reason of being a trustee or personal representative.

(3)   For the purposes of this Act a person who is a beneficiary only by reason of being an annuitant is not to be regarded as entitled to an interest in possession in land subject to the trust.

[246.109]
23.   Other interpretation provisions.—(1)   In this Act 'purchaser' has the same meaning as in Part I of the Law of Property Act 1925.

(2)   Subject to that, where an expression used in this Act is given a meaning by the Law of Property Act 1925 it has the same meaning as in that Act unless the context otherwise requires.

(3)   In this Act 'the court' means—

   (a)   the High Court, or
   (b)   a county court.

[246.110]
24. Application to Crown.—(1) Subject to subsection (2), this Act binds the Crown.
(2) This Act (except so far as it relates to undivided shares and joint ownership) does not affect or alter the descent, devolution or nature of the estates and interests of or in—

(a) land for the time being vested in Her Majesty in right of the Crown or of the Duchy of Lancaster, or
(b) land for the time being belonging to the Duchy of Cornwall and held in right or respect of the Duchy.

[246.111]
25. Amendments, repeals etc.—(1) The enactments mentioned in Schedule 3 have effect subject to the amendments specified in that Schedule (which are minor or consequential on other provisions of this Act).
(2) The enactments mentioned in Schedule 4 are repealed to the extent specified in the third column of that Schedule.
(3) Neither section 2(5) nor the repeal by this Act of section 29 of the Settled Land Act 1925 applies in relation to the deed of settlement set out in the Schedule to the Chequers Estate Act 1917 or the trust instrument set out in the Schedule to the Chevening Estate Act 1959.
(4) The amendments and repeals made by this Act do not affect any entailed interest created before the commencement of this Act.
(5) The amendments and repeals made by this Act in consequence of section 3—

(a) do not affect a trust created by a will if the testator died before the commencement of this Act, and
(b) do not affect personal representatives of a person who died before that commencement;

and the repeal of section 22 of the Partnership Act 1890 does not apply in any circumstances involving the personal representatives of a partner who died before that commencement.

[246.112]
26. Power to make consequential provision.—(1) The Lord Chancellor may by order made by statutory instrument make any such supplementary, transitional or incidental provision as appears to him to be appropriate for any of the purposes of this Act or in consequence of any of the provisions of this Act.
(2) An order under subsection (1) may, in particular, include provision modifying any enactment contained in a public general or local Act which is passed before, or in the same Session as, this Act.
(3) A statutory instrument made in the exercise of the power conferred by this section is subject to annulment in pursuance of a resolution of either House of Parliament.

[246.113]
27. Short title, commencement and extent.—(1) This Act may be cited as the Trusts of Land and Appointment of Trustees Act 1996.

(2)   This Act comes into force on such day as the Lord Chancellor appoints by order made by statutory instrument.

(3)   Subject to subsection (4), the provisions of this Act extend only to England and Wales.

(4)   The repeal in section 30(2) of the Agriculture Act 1970 extends only to Northern Ireland.

SCHEDULE 1

Section 2

PROVISIONS CONSEQUENTIAL ON SECTION 2

Minors

[246.114]
1.—(1)   Where after the commencement of this Act a person purports to convey a legal estate in land to a minor, or two or more minors, alone, the conveyance—

   (a)   is not effective to pass the legal estate, but

   (b)   operates as a declaration that the land is held in trust for the minor or minors (or if he purports to convey it to the minor or minors in trust for any persons, for those persons).

(2)   Where after the commencement of this Act a person purports to convey a legal estate in land to—

   (a)   a minor or two or more minors, and

   (b)   another person who is, or other persons who are, of full age,

the conveyance operates to vest the land in the other person or persons in trust for the minor or minors and the other person or persons (or if he purports to convey it to them in trust for any persons, for those persons).

(3)   Where immediately before the commencement of this Act a conveyance is operating (by virtue of section 27 of the Settled Land Act 1925) as an agreement to execute a settlement in favour of a minor or minors—

   (a)   the agreement ceases to have effect on the commencement of this Act, and

   (b)   the conveyance subsequently operates instead as a declaration that the land is held in trust for the minor or minors.

2.   Where after the commencement of this Act a legal estate in land would, by reason of intestacy or in any other circumstances not dealt with in paragraph 1, vest in a person who is a minor if he were a person of full age, the land is held in trust for the minor.

Family charges

3.   Where, by virtue of an instrument coming into operation after the commencement of this Act, land becomes charged voluntarily (or in consideration of marriage) or by way of family arrangement, whether immediately or after an interval, with the payment of—

(a) a rentcharge for the life of a person or a shorter period, or

(b) capital, annual or periodical sums for the benefit of a person,

the instrument operates as a declaration that the land is held in trust for giving effect to the charge.

Charitable, ecclesiastical and public trusts

4.—(1) This paragraph applies in the case of land held on charitable, ecclesiastical or public trusts (other than land to which the Universities and College Estates Act 1925 applies).

(2) Where there is a conveyance of such land—

(a) if neither section 37(1) nor section 39(1) of the Charities Act 1993 applies to the conveyance, it shall state that the land is held on such trusts, and

(b) if neither section 37(2) nor section 39(2) of that Act has been complied with in relation to the conveyance and a purchaser has notice that the land is held on such trusts, he must see that any consents or orders necessary to authorise the transaction have been obtained.

(3) Where any trustees or the majority of any set of trustees have power to transfer or create any legal estate in the land, the estate shall be transferred or created by them in the names and on behalf of the persons in whom it is vested.

Entailed interests

5.—(1) Where a person purports by an instrument coming into operation after the commencement of this Act to grant to another person an entailed interest in real or personal property, the instrument—

(a) is not effective to grant an entailed interest, but

(b) operates instead as a declaration that the property is held in trust absolutely for the person to whom an entailed interest in the property was purportedly granted.

(2) Where a person purports by an instrument coming into operation after the commencement of this Act to declare himself a tenant in tail of real or personal property, the instrument is not effective to create an entailed interest.

Property held on settlement ceasing to exist

6. Where a settlement ceases to be a settlement for the purposes of the Settled Land Act 1925 because no relevant property (within the meaning of section 2(4)) is, or is deemed to be, subject to the settlement, any property which is or later becomes subject to the settlement is held in trust for the persons interested under the settlement.

*   *   *   *   *

Note. Schedules 2 (Amendment of statutory provisions imposing trust for sale), 3 (Minor and consequential amendments) and 4 (Repeals) are not set out here, but their effect where relevant is mentioned in the notes to the main text.

TRUSTEE ACT 2000

(2000 c 29)   [23 November 2000]

PART I

THE DUTY OF CARE

[246.115]
Note. This Act implements with effect from 1 February 2001 the changes recommended in the joint report of the Law Commission and the Scottish Law Commission *Trustees' Powers and Duties* (1999) Law Com No 260, Scot Law Com 172. Part I introduces a statutory duty of care which applies to trustees in the exercise of the new powers conferred by the Act and in the other circumstances set out in Sch 1. Part II confers a wide new power of investment which gives trustees the same powers of investment as an absolute owner. Part III confers on trustees powers to acquire and manage land similar to those contained in the TLATA 1996, s 6. Part IV provides trustees with wide powers to delegate discretions to agents and to vest trust property in nominees. Part V confers a general power for trust corporations and professional trustees to charge for their services in relation to existing as well as newly created trusts. Part VI contains a number of miscellaneous provisions including a provision conferring a new trustee insurance power (by substituting a new section for the Trustee Act 1925, s 19) and a provision extending the provisions of the Act to personal representatives.

[246.116]
1.   The duty of care.—(1)   Whenever the duty under this subsection applies to a trustee, he must exercise such care and skill as is reasonable in the circumstances, having regard in particular—

    (a)   to any special knowledge or experience that he has or holds himself out as having, and

    (b)   if he acts as trustee in the course of a business or profession, to any special knowledge or experience that it is reasonable to expect of a person acting in the course of that kind of business or profession.

(2)   In this Act the duty under subsection (1) is called 'the duty of care'.

[246.117]
2.   Application of duty of care. Schedule 1 makes provision about when the duty of care applies to a trustee.

PART II

INVESTMENT

[246.118]
3.   General power of investment.—(1)   Subject to the provisions of this Part, a trustee may make any kind of investment that he could make if he were absolutely entitled to the assets of the trust.
(2)   In this Act the power under subsection (1) is called 'the general power of investment'.
(3)   The general power of investment does not permit a trustee to make investments in land other than in loans secured on land (but see also section 8).
(4)   A person invests in a loan secured on land if he has rights under any contract under which—

   (a)   one person provides another with credit, and
   (b)   the obligation of the borrower to repay is secured on land.

(5)   'Credit' includes any cash loan or other financial accommodation.
(6)   'Cash' includes money in any form.

[246.119]
4.   Standard   investment   criteria.—(1)   In   exercising   any   power   of investment, whether arising under this Part or otherwise, a trustee must have regard to the standard investment criteria.
(2)   A trustee must from time to time review the investments of the trust and consider whether, having regard to the standard investment criteria, they should be varied.
(3)   The standard investment criteria, in relation to a trust, are—

   (a)   the suitability to the trust of investments of the same kind as any particular investment proposed to be made or retained and of that particular investment as an investment of that kind, and
   (b)   the need for diversification of investments of the trust, in so far as is appropriate to the circumstances of the trust.

[246.120]
5.   Advice.—(1)   Before exercising any power of investment, whether arising under this Part or otherwise, a trustee must (unless the exception applies) obtain and consider proper advice about the way in which, having regard to the standard investment criteria, the power should be exercised.
(2)   When reviewing the investments of the trust, a trustee must (unless the exception applies) obtain and consider proper advice about whether, having regard to the standard investment criteria, the investments should be varied.
(3)   The exception is that a trustee need not obtain such advice if he reasonably concludes that in all the circumstances it is unnecessary or inappropriate to do so.
(4)   Proper advice is the advice of a person who is reasonably believed by the trustee to be qualified to give it by his ability in and practical experience of financial and other matters relating to the proposed investment.

[246.121]
6. Restriction or exclusion of this Part etc.—(1) The general power of investment is—

(a) in addition to powers conferred on trustees otherwise than by this Act, but

(b) subject to any restriction or exclusion imposed by the trust instrument or by any enactment or any provision of subordinate legislation.

(2) For the purposes of this Act, an enactment or a provision of subordinate legislation is not to be regarded as being, or as being part of, a trust instrument.

(3) In this Act 'subordinate legislation' has the same meaning as in the Interpretation Act 1978.

[246.122]
7. Existing trusts.—(1) This Part applies in relation to trusts whether created before or after its commencement.

(2) No provision relating to the powers of a trustee contained in a trust instrument made before 3rd August 1961 is to be treated (for the purposes of section 6(1)(b)) as restricting or excluding the general power of investment.

(3) A provision contained in a trust instrument made before the commencement of this Part which—

(a) has effect under section 3(2) of the Trustee Investments Act 1961 as a power to invest under that Act, or

(b) confers power to invest under that Act,

is to be treated as conferring the general power of investment on a trustee.

PART III

ACQUISITION OF LAND

[246.123]
8. Power to acquire freehold and leasehold land.—(1) A trustee may acquire freehold or leasehold land in the United Kingdom—

(a) as an investment,
(b) for occupation by a beneficiary, or
(c) for any other reason.

(2) 'Freehold or leasehold land' means—

(a) in relation to England and Wales, a legal estate in land,
(b) in relation to Scotland—

(i) the estate or interest of the proprietor of the dominium utile or, in the case of land not held on feudal tenure, the estate or interest of the owner, or

(ii) a tenancy, and

(c) in relation to Northern Ireland, a legal estate in land, including land held under a fee farm grant.

(3) For the purpose of exercising his functions as a trustee, a trustee who acquires land under this section has all the powers of an absolute owner in relation to the land.

[246.124]
9. Restriction or exclusion of this Part etc. The powers conferred by this Part are—

(a) in addition to powers conferred on trustees otherwise than by this Part, but

(b) subject to any restriction or exclusion imposed by the trust instrument or by any enactment or any provision of subordinate legislation.

[246.125]
10. Existing trusts.—(1) This Part does not apply in relation to—

(a) a trust of property which consists of or includes land which (despite section 2 of the Trusts of Land and Appointment of Trustees Act 1996) is settled land, or

(b) a trust to which the Universities and College Estates Act 1925 applies.

(2) Subject to subsection (1), this Part applies in relation to trusts whether created before or after its commencement.

PART IV

AGENTS, NOMINEES AND CUSTODIANS

Agents

[246.126]
11. Power to employ agents.—(1) Subject to the provisions of this Part, the trustees of a trust may authorise any person to exercise any or all of their delegable functions as their agent.

(2) In the case of a trust other than a charitable trust, the trustees' delegable functions consist of any function other than—

(a) any function relating to whether or in what way any assets of the trust should be distributed,

(b) any power to decide whether any fees or other payment due to be made out of the trust funds should be made out of income or capital,

(c) any power to appoint a person to be a trustee of the trust, or

(d) any power conferred by any other enactment or the trust instrument which permits the trustees to delegate any of their functions or to appoint a person to act as a nominee or custodian.

(3) In the case of a charitable trust, the trustees' delegable functions are—

(a) any function consisting of carrying out a decision that the trustees have taken;

(b) any function relating to the investment of assets subject to the trust (including, in the case of land held as an investment, managing the land and creating or disposing of an interest in the land);

(c) any function relating to the raising of funds for the trust otherwise than by means of profits of a trade which is an integral part of carrying out the trust's charitable purpose;

(d) any other function prescribed by an order made by the Secretary of State.

(4) For the purposes of subsection (3)(c) a trade is an integral part of carrying out a trust's charitable purpose if, whether carried on in the United Kingdom or elsewhere, the profits are applied solely to the purposes of the trust and either—

(a) the trade is exercised in the course of the actual carrying out of a primary purpose of the trust, or

(b) the work in connection with the trade is mainly carried out by beneficiaries of the trust.

(5) The power to make an order under subsection (3)(d) is exercisable by statutory instrument which shall be subject to annulment in pursuance of a resolution of either House of Parliament.

[246.127]
12. Persons who may act as agents.—(1) Subject to subsection (2), the persons whom the trustees may under section 11 authorise to exercise functions as their agent include one or more of their number.

(2) The trustees may not authorise two (or more) persons to exercise the same function unless they are to exercise the function jointly.

(3) The trustees may not under section 11 authorise a beneficiary to exercise any function as their agent (even if the beneficiary is also a trustee).

(4) The trustees may under section 11 authorise a person to exercise functions as their agent even though he is also appointed to act as their nominee or custodian (whether under section 16, 17 or 18 or any other power).

[246.128]
13. Linked functions etc.—(1) Subject to subsections (2) and (5), a person who is authorised under section 11 to exercise a function is (whatever the terms of the agency) subject to any specific duties or restrictions attached to the function.

For example, a person who is authorised under section 11 to exercise the general power of investment is subject to the duties under section 4 in relation to that power.

(2) A person who is authorised under section 11 to exercise a power which is subject to a requirement to obtain advice is not subject to the requirement if he is the kind of person from whom it would have been proper for the trustees, in compliance with the requirement, to obtain advice.

(3) Subsections (4) and (5) apply to a trust to which section 11(1) of the Trusts of Land and Appointment of Trustees Act 1996 (duties to consult beneficiaries and give effect to their wishes) applies.

(4) The trustees may not under section 11 authorise a person to exercise any of their functions on terms that prevent them from complying with section 11(1) of the 1996 Act.

(5) A person who is authorised under section 11 to exercise any function relating to land subject to the trust is not subject to section 11(1) of the 1996 Act.

[246.129]

14. Terms of agency.—(1)   Subject to subsection (2) and sections 15(2) and 29 to 32, the trustees may authorise a person to exercise functions as their agent on such terms as to remuneration and other matters as they may determine.

(2)   The trustees may not authorise a person to exercise functions as their agent on any of the terms mentioned in subsection (3) unless it is reasonably necessary for them to do so.

(3)   The terms are—

  (a)   a term permitting the agent to appoint a substitute;

  (b)   a term restricting the liability of the agent or his substitute to the trustees or any beneficiary;

  (c)   a term permitting the agent to act in circumstances capable of giving rise to a conflict of interest.

[246.130]

15. Asset management: special restrictions.—(1)   The trustees may not authorise a person to exercise any of their asset management functions as their agent except by an agreement which is in or evidenced in writing.

(2)   The trustees may not authorise a person to exercise any of their asset management functions as their agent unless—

  (a)   they have prepared a statement that gives guidance as to how the functions should be exercised ('a policy statement'), and

  (b)   the agreement under which the agent is to act includes a term to the effect that he will secure compliance with—

    (i)   the policy statement, or

    (ii)   if the policy statement is revised or replaced under section 22, the revised or replacement policy statement.

(3)   The trustees must formulate any guidance given in the policy statement with a view to ensuring that the functions will be exercised in the best interests of the trust.

(4)   The policy statement must be in or evidenced in writing.

(5)   The asset management functions of trustees are their functions relating to—

  (a)   the investment of assets subject to the trust,

  (b)   the acquisition of property which is to be subject to the trust, and

  (c)   managing property which is subject to the trust and disposing of, or creating or disposing of an interest in, such property.

Nominees and custodians

[246.131]

16. Power to appoint nominees.—(1)   Subject to the provisions of this Part, the trustees of a trust may—

  (a)   appoint a person to act as their nominee in relation to such of the assets of the trust as they determine (other than settled land), and

  (b)   take such steps as are necessary to secure that those assets are vested in a person so appointed.

(2)   An appointment under this section must be in or evidenced in writing.

(3)   This section does not apply to any trust having a custodian trustee or in relation to any assets vested in the official custodian for charities.

[246.132]

17. Power to appoint custodians.—(1)   Subject to the provisions of this Part, the trustees of a trust may appoint a person to act as a custodian in relation to such of the assets of the trust as they may determine.

(2)   For the purposes of this Act a person is a custodian in relation to assets if he undertakes the safe custody of the assets or of any documents or records concerning the assets.

(3)   An appointment under this section must be in or evidenced in writing.

(4)   This section does not apply to any trust having a custodian trustee or in relation to any assets vested in the official custodian for charities.

[246.133]

18. Investment in bearer securities.—(1)   If trustees retain or invest in securities payable to bearer, they must appoint a person to act as a custodian of the securities.

(2)   Subsection (1) does not apply if the trust instrument or any enactment or provision of subordinate legislation contains provision which (however expressed) permits the trustees to retain or invest in securities payable to bearer without appointing a person to act as a custodian.

(3)   An appointment under this section must be in or evidenced in writing.

(4)   This section does not apply to any trust having a custodian trustee or in relation to any securities vested in the official custodian for charities.

[246.134]

19. Persons who may be appointed as nominees or custodians.—(1)   A person may not be appointed under section 16, 17 or 18 as a nominee or custodian unless one of the relevant conditions is satisfied.

(2)   The relevant conditions are that—

    (a)   the person carries on a business which consists of or includes acting as a nominee or custodian;

    (b)   the person is a body corporate which is controlled by the trustees;

    (c)   the person is a body corporate recognised under section 9 of the Administration of Justice Act 1985.

(3)   The question whether a body corporate is controlled by trustees is to be determined in accordance with section 840 of the Income and Corporation Taxes Act 1988.

(4)   The trustees of a charitable trust which is not an exempt charity must act in accordance with any guidance given by the Charity Commissioners concerning the selection of a person for appointment as a nominee or custodian under section 16, 17 or 18.

(5)   Subject to subsections (1) and (4), the persons whom the trustees may under section 16, 17 or 18 appoint as a nominee or custodian include—

    (a)   one of their number, if that one is a trust corporation, or

    (b)   two (or more) of their number, if they are to act as joint nominees or joint custodians.

(6)   The trustees may under section 16 appoint a person to act as their nominee even though he is also—

(a)   appointed to act as their custodian (whether under section 17 or 18 or any other power), or

(b)   authorised to exercise functions as their agent (whether under section 11 or any other power).

(7)   Likewise, the trustees may under section 17 or 18 appoint a person to act as their custodian even though he is also—

(a)   appointed to act as their nominee (whether under section 16 or any other power), or

(b)   authorised to exercise functions as their agent (whether under section 11 or any other power).

[246.135]
20.   Terms of appointment of nominees and custodians.—(1)   Subject to subsection (2) and sections 29 to 32, the trustees may under section 16, 17 or 18 appoint a person to act as a nominee or custodian on such terms as to remuneration and other matters as they may determine.
(2)   The trustees may not under section 16, 17 or 18 appoint a person to act as a nominee or custodian on any of the terms mentioned in subsection (3) unless it is reasonably necessary for them to do so.
(3)   The terms are—

(a)   a term permitting the nominee or custodian to appoint a substitute;

(b)   a term restricting the liability of the nominee or custodian or his substitute to the trustees or to any beneficiary;

(c)   a term permitting the nominee or custodian to act in circumstances capable of giving rise to a conflict of interest.

Review of and liability for agents, nominees and custodians etc

[246.136]
21.   Application of sections 22 and 23.—(1)   Sections 22 and 23 apply in a case where trustees have, under section 11, 16, 17 or 18—

(a)   authorised a person to exercise functions as their agent, or

(b)   appointed a person to act as a nominee or custodian.

(2)   Subject to subsection (3), sections 22 and 23 also apply in a case where trustees have, under any power conferred on them by the trust instrument or by any enactment or any provision of subordinate legislation—

(a)   authorised a person to exercise functions as their agent, or

(b)   appointed a person to act as a nominee or custodian.

(3)   If the application of section 22 or 23 is inconsistent with the terms of the trust instrument or the enactment or provision of subordinate legislation, the section in question does not apply.

[246.137]
22.   Review of agents, nominees and custodians etc.—(1)   While the agent, nominee or custodian continues to act for the trust, the trustees—

(a)   must keep under review the arrangements under which the agent, nominee or custodian acts and how those arrangements are being put into effect,

(b)   if circumstances make it appropriate to do so, must consider whether there is a need to exercise any power of intervention that they have, and

(c)   if they consider that there is a need to exercise such a power, must do so.

(2)   If the agent has been authorised to exercise asset management functions, the duty under subsection (1) includes, in particular—

(a)   a duty to consider whether there is any need to revise or replace the policy statement made for the purposes of section 15,

(b)   if they consider that there is a need to revise or replace the policy statement, a duty to do so, and

(c)   a duty to assess whether the policy statement (as it has effect for the time being) is being complied with.

(3)   Subsections (3) and (4) of section 15 apply to the revision or replacement of a policy statement under this section as they apply to the making of a policy statement under that section.

(4)   'Power of intervention' includes—

(a)   a power to give directions to the agent, nominee or custodian;

(b)   a power to revoke the authorisation or appointment.

[246.138]
23.   Liability for agents, nominees and custodians etc.—(1)   A trustee is not liable for any act or default of the agent, nominee or custodian unless he has failed to comply with the duty of care applicable to him, under paragraph 3 of Schedule 1—

(a)   when entering into the arrangements under which the person acts as agent, nominee or custodian, or

(b)   when carrying out his duties under section 22.

(2)   If a trustee has agreed a term under which the agent, nominee or custodian is permitted to appoint a substitute, the trustee is not liable for any act or default of the substitute unless he has failed to comply with the duty of care applicable to him, under paragraph 3 of Schedule 1—

(a)   when agreeing that term, or

(b)   when carrying out his duties under section 22 in so far as they relate to the use of the substitute.

Supplementary

[246.139]
24.   Effect of trustees exceeding their powers.   A failure by the trustees to act within the limits of the powers conferred by this Part—

(a) in authorising a person to exercise a function of theirs as an agent, or

(b) in appointing a person to act as a nominee or custodian,

does not invalidate the authorisation or appointment.

[246.140]
25. Sole trustees.—(1)   Subject to subsection (2), this Part applies in relation to a trust having a sole trustee as it applies in relation to other trusts (and references in this Part to trustees—except in sections 12(1) and (3) and 19(5)— are to be read accordingly).

(2)   Section 18 does not impose a duty on a sole trustee if that trustee is a trust corporation.

[246.141]
26. Restriction or exclusion of this Part etc. The powers conferred by this Part are—

(a) in addition to powers conferred on trustees otherwise than by this Act, but

(b) subject to any restriction or exclusion imposed by the trust instrument or by any enactment or any provision of subordinate legislation.

[246.142]
27. Existing trusts. This Part applies in relation to trusts whether created before or after its commencement.

PART V

REMUNERATION

[246.143]
28. Trustee's entitlement to payment under trust instrument.—(1) Except to the extent (if any) to which the trust instrument makes inconsistent provision, subsections (2) to (4) apply to a trustee if—

(a) there is a provision in the trust instrument entitling him to receive payment out of trust funds in respect of services provided by him to or on behalf of the trust, and

(b) the trustee is a trust corporation or is acting in a professional capacity.

(2)   The trustee is to be treated as entitled under the trust instrument to receive payment in respect of services even if they are services which are capable of being provided by a lay trustee.

(3)   Subsection (2) applies to a trustee of a charitable trust who is not a trust corporation only—

(a) if he is not a sole trustee, and

(b) to the extent that a majority of the other trustees have agreed that it should apply to him.

(4)   Any payments to which the trustee is entitled in respect of services are to be treated as remuneration for services (and not as a gift) for the purposes of—

(a) section 15 of the Wills Act 1837 (gifts to an attesting witness to be void), and

(b) section 34(3) of the Administration of Estates Act 1925 (order in which estate to be paid out).

(5) For the purposes of this Part, a trustee acts in a professional capacity if he acts in the course of a profession or business which consists of or includes the provision of services in connection with—

(a) the management or administration of trusts generally or a particular kind of trust, or

(b) any particular aspect of the management or administration of trusts generally or a particular kind of trust,

and the services he provides to or on behalf of the trust fall within that description.

(6) For the purposes of this Part, a person acts as a lay trustee if he—

(a) is not a trust corporation, and

(b) does not act in a professional capacity.

[246.144]
29. Remuneration of certain trustees.—(1) Subject to subsection (5), a trustee who—

(a) is a trust corporation, but

(b) is not a trustee of a charitable trust,

is entitled to receive reasonable remuneration out of the trust funds for any services that the trust corporation provides to or on behalf of the trust.

(2) Subject to subsection (5), a trustee who—

(a) acts in a professional capacity, but

(b) is not a trust corporation, a trustee of a charitable trust or a sole trustee,

is entitled to receive reasonable remuneration out of the trust funds for any services that he provides to or on behalf of the trust if each other trustee has agreed in writing that he may be remunerated for the services.

(3) 'Reasonable remuneration' means, in relation to the provision of services by a trustee, such remuneration as is reasonable in the circumstances for the provision of those services to or on behalf of that trust by that trustee and for the purposes of subsection (1) includes, in relation to the provision of services by a trustee who is an authorised institution under the Banking Act 1987 and provides the services in that capacity, the institution's reasonable charges for the provision of such services.

(4) A trustee is entitled to remuneration under this section even if the services in question are capable of being provided by a lay trustee.

(5) A trustee is not entitled to remuneration under this section if any provision about his entitlement to remuneration has been made—

(a) by the trust instrument, or

(b) by any enactment or any provision of subordinate legislation.

(6) This section applies to a trustee who has been authorised under a power conferred by Part IV or the trust instrument—

(a)   to exercise functions as an agent of the trustees, or

(b)   to act as a nominee or custodian,

as it applies to any other trustee.

[246.145]
30.   Remuneration of trustees of charitable trusts.—(1)   The Secretary of State may by regulations make provision for the remuneration of trustees of charitable trusts who are trust corporations or act in a professional capacity.

(2)   The power under subsection (1) includes power to make provision for the remuneration of a trustee who has been authorised under a power conferred by Part IV or any other enactment or any provision of subordinate legislation, or by the trust instrument—

(a)   to exercise functions as an agent of the trustees, or

(b)   to act as a nominee or custodian.

(3)   Regulations under this section may—

(a)   make different provision for different cases;

(b)   contain such supplemental, incidental, consequential and transitional provision as the Secretary of State considers appropriate.

(4)   The power to make regulations under this section is exercisable by statutory instrument, but no such instrument shall be made unless a draft of it has been laid before Parliament and approved by a resolution of each House of Parliament.

[246.146]
31.   Trustees' expenses.—(1)   A trustee—

(a)   is entitled to be reimbursed from the trust funds, or

(b)   may pay out of the trust funds,

expenses properly incurred by him when acting on behalf of the trust.

(2)   This section applies to a trustee who has been authorised under a power conferred by Part IV or any other enactment or any provision of subordinate legislation, or by the trust instrument—

(a)   to exercise functions as an agent of the trustees, or

(b)   to act as a nominee or custodian,

as it applies to any other trustee.

[246.147]
32.   Remuneration and expenses of agents, nominees and custodians.—(1)   This section applies if, under a power conferred by Part IV or any other enactment or any provision of subordinate legislation, or by the trust instrument, a person other than a trustee has been—

(a)   authorised to exercise functions as an agent of the trustees, or

(b)   appointed to act as a nominee or custodian.

(2)   The trustees may remunerate the agent, nominee or custodian out of the trust funds for services if—

(a) he is engaged on terms entitling him to be remunerated for those services, and

(b) the amount does not exceed such remuneration as is reasonable in the circumstances for the provision of those services by him to or on behalf of that trust.

(3)   The trustees may reimburse the agent, nominee or custodian out of the trust funds for any expenses properly incurred by him in exercising functions as an agent, nominee or custodian.

[246.148]
33. Application.—(1)   Subject to subsection (2), sections 28, 29, 31 and 32 apply in relation to services provided to or on behalf of, or (as the case may be) expenses incurred on or after their commencement on behalf of, trusts whenever created.

(2)   Nothing in section 28 or 29 is to be treated as affecting the operation of—

(a) section 15 of the Wills Act 1837, or

(b) section 34(3) of the Administration of Estates Act 1925,

in relation to any death occurring before the commencement of section 28 or (as the case may be) section 29.

PART VI

MISCELLANEOUS AND SUPPLEMENTARY

[246.149]
34. Power to insure.—(1)   [*This substitutes a new section for s 19 of the Trustee Act 1925: see para* **[246.17]**.]

(2)   In section 20(1) of the Trustee Act 1925 (application of insurance money) omit 'whether by fire or otherwise'.

(3)   The amendments made by this section apply in relation to trusts whether created before or after its commencement.

[246.150]
35. Personal representatives.—(1)   Subject to the following provisions of this section, this Act applies in relation to a personal representative administering an estate according to the law as it applies to a trustee carrying out a trust for beneficiaries.

(2)   For this purpose this Act is to be read with the appropriate modifications and in particular—

(a) references to the trust instrument are to be read as references to the will,

(b) references to a beneficiary or to beneficiaries, apart from the reference to a beneficiary in section 8(1)(b), are to be read as references to a person or the persons interested in the due administration of the estate, and

(c) the reference to a beneficiary in section 8(1)(b) is to be read as a reference to a person who under the will of the deceased or under the law relating to intestacy is beneficially interested in the estate.

(3)   Remuneration to which a personal representative is entitled under section 28 or 29 is to be treated as an administration expense for the purposes of—

(a) section 34(3) of the Administration of Estates Act 1925 (order in which estate to be paid out), and

(b) any provision giving reasonable administration expenses priority over the preferential debts listed in Schedule 6 to the Insolvency Act 1986.

(4)   Nothing in subsection (3) is to be treated as affecting the operation of the provisions mentioned in paragraphs (a) and (b) of that subsection in relation to any death occurring before the commencement of this section.

*   *   *   *   *

[246.151]
39.   Interpretation.—(1)   In this Act—
　'asset' includes any right or interest;
　'charitable trust' means a trust under which property is held for charitable purposes and 'charitable purposes' has the same meaning as in the Charities Act 1993;
　'custodian trustee' has the same meaning as in the Public Trustee Act 1906;
　'enactment' includes any provision of a Measure of the Church Assembly or of the General Synod of the Church of England;
　'exempt charity' has the same meaning as in the Charities Act 1993;
　'functions' includes powers and duties;
　'legal mortgage' has the same meaning as in the Law of Property Act 1925;
　'personal representative' has the same meaning as in the Trustee Act 1925;
　'settled land' has the same meaning as in the Settled Land Act 1925;
　'trust corporation' has the same meaning as in the Trustee Act 1925;
　'trust funds' means income or capital funds of the trust.
(2)   In this Act the expressions listed below are defined or otherwise explained by the provisions indicated—

asset management functions	section 15(5)
Custodian	section 17(2)
the duty of care	section 1(2)
the general power of investment	section 3(2)
lay trustee	section 28(6)
power of intervention	section 22(4)
the standard investment criteria	section 4(3)
Subordinate legislation	section 6(3)
trustee acting in a professional capacity	section 28(5)
trust instrument	sections 6(2) and 35(2)(a)

[246.152]
40.   Minor and consequential amendments etc.—(1)   Schedule 2 (minor and consequential amendments) shall have effect.
(2)   Schedule 3 (transitional provisions and savings) shall have effect.
(3)   Schedule 4 (repeals) shall have effect.

[246.153]
41.   Power to amend other Acts.—(1)   A Minister of the Crown may by order make such amendments of any Act, including an Act extending to places outside England and Wales, as appear to him appropriate in consequence of or in connection with Part II or III.

(2)   Before exercising the power under subsection (1) in relation to a local, personal or private Act, the Minister must consult any person who appears to him to be affected by any proposed amendment.

(3)   An order under this section may—

(a)   contain such transitional provisions and savings as the Minister thinks fit;

(b)   make different provision for different purposes.

(4)   The power to make an order under this section is exercisable by statutory instrument which shall be subject to annulment in pursuance of a resolution of either House of Parliament.

(5)   'Minister of the Crown' has the same meaning as in the Ministers of the Crown Act 1975.

[246.154]

42.   Commencement and extent.—(1)   Section 41, this section and section 43 shall come into force on the day on which this Act is passed.

(2)   The remaining provisions of this Act shall come into force on such day as the Lord Chancellor may appoint by order made by statutory instrument; and different days may be so appointed for different purposes.

(3)   An order under subsection (2) may contain such transitional provisions and savings as the Lord Chancellor considers appropriate in connection with the order.

(4)   Subject to section 41(1) and subsection (5), this Act extends to England and Wales only.

(5)   An amendment or repeal in Part II or III of Schedule 2 or Part II of Schedule 4 has the same extent as the provision amended or repealed.

[246.155]

43.   Short title. This Act may be cited as the Trustee Act 2000.

SCHEDULE 1

Section 2

APPLICATION OF DUTY OF CARE

Investment

[246.156]

1.   The duty of care applies to a trustee—

(a)   when exercising the general power of investment or any other power of investment, however conferred;

(b)   when carrying out a duty to which he is subject under section 4 or 5 (duties relating to the exercise of a power of investment or to the review of investments).

Acquisition of land

2.   The duty of care applies to a trustee—

    (a)   when exercising the power under section 8 to acquire land;

    (b)   when exercising any other power to acquire land, however conferred;

    (c)   when exercising any power in relation to land acquired under a power mentioned in sub-paragraph (a) or (b).

Agents, nominees and custodians

3.—(1)   The duty of care applies to a trustee—

    (a)   when entering into arrangements under which a person is authorised under section 11 to exercise functions as an agent;

    (b)   when entering into arrangements under which a person is appointed under section 16 to act as a nominee;

    (c)   when entering into arrangements under which a person is appointed under section 17 or 18 to act as a custodian;

    (d)   when entering into arrangements under which, under any other power, however conferred, a person is authorised to exercise functions as an agent or is appointed to act as a nominee or custodian;

    (e)   when carrying out his duties under section 22 (review of agent, nominee or custodian, etc).

(2)   For the purposes of sub-paragraph (1), entering into arrangements under which a person is authorised to exercise functions or is appointed to act as a nominee or custodian includes, in particular—

    (a)   selecting the person who is to act,

    (b)   determining any terms on which he is to act, and

    (c)   if the person is being authorised to exercise asset management functions, the preparation of a policy statement under section 15.

Compounding of liabilities

4.   The duty of care applies to a trustee—

    (a)   when exercising the power under section 15 of the Trustee Act 1925 to do any of the things referred to in that section;

    (b)   when exercising any corresponding power, however conferred.

Insurance

5.   The duty of care applies to a trustee—

    (a)   when exercising the power under section 19 of the Trustee Act 1925 to insure property;

    (b)   when exercising any corresponding power, however conferred.

Reversionary interests, valuations and audit

6. The duty of care applies to a trustee—

  (a) when exercising the power under section 22(1) or (3) of the Trustee Act 1925 to do any of the things referred to there;

  (b) when exercising any corresponding power, however conferred.

Exclusion of duty of care

7. The duty of care does not apply if or in so far as it appears from the trust instrument that the duty is not meant to apply.

*   *   *   *   *

Note. Schedules 2 and 4 contain minor and consequential amendments and repeals of previous statutes which are noted, where relevant, in the earlier pages of this Section. Schedule 3 contains transitional provisions and savings.

Family provision and relief from forfeiture

INHERITANCE (PROVISION FOR FAMILY AND DEPENDANTS) ACT 1975

(1975 c 63)   [12 November 1975]

[247.1]

Note. For the law of family provision see Vol 1, para **[102.1]** et seq.

References to capital transfer tax throughout the Inheritance (Provision for Family and Dependants) Act 1975 (I(PFD)A 1975) now have effect as references to inheritance tax: see the Finance Act 1986, s 100(1)(b). For the effect of inheritance tax on an order under the I(PFD)A 1975, see the Inheritance Tax Act 1984 (ITA 1984), s 146; and see further the ITA 1984, s 29A (as inserted by the Finance Act 1989) as to the reduction of the amount of inheritance tax exemption on a deceased person's estate where an exempt beneficiary settles a claim under the I(PFD)A 1975 from his own resources.

The I(PFD)A 1975 is printed as currently in force. The Act is prospectively amended from a date to be appointed by the Family Law Act 1996 (FLA 1996), s 66(1)(2), Sch 8, para 27 (subject to savings for existing proceedings under Sch 9, para 5). No date has been appointed and in a written answer to the House of Lords on 16 January 2001 the Lord Chancellor announced that the government had decided not to implement the main provisions of Part II and would be inviting Parliament to repeal the relevant sections as soon as a legislative opportunity arose. The provisions of the FLA 1996 prospectively amending the I(PFD)A 1975 are consequential on the provisions of Part II of the 1996 Act, which are in due course to be repealed and will themselves also be repealed. The prospective amendments to the I(PFD)A 1975 introduced by the FLA 1996 have not therefore been noted below.

[247.2]

1. Application for financial provision from deceased's estate.—(1) Where after the commencement of this Act a person dies domiciled in England and Wales and is survived by any of the following persons—

(a) the wife or husband of the deceased;

(b) a former wife or former husband of the deceased who has not remarried;

[(ba) any person (not being included in paragraph (a) or (b) above) to whom subsection (1A) below applies;][1]

(c) a child of the deceased;

(d) any person (not being a child of the deceased) who, in the case of any marriage to which the deceased was at any time a party, was treated by the deceased as a child of the family in relation to that marriage;

  (e)   any person (not being a person included in the foregoing paragraphs of
        this subsection) who immediately before the death of the deceased was
        being maintained, either wholly or partly, by the deceased;

that person may apply to the court for an order under section 2 of this Act on the
ground that the disposition of the deceased's estate effected by his will or the
law relating to intestacy, or the combination of his will and that law, is not such
as to make reasonable financial provision for the applicant.
[(1A)   This subsection applies to a person if the deceased died on or after 1st
January 1996 and, during the whole of the period of two years ending
immediately before the date when the deceased died, the person was living—

  (a)   in the same household as the deceased, and
  (b)   as the husband or wife of the deceased.][2]

(2)   In this Act 'reasonable financial provision'—

  (a)   in the case of an application made by virtue of subsection (1)(a) above by
        the husband or wife of the deceased (except where the marriage with the
        deceased was the subject of a decree of judicial separation and at the date
        of death the decree was in force and the separation was continuing),
        means such financial provision as it would be reasonable in all the
        circumstances of the case for a husband or wife to receive, whether or
        not that provision is required for his or her maintenance;
  (b)   in the case of any other application made by virtue of subsection (1)
        above, means such financial provision as it would be reasonable in all the
        circumstances of the case for the applicant to receive for his
        maintenance.

(3)   For the purposes of subsection (1)(e) above, a person shall be treated as
being maintained by the deceased, either wholly or partly, as the case may be, if
the deceased, otherwise than for full valuable consideration, was making a
substantial contribution in money or money's worth towards the reasonable
needs of that person.

1   Para (ba): inserted by the LR(S)A 1995, s 2(2).
2   Sub-s (1A): inserted by the LR(S)A 1995, s 2(3).

[247.3]
2.   Powers of court to make orders.—(1)   Subject to the provisions of this
Act, where an application is made for an order under this section, the court may,
if it is satisfied that the disposition of the deceased's estate effected by his will
or the law relating to intestacy, or the combination of his will and that law, is not
such as to make reasonable financial provision for the applicant, make any one
or more of the following orders—

  (a)   an order for the making to the applicant out of the net estate of the
        deceased of such periodical payments and for such term as may be
        specified in the order;
  (b)   an order for the payment to the applicant out of that estate of a lump sum
        of such amount as may be so specified;
  (c)   an order for the transfer to the applicant of such property comprised in
        that estate as may be so specified;

(d) an order for the settlement for the benefit of the applicant of such property comprised in that estate as may be so specified;

(e) an order for the acquisition out of property comprised in that estate of such property as may be so specified and for the transfer of the property so acquired to the applicant or for the settlement thereof for his benefit;

(f) an order varying any ante-nuptial or post-nuptial settlement (including such a settlement made by will) made on the parties to a marriage to which the deceased was one of the parties, the variation being for the benefit of the surviving party to that marriage, or any child of that marriage, or any person who was treated by the deceased as a child of the family in relation to that marriage.

(2) An order under subsection (1)(a) above providing for the making out of the net estate of the deceased of periodical payments may provide for—

(a) payments of such amount as may be specified in the order,

(b) payments equal to the whole of the income of the net estate or of such portion thereof as may be so specified,

(c) payments equal to the whole of the income of such part of the net estate as the court may direct to be set aside or appropriated for the making out of the income thereof of payments under this section,

or may provide for the amount of the payments or any of them to be determined in any other way the court thinks fit.

(3) Where an order under subsection (1)(a) above provides for the making of payments of an amount specified in the order, the order may direct that such part of the net estate as may be so specified shall be set aside or appropriated for the making out of the income thereof of those payments; but no larger part of the net estate shall be so set aside or appropriated than is sufficient, at the date of the order, to produce by the income thereof the amount required for the making of those payments.

(4) An order under this section may contain such consequential and supplemental provisions as the court thinks necessary or expedient for the purpose of giving effect to the order or for the purpose of securing that the order operates fairly as between one beneficiary of the estate of the deceased and another and may, in particular, but without prejudice to the generality of this subsection—

(a) order any person who holds any property which forms part of the net estate of the deceased to make such payment or transfer such property as may be specified in the order;

(b) vary the disposition of the deceased's estate effected by the will or the law relating to intestacy, or by both the will and the law relating to intestacy, in such manner as the court thinks fair and reasonable having regard to the provisions of the order and all the circumstances of the case;

(c) confer on the trustees of any property which is the subject of an order under this section such powers as appear to the court to be necessary or expedient.

[247.4]
3. Matters to which court is to have regard in exercising powers under s 2.—(1) Where an application is made for an order under section 2 of this

Act, the court shall, in determining whether the disposition of the deceased's estate effected by his will or the law relating to intestacy, or the combination of his will and that law, is such as to make reasonable financial provision for the applicant and, if the court considers that reasonable financial provision has not been made, in determining whether and in what manner it shall exercise its powers under that section, have regard to the following matters, that is to say—

(a) the financial resources and financial needs which the applicant has or is likely to have in the foreseeable future;

(b) the financial resources and financial needs which any other applicant for an order under section 2 of this Act has or is likely to have in the foreseeable future;

(c) the financial resources and financial needs which any beneficiary of the estate of the deceased has or is likely to have in the foreseeable future;

(d) any obligations and responsibilities which the deceased had towards any applicant for an order under the said section 2 or towards any beneficiary of the estate of the deceased;

(e) the size and nature of the net estate of the deceased;

(f) any physical or mental disability of any applicant for an order under the said section 2 or any beneficiary of the estate of the deceased;

(g) any other matter, including the conduct of the applicant or any other persons, which in the circumstances of the case the court may consider relevant.

(2) Without prejudice to the generality of paragraph (g) of subsection (1) above, where an application for an order under section 2 of this Act is made by virtue of section 1(1)(a) or 1(1)(b) of this Act, the court shall, in addition to the matters specifically mentioned in paragraphs (a) to (f) of that subsection, have regard to—

(a) the age of the applicant and the duration of the marriage;

(b) the contribution made by the applicant to the welfare of the family of the deceased, including any contribution made by looking after the home or caring for the family;

and, in the case of an application by the wife or husband of the deceased, the court shall also, unless at the date of death a decree of judicial separation was in force and the separation was continuing, have regard to the provision which the applicant might reasonably have expected to receive if on the day on which the deceased died the marriage, instead of being terminated by death, had been terminated by a decree of divorce.

[(2A) Without prejudice to the generality of paragraph (g) of subsection (1) above, where an application for an order under section 2 of this Act is made by virtue of section 1(1)(ba) of this Act, the court shall, in addition to the matters specifically mentioned in paragraphs (a) to (f) of that subsection, have regard to—

(a) the age of the applicant and the length of the period during which the applicant lived as the husband or wife of the deceased and in the same household as the deceased;

(b) the contribution made by the applicant to the welfare of the family of the deceased, including any contribution made by looking after the home or caring for the family.][1]

(3)   Without prejudice to the generality of paragraph (g) of subsection (1) above, where an application for an order under section 2 of this Act is made by virtue of section 1(1)(c) or 1(1)(d) of this Act, the court shall, in addition to the matters specifically mentioned in paragraphs (a) to (f) of that subsection, have regard to the manner in which the applicant was being or in which he might expect to be educated or trained, and where the application is made by virtue of section 1(1)(d) the court shall also have regard—

  (a)   to whether the deceased had assumed any responsibility for the applicant's maintenance and, if so, to the extent to which and the basis upon which the deceased assumed that responsibility and to the length of time for which the deceased discharged that responsibility;
  (b)   to whether in assuming and discharging that responsibility the deceased did so knowing that the applicant was not his own child;
  (c)   to the liability for any other person to maintain the applicant.

(4)   Without prejudice to the generality of paragraph (g) of subsection (1) above, where an application for an order under section 2 of this Act is made by virtue of section 1(1)(e) of this Act, the court shall, in addition to the matters specifically mentioned in paragraphs (a) to (f) of that subsection, have regard to the extent to which and the basis upon which the deceased assumed responsibility for the maintenance of the applicant and to the length of time for which the deceased discharged that responsibility.

(5)   In considering the matters to which the court is required to have regard under this section, the court shall take into account the facts as known to the court at the date of the hearing.

(6)   In considering the financial resources of any person for the purposes of this section the court shall take into account his earning capacity and in considering the financial needs of any person for the purposes of this section the court shall take into account his financial obligations and responsibilities.

1   Sub-s (2A): inserted by the LR(S)A 1995, s 2(1), (4).

[247.5]
4.   Time-limit for applications. An application for an order under section 2 of this Act shall not, except with the permission of the court, be made after the end of the period of six months from the date on which representation with respect to the estate of the deceased is first taken out.

[247.6]
5.   Interim orders.—(1)   Where on an application for an order under section 2 of this Act it appears to the court—

  (a)   that the applicant is in immediate need of financial assistance, but it is not yet possible to determine what order (if any) should be made under that section; and
  (b)   that property forming part of the net estate of the deceased is or can be made available to meet the need of the applicant;

the court may order that, subject to such conditions or restrictions, if any, as the court may impose and to any further order of the court, there shall be paid to the applicant out of the net estate of the deceased such sum or sums and (if more than one) at such intervals as the court thinks reasonable; and the court may order that, subject to the provision of this Act, such payments are to be made until such date as the court may specify, not being later than the date on which the court either makes an order under the said section 2 or decides not to exercise its powers under that section.

(2) Subsections (2), (3) and (4) of section 2 of this Act shall apply in relation to an order under this section as they apply in relation to an order under that section.

(3) In determining what order, if any, should be made under this section the court shall, so far as the urgency of the case admits, have regard to the same matters as those to which the court is required to have regard under section 3 of this Act.

(4) An order made under section 2 of this Act may provide that any sum paid to the applicant by virtue of this section shall be treated to such an extent and in such manner as may be provided by that order as having been paid on account of any payment provided for by that order.

[247.7]
6. Variation, discharge etc of orders for periodical payments.—(1) Subject to the provisions of this Act, where the court has made an order under section 2(1)(a) of this Act (in this section referred to as 'the original order') for the making of periodical payments to any person (in this section referred to as 'the original recipient'), the court, on an application under this section, shall have power by order to vary or discharge the original order or to suspend any provision of it temporarily and to revive the operation of any provision so suspended.

(2) Without prejudice to the generality of subsection (1) above, an order made on an application for the variation of the original order may—

   (a) provide for the making out of any relevant property of such periodical payments and for such term as may be specified in the order to any person who has applied, or would but for section 4 of this Act be entitled to apply, for an order under section 2 of this Act (whether or not, in the case of any application, an order was made in favour of the applicant);

   (b) provide for the payment out of any relevant property of a lump sum of such amount as may be so specified to the original recipient or to any such person as is mentioned in paragraph (a) above;

   (c) provide for the transfer of the relevant property, or such part thereof as may be so specified, to the original recipient or to any such person as is so mentioned.

(3) Where the original order provides that any periodical payments payable thereunder to the original recipient are to cease on the occurrence of an event specified in the order (other than the remarriage of a former wife or former husband) or on the expiration of a period so specified, then, if, before the end of the period six months from the date of the occurrence of that event or of the expiration of that period, an application is made for an order under this section, the court shall have power to make any order which it would have had power to make if the application had been made before that date (whether in favour of the original recipient or any such person as is mentioned in subsection (2)(a) above and whether having effect from that date or from such later date as the court may specify).

(4)   Any reference in this section to the original order shall include reference to an order made under this section and any reference in this section to the original recipient shall include a reference to any person to whom periodical payments are required to be made by virtue of an order under this section.

(5)   An application under this section may be made by any of the following persons, that is to say—

  (a)   any person who by virtue of section 1(1) of this Act has applied, or would but for section 4 of this Act be entitled to apply, for an order under section 2 of this Act,
  (b)   the personal representatives of the deceased,
  (c)   the trustees of any relevant property, and
  (d)   any beneficiary of the estate of the deceased.

(6)   An order under this section may only affect—

  (a)   property the income of which is at the date of the order applicable wholly or in part for the making of periodical payments to any person who has applied for an order under this Act, or
  (b)   in the case of an application under subsection (3) above in respect of payments which have ceased to be payable on the occurrence of an event or the expiration of a period, property the income of which was so applicable immediately before the occurrence of that event or the expiration of that period, as the case may be,

and any such property as is mentioned in paragraph (a) or (b) above is in subsections (2) and (5) above referred to as 'relevant property'.

(7)   In exercising the powers conferred by this section the court shall have regard to all the circumstances of the case, including any change in any of the matters to which the court was required to have regard when making the order to which the application relates.

(8)   Where the court makes an order under this section, it may give such consequential directions as it thinks necessary or expedient having regard to the provisions of the order.

(9)   No such order as is mentioned in sections 2(1)(d), (e) or (f), 9, 10 or 11 of this Act shall be made on an application under this section.

(10)   For the avoidance of doubt it is hereby declared that, in relation to an order which provides for the making of periodical payments which are to cease on the occurrence of an event specified in the order (other than the remarriage of a former wife or former husband) or on the expiration of a period so specified, the power to vary an order includes power to provide for the making of periodical payments after the expiration of that period or the occurrence of that event.

[247.8]
7.   Payment of lump sums by instalments.—(1)   An order under section 2(1)(b) or 6(2)(b) of this Act for the payment of a lump sum may provide for the payment of that sum by instalments of such amount as may be specified in the order.

(2)   Where an order is made by virtue of subsection (1) above, the court shall have power, on an application made by the person to whom the lump sum is payable, by the personal representatives of the deceased or by the trustees of the

property out of which the lump sum is payable, to vary that order by varying the number of instalments payable, the amount of any instalment and the date on which any instalment becomes payable.

Property available for financial provision

[247.9]
8.   Property treated as part of 'net estate'.—(1)   Where a deceased person has in accordance with the provisions of any enactment nominated any person to receive any sum of money or other property on his death and that nomination is in force at the time of his death, that sum of money, after deducting therefrom any capital transfer tax payable in respect thereof, or that other property, to the extent of the value thereof at the date of the death of the deceased after deducting therefrom any capital transfer tax so payable, shall be treated for the purposes of this Act as part of the net estate of the deceased; but this subsection shall not render any person liable for having paid that sum or transferred that other property to the person named in the nomination in accordance with the directions given in the nomination.
(2)   Where any sum of money or other property is received by any person as a donatio mortis causa made by a deceased person, that sum of money, after deducting therefrom any capital transfer tax payable thereon, or that other property, to the extent of the value thereof at the date of the death of the deceased after deducting therefrom any capital transfer tax so payable, shall be treated for the purposes of this Act as part of the net estate of the deceased; but this subsection shall not render any person liable for having paid that sum or transferred that other property in order to give effect to that donatio mortis causa.
(3)   The amount of capital transfer tax to be deducted for the purposes of this section shall not exceed the amount of that tax which has been borne by the person nominated by the deceased or, as the case may be, the person who has received a sum of money or other property as a donatio mortis causa.

[247.10]
9.   Property held on a joint tenancy.—(1)   Where a deceased person was immediately before his death beneficially entitled to a joint tenancy of any property, then, if, before the end of the period of six months from the date on which representation with respect to the estate of the deceased was first taken out, an application is made for an order under section 2 of this Act, the court for the purpose of facilitating the making of financial provision for the applicant under this Act may order that the deceased's severable share of that property, at the value thereof immediately before his death, shall, to such extent as appears to the court to be just in all the circumstances of the case, be treated for the purposes of this Act as part of the net estate of the deceased.
(2)   In determining the extent to which any severable share is to be treated as part of the net estate of the deceased by virtue of an order under subsection (1) above, the court shall have regard to any capital transfer tax payable in respect of that severable share.
(3)   Where an order is made under subsection (1) above, the provisions of this section shall not render any person liable for anything done by him before the order was made.

(4) For the avoidance of doubt it is hereby declared that for the purposes of this section there may be a joint tenancy of a chose in action.

Powers of court in relation to transactions intended to defeat applications for financial provision

[247.11]
10. Dispositions intended to defeat applications for financial provision.—
(1) Where an application is made to the court for an order under section 2 of this Act, the applicant may, in the proceedings on that application, apply to the court for an order under subsection (2) below.
(2) Where on an application under subsection (1) above the court is satisfied—

(a) that, less than six years before the date of the death of the deceased, the deceased with the intention of defeating an application for financial provision under this Act made a disposition, and

(b) that full valuable consideration for that disposition was not given by the person to whom or for the benefit of whom the disposition was made (in this section referred to as 'the donee') or by any other person, and

(c) that the exercise of the powers conferred by this section would facilitate the making of financial provision for the applicant under this Act,

then, subject to the provisions of this section and of sections 12 and 13 of this Act, the court may order the donee (whether or not at the date of the order he holds any interest in the property disposed of to him or for his benefit by the deceased) to provide, for the purpose of the making of that financial provision, such sum of money or other property as may be specified in the order.
(3) Where an order is made under subsection (2) above as respects any disposition made by the deceased which consisted of the payment of money to or for the benefit of the donee, the amount of any sum of money or the value of any property ordered to be provided under that subsection shall not exceed the amount of the payment made by the deceased after deducting therefrom any capital transfer tax borne by the donee in respect of that payment.
(4) Where an order is made under subsection (2) above as respects any disposition made by the deceased which consisted of the transfer of property (other than a sum of money) to or for the benefit of the donee, the amount of any sum of money or the value of any property ordered to be provided under that subsection shall not exceed the value at the date of the death of the deceased of the property disposed of by him to or for the benefit of the donee (or if that property has been disposed of by the person to whom it was transferred by the deceased, the value at the date of that disposal thereof) after deducting therefrom any capital transfer tax borne by the donee in respect of the transfer of that property by the deceased.
(5) Where an application (in this subsection referred to as 'the original application') is made for an order under subsection (2) above in relation to any disposition, then if on an application under this subsection by the donee or by any applicant for an order under section 2 of this Act the court is satisfied—

(a) that, less than six years before the date of the death of the deceased, the deceased with the intention of defeating an application for financial provision under this Act made a disposition other than the disposition which is the subject of the original application, and

(b) that full valuable consideration for that other disposition was not given by the person to whom or for the benefit of whom that other disposition was made or by any other person,

the court may exercise in relation to the person to whom or for the benefit of whom that other disposition was made the powers which the court would have had under subsection (2) above if the original application had been made in respect of that other disposition and the court had been satisfied as to the matters set out in paragraphs (a), (b) and (c) of that subsection; and where any application is made under this subsection, any reference in this section (except in subsection (2)(b)) to the donee shall include a reference to the person to whom or for the benefit of whom that other disposition was made.

(6)   In determining whether and in what manner to exercise its powers under this section, the court shall have regard to the circumstances in which any disposition was made and any valuable consideration which was given therefor, the relationship, if any, of the donee to the deceased, the conduct and financial resources of the donee and all the other circumstances of the case.

(7)   In this section 'disposition' does not include—

(a) any provision in a will, any such nomination as is mentioned in section 8(1) of this Act or any donatio mortis causa, or

(b) any appointment of property made, otherwise than by will, in the exercise of a special power of appointment,

but, subject to these exceptions, includes any payment of money (including the payment of a premium under a policy of assurance) and any conveyance, assurance, appointment or gift of property of any description, whether made by an instrument or otherwise.

(8)   The provisions of this section do not apply to any disposition made before the commencement of this Act.

[247.12]
11.   Contracts to leave property by will.—(1)   Where an application is made to a court for an order under section 2 of this Act, the applicant may, in the proceedings on that application, apply to the court for an order under this section.

(2)   Where on an application under subsection (1) above the court is satisfied—

(a) that the deceased made a contract by which he agreed to leave by his will a sum of money or other property to any person or by which he agreed that a sum of money or other property would be paid or transferred to any person out of his estate, and

(b) that the deceased made that contract with the intention of defeating an application for financial provision under this Act, and

(c) that when the contract was made full valuable consideration for that contract was not given or promised by the person with whom or for the benefit of whom the contract was made (in this section referred to as 'the donee') or by any other person, and

(d) that the exercise of the powers conferred by this section would facilitate the making of financial provision for the applicant under this Act, then, subject to the provisions of this section and of sections 12 and 13 of this Act, the court may make any one or more of the following orders, that is to say—

(i)   if any money has been paid or any other property has been transferred to or for the benefit of the donee in accordance with the contract, an order directing the donee to provide, for the purpose of the making of that financial provision, such sum of money or other property as may be specified in the order;

(ii) if the money or all the money has not been paid or the property or all the property has not been transferred in accordance with the contract, an order directing the personal representatives not to make any payment or transfer any property, or not to make any further payment or transfer any further property, as the case may be, in accordance therewith or directing the personal representatives only to make such payment or transfer such property as may be specified in the order.

(3)   Notwithstanding anything in subsection (2) above, the court may exercise its powers thereunder in relation to any contract made by the deceased only to the extent that the court considers that the amount of any sum of money paid or to be paid or the value of any property transferred or to be transferred in accordance with the contract exceeds the value of any valuable consideration given or to be given for that contract, and for this purpose the court shall have regard to the value of property at the date of the hearing.

(4)   In determining whether and in what manner to exercise its powers under this section, the court shall have regard to the circumstances in which the contract was made, the relationship, if any, of the donee to the deceased, the conduct and financial resources of the donee and all the other circumstances of the case.

(5)   Where an order has been made under subsection (2) above in relation to any contract, the rights of any person to enforce that contract or to recover damages or to obtain other relief for the breach thereof shall be subject to any adjustment made by the court under section 12(3) of this Act and shall survive to such extent only as is consistent with giving effect to the terms of that order.

(6)   The provisions of this section do not apply to a contract made before the commencement of this Act.

[247.13]

12.   Provisions supplementary to ss 10 and 11.—(1)   Where the exercise of any of the powers conferred by section 10 or 11 of this Act is conditional on the court being satisfied that a disposition or contract was made by a deceased person with the intention of defeating an application for financial provision under this Act, that condition shall be fulfilled if the court is of the opinion that, on a balance of probabilities, the intention of the deceased (though not necessarily his sole intention) in making the disposition or contract was to prevent an order for financial provision being made under this Act or to reduce the amount of the provision which might otherwise be granted by an order thereunder.

(2)   Where an application is made under section 11 of this Act with respect to any contract made by the deceased and no valuable consideration was given or promised by any person for that contract then, notwithstanding anything in

subsection (1) above, it shall be presumed, unless the contrary is shown, that the deceased made that contract with the intention of defeating an application for financial provision under this Act.

(3)   Where the court makes an order under section 10 or 11 of this Act it may give such consequential directions as it thinks fit (including directions requiring the making of any payment or the transfer of any property) for giving effect to the order or for securing a fair adjustment of the rights of the persons affected thereby.

(4)   Any power conferred on the court by the said section 10 or 11 to order the donee, in relation to any disposition or contract, to provide any sum of money or other property shall be exercisable in like manner in relation to the personal representative of the donee, and—

    (a)   any reference in section 10(4) to the disposal of property by the donee shall include a reference to disposal by the personal representative of the donee, and

    (b)   any reference in section 10(5) to an application by the donee under that subsection shall include a reference to an application by the personal representative of the donee;

but the court shall not have power under the said section 10 or 11 to make an order in respect of any property forming part of the estate of the donee which has been distributed by the personal representative; and the personal representative shall not be liable for having distributed any such property before he has notice of the making of an application under the said section 10 or 11 on the ground that he ought to have taken into account the possibility that such an application would be made.

[247.14]
13.   Provisions as to trustees in relation to ss 10 and 11.—(1)   Where an application is made for—

    (a)   an order under section 10 of this Act in respect of a disposition made by the deceased to any person as a trustee, or

    (b)   an order under section 11 of this Act in respect of any payment made or property transferred, in accordance with a contract made by the deceased, to any person as a trustee,

the powers of the court under the said section 10 or 11 to order that trustee to provide a sum of money or other property shall be subject to the following limitation (in addition, in a case of an application under section 10, to any provision regarding the deduction of capital transfer tax) namely, that the amount of any sum of money or the value of any property ordered to be provided—

    (i)   in the case of an application in respect of a disposition which consisted of the payment of money or an application in respect of the payment of money in accordance with a contract, shall not exceed the aggregate of so much of that money as is at the date of the order in the hands of the trustee and the value at that date of any property which represents that money or is derived therefrom and is at that date in the hands of the trustee;

(ii)   in the case of an application in respect of a disposition which consisted of the transfer of property (other than a sum of money) or an application in respect of the transfer of property (other than a sum of money) in accordance with a contract, shall not exceed the aggregate of the value at the date of the order of so much of that property as is at that date in the hands of the trustee and the value at that date of any property which represents the first-mentioned property or is derived therefrom and is at that date in the hands of the trustee.

(2)   Where any such application is made in respect of a disposition made to any person as a trustee or in respect of any payment made or property transferred in pursuance of a contract to any person as a trustee, the trustee shall not be liable for having distributed any money or other property on the ground that he ought to have taken into account the possibility that such an application would be made.

(3)   Where any such application is made in respect of a disposition made to any person as a trustee or in respect of any payment made or property transferred in accordance with a contract to any person as a trustee, any reference in the said section 10 or 11 to the donee shall be construed as including a reference to the trustee or trustees for the time being of the trust in question and any reference in subsection (1) or (2) above to a trustee shall be construed in the same way.

Special provisions relating to cases of divorce, separation etc

[247.15]
14.   Provision as to cases where no financial relief was granted in divorce proceedings etc.—(1)   Where, within twelve months from the date on which a decree of divorce or nullity of marriage has been made absolute or a decree of judicial separation has been granted, a party to the marriage dies and—

(a)   an application for a financial provision order under section 23 of the Matrimonial Causes Act 1973 or a property adjustment order under section 24 of that Act has not been made by the other party to that marriage, or
(b)   such an application has been made but the proceedings thereon have not been determined at the time of the death of the deceased,

then, if an application for an order under section 2 of this Act is made by that other party, the court shall, notwithstanding anything in section 1 or section 3 of this Act, have power, if it thinks it just to do so, to treat that party for the purposes of that application as if the decree of divorce or nullity of marriage had not been made absolute or the decree of judicial separation had not been granted, as the case may be.

(2)   This section shall not apply in relation to a decree of judicial separation unless at the date of the death of the deceased the decree was in force and the separation was continuing.

[247.16]
15.   Restriction imposed in divorce proceedings, etc on application under this Act.—[(1)   On the grant of a decree of divorce, a decree of nullity of

marriage or a decree of judicial separation or at any time thereafter the court, if it considers it just to do so, may, on the application of either party to the marriage, order that the other party to the marriage shall not on the death of the applicant be entitled to apply for an order under section 2 of this Act.

In this subsection 'the court' means the High Court or, where a county court has jurisdiction by virtue of Part V of the Matrimonial and Family Proceedings Act 1984, a county court.][1]

(2)   In the case of a decree of divorce or nullity of marriage an order may be made under subsection (1) above before or after the decree is made absolute, but if it is made before the decree is made absolute it shall not take effect unless the decree is made absolute.

(3)   Where an order made under subsection (1) above on the grant of a decree of divorce or nullity of marriage has come into force with respect to a party to a marriage, then, on the death of the other party to that marriage, the court shall not entertain any application for an order under section 2 of this Act made by the first-mentioned party.

(4)   Where an order made under subsection (1) above on the grant of a decree of judicial separation has come into force with respect to any party to a marriage, then, if the other party to that marriage dies while the decree is in force and the separation is continuing, the court shall not entertain any application for an order under section 2 of this Act made by the first-mentioned party.

1   Sub-s (1): substituted by the Matrimonial and Family Proceedings Act 1984 (MFPA 1984), s 8(1).

[247.17]

15A.   Restriction imposed in proceedings under Matrimonial and Family Proceedings Act 1984 on application under this Act.—(1)   On making an order under section 17 of the Matrimonial and Family Proceedings Act 1984 (orders for financial provision and property adjustment following overseas divorces, etc) the court if it considers it just to do so, may, on the application of either party to the marriage, order that the other party to the marriage shall not on the death of the applicant be entitled to apply for an order under section 2 of this Act.

In this subsection 'the court' means the High Court or, where a county court has jurisdiction by virtue of Part V of the Matrimonial and Family Proceedings Act 1984, a county court.

(2)   Where an order under subsection (1) above has been made with respect to a party to a marriage which has been dissolved or annulled, then, on the death of the other party to that marriage, the court shall not entertain an application under section 2 of this Act made by the first-mentioned party.

(3)   Where an order under subsection (1) above has been made with respect to a party to a marriage the parties to which have been legally separated, then, if the other party to the marriage dies while the legal separation is in force, the court shall not entertain an application under section 2 of this Act made by the first-mentioned party.[1]

1   Section 15A: inserted by the MFPA 1984, s 25(3).

[247.18]

16. Variation and discharge of secured periodical payments orders made under Matrimonial Causes Act 1973.—(1) Where an application for an order under section 2 of this Act is made to the court by any person who was at the time of the death of the deceased entitled to payments from the deceased under a secured periodical payments order made under the Matrimonial Causes Act 1973, then, in the proceedings on that application, the court shall have power, if an application is made under this section by that person or by the personal representative of the deceased, to vary or discharge that periodical payments order or to revive the operation of any provision thereof which has been suspended under section 31 of that Act.

(2) In exercising the powers conferred by this section the court shall have regard to all the circumstances of the case, including any order which the court proposes to make under section 2 or section 5 of this Act and any change (whether resulting from the death of the deceased or otherwise) in any of the matters to which the court was required to have regard when making the secured periodical payments order.

(3) The powers exercisable by the court under this section in relation to an order shall be exercisable also in relation to any instrument executed in pursuance of the order.

[247.19]

17. Variation and revocation of maintenance agreements.—(1) Where an application for an order under section 2 of this Act is made to the court by any person who was at the time of the death of the deceased entitled to payments from the deceased under a maintenance agreement which provided for the continuation of payments under the agreement after the death of the deceased, then, in the proceedings on that application, the court shall have power, if an application is made under this section by that person by the personal representative of the deceased, to vary or revoke that agreement.

(2) In exercising the powers conferred by this section the court shall have regard to all the circumstances of the case, including any order which the court proposes to make under section 2 or section 5 of this Act and any change (whether resulting from the death of the deceased or otherwise) in any of the circumstances in the light of which the agreement was made.

(3) If a maintenance agreement is varied by the court under this section the like consequences shall ensue as if the variation had been made immediately before the death of the deceased by agreement between the parties and for valuable consideration.

(4) In this section 'maintenance agreement', in relation to a deceased person, means any agreement made, whether in writing or not and whether before or after the commencement of this Act, by the deceased with any person with whom he entered into a marriage, being an agreement which contained provisions governing the rights and liabilities towards one another when living separately of the parties to that marriage (whether or not the marriage has been dissolved or annulled) in respect of the making or securing of payments of the disposition or use of any property, including such rights and liabilities with respect to the maintenance or education of any child, whether or not a child of the deceased or a person who was treated by the deceased as a child of the family in relation to that marriage.

[247.20]
18. Availability of court's powers under this Act in applications under ss 31 and 36 of the Matrimonial Causes Act 1973.—(1) Where—

(a) a person against whom a secured periodical payments order was made under the Matrimonial Causes Act 1973 has died and an application is made under section 31(6) of that Act for the variation or discharge of that order or for the revival of the operation of any provision thereof which has been suspended, or

(b) a party to a maintenance agreement within the meaning of section 34 of that Act has died, the agreement being one which provides for the continuation of payments thereunder after the death of one of the parties, and an application is made under section 36(1) of that Act for the alteration of the agreement under section 35 thereof,

the court shall have power to direct that the application made under the said section 31(6) or 36(1) shall be deemed to have been accompanied by an application for an order under section 2 of this Act.

(2) Where the court gives a direction under subsection (1) above it shall have power, in the proceedings on the application under the said section 31(6) or 36(1), to make any order which the court would have had power to make under the provisions of this Act if the application under the said section 31(6) or 36(1), as the case may be, had been made jointly with an application for an order under the said section 2; and the court shall have power to give such consequential directions as may be necessary for enabling the court to exercise any of the powers available to the court under this Act in the case of an application for an order under section 2.

(3) Where an order made under section 15(1) of this Act is in force with respect to a party to a marriage, the court shall not give a direction under subsection (1) above with respect to any application made under the said section 31(6) or 36(1) by that party on the death of the other party.

Miscellaneous and supplementary provisions

[247.21]
19. Effect, duration and form of orders.—(1) Where an order is made under section 2 of this Act then for all purposes, including the purposes of the enactments relating to capital transfer tax, the will or the law relating to intestacy, or both the will and the law relating to intestacy, as the case may be, shall have effect and be deemed to have had effect as from the deceased's death subject to the provisions of the order.

(2) Any order made under section 2 or 5 of this Act in favour of—

(a) an applicant who was the former hsuband or former wife of the deceased, or

(b) an applicant who was the husband or wife of the deceased in a case where the marriage with the deceased was the subject of a decree of judicial separation and at the date of death the decree was in force and the separation was continuing, shall, in so far as it provides for the making of periodical payments, cease to have effect on the remarriage of the applicant, except in relation to any arrears due under the order on the date of the remarriage.

(3)   A copy of every order made under this Act [other than an order made under section 15(1) of this Act][1] shall be sent to the principal registry of the Family Division for entry and filing, and a memorandum of the order shall be endorsed on, or permanently annexed to, the probate or letters of administration under which the estate is being administered.

1   Words in square brackets in sub-s (3) inserted by the AJA 1982, s 52.

[247.22]
20.   Provisions as to personal representatives.—(1)   The provisions of this Act shall not render the personal representative of a deceased person liable for having distributed any part of the estate of the deceased, after the end of the period of six months from the date on which representation with respect to the estate of the deceased is first taken out, on the ground that he ought to have taken into account the possibility—

(a)   that the court might permit the making of an application for an order under section 2 of this Act after the end of that period, or

(b)   that, where an order has been made under the said section 2, the court might exercise in relation thereto the powers conferred on it by section 6 of this Act,

but this subsection shall not prejudice any power to recover, by reason of the making of an order under this Act, any part of the estate so distributed.

(2)   Where the personal representative of a deceased person pays any sum directed by an order under section 5 of this Act to be paid out of the deceased's net estate, he shall not be under any liability by reason of that estate not being sufficient to make the payment, unless at the time of making the payment he has reasonable cause to believe that the estate is not sufficient.

(3)   Where a deceased person entered into a contract by which he agreed to leave by his will any sum of money or other property to any person or by which he agreed that a sum of money or other property would be paid or transferred to any person out of his estate, then, if the personal representative of the deceased has reason to believe that the deceased entered into the contract with the intention of defeating an application for financial provision under this Act, he may, notwithstanding anything in that contract, postpone the payment of that sum of money or the transfer of that property until the expiration of the period of six months from the date on which representation with respect to the estate of the deceased is first taken out or, if during that period an application is made or an order under section 2 of this Act, until the determination of the proceedings on that application.

[247.23]
21.   Admissibility as evidence of statement made by deceased. [*Repealed by the Civil Evidence Act 1995, s 15(2), Sch 2.*]

[247.24]
22.   Jurisdiction of county courts.[1] [*Repealed by the Administration of Justice Act 1982, s 75, Sch 9, and replaced by what is now the County Courts Act 1984, s 25 (as amended).*]

1   The jurisdiction of the county court is now unlimited: see the County Courts Act 1984, s 25, as amended by the Courts and Legal Services Act 1990, s 1 and the High Court and County Courts Jurisdiction Order 1991 (SI 1991/724).

[247.25]
23.   Determination of date on which representation was first taken out. In considering for the purposes of this Act when representation with respect to the estate of a deceased person was first taken out, a grant limited to settled land or to trust property shall be left out of account, and a grant limited to real estate or to personal estate shall be left out of account unless a grant limited to the remainder of the estate has previously been made or is made at the same time.

[247.26]
24.   Effect of this Act on s 46(1)(vi) of Administration of Estates Act 1925. Section 46(1)(vi) of the Administration of Estates Act 1925, in so far as it provides for the devolution of property on the Crown, the Duchy of Lancaster or the Duke of Cornwall as bona vacantia, shall have effect subject to the provisions of this Act.

[247.27]
25.   Interpretation.—(1)   In this Act—

'beneficiary', in relation to the estate of a deceased person, means—

(a)   a person who under the will of the deceased or under the law relating to intestacy is beneficially interested in the estate or would be so interested if an order had not been made under this Act, and

(b)   a person who has received any sum of money or other property which by virtue of section 8(1) or 8(2) of this Act is treated as part of the net estate of the deceased or would have received that sum or other property if an order had not been made under this Act;

'child' includes an illegitimate child and a child en ventre sa mere at the death of the deceased;

'the court' means [unless the context otherwise requires][1] the High Court, or where a county court has jurisdiction by virtue of section 22 of this Act,[2] a county court;

'former wife' or 'former husband' means a person whose marriage with the deceased was during the lifetime of the deceased either—

(a)   dissolved or annulled by a decree of divorce or a decree of nullity of marriage granted under the law of any part of the British Islands, or

(b)   dissolved or annulled in any country or territory outside the British Islands by a divorce or annulment which is entitled to be recognised as valid by the law of England and Wales,[3]

'net estate', in relation to a deceased person, means:—

(a)   all property of which the deceased had power to dispose by his will (otherwise than by virtue of a special power of appointment) less the amount of his funeral, testamentary and administration expenses, debts and liabilities, including any capital transfer tax payable out of his estate on his death;

(b)   any property in respect of which the deceased held a general power of appointment (not being a power exercisable by will) which has not been exercised;

(c)   any sum of money or other property which is treated for the purposes of this Act as part of the net estate of the deceased by virtue of section 8(1) or (2) of this Act;

(d)   any property which is treated for the purposes of this Act as part of the net estate of the deceased by virtue of an order made under section 9 of the Act;

(e)   any sum of money or other property which is, by reason of a disposition or contract made by the deceased, ordered under section 10 or 11 of this Act to be provided for the purpose of making of the financial provision under this Act;

'property' includes any chose in action;

'reasonable financial provision' has the meaning assigned to it by section 1 of this Act;

'valuable consideration' does not include marriage or a promise of marriage;

'will' includes a codicil.

(2)   For the purposes of paragraph (a) of the definition of 'net estate' in subsection (1) above a person who is not of full age and capacity shall be treated as having power to dispose by will of all property of which he would have had power to dispose by will if he had been of full age and capacity.

(3)   Any reference in this Act to provision out of the net estate of a deceased person includes a reference to provision extending to the whole of that estate.

(4)   For the purposes of this Act any reference to a wife or husband shall be treated as including a reference to a person who in good faith entered into a void marriage with the deceased unless either—

(a)   the marriage of the deceased and that person was dissolved or annulled during the lifetime of the deceased and the dissolution or annulment is recognised by the law of England and Wales, or

(b)   that person has during the lifetime of the deceased entered into a later marriage.

(5)   Any reference in this Act to remarriage or to a person who has remarried includes a reference to a marriage which is by law void or voidable or to a person who has entered into such a marriage, as the case may be, and a marriage shall be treated for the purposes of this Act as a remarriage, in relation to any party thereto, notwithstanding that the previous marriage of that party was void or voidable.

1   Words in square brackets inserted by the MFPA 1984, s 8(2).
2   The reference to s 22 must be read as a reference to the County Courts Act 1984, s 25 (as amended): see the Interpretation Act 1978, s 17(2)(a) at para **[246.80]**.
3   Definition of 'former wife' or 'former husband' was substituted by the MFPA 1984, s 25(2).

[247.28]
26.   Consequential amendments, repeals and transitional provisions. [*The provisions of this section are omitted.*]

[247.29]
27. Short title, commencement and extent.—(1)   This Act may be cited as the Inheritance (Provision for Family and Dependants) Act 1975.
(2)   This Act does not extend to Scotland or Northern Ireland.
(3)   This Act shall come into force on 1 April 1976.

FORFEITURE ACT 1982

(1982 c 34)   [13 July 1982]

[247.30]
Note. The Forfeiture Act 1982 (FoA 1982) confers jurisdiction on the court and on the social security commissioners to modify the effect of the forfeiture rule in cases of unlawful killing other than murder, and wholly or partly restore the interest in the victim's estate or the social security benefits of which the offender would otherwise be deprived by the rule. The FoA 1982 also removes any bar to the making of an application for provision under the I(PFD)A 1975 (see paras **[247.1]**–**[247.29]**) or for financial relief under the divorce legislation. For a more detailed account of the operation of the FoA 1982 see Vol 1, paras **[9.20]**–**[9.22]**.

[247.31]
1. The 'forfeiture rule'.—(1)   In this Act, the 'forfeiture rule' means the rule of public policy which in certain circumstances precludes a person who has unlawfully killed another from acquiring a benefit in consequence of the killing.
(2)   References in this Act to a person who has unlawfully killed another include a reference to a person who has unlawfully aided, abetted, counselled or procured the death of that other and references in this Act to unlawful killing shall be interpreted accordingly.

[247.32]
2. Power to modify the rule.—(1)   Where a court determines that the forfeiture rule has precluded a person (in this section referred to as 'the offender') who has unlawfully killed another from acquiring any interest in property mentioned in subsection (4) below, the court may make an order under this section modifying the effect of that rule.
(2)   The court shall not make an order under this section modifying the effect of the forfeiture rule in any case unless it is satisfied that, having regard to the conduct of the offender and of the deceased and to such other circumstances as appear to the court to be material, the justice of the case requires the effect of the rule to be so modified in that case.
(3)   In any case where a person stands convicted of an offence of which unlawful killing is an element the court shall not make an order under this section modifying the effect of the forfeiture rule in that case unless proceedings for the purpose are brought before the expiry of the period of three months beginning with his conviction.
(4)   The interests in property referred to in subsection (1) above are—

(a) any beneficial interest in property which (apart from the forfeiture rule) the offender would have acquired—

    (i) under the deceased's will (including, as respects Scotland, any writing having testamentary effect) or the law relating to intestacy or by way of ius relicti, ius relictae or legitim;

    (ii) on the nomination of the deceased in accordance with the provisions of any enactment;

    (iii) as a donatio mortis causa made by the deceased; or

    (iv) under a special destination (whether relating to heritable or moveable property); or

(b) any beneficial interest in property which (apart from the forfeiture rule) the offender would have acquired in consequence of the death of the deceased, being property which, before the death, was held on trust for any person.

(5) An order under this section may modify the effect of the forfeiture rule in respect of any interest in property to which the determination referred to in subsection (1) above relates and may do so in either or both of the following ways, that is—

(a) where there is more than one such interest, by excluding the application of the rule in respect of any (but not all) of those interests; and

(b) in the case of any such interest in property, by excluding the application of the rule in respect of part of the property.

(6) On the making of an order under this section, the forfeiture rule shall have effect for all purposes (including purposes relating to anything done before the order is made) subject to the modifications made by the order.

(7) The court shall not make an order under this section modifying the effect of the forfeiture rule in respect of any interest in property which, in consequence of the rule, has been acquired before the coming into force of this section by a person other than the offender or a person claiming through him.

(8) In this section—

    'property' includes any chose in action or incorporeal moveable property; and

    'will' includes codicil.

[247.33]
3. Application for financial provision not affected by the rule.—(1) The forfeiture rule shall not be taken to preclude any person from making any application under a provision mentioned in subsection (2) below or the making of any order on the application.

(2) The provisions referred to in subsection (1) above are—

(a) any provision of the Inheritance (Provision for Family and Dependants) Act 1975; and

(b) sections 31(6) (variation etc of periodical payments orders) and 36(1) (variation of maintenance agreements) of the Matrimonial Causes Act 1973 and section 5(4) of the Divorce (Scotland) Act 1976 (variation etc of periodical allowances).

[247.34]

4. Commissioner to decide whether rule applies to social security benefits.—(1) Where a question arises as to whether, if a person were otherwise entitled to be eligible for any benefit or advantage under a relevant enactment, he would be precluded by virtue of the forfeiture rule from receiving the whole or part of the benefit or advantage, that question shall (notwithstanding anything in any relevant enactment) be determined by a Commissioner.

[(1A) Where a Commissioner determines that the forfeiture rule has precluded a person (in this section referred to as 'the offender') who has unlawfully killed another from receiving the whole or part of any such benefit or advantage, the Commissioner may make a decision under this subsection modifying the effect of that rule and may do so whether the unlawful killing occurred before or after the coming into force of this subsection.

(1B) The Commissioner shall not make a decision under subsection (1A) above modifying the effect of the forfeiture rule in any case unless he is satisfied that, having regard to the conduct of the offender and of the deceased and to such other circumstances as appear to the Commissioner to be material, the justice of the case requires the effect of the rule to be so modified in that case.

(1C) Subject to subsection (1D) below, a decision under subsection (1A) above may modify the effect of the forfeiture rule in either or both of the following ways—

(a) so that it applies only in respect of a specified proportion of the benefit or advantage;

(b) so that it applies in respect of the benefit or advantage only for a specified period of time.

(1D) Such a decision may not modify the effect of the forfeiture rule so as to allow any person to receive the whole or any part of a benefit or advantage in respect of any period before the commencement of this subsection.

(1E) If the Commissioner thinks it expedient to do so, he may direct that his decision shall apply to any future claim for a benefit or advantage under a relevant enactment, on which a question such as is mentioned in subsection (1) above arises by reason of the same unlawful killing.

(1F) It is immaterial for the purposes of subsection (1E) above whether the claim is in respect of the same or a different benefit or advantage.

(1G) For the purpose of obtaining a decision whether the forfeiture rule should be modified the Secretary of State may refer to a Commissioner for review any determination of a question such as is mentioned in subsection (1) above that was made before the commencement of subsections (1A) to (1F) above (whether by a Commissioner or not) and shall do so if the offender requests him to refer such a determination.

(1H) Subsections (1A) to (1F) above shall have effect on a reference under subsection (1G) above as if in subsection (1A) the words 'it has been determined' were substituted for the words 'a Commissioner determines'.]¹

(2) Regulations under this section may make such provision as appears to the Secretary of State to be necessary or expedient for carrying this section into effect; and (without prejudice to the generality of that) the regulations may, in relation to the question mentioned in subsection (1) above or any determination under that subsection [or any decision under subsection (1A) above]¹—

(a) apply any provision of any relevant enactment, with or without modifications; or exclude or contain provision corresponding to any such provision; and

(b) make provision for purposes corresponding to those for which provision may be made by regulations under [section 59 of the Social Security Administration Act 1992]² (matters relating to adjudication).

(3) The power to make regulations under this section shall be exercisable by statutory instrument which shall be subject to annulment in pursuance of a resolution of either House of Parliament.

(4) [Section 175(3) to (5) of the Social Security Contributions and Benefits Act 1992]² (provision about extent of power to make regulations) shall apply to the power to make regulations conferred by this section as it applies to the power to make regulations conferred by that Act, but as if for references to that Act there were substituted references to this section.

(5) In this section—

'Commissioner' has the same meaning as in the [Social Security Administration Act 1992]; and

'relevant enactment' means any provision of the following and any instrument made by virtue of such a provision:

the Personal Injuries (Emergency Provisions) Act 1939,

the Pensions (Navy, Army, Air Force and Mercantile Marine) Act 1939,

the Polish Resettlement Act 1947,

. . .

[the Social Security Acts 1975 to 1991,]

[the Social Security Contributions and Benefits Act 1992,]

[the Pension Schemes Act 1993]

and any other enactment relating to pensions or social security prescribed by regulations under this section.³

1   Sub-ss (1A) to (1H) and the words in the first pair of square brackets in sub-s (2) were inserted by the Social Security Act 1986, ss 76(1) to (3).

2   The words in the second pair of square brackets in sub-s (2), and the words in square brackets in sub-s (4), were substituted by the Social Security (Consequential Provisions) Act 1992, s 4, Sch 2, para 63(1), (2).

3   In sub-s (5), the words in square brackets in the definition of 'Commissioner' were substituted, and in the definition of 'relevant enactment', the entry omitted (as substituted by the Social Security Act 1986, s 86(1), Sch 10, Pt VI, para 108(b)) was repealed, and the entry relating to the Social Security Contributions and Benefits Act 1992 was added, by the Social Security (Consequential Provisions) Act 1992, ss 3, 4, Sch 1, Sch 2, para 63(3). The entry relating to the Social Security Acts 1975 to 1991 in that definition was substituted by the Statutory Sick Pay Act 1991, s 3(1)(c); and the final entry was added by the Pension Schemes Act 1993, s 190, Sch 8, para 15.

[247.35]

5.   Exclusion of murderers. Nothing in this Act or in any order made under section 2 or referred to in section 3(1) of this Act [or in any decision made under section 4(1A) of this Act] shall affect the application of the forfeiture rule in the case of a person who stands convicted of murder.

[247.36]

6.   Corresponding provision for Northern Ireland. An Order in Council under paragraph 1(1)(b) of Schedule 1 to the Northern Ireland Act 1974 (legislation for Northern Ireland in the interim period) which contains a statement that it is made only for purposes corresponding to the purposes of this Act—

    (a)   shall not be subject to paragraph 1(4) and (5) of that Schedule (affirmative resolution of both Houses of Parliament); but

    (b)   shall be subject to annulment in pursuance of a resolution of either House.

[247.37]

7. Short title, etc.—(1)   This Act may be cited as the Forfeiture Act 1982.

(2)   Section 4 of this Act shall come into force on such day as the Secretary of State may appoint by order made by statutory instrument; and sections 1 to 3 and 5 of this Act shall come into force on the expiry of the period of three months beginning with the day on which it is passed.

(3)   This Act, except section 6, does not extend to Northern Ireland.

(4)   Subject to section 2(7) of this Act, an order under section 2 of this Act or an order referred to in section 3(1) of this Act and made in respect of a person who has unlawfully killed another may be made whether the unlawful killing occurred before or after the coming into force of those sections.

Volume 2 – Cumulative Index

Index

Index

Whimsical disposition
presumptions, and, **51**.7–**51**.8
Widowed parent with adult children
entire estate by widow
  accumulation and maintenance trusts of
    residue for grandchildren, **230**.45–
    230.69
  children absolutely, to, **230**.2–**230**.15
  division of residue between children on
    trusts, **230**.16–**230**.29
  division of residue between children and
    grandchildren on trusts, **230**.30–
    230.44
  house to daughter-carer and residue to
    children, **230**.70–**230**.80
  settling residue on children with
    progressive powers to pay capital,
    230.81–**230**.94
note, **230**.1
Widowed parent with young children
entire estate by widow
  minor child on contingent trusts, to,
    229.26–**229**.36
  residence rights until youngest child
    reaches specified age, **229**.51–**229**.64
  settling residue on children with remainder
    to grandchildren, **229**.37–**229**.50
note, **229**.1
Wife
and see **Spouse**
divorce, and, **80**.3
gift of personal chattels, and, **204**.15–**204**.21
invalid marriage, in, **80**.6
subsequent marriage, by, **80**.1
surviving spouse, **80**.5
widowhood, during, **80**.2
Wild's case, **rule in**
gift to person and children, and, **85**.2
Will prepared by beneficiary
generally, **5**.4
solicitors, **5**.5
Will trusts
inheritance tax, **200**.107–**200**.118
Wills Act 1837
amendments
  1861, **244**.41–**244**.45
  1918, **244**.46–**244**.50
  1925, **244**.54
  1968, **244**.82
  1969, **244**.85
  1982, **244**.93–**244**.95

Wills Act 1837—*contd*
amendments—*contd*
  1995, **244**.130, **244**.134
definitions, **244**.3
extent, **244**.35–**244**.36
general provisions, **244**.4–**244**.34
introductory note, **244**.2
Wills Act 1861
application, **244**.45
general provisions, **244**.41–**244**.44
repeal, **244**.81
Wills Act 1963
citation, **244**.81
commencement, **244**.81
definitions, **244**.80
general provisions, **244**.75–**244**.79
Wills Act 1968
citation, **244**.83
general provisions, **244**.82
Wills Act Amendment Act 1852
definitions, **244**.41
general provisions, **244**.38–**244**.40
introductory note, **244**.37
Wills (Soldiers and Sailors) Act 1918
amendments
  1969, **244**.85
definitions, **244**.50
general provisions, **244**.46–**244**.49
Witnesses to will
blind person, and, **12**.16
capacity to benefit, and
  charging power, **9**.11
  foreign wills, **9**.12
  generally, **9**.3–**9**.9
  soldiers' wills, **9**.10
generally, **12**.16
professional privilege, and, **12**.17
Wool in store
and see **Description of property**
generally, **61**.1
Words below signature
generally, **11**.3
Written will
form of will, and, **10**.13–**10**.17
Wrong name
charitable gifts, and, **103**.3
signature of wills, and, **11**.20

Zavah
admissibility as will, and, **10**.12